Bisk Education

CPA Review™

AMERICA'S BE... ...E 1971

D0132086

GET READY TO
PASS
THE CPA EXAM

SAVE
HUNDREDS OF DOLLARS!

See coupons at back of book for special offers on AUDIO, VIDEO, ONLINE and SOFTWARE exam reviews.

▶▶▶ WITH BISK'S
ONLINE or CLASSIC
CPA REVIEW

Bisk Education
CPA REVIEW™

PASS THE CPA EXAM THE FIRST TIME — GUARANTEED!*

6 EASY STEPS TO EXAM SUCCESS...
ONLINE OR CLASSIC

STEP 1
SELECT YOUR STUDY METHOD
- **Bisk CPA Review Online** – We bring the classes to you. The hands-on guidance of a live review with the flexibility of online learning!
- **Bisk CPA Review Classic** – The CD-based alternative to our online program with the flexibility to study on your own anytime, anywhere.

STEP 2
TAKE A DIAGNOSTIC CPA EXAM
The Diagnostic CPA Exam evaluates your level of knowledge by pinpointing your strengths and weaknesses, earmarking areas for increased (or decreased) study time. This information is passed to the Bisk Personal Trainer™ so that the entire course outline is color-coded, identifying your individual needs.

STEP 3
UTILIZE THE PERSONAL TRAINER
The Bisk Personal Trainer™ feature analyzes your performance on the Diagnostic CPA Exam by matching your weakest areas against the most heavily tested exam topics (according to AICPA specifications) and automatically develops an extensive study plan just for you. Featuring practice exams with links to thousands of pages of the most comprehensive textbooks on the market, this powerful learning tool even reevaluates your needs and modifies your study plan after each study session or practice exam!

*Call for details

www.CPAexam.com/10

STEP 4

DIVE INTO THE MULTIMEDIA STUDY CENTER

- Get access to 50+ hours of streaming video lectures online or on CD.
- Take unlimited practice exams that give you right/wrong answer explanations with links to the related text.

▶ ▶ ▶ HUNDREDS OF SIMULATIONS

STEP 5

RELY ON OUR EXPERT GUIDANCE

Bisk CPA Review Online allows you to interact with professors and fellow exam candidates via email, message boards and chat rooms. With both our Online and Classic reviews, you get direct access to our editorial and technical support staffs. Plus, customer service personnel will be standing by to help with any other questions you might have!

STEP 6

FIRE UP THE CPA EXAM TEST ENGINE

The CPA Exam Test Engine allows you to practice taking an unlimited number of final exams (formatted just like the real thing) before you sit. Multiple-choice questions feature instant on-screen grading while essay questions are graded using AICPA-style keywords and phrases – helping track your study performance from start to finish and ensuring your success on the CPA Exam.

ENHANCE YOUR CPA REVIEW WITH:

MULTIMEDIA SOFTWARE (included with Bisk CPA Review Online† or Classic)

Our state-of-the-art, multimedia software covers all four exam sections and includes our popular Bisk Personal Trainer™ that evaluates your knowledge and provides a custom study program based on your progress. You get full-motion video, audio and animated graphics; plus, thousands of exam questions including simulations from our comprehensive CPA Review textbooks. (†Software features are embedded within the online classroom).

INTENSIVE DVDs

Specifically designed for the weeks right before the exam, this powerful video program will increase your retention of the most heavily tested exam topics and teach you what to study to most effectively prepare for the exam.

HOT • SPOT DVDs

Choose from 35 different topic-specific videos to help with specific areas of difficulty; each is packed with valuable tips, plus a viewer guide so you can follow along.

AUDIO TUTOR CDs

This popular lecture series, containing over 40 hours of vital exam information, puts a personal CPA review expert at your side while you drive…while you jog…whenever you can listen to an audio CD.

CALL NOW ▶ ▶ ▶ 888-CPA-BISK

Bisk Education

CPA REVIEW™

NO OTHER CPA REVIEW HAS
MORE SIMULATIONS

▶ GENERAL FEATURES

- Center-based navigation
- Expanded help system
- Home page with history links
- Increased settings options (including customizable content appearance)
- "Getting Started" section
- Tutorial-based help system
- Multiple-user support
- Ability to print every screen
- Audio help for all screens
- Web-based interface
- Earn up to 12 college credits

▶ STATISTICS FEATURES

- Color-coded statistical analysis by topic and microtopic
- Statistical charts compare all exams taken
- Statistics saved for every question and exam taken
- Summary details for all areas of study

▶ ONLINE STUDY FEATURES

◀◀ 50 HOURS OF STREAMING VIDEO

- Hundreds of simulation questions
- Bisk Personal Trainer™ (develops a personalized study plan based on exam performance)
- More than 4,000 actual CPA exam questions
- Ability to mark questions for later reference
- Thousands of pages of embedded text from our four-volume textbook series
- Recently visited areas
- Custom study (user chooses what to study)
- Global study (study any topic instantly)
- Study mode with correct and incorrect answer explanations
- Super search
- Weekly assignments, including quizzes to help keep students on track
- Study guides included
- Lecture viewer guides
- 50+ hours of streaming video lectures
- Supplemental examples help explain difficult concepts

▶ TEST FEATURES

◀◀ UNLIMITED FINAL EXAMS

- Test advisor (guides you through the test-taking process and recommends specific custom tests)
- Unlimited diagnostic exams
- Unlimited AICPA-based final exams, unique and timed
- More than 4,000 actual CPA Exam questions
- Mirrors the actual exam
- Questions chosen and weighted from topics based on the CPA Exam
- Rules-based grading of essays
- Ability to mark questions for later reference
- AICPA final exam chart

▶ ONLINE COMMUNICATION FEATURES

BETTER THAN LIVE

- Message boards for threaded discussions*
- Weekly chat sessions with your professor*
- Email interaction for one-on-one communication*
- Class news to keep you up to date*

MORE THAN 4,000 PRACTICE QUESTIONS!

▶ AVAILABLE BY SECTION OR COMPLETE SET

- Financial Accounting & Reporting
- Auditing & Attestation
- Regulation
- Business Environment & Concepts

Bisk Education, Inc. | 9417 Princess Palm Avenue | Tampa, FL 33619-8313
888-CPA-BISK | 813-621-6200 | www.CPAexam.com/10 | info@CPAexam.com

©2009 Bisk Education, Inc. All rights reserved. | SC 195842zbb1 | MCID 8792 | *Available in online review only

Microsoft Certified Solution Provider

CPA

Comprehensive Exam Review

Auditing & Attestation

Nathan M. Bisk, JD, CPA

ACKNOWLEDGEMENTS

EDITORIAL BOARD

Nathan M. Bisk, JD, CPA
Mortimer M. Caplin, LLB, JSD, LLD
Richard M. Feldheim, MBA, JD, LLM, CPA
William J. Meurer, CPA

Robert L. Monette, JD, CPA
Paul Munter, PhD, CPA
Thomas A. Ratcliffe, PhD, CPA
C. William Thomas, MBA, PhD, CPA

CONTRIBUTING EDITORS

J. Ralph Byington
PhD, CPA
University of South Carolina, Aiken

Paul Munter
PhD, CPA
KPMG

C. William Thomas
MBA, PhD, CPA
Baylor University

Anne Keaty
JD
University of Louisiana at Lafayette

Thomas A. Ratcliffe
PhD, CPA
Troy University

Mark A. Turner
DBA, CPA, CMA
Texas State University

Robert L. Monette
JD, CPA
Philadelphia CPA Review

We wish to thank the **American Institute of Certified Public Accountants** and other organizations for permission to reprint or adapt the following copyrighted © materials:

1. Uniform CPA Examination Questions and Unofficial Answers, Copyright © American Institute of Certified Public Accountants, Inc., Harborside Financial Center, 201 Plaza Three, Jersey City, NJ 07311-3881.

2. Accounting Research Bulletins, APB Opinions, Audit and Accounting Guides, Auditing Procedure Studies, Risk Alerts, Statements of Position, and Code of Professional Conduct, Copyright © American Institute of Certified Public Accountants, Inc., Harborside Financial Center, 201 Plaza Three, Jersey City, NJ 07311-3881.

3. FASB Accounting Standards and Statements of Financial Accounting Concepts, Copyright © Financial Accounting Standards Board, 401 Merrit 7, P.O. Box 5116, Norwalk, CT 06856.

4. GASB Statements, Interpretations, and Technical Bulletins, Copyright © Governmental Accounting Standards Board, 401 Merritt 7, P.O. Box 5116, Norwalk CT 06856-5116.

5. Statements on Auditing Standards, Statements on Standards for Consulting Services, Statements on Responsibilities in Personal Financial Planning Practice, Statements on Standards for Accounting and Review Services, Statements on Quality Control Standards, Statements on Standards for Attestation Engagements, and Statements on Responsibilities in Tax Practice, Copyright © American Institute of Certified Public Accountants, Inc., Harborside Financial Center, 201 Plaza Three, Jersey City, NJ 07311-3881.

6. ISB Standards, Copyright © Independence Standards Board, 6th Floor, 1211 Avenue of the Americas, New York, NY 10036-8775

© 2009, by NATHAN M. BISK, JD, CPA
Tampa, Florida 33619

THIRTY-NINTH EDITION
ALL RIGHTS RESERVED. Reproduction in any form expressly prohibited. Printed in the United States of America.

PREFACE

Our texts provide comprehensive coverage of all the topics tested on all four sections of the CPA Examination—Financial Accounting & Reporting, Auditing & Attestation, Regulation, and Business Environment & Concepts. Used effectively, our materials will enable you to achieve maximum preparedness for the Uniform CPA Examination. Here is a brief summary of the features and benefits that our texts will provide for you:

1. **Information on the Computer-Based Exam**…The Uniform CPA Examination is administered at secure testing centers on computers. See Appendix B for a full discussion of the exam process.

2. **Separate and Complete Volumes**…Each volume contains up-to-date coverage, including complete coverage of all exam changes. Our texts include the latest authoritative guidance of the AICPA, GASB, and FASB, the current tax rates, governmental and nonprofit accounting, and other topics that are tested on the exam. Our coverage is based on the most recent AICPA content specification outlines for the Uniform CPA Examination.

3. **Approximately 3,600 Pages of Text in Four Volumes**…Including a selection of more than 4,500 past CPA Examination or exclusive Bisk Education multiple-choice questions and simulations with unofficial answers. Solving these questions with immediate verification of results instills confidence and reinforces our SOLUTIONS APPROACH™ to solving exam questions.

4. **Complete Coverage**…No extra materials are required to be purchased. Our texts cover all important AICPA, FASB, GASB, and ISB authoritative guidance, including all significant regulatory materials.

5. **Detailed Summaries**…We set forth the significant testable concepts in each exam topic. These highly readable summaries are written in complete sentences using an outline format to facilitate rapid and complete comprehension. The summaries isolate and emphasize topics historically tested by the examiners.

6. **Emphasis on "How to Answer Questions" and "How to Take the Exam"**…We teach you to solve simulations using our unique and famous SOLUTIONS APPROACH™.

7. **Discussion and Development of**…AICPA grading procedures, grader orientation strategies, examination confidence, and examination success.

8. **Unique Objective Question Coverage and Unofficial Answers Updated**…We explain *why* the multiple-choice alternatives are either right or wrong. Plus, we clearly indicate the changes that need to be made in the unofficial answers to reflect current business and tax laws and AICPA, FASB, GASB, and other authoritative guidance.

9. **Writing Skills**…Each volume that covers an exam section requiring written communication responses contains a section to help you brush up on your writing skills.

10. **Indexes**…We have included an index in each volume for easy topic reference.

11. **Cross-References**…If you do decide to use our other materials, the software uses the same chapter numbering system as the book. Our video and audio programs also are referenced to those same chapters.

12. **Diagnostic Exam to Test Your Present Level of Knowledge**…And we include a practice exam to allow you to test your exam preparedness. These testing materials are designed to help you identify the exam topic areas in which you may require further concentrated study.

Our materials are designed for the candidate who has previously studied accounting. Therefore, the rate at which a candidate studies and learns (not merely reads) our material will depend on a candidate's background and aptitude. Candidates who have been out of school for a period of years may need more time to study than recent graduates. The point to remember is that all the material you will need to know to pass the exam is here, except for the professional databases available for free from www.cpa-exam.org to candidates with a notice to schedule. All you need to do is apply yourself and learn this material at a rate that is appropriate to your situation. As a final thought, keep in mind that test confidence gained through disciplined preparation equals success.

OUR EDITORIAL BOARD INCLUDES THE NATION'S LEADING CPAs, ATTORNEYS AND EDUCATORS!

The Only CPA Review Texts Developed By Full-Time Experts.

Publisher and Editor-in-Chief
NATHAN M. BISK, JD, CPA (FL), is both an attorney and certified public accountant in the State of Florida. He is a graduate of Franklin and Marshall College and the University of Florida College of Law. He is a member of the AICPA, Florida Institute of Certified Public Accountants, American Association of Attorney-CPAs, Florida Bar, American Bar Association, and American Business Law Association. His background includes public accounting experience at both Ernst & Young and Arthur Andersen & Co. He is a graduate of the two-year JET program of Merrill Lynch, Pierce, Fenner & Smith, Inc. Mr. Bisk has written and taught accounting, auditing, taxation, and business law programs since 1970.

Contributing Editor
PAUL MUNTER, PhD, CPA, is currently a partner in the Department of Professional Practice—Audit with KPMG. Previously, he served as KPMG Professor and Chairman of the Department of Accounting at the University of Miami in Coral Gables, Florida. Dr. Munter also served as the Academic Fellow in the Office of the Chief Accountant at the U.S. Securities and Exchange Commission from 2002-2003 where he worked on many of the Commission's Sarbanes-Oxley initiatives and rule-making activities.

Contributing Editor
ROBERT L. MONETTE, JD, CPA (PA), is a specialist in continuing professional education and nationally recognized as an expert on the CPA exam. He is an entrepreneur with extensive experience in business acquisitions. His background includes experience in statistical sampling, EDP auditing, financial statement analysis and taxation. Mr. Monette also has taught CPA Review in Boston, New York, New Jersey, and Philadelphia, where he has helped tens of thousands of candidates become CPAs. He is one of the expert instructors on Bisk Education's CPA Review video series and has appeared as an expert commentator in several Bisk Education CPE programs. Mr. Monette earned an undergraduate degree from Bentley College and a law degree from Villanova University.

Consulting Editor
MORTIMER M. CAPLIN, LLB, JSD, LLD, is a Senior Partner with the Washington, D.C. law firm of Caplin & Drysdale. He is a former IRS Commissioner, and served as a member of the President's Task Force on Taxation. He is a recipient of the Alexander Hamilton Award (the highest award conferred by the Secretary of the Treasury) "for outstanding and unusual leadership during service as U.S. Commissioner of Internal Revenue." For more than 30 years, Mr. Caplin has been in private practice with his present law firm, and has served as Adjunct Professor for the University of Virginia Law School. He is a nationally acclaimed author of numerous articles on tax and corporate matters.

iv

YOU WILL LEARN FROM OUR OUTSTANDING EXPERTS... WITHOUT LEAVING YOUR HOME OR OFFICE.

Consulting Editor
RICHARD M. FELDHEIM, MBA, JD, LLM, CPA (NY), is a New York CPA as well as an attorney in New York and Arizona. He holds a Master's in Tax Law from New York University Law School. Mr. Feldheim is a member of the AICPA, New York State Society of CPAs, American Bar Association, New York State Bar Association, and Association of the Bar of the City of New York. His background includes practice as both a CPA with Price Waterhouse & Co. and as a Senior Partner with the Arizona law firm of Wentworth & Lundin. He has lectured for the AICPA, the Practising Law Institute, Seton Hall University, and the University of Arizona.

Consulting Editor
THOMAS A. RATCLIFFE, PhD, CPA (TX), is the Director of Accounting and Auditing at Wilson, Price, Barranco, Blankenship & Billingsley, P.C. [Montgomery, AL]. In that role, Dr. Ratcliffe is responsible for quality control within the firm. Dr. Ratcliffe is Director Emeritus of the School of Accountancy at Troy University and also serves as accounting/auditing technical advisor to several different associations of CPA firms. Continuing his involvement in service roles within the accounting profession, Dr. Ratcliffe serves on the AICPA Council and the Auditing Standards Board. He is the former chair of the AICPA Accounting and Review Services Committee. He is also a former member of the Private Company Financial Reporting Committee.

Consulting Editor
WILLIAM J. MEURER, CPA (FL), is former Managing Partner for both the overall operations in Central Florida and the Florida Audit and Business Advisory Services sector of Arthur Andersen LLP. During his 35-year career with the firm, Mr. Meurer developed expertise in several industries, including high technology, financial services, real estate, retailing/distribution, manufacturing, hospitality, professional services, and cable television. A graduate of Regis University, Mr. Meurer is a member of both the American Institute of CPAs and the Florida Society of CPAs.

Consulting Editor
C. WILLIAM THOMAS, MBA, PhD, CPA (TX), is J.E. Bush Professor and former chairman of the Department of Accounting and Business Law at Baylor University. He is a member of the AICPA, the Texas Society of CPAs, the Central Texas Chapter of CPAs, and the American Accounting Association, where he is past Chairperson for the Southwestern Regional Audit Section. In addition, he has received recognition for special Audit Education and Curriculum projects he developed for Coopers & Lybrand. His background includes public accounting experience with KPMG Peat Marwick.

CHANGE ALERTS

SAS 115 (AU 325), *Communicating Internal Control Related Matters Identified in an Audit* (issued 10/2008)

In October 2008, the Auditing Standards Board (ASB) of the American Institute of Certified Public Accountants (AICPA) issued Statement on Auditing Standards (SAS) 115, *Communicating Internal Control Related Matters Identified in an Audit.* SAS 115 supersedes SAS 112 of the same title. It is effective for audits of financial statements for periods ending on or after December 15, 2009. Earlier implementation is permitted. (Chapter 23)

SAS 116 (AU 722), *Interim Financial Information* (issued 2/2009)

In February 2009, the ASB of the AICPA issued SAS 116, *Interim Financial Information.* It is effective for reviews of interim financial information for interim periods beginning after December 15, 2009. Early application is permitted. (Chapter 30)

PCAOB AS 6, *Evaluating Consistency of Financial Statements* (issued 9/2008)

In September 2008, the Securities and Exchange Commission (SEC) approved the Public Company Accounting Oversight Board (PCAOB) Auditing Standard (AS) 6, *Evaluating Consistency of Financial Statements.* AS 6 supersedes the PCAOB's adopted interim standards AU 420, *Consistency of Application of Generally Accepted Accounting Principles* and AU 9420, *Consistency of Application of Generally Accepted Accounting Principles: Auditing Interpretations of Section 420.* It is effective November 15, 2008. (Chapter 29)

PCAOB AS 7, *Engagement Quality Review* (issue date pending SEC approval)

In July 2009, the PCAOB adopted AS 7, *Engagement Quality Review* (EQR). AS 7, **subject to SEC approval**, will become effective for EQRs of audits and interim reviews for fiscal years beginning on or after December 15, 2009 and will supersede the PCAOB's existing concurring partner review requirement. When this volume went to press, AS 7 had not been approved by the SEC. Visit the standards section of the PCAOB's Web site (www.pcaob.org) to check its status and confirm its effective date. (Chapter 29)

SSAE 15 (AT 501), *Examination of an Entity's Internal Control Over Financial Reporting That Is Integrated With an Audit of Its Financial Statements* (issued 10/08)

In October 2008, the ASB of the AICPA issued Statement on Standards for Attestation Engagements (SSAE) 15, *An Examination of an Entity's Internal Control Over Financial Reporting That Is Integrated With an Audit of Its Financial Statements.* It is effective for integrated audits for periods ending on or after December 15, 2008. Earlier implementation is permitted. (Chapter 31)

SSARS 18 (AR 100), *Applicability of Statements on Standards for Accounting and Review Services* (issued 2/09)

In February 2009, the Accounting and Review Services Committee of the AICPA issued Statement of Standards for Accounting and Review Services (SSARS) 18, *Applicability of Statements on Standards for Accounting and Review Services.* It is effective for compilations and reviews of financial statements for periods beginning after December 15, 2009. Early application is permitted. (Chapter 31)

Editor note: Please see the change alerts pages of each chapter indicated above for additional information on the content of these new authoritative pronouncements and when they are/were eligible to be tested. Accounting and auditing pronouncements are eligible to be tested on the CPA Examination in the testing window beginning six months after a pronouncement's *effective* date, unless early application is permitted. When early application is permitted, a new pronouncement may be tested in the window beginning 6 months after the *issue* date. In this case, *both* the previous and the new pronouncements can be tested until the previous pronouncement has been superseded.

IMPORTANT ANNOUNCEMENT

***FASB Accounting Standards Codification*™**

On July 1, 2009, the Financial Accounting Standards Board (FASB) instituted a major change in the way accounting standards are organized. On that date, the *FASB Accounting Standards Codification*™ (Codification) became the single official source of authoritative, nongovernmental U.S. generally accepted accounting principles (GAAP). The Codification is effective for interim and annual periods ending after September 15, 2009. There is now only one level of authoritative GAAP that exists, other than guidance issued by the Securities and Exchange Commission (SEC). All other literature will be nonauthoritative.

The Codification content is arranged within **topics, subtopics**, and **sections**.

Topics represent a collection of related guidance. Topics reside in four main areas as follows:

- Presentation—Topics relating only to presentation matters; they do not address recognition, measurement, and derecognition matters. Examples: *Income Statement, Balance Sheet,* and *Earnings per Share*.
- Financial Statement Accounts—The Codification organizes topics in financial statement order including assets, liabilities, equity, revenue, and expenses. Examples: *Receivables, Revenue Recognition,* and *Inventory*.
- Broad Transactions—These topics relate to multiple financial statement accounts and are generally transaction-oriented. Examples: *Business Combinations, Derivatives,* and *Nonmonetary Transactions*.
- Industries—These Topics relate to accounting that is unique to an industry or type of activity. Examples: *Airlines, Software,* and *Real Estate*.

Subtopics represent subsets of a topic and are generally distinguished by type or by scope. For example, *Operating Leases* and *Capital Leases* are two subtopics of the *Leases* topic distinguished by type of lease. Each topic contains an overall subtopic that generally represents the pervasive guidance that applies to all other subtopics within the topic. Each additional subtopic represents incremental or unique guidance not contained in the overall subtopic.

Sections represent the nature of the content in a subtopic such as *Recognition, Measurement, Disclosure*, etc. The section titles and organization are the same for all subtopics. Sections are further broken down into subsections, paragraphs, and subparagraphs, depending on the specific content of each section.

To increase the utility of the Codification for public companies, relevant portions of authoritative content issued by the SEC and selected SEC staff interpretations and administrative guidance have been included for reference in the Codification, such as Regulation S-X, Financial Reporting Releases (FRR)/Accounting Series Releases (ASR), Interpretive Releases (IR), and SEC staff guidance in Staff Accounting Bulletins (SAB), EITF Topic D, and SEC Staff Observer comments. The SEC content is topically organized like all other GAAP requirements; however, it is presented separately so that Codification users can distinguish between the requirements of the SEC and other authoritative GAAP. It is important to note that the SEC sections—distinguished with an "S" preceding the section number—contain SEC content related to matters within the basic financial statements, but the Codification does not contain the entire population of SEC rules, regulations, interpretive releases, and staff guidance.

Editor note: There are links on the Codification Web site (http://asc.fasb.org) to a tutorial that demonstrates its features and functions.

COMPUTER-BASED TESTING (CBT) FORMAT

The exam is offered only in English and only in a CBT format. The AICPA provides a tutorial and sample tests for the CBT on their exam Web site (www.cpa-exam.org). You must review these before the exam because neither is available at the test centers. The AICPA recommends reviewing the tutorial before the sample tests. Exposure to both will allow you to become familiar with how to navigate through the exam, gain exposure to the exam's directions, and preview its content. The time you spend with these materials will prevent you from losing any points on the exam due to unfamiliarity with the CBT system. The simulations use both a word processor and a spreadsheet program that are similar, but not identical to commercial applications. Even if you are completely comfortable with commercial applications, you may find it unsettling to encounter different or missing functionalities on your exam day. View the tutorial and take the sample tests at least a month before taking the exam and then again a week before the exam.

AUDITING & ATTESTATION

VOLUME II of IV

TABLE OF CONTENTS

The editors strongly advise candidates to download *The Uniform CPA Examination Candidate Bulletin: Information for Applicants* from the AICPA's exam Web site (www.cpa-exam.org). It is the official handbook for exam candidates—it covers exam requirements, candidate responsibilities and other important information. Candidates should read the *Getting Started* and *Practical Advice* sections of this volume for help with devising a study plan. It's also important to keep the extent of the exam's coverage of the various topics in mind while studying. The AICPA's content specification outline which provides the approximate percentage of total exam questions associated with each area in their outline is included in the *Practical Advice* section.

QUICK TEXT REFERENCE

....

....

....

....

....

The editors strongly recommend that candidates read the entire *Getting Started, Practical Advice,* and *Writing Skills* sections of this volume. The references on this page are intended only for conveniently relocating selected parts of the volume. Add items to this list that you find yourself revisiting frequently.

FOREWORD: GETTING STARTED

Step One: Read Section One of Appendix B: Practical Advice

Section One of the *Practical Advice* section is designed to familiarize you with the CPA Examination. Included in *Practical Advice* are general comments about the exam, a schedule of exam testing windows, telephone numbers and Web site addresses of boards of accountancy, and attributes required for exam success.

Step Two: Take the Diagnostic Exam

The diagnostic exam in this foreword is designed to help you determine your strong and weak areas. This in turn will help you design your personalized training plan so you spend more time in your weak areas and do not waste precious study time in areas where you are already strong. (There are Hot•Spot™ videos and audio lectures corresponding to each chapter for more in-depth study. Call 1-888-272-2475.) You can take the diagnostic exam using either the book or the Bisk CPA Review software. If you don't mark your answers in the book; you can use the diagnostic as a second practice exam. The book provides you with a worksheet that makes self-diagnosis fast and easy. The Bisk CPA Review software scores your exam and gives you a personalized analysis of your strong and weak areas—taking the diagnostic exam allows you to get the full benefit from the software.

If you took a previous CPA exam and passed some, but not all the sections, also analyze these exam sections to help determine where you need to concentrate your efforts this time.

If you purchase a package that includes software, you will also want to go through all of the software tutorials. They are each only a few minutes long, but are loaded with valuable information. There is simply no better way to prepare to study.

Step Three: Develop a Personalized Training Plan

Based on the results from your diagnostic exams, develop your personalized training plan. If you are taking all four exam sections, are sitting for the exam for the first time, and are an "average" CPA candidate, we recommend you train for 20 weeks at a minimum of 20 hours per week. The level of intensity should increase during the final four weeks of your training and peak at 40 hours the final week before the exam. Designed to complete your study program, our Intensive™ Video Series is a concentrated and effective "cram course" that targets the information you must know to pass. The videos will refresh your memory on subjects you covered weeks earlier and clarify topics you haven't yet fully grasped. (We expect most candidates will take fewer than four sections at once. If this is the case, you should adjust these guidelines accordingly.)

You may wonder what we mean by an "average" candidate. We are referring to a candidate who has just finished (or nearly finished) academic training, attended a school that has a solid accounting curriculum, and received above average grades in accounting and other business courses. (An "average" candidate's native language is English.) Remember, "average" is a benchmark. Many candidates are not "average," so adjust your training plan accordingly.

Time Availability

	Mon.	Tues.	Wed.	Thurs.	Fri.	Sat.	Sun.
1:00 a.m.							
2:00 a.m.							
3:00 a.m.							
4:00 a.m.							
5:00 a.m.							
6:00 a.m.							
7:00 a.m.							
8:00 a.m.							
9:00 a.m.							
10:00 a.m.							
11:00 a.m.							
12:00 p.m.							
1:00 p.m.							
2:00 p.m.							
3:00 p.m.							
4:00 p.m.							
5:00 p.m.							
6:00 p.m.							
7:00 p.m.							
8:00 p.m.							
9:00 p.m.							
10:00 p.m.							
11:00 p.m.							
12:00 a.m.							

How to Find 20 Hours a Week to Study

Most CPA candidates have many other demands on their time. Consequently, your first reaction may be, "I don't have 20 hours a week to devote to training for the CPA exam." Using the chart on the previous page, we will show you how to "find" the time you need to develop your training schedule.

1. Keeping in mind what you consider to be a typical week, first mark out in black the time you know you won't be able to study. For example, mark an "X" in each block which represents time you normally sleep, have a class, work, or have some other type of commitment. Be realistic.

2. Next, in a different color, put a "C" in each block that represents commute time, an "M" in each block that represents when you normally eat, and an "E" in each block that represents when you exercise.

3. Now pick one hour each day to relax and give yourself a break. Write "BREAK" in one block for each day. Do not skip this step. By taking a break, you will study more efficiently and effectively.

4. In a third color, write "STUDY" in the remaining blocks. Count the "STUDY" blocks. Are there 20? If not, count your "C," "M," and "E" blocks; if needed, these blocks of time can be used to gain additional study time by using Bisk Education CPA Review audio lectures and video programs. For example, our audio tutor is ideal for candidates on the go. You can listen to lectures whenever you're in the car or exercising and gain valuable study time each week.

5. If you still do not have 20 "STUDY" blocks, and you scored 70% or more on your diagnostic exams, you may still be able to pass the exam even with your limited study time. If you scored less than 70% on your diagnostic exams, you still have several options: (1) reprioritize and make a block that has an "X" in it available study time; (2) concentrate on fewer exam sections; or (3) study more weeks but fewer hours per week.

How to Allocate Your 20 Weeks

Develop your overall training plan. We outline a sample training plan based on 20 hours per week and 20 weeks of study for all four sections. The time allocated to each topic was based on the length of the chapter, the difficulty of the material, and how heavily the topic is tested on the exam (see the AICPA exam content specification outline in the *Practical Advice* section of this book). Keep in mind this plan is for an "average" CPA candidate. You should customize one of these plans based on the results of your diagnostic exams and level of knowledge in each area tested. Given the AICPA examiner's stated intent to make the BEC exam integrative, we recommend candidates review for the BEC exam after, or concurrently with, other exam sections. When studying, be careful not to fall into the trap of spending too much time on an area that is rarely tested.

Sample Training Plan (all 4 sections)

Candidates should make modifications to this plan to suit their individual circumstances. For instance, this plan repeats Chapter 18. Candidates may not need to return to Chapter 18, particularly those who took a governmental accounting course. Training plans for candidates sitting for one or two sections are also included in this foreword. The Online and Classic classes incorporate different training plans within the weekly assignments. These different plans take advantage of the additional material provided for Online and Classic reviews.

		Hours
Week 1:	Read *Getting Started* and *Practical Advice* sections	1
	Take diagnostic exams (in the foreword of each text) under exam conditions	10
	Read *Writing Skills* section and get organized	1
	Chapter 1—Overview	2
	Chapter 2—Cash, Receivables & Investments	6

		Hours
Week 11:	Weekly review of weeks 1 - 10	1
	Chapter 18—Governmental Overview	3
	Chapter 19—Governmental Funds & Transactions	9
	Chapter 32—Accountant's Professional Responsibilities	3
	Chapter 33—Accountant's Legal Responsibilities	4
Week 12:	Weekly review of weeks 1 - 11	1
	Chapter 18—Governmental Overview (after Chapter 19)	3
	Chapter 20—Nonprofit Accounting	6
	Chapter 34—Contracts	8
	Chapter 35—Sales	2
Week 13:	Weekly review of weeks 1 - 12	1
	Chapter 35—Sales	4
	Chapter 36—Negotiable Instruments & Documents of Title	5
	Chapter 37—Secured Transactions	2
	Chapter 50—Economic Theory	8
Week 14:	Weekly review of weeks 1 - 13	1
	Chapter 38—Debtor & Creditor Relationships	7
	Chapter 42—Property	1
	Chapter 51—Financial Management	11
Week 15:	Weekly review of weeks 1 - 14	1
	Chapter 41—Other Regulations	2
	Chapter 42—Property	4
	Chapter 51—Financial Management	2
	Chapter 52—Decision Making	4
	Chapter 53—Cost Accounting	7
Week 16:	Weekly review of weeks 1 - 15	1+
	Chapter 39—Agency	2
	Chapter 43—Federal Taxation: Property & Other Tax Topics	5
	Chapter 44—Federal Taxation: Individuals	4
	Chapter 52—Decision Making	2
	Chapter 54—Planning & Control	6
Week 17:	Weekly review of weeks 1 - 16	1+
	Chapter 44—Federal Taxation: Individuals	6
	Chapter 46—Federal Taxation: Corporations	7
	Chapter 49—Corporations	6
Week 18:	Weekly review of weeks 1 - 17	1
	Chapter 45—Federal Taxation: Estates & Trusts	6
	Chapter 46—Federal Taxation: Corporations	3
	Chapter 47—Federal Taxation: Partnerships	5
	Chapter 48—Partnerships	5
Week 19:	Review areas in which you still feel weak	10+
	Chapter 40—Federal Securities Regulation	3
	Chapter 55—Information Technology	7
Week 20:	Take practice exams under exam conditions (see page A-1)	10
	Do final reviews and check for updating supplements	10+

Your Personalized Training Plan:

Week	Task	Diagnostic Score	Est. Hours	Date Complete	Chapter Score	Final Score
1						
2						
3						
4						
5						
6						
7						
8						
9						
10						

Week	Task	Diagnostic Score	Est. Hours	Date Complete	Chapter Score	Final Score
11						
12						
13						
14						
15						
16						
17						
18						
19						
20						

Step Four: Read the Rest of the Practical Advice Section

In Section Two of the *Practical Advice* section, we discuss examination strategies. Section Three will familiarize you with how the CPA exam is scored and tell you how you can earn additional points on the exam simply by knowing what the grader is going to seek. Section Four explains our Solutions Approach™, which will help you maximize your score. Section Five contains the AICPA exam content specification outline.

Step Five: Integrate Your Review Materials

In this step, we demonstrate how to integrate the Bisk Education CPA Review products to optimize the effectiveness of your training plan. Find the section that corresponds to the package you purchased.

Videos

The video programs are designed to supplement all of the study packages. Note how we recommend using the audio lectures in the following review plans. These recommendations also apply to the Hot•Spot™ video lectures. The videos have content similar to the Online and Classic review video lectures, but they are not exactly the same. Each Hot•Spot™ video program concentrates on a few topics. Use them to help you study the areas that are most troubling for you. Each Intensive™ video program covers one of the four exam sections. They are designed for a final, intensive review, after a candidate already has done considerable work. If time permits, use the Intensive™ programs at the very beginning (for an overview) and then set them aside until the final review one or two weeks before your exam. They contain concise, informative lectures as well as exam tips and techniques that will help you to learn the material.

Online and Classic Reviews

Our most comprehensive review packages, the Online and Classic reviews provide the discipline and learning experience of a classroom setting with the convenience of self-study. The Online reviews also provide personal attention from a faculty advisor for about seven weeks. They both include video lectures, weekly assignments, and powerful software study tools not found in other packages available on the market. These packages are intended for those candidates who want to make sure they pass the exam the first time. By using one of these packages, you are eligible to qualify for Bisk Education's money-back guarantee. Contact a customer service representative for details on the components of these packages. Candidates enrolled in an online course may contact their faculty advisor with questions about integrating materials after viewing the Web site guidance. (We strongly recommend candidates working full-time take a maximum of 2 sections concurrently.)

Book, Audio Tutor & CPA Review Multimedia

This is another comprehensive self-study review package. This combination is designed expressly for the serious CPA candidate. It is intended for those candidates who want to make sure they pass the exam the first time. By using this package, you are eligible to qualify for Bisk Education's money-back guarantee.

How to Use This Package:

1. Take the diagnostic exam using the Bisk CPA Review software. The Bisk CPA Review software scores your exam and gives you a personalized analysis of your strong and weak areas. Then view the short tutorials to learn how to use the software features to their fullest.

In chapters where you are strong (i.e., you scored 65% or better on the diagnostic exam):

2. Answer the multiple-choice questions using the Bisk CPA Review software.

3. Read the subsections of the chapter that correspond to your weak areas.

4. Listen to the audio tutor for this chapter to reinforce your weak areas and review your strong areas.

5. Using the Bisk CPA Review software, answer the multiple-choice questions you previously answered incorrectly. If you answer 70% or more correctly, move on to the next chapter. If you answer less than 70% correctly, handle this chapter as if you scored less than 65% on the diagnostic exam (see the next heading).

6. Answer at least one simulation and review written communication exercises and solutions in any other simulations.

In chapters where you are weak (i.e., you scored less than 65% on the diagnostic exam):

2. Read the chapter in the book.

3. Listen to the audio tutor on topics covered in the chapter.

4. Reread the subsections of the chapter that correspond to your weak subtopics.

5. Using the Bisk CPA Review software, answer the multiple-choice questions for this chapter. If you answer 70% or more correctly, move on to the next chapter. If you get less than 70% correct, review the subtopics where you are weak and then answer the questions you previously answered incorrectly. If you still get less than 70% correct, check the AICPA exam content specification outline in the *Practical Advice* section to see how heavily the area is tested. If an area is heavily tested, continue reviewing the material and answering multiple-choice questions until you can answer at least 70% correctly. Allocate more time than you originally budgeted, if necessary. If the area is not heavily tested, move on, but make a note to come back to this area if time allows.

6. Answer at least one simulation and review written communication exercises and solutions in any other simulations.

Book & CPA Review Multimedia

This combination allows you to use the book to review the material and the Bisk CPA Review software to practice exam questions. You can also use the book to practice exam questions when you do not have access to a computer. By using this package, you are eligible to qualify for Bisk Education's money-back guarantee.

How to Use This Package:

1. Take the diagnostic exam using the Bisk CPA Review software. The Bisk CPA Review software scores your exam and gives you a personalized analysis of your strong and weak areas. Then view the short tutorials to learn how to use the software features to their fullest.

In chapters where you are strong (i.e., you scored 65% or better on the diagnostic exam):

2. Answer the multiple-choice questions using the Bisk CPA Review software.

3. Read the subsections of the chapter that correspond to your weak areas.

4. Using the Bisk CPA Review software, answer the multiple-choice questions you previously answered incorrectly. If you answer 70% or more correctly, move on to the next chapter. If you answer less than 70% correctly, handle this chapter as if you scored less than 65% on the diagnostic exam (see the next heading).

5. Answer at least one simulation and review written communication exercises and solutions in any other simulations.

In chapters where you are weak (i.e., you scored less than 65% on the diagnostic exam):

2. Read the chapter in the book.

3. Using the Bisk CPA Review software, answer the multiple-choice questions for this chapter. If you answer 70% or more correctly, move on to the next chapter. If you get less than 70% correct, review the subtopics where you are weak and then answer the questions you previously answered incorrectly. If you still get less than 70% correct, check the AICPA exam content specification outline in the *Practical Advice* section to see how heavily the area is tested. If an area is heavily tested, continue reviewing the material and answering multiple-choice questions until you can answer at least 70% correctly. Allocate more time than you originally

budgeted, if necessary. If the area is not heavily tested, move on, but make a note to come back to this area if time allows.

4. Answer at least one simulation and review written communication exercises and solutions in any other simulations.

Book & Audio Tutor

This combination is designed for those candidates who have a strong preference for hard copy; who spend time doing other activities, such as commuting or exercising, that allow listening at the same time; or who like to reinforce what they read by listening to a lecture.

How to Use This Package:

1. Take the diagnostic exam in the foreword of your book. Using the worksheet provided, score your exam to determine your strong and weak areas.

In chapters where you are strong (i.e., you scored 65% or better on the diagnostic exam):

2. Answer the multiple-choice questions for that chapter. Using the worksheet provided, analyze your strong and weak areas.

3. Read the subsections of the chapter that correspond to your weak subtopics.

4. Listen to the audio tutor for this chapter to reinforce weak areas and review strong areas.

5. Answer the multiple-choice questions you previously answered incorrectly. If you answer 70% or more correctly, move on to the next chapter. If you answer less than 70% correctly, handle this chapter as if you scored 65% or less on the diagnostic exam (see the next heading).

6. Answer at least one simulation and review written communication exercises and solutions in any other simulations.

In chapters where you are weak (i.e., you scored less than 65% on the diagnostic exam):

2. Read the chapter in the book.

3. Listen to the audio tutor for this chapter.

4. Reread the subsections of the chapter that correspond to your weak subtopics.

5. Answer the multiple-choice questions and score yourself using the worksheet provided. If you answer 70% or more correctly, move on to the next chapter. If you answer less than 70% correctly, review the subtopics still giving you trouble and then answer the questions you previously answered incorrectly. If you still get less than 70% of the questions correct, check the AICPA exam content specification outline in the *Practical Advice* section to see how heavily the area is tested. If an area is heavily tested, continue reviewing the material and answering multiple-choice questions until you can answer at least 70% correctly. Allocate more time than you originally budgeted, if necessary. If the area is not heavily tested, move on, but make a note to come back if time allows.

6. Answer at least one simulation and review written communication exercises and solutions in any other simulations.

Step Six: Use These Helpful Hints as You Study

♦ MAKE FLASH CARDS OR TAKE NOTES AS YOU STUDY.

Make flash cards for topics that are tested heavily on the exam or that are giving you trouble. By making your own flash cards, you learn during their creation and you can tailor them to your individual learning style. You will find these very useful for weekly reviews and your final review.

Make notes and/or highlight when you read the chapters in the book. When possible, make notes when you listen to the lectures. You will find these very useful for weekly reviews and your final review.

♦ DO NOT MARK THE OBJECTIVE QUESTION ANSWERS IN THE BOOK.

Do not circle the answers to the objective questions in the book. You should work every multiple-choice question at least twice and you do not want to influence later answers by knowing how you previously answered.

Date your answer sheets to facilitate tracking your progress.

♦ MARK THE OBJECTIVE QUESTIONS YOU ANSWER INCORRECTLY OR MERELY GUESS CORRECTLY.

This will remind you to answer these questions again at a later time.

♦ SPEND YOUR WEEKLY REVIEW TIME EFFECTIVELY. DURING EACH WEEKLY REVIEW:

Answer the objective questions you previously answered incorrectly or merely guessed correctly.

Go through your flash cards or notes.

Pick at least one simulation to work. Read the written communication exercises and solutions you do not answer this week.

♦ USE THE VIDEO PROGRAMS EFFECTIVELY.

Watch the video lectures in an environment without distractions. Be prepared to take notes and answer questions just as if you were attending a live class. Frequently, the instructors will have you stop the program to work a question on your own. Be sure to do this rather than just watching the instructor work the solution.

If you are strong in a topic, we suggest you read the chapter in the book or software, then watch the related Hot•Spot™ video, and finally, answer the questions. If you are not particularly strong in a topic, watch the related video, then read the chapter and answer the questions. If you are weak in a topic, watch the related video, read the chapter, watch the video again, and then answer the questions.

♦ USE THE AUDIO TUTOR EFFECTIVELY.

Use Audio Tutor to turn nonproductive time into valuable study time. For example, play the lectures when you are commuting, exercising, getting ready for school or work, doing laundry, etc. Audio Tutor will help you to memorize and retain key concepts. It will also reinforce what you have read in the book.

Step Seven: Implement Your Training Plan

This is it! You are primed and ready. You have decided which training tools will work best for you and you know how to use them. Your goal is to obtain a passing score (75) or better on each exam section. Therefore, you should concentrate on learning new material and reviewing old material only to the extent it helps you reach this goal. Utilize the personalized training plan you developed in step three so you do not fall behind. Adjust it when necessary if you need more time in one chapter or less in another. Refer to the AICPA exam content specification outline in the *Practical Advice* section to make sure the adjustment is warranted. Above all else, remember passing the exam is an attainable goal. Good luck!

Video Cross-Reference

The video programs are designed to supplement all of our study packages. They contain concise, informative lectures, as well as exam tips and techniques to help you learn the material. The Hot•Spot™ videos concentrate on particular topics. Use them to study the areas that are most troubling for you. Each of the Intensive™ video programs covers one of the four exam sections. The Intensive™ videos are designed for a final review, after you already have done considerable work. Alternatively, the Intensive™ videos may be used as both a preview and a final review. Please see step 5 of this section and the instructions at the beginning of any Hot•Spot™ or Intensive™ viewer guide for a discussion on integrating videos into your study plan. The information below is accurate as we go to press, but it is subject to change without notice.

Video Title	Text Chapter	Approximate Time
Hot•Spot™ Cash, Receivables & Marketable Securities	2	2:30
Hot•Spot™ Inventory, Fixed Assets & Intangible Assets	3, 4, 5	2:25
Hot•Spot™ Bonds & Other Liabilities	6, 7	3:00
Hot•Spot™ Leases & Pensions	8, 9	3:05
Hot•Spot™ Owners' Equity & Miscellaneous Topics	10, 15, 16	2:10
Hot•Spot™ Revenue Recognition & Income Statement Presentation	1, 11, 12	3:55
Hot•Spot™ Accounting for Income Taxes	13	2:00
Hot•Spot™ Statement of Cash Flows	14	2:00
Hot•Spot™ Consolidations	2, 17	3:30
Hot•Spot™ Governmental & Nonprofit Accounting	18 - 20	3:50
Hot•Spot™ Audit Standards & Planning	21, 22, 29	2:45
Hot•Spot™ Internal Control	23, 27	2:00
Hot•Spot™ Audit Evidence	24, 25	2:30
Hot•Spot™ Statistical Sampling	26	1:30
Hot•Spot™ Standard Audit Reports	28	1:40
Hot•Spot™ Other Reports, Reviews & Compilations	30, 31	1:50
Hot•Spot™ Professional & Legal Responsibilities	32, 33	2:00
Hot•Spot™ Contracts	34	3:00
Hot•Spot™ Sales	35	2:20
Hot•Spot™ Commercial Paper & Documents of Title	36	2:05
Hot•Spot™ Secured Transactions	37	1:15
Hot•Spot™ Bankruptcy & Suretyship	38	2:10
Hot•Spot™ Fiduciary Relationships	39, 45	2:00
Hot•Spot™ Government Regulation of Business	40, 41	2:10
Hot•Spot™ Property & Insurance	42	1:20
Hot•Spot™ Property Taxation	43	2:05
Hot•Spot™ Individual Taxation	44	3:10
Hot•Spot™ Gross Income, Tax Liabilities & Credits	44, 46	3:00
Hot•Spot™ Corporate Taxation	46	3:00
Hot•Spot™ Partnerships & Other Tax Topics	45, 47	2:30
Hot•Spot™ Business Entities	48, 49	2:25
Hot•Spot™ Economics	50	3:25
Hot•Spot™ Financial Management	51	3:00
Hot•Spot™ Cost & Managerial Accounting	52 - 54	3:30
Hot•Spot™ Information Technology	55	3:00

Intensive™ Video Review	FAR	AUD	REG	BEC
Text Chapters	1 - 20	21 - 31	32 - 47	48 - 55
Approximate Time	9:40	4:20	5:50	4:45

Supplement to Step Three: Alternative Sample Training Plans

The editors strongly recommend that candidates develop personalized training plans. Several training plans are outlined for candidates to modify. The time allocated to each topic was based on the length of the chapter, the difficulty of the material, and how heavily the topic is tested on the exam (refer to the exam specifications found in the *Practical Advice* section). You should customize one of these plans based on the results of your diagnostic exams and level of knowledge in each area tested.

AUD Sample Training Plan (1 exam section)

		Hours
Week 1:	Read *Getting Started* and *Practical Advice* sections (if not yet done)	1
	Take diagnostic exam (in this forward) under exam conditions	3
	Read *Writing Skills* section and get organized (if not yet done)	1
	Chapter 21—Standards & Related Topics	4
	Chapter 22—Planning	7
	Chapter 23—Internal Control	4
Week 2:	Chapter 23—Internal Control	8
	Chapter 24—Evidence & Procedures	10
	Chapter 25—Audit Programs	2
Week 3:	Weekly review of weeks 1 - 2	1+
	Chapter 25—Audit Programs	5
	Chapter 26—Audit Sampling	7
	Chapter 27—Auditing IT Systems	6
	Chapter 28—Reports on Audited Financial Statements	1
Week 4:	Weekly review of weeks 1 - 3	1+
	Chapter 28—Reports on Audited Financial Statements	10
	Chapter 29—Other Auditing Standards	4
	Chapter 30—Other Types of Reports	3
	Chapter 31—Other Professional Services	2
Week 5:	Review areas in which you still feel weak	7+
	Chapter 31—Other Professional Services	5
	Take practice exam under exam conditions (see page A-1)	3
	Do final reviews and check for updating supplement	5+

UPDATING SUPPLEMENTS

Bisk Education's updating supplements are small publications available from either customer service representatives or on our CPA Review Web site (www.cpaexam.com/content/support.asp). The editors recommend checking the Web site for new supplements once a month and again a week before your exam. Version 39 updating supplements are appropriate for candidates with the 39th edition. Information from supplements of earlier editions (through the version 38 series) has been incorporated into this edition. Supplements are issued only as appropriate information becomes available.

FAR & AUD Sample Training Plan (2 exam sections)

		Hours
Week 1:	Read *Getting Started* and *Practical Advice* sections (if not yet done)	1
	Take diagnostic exams (in the forward of each text) under exam conditions	5
	Read *Writing Skills* section and get organized (if not yet done)	1
	Chapter 1—Overview	2
	Chapter 2—Cash, Receivables & Investments	10
	Chapter 3—Inventory	1

		Hours
Week 2:	Chapter 3—Inventory	4
	Chapter 4—Property, Plant & Equipment	6
	Chapter 5—Intangible Assets, R&D Costs & Other Assets	4
	Chapter 6—Bonds	6
Week 3:	Weekly review of weeks 1 - 2	1
	Chapter 7—Liabilities	6
	Chapter 8—Leases	5
	Chapter 9—Postemployment Benefits	5
	Chapter 10—Owners' Equity	3
Week 4:	Weekly review of weeks 1 - 3	1
	Chapter 10—Owners' Equity	5
	Chapter 21—Standards & Related Topics	4
	Chapter 22—Planning	7
	Chapter 23—Internal Control	3
Week 5:	Weekly review of weeks 1 - 4	1
	Chapter 23—Internal Control	9
	Chapter 24—Evidence & Procedures	10
Week 6:	Weekly review of weeks 1 - 5	1
	Chapter 11—Reporting the Results of Operations	9
	Chapter 25—Audit Programs	7
	Chapter 26—Audit Sampling	3
Week 7:	Weekly review of weeks 1 - 6	1
	Chapter 11—Reporting the Results of Operations	3
	Chapter 12—Reporting: Special Areas	6
	Chapter 26—Audit Sampling	4
	Chapter 27—Auditing IT Systems	6
Week 8:	Weekly review of weeks 1 - 7	1
	Chapter 13—Accounting for Income Taxes	6
	Chapter 14—Statement of Cash Flows	6
	Chapter 15—Financial Statement Analysis	4
	Chapter 16—Foreign Operations	3
Week 9:	Weekly review of weeks 1 - 8	1+
	Chapter 17—Consolidated Financial Statements	8
	Chapter 28—Reports on Audited Financial Statements	11
Week 10:	Weekly review of weeks 1 - 9	1+
	Chapter 18—Governmental Overview	3
	Chapter 19—Governmental Funds & Transactions	2
	Chapter 29—Other Auditing Standards	4
	Chapter 30—Other Types of Reports	3
	Chapter 31—Other Professional Services	7
Week 11:	Weekly review of weeks 1 - 10	4+
	Chapter 19—Governmental Funds & Transactions	7
	Chapter 18—Governmental Overview (after Chapter 19)	3
	Chapter 20—Nonprofit Accounting	6

		Hours
Week 12:	Review areas in which you still feel weak	10+
	Take practice exams under exam conditions (see page A-1)	5
	Do final reviews and check for updating supplements	5+

AUD & REG Sample Training Plan (2 exam sections)

Week 1:	Read *Getting Started* and *Practical Advice* sections (if not yet done)	1
	Take diagnostic exams (in the foreword of each text) under exam conditions	5
	Read *Writing Skills* section and get organized (if not yet done)	1
	Chapter 21—Standards & Related Topics	3
	Chapter 22—Planning	3
	Chapter 32—Accountant's Professional Responsibilities	3
	Chapter 33—Accountant's Legal Responsibilities	4
Week 2:	Chapter 22—Planning	3
	Chapter 23—Internal Control	11
	Chapter 24—Evidence & Procedures	6
Week 3:	Weekly review of weeks 1 - 2	1
	Chapter 24—Evidence & Procedures	4
	Chapter 25—Audit Programs	7
	Chapter 26—Audit Sampling	7
	Chapter 27—Auditing IT Systems	1
Week 4:	Weekly review of weeks 1 - 3	1
	Chapter 27—Auditing IT Systems	5
	Chapter 34—Contracts	8
	Chapter 35—Sales	6
Week 5:	Weekly review of weeks 1 - 4	1
	Chapter 36—Negotiable Instruments & Documents of Title	5
	Chapter 37—Secured Transactions	2
	Chapter 38—Debtor & Creditor Relationships	7
	Chapter 42—Property	5
Week 6:	Weekly review of weeks 1 - 5	1
	Chapter 39—Agency	2
	Chapter 41—Other Regulations	2
	Chapter 43—Federal Taxation: Property & Other Tax Topics	5
	Chapter 44—Federal Taxation: Individuals	10
Week 7:	Weekly review of weeks 1 - 6	1+
	Chapter 45—Federal Taxation: Estates & Trusts	6
	Chapter 46—Federal Taxation: Corporations	10
	Chapter 47—Federal Taxation: Partnerships	3
Week 8:	Weekly review of weeks 1 - 7	1+
	Chapter 47—Federal Taxation: Partnerships	2
	Chapter 28—Reports on Audited Financial Statements	12
	Chapter 29—Other Auditing Standards	4
	Chapter 30—Other Types of Reports	1

		Hours
Week 9:	Review areas in which you still feel weak	8+
	Chapter 30—Other Types of Reports	2
	Chapter 31—Other Professional Services	7
	Chapter 40—Federal Securities Regulation	3
Week 10:	Take practice exams under exam conditions (see page A-1)	5
	Do final reviews and check for updating supplements	15+

AUD & BEC Sample Training Plan (2 exam sections)

		Hours
Week 1:	Read *Getting Started* and *Practical Advice* sections (if not yet done)	1
	Take diagnostic exams (in the foreword of each text) under exam conditions	5
	Read *Writing Skills* section and get organized (if not yet done)	1
	Chapter 21—Standards & Related Topics	3
	Chapter 22—Planning	6
	Chapter 23—Internal Control	4
Week 2:	Chapter 23—Internal Control	7
	Chapter 24—Evidence & Procedures	10
	Chapter 25—Audit Programs	3
Week 3:	Weekly review of weeks 1 - 2	1
	Chapter 25—Audit Programs	4
	Chapter 26—Audit Sampling	7
	Chapter 27—Auditing IT Systems	2
	Chapter 54—Planning & Control	6
Week 4:	Weekly review of weeks 1 - 3	1
	Chapter 48—Partnerships	5
	Chapter 49—Corporations	3
	Chapter 55—Information Technology	7
	Chapter 27—Auditing IT Systems	4
Week 5:	Weekly review of weeks 1 - 4	1
	Chapter 49—Corporations	3
	Chapter 50—Economic Theory	8
	Chapter 51—Financial Management	8
Week 6:	Weekly review of weeks 1 - 5	1+
	Chapter 28—Reports on Audited Financial Statements	1
	Chapter 51—Financial Management	5
	Chapter 52—Decision Making	6
	Chapter 53—Cost Accounting	7
Week 7:	Weekly review of weeks 1 - 6	1+
	Chapter 28—Reports on Audited Financial Statements	11
	Chapter 29—Other Auditing Standards	4
	Chapter 30—Other Types of Reports	3
	Chapter 31—Other Professional Services	1
Week 8:	Review areas in which you still feel weak	5+
	Chapter 31—Other Professional Services	6
	Take practice exams under exam conditions (see page A-1)	5
	Do final reviews and check for updating supplements	4+

———————

DIAGNOSTIC EXAM

Editor's Note: There is only one practice (or final) exam. If you mark answers for the diagnostic exam on a separate sheet of paper, you can use these questions as a second "final" exam at the end of your review.

Problem 1 MULTIPLE-CHOICE QUESTIONS (120 to 150 minutes)

1. The third general standard requires that due professional care must be exercised in the performance of an audit and the preparation of the report. This standard is ordinarily interpreted to require
a. Thorough review of the existing safeguards over access to assets and records
b. Limited review of the indications of employee fraud and illegal acts
c. Objective review of the adequacy of the technical training and proficiency of firm personnel
d. Critical review of the judgment exercised at every level of supervision (5641)

2. A successor auditor most likely would make specific inquiries of the predecessor auditor regarding
a. Specialized accounting principles of the client's industry
b. The competency of the client's internal audit staff
c. The uncertainty inherent in applying sampling procedures
d. Disagreements with management as to auditing procedures (5620)

3. A CPA firm evaluates its personnel advancement experience to ascertain whether individuals meeting stated criteria are assigned increased degrees of responsibility. This is evidence of the firm's adherence to which element of a firm's quality control system?
a. Relevant ethical requirements
b. Human resources
c. Acceptance and continuance of client relationships and specific engagements
d. Engagement performance (7486)

4. During the initial planning phase of an audit, a CPA most likely would
a. Identify specific internal control activities that are likely to prevent fraud
b. Evaluate the reasonableness of the client's accounting estimates
c. Discuss the timing of the audit procedure with the client's management
d. Inquire of the client's attorney as to whether any unrecorded claims are probable of assertion (7798)

5. Which of the following procedures would an auditor most likely include in the initial planning of a financial statement audit?
a. Obtaining a written representation letter from the client's management
b. Examining documents to detect illegal acts having a material effect on the financial statements
c. Considering whether the client's accounting estimates are reasonable in the circumstances
d. Determining the extent of involvement of the client's internal auditors (5074)

6. The acceptable level of detection risk is inversely related to the
a. Assurance provided by substantive tests
b. Risk of misapplying auditing procedures
c. Preliminary judgment about materiality levels
d. Risk of failing to discover material misstatements (0044)

7. Which of the following procedures would an auditor most likely perform in planning a financial statement audit?
a. Inquiring of the client's legal counsel concerning pending litigation
b. Comparing the financial statements to anticipated results
c. Searching for unauthorized transactions that may aid in detecting unrecorded liabilities
d. Examining computer generated exception reports to verify the effectiveness of internal controls (5622)

8. Which of the following information discovered during an audit most likely would raise a question concerning possible illegal acts?
a. Related party transactions, although properly disclosed, were pervasive during the year.
b. The entity prepared several large checks payable to cash during the year.
c. Material internal control weaknesses previously reported to management were **not** corrected.
d. The entity was a campaign contributor to several local political candidates during the year. (6576)

9. A document in an auditor's working papers includes the following statement:

"Our audit is subject to the inherent risk that material errors and fraud, including defalcations, if they exist, will not be detected. However, we will inform you of fraud that comes to our attention, unless it is inconsequential."

The above passage is most likely from a(an)
a. Comfort letter
b. Engagement letter
c. Letter of audit inquiry
d. Representation letter (7634)

10. Which of the following most likely would **not** be considered an inherent limitation of the potential effectiveness of an entity's internal control?
a. Incompatible duties
b. Management override
c. Mistakes in judgment
d. Collusion among employees (4687)

11. Which of the following auditor concerns most likely could be so serious that the auditor concludes that a financial statement audit **cannot** be conducted?
a. The entity has **no** formal written code of conduct.
b. The integrity of the entity's management is suspect.
c. Procedures requiring segregation of duties are subject to management override.
d. Management fails to modify prescribed controls for changes in conditions. (5953)

12. Audit evidence concerning segregation of duties ordinarily is best obtained by
a. Performing tests of transactions that corroborate management's financial statement assertions
b. Observing the employees as they apply control procedures
c. Obtaining a flowchart of activities performed by available personnel
d. Developing audit objectives that reduce control risk (3906)

13. Which of the following controls most likely would be effective in offsetting the tendency of sales personnel to maximize sales volume at the expense of high bad debt write-offs?
a. Employees responsible for authorizing sales and bad debt write-offs are denied access to cash.
b. Shipping documents and sales invoices are matched by an employee who does not have authority to write off bad debts.
c. Employees involved in the credit-granting function are separated from the sales function.
d. Subsidiary accounts receivable records are reconciled to the control account by an employee independent of the authorization of credit. (2798)

14. Which of the following procedures would an auditor most likely perform to test controls relating to management's assertion about the completeness of cash receipts for cash sales at a retail outlet?
a. Observe the consistency of the employees' use of cash registers and tapes
b. Inquire about employees' access to recorded but undeposited cash
c. Trace the deposits in the cash receipts journal to the cash balance in the general ledger
d. Compare the cash balance in the general ledger with the bank confirmation request (6578)

15. For effective internal control, the accounts payable department generally should
a. Stamp, perforate, or otherwise cancel supporting documentation after payment is mailed
b. Ascertain that each requisition is approved as to price, quantity, and quality by an authorized employee
c. Obliterate the quantity ordered on the receiving department copy of the purchase order
d. Establish the agreement of the vendor's invoice with the receiving report and purchase order (5977)

16. The objectives of the internal control for a production cycle are to provide assurance that transactions are properly executed and recorded, and that
a. Production orders are prenumbered and signed by a supervisor.
b. Custody of work in process and of finished goods is properly maintained.
c. Independent internal verification of activity reports is established.
d. Transfers to finished goods are documented by a completed production report and a quality control report. (4265)

17. Which of the following circumstances most likely would cause an auditor to suspect an employee payroll fraud scheme?
a. There are significant unexplained variances between standard and actual labor cost.
b. Payroll checks are disbursed by the same employee each payday.
c. Employee time cards are approved by individual departmental supervisors.
d. A separate payroll bank account is maintained on an imprest basis. (5997)

18. Which of the following controls would an entity most likely use in safeguarding against the loss of marketable securities?
a. An independent trust company that has **no** direct contact with the employees who have record keeping responsibilities has possession of the securities.
b. The internal auditor verifies the marketable securities in the entity's safe each year on the balance sheet date.
c. The independent auditor traces all purchases and sales of marketable securities through the subsidiary ledgers to the general ledger.
d. A designated member of the board of directors controls the securities in a bank safe-deposit box. (2956)

19. Which of the following auditor concerns most likely could be so serious that the auditor concludes that a financial statement audit **cannot** be performed?
a. Management fails to modify prescribed internal controls for changes in information technology.
b. Internal control activities requiring segregation of duties are rarely monitored by management.
c. Management is dominated by one person who is also the majority stockholder.
d. There is a substantial risk of intentional misapplication of accounting principles. (7099)

20. Which of the following presumptions is correct about the reliability of audit evidence?
a. Information obtained indirectly from outside sources is the most reliable audit evidence.
b. To be reliable, audit evidence should be convincing rather than persuasive.
c. Reliability of audit evidence refers to the amount of corroborative evidence obtained.
d. An effective internal control structure provides more assurance about the reliability of audit evidence. (5120)

21. The permanent (continuing) file of an auditor's working papers most likely would include copies of the
a. Lead schedules
b. Attorney's letters
c. Bank statements
d. Debt agreements (6007)

22. In addition to evaluating the frequency of deviations in tests of controls, an auditor should also consider certain qualitative aspects of the deviations. The auditor most likely would give broader consideration to the implications of a deviation if it was
a. The only deviation discovered in the sample
b. Identical to a deviation discovered during the prior year's audit
c. Caused by an employee's misunderstanding of instructions
d. Initially concealed by a forged document (5973)

23. During an audit an internal auditor may provide direct assistance to an independent CPA in

	Obtaining an understanding of the internal control	Performing tests of controls	Performing substantive tests
a.	No	No	No
b.	Yes	No	No
c.	Yes	Yes	No
d.	Yes	Yes	Yes

(5678)

24. To which of the following matters would materiality limits **not** apply in obtaining written management representations?
a. The availability of minutes of stockholders' and directors' meetings
b. Losses from purchase commitments at prices in excess of market value
c. The disclosure of compensating balance arrangements involving related parties
d. Reductions of obsolete inventory to net realizable value (5684)

25. The objective of performing analytical procedures in planning an audit is to identify the existence of
a. Unusual transactions and events
b. Illegal acts that went undetected because of internal control weaknesses
c. Related party transactions
d. Recorded transactions that were not properly authorized (4670)

26. Which of the following ratios would an engagement partner most likely calculate when reviewing the balance sheet in the overall review stage of an audit?
a. Quick assets/current assets
b. Accounts receivable/inventory
c. Interest payable/interest receivable
d. Total debt/total assets (6366)

27. An auditor's analytical procedures performed during the overall review stage indicated that the client's accounts receivable had doubled since the end of the prior year. However, the allowance for doubtful accounts as a percentage of accounts receivable remained about the same. Which of the following client explanations most likely would satisfy the auditor?
a. The client liberalized its credit standards in the current year and sold much more merchandise to customers with poor credit ratings.
b. Twice as many accounts receivable were written off in the prior year than in the current year.
c. A greater percentage of accounts receivable were currently listed in the "more than 90 days overdue" category than in the prior year.
d. The client opened a second retail outlet in the current year and its credit sales approximately equaled the older, established outlet. (7623)

28. The primary reason an auditor requests letters of inquiry be sent to a client's attorneys is to provide the auditor with
a. The probable outcome of asserted claims and pending or threatened litigation
b. Corroboration of the information furnished by management about litigation, claims, and assessments
c. The attorneys' opinions of the client's historical experiences in recent similar litigation
d. A description and evaluation of litigation, claims, and assessments that existed at the balance sheet date (5139)

29. In performing a count of negotiable securities, an auditor records the details of the count on a security count worksheet. What other information is usually included on this worksheet?
a. An acknowledgment by a client representative that the securities were returned intact
b. An analysis of realized gains and losses from the sale of securities during the year
c. An evaluation of the client's internal control concerning physical access to the securities
d. A description of the client's procedures that prevent the negotiation of securities by just one person (6937)

30. Which of the following most likely would indicate the existence of related parties?
a. Writing down obsolete inventory just before year end
b. Failing to correct previously identified internal control structure deficiencies
c. Depending on a single product for the success of the entity
d. Borrowing money at an interest rate significantly below the market rate (2974)

31. Which of the following procedures would an auditor most likely perform in obtaining evidence about subsequent events?
a. Determine that changes in employee pay rates after year-end were properly authorized
b. Recompute depreciation charges for plant assets sold after year-end
c. Investigate changes in long-term debt occurring after year-end
d. Inquire about payroll checks that were recorded before year-end but cashed after year-end (5683)

32. In testing the existence assertion for an asset, an auditor ordinarily works from the
a. Financial statements to the potentially unrecorded items
b. Potentially unrecorded items to the financial statements
c. Accounting records to the supporting evidence
d. Supporting evidence to the accounting records (0136)

33. An auditor suspects that a client's cashier is misappropriating cash receipts for personal use by lapping customer checks received in the mail. In attempting to uncover this embezzlement scheme, the auditor most likely would compare the
a. Dates checks are deposited per bank statements with the dates remittance credits are recorded.
b. Daily cash summaries with the sums of the cash receipts journal entries.
c. Individual bank deposit slips with the details of the monthly bank statements.
d. Dates uncollectible accounts are authorized to be written off with the dates the write-offs are actually recorded. (5975)

34. Under which of the following circumstances would the use of the blank form of confirmations of accounts receivable most likely be preferable to positive confirmations?
a. The recipients are likely to sign the confirmations without devoting proper attention to them.
b. Subsequent cash receipts are unusually difficult to verify.
c. Analytical procedures indicate that few exceptions are expected.
d. The combined assessed level of inherent risk and control risk is low. (6714)

35. Which of the following strategies most likely could improve the response rate of the confirmation of accounts receivable?
a. Including a list of items or invoices that constitute the account balance
b. Restricting the selection of accounts to be confirmed to those customers with relatively large balances
c. Requesting customers to respond to the confirmation requests directly to the auditor by fax or e-mail
d. Notifying the recipients that second requests will be mailed if they fail to respond in a timely manner (6936)

36. To gain assurance that all inventory items in a client's inventory listing schedule are valid, an auditor most likely would trace
a. Inventory tags noted during the auditor's observation to items listed in the inventory listing schedule
b. Inventory tags noted during the auditor's observation to items listed in receiving reports and vendors' invoices
c. Items listed in the inventory listing schedule to inventory tags and the auditor's recorded count sheets
d. Items listed in receiving reports and vendors' invoices to the inventory listing schedule (5671)

37. An auditor vouched data for a sample of employees in a payroll register to approved clock card data to provide assurance that
a. Payments to employees are computed at authorized rates.
b. Employees work the number of hours for which they are paid.
c. Segregation of duties exists between the preparation and distribution of the payroll.
d. Internal controls relating to unclaimed payroll checks are operating effectively. (5655)

38. In confirming a client's accounts receivable in prior years, an auditor found that there were many differences between the recorded account balances and the confirmation replies. These differences, which were not misstatements, required substantial time to resolve. In defining the sampling unit for the current year's audit, the auditor most likely would choose
a. Individual overdue balances
b. Individual invoices
c. Small account balances
d. Large account balances (5667)

39. In statistical sampling methods used in substantive testing, an auditor most likely would stratify a population into meaningful groups if
a. Probability proportional to size (PPS) sampling is used.
b. The population has highly variable recorded amounts.
c. The auditor's estimated tolerable misstatement is extremely small.
d. The standard deviation of recorded amounts is relatively small. (5668)

40. For which of the following audit tests would an auditor most likely use attribute sampling?
a. Selecting accounts receivable for confirmation of account balances
b. Inspecting employee time cards for proper approval by supervisors
c. Making an independent estimate of the amount of a LIFO inventory
d. Examining invoices in support of the valuation of fixed asset additions (6236)

41. Which of the following most likely represents a significant deficiency in internal control?
a. The systems programmer designs systems for computerized applications and maintains output controls.
b. The systems analyst reviews applications of data processing and maintains systems documentation.
c. The control clerk establishes control over data received by the IT department and reconciles control totals after processing.
d. The accounts payable clerk prepares data for computer processing and enters the data into the computer. (2304)

42. An auditor who wishes to capture an entity's data as transactions are processed and continuously test the entity's computerized information system most likely would use which of the following techniques?
a. Snapshot application
b. Embedded audit module
c. Integrated data check
d. Test data generator (7030)

43. The following explanatory paragraph was included in an auditor's report to indicate a lack of consistency:

"As discussed in note T to the financial statements, the company changed its method of accounting for long-term contracts in Year 2."

How should the auditor report on this matter if the auditor concurred with the change?

	Type of opinion	Location of explanatory paragraph
a.	Unqualified	Before opinion paragraph
b.	Unqualified	After opinion paragraph
c.	Qualified	Before opinion paragraph
d.	Qualified	After opinion paragraph

(2286)

44. For which of the following events would an auditor issue a report that omits any reference to consistency?
a. A change in the method of accounting for inventories
b. A change from an accounting principle that is not generally accepted to one that is generally accepted
c. A change in the useful life used to calculate the provision for depreciation expense
d. Management's lack of reasonable justification for a change in accounting principle (6367)

45. Zero Corp. suffered a loss that would have a material effect on its financial statements on an uncollectible trade account receivable due to a customer's bankruptcy. This occurred suddenly due to a natural disaster ten days after Zero's balance sheet date, but one month before the issuance of the financial statements and the auditor's report. Under these circumstances,

	The financial statements should be adjusted	The event requires financial statement disclosure, but no adjustment	The auditor's report should be modified for a lack of consistency
a.	Yes	No	No
b.	Yes	No	Yes
c.	No	Yes	Yes
d.	No	Yes	No

(4718)

46. Which of the following events occurring after the issuance of an auditor's report most likely would cause the auditor to make further inquiries about the previously issued financial statements?
a. An uninsured natural disaster occurs that may affect the entity's ability to continue as a going concern.
b. A contingency is resolved that had been disclosed in the audited financial statements.
c. New information is discovered concerning undisclosed lease transactions of the audited period.
d. A subsidiary is sold that accounts for 25% of the entity's consolidated net income. (6032)

47. After considering an entity's negative trends and financial difficulties, an auditor has substantial doubt about the entity's ability to continue as a going concern. The auditor's considerations relating to management's plans for dealing with the adverse effects of these conditions most likely would include management's plans to
a. Increase current dividend distributions
b. Reduce existing lines of credit
c. Increase ownership equity
d. Purchase assets formerly leased (7026)

48. In which of the following situations would an auditor ordinarily choose between expressing an "except for" qualified opinion or an adverse opinion?
a. The auditor did **not** observe the entity's physical inventory and is unable to become satisfied as to its balance by other auditing procedures.
b. The financial statements fail to disclose information that is required by generally accepted accounting principles.
c. The auditor is asked to report only on the entity's balance sheet and **not** on the other basic financial statements.
d. Events disclosed in the financial statements cause the auditor to have substantial doubt about the entity's ability to continue as a going concern.

(3954)

49. Jewel, CPA, audited Infinite Co.'s prior-year financial statements. These statements are presented with those of the current year for comparative purposes without Jewel's auditor's report, which expressed a qualified opinion. In drafting the current year's auditor's report, Crain, CPA, the successor auditor, should

I. Not name Jewel as the predecessor auditor
II. Indicate the type of report issued by Jewel
III. Indicate the substantive reasons for Jewel's qualification

a. I only
b. I and II only
c. II and III only
d. I, II, and III

(6023)

50. When auditing an entity's financial statements in accordance with *Government Auditing Standards* (the "Yellow Book"), an auditor is required to report on

I. Recommendations for actions to improve operations
II. The scope of the auditor's tests of compliance with laws and regulations

a. I only
b. II only
c. Both I and II
d. Neither I nor II

(6944)

51. In an audit of internal control over financial reporting conducted in accordance with the standards of the Public Company Accounting Oversight Board (PCAOB), the auditor must communicate in writing to the audit committee
a. Significant deficiencies only
b. Material weaknesses only
c. All deficiencies in internal control over financial reporting
d. Significant deficiencies and material weaknesses

(Editors, 7949)

52. An auditor is engaged to report on selected financial data that are included in a client-prepared document containing audited financial statements. Under these circumstances, the report on the selected data should
a. Be limited to data derived from the audited financial statements
b. Be distributed only to senior management and the board of directors
c. State that the presentation is a comprehensive basis of accounting other than GAAP
d. Indicate that the data are **not** fairly stated in all material respects

(6034)

53. Which of the following procedures ordinarily should be applied when an independent accountant conducts a review of interim financial information of a nonissuer?
a. Verify changes in key account balances
b. Read the minutes of the board of directors' meeting
c. Inspect the open purchase order file
d. Perform cutoff tests for cash receipts and disbursements

(2985)

54. The financial statements of KCP America, a U.S. entity, are prepared for inclusion in the consolidated financial statements of its non-U.S. parent. These financial statements are prepared in conformity with the accounting principles generally accepted in the parent's country and are for use only in that country. How may KCP America's auditor report on these financial statements?

I. A U.S.-style report (unmodified)
II. A U.S.-style report modified to report on the accounting principles of the parent's country
III. The report form of the parent's country

	I	II	III
a.	Yes	No	No
b.	No	Yes	No
c.	Yes	No	Yes
d.	No	Yes	Yes

(0389)

55. An entity engaged a CPA to determine whether the client's Web sites meet defined criteria for standard business practices and controls over transaction integrity and information protection. In performing this engagement, the CPA should comply with the provisions of
a. Statements on Assurance Standards
b. Statements on Standards for Attestation Engagements
c. Statements on Standards for Management Consulting Services
d. Statements on Auditing Standards   (6819)

56. Which of the following is a conceptual difference between the attestation standards and generally accepted auditing standards?
a. The attestation standards provide a framework for the attest function beyond historical financial statements.
b. The requirement that the practitioner be independent in mental attitude is omitted from the attestation standards.
c. The attestation standards do not permit an attest engagement to be part of a business acquisition study or a feasibility study.
d. None of the standards of fieldwork in generally accepted auditing standards are included in the attestation standards.   (4675)

57. When providing limited assurance that the financial statements of a nonpublic entity require **no** material modifications to be in accordance with generally accepted accounting principles, the accountant should
a. Assess the risk that a material misstatement could occur in a financial statement assertion
b. Confirm with the entity's lawyer that material loss contingencies are disclosed
c. Understand the accounting principles of the industry in which the entity operates
d. Develop audit programs to determine whether the entity's financial statements are fairly presented   (5676)

58. Which of the following procedures is ordinarily performed by an accountant in a compilation engagement of a nonpublic entity?
a. Reading the financial statements to consider whether they are free of obvious mistakes in the application of accounting principles
b. Obtaining written representations from management indicating that the compiled financial statements will **not** be used to obtain credit
c. Making inquiries of management concerning actions taken at meetings of the stockholders and the board of directors
d. Applying analytical procedures designed to corroborate management's assertions that are embodied in the financial statement components   (5693)

59. Which of the following procedures would an accountant **least** likely perform during an engagement to review the financial statements of a nonpublic entity?
a. Observing the safeguards over access to and use of assets and records
b. Comparing the financial statements with anticipated results in budgets and forecasts
c. Inquiring of management about actions taken at the board of directors' meetings
d. Studying the relationships of financial statement elements expected to conform to predictable patterns   (5147)

60. Which of the following statements concerning prospective financial statements is correct?
a. Only a financial forecast would normally be appropriate for limited use.
b. Only a financial projection would normally be appropriate for general use.
c. Any type of prospective financial statement would normally be appropriate for limited use.
d. Any type of prospective financial statement would normally be appropriate for general use.   (0424)

SIMULATIONS

Problem 2 (15 to 25 minutes)

Analytical procedures consist of evaluations of financial information made by a study of plausible relationships among both financial and nonfinancial data. They range from simple comparisons to the use of complex models involving many relationships and elements of data. They involve comparisons of recorded amounts, or ratios developed from recorded amounts, to expectations developed by the auditors.

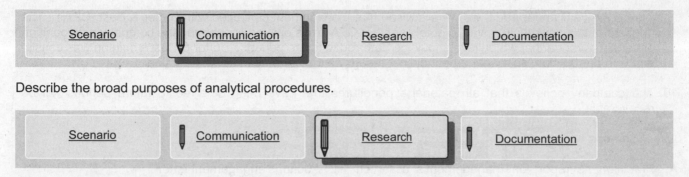

Describe the broad purposes of analytical procedures.

What authoritative reference provides guidance regarding the circumstances in which an auditor does not request the confirmation of accounts receivable during an audit?

Paragraph Reference Answer: _____

For each of the following unrelated statements, questions, excerpts, and comments taken from various parts of an auditor's working paper file, select the most likely source from the list of sources.

1. During our audit we discovered evidence of the company's failure to safeguard inventory from loss, damage, and misappropriation.

2. The company considers the decline in value of equity securities classified as available-for-sale to be temporary.

3. Was the difference of opinion on the accrued pension liabilities that existed between the engagement personnel and the actuarial specialist resolved in accordance with firm policy and appropriately documented?

4. Our audit is designed to provide reasonable assurance of detecting misstatements that, in our judgment, could have a material effect on the financial statements taken as a whole. Consequently, our audit will not necessarily detect all misstatements that exist due to error, fraudulent financial reporting, or misappropriation of assets.

5. There have been no communications from regulatory agencies concerning noncompliance with or deficiencies in financial reporting practices.

6. Nothing came to our attention that caused us to believe that at October 31, Year 1, there was any change in the capital stock, increase in long-term debt, or decrease in consolidated net current assets or stockholders' equity as compared with the amounts shown in the September 30, Year 1 unaudited condensed consolidated balance sheet.

7. It is our opinion that the possible liability to the company in this proceeding is nominal in amount.

8. As discussed in Note 4 to the financial statements, the company experienced a net loss for the year ended July 31, Year 1, and is currently in default under substantially all of its debt agreements. In addition, on September 25, Year 1, the company filed a prenegotiated voluntary petition for relief under Chapter 11 of the U.S. Bankruptcy Code. These matters raise substantial doubt about the company's ability to continue as a going concern.

9. During the year under audit, we were advised that management consulted with Better & Best, CPAs. The purpose of this consultation was to obtain another CPA firm's opinion concerning the company's recognition of certain revenue that we believe should be deferred to future periods. Better & Best's opinion was consistent with our opinion, so management did not recognize the revenue in the current year.

10. The company believes that all material expenditures that have been deferred to future periods will be recoverable.

List of Sources

A. Practitioner's report on management's assertion about an entity's compliance with specified requirements

B. Auditor's communications on significant deficiencies and material weaknesses

C. Audit inquiry letter to legal counsel

D. Lawyer's response to audit inquiry letter

E. Audit committee's communication to the auditor

F. Auditor's communication to the audit committee (other than with respect to significant deficiencies)

G. Report on the application of accounting principles

H. Auditor's engagement letter

I. Letter for underwriters

J. Accounts receivable confirmation request

K. Request for bank cutoff statement

L. Explanatory paragraph of an auditor's report on financial statements

M. Partner's engagement review notes

N. Management representation letter

O. Successor auditor's communication with predecessor auditor

P. Predecessor auditor's communication with successor auditor

(6946)

Problem 3 (20 to 30 minutes)

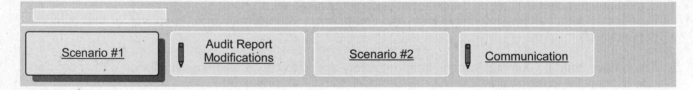

*   The auditor is independent.
*   The auditor previously expressed an unqualified opinion on the prior year's financial statements.
*   Only single-year (not comparative) statements are presented for the current year.
*   The conditions for an unqualified opinion exist unless contradicted in the factual situations.
*   The conditions stated in the factual situations are material.
*   No report modifications are to be made except in response to the factual situation.

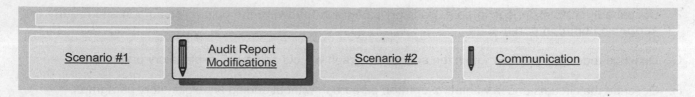

The following items present various independent factual situations an auditor might encounter in conducting an audit. The list represents the report modifications (if any) that would be necessary. For each situation, select one response. Select, as the **best** answer for each item, the action the auditor normally would take.

1. In auditing the long-term investments account, an auditor is unable to obtain audited financial statements for an investee located in a foreign country. The auditor concludes that sufficient appropriate audit evidence regarding this investment cannot be obtained.

2. Due to recurring operating losses and working capital deficiencies, an auditor has substantial doubt about an entity's ability to continue as a going concern for a reasonable period of time. However, the financial statement disclosures concerning these matters are adequate.

3. A principal auditor decides to take responsibility for the work of another CPA who audited a wholly owned subsidiary of the entity and issued an unqualified opinion. The total assets and revenues of the subsidiary represent 17% and 18%, respectively, of the total assets and revenues of the entity being audited.

4. An entity issues financial statements that present financial position and results of operations but omits the related statement of cash flows. Management discloses in the notes to the financial statements that it does not believe the statement of cash flows to be a useful financial statement.

5. An entity changes its method of pricing inventory from LIFO to FIFO. The auditor concurs with the change although it has a material effect on the comparability of the entity's financial statements.

6. An entity is a defendant in a lawsuit alleging infringement of certain patent rights. However, the ultimate outcome of the litigation cannot be reasonably estimated by management. The auditor believes there is a reasonable possibility of a significant material loss, but the lawsuit is adequately disclosed in the notes to the financial statements.

7. An entity discloses in the notes to the financial statements certain lease obligations. The auditor believes that the failure to capitalize these leases is a departure from generally accepted accounting principles.

<u>*Report Modifications*</u>

A. Describe the circumstances in an explanatory paragraph **preceding** the opinion paragraph **without modifying** the three standard paragraphs.

B. Describe the circumstances in an explanatory paragraph **following** the opinion paragraph **without modifying** the three standard paragraphs.

C. Describe the circumstances in an explanatory paragraph **preceding** the opinion paragraph and **modify** the **opinion** paragraph.

D. Describe the circumstances in an explanatory paragraph **following** the opinion paragraph and **modify** the **opinion** paragraph.

E. Describe the circumstances in an explanatory paragraph **preceding** the opinion paragraph and **modify** the **scope** and **opinion** paragraphs.

F. Describe the circumstances in an explanatory paragraph **following** the opinion paragraph and **modify** the **scope** and **opinion** paragraphs.

G. Describe the circumstances within the **scope** paragraph without adding an explanatory paragraph.

H. Describe the circumstances within the **opinion** paragraph without adding an explanatory paragraph.

I. Describe the circumstances within the **scope** and **opinion** paragraphs without adding an explanatory paragraph.

J. Issue the **standard** auditor's report **without modification.**

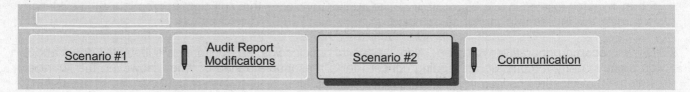

Post, CPA, accepted an engagement to audit the financial statements of General Co., a new client. General is a publicly held retailing entity that recently replaced its operating management. In the course of applying auditing procedures, Post discovered that General's financial statements may be materially misstated due to the existence of fraud.

a. Describe Post's responsibilities for reporting on General's financial statements and other communications if Post concludes that General's financial statements are materially affected by fraud.

b. Describe the circumstances in which Post may have a duty to disclose fraud to third parties outside General's management and its audit committee.

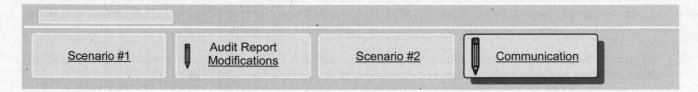

What authoritative reference provides guidance on an engagement to report on only one basic financial statement, but not the others, although the auditor's access to information and application of procedures is not limited in scope?

Paragraph Reference Answer: _____   (6719)

ANSWERS TO MULTIPLE-CHOICE QUESTIONS

The editors strongly recommend that candidates **not** spend much time on the answers to specific questions that they answered incorrectly on the diagnostic exam, particularly at the beginning of their review. Instead, study the related chapter. After studying the related chapter(s), question-specific explanations will make more sense.

1. (d) The third general standard states, "The auditor must exercise due professional care in the performance of the audit and the preparation of the report." The exercise of due care requires critical review at every level of supervision of the work done and the judgment exercised by those assisting in the audit. Safeguards over assets and records and review of indications of fraud and illegal acts are internal control issues specific to one audit. Objective review of the adequacy of the training and proficiency of personnel is a quality control issue. (5641)

2. (d) A successor should ask about *disagreements with management as* to accounting principles, *auditing procedures*, or other significant matters. Other matters subject to inquiry should include information that might bear on the integrity of management; the predecessor's communications to those charged with governance regarding fraud and illegal acts by the client; the predecessor's communications to management and those charged with governance regarding significant deficiencies and material weaknesses in internal control; and the predecessor's understanding of the reasons for the change in auditors. The auditor would use other sources for learning specialized accounting principles of the client's industry and the inherent uncertainty in applying sampling procedures. The competency of the client's internal audit staff should be an evaluation made by the current auditor. (5620)

3. (a) The evaluation of personnel advancement provides evidence of adherence to the human resources element of a firm's quality control system. (7486)

4. (c) In the planning phase of an audit a CPA most likely would coordinate with client personnel, requiring a discussion of the timing of audit procedures, such as a physical count of inventory. An auditor would identify specific internal control activities that are likely to prevent fraud during the review of internal control or when fraud factors are discovered. An auditor would evaluate the reasonableness of a client's accounting estimates and inquire of a client's attorney regarding unrecorded claims when collecting evidence. (7798)

5. (d) Of the procedures listed, an auditor is most likely to determine the extent of involvement of the client's internal auditors in the initial planning of a financial statement audit. A written representation letter from the client's management is obtained at the end of an audit, not the beginning. Examining documents and considering the reasonableness of estimates are procedures that are done during the audit. (5074)

6. (a) Detection risk relates to the substantive audit procedures and is managed by the auditor's response to risk of material misstatement. For a given level of audit risk, detection risk should bear an inverse relationship to the risk of material misstatement at the relevant assertion level. The greater the risk of material misstatement, the less the detection risk that an be accepted by the auditor. Conversely, the lower the risk of material misstatement, the greater the detection risk that can be accepted by the auditor. However, the auditor should perform substantive procedures for all relevant assertions related to material classes of transactions, account balances, and disclosures. The risk of misapplying audit procedures is a part of detection risk. The acceptable level of detection risk is unrelated to the preliminary judgment about materiality levels. The risk of failing to discover material misstatements during an audit is detection risk. (0044)

7. (b) The purpose of applying analytical procedures in planning the audit is to assist in planning the nature, timing, and extent of auditing procedures that will be used to obtain audit evidence for specific account balances or classes of transactions. Inquiry of the client's legal counsel is an audit procedure that would be performed near the end of the audit engagement. Answer (c) is a substantive audit procedure that would be performed later in the audit engagement to support management's assertion of completeness. The auditor determines whether controls have been placed in operation, i.e., whether the entity is using the control, as part of the understanding of internal control necessary to plan the audit. Answer (d) is an example of testing the operating *effectiveness* of a control. Whether a control has been placed in operation at a point in time is different from its operating *effectiveness* over a period of time. The auditor evaluates the operating *effectiveness* of controls as part of assessing control risk. (5622)

8. (b) Large cash payments are unusual in normal, legal business practice. Cash transactions have the attribute of anonymity, which is useful for hiding illegal acts. Properly disclosed related party

transactions and contributions to several local candidates, in and of themselves, do not suggest the occurrence of illegal acts. Internal control procedures are subject to cost/benefit constraints. An entity may appropriately decide that a major weakness is too costly to alleviate. (6576)

9. (b) SAS 108 states, "An understanding with the client regarding an audit of the financial statements generally includes the following matters...The auditor is responsible for conducting the audit in accordance with generally accepted auditing standards. Those standards require that the auditor obtain reasonable rather than absolute assurance about whether the financial statements are free of material misstatement, whether caused by error or fraud. Accordingly, a material misstatement may remain undetected. Also, an audit is not designed to detect error or fraud that is immaterial to the financial statements. If, for any reason, the auditor is unable to complete the audit or is unable to form or has not formed an opinion, he or she may decline to express an opinion or decline to issue a report as a result of the engagement...These matters should be communicated in the form of an engagement letter." A comfort letter is provided to an underwriter by an auditor; typically an auditor informs the client of fraud, not the underwriter. A letter of audit inquiry is sent to a third party such as a vendor, customer, or attorney; typically an auditor informs the client of fraud, not third parties such as these. A representation letter is addressed by management to the auditor; management is unlikely to use the phrase "our audit." (7634)

10. (a) While incompatible duties can be segregated and therefore controlled, the possibility of management override and collusion among employees to circumvent controls will still exist. Mistakes in judgment also cannot be controlled. (4687)

11. (b) Concerns about the integrity of the entity's management may be so serious as to cause the auditor to conclude that the risk of management misrepresentation in the financial statements is such that an audit cannot be conducted. Answers (a), (c), and (d) should be considered by the auditor but are not necessarily serious enough to raise an auditability question. (5953)

12. (b) Audit evidence is more reliable when it is obtained directly by the auditor rather than evidence obtained indirectly or by inference (SAS 106). Performing tests of transactions tests segregation of duties from the past which may not be operating currently. A flowchart reflects the ideal operating conditions of the company, established at a point in time, which may not be representative of the actual processing procedures being performed. Audit objectives cannot in themselves reduce control risk. (3906)

13. (c) The most effective control in offsetting the tendency of sales personnel to maximize sales volume at the expense of high bad debt write-offs would be the segregation of duties of those employees involved in credit-granting and sales functions. If this segregation exists, credit-granting employees should help to screen out those potential customers likely to result in high bad-debt write-offs. (2798)

14. (a) Assertions about completeness are tested by testing whether or not all cash is recorded. If employees consistently use cash registers and tapes, it is likely that all cash is recorded. Inquiry about employees' access to undeposited recorded cash, comparing the cash receipts journal to the general ledger, and comparing the cash balance in the general ledger with the bank confirmation request, test assertions about only *recorded* cash. (6578)

15. (d) The agreement of the documents will verify that the goods were ordered (purchase order), received (receiving report), and the company has been billed (vendor's invoice). The individual signing the checks, not accounts payable, should stamp, perforate, or otherwise cancel the supporting documentation. The purchasing department, not accounting, is involved with the approval of purchase requisitions and blanking out the quantity ordered on the receiving department copy of the purchase order. (5977)

16. (b) Controlling the access to assets is an important objective of proper inventory control. Answers (a), (c), and (d) are procedures for satisfying inventory control objectives—not actual internal control objectives. (4265)

17. (a) Significant unexplained variances between standard and actual labor cost could cause an auditor to suspect a payroll fraud scheme. Payroll checks disbursed by the same employee each payday (as long as that person has no other payroll responsibilities), employee time cards being approved by individual departmental supervisors, and a separate payroll bank account maintained on an imprest basis are proper internal control procedures. (5997)

18. (a) Of the choices given, the strongest internal control in safeguarding against the loss of marketable securities would be the use of an independent trust company that has no direct contact with the employees who have record keeping responsibilities. The fact that only the trust company has access to the securities should prevent unauthorized entity personnel with record keeping responsibility

from conspiring or colluding to misappropriate securities. In determining appropriate controls in safeguarding an asset against loss, the auditor would start with those controls involving access to the asset in question. Neither verifying the securities in the safe nor tracing all purchases and sales provides evidence as to who has access to, or custody of, the marketable securities. Allowing just one person access to an asset enables the individual to take the asset without being discovered. (2956)

19. (d) Concerns about the integrity of the entity's management may be so serious as to cause the auditor to conclude that the risk of management misrepresentations in the financial statements is such that an audit cannot be conducted. Answers (a), (b), and (c) may be considerations, but are not necessarily so serious as to cause an auditor to question whether the entity can be audited. (7099)

20. (d) According to SAS 106, "Audit evidence that is generated internally is more reliable when the related controls imposed by the entity are effective." Information obtained directly, not indirectly, from outside sources would provide the most reliable evidence. SAS 106 states, "the auditor may find it necessary to rely on audit evidence that is persuasive rather than conclusive." The reliability of audit evidence refers to its source and nature and is dependent on the individual circumstances under which it is obtained. (5120)

21. (d) Permanent files contain items of continuing interest, such as debt agreements, internal control flowcharts, and articles of incorporation. The other items are of temporary interest only. (6007)

22. (d) Evidence that a deviation was covered up in a fraudulent manner would require the auditor to consider the implications of the deviation more closely. Answers (a), (b), and (c) give no causes for added concern. (5973)

23. (d) In performing an audit, the auditor may request direct assistance from the internal auditors including assistance in obtaining an understanding of internal control or in performing tests of controls or substantive tests. (5678)

24. (a) Management's representations may be limited to matters that are considered material. Materiality limitations would not apply to those representations that are not directly related to amounts included in the financial statements, such as the availability of minutes of stockholders' and directors' meetings. Answers (b), (c), and (d) relate directly to amounts in the financial statements and thus materiality limits would apply. (5684)

25. (a) The objective of the procedures is to identify such things as the existence of unusual transactions and events. Answers (b), (c), and (d) would not necessarily be discovered in the performance of analytics, but more likely would be discovered during substantive tests. (4670)

26. (d) The overall review of the audit is concerned with the big picture. The other answer options are analytical procedures that likely are performed during earlier stages, or not at all. (6366)

27. (d) Increased sales to comparable customers would double accounts receivable (A/R) without a change in the allowance for doubtful accounts as a percentage of A/R. The client should increase this percentage if it has more customers with poor credit ratings. With no other changes, if twice as many A/R were written off previously or if more A/R are old, it suggests the current write-offs are inadequate. (7623)

28. (b) The letter of inquiry to the client's attorney is the primary means the auditor has to obtain corroboration of information furnished by management concerning litigation, claims, and assessments. The terms mentioned in answers (a) and (c) might be covered by the attorney, but are not the primary reasons the auditor makes the request. The items in answer (d) normally are furnished by management (or management may request that the attorney prepare the description and evaluation); they are not the primary reason that the auditor sends a letter of inquiry. (5139)

29. (a) A physical count of assets that could be stolen readily (negotiable securities or gems, for instance) should include acknowledgement that the assets are again in the client's custody, if they are handled by the auditor. Sold securities would not be counted, so an analysis of realized gains and losses is not related closely to a count. An evaluation of control policies concerning physical access or negotiation generally would be documented with other control evaluations, not with substantive tests. (6937)

30. (d) Transactions that because of their nature may be indicative of the existence of related parties include: (a) Borrowing or lending on an interest-free basis or at a rate of interest significantly above or below market rates prevailing at the time of the transaction; (b) selling real estate at a price that differs significantly from its appraised value; (c) exchanging property for similar property in a nonmonetary transaction; (d) making loans with no scheduled terms for when or how the funds will be repaid. (2974)

31. (c) The auditor should perform other auditing procedures with respect to the period after the balance sheet date for the purpose of ascertaining the occurrence of subsequent *events* that may require adjustment or disclosure including investigating changes in long-term debt after year-end. Other procedures are applied to transactions occurring after the balance sheet date for the purpose of assurance that proper cutoffs have been made, and for the purpose of obtaining information to aid in the evaluation of the assets and liabilities as of the balance sheet date. Answers (a), (b), and (d) would not provide evidence about subsequent events as (a) is a test of controls and (b) and (d) are not common procedures. (5683)

32. (c) In testing the existence assertion for an asset, the auditor would start with the accounting records themselves to determine that the assets recorded on the client's books do exist. Further evidence of the asset existence would then be found in the supporting evidence. (0136)

33. (a) Lapping involves the theft of one customer's payment and subsequently crediting the customer with payment made by another customer. Future remittances may be deposited but would be credited to the account from which funds were stolen, thus comparison of remittance dates would detect the scheme. Answers (b), (c), and (d) occur after the theft and would not show differences to pursue. (5975)

34. (a) Blank A/R confirmations request that the customers supply the amount owed, if any. By having the customers provide the information, the auditor increases the likelihood that customers did examine their records. Positive confirmations have the amount that the customers owe provided by the client, typically invoice-by-invoice. The invoice-by-invoice form simplifies verifying subsequent cash receipts as compared to a single sum owed. Negative confirmations request the customer to return the confirmation, with corrections, only if their records differ. They usually are used if the combined assessed level of inherent risk and control risk is low, i.e., if few exceptions are expected. (6714)

35. (a) Providing additional information may make the task of confirming debts appear easier to the client's customers' employees, resulting in a response getting prepared and approved, rather than indefinitely waiting in a stack for a supervisor to examine and then approve. Customers with large balances may have the worse response rate. The use of fax or e-mail may impact the response time, but probably not the response rate. The threat of a second request will probably have no more positive impact than the first request had, and may annoy the client's customers. (6936)

36. (c) To gain assurance that all items in a client's inventory listing schedule are valid, an auditor most likely would trace items listed in the listing schedule to inventory tags and the auditor's recorded count sheets. To trace the inventory tags to the listing schedule and to trace items listed in receiving reports and vendors' invoices to the listing schedule would provide assurance that all the inventory items are on the schedule, but would not give assurance that all of the items on the schedule are valid; some items on the schedule may not exist. Tracing tags to receiving reports and vendors' invoices does not involve the inventory listing schedule and thus does not provide any assurances related to the listing schedule. (5671)

37. (b) To test for the appropriate number of hours worked, the auditor examines clock card data. To test for answer (a), the auditor checks personnel records. To test for answers (c) and (d), the auditor uses inquiries and observation. (5655)

38. (b) It is easiest to reconcile differences and for customers to research the auditor's questions on an individual invoice level. The designation of a sampling unit depends on the type of applied auditing procedures. The auditor considers which sampling unit leads to the most efficient and effective application, given the circumstances. In the case of a high number of expected differences in amounts for accounts receivable confirmations, if the auditor selects the customer balance as a sampling unit, the auditor may need to test each individual transaction supporting that balance in the event of a contradictory report from the customer. (5667)

39. (b) Stratified sampling can be particularly useful in reducing the overall sample size on populations that have a wide range of dollar values (or highly variable recorded amounts). The primary objective is to decrease the effect of variance in the total population, thereby reducing sample size. PPS sampling insures items with large amounts all make it into the sample, but not by stratifying the population. The estimated tolerable misstatement and standard deviation are irrelevant to a decision to stratify. (5668)

40. (b) In performing tests of controls, the auditor is frequently interested in determining the rate of deviation from prescribed internal control policies and procedures. The sampling plan generally used in this situation is attribute sampling. (6236)

41. (a) A weakness in internal control exists where an individual is in a position to both perpetrate and conceal an error or fraud. Hence, a systems programmer should not be given any control over the review or distribution of the output of the IT system. (2304)

42. (b) Embedded audit modules are coded into a client's application to collect data for the auditor. Integrated data checks and test data generators involve auditor-controlled fictitious data. Snapshot applications capture screen images. (7030)

43. (b) If there has been a change in accounting principles or in the method of their application that has a material effect on the comparability of the company's financial statements, the auditor should refer to the change in an explanatory paragraph of her/his report. Such explanatory paragraph (following the opinion paragraph) should identify the nature of the change and refer the reader to the note in the financial statements that discusses the change in detail. (2286)

44. (c) Consistency is only mentioned when it is absent in the financial statements. A change in the useful life used to calculate the provision for depreciation expense is merely a change in estimate and does not require comment by the auditor. The other three answer options would require a comment that the financial statements were not consistent with the prior period. (6367)

45. (d) The second type of subsequent event, including losses on receivables resulting from conditions arising subsequent to the balance sheet date, provides evidence with respect to conditions that did not exist at the balance sheet date, but arose subsequently. These events should not result in adjustment of the financial statements. Some, however, may be of such a nature that disclosure is required to keep the financial statements from being misleading. Consistency is implied in the auditor's report, and a subsequent event does not give rise to a report modification for consistency. (4718)

46. (c) When the auditor becomes aware of information which relates to financial statements previously reported on not known at the date of her/his report, s/he should follow up on the information. Answers (a), (b), and (d) do not fit this requirement. (6032)

47. (c) In this situation, an auditor's consideration of management's plans may include plans to dispose of assets, restructure debt, reduce expenditures, and increase ownership equity. (7026)

48. (b) When financial statements are materially affected by a departure from GAAP and the auditor has audited the statements in accordance with generally accepted auditing standards, s/he should express a qualified opinion. In deciding whether the effects of a departure from GAAP are sufficiently material to require either a qualified or adverse opinion, one factor to be considered is the dollar magnitude of such effects. Answer (a) represents a scope limitation which would result in a disclaimer of opinion. Answer (c) is an example of an "except for" qualified opinion, but not an adverse opinion. Answer (d) is an example of a situation where an explanatory paragraph would be added to an unqualified opinion. (3954)

49. (d) If the financial statements of a prior period have been audited by a predecessor auditor whose report is not presented, the successor auditor should indicate in the introductory paragraph of her/his report (a) that the financial statements of the prior period were audited by another auditor, (b) the date of her/his report, (c) the type of report issued by the predecessor auditor, and (d) if the report was other than a standard report, the substantive reasons therefore. (6023)

50. (b) In an audit in accordance with GAS, an auditor is required to report on the auditor's test of the entity's compliance with applicable laws and regulations. Among the basic elements of such a report is a statement that the standards require that the auditor plan and perform the audit to obtain reasonable assurance about whether the financial statements are free of material misstatement. Recommendations for actions to improve operations are a side-benefit of an audit and are not required. (6944)

51. (d) The auditor must communicate, in writing, to the audit committee, all significant deficiencies and material weaknesses identified during the audit. (7949)

52. (a) An auditor's report on information accompanying the basic financial statements (BFS) should include either an opinion on whether the accompanying information is fairly stated in all material respects in relation to the BFS taken as a whole or a disclaimer of opinion. The report should be limited to data that are derived from financial statements audited by that auditor. There is no restriction on the distribution. The basis of accounting is not necessarily other than GAAP. The data generally are indicated as fairly stated in all material respects. (6034)

53. (b) The procedures for a review of interim financial information include reading the minutes of

meetings of stockholders, board of directors, and committees of the board of directors to identify actions that may affect the interim financial information. Answers (a), (c), and (d) are not among the procedures normally applied in a review of interim financial information. (2985)

54. (d) If financial statements prepared in conformity with accounting principles generally accepted in another country are prepared for use *only* outside the United States, the auditor may report using either (1) a U.S.-style report modified to report on the accounting principles of another country, or (2) if appropriate, the report form of the other country. An unmodified U.S.-style report would be inappropriate in this situation. (0389)

55. (b) Attestation engagements involve the expression of a written report on an assertion by another party. Statements on Auditing Standards apply to financial statement audits of nonissuers. The other two alternatives do not exist. (6819)

56. (a) An attest engagement may be part of a larger engagement, such as a feasibility study, that includes an examination of prospective financial information. Answer (b) represents the fourth general standard for attestations. The two attestation fieldwork standards are the same as the first and third standards of fieldwork for audits. (4675)

57. (c) In a review of financial statements, where the CPA expresses limited assurance that the financial statements do not contain material deviations from GAAP, the accountant is required to obtain a knowledge of the accounting principles and practices of the industry in which the entity operates. This is required so that the CPA can determine and apply proper inquiry and analytics. The CPA does not need to apply the procedures listed in the other answers for a review. (5676)

58. (a) Before submission, the accountant should read the compiled financial statements and consider whether such financial statements appear to be appropriate in form and free from obvious material errors. In this context, the term *error* refers to mistakes in the compilation of financial statements, including arithmetical or clerical mistakes, and mistakes in the application of accounting principles, including inadequate disclosure. A representation letter from members of management usually is not obtained in a compilation engagement. Inquiries of management concerning actions taken at meetings of the stockholders and the board of directors is a procedure normally used in a review engagement, and is not necessary in a compilation engagement. The accountant is not required to make inquiries or perform other procedures to verify, corroborate, or review information supplied by the entity. (5693)

59. (a) Procedures for conducting a review of financial statements generally are limited to analytical procedures and inquiries. The practitioner does not need to observe internal controls. (5147)

60. (c) Any type of prospective financial statements that would be useful in the circumstances would normally be appropriate for limited use. Thus, the presentation may be a financial forecast or a financial projection. Only the financial forecast is appropriate for general use. (0424)

SIMULATION SOLUTIONS

Solution 2

Response #1: Communication (3 points)

Analytical procedures are used for these broad purposes:

- To assist the auditor in **planning the nature, timing, and extent** of other auditing procedures.
- As a **substantive test** to obtain **audit evidence** about particular **assertions** related to account balances or classes of transactions.
- As an **overall review** of the financial information in the final review stage of the audit.

Response #2: Research (1 point)

Paragraph Reference Answer: AU 330.34

Guidance: AU 330.34 states, "For the purpose of this section, accounts receivable means (a) The entity's claims against customers that have arisen from the sale of goods or services in the normal course of business, and (b) A financial institution's loans. Confirmation of accounts receivable is a generally accepted auditing procedure. As discussed in paragraph .06, it is generally presumed that evidence obtained from third parties will provide the auditor with higher-quality audit evidence than is typically available from within the entity. Thus, there is a presumption that the auditor will request the confirmation of accounts receivable during an audit unless one of the following is true:

- Accounts receivable are immaterial to the financial statements.
- The use of confirmations would be ineffective.
- The auditor's combined assessed level of inherent and control risk is low, and the assessed level, in conjunction with the evidence expected to be provided by analytical procedures or other substantive tests of details, is sufficient to reduce audit risk to an acceptably low level for the applicable financial statement assertions. In many situations, both confirmation of accounts receivable and other substantive tests of details are necessary to reduce audit risk to an acceptably low level for the applicable financial statement assertions."

Response #3: Documentation (6 points)

1. B

The auditor's communication to the audit committee regarding significant deficiencies and material weaknesses includes a description of the conditions noted.

2. N

Management is a knowledgeable source of the company's viewpoint, beliefs, intentions, and occurrence of events.

3. M

An auditor's review notes include reminders of select conditions to allow a double check to ensure that all matters are resolved appropriately.

4. H

Appropriate places for disclaimers are the engagement letter and post-engagement reports. The statement speaks of the audit in the future ("Consequently, our audit will not…") from the perspective of the auditor.

5. N

See the explanation to #2.

6. I

Letters to underwriters may contain negative assurance, which is used in few instances. A practitioner's report on a management assertion would not be discussing stockholder's equity in relation to previous unaudited financial statements; it would discuss the practitioner's work in relation to management's assertion.

7. D

An opinion regarding liability related to a proceeding is usually from a lawyer in response to an audit inquiry letter. The management representation letter usually has a less specific statement of all possible liabilities being included in the financial statements as appropriate. These are the two parties most likely to be knowledgeable about proceedings related to the client.

8. L

The phrases *substantial doubt* and *ability to continue as a going concern* are required in the auditor's report when there is a going concern uncertainty.

9. F

The auditor's communication to the audit committee should include any disagreements, whether or not resolved, with management about matters that, individually or in the aggregate, could have a significant impact on the financial statements.

10. N

See the explanation to #2.

(6946)

Solution 3

Response #1: Audit Report Modifications (5 points)

1. E

When a qualified opinion results from a limitation on the scope of the audit or an insufficiency of audit evidence, the situation should be described in an explanatory paragraph preceding the opinion paragraph and referred to in both the scope and opinion paragraphs of the auditor's report.

2. B

If, after considering identified conditions and events and management's plans, the auditor concludes that substantial doubt about the entity's ability to continue as a going concern for a reasonable period of time remains, the audit report should include an explanatory paragraph (following the opinion paragraph) to reflect that conclusion. Inadequate disclosure with respect to an entity's ability to continue as a going concern is a departure from GAAP, resulting in either an "except for" qualified opinion or an adverse opinion. In this case, however, because it was concluded that financial statement disclosures were adequate, an unqualified opinion with an explanatory paragraph is appropriate.

3. J

If the auditor decides that it is appropriate for her/him to serve as the principal auditor, s/he must then decide whether to make reference in her/his report to the audit performed by another auditor. If the principal auditor decides to assume responsibility for the work of the other auditor insofar as that work relates to the principal auditor's expression of an opinion taken as a whole, no reference should be made to the other auditor's work or report.

4. C

The auditor is not required to prepare a basic financial statement and include it in her/his report if the company's management declines to present the statement. Accordingly, the auditor should issue an "except for" qualified opinion. The circumstances surrounding the qualification are to be reported in a separate paragraph preceding the opinion paragraph. The opinion paragraph should then be modified using the appropriate "except for" wording, making reference to the separate explanatory paragraph.

5. B

Changes in accounting principle having a material effect on the financial statements require recognition in the independent auditor's report through the addition of an explanatory paragraph (following the opinion paragraph). Such explanatory paragraph should identify the nature of the change and refer the reader to the note in the financial statements that discusses the change in detail.

6. J

Circumstances that may require the auditor to add an explanatory paragraph to a standard report, while not precluding an unqualified opinion, do not include an uncertainty. An emphasis paragraph may be added. However, emphasis paragraphs are never required; they may be added solely at the auditor's discretion.

7. C

The auditor should disclose, in a separate explanatory paragraph preceding the opinion paragraph, all the substantive reasons for a departure from generally accepted accounting principles and that the opinion paragraph should include appropriate qualifying language.

Response #2: Communication (4 points)

a. If Post concludes that General's financial statements **are materially affected** by fraud, Post should insist that the **financial statements be revised** and, if they are not, express a **qualified or** an **adverse** opinion on the financial statements, disclosing all the substantive reasons for such an opinion. Additionally, Post should adequately inform General's audit committee or its board of directors about the fraud.

b. Post may have a duty to disclose fraud to **third parties** outside General's management and its audit committee in the following circumstances:

- When General reports an **auditor change** under the appropriate securities law.
- When a **successor auditor appropriately makes inquiries** of a predecessor auditor.
- When responding to a **subpoena.**
- When **communicating with a funding or other specified agency,** as required for entities that

receive financial assistance from a government agency.

Response #3: Research (1 point)

Paragraph Reference Answer: AU 508.33

Guidance: AU 508.33 states, "*Limited reporting engagements.* The auditor may be asked to report on one basic financial statement and not on the others. For example, he or she may be asked to report on the balance sheet and not on the statements of income, retained earnings or cash flows. These engagements do not involve scope limitations if the auditor's access to information underlying the basic financial statements is not limited and if the auditor applies all the procedures he considers necessary in the circumstances; rather, such engagements involve limited reporting objectives."

(6719)

PERFORMANCE BY TOPICS

Diagnostic exam question numbers corresponding to each chapter of the Auditing & Attestation text are listed below. To assess your preparedness for the CPA exam, record the number and percentage of questions you correctly answered in each topic area. Multiple-choice questions are worth one point. The multiple-choice question point distribution (not counting the simulations) approximates that of the exam.

Chapter 21:
Standards &
Related Topics

Question #	Correct	√
1		
2		
3		
# Questions	3	
# Correct		
% Correct		

Chapter 22: Planning

Question #	Correct	√
4		
5		
6		
7		
8		
9		
# Questions	6	
# Correct		
% Correct		

Chapter 23:
Internal Control

Question #	Correct	√
10		
11		
12		
13		
14		
15		
16		
17		
18		
19		
# Questions	10	
# Correct		
% Correct		

Chapter 24:
Evidence & Procedures

Question #	Correct	√
20		
21		
22		
23		
24		
25		
26		
27		
28		
29		
30		
# Questions	11	
# Correct		
% Correct		

Chapter 25:
Audit Programs

Question #	Correct	√
31		
32		
33		
34		
35		
36		
37		
# Questions	7	
# Correct		
% Correct		

Chapter 26:
Audit Sampling

Question #	Correct	√
38		
39		
40		
# Questions	3	
# Correct		
% Correct		

Chapter 27:
Auditing IT Systems

Question #	Correct	√
41		
42		
# Questions	2	
# Correct		
% Correct		

Chapter 28:
Reports on Audited
Financial Statements

Question #	Correct	√
43		
44		
45		
46		
47		
48		
49		
# Questions	7	
# Correct		
% Correct		

Chapter 29:
Other Auditing Standards

Question #	Correct	√
50		
51		
# Questions	2	
# Correct		
% Correct		

Chapter 30:
Other Types of Reports

Question #	Correct	√
52		
53		
54		
# Questions	3	
# Correct		
% Correct		

Chapter 31: Other
Professional Services

Question #	Correct	√
55		
56		
57		
58		
59		
60		
# Questions	6	
# Correct		
% Correct		

PERFORMANCE BY AICPA CONTENT SPECIFICATIONS OUTLINE

Diagnostic exam question numbers corresponding to each section of the AICPA Auditing and Attestation Content Specifications Outline are listed below. To assess your preparedness for the CPA exam, record the number and percentage of questions you correctly answered in each topic area. To simplify the self-evaluation, the simulations are excluded from the Performance By AICPA Content Specifications Outline. Multiple-choice questions are worth one point. The multiple-choice question point distribution (not counting the simulations) approximates that of the exam.

CSO I: Plan the engagement, evaluate the prospective client and engagement, decide whether to accept or continue the client and the engagement, and enter into an agreement with the client (22%–28%)

Question #	Correct √
1	
2	
3	
4	
5	
6	
7	
9	
11	
19	
22	
23	
25	
30	
55	
56	
# Questions	16
# Correct	
% Correct	

CSO II: Consider internal control in both manual and computerized environments (12%–18%)

Question #	Correct √
10	
12	
13	
14	
15	
16	
17	
18	
41	
# Questions	9
# Correct	
% Correct	

CSO III: Obtain and document information to form a basis for conclusions (32%–38%)

Question #	Correct √
8	
24	
28	
29	
31	
32	
33	
34	
35	
36	
37	
38	
39	
40	
42	
45	
53	
57	
58	
59	
# Questions	20
# Correct	
% Correct	

CSO IV: Review the engagement to provide reasonable assurance that objectives are achieved and evaluate information obtained to reach and to document engagement conclusions (8%–12%)

Question #	Correct √
20	
21	
26	
27	
47	
# Questions	5
# Correct	
% Correct	

CSO V: Prepare communications to satisfy engagement objectives (12%–18%)

Question #	Correct √
43	
44	
46	
48	
49	
50	
51	
52	
54	
60	
# Questions	10
# Correct	
% Correct	

CHAPTER 21

STANDARDS & RELATED TOPICS

CHAPTER 21

STANDARDS & RELATED TOPICS

I. Audit Function Overview

A. Responsibilities

The independent auditor is responsible for performing an audit in accordance with generally accepted auditing standards (GAAS). The objective of the audit is the expression of an opinion as to whether, in all material respects, the financial position, results of operations, and cash flows are presented fairly in conformity with generally accepted accounting principles (GAAP). The auditor's responsibility to express an opinion on the financial statements is stated explicitly in the introductory paragraph of the auditor's report.

1. **Management** Management is responsible for the contents of financial statements, even if the statements are prepared and/or audited by CPAs. Financial statements are management's representations of the effects of transactions and events that have affected the organization's financial position and results of operations. Management is also responsible for establishing and maintaining effective internal control and for developing accounting policies.

2. **Users** Financial statement users should recognize that the accounting process necessitates the use of estimates and evaluations that affect the fairness of the financial statements. They also should understand the meaning and significance of the auditor's report.

B. Audit Function

The auditor independently accumulates and evaluates audit evidence of an economic entity for the purpose of reporting on the degree of correspondence between the information produced and the established criteria (e.g., GAAP).

Exhibit 1 ▶ Comparison of Financial Accounting & Auditing

Note that financial accounting is a **process of aggregation.** *Individual transactions are first recorded in journals; subsequently, the data in journals are classified in ledgers; and finally, the data in ledgers are summarized in the financial statements.*

1. **Vouching** Did the transactions summarized in the financial statements actually occur? The auditor makes this determination by vouching items from the financial statements back to the

accounts and ultimately to the original transaction documents. This is a downward process in Exhibit 1.

2.   **Tracing** Have all transactions that occurred during the period been recorded properly in the accounts and summarized in the financial statements? (Are the financial statements complete?) The auditor makes this determination by tracing items from original transaction documents to the accounts and ultimately to the financial statements. This is an upward process in Exhibit 1.

C.   **Audit Process Steps**

1.   **Establish Understanding With Client** The auditor should establish an understanding with the client regarding the engagement services, including the objectives, scope, and limitations of the engagement, as well as the auditor's and management's responsibilities. The auditor should document the understanding in an engagement letter.

2.   **Obtain Understanding of the Entity & Its Environment, Including Internal Control** The auditor should perform risk assessment procedures to obtain this understanding. The nature, extent, and timing of these procedures depend on the size and complexity of the entity as well as the auditor's previous experience with the entity, if any. This process should include a discussion(s) among the audit team concerning the susceptibility of the financial statements to material misstatements.

3.   **Assess the Risks of Material Misstatement** The auditor will identify and evaluate the risks of material misstatement at the financial statement and *relevant assertion* levels. This will include identifying risks and potential misstatements, as well as considering the materiality and probability of potential misstatements.

     Relevant Assertions In representing that the financial statements are fairly presented in conformity with GAAP, management implicitly or explicitly makes assertions regarding the recognition, measurement, presentation, and disclosure of information in the financial statements and related disclosures. *Relevant assertions* are assertions that have a meaningful bearing on whether an account is fairly stated. For example, valuation may not be relevant to a cash account unless currency translation is involved; however, existence and completeness are always relevant. (For more information about relevant assertions see the section of Chapter 24 on the use of assertions in obtaining audit evidence.)

4.   **Design & Perform Procedures to Address the Risks of Material Misstatement** The auditor uses the knowledge provided by the understanding of the entity and its environment and the assessed risks of material misstatement in determining the nature, extent, and timing of further audit procedures. Further audit procedures include testing the operating effectiveness of controls and substantive procedures. While tests of controls are optional, substantive procedures are required for all relevant assertions related to each material class of transactions, account balance, and disclosure.

5.   **Evaluate Audit Evidence** Based on procedures performed, the auditor analyzes the accumulated audit evidence to determine whether the assessments of the risks of material misstatement at the relevant assertion level are still appropriate. The auditor may need to reevaluate the planned audit procedures to obtain sufficient appropriate audit evidence to support the opinion on the financial statements.

6.   **Form Opinion & Issue Audit Report** The audit report will describe the scope of the audit and state the auditor's conclusion regarding the fairness of the financial statements and related disclosures. Before issuing the audit report, the lead audit partner will perform a final review of the workpapers to ensure that the appropriate type of opinion will be expressed.

Concurring Partner Review For public companies (issuers), there also must be a second, or concurring, partner review. On the basis of this review, the concurring partner reviewer should conclude that no matters have come to her/his attention that would cause the reviewer to believe that the financial statements are not in conformity with GAAP in all material respects or that the firm's audit was not performed in accordance with GAAS.

Editor note: Subject to Securities and Exchange Commission (SEC) approval, the concurring partner review requirement will be superseded by the Public Accounting Oversight Board (PCAOB) Auditing Standard (AS) 7, *Engagement Quality Review* (EQR), adopted by the PCAOB in July 2009. When this volume went to press, AS 7 had not been approved by the SEC. If approved by the SEC, AS 7 will become effective for both the EQRs of audits and interim reviews for fiscal years beginning on or after December 15, 2009. See Chapter 29 of this volume for more information.

D.   **Definitions**

1.   **Financial Statement Audit** This is the audit discussed above and throughout the remainder of the text unless otherwise indicated. Its objective is to express an opinion on the fairness, in all material respects, with which the financial statements present the organization's financial position, results of operations, and cash flows in conformity with GAAP.

2.   **Compliance Audit** The purpose of this type of audit is to evaluate an organization's compliance with a defined set of specifications. Common examples include Internal Revenue Service audits to determine whether a taxpayer has complied with applicable provisions of the Internal Revenue Code; audits of governmental units to verify their compliance with applicable state and federal regulations; and verification audits by a CPA to determine a client's compliance with the provisions of a bond or loan indenture.

3.   **Operational Audit** These audits, usually performed by internal auditors, evaluate the efficiency and effectiveness of some part of an organization in achieving its specific goals in relation to the general goals of an organization. This type of audit involves an evaluation of operating procedures and methods, and usually requires the auditor to issue a report to management recommending ways to improve efficiency and/or effectiveness. A common example would be a review by government auditors to determine the effectiveness and continued utility of specific government-funded programs. This type of audit usually is not concerned with financial information.

4.   **Audit Program (Plan)** This is a detailed list of audit procedures to be performed to satisfy audit objectives. Informally, sometimes this phrase refers to the substantive tests for a particular account or transaction cycle.

5.   **External Auditors** These are independent CPAs who provide a professionally competent evaluation (audit) of the financial statements of a client. Consistent with their external audit and advisory responsibilities, CPAs are certified and licensed by the individual states or territories in which they practice, and many belong to the American Institute of Certified Public Accountants (AICPA). The terms "CPA" and "auditor" frequently are used interchangeably. In this text, unless otherwise indicated, the term "auditor" signifies a CPA who is independent of the client.

Exhibit 2 ▶ Important Characteristics of Audits & Auditors

Independence	Auditors represent neither the financial statement preparers (management) nor the financial statement users (investors, creditors, etc.).
Materiality	An audit is directed toward the discovery of material misstatements or omissions in the financial statements. Materiality involves professional judgment and is influenced by the auditor's perception of the needs of a reasonable person relying on the financial statements. Materiality judgments are made in light of the surrounding circumstances and involve both quantitative and qualitative considerations.
Selective Testing	Auditors base their opinions on selective testing; they rarely examine all of the items in an individual account or in the financial statements.
Audit Risk	Audit risk is a key consideration in an audit. Audit risk is a function of both the risk that the financial statements prepared by management are materially misstated and the risk that the auditor will not detect the misstatement. The auditor should perform the audit to reduce audit risk to a low enough level that is appropriate, in the auditor's judgment, to allow the expression of an opinion on the financial statements or if circumstances require, a disclaimer of an opinion. An auditor's report provides reasonable, not absolute, assurance as to whether the financial statements adhere to the established criteria. This is because audit risk cannot be eliminated due to the nature of audit evidence and the characteristics of fraud.
Overall Opinion	The auditor's opinion relates to the financial statements taken as a whole as stated in the fourth reporting standard. *Taken as a whole* can apply to a complete set of financial statements or to an individual financial statement. (An auditor may express an unqualified opinion on one of the financial statements and a different type of opinion or a disclaimer on another, if warranted.)
Presentation	An audit is concerned with financial statement presentation; it is not concerned with the effectiveness of management, or the advisability of investing in the organization.

6. **Internal Auditors** Internal auditors work full time for the organization or entity. Some internal auditors perform financial statement audits, while others perform compliance or operational audits. Internal auditors are not independent in the same sense as an external auditor, so they cannot issue an audit report for stockholders or other interested outside parties. For an internal audit function to be effective, it is important that it be directed to a level of the organization that is above the level being audited. For example, if the internal auditors report to the audit committee of the board of directors, the internal audit function would be organizationally independent from a particular plant audited by the internal audit staff.

7. **Governmental Auditors** These are auditors who work for the federal, state, or local government. Two of the most commonly mentioned are the following:

   a. **Government Accountability Office (GAO) Auditors** GAO auditors conduct audits for Congress. While they do a considerable number of compliance audits, they also perform an increasing amount of operational-type audit work.

   b. **Internal Revenue Agents** These are auditors who conduct compliance audits for the Internal Revenue Service.

8. **Those Charged With Governance** The term *those charged with governance* refers to the person(s) with responsibility for overseeing the strategic direction of the entity and obligations

related to the accountability of the entity, including overseeing the entity's financial reporting process. This term includes the board of directors and audit committees.

9. **Audit Committees** These are special committees formed by the client's board of directors to assist in oversight responsibilities. In general, responsibilities include monitoring the financial reporting process and related internal controls as well as communicating with internal and external auditors.

II. Generally Accepted Auditing Standards (GAAS)

A. **Codification of Professional Standards**
The AICPA's Codification of Professional Standards is a copyrighted topical codification of Statements on Auditing Standards (SASs) and other standards. The codification abbreviations are used throughout this volume, along with section and paragraph reference numbers. The codification is segregated into broad areas of interest, typically by type of service, as follows:

1. U.S. Auditing Standards [AU]

2. Attestation Standards [AT]

3. Accounting & Review Services [AR]

4. Code of Professional Conduct [ET]

5. Bylaws of the American Institute of Certified Public Accountants [BL]

6. Consulting Services [CS]

7. Quality Control [QC]

8. Peer Review [PR]

9. Tax Services [TS]

10. Personal Financial Planning [PFP]

11. Continuing Professional Education [CPE]

B. **Applicability of Professional Standards**

1. **Issuers** As a result of the passage of the Sarbanes-Oxley Act of 2002 (Act), auditing and related professional practice standards to be used in the performance of and reporting on audits of the financial statements of public companies are now established by the Public Company Accounting Oversight Board (PCAOB) and approved by the Securities and Exchange Commission (SEC). The term *public companies* is a general reference to the entities subject to the securities laws. The Act refers to these companies as *issuers*. (Accordingly, *nonissuers* are those entities not subject to the Act or the rules of the SEC.) The PCAOB adopted, on an initial, transitional basis, the professional standards of auditing, attestation, quality control, ethics, and independence issued by the AICPA that were in existence on April 16, 2003. See Chapter 29 for more information about auditing standards and related rules issued by the PCAOB. There are also references throughout this volume to pertinent differences between standards for nonissuers vs. issuers.

2. **Nonissuers** Nonissuers are those entities not subject to the Act or the rules of the SEC. For audits of nonissuers, the preparation and issuance of audit reports must be conducted in accordance with the AICPA Code of Professional Conduct and the standards promulgated by the AICPA Auditing Standards Board (ASB).

C.   Observations on GAAS (AU 150)
An independent auditor is required to plan, conduct and report the results of an audit in accordance with GAAS. The standards provide measures of quality of the auditor's performance and audit objectives.

Exhibit 3 ▶ Generally Accepted Auditing Standards Mnemonic

T	Training
I	Independence
P	Performance
S	Supervision & planning
E	Entity & its environment
E	Evidence
A	Accounting = U.S. GAAP
C	Consistency
D	Disclosure
E	Expressing an opinion

1.   **Foundation** The concepts of materiality and audit risk underlie the application of GAAS, especially the standards of fieldwork and reporting. Materiality and audit risk need to be considered when determining the nature, extent, and timing of audit procedures to be performed, as well as evaluating the results of those procedures. (See Exhibit 2.)

2.   **Statements on Auditing Standards** SASs are detailed statements issued by the Auditing Standards Board (ASB) of the AICPA. These statements are the primary body of GAAS. Auditing standards are not the same as auditing procedures.

   a.   **Procedures** Procedures relate to the acts to be performed; for example, the confirmation of a predetermined number of accounts receivable. Auditing procedures will vary from engagement to engagement.

   b.   **Standards** Standards provide the objectives that audit procedures are to attain and measures of the quality of procedures to be performed. Auditing standards do not vary from engagement to engagement.

3.   **Professional Requirements (AU 120)** The SASs contain professional requirements along with related guidance. There are two kinds of requirements:

   a.   **Unconditional Requirements** The auditor is required to comply with an unconditional requirement in all cases in which the requirement applies. The words *must* or *is required* indicate an unconditional requirement.

   b.   **Presumptively Mandatory Requirements** The auditor is also required to comply with a presumptively mandatory requirement in all cases in which the requirement applies. However, in rare circumstances, the auditor may depart from such a requirement provided the auditor documents the justification for the departure and how the alternative procedures performed were sufficient to achieve the objectives of that requirement. The word *should* indicates a presumptively mandatory requirement.

D.   General Standards (TIP)
The general standards are personal in nature. They relate to the qualifications of the auditor and the quality of the work performed.

1.   **Technical Training & Proficiency** The auditor must have adequate technical training and proficiency to perform the audit.

2. **Independence** The auditor must maintain independence in mental attitude in all matters relating to the audit.

3. **Due Professional Care** The auditor must exercise due professional care in the performance of the audit and the preparation of the report.

E. **Standards of Fieldwork (SEE)**
Audit documentation should be sufficient to show that the standards of fieldwork have been observed.

1. **Adequate Planning & Supervision** The auditor must adequately plan the work and must properly supervise any assistants.

2. **Understanding the Entity & Its Environment** The auditor must obtain a sufficient understanding of the entity and its environment, including its internal control, to assess the risk of material misstatement of the financial statements whether due to error or fraud, and to design the nature, extent, and timing of further audit procedures.

3. **Sufficient Appropriate Audit Evidence** The auditor must obtain sufficient appropriate audit evidence by performing audit procedures to afford a reasonable basis for an opinion regarding the financial statements under audit.

F. **Standards of Reporting (ACDE)**

1. **Accounting in Conformity With U.S. GAAP** The auditor must state in the auditor's report whether the financial statements are presented in accordance with generally accepted accounting principles (GAAP).

2. **Consistency** The auditor must identify in the auditor's report those circumstances in which such principles have not been consistently observed in the current period in relation to the preceding period.

3. **Adequate Informative Disclosure** When the auditor determines that informative disclosures are not reasonably adequate, the auditor must so state in the auditor's report.

4. **Expression of Opinion** The auditor must either express an opinion regarding the financial statements, taken as a whole, or state that an opinion cannot be expressed, in the auditor's report. When the auditor cannot express an overall opinion, the auditor should state the reasons therefor in the auditor's report. In all cases where an auditor's name is associated with financial statements, the auditor should clearly indicate the character of the auditor's work, if any, and the degree of responsibility the auditor is taking, in the auditor's report.

III. General Standards

A. **Training & Proficiency of the Independent Auditor (AU 210)**
The auditor holds her/himself out as being proficient in accounting and auditing. This requires academic training and professional experience. Training is an ongoing process that includes remaining current with new developments taking place in business and in the accounting profession.

Exhibit 4 ▸ The First General Standard

The auditor must have adequate technical training and proficiency to perform the audit.

B. **Independence (AU 220)**
The attitude implied by independence is that of judicial impartiality or fairness toward clients and others who rely upon the independent auditor's report. The auditor's objective is to ensure that the general public maintains confidence in the independence of the auditor. Independence in attitude also implies the auditor is without bias towards the client. The SEC also has adopted independence

requirements for auditors who report on financial statements filed with it that differ from the AICPA requirements in some respects. The restrictions imposed by the Sarbanes-Oxley Act of 2002 also apply, as discussed in Chapter 29 of this volume.

Exhibit 5 ▶ The Second General Standard

> The auditor must maintain independence in mental attitude in all matters relating to the audit.

1. **Disclose** The auditors of publicly owned companies (issuers) must disclose, in writing, to those charged with governance, all relationships between the auditor and its related entities and the client entity and its related entities that, in the auditor's judgment, may be considered to bear on independence. Auditors of nonissuers may determine, in certain situations, that it is appropriate to communicate this same information.

2. **Confirm** The auditor must confirm in writing that, in the auditor's judgment, it is independent of the client entity according to the federal securities statutes, in conjunction with SEC filings.

3. **Discuss** The auditors of issuers must discuss the auditor's independence with those charged with governance.

C. Due Care in the Performance of Work (AU 230)

Each person within an independent auditor's organization has the responsibility to exercise due care and to adhere to the standards of fieldwork and reporting. This responsibility necessitates critical review by supervisors of the work done and judgment exercised by those assisting in the audit.

Exhibit 6 ▶ The Third General Standard

> The auditor must exercise due professional care in the performance of the audit and the preparation of the report.

1. **Professional Skepticism** Due professional care requires the auditor to exercise professional skepticism. Professional skepticism is an attitude that includes a questioning mind and a critical assessment of audit evidence.

2. **Reasonable Assurance** In exercising due care, the auditor must plan and perform the audit to obtain sufficient appropriate audit evidence so that audit risk will be limited to a low level. The high, but not absolute, level of assurance that is intended to be obtained by the auditor is expressed in the auditor's report as obtaining reasonable assurance about whether the financial statements are free of material misstatement (whether caused by error or fraud).

3. **Fraud** An auditor commits a type of fraud if the auditor alleges possessing the degree of skill commonly possessed by other auditors when the auditor actually does not possess such skill.

4. **Not Infallible** Due care does not guarantee infallibility in either performance or in matters of pure judgment.

IV. Quality Control Standards (QC 10, SQCS 7)

A. Overview

1. **Purpose** This Statement on Quality Control Standards (SQCS) applies to quality control for a CPA firm's accounting and auditing practice. It describes the elements of a quality control system and provides guidance for the design, implementation, and maintenance of the system. A firm must establish a system of quality control to provide the firm with reasonable assurance that the firm and its personnel comply with professional standards and applicable

regulatory and legal requirements and issue appropriate reports. A system of quality control consists of policies and procedures designed to meet these objectives and monitor compliance. The nature and extent of the policies and procedures depend on such factors as a firm's size, the degree of operating autonomy that its personnel are allowed, the nature of its practice, its organization, and appropriate cost-benefit considerations. A U.S. firm should have a system of quality control that provides reasonable assurance that work performed by its foreign offices or by its domestic or foreign affiliates meets U.S. professional standards.

Editor note: SQCS 7 became effective on January 1, 2009. It superseded all SQCS that were in existence on that date.

2. **Relationship of GAAS & SQCS** GAAS relate to the conduct of individual audit engagements. The SQCS relates to the conduct of a CPA firm's accounting and audit practice as a whole which is composed of individual audit and accounting engagements, thus GAAS and this SQCS are related. The SQCS may affect the conduct of individual engagements as well as a firm's practice as a whole. Deficiencies in individual engagements do not, in and of themselves, indicate that a firm's system of quality control is insufficient to provide it with reasonable assurance that its personnel comply with applicable professional standards. And although an effective quality control system is conducive to compliance with GAAS, deficiencies in or noncompliance with a firm's quality control system do not, in and of themselves, indicate that an engagement was not performed in accordance with GAAS.

3. **Definitions**

    a. **Accounting & Auditing Practice** "A practice that performs engagements covered by this section, which are audit, attestation, compilation, review and any other services for which standards have been established by the AICPA Auditing Standards Board or the AICPA Accounting and Review Services Committee under Rules 201 or 202 of the AICPA Code of Professional Conduct (ET sections 201-202). Although standards for other engagements may be established by other AICPA technical committees, engagements performed in accordance with those standards are not encompassed in the definition of an accounting and auditing practice."

    b. **Engagement Documentation** "The record of work performed, results obtained, and conclusions the practitioner reached, also known as working papers or workpapers."

    c. **Engagement Partner** "An individual responsible for supervising engagements covered by this section and signing or authorizing an individual to sign the report on such engagements, and who, where required, has the appropriate authority from a professional, legal or regulatory body. Firms may use different titles to refer to individuals with this authority."

    d. **Engagement Quality Control Review** "A process designed to provide an objective evaluation, by an individual or individuals who are not members of the engagement team, of the significant judgments the engagement team made and the conclusions they reached in formulating the report."

    e. **Engagement Quality Control Reviewer** "A partner, other person in the firm, qualified external person, or a team made up of such individuals, none of whom is part of the engagement team, with sufficient and appropriate experience and authority to perform the engagement quality control review."

    f. **Engagement Team** "All personnel performing the engagement, excluding those who perform the engagement quality control review. The engagement team (i) includes all employees and contractors retained by the firm who perform engagement procedures, irrespective of their functional classification (for example, audit, tax, or management consulting services) and (ii) excludes specialists as discussed in AU section 336,

Using the Work of a Specialist, and individuals who perform only routine clerical functions, such as word processing and photocopying."

g.   **Firm** "A form of organization permitted by law or regulation whose characteristics conform to resolutions of the Council of the American Institute of Certified Public Accountants that is engaged in the practice of public accounting."

h.   **Inspection** "A retrospective evaluation of the adequacy of the firm's quality control policies and procedures, its personnel's understanding of those policies and procedures and the extent of the firm's compliance with them. Inspection is an element of monitoring."

i.   **Monitoring** "A process comprising an ongoing consideration and evaluation of the firm's system of quality control, the objective of which is to enable the firm to obtain reasonable assurance that its system of quality control is designed appropriately and operating effectively."

j.   **Partner** "An individual with authority to bind the firm with respect to the performance of a professional services engagement. For purposes of this definition, partner may include an employee with this authority who has not assumed the risks and benefits of ownership. Firms may use different titles to refer to individuals with this authority."

k.   **Personnel** "All individuals who perform professional services for which the firm is responsible, whether or not they are CPAs."

l.   **Professional Requirements** The SQCS uses two categories of professional requirements, identified by specific terms, to describe the degree of responsibility they impose on firms—*unconditional requirements* and *presumptively mandatory requirements*—which are defined in a fashion similar to the same terms in AU 120.

m.   **Professional Standards** "Standards established by the AICPA Auditing Standards Board or the AICPA Accounting and Review Services Committee under Rules 201 or 202 of the AICPA Code of Professional Conduct or other standard setting bodies that set auditing and attest standards applicable to the engagement being performed."

n.   **Qualified External Person** "An individual outside the firm with the capabilities and competence to act as an engagement partner."

o.   **Reasonable Assurance** The SQCS defines reasonable assurance in a fashion similar to AU 230, i.e., a high, but not absolute level of assurance.

p.   **Relevant Ethical Requirements** "Ethical requirements to which the firm and its personnel are subject, which consist of the AICPA Code of Professional Conduct together with rules of state boards of accountancy and applicable regulatory agencies, which may be more restrictive."

q.   **Staff** "Personnel, other than partners and engagement partners, including any specialists who are employees of the firm."

4.   **Communication of Polices & Procedures** Although communication is enhanced if in writing, it is not required. In addition to the policies and procedures of the quality control system, the objectives they are designed to achieve should also be communicated. Feedback from personnel should be encouraged.

5.   **Documentation of Policies & Procedures** Quality control policies and procedures should be documented. The extent of the documentation depends on the size, structure and nature of the firm's practice. Usually, it would be expected that a large firm would have more

documentation than a small firm and that a multi-office firm's documentation would be more extensive than that of a single-office firm.

B.   Elements of a Quality Control System
Each of the following interrelated elements should be included in quality control policies and procedures: leadership responsibilities for quality within the firm; relevant ethical requirements; acceptance & continuance of client relationships & specific engagements; human resources; engagement performance; and monitoring.

1.   **Leadership Responsibilities** A firm's quality control policies and procedures should require that a firm's leadership assume ultimate responsibility for the quality control system. Additionally, the person(s) assigned operational responsibility for quality control should be qualified and given the necessary authority. The policies and procedures should support a culture within the firm that recognizes that quality is essential and this should be reflected in the firm's business strategy. The standard refers to this as the *tone at the top.* Accordingly, these policies should be established:

a.   Management responsibilities should be assigned so that commercial considerations do not override the quality of work performed.

b.   Performance evaluations, compensation (including incentives), and advancement of personnel should be geared to demonstrate the firm's commitment to the objectives of the quality control system.

c.   Sufficient and appropriate resources should be devoted to the development, communication, and support of its quality control procedures.

2.   **Relevant Ethical Requirements** Policies and procedures should be designed to obtain reasonable assurance that the firm and its personnel comply with relevant ethical requirements.

a.   **Fundamental Principles** The AICPA Code of Professional Conduct establishes these fundamental principles of professional ethics: responsibilities; the public interest; integrity; objectivity and independence; due care; scope and nature of services.

b.   **Independence**

(1)   **Objectives** The objectives of a firm's policies and procedures on independence should be:

(a)   Communication of the firm's independence requirements to its personnel and, as needed, to others

(b)   The identification and evaluation of circumstances and relationships that put independence at risk and the elimination of those risks with safeguards, if possible, and if not, withdrawal from the engagement

(2)   **Policies & Procedures** The firm's policies and procedures on independence and objectivity and should include processes in place or requirements that:

(a)   It is notified of any breaches of independence

(b)   Any regulatory requirements for rotation of personnel are met

(c)   At least annually, a firm should obtain written confirmation of compliance with its policies and procedures on independence from all personnel.

3.   **Acceptance & Continuance of Clients & Engagements**

a.   **Requirements** A firm should accept and continue relationships and engagements only when it

      (1) Has considered the integrity of the client and the risks associated with providing services in the particular circumstances. Factors to consider include the nature of the client's operations, including its business practices and the attitude of the client's management and those charged with governance about internal control or such matters as the aggressive interpretation of accounting standards

      (2) Is competent to perform the engagement and has the capabilities and resources to do so

      (3) Can comply with legal and ethical requirements

  b. **Understanding With the Client** An understanding (oral or written per the requirements of other professional standards) with the client about the nature, scope, and limitations of the services to be provided should be obtained to minimize the risk of misunderstandings.

  c. **Documentation** The resolution of significant issues that arise should be documented.

4. **Human Resources** A firm needs to have personnel who can accomplish the objectives of a system of quality control, i.e., perform its engagements in accordance with professional standards and regulatory and legal requirements, and issue appropriate reports. Accordingly, human resources policies and procedures should address: recruitment and hiring; determining capabilities and competencies; assigning personnel to engagements; professional development; and performance evaluation, compensation and advancement.

  a. **Recruitment & Hiring** Processes should be in place that enable a firm to select individuals of integrity who have the competencies to perform the firm's work and the capacity for further development.

  b. **Determining Capabilities & Competencies** Capabilities and competencies are measured in qualitative rather than quantitative terms and can be developed via a variety of methods.

      (1) **Engagement Partner** Polices and procedures should provide reasonable assurance that the firm's engagement partners have the competencies needed to fulfill their responsibilities. Usually these competencies will be gained by experience in the types of engagements covered by this standard (in the practice of public accounting), but they can also be gained from other types of relevant experience. If needed, the experience of an engagement partner can be supplemented by continuing professional education and consultation. The competency requirements are broad, varied and interrelated. They include:

         (a) Understanding of the role of a system of quality control and the Code of Professional Conduct

         (b) Understanding of the service to be performed

         (c) Technical proficiency

         (d) Familiarity with the industry

         (e) Professional judgment

         (f) Understanding the organization's information technology systems

      (2) **Uniform Accountancy Act** A firm's compliance with this standard is intended to meet the competency requirements of the Uniform Accountancy Act (UAA). CPAs are required to meet the legal requirements of the applicable licensing jurisdiction governing public accounting, which may incorporate parts of the UAA.

c.   **Assignment of Personnel to Engagements**

(1)   **Engagement Partner** The firm should establish policies and procedures that require that the responsibilities of the engagement partner are clearly defined and communicated to that person and likewise, that the identity and role of the engagement partner are communicated to the client's management and those charged with governance. The SQCS includes a recommendation that systems be established to monitor the workload and availability of engagement partners to ensure that they have time to adequately perform their assignments.

(2)   **Staff** Consideration of the nature and extent of supervision is important—factors to consider for this as well as for the selection of the team are similar to the competency requirements of the engagement partner covered in the previous section. Teamwork and training are important so that less experienced members can be brought along.

d.   **Professional Development** Policies and procedures should promote the need for all levels of personnel to participate in both general and industry-specific professional development activities in order to fulfill their responsibilities and meet the continuing professional education requirements of the AICPA and regulatory agencies. The importance of passing the CPA exam should be stressed.

e.   **Performance Evaluation, Compensation & Advancement** Recognition and reward should be given to personnel who demonstrate a commitment to ethical principles as well as to professional development and maintenance of competence. The size and circumstances of the firm have a bearing on the degree of formality used to evaluate personnel. Policies and procedures should provide that personnel selected for advancement have the qualifications to assume their new responsibilities.

5.   **Engagement Performance** Policies and procedures should be designed to provide the firm with reasonable assurance that engagements are consistently performed in accordance with professional standards and regulatory and legal requirements and that appropriate reports are issued. Engagement performance, supervision, and review responsibilities should be addressed.

a.   **Documentation** Policies and procedures should be established to ensure the confidentiality, safe custody, integrity, accessibility, retention, and retrievability of engagement documentation.

b.   **Consultation** Policies and procedures should ensure that consultation takes place when appropriate; sufficient resources are available to enable it to take place; all relevant facts are provided to those consulted; and the conclusions reached should be documented and implemented.

c.   **Resolution of Differences of Opinion** A firm should have policies and procedures in place for resolving differences of opinion within the engagement team and between the team and others, including the engagement quality control reviewer. The report should not be released until all issues are resolved. The resolution should be documented and implemented.

d.   **Engagement Quality Control Review** Criteria should be developed to determine when an engagement quality control review should be performed. The review should be completed before the report is released. Accordingly, the review should be conducted in a timely manner and may be done at appropriate stages during the engagement. The involvement of the quality control reviewer does not result in the transfer of any responsibility for the engagement from the engagement partner. The extent of the review may depend, among other things, on the complexity of the engagement and the degree of risk that the report may not be appropriate.

(1) Components of the Engagement Quality Control Review The review should include:

    (a) An evaluation of the significant judgments made by the engagement team and the conclusions reached in formulating the report; this should include a selection of related engagement documentation for review

    (b) The reading of the financial statements or other subject matter information to determine if the report is appropriate

    (c) A discussion with the engagement partner regarding significant findings and issues

(2) Independence & Objectivity of the Review Even though the engagement quality control reviewer is not a member of the engagement team, the reviewer should also satisfy the independence requirements relating to the engagements reviewed. Additionally, when there are enough partners in a firm to make it practicable, the reviewer should not be selected by the engagement partner. Consultation during the engagement with the quality control reviewer by the engagement team to assure the acceptability of a judgment or concerning other matters does not necessarily impair the quality control reviewer's objectivity. However, should the nature and extent of such consultations become significant, both parties need to exercise caution to preserve the reviewer's objectivity. The reviewer should be replaced by the firm if impairment does occur.

(3) Documentation of the Review There should be documentation that the firm's engagement quality control review procedures have been followed; that the review was completed before the report was released; and that the reviewer is not aware of any significant unresolved matters.

6. Monitoring

a. Purpose The purpose of monitoring procedures is to provide a comprehensive evaluation of adherence to all applicable professional standards and regulatory and legal requirements and the firm's quality control policies and procedures; and whether the quality control system has been appropriately designed and effectively implemented so that appropriate reports are issued.

b. Assignment of Responsibility Firms should assign responsibility for monitoring to a person of appropriate authority and experience and assign performance of monitoring to qualified personnel. They are required to evaluate deficiencies and communicate recommendations for remedial action.

c. Procedures

(1) Monitoring procedures include assessment of:

    (a) Appropriateness of the firm's guidance materials and any practice aids

    (b) New developments in professional standards and regulatory and legal requirements, and how they are reflected in the firm's policies and procedures

    (c) Compliance with policies and procedures on independence

    (d) Decisions related to acceptance and continuance of client relationships and specific engagements

(e)   Firm personnel's understanding of the firm's quality control policies and procedures, and their implementation

(f)   Selected administrative and personnel records pertaining to the quality control elements

(2)   Monitoring procedures can be accomplished through the performance of

(a)   Engagement quality control reviews

(b)   Postissuance reviews of engagement working papers, reports, and clients' financial statements for selected engagements

(c)   Inspection procedures (with or without prior notification to the engagement team), the nature and extent of which partially depends on the existence and effectiveness of other monitoring procedures, including the scope or conclusions of peer reviews or regulatory inspections (Note: a peer review does not substitute for all monitoring procedures, but it can substitute for the inspection of engagement working papers, reports, and client's financial statements for some or all of the engagements for the period covered by the peer review.)

d.   **Small Firms**   Monitoring of one's own compliance with the firm's policies and procedures may be necessary in small firms. To effectively monitor one's own compliance with the firm's policies and procedures, one must be able to critically review her/his own performance, assess her/his own strengths and weaknesses, and maintain an attitude of continual improvement. Circumstances and the degree of risk on noncompliance may indicate the need to have an outside individual monitor compliance.

e.   **Deficiencies**   Any system of quality control has inherent limitations that can reduce its effectiveness. As stated previously, deficiencies in individual engagements do not, in and of themselves, indicate that the firm's system of quality control is insufficient to provide it with reasonable assurance that its personnel comply with applicable standards. The firm should determine if deficiencies identified by the monitoring activities are systemic, repetitive, or significant and thus merit prompt corrective action. The firm should communicate to relevant engagement partners and other appropriate personnel deficiencies noted as a result of the monitoring process and recommendations for remedial action. If the deficiencies resulted in an inappropriate report or procedures were omitted during an engagement, in addition to determining what further action is needed to comply with professional standards and regulatory and legal requirements, the firm may consider obtaining legal advice.

f.   **Communication**   At least annually, the firm should communicate the results of the monitoring of its quality control process to relevant engagement partners and other personnel, including the firm's leadership. The communication should be thorough enough to provide a basis for their reliance on the system of quality control. The information should include:

(1)   A description of the monitoring procedures performed

(2)   The conclusions drawn from the monitoring procedures

(3)   A description of any systemic, repetitive, or other significant deficiencies and of the corrective actions taken

g.   **Documentation**   Policies and procedures should be established to document:

(1)   Monitoring procedures, including the selection method of completed engagements to be inspected

(2) A record of the evaluation of adherence to professional standards and regulatory and legal requirements; whether the quality control system has been appropriately designed and effectively implemented; and whether as a result of the foregoing, that appropriate reports are issued

(3) Identification and evaluation of the deficiencies and the basis for determining if further action was needed

h. Complaints & Allegations of Noncompliance Policies and procedures should be established for dealing with complaints and allegations of noncompliance with professional standards or with the firm's system of quality control. There should be clearly defined channels for personnel to use to communicate concerns without fear of reprisal. Complaints and allegations and the responses to them should be documented.

C. Documentation of the Operation of a Quality Control System
Documentation of the operation of quality control policies and procedures should be sufficient to provide evidence of the operation of each element of the quality control system. The form and content of documentation is a matter of judgment and depends on a variety of factors, for example, the size of the firm and the nature and complexity of its practice and organization. The retention period may be longer than that needed for monitoring and peer review activities if required by law or regulation.

V. Communications Between Predecessor & Successor Auditors (AU 315, SAS 84 & 93)

A. Overview
AU 315 provides guidance relating to communications between the predecessor and successor auditors when a change in auditors has taken place or is in process. Generally, the requirements of this guidance do not apply when the most recently audited financial statements are more than two years prior to the beginning of the period to be audited by the successor auditor.

1. **Predecessor Auditor** A predecessor auditor is one who has reported on the most recent audited financial statements; was engaged to perform, but did not complete, an audit; has resigned or has been terminated; or previously reported on financial statements that a client wants reaudited. A CPA who performed a review or compilation, instead of an audit, is not a predecessor auditor.

2. **Successor Auditor** A successor auditor is one who has provisionally accepted an engagement or has been asked to make a proposal for an engagement.

3. **Reaudit** A reaudit is an engagement to audit and report on financial statements that have previously been audited and reported on by another auditor.

B. Communications
The successor has the responsibility to initiate communication. Either written or oral communication is permissible. The information communicated should be kept confidential, regardless of whether or not the successor accepts the engagement.

1. **Before Successor Accepts Engagement** The successor auditor should attempt certain communications **before** accepting the engagement.

a. **Permission** The AICPA Code of Professional Conduct precludes an auditor from disclosing confidential information without the client's consent, so the successor must ask the prospective client to authorize the predecessor to respond promptly and fully to the successor's inquiries. If a prospective client refuses to permit the predecessor to respond or limits the response, the successor auditor should inquire as to the reasons and consider the implications of that refusal in deciding whether to accept the engagement.

      b.   **Inquiries** These inquiries should *relate to matters that will help the successor to decide whether to accept the engagement.* Matters covered by inquiries should include:

          (1)   Information that might bear on the integrity of management

          (2)   Disagreements with management on accounting principles, auditing procedures, or other significant matters

          (3)   Communications to those charged with governance regarding fraud and illegal acts by clients

          (4)   Communications regarding significant deficiencies and material weaknesses in internal control

          (5)   The predecessor's understanding as to the reasons for the change in auditors.

      c.   **Response** The predecessor should respond promptly and fully. If the predecessor decides not to respond fully (due to unusual circumstances such as impending litigation), the predecessor should clearly state that a limited response is being given. The successor should consider the implications of receiving a limited response in deciding whether to accept the engagement.

   2.   **Review of Workpapers** Other communications prior to, or subsequent to, acceptance of the engagement are concerned with assisting the successor with planning the audit, such as evaluations of consistency in applying accounting principles, inquiries into audit areas that required an inordinate amount of time, and problems that arose because of the condition of accounting systems or records.

   3.   **Revision** During the course of the audit, the successor may become aware of information that leads to a belief that the financial statements reported on by the predecessor may require revision. The successor should ask the client to arrange a meeting with the client, the predecessor, and the successor to resolve the matter. If the client refuses or if the successor is not satisfied, the successor should evaluate possible implications for the current engagement and whether to resign. Further, the successor auditor may want to consider consulting an attorney.

C.   **Release of Workpapers**

Ultimately, the predecessor determines what workpapers the successor may review or copy. A predecessor might not care to release workpapers containing matters pertaining to pending litigation or potentially fraudulent client representations.

   1.   **Signed Statement** Generally though, the successor auditor may be able to gain broader access by offering additional assurances. The successor can sign a statement that acknowledges the successor's responsibility to keep the information confidential and consents to use the workpapers solely for purposes of planning the successor's audit; not to comment on the performance of the predecessor's audit; not to provide expert testimony on the quality of the predecessor's audit; and not to use the workpapers as audit evidence in the successor's audit.

   2.   **Use** The successor auditor uses the predecessor's workpapers as a start for obtaining confidence in the beginning balances. (The predecessor's work does not replace the need for some testing.) This can encompass a review of virtually all of the predecessor's workpapers. The successor should **not** make any reference to the predecessor's work as a basis for the successor's own opinion. The nature, extent, and timing of audit procedures, as well as the opinion the successor auditor reaches, are solely that auditor's responsibility.

CHAPTER 21—STANDARDS & RELATED TOPICS

Problem 21-1 MULTIPLE CHOICE QUESTIONS (36 to 45 minutes)

1. Which of the following statements is correct concerning an auditor's responsibilities regarding financial statements?
a. An auditor may not draft an entity's financial statements based on information from management's accounting system.
b. The adoption of sound accounting policies is an implicit part of an auditor's responsibilities.
c. An auditor's responsibilities for audited financial statements are confined to the expression of the auditor's opinion.
d. Making suggestions that are adopted about an entity's internal control environment impairs an auditor's independence.   (R/03, AUD, #8, 7630)

2. After fieldwork audit procedures are completed, a partner of the CPA firm who has not been involved in the audit performs a second or wrap-up working paper review. This second review usually focuses on
a. The fair presentation of the financial statements in conformity with GAAP
b. Fraud involving the client's management and its employees
c. The materiality of the adjusting entries proposed by the audit staff
d. The communication of internal control weaknesses to the client's audit committee
(11/94, AUD, #5, amended, 5078)

3. Which of the following best describes what is meant by the term generally accepted auditing standards?
a. Procedures to be used to gather evidence to support financial statements
b. Measures of the quality of the auditor's performance
c. Pronouncements issued by the Auditing Standards Board
d. Rules acknowledged by the accounting profession because of their universal application
(11/91, AUD, #9, 7485)

4. GAAS require the auditor to document in the workpapers the justification for a departure from a presumptively mandatory requirement. What language indicates a presumptively mandatory requirement?
a. "must" or "is required"
b. "could"
c. "may consider"
d. "should"   (Editors, 8263)

5. The second standard of fieldwork requires the auditor to obtain an understanding of
a. Internal control
b. The internal audit function
c. The entity and its environment, including internal control
d. The control environment   (Editors, 8261)

6. Which of the following factors most likely would lead a CPA to conclude that a potential audit engagement should **not** be accepted?
a. There are significant related party transactions that management claims occurred in the ordinary course of business.
b. Internal control activities requiring the segregation of duties are subject to management override.
c. Management continues to employ an inefficient system of information technology to record financial transactions.
d. It is unlikely that sufficient appropriate evidence is available to support an opinion on the financial statements.   (R/06, AUD, #43, amended, 8161)

7. The third general standard requires that due care is to be exercised in the performance of an audit. This standard is ordinarily interpreted to require
a. Thorough review of the existing safeguards over access to assets and records
b. Limited review of the indications of employee fraud and illegal acts
c. Objective review of the adequacy of the technical training and proficiency of firm personnel
d. Critical review of the judgment exercised at every level of supervision   (5/95, AUD, #23, 5641)

8. One of a CPA firm's basic objectives is to provide professional services that conform with professional standards. Reasonable assurance of achieving this basic objective is provided through
a. A system of quality control
b. A system of peer review
c. Continuing professional education
d. Compliance with generally accepted reporting standards   (11/92, AUD, #3, 2937)

9. Which of the following factors most likely would cause a CPA **not** to accept a new audit engagement?
a. The prospective client's unwillingness to permit inquiry of its legal counsel
b. The inability to review the predecessor auditor's working papers
c. The CPA's lack of understanding of the prospective client's operations and industry
d. The indications that management has not investigated employees in key positions before hiring them (R/03, AUD, #11, 7633)

10. Which of the following is **not** a factor a CPA firm should take into consideration when deciding whether to undertake or continue client relationships and engagements?
a. The possibility of the existence of related party transactions
b. The client's integrity
c. The firm's ability to perform the engagement
d. The firm's ability to comply with legal and ethical requirements (Editors, 9046)

11. Would the following factors ordinarily be considered in planning an audit engagement's personnel requirements?

	Opportunities for on-the-job training	Continuity and periodic rotation of personnel
a.	Yes	Yes
b.	Yes	No
c.	No	Yes
d.	No	No

(5/95, AUD, #6, 5624)

12. Which of the following factors most likely would lead a CPA to conclude that a potential audit engagement should be rejected?
a. The details of most recorded transactions are not available after a specified period of time.
b. Internal control activities requiring the segregation of duties are subject to management override.
c. It is unlikely that sufficient appropriate audit evidence is available to support an opinion on the financial statements.
d. Management has a reputation for consulting with several accounting firms about significant accounting issues. (R/00, AUD, #2, amended, 6927)

13. Which of the following factors most likely would cause a CPA to **not** accept a new audit engagement?
a. The prospective client has already completed its physical inventory count.
b. The CPA lacks an understanding of the prospective client's operations and industry.
c. The CPA is unable to review the predecessor auditor's working papers.
d. The prospective client is unwilling to make all financial records available to the CPA. (R/01, AUD, #2, 7017)

14. A successor auditor ordinarily should request to review the predecessor's working papers relating to

	Contingencies	Internal control
a.	Yes	Yes
b.	Yes	No
c.	No	Yes
d.	No	No

(R/02, AUD, #2, 7092)

15. A successor auditor most likely would make specific inquiries of the predecessor auditor regarding
a. Specialized accounting principles of the client's industry
b. The competency of the client's internal audit staff
c. The uncertainty inherent in applying sampling procedures
d. Disagreements with management as to auditing procedures (5/95, AUD, #2, 5620)

16. In auditing the financial statements of Star Corp., Land discovered information leading Land to believe that Star's prior year's financial statements, which were audited by Tell, require substantial revisions. Under these circumstances, Land should
a. Notify Star's audit committee and stockholders that the prior year's financial statements **cannot** be relied on
b. Request Star to arrange a meeting among the three parties to resolve the matter
c. Notify Tell about the information and make inquiries about the integrity of Star's management
d. Request Star to reissue the prior year's financial statements with the appropriate revisions (5/95, AUD, #18, amended, 5636)

17. A successor auditor should make specific and reasonable inquiries of the predecessor auditor regarding the predecessor's
a. Understanding of the reasons for the change in auditors
b. Methodology used in applying sampling techniques
c. Opinion on subsequent events that have occurred since the balance sheet date
d. Perception of the competency and reliance on the client's internal audit function
(R/05, AUD, #37, 7832)

18. A successor auditor is required to attempt communication with the predecessor auditor prior to
a. Performing tests of controls
b. Testing beginning balances for the current year
c. Making a proposal for the audit engagement
d. Accepting the engagement
(R/06, AUD, #19, 8137)

Problem 21-2 ADDITIONAL MULTIPLE CHOICE QUESTIONS (22 to 28 minutes)

19. Which of the following elements underlies the application of generally accepted auditing standards, particularly the standards of fieldwork and reporting?
a. Internal control
b. Corroborating evidence
c. Materiality and audit risk
d. Quality control (Editors, 0015)

20. An auditor strives to achieve independence in appearance in order to
a. Maintain public confidence in the profession
b. Become independent in fact
c. Maintain an unbiased mental attitude
d. Comply with the generally accepted auditing standards of fieldwork (Editors, 0020)

21. Because an audit in accordance with generally accepted auditing standards is influenced by the possibility of material misstatements, the auditor should conduct the audit with an attitude of
a. Objective judgment
b. Conservative advocacy
c. Professional responsiveness
d. Professional skepticism (Editors, 0213)

22. Which of the following categories is included in generally accepted auditing standards?
a. Standards of review
b. Standards of planning
c. Standards of fieldwork
d. Standards of evidence (R/07, AUD, #1, 8373)

23. The nature and extent of a CPA firm's quality control policies and procedures will depend on various factors including its

	Size	*Operating Characteristics*
a.	Yes	Yes
b.	Yes	Yes
c.	Yes	No
d.	No	Yes

(5/95, AUD, #5, amended, 5623)

24. Which of the following should be considered in establishing a CPA firm's quality control policies and procedures?

	Performance Evaluation, Compensation & Advancement	*Professional Development*	*Recruitment & Hiring*
a.	Yes	Yes	No
b.	Yes	Yes	Yes
c.	No	No	Yes
d.	Yes	No	Yes

(Editors, amended, 0009)

25. Which of the following factors most likely would cause a CPA to decide not to accept a new audit engagement?
a. The CPA's lack of understanding of the prospective client's internal auditor's computer-assisted audit techniques
b. Management's disregard of its responsibility to maintain an adequate internal control environment
c. The CPA's inability to determine whether related party transactions were consummated on terms equivalent to arm's-length transactions
d. Management's refusal to permit the CPA to perform substantive tests before the year-end
(R/00, AUD, #3, 6928)

26. Which of the following is an element of a CPA firm's quality control system that should be considered in establishing its quality control policies and procedures?

a. Complying with laws and regulations
b. Using statistical sampling techniques
c. Relevant ethical requirements
d. Considering audit risk and materiality

(5/94, AUD, #15, amended, 4680)

27. Before accepting an engagement to audit a new client, a CPA is required to obtain

a. An understanding of the prospective client's industry and business
b. A management representation letter
c. A preliminary understanding of the prospective client's control environment
d. The prospective client's consent to make inquiries of the predecessor auditor

(5/97, AUD, #2, amended, 6391)

28. A successor auditor should request the new client to authorize the predecessor auditor to allow a review of the predecessor's

	Engagement letter	*Working papers*
a.	Yes	Yes
b.	Yes	No
c.	No	Yes
d.	No	No

(R/03, AUD, #10, 7632)

29. Ordinarily, the predecessor auditor permits the successor auditor to review the predecessor's working paper analyses relating to

	Contingencies	*Balance sheet accounts*
a.	Yes	Yes
b.	Yes	No
c.	No	Yes
d.	No	No

(11/98, AUD, #19, 6710)

SIMULATION

Problem 21-3 (40 to 50 minutes)

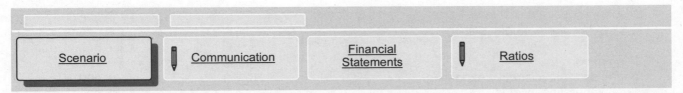

Feiler, the sole owner of a small hardware business, has been told that the business should have financial statements reported on by an independent CPA. Feiler, having some bookkeeping experience, has personally prepared the company's financial statements and does not understand why such statements should be audited by a CPA. Feiler has asked you to explain why an audit is considered important.

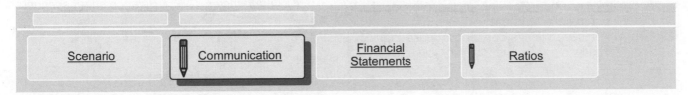

In a letter to Feiler, describe (a) the objectives of an independent audit and (b) five ways in which an independent audit may be beneficial to his company.

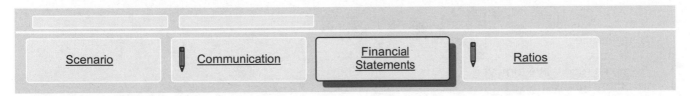

The following financial statements were prepared by Feiler Hardware for the year ended December 31, Year 5. Sales represent net credit sales. The total assets, the receivables, and inventory balances at December 31, Year 5, were the same as at December 31, Year 4.

Feiler Hardware
Balance Sheet
December 31, Year 5

Assets		Liabilities and Capital	
Cash	$ 60,000	Accounts payable	$ 40,000
Receivables	100,000	Notes payable	25,000
Inventory	150,000	Other current liabilities	35,000
Total current assets	$310,000	Total current liabilities	$100,000
Plant and equipment—net	190,000	Long-term debt	87,500
		Feiler, Capital	312,500
Total assets	$500,000	Total liabilities and capital	$500,000

Feiler Hardware
Income Statement
Year Ended December 31, Year 5

Sales		$750,000
Less Cost of goods sold		450,000
Gross margin		$300,000
Selling expenses	$60,000	
General and administrative expenses	75,000	135,000
Operating income		$165,000
Less interest expense		10,000
Income before taxes		$155,000
Less federal income taxes		55,000
Net income		$100,000

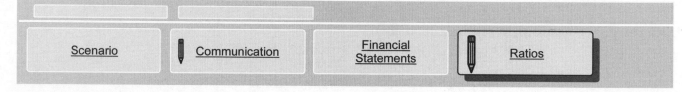

Each of the following represent financial ratios calculated from the prior year's financial statements. For each ratio, calculate the current year's ratio from the financial statements presented. Calculations should be rounded, if necessary, to the same number of places as the prior year's ratios.

	Ratio	Year 5	Year 4
1.	Current ratio		2.5
2.	Quick ratio		1.3
3.	Accounts receivable turnover		9.0
4.	Inventory turnover		1.5

Analytical procedures are evaluations of financial information made by a study of plausible relationships among financial and nonfinancial data. Understanding and evaluating such relationships are essential to the audit process. For each observed change, select the most likely explanations from the accompanying list.

<u>Observed Changes</u>

1. Inventory turnover increased substantially from the prior year. (3 explanations)

2. Accounts receivable turnover decreased substantially from the prior year. (3 explanations)

Explanations

A. Items shipped on consignment during the last month of the year were recorded as sales.

B. A significant number of credit memos for returned merchandise that were issued during the last month of the year were not recorded.

C. Year-end purchases of inventory were overstated by incorrectly including items received in the first month of the subsequent year.

D. Year-end purchases of inventory were understated by incorrectly excluding items received before the year end.

E. A larger percentage of sales occurred during the last month of the year, as compared to the prior year.

F. A smaller percentage of sales occurred during the last month of the year, as compared to the prior year.

G. The same percentage of sales occurred during the last month of the year, as compared to the prior year.

H. Sales increased at the same percentage as cost of goods sold, as compared to the prior year.

I. Sales increased at a greater percentage than cost of goods sold increased, as compared to the prior year.

J. Sales increased at a lower percentage than cost of goods sold increased, as compared to the prior year.

Analytics   Research

Note: The editors recommend that candidates who are unfamiliar with researching the AICPA's database of professional literature review the sample research question in the **Practical Advice** appendix before answering their first research question. Candidates typically should start developing their research skills at least a month before their exams.

What authoritative reference provides guidance on fieldwork to a current-year auditor who has not observed the physical count of the inventory in a prior year?

Paragraph Reference Answer: _____

(5/96, AUD, #2, amended, 8067)

Solution 21-1 MULTIPLE CHOICE ANSWERS

GAAS

1. (c)   The financial statements are management's responsibility. The auditor's responsibility is to express an opinion on the financial statements. Management is responsible for adopting sound accounting policies and for establishing and maintaining internal control. The independent auditor may make suggestions about the form or content of the financial statements or draft them, in whole or in part, based on information from management during the performance of the audit. However, the auditor's responsibility for the financial statements audited is confined to the expression of an opinion on them. The audit of financial statements requires CPAs to review many aspects of an organization's activities and procedures. Consequently, they can advise clients of needed improvements in internal control and make constructive suggestions on financial, tax, and other operating matters.   (7630)

2. (a)   The secondary review partner usually focuses on the fair presentation of the financial statements in accordance with GAAP. Answers (b), (c), and (d) are usually done by staff directly involved in the audit.   (5078)

3. (b)   Auditing standards provide a measure of audit quality. Auditing standards are issued by the Auditing Standards Board, but that does not describe what is meant by generally accepted auditing standards. Auditing procedures relate to

the acts to be performed during an audit to comply with auditing standards. (7485)

4. (d) The word *should* indicates a presumptively mandatory requirement. The auditor is required to comply with a presumptively mandatory requirement in all cases in which the requirement applies. However, in rare circumstances, the auditor may depart from such a requirement provided the auditor documents in the workpapers the justification for the departure and the alternative procedures performed to achieve the objectives of that requirement. The words *must* or *is required* indicate an unconditional requirement. The auditor is required to comply with an unconditional requirement in all cases in which the requirement applies. The words *may, might,* and *could* are used to describe actions and procedure included in explanatory material in the standards.
(8263)

5. (c) The second standard of fieldwork states: "The auditor must obtain a sufficient understanding of the entity and its environment, including its internal control, to assess the risk of material misstatement of the financial statements whether due to error or fraud, and to design the nature, timing, and extent of further audit procedures." (8261)

6. (d) If sufficient appropriate evidence is not available to support an opinion on the financial statements then an audit cannot be performed. Significant related party transactions need to be disclosed. Many internal control activities are subject to management override. The costs of a new efficient information system may outweigh its benefits. (8161)

7. (d) The third general standard states, "The auditor must exercise due professional care in the performance of the audit and the preparation of the report." The exercise of due care requires critical review at every level of supervision of the work done and the judgment exercised by those assisting in the audit. Safeguards over assets and records and review of indications of fraud and illegal acts are internal control issues. Objective review of the adequacy of the training and proficiency of personnel is a quality control issue. (5641)

Quality Control

8. (a) A system of quality control should provide the firm with reasonable assurance that its personnel comply with professional standards and applicable regulatory and legal requirements, and that the reports issued are appropriate in the circumstances. A peer review provides information on whether a CPA firm is following an appropriate quality control system and would not by itself provide

reasonable assurance that a CPA firm is providing professional services that conform with professional standards. Continuing professional education is only one of the policies and procedures concerned with the human resources element of quality control. Compliance with generally accepted reporting standards is only one part of the basic objective of providing professional services that conform with professional standards. (2937)

9. (a) Auditors typically inquire of the client's legal counsel regarding litigation, claims, and assessments. The prospective client's unwillingness to permit such inquiry casts doubt on the reliability of management representations. Further, such a scope limitation usually results in a disclaimer of opinion; ethics require auditors to accept only engagements they can reasonably expect to complete. There may be legitimate reasons why an auditor is unable to review a predecessor's working papers or why management doesn't investigate employees in key positions before hiring them. There is no need for the auditor to understand the prospective client's industry before the audit is begun as long as the auditor can reasonably expect to gain such understanding in a timely manner. (7633)

10. (a) The standards require that a firm's quality control policies and procedures regarding the acceptance and continuance of clients and engagements take answers (b), (c), and (d) into consideration. In the absence of evidence to the contrary, related party transactions should not be assumed to be outside of the ordinary course of business. The auditor is concerned with complying with GAAS to identify related party transactions and determining that they are accounted for and disclosed according to GAAP. (9046)

11. (a) The auditor uses professional judgment in planning an audit engagement's personnel requirements; the auditor has final responsibility and may delegate portions of the audit functions to other firm personnel, referred to in the code as "assistants." Opportunities for on-the-job training as well as continuity and periodic rotation of personnel are all valid factors the auditor may consider in this task. (5624)

12. (c) If sufficient appropriate audit evidence is not available to support an opinion, an audit cannot be performed. In many online systems, most routine transaction details are not available after a specified period of time. Internal control is usually subject to management override. Consultation with several accounting firms reflects management's concern over proper accounting and reporting. (6927)

13. (d)   Unwillingness to make available all financial records heightens the risk associated with an audit client. Inventory assertions may be confirmed by alternative audit procedures. A CPA may gain an understanding of the client's operations and industry from audit guides and other publications. Review of the predecessor auditor's workpapers is not necessary prior to accepting an audit engagement.   (7017)

Predecessor & Successor Auditors

14. (a)   The predecessor auditor should ordinarily permit the successor auditor to review working papers, including documentation of planning, *internal control*, audit results, and other matters of continuing accounting and auditing significance, such as the working paper analysis of balance sheet accounts, and those relating to *contingencies*.   (7092)

15. (d)   A successor should ask about *disagreements with management as* to accounting principles, *auditing procedures*, or other significant matters. Other matters subject to inquiry should include information that might bear on the integrity of management; the predecessor's communications to those charged with governance regarding fraud and illegal acts by the client; the predecessor's communications to management and those charged with governance regarding significant deficiencies and material weaknesses in internal control; and the predecessor's understanding of the reasons for the change in auditors. The auditor would use other sources for learning specialized accounting principles of the client's industry and the inherent uncertainty in applying sampling procedures. The competency of the client's internal audit staff should be an evaluation made by the current auditor.   (5620)

16. (b)   If during an audit, the successor auditor becomes aware of information that leads the auditor to believe the financial statements reported on by the predecessor auditor may require revision, the successor auditor should request the client to arrange a meeting among the three parties to resolve the matter. If the client refuses or if the successor is not satisfied after the meeting, the successor auditor should evaluate any implications on the current engagement and whether resignation from the engagement is appropriate as well as consider consulting with an attorney in determining an appropriate course of action.   (5636)

17. (a)   A successor should ask about the predecessor's *understanding of the reasons for the change in auditors*. Other matters subject to inquiry should include information that might bear on the integrity of management; disagreements the predecessor had with management as to accounting principles, auditing procedures, or other significant matters; the predecessor's communications to those charged with governance regarding fraud and illegal acts by the client; and the predecessor's communications to management and those charged with governance regarding significant deficiencies and material weaknesses in internal control. Appropriate inquires should help the successor to decide whether to accept the engagement—the other answer alternatives do not meet this objective. Additionally the nature, timing, and extent of the audit work performed and the conclusions reached are matters solely for the successor auditor's judgment.   (7832)

18. (d)   A successor auditor should attempt certain communications before accepting the engagement.   (8137)

Solution 21-2 ADDITIONAL MULTIPLE CHOICE ANSWERS

GAAS

19. (c)   *Materiality* and *audit risk* underlie the application of the 10 standards and the SASs, particularly those related to fieldwork and reporting. An understanding of internal control and sufficient evidence are requirements of GAAS, not elements of GAAS application. Quality control is not part of GAAS. It is promulgated by the AICPA in Statements on Quality Control Standards.   (0015)

20. (a)   It is of utmost importance to the profession that the general public maintain confidence in the independence of independent auditors. Public confidence would be impaired by evidence that independence was actually lacking, and it might also be impaired by the existence of circumstances which reasonable people might believe likely to influence independence.   (0020)

21. (d)   Due professional care requires the auditor to exercise professional skepticism. Professional skepticism is an attitude that includes a questioning mind and a critical assessment of audit evidence.   (0213)

22. (c)   Standards of fieldwork is one of the three categories of the ten generally accepted auditing standards (GAAS). The other two categories are general standards and standards of reporting. (8373)

Quality Control

23. (a) Factors which impact the nature and extent of a firm's quality control policies and procedures depend on various factors including its size and operating characteristics. (5623)

24. (b) A firm shall consider each of the elements of quality control, to the extent applicable to its practice, in establishing its quality control policies and procedures. Performance evaluation, compensation, and advancement; professional development: and recruitment and hiring decisions are part of the human resources element of a quality control system. The human resources element should also address the determination of capabilities and competencies and the assignment of personnel to engagements. (0009)

25. (b) Management's carelessness regarding an adequate internal control environment may make it improbable that an auditor will be able to collect sufficient appropriate audit evidence to form an opinion. An auditor need not understand the internal auditor's techniques, particularly before accepting an engagement. The auditor merely needs to determine if related party transactions are properly disclosed, not whether they occur similarly to arm's-length transactions. Performing substantive tests at year-end is adequate if all records are available. (6928)

26. (c) Relevant ethical requirements is one of the elements that should be addressed by a firm's system of quality control. Answer (a) is not an *element* of a system of quality control. Answers (b) and (d) would be associated with auditing requirements and procedures. (4680)

Predecessor & Successor Auditors

27. (d) If a prospective client refuses to permit a predecessor auditor to respond to a successor's questions, the successor auditor should inquire as to the reasons and consider the implications of that refusal in deciding whether to accept that engagement. The alternative answers may be done after accepting an engagement to audit a client. (6391)

28. (c) The successor auditor should request that the client authorize the predecessor auditor to allow a review of the predecessor auditor's working papers. It is customary in such circumstances for the predecessor auditor to be available to the successor auditor and make available for review certain working papers. The predecessor auditor should determine which working papers are to be made available for review and which may be copied. The predecessor auditor should ordinarily permit the successor auditor to review working papers, including documentation of planning, internal control, audit results, and other matters of continuing accounting and auditing significance, such as the working paper analysis of balance sheet accounts, and those relating to contingencies. While, in a broad sense, an engagement letter could be considered part of the predecessor's working papers, as the predecessor's engagement letter could shed little light on the previous audit, there is little point in a successor reviewing it. (7632)

29. (a) The working papers the predecessor would ordinarily make available would include analysis of balance sheet accounts and those relating to contingencies. (6710)

PERFORMANCE BY SUBTOPICS

Each category below parallels a subtopic covered in Chapter 21. Record the number and percentage of questions you correctly answered in each subtopic area.

GAAS

Question #	Correct √
1	
2	
3	
4	
5	
6	
7	

Questions   7

Correct   _____
% Correct

Quality Control

Question #	Correct √
8	
9	
10	
11	
12	
13	

Questions   6

Correct   _____
% Correct   _____

Predecessor & Successor Auditors

Question #	Correct √
14	
15	
16	
17	
18	

Questions   5

Correct   _____
% Correct   _____

SIMULATION SOLUTION

Solution 21-3

Response #1: Communication (6 points)

a. You should explain to Feiler that an independent audit is an audit of the financial statements in accordance with certain **generally accepted auditing standards.** The objective of an ordinary audit is **to render an opinion on the fairness, in all material respects**, with which the financial statements **present financial position, results of operations, and cash flows in conformity with generally accepted accounting principles.** The auditor, after an objective **evidence-gathering audit**, expresses an opinion and "bears witness" to the fair presentation of financial statements. An independent expert is needed to lend **credibility** to the financial statements. It would not be meaningful for a company to report on itself without the **attestation of an independent party** because the company, itself, might not be **objective.**

b. You should inform Feiler of five of the following ways in which an independent audit can be beneficial:

1. To serve as a basis for the **extension of credit**.
2. To supply **credit rating agencies** with required information.
3. To serve as a basis for preparation of **tax returns**.
4. To **establish amounts of losses** from fire, theft, burglary, and so forth.
5. To **determine amounts receivable or payable** under
   a. Agreements for **bonuses** based on profits.
   b. **Contracts** for sharing expenses.
   c. **Cost-plus contracts**.

6. To provide data for proposed changes in financial structure or to supply proper financial data in the event of a proposed **sale or merger**.
7. To serve as a **basis for changes** in accounting or recording practices.
8. To serve as a basis for action in **bankruptcy** and insolvency cases.
9. To determine proper execution of **trust agreements**.
10. To furnish **estates** with information in order to obtain proper settlements and avoid costly litigation.
11. To provide a **review** of many aspects of the organization's **activities and procedures**.
12. To establish and/or improve **internal control** policies and procedures.
13. To provide important aid in case of **tax audits, court actions**, and so forth.
14. To **discourage employees from planning errors**, fraud, and so forth, by making them aware of auditor presence.
15. To provide **industry-wide comparisons**.
16. To provide a realistic look at **inventories**.
17. To review adequacy of **insurance coverage**.
18. To provide the **professional knowledge** of an external auditor, which is generally superior to the client's bookkeeping experience.

Response #2: Ratios (2 points)

1. 3.1

The current ratio is total current assets divided by total current liabilities. ($310,000 / $100,000 = 3.1)

2. 1.6

The quick (or acid-test) ratio is cash plus marketable securities plus net receivables divided by current liabilities. [($60,000 + $100,000) / $100,000 = 1.6]

3. 7.5

Accounts receivable turnover is net credit sales divided by average net receivables. {$750,000 / [($100,000 + $100,000) / 2] = 7.5}

4. 3.0

Inventory turnover is cost of goods sold divided by average inventory. {$450,000 / [($150,000 + $150,000) / 2] = 3.0}

Response #3: Analytics (6 points)

1. A, B, D

Inventory turnover is cost of goods sold divided by average inventory. When cost of goods sold is overstated, this ratio will increase. Due to recording consignment items shipped during the last month as sales, the cost of goods sold is overstated. Due to not recording a significant number of credit memos for returned merchandise, the cost of goods sold is overstated. When average inventory is understated, this ratio will increase. Due to the incorrect understatement of inventory from the exclusion of inventory received before year-end, average inventory is understated.

2. A, B, E

Accounts receivable turnover is net credit sales divided by average net receivables. This ratio will decrease when net credit sales decreases or average net receivables increases. Due to recording consignment items shipped during the last month as sales, sales and accounts receivable are both overstated by the same amount. However, proportionately, accounts receivables increases more than net credit sales, decreasing the ratio. Due to not recording a significant number of credit memos for returned merchandise, sales and accounts receivable are disproportionately overstated. A larger percentage of sales occurring during the last month of the year, as compared to the prior year, increases the amount in accounts receivable. This increases average accounts receivable, as compared to last year, without increasing sales, as compared to last year.

Response #4: Research (1 point)

Paragraph Reference Answer: AU 331.13

Guidance: AU 331.13 states, "The independent auditor may be asked to audit financial statements covering the current period and one or more periods for which he had not observed or made some physical counts of prior inventories. He may, nevertheless, be able to become satisfied as to such prior inventories through appropriate procedures, such as tests of prior transactions, reviews of the records of prior counts, and the application of gross profit tests, provided that he has been able to become satisfied as to the current inventory."

(8067)

CHAPTER 22

PLANNING

CHAPTER 22

PLANNING

I. Planning & Supervision (AU 311, SAS 108)

A. Appointment of the Independent Auditor

Exhibit 1 ▶ The First Standard of Fieldwork

> The auditor must adequately plan the work and must properly supervise any assistants.

1. **Early** An early appointment is advantageous. It allows the auditor to plan the audit prior to the balance sheet date.

2. **Near Year-End** Before accepting an engagement near or after the close of the accounting period, the auditor should consider whether it will be possible to perform an adequate audit that will support an unqualified opinion. If not, the auditor should discuss with the client the possibility of either a qualified opinion or a disclaimer of an opinion.

B. Understanding With the Client
The auditor should establish an understanding with the client regarding the objectives, scope, and limitations of the services to be performed and document it in an engagement letter to the client. The letter should also delineate the responsibilities of the auditor versus those of management. Such an understanding reduces the chance that either party will misinterpret the needs or expectations of the other.

1. **Engagement Letter Requirements** The engagement letter should generally include the following matters.

    a. The objective of the audit is the expression of an opinion on the financial statements.

    b. Management's responsibilities include

    (1) The entity's financial statements as well as the selection and application of accounting policies;

    (2) Establishing and maintaining effective internal control over financial reporting;

    (3) Designing and implementing programs and controls to prevent and detect fraud;

    (4) Identifying and ensuring compliance with applicable laws and regulations;

    (5) Making all financial records and related information available to the auditor;

    (6) Providing the auditor with a letter at the conclusion of the engagement that confirms certain representations made during the audit;

    (7) Adjusting the financial statements to correct material misstatements; and

    (8) Affirming to the auditor in the representation letter that the effects of any uncorrected misstatements aggregated by the auditor during the current engagement and pertaining to the latest period presented are immaterial, both individually and in the aggregate, to the financial statements taken as a whole.

c. The auditor

(1) Is responsible for conducting the audit in accordance with GAAS. GAAS require the auditor to obtain reasonable rather than absolute assurance about whether the financial statements are free of material misstatement, whether caused by error or fraud; consequently, a material misstatement may remain undetected.

(2) Is not required to search for significant deficiencies in internal control, however, the auditor is responsible for ensuring that those charged with governance are aware of any significant deficiencies that come to the auditor's attention.

(3) May decline to express an opinion or decline to issue a report If unable to complete the audit or is unable to or has not formed an opinion.

d. An audit

(1) Includes obtaining an understanding of the entity and its environment, including its internal control, sufficient to assess the risks of material misstatement of the financial statements and to design the nature, extent, and timing of further audit procedures.

(2) Is not designed to detect error or fraud that is immaterial to the financial statements.

(3) Is not designed to provide assurance on internal control or to identify significant deficiencies.

2. **Optional** The engagement letter may also include other matters such as: overall audit strategy; involvement of specialists, internal auditors, and/or predecessor auditors; fees and billing; liability issues; access to the auditor's workpapers; and any additional services to be provided.

C. **Planning**
Planning involves the development of an overall strategy for the expected conduct, organization, and staffing of the audit. The nature, extent, and timing of planning vary with the size and complexity of the entity and the auditor's experience with and knowledge of the entity and its environment, including internal control. The auditor must plan the audit to be responsive to the assessment of the risk of material misstatement (RMM). Planning begins with engagement acceptance and continues throughout the audit because evidence gathered may require the revision of the overall audit strategy. The auditor should update and document any significant changes to the overall audit strategy.

1. **Preliminary Engagement Activities** The auditor should perform the following procedures at the beginning of the audit engagement. Their purpose is to consider any events or circumstances that may either adversely affect the auditor's ability to plan and perform the engagement to reduce audit risk to an acceptably low level or pose an unacceptable level of risk to the auditor. (Performance of these procedures should also be part of a CPA firm's system of quality control—see Chapter 21.)

a. Procedures regarding both the continuance of the client relationship and the specific audit engagement

b. Evaluation of the auditor's compliance with ethical requirements, including independence

2. **Overall Audit Strategy** In establishing the overall audit strategy, the auditor should:

   a. **Characteristics That Define Scope** Determine the characteristics of the engagement that define its scope, such as the basis of reporting, industry-specific reporting requirements, and the locations of the entity.

   b. **Reporting Objectives / Required Communications / Deadlines** Determine the reporting objectives of the engagement to plan the timing of the audit and the nature of required communications, such as deadlines for interim and final reporting as well as key dates for expected communications with management and those charged with governance.

   c. **Key Factors that Define the Focus of Audit** Consider the important factors that will determine the focus of the audit team's efforts, such as:

      (1) Determination of materiality levels;

      (2) Preliminary identification of areas where there may be higher risks of material misstatement;

      (3) Preliminary identification of material locations and account balances;

      (4) Evaluation of whether the auditor plans to perform tests of controls; and

      (5) Identification of recent significant entity-specific, industry, or financial reporting developments.

   d. **Examples of Matters to Consider** In establishing the overall audit strategy, the auditor may consider the following matters:

      (1) Scope of Engagement

      - Basis of reporting, including any need to reconcile to another basis of reporting
      - Industry-specific reporting requirements
      - Expected audit coverage, including the number and locations to be included
      - Nature of the control relationships between a parent and its subsidiaries that determine how the group is to be consolidated
      - Extent to which locations are audited by other auditors
      - Nature of the subsidiaries or divisions to be audited, including need for specialized knowledge
      - Reporting currency to be used, including any need for currency translation
      - Need for statutory or regulatory audit requirements
      - Availability of internal auditors and the extent of the auditor's potential reliance on such work
      - Entity's use of service organizations
      - Expected use of audit evidence obtained in prior audits
      - Effect of IT on audit procedures
      - Coordination of the expected coverage and timing of the audit work with any reviews of interim financial information and the effect on the audit of the information obtained during such reviews
      - Discussion of matters that may affect the audit with firm personnel responsible for performing other services for the entity
      - Availability of client personnel and data

     (2)   **Reporting Objectives, Timing & Communications Required**

- Entity's timetable for reporting, including interim periods
- Organization of meetings with management and those charged with governance to discuss the nature, extent, and timing of the audit work
- Discussion with management and those charged with governance regarding the expected type and timing of reports to be issued and other communications
- Discussion with management concerning the expected communications on the status of audit work throughout the engagement and the expected deliverables resulting from the audit procedures
- Communication with auditors of other locations regarding the expected types and timing of reports as well as other communications
- Expected nature and timing of communications among audit team members, including team meetings and timing of the review of work performed
- Whether there are any other expected communications with third parties, including any statutory or contractual reporting responsibilities arising from the audit

     (3)   **Scope of the Audit**

- Setting materiality for planning purposes
- Setting and communicating materiality for auditors of other locations
- Reconsidering materiality as audit procedures are performed during the course of the audit
- Identifying the material locations and account balances
- Audit areas where there is a higher RMM
- Effect of the assessed RMM at the overall financial statement level on scope, supervision, and review
- Selection of the audit team and the assignment of audit work to the team members, including assignment of experienced members to areas where there may be higher risks of material misstatement
- Engagement time budgeting
- Manner in which the auditor emphasizes to team members the need to maintain a questioning mind and to exercise professional skepticism in gathering and evaluating audit evidence
- Results of previous audits that involved evaluating the operating effectiveness of internal control, including the nature of identified weaknesses and actions taken to address them
- Management's commitment to the design and operation of internal control
- Volume of transactions, which may be a factor in determining whether it is more effective for the auditor to rely on internal control
- Importance attached to internal control throughout the entity
- Significant business developments, including changes in IT, business processes, and key management as well as acquisitions, mergers, and divestments.
- Significant industry developments
- Significant accounting changes
- Other significant relevant developments

3.   **Audit Plan** Once the audit strategy has been established, the auditor will be able to develop a more detailed audit plan (set of audit programs) that addresses specific audit objectives. The audit plan documents the nature, extent, and timing of audit procedures to be performed to obtain sufficient appropriate audit evidence to reduce audit risk to an acceptably low level. That said, the two planning activities are interrelated and thus are not necessarily discrete or sequential. The auditor should document any changes to the original audit plan. The audit plan should include:

a.   **Risk Assessment Procedures** A description of the nature, extent, and timing of planned risk assessment procedures sufficient to assess the risks of material misstatement. This may occur early in the audit process.

b.   **Further Audit Procedures** A description of the nature, extent, and timing of planned further audit procedures at the relevant assertion level (see editor note at end of this "audit plan" section) for each material class of transactions, account balance, and disclosure. The plan for further audit procedures reflects the auditor's decision whether to test the operating effectiveness of controls and the nature, extent, and timing of planned substantive procedures.

The planning of specific further audit procedures depends on the outcome of the risk assessment procedures. Also, the auditor may begin to perform some further audit procedures before the planning of others is completed.

c.   **Other Procedures** A description of other audit procedures to be performed in order to comply with GAAS.

Editor note: In representing that the financial statements are fairly presented in conformity with GAAP, management implicitly or explicitly makes assertions regarding the recognition, measurement, presentation, and disclosure of information in the financial statements and related disclosures. *Relevant assertions* are assertions that have a meaningful bearing on whether an account is fairly stated. For example, valuation may not be relevant to a cash account unless currency translation is involved; however, existence and completeness are always relevant. (For more information about relevant assertions see the section of Chapter 24 on the use of assertions in obtaining audit evidence.)

4.   **Determining Involvement of Specialists** The auditor should consider whether specialized skills are needed in performing the audit.

a.   **Responsibilities** If the use of a specialist is planned, the auditor should determine whether that professional will effectively function as a member of the audit team. For example, a tax practitioner or a professional with valuation skills employed by the audit firm may be used to perform audit procedures as part of the audit team. If such a professional is part of the audit team, the auditor's responsibilities for supervising that professional are equivalent to those for other assistants.

b.   **Information Technology (IT) Specialists** In determining whether an IT professional is needed on the audit team, the auditor should consider such factors as: (1) the complexity of the entity's systems and IT controls and the manner in which they are used; (2) the significance of changes made to existing systems or the implementation of new systems; (3) the extent to which data is shared among systems; (4) the extent of the entity's participation in electronic commerce; (5) the entity's use of emerging technologies; and (6) the significance of audit evidence that is only available in electronic form.

D.   Communication

The auditor is required to communicate with those charged with governance an overview of the planned scope and timing of the audit.

E.   Supervision

Supervision involves directing assistants in accomplishing the audit objectives and determining whether those objectives were accomplished. The extent of supervision required will vary depending on the complexity of the subject matter, the qualifications of the persons performing the work, and other factors or circumstances.

For purposes of this discussion *assistants* are audit firm personnel other than the auditor with final responsibility for the audit. The term *auditor* refers to either the auditor with final responsibility for the audit or assistants.

1. **Communication Between Auditor & Assistants**

    a. **Responsibilities / Audit Objectives** The auditor should inform assistants of their responsibilities and the objectives of the audit procedures they are to perform in sufficient detail.

    b. **Significant Accounting & Auditing Questions** The assistants should be instructed to bring significant accounting and auditing questions to the auditor's attention.

    c. **Report Difficulties** Assistants should be directed to report difficulties encountered in performing the audit, such as missing documents or resistance from client personnel in providing access to information or in responding to inquiries.

    d. **Material Misstatement / Fraud Discussion** The auditor should discuss with members of the audit team the susceptibility of the entity's financial statements to material misstatement due to error or fraud, with special emphasis on fraud. The purpose of the discussion is to help the audit team members to understand the entity and its environment, including control and how the entity's risks may affect the audit. The discussion should emphasize the need to maintain a questioning mind and to exercise professional skepticism in gathering and evaluating evidence.

2. **Review Assistants' Work** The auditor should review the work performed by each assistant to

    a. **Confirm Performance / Documentation** Be sure it was performed and documented adequately and

    b. **Confirm Consistency With Audit Report** Evaluate whether the results obtained are consistent with the conclusions to be presented in the audit report.

3. **Disagreements** Both the auditor and the assistants should be aware of the procedures to be followed when differences of opinion arise on accounting and auditing issues. The procedures should allow assistants to document their disagreements with the conclusions reached if, after appropriate consultation, assistants believe it necessary to disassociate themselves from the issue's resolution. The basis for the resolution should also be documented.

II. Audit Risk & Materiality in Conducting an Audit (AU 312, SAS 107)

Audit risk and materiality affect the application of GAAS and should be considered together in designing the nature, extent, and timing of audit procedures and evaluating the results of those procedures.

A. Nature of Audit Risk
Audit risk is the risk that an auditor may unknowingly fail to modify the opinion on financial statements that are misstated materially. The existence of audit risk is acknowledged in the auditor's standard report by the statement that the auditor obtains reasonable [not absolute] assurance about whether the financial statements are free of material misstatement. The auditor should plan the audit so that audit risk will be reduced to a low level that is appropriate, in the auditor's judgment, for expressing an opinion on the financial statements.

The auditor should consider audit risk in relation to

* The relevant assertions related to individual account balances, classes of transactions, and disclosures and

* At the overall financial statement level.

B. **Nature of Materiality**

1. **Nature** Some matters are important for the fair presentation of financial statements, while others are not. The auditor plans and performs the audit to obtain reasonable assurance that material misstatements, whether caused by error or fraud, are detected.

2. **Auditor's Judgment / Reasonable Person Standard** The auditor's materiality judgments involve both quantitative and qualitative considerations and the auditor's perception of the needs of users of the financial statements. A misstatement is material if it is one that would change or influence the judgment of a reasonable person relying on the financial statements.

    Editor's note: Although the auditor should be alert for misstatements that could be qualitatively material, it is usually not practical to design audit procedures to detect them.

3. **User Profile** An auditor of financial statements considers the needs of users in general (as a group) rather than the needs of specific users. Users are assumed to:

    a. Have an appropriate knowledge of business and economic activities and accounting practices;

    b. Have a willingness to study the information in the financial statements with appropriate diligence;

    c. Understand that financial statements are prepared and audited to levels of materiality;

    d. Recognize the uncertainties inherent in the measurement of amounts based on the use of estimates, judgment, and the consideration of future events; and

    e. Make appropriate economic decisions on the basis of the information in the financial statements.

C. **Nature & Causes of Misstatements**
    There are two types of misstatements.

1. **Known Misstatements** These are misstatements specifically identified during the audit arising from the incorrect selection or misapplication of accounting principles or misstatements of facts.

2. **Likely Misstatements** Likely misstatements are those that

    a. Arise from differences between management's and the auditor's judgments concerning accounting estimates that the auditor considers unreasonable or inappropriate or

    b. The auditor considers likely to exist based on an extrapolation from audit evidence, for example, the projection of the results of a sample to the relevant population.

3. **Causes of Misstatements** Misstatements result from errors or fraud. This distinction affects the auditor's response to misstatements. The auditor has no responsibility to plan the audit to detect immaterial misstatements. However, if misstatements due to fraud are detected, the auditor should consider the implications for the integrity of management and employees and the possible effects on other aspects of the audit even if the misstatements are not material.

    a. **Errors** Errors are unintentional mistakes of amounts or disclosures in financial statements.

    b. **Fraud** Fraud is an intentional act involving the use of deception to obtain an unjust or or illegal advantage committed by employees, management, those charged with governance, or third parties. There are two types of fraudulent misstatements that are relevant in an audit of financial statements (for more information see the section on fraud in this chapter). They are misstatements arising from:

    (1)   Fraudulent financial reporting

    (2)   Misappropriation of assets (theft)

c.   **Types of Misstatements**

    (1)   An inaccuracy in gathering or processing data

    (2)   Misapplication of GAAP in regard to the amount, classification, or presentation of a financial statement item

    (3)   Omission of a financial statement item

    (4)   A financial statement disclosure that is not presented in conformity with GAAP

    (5)   Omission of a financial statement disclosure required by GAAP

    (6)   An incorrect accounting estimate

    (7)   The auditor's evaluation of management's judgment concerning an accounting estimate or the selection or application of an accounting principle as unreasonable or inappropriate

D.   **Financial Statement Level Considerations**

1.   **Purposes** The auditor must consider audit risk and determine a materiality level for the financial statements taken as a whole for the purposes of

    a.   Determining the extent and nature of risk assessment procedures

    b.   Identifying and assessing the risks of material misstatement

    c.   Determining the nature, extent, and timing of further audit procedures; and

    d.   Evaluating whether the financial statements taken as a whole are presented fairly.

2.   **Pervasive Risks** At the overall financial statement level, the auditor should consider risks of material misstatement that relate pervasively to the financial statements taken as a whole and potentially affect many relevant assertions. Risks of this nature often relate to the entity's control environment and are not necessarily identifiable with specific assertions at the account balance, class of transactions, or disclosure level. Such risks may be especially relevant to the consideration of the risk of fraud.

3.   **Multiple Locations / Components** The auditor should consider the extent to which audit procedures should be performed at selected locations or components. The factors an auditor should consider regarding the selection of a particular location or component include (a) the nature and amount of assets and transactions; (b) the degree of centralization of records or information processing; (c) the effectiveness of the control environment, particularly with respect to management's direct control over the exercise of authority delegated to others and its ability to effectively supervise activities at a particular location; (d) the frequency, timing, and scope of the entity's monitoring activities; (e) judgments about materiality of a particular component or location; and (f) risks associated with the location or component, such as political or economic instability.

E. **Individual Account Balance, Class of Transactions & Disclosure Level Considerations**

1. **Risk / Materiality Relationship** There is usually an inverse relationship between audit risk and materiality considerations. The risk that relevant assertions related to a particular account balance, class of transactions, or disclosure could be misstated by a very large amount may be very low, but the risk that it could be misstated by a small amount may be very high.

2. **Auditor Response to Risk / Materiality Judgments** Everything else being equal, a decrease in either the acceptable level of audit risk or the perceived materiality level of an account balance, class of transactions, or disclosure would require the auditor to do one or more of the following.

   a. Select a more effective auditing procedure (nature).

   b. Increase the extent of a particular auditing procedure (extent).

   c. Perform auditing procedures closer to the balance sheet date (timing).

3. **Materiality** In planning the nature, extent and timing of audit procedures for a specific account balance, class of transactions, or disclosure, the auditor is concerned with detecting misstatements that could be material when aggregated with misstatements in other balances, classes, or disclosures to the financial statements taken as a whole.

4. **Audit Risk Components** The risk that relevant assertions related to account balances, classes of transactions, or disclosures are misstated has two components: inherent risk and control risk. The combination of these two risks is known as the risk of material misstatement (RMM). The RMM combined with the auditor's detection risk make up audit risk. These components may be assessed in quantitative terms (such as percentages) or nonquantitative terms (such as high, medium, or low).

   The general relationship between audit risk and its components is expressed in the following model. This is not a mathematical formula nor does does it include all factors that may influence the assessment of audit risk. The standard setters included it because they thought this form of representation might prove useful.

   Exhibit 2 ▶ Audit Risk Model

	AR	= RMM × DR	or	AR	= (IR × CR) × (AP × TD)
where:	AR	= Audit Risk	IR	=	Inherent Risk
	RMM	= Risk of Material Misstatement	CR	=	Control Risk
			AP	=	Substantive Analytical Procedures Risk
	DR	= Detection Risk	TD	=	Tests of Details Risk

   a. **Risk of Material Misstatement (RMM)** The RMM (consisting of inherent risk and control risk) is the risk that the relevant assertions related to balances, classes, or disclosures contain misstatements that could be material to the financial statements when aggregated with other misstatements. The RMM rests within the entity, independent of the audit.

   The auditor should assess the RMM at the relevant assertion level as a basis for further audit procedures. This assessment is not a precise measurement of risk—it is a judgment. The auditor should make the assessment by performing:

   - Risk assessment procedures to obtain an understanding of the entity and its environment, including its internal control; and

- Tests of controls, where appropriate, to obtain evidence about their operating effectiveness.

(1) **Inherent Risk (IR)** Inherent risk is the susceptibility of a relevant assertion to a material misstatement, assuming there are no related controls. Some items can pose more risk simply due to their nature, for example, cash has a lot of inherent risk because it is more susceptible to theft than most items. Complex calculations have more inherent risk than simple calculations. Accounts consisting of estimates that are subject to significant measurement uncertainty have more inherent risk than do accounts consisting of relatively routine, factual data. External factors that give rise to business risk can influence inherent risk, for example, technological developments could make a particular product obsolete, causing inventory to be more susceptible to overstatement.

(2) **Control Risk (CR)** Control risk is the risk that a material misstatement that could occur in a relevant assertion will not be prevented or detected on a timely basis by the entity's internal controls. This risk is a function of the effectiveness of the design and operation of internal controls related to the preparation of the financial statements. Some control risk will always exist because of the inherent limitations of any entity's internal control system. These include breakdowns in controls that can occur due to human fallibility or circumvention of controls either by collusion or inappropriate management override.

b. **Detection Risk (DR)** It is the risk that the auditor will not detect a material misstatement that exists in a relevant assertion. It is nearly always present to some degree because an auditor rarely examines 100 percent of an account balance or class of transactions. Detection risk is also a function of the effectiveness of an auditing procedure and its application by the auditor, i.e., the auditor can select an inappropriate procedure, misapply a procedure, or misinterpret the audit results.

(1) Detection risk relates to substantive procedures. It can be broken down (disaggregated) into the additional components of tests of details risk (TD) and substantive analytical procedures risk (AP).

(2) Detection risk is managed by the auditor's response to the RMM. It should bear an inverse relationship to the RMM, i.e., if the auditor perceives an increase in the RMM, the auditor should accept less detection risk. Conversely, the lower the RMM, the greater the detection risk than can be accepted by the auditor.

Accordingly, the level of detection risk also has an inverse relationship with the amount of substantive testing needed. If the auditor decreases the acceptable level of detection risk, more substantive testing will be in order and vice versa. However, the auditor should perform substantive procedures for all relevant assertions related to all material account balances, classes of transactions, and disclosures regardless of the level of risk.

And there is a direct relationship between the RMM and the amount of substantive testing needed.

Exhibit 3 ▶ Risk Relationships

Inherent Risk and Control Risk (RMM)	Acceptable Level of Detection Risk	Substantive Tests
Increase	Decrease	Increase
Decrease	Increase	Decrease

Editor note: A change in substantive tests means to alter the nature, extent, or timing of such tests.

c. **How the RMM & Detection Risk Differ** Inherent risk and control risk (RMM) differ from detection risk in that they are the entity's risks and exist independently of the audit, whereas detection risk relates to the auditor's procedures and can be altered by adjusting the nature, extent, and timing of substantive procedures. Thus, the auditor assesses inherent risk and control risk (RMM). Detection risk is a function of the nature, extent, and timing of audit procedures, and, as such, may be changed by the auditor.

F. **Determining Materiality When Planning the Audit**

1. **Financial Statement Level** The auditor should determine a materiality level for the financial statements taken as a whole when establishing the overall audit strategy. Determining a materiality level for the financial statements taken as a whole helps the auditor identify and assess the risks of material misstatements as well as plan the nature, extent, and timing of further audit procedures.

   a. **Benchmarks** Determining materiality is a matter of professional judgment. The auditor may apply a percentage to a chosen benchmark to aid in determining overall materiality. Depending on the nature and circumstances of the entity, appropriate benchmarks might include: total revenues, gross profit, and other categories of reported income. For asset-based entities (e.g., an investment fund), an appropriate benchmark might be net assets. When identifying an appropriate benchmark, the auditor may consider the following factors.

      (1) The elements of the financial statements (e.g., assets, liabilities, etc.) and the financial statement measures defined by GAAP (e.g., financial positlon), or other specific requirements

      (2) Whether there are financial statement items, for the particular entity, that users' tend to focus on

      (3) The nature of the entity and the industry in which it operates

      (4) The size of the entity, nature of its ownership, and the way it is financed

   b. **Considerations** In determining materiality, the auditor should consider (a) prior periods' financial results and financial positions, (b) the period-to-date financial results and financial position, and (c) budgets or forecasts for the current period. The auditor should take into account any significant changes in the entity's circumstances (e.g., a significant business acquisition) and relevant changes in the economy or the industry in which the entity operates. For example, if an auditor usually determines materiality for a specific entity based on a percentage of profit, but there are circumstances that gave rise to an exceptional increase in profit, the auditor may conclude that a normalized profit figure based on past results is a more appropriate benchmark.

2. **Misstatements of Lesser Amounts** The materiality level determined for the financial statements taken as a whole is not a threshold below which identified misstatements are always considered to be immaterial.

   a. **Specific Circumstances** Specific circumstances of the entity may cause misstatements of particular items to be considered material by users of the financial statements even if they are below the determined materiality level. Factors to consider when identifying such items include

      (1) Whether accounting standards, laws, or regulations affect users' expectations regarding the measurement or disclosure of certain items (for example, related party transactions or compensation of management or those charged with governance)

(2) The key disclosures in relation to the industry and the entity's environment (for example, research and development costs for a pharmaceutical company)

(3) Whether attention is focused on the financial performance of a particular subsidiary or division that is separately disclosed in the consolidating financial statements (for example, a newly acquired business)

The views of management and and those charged with governance may be helpful to the auditor in gaining or confirming an understanding of user needs.

b. Tolerable Misstatement Determination

(1) Definition When planning a test of details, tolerable misstatement (or tolerable error) is the maximum monetary misstatement that the auditor is willing to accept in a particular account balance or class of transactions.

(2) Purpose The auditor normally sets the levels of tolerable misstatement lower than the materiality levels. In doing so, the auditor acknowledges the possibility that some misstatements of even lesser amounts (than those identified due to specific circumstances) could, when aggregated, result in the material misstatement of the financial statements.

Setting the tolerable misstatement for a specific audit procedure at less than the financial statement materiality level allows the auditor to use it as a tool to design the audit so that tolerable misstatement, combined for all of the tests in the audit, does not exceed materiality for the financial statements. (See Chapter 25, *Audit Sampling*, for more information on tolerable misstatement.)

3. Changes in Materiality During the audit, the auditor may become aware of additional factors that change the auditor's judgment about materiality. Thus, when evaluating audit findings, the auditor may use a different level of materiality than that used for planning purposes. If the auditor decides to lower the level of materiality, the auditor should reconsider the related levels of tolerable misstatement and the appropriateness of the nature, extent, and timing of further audit procedures.

4. When Aggregated Misstatements Approach the Materiality Level When aggregated misstatements (known and likely) approach the materiality level, the auditor should determine if there is an unacceptable level of risk that undetected misstatements could cause the materiality level to be exceeded. If so, the auditor should reconsider the nature and extent of further audit procedures.

5. Documentation Requirements The auditor should document the levels of materiality and tolerable misstatement, including any changes, and the basis on which those levels were determined.

G. Communication of Misstatements to Management
The auditor must communicate all nontrivial misstatements (distinguishing between known and likely ones) to the appropriate level of management on a timely basis.

1. Known Misstatements The auditor should request that management record adjustments needed to correct all known misstatements, including the effect of prior period misstatements.

2. Likely Misstatements

a. If the auditor evaluates the amount of likely misstatement from a sample in an account balance, class of transactions, or disclosure as material, either individually or in aggregate with other misstatements, the auditor should request management to examine the entire population in order to find any additional corrections needed. Afterwards, the auditor should reevaluate the amount of likely misstatement which may include performing additional audit procedures.

b. If the auditor has identified a likely misstatement involving differences in estimates, the auditor should request management to review the assumptions and methods used in developing management's estimate. Afterwards, the auditor should reevaluate the amount of likely misstatement which may include performing additional audit procedures.

c. If an analytical procedure indicates that a misstatement might exist, but not its approximate amount, the auditor should request management to investigate and, if necessary, should expand audit procedures to determine whether a misstatement exists.

3. Documentation Requirements The auditor should document all known and likely misstatements identified by the auditor during the audit, other than those that are trivial, that have been corrected by management.

4. No Adjustment If management decides not to correct some or all of the known and likely misstatements, the auditor should obtain an understanding of management's reasons and should take that into account when considering the qualitative aspects of the entity's accounting practices and the implications for the auditor's report.

H. Evaluating Misstatements
The auditor should not assume that a misstatement is an isolated occurrence. The auditor should consider whether the overall audit strategy and the audit plan need to be revised if the nature of misstatements and the circumstances of their occurrence are indicative that other misstatements may exist that, when aggregated with identified misstatements, could be material.

1. Quantitative Evaluation of Misstatements

a. Uncorrected Misstatements In evaluating whether the financial statements are presented fairly, the auditor must consider the effects, both individually and in the aggregate, of all uncorrected known and likely misstatements.

(1) Individually Before considering the aggregated effect, the auditor should consider each uncorrected misstatement separately to evaluate:

- Its effect in relation to the relevant individual account balances, classes of transactions, or disclosures, including whether materiality levels for particular items of lesser amounts due to specific circumstances of the entity have been exceeded

- Whether it is appropriate to offset misstatements, for example, misstatements of items within the same account balance

- The effect of misstatements related to prior periods on the current period's financial statements; in prior periods, misstatements may not have been corrected by the entity because they did not cause those financial statements to be materially misstated.

(2) Aggregate Uncorrected misstatements should be aggregated in a manner that allows the auditor to determine whether, in relation to individual amounts, subtotals, or totals in the financial statements, they materially misstate the financial statements taken as a whole.

(3) Documentation Requirements The auditor should document

- A summary of uncorrected misstatements, other than those that are trivial, related to known and likely misstatements

- The auditor's conclusion as to whether uncorrected misstatements, individually or in aggregate, do or do not cause the financial statements to be materially misstated, and the basis for that conclusion

b. **Use of Estimates to Manipulate Earnings** The auditor should evaluate whether the aggregated differences between estimates supported by audit evidence and those included in the financial statements, while individually reasonable, indicate a possible bias on the part of management, if when considered as whole, their effect is to increase income. Or if estimates are clustered at one end of the acceptable range in the prior year and at the other end in the current year, it may be that management is using the swing to manipulate earnings to conform to expectations. The auditor should consider whether these conditions should be communicated to those charged with governance.

2. **Qualitative Evaluation of Misstatements** Factors to consider include

- The potential effect of the misstatement on trends, especially trends in profitability
- A misstatement that changes a loss into income or vice versa
- The potential effect of the misstatement on the entity's compliance with loan covenants, other contractual agreements, and regulatory provisions
- The existence of statutory or regulatory reporting requirements that affect materiality thresholds
- The misstatement masks a change in earnings or other trends, especially in the context of general economic and industry conditions
- A misstatement that has the effect of increasing management's compensation, for example, by satisfying the requirements for the award of bonuses or other forms of incentive compensation
- The sensitivity of the circumstances surrounding the misstatement, for example, the implications of misstatements involving fraud and possible illegal acts, violations of contractual provisions, and conflicts of interest
- The significance of the financial statement element affected by the misstatement, for example, a misstatement affecting recurring earnings as contrasted to one involving a nonrecurring charge or credit, such as an extraordinary item
- The effects of misclassifications, for example, misclassification between operating and nonoperating income or recurring and nonrecurring income items or a misclassification between fundraising costs and program activity costs in a not-for-profit organization
- The significance of the misstatement relative to reasonable user needs
- The definitive character of the misstatement, for example, the precision of an error that is objectively determinable as contrasted with a misstatement that unavoidably involves a degree of subjectivity through estimation, allocation, or uncertainty
- The motivation of management with respect to the misstatement, for example, (1) an indication of a possible pattern of bias by management when developing and accumulating accounting estimates, (2) a misstatement precipitated by management's continued unwillingness to correct weaknesses in the financial reporting process, or (3) the intentional decision not to follow generally accepted accounting principles
- The cost of making the correction; it may not be cost-beneficial for the client to develop a system to calculate a basis to record the effect of an immaterial misstatement; on the other hand, if management appears to have developed a system to calculate an amount that represents an immaterial misstatement, it may reflect a motivation of management as noted above
- The existence of offsetting effects of individually significant but different misstatements
- The likelihood that a misstatement that is currently immaterial may have a material effect in future periods because of a cumulative effect that builds over several periods
- The risk that possible additional undetected misstatements would affect the auditor's evaluation

III. Understanding the Entity & Its Environment (AU 314, SAS 109)

A. Second Standard of Fieldwork

Exhibit 4 ▶ The Second Standard of Fieldwork

> The auditor must obtain a sufficient understanding of the entity and its environment, including its internal control, to assess the risk of material misstatement of the financial statements whether due to error or fraud, and to design the nature, extent, and timing of further audit procedures.

B. Risk Assessment Procedures

The auditor should perform risk assessment procedures to gain an understanding of the entity and its environment, including its internal control. The nature, extent, and timing of these procedures depend on the circumstances of the engagement, such as the size and complexity of the entity as well as the auditor's experience with the entity. The auditor may choose to perform risk assessment procedures concurrently with tests of controls and/or substantive procedures. These procedures include:

1. **Inquiries** The auditor is required to make inquiries of management and others within the entity. Much of the information needed can be obtained from management and those responsible for financial reporting. However, inquiries of others within the entity, such as internal auditors, and other employees with different levels of authority, may be useful in providing the auditor with different perspectives in identifying risks of material misstatement.

2. **Analytics** The auditor should apply analytics in planning the audit to assist in understanding the entity and its environment as well as to identify areas that may represent specific risks. In performing analytics as risk assessment procedures, the auditor should develop expectations about plausible relationships that are reasonably expected to exist. When comparison of those expectations with recorded amounts or ratios reveals unusual or unexpected relationships, the auditor should consider those results in identifying risks of material misstatement. However, when analytics use data aggregated at a high level, the results of those analytics may provide only a broad initial indication about whether a material misstatement exists. Accordingly, the auditor should consider the results of such analytics along with other information gathered in identifying the risks of material misstatement.

3. **Observation & Inspection** Observation and inspection may support inquiries of management and others as well as provide information about the entity and its environment. Such procedures ordinarily include:

   a. Observation of entity activities and operations.

   b. Inspection of documents (such as business plans and strategies), records, and internal control manuals.

   c. Reading reports prepared by management (such as quarterly management reports and interim financial statements), those charged with governance (such as minutes of board of directors' meetings), and internal audit.

   d. Visits to the entity's premises.

   e. Tracing transactions through the information system relevant to financial reporting. This may be performed as part of a walk-through.

4. **Prior-Period Information** If the auditor uses information about the entity and its environment obtained in prior periods, the auditor should determine whether changes have occurred that may affect the relevance of such information in the current audit. Previous experience with the entity contributes to the understanding of the entity. For example, procedures performed in previous audits ordinarily provide information about the entity's organizational

structure, business, and controls, as well as past misstatements and whether they were corrected on a timely basis. However, such information may be irrelevant due to changes in the entity or its environment. The auditor should make inquiries and perform other appropriate audit procedures, such as walk-throughs, to determine whether changes have occurred.

5. **Fraud Risk** The auditor should specifically assess the RMM due to fraud and consider that assessment in designing audit procedures. The results of the fraud risk assessment provide only a broad initial indication about whether a material misstatement due to fraud may exist. Therefore, the auditor should consider the results of the fraud risk assessment along with other information gathered in identifying the risks of material misstatement.

6. **Other Information** The auditor also should consider other relevant information such as that obtained from the auditor's client acceptance or continuance process, or, where practicable, experience gained on other engagements performed for the entity.

C. **Audit Team Discussion**
The audit team should discuss the susceptibility of the financial statements to material misstatement. This discussion may be held concurrently with the required fraud risk discussion.

1. **Objective** The objective of this discussion is to gain a better understanding of the potential for material misstatements resulting from fraud or error in the specific areas assigned to the audit team, and to understand how the results of procedures performed may affect other aspects of the audit, including decisions about the nature, extent, and timing of further audit procedures.

2. **Topics** The discussion is an opportunity for more experienced team members to share their insights based on their knowledge of the entity. It is also a time for the team members to exchange information about the entity's business risks as well as to discuss how and where the financial statements may be susceptible to material misstatement due to error or fraud. There should be an emphasis on the need to exercise professional skepticism throughout the engagement, to be alert to indications of material misstatement due to fraud or error, and to be rigorous in following up on such indications. Additional critical issues to be discussed include: areas of significant audit risk; areas susceptible to management override of controls; unusual accounting procedures used; important control systems; materiality at the financial statement and account level; and how materiality will be used to determine the extent of testing. The application of GAAP in light of the entity's accounting policies also should be addressed.

D. **Areas of Understanding**
The auditor should obtain an understanding of the entity and its environment in the following areas:

1. **Industry, Regulatory & Other External Factors** This includes (1) industry conditions, such as competitors, supplier and customer relationships, and technological developments; (2) the regulatory environment, including relevant accounting pronouncements, the legal and political environment, and environmental requirements pertaining to the entity, among other matters; as well as (3) other external factors, such as general economic conditions.

2. **Nature of the Entity** This refers to the entity's operations, ownership, governance, types of investments, organizational structure, and financing. Understanding the nature of an entity enables the auditor to understand the entity's classes of transactions, account balances, and disclosures to be expected.

   a. **Complex Structures** The existence of subsidiaries or other components gives rise to additional risks of material misstatement such as: consolidation difficulties; the allocation of goodwill to subsidiaries, and its impairment; whether investments are joint ventures, subsidiaries, or investments accounted for using the equity method; and whether special-purpose entities are accounted for appropriately.

b. **Related Parties** It is important to understand the relationships between the owners, management, and other key personnel as well as their relations with other people or entities to determine whether related-party transactions have been identified and accounted for appropriately.

3. **Objectives, Strategies & Related Business Risks** In response to industry, regulatory and other internal and external factors, the entity develops objectives (overall plans for the entity) and strategies to achieve those objectives.

a. **Business Risks** Business risks result from significant conditions, events, actions, or inactions that could interfere with the entity's ability to achieve its objectives and execute its strategies. Inappropriate objectives and strategies also represent business risks. Not all business risks give rise to risks of material misstatement; however, most business risks will affect the financial statements in some way either immediately or in the future. Long-term consequences may need to be considered when assessing going concern issues; for example, a decline in the industry may affect the entity's ability to continue as a going concern. The auditor does not, however, have a responsibility to identify or assess all business risks.

b. **Sources** As part of internal control, management usually identifies business risks and develops approaches to address them. However, smaller entities often do not set their objectives and strategies, or manage the related business risks, through formal plans or processes; therefore, there may not be any documentation of such matters. In such cases, the auditor may use inquiries of management and observation to obtain an understanding of how the entity responds to such matters.

4. **Measurement & Review of the Entity's Financial Performance** Review of performance measures highlights aspects of the entity's performance that management and others consider important. Whether external or internal, such performance measures create pressures on the entity that could motivate management to take actions that either improve the business performance or misstate the financial statements. Internally generated information used by management may include key performance indicators; budgets; variance analysis; subsidiary, divisional, departmental, or other level performance reports; as well as comparisons of the entity's performance with that of competitors. External information, such as analysts' reports and credit rating agency reports, may be obtained from the client or Web sites.

5. **Internal Control** The auditor should obtain an understanding of the five components of internal control by performing risk assessment procedures to evaluate the design and implementation of relevant controls. The auditor's knowledge should be sufficient to:

a. Identify types of potential misstatements.

b. Consider factors that affect the risks of material misstatement.

c. Design tests of controls, when applicable, and substantive procedures.

E. **Documentation**

1. **Discussion** The auditor should document the discussion concerning the susceptibility of the financial statements to material misstatement due to error or fraud, including (a) how and when the discussion took place, (b) the subject matter discussed, (c) who participated in the discussion, and (d) significant decisions regarding planned responses at the financial statement and relevant assertion levels.

2. **Understanding** The auditor also should document (a) key elements of the understanding obtained regarding each of the five aspects outlined above (section III. D), including each of the five components of internal control; (b) the sources of information from which the understanding was obtained; and (c) the risk assessment procedures performed.

IV. **Consideration of Fraud in a Financial Statement Audit (AU 316, SAS 99)**

A. **Fraud Overview**

1. **Responsibilities**

a. **Management and Those Charged With Governance** It is management's responsibility to design and implement programs and controls to prevent, deter, and detect fraud. Management and those charged with governance should set the proper "tone at the top" for the entity.

b. **Auditor**

(1) **Reasonable Assurance** The auditor has a responsibility to plan and perform the audit to obtain reasonable assurance about whether the financial statements are free of material misstatement, whether caused by error or fraud. Because absolute assurance is not attainable, even a properly designed and executed audit may not detect a material misstatement resulting from fraud.

(2) **Focus on Misstatements of Financial Statements** Auditors do not make legal determinations of whether fraud has occurred—the auditor is interested in acts that result in a material misstatement of the financial statements.

2. **Fraud Characteristics** Fraud is primarily differentiated from error by whether the resulting misstatement in the financial statements is intentional or unintentional. Fraud is an intentional act that causes a misstatement. Misstatements due to fraud are difficult to detect because fraud is usually concealed.

a. **Types of Misstatements** There are two types of misstatements relevant to an auditor's consideration of fraud—those arising from fraudulent financial reporting and misappropriation of assets.

(1) **Fraudulent Financial Reporting** Misstatements arising from fraudulent financial reporting are intentional misstatements or omissions of amounts or disclosures in financial statements designed to deceive financial statement users. It may be accomplished by

- Manipulation, falsification, or alteration of accounting records or supporting documents from which financial statements are prepared;

- Misrepresentation in or intentional omission from the financial statements of events, transactions, or other significant information; or

- Intentional misapplication of accounting principles relating to amounts, classification, manner of presentation, or disclosure.

Material misstatements due to fraudulent financial reporting often result from an overstatement of revenues (for example, through premature revenue recognition or recording fictitious revenues) or an understatement of revenues (for example, through improperly shifting revenues to a later period). Therefore, the auditor should ordinarily presume that there is a RMM due to fraud relating to revenue recognition. If an auditor finds this not to be the case, the auditor should document the reasons supporting this conclusion.

(2) **Misappropriation of Assets** Misstatements arising from misappropriation of assets involve the theft of an entity's assets where the effect causes the financial statements to be misstated. It can be accomplished in various ways—including embezzling receipts, stealing assets, or causing an entity to pay for

goods or services that have not been received. It is sometimes referred to as defalcation or theft.

b. **Attributes** The auditor should consider the following attributes of the RMM due to fraud to identify whether and how a risk is relevant to the audit.

(1) **Type** Whether it involves fraudulent financial reporting or misappropriation of assets

(2) **Significance** Whether it is of a magnitude that could lead to result in a possible material misstatement of the financial statements

(3) **Likelihood** The likelihood that it will result in a material misstatement in the financial statements

(4) **Pervasiveness** Whether the potential risk is pervasive to the financial statements as a whole or specifically related to a particular assertion, account, or class of transactions

c. **Conditions Conducive to Fraud** Three conditions generally are present when fraud occurs. (See the section on fraud risk factors within the *Assessment of the Risk of Material Misstatement Due to Fraud* section of this chapter for examples of circumstances or events that can create these conditions.)

(1) **Incentive / Pressure** Management or other employees have an incentive or are under pressure, which provides a reason to commit fraud.

(2) **Opportunity** Circumstances exist—for example, the absence of controls, ineffective controls, or the ability of management to override controls—that provide an opportunity for a fraud to be perpetrated.

(3) **Attitude / Rationalization** Those involved are able to rationalize committing a fraudulent act.

B. Assessment of the Risk of Material Misstatement Due to Fraud

1. **Professional Skepticism** Due professional care requires the auditor to exercise professional skepticism. The auditor should conduct the engagement with a mindset that recognizes the possibility that a material misstatement due to fraud could be present, regardless of any past experience with the entity or the auditor's belief about management's honesty and integrity. The auditor should be aware that management is often in the best position to perpetrate fraud. Such an attitude is demonstrated by designing audit procedures to obtain more reliable evidence for certain account balances and classes of transactions and/or the related assertions; and obtaining corroboration of management's assertions or representations from independent sources.

2. **Audit Team Discussion About the RMM Due to Fraud** Members of the audit team should have a brainstorming session which includes the auditor with final responsibility for the audit. The discussion should cover how and where the financial statements may be susceptible to fraud; how management could perpetrate and conceal fraudulent financial reporting; and how assets could be misappropriated. Factors affecting the entity that could create the three conditions conducive to fraud (see preceding section) should be covered. Management override of controls should also be considered. Finally, the team should plan a response to the entity's susceptibility to fraud.

How and when this discussion occurred should be documented. The record should include the names of the participants and the subject matter discussed.

Communication among the audit team members about the RMM due to fraud should continue throughout the audit.

3. **Obtaining Information to Identify the RMM Due to Fraud**

   a. **Inquiries of Those Charged With Governance** The auditor should inquire directly of those charged with governance regarding their views about the risks of fraud and whether they have knowledge of any fraud or suspected fraud affecting the entity If the audit committee is charged with the oversight of the entity's assessment of fraud and the controls established to mitigate those risks, the auditor should obtain an understanding of how the audit committee fulfills that responsibility.

   b. **Inquiries of Management** The auditor should inquire of management as to the risks of fraud and how they are addressed. This should include

      (1) Whether management has knowledge of any fraud or suspected fraud affecting the entity;

      (2) Whether management is aware of any allegations of fraud or suspected fraud received from employees, former employees, analysts, regulators, etc.;

      (3) Management's understanding about the risks of fraud in the entity, including any specific fraud risks the entity has identified or account balances or classes of transactions for which a risk of fraud may be likely to exist;

      (4) Programs and controls to mitigate specific fraud risks the entity has identified, or that otherwise help to prevent, deter, and detect fraud, and how management monitors those programs and controls and reports on them to those charged with governance;

      (5) For an entity with multiple locations, the nature and extent of monitoring of these, and whether there are any among them for which a risk of fraud may be more likely to exist; and

      (6) Whether and how management communicates to employees its views on business practices and ethical behavior;

   c. **Inquires of Others** The auditor should inquire of others within the entity about the existence or suspicion of fraud.

      (1) Internal auditors should be asked whether they have performed any procedures to detect fraud, and if these resulted in the discovery of any fraud, how management responded to their findings.

      (2) The auditor should use professional judgment to determine those others within the entity to whom inquiries should be directed and the extent of such inquiries. To make this determination, the auditor should consider those who may have additional knowledge about or be able to corroborate risks of fraud identified in the discussions with management or those charged with governance.

      An example of others the auditor may approach include employees involved in the handling of complex or unusual transactions. Talking with in-house legal counsel is also often helpful. And to gain additional perspective, the auditor may wish to talk with personnel in operations or at least **not** involved in the financial reporting process.

   d. **Analytical Procedure Results** The auditor should consider any unusual or unexpected relationships, particularly those involving revenue accounts, that have been identified in performing analytical procedures—during the planning or overall review stage of the audit or as a substantive test.

Although often helpful in identifying the RMM due to fraud, because analytical procedures generally use data aggregated at a high level, their results must be considered along with other evidence.

e. **Fraud Risk Factors** The auditor should consider evidence that indicates the existence of the three conditions that are conducive to fraud (covered earlier in this section—incentives or pressures to perpetrate fraud; opportunities to carry out the fraud; and attitudes or rationalizations to justify a fraudulent action). All three do not need to be evident for the auditor to conclude there may be risks. Circumstances or events that can create these conditions are known as fraud risk factors. Fraud risk factors do not necessarily indicate the existence of fraud, but they are often present where fraud exists.

(1) **Examples of Risk Factors Relating to Misstatements Due to Fraudulent Financial Reporting**

- **Incentives / Pressures**

    - Financial stability or profitability is threatened by economic, industry, or entity operating conditions, such as or as indicated by (1) a high degree of competition or market saturation, accompanied by declining margins; (2) a high vulnerability to rapid changes, such as changes in technology, product obsolescence, or interest rates; (3) significant declines in customer demand and increasing business failures in either the industry or overall economy; (4) operating losses making the threat of bankruptcy, foreclosure, or hostile takeover imminent; (5) recurring negative cash flows from operations and an inability to generate cash flows from operations while reporting earnings and earnings growth; (6) rapid growth or unusual profitability, especially compared to that of other companies in the same industry; or (7) new accounting, statutory, or regulatory requirements.

    - Excessive pressure exists for management to meet the requirements or expectations of third parties due to (1) profitability or trend level expectations of investment analysts, institutional investors, significant creditors, or other external parties (particularly expectations that are unduly aggressive or unrealistic), including expectations created by management in, for example, overly optimistic press releases or annual report messages; (2) the need to obtain additional debt or equity financing to stay competitive—including financing of major research and development or capital expenditures; (3) a marginal ability to meet exchange listing requirements or debt repayment or other debt covenant requirements; or (4) perceived or real adverse effects of reporting poor financial results on significant pending transactions, such as business combinations or contract awards.

    - Information available indicates that management's or those charged with governance's personal financial situation is threatened by the entity's financial performance arising from (1) significant financial interests in the entity; (2) significant portions of their compensation (for example, bonuses, stock options, and earn-out arrangements) being contingent upon achieving aggressive targets for stock price, operating results, financial position, or cash flow; or (3) personal guarantees of debts of the entity.

- There is excessive pressure on management or operating personnel to meet financial targets set up by those charged with governance or management, including sales or profitability incentive goals.

- **Opportunities**

  - The nature of the industry or the entity's operations provides opportunities to engage in fraudulent financial reporting that can arise from (1) significant related-party transactions not in the ordinary course of business or with related entities not audited or audited by another firm; (2) a strong financial presence or ability to dominate a certain industry sector that allows the entity to dictate terms or conditions to suppliers or customers that may result in inappropriate or non-arm's-length transactions; (3) assets, liabilities, revenues, or expenses based on significant estimates that involve subjective judgments or uncertainties that are difficult to corroborate; (4) significant, unusual, or highly complex transactions, especially those close to period end that pose difficult "substance over form" questions; (5) significant operations located or conducted across international borders in jurisdictions where differing business environments and cultures exist; or (6) significant bank accounts or subsidiary or branch operations in tax-haven jurisdictions for which there appears to be no clear business justification.

  - There is ineffective monitoring of management as a result of (1) domination of management by a single person or small group (in a nonowner-managed business) without compensating controls; or (2) Ineffective oversight over the financial reporting process and internal control by those charged with governance.

  - There is a complex or unstable organizational structure, as evidenced by (1) difficulty in determining the organization or individuals that have controlling interest in the entity; (2) overly complex organizational structure involving unusual legal entities or managerial lines of authority; or (3) high turnover of senior management, counsel, or board members.

  - Internal control components are deficient as a result of (1) inadequate monitoring of controls, including automated controls and controls over interim financial reporting (where external reporting is required); (2) high turnover rates or employment of ineffective accounting, internal audit, or information technology staff; or (3) ineffective accounting and information systems, including situations involving significant deficiencies or material weaknesses in internal control.

- **Attitudes / Rationalizations**

  - Ineffective communication, implementation, support, or enforcement of the entity's values or ethical standards by management or the communication of inappropriate values or ethical standards

- Nonfinancial management's excessive participation in or preoccupation with the selection of accounting principles or the determination of significant estimates

- Known history of violations of securities laws or other laws and regulations, or claims against the entity, its senior management, or board members alleging fraud or violations of laws and regulations

- Excessive interest by management in maintaining or increasing the entity's stock price or earnings trend

- A practice by management of committing to analysts, creditors, and other third parties to achieve aggressive or unrealistic forecasts

- Management failing to correct known significant deficiencies or material weaknesses in internal control on a timely basis

- An interest by management in employing inappropriate means to minimize reported earnings for tax-motivated reasons

- Recurring attempts by management to justify marginal or inappropriate accounting on the basis of materiality

- The relationship between management and the current or predecessor auditor is strained, as exhibited by (1) frequent disputes with the current or predecessor auditor on accounting, auditing, or reporting matters; (2) unreasonable demands on the auditor, such as unreasonable time constraints regarding the completion of the audit or the issuance of the auditor's report; (3) formal or informal restrictions on the auditor that inappropriately limit access to people or information or the ability to communicate effectively with those charged with governance; or (4) domineering management behavior in dealing with the auditor, especially involving attempts to influence the scope of the auditor's work or the selection or continuance of personnel assigned to or consulted on the audit engagement.

(2) **Examples of Risk Factors Relating to Misstatements Due to Misappropriation of Assets**

- **Incentives / Pressures**

  - Personal financial obligations may create pressure on management or employees with access to cash or other assets susceptible to theft to misappropriate those assets.

  - Adverse relationships between the entity and employees with access to cash or other assets susceptible to theft may motivate those employees to misappropriate those assets. For example, adverse relationships may be created by (1) known or anticipated future employee layoffs; (2) recent or anticipated changes to employee compensation or benefit plans; or (3) promotions, compensation, or other rewards inconsistent with expectations.

- **Opportunities**

  - Certain characteristics or circumstances may increase the susceptibility of assets to misappropriation. For example, opportunities to misappropriate assets increase when there are (1) large amounts of cash on hand or processed; (2) inventory items that are small in size, of high value, or in high demand; (3) easily convertible assets, such as bearer bonds, diamonds, or computer chips; or (4) fixed assets that are small in size, marketable, or lacking observable identification of ownership.

- Inadequate internal control over assets may increase the susceptibility of misappropriation of those assets. For example, misappropriation of assets may occur because there is / are (1) inadequate segregation of duties or independent checks; (2) inadequate management oversight of employees responsible for assets, for example, inadequate supervision or monitoring of remote locations; (3) inadequate job applicant screening of employees with access to assets; (4) inadequate record keeping with respect to assets; (5) an inadequate system of authorization and approval of transactions (for example, in purchasing); (6) inadequate physical safeguards over cash, investments, inventory, or fixed assets; (7) a lack of complete and timely reconciliations of assets; (8) a lack of timely and appropriate documentation of transactions, for example, credits for merchandise returns; (9) a lack of mandatory vacations for employees performing key control functions; (10) inadequate management understanding of information technology, which enables information technology employees to perpetrate a misappropriation; or (11) inadequate access controls over automated records, including controls over and review of computer systems event logs.

- **Attitudes / Rationalizations**

  - Disregard for the need for monitoring or reducing risks related to misappropriations of assets

  - Disregard for internal control over misappropriation of assets by overriding existing controls or by failing to correct known internal control deficiencies

  - Behavior indicating displeasure or dissatisfaction with the company or its treatment of the employee

  - Changes in behavior or lifestyle that may indicate assets have been misappropriated

f. **Other Information Gained Throughout the Audit** Information from reviews of interim financial statements or from procedures relating to the acceptance and continuance of clients and engagements may be helpful in assessing the RMM due to fraud. Inherent risks of assertions or those identified at the account balance or class of transaction level should also be considered in relation to the RMM due to fraud.

The auditor's assessment of the RMM due to fraud should be ongoing throughout the audit. Conditions may be identified during fieldwork that change or support a judgment regarding the assessment of the risks, such as discrepancies in the accounting records; conflicting or missing audit evidence; and problematic or unusual relationships between the auditor and management

g. **Consideration of the Entity's Controls That Address Fraud** The auditor should consider whether such programs and controls mitigate the identified risks of material misstatement due to fraud or whether specific control deficiencies may exacerbate the risks.

h.   **Final Review** At or near the completion of fieldwork, the auditor should evaluate whether the accumulated results of auditing procedures and other observations affect the assessment of the RMM due to fraud made earlier in the audit. This evaluation primarily is a qualitative matter based on the auditor's judgment. Such an evaluation may provide further insight about the RMM due to fraud and whether there is a need to perform additional or different audit procedures. As part of this evaluation, the auditor with final responsibility for the audit should ascertain that there has been appropriate communication with the other audit team members throughout the audit regarding information or conditions indicative of RMM due to fraud.

C.   **Response to the Risk of Material Misstatement Due to Fraud**

1.   **Overall Response** Judgments about the RMM due to fraud have an overall effect on how the audit is conducted.

a.   **Assignment of Personnel & Supervision** The knowledge, skill, and ability of personnel assigned significant engagement responsibilities should be commensurate with the auditor's assessment of the RMM due to fraud.

b.   **Accounting Principles** The auditor should consider management's selection and application of significant accounting principles, particularly those related to subjective measurements and complex transactions, to determine if their collective application indicates a bias that may create such a material misstatement of the financial statements.

c.   **Predictability of Auditing Procedures** The auditor should incorporate an element of unpredictability in the selection of auditing procedures from year to year—for example, performing substantive tests of selected account balances and assertions not otherwise tested due to their materiality or risk, adjusting the timing of testing from that otherwise expected, using differing sampling methods, and performing procedures at different locations or at locations on an unannounced basis.

2.   **Responses Involving the Nature, Extent, & Timing of Audit Procedures** The auditing procedures performed in response to identified RMM due to fraud will vary depending upon the types of risks identified and the account balances, classes of transactions, and related assertions that may be affected. These procedures may involve both substantive tests and tests of the operating effectiveness of the entity's programs and controls. However, because management may have the ability to override controls that otherwise appear to be operating effectively, it is unlikely that audit risk can be reduced to an appropriately low level by performing only tests of controls.

The auditor's responses to address specifically identified RMM due to fraud may include changing the nature, extent, and timing of auditing procedures in the following ways.

a.   **Nature** The nature of auditing procedures may need to be changed to obtain evidence that is more reliable or to obtain additional corroborative information. Also, physical observation or inspection of certain assets may become more important.

b.   **Extent** The extent of the procedures applied should reflect the assessment of the RMM due to fraud. For example, increasing sample sizes or performing analytical procedures at a more detailed level may be appropriate.

c.   **Timing** The timing of substantive tests may need to be modified. For example, the auditor might conclude that substantive testing should be performed at or near the end of the reporting period.

3.   **Responses to Further Address the Risk of Management Override of Controls** Management is in a unique position to perpetrate fraud because of its ability manipulate accounting records and prepare fraudulent financial statements by overriding established

controls. By its nature, management override of controls can occur in unpredictable ways. Accordingly, in addition to overall responses and responses that address specifically identified risks of material misstatement due to fraud, further audit procedures should be performed to address the risk of management override of controls. The results of these procedures should be documented. These include

    a.   **Examining Journal Entries** Material misstatements of financial statements due to fraud often involve the manipulation of the financial reporting process by recording inappropriate or unauthorized journal entries; or making adjustments to amounts reported in the financial statements that are not reflected in formal journal entries, such as through consolidating adjustments, report combinations, and reclassifications. Accordingly, the auditor should examine journal entries and other adjustments for evidence of possible material misstatement due to fraud. The selection of the appropriate journal entries should be based on the auditor's understanding and the nature of the entity's financial reporting process and influenced by the assessment of the effectiveness of the related controls. Other selection factors include the characteristics of the journal entries and the nature and complexity of the affected accounts. Special attention should be paid to journal entries processed outside of the normal course of business.

    b.   **Reviewing Accounting Estimates for Biases** Fraudulent financial reporting often is accomplished through intentional misstatement of accounting estimates. The auditor should consider whether differences between estimates supported by the audit evidence and those included in the financial statements, even if they are individually reasonable, indicate a possible bias, in which case the auditor should reconsider the estimates taken as a whole.

        The auditor should also compare current year estimates to the prior year's to determine (with the aid of hindsight) if there are indications of bias. The significant accounting estimates selected for testing should include those that are based on highly sensitive assumptions or are otherwise significantly affected by judgments made by management.

    c.   **Evaluating the Business Rationale for Significant Unusual Transactions** The auditor should gain an understanding of the business rationale for such transactions and whether that rationale (or the lack thereof) suggests that the transactions may have been entered into to engage in fraudulent financial reporting or conceal misappropriation of assets.

4.   **Withdrawal** The auditor may conclude that it would not be practicable to design auditing procedures that sufficiently address the RMM due to fraud. In that case, withdrawal from the engagement with communication to the appropriate parties may be an appropriate course of action.

D. Evaluation of Evidence

1.   **Immaterial Misstatements Due to Fraud** Even if the misstatements due to fraud are not material to the financial statements, the auditor should evaluate the implications for the integrity of management and employees and the possible effects on other aspects of the audit. The auditor should reevaluate the assessment of the RMM due to fraud and its resulting impact on the nature, extent, and timing of the tests of balances or transactions and the assessment of the effectiveness of controls if control risk was assessed below the maximum.

2.   **Material Misstatements Due to Fraud** If the auditor believes that the misstatement is or may be the result of fraud, and either has determined that the effect could be material to the financial statements or has been unable to evaluate whether the effect is material, the auditor should

a. **Obtain Additional Evidence** Attempt to obtain additional audit evidence to determine whether material fraud has occurred or is likely to have occurred;

b. **Effect on Financial Statements & Audit Report** If fraud has occurred, determine its effect on the financial statements and the auditor's report;

c. **Impact on Other Aspects of the Audit** Consider the implications for other aspects of the audit;

d. **Discuss with Management & Those Charged With Governance** Discuss the matter and the approach for further investigation with a level of management that is at least one level above those involved, and with senior management and those charged with governance; and

e. **Legal Counsel** If appropriate, suggest that the client consult with legal counsel.

3. **Withdrawal** The auditor's consideration of the RMM and the results of audit tests may indicate such a significant RMM due to fraud that the auditor should consider withdrawing from the engagement and communicating the reasons for withdrawal to those charged with governance. Whether to withdraw may depend on the implications about the integrity of management and the diligence and cooperation of management or the board of directors in investigating the circumstances and taking appropriate action. The auditor may wish to consult with legal counsel when considering withdrawal from an engagement.

E. **Communications**

1. **Those Charged With Governance & Management** The auditor should report any fraud involving senior management or fraud causing a material misstatement of the financial statements directly to those charged with governance.

   The appropriate level of management must be informed whenever the auditor detects evidence of possible fraud, even if the matter is insignificant. The auditor should reach an agreement with those charged with governance about the nature and extent of communications regarding fraud by lower level employees.

   If the auditor's assessment of the RMM due to fraud has identified risks that have continuing control implications that could represent significant deficiencies or material weaknesses in internal control the auditor is required to communicate those, in writing, to management and those charged with governance.

2. **Outside Parties** The auditor's ethical and legal obligations generally preclude the auditor from the disclosure of possible fraud to outside parties, however there are exceptions. In the following circumstances, an auditor may need to disclose information. The auditor may want to consult with legal counsel beforehand.

   a. To comply with legal and regulatory requirements

   b. To a successor auditor making inquiries in accordance with AU 315, *Communications Between Predecessor and Successor Auditors*

   c. In response to a subpoena

   d. To a funding agency or other specified agency in accordance with requirements for the audits of entities that receive governmental financial assistance

F. **Documentation** The auditor should document

1. The discussion among engagement personnel in planning the audit regarding the susceptibility of the entity's financial statements to material misstatement due to fraud, including

how and when the discussion occurred, the audit team members who participated, and the subject matter discussed

2. The procedures performed to obtain information necessary to identify and assess the RMM due to fraud

3. Specific RMM due to fraud that were identified, and a description of the auditor's response to those risks

4. If the auditor has not identified in a particular circumstance, improper revenue recognition as a RMM due to fraud, the reasons supporting the auditor's conclusion

5. The results of the procedures performed to further address the risk of management override of controls

6. Other conditions and analytical relationships that caused the auditor to believe that additional auditing procedures or other responses were required and any further responses the auditor concluded were appropriate, to address such risks or other conditions

7. The nature of the communications about fraud made to management, those charged with governance, and others

V. Assessing the Risks of Material Misstatement (AU 314, SAS 109 continued)

A. Steps
The auditor should identify and evaluate the risks of material misstatement at the relevant assertions level as well as at the financial statement level. More specifically, the auditor should:

1. **Identify Risks** Identify risks throughout the process of obtaining an understanding of the entity and its environment, including related internal controls, as well as while considering the classes of transactions, account balances, and disclosures in the financial statements.

2. **Identify Potential Misstatements** Relate the identified risks to types of potential misstatements that could occur at the relevant assertion level.

3. **Consider Materiality** Consider whether any identified risks are so significant that they could cause a material misstatement of the financial statements.

4. **Consider Probability** Consider the probability that identified risks will cause a material misstatement of the financial statements.

B. Support
The auditor should use the information gathered from risk assessment procedures, including the audit evidence obtained in evaluating the design and implementation of controls, as evidence to support the risk assessment. The auditor should use the risk assessment to determine the nature, extent, and timing of further audit procedures. If the risk assessment is based on an expectation that controls are operating effectively to prevent or detect material misstatements, the auditor should test the operating effectiveness of controls that have been determined to be suitably designed to prevent or detect material misstatements.

C. Pervasiveness
The auditor should determine whether the identified risks relate to specific relevant assertions related to classes of transactions, account balances, and disclosures, or whether they are more pervasive and relate to the financial statements taken as a whole. For example, a weak control environment creates risks that are not likely to be confined to specific assertions, but rather relate to the financial statements as a whole.

D. Significant Risks

The auditor should use professional judgment to determine which identified risks are *significant risks* that require special audit consideration. The auditor should consider inherent risk to determine whether the nature of the risk, the materiality of the potential misstatement including the likelihood of multiple misstatements, and the probability of occurrence are such that they require special audit consideration.

1. **Nature** In considering the nature of identified risks, the auditor should consider the following:

    a. Whether the risk is a risk of fraud.

    b. Whether the risk is related to recent significant economic, accounting, or other developments and, therefore, requires specific attention.

    c. The complexity of transactions.

    d. Whether the risk involves significant transactions with related parties.

    e. The degree of subjectivity involved in the measurement of financial information related to the risks, especially those involving a wide range of measurement uncertainty.

    f. Whether the risk involves significant nonroutine or unusual transactions that are outside the normal course of business.

2. **Nonroutine Transactions** Nonroutine transactions are transactions that are unusual, either due to size or nature, and therefore, occur infrequently. The risks of material misstatement related to nonroutine transactions may be greater when the following circumstances are involved: (a) greater management intervention to specify accounting treatment; (b) greater manual intervention for data collection and processing; (c) complex calculations or accounting principles; (d) difficult implementation of effective controls over the risks due to the nature of the transaction; and (e) significant related-party transactions.

3. **Judgmental Matters** Judgmental matters may include the development of accounting estimates for which there is significant measurement uncertainty. The risks of material misstatement related to judgmental matters requiring the development of accounting estimates may be greater when the following matters are involved: (a) accounting principles for estimates or revenue recognition are subject to different interpretations; or (b) required judgment is subjective, complex, or requires assumptions about the effects of future events.

E. Risks Requiring Tests of Controls

The auditor should identify those risks for which it is not possible or practicable to obtain sufficient audit evidence from substantive procedures alone. Such risks may concern routine transactions that are often highly automated with little or no manual intervention. In these cases, audit evidence may be available only in electronic form; therefore, its appropriateness and sufficiency often depend on the operating effectiveness of controls over its completeness and accuracy.

F. Risk Assessment Revision

The auditor's assessment of the risks of material misstatement is based on audit evidence available; therefore, as additional audit evidence is obtained, this risk assessment may need to be revised during the course of the audit. For example, in performing tests of controls, the auditor may obtain audit evidence that controls are not operating effectively. Also, while performing substantive procedures, the auditor may detect more misstatements than is consistent with the auditor's original risk assessment. Thus, in these circumstances, the auditor should modify the assessment and adjust further audit procedures accordingly.

G. Documentation

The auditor should document: (1) the assessment of the risks of material misstatement at the financial statement and relevant assertion levels; (2) the basis for that assessment; (3) significant risks identified and related controls evaluated; as well as (4) risks identified that require tests of controls to obtain sufficient audit evidence and the related controls evaluated.

VI. Responding to Assessed Risks (AU 318, SAS 110)

A. Financial Statement Level

The auditor should develop overall responses to address the assessed risks of material misstatement at the financial statement level. Some responses to consider include:

1. **Professional Skepticism** More emphasis on the need to maintain professional skepticism in gathering and evaluating audit evidence.

2. **Assignments** Assignment of more experienced staff or those with specialized skills or the use of specialists.

3. **Supervision** Increase supervision.

4. **Unpredictability** Incorporation of more unpredictable elements in further audit procedures.

5. **General Changes** General changes to the nature, extent, or timing of further audit procedures. An example of this would be to perform substantive procedures at the end of the period instead of at an interim date in response to weaknesses in the control environment. Other general changes may include seeking more extensive audit evidence from substantive procedures, modifying the nature of audit procedures to obtain more persuasive audit evidence, or increasing the number of locations to be included in the audit scope.

B. Relevant Assertion Level

The auditor should design and perform further audit procedures whose nature, extent, and timing are responsive to the assessed risks of material misstatement at the relevant assertion level. In designing further audit procedures, the auditor should consider such matters as: the significance of the risk; the probability that a material misstatement will occur; the characteristics of the class of transactions, account balance, or disclosure involved; the nature of specific controls, including whether they are manual or automated; and whether the auditor expects to obtain audit evidence to determine if the entity's controls are effective in preventing or detecting material misstatements.

1. **Audit Approach** Performing substantive procedures alone may be appropriate for specific relevant assertions and risks; hence, the auditor may ignore the effect of controls. This may be because risk assessment procedures have not identified any effective controls relevant to the assertion or because testing the operating effectiveness of controls would not be efficient. However, the auditor must be satisfied that performing only substantive procedures for specific assertions would be effective in reducing detection risk to an acceptably low level. A combined approach using both tests of controls and substantive tests is often most effective.

   a. Regardless of the audit approach selected, the auditor should design and perform substantive procedures for all relevant assertions related to each material class of transactions, account balance, and disclosure. Also, analytical procedures alone may not be sufficient in some instances.

   b. Sometimes small entities do not have many control activities that can be identified by the auditor. In these circumstances, further audit procedures will most likely consist primarily of substantive procedures.

2. **Nature** The nature of procedures refers to whether they are tests of controls or substantive procedures as well as their type (i.e., inspection, observation, inquiry, confirmation, recalculation, reperformance, or analytical procedures). The nature of audit procedures is the most important consideration in responding to assessed risks.

a. **Appropriateness** Some audit procedures are more appropriate for some assertions than others. For example, in relation to revenue, tests of controls may be more appropriate to test the completeness assertion, whereas substantive procedures may more appropriate to test the occurrence assertion.

b. **Basis** The selection of audit procedures should be based on the risk assessment; thus, the higher the risk, the more reliable and relevant the audit evidence should be. This will effect the type and combination of audit procedures. The auditor should consider both the inherent risk and control risk of each class of transactions, account balance, or disclosure. For example, if the auditor determines that there is low inherent risk regardless of the related controls, substantive analytical procedures alone may provide sufficient appropriate audit evidence. Alternatively, if the auditor expects there is low control risk because an entity has effective controls and the auditor intends to design substantive procedures based on the operating effectiveness of those controls, then the auditor should perform tests of controls also.

3. **Timing** This refers to when audit procedures are performed as well as the period or date for which the audit evidence is applicable.

   a. **Interim Date** The auditor may perform further audit procedures at an interim date or at the end of the period. The higher the RMM, the more effective it may be to perform substantive procedures nearer to, or at, the period end. It may also be effective to perform audit procedures at unpredictable times. However, while performing audit procedures at an interim date, the auditor may detect significant issues at an early stage of the audit. This will give management more time to resolve such issues or the auditor more time to adjust the audit approach to address such issues. If the auditor performs tests of controls or substantive procedures at an interim date, the auditor will need to consider the additional evidence for the remaining period that is necessary.

   b. **Period End** Certain procedures can be performed only at or after period end such as agreeing the financial statements to the accounting records.

   c. **Additional Considerations** The auditor also should consider the following factors when planning the timing of audit procedures:

      (1) The control environment.

      (2) When relevant information is available. For example, electronic files may only be available for a short amount of time.

      (3) The nature of the risk. For example, if there is a risk of overstatement of revenues to meet earnings expectations by subsequent creation of false sales agreements, the auditor may examine contracts available on the date of the period end.

      (4) The period or date to which the audit evidence will relate.

4. **Extent** This refers to the quantity of a specific audit procedure to be performed; for example, a sample size or the number of observations of a control activity may vary. The extent of an audit procedure is a matter of professional judgment. In making this judgment, the auditor should consider (a) the tolerable misstatement, (b) the assessed RMM, and (c) the degree of assurance the auditor plans to obtain. Generally, the extent of audit procedures should increase as the RMM increases.

C. **Documentation**
The auditor should document: (1) the overall responses to address the assessed risks of misstatement at the financial statement level; (2) the nature, extent, and timing of the further audit procedures; (3) the connection of those procedures with the assessed risks at the relevant assertion

level; (4) the results of the audit procedures; and (5) the conclusions reached concerning the use of audit evidence about the operating effectiveness of controls that was obtained in a prior audit.

VII. Illegal Acts by Clients (AU 317, SAS 54)

A. Illegal Acts

Illegal acts are defined as violations of laws or governmental regulations by management or employees acting on behalf of an entity. Illegal acts by clients do not include personal misconduct by the entity's personnel unrelated to their business activities.

1. **Focus on Effect of Illegal Acts on the Financial Statements** Illegal acts vary considerably in their relation to the financial statements. Generally, the further removed an illegal act is from the events and transactions ordinarily reflected in financial statements, the less likely the auditor is to become aware of the act or to recognize its possible illegality. Generally, the auditor leaves the determination of the legality of an act to an expert qualified to practice law or to a court of law.

2. **Direct Versus Indirect Effect on the Financial Statements**

    a. **Direct Effect on the Financial Statements** The auditor considers laws and regulations that have a direct and material effect on the determination of financial statement amounts, for example, tax laws. The nature of the auditor's responsibility to detect and report misstatements resulting from illegal acts having a direct and material effect on the financial statements is the same as that for misstatements caused by error or fraud.

    b. **Indirect Effect on the Financial Statements** Entities may be affected by many other laws or regulations, including those related to securities trading, occupational safety and health, food and drug administration, environmental protection, equal employment, and price-fixing or other antitrust violations. Generally, these laws and regulations relate more to an entity's operating aspects than to its financial and accounting aspects, and their financial statement effect is indirect. Their indirect effect is normally the result of the need to disclose a contingent liability because of the allegation or determination of illegality.

    Normally, an audit in accordance with GAAS does not include audit procedures specifically designed to detect illegal acts. If information comes to the auditor's attention that provides evidence concerning the existence of possible illegal acts that could have a material indirect effect on the financial statements, the auditor should apply audit procedures specifically directed to ascertaining whether an illegal act has occurred. However, because of the characteristics of "indirect effect" illegal acts, an audit made in accordance with GAAS provides no assurance that illegal acts will be detected or that any contingent liabilities that may result will be disclosed.

3. **Red Flags** In applying audit procedures, the auditor may encounter information (or "red flags") that may raise a question concerning possible illegal acts, such as the following:

    a. Unauthorized or improperly recorded transactions

    b. Investigation by a governmental agency

    c. Large payments for unspecified services to consultants

    d. Excessive sales commissions or agents' fees

    e. Unusually large cash payments

    f. Unexplained payments to government officials or employees

g.   Failure to file tax returns

h.   Forced to discontinue operations in a foreign country

4.   **Relation to Financial Statements** Generally, the further removed an illegal act is from the events and transactions reflected in the financial statements, the less likely the auditor is to become aware of the act. The auditor normally considers only those laws and regulations having a direct and material effect on the financial statement amounts. The auditor is required to consider illegal acts that could have a direct and material effect on the financial statements (e.g., violations of tax law) and consider that in the design of substantive tests.

a.   **Indirect** An entity may be affected by many laws or regulations relating more to its operating aspects than to the financial statements. An auditor ordinarily does not have sufficient basis for recognizing possible violations of laws and regulations (for example, shipping regulations for tractor-trailers or maritime vessels).

b.   **Notification** The auditor may not become aware of illegal acts that could have an indirect effect on the financial statements unless the client discloses such information, or there is evidence of a governmental agency investigation or enforcement proceeding in the records normally inspected in an audit. Examples would include price-fixing, equal employment violations, and occupational safety and health violations.

B.   **Procedures**
Normally, an audit conducted in accordance with GAAS does not include procedures specifically designed to detect illegal acts. During the course of an audit, however, other audit procedures may bring illegal acts to the auditor's attention. Such procedures may include the following: reading minutes; inquiring of client's management and legal counsel concerning litigation, claims, and assessments; and performing substantive tests of details of transactions or balances. The auditor also should make inquiries of management concerning the client's compliance with laws and regulations, and the client's policies to prevent illegal acts. The auditor should obtain written representations from management concerning the absence of violations or possible violations of laws or regulations whose effects must be considered for disclosure in the financial statements or as a basis for recording a loss contingency.

1.   **Possible Illegal Act** If a possible illegal act has occurred, the auditor should obtain an understanding of the act, the circumstances under which it occurred, and sufficient information to evaluate its effect on the financial statements. The auditor may wish to consult with the client's legal counsel or other specialists regarding the possible illegal act and its effects, and additional procedures may be applied, if necessary, to obtain further understanding of the acts.

2.   **Additional Procedures** Additional audit procedures may include the following:

a.   Examining supporting documents, such as invoices, canceled checks, and agreements, and comparing them with accounting records

b.   Confirming significant information concerning the matter with the other party to the transaction or with intermediaries, such as banks or lawyers

c.   Determining whether the transaction has been authorized properly

d.   Considering whether other similar transactions or events may have occurred, and applying procedures to identify them

C.   **Financial Statement Effect**
When an illegal act has occurred, the auditor should consider both the quantitative and qualitative materiality of the act on the financial statements as well as the implications for other aspects of the audit, such as the reliability of representations of management. The illegal act may involve contingent liabilities that must be disclosed. The auditor should consider whether material revenue or

earnings are derived from transactions involving illegal acts, or if illegal acts create significant unusual risks associated with material revenue or earnings.

D.   Audit Committee

The auditor should ascertain that the audit committee, or those with equivalent authority, are adequately informed about illegal acts that come to the auditor's attention. The communication should describe the act, the circumstances, and the effect on the financial statements. The communication may be written or oral. If oral, the communication should be documented. The auditor need not communicate inconsequential matters.

E.   Auditor's Report

If the client refuses to accept the auditor's report as modified, the auditor should withdraw from the engagement and indicate the reasons for doing so in writing to the audit committee or board of directors.

1.   **Not Disclosed**   If the auditor concludes that an illegal act having a material effect on the financial statements has occurred, and the act has not been accounted for or disclosed properly, the auditor should express a qualified opinion or an adverse opinion, depending on the materiality.

2.   **Scope Limitation**   If the auditor is precluded by the client from obtaining sufficient audit evidence to determine whether an illegal act that could be material has, or is likely to have, occurred, (i.e., a scope limitation), the auditor should disclaim an opinion on the financial statements.

F.   Other Considerations

The auditor may decide that withdrawal is necessary when the client does not take remedial action that the auditor considers necessary, even when the illegal act is not material to the financial statements.

1.   **Management Integrity**   The auditor should consider the implications of an illegal act in relation to other aspects of the audit, particularly the reliability of management representations.

2.   **Outside Parties**   The auditor may wish to consult with legal counsel before discussing illegal acts with outside parties. Disclosure of illegal acts to outside parties may be necessary in certain circumstances, such as

a.   When the entity reports an auditor change under the appropriate securities law on Form 8-K. Also see Private Securities Litigation Reform Act of 1995.

b.   To an auditor making inquiries in accordance with SAS 84, *Communications Between Predecessor and Successor Auditors.*

c.   In response to a subpoena.

d.   To a funding agency or other specified agency in accordance with requirements for the audits of entities that receive governmental financial assistance.

3.   **Private Securities Litigation Reform Act of 1995**   Auditors must include procedures to (1) detect illegal acts that would have a direct and material effect on the financial statements, (2) identify related-party transactions that would have a material effect on the financial statements, and (3) evaluate an issuer's ability to continue as a going concern.

a.   **Reports to Entity**   An auditor who becomes aware of possible illegal activities shall inform the entity's management and assure that the audit committee or the board of directors is adequately informed. If the auditor concludes that the illegal act has a material effect on the financial statements and management has not taken appropriate remedial actions, and departure from a standard report seems reasonable, the auditor shall report this directly to the board of directors.

b. **Reporting to SEC** The entity is required to notify the SEC no later than 1 business day after receipt of such report. If the entity fails to notify the SEC within 1 business day, the auditor must resign from the engagement and/or report to the SEC within 1 business day.

4. **Foreign Corrupt Practices Act of 1977 (FCPA)** The antibribery provisions of the FCPA make it illegal for a U.S. person or company, and any foreign company or person acting while in the U.S., to bribe a foreign government official for the purpose of obtaining or retaining business. Companies are subject to a fine of up to $2,000,000, while individuals are subject to a maximum fine of $100,000 and/or up to 5 years imprisonment. Fines imposed on individuals cannot be paid by companies. In addition, civil penalties may be imposed.

a. **Management** Additionally, the FCPA requires companies whose securities are listed in the U.S. (issuers registered with the SEC) to maintain records which accurately reflect the transactions and dispositions of assets of the company and to maintain a system of internal accounting control sufficient to provide reasonable assurance that (1) transactions are executed in accordance with management's authorization, (2) transactions are recorded properly in conformity with GAAP, (3) access to assets is restricted to those authorized by management, and (4) the recorded accountability for assets periodically is compared to, and reconciled with, the existing assets.

b. **Auditor** The FCPA does not require the auditor to issue a special report on internal control.

G. **Responsibilities in Other Circumstances**
An auditor may accept an engagement that entails, by agreement with the client, a greater responsibility for detecting illegal acts than a typical audit. For example, an auditor may be engaged to test and report on compliance with specific government regulations.

VIII. **Communication With Those Charged With Governance (AU 380, SAS 114)**

A. **Definitions**

1. **Those Charged With Governance** Persons with responsibility for overseeing the strategic direction of the entity and obligations related to the accountability of the entity are defined as those charged with governance. This includes overseeing the financial reporting process. (The term *those charged with governance* encompasses the terms *board of directors* and *audit committee.*)

2. **Management** Those responsible for achieving the objectives of the entity and who have the authority to establish policies and make decisions by which those objectives are to be pursued are termed management. Their responsibilities include the financial statements and the system of internal control over financial reporting.

B. **Matters to Be Communicated to Those Charged With Governance**
Matters related to the financial statements that are significant and relevant to the responsibilities of those charged with governance in overseeing the financial reporting process must be communicated by the auditor. However, communication by the auditor does not relieve management of their responsibility to communicate matters of interest to those charged with governance.

1. **GAAS** The auditor should communicate the auditor's responsibilities under GAAS, including that:

a. **Opinion** The auditor is responsible for forming and expressing an opinion about whether the financial statements that have been prepared by management with the oversight of those charged with governance are presented fairly, in all material respects, in conformity with GAAP.

b.   **Responsibilities**   The audit does not relieve either management or those charged with governance of their responsibilities.

c.   **Independence**   The auditor may determine that it is appropriate to communicate circumstances or relationships that in the auditor's professional judgment may reasonably be thought to bear on independence and that the auditor gave significant consideration to in reaching the conclusion that independence has not been impaired.

2.   **Overview**   An overview of the planned scope and timing of the audit should be communicated.   The auditor must exercise professional judgment in determining the nature and extent of this communication.   For example, communicating the nature and timing of specific audit procedures may make them too predictable.

3.   **Significant Findings**   The auditor should communicate significant findings from the audit, including:

a.   The auditor's views about qualitative aspects of the entity's significant accounting practices, including accounting policies, accounting estimates, and financial statement disclosures

b.   Significant difficulties, if any, encountered during the audit

c.   Uncorrected misstatements, other than those the auditor believes are trivial, if any

d.   Disagreements with management, if any

e.   Other findings or issues, if any, arising from the audit that are, in the auditor's professional judgment, significant and relevant to those charged with governance regarding their oversight of the financial reporting process

And, unless all of those charged with governance are involved in managing the entity, the auditor also should communicate:

f.   Material, corrected misstatements that were brought to the attention of management as a result of audit procedures

g.   Representations the auditor is requesting from management

h.   Management's consultations with other accountants

i.   Significant issues, if any, arising from the audit that were discussed, or the subject of correspondence, with management

C.   **The Communication Process**
It is important that the communication process be effective and two-way, so the auditor should communicate with those charged with governance the form, timing, and expected general content of the communications.   If the two-way communication is not adequate, the auditor should consider the effect, if any, on the auditor's assessment of the risks of material misstatements.   The auditor must exercise professional judgment as to whether the communication is oral or in writing.

D.   **Documentation**
The auditor should document matters communicated orally and retain those in writing.

CHAPTER 22—PLANNING

Problem 22-1 MULTIPLE CHOICE QUESTIONS (76 to 95 minutes)

1. An auditor's engagement letter should include a statement regarding
a. Management's responsibility to provide certain written representations to the auditor
b. Conditions under which the auditor may modify the preliminary judgment about materiality
c. Internal control activities that would reduce the auditor's assessment of control risk
d. Materiality matters that could modify the auditor's preliminary assessment of fraud risk
(R/05, AUD, #35, amended, 7830)

2. An auditor is required to establish an understanding with a client regarding the services to be performed for each engagement. This understanding generally includes
a. The auditor's responsibility for determining the preliminary judgments about materiality and audit risk factors
b. Management's responsibility for identifying mitigating factors when the auditor has doubt about the entity's ability to continue as a going concern
c. The auditor's responsibility for ensuring that the audit committee is aware of any significant deficiencies and material weaknesses that come to the auditor's attention
d. Management's responsibility for providing the auditor with an assessment of the risk of material misstatement due to fraud
(R/06, AUD, #12, 8130)

3. During the initial planning phase of an audit, a CPA most likely would
a. Identify specific internal control activities that are likely to prevent fraud
b. Evaluate the reasonableness of the client's accounting estimates
c. Discuss the timing of the audit procedure with the client's management
d. Inquire of the client's attorney as to whether any unrecorded claims are probable of assertion
(5/98, AUD, #2, 7798)

4. In developing a preliminary audit strategy, an auditor should consider
a. Whether the allowance for sampling risk exceeds the achieved upper precision limit
b. Findings from substantive tests performed at interim dates
c. Whether the inquiry of the client's attorney identifies any litigation, claims, or assessments **not** disclosed in the financial statements
d. Potential risks of material misstatement
(11/91, AUD, #8, amended, 2276)

5. An auditor should design the written audit plan (or program) so that
a. All material transactions will be selected for substantive testing.
b. Substantive tests prior to the balance sheet date will be minimized.
c. The audit procedures selected will achieve specific audit objectives.
d. Each account balance will be tested under either tests of controls or tests of transactions.
(5/95, AUD, #16, amended, 5634)

6. Which of the following procedures would an auditor most likely include in the initial planning of a financial statement audit?
a. Obtaining a written representation letter from the client's management
b. Examining documents to detect illegal acts having a material effect on the financial statements
c. Considering whether the client's accounting estimates are reasonable in the circumstances
d. Determining the extent of involvement of the client's internal auditors (11/94, AUD, #1, 5074)

7. Prior to commencing fieldwork, an auditor usually discusses the general audit strategy with the client's management. Which of the following details do management and the auditor usually agree upon at this time?
a. The specific matters to be included in the communication with the audit committee
b. The minimum amount of misstatements that may be considered to be significant deficiencies and material weaknesses
c. The schedules and analyses that the client's staff should prepare
d. The effects that inadequate controls may have over the safeguarding of assets
(R/06, AUD, #7, 8125)

8. The audit work performed by each assistant should be reviewed to determine whether it was adequately performed and to evaluate whether the
a. Audit procedures performed are approved in the professional standards.
b. Auditor's system of quality control has been maintained at a high level.
c. Results are consistent with the conclusions to be presented in the auditor's report.
d. Audit has been performed by persons having adequate technical training and proficiency as auditors. (11/91, AUD, #5, amended, 2273)

9. The in-charge auditor most likely would have a supervisory responsibility to explain to the staff assistants
a. That immaterial fraud is **not** to be reported to the client's audit committee
b. How the results of various auditing procedures performed by the assistants should be evaluated
c. Why certain documents are being transferred from the current file to the permanent file
d. What benefits may be attained by the assistant's adherence to established time budgets
(5/95, AUD, #7, amended, 5625)

10. A difference of opinion regarding the results of a sample cannot be resolved between the assistant who performed the auditing procedures and the in-charge auditor. The assistant should
a. Accept the judgment of the more experienced in-charge auditor
b. Refuse to perform any further work on the engagement
c. Document the disagreement and ask to be disassociated from the resolution of the matter
d. Notify the client that a serious audit problem exists (Editors, 0209)

11. Which of the following statements is **not** correct about materiality?
a. The concept of materiality recognizes that some matters are important for fair presentation of financial statements in conformity with GAAP, while other matters are **not** important.
b. An auditor considers materiality for planning purposes in terms of the largest aggregate level of misstatements that could be material to any one of the financial statements.
c. An auditor's consideration of materiality is influenced by the auditor's perception of the needs of a reasonable person who will rely on the financial statements.
d. Materiality judgments are made in light of surrounding circumstances and necessarily involve both quantitative and qualitative judgments.
(11/94, AUD, #11, amended, 5084)

12. Holding other planning considerations equal, a decrease in the amount of misstatements in a class of transactions that an auditor could tolerate most likely would cause the auditor to
a. Apply the planned substantive tests prior to the balance sheet date
b. Perform the planned auditing procedures closer to the balance sheet date
c. Increase the assessed level of control risk for relevant financial statement assertions
d. Decrease the extent of auditing procedures to be applied to the class of transactions
(11/97, AUD, #11, 6574)

13. Inherent risk and control risk differ from detection risk in that inherent risk and control risk are
a. Functions of the client and its environment, while detection risk is not
b. Changed at the auditor's discretion, while detection risk is not
c. Considered at the individual account-balance level, while detection risk is not
d. Elements of audit risk, while detection risk is not
(Editors, 2810)

14. On the basis of audit evidence gathered and evaluated, an auditor decides to increase the assessed level of control risk from that originally planned. To achieve an overall audit risk level that is substantially the same as the planned audit risk level, the auditor would
a. Decrease substantive testing
b. Decrease detection risk
c. Increase inherent risk
d. Increase materiality levels
(11/94, AUD, #10, 5083)

15. The acceptable level of detection risk is inversely related to the
a. Assurance provided by substantive tests
b. Risk of misapplying auditing procedures
c. Preliminary judgment about materiality levels
d. Risk of failing to discover material misstatements
(5/91, AUD, #26, 0044)

16 Which of the following would an auditor most likely use in determining the auditor's preliminary judgment about materiality?
a. The results of the initial assessment of control risk
b. The anticipated sample size for planned substantive tests
c. The entity's financial statements of the prior year
d. The assertions that are embodied in the financial statements (11/97, AUD, #10, 6573)

17. Which of the following procedures would an auditor most likely perform in planning a financial statement audit?
a. Inquiring of the client's legal counsel concerning pending litigation
b. Comparing the financial statements to anticipated results
c. Searching for unauthorized transactions that may aid in detecting unrecorded liabilities
d. Examining computer generated exception reports to verify the effectiveness of internal controls
(5/95, AUD, #4, amended, 5622)

18. In planning an audit, the auditor's knowledge about the design of relevant internal control policies and procedures should be used to
a. Identify the types of potential misstatements that could occur
b. Assess the operational efficiency of internal control
c. Determine whether controls have been circumvented by collusion
d. Document the assessed level of control risk
(11/95, AUD, #2, amended, 5951)

19. When obtaining an understanding of the entity and its environment, including its internal control, the auditor is required to document

I. The discussion concerning the susceptibility of the financial statements to material misstatement
II. The risk assessment procedures performed

a. I only
b. II only
c. Both I and II
d. Neither I nor II
(Editors, 8266)

20. Which of the following statements describes why a properly designed and executed audit may **not** detect a material misstatement in the financial statements resulting from fraud?
a. Audit procedures that are effective for detecting an unintentional misstatement may be ineffective for an intentional misstatement that is concealed through collusion.
b. An audit is designed to provide reasonable assurance of detecting material errors, but there is **no** similar responsibility concerning fraud.
c. The factors considered in assessing control risk indicated an increased risk of intentional misstatements, but only a low risk of unintentional errors in the financial statements.
d. The auditor did not consider factors influencing audit risk for account balances that have effects pervasive to the financial statements taken as a whole.
(11/91, AUD, #10, amended, 2278)

21. Which of the following factors most likely would heighten an auditor's concern about the risk of fraudulent financial reporting?
a. Large amounts of liquid assets that are easily convertible into cash
b. Low growth and profitability as compared to other entities in the same industry
c. Financial management's participation in the initial selection of accounting principles
d. An overly complex organizational structure involving unusual lines of authority
(R/01, AUD, #3, 7018)

22. Which of the following circumstances most likely would cause an auditor to suspect that there are material misstatements in an entity's financial statements?
a. The entity's management places **no** emphasis on meeting publicized earnings projections
b. Significant differences between the physical inventory count and the accounting records are **not** investigated
c. Monthly bank reconciliations ordinarily include several large outstanding checks
d. Cash transactions are electronically processed and recorded, leaving **no** paper audit trail
(R/03, AUD, #7, 7629)

23. If the business environment is experiencing a recession, the auditor most likely would focus increased attention on which of the following accounts?
a. Purchase returns and allowances
b. Allowance for doubtful accounts
c. Common stock
d. Noncontrolling interest of a subsidiary purchased during the year
(R/06, AUD, #23, 8141)

24. Which of the following circumstances would an auditor most likely consider a risk factor relating to misstatements arising from fraudulent financial reporting?
a. Several members of management have recently purchased additional shares of the entity's stock.
b. Several members of the board of directors have recently sold shares of the entity's stock.
c. The entity distributes financial forecasts to financial analysts that predict conservative operating results.
d. Management is interested in maintaining the entity's earnings trend by using aggressive accounting practices.
(R/06, AUD, #37, 8155)

25. Disclosure of possible fraud to parties other than a client's senior management and its audit committee ordinarily is not part of an auditor's responsibility. However, to which of the following outside parties may a duty to disclose that possible fraud exists?

	To the SEC when the client reports an auditor change	To a successor auditor when the successor makes appropriate inquiries	To a funding agency from which the client receives governmental financial assistance
a.	Yes	Yes	No
b.	Yes	No	Yes
c.	No	Yes	Yes
d.	Yes	Yes	Yes

(5/90, AUD, #55, amended, 0163)

26.   When assessing the risk of material misstatement, an auditor is required to document

    I.   The basis for the assessment
    II.   Significant risks identified and the related controls that were evaluated

a. I only
b. II only
c. Both I and II
d. Neither I nor II   (Editors, 8265)

27.   Regardless of the assessed level of control risk, an auditor would perform some
a. Tests of controls to determine the effectiveness of internal control policies
b. Analytical procedures to verify the design of internal control procedures
c. Substantive tests to restrict detection risk for significant transaction classes
d. Dual-purpose tests to evaluate both the risk of monetary misstatement and preliminary control risk   (11/93, AUD, #23, 4260)

28.   After obtaining an understanding of the entity and its environment and assessing the risk of material misstatement, an auditor decided to perform tests of controls. The auditor most likely decided that
a. It would be efficient to perform tests of controls that would result in a reduction in planned substantive tests.
b. Additional evidence to support a further reduction in control risk is not available.
c. An increase in the assessed level of control risk is justified for certain financial statement assertions.
d. There were many internal control weaknesses that could allow errors to enter the accounting system.   (5/95, AUD, #33, amended, 5651)

29.   As the acceptable level of detection risk increases, an auditor may
a. Increase the assessed level of control risk
b. Change the assurance provided by tests of controls by using a larger sample size than planned
c. Change the timing of substantive tests from year-end to an interim date
d. Change the nature of substantive tests from a less effective to a more effective procedure
         (11/92, AUD, #10, amended, 2944)

30.   Which of the following information discovered during an audit most likely would raise a question concerning possible illegal acts?
a. Related party transactions, although properly disclosed, were pervasive during the year.
b. The entity prepared several large checks payable to cash during the year.
c. Material internal control weaknesses previously reported to management were **not** corrected.
d. The entity was a campaign contributor to several local political candidates during the year.
         (11/97, AUD, #13, 6576)

31.   Which of the following procedures would **least** likely result in the discovery of possible illegal acts?
a. Reading the minutes of the board of directors' meetings
b. Making inquiries of the client's management
c. Performing tests of details of transactions
d. Reviewing an internal control questionnaire
         (R/05, AUD, #25, 7820)

32.   When an auditor becomes aware of a possible illegal act by a client, the auditor should obtain an understanding of the nature of the act to
a. Evaluate the effect on the financial statements
b. Determine the reliability of management's representations
c. Consider whether other similar acts may have occurred
d. Recommend remedial actions to the audit committee   (11/92, AUD, #4, 2938)

33.   If information comes to an auditor's attention that implies the existence of possible illegal acts that could have a material, but indirect effect on the financial statements, the auditor should next
a. Apply audit procedures specifically directed to ascertaining whether an illegal act has occurred
b. Seek the advice of an informed expert qualified to practice law as to possible contingent liabilities
c. Discuss the evidence with the client's audit committee, or others with equivalent authority and responsibility
d. Report the matter to an appropriate level of management at least one level above those involved
         (Editors, 0172)

34. Which of the following relatively small misstatements most likely could have a material effect on an entity's financial statements?
a. An illegal payment to a foreign official that was not recorded
b. A piece of obsolete office equipment that was not retired
c. A petty cash fund disbursement that was not properly authorized
d. An uncollectible account receivable that was not written off (5/95, AUD, #9, 5627)

35. An auditor who discovers that a client's employees paid small bribes to municipal officials most likely would withdraw from the engagement if
a. The payments violated the client's policies regarding the prevention of illegal acts.
b. The client receives financial assistance from a federal government agency.
c. Documentation that is necessary to prove that the bribes were paid does not exist.
d. Management fails to take the appropriate remedial action. (R/00, AUD, #6, 6931)

36. Under the Private Securities Litigation Reform Act of 1995, Baker, CPA, reported certain uncorrected illegal acts to Supermart's board of directors. Baker believed that failure to take remedial action would warrant a qualified audit opinion because the illegal acts had a material effect on Supermart's financial statements. Supermart failed to take appropriate remedial action and the board of directors refused to inform the SEC that it had received such notification from Baker. Under these circumstances, Baker is required to
a. Withhold an audit opinion until Supermart takes appropriate remedial action
b. Deliver a report concerning the illegal acts to the SEC within one business day
c. Notify the stockholders that the financial statements are materially misstated
d. Resign from the audit engagement within ten business days (R/99, AUD, #4, 6820)

37. Which of the following matters would an auditor most likely communicate to an entity's audit committee?
a. A list of negative trends that may lead to working capital deficiencies and adverse financial ratios
b. The level of responsibility assumed by management for the preparation of the financial statements
c. Difficulties encountered in achieving a satisfactory response rate from the entity's customers in confirming accounts receivables
d. The effects of significant accounting policies adopted by management in emerging areas for which there is **no** authoritative guidance (R/02, AUD, #5, 7095)

38. An auditor's communication with the audit committee is required to include the
a. Basis for the auditor's preliminary judgment about materiality
b. Justification for the auditor's selection of sampling methods
c. Discussion of disagreements with management about matters that significantly impact the entity's financial statements
d. Assessment of the quality of the entity's earnings as compared to the previous year (R/05, AUD, #39, 7834)

Problem 22-2 ADDITIONAL MULTIPLE CHOICE QUESTIONS (74 to 93 minutes)

39. An auditor is required to establish an understanding with a client regarding the services to be performed for each engagement. This understanding generally includes
a. Management's responsibility for errors and the illegal activities of employees that may cause material misstatement
b. The auditor's responsibility for ensuring that the audit committee is aware of any significant deficiencies that come to the auditor's attention
c. Management's responsibility for providing the auditor with an assessment of the risk of material misstatement due to fraud
d. The auditor's responsibility for determining preliminary judgments about materiality and audit risk factors (R/99, AUD, #6, amended, 6822)

40. Which of the following statements would least likely appear in an auditor's engagement letter?
a. Fees for our services are based on our regular per diem rates, plus travel and other out-of-pocket expenses.
b. During the course of our audit we may observe opportunities for economy in, or improved controls over, your operations.
c. Our engagement is subject to the risk that material errors or irregularities, including fraud and defalcations, if they exist, will **not** be detected.
d. After performing our preliminary analytical procedures we will discuss with you the other procedures we consider necessary to complete the engagement. (5/95, AUD, #3, 5621)

41. An auditor's engagement letter should include
a. Management's acknowledgment of its responsibility for maintaining effective internal control
b. The auditor's preliminary assessment of the risk factors relating to misstatements arising from fraudulent financial reporting
c. A reminder that management is responsible for illegal acts committed by employees
d A request for permission to contact the client's lawyer for assistance in identifying litigation, claims, and assessments
(R/02, AUD, #3, amended, 7093)

42. A document in an auditor's working papers includes the following statement:

"Our audit is subject to the inherent risk that material errors and fraud, including defalcations, if they exist, will not be detected. However, we will inform you of fraud that comes to our attention, unless it is inconsequential."

The above passage is most likely from a(an)
a. Comfort letter
b. Engagement letter
c. Letter of audit inquiry
d. Representation letter (R/03, AUD, #12, 7634)

43. The element of the audit planning process most likely to be agreed upon with the client before implementation of the audit strategy is the determination of the
a. Evidence to be gathered to provide a sufficient basis for the auditor's opinion
b. Procedures to be undertaken to discover litigation, claims, and assessments
c. Pending legal matters to be included in the inquiry of the client's attorney
d. Timing of inventory observation procedures to be performed (5/95, AUD, #1, 5619)

44. Which of the following procedures would an auditor most likely include in the initial planning phase of a financial statement audit?
a. Obtain an understanding of the entity's risk assessment process
b. Identify specific internal control activities designed to prevent fraud
c. Evaluate the reasonableness of the entity's accounting estimates
d. Perform cutoff tests of the entity's sales and purchases (11/98, AUD, #18, amended, 6709)

45. Audit programs should be designed so that
a. Most of the required procedures can be performed as interim work.
b. Inherent risk is assessed at a sufficiently low level.
c. The auditor can make constructive suggestions to management.
d. The audit evidence gathered supports the auditor's conclusions. (11/94, AUD, #16, 5089)

46. Which of the following factors would a CPA ordinarily consider in the planning stage of an audit engagement?

I. Financial statement accounts likely to contain a misstatement
II. Conditions that require extension of audit tests

a. I only
b. II only
c. Both I and II
d. Neither I nor II (R/02, AUD, #12, 7102)

47. In designing written audit programs, an auditor should establish specific audit objectives that relate primarily to the
a. Timing of audit procedures
b. Cost-benefit of gathering evidence
c. Selected audit techniques
d. Financial statement assertions
(5/94, AUD, #8, 4673)

48. The senior auditor responsible for coordinating the fieldwork usually schedules a preaudit conference with the audit team primarily to
a. Give guidance to the staff regarding both technical and personnel aspects of the audit
b. Provide an opportunity to document staff disagreements regarding technical issues
c. Establish the need for using the work of specialists and internal auditors
d. Discuss staff suggestions concerning the establishment and maintenance of time budgets
(11/94, AUD, #4, amended, 5077)

49. Prior to commencing fieldwork, an auditor usually discusses the general audit strategy with the client's management. Which of the following matters does the auditor and management agree upon at this time?
a. The appropriateness of the entity's plans for dealing with adverse economic conditions.
b. The determination of the fraud risk factors that exist within the client's operations.
c. The control weaknesses to be included in the communication with the audit committee.
d. The coordination of the assistance of the client's personnel in data preparation.
(R/07, AUD, #10, 8382)

50. An auditor's engagement letter most likely would include a statement that
a. Lists potential control deficiencies discovered during the prior-year's audit.
b. Explains the analytical procedures that the auditor expects to apply.
c. Describes the auditor's responsibility to evaluate going-concern issues.
d. Limits the auditor's responsibility to detect errors and fraud. (R/07, AUD, #11, amended, 8383)

51. An audit supervisor reviewed the work performed by the staff to determine if the audit was adequately performed. The supervisor accomplished this by primarily reviewing which of the following?
a. Checklists
b. Working papers
c. Analytical procedures
d. Financial statements (R/07, AUD, #23, 8395)

52. The risk that an auditor will conclude, based on substantive tests, that a material error does **not** exist in an account balance when, in fact, such error does exist is referred to as
a. Sampling risk
b. Detection risk
c. Nonsampling risk
d. Inherent risk (11/91, AUD, #7, 2275)

53. When an auditor increases the assessed level of control risk because certain control activities were determined to be ineffective, the auditor most likely would increase the
a. Level of detection risk
b. Extent of tests of details
c. Level of inherent risk
d. Extent of tests of controls (R/05, AUD, #4, 7799)

54. Inherent risk and control risk differ from detection risk in that they
a. Arise from the misapplication of auditing procedures
b. May be assessed in either quantitative or nonquantitative terms
c. Exist independently of the financial statement audit
d. Can be changed at the auditor's discretion
(11/94, AUD, #8, 5081)

55. Which of the following audit risk components may be assessed in nonquantitative terms?

	Control risk	Detection risk	Inherent risk
a.	Yes	Yes	No
b.	Yes	No	Yes
c.	Yes	Yes	Yes
d.	No	Yes	Yes

(5/95, AUD, #10, 5628)

56. Which of the following would an auditor most likely use in determining the auditor's preliminary judgment about materiality?
a. The anticipated sample size of the planned substantive tests
b. The entity's annualized interim financial statements
c. The results of the internal control questionnaire
d. The contents of the management representation letter (5/95, AUD, #11, 5629)

57. In planning an audit of a new client, an auditor most likely would consider the methods used to process accounting information because such methods
a. Influence the design of internal control
b. Affect the auditor's preliminary judgment about materiality levels
c. Assist in evaluating the planned audit objectives
d. Determine the auditor's acceptable level of audit risk (11/94, AUD, #7, amended, 5080)

58. The primary objective of procedures performed to obtain an understanding of the entity and its environment, including its internal control, is to provide an auditor with
a. Knowledge necessary to assess the risk of material misstatement and design further audit procedures
b. An evaluation of the consistency of application of management's policies
c. A basis for modifying tests of controls
d. Audit evidence to use in assessing inherent risk
(Editors, 5642)

59. Which of the following statements reflects an auditor's responsibility for detecting errors and fraud?
a. An auditor is responsible for detecting employee errors and simple fraud, but not for discovering fraud involving employee collusion or management override.
b. An auditor should plan the audit to detect errors and fraud that are caused by departures from GAAP.
c. An auditor is not responsible for detecting errors and fraud unless the application of GAAS would result in such detection.
d. An auditor should design the audit to provide reasonable assurance of detecting errors and fraud that are material to the financial statements.
(5/95, AUD, #15, amended, 5633)

60. Which of the following circumstances most likely would cause an auditor to suspect that there are material misstatements in an entity's financial statements?
a. Senior financial management participates in the selection of accounting principles and the determination of significant estimates.
b. Supporting accounting records and files that should be readily available are **not** produced promptly when requested.
c. Related party transactions take place in the ordinary course of business with an entity that is audited by another CPA firm.
d. Senior management has an excessive interest in upgrading the entity's information technology capabilities. (R/05, AUD, #31, 7826)

61. Which of the following factors most likely would cause an auditor to question the integrity of management?
a. Management has an aggressive attitude toward financial reporting and meeting profit goals.
b. Audit tests detect material fraud that was known to management, but **not** disclosed to the auditor.
c. Managerial decisions are dominated by one person who is also a stockholder.
d. Weaknesses in internal control reported to the audit committee are not corrected by management. (R/03, AUD, #9, 7631)

62. Which of the following procedures would an auditor most likely perform during the overall review stage of an audit of an entity's financial statements?
a. Obtain assurance from the entity's attorney that all material litigation has been disclosed in the financial statements
b. Verify the clerical accuracy of the entity's proof of cash and its bank cutoff statement
c. Determine whether inadequate provisions for the safeguarding of assets have been corrected
d. Consider whether the results of audit procedures affect the assessment of the risk of material misstatement due to fraud (R/01, AUD, #12, 7027)

63. Which of the following statements is correct concerning an auditor's responsibility to report fraud?
a. The auditor is required to communicate to the client's audit committee all minor fraudulent acts perpetrated by low-level employees, even if the amounts involved are inconsequential.
b. The disclosure of material management fraud to principal stockholders is required when both senior management and the board of directors fail to acknowledge the fraudulent activities.
c. Fraudulent activities involving senior management of which the auditor becomes aware should be reported directly to the SEC.
d. The disclosure of fraudulent activities to parties other than the client's senior management and its audit committee is not ordinarily part of the auditor's responsibility. (R/05, AUD, #14, 7809)

64. Which of the following characteristics most likely would heighten an auditor's concern about the risk of material misstatement arising from fraudulent financial reporting?
a. There is a lack of interest by management in maintaining an earnings trend.
b. Computer hardware is usually sold at a loss before being fully depreciated.
c. Management had frequent disputes with the auditor on accounting matters.
d. Monthly bank reconciliations usually include several large checks outstanding.
(R/07, AUD, #48, 8420)

65. An auditor may decide to perform only substantive procedures for specific assertions because the auditor believes
a. Control policies and procedures are unlikely to pertain to the assertions.
b. The entity's control environment, monitoring, and control activities are interrelated.
c. Sufficient audit evidence to support the assertions is likely to be available.
d. More emphasis on tests of controls than substantive tests is warranted.
(11/93, AUD, #21, amended, 4258)

66. An auditor uses the assessed risk of material misstatement to
a. Evaluate the effectiveness of the entity's internal control policies and procedures
b. Identify transactions and account balances where inherent risk is at the maximum
c. Indicate whether materiality thresholds for planning and evaluation purposes are sufficiently high
d. Determine the acceptable level of detection risk for financial statement assertions
(5/94, AUD, #24, amended, 4689)

67. An auditor would most likely question whether a client has committed illegal acts if the client has
a. Been forced to discontinue operations in a foreign country
b. Been an annual donor to a local political candidate
c. Disclosed several subsequent events involving foreign operations in the notes to the financial statements
d. Failed to correct material weaknesses in internal control that were reported after the prior year's audit
(Editors, 0189)

68. Jones, CPA, is auditing the financial statements of XYZ Retailing Inc. What assurance does Jones provide that direct effect illegal acts that are material to XYZ's financial statements, and illegal acts that have a material, but indirect, effect on the financial statements, will be detected?

	Direct effect illegal acts	Indirect effect illegal acts
a.	Reasonable	None
b.	Reasonable	Limited
c.	Limited	None
d.	Limited	Limited

(5/94, AUD, #6, amended, 4671)

Items 69 and 70 are based on the following:

During the annual audit of Ajax Corp., a publicly held company, Jones, CPA, a continuing auditor, determined that illegal political contributions had been made during each of the past seven years, including the year under audit. Jones notified the board of directors about the illegal contributions, but they refused to take any action because the amounts involved were immaterial to the financial statements.

69. Jones should reconsider the intended degree of reliance to be placed on the
a. Letter of audit inquiry to the client's attorney
b. Prior years' audit programs
c. Management representation letter
d. Preliminary judgment about materiality levels
(11/94, AUD, #12, 5085)

70. Since management took no action, Jones should
a. Report the illegal contributions to the Securities and Exchange Commission
b. Issue an "except for" qualified opinion or an adverse opinion
c. Disregard the political contributions since the board of directors were notified and the amounts involved were immaterial
d. Consider withdrawing from the engagement or dissociating from any future relationship with Ajax Corp
(Editors, 7487)

71. Morris, CPA, suspects that a pervasive scheme of illegal bribes exists throughout the operations of Worldwide Import-Export Inc., a new audit client. Morris notified the audit committee and Worldwide's legal counsel, but neither could assist Morris in determining whether the amounts involved were material to the financial statements or whether senior management was involved in the scheme. Under these circumstances, Morris should
a. Express an unqualified opinion with a separate explanatory paragraph
b. Disclaim an opinion on the financial statements
c. Express an adverse opinion of the financial statements
d. Issue a special report regarding the illegal bribes
(5/90, AUD, #57, 0165)

72. Which of the following statements is correct regarding the auditor's consideration of the possibility of illegal acts by clients?
a. The auditor has a responsibility to plan and perform the audit to obtain reasonable assurance that **no** illegal acts have been committed by clients.
b. The auditor's training, experience, and understanding of the client should be used to provide a basis for the determination as to whether illegal acts have occurred.
c. If specific information concerning an illegal act comes to the auditor's attention, the auditor should apply audit procedures specifically directed to ascertaining whether an illegal act has occurred.
d. If an illegal act has occurred, the auditor should express a qualified opinion or an adverse opinion on the financial statements taken as a whole.
(R/07, AUD, #50, 8422)

73. An auditor would **least** likely initiate a discussion with a client's audit committee concerning

a. The methods used to account for significant unusual transactions
b. The maximum dollar amount of misstatements that could exist without causing the financial statements to be materially misstated
c. Indications of fraud and illegal acts committed by a corporate officer that were discovered by the auditor
d. Disagreements with management as to accounting principles that were resolved during the current year's audit   (5/95, AUD, #19, 5637)

74. In identifying matters for communication with an entity's audit committee, an auditor most likely would ask management whether

a. The turnover in the accounting department was unusually high.
b. It consulted with another CPA firm about accounting matters.
c. There were any subsequent events of which the auditor was unaware.
d. It agreed with the auditor's assessed level of control risk.   (5/96, AUD, #6, 6238)

75. Which of the following matters is an auditor **not** required to communicate to an entity's audit committee?

a. Significant adjustments arising from the audit that were recorded by management
b. The basis for the auditor's conclusions about the reasonableness of management's sensitive accounting estimates
c. The level of responsibility assumed by the auditor under generally accepted auditing standards
d. The degree of reliance the auditor placed on the management representation letter
    (R/03, AUD, #15, 7637)

SIMULATIONS

Problem 22-3 (40 to 50 minutes)

Company Profile | Financial Information | Risk Factors | Analytical Results

Company

The year under audit is year 2. Scott, Inc. (Scott) is a manufacturer of handmade glycerine soap and candles. The company has been in business for 15 years and has its headquarters in Yorba Linda, California. Historically, Scott's revenues arose predominantly from sales within North America, where its products have an excellent reputation.

Marketing

Scott is divided into two divisions, which serve the major markets for the company's products. One division focuses on sales to department stores. The other division focuses on placing company products in small specialty shops. Currently, each division generates about half of Scott's revenues and net income.

Scott experienced record profitability in Year 1 and management anticipated that Year 2 would be another banner year. However, sales declined in Year 2 because of regional economic conditions related to a recent recession, and the financial results for Year 2 did not meet management's expectations. Sales for Year 2 decreased 5% compared to Year 1 and gross profit also declined due to increases in manufacturing costs. Management, after reviewing its operations for Year 2, recognized that its domestic sales growth had slowed in the past several years and its manufacturing costs had increased. As a result, the company adopted a new business plan with a global focus for marketing its products. During Year 2, Scott opened up new markets in Australia and Japan with production at each of these locations.

Management

Management realized it must strictly control all costs to make its overall operations more efficient. As a result, Scott announced that it would make a series of restructuring changes as of the end of Year 2 as part of its overall business plan. During Year 2, the company issued long-term debt with complex financial covenants. The debt was incurred to purchase property, plant and equipment. The company also issued additional common stock during Year 2.

Senior management at the company experienced significant turnover in recent years. The CEO has been with the company for only one year. The CEO was hired from a major competitor after the previous CEO left to take a position with a large manufacturing company in the Northeast. In another management change, the company's CFO retired, and the current CFO was hired only six months ago. The new CFO was an audit manager from the predecessor audit firm.

Engagement

Scott switched from a regional audit firm to an international audit firm, because the company added factories and employees overseas. There have been no internal disagreements over accounting issues in any of the prior three years.

| Company Profile | Financial Information | Risk Factors | Analytical Results |

Scott, Inc.
Consolidated Balance Sheets
December 31, Year 2 and Year 1

	Year 2	Year 1
Assets		
Current assets		
Cash and cash equivalents	$ 3,385,000	$ 6,620,000
Receivables—net	2,964,000	3,124,000
Inventory	3,158,000	3,016,000
Other current assets	639,000	1,379,000
Total current assets	10,146,000	14,139,000
Property, plant and equipment—net	25,900,000	22,000,000
Other assets	800,000	800,000
Total assets	$36,846,000	$36,939,000

Liabilities and Stockholders' Equity		
	Year 2	Year 1
Current liabilities		
Current portion of long-term debt	$ 1,200,000	$ 1,200,000
Accounts payable	3,300,000	11,200,000
Other current liabilities	516,000	1,459,000
Total current liabilities	5,016,000	13,859,000
Long-term debt	19,500,000	16,500,000
Total liabilities	24,516,000	30,359,000
Stockholders' equity		
Common stock	7,280,000	3,280,000
Retained earnings	5,050,000	3,300,000
Total stockholders' equity	12,330,000	6,580,000
Total liabilities and stockholders' equity	$36,846,000	$36,939,000

Scott, Inc.
Consolidated Income Statements
For the years ended December 31, Year 2 and Year 1

	Year 2	Year 1
Sales	$19,672,000	$20,730,000
Cost of goods sold	12,197,000	12,231,000
Gross profit on sales	7,475,000	8,499,000
Other operating expenses		
Selling expenses	1,978,000	2,151,000
General administrative	1,377,000	1,248,000
Total other operating expenses	3,355,000	3,399,000
Income from operations before interest expense	4,120,000	5,100,000
Interest expense	1,250,000	1,300,000
Income before taxes	2,870,000	3,800,000
Provision for income taxes	1,120,000	1,520,000
Net income	$ 1,750,000	$ 2,280,000

Scott, Inc.
Consolidated Statements of Cash Flows
For the years ended December 31, Year 2 and Year 1

	Year 2	Year 1
Cash flows from operating activities:		
Net income (loss)	$ 1,750,000	$ 2,280,000
Adjustments to reconcile net income (loss) to cash provided by (used for) operating activities:		
Depreciation and amortization	2,000,000	1,900,000
Changes in certain assets and liabilities:		
Decrease (increase) in receivables	160,000	76,000
Decrease (increase) in inventory	(142,000)	(116,000)
Decrease (increase) in other current assets	740,000	
Decrease (increase) in other assets		
Increase (decrease) in accounts payable	(7,900,000)	760,000
Increase (decrease) in other current liabilities	(943,000)	500,000
Net cash provided by (used for) operating activities	(4,335,000)	5,400,000
Cash flows from investing activities:		
Purchase of property, plant and equipment	(5,900,000)	(2,900,000)
Net cash provided by (used for) investing activities	(5,900,000)	(2,900,000)
Cash flows from financing activities:		
Proceeds from issuance of long-term debt	4,200,000	
Principal payments on long-term debt	(1,200,000)	(1,100,000)
Proceeds from issuance of common stock	4,000,000	
Net cash provided by (used for) financing activities	7,000,000	(1,100,000)
Net increase (decrease) in cash and cash equivalents	(3,235,000)	1,400,000
Cash and cash equivalents at beginning of year	6,620,000	5,220,000
Cash and cash equivalents at end of year	$ 3,385,000	$ 6,620,000

Company Profile | Financial Information | Risk Factors | Analytical Results

Based on the information in Scott's Company Profile, which of the following is the factor most likely to increase audit risk? Select only one factor.

A. The company has begun to focus on a strategic advertising plan so it may expand its domestic market into other states.	
B. During year 2, management issued additional long-term debt with complex financial covenants.	
C. Scott is divided into two divisions, which serve the major markets of the company's products.	
D. The new CFO was an audit manager from the predecessor audit firm.	

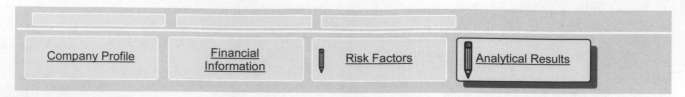

The table below presents some ratios that were considered significant in the current and prior year's audit of Scott. Compare the values for each ratio. Then select the most likely explanation for the analytical results. An explanation may be used once, more than once, or not at all. (You should **not** recalculate ratios.)

Ratio	Year 2	Year 1	Explanations
1. Debt to equity	1.99	4.61	
2. Gross profit percentage	38.00%	41.00%	

Selection List

A. Sales decreased as compared to the prior year.

B. Manufacturing costs increased during the year at a greater rate than sales increased.

C. Proceeds from the sale of stock and issuance of debt were used to pay payables on a more current basis.

D. Capital stock was issued during the year.

E. The company may have accumulated excess and obsolete inventory.

F. Manufacturing cost decreased less than sales decreased during the year.

The auditor in the Scott engagement has chosen to increase attention on the financial statement assertion of valuation. Procedures that might be used in an audit are listed below. From the following list, choose the two procedures that would be most appropriate to perform in an audit that is giving increased attention to the **valuation assertion.** Only **two** procedures may be chosen.

Selection List

A. Observing the client count the physical inventory

B. Testing shipping and receiving cutoff procedures

C. Obtaining confirmation from lenders regarding inventories pledged under loan agreements

D. Examining paid vendors' invoices

E. Obtaining confirmation of inventories at locations outside the entity

F. Examining an analysis of inventory turnover

G. Tracing test counts recorded during the physical inventory observation to the inventory listing

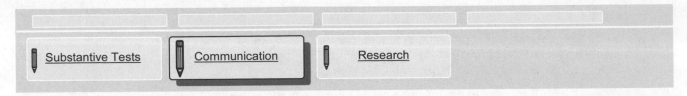

Your firm has been doing the audit for Scott, Inc. for two years. At the beginning of the year, Scott's board of directors was composed of family members owning stock in the company. However, by the end of the year, a majority of the board of directors is now non-family members with extensive financial management experience. In a memorandum to your audit team, explain the impact of the composition of the new board of directors on audit risk.

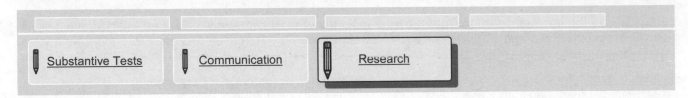

Management informed your firm's engagement partner that a prospective lender made a preliminary request for a CPA's letter regarding the company's solvency. The partner requested that you find guidance, if any, in AICPA Professional Standards regarding CPA reports on matters relating to solvency.

Paragraph(s) Reference Answer: _____

(R/05, AUD, amended, 7846)

Problem 22-4 (15 to 25 minutes)

Green, CPA, is considering audit risk at the financial statement level in planning the audit of National Federal Bank (NFB) Company's financial statements for the year ended December 31, Year 1. Audit risk at the financial statement level is influenced by the risk of material misstatements, which may be indicated by a combination of factors related to management, the industry, and the entity. In assessing such factors, Green has gathered the following information concerning NFB's environment.

Company profile

NFB is a federally insured bank that has been consistently more profitable than the industry average by marketing mortgages on properties in a prosperous rural area, which has experienced considerable growth in recent years. NFB packages its mortgages and sells them to large mortgage investment trusts. Despite recent volatility of interest rates, NFB has been able to continue selling its mortgages as a source of new lendable funds.

NFB's board of directors is controlled by Smith, the majority stockholder, who also acts as the chief executive officer. Management at the bank's branch offices has authority for directing and controlling NFB's operations and is compensated based on branch profitability. The internal auditor reports directly to Harris, a minority shareholder, who also acts as chairman of the board's audit committee. The accounting department has experienced little turnover in personnel during the five years Green has audited NFB. NFB's formula consistently underestimates the allowance for loan losses, but its controller has always been receptive to Green's suggestions to increase the allowance during each engagement.

Recent developments

During Year 1, NFB opened a branch office in a suburban town thirty miles from its principal place of business. Although this branch is not yet profitable due to competition from several well-established regional banks, management believes that the branch will be profitable by Year 3.

Also, during Year 1, NFB increased the efficiency of its accounting operations by installing a new, sophisticated computer system.

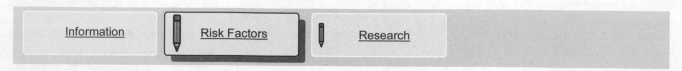

Based only on the information above, describe the factors that most likely would have an effect on the risk of material misstatements. Indicate whether each factor increases or decreases the risk. Use the format illustrated below.

Environmental factor	Effect on risk of material misstatements
Branch management has authority for directing and controlling operations	Increase

What authoritative reference recognizes that although fraudulent journal entries often are made at the end of a reporting period, the auditor should consider whether there is a need to test journal entries throughout the reporting period under audit?

Paragraph Reference Answer: _____

(5/91, AUD, #5, amended, 9034)

Problem 22-5 (15 to 25 minutes)

Recently there has been a significant number of highly publicized cases of alleged or actual management fraud involving the misstatement of financial statements. Although most client managements possess unquestioned integrity, a very small number, given sufficient incentive and opportunity, may be predisposed to fraudulently misstate reported financial condition and operating results.

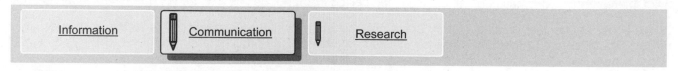

a. What distinguishes management fraud from a defalcation?

b. What are an auditor's responsibilities under generally accepted auditing standards to detect management fraud?

c. What are the characteristics of management fraud that an auditor should consider to fulfill the auditor's responsibilities under generally accepted auditing standards related to detecting management fraud?

d. Three factors that heighten an auditor's concern about the existence of management fraud include (1) an intended public placement of securities in the near future, (2) management remuneration dependent on operating results, and (3) a weak internal control environment evidenced by lack of concern for basic controls and disregard of the auditor's recommendations. What other factors should heighten an auditor's concern about the existence of management fraud?

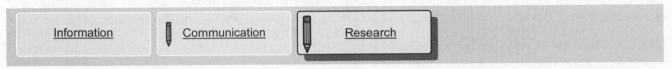

What authoritative reference provides a minimum list of matters subject to inquiry of a predecessor auditor by a successor auditor?

Paragraph Reference Answer: _____

(11/95, AUD, #4, amended, 9035)

Problem 22-6 (20 to 25 minutes)

Kent, CPA is the engagement partner on the financial statement audit of Super Computer Services Co. (SCS) for the year ended April 30, Year 7. On May 6, Year 7, Smith, the senior auditor assigned to the engagement, had the following conversation with Kent concerning the planning phase of the audit:

Kent: Do you have all the audit programs updated yet for the SCS engagement?

Smith: Mostly, I still have work to do on the fraud risk assessment.

Kent: Why? Our "errors and irregularities" program from last year is still OK. It's passed peer review several times. Besides, we don't have specific duties regarding fraud. If we find it, we'll deal with it then.

Smith: I don't think so. That new CEO, Mint, has almost no salary, mostly bonuses and stock options. Doesn't that concern you?

Kent: No, Mint's employment contract was approved by the Board of Directors just three months ago. It was passed unanimously.

Smith: I guess so, but Mint told those stock analysts that SCS's earnings would increase 30% next year. Can Mint deliver numbers like that?

Kent: Who knows? We're auditing the Year 7 financial statements, not Year 8. Mint will probably amend that forecast every month between now and next May.

Smith: Sure, but all this may change our other audit programs.

Kent: No, it won't. The programs are fine as is. If you find fraud in any of your tests, just let me know. Maybe we'll have to extend the tests. Or maybe we'll just report it to the audit committee.

Smith: What would they do? Green is the audit committee's chair, and remember, Green hired Mint. They've been best friends for years. Besides, Mint is calling all the shots now. Brown, the old CEO, is still on the Board, but Brown's never around. Brown's even been skipping the Board meetings. Nobody in management or on the Board would stand up to Mint.

Kent: That's nothing new. Brown was like that years ago. Brown caused frequent disputes with Jones, CPA, the predecessor auditor. Three years ago, Jones told Brown how ineffective the internal audit department was then. Next thing you know, Jones is out and I'm in. Why bother? I'm just as happy that those understaffed internal auditors don't get in our way. Just remember, the bottom line is...are the financial statements fairly presented? And they always have been. We don't provide any assurances about fraud. That's management's job.

Smith: But what about the lack of segregation of duties in the cash disbursements department? That clerk could write a check for anything.

Kent: Sure. That's a significant deficiency every year and probably will be again this year. But we're talking cost-effectiveness here, not fraud. We just have to do lots of testing on cash disbursements and report it again.

Smith: What about the big layoffs coming up next month? It's more than a rumor. Even the employees know it's going to happen, and they're real uptight about it.

Kent: I know, it's the worst kept secret at SCS, but we don't have to consider that now. Even if it happens, it will only improve next year's financial results. Brown should have let these people go years ago. Let's face it, how else can Mint even come close to the 30% earnings increase next year?

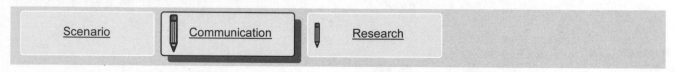

a. Describe the fraud risk factors that are indicated in the accompanying dialogue.

b. Describe Kent's misconceptions regarding the consideration of fraud in the audit of SCS's financial statements that are contained in the dialogue above and explain why each is a misconception.

c. Describe an auditor's working paper documentation requirements regarding the assessment of the risk of material misstatement due to fraud.

What authoritative reference provides guidance when an auditor's analytics indicate that a misstatement in financial statements might exist, but not its amount?

Paragraph Reference Answer: _____

(5/98, AUD, #2, amended, 6635)

Solution 22-1 MULTIPLE CHOICE ANSWERS

Planning & Supervision

1. (a) The AICPA's sample engagement letter states, "At the conclusion of our audit, we will request certain written representations from you about the financial statements and matters related thereto." Auditors generally do not discuss preliminary judgments about materiality or fraud risk with the client. Internal control activities that would reduce the auditor's assessment of control risk generally would be discussed later in the audit, when the auditor has greater familiarity with the internal controls in place, typically when making recommendations to improve internal controls. (7830)

2. (c) The understanding with the client generally includes the auditor's responsibility for communicating significant deficiencies and material weaknesses, if the auditor becomes aware of any. Preliminary judgments about materiality and audit risk factors are not required to be understood by the client. It is the auditor's responsibility to identify mitigating factors when there is going concern doubt as well as to assess the risk of material misstatement due to fraud. (8130)

3. (c) In the planning phase of an audit a CPA most likely would coordinate with client personnel, requiring a discussion of the timing of audit procedures, such as a physical count of inventory. An auditor would identify specific internal control activities that are likely to prevent fraud during the review of internal control or when fraud factors are discovered. An auditor would evaluate the reasonableness of a client's accounting estimates and inquire of a client's attorney regarding unrecorded claims when collecting evidence. (7798)

4. (d) In establishing the overall audit strategy, the auditor should consider the important factors that will determine the focus of the audit teams' efforts, such as the determination of appropriate materiality levels and preliminary identification of areas where there may be higher risks of material misstatement. When the auditor is developing a preliminary audit strategy, the auditor has not performed sampling procedures or interim tests, nor made inquiries of the client's attorney. (2276)

5. (c) The auditor should prepare a written audit plan (or program). The audit plan should detail the nature, timing, and extent of the audit procedures that are necessary to accomplish the objectives of the audit. (SAS 108). All material transactions and all account balances are not required to be tested in all circumstances. Minimizing substantive tests prior to the balance sheet date is not required. (5634)

6. (d) Of the procedures listed, an auditor is most likely to determine the extent of involvement of the client's internal auditors in the initial planning of a financial statement audit. A written representation letter from the client's management is usually obtained at the end of an audit, not the beginning. Examining documents and considering the reasonableness of estimates are procedures that are done during the audit. (5074)

7. (c) Among other procedures performed during the planning of the audit, the auditor may discuss the general audit strategy concerning the type, scope, and timing of the audit with the entity's management, audit committee, or board of directors as well as coordinate any assistance of the entity's personnel in data preparation that is needed. (8125)

8. (c) The work performed by each assistant, including audit documentation, should be reviewed to determine whether it was adequately performed and documented and to evaluate the results, relative to the conclusions to be presented in the auditor's report. The standards are guidelines for auditing procedures which are applied based on the auditor's

professional judgment. The quality control standards do not state that quality control must be maintained at a high level, rather, a firm must establish a system of quality control designed to provide the firm with reasonable assurance that the firm and its personnel comply with professional standards and applicable regulatory and legal requirements, and that the firm or engagement partners issue reports that are appropriate in the circumstances. The question concerns the reason for reviewing fieldwork, not the auditor's qualifications. (2273)

9. (b) The auditor should inform assistants of their responsibilities and the objective(s) of the audit procedures they are to perform. This would also serve to inform them of the basis of how the results of the audit procedures should be evaluated. It is very unlikely that staff assistants would report to the client's audit committee. Answers (c) and (d) are less vital duties than audit procedure evaluation. (5625)

10. (c) Procedures should enable an assistant to document her/his disagreement with the conclusions reached if, after appropriate consultation, s/he believes it necessary to disassociate her/himself from the resolution of the matter. An assistant can disagree with the in-charge auditor—the matter should be addressed in some manner. An assistant is not precluded from working on the audit if s/he has a difference of opinion concerning auditing or accounting issue(s). The assistant should not, on her/his own, notify the client that a serious audit problem exists. (0209)

Audit Risk & Materiality

11. (b) The auditor must determine a materiality level for the financial statements taken as a whole. The concept of materiality recognizes that some matters affect the fair presentation of financial statements, while others do not. Materiality judgments involve both quantitative and qualitative considerations. In making the assessment of materiality, an auditor should consider the needs of a reasonable person who would rely on the financial statements. (5084)

12. (b) If an auditor must decrease detection risk, the auditor should change the nature, extent, or timing of audit procedures. Performing procedures closer to the balance sheet date allows less opportunity for misstatements due to roll-forward adjustments to the auditor's interim work. An increase in the assessed level of control risk will cause a decrease in the amount of misstatements that an auditor can tolerate. A decrease in the tolerable amount of

misstatements would increase, not decrease, the extent of auditing procedures. (6574)

13. (a) Inherent risk is the susceptibility of an assertion to a material misstatement, assuming that there are no related controls. Control risk is the risk that a material misstatement that could occur in an assertion will not be prevented or detected on a timely basis by the entity's internal control. Detection risk is the risk that the auditor will not detect a material misstatement that exists in an assertion. Thus, inherent risk and control risk are functions of the client and its environment while detection risk is not. Inherent risk, control risk, and detection risk are all a part of audit risk. Inherent risk and control risk differ from detection risk in that they exist independently of the audit of financial statements, whereas detection risk relates to the auditor's procedures and can be changed at the auditor's discretion. All of the elements of audit risk should be considered in relation to individual account balances, classes of transactions and disclosures; and at the overall financial statement level. (2810)

14. (b) Detection risk has an inverse relationship to control risk. Therefore, if an auditor decides to *increase* the assessed level of control risk from the originally planned level, in order to achieve an equivalent overall level of risk, the detection risk must be *decreased*. (5083)

15. (a) Detection risk relates to the substantive audit procedures and is managed by the auditor's response to the risk of material misstatement. For a given level of audit risk, detection risk should bear an inverse relationship to the risk of material misstatement at the relevant assertion level. The greater the risk of material misstatement, the less the detection risk that can be accepted by the auditor. Conversely, the lower the risk of material misstatement, the greater the detection risk that can be accepted by the auditor. However, the auditor should perform substantive procedures for all relevant assertions related to material classes of transactions, account balances, and disclosures. The risk of misapplying audit procedures is a part of detection risk. The acceptable level of detection risk is unrelated to the preliminary judgment about materiality levels. The risk of failing to discover material misstatements during an audit is detection risk. (0044)

16. (c) In determining materiality, the auditor should consider, among other things, prior-periods' financial results and financial positions. Materiality impacts the evaluation of the alternative answers, rather than the reverse. (6573)

Entity & Its Environment

17. (b) The purpose of applying analytical procedures in planning the audit, for example, comparing recorded amounts to anticipated results, is to assist the auditor in planning the nature, timing, and extent of auditing procedures that will be used to obtain audit evidence for account balances or classes of transactions. Inquiry of the client's legal counsel is an audit procedure that would be performed near the end of the audit engagement. Answer (c) is a substantive audit procedure that would be performed later in the audit engagement to support management's assertion of completeness. The auditor determines whether controls have been placed in operation, i.e., whether the entity is using the control, as part of the understanding of internal control necessary to plan the audit. Answer (d) is an example of testing the operating effectiveness of a control. Whether a control has been placed in operation at a point in time is different from its operating effectiveness over a period of time. The auditor evaluates the operating *effectiveness* of controls as part of assessing control risk. (5622)

18. (a) The auditor should use the knowledge obtained in evaluating the design and implementation of controls to identify types of potential misstatements; consider factors that affect the risks of material misstatement; and design tests of controls, when applicable, and substantive procedures. (5951)

19. (c) The auditor should document both the discussion among the audit team regarding the susceptibility of the entity's financial statements to material misstatement and the risk assessment procedures performed. (8266)

Errors & Fraud

20. (a) Due to the characteristics of fraud, even a properly designed and planned audit may not detect a material misstatement resulting from fraud. Audit procedures that are effective for detecting *un*intentional misstatements may be ineffective for detecting *intentional* misstatements concealed through collusion. (2278)

21. (d) An overly complex organizational structure as an operating characteristic is a risk factor of fraudulent financial reporting. (7018)

22. (b) Failure to investigate discrepancies between physical inventory count and accounting records reveals, at best, a careless attitude, even if such discrepancies are due to innocent errors. Undue emphasis by management on meeting

publicized earnings projections indicates a questionable control environment; the opposite attitude rarely indicates a problem. Monthly bank reconciliations with large outstanding checks and cash transactions processed and recorded electronically without paper documentation are often part of normal proper operations. (7629)

23. (b)   The auditor should take into consideration such specific conditions in identifying areas of the financial statements that are especially susceptible to misstatement. The allowance for doubtful accounts may increase substantially in a recession; therefore, the auditor most likely would focus increased attention on this account due to its susceptibility to understatement during a recession. In declining economic conditions, the client may be tempted to overstate accounts receivable by understating the allowance for doubtful accounts. Answers (a), (c), and (d) are not likely to be affected by a recession. (8141)

24. (d)   The fact that management is interested in maintaining the entity's earnings trend by using aggressive accounting practices indicates that management may have an incentive to engage in fraudulent financial reporting also. Stock transactions of management or the board of directors are not ordinarily considered fraud risk factors. Aggressive financial forecasts as opposed to conservative financial forecasts would be considered a fraud risk factor. (8155)

25. (d)   Disclosure of possible fraud to parties other than the client's senior management and its audit committee ordinarily is not part of the auditor's responsibility, and ordinarily would be precluded by the auditor's ethical or legal obligation of confidentiality unless the matter is reflected in the auditor's report. The auditor should recognize, however, that in the following circumstances a duty to disclose outside the client may exist: (a) when the entity reports an auditor change under the appropriate securities law on Form 8-K, (b) to a successor auditor when the successor makes inquiries in accordance with AU 315, (c) in response to a subpoena, and (d) to a funding agency or other specified agency in accordance with requirements for the audits of entities that receive governmental financial assistance. (0163)

Assessing & Responding to RMM

26. (c)   The auditor should document: (1) the assessment of the risks of material misstatement at the financial statement and relevant assertion levels; (2) the basis for that assessment; (3) significant risks identified and related controls evaluated; as well as

(4) risks identified that require tests of controls to obtain sufficient audit evidence and the related controls evaluated. (8265)

27. (c)   Regardless of the assessed risk of material misstatement, the auditor should design and perform substantive procedures for all relevant assertions related to each material class of transactions, account balance, and disclosure. The auditor should perform tests of controls when the auditor's risk assessment includes an expectation of the operating effectiveness of controls or when it is not possible or practicable to reduce detection risk at the relevant assertion level to an acceptably low level with audit evidence obtained from substantive procedures alone. Analytical procedures are required to be used in the planning stage of the audit (and in the final review stage); however, they would not be performed to verify the design of internal control procedures. A dual-purpose test is a procedure that is designed to test both the operating effectiveness of the control(s) and details of the same transaction; this is efficient, but not required. (4260)

28. (a)   The auditor's assessment of the identified risks at the relevant assertion level provides a basis for considering the appropriate audit approach for designing and performing further audit procedures. In some cases, the auditor may determine that performing only substantive procedures is appropriate for specific relevant assertions and risks. In those circumstances, the auditor may exclude the effect of controls from the relevant risk assessment. This may be because the auditor's risk assessment procedures have not identified any effective controls relevant to the assertion or because testing the operating effectiveness of controls would be inefficient. If evidence is not available, tests of controls are not performed. As the assessed level of control risk increases, the auditor is less likely to test controls. If the auditor is aware of many internal control weaknesses, the assessed level of control risk will be high, and controls will not be tested. (5651)

29. (c)   As the risk of material misstatement decreases, which consists of inherent risk and control risk, detection risk increases; therefore, the auditor may decrease the assurance obtained from substantive procedures by altering their nature, timing, and extent. Answers (b) and (d) would tend to increase assurance obtained from procedures performed. (2944)

Illegal Acts by Clients

30. (b)   Large cash payments are unusual in normal, legal business practice. Cash transactions have the attribute of anonymity, which is useful for

hiding illegal acts. Properly disclosed related party transactions and contributions to several local candidates, in and of themselves, do not suggest the occurrence of illegal acts. Internal control procedures are subject to cost/benefit constraints. An entity may appropriately decide that a major weakness is too costly to alleviate. (6576)

31. (d) Management and other employees are unlikely to implicate themselves in wrongdoing on an internal control questionnaire that they know is designed expressly for audit purposes. Reading the minutes of the board of directors' (BOD) meetings, making inquiries of the client's management, or performing tests of details of transactions is more likely to reveal possible illegal acts. Minutes of the BOD meetings are recorded with considerable BOD scrutiny and over a long period. Close scrutiny makes it difficult to falsify minutes. Also, wrongdoers might not think to falsify minutes sufficiently far enough in advance of possible illegal acts to mask motivations or opportunities for performing illegal acts. Inquiries of the client's management can target issues raised during those same inquiries. Also, body language, voice tone, and other intangibles noticed during a face-to-face discussion may indicate possible illegal acts to an alert interviewer. Tests of details of transactions may reveal unauthorized or improperly recorded transactions, investigation by a governmental agency, large payments for unspecified service to consultants, excess commissions or agents' fees, unusually large cash payments, or other "red flags." (7820)

32. (a) When the auditor becomes aware of information concerning a possible illegal act, the auditor should obtain an understanding of the nature of the act, the circumstances in which it occurred, and sufficient other information to evaluate the effect on the financial statements. Obtaining an understanding of the act will not necessarily affect the reliability of management's representations. Consideration of whether other similar acts may have occurred is an additional procedure used, if necessary, by the auditor to obtain further understanding of the nature of the acts. It would not be considered until after the auditor determined the effect of the act on the financial statements. While the occurrence of illegal acts will be communicated to the audit committee, the auditor will not necessarily recommend remedial actions. (2938)

33. (a) If information comes to the auditor's attention that provides evidence concerning possible illegal acts that could have a material indirect effect on the financial statements, the auditor should apply audit procedures specifically directed to determining whether an illegal act has occurred. Only after

determining that an illegal act has occurred would the auditor contemplate the steps in the alternatives. (0172)

34. (a) The auditor should consider the implications of an illegal act in relation to other aspects of the audit, particularly the reliability of representations of management. A relatively small misstatement of fixed assets, an improperly authorized petty cash fund disbursement, or an uncollectible account receivable that was not written off have less impact on the financial statements taken as a whole and, by themselves, do not tend to place doubt on the integrity of management. (5627)

35. (d) If management fails to take appropriate remedial action when informed of illegal acts, management's integrity and representations may be questionable. The auditor should consider withdrawal if illegal payments do not violate the client's policies. If the client receives financial assistance from the government, the discovery of illegal acts may increase the auditor's reporting responsibilities. It is not in employees' interests to document their illegal acts, so it would not be surprising that documentation might not exist. (6931)

36. (b) An auditor who becomes aware of possible illegal activities shall inform the entity's management. If the auditor concludes that the illegal act has a material effect on the financial statements and management has not taken appropriate remedial actions, and departure from a standard report seems reasonable, the auditor shall directly report this to the board of directors. The entity is required to notify the SEC no later than 1 business day after receipt of such report. If the entity fails to notify the SEC within 1 business day, the auditor must resign from the engagement and/or report to the SEC within 1 business day. (6820)

Communications With Audit Committee

37. (d) The auditor should inform the audit committee of selection of or changes in significant accounting policies, whether or not they pertain to emerging areas for which there is no authoritative guidance or to everyday transactions. The auditor is not responsible for financial analysis, such as a list of negative trends. Management's responsibility for financial statements is the same for every company; further, it is redundant to repeat it in communications to the audit committee when it is included in the audit report. The auditor reports difficulties working with management, not customers, to the audit committee. (7095)

38. (c) The auditor must inform the audit committee of any disagreements, whether or not resolved, with management about matters that, individually or in the aggregate, could have a significant impact on the financial statements. The auditor rarely discusses either the basis for the auditor's judgment about materiality or justification for sampling methods selection with the client's management or audit committee. The auditor must discuss the auditor's judgment about the quality of a public company's accounting principles and underlying estimates in the financial statements with the audit committee, not the quality of earnings. (7834)

Solution 22-2 ADDITIONAL MULTIPLE CHOICE ANSWERS

Planning & Supervision

39. (b) The auditor is responsible for ensuring that those charged with governance are aware of any significant deficiencies that come to her/his attention. Management is unlikely to take responsibility for errors and illegal activities of employees. The auditor assesses the risk of material misstatement due to fraud. The auditor's preliminary judgments about materiality and audit risk factors generally are not discussed with the client. (6822)

40. (d) In an engagement letter, the firm and the client indicate their mutual understanding and agree to the nature and terms of the engagement. Answer (a) would be included as part of the terms of the engagement. Answer (b) would be included to indicate the nature of the services the client could expect in the engagement. Answer (c) would be included to establish the mutual understanding of some of the limitations inherent in an audit due to less than 100% testing of all accounts. The auditor would usually not outline to the client the specific procedures to be performed during the audit. (5621)

41. (a) An understanding with the client regarding an audit of the financial statements generally includes a statement that management is responsible for establishing and maintaining effective internal control over financial reporting. An engagement letter should document this understanding. At the point at which an engagement letter usually is sent, the auditor typically has not performed any assessment of risk factors relating to misstatements arising from any circumstances. Management's liability for employee acts is not a part of audit engagement terms. It is appropriate for the client to understand the auditor will request permission to contact the client's lawyer for assistance in identifying litigation, claims, and assessments; however, this permission typically is requested separately from the engagement letter. (7093)

42. (b) SAS 108 states, "An understanding with the client regarding an audit of the financial statements generally includes the following matters...The auditor is responsible for conducting the audit in accordance with generally accepted auditing standards. Those standards require that the auditor obtain reasonable rather than absolute assurance about whether the financial statements are free of material misstatement, whether caused by error or fraud. Accordingly, a material misstatement may remain undetected. Also, an audit is not designed to detect error or fraud that is immaterial to the financial statements. If, for any reason, the auditor is unable to complete the audit or is unable to form or has not formed an opinion, he or she may decline to express an opinion or decline to issue a report as a result of the engagement...These matters should be communicated in the form of an engagement letter." A comfort letter is provided to an underwriter by an auditor; typically an auditor informs the client of fraud, not the underwriter. A letter of audit inquiry is sent to a third party such as a vendor, customer, or attorney; typically an auditor informs the client of fraud, not third parties such as these. A representation letter is addressed by management to the auditor; management is unlikely to use the phrase "our audit." (7634)

43. (d) The element of the audit planning process most likely to be agreed upon with the client before implementation of the audit strategy is the timing of inventory observation procedures to be performed. Evidence to be gathered to provide a sufficient basis for the auditor's opinion is solely a matter of auditor judgment. The procedures to be undertaken to discover litigation, claims, and assessments are determined by the auditor. Pending legal matters to be included in the inquiry of the client's attorney are more likely to be discussed after implementation of the audit strategy. (5619)

44. (a) Gaining an understanding of the entity and its environment, including internal control, is the first of these four procedures to be performed in an audit. The entity's risk assessment process is part of its internal control. The auditor identifies specific activities designed to prevent fraud when considering

relying on internal control. The other two options are substantive procedures. (6709)

45. (d) The primary purpose of the audit is to gather sufficient evidence to support the auditor's conclusions. The design of the audit program has no effect on inherent risk. Procedures *may* be performed prior to the balance sheet date only if the effectiveness of interim work is not likely to be impaired. Suggestions to management are secondary considerations in an audit. (5089)

46. (c) Planning involves the development of an overall strategy for the expected conduct, organization, and staffing of the audit. The auditor must plan the audit to be responsive to the assessment of the risk of material misstatement. In establishing the overall audit strategy, the auditor should consider the important factors that will determine the focus of the audit team's efforts, such as (1) determination of appropriate materiality levels, (2) preliminary identification of areas where there may be higher risks of material misstatement, (3) preliminary identification of material locations and account balances, (4) evaluation of whether the auditor plans to perform tests of controls, and (5) identification of recent significant entity-specific, industry, financial reporting, or other relevant developments. (7102)

47. (d) According to SAS 108, "Once the audit strategy has been established, the auditor is able to start the development of a more detailed audit plan to address the various matters identified in the audit strategy, taking into account the need to achieve the audit objectives....The audit plan [or program] should include [a] description of the nature, timing, and extent of planned further audit procedures at the relevant assertion level for each material class of transactions, account balance, and disclosure." Answers (a), (b), and (c) are all considerations of the substantive and analytical procedures necessary to satisfy the audit objectives. (4673)

48. (a) In a preaudit conference, a senior auditor would most likely discuss the technical and personnel aspects of a job. Feedback from the staff would occur later. Establishing the need for specialists and the use of internal auditors is done during the planning stage. Answer (b) is done during fieldwork. (5077)

Audit Risk & Materiality

49. (d) Planning involves the development of an overall strategy for the expected conduct, organization, and staffing of the audit. To consider the appropriateness of the entity's plans for dealing with adverse economic conditions effectively, the auditor should be familiar with the entity and the conditions it is likely to encounter; such familiarity is enhanced by fieldwork. The fraud risk factors that exist within the client's operations and the control weaknesses to be included in the communication with the audit committee are unlikely to be known prior to commencing fieldwork. (8382)

50. (d) The engagement letter documents the understanding with the client regarding the services to be performed for each engagement. The understanding should include the objectives of the engagement, management's responsibilities, the auditor's responsibilities, and *limitations* of the engagement. Matters that should be communicated in the form of an engagement letter include a statement that the auditor is responsible for conducting the audit in accordance with GAAS. Those standards require that the auditor obtain reasonable rather than absolute assurance about whether the financial statements are free of material misstatement, whether caused by error or fraud. Accordingly, a material misstatement may remain undetected. Also, an audit is not designed to detect error or fraud that is immaterial to the financial statements. Potential control deficiencies typically would not be mentioned. The analytical procedures that the auditor expects to apply would be documented in the audit plan, not the engagement letter. The engagement letter could describe the auditor's responsibility to evaluate going-concern issues, but it is not required to be included. (8383)

51. (b) The work performed by each assistant, including the audit documentation, should be reviewed to determine whether it was adequately performed and documented and to evaluate the results, relative to the conclusions to be presented in the auditor's report. Checklists, worksheets documenting analytical procedures, and financial statements are each a part of working papers; a review of only one of these parts most likely would be insufficient. (8395)

52. (b) Detection risk is the risk that the auditor will not detect a material misstatement that exists in an assertion. Inherent risk is the susceptibility of an assertion to a material misstatement assuming that there are no related controls. Sampling risk arises from the possibility that, when a test of controls or a substantive test is restricted to a sample, the auditor's conclusions may be different from the conclusions s/he would reach if the test were applied in the same way to all items in the account balance or class of transactions. Nonsampling risk includes all the aspects of audit risk that are not due to sampling. (2275)

53. (b)   As the assessed level of control risk increases, the acceptable level of detection risk decreases. To decrease detection risk, an auditor changes the nature, extent, or timing of tests of details. To decrease detection risk, an auditor increases the extent of test of details. The level of inherent risk doesn't change, although an auditor may change the assessment of the level of inherent risk. As inherent risk is the susceptibility of an assertion to misstatement, assuming no related internal controls, the assessment of inherent risk level rarely changes due to a change in control risk. Increased testing of controls that the auditor already has determined to be ineffective provides no benefit.   (7799)

54. (c)   Inherent risk and control risk *exist independently of the financial statement audit*. They are the entity's risks and cannot be changed at the auditor's discretion. Detection risk is the risk that an auditor will not detect a material misstatement—it, not inherent risk or control risk, can arise from the misapplication of auditing procedures. All three risks can be assessed in quantitative terms, such as percentages, or nonquantitative terms, such as high, medium, or low risk.   (5081)

55. (c)   All three components of audit risk (control risk, detection risk, and inherent risk) may be assessed in quantitative terms, such as percentages, or nonquantitative terms, such as high, medium, or low risk.   (5628)

56. (b)   In determining materiality, the auditor should consider (1) prior-periods' financial results and financial positions, (2) the period-to-date financial results and financial position, and (3) budgets or forecasts for the current period. The auditor should take into account any significant changes in the entity's circumstances and relevant changes in the economy or the industry in which the entity operates. The anticipated sample size of the planned tests and the internal control questionnaire are, if anything, dependent on materiality, not vice versa. The contents of the management representation letter are not always known during the planning stages of the audit.   (5629)

Entity & Its Environment

57. (a)   The auditor should obtain sufficient knowledge about the accounting system because the methods influence the design of internal control. Materiality levels, audit objectives, and an auditor's acceptable level of audit risk are independent of the methods used to process accounting information.   (5080)

58. (a)   The second standard of fieldwork states, "The auditor must obtain a sufficient understanding of the entity and its environment, including its internal control, to assess the risk of material misstatement of the financial statements whether due to error or fraud, and to design the nature, timing and extent of further audit procedures." The other choices are intermediate considerations.   (5642)

Errors & Fraud

59. (d)   The auditor has a responsibility to plan and perform the audit to obtain reasonable assurance about whether the financial statements are free of material misstatements, whether caused by error or fraud.   (5633)

60. (b)   When supporting accounting records and files that should be readily available are not produced promptly when requested, it suggests either a hostile staff (poor control environment) or a poor information and communication system. Senior financial management should participate in the selection of accounting principles and determination of significant estimates. Related party transactions do not, in themselves, indicate misstatements. Management's excessive interest in updating the IT capabilities may lead to poor financial performance by the entity, but not necessarily misstatements in the financial statements.   (7826)

61. (b)   As management signs a representation letter that includes a statement that all known fraud has been reported to the auditor, if an auditor discovers fraud known to management, but undisclosed to the auditor, the auditor has evidence that management has lied regarding audit information at least once. This impairs reliance on other management statements. While an aggressive attitude toward meeting profit goals is suggestive of incentive and management decision dominated by one person may provide opportunity to commit fraud, they are not as important as actual known management deception. Some weaknesses in internal control may be knowingly left uncorrected due to cost-benefit considerations.   (7631)

62. (d)   Auditors should obtain assurance from the entity's attorney, verify clerical accuracy, and determine whether inadequate asset safeguards are corrected during the evidence gathering stage of the audit. Considering whether audit results affect the assessment of fraud risk is an overall review stage procedure.   (7027)

63. (d) The auditor must inform the audit committee directly regarding fraud possibly concerning senior management or causing a material misstatement of the financial statements. The auditor may need to disclose information: when legal and regulatory compliance requirements exist; to a successor auditor; in response to a subpoena; or to a funding agency or other specific agency in accordance with requirements for the audits of entities that receive financial assistance from a governmental agency. Typically, the auditor reports directly to the SEC only when the audit committee fails to do so. (7809)

64. (c) A strained relationship between management and auditors is one of the risk factors of fraud due to fraudulent financial reporting. A lack of interest in maintaining an earnings trend tends to reduce the risk of fraud due to fraudulent financial reporting. It may be in an entity's best interest to sell computer hardware before it is depreciated fully. The mere existence of outstanding checks of any amount in monthly bank reconciliations is a normal occurrence. (8420)

Assessing & Responding to RMM

65. (a) In some cases, the auditor may determine that performing only substantive procedures is appropriate for specific relevant assertions and risks. In those circumstances, the auditor may exclude the effect of controls from the relevant risk assessment. This may be because the auditor's risk assessment procedures have not identified any effective controls relevant to the assertion or because testing the operating effectiveness of controls would be inefficient. (4258)

66. (d) The auditor should design and perform further audit procedures whose nature, timing, and extent are responsive to the assessed risks of material misstatement at the relevant assertion level. Detection risk is a function of the effectiveness of an auditing procedure and its application by the auditor; therefore, the assessed risk of material misstatement will determine the acceptable level of detection risk and hence the appropriate audit procedures to be performed. The effectiveness of internal control, inherent risk, and materiality thresholds are all factors that help the auditor assess the risk of material misstatement. (4689)

Illegal Acts by Clients

67. (a) Forced discontinuance of operations in a foreign country may indicate illegal acts. Annual donations to a local politician generally are not illegal. Management may elect not to correct material weaknesses if the cost of correction would exceed the benefit. Disclosure of subsequent events generally would not cause the auditor to question whether illegal acts have occurred. (0189)

68. (a) The auditor's responsibility to detect and report misstatements resulting from illegal acts having a direct material effect on the financial statements is the same as that for misstatements caused by error or fraud. (The auditor should plan and perform the audit to obtain reasonable assurance about whether the financial statements are free of material misstatement, whether caused by error or fraud.) Due to the nature of illegal acts, an audit made in accordance with generally accepted auditing standards provides no assurance that illegal acts that could have an indirect material effect on the financial statements will be detected or any contingent liabilities that may result will be disclosed. (4671)

69. (c) The auditor should consider the implications of an illegal act in relation to other aspects of the audit, particularly the reliability of representations of management. (5085)

70. (d) The auditor may conclude that withdrawal is necessary when the client does not take the remedial action that the auditor considers necessary in the circumstances even when the illegal act is not material to the financial statements. (7487)

71. (b) When the auditor is unable to conclude whether the financial statements are materially misstated due to an illegal act, s/he should disclaim an opinion or issue a qualified opinion on the financial statements. (0165)

72. (c) If a possible illegal act has occurred the auditor should obtain an understanding of the act, the circumstances under which it occurred, and sufficient information to evaluate its effect on the financial statements. Normally, an audit conducted in accordance with GAAS does not include procedures specifically designed to detect illegal acts not having a direct and material effect on the financial statements. An auditor's training, experience, and understanding of the client probably would be insufficient to provide a basis of the determination as to whether illegal acts have occurred; consultation with legal counsel or other specialists may be necessary. Not all illegal acts would require an auditor to express a qualified opinion or an adverse opinion on the financial statements taken as a whole. (8422)

Communications With Audit Committee

73. (b) While the amount of misstatements that would be material may be discussed with the audit

committee, the auditor *must* report both the methods used to account for significant unusual transactions and disagreements with management, whether or not satisfactorily resolved. The auditor also has the responsibility to report significant deficiencies and material weaknesses. An indication of fraud and illegal acts is an example of a possible significant deficiency or material weakness. (5637)

74. (b) In some cases, management may decide to consult with other accountants about auditing and accounting matters. When the auditor is aware that such consultation has occurred, s/he should discuss with the audit committee her/his views about significant matters that were the subject of such consultation. The rate of turnover being too high and the auditor's assessed level of control risk are judgments of the auditor. The question of subsequent events would be less likely to be discussed than accounting consultations when an auditor is identifying matters for communication with an entity's audit committee. (6238)

75. (d) The auditor should inform the audit committee about adjustments arising from the audit that could, in her/his judgment, either individually or in the aggregate, have a significant effect on the entity's financial reporting process. The auditor should determine that the audit committee is informed about the process used by management in formulating particularly sensitive accounting estimates and about the basis for the auditor's conclusions regarding the reasonableness of those estimates. In order for the audit committee to understand the nature of the assurance provided by an audit, the auditor should communicate the level of responsibility assumed for these matters under generally accepted auditing standards. (7637)

PERFORMANCE BY SUBTOPICS

Each category below parallels a subtopic covered in Chapter 22. Record the number and percentage of questions you correctly answered in each subtopic area.

Planning & Supervision

Question #	Correct √
1	
2	
3	
4	
5	
6	
7	
8	
9	
10	
# Questions	10
# Correct	
% Correct	

Audit Risk & Materiality

Question #	Correct √
11	
12	
13	
14	
15	
16	
# Questions	6
# Correct	
% Correct	

Entity & Its Environment

Question #	Correct √
17	
18	
19	
# Questions	3
# Correct	
% Correct	

Errors & Fraud

Question #	Correct √
20	
21	
22	
23	
24	
25	
# Questions	6
# Correct	
% Correct	

Assessing & Responding to RMM

Question #	Correct √
26	
27	
28	
29	
# Questions	4
# Correct	
% Correct	

Illegal Acts by Clients

Question #	Correct √
30	
31	
32	
33	
34	
35	
36	
# Questions	7
# Correct	
% Correct	

Communications With Audit Committee

Question #	Correct √
37	
38	
# Questions	2
# Correct	
% Correct	

SIMULATION SOLUTIONS

Solution 22-3 (10 points)

Response #1: Risk Factors (1 point)

Answer: B

The auditor will need to focus more attention on the complex financial covenants to determine whether there have been any violations and whether they need to be disclosed in the financial statements.

Response #2: Analytical Results (4 points)

1. D

The debt to equity ratio equals total liabilities divided by shareholder's equity. Therefore, if capital stock was issued during the year, equity would increase, thereby decreasing the ratio.

2. F

Gross profit percentage equals sales less the cost of goods sold divided by sales. If manufacturing cost decreased less than sales decreased during the year, then the numerator would decrease more in proportion to the denominator, thereby decreasing the percentage.

Response #3: Substantive Tests (4 points)

Answers: D, F

Examining paid vendors' invoices would allow the auditor to determine whether liabilities are valued accurately in the financial statements. Also, examining an analysis of inventory turnover would allow the auditor to determine whether there may be slow moving or obsolete inventory.

Response #4: Communication (5 points)

Expected response should include:

An independent board of directors should reduce the likelihood that the financial statements are materially misstated.

1) objectivity (lack of conflicts of interest)

2) competency (prior experience working with financial data)

3) provides a safety valve—can communicate with the audit committee rather than directly with the owners

Response #5: Research (1 point)

Answer: AT 9101.23

Guidance: AT 9101.23 states

"2. Responding to Requests for Reports on Matters Relating to Solvency

Question—Lenders, as a requisite to the closing of certain secured financings in connection with leveraged buyouts (LBOs), recapitalizations and certain other financial transactions, have sometimes requested written assurance from an accountant regarding the prospective borrower's solvency and related matters. The lender is concerned that such financings not be considered to include a fraudulent conveyance or transfer under the Federal Bankruptcy Code or the relevant state fraudulent conveyance or transfer statute. If the financing is subsequently determined to have included a fraudulent conveyance or transfer, repayment obligations and security interests may be set aside or subordinated to the claims of other creditors."

(7846)

Solution 22-4

Response #1: Risk Factors (9 points)

The factors most likely to have an effect on the risk of material misstatements and their resulting effect include the following:

Environmental factor	Effect on risk of material misstatements
Governmental regulation over the banking industry is extensive.	Decrease
NFB operates profitably in a growing prosperous area.	Decrease
Overall **demand for the industry's product** is high.	Decrease
Interest rates have been **volatile** recently.	Increase
The **availability of funds** for additional mortgages is **promising**.	Decrease
The **principal shareholder** is also the **chief executive officer** and controls the board of directors.	Increase
Branch **management is compensated based on branch profitability**.	Increase
The **internal auditor reports directly to the chairman of the board's audit committee**, a minority shareholder.	Decrease

Environmental factor	Effect on risk of material misstatements
The **accounting department** has experienced **little turnover** in personnel recently.	Decrease
NFB is a **continuing audit client**.	Decrease
Management **fails to establish proper procedures** to provide reasonable assurance of reliable **accounting estimates**.	Increase
Management **fails to establish proper procedures** to provide reasonable assurance of reliable **accounting estimates**.	Increase
Management has been receptive to Green's **suggestions** relating to accounting adjustments.	Decrease
NFB recently **opened a new branch** office that is **not yet profitable**.	Increase
NFB recently installed a **new sophisticated computer system**.	Increase

Response #2: Research (1 point)

Paragraph Reference Answer: AU 316.62

Guidance: AU 316.62 states, "Because fraudulent journal entries often are made at the end of a reporting period, the auditor's testing ordinarily should focus on the journal entries and other adjustments made at that time. However, because material misstatements in financial statements due to fraud can occur throughout the period and may involve extensive efforts to conceal how it is accomplished, the auditor should consider whether there also is a need to test journal entries throughout the period under audit."

(9034)

Solution 22-5

Response #1: Communication (9 points)

a. Management fraud is the **deliberate falsification** or alteration of accounting records or documents committed by management to **intentionally** render the financial statements **misleading**. A defalcation is the misappropriation of an entity's assets by an employee through **embezzlement**, the **falsification** of documents, or **violation** of policy.

b. Under GAAS an auditor is **responsible to assess the risk** that management fraud may cause the financial statements to be materially misstated. Based on that assessment, the **auditor should design the audit to provide reasonable assurance** of detecting management fraud that is material to the financial statements.

c. The characteristics of management fraud that an auditor should consider include the **materiality of the effect on the financial statements**, the level of **management** involved, the **extent and skillfulness of any concealment**, the **relationship to established control procedures**, and **the specific financial statements affected**.

d. Among the other factors that should heighten an auditor's concern about the existence of management fraud are the following:

- **Potential sale** of the entity.
- Undertaking an aggressive acquisition program **using the entity's stock as consideration**.
- Indications that the entity will fall short of meeting **earnings or sales forecasts**.
- Indications of **financial distress** such as insufficient working capital, high debt, slow collection of receivables, or other going concern problems.
- **Unfavorable industry conditions**.
- The existence of **related party transactions**.
- A CEO who **dominates the board of directors**.

Response #2: Research (1 point)

Paragraph Reference Answer: AU 315.09

Guidance: AU 315.09 states, "The successor auditor should make specific and reasonable inquiries of the predecessor auditor regarding matters that will assist the successor auditor in determining whether to accept the engagement. Matters subject to inquiry should include

- Information that might bear on the integrity of management.
- Disagreements with management as to accounting principles, auditing procedures, or other similarly significant matters.
- Communications to those charged with governance regarding fraud and illegal acts by clients.
- Communications to management and those charged with governance regarding significant deficiencies and material weaknesses in internal control.
- The predecessor auditor's understanding as to the reasons for the change of auditors.

The successor auditor may wish to consider other reasonable inquiries."

(9035)

Solution 22-6

Response #1: Communication (17 points)

a. There are many fraud risk factors that are indicated in the dialogue. Among the fraud risk factors are the following:

- A significant portion of Mint's compensation is represented by **bonuses and stock options**. Although this arrangement has been approved by SCS's Board of Directors, this may be a motivation for Mint, the new CEO, to engage in fraudulent financial reporting.

- Mint's statement to the stock analysts that SCS's earnings would increase 30% next year may be both an **unduly aggressive and unrealistic forecast**. That forecast may tempt Mint to intentionally misstate certain ending balances this year that would increase the profitability of the next year.

- SCS's audit committee may not be **sufficiently objective** because Green, the chair of the audit committee, hired Mint, the new CEO, and they have been best friends for years.

- **One individual,** Mint, appears to **dominate management** without any compensating controls. Mint seems to be making all the important decisions without any apparent input from other members of management or resistance from the Board of Directors.

- There were frequent disputes between Brown, the prior CEO, who like Mint apparently dominated management and the Board of Directors, and Jones, the predecessor auditor. This fact may indicate that an **environment** exists in which management will be reluctant to make any changes that Kent suggests.

- Management seems to be satisfied with an understaffed and ineffective internal audit department. This situation displays an **inappropriate attitude** regarding the internal control environment.

- Management has failed to properly monitor and correct a significant deficiency in its internal control—the lack of segregation of duties in cash disbursements. This **disregard for the control environment** is also a risk factor.

- Information about anticipated future layoffs has spread among the employees. This information may cause an increase in the risk of material misstatement arising from the misappropriation of assets by **dissatisfied employees**.

b. Kent has many misconceptions regarding the consideration of fraud in the audit of SCS's financial statements that are contained in the dialogue. Among Kent's misconceptions are the following:

- Kent states that an auditor does not have specific duties regarding fraud. In fact, an auditor has a responsibility to **specifically assess** the risk of material misstatement due to fraud and to **consider that assessment** in designing the audit procedures to be performed. Furthermore, the audit team must **brainstorm** on ways in which **fraud** could **occur** at this client. Editor's note: *consider, evaluate,* and *speculate* are less acceptable alternatives for *brainstorm,* as *brainstorm* is used in SAS 99.

- Kent is not concerned about Mint's employment contract. Kent should be concerned about a CEO's contract that is based primarily on **bonuses and stock options** because such an arrangement may indicate a **motivation** for management to engage in fraudulent financial reporting.

- Kent does not think that Mint's forecast for the next year has an effect on the financial statement audit for the current year. However, Kent should consider the possibility that Mint may **intentionally misstate** the current ending balances to increase the reported profit in the next year.

- Kent believes that the audit programs are fine as is. Actually, Kent should **modify** the audit programs because of the many risk factors that are present in the SCS audit.

- Kent is not concerned that the internal audit department is ineffective and understaffed. In fact, Kent should be concerned that SCS has **permitted this situation to continue** because it represents a risk factor relating to misstatements arising from fraudulent financial reporting and/or the misappropriation of assets.

- Kent states that an auditor provides no assurances about fraud because that's management's job. In fact, an auditor has a responsibility to **plan and perform** an audit to obtain **reasonable assurance** about whether the financial statements are free of material misstatement, **whether caused by error or fraud**.

- Kent is not concerned that the prior year's significant deficiency has not been corrected. However, Kent should be concerned that the **lack of segregation of duties** in the cash disbursements department represents a risk factor relating to misstatements arising from the misappropriation of assets.

- Kent does not believe that the rumors about big layoffs in the next month have an effect on audit planning. In planning the audit, Kent should consider this risk factor because it may cause an increase in the risk of material misstatement arising from the misappropriation of assets by **dissatisfied employees**.

c. In planning a financial statement audit, the auditor should **document** in the working papers evidence of the performance of the assessment of the **risk of material misstatement due to fraud**. Where risk factors are identified, the documentation should include those **risk factors identified** and the **auditor's response** to those risk factors, individually or in combination. In addition, during the performance of the audit, the auditor may identify fraud risk factors or other conditions that cause the auditor to believe that an **additional response** is required. The auditor should document such risk factors or other conditions,

and any further response that the auditor concludes is appropriate.

Response #2: Research (1 point)

Paragraph Reference Answer: AU 312.54

Guidance: AU 312.54 states, "When the auditor tests relevant assertions related to an account balance or a class of transactions by a substantive analytical procedure, the auditor might not specifically identify misstatements but would obtain only an indication of whether misstatement might exist in the balance or class and possibly its approximate magnitude. If the substantive analytical procedure indicates that a misstatement might exist, but not its approximate amount, the auditor should request management to investigate and, if necessary, should expand his or her audit procedures to enable him or her to determine whether a misstatement exists in the account balance or class of transactions."

(6635)

CHANGE ALERT

SAS 115 (AU 325), *Communicating Internal Control Related Matters Identified in an Audit* **(issued 10/2008)**

In October 2008, the Auditing Standards Board of the American Institute of Certified Public Accountants issued Statement on Auditing Standards (SAS) 115, *Communicating Internal Control Related Matters Identified in an Audit.*

This statement supersedes SAS 112 of the same title and was issued to incorporate the revisions of the definitions of the different kinds of deficiencies in internal control and align the related guidance for evaluating deficiencies in internal control with Statement on Standards for Attestation Engagements 15, *An Examination of an Entity's Internal Control Over Financial Reporting That Is Integrated With an Audit of Its Financial Statements.*

This statement is effective for audits of financial statements for periods ending on or after December 15, 2009. Earlier implementation is permitted.

This statement is eligible to be tested beginning in the April-May 2009 exam window.

CHAPTER 23

INTERNAL CONTROL

CHAPTER 23

INTERNAL CONTROL

I. Overview

A. Definition

Internal control is a process—effected by those charged with governance, management and other personnel—designed to provide reasonable assurance about the achievement of the entity's objectives with regard to reliability of financial reporting, effectiveness and efficiency of operations, and compliance with applicable laws and regulations. Internal control consists of five interrelated components.

B. Components of Internal Control

Exhibit 1 ▶ Components of Internal Control Mnemonic

C	**C**ontrol Activities
R	**R**isk Assessment
I	**I**nformation & Communication Systems
M	**M**onitoring
E	Control **E**nvironment

1. **Control Activities** Control activities are those policies and procedures established to provide reasonable assurance that management decisions are executed. Control activities may have various objectives and are found at several levels. Control activities relevant to an audit are categorized as practices that relate to the following:

    a. **Performance Reviews** This includes reviewing and analyzing the actual performance of the entity; relating different sets of data (operating or financial) to one another, while analyzing the relationships and investigative and corrective actions; as well as comparing internal data with external information and reviewing functional or activity performance.

    b. **Information Processing** Controls are performed to check accuracy, completeness, and authorization of transactions. The two broad groupings of information systems control activities are application controls and general controls.

    c. **Physical Controls** These involve physical security of assets, including limited access to assets and records; authorization for access to computer programs and data files; and periodic counting and comparison with amounts shown on control records.

    d. **Segregation of Duties** Incompatible functions place a person in the position to both perpetrate and conceal errors or fraud in the normal course of her/his duties. Therefore, a well designed plan of organization separates the duties of authorization, record keeping, and custody of assets.

2. **Risk Assessment** For financial reporting purposes, risk assessment is an entity's (not an auditor's) identification, analysis, and management of risks relevant to the preparation of financial statements that are presented fairly in conformity with GAAP. Risks relevant to financial reporting include external and internal events that may occur and adversely affect an entity's ability to process and report financial data consistent with management's assertions.

3. **Information & Communication** This refers to the identification, retention, and transfer of information in a timely manner enabling personnel to execute their responsibilities.

    a. **Information** The quality of information impacts management's capacity to make decisions to direct the entity's activities and prepare financial statements. The information system of concern to the auditor, including the accounting system, is composed of the procedures and records established to record, process, summarize, and report transactions as well as maintain accountability for the corresponding assets, liabilities, and equity.

    b. **Communication** Communication includes establishing individual duties and responsibilities relating to internal control and making them known to involved personnel.

4. **Monitoring** Monitoring is a process that evaluates the quality of internal control performance over time. Monitoring also includes initiating appropriate corrective actions. The process is achieved through separate evaluations or ongoing activities. Customer complaints and other external communication may indicate areas of concern.

    a. **Management** Monitoring is a responsibility of management. Management must monitor internal control to consider whether it is being implemented as planned and that it is modified appropriately as changes occur. Internal auditors, or personnel with similar duties, may contribute to monitoring.

    b. **Necessity** Monitoring is necessary, due to the tendency of internal control to break down over time.

5. **Control Environment** The control environment is the foundation for all other components of internal control. It sets the tone of an organization that influences the control consciousness of its people. In other words, it establishes the overall attitude, awareness, and actions of the board of directors, management, employees, and others concerning the importance and emphasis of internal control in the entity. The following elements make up the control environment:

    a. Communication and enforcement of integrity and ethical values

    b. Management's commitment to competence

    c. Participation of those charged with governance

    d. Management's philosophy and operating style

    e. The entity's organizational structure

    f. Methods of assigning authority and responsibility

    g. Human resource policies and practices

II. Understanding of Internal Control (AU 314, SAS 109 continued)

A. General Considerations

1. **Responsibility** It is management's responsibility to establish and maintain internal control.

2. **Perspective** The classification of internal control into five components establishes a framework for evaluation of an entity's internal control, but it is not necessarily how the entity implements internal control. The auditor's main concern is whether, and how, a specific control prevents, detects, and corrects material misstatements in relevant assertions, rather than its classification into any particular component.

3. **Accounting Policies** The auditor should obtain an understanding of the entity's selection and application of accounting policies and should consider whether they are appropriate and consistent with GAAP, or an other comprehensive basis of accounting (OCBOA), as well as accounting policies used in the industry. The understanding should include: the methods used to account for significant and unusual transactions; the effect of significant accounting policies in controversial or emerging areas that lack authoritative guidance; and changes in accounting policies. The auditor should also identify new financial reporting standards or regulations applicable to the entity and consider when and how the entity will adopt them.

4. **Inherent Limitations** Inherent limitations exist with respect to the effectiveness of an entity's internal control. The best designed and operated system of internal control can provide only reasonable assurance regarding accomplishment of control objectives.

   a. **Errors (Inadvertent)** Mistakes may occur in the application of certain policies and procedures due to misunderstanding of instructions or personal carelessness.

   b. **Fraud (Intentional)** Controls can be circumvented by collusion or management override. The potential for override of controls by management depends on the control environment to a great extent.

5. **Smaller Entities** The extent of segregation of duties may be limited in smaller entities due to fewer employees. However, even in a very small entity, it can be practicable to implement some degree of segregation of duties or other form of simple but effective controls for vital areas.

6. **Identifying Internal Controls** The auditor should identify the controls that are likely to prevent or detect and correct material misstatements in specific relevant assertions. Generally, the auditor gains an understanding of controls and relates them to relevant assertions in the context of processes and systems in which they exist. This is useful because individual control activities do not usually address a specific risk by themselves.

7. **Relationship** Controls can be directly or indirectly related to an assertion. The more indirect the relationship, the less effective that control may be in reducing control risk for that assertion.

8. **Auditability** The auditor's understanding of internal control may cause concerns about the auditability of an entity's financial statements. Doubts as to the integrity of management may cause the auditor to conclude that an audit cannot be completed. Also, the condition and reliability of the entity's records may cause concern regarding the sufficiency of audit evidence available. In such cases, the auditor may need to consider a qualified opinion or disclaimer of opinion. However, some circumstances may require the auditor to withdraw from the engagement.

B. **Relevance**
   There is a direct relationship between an entity's *objectives* and the internal controls *components* it implements. The auditor need consider only the objectives and related controls relevant to the audit. Not all categories of objectives and related controls are relevant to a financial statement audit. Even though internal control components may apply to the entire entity or to only a portion of its divisions or operations, it might not be essential for the auditor to obtain an understanding of internal control concerning all of an entity's divisions and operations.

   1. **Relevant Controls** Controls including those that pertain to the entity's ability to produce financial statements for external use in accordance with GAAP, or OCBOA, are relevant to the audit. It is not necessary to assess all controls related to assessing the risks of material misstatement. This is a matter of professional judgment. However, the auditor should evaluate the design and implementation of related controls for all *significant risks* and for risks that substantive procedures alone do not provide sufficient audit evidence. When using professional judgment to decide which controls should be assessed, the auditor should consider the circumstances, the applicable component, and factors such as:

a.   Materiality

b.   The size of the entity

c.   The nature of the entity's business, including its organization and ownership characteristics

d.   The diversity and complexity of its operations

e.   Its applicable legal and regulatory requirements

f.   The nature and complexity of the systems that are part of the entity's internal control, including the use of service organizations

2.   **Significant Risks** *Significant risks* are risks that require special audit consideration (see Chapter 22). Therefore, the auditor should evaluate the design and implementation of related controls for all *significant risks*. However, risks related to significant nonroutine or judgmental matters are less likely to be subject to routine controls. This means the auditor will need to consider how management responds to the risks and whether appropriate control activities have been implemented to address the risks. Appropriate control activities may consist of a review of assumptions by senior management or experts; formal processes for estimations; or approval by the audit committee, or equivalent.

3.   **Other Risks Requiring Tests of Controls** The auditor should obtain an understanding of controls over those risks for which it is not possible or practicable to obtain sufficient audit evidence from substantive procedures alone. Such risks may concern routine transactions that are often highly automated with little or no manual intervention. In such cases, audit evidence may be available only in electronic form; therefore, its appropriateness and sufficiency often depend on the operating effectiveness of controls over its completeness and accuracy.

4.   **Partially Relevant Controls** Controls pertaining to data the auditor uses to apply or evaluate auditing procedures such as those related to the operations and compliance objectives or the completeness and accuracy of information may also be relevant to the audit. For example, an auditor may use production statistics in analytical procedures. Also, controls related to compliance with tax laws may have a direct and material effect on the financial statements.

5.   **Irrelevant Controls** Some controls such as those concerned with adherence to health and safety regulations or the effectiveness, economy, and efficiency of certain management decision-making processes (the appropriate price to charge for its products, etc.) are irrelevant to the audit and do not need to be considered.

6.   **Overlapping Controls** Internal control over safeguarding assets to reduce unauthorized procurement, use, or disposition of assets may involve controls related to both financial reporting and operations objectives. For example, use of a lockbox system for collecting payments or passwords for restricted access to payroll records may be relevant to the audit; while controls reducing raw material waste in production usually are irrelevant to the audit.

C.   **Depth of Understanding**
Obtaining an understanding of internal control consists of evaluating the design and implementation of controls.

1.   **Design** To evaluate the design of a control, the auditor should consider whether the control, individually or in combination with other controls, is able to effectively prevent or detect and correct material misstatements.

2.   **Implementation** To evaluate the implementation of a control means to determine whether a control is actually being used by the entity. In determining whether to consider implementation of a control, the auditor should first consider the design of the control. If the control is designed improperly, it may represent a material weakness in the entity's internal control;

therefore, the auditor should consider whether to communicate this to the audit committee and management.

3. **Procedures** The auditor should perform risk assessment procedures (covered in Chapter 22) to obtain an understanding of internal control. More specifically, procedures to obtain evidence about the design and implementation of controls may include:

   a. Inquiring of entity personnel; inquiries alone are not sufficient to evaluate the design and implementation of a control

   b. Observing the application of specific controls

   c. Inspecting documents and reports

   d. Tracing transactions relevant to financial reporting through the information system

4. **Sufficiency** Obtaining this understanding is not sufficient to serve as testing the operating effectiveness of controls, unless there is some automation that provides for the consistent operation of the control. For example, obtaining audit evidence about the implementation of a manual control at a point in time does not provide audit evidence about the operating effectiveness of the control at other times during the period under audit. However, because IT processing is inherently consistent generally, procedures to determine implementation of an automated control may serve as a test of that control's operating effectiveness.

D. **Understanding of Components of Internal Control**

1. **Control Environment** The auditor should obtain sufficient knowledge of the control environment to understand management's and the board of directors' attitude, awareness, and actions concerning the control environment. The auditor should concentrate on the implementation of controls rather than the form, because appropriate controls may exist but not be enforced. In evaluating the design of the entity's control environment, the auditor should consider all elements of the control environment and how they are incorporated. The responsibilities of the board of directors and its committees, particularly the audit committee, are extremely important.

2. **Risk Assessment** The auditor should obtain sufficient familiarity of the client's risk assessment process to discern how management evaluates risks relevant to financial reporting objectives and elects actions to mitigate those risks. In evaluating the design and implementation of the entity's risk assessment process, the auditor should consider how management identifies business risks relevant to financial reporting, determines the significance of those risks, assesses the probability of their occurrence, and elects actions to mitigate them. An entity's perspective when assessing risk differs from the auditor's evaluation of audit risk. The entity seeks to identify, evaluate, and manage risks that impact the entity's objectives. The auditor evaluates risks to assess the potential for material misstatement of the financial statements.

3. **Information & Communication** The auditor should obtain a sufficient understanding of the process the entity employs to communicate duties, responsibilities, and material matters pertaining to financial reporting. The auditor's understanding of communication also includes communications between management and the board of directors, particularly the audit committee, as well as external communications pertaining to financial reporting matters, such as those with regulatory authorities. The auditor should obtain sufficient knowledge about the information system pertaining to financial reporting to understand the following:

   a. The classes of transactions in the entity's operations that are significant to the financial statements and how those transactions originate within the entity's business processes.

b. The procedures by which transactions are initiated, authorized, recorded, processed, and reported in the financial statements as well as how incorrect processing of transactions is resolved.

c. The accounting records, supporting information, and specific accounts in the financial statements involved in the processing and reporting of transactions.

d. How the information system captures events and conditions, other than classes of transactions, that are significant to the financial statements.

e. The financial reporting process used to prepare the entity's financial statements, including significant accounting estimates and disclosures.

4. **Control Activities** The process of obtaining an understanding of control activities usually overlaps with obtaining knowledge of other components. The understanding gained regarding the existence of control activities while considering other components will indicate if additional understanding of control activities is warranted. Audit planning does **not** demand knowledge of control activities related to every account balance, transaction class, or disclosure component in the financial statements.

5. **Monitoring** The auditor should obtain sufficient understanding of the major types of activities the entity employs to monitor internal control pertaining to financial reporting, including the manner in which those activities are used to take appropriate corrective actions. The auditor also should obtain an understanding of the sources of information used in monitoring activities, as well as management's basis for determining that the sources are reliable. If management assumes, without a basis for that assumption, that data produced from the entity's information system is reliable, errors may exist that could potentially lead management to incorrect conclusions.

E. Documentation

The auditor should document the following regarding the understanding of internal control: (a) key elements of the understanding obtained regarding the five components of internal control; (b) the sources of information from which the understanding was obtained; and (c) the risk assessment procedures performed. The form and extent of documentation is influenced by the size and complexity of the entity, as well as the nature of the entity's internal control. For a large, complex entity, this may include flowcharts, questionnaires, or decision tables. For a small, simple entity, a memorandum may be sufficient.

F. Tools

1. **Flowchart Approach** An internal control flowchart is a graphic representation of a portion of a company's internal control. It shows the segregation of functions, document flows, controls, etc.

Exhibit 2 ▸ Common Flowchart Symbols

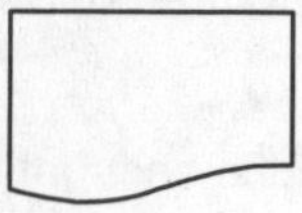

DOCUMENT: Paper documents and reports of all kinds, e.g., sales invoices, purchase orders, employee paychecks, and computer-prepared error listings.

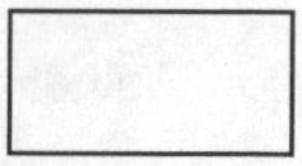

COMPUTER OPERATION/PROCESS: Execute defined operations resulting in some change in the information or the determination of flow direction, e.g., checking customer's credit limit.

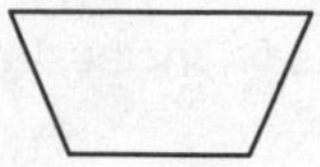

MANUAL OPERATION: Off-line process that is performed manually, e.g., preparing a three-part sales invoice or manually posting to customer accounts.

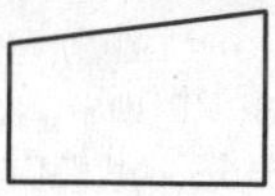

MANUAL INPUT: Represents input entered manually at the time of processing, e.g., using a keyboard.

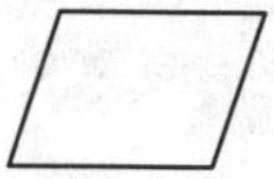

INPUT/OUTPUT: General input/output symbol, e.g., general ledger, can be used regardless of the type of medium or data.

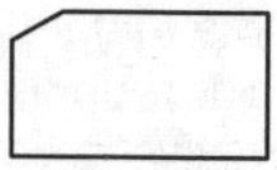

PUNCHED CARD: Input/output function in which the medium is a punched card, e.g., payroll earnings card.

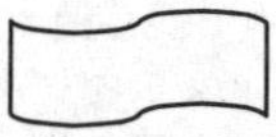

PUNCHED TAPE: Input/output function in which the medium is punched tape.

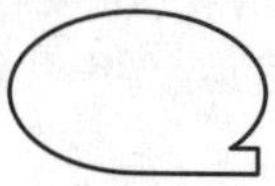

MAGNETIC TAPE: Input/output function in which the medium is magnetic tape, e.g., master payroll data file.

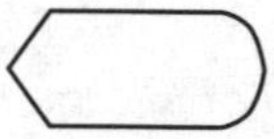

DISPLAY: Input/output device in which the information is displayed at the time of processing for human use, e.g., display customer number.

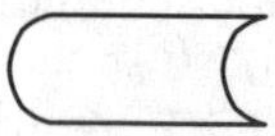

ONLINE STORAGE: Storage that is connected to and under the control of the computer, e.g., disk, drum, magnetic tape, etc.

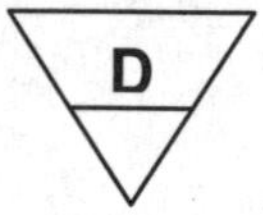

OFF-LINE STORAGE: Any off-line storage of information regardless of the medium on which the information is recorded. This includes filing documents such as sales invoices and purchase orders. An "A" signifies an alphabetic file, an "N" is for a numeric file, and a "D" indicates a file organized by date.

OFF-PAGE CONNECTOR: Designates entry to or exit from a page. For example, it can be used to indicate sending a copy of an invoice to a customer.

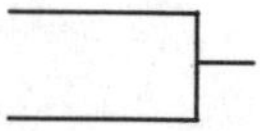

ANNOTATION: Provides additional information.

DECISION: Determines next action. Used in program flowcharts, e.g., is A = B?

a.   **Advantages** The internal control flowchart is a graphic representation of a series of sequential processes. It shows the steps required and the flow of documents from person to person in carrying out the functions depicted. Therefore, the tendency to overlook the controls existing between functions or departments is minimized. Another advantage is that the flowchart clearly communicates the structure. The use of a flowchart is especially useful in the evaluation of electronic IT systems because it avoids much of the terminology that would be present in a narrative. Finally, constructing a flowchart requires the auditor to completely understand the structure.

b. **Disadvantage** It may be more time consuming to construct a flowchart rather than to fill out an internal control questionnaire.

2. **Questionnaire Approach** An internal control questionnaire is simply an enumeration of the matters to be investigated in the auditor's consideration of internal control. It should be designed by persons who are fully conversant with the problems of internal control and who have experience in the kind of structure being reviewed.

    a. **Sample Questions** While the size and scope of internal control questionnaires will vary, some possible questions for an accounts receivable system are as follows:

        (1) Are the following functions performed by employees other than accounts receivable bookkeepers?

            (a) Handling cash and maintaining cash records

            (b) Opening incoming mail

            (c) Credit and collection

            (d) Review and mailing of statements to customers

        (2) Are the accounts receivable ledgers unavailable to the cashier?

        (3) Are the subsidiary ledgers regularly balanced with the control accounts?

        (4) Are the subsidiary ledgers occasionally balanced with the control accounts by someone other than the accounts receivable bookkeepers?

        (5) Are aged trial balances of accounts receivable regularly prepared and submitted for executive approval?

        (6) Are statements sent at regular intervals to all customers?

    b. **Advantages** One advantage of the internal control questionnaire is that it is easy to complete. Another advantage is that the comprehensive list of questions provides assurance that relevant points will be covered. Also, weaknesses are obvious because they are usually the "no" answers.

    c. **Disadvantage** A possible problem is that if the questionnaire is too general, it may not be adequate to evaluate an entity's internal control.

3. **Narrative (Memorandum) Approach** The auditor determines what the prescribed system of internal control is, and then writes it out in the auditor's own words.

    a. **Advantages** The narrative is tailor-made for each engagement. Another advantage is that it requires a detailed analysis of the client's internal control because the auditor must thoroughly understand the structure in order to describe it.

    b. **Disadvantages** The narrative approach is very time consuming. It does not have built-in safeguards to prevent the auditor from overlooking some aspect of internal control—weaknesses are not always obvious and might not be detected by this approach.

III. Tests of Controls (AU 318, SAS 110 continued)

    A. **General Requirements & Considerations**
The auditor should perform tests of controls when: (1) the auditor's risk assessment includes an expectation of the operating effectiveness of controls or (2) when it is not possible or practicable to reduce detection risk at the relevant assertion level to an acceptably low level with audit evidence obtained from substantive procedures alone.

1. **Testing Operating Effectiveness** Tests of the operating effectiveness of controls are performed only on those controls determined to be capable of preventing or detecting a material misstatement.

2. **Operating Effectiveness vs. Implementation** Testing the operating effectiveness of controls is not the same as obtaining audit evidence that controls have been implemented. When performing risk assessment procedures, the auditor obtains evidence of implementation by determining that relevant controls exist and that the entity is using them. When performing tests of controls, the auditor obtains evidence that controls are operating effectively. This includes obtaining audit evidence about (a) how controls were applied at relevant times during the period under audit, (b) the consistency with which they were applied, and (c) by whom or by what means they were applied. If substantially different controls were used at different times during the period under audit, the auditor should consider each separately.

3. **Concurrent Performance** The auditor may determine that it is efficient to test the operating effectiveness of controls at the same time as evaluating their design and implementation. Even though some risk assessment procedures may not have been specifically designed as tests of controls, they may serve as tests of controls if they provide audit evidence about the operating effectiveness of controls. Nevertheless, the auditor will need to evaluate the sufficiency of the audit evidence provided by those audit procedures.

B. **Nature**

The auditor should select procedures to obtain assurance about the operating effectiveness of controls. As the planned level of assurance increases, the more reliable or extensive audit evidence should be. When the audit approach consists primarily of tests of controls, the auditor should obtain a higher level of assurance about the operating effectiveness of controls. Tests of the operating effectiveness of controls generally include: (1) inquiries of appropriate entity personnel; (2) inspection of documents, reports, or electronic files, indicating performance of the control; (3) observation of the application of the control; and (4) reperformance of the application of the control by the auditor.

1. **Combination of Procedures** The auditor should use a combination of audit procedures to obtain sufficient appropriate audit evidence concerning the operating effectiveness of controls; inquiry alone is not sufficient. Typically, inquiry combined with inspection or reperformance provides more assurance than inquiry combined with observation only. Also, because an observation pertains to only the point in time at which it is made, the auditor should supplement an observation with inquiries of entity personnel and may also need to inspect documentation regarding the operation of such controls at other times during the period under audit.

2. **Design** In designing tests of controls, the auditor should consider the need to obtain audit evidence concerning the operating effectiveness of controls directly related to relevant assertions as well as other indirect controls on which these controls depend. For example, the auditor should consider controls related to the accuracy and completeness of information when other controls depend on that information to operate effectively. Such controls may be IT general and application controls.

3. **Dual-Purpose Tests** The auditor may design a test of controls to be performed concurrently with a test of details on the same transaction. Because the objectives of the tests are different, the auditor should carefully consider the design and evaluation of such tests in order to accomplish both objectives. For example, the auditor may examine an invoice to determine whether it has been approved and to provide substantive evidence of a transaction. Furthermore, when performing such tests the auditor should consider whether the extent (e.g., sample size) of substantive procedures should be increased from that originally planned if controls are found to be ineffective.

4. **Results of Substantive Procedures** The lack of misstatements detected by substantive procedures does not provide audit evidence that related controls are effective. On the other

hand, misstatements detected by substantive procedures should be considered when assessing the operating effectiveness of related controls. When a material misstatement is detected by the auditor that was not identified by the entity, it should be regarded as at least a significant deficiency and a strong indicator of a material weakness in internal control.

C.   Timing
The timing of tests of controls depends on the auditor's objective and the period of reliance on those controls.

1.   **Reliance**   The auditor should test controls at a point in time, or throughout the period, depending on when the auditor intends to rely on those controls. For example, evidence relating to only a point in time may be sufficient when testing controls over the counting of physical inventory at the end of the period. However, this may be insufficient if the auditor needs evidence concerning a period of time. In this case, the auditor also should perform tests that provide evidence that the control operated effectively at relevant times during the period. For example, the operation of a control embedded in a computer program may be tested at a particular point in time; then the auditor may perform tests of general controls pertaining to the modification and use of that computer program to obtain evidence concerning the consistent operation of the control during the audit period.

2.   **Interim Tests**   When the auditor performs tests of controls during an interim period, the auditor should determine what additional audit evidence should be obtained for the remaining period.

   a.   **Considerations**   In determining the additional evidence needed, the auditor should consider: (1) the significance of the assessed risks of material misstatement at the relevant assertion level, (2) the specific controls that were tested during the interim period, (3) the amount of audit evidence obtained concerning the operating effectiveness of those controls, (4) the length of the remaining period, (5) the extent to which the auditor intends to reduce further substantive procedures based on the reliance of controls, and (6) the control environment.

   b.   **Significant Changes**   The auditor should obtain audit evidence about the nature and extent of any significant changes in internal control, including changes in the information system, processes, and personnel that occur in the remaining period.

   c.   **Examples**   Additional audit evidence may be obtained by extending the testing of the operating effectiveness of controls to the remaining period, or by testing the entity's monitoring of controls.

3.   **Prior Audit Evidence**   If the auditor plans to use prior period audit evidence about the operating effectiveness of controls, the auditor should obtain audit evidence concerning whether there have been changes in those controls since the prior audit.

   a.   **Controls With Changes**   If the auditor plans to rely on controls that have changed since they were last tested, the auditor should test the operating effectiveness of such controls in the current audit.

   b.   **Controls Without Changes**   If the auditor plans to rely on controls that have not changed since they were last tested, the auditor should test the operating effectiveness of such controls at least once every three years. This rule does not apply to controls that mitigate a significant risk. Generally, as the risk of material misstatement or the reliance on controls increases, the time that is allowed to elapse should decrease.

   c.   **Considerations**   In considering whether it is appropriate to use prior period audit evidence concerning the operating effectiveness of controls and the amount of time that may elapse before retesting a control, the auditor should consider:

(1) The effectiveness of other components of internal control, including the control environment, the entity's monitoring of controls, and the entity's risk assessment process.

(2) The risks arising from the characteristics of the control, including whether controls are manual or automated.

(3) The effectiveness of IT general controls.

(4) The effectiveness of the control and its application by the entity, including the nature and extent of deviations in the application of the control from tests of operating effectiveness in prior audits.

(5) Whether the lack of a change in a particular control poses a risk due to changing circumstances.

(6) The risk of material misstatement and the extent of reliance on the control.

d. **Substantial Reliance on Prior Audits** If the auditor uses audit evidence obtained in prior audits for several controls, the auditor should plan to test a sufficient portion of the controls in each audit period, so that at a minimum, each control is tested at least every third audit.

e. **Controls Mitigating Significant Risks** While the auditor should *consider* information obtained in prior audits in designing tests of controls, the auditor should **not** *rely* on prior audit evidence concerning the operating effectiveness of controls intended to mitigate a significant risk. If the auditor plans to rely on the operating effectiveness of such controls, the auditor should test the operating effectiveness of those controls in the current period.

D. **Extent**

The auditor should design tests of controls to obtain sufficient appropriate audit evidence that the controls are operating effectively throughout the period of reliance. In determining the extent of tests of controls, the auditor may consider the following factors:

1. The frequency of performance of the control during the period.

2. The length of time the auditor is relying on the operating effectiveness of the control.

3. The relevance and reliability of the audit evidence to be obtained in supporting that the control prevents, or detects and corrects, material misstatements at the relevant assertion level.

4. The extent to which audit evidence is obtained from tests of other controls related to the relevant assertion.

5. The extent to which the auditor plans to rely on the operating effectiveness of the control to reduce substantive procedures. The extent of tests of controls should increase as the auditor increases reliance on the operating effectiveness of controls.

6. The expected deviation from the control. The extent of tests of controls should increase as the expected deviation rate increases. However, the rate of expected deviation may be so high as to indicate that the performance of tests of controls will not be sufficient to reduce the control risk at the relevant assertion level.

IV. **Communicating Internal Control Related Matters Identified in an Audit (AU 325, SAS 115)**

A. **Overview**

AU 325 provides guidance on communicating matters related to an entity's internal control over financial reporting *identified in an audit of financial statements;* it is applicable even when an auditor disclaims an opinion.

It is **not** the auditor's duty to search for deficiencies in internal control. However, the auditor may notice deficiencies as a consequence of performing audit procedures.

B.   Definitions

1.   **Deficiency in Internal Control**   A *deficiency in internal control* exists when the design or operation of a control does not allow management or employees, in the normal course of performing their assigned functions, to prevent or detect and correct misstatements on a timely basis.

    a.   **Design**   A deficiency in *design* exists when a control necessary to meet the control objective is missing or an existing control is not properly designed so that even if the control operates as designed, the control objective would not be met.

    b.   **Operation**   A deficiency in *operation* exists when a properly designed control does not operate as designed or the person performing the control does not possess the necessary authority or competence to perform the control effectively.

2.   **Significant Deficiency**   A *significant deficiency* is a deficiency, or combination of deficiencies in internal control, that is less severe than a material weakness, yet important enough to merit attention by those charged with governance.

3.   **Material Weakness**   A *material weakness* is a deficiency, or combination of deficiencies in internal control, such that there is a reasonable possibility that a material misstatement of the entity's financial statements will not be prevented, or detected and corrected on a timely basis.

C.   Evaluating Deficiencies in Internal Control
The auditor must evaluate deficiencies in internal control and determine whether they are significant deficiencies or material weaknesses. In making this determination, the auditor should consider the likelihood and magnitude of a possible misstatement. Thus, the significance of a deficiency in internal control depends on the potential for a misstatement, not on whether a misstatement actually has occurred.

1.   **Risk Factors**   Risk factors that affect whether there is a reasonable possibility that a deficiency will cause a misstatement to occur include: the nature of the financial statement accounts, classes of transactions, disclosures, and assertions involved; the susceptibility of the item to loss or fraud; the subjectivity, complexity, or degree of judgment required to determine the amount involved; the effect other controls or deficiencies have on the control; and possible future consequences of the deficiency.

2.   **Multiple Deficiencies in Internal Control**   Multiple deficiencies in internal control that affect the same account balance or disclosure increase the likelihood of misstatement and may, in combination, constitute a significant deficiency or material weakness, even though such deficiencies are individually insignificant. Therefore, the auditor should evaluate individual deficiencies in internal control that affect the same account balance, disclosure, relevant assertion, or component of internal control, to determine whether they collectively result in a significant deficiency or material weakness.

3.   **Compensating Controls**   The auditor may consider the possible mitigating effects of effective compensating controls that have been tested and evaluated as part of the audit. A compensating control is a control that limits the severity of a deficiency in internal control and keeps it from rising to the level of a significant deficiency or, in some instances, a material weakness. However, it does not eliminate the deficiency.

4.   **Indicators of Material Weaknesses**   Indicators of material weaknesses include: Identification of fraud, whether or not material, carried out by senior management; restatement of previously issued financial statements to correct a material misstatement due to error or fraud; identification by the auditor of a material misstatement that would not have been

detected by the entity's internal controls; and ineffective oversight of the entity's financial reporting and internal control by those charged with governance.

D. Communication

Deficiencies in internal control that are identified and determined to be significant deficiencies or material weaknesses must be communicated in writing to management and those charged with governance in every audit. This requirement includes significant deficiencies and material weaknesses that were previously communicated to management and those charged with governance that have not yet been remediated.

1. **Timing** The required written communication is best made by the report release date (the date the auditor grants the entity permission to use the auditor's report in connection with the financial statements), but should be made no later than 60 days after the report release date.

    In some circumstances, early communication to management or those charged with governance may be important due to their significance or the need for timely follow-up action. Therefore, the auditor may decide to communicate certain identified significant deficiencies and material weaknesses *during* the audit. Such matters do not have to be communicated in writing initially, however, even if they are remediated during the audit, they must be included in the final required written communication.

2. **Known Deficiencies** The existence of certain significant deficiencies or material weaknesses may already be known to management and may represent a conscious decision to accept the risk because of cost or other considerations. The auditor's responsibility to communicate significant deficiencies and material weaknesses exists regardless of management's decisions.

3. **Required** The written communication should:

    a. State that the purpose of the auditor's consideration of internal control was to express an opinion on the financial statements, but not to express an opinion on the effectiveness of the entity's internal control over financial reporting (ICFR).

    b. State that the auditor is not expressing an opinion on the effectiveness of internal control.

    c. State that the auditor's consideration of internal control was not designed to identify all deficiencies in internal control that might be significant deficiencies or material weaknesses.

    d. Include the definition of the terms *material weakness* and, where relevant, *significant deficiency*.

    e. Identify the matters that are considered to be significant deficiencies and those that are considered to be material weaknesses.

    f. State that the communication is intended solely for the information and use of management, those charged with governance, and others within the organization and is not intended to be and should not be used by anyone other than these specified parties. If an entity is required to furnish such auditor communications to a governmental authority, specific reference to such governmental authorities may be made.

Exhibit 3 ▶ Illustrative Written Communication

In planning and performing our audit of the financial statements of ABC Company (the "Company") as of and for the year ended December 31, 20XX, in accordance with auditing standards generally accepted in the United States of America, we considered the Company's internal control over financial reporting (internal control) as a basis for designing our auditing procedures for the purpose of expressing our opinion on the financial statements, but not for the purpose of expressing an opinion on the effectiveness of the Company's internal control. Accordingly, we do not express an opinion on the effectiveness of the Company's internal control.

Our consideration of internal control was for the limited purpose described in the preceding paragraph and was not designed to identify all deficiencies in internal control that might be significant deficiencies or material weaknesses and therefore, there can be no assurance that all deficiencies, significant deficiencies, or material weaknesses have been identified. However, as discussed below, we identified certain deficiencies in internal control that we consider to be material weaknesses [*and other deficiencies that we consider to be significant deficiencies*].

A deficiency in internal control exists when the design or operation of a control does not allow management or employees, in the normal course of performing their assigned functions, to prevent, or detect and correct misstatements on a timely basis. A material weakness is a deficiency, or a combination of deficiencies, in internal control, such that there is a reasonable possibility that a material misstatement of the entity's financial statements will not be prevented, or detected and corrected on a timely basis. [*We consider the following deficiencies in the Company's internal control to be material weaknesses:*]

[*Describe the material weaknesses that were identified.*]

[*A significant deficiency is a deficiency, or combination of deficiencies, in internal control that is less severe than a material weakness, yet important enough to merit attention by those charged with governance. We consider the following deficiencies in the Company's internal control to be significant deficiencies:*]

[*Describe the significant deficiencies that were identified.*]

This communication is intended solely for the information and use of management, [*identify the body or individuals charged with governance*], others within the organization, and [*identify any specified governmental authorities*] and is not intended to be and should not be used by anyone other than these specified parties.

4. **Optional** The auditor may include additional statements in the required written communication regarding the general inherent limitations of internal control or the specific nature and extent of the auditor's consideration of internal control during the audit.

   Additionally, nothing precludes the auditor from communicating other matters (orally or in writing) that the auditor believes to be of potential benefit to the entity. For example, the auditor could make recommendations for operational or administrative efficiency, or for improving internal control. The auditor could also communicate information about deficiencies in internal control that are not significant deficiencies or material weaknesses. If these matters are communicated orally, the auditor should document the communication.

5. **No Material Weaknesses Identified** The auditor may issue a communication indicating that no *material weaknesses* were identified during the audit of the financial statements for the client to submit to governmental authorities. However, the auditor should **not** issue a written communication stating that no *significant deficiencies* were identified during the audit.

6. **Management's Response** Management may wish or be required to prepare a written response to the auditor's communication. If such a response is included in a document containing the auditor's written communication, the auditor may add a paragraph to the auditor's written communication disclaiming an opinion on such information.

V. Internal Control Objectives & Procedures for Specific Transaction Cycles

    A.   Objectives of Internal Control
    A well designed internal control should ensure five objectives.

        1.   Authorization The starting point for establishing accounting control of transactions is appropriate authorization. Obtaining reasonable assurance of appropriate general or specific authorization requires independent evidence that authorizations are issued by persons acting within the scope of their authority and that transactions conform with the terms of the authorizations.

        2.   Validity Controls should provide reasonable assurance relative to the validity or existence of assets and liabilities at a given date and whether recorded transactions have occurred during a given period.

        3.   Proper Recording The objective of internal control with respect to the proper recording of transactions encompasses several sub-objectives. These include the following:

            a.   Completeness Transactions are not omitted from the accounting records.

            b.   Valuation Transactions are recorded at the actual amounts at which they transpired.

            c.   Classification Transactions are classified in the appropriate accounts.

            d.   Timing Transactions are recorded in the accounting period in which they occurred. Additionally, they are recorded as promptly as practicable when recording is necessary to maintain accountability.

        4.   Accountability & Comparison The accountability objective of internal control is to assure the availability of information necessary to follow assets from the time of their acquisition until their disposition. This requires maintaining records for accountability of assets and periodic comparison of these records with the related assets. The purpose of comparing recorded accountability with assets is to determine whether the actual assets agree with the recorded accountability. Consequently, it is related closely to the above discussion of proper recording of transactions.

        5.   Protection & Limited Access Controls should provide adequate protection of assets. Such protection is facilitated through segregation of incompatible functions and requires that access to assets be limited to authorized personnel. Access to assets includes both direct physical access and indirect access through documents that authorize use or disposition of assets.

    B.   Source Documents & Accounting Records
    To determine the correct test of an internal control or to identify an internal control weakness, you must understand how source documents and accounting records relate to each other and what type of internal controls should exist.

        1.   Segregation Remember that the authorization of a transaction, its record keeping, and the custody of the related asset should all be separated. If any person or department was responsible for more than one of these functions, an internal control weakness would exist. For example, in the payroll function:

            **a.   **The personnel department should authorize pay rates (authorization).

            **b.   **The timekeeping department should prepare attendance and timekeeping data (record keeping).

            **c.   **The payroll department prepares the payroll (record keeping).

            **d.   **The treasurer's department prepares the payroll checks and distributes them to employees (custody).

2. **Tracking** Source documents should be prenumbered and controlled so that they all can be accounted for.

3. **Reconciliation** Subsidiary ledgers should be reconciled to general ledgers.

4. **Perspective** When considering a question about testing an internal control, first determine what is being asked.

    a. Tracing from a source document to the recorded entry tests the completeness assertion by looking for understatements.

    b. Vouching from a recorded entry to the source document tests the existence assertion by looking for overstatements.

C. **Policies & Procedures Within Transaction Cycles**
    This section examines the five transaction cycles more closely by relating specific internal control policies and procedures within the cycles to the objectives of internal control. Additionally, for each control, an audit test of controls is suggested to evaluate the effectiveness of the policies and procedures.

    1. **Transaction Cycles** Internal control objectives can be analyzed based on specific business activities or logical groups of transactions. Groupings of similar transactions or functions of an entity are known as transaction cycles. Dividing the audit into transaction cycles is known as the cycle approach. The cycle approach combines similar transactions with the ledger balances that result from those transactions. This is more efficient than treating each account balance as a separate segment. Although classification is somewhat arbitrary, the following is representative of the cycles of most businesses:

        a. Sales, Receivables & Cash Receipts Cycle

        b. Purchases, Payables & Cash Disbursements Cycle

        c. Inventory & Production Cycle

        d. Personnel & Payroll Cycle

        e. Property, Plant & Equipment Cycle

    2. **Universal Procedures** Several internal control policies and procedures are common to most, if not all, transaction cycles. Listed in the Appendix at the end of this chapter are general internal control questions that can be asked for most of the transaction cycles indicated. These questions are presented in this format to help you become familiar with the general questions. Specific internal control questions applicable to the individual transaction cycles are included under the transaction cycle titles in the Appendix of this chapter. Questions generally should be worded to require a yes or no answer.

    3. **Sales, Receivables & Cash Receipts Cycle**

Objective	*Internal Control*	*Test of Controls*
Authorization	Credit approval occurs before shipment is authorized.	Examine appropriate document for approval.
	Existence of a cash discount policy.	Discuss policy with management. Review sales orders for evidence of compliance.
	Approval of cash discounts and adjustments.	Examine remittance advices for proper approval.
	Sales prices are from authorized price list or executed contract.	Compare sales invoice prices to appropriate price list or contract.

Objective	Internal Control	Test of Controls
Validity	Prenumbered sales invoices.	Account for numerical sequence of sales invoices.
	Sales are supported by authorized shipping documents and approved customer orders.	Examine supporting bills of lading and customer orders.
	Monthly statements are mailed to customers.	Observe mailing of statements.
	Independent follow-up of customer complaints.	Examine customer correspondence files.
	Separation of the functions of cash handling and record keeping.	Observation. Discuss with management and review employee job descriptions.
	Shipment is acknowledged by shipping department.	Examine acknowledgment on sales order copy.
Proper Recording	Shipping documents are prenumbered (Completeness).	Accounting for numerical sequence of shipping documents. Trace documents to recording of sales and accounts receivable subsidiary ledger.
	A chart of accounts is used and is adequate (Classification).	Review adequacy and use of proper accounts. Examine sales documents to determine if sales transactions are properly classified.
	Cash receipts are recorded immediately and deposited on a daily basis (Timing).	Observation. Trace totals to duplicate deposit slips.
	Sales invoices and credit memoranda are prenumbered (Completeness).	Account for numerical sequence of sales invoices and credit memoranda.
	Internal verification of invoice preparation and posting (Valuation, Completeness, Classification).	Observation. Discuss policy with management.
Accountability and Comparison	Independent reconciliation of bank statements.	Observation. Review bank reconciliation.
	Cash register totals are verified by persons not having access to cash or cash records.	Examine documentation of verification.
	Cash receipts are recorded immediately to establish accountability.	Observe the cash receiving process.
	A list of checks is prepared as the mail is opened.	Observation. Compare check listing total to duplicate deposit slip.
Protection and Limited Access	Persons receiving or otherwise handling cash are bonded.	Discuss with management. Review appropriate documentation of bonding.
	Checks are immediately endorsed.	Observation.
	Separation of cash handling and record keeping functions.	Observation. Discuss with management and review employee job descriptions.

4.   Purchases, Payables & Cash Disbursements Cycle

Objective	*Internal Control*	*Test of Controls*
Authorization	Appropriate approval is required for all purchases.	Examine supporting documentation for indication of approval (purchase requisition and order).
	Payment approval required before check signing.	Observation. Examine documentation for indication of approval.
	Authorized signatures on checks. Two signatures on large checks.	Select a sample of large disbursements from the cash disbursements journal and examine the correlating canceled checks for two signatures.
Validity	Purchases are supported by purchase requisition, purchase order, receiving report, and vendor invoice.	Examine supporting documentation of vouchers.
	Documentation is canceled to prevent reuse.	Examine documentation for indication of cancellation.
	Receiving reports are prenumbered.	Account for numerical sequence of receiving reports.
	Receiving reports are required before approval of invoice for payment.	Discuss policy with management. Observation. Compare payment approval and receiving report dates.
Proper Recording	Vouchers are prenumbered (Completeness).	Account for numerical sequence of vouchers.
	Internal verification of vendor invoice amounts and calculations. (Valuation).	Examine invoice copy for indication of clerical accuracy verification.
	Transactions are recorded as soon as possible after receiving goods. (Timing).	Compare purchases journal dates to receiving report and invoice dates. (Observation).
	Purchase orders are prenumbered (Completeness).	Account for numerical sequence of purchase orders.
	A chart of accounts is used and is adequate (Classification).	Review adequacy and use of proper accounts. Examine sales documents to determine if sales transactions are properly classified.
Accountability and Comparison	Independent reconciliation of bank statement.	Observation. Review bank reconciliation.
	Checks are signed only with appropriate support, by the treasurer, and the treasurer mails the checks.	Observation. Examine canceled check signatures.
	Monthly suppliers' statements are compared to accounts payable.	Examine statements for indication of agreement.
	Receiving department examines quantity and quality of merchandise upon receipt.	Examine copies of receiving reports and purchase orders for indication of goods received.

Objective	Internal Control	Test of Controls
Accountability and Comparison (cont.)	Accountability is established for unused and voided checks.	Discuss policy with management.
Protection and Limited Access	Separation of functions between accounts payable and custody of signed checks.	Observation. Review employee job descriptions.
	Checks are prenumbered.	Account for numerical sequence of checks.
	Mechanical check protector is used.	Examine check copies for evidence of check protector use.
	Separation of purchasing department functions from receiving and record keeping.	Observation. Review employee job descriptions.
	Physical control of unused checks is properly and securely maintained.	Observation. Discuss policy with management.

5. Inventory & Production Cycle

Objective	Internal Control	Test of Controls
Authorization	Movement of inventory items is authorized by requisitions.	Examine requisitions for indication of approval. Inquire of client personnel.
	Inventory purchases are appropriately authorized.	Select a sample of recorded purchases and vouch to documents authorizing purchase.
	Write-offs and write-downs of obsolete inventory are appropriately authorized.	Examine appropriate documentation for indication of authorization.
Validity	Receiving prepares prenumbered receiving reports.	Account for numerical sequence of receiving reports.
	Payment for inventory is approved only after verification of quantity and prices of vendor invoice.	Examine documentation for indication of verification.
Proper Recording	Merchandise receiving reports are matched with vendor invoices (Valuation, Completeness).	Examine vendor invoice copy for indication of agreement with receiving report.
	Purchase orders are prenumbered (Completeness).	Account for numerical sequence of purchase orders.
	Shipping or transfer reports are prenumbered (Completeness).	Account for numerical sequence of reports.
	Movement of inventory items is accounted for on a timely basis by authorized requisitions (Timing, Completeness, Classification).	Compare dates recorded for shipping reports of transferor with receiving report and requisition data of receiving department.
	Clerical accuracy of vendor invoices is checked prior to payment (Valuation).	Examine invoice for indication of accuracy check.

Objective	*Internal Control*	*Test of Controls*
Accountability and Comparison	Receiving department indicates description and quantity of inventory received on prenumbered receiving reports.	Examine receiving reports.
	Perpetual inventory records maintained for large dollar value items.	Review inventory records. Discuss policy with management.
	Periodic comparison made between inventory records and physical inventory.	Review inventory records for indication of agreement with physical count.
Protection and Limited Access	Inventory is stored under the control of a custodian. Access is limited.	Observation. Discuss procedures with management and custodian.
	Inventory purchasers and handlers are bonded.	Review appropriate documentation of bonding.
	Inventory records are maintained separate from the functions of shipping, receiving, and custody.	Observation.
	Physical safeguards against theft and fire exist.	Examine physical safeguards.
	Insurance coverage on inventory is adequate.	Review insurance policies.

6. Personnel & Payroll Cycle

Objective	*Internal Control*	*Test of Controls*
Authorization	Employment is authorized before hiring.	Review hiring policies and verify the hiring authorization of a sample of employees.
	Payment rates (including commissions and bonuses) and hours to be worked are authorized at the appropriate levels.	Examine approval for rates or union contracts and approval for hours to be worked.
	Deduction authorizations are obtained for each payroll deduction.	Review personnel file for authorizations.
	Personnel department authorizes all changes to payroll master file.	Review change authorizations for sample of changes made during the year.
	Authorized signature(s) required on payroll checks.	Examine payroll checks for evidence of appropriate signature(s).
Validity	Time clock is used to record time worked by employees.	Observation.
	Department head or foreman approves and signs time cards.	Examine time cards for indication of approval.
	A paymaster (with no other payroll responsibilities) distributes payroll checks.	Observation. Discuss policy with management.

Objective	*Internal Control*	*Test of Controls*
Validity (Cont.)	Personnel department keeps personnel files on each employee.	Review personnel files.
	Terminations are properly documented.	Review personnel files.
Proper Recording	Accounting procedures require recording payroll transactions as timely as possible (Timing).	Compare time card dates with recording date and paycheck dates for proper timing.
	Job time tickets are reconciled to time clock cards.	Examine job time tickets for indication of reconciliation and/or approval.
	An adequate chart of accounts is maintained including appropriate payroll accounts (Classification).	Review adequacy and use of proper accounts.
	Calculation and amounts of payroll are internally verified. (Completeness, Valuation).	Examine indication of internal verification.
	Account classification of payroll-related transactions is internally verified (Classification).	Review reconciliation of monthly payroll with labor distribution.
Accountability and Comparison	Independent reconciliation of bank statement for imprest payroll account.	Observation. Review reconciliation of bank statement.
	Unclaimed payroll checks are returned to a person responsible for their custody (e.g., internal audit).	Discuss policy with management. Observe distribution of paychecks. Inquire of client personnel.
	Accountability is established for unused and voided payroll account checks.	Discuss policy with management and personnel responsible for check accountability (Observation).
Protection and Limited Access	Separation of personnel, payroll, and timekeeping functions.	Observation. Discuss functions with management.
	Use of a separate imprest payroll account.	Review separate documentation such as bank statements.
	Payroll checks are prenumbered.	Account for numerical sequence of payroll checks.
	Treasurer signs payroll checks.	Observation. Examine canceled payroll checks.

7. **Property, Plant & Equipment Cycle**

Objective	*Internal Control*	*Test of Controls*
Authorization	Authorization is required for all purchases over a certain amount.	Discuss policy with management. Review documentation of a sample of large purchases for indication of approval.
Validity	Major purchases require authorization by the board of directors.	Examine documentation of major purchases for approval by board. Review minutes of board meetings.

Objective	*Internal Control*	*Test of Controls*
Validity (Cont.)	Movements or sales of equipment have prior approval.	Examine appropriate documentation for existence of approval.
	Abandonments are reported to accounting department by foremen.	Discuss abandonment policy with management and foremen.
	Purchases are supported by appropriate authorizations, purchase order, receiving report, and vendor invoice.	Examine acquisition files for supporting documentation.
	Policies exist for classification of fixed assets, including a policy for expensing or capitalizing items (Classification).	Examine written policies. Vouch a selected sample of capitalized and expensed disbursements for compliance with policies.
	Policies exist for asset life estimations and depreciation tables used (Valuation, Timing).	Review written policies. Discuss with management. Vouch a sample of items for compliance with policies.
	Depreciation charges are recorded in subsidiary ledgers and amounts are internally verified periodically (Valuation, Completeness).	Examine subsidiary ledgers for appropriate depreciation charges and evidence of internal verification.
	Accounting procedures require timely recording of purchases and associated depreciation (Timing).	Compare receiving report dates, invoice dates, and recording dates for appropriate timing.
Accountability and Comparison	Subsidiary ledgers exist and are used.	Verify the existence of subsidiary ledgers and review entry detail for appropriateness.
	The responsibility for small tools is assigned to individual foremen.	Review tool responsibility with management and foremen. Examine the internal verification of the existence of tools.
	Internal verification is performed to examine existence and condition of fixed assets on a periodic basis.	Discuss policy with internal audit. Examine records for indication of verification.
Protection and Limited Access	Equipment has identification numbers to protect against loss.	Examine assets for existence of identification numbers.
	Insurance coverage on property, plant, and equipment is adequate.	Review insurance policies for adequacy of coverage.
	Physical safeguards are available for protection of assets from fire and theft (e.g., fire extinguishers, burglar alarms, etc.).	Examine physical safeguards for adequacy.

VI. General Internal Control Questionnaires

A. Control Environment

This questionnaire's objective is to determine if responsibilities are defined and authority is assigned to specific individuals to permit identification of whether persons are acting within the scope of their authority.

Management Philosophy and Operating Style

1. Does management have clear objectives in terms of budget, profit, and other financial and operating goals?

2. Are policies

    a. Clearly written?

    b. Communicated throughout the entity?

    c. Actively monitored?

3. Does management adequately consider the effects of taking business risks?

Organizational Structure

1. Is the organization of the entity clearly defined in terms of lines of authority and responsibility?

2. Does the entity have a current organization chart?

3. Are policies and procedures for authorization of transactions established at adequately high levels?

Audit Committee

1. Does the board of directors have an audit committee?

2. Does the audit committee take an active role in overseeing the entity's accounting and financial reporting policies and practices?

3. Does the audit committee

    a. Hold regular meetings?

    b. Appoint members with adequate qualifications?

    c. Adequately assist the board in meeting its fiduciary responsibilities?

    d. Assist the board in maintaining a direct line of communication with the internal and external auditors?

Methods of Assigning Authority and Responsibility

1. Does the entity have code of conduct and conflict of interest requirements?

2. Are employees given job descriptions which delineate specific duties, reporting relationships, and constraints?

3. Has the entity developed computer systems documentation which indicates procedures for authorizing transactions and approving systems changes?

Management Control Methods

1. Are there regular meetings of the board of directors and are minutes of such meetings prepared on a timely basis?

2. Does the entity have in place planning and reporting systems that

    a. Identify variances from planned performance?

     b. Communicate variances to the appropriate management level?

     c. Adequately investigate variances?

     d. Allow management to take appropriate and timely corrective action?

3. Has the company established a records retention policy and made arrangements for the storage of the information?

Internal Audit Function

1. Does the entity have an internal audit function?

2. If the entity has an internal audit function

     a. Is the internal auditor independent of the activities s/he audits?

     b. Is the internal audit function adequately staffed?

     c. Does the internal auditor document internal control and perform tests of controls?

     d. Does the internal auditor perform substantive tests of the details of transactions and account balances?

     e. Does the internal auditor document the planning and execution of her/his work?

     f. Does the internal auditor render written reports on her/his findings and conclusions?

     g. Are the internal auditor's reports submitted to the board or to a similar committee?

3. Does management take timely action to correct conditions reported by the internal auditor?

Personnel Policies and Procedures

1. Are employees adequately trained?

2. Is performance systematically evaluated?

3. Does the entity dismiss employees on a timely basis for critical violations of control policies?

4. Are employees in positions of trust bonded?

5. Are employees required to take mandatory vacations?

6. Is access to records limited to authorized persons?

B. Accounting System
This questionnaire's objective is to determine if accounting policies and procedures are determined in accordance with management's authorization.

- Access to the accounting and financial records is limited to minimize opportunity for errors and fraud, and to provide reasonable protection from physical hazards.
- Accounting entries are initiated and approved in accordance with management's authorization.
- Accounting entries are appropriately accumulated, classified, and summarized.
- The general ledger and related records permit preparation of financial statements in conformity with GAAP.
- Financial statements with related disclosures are prepared and released in accordance with management's authorization.

- Individuals at appropriate levels consider reliable information in making estimates and judgments required for preparation of the financial statements and related disclosures.

General Accounting

1. Does the entity have adequate written statements and explanations of its accounting policies and procedures, such as

   a. Chart of accounts?

   b. Assignment of responsibilities and delegation of authority?

   c. Explanations of documentation and approval requirements for various types of transactions and journal entries?

2. Is access to the general ledger and related records restricted to those who are assigned general ledger responsibilities?

3. Is appropriate insurance coverage maintained (such as loss of records coverage and fidelity bonding of employees in positions of trust) in accordance with management's authorization?

4. Are all journal entries reviewed and approved?

5. Are all journal entries explained and supported?

6. Are individuals who review and approve journal entries independent of initiation of the entries they are authorized to approve?

Preparation of Financial Statements

1. Are the general ledger accounts arranged in orderly groupings which are conducive to efficient statement preparation?

2. Are there adequate instructions and procedures for

   a. Assignment of specific preparation and review responsibilities?

   b. Accumulation of information on intercompany transactions?

   c. Accumulation of information for footnote disclosure?

3. Are estimates and adjustments to provide valuation allowances reviewed and approved by appropriate levels in the organization independent of the persons originating the estimates and adjustments?

4. Are procedures adequate for the review and comparison of working papers to source data, and comparison of elimination and reclassification entries to those made in prior periods?

5. Are financial statements subjected to overall review and comparisons with the prior period and with budgeted amounts by appropriate levels of management?

VII. Transaction Cycle Internal Control Questionnaires

A. Revenues & Receivables

This questionnaire's objectives are to determine if the types of goods and services provided, the manner in which they will be provided, and the customers to which they will be provided are in accordance with management's authorization.

- The prices and other terms of sales are established in accordance with management's authorization.

- Credit terms and limits are established.
- Goods delivered and services provided are based on orders which have been approved.
- Deliveries of goods and services result in preparation of accurate and timely billings.
- Sales related deductions and adjustments are made in accordance with management's authorization.

1. Are sales orders approved before shipment?

2. Do approved sales orders record the terms of sales in detail?

3. Are unfilled sales commitments periodically reviewed?

4. Is current information on prices, discounts, sales taxes, freight, warranties, and returned goods clearly communicated to the sales and billing personnel (i.e., approved sales catalogs, manuals, and price lists)?

5. Is the credit of prospective customers investigated before it is extended to them?

6. Is there a periodic review of credit limits?

7. Are shipping documents prepared for all shipments?

8. Are goods shipped based on documented sales orders which have been approved?

9. Are shipping documents subjected to

   a. Timely communication to persons who physically perform the shipping function?

   b. Timely communication to persons who perform the billing function?

10. Are quantities of goods shipped verified by double counting or comparison with counts by common carriers?

11. Are shipping documents compared with billings to determine that all goods shipped are billed and accounted for?

12. Are sales invoices prepared for all shipments of goods?

13. Are sales invoices

   a. Matched with approved sales orders?

   b. Matched with shipping documents?

14. Are credit memos

   a. Prenumbered and accounted for?

   b. Matched with applicable receiving reports for returns?

   c. Approved by a responsible employee independent of the person preparing the credit memo?

15. Are monthly statements reviewed and mailed by a responsible employee who is independent of the accounts receivable and cash functions?

16. Is an aging schedule of past due accounts prepared monthly?

17. Is there documentation of review and analysis of accounts receivable balances for determining valuation allowances and any specific balances to be written-off?

18. Are valuation allowances and write-offs approved?

B. Cash Receipts

This questionnaire's objectives are to determine if access to cash receipts records, accounts receivable records, and billing and shipping records is controlled to prevent the taking of unrecorded cash receipts or abstraction of recorded cash receipts.

- Detailed transaction and account balance records are reconciled with control accounts and bank statements at least monthly for the timely detection and correction of errors.
- All cash receipts are recorded at the correct amounts in the period in which received and are classified and summarized properly.

1. Does the person who opens the mail

    a. Place restrictive endorsements on all checks received so they are for deposit only?

    b. List all remittances and prepare totals daily?

    c. Forward all remittances to the person who prepares and makes a daily bank deposit?

2. Are currency receipts forwarded daily to the person who prepares the daily bank deposit?

3. Is a summary listing of daily currency receipts forwarded to a person independent of physical handling of remittances and accounts receivable?

4. Are each day's receipts deposited intact daily?

5. Are all employees who handle receipts adequately bonded?

6. Does company policy prohibit the cashing of any accommodation checks (payroll, personal) out of collections?

7. Are bank chargebacks received directly from the bank and investigated by a person independent of the physical handling of collections and posting of accounts receivable subsidiary ledgers?

8. Are entries to the cash receipts journal compared with

    a. Duplicate deposit slips authenticated by the bank?

    b. Deposits per the bank statement?

    c. Listings prepared when the mail is opened?

9. Is information from remittance documentation adequate for the accurate posting of credits to individual accounts receivable subsidiary records or accounts such as investment income, rents, and sales of property?

10. Are details of collections posted to subsidiary accounts receivable records by a person independent of the general ledger functions, physical handling of collections, and receipt and investigation of bank chargebacks?

C. Purchases & Accounts Payable

This questionnaire's objectives are to determine if the types of goods and services to be obtained, the manner in which they are obtained, the vendors from which they are obtained, the quantities to be obtained, and the prices and terms initiated and executed are in accordance with management's authorization.

- Adjustments to vendor accounts and account distributions are made in accordance with management's authorization.

- All goods and services received are accounted for accurately and on a timely basis.
- Only authorized goods and services are accepted and paid for.
- Amounts payable for goods and services received are recorded accurately at the correct amounts in the appropriate period and classified properly.
- Access to purchasing, receiving, and accounts payable records is controlled to prevent or detect duplicate or improper payments.

1. Are written purchase orders used for all commitments and do those orders include the vendor description, quantity, quality, price, terms, and delivery requirements for the goods or services ordered?

2. Is there a record of open purchase commitments?

3. Are open purchase orders periodically reviewed and investigated?

4. Are goods received inspected for condition and independently counted for comparison with the applicable purchase order?

5. Are receiving reports prepared promptly for all goods received?

6. Do receiving reports provide for recording of

   a. Description, quantity, and acceptability of goods?

   b. Date on which the goods or services are received?

   c. Signature of the individual approving the receipt?

7. Are receiving reports subjected to

   a. Accounting for all receiving reports used?

   b. Distribution for timely matching of copies with purchase orders and vendor invoices?

8. Is control established over all invoices received?

9. Are duplicate invoices stamped or destroyed as a precaution against duplicate payment?

10. Are vendors' invoices, prior to payment, compared in detail to purchase orders and receiving reports?

11. Are all available discounts taken?

12. Are there procedures for periodic review and investigation of unprocessed invoices, unmatched purchase orders, and receiving reports to provide for follow-up and proper accruals, and to result in a proper cutoff for financial reporting purposes?

13. Are vendors' statements reviewed for, and proper follow-up made of, overdue items?

D. **Payroll**
This questionnaire's objectives are to determine if employees are hired and retained only at rates and benefits determined by management's authorization.

- Payroll withholdings and deductions are based on evidence of appropriate authorization.
- Compensation is made only to company employees at authorized rates and for services rendered.
- Gross pay, withholdings, deductions, and net pay are computed correctly using authorized rates and properly authorized withholding exemptions and deductions.
- Payroll costs and related liabilities are accumulated, classified, and summarized correctly in the accounts in the proper period.

- Comparisons are made of personnel, payroll, and work records at reasonable intervals for timely detection and correction of errors.
- Net pay and related withholdings and deductions are remitted to the appropriate employees when due.
- Functions are assigned so that no single individual is in a position to both perpetrate and conceal errors and fraud in the normal course of their duties.
- Access to personnel and payroll records is limited.

1. Are all new hires, rates of pay and changes thereto, changes in position, and terminations based on written authorizations by management's criteria?

2. Are appropriate written authorizations obtained from employees for all payroll deductions and withholding exemptions?

3. Are personnel files maintained on individual employees which include appropriate written authorizations for rates of pay, payroll deductions, and withholding exemptions?

4. Are methods for determining premium pay rates for matters such as overtime, night shift work, and employee benefits determined in accordance with management's authorizations?

5. Do employees who perform the payroll processing function receive timely notification of wage and salary rate changes, new hires, changes in position, terminations, and changes in authorized deductions and withholding exemptions?

6. Is there an adequate chart of accounts for determining account distributions for wages and related taxes and controlling liabilities for payroll deductions and taxes withheld?

7. Are clerical operations in the preparation of payrolls verified by re-performance or reconciliation with independent controls over source data?

8. Are piece rate records reconciled with production records, or salespeople's commission records reconciled with recorded sales, or total production hours reconciled with production statistics?

9. Are payroll checks drawn on a separate imprest account, and are deposits equal to the amount of net pay?

10. Is responsibility for custody and follow-up of unclaimed wages assigned to a responsible person independent of personnel, payroll processing, and cash disbursement functions?

11. Are procedures adequate to result in timely and accurate preparation and filing of payroll tax returns and payment of accumulated withholdings and related accrued taxes?

12. Are personnel and payroll records reasonably safeguarded (locked file cabinets, work areas with limited access)?

E. Cash Disbursements

This questionnaire's objectives are to determine if functions are assigned so that no single individual is in a position to both perpetrate and conceal errors or fraud in the normal course of their duties.

- Disbursements are made only for expenditures incurred in accordance with management's authorization.
- Adjustments to cash accounts are made only in accordance with management's authorizations.
- Disbursements are recorded at correct amounts in the appropriate period and are classified properly in the accounts.
- Access to cash and disbursement records is restricted to minimize opportunities for irregular or erroneous disbursements.

- Comparison of detail records, control accounts, and bank statements are made at reasonable intervals for detection and appropriate disposition of errors or fraud.

1. Are bank accounts and check signers authorized by the board of directors?

2. Are approved supporting documents presented with the checks to the check signer?

3. Is a mechanical check protector used to inscribe amounts on checks to protect against alteration?

4. Are supporting documents for checks canceled to avoid reuse?

5. Are signed checks independently mailed directly after signing without being returned to persons involved in the invoice processing and check preparation functions?

6. Are all voided checks retained and mutilated?

7. Are there written policies that prohibit making checks payable to cash or bearer, and signing blank checks?

8. Are dual signatures required for large disbursements, and are the signers independent of one another?

9. If a check-signing machine is used, are the keys, signature plate, and operation of the signing machine under control at all times of the official whose signature is on the plate? Are employees who have custody of them independent of voucher and check preparation functions, and are they denied access to blank checks?

10. If cash funds are maintained on the premises, they should be kept on an imprest basis; and

    a. Are they kept in a safe place?

    b. Are they reasonable in amount?

    c. Are they controlled by one custodian?

    d. Are disbursements supported by vouchers?

    e. Are vouchers approved with management's authorization?

    f. Are cash funds on a surprise basis counted by someone other than the custodian?

    g. Is the custodian independent of cash receipts?

    h. Does the custodian have no access to accounting records?

    i. Are reimbursements of the cash fund remitted by checks made payable to the order of the custodian?

11. Are old outstanding checks investigated, controlled, and their proper disposition arranged?

F. **Inventory & Cost of Sales**
    This questionnaire's objectives are to determine if all production activity and accounting therefore is determined in accordance with management's general or specific authorizations.

    - Resources obtained and used in the production process and completed results are recorded accurately on a timely basis.
    - Transfer of finished products to customers and other dispositions such as sales of scrap are recorded accurately.

- Inventory, production costs, and costs of sales are accumulated and classified in the accounts to maintain accountability for costs and permit preparation of statements in conformity with GAAP.
- Inventory is protected from unauthorized use or removal.
- Recorded balances of inventory are substantiated and evaluated at reasonable intervals by comparison with quantities on hand.

1. Are production goals and schedules based on accompanying sales forecasts?

2. Are methods and materials to be used based upon product engineering plans and specifications?

3. Does the company have budgeted inventory levels and predetermined reorder points authorized by management?

4. Does the company have policies for identification and disposition of excess or obsolete inventory?

5. Are all adjustments to inventory and cost of sales made in accordance with management's authorizations?

6. Are all dispositions of obsolete or excess inventory approved?

7. Does the chart of accounts provide adequate general ledger control accounts and subsidiary detail for the accumulation and classification of costs of materials, direct labor, and overhead?

8. Is access to the detailed inventory records and control accounts limited to persons responsible for their maintenance, oversight, and internal audit?

9. Are there physical safeguards against theft, fire, and flooding?

10. Is insurance coverage of the inventory maintained and reviewed periodically for adequacy?

11. Do detailed written inventory procedures and instructions exist that have been approved and are they adequately communicated to the persons who perform the physical counts?

12. Are inventory physical counts performed by persons whose duties do not include the physical custody and detailed record keeping of inventory or maintenance of control accounts?

13. Are differences in physical counts and detailed records investigated?

14. Are adjustments of the inventory detail records and control accounts given prior approval by management?

15. Are dispositions of obsolete or excess inventories made in accordance with criteria authorized by management?

G. **Property, Plant & Equipment**

This questionnaire's objectives are to determine if additions and related accumulation of depreciation, retirements, and dispositions of property, plant and equipment (PPE) are made in accordance with management's authorization.

- Transactions involving PPE and depreciation are recorded, accumulated, and classified accurately in detail and in control accounts to maintain accountability for the assets.
- PPE are reasonably safeguarded from loss.

1. Are work order forms approved by management for property additions?

2. Are contracts and agreements signed by individuals in accordance with appropriately documented designation by the board of directors?

3. Are detailed records maintained for PPE indicating a description of the assets; their location, cost, acquisition date, date of service, depreciable life, and method of depreciation used?

4. Are PPE insured and coverage reviewed periodically for additions, disposals, and adequacy?

5. Is there a written capitalization/expense policy for PPE purchases?

H. Stockholders' Equity & Capital Accounts

This questionnaire's objectives are to determine if capital transactions are authorized and approved in conformity with the entity's governing document (corporate charter, partnership agreement).

- Transactions and obligations are recorded promptly and accurately.
- Access to records, agreements, and negotiable documents is permitted only in accordance with management's authorization.
- Records, agreements, and documents are subjected to adequate physical safeguards and custodial procedures.
- Dividends are disbursed accurately and in conformity with decisions of the board of directors.

1. Are authorizations and approvals for specific capital transactions appropriately recorded?

2. Are two officials authorized by the board required to sign and countersign stock certificates?

3. Are all stock certificates prepared and approved before issuance within management's authorization?

4. Are appropriate control records maintained for each class of stock on information such as number of shares authorized, issued and outstanding, and the number of shares subject to options, warrants, and conversion privileges?

5. Are timely detailed records maintained on specific stock certificates issued and outstanding for each class of capital stock and the identity of holders of record and the number of shares for each certificate?

6. Are detailed stock certificate records reconciled at reasonable intervals with the control records and the general ledger?

7. Are reconciliations of detailed records with the control records and general ledger performed by persons independent of custody of unissued stock certificates, maintenance of the detailed records, and cash functions?

8. Are unissued stock certificates, reacquired certificates and detailed stockholder records subject to reasonable physical safeguards?

9. Are stock certificates prenumbered so that all certificates (unissued, issued, and retired) may be accounted for?

10. Are retired stock certificates examined for proper endorsement and effectively canceled by a person whose duties do not include maintenance of the detailed stockholder records?

11. Are treasury stock certificates registered in the name of the company and recorded to be readily distinguished from other outstanding shares?

12. Are dividends declared recorded in the minutes of the board of directors meetings?

13. Do procedures result in an accurate cutoff and accurate listing of stockholders as of the record date?

14. Are total dividends disbursed reconciled to total outstanding shares as of the record date?

VIII. Appendix: General Internal Control Questions

General Control Questions	Cash Receipts	Cash Disbursements	Payroll
1. Are forms used that are prenumbered?	Prenumbered Receipts, Cash Register tapes by date	Prenumbered Checks	Prenumbered Payroll Checks
2. Is adequate control maintained of unissued forms to prevent misuse?	Unused Blank Receipts controlled	Unused Blank Checks controlled	Unused Blank Payroll Checks controlled
3. Are policies and procedures in place for the authorization of transactions?	Remittance listing prepared by designated mail opener.	Check signers authorized by board of directors. Authorization for bank accounts to be maintained.	Payroll approved in writing by responsible employee prior to issuance of paychecks.
4. Is approval of transaction obtained prior to processing?	Comparison of remittance listing and validated deposit slip before processing.	Invoice matched to approved receiving report and approved purchase order. Disbursements and bank transfers approved.	Supervisor reviews and approves time cards.
5. Is a proper segregation of duties maintained to reduce potential errors and fraud?	Employee responsible for preparing remittance lists independent of billing, cash disbursement, and general ledger functions. Employee making deposit independent of cash disbursement, billing, and general ledger functions.	Employee performing bank reconciliation independent of invoice processing, cash disbursements, cash receipts, petty cash, and general ledger functions.	Payroll checks signed by treasurer. Payroll checks distributed by person independent of personnel, payroll preparation, time—keeping, and check preparation.
6. Are all prenumbered forms accounted for?	Detail Cash Receipts Journal	Outstanding check list maintained.	Payroll Journal, Outstanding check list maintained.
7. Is a detailed record of transactions maintained?	Cash Receipts Journal	Check Register, Cash Disbursements Journal	Payroll Journal
8. Are periodic (monthly, annual) reconciliations made between source documents, quantities on hand, subsidiary ledgers, and the general ledger?	Trace cash receipts journal total to bank statement and/or validated deposit slips.	Bank reconciliations, Cash Disbursements Journal reconciled to general ledger.	Time card hours reconciled to job time tickets.
9. Is access to assets and/or accounting records limited?	Mail received by same person daily who is independent of cash, billings, general ledger and shipping functions.	Bank statement received directly by person who will reconcile.	Payroll records and Personnel files kept in locked file cabinets.
10. Are transactions and source documents checked for clerical accuracy?	Remittance list footed and agreed to validated deposit slip.	Checks compared to approved invoice and supporting documents before signing. Discounts, if available, have been taken.	Time card totals checked by supervisor.
11. Is there a proper cutoff of transactions for accurate reporting?	Bank reconciliations are prepared and approved on a timely basis.	Bank reconciliations are prepared and approved on a timely basis.	Bank reconciliations are prepared and approved on a timely basis.

Inventory	Cost of Sales	Fixed Assets	Accounts Receivable	Accounts Payable
Prenumbered: Shipping Documents, Purchase Orders, Receiving Reports	Prenumbered Inventory Requisitions	Prenumbered Purchase Orders	Prenumbered Invoices	Prenumbered Vouchers
Unused Purchase Orders, Receiving Reports, Shipping Documents controlled.	Unused Inventory Requisitions controlled.	Unused Purchased Orders controlled	Unused Invoices controlled	Unused Vouchers controlled
Purchases made in accordance with vendor acceptability. Customer Acceptance/Terms of Sale, credit clearance all preestablished.	Pre-established overhead rates, requisition processing controls	Additions/Retirements have authorization in Board of Directors meeting minutes.	Invoices prepared from approved shipping reports and matching vendor purchase orders.	Authorization by Board of Directors for large purchases (contracts).
Approved purchase order, Approved inventory requisitions, sales orders approved before shipment	Inventory requisitions, overhead rate changes and personnel rate changes are properly approved.	Approval of additions and retirements in writing; Board minutes, manager approval.	Approval noted on invoice.	Invoices and supporting documents approved before payment.
Credit, Sales, Shipping, Billing, Collections, receiving, and general accounting all independent of one another.	Authority to approve inventory requisitions assigned to employees independent of physical custody, and maintenance of inventory records and inventory control accounts.	Responsibility for physical custody assigned to employees independent of maintaining detailed property records and general ledger functions.	Individual responsible for accounts receivable function is independent of cash and general ledger functions.	Vendors' invoices processed by employee independent of purchasing, receiving, shipping, and cash functions.
Purchase Orders, Shipping Documents, Receiving Reports	Work Orders, Inventory Requisitions	Physical asset identi-fication plates numbered consecutively	Numbered sales invoices properly filed.	Numbered vouchers and Purchase Orders maintained in open, pending, or paid files.
Shipment Log, Receiving Log, Purchases Journal	Work-in-Process and Finished Goods journals	Detailed listing of fixed assets maintained	Sales Invoice Register	Purchases Journal and Accounts Payable Subsidiary Ledger maintained
Inventory physically counted annually. Inventory detail records and control accounts reconciled to physical count. Perpetual records reconciled to general ledger and physical counts.	Cost accounting system reconciled to general ledger.	Detailed records of assets compared to actual PPE on hand, and reconciled to general ledger.	Accounts receivable subsidiary ledger reconciled to general ledger control account.	Accounts payable sub-sidiary ledger reconciled with general ledger control account.
Finished goods and merchandise are restricted so that withdrawals are based on approved sales orders.	Releases from storage of raw materials and supplies based upon approved requisitions.	Physical controls such as fences, burglar alarms, fire alarms, security guards, and requisitioning procedures for the use of portable equipment.	Passwords used on computer system limiting data entry to designated individuals.	Passwords used on computer system limiting data entry to designated individuals.
Receiving Reports, Shipping Documents, Purchase Orders	Inventory Requisitions checked	Invoices compared to approved purchase order and totals including taxes and freight are checked for reasonableness.	Sales Invoices	Vendors' Invoices
Inventory received included, goods on consignment included, goods sold but not shipped excluded from inventory totals.	See Inventory	Cash receipts and dis-bursements checked and compared to bank reconciliation for cutoff.	Shipping documents and related billings compared for proper cutoff.	Receiving reports or service dates and vendor invoices compared prior to recording.

The CPA Examination

The CPA exam is designed as a licensing requirement to measure the technical competence of CPA candidates. Although licensing occurs at the state or territory level (usually by a board of accountancy), the exam is uniform at all sites and has national acceptance. Passing the CPA exam in one jurisdiction generally allows a candidate to obtain a reciprocal certificate or license in another jurisdiction if they meet that jurisdiction's requirements.

Boards of accountancy also rely upon other means to ensure that candidates possess the necessary technical and character attributes, including interviews, letters of reference, affidavits of employment, ethics exams, and educational requirements. Each board's contact information is listed in the *Practical Advice* appendix of this volume and on the Web site of the National Association of the State Boards of Accountancy (www.nasba.org).

The CPA exam is essentially an academic exam that tests the breadth of material covered by good accounting curricula. It emphasizes the body of knowledge required for the practice of public accounting. It is to your advantage to take the exam as soon as possible after completing the formal education requirements.

We recommend that most candidates study for two exam sections at once because there are synergies to be gained. All sections of the exam share some common subjects (particularly Financial Accounting & Reporting and Auditing & Attestation); so as you study for one section, you are also studying, in part, for the others. This advice may not apply to all candidates. Some candidates with full-time jobs and other responsibilities may find that studying for just one exam section at a time is best for them.

More helpful exam information is included in the *Practical Advice* appendix in this volume.

CHAPTER 23—INTERNAL CONTROL

Problem 23-1 MULTIPLE CHOICE QUESTIONS (132 to 165 minutes)

1. Management's attitude toward aggressive financial reporting and its emphasis on meeting projected profit goals most likely would significantly influence an entity's control environment when
a. External policies established by parties outside the entity affect its accounting practices.
b. Management is dominated by one individual who is also a shareholder.
c. Internal auditors have direct access to the board of directors and the entity's management.
d. The audit committee is active in overseeing the entity's financial reporting policies.
(5/97, AUD, #1, 6390)

2. Proper segregation of duties reduces the opportunities to allow persons to be in positions to both
a. Journalize entries and prepare financial statements
b. Record cash receipts and cash disbursements
c. Establish internal controls and authorize transactions
d. Perpetuate and conceal errors and fraud
(11/94, AUD, #26, amended, 5099)

3. Which of the following is **not** a component of an entity's internal control?
a. Control risk
b. Control activities
c. The information and communication systems
d. The control environment   (Editors, 0086)

4. Which of the following are considered control environment factors?

	Detection risk	Personnel policies and practices
a.	Yes	Yes
b.	Yes	No
c.	No	Yes
d.	No	No

(11/94, AUD, #29, 5102)

5. Which of the following is a management control method that most likely could improve management's ability to supervise company activities effectively?
a. Monitoring compliance with internal control requirements imposed by regulatory bodies
b. Limiting direct access to assets by physical segregation and protective devices
c. Establishing budgets and forecasts to identify variances from expectations
d. Supporting employees with the resources necessary to discharge their responsibilities
(11/95, AUD, #6, 5955)

6. Which of the following events most likely would indicate the existence of related parties?
a. Granting stock options to key executives at favorable prices
b. High turnover of senior management and members of the board of directors
c. Failure to correct internal control weaknesses on a timely basis
d. Selling real estate at a price significantly different from appraised value
(R/06, AUD, #41, 8159)

7. Proper segregation of duties reduces the opportunities to allow any employee to be in a position to both
a. Journalize cash receipts and disbursements and prepare the financial statements
b. Monitor internal controls and evaluate whether the controls are operating as intended
c. Adopt new accounting pronouncements and authorize the recording of transactions
d. Record and conceal fraudulent transactions in the normal course of assigned tasks
(R/06, AUD, #40, 8158)

8. Which of the following most likely would **not** be considered an inherent limitation of the potential effectiveness of an entity's internal control?
a. Incompatible duties
b. Management override
c. Mistakes in judgment
d. Collusion among employees
(5/94, AUD, #22, amended, 4687)

9. In the consideration of an entity's internal control, the auditor is basically concerned that the controls provide reasonable assurance that
a. Operational efficiency has been achieved in accordance with management plans.
b. Errors and fraud have been prevented or detected.
c. Management cannot override the controls.
d. Controls have not been circumvented by collusion. (Editors, 7488)

10. Which of the following auditor concerns most likely could be so serious that the auditor concludes that a financial statement audit **cannot** be conducted?
a. The entity has no formal written code of conduct.
b. The integrity of the entity's management is suspect.
c. Procedures requiring segregation of duties are subject to management override.
d. Management fails to modify prescribed controls for changes in conditions.
(11/95, AUD, #4, 5953)

11. Which of the following factors would most likely be considered an inherent limitation to an entity's internal control?
a. The complexity of the information processing system
b. Human judgment in the decision making process
c. The ineffectiveness of the board of directors
d. The lack of management incentives to improve the control environment (R/06, AUD, #18, 8136)

12. Which of the following factors would **least** likely affect the extent of the auditor's consideration of the client's internal controls?
a. The amount of time budgeted to complete the engagement
b. The size and complexity of the client
c. The nature of specific relevant controls
d. The auditor's prior experience with client operations (R/06, AUD, #20, 8138)

13. An auditor would most likely be concerned with internal control policies and procedures that provide reasonable assurance about the
a. Methods of assigning production tasks to employees
b. Appropriate prices the entity should charge for its products
c. Efficiency of management's decision-making process
d. Entity's ability to process and summarize financial data (Editors, 2303)

14. In obtaining an understanding of an entity's internal control in a financial statement audit, an auditor is **not** obligated to
a. Determine whether the control procedures have been implemented
b. Perform procedures to understand the design of the internal control policies
c. Document the understanding of the entity's internal control
d. Search for significant deficiencies in the operation of the entity's internal control
(11/93, AUD, #19, amended, 4256)

15. In obtaining an understanding of an entity's internal control, an auditor is required to obtain knowledge about the

	Operating effectiveness of policies and procedures	Design of policies and procedures
a.	Yes	Yes
b.	No	Yes
c.	Yes	No
d.	No	No

(5/93, AUD, #12, amended, 3908)

16. When obtaining an understanding of an entity's internal control, an auditor should concentrate on the implementation of the procedures because
a. The procedures may be operating effectively but may not be documented.
b. Management may implement procedures whose costs exceed their benefits.
c. The procedures may be so inappropriate that no reliance is contemplated by the auditor.
d. Management may establish appropriate procedures but not enforce compliance with them.
(5/94, AUD, #21, amended, 4686)

17. An auditor should obtain sufficient knowledge of an entity's accounting system to understand the
a. Safeguards used to limit access to computer facilities
b. Process used to prepare significant accounting estimates
c. Procedures used to assure proper authorization of transactions
d. Policies used to detect the concealment of fraud
(5/94, AUD, #20, amended, 4685)

18. The objective of tests of details of transactions performed as tests of controls is to
a. Monitor the design and use of entity documents such as prenumbered shipping forms
b. Determine whether internal controls have been implemented
c. Detect material misstatements in the account balances of the financial statements
d. Evaluate whether internal control procedures operated effectively
(11/94, AUD, #42, amended, 5115)

19. Which of the following types of evidence would an auditor most likely examine to determine whether internal control policies and procedures are operating as designed?
a. Gross margin information regarding the client's industry
b. Confirmations of receivables verifying account balances
c. Client records documenting the use of computer programs
d. Anticipated results documented in budgets or forecasts (11/95, AUD, #11, amended, 5958)

20. Audit evidence concerning segregation of duties ordinarily is best obtained by
a. Performing tests of transactions that corroborate management's financial statement assertions
b. Observing the employees as they apply control procedures
c. Obtaining a flowchart of activities performed by available personnel
d. Developing audit objectives that reduce control risk (5/93, AUD, #10, 3906)

21. Which of the following statements is correct concerning the use of prior audit evidence regarding the operating effectiveness of controls?
a. If the auditor plans to rely on controls that have changed since they were last tested, the auditor should test those controls at least once every three years.
b. If the auditor uses prior audit evidence for several controls, the auditor should test a sufficient portion of them in each audit so that each is tested every third audit.
c. If the auditor plans to rely on controls that have not changed since they were last tested, the auditor should test those controls at least every other year.
d. If the auditor plans to rely on controls that mitigate a significant risk, those controls should be tested at least every other year. (Editors, 8267)

22. Which of the following is true regarding significant deficiencies and material weaknesses in an audit of financial statements?
a. Auditors must search for them.
b. Auditors must communicate them to management and those charged with governance.
c. They must be included in the financial statements.
d. They must be disclosed in the notes to the financial statements.
(R/06, AUD, #24, amended, 8142)

23. A significant deficiency in internal control exists when
a. The design or operation of a control does not allow management or employees, in the normal course of performing their assigned functions, to be able to prevent, or detect and correct misstatements on a timely basis.
b. The person performing the control does not possess the necessary authority or competence to perform the control effectively.
c. There is a deficiency, or a combination of deficiencies, that is less severe than a material weakness, yet important enough to merit attention by those charged with governance.
d. The auditor finds evidence that a misstatement of the financial statements actually occurred as a direct result of a missing control. (Editors, 9036)

24. Which of the following statements is correct concerning deficiencies in internal control in an audit?
a. An auditor is required to search for deficiencies in internal control during an audit.
b. All significant deficiencies are also considered to be material weaknesses.
c. An auditor may communicate deficiencies during an audit in addition to after the audit's completion.
d. An auditor may report that no significant deficiencies were noted during an audit.
(5/95, AUD, #38, amended, 5656)

25. Which of the following is **least** likely to indicate the existence of a material weakness in internal control?
a. Fraud on the part of senior management
b. Previously issued financial statements were restated to reflect the correction of a material misstatement due to error or fraud
c. Those charged with governance exercise ineffective oversight of the entity's financial reporting and internal control
d. There is substantial doubt about the entity's ability to continue as a going concern.
(Editors, 9037)

26. Which of the following statements is correct concerning an auditor's required communication of significant deficiencies and material weaknesses identified during an audit of financial statements?
a. A significant deficiency previously communicated during the prior year's audit that remains uncorrected causes a scope limitation.
b. An auditor should perform tests of controls on significant deficiencies before communicating them to the client.
c. An auditor's written communication on deficiencies in internal control should include a restriction on the use of the communication.
d. An auditor should communicate significant deficiencies after tests of controls, but before commencing substantive tests.
(11/94, AUD, #45, amended, 5118)

27. Which of the following statements should **not** be included in a written communication regarding significant deficiencies and material weaknesses identified in an audit of financial statements?
a. The auditor's consideration of internal control was not designed to identify all deficiencies in internal control that might be significant deficiencies or material weaknesses.
b. There were no significant deficiencies identified during the audit.
c. A material weakness is a deficiency, or combination of deficiencies, in internal control, such that there is a reasonable possibility that a material misstatement of the entity's financial statements will not be prevented, or detected and corrected on a timely basis.
d. The purpose of the auditor's consideration of internal control was to express an opinion on the financial statements, but not to express an opinion on the effectiveness of the entity's internal control. (Editors, 2957)

28. A deficiency in internal control exists when misstatements of the financial statements may occur and not be prevented, detected, or corrected on a timely basis by
a. Outside consultants who issue a special-purpose report on internal control
b. Management or employees in the normal course of performing their assigned functions
c. Management when reviewing interim financial statements and reconciling account balances
d. An independent auditor during the testing of controls phase of the consideration of internal control
(Editors, 7489)

29. Which of the following procedures most likely would **not** be an internal control procedure designed to reduce the risk of errors in the billing process?
a. Comparing control totals for shipping documents with corresponding totals for sales invoices
b. Using computer programmed controls on the pricing and mathematical accuracy of sales invoices
c. Matching shipping documents with approved sales orders before invoice preparation
d. Reconciling the control totals for sales invoices with the accounts receivable subsidiary ledger
(11/94, AUD, #36, 5109)

30. Tracing shipping documents to prenumbered sales invoices provides evidence that
a. No duplicate shipments or billings occurred.
b. Shipments to customers were properly invoiced.
c. All goods ordered by customers were shipped.
d. All prenumbered sales invoices were accounted for. (5/95, AUD, #32, 5650)

31. Proper authorization of write-offs of uncollectible accounts should be approved in which of the following departments?
a. Accounts receivable
b. Credit
c. Accounts payable
d. Treasurer (11/94, AUD, #35, 5108)

32. Which of the following controls most likely would be effective in offsetting the tendency of sales personnel to maximize sales volume at the expense of high bad debt write-offs?
a. Employees responsible for authorizing sales and bad debt write-offs are denied access to cash.
b. Shipping documents and sales invoices are matched by an employee who does not have authority to write off bad debts.
c. Employees involved in the credit-granting function are separated from the sales function.
d. Subsidiary accounts receivable records are reconciled to the control account by an employee independent of the authorization of credit.
(5/92, AUD, #45, 2798)

33. Which of the following internal controls most likely would reduce the risk of diversion of customer receipts by an entity's employees?
a. A bank lockbox system
b. Prenumbered remittance advices
c. Monthly bank reconciliations
d. Daily deposit of cash receipts
(11/95, AUD, #12, 5959)

34. An auditor who uses a transaction cycle approach to assessing control risk most likely would test control activities related to transactions involving the sale of goods to customers with the
a. Collection of receivables
b. Purchase of merchandise inventory
c. Payment of accounts payable
d. Sale of long-term debt   (R/06, AUD, #26, 8144)

35. Management's emphasis on meeting projected profit goals most likely would significantly influence an entity's control environment when
a. Internal auditors have direct access to the entity's board of directors.
b. A significant portion of management compensation is represented by stock options.
c. External policies established by parties outside the entity affect accounting policies.
d. The audit committee is active in overseeing the entity's financial reporting policies.
(R/06, AUD, #42, 8160)

36. Which of the following procedures would an auditor most likely perform to test controls relating to management's assertion about the completeness of cash receipts for cash sales at a retail outlet?
a. Observe the consistency of the employees' use of cash registers and tapes
b. Inquire about employees' access to recorded but undeposited cash
c. Trace the deposits in the cash receipts journal to the cash balance in the general ledger
d. Compare the cash balance in the general ledger with the bank confirmation request
(11/97, AUD, #15, 6578)

37. Which of the following fraudulent activities most likely could be perpetrated due to the lack of effective internal controls in the revenue cycle?
a. Merchandise received is not promptly reconciled to the outstanding purchase order file.
b. Obsolete items included in inventory balances are rarely reduced to the lower of cost or market value.
c. The write-off of receivables by personnel who receive cash permits the misappropriation of cash.
d. Fictitious transactions are recorded that cause an understatement of revenue and overstatement of receivables.   (R/06, AUD, #44, 8162)

38. Sound internal control procedures dictate that immediately upon receiving checks from customers by mail, a responsible employee should
a. Add the checks to the daily cash summary
b. Verify that each check is supported by a pre-numbered sales invoice
c. Prepare a duplicate listing of checks received
d. Record the checks in the cash receipts journal
(5/95, AUD, #30, 5648)

39. Which of the following internal control procedures is **not** usually performed in the vouchers payable department?
a. Matching the vendor's invoice with the related receiving report
b. Approving vouchers for payment by having an authorized employee sign the vouchers
c. Indicating the asset and expense accounts to be debited
d. Accounting for unused prenumbered purchase orders and receiving reports
(11/94, AUD, #40, 5113)

40. For effective internal control, the Accounts Payable Department generally should
a. Stamp, perforate, or otherwise cancel supporting documentation after payment is mailed
b. Ascertain that each requisition is approved as to price, quantity, and quality by an authorized employee
c. Obliterate the quantity ordered on the Receiving Department copy of the purchase order
d. Establish the agreement of the vendor's invoice with the receiving report and purchase order
(11/95, AUD, #30, 5977)

41. When the shipping department returns non-conforming goods to a vendor, the purchasing department should send to the accounting department the
a. Unpaid voucher
b. Debit memo
c. Vendor invoice
d. Credit memo   (11/92, AUD, #16, 2950)

42. To provide assurance that each voucher is submitted and paid only once, an auditor most likely would examine a sample of paid vouchers and determine whether each voucher is
a. Supported by a vendor's invoice
b. Stamped "paid" by the check signer
c. Prenumbered and accounted for
d. Approved for authorized purchases
(5/95, AUD, #34, 5652)

43. The authority to accept incoming goods in receiving should be based on a(an)
a. Vendor's invoice
b. Materials requisition
c. Bill of lading
d. Approved purchase order
(5/93, AUD, #17, 3913)

44. In testing controls over cash disbursements, an auditor most likely would determine that the person who signs checks also
a. Reviews the monthly bank reconciliation
b. Returns the checks to accounts payable
c. Is denied access to the supporting documents
d. Is responsible for mailing the checks
(11/95, AUD, #29, 5976)

45. Which of the following questions would most likely be included in an internal control questionnaire concerning the completeness assertion for purchases?
a. Is an authorized purchase order required before the receiving department can accept a shipment or the vouchers payable department can record a voucher?
b. Are purchase requisitions prenumbered and independently matched with vendor invoices?
c. Is the unpaid voucher file periodically reconciled with inventory records by an employee who does not have access to purchase requisitions?
d. Are purchase orders, receiving reports, and vouchers prenumbered and periodically accounted for? (5/92, AUD, #46, 2799)

46. Which of the following questions would an auditor most likely include on an internal control questionnaire for notes payable?
a. Are assets that collateralize notes payable critically needed for the entity's continued existence?
b. Are two or more authorized signatures required on checks that repay notes payable?
c. Are the proceeds from notes payable used for the purchase of noncurrent assets?
d. Are direct borrowings on notes payable authorized by the board of directors?
(11/93, AUD, #32, 4269)

47. An auditor generally tests the segregation of duties related to inventory by
a. Personal inquiry and observation
b. Test counts and cutoff procedures
c. Analytical procedures and invoice recomputation
d. Document inspection and reconciliation
(5/95, AUD, #31, 5649)

48. Sound internal control procedures dictate that defective merchandise returned by customers should be presented initially to the
a. Accounts receivable supervisor
b. Receiving clerk
c. Shipping department supervisor
d. Sales clerk (5/93, AUD, #20, 3916)

49. Which of the following internal control procedures most likely would prevent direct labor hours from being charged to manufacturing overhead?
a. Periodic independent counts of work in process for comparison to recorded amounts
b. Comparison of daily journal entries with approved production orders
c. Use of time tickets to record actual labor worked on production orders
d. Reconciliation of work-in-process inventory with periodic cost budgets (5/94, AUD, #32, 4697)

50. Which of the following internal control procedures most likely would be used to maintain accurate inventory records?
a. Perpetual inventory records are periodically compared with the current cost of individual inventory items
b. A just-in-time inventory ordering system keeps inventory levels to a desired minimum
c. Requisitions, receiving reports, and purchase orders are independently matched before payment is approved
d. Periodic inventory counts are used to adjust the perpetual inventory records
(5/94, AUD, #33, 4698)

51. The objectives of the internal control for a production cycle are to provide assurance that transactions are properly executed and recorded, and that
a. Production orders are prenumbered and signed by a supervisor.
b. Custody of work in process and of finished goods is properly maintained.
c. Independent internal verification of activity reports is established.
d. Transfers to finished goods are documented by a completed production report and a quality control report. (11/93, AUD, #28, amended, 4265)

52. In obtaining an understanding of a manufacturing entity's internal control concerning inventory balances, an auditor most likely would
a. Analyze the liquidity and turnover ratios of the inventory
b. Perform analytical procedures designed to identify cost variances
c. Review the entity's descriptions of inventory policies and procedures
d. Perform test counts of inventory during the entity's physical count
(11/95, AUD, #32, amended, 5979)

53. An auditor most likely would **not** rely on controls if the payroll department supervisor is responsible for
a. Examining authorization forms for new employees
b. Comparing payroll registers with original batch transmittal data
c. Authorizing payroll rate changes for all employees
d. Hiring all subordinate payroll department employees (5/94, AUD, #29, amended, 4694)

54. The purpose of segregating the duties of hiring personnel and distributing payroll checks is to separate the
a. Human resources function from the controllership function
b. Administrative controls from the internal accounting controls
c. Authorization of transactions from the custody of related assets
d. Operational responsibility from the record keeping responsibility (11/93, AUD, #30, 4267)

55. In determining the effectiveness of an entity's policies and procedures relating to the existence or occurrence assertion for payroll transactions, an auditor most likely would inquire about and
a. Observe the segregation of duties concerning personnel responsibilities and payroll disbursement
b. Inspect evidence of accounting for prenumbered payroll checks
c. Recompute the payroll deductions for employee fringe benefits
d. Verify the preparation of the monthly payroll account bank reconciliation
(11/95, AUD, #31, 5978)

56. Which of the following is a control procedure that most likely could help prevent employee payroll fraud?
a. The personnel department promptly sends employee termination notices to the payroll supervisor.
b. Employees who distribute payroll checks forward unclaimed payroll checks to the absent employees' supervisors.
c. Salary rates resulting from new hires are approved by the payroll supervisor.
d. Total hours used for determination of gross pay are calculated by the payroll supervisor.
(11/95, AUD, #15, 5962)

57. Which of the following circumstances most likely would cause an auditor to suspect an employee payroll fraud scheme?
a. There are significant unexplained variances between standard and actual labor cost.
b. Payroll checks are disbursed by the same employee each payday.
c. Employee time cards are approved by individual departmental supervisors.
d. A separate payroll bank account is maintained on an imprest basis. (11/95, AUD, #50, 5997)

58.   Which of the following flowcharts indicates that new equipment transactions and the old equipment file have been used to prepare equipment labels, prepare a printed equipment journal, and generate a new equipment file?

a.

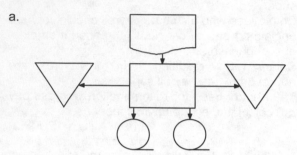

b.

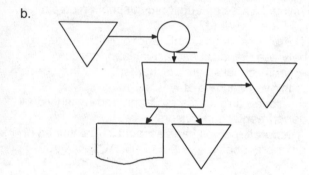

c.

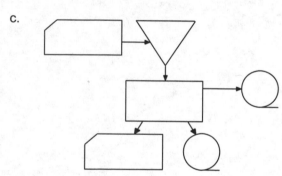

d.

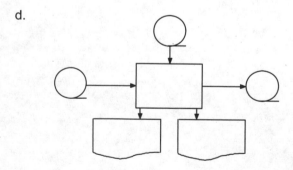

(Editors, 7490)

59.   Equipment acquisitions that are misclassified as maintenance expense most likely would be detected by an internal control procedure that provides for
a.   Segregation of duties of employees in the accounts payable department
b.   Authorization by the board of directors of significant equipment acquisitions
c.   Investigation of variances within a formal budgeting system
d.   Independent verification of invoices for disbursements recorded as equipment acquisitions
(11/93, AUD, #34, amended, 4271)

60.   Which of the following internal control procedures most likely would justify a reduced assessed level of control risk concerning property, plant and equipment acquisitions?
a.   Periodic physical inspection of property, plant and equipment by the internal audit staff
b.   Comparison of current year property, plant and equipment account balances with prior year actual balances
c.   The review of prenumbered purchase orders to detect unrecorded trade-ins
d.   Approval of periodic depreciation entries by a supervisor independent of the accounting department   (5/93, AUD, #21, 3917)

61.   A weakness in internal control over recording retirements of equipment may cause an auditor to
a.   Inspect certain items of equipment in the plant and trace those items to the accounting records
b.   Review the subsidiary ledger to ascertain whether depreciation was taken on each item of equipment during the year
c.   Trace additions to the "other assets" account to search for equipment that is still on hand but no longer being used
d.   Select certain items of equipment from the accounting records and locate them in the plant
(Editors, 0081)

62.   Which of the following questions would an auditor **least** likely include on an internal control questionnaire concerning the initiation and execution of equipment transactions?
a.   Are requests for major repairs approved at a higher level than the department initiating the request?
b.   Are prenumbered purchase orders used for equipment and periodically accounted for?
c.   Are requests for purchases of equipment reviewed for consideration of soliciting competitive bids?
d.   Are procedures in place to monitor and properly restrict access to equipment?
(11/94, AUD, #41, 5114)

63. Which of the following controls would an entity most likely use in safeguarding against the loss of marketable securities?
a. An independent trust company that has no direct contact with the employees who have record keeping responsibilities has possession of the securities.
b. The internal auditor verifies the marketable securities in the entity's safe each year on the balance sheet date.
c. The independent auditor traces all purchases and sales of marketable securities through the subsidiary ledgers to the general ledger.
d. A designated member of the board of directors controls the securities in a bank safe-deposit box.
(11/92, AUD, #22, 2956)

64. When an entity uses a trust company as custodian of its marketable securities, the possibility of concealing fraud most likely would be reduced if the
a. Trust company has no direct contact with the entity employees responsible for maintaining investment accounting records.
b. Securities are registered in the name of the trust company, rather than the entity itself.
c. Interest and dividend checks are mailed directly to an entity employee who is authorized to sell securities.
d. Trust company places the securities in a bank safe-deposit vault under the custodian's exclusive control. (5/94, AUD, #34, 4699)

65. Which of the following controls would a company most likely use to safeguard marketable securities when an independent trust agent is **not** employed?
a. The investment committee of the board of directors periodically reviews the investment decisions delegated to the treasurer.
b. Two company officials have joint control of marketable securities, which are kept in a bank safe-deposit box.
c. The internal auditor and the controller independently trace all purchases and sales of marketable securities from the subsidiary ledgers to the general ledger.
d. The chairman of the board verifies the marketable securities which are kept in a bank safe-deposit box, each year on the balance sheet date.
(11/95, AUD, #16, 5963)

66. Which **two** of the following procedures most likely would give the greatest assurance that securities held as investments are safeguarded?
a. There is no access to securities between the year-end and the date of the auditor's security count.
b. Proceeds from the sale of investments are received by an employee who does not have access to securities.
c. Investment acquisitions are authorized by a member of the Board of Directors before execution.
d. Custody of investment securities is assigned to an outside agent such as a brokerage house.
e. Access to securities requires the signatures and presence of two designated officials.
(5/93, AUD, #22, amended, 3918)

Problem 23-2 ADDITIONAL MULTIPLE CHOICE QUESTIONS (52 to 65 minutes)

67. The overall attitude and awareness of an entity's board of directors concerning the importance of internal control usually is reflected in its
a. Computer-based controls
b. System of segregation of duties
c. Control environment
d. Safeguards over access to assets
(5/95, AUD, #25, amended, 5643)

68. In an audit of financial statements, an auditor's primary consideration regarding an internal control policy or procedure is whether the policy or procedure
a. Reflects management's philosophy and operating style
b. Affects management's financial statement assertions
c. Provides adequate safeguards over access to assets
d. Enhances management's decision-making processes (11/94, AUD, #28, 5101)

69. Proper segregation of functional responsibilities in an effective internal control structure calls for separation of the functions of
a. Authorization, payment, and recording
b. Authorization, recording, and custody
c. Custody, execution, and reporting
d. Authorization, execution, and payment
(Editors, 0092)

70. When considering internal control, an auditor should be aware of the concept of reasonable assurance, which recognizes that
a. Internal control policies and procedures may be ineffective due to mistakes in judgment and personal carelessness.
b. Adequate safeguards over access to assets and records should permit an entity to maintain proper accountability.
c. Establishing and maintaining internal control is an important responsibility of management.
d. The cost of an entity's internal control should not exceed the benefits expected to be derived.
(5/95, AUD, #26, amended, 5644)

71. Which of the following auditor concerns most likely could be so serious that the auditor concludes that a financial statement audit **cannot** be performed?
a. Management fails to modify prescribed internal controls for changes in information technology.
b. Internal control activities requiring segregation of duties are rarely monitored by management.
c. Management is dominated by one person who is also the majority stockholder.
d. There is a substantial risk of intentional misapplication of accounting principles.
(R/02, AUD, #9, 7099)

72. Which of the following procedures most likely would provide an auditor with evidence about whether an entity's internal control activities are suitably designed to prevent or detect material misstatements?
a. Reperforming the activities for a sample of transactions
b. Performing analytical procedures using data aggregated at a high level
c. Vouching a sample of transactions directly related to the activities
d. Observing the entity's personnel applying the activities
(5/97, AUD, #4, 6393)

73. Which of the following is an inherent limitation in internal control?
a. Incompatible duties
b. Lack of segregation of duties
c. Faulty human judgment
d. Lack of an audit committee
(R/07, AUD, #5, 8377)

74. Which of the following audit techniques ordinarily would provide an auditor with the **least** assurance about the operating effectiveness of an internal control activity?
a. Inquiry of client personnel
b. Inspection of documents and reports
c. Observation of client personnel
d. Preparation of system flowcharts
(R/05, AUD, #15, 7810)

75. After testing a client's internal control activities, an auditor discovers a material weakness in the operation of a client's internal controls. Under these circumstances the auditor most likely would
a. Issue a disclaimer of opinion about the internal controls as part of the auditor's report
b. Increase the assessment of control risk and increase the extent of substantive tests
c. Issue a qualified opinion of this finding as part of the auditor's report
d. Withdraw from the audit because the internal controls are ineffective
(R/07, AUD, #3, amended, 8375)

76. The ultimate purpose of assessing control risk is to contribute to the auditor's evaluation of the risk that
a. Specific internal control activities are not operating as designed.
b. The collective effect of the control environment may not achieve the control objectives.
c. Tests of controls may fail to identify activities relevant to assertions.
d. Material misstatements may exist in the financial statements.
(R/07, AUD, #30, 8402)

77. Which of the following factors should an auditor consider in evaluating the severity a deficiency in internal control to determine if it should be communicated to management and those charged with governance, i.e., that it is a significant deficiency or a material weakness?

I. Magnitude of the potential misstatement
II. Likelihood of the misstatement

a. I only
b. II only
c. Both I and II
d. Neither I nor II
(Editors, 7105)

78. An auditor's written communication regarding significant deficiencies and material weaknesses identified during a financial statement audit should
a. Include a brief description of the tests of controls performed in searching for significant deficiencies and material weaknesses
b. Indicate that the purpose of the auditor's consideration of internal control was to express an opinion on the financial statements but not to express an opinion on the effectiveness of internal control
c. Include a paragraph describing management's assertion concerning the effectiveness of internal control
d. Indicate that the deficiencies should be disclosed in the annual report to the entity's shareholders   (11/95, AUD, #35, amended, 5982)

79. Which of the following procedures concerning accounts receivable would an auditor most likely perform to obtain audit evidence to support the operating effectiveness of a control?
a. Observing an entity's employee prepare the schedule of past due accounts receivable
b. Sending confirmation requests to an entity's principal customers to verify the existence of accounts receivable
c. Inspecting an entity's analysis of accounts receivable for unusual balances
d. Comparing an entity's uncollectible accounts expense to actual uncollectible accounts receivable   (5/96, AUD, #2, amended, 6234)

80. To determine whether internal control relative to the revenue cycle of a wholesaling entity is operating effectively in minimizing the failure to prepare sales invoices, an auditor most likely would select a sample of transactions from the population represented by the
a. Sales order file
b. Customer order file
c. Shipping document file
d. Sales invoice file   (R/05, AUD, #20, 7815)

81. Employers bond employees who handle cash receipts because fidelity bonds reduce the possibility of employing dishonest individuals and
a. Protect employees who make unintentional errors from possible monetary damages resulting from their errors.
b. Deter dishonesty by making employees aware that insurance companies may investigate and prosecute dishonest acts.
c. Facilitate an independent monitoring of the receiving and depositing of cash receipts.
d. Force employees in positions of trust to take periodic vacations and rotate their assigned duties.
     (5/90, AUD, #35, 0073)

82. Which of the following fraudulent activities most likely could be perpetrated due to the lack of effective internal controls in the revenue cycle?
a. Fictitious transactions may be recorded that cause an understatement of revenues and an overstatement of receivables.
b. Claims received from customers for goods returned may be intentionally recorded in other customers' accounts.
c. Authorization of credit memos by personnel who receive cash may permit the misappropriation of cash.
d. The failure to prepare shipping documents may cause an overstatement of inventory balances.
     (11/97, AUD, #14, 6577)

83. For the most effective internal control, monthly bank statements should be received directly from the banks and reviewed by the
a. Cash disbursements accountant
b. Cash receipts accountant
c. Controller
d. Internal auditor   (Editors, 0111)

84. Mailing disbursement checks and remittance advices should be controlled by the employee who
a. Matches the receiving reports, purchase orders, and vendors' invoices
b. Signs the checks last
c. Prepares the daily voucher summary
d. Agrees the check register to the daily check summary   (5/93, AUD, #18, 3914)

85. Which of the following internal control procedures is **not** usually performed in the treasurer's department?
a. Verifying the accuracy of checks and vouchers
b. Controlling the mailing of checks to vendors
c. Approving vendors' invoices for payment
d. Canceling payment vouchers when paid
     (11/93, AUD, #27, 4264)

86. Which of the following controls would be most effective in assuring that recorded purchases are free of material errors?
a. The Receiving Department compares the quantity ordered on purchase orders with the quantity received on receiving reports
b. Vendors' invoices are compared with purchase orders by an employee who is independent of the Receiving Department
c. Receiving reports require the signature of the individual who authorized the purchase
d. Purchase orders, receiving reports, and vendors' invoices are independently matched in preparing vouchers   (11/90, AUD, #51, 7491)

87. Which of the following events occurring in the year under audit would most likely indicate that internal controls utilized in previous years may be inadequate in the year under audit?
a. The entity announced that the internal audit function would be eliminated after the balance sheet date.
b. The audit committee chairperson unexpectedly resigned during the year under audit.
c. The chief financial officer waived approvals on all checks to one vendor to expedite payment.
d. The frequency of accounts payable check runs was changed from biweekly to weekly.
(R/05, AUD, #48, 7843)

88. Independent internal verification of inventory occurs when employees who
a. Issue raw materials obtain material requisitions for each issue and prepare daily totals of materials issued.
b. Compare records of goods on hand with physical quantities do not maintain the records or have custody of the inventory.
c. Are independent of issuing production orders update records from completed job cost sheets and production cost reports on a timely basis.
d. Obtain receipts for the transfer of completed work to finished goods prepare a completed production report. (Editors, 0089)

89. Which of the following most likely would be an internal control procedure designed to detect errors and fraud concerning the custody of inventory?
a. Periodic reconciliation of work in process with job cost sheets
b. Segregation of functions between general accounting and cost accounting
c. Independent comparisons of finished goods records with counts of goods on hand
d. Approval of inventory journal entries by the storekeeper (5/91, AUD, #29, amended, 7492)

90. What is the most likely course of action that an auditor would take after determining that performing substantive tests on inventory will take **less** time than performing tests of controls?
a. Assess control risk at the minimum level
b. Perform both tests of controls and substantive tests on inventory
c. Perform only substantive tests on inventory
d. Perform only tests of controls on inventory
(R/07, AUD, #47, 8419)

91. Which of the following departments most likely would approve changes in pay rates and deductions from employee salaries?
a. Personnel
b. Treasurer
c. Controller
d. Payroll (11/93, AUD, #31, 4268)

92. Which of the following procedures represents a weakness in internal controls for payroll?
a. The payroll clerk distributes signed payroll checks. Undistributed checks are returned to the payroll department.
b. The accounting department wires transfers funds to the payroll bank account. The transfer is based on totals from the payroll department summary.
c. The payroll department prepares checks using a signature plate. The treasurer supervises the process before payroll checks are distributed.
d. The payroll department prepares checks. The chief financial officer signs the payroll checks.
(R/05, AUD, #36, 7831)

SIMULATIONS

Problem 23-3 (10 to 20 minutes)

Field, CPA, is auditing the financial statements of Miller Mailorder, Inc. (MMI) for the year ended January 31, Year 1. Field has compiled a list of possible errors and fraud that may result in the misstatement of MMI's financial statements.

| Scenario | Errors & Fraud | Communication | Research |

For each possible error and fraud listed, select one internal control procedure from the answer list that, if properly designed and implemented, most likely could assist MMI in preventing or detecting the errors and fraud.

Possible Errors & Fraud

1. Invoices for goods sold are posted to incorrect customer accounts.

2. Goods ordered by customers are shipped, but are not billed to anyone.

3. Invoices are sent for shipped goods, but are not recorded in the sales journal.

4. Invoices are sent for shipped goods and are recorded in the sales journal, but are not posted to any customer account.

5. Credit sales are made to individuals with unsatisfactory credit ratings.

6. Goods are removed from inventory for unauthorized orders.

7. Goods shipped to customers do not agree with goods ordered by customers.

8. Invoices are sent to allies in a fraudulent scheme and sales are recorded for fictitious transactions.

Internal Control Procedures

A. Shipping clerks compare goods received from the warehouse with the details on the shipping documents.

B. Approved sales orders are required for goods to be released from the warehouse.

C. Monthly statements are mailed to all customers with outstanding balances.

D. Shipping clerks compare goods received from the warehouse with approved sales orders.

E. Customer orders are compared with the inventory master file to determine whether items ordered are in stock.

F. Daily sales summaries are compared with control totals of invoices.

G. Shipping documents are compared with sales invoices when goods are shipped.

H. Sales invoices are compared with the master price file.

I. Customer orders are compared with an approved customer list.

J. Sales orders are prepared for each customer order.

K. Control amounts posted to the accounts receivable ledger are compared with control totals of invoices.

L. Sales invoices are compared with shipping documents and approved customer orders before invoices are mailed.

M. Prenumbered credit memos are used for granting credit for goods returned.

N. Goods returned for credit are approved by the supervisor of the sales department.

O. Remittance advices are separated from the checks in the mailroom and forwarded to the accounting department.

P. Total amounts posted to the accounts receivable ledger from remittance advices are compared with the validated bank deposit slip.

Q. The cashier examines each check for proper endorsement.

R. Validated deposit slips are compared with the cashier's daily cash summaries.

S. An employee, other than the bookkeeper, periodically prepares a bank reconciliation.

T. Sales returns are approved by the same employee who issues receiving reports evidencing actual return of goods.

An auditor is required to obtain a sufficient understanding of each of the components of an entity's internal control. This is necessary to plan the audit of the entity's financial statements and to assess the risk of material misstatement. For what purposes should an auditor's understanding of internal control components be used in planning an audit?

What authoritative reference provides guidance for the general consideration of whether to perform tests of controls or substantive procedures at an interim date vs. the period end?

Paragraph Reference Answer: _____

(5/95, AUD, #3, amended, 5725)

Problem 23-4 (15 to 20 minutes)

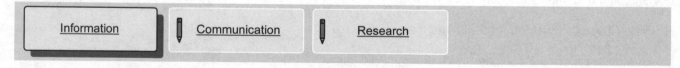

Smith, CPA, has been engaged to audit the financial statements of Reed, Inc., a publicly held retailing company. Before assessing the risk of material misstatement, Smith is required to obtain an understanding of Reed's control environment.

a. Identify additional control environment factors (excluding the factor illustrated in the example below) that establish, enhance, or mitigate the effectiveness of specific policies and procedures.

b. For the control environment factors identified in a., describe the components that could be of interest to the auditor.

Use the following format:

Management Philosophy & Operating Style

Management philosophy and operating style characteristics may include the following: management's approach to taking and monitoring business risks; management's attitudes and actions toward financial reporting; and management's emphasis on meeting budget, profit, and other financial and operating goals.

What authoritative reference provides guidance as to what an auditor should consider when evaluating whether deficiencies in internal control are significant deficiencies or material weaknesses, either individually or in combination?

Paragraph Reference Answer: _____

(11/91, AUD, #3, amended, 5726)

Problem 23-5 (25 to 35 minutes)

Smith, CPA, is the supervising partner of the financial statement audit of Digit Sales Co., a publicly-held entity that files reports with the SEC. Hall, the senior auditor assigned to the engagement, had the following conversation with Smith at the end of the fieldwork:

Smith: Don't you think that Digit's board of directors would be surprised with those huge inventory adjustments that we had Digit book last week?

Hall: I guess so, but what about that new assistant controller, Green? What incompetence!

Smith: Well, I suppose Green has a bit to learn about GAAP, but I was really upset when Dodd, the controller, contacted that other CPA firm about the contingent liability I wanted booked.

Hall: Which one was that?

Smith: You know, the employment discrimination suit filed by the union.

Hall: Oh, now I remember. Digit's going to lose that one big time.

Smith: Right! You know it. I know it. The lawyer knows it. Even Dodd knows it, but it wasn't booked until the other CPAs agreed with me.

Hall: Well, the important thing is that they did book it. I was more upset about their two-week delay in having the financial statements completed on time.

Smith: I know it cost us a lot of time, but Dodd was never late on that before. Maybe I should change the dates on next year's engagement letter rather than complain to the board.

Hall: How about that large receivable?

Smith: What a joke! Dodd wouldn't write that overdue account off and Digit doesn't even sell that model any-more. At least Green was on our side.

Hall: They never did collect a penny on that account.

Smith: I heard that the customer finally filed for bankruptcy last month.

Hall: At least Dodd finally booked the write-off after that poorly-timed vacation.

Smith: I suppose so, but I still can't believe that Dodd took two weeks off near the end of our fieldwork.

Hall: Actually, that was great. With Dodd gone, Green booked that inventory adjustment without much of a battle.

Smith: Sure, but we couldn't finish the fieldwork until Dodd signed the rep letter and booked that receivable write-off. The report was late and it caused me grief with our managing partner.

Hall: But that's not fair. It wasn't our fault. The bottom line is they got a clean opinion and this job is history.

Smith: Not really. We haven't communicated with the audit committee yet.

Hall: What do we have to tell them? They got an unqualified opinion...and remember, there were only a few significant deficiencies. I'm out of here.

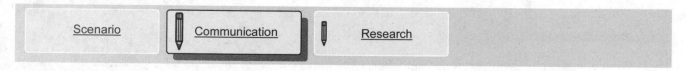

a. From Smith and Hall's discussion, what specific matters is Smith required to communicate to Digit's audit committee? Do not include matters that are not required to be communicated under GAAS.

b. What other matters (omitted from the discussion above) is Smith required to communicate to Digit's audit committee under GAAS?

What authoritative reference provides guidance as to the determination of which of the risks identified are *significant risks* that require special audit consideration?

Paragraph Reference Answer: _____

(11/96, AUD, #3, amended, 6386)

Problem 23-6 (15 to 20 minutes)

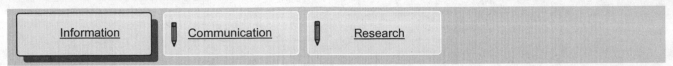

Harris, CPA, has accepted an engagement to audit the financial statements of Grant Manufacturing Co., a new client. Grant has an adequate control environment and a reasonable segregation of duties. Harris is about to assess control risk for the assertions related to Grant's property and equipment.

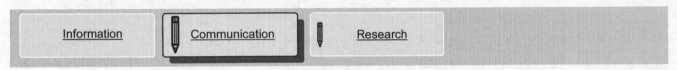

Describe the key internal control policies and procedures related to Grant's property, equipment and related transactions (additions, transfers, major maintenance and repairs, retirements, and dispositions) that Harris may consider in assessing control risk.

What authoritative reference defines Inherent risk and control risk?

Paragraph Reference Answer: _____

(5/92, AUD, #3, amended, 5727)

Problem 23-7 (15 to 25 minutes)

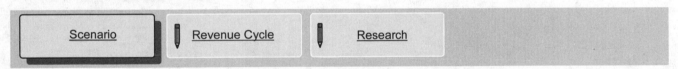

The accompanying flowchart depicts the activities relating to the sales, shipping, billing, and collecting processes used by Newton Hardware, Inc.

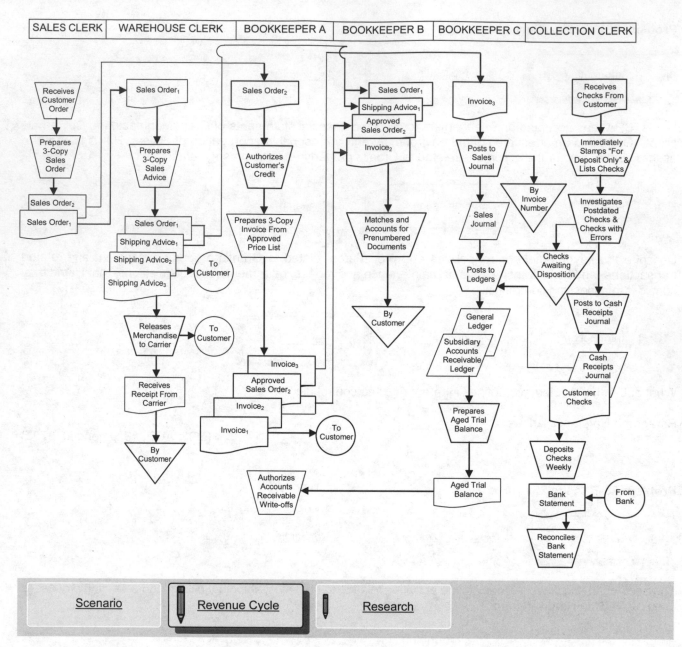

Identify the weaknesses in internal control relating to the activities of (a) the warehouse clerk, (b) bookkeeper A, and (c) the collection clerk. Do not identify weaknesses relating to the sales clerk or bookkeepers B and C. Do not discuss recommendations concerning the correction of these weaknesses.

What authoritative reference reminds auditors that an audit of financial statements is a cumulative and iterative process because as the auditor performs planned audit procedures, the audit evidence obtained may cause the auditor to revise her/his risk assessment?

Paragraph Reference Answer: _____

(5/88, AUD, #4, amended 5728)

Problem 23-8 (15 to 25 minutes)

An auditor's working papers include the narrative description below of the cash receipts and billing portions of Southwest Medical Center's internal control. Southwest is a healthcare provider that is owned by a partnership of five physicians. It employs 11 physicians, including the five owners, 20 nurses, five laboratory and X-ray technicians, and four clerical workers. The clerical workers perform such tasks as reception, correspondence, cash receipts, billing, accounts receivable, bank deposits, and appointment scheduling. These clerical workers are referred to in the narrative as "office manager," "clerk #1," "clerk #2," and "clerk #3." Assume that the narrative is a complete description of the system.

NARRATIVE

About two-thirds of Southwest's patients receive medical services only after insurance coverage is verified by the office manager and communicated to the clerks. Most of the other patients pay for services by cash or check when services are rendered, although the office manager extends credit on a case-by-case basis to about 5% of the patients.

When services are rendered, the attending physician prepares a prenumbered service slip for each patient and gives the slip to clerk #1 for pricing. Clerk #1 completes the slip and gives the completed slip to clerk #2 and a copy to the patient.

Using the information on the completed slip, clerk #2 performs one of the following three procedures for each patient.

- Clerk #2 files an insurance claim and records a receivable from the insurance company if the office manager has verified the patient's coverage; or
- Clerk #2 posts a receivable from the patient on clerk #2's PC if the office manager has approved the patient's credit; or
- Clerk #2 receives cash or a check from the patient as the patient leaves the medical center, and clerk #2 records the cash receipt.

At the end of each day, clerk #2 prepares a revenue summary.

Clerk #1 performs correspondence functions and opens the incoming mail. Clerk #1 gives checks from insurance companies and patients to clerk #2 for deposit. Clerk #2 posts the receipt of patients' checks on clerk #2's PC patient receivable records and insurance companies' checks to the receivables from the applicable insurance companies. Clerk #1 gives mail requiring correspondence to clerk #3.

Clerk #2 stamps all checks "for deposit only" and each day prepares a list of checks and cash to be deposited in the bank. (This list also includes the cash and checks personally given to clerk #2 by patients.) Clerk #2 keeps a copy of the deposit list and gives the original to clerk #3.

Clerk #3 personally makes the daily bank deposit and maintains a file of the daily bank deposits. Clerk #3 also performs appointment scheduling for all of the doctors and various correspondence functions. Clerk #3 also maintains a list of patients whose insurance coverage the office manager has verified.

When insurance claims or patient receivables are not settled within 60 days, clerk #2 notifies the office manager. The office manager personally inspects the details of each instance of nonpayment. The office manager converts insurance claims that have been rejected by insurance companies into patient receivables. Clerk #2 records these patient receivables on clerk #2's PC and deletes these receivables from the applicable insurance companies. Clerk #2 deletes the patient receivables that appear to be uncollectible from clerk #2's PC when authorized by the office manager. Clerk #2 prepares a list of patients with uncollectible balances and gives a copy of the list to clerk #3, who will not allow these patients to make appointments for future services.

Once a month an outside accountant posts clerk #2's daily revenue summaries to the general ledger, prepares a monthly trial balance and monthly financial statements, accounts for the prenumbered service slips, files payroll forms and tax returns, and reconciles the monthly bank statements to the general ledger. This accountant reports directly to the physician who is the managing partner.

All four clerical employees perform their tasks on PCs that are connected through a local area network. Each PC is accessible with a password that is known only to the individual employee and the managing partner. Southwest uses a standard software package that was acquired from a software company and that cannot be modified by Southwest's employees. None of the clerical employees have access to Southwest's check-writing capabilities.

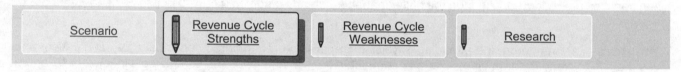

Using only the information in the narrative, describe the strengths in Southwest's internal control.

Using only the information in the narrative, describe the weaknesses in Southwest's internal control that could permit material misstatements to occur in the financial statements. In addition, for each weakness, identify one internal control activity that most likely could help correct that weakness. Use the following format.

Weaknesses	Internal control activities

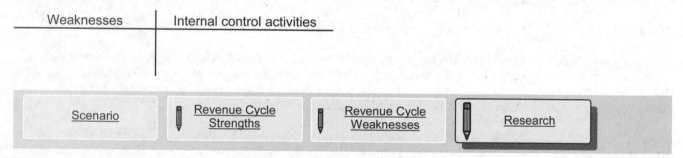

What authoritative reference provides guidance when the auditor has determined that it is not possible or practicable to reduce detection risk at the relevant assertion level to an acceptably low level with audit evidence obtained only from substantive procedures?

Paragraph Reference Answer: _____

(11/98, AUD, #3, amended, 5729)

Problem 23-9 (15 to 25 minutes)

| Scenario | Disbursements Cycle | Research |

The accompanying flowchart depicts the activities relating to the purchasing, receiving, and accounts payable departments of Model Company, Inc.

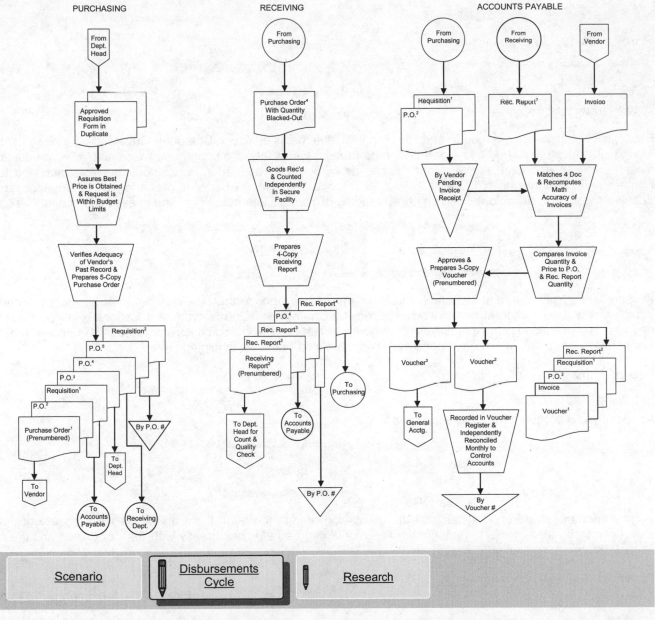

| Scenario | Disbursements Cycle | Research |

Based only on the flowchart, describe the internal control procedures (strengths) that most likely would provide reasonable assurance that specific internal control objectives for the financial statement assertions regarding purchases and accounts payable will be achieved. Do not describe weaknesses in internal control.

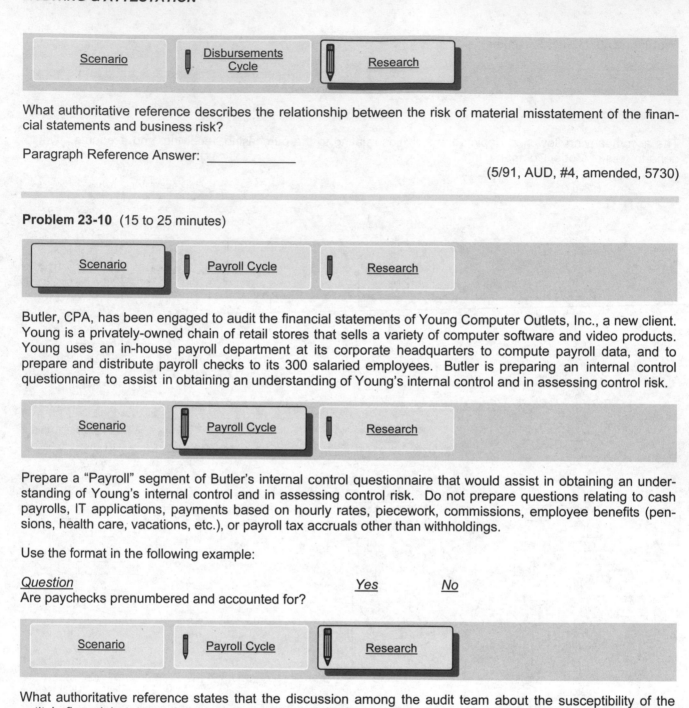

What authoritative reference describes the relationship between the risk of material misstatement of the financial statements and business risk?

Paragraph Reference Answer: _____

(5/91, AUD, #4, amended, 5730)

Problem 23-10 (15 to 25 minutes)

Butler, CPA, has been engaged to audit the financial statements of Young Computer Outlets, Inc., a new client. Young is a privately-owned chain of retail stores that sells a variety of computer software and video products. Young uses an in-house payroll department at its corporate headquarters to compute payroll data, and to prepare and distribute payroll checks to its 300 salaried employees. Butler is preparing an internal control questionnaire to assist in obtaining an understanding of Young's internal control and in assessing control risk.

Prepare a "Payroll" segment of Butler's internal control questionnaire that would assist in obtaining an understanding of Young's internal control and in assessing control risk. Do not prepare questions relating to cash payrolls, IT applications, payments based on hourly rates, piecework, commissions, employee benefits (pensions, health care, vacations, etc.), or payroll tax accruals other than withholdings.

Use the format in the following example:

Question   *Yes*   *No*
Are paychecks prenumbered and accounted for?

What authoritative reference states that the discussion among the audit team about the susceptibility of the entity's financial statements to material misstatements can be held concurrently with the discussion about the financial statement's susceptibility to fraud?

Paragraph Reference Answer: _____

(5/93, AUD, #3, amended, 5731)

Solution 23-1 MULTIPLE CHOICE ANSWERS

Components of Internal Control

1. (b) The control environment reflects the overall attitude, awareness, and actions of the board of directors, management, owners and others concerning the importance of control and its emphasis in the entity. If management is dominated by one individual who is also a shareholder, aggressive reporting and the achievement of profit goals may be overemphasized to the detriment of proper reporting. Answers (a), (c), and (d) represent examples of positive control environment influences.   (6390)

2. (d) Assigning different people the responsibilities of authorizing transactions, recording transactions, and maintaining custody of assets is intended to reduce the opportunities to allow any person to be in a position to both perpetrate and conceal errors or fraud in the normal course of her/his duties. Answers (a) and (b) list tasks that are record keeping. Answer (c) lists tasks that are both authorization.   (5099)

3. (a) Internal control consists of five interrelated components: control environment, risk assessment, information and communication systems, control activities, and monitoring. Control risk is one of the three components of audit risk.   (0086)

4. (c) The control environment sets the tone of an organization, influencing the control consciousness of its people. Factors include management's philosophy and operating style, personnel policies and practices, etc. Detection risk is an element of audit risk, not a factor of the control environment.   (5102)

5. (c) Performance reviews is a category of control activities that includes reviewing and analyzing actual performance versus budgets, forecasts, and prior-period performance.   (5955)

6. (d) Selling real estate at a price considerably different from its appraised value may indicate the existence of related parties. Granting stock options to key executives at favorable prices is a common method of compensation. While high turnover of senior management and members of the board of directors may be a cause for concern, it usually does not provide indications of related parties. Failure to correct internal control weaknesses is often due to cost/benefit considerations.   (8159)

7. (d) The purpose of segregation of duties is to eliminate incompatible functions. Incompatible functions place a person in the position to both perpetrate and conceal errors or fraud in the normal course of her/his duties. Therefore, a well designed plan of organization separates the duties of authorization, record keeping, and custody of assets. The tasks in answer (a) are both record keeping duties. The tasks in answer (b) are both internal control functions. The tasks in answer (c) are both authorization duties.   (8158)

Understanding of Internal Control

8. (a) While incompatible duties can be segregated and therefore controlled, the possibility of management override and collusion among employees to circumvent controls will still exist. Mistakes in judgment also cannot be controlled.   (4687)

9. (b) The auditor's primary consideration is whether, and how, a specific control prevents, or detects and corrects, material misstatements in relevant assertions related to classes of transactions, account balances, or disclosures. An auditor is usually concerned with the operating effectiveness of controls as apposed to operating efficiency. Answers (c) and (d) are inherent limitations of internal control.   (7488)

10. (b) Concerns about the integrity of the entity's management may be so serious as to cause the auditor to conclude that the risk of management misrepresentations in the financial statements is such that an audit cannot be conducted. Answers (a), (c), and (d) should be considered by the auditor but are not necessarily serious enough to raise an auditability question.   (5953)

11. (b) Human judgment in the decision making process is usually considered an inherent limitation because mistakes may occur in the application of certain policies and procedures due to misunderstanding of instructions or personal carelessness. The complexity of the information processing system is not in itself an inherent limitation; it is the incorrect use of the complex system by humans that causes the majority of errors. The ineffectiveness of the board of directors and the lack of management incentives to improve the control environment are correctible weaknesses in internal control; they are not inherent.   (8136)

12. (a) The nature, timing, and extent of procedures the auditor chooses to perform in the consideration of internal control will vary depending on the size and complexity of the entity, previous experience with the entity, the nature of the specific controls used by the entity including the entity's use

of IT, the nature and extent of changes in systems and operations, and the nature of the entity's documentation of specific controls. (8138)

13. (d) Ordinarily, controls that are relevant to an audit pertain to the entity's objective of preparing financial statements that are fairly presented in conformity with generally accepted accounting principles, including the management of risk that may give rise to a risk of material misstatement in those financial statements. (2303)

14. (d) While the auditor should be alert to significant deficiencies, the auditor is not obligated to search for them. Obtaining an understanding of internal control involves evaluating the design of a control and determining whether it has been implemented. This understanding should be documented. (4256)

15. (b) Obtaining an understanding of internal control consists of evaluating the design and implementation of controls. This is not the same as testing the operating effectiveness of controls. The auditor only tests the operating effectiveness of controls when: (1) the auditor's risk assessment includes an expectation of the operating effectiveness of controls or (2) when it is not possible or practicable to reduce detection risk at the relevant assertion level to an acceptably low level with audit evidence obtained from substantive procedures alone. (3908)

16. (d) When obtaining an understanding of an entity's internal control, an auditor should concentrate on the implementation of procedures because *management may establish appropriate procedures but not enforce compliance with them.* Depending on the size of the entity, written policies may not be necessary. The implementation of procedures whose costs exceed their benefits would not affect the auditor's assessment of the performance of control procedures. An auditor should consider the design (appropriateness) of a control in determining whether to consider its implementation, thus as the question asks the reason for the auditor's concentration on the implementation of controls, an inappropriate control is not directly related to the question. (4686)

17. (b) The information system relevant to financial reporting objectives, which includes the accounting system, consists of the procedures and records established to authorize, process, and report an entity's transactions. The auditor should obtain sufficient knowledge of the information system, including the related business processes relevant to financial reporting, to understand the financial reporting process used to prepare the entity's financial statements, *including significant accounting estimates* and disclosures. Safeguards used to limit

access to computer facilities, procedures used to assure proper authorization of transactions, and policies used to detect the concealment of fraud are all examples of control policies and procedures. (4685)

Tests of Controls

18. (d) The auditor may design a test of controls to be performed concurrently with a test of details on the same transaction. The objective of tests of controls is to evaluate whether a control operated effectively. Answer (a) would be a substantive test rather than a test of controls. Answer (b) is an objective of obtaining an understanding of an entity's internal control. Answer (c) is the objective of substantive procedures. (5115)

19. (c) When a client has documentation regarding the use of computer programs, it is an effective internal control. Answer (b) is a substantive procedure. Answers (a) and (d) are analytical procedures. (5958)

20. (b) Audit evidence is more reliable when it is obtained directly by the auditor rather than evidence obtained indirectly or by inference. Performing tests of transactions tests segregation of duties from the past which may not be operating currently. A flowchart reflects the ideal operating conditions of the company, established at a point in time, which may not be representative of the actual processing procedures being performed. Audit objectives cannot in themselves reduce control risk. (3906)

21. (b) When the auditor determines that it is appropriate to use audit evidence obtained in prior audits for a number of controls, the auditor should plan to test a sufficient portion of the controls in each audit period, so that at a minimum, each control is tested at least every third audit. If the auditor plans to rely on controls that have changed since they were last tested, the auditor should test those controls in the current audit. If the auditor plans to rely on controls that have not changed since they were last tested, the auditor should test those controls at least every three years. If the auditor plans to rely on controls that mitigate a significant risk, those controls should be tested in the current period. (8267)

Communicating Internal Control Related Matters

22. (b) If the auditor finds significant deficiencies or material weaknesses as a consequence of performing audit procedures in an audit of financial statements, the auditor is required to communicate them in writing to management and those charged with governance. It is not the auditor's duty to search for them or to express an opinion on the

effectiveness of internal control. They are not required to be included in the financial statements or the footnotes. (8142)

23. (c) A significant deficiency is a deficiency in internal control, or combination of deficiencies in internal control, that is less severe than a material weakness, yet important enough to merit attention by those charged with governance. Answer (a) is the definition of a deficiency in internal control. Answer (b) describes one of the conditions for a deficiency in the operation of a control to exist (the other condition is when a properly designed control does not operate as designed). Answer (d) is false; the severity of a deficiency in internal control (taken into consideration by the auditor in the determination of whether a deficiency is either a significant deficiency or a material weakness) does not depend on whether a misstatement actually occurred. (9036)

24. (c) *An auditor may communicate some deficiencies during an audit in addition to after the audit's completion* due to their significance and the need for timely corrective action. Such early communication is not required to be in writing. However, all significant deficiencies and material weaknesses should ultimately be reported in the required written communication to management and those charged with governance even if they were remediated during the audit. (The required written communication is best made by the audit report release date, but should be made no later than 60 days following this date.) In an audit of financial statements, the auditor is not required to search for deficiencies in internal control. All material weaknesses are significant deficiencies, but not all significant deficiencies are material weaknesses. An auditor should not issue a written communication stating that no significant deficiencies were identified during the audit. (Management or those charged with governance may request that the auditor issue a communication indicating that no material weaknesses were identified to submit to a governmental authority. This is allowable.) (5656)

25. (d) Answers (a) – (c) are listed as indicators of material weaknesses by the standard setters. Their list also includes the identification by the auditor of a material misstatement of the financial statements in circumstances that indicate that the misstatement would not have been detected by the entity's internal control. Substantial doubt about the entity's ability to continue as a going concern does not indicate the existence of a material weakness in internal control. (9037)

26. (c) The written communication regarding significant deficiencies and material weaknesses

identified during an audit of financial statements should include a restriction on its use. Significant deficiencies do not create scope limitations; management may have made a conscious decision to accept the degree of risk due to cost or other considerations. The auditor is not required to perform tests of controls on significant deficiencies; however, performing tests of controls in an audit may reveal significant deficiencies. The required written communication is best made by the audit report release date, but should be made no later than 60 days after this date. In some circumstances, the auditor may decide to communicate certain identified significant deficiencies and material weaknesses during the audit; however these should ultimately be included in the formal final written communication even if remediated during the audit. (5118)

27. (b) The auditor should not issue an written communication stating that no significant deficiencies were identified during an audit. The other answer alternatives are all examples of items that should be included in the written communication regarding significant deficiencies and material weaknesses identified during an audit of financial statements. (2957)

28. (b) A deficiency in internal control exists when the design or operation of a control does not allow management or employees, in the normal course of performing their assigned functions, to prevent, detect, or correct misstatements on a timely basis. (7489)

Revenue Cycle

29. (d) Answers (a), (b), and (c) are all controls applicable to the billing process. Answer (d) is a control used *after* the billing process. (5109)

30. (b) Tracing from shipping documents to sales invoice provides evidence that *shipments to customers were properly invoiced.* (5650)

31. (d) The treasury department is independent of record keeping and custodial functions for accounts receivable. Incompatible functions are those that place any person in a position to both perpetrate and conceal errors or fraud in the normal course of her/his duties. Therefore, a well-designed plan of organization separates the duties of authorization, record keeping, and custody of assets. Answer (a) would not separate the authorization and record keeping functions. Credit authorization and write-off of accounts by the same department could allow for an employee defalcation scheme. The A/P department would not have adequate information to make such a recommendation which could result in error or fraud concealment. (5108)

32. (c)   The most effective control in offsetting the tendency of sales personnel to maximize sales volume at the expense of high bad debt write-offs would be the segregation of duties of those employees involved in credit-granting and sales functions. If this segregation exists, credit-granting employees should help to screen out those potential customers likely to result in high bad-debt write-offs.   (2798)

33. (a)   A bank lockbox system assures accountability control as cash enters the client's cash receipts system. Answers (b), (c), and (d) are controls imposed after cash is captured in the system.   (5959)

34. (a)   The cycle approach combines similar transactions with the ledger balances that result from those transactions. Receivables result from the sale of goods; therefore, it is logical and more efficient to test these items together.   (8144)

35. (b)   Management's emphasis on meeting projected profit goals most likely would significantly influence the control environment when a significant portion of management compensation is represented by stock options because it provides an incentive to commit fraud. Answers (a), (c), and (d) would mitigate this risk factor.   (8160)

36. (a)   Assertions about completeness are tested by testing whether or not all cash is recorded. If employees consistently use cash registers and tapes, it is likely that all cash is recorded. Inquiry about employees' access to undeposited recorded cash, comparing the cash receipts journal to the general ledger, and comparing the cash balance in the general ledger with the bank confirmation request, test assertions about only *recorded* cash.   (6578)

37. (c)   Segregation of duties prevents an employee from committing fraud and subsequently concealing it. Proper segregation of duties separates the functions of record keeping, custody and authorization. Answers (a) and (b) are not necessarily fraudulent activities. Fictitious transactions that overstate receivables also tend to overstate revenue, not understate it.   (8162)

38. (c)   By immediately recording the receipt of the checks, the employee provides evidence of the existence of cash. While the procedures in answers (a), (b), and (d) are appropriate, preparing a duplicate listing of the checks is of immediate concern.   (5648)

Disbursements Cycle

39. (d)   Accounting for unused purchase orders and receiving reports by the same department does not provide sufficient segregation of duties for the authorization, custody, and reporting functions of an effective internal control system. The lack of segregation of these items could result in an employee defalcation scheme. Answers (a), (b), and (c) each represent a procedure that is usually performed in the vouchers payable department.   (5113)

40. (d)   The agreement of the documents will verify that the goods were ordered (purchase order), received (receiving report), and the company has been billed (vendor's invoice). The individual signing the checks, not accounts payable, should stamp, perforate, or otherwise cancel the supporting documentation. The purchasing department, not accounting, is involved with the approval of purchase requisitions and blanking out the quantity ordered on the receiving department copy of the purchase order.   (5977)

41. (b)   When the shipping department returns nonconforming goods to a vendor, the purchasing department should send a debit memo to the accounting department. This enables the accounting department to make the appropriate adjustment to the vendor's account. Answers (a) and (c) are incorrect because the accounting department would have no use for the unpaid voucher and the vendor invoice. A credit memo would be provided by the vendor, not by the purchasing department.   (2950)

42. (b)   By immediately stamping "paid" on the paid voucher, the check signer prevents the voucher from being paid again. While each of the items in answers (a), (c), and (d) is a recommended practice, none prevent the voucher from being paid again.   (5652)

43. (d)   A good internal control system will include the segregation of duties, such as the comparison of an approved purchase order to items received. Answers (a) and (c) represent documentation included with the order as it is received, without any indication of authorization. Answer (b) represents a form used when goods and materials are taken from inventory to be used or shipped.   (3913)

44. (d)   A control for cash disbursements is for the person who signs the checks to compare them to supporting documents, cancel the documents, and to mail the checks. The person who signs checks should have access to the supporting documents in order to validate their legitimacy. Reconciliation of the monthly bank statement is a control that should be done by a person independent of cash transactions. Checks should not be returned or given to anyone with cash disbursement responsibilities.   (5976)

45. (d) Assertions about completeness deal with whether all transactions and accounts that should be presented in the financial statements are so included. One step in assuring this is the periodic reconciliation of prenumbered purchase orders, receiving reports, and vouchers. (2799)

46. (d) Approved borrowings by the board of directors indicate that transactions must be approved before the recording and custody functions can take place. This is also performed by a party independent of the recording and custody functions. (4269)

Inventory & Production Cycle

47. (a) To test for appropriate segregation of duties, the auditor observes and makes inquiries. The procedures in answers (b), (c), and (d) are not applicable to testing for segregation of duties. (5649)

48. (b) For sound internal controls, all receipts for goods, including returned goods or materials, should be handled by the receiving clerk. Receiving reports should be prepared for all items received. Employees who have recording responsibilities should not also have custody of the related assets. (3916)

49. (c) Use of time tickets indicates the amount of actual labor employed during the day on a given job. An internal control procedure requiring the use of charging the actual time to the job in progress would help prevent mistakes in the recording of direct and indirect labor. Answers (a) and (d) would indicate variances after improperly charging direct labor to factory overhead, but would be poor preventative measures. Answer (b) would have no effect on identifying misposted direct labor. (4697)

50. (d) Assertions about existence or occurrence deal with whether assets or liabilities of the entity exist at a given date and whether recorded transactions have occurred during a given period. Periodically comparing goods on hand with perpetual inventory records would assist in identifying potential errors. Answer (a) addresses the valuation of the inventory. Answer (b) would not identify variances in actual inventory compared to recorded amounts. Answer (c) represents examples of controls necessary for the proper segregation of duties in purchasing inventory. (4698)

51. (b) Controlling the access to assets is an important objective of proper inventory control. The other answer alternatives are procedures for satisfying inventory control objectives—not actual internal control objectives. (4265)

52. (c) To obtain an understanding of a manufacturer's internal control concerning inventory balances, an auditor would review the entity's descriptions of inventory policies and procedures. Analyzing inventory ratios, performing cost variance analytical procedures, and performing inventory test counts are substantive procedures. (5979)

Personnel & Payroll Cycle

53. (c) Incompatible functions are those that place any person in a position to both perpetrate and conceal errors or fraud in the normal course of her/ his duties. Therefore, a well-designed plan of organization separates the duties of authorization, record keeping, and asset custody. Authorizing payroll rate changes for all employees would be incompatible with record keeping. Examining authorization forms for new employees is not the same as authorization; therefore, the payroll department supervisor would only be in control of record keeping. While hiring all subordinate payroll department employees would not be a compatible function with record keeping, it is not as serious as authorizing pay rate changes for all employees. (4694)

54. (c) Incompatible functions are those that place any person in a position to both perpetrate and conceal errors or fraud in the normal course of her/his duties. A well-designed organization plan separates authorization, record keeping, and asset custody. (4267)

55. (a) Observing the segregation of duties concerning personnel responsibilities and payroll disbursement is a common audit procedure relating to the existence or occurrence assertion for payroll transactions. Inspecting evidence of accounting for prenumbered payroll checks would provide evidence related to the completeness assertion. Recomputing the payroll deductions for employee fringe benefits would provide evidence related to the valuation and the rights and obligations assertions. An auditor would likely review payroll checks and bank reconciliations to determine that all checks were cashed as part of obtaining evidence for the existence or occurrence assertion and not just verify the preparation of the monthly payroll account bank reconciliation. (5978)

56. (a) By promptly notifying the payroll supervisor of employee terminations, the personnel department would avoid a terminated employee from continuing to be paid. Unclaimed payroll checks should be forwarded to the Treasurer's office. Salary rates should be controlled in the personnel office. Total hours should be determined and approved prior to getting to the payroll department. Although

answers (c) and (d) are good controls, they would not prevent employee payroll fraud. (5962)

57. (a) Significant unexplained variances between standard and actual labor cost could cause an auditor to suspect a payroll fraud scheme. Payroll checks disbursed by the same employee each payday (as long as that person has no other payroll responsibilities), employee time cards being approved by individual departmental supervisors, and a separate payroll bank account maintained on an imprest basis are proper internal control procedures. (5997)

PP&E Cycle

58. (d) The requirement is to find the flowchart indicating two forms of input (new transactions and the old file) being processed to generate three forms of output (labels, printed journal, and a new file). Answer (a) shows only one input with four forms of output. Answer (b) represents a manual process while the facts indicate that a printed journal is to be generated. Answer (c) shows a punched card as one of the output items when labels, a printed journal, and a new file should be represented in the output. (7490)

59. (c) The investigation of variances within a formal budgeting system would identify any unusual and unanticipated fluctuations in the repair and maintenance accounts when asset acquisitions are recorded there incorrectly. The segregation of duties is a good control; however, answer (a) would not ensure that equipment acquisitions were not misclassified. Answer (b) is a good internal control, but would not ensure that equipment purchases were recorded properly because these invoices only represent those acquisitions which are already properly recorded as fixed assets. Answer (d) would not prevent the recording of an acquisition to the repair and maintenance accounts, nor would it serve to identify misclassifications. (4271)

60. (a) The periodic inspection of physical equipment and comparison to what is recorded by the internal auditor (who does not participate actively in the acquisition or disposal process) may allow for a reduction in the scope of the auditor's tests of asset acquisitions. The comparison of account balances and entries is an analytical procedure that would highlight unusual and unanticipated fluctuations; however, it would not indicate acquisitions that were not approved. The review of prenumbered purchase orders would indicate trade-ins or retirements of fixed assets in exchange for new assets; thus, there would be no change in the quantity of fixed assets on hand. (3917)

61. (d) A weakness in internal control over recording retirements of equipment (which could result in an overstatement) may cause an auditor to *select certain items of equipment from the accounting records and locate them in the plant* to make sure that they exist and are useful (unretired) assets. Inspecting certain items of equipment in the plant and then identifying those items in the accounting records would not locate assets which appear on the books even though they have been retired because none of the equipment traced would be retired equipment. (If an auditor failed to find equipment from the plant in the accounting records, an understatement would have been discovered.) If retired equipment that was not fully depreciated was not removed from the records, the related depreciation calculation would not reveal its retirement. Additions to the "other assets" account should have nothing to do with the failure to record retirements of equipment. (0081)

62. (d) The procedures in place to monitor and properly restrict access to equipment would more likely be *observed* by the auditor than be part of a questionnaire, as this is very important. Answer (a) represents the authorization function of the control structure, which would be included on the internal control questionnaire. Answer (b) represents a procedure to test the accounting and recording function of the control structure, which the auditor would include in an internal control questionnaire. Requests for competitive bids reduce the possibility of an individual's personal gain at the expense of the business in unusual and material transactions. (5114)

Investing Cycle

63. (a) Of the choices given, the strongest internal control in safeguarding against the loss of marketable securities would be the use of an independent trust company that has no direct contact with the employees who have record keeping responsibilities. The fact that only the trust company has access to the securities should prevent unauthorized entity personnel with record keeping responsibility from conspiring or colluding to misappropriate securities. In determining appropriate controls in safeguarding an asset against loss, the auditor would start with those controls involving access to the asset in question. Neither verifying the securities in the safe nor tracing all purchases and sales provides evidence as to who has access to, or custody of, the marketable securities. Allowing just one person access to an asset enables the individual to take the asset without being discovered. (2956)

64. (a) The fact that only the trust company has access to the securities should prevent unauthorized

entity personnel with record keeping responsibility from conspiring or colluding to misappropriate the securities. Trust company employees or management potentially could sell or otherwise mismanage the assets. Answers (c) and (d) put custody and record keeping functions in the hands of one party which could result in unauthorized transactions.

(4699)

65. (b) A bank safe-deposit box with two company officials in control of the assets provides strong physical control over the securities. Answers (a) and (c) would not safeguard the physical marketable security. Answer (d) does not provide for dual control throughout the year, as is preferred. (5963)

66. (d, e) Custody of investment securities usually is maintained on company premises or assigned to an outside agent such as a brokerage house. Good controls dictate that at least two officers should sign for, and be present to access, these investments to prevent unauthorized sales. Having no access to securities between the year-end and the date of the auditor's security count provides no guarantee that unauthorized access to the investments during the time period indicated did not occur. Having proceeds from the sale of investments received by an employee who does not have access to securities and investment acquisitions authorized by a member of the Board of Directors before execution are good controls, but do not address the physical control of the assets. (3918)

Solution 23-2 ADDITIONAL MULTIPLE CHOICE ANSWERS

Components of IC

67. (c) The auditor should obtain sufficient knowledge of the control environment to understand the attitudes, awareness, and actions of those charged with governance concerning the entity's internal control and its importance in achieving reliable financial reporting. Computer-based controls, the system of segregation of duties, and safeguards over access to assets are day-to-day details with which board members are unlikely to have as much influence (unless they are also officers). (5643)

68. (b) In an audit of financial statements, an auditor's primary consideration is whether, and how, a specific control prevents, or detects and corrects, material misstatements in relevant assertions related to classes of transactions, account balances, or disclosures. Management's philosophy and operating style are elements of the control environment that would influence policies and procedures, but are not the auditor's primary consideration. Whether controls provide adequate safeguards over access to assets is not relevant to all controls (as is answer "b") nor is it the auditor's primary consideration. And again, the enhancement of management's decision-making processes is not an auditor's primary consideration.

(5101)

69. (b) Incompatible functions are those that place any person in a position to both perpetrate and conceal errors or fraud in the normal course of their duties. Therefore, a well-designed plan of organization separates the duties of authorization, record keeping, and custody of assets. (0092)

Understanding of IC

70. (a) Internal control, no matter how well designed and operated, can provide an entity with reasonable, but not absolute, assurance about achieving an entity's objectives. The likelihood of achievement is affected by limitations inherent to internal control. These include the realities that human judgment in decision making can be faulty and that breakdowns in internal control can occur because of human failures such as simple errors or mistakes. While answers (b), (c), and (d) are generally true statements, they are not included in the concept of reasonable assurance. (5644)

71. (d) Concerns about the integrity of the entity's management may be so serious as to cause the auditor to conclude that the risk of management misrepresentations in the financial statements is such that an audit cannot be conducted. Answers (a), (b), and (c) may be considerations, but are not necessarily so serious as to cause an auditor to question whether the entity can be audited. (7099)

72. (d) Observing the entity's personnel applying the activities provides evidence about the design and implementation of internal control activities. Entity personnel may have trouble implementing poorly designed activities. Reperformance alone would not provide evidence about whether and how the activities are actually performed. The procedures in answers (b) and (c) might detect misstatements, but would not provide much information about internal controls. (6393)

73. (c) Internal control, no matter how well designed and operated, can provide an entity with reasonable, but not absolute, assurance about

achieving an entity's objectives. The likelihood of achievement is affected by limitations inherent to internal control. These include the realities that human judgment in decision making can be faulty. An inherent quality is part of the very nature of something and thus is not considered alterable as are incompatible duties, lack of segregation of duties or the lack of an audit committee. (8377)

Tests of Controls

74. (d) The CPA examiners generally recognize four types of tests of internal controls to determine the degree of operating effectiveness: inquiries of appropriate entity personnel, inspection of documents and reports, observation of the application of specific internal control policies and procedures, and re-performance of the application of the policy or procedures by the auditor. System flowcharts may document the auditor's understanding of internal control, but flowchart preparation provides little assurance about the documented activity's operating effectiveness. (7810)

75. (b) An audit is a cumulative and iterative process. As the auditor performs planned audit procedures, the audit evidence obtained may cause the auditor to modify the nature, timing or extent of other planned audit procedures. In particular, the risk assessment may be based on an expectation that controls are operating effectively. If, after testing a client's internal control activities, the auditor discovers a material weakness in the operation of a client's internal controls, the auditor most likely would increase the assessment of control risk and increase the extent of substantive procedures in order to obtain more audit evidence rather than withdraw from the audit. In an audit of financial statements, the auditor is not required to perform procedures to identify deficiencies in internal control or to express an opinion on the effectiveness of the entity's internal control. (8375)

76. (d) The purpose of an audit is to express an opinion on the financial statements; an auditor assesses control risk as part of an evaluation of the likelihood that material misstatements exist in the financial statements. (8402)

Communicating Internal Control Related Matters

77. (c) The severity of a deficiency in internal control is dependent on the magnitude of the potential misstatement that could result from the deficiency or deficiencies and whether there is a reasonable possibility (the likelihood) that the entity's controls will fail to prevent, or detect and correct a misstatement of an account balance or disclosure.

It's also important to note that whether a misstatement actually occurred is not relevant to the determination of a control deficiency's severity. (7105)

78. (b) The written communication regarding significant deficiencies and material weaknesses identified during a financial statement audit should (1) include a statement that indicates that the auditor's consideration of internal control was to express an opinion on the financial statements, but not to express an opinion on the effectiveness of the entity's internal control; (2) state that the auditor is not expressing an opinion on the effectiveness of internal control; (3) state that the auditor's consideration of internal control was not designed to identify all deficiencies in internal control that might be significant deficiencies or material weaknesses; (4) include the definition of the terms *material weakness* and, where relevant, *significant deficiency;* (5) identify the matters that are considered to be significant deficiencies and those that are considered to be material weaknesses; and (6) state that the communication is intended solely for the information and use of management, those charged with governance, and others within the organization and is not intended to be and should not be used by anyone other than these specified parties. (If an entity is required to furnish the auditor's written communication to a governmental authority, a specific reference to the governmental authority may be made.) (5982)

Revenue Cycle

79. (a) Observation of an entity's preparation of a schedule is a test of a control. Confirmation requests, inspection of an analysis of accounts receivables, and comparison of an entity's uncollectible accounts expense to actual uncollectible accounts receivables are all substantive procedures. (6234)

80. (c) For each shipment, there should be a sales invoice. If the auditor selects a sample of transactions from the shipping document file and does not find corresponding sales invoices, the auditor knows the controls are ineffective. For each sales order and customer order, there may or may not be a sales invoice, depending on whether the product was shipped. When testing to see if there is a failure to produce sales invoices, by selecting a sample from the sales invoice file, an auditor would guarantee to get only transactions where this failure did not occur. (7815)

81. (b) In addition to indemnification in case of loss, fidelity bonds provide a psychological deterrent to employees considering defalcations. The insurance company's investigation before an employee is

bonded tends to discourage those with intentions of committing defalcations from accepting jobs requiring bonds. A further deterrent is the employee's knowledge that the insurance company will prosecute in an effort to recover a loss, whereas an employer might forego prosecution. (0073)

82. (c) One of the most effective means of detecting or preventing fraud is the segregation of duties involving authorization, custody, and record keeping. Authorization of credit memos by personnel who receive cash (custody) is not segregation of duties. The recording of fictitious transactions and failure to prepare shipping documents resulting in an overstatement of inventory likely would be discovered during reconciliations. Return claims applied to inappropriate accounts likely would be discovered by customers when monthly statements are issued.

(6577)

83. (d) Internal verifications of cash balances generally should be made monthly. Recorded cash on hand and petty cash balances should be compared with cash counts and recorded bank balances should be reconciled to balances shown on bank statements. These verifications should be made by personnel who are not otherwise involved in executing or recording cash transactions to maintain a segregation of functions. The cash receipts accountant, the cash disbursements accountant, and the controller should not reconcile the monthly statements as they are involved in the executing or recording of cash transactions. (0111)

Disbursements Cycle

84. (b) Good internal controls require that the person who last signs the checks keep control of them until they are mailed. Answers (a), (c), and (d) do not provide sufficient segregation of duties for the authorization, custodial, and reporting functions of an effective internal control system. (3914)

85. (c) Incompatible functions are those that place any person in a position to both perpetrate and conceal errors or fraud in the normal course of her/his duties. Therefore, a well-designed plan of organization separates the duties of authorization, record keeping, and custody of assets. The treasurer generally would perform the other procedures. (4264)

86. (d) The most effective controls over recorded purchases occur when supporting forms such as purchase orders, receiving reports, and vendor invoices are compared independently for agreement. For good control, the receiving department should not know the quantity ordered. Answer (b) is a step in the right direction, but does

not encompass as many independent comparisons as does answer (d). Answer (c) is an example of incompatible functions. Assets should not be checked in and recorded by the person who authorized their purchase. (7491)

87. (c) The chief financial officer's willingness to override the internal controls reveals a management philosophy that values meeting goals higher than working within established procedures. Little time would be saved by adhering to approval procedures at most entities, indicating, at best, poor organization regarding the transactions. Elimination of the internal audit function, in itself, doesn't indicate that controls are now inadequate, although this is a second-best answer. As the audit committee chair is unlikely to have been in a position to commit a disreputable act with regard to the entity under audit, the chair's resignation probably doesn't indicate personal misconduct. If an audit committee chair resigned in protest of entity misconduct, the chair likely would have informed the auditor directly of the reasons for the resignation. Check-run frequency rarely effects the quality of internal controls. (7843)

88. (b) Incompatible functions are those that place any person in a position to both perpetrate and conceal errors or fraud in the normal course of their duties. A well-designed plan of organization separates the duties of authorization, record keeping, and custody of assets. Answers (a) and (d) do not separate custody and record keeping. Answer (c) does not provide verification of inventory. (0089)

Inventory & Production Cycle

89. (c) An independent comparison of finished goods records with counts of goods on hand is designed to detect errors and fraud concerning inventory custody as it provides an independent reconciliation of the two amounts. Answers (a) and (b) do not consider the inventory itself nor inventory custody. The storekeeper should not have both access and authorization. (7492)

90. (c) An auditor need consider only the objectives and related controls relevant to the audit. An auditor performs tests of the design and operation of internal controls to determine if the auditor may rely upon them. If the auditor has determined that it will take less time to perform substantive tests than it will to perform tests of controls, there is no reason to assess control risk or perform any tests of controls on inventory. Control risk may be assessed at a minimum level only after testing controls and finding them strong. (8419)

Personnel & Payroll Cycle

91. (a) The authorization of a transaction, its record keeping, and the custody of the related asset should all be separated. In a payroll function, the treasurer's department prepares and distributes payroll checks to employees (custody), the controller reviews the payroll, and the payroll department prepares the payroll (record keeping). (4268)

92. (a) An important internal control is the separation of the duties of authorization, record keeping, and custody. As the payroll department prepares the payroll (record keeping) and has custody of the related assets, a payroll clerk is in a position to both perpetrate and conceal misappropriation of assets. Having the accounting department wire transfer funds (authorization) based on total from a payroll summary (record keeping) may be unusual, but the two mentioned types of duties are separated. With the treasurer supervises the use of a signature plate (custody) by the payroll department to prepare checks (record keeping), segregation of duties is maintained. With the chief financial officer signing checks (custody) prepared by the payroll department (record keeping), segregation of duties is maintained. (7831)

PERFORMANCE BY SUBTOPICS

Each category below parallels a subtopic covered in Chapter 23. Record the number and percentage of questions you correctly answered in each subtopic area.

Components of IC

Question #	Correct √
1	
2	
3	
4	
5	
6	
7	
# Questions	7
# Correct	
% Correct	

Understanding of IC

Question #	Correct √
8	
9	
10	
11	
12	
13	
14	
15	
16	
17	
# Questions	10
# Correct	
% Correct	

Tests of Controls

Question #	Correct √
18	
19	
20	
21	
# Questions	4
# Correct	
% Correct	

Communicating Internal Control Related Matters

Question #	Correct √
22	
23	
24	
25	
26	
27	
28	
# Questions	7
# Correct	
% Correct	

Revenue Cycle

Question #	Correct √
29	
30	
31	
32	
33	
34	
35	
36	
37	
38	
# Questions	10
# Correct	
% Correct	

Disbursements Cycle

Question #	Correct √
39	
40	
41	
42	
43	
44	
45	
46	
# Questions	8
# Correct	
% Correct	

Inventory & Production Cycle

Question #	Correct √
47	
48	
49	
50	
51	
52	
# Questions	6
# Correct	
% Correct	

Personnel & Payroll Cycle

Question #	Correct √
53	
54	
55	
56	
57	
# Questions	5
# Correct	
% Correct	

PP&E Cycle

Question #	Correct √
58	
59	
60	
61	
62	
# Questions	5
# Correct	
% Correct	

Investing Cycle

Question #	Correct √
63	
64	
65	
66	
# Questions	4
# Correct	
% Correct	

SIMULATION SOLUTIONS

Solution 23-3

Response #1: Errors & Fraud (5 points)

1. C

The error of posting a customer's invoice to the wrong account would be detected when a monthly statement was received, indicating a balance due, when no payment is owed.

2. G

Before goods are shipped from the warehouse, an employee should determine that a valid sales invoice exists that matches the shipping documents and actual shipment being made. This would prevent shipments being made that did not result from a customer order.

3. F

To prevent having unrecorded sales, the company should make a comparison each day of the total sales invoices with the daily sales summaries. This comparison would detect differences between the total sales made and recorded.

4. K

Unrecorded accounts receivable would be prevented by comparing the control total of sales invoices to the control total amount posted to the accounts receivable ledger. Any differences would indicate possible errors in the recording function and require a reconciliation, which would detect unposted customer sales.

5. I

Requiring employees to use an approved customer list before making credit sales to customers would prevent the company from allowing sales to be made to uncreditworthy customers.

6. B

An internal control procedure that would prevent goods being removed from the warehouse when a bona fide sale does not exist would be the requirement that an approved sales order be received in the warehouse before the goods could be released from the warehouse.

7. D

The company should implement an internal control procedure to prevent shipping Customer A's order to Customer B. A control procedure to prevent such errors would be to have the shipping clerk compare the order received from the warehouse and prepared for shipping to the approved customer sales order.

8. L

The company would be able to prevent a fraudulent sales scheme where sales were recorded for fictitious transactions if certain control procedures were in place. For example, requiring an employee not in the sales department to compare customer sales invoices to shipping documents and approved customer orders before invoices were recorded and sent would prevent other than bona fide sales transactions from being recorded.

Response #2: Communication (4 points)

In **planning** an audit, an auditor's understanding of the internal control structure elements should be used to **identify** the types of **potential misstatements** that could occur, to consider the factors affecting the risk of material misstatement, and to influence the design of substantive tests.

Response #3: Research (1 point)

Paragraph Reference Answer: AU 318.16

Guidance: AU 318.16 states, "The auditor may perform tests of controls or substantive procedures at an interim date or at period end. The higher the risk of material misstatement, the more likely it is that the auditor may decide it is more effective to perform substantive procedures nearer to, or at, the period end rather than at an earlier date, or to perform audit procedures unannounced or at unpredictable times (for example, performing audit procedures at selected locations on an unannounced basis). On the other hand, performing audit procedures before the period end may assist the auditor in identifying significant matters at an early stage of the audit, and consequently resolving them with the assistance of management or developing an effective audit approach to address such matters. If the auditor performs tests of the operating effectiveness of controls or substantive procedures before period end, the auditor should consider the additional evidence that is necessary for the remaining period."

(5725)

Solution 23-4

Response #1: Communication (9 points)

The control environment factors (excluding the factor illustrated in the example) that establish, enhance, or mitigate the effectiveness of specific policies and procedures, and their components are

Organizational Structure

An entity's organizational structure provides the **overall framework** for planning, directing, and controlling operations. An organizational structure includes consideration of the form and nature of an entity's **organizational units**, including the **data processing organization**, and **related management** functions and **reporting relationships**. In addition, the organizational structure should **assign authority and responsibility** within the entity in an appropriate manner.

Audit Committee/Board of Directors

An effective audit committee takes an **active role** in **overseeing** an entity's accounting and financial **reporting policies and practices**. The committee should **assist the board** of directors in fulfilling its **fiduciary and accountability responsibilities** and should help maintain a direct line of communication between the board and the entity's external and internal auditors.

Methods of Assigning Authority and Responsibility

These methods affect the understanding of reporting relationships and responsibilities established within the entity. Methods of assigning authority and responsibility include consideration of

- **Entity policy regarding** such matters as **acceptable business practices**, conflicts of interest, and **codes of conduct**.
- Assignment of responsibility and delegation of authority to deal with such matters as organizational goals and objectives, operating functions, and regulatory requirements.
- Employee **job descriptions** delineating specific duties, reporting relationships, and constraints.
- **Computer systems documentation** indicating the procedures for authorizing transactions and approving system changes.

Internal Audit Function

The internal audit function is established within an entity to **examine and evaluate the adequacy** and **effectiveness of other internal control policies and procedures**. Establishing an effective internal audit function includes consideration of its **authority** and **reporting relationships**, the **qualifications** of its staff, and its **resources**.

Management Control Methods

These methods affect management's direct control over the exercise of authority delegated to others and its ability to effectively supervise overall company activities. Management control methods include consideration of

- **Establishing planning and reporting systems** that set forth management's plans and the results of actual performance. Such systems may include **business planning; budgeting,** forecasting, and profit planning; and responsibility accounting.
- Establishing **methods that identify** the status of **actual performance and exceptions from planned performance,** as well as communicating them to the appropriate levels of management.
- Using such methods at appropriate management levels to **investigate variances from expectations** and to take appropriate and timely **corrective action**.
- Establishing and **monitoring** policies **for** developing and **modifying accounting systems** and **control procedures**, including the development, modification, and use of any related computer programs and data files.

Personnel Policies & Practices

These polices and practices affect an entity's ability to employ sufficient competent personnel to accomplish its goals and objectives. **Personnel policies** and practices include consideration of an entity's policies and procedures for **hiring, training, evaluating, promoting,** and **compensating** employees, and giving them the resources necessary to **discharge** their assigned responsibilities.

External Influences

These are influences established and exercised by parties outside an entity that affect an entity's operations and practices. They include monitoring and **compliance requirements** imposed by legislative and regulatory bodies, such as examinations by bank regulatory agencies. They also include review and **follow-up by parties outside the entity** concerning entity actions. External influences are ordinarily outside an entity's authority. Such influences, however, may **heighten management's consciousness** of and attitude towards the conduct and reporting of an entity's operations and may also prompt management to establish specific internal control policies or procedures.

Paragraph Reference Answer: AU 325.08

Guidance: AU 325.08 states, "The auditor should evaluate the severity of each deficiency in internal control identified during the audit to determine whether the deficiency, individually or in combination, is a significant deficiency or a material weakness. The severity of a deficiency depends on the magnitude of the potential misstatement resulting from the deficiency or deficiencies; and whether there is a reasonable possibility that the entity's controls will fail to prevent, or detect and correct a misstatement of an account balance or disclosure. The severity of a deficiency does not depend on whether a misstatement actually occurred."

(5726)

Solution 23-5

a. Smith should inform Digit's audit committee about the inventory **adjustments arising from the audit**. These adjustments probably have a significant effect on the financial statements and should be included in the required matters to be communicated to the audit committee.

Dodd's consultation with another CPA firm concerning the previously unrecorded contingent liability should also be discussed with the audit committee. Smith should make the audit committee aware of Smith's views about any **significant matters that were the subject of that consultation**.

Smith should also inform the audit committee of any **serious difficulties encountered in dealing with management** related to the performance of the audit. Specifically, the two-week delay in completing the financial statements and the unavailability of Dodd, the controller, near the end of the fieldwork should be reported to the audit committee.

Smith's **disagreement** with Dodd over the write-off of the overdue account receivable, **even though satisfactorily resolved**, should also be discussed with the audit committee.

Finally, the **significant deficiencies** that Smith became aware of during the audit should be communicated to the audit committee.

b. In order for Digit's audit committee to understand the nature of the assurance that an audit provides,

Smith should communicate the **level of responsibility assumed under generally accepted auditing standards**. The audit committee should understand that an audit is designed to obtain **reasonable, rather than absolute, assurance** about the financial statements.

Smith should also determine that Digit's audit committee is informed about the initial selection of and changes in **significant accounting policies and their application**. The audit committee would be interested in the methods Digit uses to account for **significant unusual transactions** and accounting policies in controversial or emerging areas for which there is no authoritative guidance or consensus.

The audit committee should also be informed about the **accounting estimates** that are based upon management's judgments, the processes used to formulate particularly sensitive estimates, and the basis for Smith's conclusions regarding the reasonableness of those estimates.

Additionally, Smith should discuss with the audit committee Smith's responsibility for **other information in documents containing audited financial statements**, such as the "Management's Discussion and Analysis of Financial Condition and Results of Operations" that is presented in the annual report to shareholders. Smith should also discuss any procedures performed and the results.

Smith should also discuss with the audit committee any **major issues** that were discussed with management in connection with the recurring retention of Smith's CPA firm, including discussions regarding the application of accounting principles and auditing standards.

Finally, Smith should be assured that the audit committee is informed about any **fraud** and **illegal acts** that Smith becomes aware of during the audit unless those matters are clearly inconsequential. However, if senior management is involved in fraud or an illegal act, Smith should communicate directly with the audit committee.

Paragraph Reference Answer: AU 314.111

Guidance: AU 314.111 states, "The determination of significant risks, which arise on most audits, is a matter for the auditor's professional judgment. In exercising this judgment, the auditor should consider inherent risk to determine whether the nature of the risk, the likely magnitude of the potential misstatement including the possibility that the risk may give rise to multiple misstatements, and the likelihood of the risk occurring are such that they require special audit consideration. Routine, noncomplex transactions that are subject to systematic processing are less likely to give rise to significant risks because they have lower inherent risks. On the other hand, significant risks are often derived from business risks that may result in a material misstatement. In considering the nature of the risks, the auditor should consider a number of matters, including the following:

- Whether the risk is a risk of fraud
- Whether the risk is related to recent significant economic, accounting, or other developments and, therefore, requires specific attention
- The complexity of transactions
- Whether the risk involves significant transactions with related parties
- The degree of subjectivity in the measurement of financial information related to the risks, especially those involving a wide range of measurement uncertainty
- Whether the risk involves significant nonroutine transactions that are outside the normal course of business for the entity, or that otherwise appear to be unusual"

(6386)

Solution 23-6

Response #1: Communication (9 points)

The key internal control policies and procedures related to Grant's property, equipment, and related transactions that Harris may consider in assessing control risk include the following:

- Advance **approval** in accordance with management's criteria is required for property and equipment transactions.
- Approval authority for transactions above an established dollar value is required at a higher level, such as the **board of directors**.
- Property and equipment transactions are **adequately documented**.
- There are **written policies covering capitalizing expenditures**, classifying **leases**, and determining estimated **useful lives**, salvage values, and methods of depreciation and amortization.
- There are adequate policies and procedures to determine whether property and equipment are received and properly recorded, such as a system that **matches** purchase orders, receiving reports, and vendors' invoices.
- There are adequate procedures to determine whether **dispositions** of property and equipment are **properly accounted for** and proceeds, if

any, are received in accordance with management's authorization.
- A property and equipment **subsidiary ledger is maintained** showing additions, retirements, and depreciation, and the ledger is periodically reconciled.
- Property and equipment is **physically inspected** and **reconciled** at reasonable intervals with independently maintained property and equipment records.
- An **annual budget** is prepared and monitored to forecast and **control acquisitions and retirements** of property and equipment.
- Reporting procedures assure prompt **identification and analysis of variances** between **authorized expenditures and actual costs**.
- Property and equipment is protected by adequate **safeguards**.
- Property and equipment is **insured** in accordance with management's authorization.
- Documents evidencing **title and property rights** are periodically **compared with** the detailed property records.
- The **entity employs internal auditors** to test whether the internal control structure policies and procedures are operating effectively.

Response #2: Research (1 point)

Paragraph Reference Answer: AU 312.21

Guidance: AU 312.21 states, "The risk that the relevant assertions related to account balances, classes of transactions, or disclosures are misstated consists of the following two components: *Inherent risk* (IR) is the susceptibility of a relevant assertion to a misstatement that could be material, either individually or when aggregated with other misstatements, assuming that there are no related controls. The risk of such misstatement is greater for some assertions and related account balances, classes of transactions, and disclosures than for others. For example, complex calculations are more likely to be misstated than simple calculations. Cash is more susceptible to theft than an inventory of coal. Accounts consisting of amounts derived from accounting estimates that are subject to significant measurement uncertainty pose greater risks than do accounts consisting of relatively routine, factual data. External circumstances giving rise to business risks also influence inherent risk. For example, technological developments might make a particular product obsolete, thereby causing inventory to be more susceptible to overstatement. In addition to those circumstances that are peculiar to a specific relevant assertion, factors in the entity and its environment that relate to several or all of the classes of transaction, account balances, or disclosures may influence the inherent risk related to a specific relevant assertion. These latter factors include, for example, a lack of sufficient working capital to continue operations or a declining industry characterized by a large number of business failures. *Control risk* (CR) is the risk that a misstatement that could occur in a relevant assertion and that could be material, either individually or when aggregated with other misstatements, will not be prevented or detected on a timely basis by the entity's internal control. That risk is a function of the effectiveness of the design and operation of internal control in achieving the entity's objectives relevant to preparation of the entity's financial statements. Some control risk will always exist because of the inherent limitations of internal control."

(5727)

Solution 23-7

Response #1: Revenue Cycle (9 points)

The weaknesses in Newton Hardware's internal controls include these:

Warehouse Clerk

- **Initiates posting to inventory records** by preparation of shipping advice.
- **Releases merchandise** to customers **before** proper **approvals** of customers' credit.
- Does **not retain a copy of the shipping advice** for comparison with receipt from carrier.

Bookkeeper A

- **Authorizes customers' credit and prepares source documents** for posting to customers' accounts.
- **Prepares invoices without notice** that the merchandise was actually shipped and the date it was shipped.
- **Authorizes write-offs** of customer accounts receivable and authorizes **customers' credit**.

Collection Clerk

- **Receives directly** and **records** customers' checks.
- **Does not deliver checks** excluded from the deposit to an employee independent of the bank deposit for review and disposition.
- Initiates posting of receipts to subsidiary accounts receivable ledger and has **initial access to cash receipts**.
- Does **not deposit** cash receipts **promptly**.
- **Reconciles bank statement** and has initial access to cash receipts.

Response #2: Research (1 point)

Paragraph Reference Answer: AU 318.71

Guidance: AU 318.71 states, "An audit of financial statements is a cumulative and iterative process. As the auditor performs planned audit procedures, the audit evidence obtained may cause the auditor to modify the nature, timing, or extent of other planned audit procedures. Information may come to the auditor's attention that differs significantly from the information on which the risk assessments were based. For example, the extent of misstatements that the auditor detects by performing substantive procedures may alter the auditor's judgment about the risk assessments and may indicate a material weakness in internal control. In addition, analytical procedures performed at the overall review stage of the audit may indicate a previously unrecognized risk of material misstatement. In such circumstances, the auditor should reevaluate the planned audit procedures based on the revised consideration of assessed risks for all or some of the relevant assertions related to classes of transactions, account balances, or disclosures."

(5728)

Solution 23-8

Response #1: Revenue Cycle Strengths (5 points)

There are many strengths in Southwest's internal control that an auditor most likely could consider in assessing control risk. Among the strengths are the following:

- Insurance **coverage for patients is verified** and communicated to the clerks by the office manager before medical services are rendered.
- The physician who renders the medical services documents the services on a **prenumbered service slip** that is used for recording revenue and as a receipt for the patient.
- Patients with uncollectible balances are prevented from making future appointments or receiving additional services because **the clerk** (clerk #3) **who makes appointments receives a list of patients with uncollectible balances**.
- **Prenumbered service slips are accounted for on a monthly basis** by the outside accountant who is independent of the revenue generating and revenue recording functions.
- The **bank reconciliation is prepared monthly** by the outside accountant who is independent of the revenue generating and revenue recording functions.
- **Computer passwords** are only known to the individual employees and the managing partner

who has no duties in the revenue recording functions.

- Computer **software cannot be modified** by Southwest's employees.

- None of the employees who perform duties in the revenue generating and revenue recording areas have **access to check-writing capabilities**.

Response #2: Revenue Cycle Weaknesses (4 points)

There are many weaknesses in Southwest's internal control that could permit material misstatements to occur in the financial statements. The following are the weaknesses and the internal control activities that most likely could help correct the weaknesses:

Weaknesses	*Internal control activities*
The office manager does not extend credit on the basis of a formal credit search, established credit limits, or any objective criteria.	**Objective credit limits** should be established and a formal credit search should be performed.
The office manager approves the extension of credit to patients and also approves the write-off of uncollectible patient receivables.	The **approval of credit and the write-off of patient receivables should be segregated.** One of the partners should be assigned the task of deciding which patient receivables should be written off.
There is no independent verification of clerk #1's pricing procedures.	The **verification of clerk #1's pricing procedures** should be assigned to another employee, such as clerk #3.
Clerk #2 performs numerous **incompatible functions**. For example, clerk #2: • **Receives cash and check directly from patients**; • **Receives check through the mail** from patients and insurance companies; • Prepares the **daily revenue summary**; • Prepares the daily bank deposit; • Maintains the accounts receivable records and **can add or delete information on the PC without proper authorization**; • Notifies the office manager when insurance claims and patient receivables are **not settled within 60 days**; and • Prepares the **list of patients with uncollectible balances**.	• The preparation of the daily revenue summary and the daily bank deposit should be assigned to an employee who does not receive cash directly from patients and check from patients and insurance companies. • The checks received through the mail should be stamped by clerk #1 who opens the mail and the remittance advices or copies of the checks or a list of the checks should be given to clerk #2. • The recording of accounts receivable and the deleting of uncollectible accounts should be assigned to an employee who does not have access to cash and checks. • The office manager should be notified by an employee who does not maintain the accounts receivable records when insurance claims and patient receivables are not settled within 60 days. • The preparation of the list of patients with uncollectible balances should be assigned to an employee who does not maintain the accounts receivable records.
No aged trial balance of patient receivables is prepared and reconciled to the general ledger.	An aged trial balance of patient receivables should be prepared and reconciled to the general ledger by someone other than clerk #2, such as the outside accountant, and reviewed by one of the partners.
Rejected insurance claims are **automatically converted to patient receivables without any follow-up** or investigation. In addition, there is no investigation of other unsettled insurance claims that are over 60 days.	Rejected insurance claims and other unsettled insurance claims over 60 days should be reviewed by one of the partners, and formal follow-up procedures to discover why claims were rejected or are unsettled should be implemented.

Weaknesses

Uncollectible patient receivables are not determined on the basis of established objective criteria. In addition, there is no follow-up on uncollectible accounts, such as the use of phone calls, letters, or collection agencies.

Response #3: Research (1 point)

Paragraph Reference Answer: AU 318.24

Guidance: AU 318.24 states, "When, in accordance with paragraph .117 of section 314, *Understanding the Entity and Its Environment and Assessing the Risks of Material Misstatement,* the auditor has determined that it is not possible or practicable to reduce the detection risks at the relevant assertion level to an acceptably low level with audit evidence obtained only from substantive procedures, he or she should perform tests of controls to obtain audit evidence about their operating effectiveness. For example, as discussed in paragraphs .119 and .120 of section 314, the auditor may find it impossible to design effective substantive procedures that by themselves provide sufficient appropriate audit evidence at the relevant assertion level when an entity conducts its business using information technology (IT) and no documentation of transactions is produced or maintained, other than through the IT system."

(5729)

Solution 23-9

Response #1: Disbursements Cycle (9 points)

The internal control procedures that most likely would provide reasonable assurance that specific control objectives for the financial statement assertions regarding purchases and accounts payable will be achieved are:

1. Proper **authorization of requisitions** by department head is required before purchase orders are prepared.

2. Purchasing department assures that **requisitions are within budget limits** before purchase orders are prepared.

3. The adequacy of each **vendor's** past record as a supplier is **verified**.

4. Secure facilities **limit access** to the goods during the receiving activity.

5. Receiving department makes a **blind count** of the goods received, independently of any other department.

Internal control activities

Objective write-off criteria should be established and **follow-up procedures** should be implemented such as the use of phone calls, letters, and collection agencies.

6. The requisitioning department head **independently verifies** the quantity and quality of the goods received.

7. **Requisitions, purchase orders,** and **receiving reports** are **matched with vendor invoices** as to quantity and price.

8. Accounts payable department **recomputes** the **mathematical accuracy** of each **invoice**.

9. The **voucher register** is **independently reconciled** to the **control accounts monthly**.

10. All **supporting documentation is required** for payment and is made available to the treasurer.

11. The purchasing, receiving, and accounts payable **functions are segregated**.

Response #2: Research (1 point)

Paragraph Reference Answer: AU 314.30

Guidance: AU 314.30 states, "Business risk is broader than the risk of material misstatement of the financial statements, although it includes the latter. For example, a new entrant to the marketplace with the competitive advantage of brand recognition and economies of scale may represent a business risk to a manufacturer's ability to garner as much shelf space at retailers and compete on price. The potential risk of material misstatement of the financial statements related to such business risk might be obsolescence or overproduction of inventory that could only be sold at discounted amounts. Business risk particularly may arise from change or complexity, although a failure to recognize the need for change may also give rise to risk. Change may arise, for example, from the development of new products that may fail; from an inadequate market, even if successfully developed; or from flaws that may result in liabilities and reputation risk. As an example of complexity, the conduct and management of long-term engineering projects (such as ship construction or the building of a suspension bridge) give rise to risks in the areas of percentage of completion, pricing, costing, design, and performance control. An understanding of business risks increases the likelihood of identifying risks of material misstatement. However, the auditor does not have a responsibility to identify or assess all business risks."

(5730)

Solution 23-10

Young Computer Outlets, Inc.
Payroll
Internal Control Questionnaire

Question	Yes	No

1. Are **payroll changes** (hires, separations, salary changes, overtime, bonuses, promotions, etc.) properly **authorized and approved**?

2. Are discretionary payroll **deductions and withholdings authorized** in writing by employees?

3. Are the employees who perform each of the following payroll functions **independent** of the other five functions?

- **personnel and approval of payroll changes**
- **preparation** of payroll data
- **approval** of payroll
- **signing** of paychecks
- **distribution** of paychecks
- **reconciliation** of payroll account

4. Are changes in standard data on which payroll is based (hires, separations, salary changes, promotions, deduction and withholding changes, etc.) **promptly input** to the system to process the payroll?

5. Is gross pay determined by using **authorized salary rates and time and attendance records**?

6. Is there a **suitable chart of accounts** and/or established guidelines for determining salary account distribution and for recording payroll withholding liabilities?

7. Are **clerical operations** in payroll preparation **verified**?

8. Is **payroll preparation and recording reviewed** by supervisors or internal audit personnel?

Question	Yes	No

9. Are **payrolls approved** by a responsible official **before** payroll checks are **issued**?

10. Are payrolls disbursed through an **imprest account**?

11. Is the payroll **bank account reconciled monthly** to the general ledger?

12. Are payroll **bank reconciliations** properly **approved** and differences promptly followed up?

13. Is the custody and follow-up of **unclaimed salary checks** assigned to a responsible official?

14. Are **differences reported by employees followed up on a timely basis** by persons not involved in payroll preparation?

15. Are there **procedures** (e.g., tickler files) to assure **proper and timely payment of withholdings** to appropriate bodies and to file required information returns?

16. Are employee **compensation records reconciled to control accounts**?

17. Is **access** to personnel and payroll records, checks, forms, signature plates, etc. **limited**?

Paragraph Reference Answer: AU 314.14

Guidance: AU 314.14 states, "The members of the audit team, including the auditor with final responsibility for the audit, should discuss the susceptibility of the entity's financial statements to material misstatements. This discussion could be held concurrently with the discussion among the audit team that is specified by to discuss the susceptibility of the entity's financial statements to fraud. When the entire engagement is performed by a single auditor, the auditor should consider and document the susceptibility of the entity's financial statements to material misstatements. In these circumstances, the auditor should consider other factors that may be necessary in the engagement, such as personnel possessing specialized skills."

(5731)

CHAPTER 24

EVIDENCE & PROCEDURES

CHAPTER 24

EVIDENCE & PROCEDURES

I. Audit Evidence (AU 326, SAS 106)

A. Concept of Audit Evidence

Exhibit 1 ▸ The Third Standard of Fieldwork

> The auditor must obtain sufficient appropriate audit evidence by performing audit procedures to afford a reasonable basis for an opinion regarding the financial statements under audit.

1. **Definition** *Audit evidence* is all the information used by the auditor in arriving at the conclusions on which the audit opinion is based, including the information contained in the accounting records underlying the financial statements and other information. This includes evidence obtained from audit procedures performed during the audit and may include evidence obtained from other sources, such as prior audits and quality control procedures for client acceptance and continuance.

2. **Sources** Audit evidence should be obtained through testing the accounting records. However, because accounting records alone do not provide sufficient appropriate audit evidence, the auditor should obtain other audit evidence. This may consist of (a) minutes of meetings; (b) confirmations from third parties; (c) industry analysts' reports; (d) comparable data about competitors (benchmarking); (e) controls manuals; (f) information obtained through other audit procedures; and (g) information developed by or available to the auditor that permits the auditor to reach conclusions through valid reasoning.

3. **Accounting Records** Accounting records generally include (a) the records of initial entries and supporting records, such as checks and records of electronic fund transfers; (b) invoices; (c) contracts; (d) the general and subsidiary ledgers, journal entries, and other adjustments to the financial statements that are not reflected in formal journal entries; and (e) records such as worksheets and spreadsheets supporting cost allocations, computations, reconciliations, and disclosures.

B. Sufficient Appropriate Audit Evidence
The auditor should consider the sufficiency and appropriateness of audit evidence to be obtained when assessing risks and designing further audit procedures.

1. **Sufficiency & Appropriateness** *Sufficiency* measures the quantity of audit evidence. *Appropriateness* measures the quality of audit evidence, that is, its relevance and reliability. The quantity of audit evidence needed is affected by the risk of misstatement. This means as risk increases, audit evidence required increases. The quantity also is affected by the quality of such evidence. This means as the quality of evidence increases, the quantity of evidence may be able to be decreased. However, merely obtaining more audit evidence may not compensate for audit evidence of lower quality. The auditor should exercise professional judgment and professional skepticism in evaluating the sufficiency and appropriateness of audit evidence to support the audit opinion.

   a. **Relevance** Certain audit procedures may provide relevant audit evidence pertaining to some assertions and not others. The auditor can not substitute audit evidence related to a specific assertion for evidence concerning another assertion; that is, the evidence must be relevant to the assertion it supports.

b. **Reliability** The reliability of audit evidence is dependent on its source, nature, and the circumstances under which it is obtained. While recognizing that exceptions may exist, the following generalizations can be made:

(1) Audit evidence is more reliable when it is obtained from knowledgeable independent sources outside the entity.

(2) Internally generated audit evidence is more reliable when the related internal controls are effective.

(3) Audit evidence obtained directly by the auditor is more reliable than evidence obtained indirectly or by inference.

(4) Audit evidence is more reliable when it exists in documentary form (paper, electronic, or other medium).

(5) Audit evidence provided by original documents is more reliable than audit evidence provided by photocopies or facsimiles.

2. **Accuracy & Completeness** The auditor should obtain audit evidence about the accuracy and completeness of information produced by the entity's information system when that information is used in performing audit procedures. For example, if the auditor uses data obtained from the entity's information system in performing analytical procedures, the auditor should obtain audit evidence concerning the accuracy and completeness of that data.

3. **Corroborative Evidence** The auditor ordinarily obtains more assurance from consistent audit evidence obtained from different sources or of a different nature than from items of audit evidence considered individually. For example, corroborating information obtained from a source independent of the entity may increase the assurance the auditor obtains from a management representation.

4. **Cost Constraints** The relationship between the cost of obtaining audit evidence and the usefulness of the information may be considered. However, the degree of difficulty or expense involved in testing a particular item is not, by itself, a valid basis for omitting the procedure for which there is no appropriate alternative.

5. **Persuasive Evidence** The auditor may need to rely on audit evidence that is persuasive rather than conclusive. However, to obtain reasonable assurance, the auditor must not be satisfied with audit evidence that is less than persuasive.

C. **Use of Assertions in Obtaining Audit Evidence**

1. **Nature of Assertions** Assertions are representations made by management that are embodied in the financial statements being audited. Assertions used by the auditor fall into the following categories:

a. **Classes of Transactions & Events** The following assertions are relevant to classes of transactions and events:

(1) **Occurrence** Transactions and events that have been recorded have occurred and pertain to the entity.

(2) **Completeness** All transactions and events that should have been recorded have been recorded.

(3) **Accuracy** Amounts and other data relating to recorded transactions and events have been recorded appropriately.

        (4)   **Cutoff** Transactions and events have been recorded in the correct accounting period.

        (5)   **Classification** Transactions and events have been recorded in the proper accounts.

    b.   **Account Balances** The following assertions are relevant to ending account balances:

        (1)   **Existence** Assets, liabilities, and equity interests actually exist.

        (2)   **Rights & Obligations** The entity holds or controls the rights to assets, and liabilities are the obligations of the entity.

        (3)   **Completeness** All assets, liabilities, and equity interests that should have been recorded have been recorded.

        (4)   **Valuation & Allocation** Assets, liabilities, and equity interests are included in the financial statements at appropriate amounts and any resulting valuation or allocation adjustments are recorded appropriately.

    c.   **Presentation & Disclosure** The following assertions are relevant to the presentation and disclosure in the financial statements:

        (1)   **Occurrence & Rights & Obligations** Disclosed events and transactions have occurred and pertain to the entity.

        (2)   **Completeness** All disclosures that should have been included in the financial statements have been included.

        (3)   **Classification & Understandability** Financial information is appropriately presented and described and disclosures are clearly expressed.

        (4)   **Accuracy & Valuation** Financial and other information are disclosed fairly and at appropriate amounts.

2.   **Relevant Assertions** The auditor should use relevant assertions in assessing risks by considering the different types of potential misstatements that may occur, and then designing further audit procedures that are responsive to the assessed risks. To identify relevant assertions, the auditor should determine the source of likely potential misstatements in each significant class of transactions, account balance, and presentation and disclosure. In determining whether a particular assertion is relevant, the auditor should evaluate:

    a.   The nature of the assertion

    b.   The volume of transactions or data related to the assertion

    c.   The nature and complexity of the systems by which the entity processes and controls information supporting the assertion

D.   **Audit Procedures for Obtaining Audit Evidence**

1.   **Procedures** The auditor should obtain audit evidence to draw reasonable conclusions on which to base the opinion by performing the following procedures:

    a.   **Risk Assessment Procedures** Obtain an understanding of the entity and its environment, including its internal control, to assess the risks of material misstatement at the financial statement and relevant assertion levels. Risk assessment procedures must be supplemented by tests of controls, when necessary, and substantive procedures.

b. **Tests of Controls** When necessary, or when the auditor has determined to do so, test the operating effectiveness of controls in preventing or detecting material misstatements at the relevant assertion level. Tests of controls are necessary in two circumstances. When the auditor's risk assessment includes an expectation of the operating effectiveness of controls, the auditor should test those controls to support the risk assessment. Also, when the substantive procedures alone do not provide sufficient appropriate audit evidence, the auditor should perform tests of controls to obtain audit evidence about the operating effectiveness of IC.

c. **Substantive Procedures** Substantive procedures detect material misstatements at the relevant assertion level through tests of details and substantive analytical procedures. The auditor should design and perform substantive procedures for all relevant assertions related to each material class of transactions, account balance, and disclosure regardless of the assessed risk of material misstatement.

2. **Types of Procedures** The following procedures, or combinations of them, may be used as risk assessment procedures, test of controls, or substantive procedures, depending on the context in which they are applied: (a) inspection of records or documents; (b) inspection of tangible assets; (c) observation; (d) inquiry; (e) confirmation; (f) recalculation; (g) reperformance; or (h) analytics.

E. **Evaluating Audit Evidence (SAS 110 continued)**

1. **Risk Assessments** The auditor should determine, based on audit evidence obtained, whether the risk assessments at the relevant assertion level are still appropriate.

2. **Planned Audit Procedures** As an audit is a cumulative and iterative process, audit evidence obtained during the audit may cause the auditor to change the nature, timing, or extent of other planned audit procedures. Such evidence may indicate that risk assessments need to be revised. In this case, the auditor should reevaluate the planned audit procedures based on the revised risk assessments for all or some relevant assertions.

a. **Deviations From Controls** If deviations are detected in testing the operating effectiveness of controls, the auditor should make specific inquiries to understand these deviations and their potential consequences. The auditor also should consider whether any detected misstatements change the auditor's judgment of the effectiveness of related controls. Furthermore, the auditor should determine whether: (1) reliance on the controls is appropriate based on the tests of controls performed, (2) additional tests of controls are necessary, or (3) the potential risks need to be addressed using substantive procedures.

b. **Fraud or Error** The auditor cannot assume that an instance of fraud or error is an isolated occurrence; thus, the auditor should consider how that instance affects the assessed risks of material misstatement. The auditor should determine whether audit risk has been reduced to an appropriately low level and whether the nature, timing, and extent of audit procedures need to be reconsidered.

3. **Developing an Opinion** The auditor should use professional judgment to conclude whether sufficient appropriate audit evidence has been obtained to reduce the risk of material misstatement in the financial statements to an appropriately low level. The auditor should evaluate all relevant audit evidence, regardless of whether it supports or contradicts the relevant assertions, when developing an opinion on the financial statements. If the auditor is unable to obtain sufficient appropriate audit evidence, the auditor should express a qualified opinion or a disclaimer of opinion.

II. Internal Audit Function (AU 322, SAS 65)

    A.   Internal Auditors
An external auditor usually will perform financial audits to enable the auditor to attest to the fairness of an entity's financial statements. Internal auditors also may perform financial audits as well as procedural and operational audits beyond the scope of the external audit. Therefore, a comprehensive internal audit program may be more detailed and cover more areas than an independent auditor's program.

        1.   External Auditor The auditor maintains independence from the entity to fulfill the responsibility to obtain sufficient appropriate audit evidence matter to provide a reasonable basis for the opinion on the entity's financial statements.

        2.   Internal Auditor Internal auditors maintain objectivity with respect to the activity being audited to fulfill the responsibility for providing analyses, evaluations, recommendations, and other information to the entity's management and board of directors or to others with equivalent authority.

    B.   Internal Audit
When obtaining an understanding of internal control, the auditor should obtain an understanding of the internal audit function sufficient to identify those internal audit activities that are relevant to planning the audit.

        1.   Procedures The auditor ordinarily should make inquiries of appropriate management and internal audit personnel about the internal auditors' (a) organizational status within the entity; (b) application of professional standards; (c) audit plan, including the nature, timing, and extent of audit work; (d) access to records; and (e) whether there are limitations on the scope of their activities.

        2.   Relevance Internal audit activities relevant to an audit of the entity's financial statements are those that provide evidence about the design and effectiveness of internal control policies and procedures that pertain to the entity's ability to record, process, summarize, and report financial data consistent with the assertions embodied in the financial statements, or that provide direct evidence about potential misstatements of such data. The following procedures help the auditor assess the relevancy of internal audit activities: (a) considering knowledge from prior year audits, (b) reviewing how the internal auditors allocate their audit resources to financial or operating areas in response to their risk assessment process, and (c) obtaining detailed information about the scope of internal audit activities.

        3.   Consideration of Internal Auditors' Work The auditor may conclude that some of the internal auditors' activities are relevant to the audit and that it would be efficient to consider how the internal auditors' work might affect the nature, timing, and extent of audit procedures. In that case, the auditor should assess the competence and objectivity of the internal auditors in light of the intended effect of the internal auditors' work on the audit.

           a.   Competence

               (1)   Education level and professional experience

               (2)   Professional certification and continuing education

               (3)   Evaluation of internal auditors' performance

               (4)   Supervision and review of internal auditors' activities

               (5)   Quality of working paper documentation, reports, and recommendations

     b.   **Objectivity**

        (1)   The organizational status of the internal auditor

        (2)   The organizational level to which the internal auditor reports (the higher, the more objective)

        (3)   Amount of access to the board of directors or audit committee

        (4)   Whether the board of directors, the audit committee, or the owner-manager oversees employment of the internal auditors

        (5)   Policies to maintain internal auditor's objectivity about areas audited

4.   **Coordination With Internal Auditors** Work is coordinated by (a) holding periodic meetings, (b) scheduling audit work, (c) arranging access to internal auditors' working papers, (d) reviewing audit reports, and (e) discussing possible audit issues.

5.   **Effectiveness of Internal Auditors' Work** Involves determining whether the scope of work is appropriate; audit programs are adequate; working papers adequately document work performed, including evidence of supervision and review; conclusions are appropriate; and reports are consistent with the results of the work performed.

C.   **Direct Assistance**
If the internal auditors provide direct assistance, the auditor should inform the internal auditors of their responsibilities, the objectives of the procedures, and matters that may affect the nature, timing, and extent of audit procedures.

    1.   **Supervision** The external auditor should assess the internal auditors' competence and objectivity, and supervise, review, evaluate, and test the work performed. The external auditor should test the internal auditors' work by examining some of the controls, transactions, or balances that the internal auditors examined, or similar evidence not actually examined by the internal auditors.

    2.   **Guidance** The internal auditors also should be informed of the need to bring all significant accounting and auditing issues identified to the external auditor's attention.

III. Management Representations (AU 333, SAS 85)

A.   **Written Representations**
In order to comply with GAAS, the auditor must obtain certain written representations from management. These are part of the audit evidence but are not a substitute for the application of auditing procedures. Written representations (1) confirm the oral representations that were given to the auditor during the engagement, (2) serve as documentation of the continuing appropriateness of the representations, and (3) reduce the chance of misunderstanding concerning matters covered by the representations.

    1.   **Corroboration** The auditor frequently performs auditing procedures in order to corroborate the substance of the written representations. In some cases, however, there cannot be any corroboration.

    2.   **Reliance** It is reasonable for the auditor to rely on the written representations of management unless audit procedures provide audit evidence that indicates otherwise. However, the auditor must maintain an appropriate level of professional skepticism.

    3.   **Contradictory Evidence** In cases where management representations are contradicted by other audit evidence, the auditor should investigate the circumstances and consider the reliability of the representations being made. Based on the circumstances, the auditor should consider whether reliance on management's representations relating to other aspects of the financial statements is appropriate and justified.

4. **Update** An updating management representation letter should state (a) whether any information has come to management's attention that would cause them to believe that any of the previous representations should be modified, and (b) whether any events have occurred subsequent to the balance sheet date of the latest financial statements reported on by the auditor that would require adjustment to or disclosure in those financial statements. An auditor should obtain updating representation letters from management in the following circumstances:

   a. **Reissuance** When a predecessor auditor is requested by a former client to reissue the report on the financial statements of a prior period that are to be presented on a comparative basis with audited financial statements of a subsequent period.

   b. **SEC Filings** When performing subsequent events procedures in connection with filings under the Securities Act of 1933.

B. **Requirements**
Written representations from management must be obtained for all financial statements and periods covered by the auditor's report. For example, when comparative financial statements are presented, the written representations obtained at the completion of the most recent audit should address all periods being presented. Representations specifically required for all audits are noted in the sample representation letter in Exhibit 2.

1. **Adapt** The specific written representations obtained by the auditor depend on the circumstances of the particular engagement and the nature and basis of the financial statement presentation (e.g., whether the financial statements are based on GAAP or OCBOA). The representation letter ordinarily is tailored to include additional appropriate representations from management relating to matters specific to the entity's business or industry.

2. **Duration** If current management was not present during all periods covered by the auditor's report, the auditor should still obtain written representations from current management on all such periods.

3. **Subsidiary** If the independent auditor performs an audit of the financial statements of a subsidiary, but does not audit those of the parent company, the auditor may want to obtain representations from management of the parent company concerning matters that may affect the subsidiary (for instance, related-party transactions or the parent company's intention to provide continuing financial support to the subsidiary).

4. **Address** The written representations should be addressed to the auditor.

5. **Dates** The representations should be made as of the date of the auditor's report. If the auditor *dual dates* the report, the auditor should consider whether obtaining additional representations relating to the subsequent event is appropriate.

6. **Signatures** The letter should be signed by those members of management with overall responsibility for financial and operating matters whom the auditor believes are responsible for and knowledgeable about (directly or through others in the organization) the matters covered by the representations. Such members of management normally include the chief executive officer and chief financial officer (or others with equivalent positions in the entity). In certain circumstances, the auditor may want to obtain written representations from other individuals. For example, the auditor may want to obtain written representations about the completeness of the minutes of the meetings of stockholders, directors, and committees of directors from the person responsible for keeping such minutes.

Exhibit 2 ▶ Management Representation Letter

[*Date*]

To [*Independent Auditor*]

We are providing this letter in connection with your audit(s) of the [*identification of financial statements*] of [*name of entity*] as of [*dates*] and for the [*period*s] for the purpose of expressing an opinion as to whether the [*consolidated*] financial statements present fairly, in all material respects, the financial position, results of operations, and cash flows of [*name of entity*] in conformity with accounting principles generally accepted in the United States of America. We confirm that we are responsible for the fair presentation in the [*consolidated*] financial statements of financial position, results of operations, and cash flows in conformity with generally accepted accounting principles.

Certain representations in this letter are described as being limited to matters that are material. Items are considered material, regardless of size, if they involve an omission or misstatement of accounting information that, in the light of surrounding circumstances, makes it probable that the judgment of a reasonable person relying on the information would be changed or influenced by the omission or misstatement.

We confirm, to the best of our knowledge and belief, [*as of (**date of auditor's report**)*,] the following representations made to you during your audit(s).

1. The financial statements referred to above are fairly presented in conformity with accounting principles generally accepted in the United States of America.

2. We have made available to you all

    a. Financial records and related data

    b. Minutes of the meetings of stockholders, directors, and committees of directors, or summaries of actions of recent meetings for which minutes have not yet been prepared

3. There have been no communications from regulatory agencies concerning noncompliance with or deficiencies in financial reporting practices.

4. There are no material transactions that have not been properly recorded in the accounting records underlying the financial statements.

5. We believe that the effects of the uncorrected financial statement misstatements summarized in the accompanying schedule are immaterial, both individually and in the aggregate, to the financial statements taken as a whole.

6. We acknowledge our responsibility for the design and implementation of programs and controls to prevent and detect fraud.

7. We have no knowledge of any fraud or suspected fraud affecting the entity involving

    a. Management

    b. Employees who have significant roles in internal control

    c. Others where the fraud could have a material effect on the financial statements

8. We have no knowledge of any allegations of fraud or suspected fraud affecting the entity received in communications from employees, former employees, analysts, regulators, short sellers, or others.

9. The company has no plans or intentions that may materially affect the carrying value or classification of assets and liabilities.

10. The following have been properly recorded or disclosed in the financial statements:

    a. Related-party transactions, including sales, purchases, loans, transfers, leasing arrangements, and guarantees, and amounts receivable from or payable to related parties

    b. Guarantees, whether written or oral, under which the company is contingently liable

    c. Significant estimates and material concentrations known to management that are required to be disclosed in accordance with Financial Accounting Standards Board (FASB) *Accounting Standards Codification* (ASC) 275, *Risks and Uncertainties*. [*Significant estimates are estimates at the balance sheet date that could change materially within the next year. Concentrations refer to volumes of business, revenues, available sources of supply, or markets or geographic areas for which events could occur that would significantly disrupt normal finances within the next year.*]

11. There are no

    a. Violations or possible violations of laws or regulations whose effects should be considered for disclosure in the financial statements or as a basis for recording a loss contingency

    b. Unasserted claims or assessments that our lawyer has advised us are probable of assertion and must be disclosed in accordance with FASB ASC 450, *Contingencies*

    c. Other liabilities or gain or loss contingencies that are required to be accrued or disclosed by FASB ASC 450

12. The company has satisfactory title to all owned assets, and there are no liens or encumbrances on such assets nor has any asset been pledged as collateral.

13. The company has complied with all aspects of contractual agreements that would have a material effect on the financial statements in the event of noncompliance.

[*Add additional representations that are unique to the entity's business or industry.*]

To the best of our knowledge and belief, no events have occurred subsequent to the balance sheet date and through the date of this letter that would require adjustment to or disclosure in the aforementioned financial statements.

_____

[*Name of Chief Executive Officer and Title*]

_____

[*Name of Chief Financial Officer and Title*]

C. Materiality

Management's representations may be limited to matters that are considered either individually or collectively material to the financial statements, provided management and the auditor have reached an understanding on materiality for this purpose. Materiality may be different for different representations. A discussion of materiality may be included explicitly in the representation letter, in either qualitative or quantitative terms. Materiality considerations would not apply to those representations that are not directly related to amounts included in the financial statements. In addition, because of the possible effects on other aspects of the audit, materiality would not be relevant with respect to knowledge of fraud or suspected fraud involving management or those employees who have significant roles in internal control.

D. Scope Limitation

Management's refusal to furnish written representations constitutes a limitation on the scope of the audit sufficient to preclude an unqualified opinion and ordinarily is sufficient to cause an auditor to disclaim an opinion on the financial statements or withdraw from the engagement. Further, the auditor should consider the effects of the refusal on the reliability of other management representations.

1. **Qualified Opinion** Based on the nature of the representations not obtained or the circumstances of the refusal, the auditor may conclude that a qualified opinion is appropriate.

2. **Audit Procedures Restricted** If the auditor is precluded from performing procedures that are necessary in the circumstances with respect to a matter that is material to the financial statements, even though management has given representations concerning the matter, there is a limitation on the scope of the audit. In this case, the auditor should qualify or disclaim an opinion.

IV. Analytics (AU 329, SAS 56)

A. Overview

Analytics, or analytical procedures, consist of evaluations of financial information made by a study of plausible relationships among both financial and nonfinancial data. The procedures range from simple comparisons to complex models. To utilize analytics effectively, the auditor must understand financial relationships and have knowledge of the client and its industry.

1. **Purpose**

    a. To assist the auditor in **planning** the nature, timing, and extent of substantive tests. (This is **required** by GAAS.) Analytics should focus on enhancing the auditor's understanding of the client's business and the transactions and events that have occurred since the last audit date, and identifying areas that may represent specific risks relevant to the audit. Analytical procedures used in planning the audit generally use data aggregated at a high level.

    b. As a substantive test to obtain audit evidence about particular assertions related to account balances or classes of transactions. (**Not** required by GAAS, but commonly used.)

    c. As an overall **review** of the financial information in the final review stage of the audit. (This also is **required** by GAAS.)

2. **Expectations** Analytics involve comparisons of recorded amounts, or ratios developed from recorded amounts, to expectations developed by the auditor. The auditor develops expectations by identifying relationships that reasonably are expected to exist from understanding the client and the industry in which the client operates. The following are examples of sources of information for developing expectations:

    a. Financial information for comparable prior periods giving consideration to known changes

    b. Anticipated results; for example, forecasts including extrapolations from interim data

    c. Relationships among elements of financial information within the period

    d. Information regarding the industry in which the client operates; for example, gross margin information

    e. Relationships of financial information with relevant nonfinancial information

3. **Benford's Law** Application of Benford's Law is an example of a complex analytical procedure. Benford's Law is a numerical probability theory establishing the frequency of the appearance of digits in naturally occurring sets of numbers. A common assumption is that in a sample of numbers from any population, all numbers have an equal probability of appearing. Many people do not create convincing dummy data sets because they are unaware of

the unequal probability of the appearance of numbers 1 through 9. Benford's Law predicts the following approximate frequencies of occurrence as first digits: 1, 30%; 2, 18%; 3, 12%; 4, 10%; 5, 8%; 6, 7%; 7, 6%; 8, 5%; and 9, 4%. (The law predicts more, but that level of detail is beyond this discussion.) Large and varied populations of numbers adhere more closely to the distribution predicted by Benford's Law than small samples.

Exhibit 3 ▶ Benford's Law

> A manager's ceiling for invoice approval is $5,000. Anomalies in the occurrence of 5, 6, 7, 8, and 9 as first digits would be expected. A higher than expected level of occurrence of 4 as a first digit (i.e., invoices at $4,001 to $4,999) suggest that purchases were intentionally divided into component parts to avoid higher level approval procedures. If 4 occurs more frequently than expected, the manager's spending warrants further scrutiny.

    a. Seemingly divergent sets of numbers (such as utility bills of a given region, numbers on a newspaper page, and sport statistics) all adhere to Benford's Law. Computer software based on Benford's Law is a powerful device for detecting financial errors (including those due to software bugs), as well as fraud.

    b. False positives do occur. Innocent anomalies can be created by "unnatural" external factors. Thresholds and ceilings are some factors that may cause anomalies. For instance, an HMO's fee schedule can create clustering, and hence, noncompliant number repetition, in a medical office's billing.

B. Used in Overall Review

Analytics are used in the overall review stage to assist the auditor in assessing conclusions reached and in evaluating the overall financial statement presentation. The overall review generally would include reading the financial statements and notes and considering the adequacy of evidence gathered in response to unusual or unexpected balances identified in planning the audit or in the course of the audit, and unusual or unexpected balances or relationships that were not identified previously. The results of an overall review may indicate that additional evidence may be needed. Also, use of analytics in the overall review helps the auditor in the going concern assessment.

C. Used as Substantive Tests

The auditor's reliance on substantive tests to achieve an audit objective related to a particular assertion (management representation) may be derived from tests of details, from analytics, or from a combination of both.

    1. Effectiveness & Efficiency The expected effectiveness and efficiency of an analytical procedure in identifying potential misstatements depends on, among other things, the nature of the assertion, the plausibility and predictability of the relationship, the availability and reliability of the data used to develop the expectation, and the precision of the expectation. For example, the auditor may use inventory turnover figures to evaluate inventory salability.

    2. Significant Differences In planning the analytical procedures used as substantive tests, the auditor should consider the amount of difference from the expectation that can be accepted without further investigation. The auditor should evaluate significant unexpected differences. If an explanation for a difference cannot be obtained, the auditor should obtain sufficient evidence about the assertion by performing other audit procedures to determine whether the difference is likely to be a misstatement.

D. Plausibility, Predictability & Precision

A basic premise underlying the application of analytics is that plausible relationships among data reasonably may be expected to exist and continue in the absence of known conditions to the contrary. The expectation should be precise enough to provide the desired level of assurance that differences that may be potential material misstatements, individually or when aggregated with other misstatements, would be identified for the auditor to investigate. The auditor's identification and consideration of factors that significantly affect the amount being audited and the level of detail of data used to develop expectations affect the precision of the expectations. Greater detail of data increases reliability of expectations. For example, using monthly amounts generally will be more effective than annual amounts.

1. Relationships are more predictable in a stable environment, while relationships in a dynamic environment lose predictability.

2. Relationships involving income statement accounts usually are more predictable than those involving only balance sheet accounts because income statement accounts represent transactions over a period, while balance sheet accounts represent amounts as of a point in time.

E. Reliability

The reliability of the data used by the auditor to develop expectations should be appropriate for the desired level of assurance from the analytical procedures. The auditor should assess the reliability of the data by considering the source of the data and the conditions under which it was gathered. The following factors influence the auditor's consideration of the reliability of data:

1. Whether the data was obtained from independent sources outside the entity or from sources within the entity

2. Whether sources within the entity were independent of those who are responsible for the amount being audited

3. Whether the data was developed under a reliable system with adequate controls

4. Whether the data was subjected to audit testing in the current or prior year

5. Whether the expectations were developed using data from a variety of sources

V. Using a Specialist's Work (AU 336, SAS 73)

A. Decision to Use a Specialist's Work

The auditor is not expected to have the expertise of a person trained for, or qualified to engage in, the practice of another profession or occupation. An auditor may encounter complex or subjective matters that may require special skill or knowledge and require using the work of a specialist to obtain appropriate audit evidence. Examples of the types of matters that may decide the auditor to use the work of a specialist include:

1. **Valuation** Valuation (i.e., special-purpose inventories, high-technology materials or equipment, pharmaceutical products, complex financial instruments, real estate, restricted securities, works of art, and environmental contingencies)

2. **Specialized Techniques** Determination of quantities or amounts derived by using specialized techniques or methods (i.e., actuarial determinations for employee benefits obligations and disclosures, and determination of insurance loss reserves)

3. **Interpretation** Interpretation of technical requirements, regulations, or agreements (i.e., the potential significance of contracts or other legal documents, or legal title to property)

B. Selection

The auditor should evaluate the professional qualifications of the specialist to determine that the specialist possesses the necessary skill or knowledge in the particular field.

1. **Definition** A specialist is a person (or firm) possessing special skill or knowledge in a particular field other than accounting or auditing. Specialists include, but are not limited to, actuaries, appraisers, engineers, environmental consultants, and geologists. Additionally, an attorney engaged in situations other than to provide services to a client concerning litigation, claims, or assessments is considered a specialist.

    2.   Considerations

        a.   The professional certification, license, or other recognition of competence

        b.   The reputation and standing of the specialist in the views of peers and others

        c.   The specialist's experience in the type of work under consideration

    3.   Engaged by Management Management may engage or employ a specialist and the auditor may use that specialist's work as audit evidence in performing substantive tests to evaluate material financial statement assertions. Alternatively, management may engage a specialist employed by the auditor's firm to provide advisory services.

    4.   Engaged by Auditor The auditor may engage a specialist and use that specialist's work as audit evidence in performing substantive tests to evaluate material financial statement assertions.

C.   Understanding
The auditor should obtain an understanding of the nature of the work performed or to be performed by the specialist. This understanding should cover the following:

    1.   Appropriateness, Objectives & Scope of the Specialist's Work The appropriateness of using the specialist's work for the intended purpose.

    2.   Specialist's Relationship to Client The auditor should evaluate circumstances that might impair the objectivity of the specialist. Such circumstances include situations in which the client has the ability (through employment, family relationship, or otherwise) to control, directly or indirectly, or significantly influence the specialist.

        a.   **No Relationship** The specialist's work usually will provide the auditor with greater assurance when there is no relationship.

        b.   **Relationship** The auditor should assess the risk that the specialist's objectivity might be impaired. If the relationship might impair the specialist's objectivity, the auditor should perform additional procedures or engage another specialist.

    3.   Methods Used The appropriateness and reasonableness of methods and assumptions used and their application are the responsibility of the specialist.

        a.   The auditor should obtain an understanding to determine whether the findings are suitable for corroborating the assertions in the financial statements. The auditor should consider whether the specialist's findings support the related assertions in the financial statements and make appropriate tests of data provided to the specialist.

        b.   Ordinarily, the auditor would use the work of the specialist unless the auditor believes that the findings are unreasonable, in which case, the auditor should apply additional procedures.

    4.   Comparison of Methods or Assumptions With Those Used in Preceding Period

    5.   Form & Content of a Specialist's Findings

D.   Auditor's Conclusions
If the auditor determines that the specialist's findings support the related assertions in the financial statements, the auditor may reasonably conclude that sufficient appropriate audit evidence has been obtained.

    1.   Indeterminate If there is a material difference between the specialist's findings and the assertions in the financial statements, the auditor should apply additional procedures. If the auditor is unable to resolve the matter, the auditor should obtain the opinion of another specialist, unless it appears that the matter cannot be resolved. A matter that has not been resolved ordinarily will cause the auditor to qualify the opinion or disclaim an opinion.

2. **Disagreement** The auditor may conclude that the assertions in the financial statements are not in conformity with GAAP. In that event, the auditor expresses a qualified or adverse opinion.

E. **Effect on Auditor's Report**
Normally, the auditor should not refer to the work or findings of the specialist. Such a reference might be misunderstood to be a qualification of the auditor's opinion or a division of responsibility, neither of which is intended. Further, there may be an inference that the auditor making such reference performed a more thorough audit than an auditor not making such reference. Reporting alternatives are:

1. **Unqualified Opinion, Standard Report** No reference to the specialist

2. **Unqualified Opinion, Explanatory Paragraph Added to Report** Refer to specialist in explanatory paragraph **only** if doing so will help clarify the reason for the explanatory paragraph.

3. **Qualified or Disclaimer of Opinion** Scope limitation, the auditor is unable to obtain sufficient appropriate audit evidence—no reference to the specialist

4. **Qualified or Adverse Opinion** Auditor concludes there is a departure from GAAP—refer to specialist in explanatory paragraph only if doing so will help clarify the reason for the qualification or adverse opinion.

VI. Inquiry of Client's Lawyer (AU 337, SAS 12)

A. **Accounting**
Management has the responsibility to adopt policies and procedures that will identify, evaluate, and account for litigation, claims, and assessments as a basis for the preparation of financial statements in conformity with GAAP.

B. **Auditing**
The auditor should obtain audit evidence relating to (1) the existence of conditions or circumstances that indicate a possible loss from litigation, claims, and assessments, (2) the period in which the underlying cause for legal action occurred, (3) the probability of an unfavorable outcome, and (4) the amount or range of the potential loss.

1. **Procedures** Management is the primary source of information. The auditor should perform the following:

    a. Inquire of, and discuss with, management the client's policies and procedures for identifying, evaluating, and accounting for litigation, claims, and assessments.

    b. Obtain from management a description and evaluation of litigation, claims, and assessments that existed at the balance sheet date and to the date until management furnishes the information. Further, the auditor should obtain assurance, in writing, that the client disclosed all matters that are required to be disclosed FASB ASC 450, *Contingencies.*

    c. Examine appropriate documents in the possession of the client that relate to these contingencies, including correspondence and invoices from lawyers.

     d.   Obtain assurance from management, ordinarily in writing, that it has disclosed all unasserted claims the lawyer feels are probable of assertion and that must be disclosed in accordance with FASB ASC 450, *Contingencies*.

         (1)   **Inform Lawyer** With the **client's permission,** the auditor should inform the lawyer that the client has given the auditor this assurance.

         (2)   **Other Audit Procedures** The auditor will find that some of the regular audit procedures (e.g., reading the minutes of the board of directors meetings, sending bank confirmations, reading contracts and loan agreements, and inspecting documents for guarantees by the client) also may disclose possible litigation, claims, and assessments.

2.   **Letter of Audit Inquiry to Client's Lawyer** The auditor should request client management to send a letter of inquiry to those lawyers consulted by management concerning litigation, claims, and assessments (however, the letter should be mailed physically by the auditor). This serves to corroborate the information furnished by management. Additionally, this corroboration may be provided by information from inside legal counsel. However, such information is not a substitute for information that outside counsel refuses to furnish.

Exhibit 4 ▶ Sample Inquiry Letter to Legal Counsel

In connection with an audit of our financial statements at (balance sheet date) and for the (period) then ended, management of the Company has prepared, and furnished to our auditors (name and address of auditors), a description and evaluation of certain contingencies, including those set forth below involving matters with respect to which you have been engaged and to which you have devoted substantive attention on behalf of the Company in the form of legal consultation or representation. These contingencies are regarded by management of the Company as material for this purpose (management may indicate a materiality limit if an understanding has been reached with the auditor). Your response should include matters that existed at (balance sheet date) and during the period from that date to the date of your response.

Pending or Threatened Litigation (excluding unasserted claims)

[Ordinarily the information would include the following: (1) the nature of the litigation, (2) the progress of the case to date, (3) how management is responding or intends to respond to the litigation (for example, to contest the case vigorously or to seek an out-of-court settlement), and (4) an evaluation of the likelihood of an unfavorable outcome and an estimate, if one can be made, of the amount or range of potential loss.] Please furnish to our auditors such explanation, if any, that you consider necessary to supplement the foregoing information, including an explanation of those matters as to which your views may differ from those stated and an identification of the omission of any pending or threatened litigation, claims, and assessments or a statement that the list of such matters is complete.

Unasserted Claims and Assessments (considered by management to be probable of assertion, and that, if asserted, would have at least a reasonable possibility of an unfavorable outcome)

[Ordinarily management's information would include the following: (1) the nature of the matter, (2) how management intends to respond if the claim is asserted, and (3) an evaluation of the likelihood of an unfavorable outcome and an estimate, if one can be made, of the amount or range of potential loss.] Please furnish to our auditors such explanation, if any, that you consider necessary to supplement the foregoing information, including an explanation of those matters as to which your views may differ from those stated.

We understand that whenever, in the course of performing legal services for us with respect to a matter recognized to involve an unasserted possible claim or assessment that may call for financial statement disclosure, if you have formed a professional conclusion that we should disclose or consider disclosure concerning such possible claim or assessment, as a matter of professional responsibility to us, you will so advise us and will consult with us concerning the question of such disclosure and the applicable requirements of Financial Accounting Standards Board *Accounting Standards Codification* 450, *Contingencies*. Please specifically confirm to our auditors that our understanding is correct.

Please specifically identify the nature of and reasons for any limitation on your response.

[The auditor may request the client to inquire about additional matters, for example, unpaid or unbilled charges or specified information on certain contractually assumed obligations of the company, such as guarantees of indebtedness of others.]

a. **Contents** Some of the matters that should be covered in a letter of audit inquiry include:

(1) Identification of the company, subsidiaries, and audit date

(2) A management-prepared list and evaluation of pending or threatened litigation, claims, and assessments with which the lawyer has been substantially involved; if management prefers, they may request the lawyer to prepare the list; the lawyer is asked either to furnish the following information or to comment as to where the lawyer's views differ from management's:

(a) A description of the matter, progress to date, and the action the company plans to take

(b) An evaluation of the likelihood of an unfavorable outcome and, if possible, an estimate of the amount or range of potential loss

(c) An identification of any missing items or a statement that the list is complete

(3) A management-prepared list describing and evaluating unasserted claims and assessments that management considers are probable of assertion and that have at least a reasonable probability of unfavorable outcome. For example, due to client negligence, a customer may have suffered a serious injury. It is possible the client may expect a lawsuit and may have consulted the lawyer in that regard. The lawyer is requested to comment on those areas where the lawyer's views differ from those of management.

(4) A statement that management understands that it will be notified by the lawyer when an unasserted claim or assessment requiring financial disclosure per FASB ASC 450, *Contingencies*, comes to the attention of the lawyer. The communication includes a request that the lawyer confirm this understanding.

(5) A request that the lawyer specifically indicate the nature of, and the reason for, any limitations on the response.

b. **Materiality** No inquiry needs to be made concerning matters not considered material as long as the auditor specifies a materiality amount in the letter.

c. **Conference** If the client's lawyers provide the auditor with the information in a conference, the auditor should document the information received.

> **d.** **Change of Lawyers** If there has been a change or resignation of lawyers, the auditor should consider the need to inquire of the reasons for the change. Lawyers may be required to resign when clients fail to follow their advice on matters of disclosure.
>
> **e.** **Dates** The client's letter should specify the date by which the lawyer's response should be sent to the auditor and also should request the lawyer to specify the effective date of the response. (If the lawyer's response does not specify an effective date, the auditor can assume it is the date of the response.) The latest date of the period covered by the lawyer's response (the "effective date") should be as close as possible to the date of the auditor's report. Consequently, specifying the effective date of the lawyer's response to reasonably approximate the expected date of the auditor's report will in most instances eliminate the need for an updated response from the lawyer.

3. **Lawyer's Response Limited** The lawyer may limit the response to those matters that the lawyer had been involved with substantially and that are considered to be material (provided the lawyer and the auditor have agreed on what will be considered material). The refusal of a lawyer to furnish the information requested in an inquiry letter is a limitation on the scope of the audit that is sufficient to preclude an unqualified opinion if not satisfactorily resolved.

4. **Other Limitations on a Lawyer's Response** Due to the inherent uncertainties present, the lawyer may feel unable to respond to the likelihood of an unfavorable outcome and/or to the amount or range of potential loss on one or more items. The auditor then is faced with an uncertainty that will be resolved in the future but that cannot be reasonably estimated at the present time. If the effect on the financial statements could be material, the auditor may add an explanatory paragraph to the report to emphasize the uncertainty.

5. **Communications Prohibited** The refusal of a client to allow necessary communications with a lawyer is a scope limitation that usually results in a disclaimer of opinion.

VII. Audit Documentation (AU 339, SAS 103)

A. **Overview**
Auditors should prepare and maintain audit documentation, or working papers. Working papers' form and content are designed to meet the circumstances of a particular audit. Audit documentation is the principal record of procedures applied, evidence obtained, and conclusions reached by the auditor. The quantity, type, and content of audit documentation are matters of professional judgment. Audit documentation serves two main purposes. It provides the principal support for (1) the opinion expressed, or disclaimer of opinion, and (2) the representation in the auditor's report that the audit was performed in accordance with U.S. GAAS.

1. **Additional Objectives** Audit documentation serves a number of other purposes:

a. Assists planning and performance of the audit

b. Assists new auditors to an engagement and review the prior year's documentation to understand the work performed as an aid in planning and performing the current engagement

c. Assists supervision and review

d. Demonstrates accountability for procedures performed, evidence examined, and conclusions reached

e. Maintains a record of matters of continuing significance to future audits

f. Enables quality control reviews, and inspections (peer reviews)

g. Assists successor auditors who review a predecessor auditor's workpapers

2. **Tick Marks** Auditors often use a mark to refer the reader of a schedule or other working paper to a note that is applicable to more than one item on the working paper. In this way, a note only has to be written once, rather than each time it is applicable. Thus, these "tick marks" merely are abbreviated notes. There is no industry-wide standard for tick marks, so a legend indicating what each mark signifies (similar to a map legend) is important for complete documentation.

3. **Ownership** Audit documentation is the property of the auditor.

4. **Confidentiality** The auditor has an ethical, and possibly legal, obligation to maintain the confidentiality of client information. Reasonable procedures to prevent unauthorized access to audit documentation should be adopted.

5. **Documentation Completion Date** The auditor should complete the final audit file on a timely basis, but within 60 days following the report release date.

6. **Retention** The auditor should adopt procedures to retain audit documentation for a period sufficient to satisfy legal or regulatory requirements, and to meet practice needs. However, such period should be at least 5 years from the report release date. Under the provisions of the Sarbanes-Oxley Act of 2002, sufficient documentation to support the opinion expressed in the audit report of a public company must be retained for seven years. Items that do not need to be retained include: superseded drafts of workpapers or financial statements, notes that reflect incomplete or preliminary thinking, previous copies of documents corrected for errors, and duplicates of documents. After the documentation completion date the auditor must not delete or discard any documentation from the final audit file before the end of the specified retention period. Also, the auditor must appropriately document any additions to the audit file after the documentation completion date.

B. **Form, Content & Extent**
    The form, content, and extent of workpapers depend on the particular circumstances of the audit, audit methodology, and tools used. Workpapers should include, for example, audit programs, analyses, memoranda, summaries of significant findings or issues, letters of confirmation and representation, checklists, abstracts or copies of important documents, correspondence (including e-mail) of significant findings or issues, and schedules of work performed. Important documents may include significant contracts or agreements if they are needed for an experienced auditor to understand the work performed and conclusions reached.

    1. **Experienced Auditor** Audit documentation should be sufficient to enable an experienced auditor, with no prior connection to the audit, to understand:

        a. The nature, timing, extent, of procedures performed

        b. The results of procedures and the evidence obtained

        c. The conclusions reached on significant matters

        d. That the accounting records reconcile with the financial statements or other information being reported on

    2. **Oral Explanations** On their own, oral explanations do not constitute sufficient support for the audit work performed or the conclusions reached. However, they may be used to clarify or explain information contained in the audit documentation.

    3. **Significant Findings or Issues** The auditor should document significant findings or issues, actions taken to address them, and the basis for final conclusions. The auditor should document any discussions, including responses, with management or others within the entity about significant findings or issues on a timely basis. If the auditor identifies evidence that contradicts or is inconsistent with the auditor's final conclusions concerning a significant

finding or issue, the auditor should document how the contradictory or inconsistent evidence was addressed in forming the conclusion.

4. **Nature & Extent** In determining the form, content, and extent of documentation, the auditor should consider:

    a.   The nature of the auditing procedures performed

    b.   The identified risk of material misstatement

    c.   The extent of judgment involved

    d.   The significance of the evidence obtained

    e.   The nature and extent of exceptions identified

    f.   The need to document a conclusion, or its basis, if not readily determinable from the workpapers

5. **Identification of Preparer & Reviewer** In documenting the nature, timing, and extent of audit procedures performed, the auditor should record:

    a.   Who performed the procedures and the date they were completed

    b.   Who reviewed the workpapers and the date of such review

VIII. Related Parties (AU 334, SAS 45)

A. **Accounting Considerations**
Related-party transactions should be disclosed adequately and properly in conformity with GAAP. Recognition should be given to their economic substance rather than merely their legal form. Examples of related-party transactions include parent-subsidiary transactions and transactions among subsidiaries of a common parent. Transactions between related parties are considered related-party transactions even if they are not given accounting recognition (e.g., a parent providing free services to a subsidiary). Transactions that may indicate the existence of related-party transactions include the following:

1. **Loans** Borrowing or lending money without charging interest or at an interest rate significantly different from current market rates or making loans without scheduled repayment terms

2. **Sales** Selling real estate at a price considerably different from its appraised value or exchanging property for similar property in a nonmonetary transaction

B. **Audit Procedures**
The auditor should be aware of the possible existence of such transactions and of any common ownership or management control relationships and may decide there is a need for additional procedures to determine their existence in certain cases. The auditor should be aware that business structure and operating style occasionally are designed deliberately to obscure related-party transactions. The auditor should gain an understanding of management and the business in order to evaluate the possible existence of related-party transactions. Related-party transactions should **not** be assumed to be outside of the normal course of business unless there is applicable evidence.

1. **Motivating Condition Examples**

    a.   Lack of sufficient working capital or credit to continue in business

    b.   An urgent desire for a favorable earnings record to support the company's stock price

    c.   An overly optimistic earnings forecast

d.   Significant litigation, especially between stockholders and management

e.   Excess capacity or a declining industry with a large number of business failures

f.   Dependence on a single (or a relatively few) products, customers, or transactions for the ongoing success of the business

g.   Significant dangers of obsolescence from operating in a high technology industry

2.   **Determining Existence of Related Parties**   The auditor should test material transactions between related parties and the client.   To discover the existence of less obvious relationships, the auditor may apply one or more specific procedures, such as the following:

a.   Evaluation of the company's procedures for identifying and properly accounting for related party transactions.

b.   Request of appropriate management personnel the names of all related parties and inquire whether any transaction occurred with these parties during the period (should be documented in the management representation letter).

c.   Review the workpapers from prior years for the names of known related parties.   Inquire of the predecessor, principal, or other auditors of related parties as to their knowledge of existing relationships.

d.   Determine the names of all pensions and trusts established for the benefit of employees and the names of their officers and trustees.   They will be considered related parties if managed by or under the trusteeship of the client's management.

e.   Review SEC filings, etc., for the names of related parties and for other businesses in which officers and directors occupy directorship or management positions.   Review stockholder listings of closely held companies to identify principal stockholders.

f.   Review the period's material investment transactions to determine if any related party transactions were created.

3.   **Identifying Material Related-Party Transactions**   The following procedures may help the auditor identify material transactions with known related parties or that may indicate previously undetermined relationships:

a.   Provide the names of related parties to the audit staff so they can watch for transactions with those parties.

b.   Review the minutes of the board of directors' meetings (and other executive or operating committees) to see if any material transactions were authorized or discussed.

c.   Review invoices from law firms that have performed regular or special services.

d.   Review "conflict-of-interests" statements obtained by the company from its management.

e.   Review the extent and nature of transactions with major customers, suppliers, etc. Review loans receivable and payable confirmations to see if any are guaranteed by parties that may be considered related parties.

f.   Consider whether nonmonetary transactions, such as free accounting or management expertise, are being provided but not recorded.

g. Review the accounting records for large, unusual, or nonrecurring transactions or balances. Special attention should be paid to transactions that are recognized at or near the end of the reporting period.

h. Review confirmations of compensating balance arrangements.

4. **Examining Transactions** Once related-party transactions have been identified, the auditor should apply whatever procedures considered necessary to obtain reasonable satisfaction as to their purpose, nature, and effect on the financial statements. In extending inquiry beyond the range of management, the auditor should perform the following:

   a. Obtain an understanding of the business purpose of the transaction.

      (1) Examine pertinent documents such as invoices, contracts, and receiving and shipping documents.

      (2) Determine whether appropriate officials, such as the board of directors, have approved the transaction.

      (3) Test the amounts to be disclosed (or considered to be disclosed) in the financial statements for reasonableness.

      (4) Consider having intercompany balances audited on the same date. The auditors then would exchange relevant information.

      (5) Inspect or confirm the transferability and value of collateral.

   b. Perform additional procedures needed to fully understand the particular transaction.

      (1) Confirm the amounts and terms of the transactions (including guarantees) with the other parties.

      (2) Inspect evidence that is in the possession of the other party (or parties) to the transaction.

      (3) Confirm or discuss significant information with such intermediaries as banks, guarantors, or attorneys.

      (4) If there is reason to believe that transactions lacking substance were conducted with any unfamiliar customers, businesses, etc., the auditor should refer to trade journals, credit agencies, etc., to verify the lack of substance.

      (5) Obtain information on the financial capability of the other party (parties) with respect to material uncollected balances, guarantees, and other obligations.

C. **Disclosure**
The auditor must evaluate the sufficiency and appropriateness of evidence concerning related parties. This evaluation involves all the information available so that, using professional judgment, the auditor can determine the adequacy of the related-party disclosures.

1. **Difficulty** Unless a transaction with a related party is of a routine nature, it generally is **not** possible to determine whether a particular transaction would have taken place had the parties not been related. As a result, it is quite difficult to determine if the terms were equivalent to those that prevail in arm's-length transactions.

2. **Representation** If the financial statements contain a representation that a material transaction was carried out at arm's-length bargaining and the representation is unsubstantiated by management, the auditor should, depending upon the materiality of the unsubstantiated representations, express a qualified or adverse opinion due to a departure from GAAP.

CHAPTER 24—EVIDENCE & PROCEDURES

Problem 24-1 MULTIPLE CHOICE QUESTIONS (126 to 158 minutes)

1. The best primary audit evidence regarding year-end bank balances is documented in the
a. Standard bank confirmations
b. Interbank transfer schedule
c. Bank reconciliations
d. Bank deposit lead schedule   (Editors, 0146)

2. Which of the following procedures would provide the most reliable audit evidence?
a. Inquiries of the client's internal audit staff held in private
b. Inspection of prenumbered client purchase orders filed in the vouchers payable department
c. Analytical procedures performed by the auditor on the entity's trial balance
d. Inspection of bank statements obtained directly from the client's financial institution
(5/93, AUD, #26, 3922)

3. Which of the following presumptions is correct about the reliability of audit evidence?
a. Information obtained indirectly from outside sources is the most reliable audit evidence.
b. To be reliable, audit evidence should be convincing rather than persuasive.
c. Reliability of audit evidence refers to the amount of corroborative evidence obtained.
d. An effective internal control structure provides more assurance about the reliability of audit evidence.   (11/94, AUD, #47, amended, 5120)

4. The most reliable procedure for an auditor to use to test the existence of a client's inventory at an outside location would be to
a. Observe physical counts of the inventory items
b. Trace the total on the inventory listing to the general ledger inventory account
c. Obtain a confirmation from the client indicating inventory ownership
d. Analytically compare the current-year inventory balance to the prior-year balance
(R/06, AUD, #21, 8139)

5. An auditor scans a client's investment records for the period just before and just after the year end to determine that any transfers between categories of investments have been properly recorded. The primary purpose of this procedure is to obtain evidence about management's financial statement assertions of
a. Rights and obligations, and existence or occurrence
b. Valuation and allocation, and rights and obligations
c. Existence or occurrence, and classification
d. Classification, and valuation and allocation
(R/05, AUD, #29, amended, 7824)

6. A client uses a suspense account for unresolved questions whose final accounting has not been determined. If a balance remains in the suspense account at year end, the auditor would be most concerned about
a. Suspense debits that management believes will benefit future operations
b. Suspense debits that the auditor verifies will have realizable value to the client
c. Suspense credits that management believes should be classified as "Current liability"
d. Suspense credits that the auditor determines to be customer deposits   (11/96, AUD, #13, 6365)

7. An entity's income statements were misstated due to the recording of journal entries that involved debits and credits to an unusual combination of expense and revenue accounts. The auditor most likely could have detected this misstatement by
a. Tracing a sample of journal entries to the general ledger
b. Evaluating the effectiveness of internal control policies and procedures
c. Investigating the reconciliations between controlling accounts and subsidiary records
d. Performing analytical procedures designed to disclose differences from expectations
(11/94, AUD, #14, amended, 5087)

8. An auditor may achieve audit objectives related to particular assertions by
a. Performing analytical procedures
b. Adhering to a system of quality control
c. Preparing auditor working papers
d. Increasing the level of detection risk
(11/95, AUD, #38, 5985)

9. In addition to evaluating the frequency of deviations in tests of controls, an auditor should also consider certain qualitative aspects of the deviations. The auditor most likely would give broader consideration to the implications of a deviation if it was

a. The only deviation discovered in the sample
b. Identical to a deviation discovered during the prior year's audit
c. Caused by an employee's misunderstanding of instructions
d. Initially concealed by a forged document

(11/95, AUD, #26, 5973)

10. Which of the following circumstances most likely would cause an auditor to suspect that material misstatements exist in a client's financial statements?

a. The assumptions used in developing the prior year's accounting estimates have changed.
b. Differences between reconciliations of control accounts and subsidiary records are not investigated.
c. Negative confirmation requests yield fewer responses than in the prior year's audit.
d. Management consults with another CPA firm about complex accounting matters.

(R/02, AUD, #7, 7097)

11. In assessing the objectivity of internal auditors, an independent auditor should

a. Evaluate the quality control program in effect for the internal auditors
b. Examine documentary evidence of the work performed by the internal auditors
c. Test a sample of the transactions and balances that the internal auditors examined
d. Determine the organizational level to which the internal auditors report   (11/95, AUD, #1, 5950)

12. The work of internal auditors may affect the independent auditor's

I. Procedures performed in obtaining an understanding of internal control
II. Procedures performed in assessing the risk of material misstatement
III. Substantive procedures performed in gathering direct evidence

a. I and II only
b. I and III only
c. II and III only
d. I, II, and III   (11/95, AUD, #53, amended, 6000)

13. In assessing the competence and objectivity of an entity's internal auditor, an independent auditor **least** likely would consider information obtained from

a. Discussions with management personnel
b. External quality reviews of the internal auditor's activities
c. Previous experience with the internal auditor
d. The results of analytical procedures

(11/94, AUD, #68, 5141)

14. In assessing the competence of an internal auditor, an independent CPA most likely would obtain information about the

a. Quality of the internal auditor's working paper documentation
b. Organization's commitment to integrity and ethical values
c. Influence of management on the scope of the internal auditor's duties
d. Organizational level to which the internal auditor reports   (R/99, AUD, #16, 6832)

15. In assessing the competence of a client's internal auditor, an independent auditor most likely would consider the

a. Internal auditor's compliance with professional internal auditing standards
b. Client's policies that limit the internal auditor's access to management salary data
c. Evidence supporting a further reduction in the assessed level of control risk
d. Results of ratio analysis that may identify unusual transactions and events.

(R/06, AUD, #9, 8127

16. For which of the following judgments may an independent auditor share responsibility with an entity's internal auditor who is assessed to be both competent and objective?

	Assessment of inherent risk	Assessment of control risk
a.	Yes	Yes
b.	Yes	No
c.	No	Yes
d.	No	No

(5/96, AUD, #3, 6235)

17. During an audit an internal auditor may provide direct assistance to an independent CPA in

	Obtaining an understanding of internal control	Performing tests of controls	Performing substantive tests
a.	No	No	No
b.	Yes	No	No
c.	Yes	Yes	No
d.	Yes	Yes	Yes

(5/95, AUD, #60, amended, 5678)

18. A purpose of a management representation letter is to reduce
a. Audit risk to an aggregate level of misstatement that could be considered material
b. An auditor's responsibility to detect material misstatements only to the extent that the letter is relied on
c. The possibility of a misunderstanding concerning management's responsibility for the financial statements
d. The scope of an auditor's procedures concerning related party transactions and subsequent events   (5/93, AUD, #32, 3928)

19. When considering the use of management's written representations as audit evidence about the completeness assertion, an auditor should understand that such representations
a. Complement, but do not replace, substantive tests designed to support the assertion
b. Constitute sufficient evidence to support the assertion when considered in combination with the assessment of control risk
c. Replace the assessment of control risk as evidence to support the assertion
d. Are not part of the audit evidence considered to support the assertion   (Editors, 0218)

20. Key Co. plans to present comparative financial statements for the years ended December 31, Year 7, and Year 8, respectively. Smith, CPA, audited Key's financial statements for both years and plans to report on the comparative financial statements on May 1, Year 9. Key's current management team was not present until January 1, Year 8. What period of time should be covered by Key's management representation letter?
a. January 1, Year 7, through December 31, Year 8.
b. January 1, Year 7, through May 1, Year 9.
c. January 1, Year 8, through December 31, Year 8.
d. January 1, Year 8, through May 1, Year 9.
(R/99, AUD, #26, amended, 6842)

21. For which of the following matters should an auditor obtain written management representations?
a. Management's cost-benefit justifications for not correcting internal control weaknesses
b. Management's knowledge of future plans that may affect the price of the entity's stock
c. Management's compliance with contractual agreements that may affect the financial statements
d. Management's acknowledgment of its responsibility for employees' violations of laws
(R/99, AUD, #25, 6841)

22. Which of the following matters most likely would be included in a management representation letter?
a. An assessment of the risk factors concerning the misappropriation of assets
b. An evaluation of the litigation that has been filed against the entity
c. A confirmation that the entity has complied with contractual agreements
d. A statement that all material internal control weaknesses have been corrected
(R/06, AUD, #46, 8164)

23. To which of the following matters would materiality limits **not** apply in obtaining written management representations?
a. The availability of minutes of stockholders' and directors' meetings
b. Losses from purchase commitments at prices in excess of market value
c. The disclosure of compensating balance arrangements involving related parties
d. Reductions of obsolete inventory to net realizable value   (5/95, AUD, #66, 5684)

24. To which of the following matters would materiality limits **not** apply when obtaining written client representations?
a. Violations of state labor regulations
b. Disclosure of line-of-credit arrangements
c. Information about related party transactions
d. Instances of fraud involving management
(R/06, AUD, #6, 8124)

25. A scope limitation sufficient to preclude an unqualified opinion always will result when management

a. Prevents the auditor from reviewing the working papers of the predecessor auditor
b. Engages the auditor after the year-end physical inventory is completed
c. Requests that certain material accounts receivable not be confirmed
d. Refuses to acknowledge its responsibility for the fair presentation of the financial statements in conformity with GAAP   (R/00, AUD, #16, 6941)

26. Which of the following statements ordinarily is **not** included among the written client representations made by the chief executive officer and the chief financial officer?

a. "Sufficient audit evidence has been made available to the auditor to permit the issuance of an unqualified opinion."
b. "There are no unasserted claims or assessments that our lawyer has advised us are probable of assertion and must be disclosed."
c. "We have no plans or intentions that may materially affect the carrying value or classification of assets and liabilities."
d. "No events have occurred subsequent to the balance sheet date that would require adjustment to, or disclosure in, the financial statements."
    (R/06, AUD, #4, 8122)

27. Which of the following would **not** be considered an analytical procedure?

a. Estimating payroll expense by multiplying the number of employees by the average hourly wage rate and the total hours worked
b. Projecting an error rate by comparing the results of a statistical sample with the actual population characteristics
c. Computing accounts receivable turnover by dividing credit sales by the average net receivables
d. Developing the expected current year sales based on the sales trend of the prior five years
    (5/95, AUD, #48, 5666)

28. Analytical procedures used in planning an audit should focus on

a. Reducing the scope of tests of controls and substantive tests
b. Providing assurance that potential material misstatements will be identified
c. Enhancing the auditor's understanding of the client's business
d. Assessing the adequacy of the available audit evidence   (5/95, AUD, #8, 5626)

29. An auditor compares annual revenues and expenses with similar amounts from the prior year and investigates all changes exceeding 10%. This procedure most likely could indicate that

a. Fourth quarter payroll taxes were properly accrued and recorded, but were not paid until early in the subsequent year.
b. Unrealized gains from increases in the value of available-for-sale securities were recorded in the income account for trading securities.
c. The annual provision for uncollectible accounts expense was inadequate because of worsening economic conditions.
d. Notice of an increase in property tax rates was received by management, but was not recorded until early in the subsequent year.
    (R/06, AUD, #28, 8146)

30. An auditor discovered that a client's accounts receivable turnover is substantially lower for the current year than for the prior year. This may indicate that

a. Obsolete inventory has not yet been reduced to fair market value.
b. There was an improper cutoff of sales at the end of the year.
c. An unusually large receivable was written off near the end of the year.
d. The aging of accounts receivable was improperly performed in both years.
    (R/06, AUD, #45, 8163)

31. Which of the following ratios would an engagement partner most likely calculate when reviewing the balance sheet in the overall review stage of an audit?

a. Quick assets/current assets
b. Accounts receivable/inventory
c. Interest payable/interest receivable
d. Total debt/total assets   (11/96, AUD, #14, 6366)

32. An auditor most likely would apply analytical procedures in the overall review stage of an audit to

a. Enhance the auditor's understanding of subsequent events
b. Identify auditing procedures omitted by the staff accountants
c. Determine whether additional audit evidence may be needed
d. Evaluate the effectiveness of the internal control activities   (R/06, AUD, #39, 8157)

33. Which of the following nonfinancial information would an auditor most likely consider in performing analytical procedures during the planning phase of an audit?
a. Turnover of personnel in the accounting department
b. Objectivity of audit committee members
c. Square footage of selling space
d. Management's plans to repurchase stock
(5/97, AUD, #3, 6392)

34. An auditor's analytical procedures most likely would be facilitated if the entity
a. Segregates obsolete inventory before the physical inventory count
b. Uses a standard cost system that produces variance reports
c. Corrects material weaknesses in internal control before the beginning of the audit
d. Develops its data from sources solely within the entity
(11/95, AUD, #41, 5988)

35. Which of the following factors would **least** influence an auditor's consideration of the reliability of data for purposes of analytical procedures?
a. Whether the data were processed in an IT system or in a manual accounting system
b. Whether sources within the entity were independent of those who are responsible for the amount being audited
c. Whether the data were subjected to audit testing in the current or prior year
d. Whether the data were obtained from independent sources outside the entity or from sources within the entity (5/90, AUD, #2, amended, 0151)

36. An auditor's analytical procedures performed during the overall review stage indicated that the client's accounts receivable had doubled since the end of the prior year. However, the allowance for doubtful accounts as a percentage of accounts receivable remained about the same. Which of the following client explanations most likely would satisfy the auditor?
a. The client liberalized its credit standards in the current year and sold much more merchandise to customers with poor credit ratings.
b. Twice as many accounts receivable were written off in the prior year than in the current year.
c. A greater percentage of accounts receivable were currently listed in the "more than 90 days overdue" category than in the prior year.
d. The client opened a second retail outlet in the current year and its credit sales approximately equaled the older, established outlet.
(R/03, AUD, #1, 7623)

37. Which of the following comparisons would an auditor most likely make in evaluating an entity's costs and expenses?
a. The current year's accounts receivable with the prior year's accounts receivable
b. The current year's payroll expense with the prior year's payroll expense
c. The budgeted current year's sales with the prior year's sales
d. The budgeted current year's warranty expense with the current year's contingent liabilities
(11/97, AUD, #17, 6580)

38. Analytical procedures performed during an audit indicate that accounts receivable doubled since the end of the prior year. However, the allowance for doubtful accounts as a percentage of accounts receivable remained about the same. Which of the following client explanations would satisfy the auditor?
a. A greater percentage of accounts receivable are listed in the "more than 120 days overdue" category than in the prior year.
b. Internal control activities over the recording of cash receipts have been improved since the end of the prior year.
c. The client opened a second retail outlet during the current year and its credit sales approximately equaled the older outlet.
d. The client tightened its credit policy during the current year and sold considerably less merchandise to customers with poor credit ratings.
(R/06, AUD, #15, 8133)

39. Which of the following statements is correct concerning an auditor's use of the work of a specialist?
a. The auditor need not obtain an understanding of the methods and assumptions used by the specialist.
b. The auditor may not use the work of a specialist in matters material to the fair presentation of the financial statements.
c. The reasonableness of the specialist's assumptions and their applications are strictly the auditor's responsibility.
d. The work of a specialist who has a contractual relationship with the client may be acceptable under certain circumstances.
(11/95, AUD, #54, 6001)

40. In using the work of a specialist, an auditor may refer to the specialist in the auditor's report if, as a result of the specialist's findings, the auditor
a. Becomes aware of conditions causing substantial doubt about the entity's ability to continue as a going concern.
b. Desires to disclose the specialist's findings, which imply that a more thorough audit was performed.
c. Is able to corroborate another specialist's earlier findings that were consistent with management's representations.
d. Discovers significant deficiencies in the design of the entity's internal control that management does not correct.
(5/95, AUD, #62, amended, 5680)

41. The scope of an audit is **not** restricted when an attorney's response to an auditor as a result of a client's letter of audit inquiry limits the response to
a. Matters to which the attorney has given substantive attention in the form of legal representation
b. An evaluation of the likelihood of an unfavorable outcome of the matters disclosed by the entity
c. The attorney's opinion of the entity's historical experience in recent similar litigation
d. The probable outcome of asserted claims and pending or threatened litigation
(11/90, AUD, #19, 0138)

42. The primary source of information to be reported about litigation, claims, and assessments is the
a. Client's lawyer
b. Court records
c. Client's management
d. Independent auditor   (11/93, AUD, #39, 4276)

43. A lawyer's response to an auditor's inquiry concerning litigation, claims, and assessments may be limited to matters that are considered individually or collectively material to the client's financial statements. Which parties should reach an understanding on the limits of materiality for this purpose?
a. The auditor and the client's management
b. The client's audit committee and the lawyer
c. The client's management and the lawyer
d. The lawyer and the auditor
(R/99, AUD, #24, 6840)

44. "In connection with an audit of our financial statements, management has prepared, and furnished to our auditors a description and evaluation of certain contingencies." The foregoing passage most likely is from a(an)
a. Audit inquiry letter to legal counsel
b. Management representation letter
c. Audit committee's communication to the auditor
d. Financial statement footnote disclosure
(R/05, AUD, #22, 7817)

45. If a client will **not** permit inquiry of outside legal counsel, the auditor's report ordinarily will contain a(an)
a. Adverse opinion
b. Disclaimer of opinion
c. Unqualified opinion with a separate explanatory paragraph
d. Qualified opinion   (R/05, AUD, #1, 7796)

46. The primary reason an auditor requests letters of inquiry be sent to a client's attorneys is to provide the auditor with
a. The probable outcome of asserted claims and pending or threatened litigation
b. Corroboration of the information furnished by management about litigation, claims, and assessments
c. The attorneys' opinions of the client's historical experiences in recent similar litigation
d. A description and evaluation of litigation, claims, and assessments that existed at the balance sheet date   (11/94, AUD, #66, 5139)

47. Which of the following is an audit procedure that an auditor most likely would perform concerning litigation, claims, and assessments?
a. Request the client's lawyer to evaluate whether the client's pending litigation, claims, and assessments indicate a going concern problem
b. Examine the legal documents in the client's lawyer's possession concerning litigation, claims, and assessments to which the lawyer has devoted substantive attention
c. Discuss with management its policies and procedures adopted for evaluating and accounting for litigation, claims, and assessments
d. Confirm directly with the client's lawyer that all litigation, claims, and assessments have been recorded or disclosed in the financial statements
(11/95, AUD, #55, 6002)

48. Which of the following statements extracted from a client's lawyer's letter concerning litigation, claims, and assessments most likely would cause the auditor to request clarification?
a. "I believe that the plaintiff will have problems establishing any liability."
b. "I believe that this action has only a remote chance in establishing any liability."
c. "I believe that the plaintiff's case against the company is without merit."
d. "I believe that the company will be able to defend this action successfully."
(R/06, AUD, #38, 8156)

49. An auditor's working papers serve mainly to
a. Provide the principal support for the auditor's report
b. Satisfy the auditor's responsibilities concerning the Code of Professional Conduct
c. Monitor the effectiveness of the CPA firm's quality control procedures
d. Document the level of independence maintained by the auditor   (5/95, AUD, #71, 5689)

50. Which of the following sets of information does an auditor usually confirm on one form?
a. Accounts payable and purchase commitments
b. Cash in bank and collateral for loans
c. Inventory on consignment and contingent liabilities
d. Accounts receivable and accrued interest receivable   (11/95, AUD, #40, 5987)

51. Which of the following is **not** required documentation in an audit in accordance with generally accepted auditing standards?
a. A written engagement letter formalizing the level of service to be rendered
b. A flowchart depicting the segregation of duties and authorization of transactions
c. A written audit program describing the necessary procedures to be performed
d. Written representations from management
(Editors, 2321)

52. In creating lead schedules for an audit engagement, a CPA often uses automated workpaper software. What client information is needed to begin this process?
a. Interim financial information such as third quarter sales, net income, and inventory and receivables balances
b. Specialized journal information such as the invoice and purchase order numbers of the last few sales and purchases of the year
c. General ledger information such as account numbers, prior-year account balances, and current-year unadjusted information
d. Adjusting entry information such as deferrals and accruals, and reclassification journal entries
(5/98, AUD, #11, 6628)

53. "There have been no communications from regulatory agencies concerning noncompliance with, or deficiencies in, financial reporting practices that could have a material effect on the financial statements." The foregoing passage is most likely from a
a. Report on internal control
b. Special report
c. Management representation letter
d. Letter for underwriters   (5/97, AUD, #8, 6397)

54. In performing a count of negotiable securities, an auditor records the details of the count on a security count worksheet. What other information is usually included on this worksheet?
a. An acknowledgment by a client representative that the securities were returned intact
b. An analysis of realized gains and losses from the sale of securities during the year
c. An evaluation of the client's internal control concerning physical access to the securities
d. A description of the client's procedures that prevent the negotiation of securities by just one person   (R/00, AUD, #12, 6937)

55. Which of the following factors would **least** likely affect the quantity and content of an auditor's working papers?
a. The condition of the client's records
b. The assessed risk of material misstatement
c. The nature of the auditor's report
d. The content of the representation letter
(11/94, AUD, #73, amended, 5146)

56. The permanent (continuing) file of an auditor's working papers most likely would include copies of the
a. Lead schedules
b. Attorney's letters
c. Bank statements
d. Debt agreements   (11/95, AUD, #60, 6007)

57. The audit working paper that reflects the major components of an amount reported in the financial statements is the
a. Interbank transfer schedule
b. Carryforward schedule
c. Supporting schedule
d. Lead schedule   (11/91, AUD, #52, 2320)

58. An auditor ordinarily uses a working trial balance resembling the financial statements without footnotes, but containing columns for
a. Cash flow increases and decreases
b. Audit objectives and assertions
c. Reclassifications and adjustments
d. Reconciliations and tick marks
          (11/94, AUD, #72, 5145)

59. Which of the following procedures most likely could assist an auditor in identifying related party transactions?
a. Performing tests of controls concerning the segregation of duties
b. Evaluating the reasonableness of management's accounting estimates
c. Reviewing confirmations of compensating balance arrangements
d. Scanning the accounting records for recurring transactions   (R/05, AUD, #16, 7811)

60. When auditing related party transactions, an auditor places primary emphasis on
a. Ascertaining the rights and obligations of the related parties
b. Confirming the existence of the related parties
c. Verifying the valuation of the related party transactions
d. Evaluating the disclosure of the related party transactions   (5/95, AUD, #68, 5686)

61. An auditor searching for related party transactions should obtain an understanding of each subsidiary's relationship to the total entity because
a. The business structure may be deliberately designed to obscure related party transactions.
b. Intercompany transactions may have been consummated on terms equivalent to arm's-length transactions.
c. This may reveal whether particular transactions would have taken place if the parties had not been related.
d. This may permit the audit of intercompany account balances to be performed as of concurrent dates.   (Editors, 0185)

62. After determining that a related party transaction has, in fact, occurred, an auditor should
a. Add a separate paragraph to the auditor's standard report to explain the transaction
b. Perform analytical procedures to verify whether similar transactions occurred, but were not recorded
c. Obtain an understanding of the business purpose of the transaction
d. Substantiate that the transaction was consummated on terms equivalent to an arm's-length transaction   (11/94, AUD, #69, 5142)

63. An auditor most likely would modify an unqualified opinion if the entity's financial statements include a footnote on related party transactions
a. Disclosing loans to related parties at interest rates significantly below prevailing market rates
b. Describing an exchange of real estate for similar property in a nonmonetary related party transaction
c. Stating that a particular related party transaction occurred on terms equivalent to those that would have prevailed in an arm's-length transaction
d. Presenting the dollar-volume of related party transactions and the effects of any change in the method of establishing terms from prior periods
          (5/93, AUD, #44, 3940)

Problem 24-2 ADDITIONAL MULTIPLE CHOICE QUESTIONS (60 to 75 minutes)

64. Which of the following types of audit evidence is the most persuasive?
a. Prenumbered client purchase order forms
b. Client work sheets supporting cost allocations
c. Bank statements obtained from the client
d. Management representation letter
(5/95, AUD, #39, amended, 5657)

65. Which of the following circumstances most likely would cause an auditor to consider whether material misstatements exist in an entity's financial statements?
a. Management places little emphasis on meeting earnings projections.
b. The board of directors makes all major financing decisions.
c. Significant deficiencies previously communicated to management are not corrected.
d. Transactions selected for testing are not supported by proper documentation.
(11/94, AUD, #13, amended, 5086)

66. Which of the following procedures would yield the most appropriate evidence?
a. A scanning of trial balances
b. An inquiry of client personnel
c. A comparison of beginning and ending retained earnings
d. A recalculation of bad debt expense
(R/06, AUD, #25, 8143)

67. An auditor observes the mailing of monthly statements to a client's customers and reviews evidence of follow-up on errors reported by the customers. This test of controls most likely is performed to support management's financial statement assertions of

	Classification and Understandability	Existence or occurrence
a.	Yes	Yes
b.	Yes	No
c.	No	Yes
d.	No	No

(R/06, AUD, #1, 8119)

68. At the conclusion of an audit, an auditor is reviewing the evidence gathered in support of the financial statements. With regard to the valuation of inventory, the auditor concludes that the evidence obtained is not sufficient to support management's representations. Which of the following actions is the auditor most likely to take?
a. Consult with the audit committee and issue a disclaimer of opinion
b. Consult with the audit committee and issue a qualified opinion
c. Obtain additional evidence regarding the valuation of inventory
d. Obtain a statement from management supporting their inventory valuation
(R/07, AUD, #22, 8394)

69. The auditor's inventory observation test counts are traced to the client's inventory listing to test for which of the following financial statement assertions?
a. Completeness
b. Rights & obligations
c. Valuation or allocation
d. Classification & understandability
(R/07, AUD, #24, amended, 8396)

70. After making inquiries about credit granting policies, an auditor selects a sample of sales transactions and examines evidence of credit approval. This test of controls most likely supports management's financial statement assertion(s) of

	Rights and obligations	Valuation and allocation
a.	Yes	Yes
b.	Yes	No
c.	No	Yes
d.	No	No

(R/07, AUD, #31, 8403)

71. Which of the following procedures would an auditor most likely perform in auditing the statement of cash flows?
a. Reconcile the amounts included in the statement of cash flows to the other financial statements' amounts
b. Vouch a sample of cash receipts and disbursements for the last few days of the current year
c. Reconcile the cutoff bank statement to the proof of cash to verify the accuracy of the year-end cash balance
d. Confirm the amounts included in the statement of cash flows with the entity's financial institution
(R/07, AUD, #36, 8408)

72. Miller Retailing, Inc., maintains a staff of three full-time internal auditors who report directly to the controller. In planning to use the internal auditors to provide assistance in performing the audit, the independent auditor most likely will
a. Place limited reliance on the work performed by the internal auditors
b. Decrease the extent of the tests of controls needed to support the assessed level of detection risk
c. Increase the extent of the procedures needed to reduce control risk to an acceptable level
d. Avoid using the work performed by the internal auditors   (5/90, AUD, #28, 0157)

73. In assessing the objectivity of internal auditors, the independent CPA who is auditing the entity's financial statements most likely would consider the
a. Internal auditing standards developed by The Institute of Internal Auditors
b. Tests of internal control activities that could detect errors and fraud
c. Materiality of the accounts recently inspected by the internal auditors
d. Results of the tests of transactions recently performed by the internal auditors
            (R/02, AUD, #18, 7108)

74. The date of the management representation letter should be as of the date of the
a. Balance sheet
b. Latest interim financial information
c. Auditor's report
d. Latest related party transaction
            (5/95, AUD, #67, 5685)

75. Which of the following expressions most likely would be included in a management representation letter?
a. No events have occurred subsequent to the balance sheet date that require adjustment to, or disclosure in, the financial statements.
b. There are no significant deficiencies identified during the prior-year's audit of which the audit committee of the board of directors is unaware.
c. We do not intend to provide any information that may be construed to constitute a waiver of the attorney-client privilege.
d. Certain computer files and other required audit evidence may exist only for a short period of time and only in computer-readable form.
            (R/05, AUD, #6, amended, 7801)

76. For all audits of financial statements made in accordance with generally accepted auditing standards, the use of analytical procedures is required to some extent

	In the planning stage	As a substantive test	In the review stage
a.	Yes	No	Yes
b.	No	Yes	No
c.	No	Yes	Yes
d.	Yes	No	No

(11/90, AUD, #22, 0141)

77. An auditor's decision either to apply analytical procedures as substantive tests or to perform tests of transactions and account balances usually is determined by the
a. Availability of data aggregated at a high level
b. Auditor's familiarity with industry trends
c. Timing of tests performed after the balance sheet date
d. Relative effectiveness and efficiency of the tests
            (11/92, AUD, #31, amended, 2965)

78. To be effective, analytical procedures in the overall review stage of an audit engagement should be performed by
a. The staff accountant who performed the substantive auditing procedures
b. The managing partner who has responsibility for all audit engagements at that practice office
c. A manager or partner who has a comprehensive knowledge of the client's business and industry
d. The CPA firm's quality control manager or partner who has responsibility for the firm's peer review program   (R/01, AUD, #10, 7025)

79. Analytical procedures performed in the overall review stage of an audit suggest that several accounts have unexpected relationships. The results of these procedures most likely would indicate that
a. Fraud exists among the relevant account balances.
b. Internal control activities are not operating effectively.
c. Additional tests of details are required.
d. The communication with the audit committee should be revised.
            (5/97, AUD, #9, amended, 6398)

80. The accounts receivable turnover ratio increased significantly over a two-year period. This trend could indicate that
a. The accounts receivable aging has deteriorated.
b. The company has eliminated its discount policy.
c. The company is more aggressively collecting customer accounts.
d. Customer sales have substantially decreased.
(R/05, AUD, #47, 7842)

81. Analytical procedures performed in the final review stage of an audit generally would include
a. Reassessing the factors that assisted the auditor in deciding on preliminary materiality levels and audit risk
b. Considering the adequacy of the evidence gathered in response to unexpected balances identified in planning
c. Summarizing uncorrected misstatements specifically identified through tests of details of transactions and balances
d. Calculating projected uncorrected misstatements estimated through audit sampling techniques
(R/05, AUD, #18, 7813)

82. Which two of the following tend to be most predictable for purposes of analytical procedures applied as substantive tests?
a. Data subject to audit testing in the prior year
b. Transactions subject to management discretion
c. Relationships involving income statement accounts
d. Relationships involving amounts from stable environments
e. Relationships involving balance sheet accounts
(5/92, AUD, #20, amended, 2773)

83. An auditor compares current annual revenues and expenses with those of the prior year and investigates all changes exceeding 10%. By this procedure the auditor would be most likely to learn that
a. An increase in property tax rates has not been recognized in the client's accrual.
b. The client changed its capitalization policy for small tools in the current year.
c. Fourth quarter payroll taxes were not paid.
d. The current provision for uncollectible accounts is inadequate because of worsening economic conditions. (Editors, 7493)

84. Analytical procedures used in the overall review stage of an audit generally include
a. Gathering evidence concerning account balances that have not changed from the prior year
b. Retesting control procedures that appeared to be ineffective during the assessment of control risk
c. Considering unusual or unexpected account balances that were not previously identified
d. Performing tests of transactions to corroborate management's financial statement assertions
(5/95, AUD, #47, 5665)

85. Which of the following factors would most likely influence an auditor's consideration of the reliability of data when performing analytical procedures?
a. Whether the data were developed in a computerized or a manual accounting system
b. Whether the data were prepared on the cash basis or in conformity with GAAP
c. Whether the data were developed under a system with adequate controls
d. Whether the data were processed in an online system or a batch entry system
(R/07, AUD, #16, 8388)

86. Which of the following is an analytical procedure that an auditor most likely would perform when planning an audit?
a. Confirming bank balances with the financial institutions
b. Scanning accounts receivable for amounts over credit limits
c. Recalculating inventory extensions of physical inventory counts
d. Comparing the current-year account balances for conformity with predictable patterns
(R/07, AUD, #25, 8397)

87. Which of the following procedures would a CPA most likely perform in the planning stage of a financial statement audit?
a. Obtain representations from management regarding the availability of all financial records
b. Communicate with the audit committee concerning the prior year's audit adjustments
c. Make inquiries of the client's attorney regarding pending and threatened litigation and assessments
d. Compare recorded financial information with anticipated results from budgets and forecasts
(R/07, AUD, #42, 8414)

88. An auditor intends to use the work of an actuary who has a relationship with the client. Under these circumstances, the auditor
a. Is required to disclose the contractual relationship in the auditor's report
b. Should assess the risk that the actuary's objectivity might be impaired
c. Is not permitted to rely on the actuary because of a lack of independence
d. May communicate this matter to management as a control deficiency
(R/07, AUD, #40, amended, 8412)

89. Which of the following statements extracted from a client's lawyer's letter concerning litigation, claims, and assessments most likely would cause the auditor to request clarification?
a. "I believe that the possible liability to the company is nominal in amount"
b. "I believe that the action can be settled for less than the damages claimed"
c. "I believe that the plaintiff's case against the company is without merit"
d. "I believe that the company will be able to defend this action successfully" (11/96, AUD, #12, 6364)

90. A client's lawyer is unable to form a conclusion about the likelihood of an unfavorable outcome of pending litigation because of inherent uncertainties. If the litigation's effect on the client's financial statements could be material, the auditor most likely would
a. Issue a qualified opinion in the auditor's report because of the lawyer's scope limitation
b. Withdraw from the engagement because of the lack of information furnished by the lawyer
c. Disclaim an opinion on the financial statements because of the materiality of the litigation's effect
d. Add an explanatory paragraph to the auditor's report because of the uncertainty
(5/95, AUD, #64, 5682)

91. Which of the following factors most likely would cause a CPA to decline to accept a new audit engagement?
a. The CPA does not understand the entity's operations and industry.
b. Management acknowledges that the entity has had recurring operating losses.
c. The CPA is unable to review the predecessor auditor's working papers.
d. Management is unwilling to permit inquiry of its legal counsel. (R/07, AUD, #12, 8384)

92. "There are no violations or possible violations of laws or regulations whose effects should be considered for disclosure in the financial statements or as a basis for recording a loss contingency." The foregoing passage most likely is from a (an)
a. Client engagement letter
b. Report on compliance with laws and regulations
c. Management representation letter
d. Attestation report on an entity's internal control
(11/94, AUD, #64, amended, 5137)

93. Which of the following most likely would indicate the existence of related parties?
a. Writing down obsolete inventory just before year-end
b. Failing to correct previously identified internal control structure deficiencies
c. Depending on a single product for the success of the entity
d. Borrowing money at an interest rate significantly below the market rate (11/92, AUD, #40, 2974)

SIMULATIONS

Problem 24-3 (15 to 20 minutes)

Analytical procedures consist of evaluations of financial information made by a study of plausible relationships among both financial and nonfinancial data. They range from simple comparisons to the use of complex models involving many relationships and elements of data. They involve comparisons of recorded amounts, or ratios developed from recorded amounts, to expectations developed by the auditors.

For each of the following unrelated statements, questions, excerpts, and comments taken from various parts of an auditor's working paper file, select the most likely source from the list of sources.

List of Sources

A. Practitioner's report on management's assertion about an entity's compliance with specified requirements	I. Letter for underwriters
B. Auditor's communications on significant deficiencies	J. Accounts receivable confirmation request
C. Audit inquiry letter to legal counsel	K. Request for bank cutoff statement
D. Lawyer's response to audit inquiry letter	L. Explanatory paragraph of an auditor's report on financial statements
E. Audit committee's communication to the auditor	M. Partner's engagement review notes
F. Auditor's communication to the audit committee (other than with respect to significant deficiencies)	N. Management representation letter
G. Report on the application of accounting principles	O. Successor auditor's communication with predecessor auditor
H. Auditor's engagement letter	P. Predecessor auditor's communication with successor auditor

1. During our audit we discovered evidence of the company's failure to safeguard inventory from loss, damage, and misappropriation.

2. The company considers the decline in value of equity securities classified as available-for-sale to be temporary.

3. Was the difference of opinion on the accrued pension liabilities that existed between the engagement personnel and the actuarial specialist resolved in accordance with firm policy and appropriately documented?

4. Our audit is designed to provide reasonable assurance of detecting misstatements that, in our judgment, could have a material effect on the financial statements taken as a whole. Consequently, our audit will not necessarily detect all misstatements that exist due to error, fraudulent financial reporting, or misappropriation of assets.

5. There have been no communications from regulatory agencies concerning noncompliance with or deficiencies in financial reporting practices.

6. Nothing came to our attention that caused us to believe that at October 31, Year 1, there was any change in the capital stock, increase in long-term debt, or decrease in consolidated net current assets or stockholders' equity as compared with the amounts shown in the September 30, Year 1 unaudited condensed consolidated balance sheet.

7. It is our opinion that the possible liability to the company in this proceeding is nominal in amount.

→

8. As discussed in Note 4 to the financial statements, the company experienced a net loss for the year ended July 31, Year 1, and is currently in default under substantially all of its debt agreements. In addition, on September 25, Year 1, the company filed a prenegotiated voluntary petition for relief under Chapter 11 of the U.S. Bankruptcy Code. These matters raise substantial doubt about the company's ability to continue as a going concern.

9. During the year under audit, we were advised that management consulted with Better & Best, CPAs. The purpose of this consultation was to obtain another CPA firm's opinion concerning the company's recognition of certain revenue that we believe should be deferred to future periods. Better & Best's opinion was consistent with our opinion, so management did not recognize the revenue in the current year.

10. The company believes that all material expenditures that have been deferred to future periods will be recoverable.

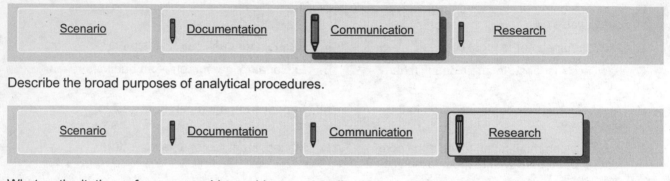

Describe the broad purposes of analytical procedures.

What authoritative reference provides guidance regarding the circumstances in which an auditor does not request the confirmation of accounts receivable during an audit?

Paragraph Reference Answer: _____

(R/00, AUD, #2, amended, 6946)

Problem 24-4 (20 to 30 minutes)

| Scenario | Documentation | Communication | Research |

Analytical procedures consist of evaluations of financial information made by a study of plausible relationships among both financial and nonfinancial data. They range from simple comparisons to the use of complex models involving many relationships and elements of data. They involve comparisons of recorded amounts, or ratios developed from recorded amounts, to expectations developed by the auditors.

For each of the following unrelated statements, questions, excerpts, and comments taken from various parts of an auditor's working paper file, select the most likely source from the list of sources.

List of Sources

A. Practitioner's report on management's assertion about an entity's compliance with specified requirements

B. Auditor's communications on significant deficiencies

C. Audit inquiry letter to legal counsel

D. Lawyer's response to audit inquiry letter

E. Audit committee's communication to the auditor

F. Auditor's communication to the audit committee (other than with respect to significant deficiencies)

G. Report on the application of accounting principles

H. Auditor's engagement letter

I. Letter for underwriters

J. Accounts receivable confirmation request

K. Request for bank cutoff statement

L. Explanatory paragraph of an auditor's report on financial statements

M. Partner's engagement review notes

N. Management representation letter

O. Successor auditor's communication with predecessor auditor

P. Predecessor auditor's communication with successor auditor

1. Our use of professional judgment and the assessment of audit risk and materiality for the purpose of our audit mean that matters may have existed that would have been assessed differently by you. We make no representation as to the sufficiency or appropriateness of the information in our working papers for your purposes.

2. Indicate in the space provided below whether this information agrees with your records. If there are exceptions, please provide any information that will assist the auditor in reconciling the difference.

3. Blank checks are maintained in an unlocked cabinet along with the check-signing machine. Blank checks and the check-signing machine should be locked in separate locations to prevent the embezzlement of funds.

4. Our audit cannot be relied upon to disclose significant deficiencies in the design or operation of internal control. Nevertheless, we will communicate to you all significant deficiencies and potential areas for improvement that we become aware of during the course of our audit.

5. The timetable set by management to complete our audit was unreasonable considering the failure of the company's personnel to complete schedules on a timely basis and delays in providing necessary information.

6. Several employees have disabled the anti-virus detection software on their PCs because the software slows the processing of data and occasionally rings false alarms. The company should obtain anti-virus software that runs continuously at all system entry points and that cannot be disabled by unauthorized personnel.

7. In connection with an audit of our financial statements, management has prepared, and furnished to our auditors, a description and evaluation of certain contingencies.

8. The company has no plans or intentions that may materially affect the carrying value or classification of assets and liabilities.

9. In planning the sampling application, was appropriate consideration given to the relationship of the sample to the audit objective and to preliminary judgments about materiality levels?

a. Identify the sources of information from which an auditor develops expectations for analytical procedures.

b. Describe the factors that influence an auditor's consideration of the reliability of data for purposes of achieving audit objectives.

What authoritative reference provides guidance on who is ultimately responsible for an audit firm's quality control system?

Paragraph Reference Answer: _____

(R/00, AUD, #2, amended, 6956)

Problem 24-5 (15 to 20 minutes)

Analytical procedures are evaluations of financial information made by a study of plausible relationships among financial and nonfinancial data. Understanding and evaluating such relationships are essential to the audit process. The following financial statements were prepared by Holiday Manufacturing Co. for the year ended December 31, Year 5. Also presented are various financial statement ratios for Holiday as calculated from the prior year's financial statements. Sales represent net credit sales. The total assets and the receivables and inventory balances at December 31, Year 5, were the same as at December 31, Year 4.

Holiday Manufacturing Co.
Balance Sheet
December 31, Year 5

Assets		Liabilities and Capital	
Cash	$ 240,000	Accounts payable	$ 160,000
Receivables	400,000	Notes payable	100,000
Inventory	600,000	Other current liabilities	140,000
Total current assets	$1,240,000	Total current liabilities	$ 400,000
Plant and equipment—net	760,000	Long-term debt	350,000
		Common stock	750,000
		Retained earnings	500,000
Total assets	$2,000,000	Total liabilities and capital	$2,000,000

Holiday Manufacturing Co.
Income Statement
Year Ended December 31, Year 5

Sales		$3,000,000
Cost of goods sold		
Material	$800,000	
Labor	700,000	
Overhead	300,000	1,800,000
Gross margin		$1,200,000
Selling expenses	$240,000	
General and administrative expenses	300,000	540,000
Operating income		$ 660,000
Less interest expense		40,000
Income before taxes		$ 620,000
Less federal income taxes		220,000
Net income		$ 400,000

Each of the following represent financial ratios that the auditor calculated during the prior year's audit. For each ratio, calculate the current year's ratio from the financial statements presented and select the answer from the list. Calculations should be rounded, if necessary, to the same number of places as the prior year's ratios.

	Ratio	Year 5	Year 4	List: Ratio Calculations
1.	Current ratio		2.5	A. 0.6 H. 3.1 O. 13%
2.	Quick ratio		1.3	B. 0.7 I. 4.5 P. 22%
3.	Accounts receivable turnover		5.5	C. 1.0 J. 5.0 Q. 28%
4.	Inventory turnover		2.5	D. 1.5 K. 7.5 R. 33%
5.	Total asset turnover		1.2	E. 1.6 L. 10.0 S. 38%
6.	Gross margin percentage		35%	F 2.0 M. 15.5 T. 40%
7.	Net operating margin percentage		25%	G. 3.0 N. 16.5 U. 60%
8.	Times interest earned		10.3	V. 67%
9.	Total debt to equity percentage		50%	

Most of an auditor's work in forming an opinion on financial statements consists of obtaining and evaluating audit evidence concerning the financial statement assertions.

a.   What is the definition of "financial statement assertions?" Do not list the assertions.

b.   What is the relationship between audit objectives and financial statement assertions?

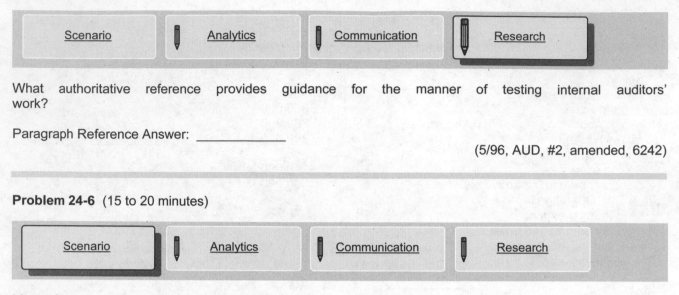

What authoritative reference provides guidance for the manner of testing internal auditors' work?

Paragraph Reference Answer: _____

(5/96, AUD, #2, amended, 6242)

Problem 24-6 (15 to 20 minutes)

Most of an auditor's work in forming an opinion on financial statements consists of obtaining and evaluating audit evidence concerning the financial statement assertions.

| Scenario | | Analytics | | Communication | | Research |

Each of the following items represent an auditor's observed changes, independent of each other, in certain financial statement ratios or amounts from the prior year's ratios or amounts. For each observed change, select the most likely explanation or explanations from the accompanying list.

Auditor's Observed Changes

1. Allowance for doubtful accounts increased from the prior year, but allowance for doubtful accounts as a percentage of accounts receivable decreased from the prior year. (3 explanations)

2. Long-term debt increased from the prior year, but interest expense increased a larger-than proportionate amount than long-term debt. (1 explanation)

3. Operating income increased from the prior year although the entity was less profitable than in the prior year. (2 explanations)

4. Gross margin percentage was unchanged from the prior year although gross margin increased from the prior year. (1 explanation)

Explanations

A. Items shipped on consignment during the last month of the year were recorded as sales.

I. Sales increased at a greater percentage than cost of goods sold increased, as compared to the prior year.

B. A significant number of credit memos for returned merchandise that were issued during the last month of the year were not recorded.

J. Sales increased at a lower percentage than cost of goods sold increased, as compared to the prior year.

C. Year-end purchases of inventory were overstated by incorrectly including items received in the first month of the subsequent year.

K. Interest expense decreased, as compared to the prior year.

D. Year-end purchases of inventory were understated by incorrectly excluding items received before the year end.

L. The effective income tax rate increased, as compared to the prior year.

E. A larger percentage of sales occurred during the last month of the year, as compared to the prior year.

M. The effective income tax rate decreased, as compared to the prior year.

F. A smaller percentage of sales occurred during the last month of the year, as compared to the prior year.

N. Short-term borrowing was refinanced on a long-term basis at the same interest rate.

G. The same percentage of sales occurred during the last month of the year, as compared to the prior year.

O. Short-term borrowing was refinanced on a long-term basis at lower interest rates.

H. Sales increased at the same percentage as cost of goods sold, as compared to the prior year.

P. Short-term borrowing was refinanced on a long-term basis at higher interest rates.

a. What is the relationship between audit objectives and audit procedures?

b. What are an auditor's primary considerations when selecting particular audit procedures to achieve audit objectives?

What authoritative reference provides guidance for the evaluation of significant unexpected differences resulting from analytical procedures performed by the auditor?

Paragraph Reference Answer: _____

(5/96, AUD, #2, amended, 6243)

Problem 24-7 (15 to 25 minutes)

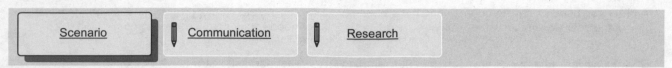

Hart, an assistant accountant with the firm of Better & Best, CPAs, is auditing the financial statements of Tech Consolidated Industries, Inc. The firm's audit program calls for the preparation of a written management representation letter.

a. 1. In an audit of financial statements, in what circumstances is the auditor required to obtain a management representation letter?

   2. What are the purposes of obtaining the letter?

b. 1. To whom should the representation letter be addressed and as of what date should it be dated?

   2. Who should sign the letter and what would be the effect of their refusal to sign the letter?

c. In what respects may an auditor's other responsibilities be relieved by obtaining a management representation letter?

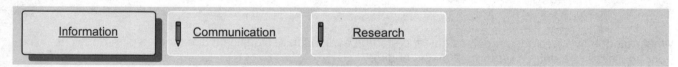

What authoritative reference provides guidance to a successor auditor if s/he becomes aware of information that leads him or her to believe that financials statements reported on by the predecessor auditor may require revision and yet the client refuses to inform the predecessor auditor?

Paragraph Reference Answer: _____

(11/93, AUD, #4, amended, 6244)

Problem 24-8 (15 to 25 minutes)

Kent, CPA, is engaged in the audit of Davidson Corp.'s financial statements for the year ended December 31, Year 9. Kent is about to commence auditing Davidson's employee pension expense, but Kent's preliminary inquiries concerning Davidson's defined benefit pension plan lead Kent to believe that some of the actuarial computations and assumptions are so complex that they are beyond the competence ordinarily required of an auditor. Kent is considering engaging Park, an actuary, to assist with this portion of the audit.

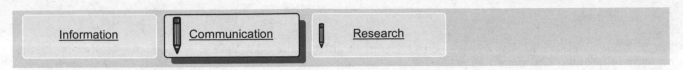

a. What are the factors Kent should consider in the process of selecting Park?

b. What are the matters that should be understood among Kent, Park, and Davidson's management as to the nature of the work to be performed by Park?

c. May Kent refer to Park in the auditor's report if Kent decides to issue an unqualified opinion? Why?

d. May Kent refer to Park in the auditor's report if Kent decides to issue other than an unqualified opinion as a result of Park's findings? Why?

What authoritative reference notes that an audit performed in accordance with auditing standards generally accepted in the United States cannot be expected to provide assurance that all related party transactions will be revealed?

Paragraph Reference Answer: _____

(5/90, AUD, #5, amended, 6245)

Problem 24-9 (15 to 25 minutes)

Your firm is auditing the financial statements of Consolidated Industries Co. for the year ended December 31, Year 5. On April 2, Year 6, an inquiry letter to J. J. Young, Consolidated's outside attorney, was drafted to corroborate the information furnished to you by management concerning pending and threatened litigation, claims, and assessments, and unasserted claims and assessments. On May 6, Year 6, C. R. Brown, Consolidated's Chief Financial Officer, gave you a draft of the inquiry letter below for your review before mailing it to Young.

May 6, Year 6
J. J. Young, Attorney at Law
123 Main Street
Anytown, USA

Dear J. J. Young:

In connection with an audit of our financial statements at December 31, Year 5, and for the year then ended, management of the Company has prepared, and furnished to our auditors, Cole & Cole, CPAs, 456 Broadway, Anytown, USA, a description and evaluation of certain contingencies, including those set forth below involving matters with respect to which you have been engaged and to which you have devoted substantive attention on behalf of the Company in the form of legal consultation or representation. Your response should include matters that existed at December 31, Year 5. Because of the confidentiality of all these matters, your response may be limited

In November Year 5, an action was brought against the Company by an outside salesman alleging breach of contract for sales commissions and pleading a second cause of action for an accounting with respect to claims for fees and commissions. The causes of action claim damages of $300,000, but the Company believes it has meritorious defenses to the claims. The possible exposure of the Company to a successful judgment on behalf of the plaintiff is slight. In July Year 1, an action was brought against the Company by Industrial Manufacturing Co. (Industrial) alleging patent infringement and seeking damages of $20,000,000. The action in U. S. District Court resulted in a decision on October 16, Year 5, holding that the Company infringed seven Industrial patents and awarded damages of $14,000,000. The Company vigorously denies these allegations and has filed an appeal with the U. S. Court of Appeals for the Federal Circuit. The appeal process is expected to take approximately two years, but there is some chance that Industrial may ultimately prevail.

Please furnish to our auditors such explanation, if any, that you consider necessary to supplement the foregoing information, including an explanation of those matters as to which your views may differ from those stated and an identification of the omission of any pending or threatened litigation, claims, and assessments or a statement that the list of such matters is complete. Your response may be quoted or referred to in the financial statements without further correspondence with you.

You also consulted on various other matters considered pending or threatened litigation. However, you may not comment on these matters because publicizing them may alert potential plaintiffs to the strengths of their cases. In addition, various other matters probable of assertion that have some chance of an unfavorable outcome, as of December 31, Year 5, are unasserted claims and assessments.

C. R. Brown
Chief Financial Officer

In a memo to Brown, describe the omissions, ambiguities, and inappropriate statements and terminology in Brown's letter.

What authoritative reference notes that once a management representation conflicts with other audit evidence, an auditor should consider whether reliance on management representations relating to other aspects continues to be appropriate and justified?

Paragraph Reference Answer: _____

(5/93, AUD, #5, amended, 6246)

Problem 24-10 (15 to 25 minutes)

Temple, CPA, is auditing the financial statements of Ford Lumber Yards, Inc. a privately held corporation with 300 employees and five stockholders, three of whom are active in management. Ford has been in business for many years, but has never had its financial statements audited. Temple suspects that the substance of some of Ford's business transactions differ from their form because of the pervasiveness of related party relationships and transactions in the local building supplies industry.

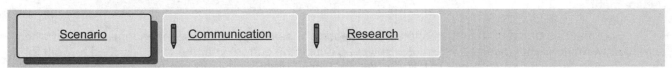

Describe the audit procedures Temple should apply to identify related party relationships and transactions.

What authoritative reference provides guidance concerning written representations from management that was not present during all the periods covered by the auditor's report?

Paragraph Reference Answer: _____

(11/88, AUD, #2, amended, 6247)

Problem 24-11 (15 to 25 minutes)

Young, CPA, is considering the procedures to be applied concerning a client's loss contingencies relating to litigation, claims, and assessments.

What substantive audit procedures should Young apply when testing for loss contingencies relating to litigation, claims, and assessments?

What authoritative reference provides guidance regarding questioning internal audit personnel about the risks of fraud in an audit of financial statements?

Paragraph Reference Answer: _____

(5/88, AUD, #3, amended, 3033)

Problem 24-12 (40 to 50 minutes)

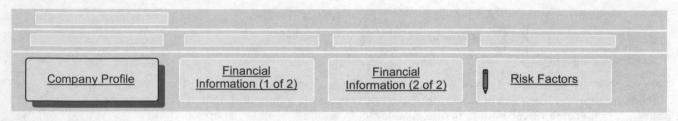

| Company Profile | Financial Information (1 of 2) | Financial Information (2 of 2) | Risk Factors |

Company

Pacific Gourmet, Inc. (Pacific Gourmet) is a retailer of fine food, wine, and related products. The company has been in operation for fifteen years and consists of three core business operations: product sales in its retail store, product sales to food and specialty stores, and food services. The company was started as a local family business and has received additional funding over the years from several private investors.

Pacific Gourmet has a wholly owned subsidiary, which provides food services to corporate clients around the country. In addition, the company also holds investments in several private companies with whom it does business. On January 31, Year 1, Pacific Gourmet guaranteed a $15 million debt obligation of one of these investments—Vineyard Partners—for a period of five years. The Company owns 15% interest in Vineyard Partners.

Marketing

The company experienced significant sales growth during its history and continues to expand its product offerings and market reach. Pacific Gourmet focuses its marketing efforts on demographic groups not typically affected by fluctuations in the economy and thus continues to maintain consistent revenue growth. However, Pacific Gourmet sustained a significant decline in its gross margin on product sales due to an increase in the cost of raw materials and failure to monitor compliance with budgetary guidelines.

Management

Pacific Gourmet has a senior management team composed of seasoned business managers—many of whom have been with the company since inception. However, during the current year the CFO resigned to work for a competitor and recruited several key Pacific Gourmet financial professionals to join him at his new company. After several months of searching, a new CFO with a background in retail finance was hired.

In addition, the accounting department is currently understaffed due to staff turnover. Further, the new CFO is redesigning the accounting policies and procedures and is replacing the general ledger software to improve the effectiveness of the company's financial reporting systems.

Engagement

Pacific Gourmet uses an independent audit firm for its annual audits, which must be provided to investors and lenders under the company's debt covenants. The company's management maintains a strong professional relationship with the audit engagement team. However, there was a disagreement between the auditors and the new CFO in the current year regarding the $15 million-debt guarantee.

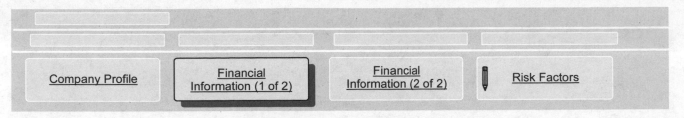

| Company Profile | Financial Information (1 of 2) | Financial Information (2 of 2) | Risk Factors |

Pacific Gourmet, Inc. and Subsidiary
Consolidated Balance Sheets
December 31, Year 2 and Year 1

	Year 2	Year 1
Assets		
Current assets		
Cash and cash equivalents	$ 54,280,000	$ 42,500,000
Receivables - net	12,000,000	10,000,000
Inventory	12,000,000	10,000,000
Other current assets	7,000,000	5,000,000
Total current assets	85,280,000	67,500,000
Property, plant and equipment - net	23,000,000	25,000,000
Other assets	30,000,000	30,000,000
Total assets	$138,280,000	$122,500,000
Liabilities and Stockholders' Equity		
Current liabilities		
Accounts payable	$ 23,000,000	$ 20,000,000
Current portion of long-term debt	1,000,000	1,000,000
Other current liabilities	965,000	1,000,000
Total current liabilities	24,965,000	22,000,000
Long-term debt	13,000,000	14,000,000
Total liabilities	37,965,000	36,000,000
Stockholders' equity		
Common stock	100,000	100,000
Additional paid-in capital	9,900,000	9,900,000
Retained earnings	90,315,000	76,500,000
Total Stockholders' equity	100,315,000	86,500,000
Total liabilities and stockholders' equity	$138,280,000	$122,500,000

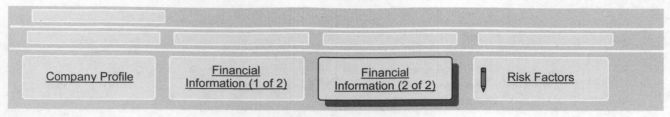

| Company Profile | Financial Information (1 of 2) | Financial Information (2 of 2) | Risk Factors |

Pacific Gourmet, Inc. and Subsidiary
Consolidated Income Statements
For the years ended December 31, Year 2 and Year 1

	Year 2	Year 1
Sales	$100,850,000	$ 95,600,000
Cost of goods sold	55,000,000	42,500,000
Gross profit on sales	45,850,000	53,100,000
Expenses		
Selling expenses	17,600,000	15,000,000
General and administrative	6,015,000	5,000,000
Interest expense	1,120,000	1,200,000
Total expense	24,735,000	21,200,000
Income before taxes	21,115,000	31,900,000
Provision for income taxes	7,300,000	7,500,000
Net income	$ 13,815,000	$ 24,400,000

Pacific Gourmet, Inc. and Subsidiary
Consolidated Statement of Cash Flows
For the Year ended December 31, Year 2

Cash flows from operating activities:	$13,815,000
Net income (loss)	
Adjustments to reconcile net income (loss) to cash provided by	
(used for) operating activities	
Depreciation	1,500,000
Changes in certain assets and liabilities:	
Decrease (increase) in receivables	(2,000,000)
Decrease (increase) in inventory	(2,000,000)
Decrease (increase) in other current assets	(2,000,000)
Increase (decrease) in accounts payable	3,000,000
Increase (decrease) in other current liabilities	(35,000)
Net Cash provided by (used for) operating activities	12,280,000
Cash flows from investing activities:	
Proceeds from sales of property, plant and equipment	500,000
Net cash provided by (used for) investing activities	500,000
Cash flows from financing activities:	
Principal payments on long-term debt	(1,000,000)
Net cash provided by (used for) financing activities	(1,000,000)
Net increase (decrease) in cash and cash equivalents	11,780,000
Cash and cash equivalents at beginning of year	42,500,000
Cash and cash equivalents at end of year	$54,280,000

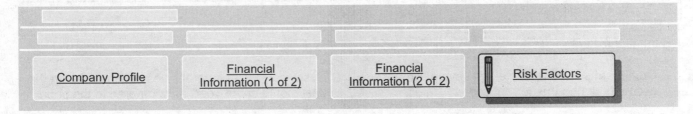

Company Profile	Financial Information (1 of 2)	Financial Information (2 of 2)	Risk Factors

Based on the information in the Pacific Gourmet's Company Profile, which factor is most likely to increase audit risk? Select only one factor.

A. The company was started as a local family business and has received additional funding over the years from several investors.	
B. The new CFO is redesigning the company's accounting policies and procedures.	
C. The company consists of three core business operations: product sales in its retail store, product sales to food and specialty stores, and food services.	
D. The company experienced significant sales growth during its history and continues to expand its product offerings and market reach.	

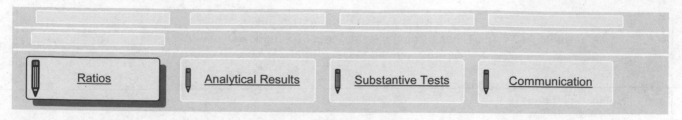

Use the data in Pacific Gourmet's financial statements to calculate for year 2 the analytical ratios indicated in the table below to 2 decimal places. (For turnover ratios, year-end balances should be used. All calculations are based on a 365-day year.)

Ratio	Year 2	Year 1
1. Current ratio		3.07
2. Return on equity		28.21%

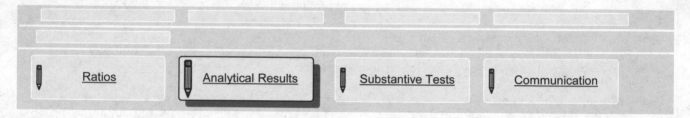

The table below presents several ratios that were considered significant in the current and prior year's audits of Pacific Gourmet. Compare the values for each ratio. Then select the most likely explanation for the analytical results. An explanation may be used once, more than once or not at all. (You should not recalculate ratios. Turnover ratios are based on average balances.)

Ratio	Year 2	Year 1	Explanations
1. Days sales in accounts receivable	40	39	
2. Operating profit margin	22.05%	34.62%	

Explanations

A. Credit terms were restricted on several large accounts during the current year.

B. Operating expenses increased at a higher rate than sales revenue.

C. Sales revenue increased at a higher rate than operating expenses.

D. A smaller percentage of sales occurred during the last month of the year, as compared to the prior year.

E. A larger percentage of sales occurred during the last month of the year, as compared to the prior year.

F. Sales increased as compared to the prior year.

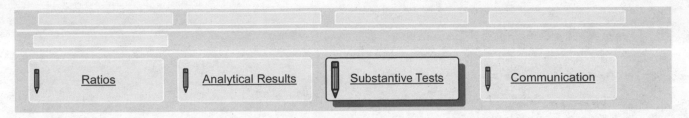

The auditor determines that both of the following objectives will be part of Pacific Gourmet's audit. For each of the following audit objectives, select the substantive test that would most likely provide support for the objective. A substantive test may be used once, more than once, or not at all.

Objective	Substantive Tests
1. Verify existence of accounts receivable.	
2. Determine that inventory balance is accurately stated.	

Selection List

A. Perform tests of subsequent cash receipts after the balance sheet date.

B. Review and assess an aging schedule of accounts receivable.

C. Compare recognized revenue to related industry statistics.

D. Tour the storage facility for inventory to determine adequacy of security controls.

E. Perform shipping cutoff procedures.

F. Review payments to vendors subsequent to year-end.

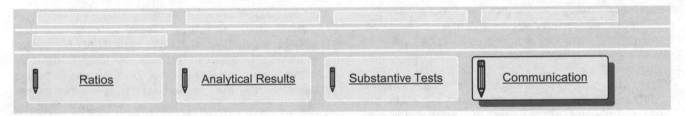

Pacific Gourmet has recommended your firm to Sparkle Co. Consequently, your CPA firm has been engaged to audit the financial statements of Sparkle Co., a nonpublic entity. During fieldwork, Sparkle's management requests that you change the engagement to a review of financial statements in accordance with *Statements on Standards for Accounting and Review Services* (SSARS). In a memorandum to your firm's engagement partner, explain the circumstances under which such a change of engagements may be considered.

REMINDER: On the actual exam your response will be graded for both technical content and writing skills. Technical content will be evaluated for information that is helpful to the intended reader and clearly relevant to the issue. Writing skills will be evaluated for development, organization, and the appropriate expression of ideas in professional correspondence. Use a standard business memo or letter format with a clear beginning, middle, and end. Do not convey information in the form of a table, bullet point list, or other abbreviated presentation.

Research

During the audit of the Pacific Gourmet financial statements, the auditor finds that Pacific Gourmet failed to present a statement of cash flows. Pacific Gourmet's management has declined to correct this violation of generally accepted accounting principles because they believe that complying with GAAP would confuse those relying on the financial statements.

This is the only qualification that the auditor wishes to include in the standard auditor's report. What is the citation that addresses this issue?

Paragraph Reference Answer: _____

(R/06, AUD, #51, 8169)

Solution 24-1 MULTIPLE CHOICE ANSWERS

Audit Evidence

1. (a) The bank confirmations provide the best primary evidence of the year-end bank balance. In an audit engagement, the best evidence is from an independent third party. If no confirmation is present, a bank reconciliation would provide primary evidence. Neither a bank deposit lead schedule nor an interbank transfer schedule is primary evidence by itself. (0146)

2. (d) Audit evidence is more reliable when it is obtained from independent sources outside the entity. Answers (a), (b), and (c) are examples of auditing procedures performed on information obtained from within the entity. (3922)

3. (d) Audit evidence that is generated internally is more reliable when the related controls imposed by the entity are effective. Information obtained directly, not indirectly, from outside sources would provide the most reliable evidence. The auditor may find it necessary to rely on audit evidence that is persuasive rather than conclusive. The reliability of audit evidence refers to its source and nature and is dependent on the individual circumstances under which it is obtained. (5120)

4. (a) The independent auditor's direct personal knowledge, obtained through physical examination, observation, computation, and inspection, is more persuasive than information obtained indirectly. (8139)

5. (d) Classification concerns whether financial information is appropriately presented in the proper accounts within the financial statements.

Valuation and allocation deals with whether assets, liabilities, and equity interests are valued properly and any resulting valuation or allocation adjustments are appropriately recorded. When accounting for investments, the classification has an impact on the appropriate method of valuation in the financial statements. Rights and obligations concerns whether, at a given date, recorded assets indeed represent rights of the entity and liabilities represent obligations. Reviewing investment records regarding transfers between categories (internal documents) provides little evidence that ownership rights in the investments still exists at the balance sheet date, that the investment is not pledged as loan collateral, that the investments exist at the balance sheet date, or that an external transaction involving the investment occurred during the period. (7824)

6. (a) Suspense debits that management believes will benefit future operations are assets. The auditor is most concerned that assets are not overstated and that liabilities are not understated. Suspense debits that the auditor verifies will have realizable value to the client are, insofar as the auditor knows, correct. Thus, for these items, there would be no overstatement. The other two answer options contain items that, if incorrect, would overstate *liabilities*. (6365)

7. (d) Performing analytical procedures designed to disclose differences from expectations would be the most likely way to detect unusual entries. The other answer alternatives are not as likely to detect journal entries with unusual combinations of accounts. (5087)

8. (a) One of the uses of analytics is as a substantive test to obtain audit evidence about particular assertions. In the process of achieving objectives, auditors adhere to a system of quality control, prepare working papers, and may possibly increase the level of detection risk; however, none of these actually cause the auditor to achieve audit objectives. (5985)

9. (d) Evidence that a deviation was covered up in a fraudulent manner would require the auditor to consider the implications of the deviation more closely. Answers (a), (b), and (c) give no causes for added concern. (5973)

10. (b) Unreconciled differences between control and subsidiary accounts indicate a disregard for common accounting safeguards. Assumptions used in developing estimates should change with changing circumstances. A lower response rate for negative confirmation requests indicates fewer customer account misstatements. Consultation with a CPA firm about complex accounting matters often indicates conscientious accounting and reporting. (7097)

Internal Auditors

11. (d) When assessing the internal auditor's objectivity, the auditor should obtain information about the organizational status of the internal auditor including the organizational level to which the internal auditor reports. Answers (a), (b), and (c) provide an indication of competency, not objectivity. (5950)

12. (d) The internal auditors' work may affect the nature, timing, and extent of the audit, including: procedures the auditor performs when obtaining an understanding of the entity's internal control structure; procedures the auditor performs when assessing risk; and substantive procedures the auditor performs. (6000)

13. (d) Answers (a), (b), and (c) are all items the auditor considers in assessing the internal auditor's competence and objectivity. (5141)

14. (a) The quality of internal auditors' documentation reflects on their competence. The other answers are concerned with objectivity. (6832)

15. (a) In assessing competence and objectivity, the auditor usually considers information obtained from previous experience with the internal audit function, from discussions with management personnel, and from a recent external quality review, if performed, of the internal audit function's activities. The auditor may also use professional internal auditing standards as criteria in making the assessment. (8127)

16. (d) The responsibility to report on the financial statements rests solely with the independent auditor. Because the auditor has the ultimate responsibility to express an opinion on the financial statements, judgments about assessments of inherent and control risks, the materiality of misstatements, the sufficiency of test performed, the evaluation of significant accounting estimates, and other matters affecting the auditor's report should always be those of the auditor. (6235)

17. (d) In performing an audit, the auditor may request direct assistance from the internal auditors including assistance in obtaining an understanding of internal control or in performing tests of controls or substantive tests. (5678)

Management Representations

18. (c) Written representations from management reduce the possibility of a misunderstanding concerning management's responsibility for the financial statements. The auditor does not reduce audit risk or the scope of procedures performed based on representations made in the management representation letter. A representation letter does not reduce the auditor's responsibility to detect material misstatements in the audit. (3928)

19. (a) During an audit, management makes many representations to the auditor in response to specific inquiries or through the financial statements. Such representations from management are part of the audit evidence the independent auditor obtains, but they are not a substitute for the application of those auditing procedures necessary to afford a reasonable basis for an opinion regarding the financial statements under audit. Written representations from management ordinarily confirm representations given to the auditor, indicate and document the continuing appropriateness of such representations, and reduce the possibility of misunderstanding concerning the matters that are the subject of the representations. (0218)

20. (b) If comparative financial statements are reported on, the written representations obtained at the completion of the most recent audit should

address all periods being reported on. The representations should be made as of the date of the auditor's report. If current management was not present during all periods covered by the auditor's report, the auditor should nevertheless obtain written representations from current management on all such periods. (6842)

21. (c) Compliance with aspects of contractual agreements that may affect the financial statements is a matter ordinarily included in management representations. Management's justifications for not correcting control weaknesses are primarily of concern to the audit committee, not the auditor. Generally, the auditor is not concerned with forecasts of the entity's stock price. Management is unlikely to acknowledge any responsibility for employees' violations of laws—merely responsibility for having reasonable controls in place. (6841)

22. (c) Compliance with contractual agreements that may affect the financial statements is a matter ordinarily included in management representations. It is the auditor's responsibility to assess the risk factors concerning the misappropriation of assets. An evaluation of the litigation that has been filed against the entity is a matter to be covered in a lawyer's response to a letter of audit inquiry. Management is not required to correct all material internal control weaknesses. (8164)

23. (a) Management's representations may be limited to matters that are considered material. Materiality limitations would not apply to those representations that are not directly related to amounts included in the financial statements, such as the availability of minutes of stockholders' and directors' meetings. Answers (b), (c), and (d) relate directly to amounts in the financial statements and thus materiality limits would apply. (5684)

24. (d) Because of the possible effects of fraud and the importance of management integrity on other aspects of the audit, materiality limits do not apply with respect to fraud involving management. This means that no incident involving management fraud may be ignored no matter how minor it may seem. Some instances of answers (a), (b), and (c) may not be significant enough to matter. (8124)

25. (d) An unqualified opinion requires written management representations. Alternative procedures may be used when the client prevents the auditor from reviewing the predecessor's working papers, engages the auditor after the year-end physical inventory is completed, or requests that certain material A/R not be confirmed. (6941)

26. (a) Management is required to make all financial records and related data available to the auditor. It is up to the auditor to gather sufficient audit evidence to support the opinion on the financial statements. The other three statements are required to be included in the management representation letter. (8122)

Analytics

27. (b) Analytical procedures consist of evaluations of financial information made by a study of plausible relationships among both financial and non-financial data. Projecting an error rate is not such an evaluation. (5666)

28. (c) The purpose of applying analytical procedures in planning the audit is to assist in planning the nature, timing, and extent of auditing procedures that will be used to obtain audit evidence for specific account balances or classes of transactions. To accomplish this, the analytical procedures used in planning the audit should focus on enhancing the auditor's understanding of the client's business and the transactions and events that have occurred since the last audit date. Consideration of reductions in the scope of test of controls and substantive tests occurs after the auditor understands the client's business. The audit as a whole provides reasonable assurance that potential material misstatements will be identified. Assessing the adequacy of available audit evidence can occur only after examination of audit evidence, not in the planning stage. (5626)

29. (b) This procedure would most likely provide indications of any material improper entries in the revenue and expense accounts. This procedure would not indicate when something was paid. The auditor did not expect much change as the question states that similar amounts from the prior year were used as the expectation to compare. That is, if the auditor did not consider increased property taxes or a change in uncollectible accounts in his/her expectation, then those changes that should have been recorded, but weren't, would not be detected. (8146)

30. (b) If the client did not properly cutoff sales at the end of the year, then A/R would be overstated as well as sales. A/R turnover equals net credit sales divided by average net accounts receivable. Therefore, if net credit sales is overstated and average net receivables is overstated disproportionately, the turnover would be lower than expected when compared to the prior year. Answers (a) and (d) would not affect A/R turnover. A/R turnover would increase if a large receivable were written off near the end of the year. (8163)

31. (d) The overall review of the audit is concerned with the big picture. The other answer options are analytical procedures that likely are performed during earlier stages, or not at all. (6366)

32. (c) Analytics are used in the overall review stage to assist the auditor in assessing conclusions reached and in evaluating the overall financial statement presentation. The overall review generally would include reading the financial statements and notes and considering the adequacy of evidence gathered in response to unusual or unexpected balances. The results of these procedures may indicate that additional evidence may be needed. Procedures to achieve the objectives in answers (a) and (d) would be performed before the overall review stage. The auditor would examine the workpapers to determine if any procedures were omitted. (8157)

33. (c) Analytics are concerned with plausible relationships. The square footage of selling space might be used to compared retail revenues and expenses to industry figures and prior year performance. Personnel turnover and objectivity of audit committee members are concerned with the control environment. Management plans are considered when evaluating the control environment, valuation, and disclosure. (6392)

34. (b) The use of a standard cost system that produces variance reports allows the auditor an opportunity to compare the output from the standard cost system with the financial information presented by management. Segregating obsolete inventory before the physical inventory count would likely facilitate inventory procedures, but not necessarily the analytical procedures. The auditor should assess the reliability of the data by considering the source of the data and the conditions under which it was gathered. Stronger internal controls and independent sources enhance the reliability of data used in analytics, but (b) is the best answer. (5988)

35. (a) Whether the data were processed in an IT system or in a manual accounting system generally would not influence the auditor's consideration of the reliability of data for purposes of analytics. Factors that do influence the reliability of data include whether the data was obtained from independent sources outside the entity or from sources within the entity; whether sources within the entity were independent of those who are responsible for the amount being audited; whether the data was developed under a reliable system with adequate controls; whether the data was subjected to audit testing in the current or prior year; and whether the expectations were developed using data from a variety of sources. (0151)

36. (d) Increased sales to comparable customers would double accounts receivable (A/R) without a change in the allowance for doubtful accounts as a percentage of A/R. The client should increase this percentage if it has more customers with poor credit ratings. With no other changes, if twice as many A/R were written off previously or if more A/R are old, it suggests the current write-offs are inadequate. (7623)

37. (b) Analytics involve evaluations of information made by a study of plausible relationships. The relationship between two consecutive years' payroll expenses is related more closely than warranty expense and contingent liabilities. A/R and sales are not the primary accounts likely to be examined in evaluating an entity's costs and expenses. (6580)

38. (c) Increased sales to comparable customers would double accounts receivable (A/R) without a change in the allowance for doubtful accounts as a percentage of A/R. The allowance for doubtful accounts as a percentage should increase if a greater percentage of A/R is overdue this year. Improved internal control over cash receipts would tend to decrease accounts receivable balances. The allowance for doubtful accounts as a percentage should decrease if the client has less customers with poor credit ratings. (8133)

Using the Work of a Specialist

39. (d) When a specialist does not have a relationship with the client, the specialist's work usually will provide the auditor with greater assurance of reliability. However, the work of a specialist having a relationship to the client may be acceptable under certain circumstances. The appropriateness and reasonableness of methods and assumptions used and their application are the responsibility of the specialist. The auditor should obtain an understanding of the methods or assumptions used by the specialist, and evaluate whether the specialist's findings support the related assertions in the financial statements. An auditor may encounter complex or subjective matters potentially material to the financial statements. Such matters may require special skill or knowledge that, in the auditor's judgment, require using the work of a specialist. (6001)

40. (a) The auditor may decide to add explanatory language to his or her standard report or depart from an unqualified opinion. Reference to and identification of the specialist may be made in the auditor's report if such reference will facilitate an understanding of the reason for the explanatory paragraph or the departure from the unqualified opinion.

Q&A
24-55

If, as a result of the use of a specialist, the auditor concludes that conditions exist that cause substantial doubt about the entity's ability to continue as a going concern and the auditor believes a reference to the specialist will facilitate an understanding of the reason for the reference to this conclusion, the auditor may refer to the specialist in the auditor's report. Disclosure of the specialist's findings, implying that a more thorough audit was performed, is not appropriate. If a specialist's findings are consistent with management's representations and corroborate another specialist's earlier findings, there would be no need to disclose the findings of the specialist for the reasons above. Internal control is generally not a matter that would require the use of a specialist. (5680)

Inquiry of Client's Lawyer

41. (a) A lawyer may limit his response to matters to which s/he has given substantive attention in the form of legal consultation or representation. Answers (b), (c) and (d) are sufficient to cause a scope limitation. (0138)

42. (c) As the events or conditions that should be considered in accounting for and reporting litigation, claims, and assessments are matters within the direct knowledge, and often control of, an entity's management, that management is the primary source of information about such matters. Although a letter of audit inquiry to the client's lawyer is the auditor's primary means of obtaining *corroboration* of the information furnished by management concerning litigation, claims, and assessments, it is not the primary means of obtaining that information. (4276)

43. (d) A lawyer's response may be limited to matters that are considered individually or collectively material to the financial statements provided the lawyer and auditor have reached an understanding on the limits of materiality for this purpose. (6840)

44. (a) The passage is a quote from a sample inquiry letter to legal counsel. It is rare to refer to "our auditors" in a letter to that auditor; it is more likely that a third party is being addressed using this language. Management's representation letter states that the financial statements are presented fairly in conformity with GAAP and that, "there are no...other liabilities or gain or loss contingencies that are required to be accrued or disclosed...." That information was furnished to auditors generally is inappropriate for footnotes to financial statement. (7817)

45. (b) When restrictions that significantly limit the scope of the audit are imposed by the client,

ordinarily the auditor should disclaim an opinion on the financial statements. (7796)

46. (b) The letter of inquiry to the client's attorney is the primary means the auditor has to obtain corroboration of information furnished by management concerning litigation, claims, and assessments. The terms mentioned in answers (a) and (c) might be covered by the attorney, but are not the primary reasons the auditor makes the request. The items in answer (d) normally are furnished by management (or management may request that the attorney prepare the description and evaluation); they are not the primary reason that the auditor sends a letter of inquiry. (5139)

47. (c) As the events that should be considered in the financial accounting for and reporting of litigation, claims, and assessments are matters within the direct knowledge and, often, control of management of an entity, management is the primary source of information about such matters. Accordingly, the independent auditor's procedures should include inquiry and discussion with management concerning the policies and procedures adopted for identifying, evaluating, and accounting for litigation, claims, and assessments. A letter of audit inquiry to the client's lawyer is the auditor's primary means of obtaining corroboration of the information furnished by management concerning litigation, claims, and assessments. However, the lawyer does not evaluate the client's ability to continue as a going concern or whether all litigation, claims, and assessments have been recorded or disclosed in the financial statements. Examination of documents in the client's lawyer's possession is an atypical procedure. (6002)

48. (a) Only the statement in answer (a) would require further clarification. The statements in answers (b), (c), and (d) clearly indicate the probability of an unfavorable outcome. (8156)

Workpapers

49. (a) Audit documentation (working papers) *provides the principal support for the* representation in the *auditor's report* that the audit was performed in accordance with GAAS and for the opinion expressed regarding the financial information or the assertion to the effect that an opinion cannot be expressed. (5689)

50. (b) A standard confirmation request sent to a financial institution at which the client has both a checking or savings account and a loan would include requests on one form regarding the cash balance and the loan balance and, in addition, a description of the loan collateral. While confirmation of accounts

receivable is a generally accepted auditing procedure, confirmation of accounts payable is not. It generally is used only in cases of suspected fraud, sloppy or missing records, or suspected understatements. An entity holding inventory on consignment generally would not have information related to contingent liabilities. Accrued interest receivable most likely would be related to notes receivable rather than accounts receivable. (5987)

51. (b) The auditor is required to document her/his understanding of the entity's internal control. However, the form and extent of documentation is influenced by the size and complexity of the entity, as well as the nature of the entity's controls. Therefore, a flowchart depicting the segregation of duties and authorization of transactions is not necessarily required. Answers (a), (c), and (d) are required in all audits. (2321)

52. (c) Lead schedules generally summarize information, such as a summary of all cash accounts with debits and credits summarized into major categories and information about beginning and ending balances. (6628)

53. (c) Whether there have been communications from regulatory agencies concerning noncompliance with or deficiencies in financial reporting practices should be addressed in a management representation letter. A report on internal control or another special report generally would not discuss communications from other entities. Letters for underwriters concentrate on financial statements more than internal control. (6397)

54. (a) A physical count of assets that could be stolen readily (negotiable securities or gems, for instance) should include acknowledgement that the assets are again in the client's custody, if they are handled by the auditor. Sold securities would not be counted, so an analysis of realized gains and losses is not related closely to a count. An evaluation of control policies concerning physical access or negotiation generally would be documented with other control evaluations, not with substantive tests. (6937)

55. (d) The matters noted in answers (a), (b), and (c) would all have a significant impact on the quantity and content of the auditor's working papers. While the content of the representation letter may affect the quantity and content of the auditor's workpapers, the effect is minimal. (5146)

56. (d) Permanent files contain items of continuing interest, such as debt agreements, internal

control flowcharts, and articles of incorporation. The other items are of temporary interest only. (6007)

57. (d) Workpapers for each asset, liability, and equity account begin with a lead schedule summarizing the account's balance per the general ledger, and then showing adjusting and reclassification entries, and the final balance per audit. The lead schedule also includes the auditor's conclusion about whether the account is stated fairly. (2320)

58. (c) Working trial balances contain reclassification and adjustments columns. The items in answers (a), (b), and (d) are included in the audit workpapers, but are not included in the working trial balance. (5145)

Related Parties

59. (c) Business structure and operating style occasionally are designed deliberately to obscure relationships. Because compensating balance arrangements and nonmonetary transactions obscure the form of transactions, they are suspect. Compensating balance arrangements involve related parties more often than the other answer options. Segregation of duties applies whether the parties to a transaction are related or not. Reasonable and unreasonable accounting estimates both exist with and without related parties present. Entities frequently have recurring transactions with independent entities. (7811)

60. (d) An auditor should place primary emphasis on *evaluating the* adequacy of *the disclosure of the related party transactions.* The other answer alternatives are among the possible procedures used to evaluate the adequacy of related party disclosures. (5686)

61. (a) When searching for related party transactions, the auditor should obtain an understanding of each subsidiary's relationship to the total entity because business structure and operating style are occasionally deliberately designed to obscure related party transactions. Answers (b), (c), and (d) are not reasons for an auditor to obtain an understanding of each subsidiary's relationship to the total entity. (0185)

62. (c) After identifying related party transactions, the auditor should obtain an understanding of the business purpose of the transactions. The other answers are all procedures that may be performed later. (5142)

63. (c) Except for routine transactions, it will generally not be possible to determine whether a particular transaction would have taken place if the parties had not been related, or assuming it would have taken place, what the terms and manner of settlement would have been. Accordingly, it is difficult to substantiate representations that a transaction was consummated on terms equivalent to those that prevail in arm's-length transactions. If such a representation is included in the financial statements and the auditor believes that the representation is unsubstantiated by management, s/he should express a qualified or adverse opinion because of a departure from GAAP, depending on materiality. The disclosure of loans below market value is additional support for items included in the financial statements. Describing the exchange of real estate or presenting the dollar volume of related party transactions and any changes in the method of establishing terms from prior periods are all typical disclosure items that should be included in the financial statements for them to be in conformity with GAAP. (3940)

Solution 24-2 ADDITIONAL MULTIPLE CHOICE ANSWERS

Audit Evidence

64. (c) Despite being handled by the client, bank statements originate outside the entity and therefore are the most persuasive of the choices. Both purchase orders and work sheets originate within the client. Management's *representation* letter only documents the client's oral representations. (5657)

65. (d) The auditor most likely would consider whether material misstatements exist when transactions selected for testing are not supported by proper documentation. Reduced emphasis on meeting earnings projections would be a factor *decreasing* the likelihood of earnings overstatements and assets (the most frequent misstatement). Having the board of directors make major financing decisions would decrease the incentive for management to use questionable reporting by reducing the amount of management's responsibility. Significant deficiencies previously communicated to management may not have been corrected because of an unfavorable cost-benefit relationship. (5086)

66. (d) Appropriate evidence is both valid and relevant. The validity of audit evidence is highly dependent upon the circumstances under which it is obtained. The independent auditor's direct personal knowledge, obtained through physical examination, observation, computation, and inspection, is more persuasive than information obtained indirectly. (8143)

67. (c) The existence or occurrence assertions concern whether assets or liabilities exist as of the financial statement date and whether recorded transactions actually occurred during a reporting period. Even though this is a test of controls, this procedure also provides evidence that customers' balances actually exist. The presentation and disclosure assertions concern proper classification, description, and disclosure in the financial statements. (8119)

68. (c) Evidence obtained during an audit may cause the auditor to change the nature, extent, or timing of other planned audit procedures. A disclaimer of opinion or a qualified opinion would be issued if the auditor could not obtain sufficient evidence; there is no indication that that is the case in this situation. A statement from management supporting their inventory valuation is merely another management representation and likely would be an insufficient substitute for additional audit procedures. (8394)

69. (a) Tracing the auditor's inventory observations test counts to the client's inventory listings is testing to see if all assets that should have been recorded have been recorded, i.e., completeness. Rights and obligations would be concerned with, for example, whether the inventory was pledged as collateral or under contract to be sold for other than market value. Valuation or allocation would be concerned with, for example, the value assigned to the inventory and whether its historical cost is under market value as of the balance sheet date. Classification and understandability would be concerned with, for example, whether the inventory was appropriately in short-term assets. (8396)

70. (c) If credit is granted in accordance with policies, there is a greater chance that accounts receivable are correctly valued as allowance account amounts are based on the assumption that those policies are followed. Confirming that credit is granted in accordance with policies provides little evidence as to the rights and obligations connected with those sales. (8403)

71. (a) Reconciling the amount included in the statement of cash flows to other statements is a basic procedure. Relationships among elements of financial information within the period are one source of expectations regarding relationships that reasonably are expect to exist. The other procedures generally

are involved in auditing the balance in the cash accounts, not necessarily the statement of cash flows. (8408)

Internal Auditors

72. (a) If the independent auditor decides that the work performed by internal auditors may have a bearing on her/his own procedures, s/he should assess the competence and objectivity of internal auditors and evaluate their work. When assessing the internal auditor's objectivity, the auditor should determine the organizational status of the internal auditor responsible for the internal audit function. In this case, the independent auditor would place limited reliance on the work performed by the internal auditors because the internal auditors report to the controller and thus may be reluctant to report weaknesses in the controller's activities. The independent auditor performs tests of controls to assess the level of control risk and then will use the work of the internal auditors, if appropriate, to decrease the substantive tests. The auditor is not precluded from using the work of internal auditors as long as, in his or her judgment, he or she is satisfied with their competence and objectivity. (0157)

73. (a) Considering professional standards and whether an internal auditor meets them provides an indication regarding his or her objectivity. Neither the tests of activities that could detect errors and fraud, materiality of recently inspected accounts, nor the results of tests performed by internal auditors influence an internal auditor's objectivity. An internal auditor may concentrate appropriately on compliance testing, rather than tests of errors and fraud. The accounts to be audited may be selected by people other than the auditors. A biased internal auditor conceivably might be unusually careful in work performed just before the external audit. (7108)

Management Representations

74. (c) The management representation letter should be dated as of the date of the auditor's report. (5685)

75. (a) The last paragraph of the AICPA's illustrative management representation letter states: "To the best of our knowledge and belief, no events have occurred subsequent to the balance sheet date and through the date of this letter that would require adjustment to, or disclosure in, the aforementioned financial statements." The auditor, not management, is responsible for reporting significant deficiencies to the audit committee. Statements regarding the attorney-client privilege generally are made by attorneys, not client management. That certain computer

files may exist only for a short period of time is more appropriately noted at the beginning of the audit; a management representation letter should be dated as of the date of the auditor's report. (7801)

Analytics

76. (a) GAAS require that analytics are to be used to some extent in all audits in the planning of the audit and in the final review stages. The use of analytics as a substantive test is not mandated, but it should be noted that analytics can be more effective or efficient than tests of details for achieving certain substantive testing objectives. (0141)

77. (d) The auditor's reliance on substantive tests to achieve an audit objective related to a particular assertion may be derived from tests of details, from analytical procedures, or from a combination of both. The decision about which procedure or procedures to use to achieve a particular audit objective is based on the auditor's judgment on the expected effectiveness and efficiency of the available procedures. An auditor's decision whether to apply analytics or to perform tests of transactions and account balances is not determined solely by the availability of data aggregated at a high level, the auditor's familiarity with industry trends, or the timing of tests performed after the balance sheet date. (2965)

78. (c) Understanding financial relationships is essential to evaluating the results of analytics and usually requires knowledge of the client and the industry. The staff accountant may not be objective regarding his or her own work and may have limited industry knowledge. It would not be practicable for the managing partner who has responsibility for all audit engagements at that practice office to perform this procedure for all audits. A firm's quality control manager is not a member of the engagement team and thus may not participate in this manner in the engagement. (7025)

79. (c) Unexpected relationships discovered through analytics indicate additional investigation is appropriate. To assume that fraud exists in the relevant accounts or to revise communications with the audit committee without further investigation would be an over-reaction. Analytics are a substantive test, not a test of internal control. (6398)

80. (c) A basic premise underlying the application of analytics is that plausible relationships among data reasonably may be expected to exist and continue in the absence of known conditions to the contrary. The accounts receivable (A/R) turnover formula is net credit sales divided by average net A/R. In other words, A/R turnover is a measure of

how many times in a year an entity collects what its credit sales. If the ratio increased, either average net A/R decreased or net credit sales increased. An increase in collections results in decreased average net A/R. The A/R aging is said to have deteriorated when collection times lengthen, an unusual circumstance if average net A/R decreased in proportion to sales. The elimination of a discount policy might decrease sales, but its relative impact on net credit sales and average net A/R is not known; in the absence of information to the contrary, assume that this did not have a significant impact on the ratio. A decrease in net credit sales would decrease the ratio. (7842)

81. (b) The final review stage of the audit provides an overall review of financial information in light of the audit opinion expressed. A final consideration of the adequacy of evidence is appropriate for this stage. Factors that determined the preliminary materially and audit risk levels would have been reassessed before arriving at final materially and audit risk levels. Summarizing specified uncorrected misstatements and calculating projected uncorrected misstatements estimated through sampling techniques is done before deciding on an audit opinion. (7813)

82. (c, d) As higher levels of assurance are desired from analytical procedures, more predictable relationships are required to develop the expectation. Relationships in a stable environment are usually more predictable than relationships in a dynamic or unstable environment. Relationships involving income statement accounts tend to be more predictable than relationships involving only balance sheet accounts since income statement accounts represent transactions over a period of time, whereas balance sheet accounts represent amounts as of a point in time. Relationships involving transactions subject to management discretion are sometimes less predictable. (2773)

83. (b) A comparison of revenues and expenses with those of the prior year is likely to reveal a change in the capitalization policy for small tools. For instance, if tools costing less than $25 formerly were expensed and the policy is changed to $100, this is likely to show a substantial increase in the amount of tools expensed during the period. Answer (c) concerns a liability account, *Payroll Taxes Payable,* not a revenue or expense account. Failure to recognize the property tax increase would make the account balances comparable and so the auditor would *not* investigate. (7493)

84. (c) The objective of analytical procedures used in the overall review stage of the audit is to assist the auditor in assessing the conclusions reached and in the evaluation of the overall financial statement presentation. The overall review would generally include reading the financial statements and notes and *considering unusual or unexpected balances or relationships that were not previously identified.* The other answer alternatives are done before the overall review stage. (5665)

85. (c) The following factors influence the auditor's consideration of the reliability of data for purposes of achieving audit objectives: whether the data was obtained from independent sources outside the entity or from sources within the entity; whether sources within the entity were independent of those who are responsible for the amount being audited; whether the data was developed under a reliable system with adequate controls; whether the data was subjected to audit testing in the current or prior year; and whether the expectations were developed using data from a variety of sources. Whether the data was processed in an IT system or in a manual accounting system, whether the data was prepared on the cash basis or in conformity with GAAP, and whether the data was processed in an online system or a batch entry system generally would not influence the auditor's consideration of the reliability of data for purposes of analytics. (8388)

86. (d) Analytics involve comparisons of recorded amounts or ratios developed from recorded amounts to expectations developed by the auditor. Comparing current year account balances for conformity with predictable patterns assists the author's understanding of the client's business and events that have occurred since the last audit date and identifies areas that may represent specific risks relevant to the audit. Confirming bank balances with financial institutions, scanning accounts receivable for amounts over credit limits, and recalculating inventory extensions of physical inventory counts generally are not considered analytics. (8397)

87. (d) The auditor is required to perform analytics in the planning stage of the audit. These procedures assist the auditor in planning the nature, extent, and timing of substantive tests; thus, they should focus on enhancing the auditor's understanding of the client's business and the transactions and events that have occurred since the last audit and identifying areas that may represent specific risks relevant to the audit. Analytics involve comparisons of recorded amounts or ratios developed from recorded amounts to expectations developed by the auditor. Comparison of recorded financial information with anticipated results from budgets and forecasts is appropriate for this planning stage. Representations from management are dated the same date as the

auditor's report. Communication regarding the prior year's audit adjustments typically occurs near the end of the audit for that year. Inquiry of the client's attorney tends to occur after the planning stage, as part of the substantive tests. (8414)

Using the Work of a Specialist

88. (b) An auditor may use the work of a specialist who has a relationship with the client, but must assess the risk that the specialist might not be objective. If the relationship might impair the specialist's objectivity, the auditor should perform additional procedures or engage another specialist. Normally, an auditor should not refer to the work or findings of the specialist. In expressing an unqualified opinion, the auditor may refer to the specialist in an explanatory paragraph only if doing so will help clarify the reason for the explanatory paragraph. If there is a material departure from GAAP, the auditor may refer to the specialist in an explanatory paragraph only if doing so will help clarify the reason for the qualified or adverse opinion. Control deficiencies result from the client's actions or inactions, not the auditor's actions. (8412)

Inquiry of Client's Lawyer

89. (b) The response in answer (b) is vague and probably would need clarification. The other answer options indicate that the client probably doesn't have any material liability concerning the matters discussed. (6364)

90. (d) When a client's lawyer is unable to form a conclusion about the likelihood of an unfavorable outcome of pending litigation because of inherent uncertainties and the effect on the financial statements could be material, the auditor ordinarily will conclude that an explanatory paragraph should be added to the report. (5682)

91. (d) The refusal of a client to allow necessary communications with a lawyer is a scope limitation that usually results in a disclaimer of opinion; knowing that an audit could not be performed, a CPA could not accept the engagement. A CPA need not understand a client's operations and industry when accepting an engagement if the CPA reasonably can expect to gain an appropriate understanding. Recurring operating losses do not prohibit audit completion. An *inquiry* of the predecessor auditor is a necessary procedure because the predecessor auditor may be able to provide information that will assist the successor auditor in determining whether to accept the engagement. However, the review of the predecessor auditor's working papers assists the successor auditor in the planning of the engagement. The successor auditor may initiate this after accepting the engagement. Furthermore, although the predecessor auditor should ordinarily permit the successor auditor to review the working papers, the extent, if any, to which a predecessor auditor permits access to working papers, is a matter of judgment. (8384)

Workpapers

92. (c) The management representation letter should address that there are no violations or possible violations of laws or regulations whose effects should be considered for disclosure in the financial statements or as a basis for recording a loss contingency. (5137)

Related Parties

93. (d) Transactions that because of their nature may be indicative of the existence of related parties include borrowing or lending on an interest-free basis or at a rate of interest significantly above or below market rates prevailing at the time of the transaction; selling real estate at a price that differs significantly from its appraised value; exchanging property for similar property in a nonmonetary transaction; and making loans with no scheduled terms for when or how the funds will be repaid. (2974)

PERFORMANCE BY SUBTOPICS

Each category below parallels a subtopic covered in Chapter 24. Record the number and percentage of questions you correctly answered in each subtopic area.

Audit Evidence

Question #	Correct √
1	
2	
3	
4	
5	
6	
7	
8	
9	
10	
# Questions	10

Correct _____
% Correct

Internal Auditors

Question #	Correct √
11	
12	
13	
14	
15	
16	
17	
# Questions	7

Correct _____
% Correct

Management Representations

Question #	Correct √
18	
19	
20	
21	
22	
23	
24	
25	
26	
# Questions	9

Correct _____
% Correct

Analytics

Question #	Correct √
27	
28	
29	
30	
31	
32	
33	
34	
35	
36	
37	
38	
# Questions	12

Correct _____
% Correct _____

Using the Work of a Specialist

Question #	Correct √
39	
40	
# Questions	2

Correct _____
% Correct

Inquiry of Client's Lawyer

Question #	Correct √
41	
42	
43	
44	
45	
46	
47	
48	
# Questions	8

Correct _____
% Correct _____

Workpapers

Question #	Correct √
49	
50	
51	
52	
53	
54	
55	
56	
57	
58	
# Questions	10

Correct _____
% Correct _____

Related Parties

Question #	Correct √
59	
60	
61	
62	
63	
# Questions	5

Correct _____
% Correct _____

SIMULATION SOLUTIONS

Solution 24-3

Response #1: Documentation (6 points)

1. B

The auditor's report to the audit committee regarding significant deficiencies includes a description of the conditions noted.

2. N

Management is a knowledgeable source of the company's viewpoint, beliefs, intentions, and occurrence of events.

3. M

An auditor's review notes include reminders of select conditions to allow a double check to ensure that all matters are resolved appropriately.

4. H

Appropriate places for disclaimers are the engagement letter and post-engagement reports. The statement speaks of the audit in the future ("Consequently, our audit will not...") from the perspective of the auditor.

5. N

Management is a knowledgeable source of the company's viewpoint, beliefs, intentions, and occurrence of events.

6. I

Letters to underwriters may contain negative assurance, which is used in few instances, certainly not in a report on significant deficiencies. A practitioner's report on a management assertion would not be discussing stockholder's equity in relation to previous unaudited financial statements; it would discuss the practitioner's work in relation to management's assertion.

7.   D

An opinion regarding liability related to a proceeding is usually from a lawyer in response to an audit inquiry letter. The management representation letter usually has a less specific statement of all possible liabilities being included in the financial statements as appropriate. These are the two parties most likely to be knowledgeable about proceedings related to the client.

8.   L

The phrases *substantial doubt* and *ability to continue as a going concern* are required in the auditor's report when there is a going concern uncertainty.

9.   F

The auditor's communication to the audit committee should include any disagreements, whether or not resolved, with management about matters that, individually or in the aggregate, could have a significant impact on the financial statements.

10.   N

Management is a knowledgeable source of the company's viewpoint, beliefs, intentions, and occurrence of events.

Response #2: Communication (3 points)

Analytical procedures are used for these broad purposes:

- To assist the auditor in **planning the nature, timing, and extent** of other auditing procedures.
- As a **substantive test** to obtain **audit evidence** about particular **assertions** related to account balances or classes of transactions.
- As an **overall review** of the financial information in the final review stage of the audit.

Response #3: Research (1 point)

Paragraph Reference Answer: AU 330.34

Guidance: AU 330.34 states, "For the purpose of this section, accounts receivable means (a) The entity's claims against customers that have arisen from the sale of goods or services in the normal course of business, and (b) A financial institution's loans. Confirmation of accounts receivable is a generally accepted auditing procedure. As discussed in paragraph .06, it is generally presumed that

evidence obtained from third parties will provide the auditor with higher-quality audit evidence than is typically available from within the entity. Thus, there is a presumption that the auditor will request the confirmation of accounts receivable during an audit unless one of the following is true:

- Accounts receivable are immaterial to the financial statements.
- The use of confirmations would be ineffective.
- The auditor's combined assessed level of inherent and control risk is low, and the assessed level, in conjunction with the evidence expected to be provided by analytical procedures or other substantive tests of details, is sufficient to reduce audit risk to an acceptably low level for the applicable financial statement assertions. In many situations, both confirmation of accounts receivable and other substantive tests of details are necessary to reduce audit risk to an acceptably low level for the applicable financial statement assertions."

(6946)

Solution 24-4

Response #1: Documentation (4 points)

1.   P

The client, a CPA performing a review, and a successor auditor are most likely to be the external viewers of workpapers. Typically, each successor will try to view a predecessor's workpapers, but the opposite will be rare. A client is the most atypical user of the three. Further, there is no answer option with a communication regarding the client or reviewer viewing the workpapers.

2.   J

A confirmation request seeks an indication of agreement between provided information with another's records. The language in this statement is more suitable to an accounts receivable confirmation (a relatively straight-forward matter of matching amounts) than an inquiry of legal counsel (a relatively complex matter requiring the judgment by counsel, and thus a more complex letter of inquiry).

3.   B

The auditor's report to the audit committee regarding significant deficiencies includes a description of the conditions noted.

4. H

The statement speaks of the future ("...we will communicate to you....") from the perspective of the auditor. It is most likely that an auditor would send this message to management. The appropriate place for this disclaimer is in the engagement letter.

5. F

The auditor's communication to the audit committee should include any serious difficulties encountered in dealing with management related to the performance of the audit.

6. B

The auditor's report to the audit committee regarding significant deficiencies includes a description of the conditions noted.

7. C

This statement is from the entity's management ("our financial statements") to a party (other than the auditor) who is knowledgeable about the company's contingent liabilities. In connection with audits, lawyers frequently are asked to provide their opinion of contingent liabilities related to the services that they provide to clients.

8. N

Management is a knowledgeable source of the company's viewpoint, beliefs, intentions, and occurrence of events.

9. M

An auditor's review notes include reminders to check on issues where mistakes have a relatively high probability of being made.

Response #2: Communication (5 points)

a. An auditor's expectations are developed from the following sources of information:

- Financial information for **comparable prior periods** giving consideration to known changes.
- **Anticipated results**—for example, budgets, forecasts, and extrapolations.
- **Relationships** among elements of financial information **within the period**.
- **Information regarding the industry** in which the client operates.
- **Relationships** of financial information **with** relevant **nonfinancial information**.

b. The factors that influence an auditor's consideration of the reliability of data for purposes of achieving audit objectives are whether the

- Data were **obtained from independent sources** outside the entity or from sources within the entity.
- **Sources within the entity were independent** of those who are responsible for the amount being audited.
- Data were **developed under a reliable system** with adequate controls.
- Data were **subjected to audit testing** in the current or prior year.
- Expectations were developed using data from a **variety** of sources.

Response #3: Research (1 point)

Paragraph Reference Answer: QC 10.15

Guidance: QC 10.15 states, "The firm should promote an internal culture based on the recognition that quality is essential in performing engagements and should establish policies and procedures to support that culture. Such policies and procedures should require the firm's leadership (managing partner or board of managing partners, chief executive officer, or equivalent) to assume ultimate responsibility for the firm's system of quality control."

(6956)

Solution 24-5

Response #1: Analytics (5 points)

1. H

The current ratio is total current assets divided by total current liabilities. ($1,240,000 / $400,000 = 3.1)

2. E

The quick (or acid-test) ratio is cash plus marketable securities plus net receivables divided by current liabilities. [($240,000 + $400,000) / $400,000 = 1.6]

3. K

Accounts receivable turnover is net credit sales divided by average net receivables. {$3,000,000 / [($400,000 + $400,000) / 2] = 7.5}

4. G

Inventory turnover is cost of goods sold divided by average inventory. {$1,800,000 / [($600,000 + $600,000) / 2] = 3.0}

5. D

Total asset turnover is sales divided by total assets. ($3,000,000 / $2,000.000 = 1.5)

6. T

Gross margin percentage is the gross margin divided by sales, expressed as a percentage. ($1,200,000 / $3,000,000 = 0.4 = 40%)

7. P

Net operating margin percentage is operating income divided by sales, expressed as a percentage. [($660,000 / $3,000,000 = .22 = 22%)]

8. N

Times interest earned is income before income taxes and interest charges divided by interest charges. $660,000 / $40,000 = 16.5]

9. U

Total debt to equity percentage is total liabilities divided by owners' equity, expressed as a percentage. [($400,000 + $350,000) / ($750,000 + $500,000) = 0.6 = 60%]

Response #2: Communication (4 points)

a. Financial statement assertions are **representations by management** that are embodied in financial statement components.

b. In obtaining **audit evidence in support of financial statement assertions**, an auditor develops specific audit objectives in the light of those assertions.

Response #3: Research (1 point)

Paragraph Reference Answer: AU 322.26

Guidance: AU 322.26 states, "In making the evaluation, the auditor should test some of the internal auditors' work related to the significant financial statement assertions. These tests may be accomplished by either (a) examining some of the controls, transactions, or balances that the internal auditors examined or (b) examining similar controls, transactions, or balances not actually examined by the internal auditors. In reaching conclusions about the internal auditors' work, the auditor should compare the results of his or her tests with the results of the internal auditors' work. The extent of this testing will depend on the circumstances and should be sufficient to enable the auditor to make an evaluation of the overall quality and effectiveness of the internal audit work being considered by the auditor."

(6242)

Solution 24-6

Response #1: Analytics (5 points)

1. A, B, E

The allowance for doubtful accounts as a percentage of accounts receivable will decrease when the allowance for doubtful accounts decreases proportionately less than the accounts receivable does or when accounts receivable increases. Due to recording consignment items shipped during the last month as sales, accounts receivable is overstated. Due to not recording a significant number of credit memos for returned merchandise, accounts receivable is overstated. However, these occurrences do not impact the allowance for doubtful accounts. A larger percentage of sales occurring during the last month of the year, as compared to the prior year, increases the amount in accounts receivable. This increases average accounts receivable, as compared to last year, without increasing the allowance for doubtful accounts, as compared to last year.

2. P

The rate of interest paid will increase the proportionate amount of interest expense even with the same amount of debt.

3. L, P

Operating income does not include interest or income tax expense; the rates for these apparently increased.

4. H

Percentages measure proportional changes. The items being compared must have changed proportionately if the percentage did not change.

Response #2: Communication (4 points)

a. There is not necessarily a one-to-one relationship between audit objectives and procedures. Some **auditing procedures may relate to more than one objective**. On the other hand, a **combination of auditing procedures may be needed to achieve a single objective**. The procedures adopted should be **adequate** to achieve the audit objectives.

b. The selection of audit procedures should be based on the assessed **risk of material misstatement**. The higher the risk, the more **reliable** and relevant the **audit evidence** obtained should be. The auditor should consider both the **inherent risks** and **control risk** of each class of transactions, account balance, or disclosure.

Response #3: Research (1 point)

Paragraph Reference Answer: AU 329.21

Guidance: AU 329.21 states, "The auditor should evaluate significant unexpected differences. Reconsidering the methods and factors used in developing the expectation and inquiry of management may assist the auditor in this regard. Management responses, however, should ordinarily be corroborated with other audit evidence. In those cases when an explanation for the difference cannot be obtained, the auditor should obtain sufficient appropriate audit evidence about the assertion by performing other audit procedures to satisfy himself as to whether the difference is a likely misstatement. In designing such other procedures, the auditor should consider that unexplained differences may indicate an increased risk of material misstatement. (See section 316, *Consideration of Fraud in a Financial Statement Audit.*)."

(6243)

Solution 24-7

Response #1: Communication (9 points)

a. 1. An auditor is required to obtain a written management representation letter as part of **every audit performed in accordance with generally accepted auditing standards**.

2. The **purposes** of obtaining a written management representation letter are to:

- **Confirm** the **oral representations** given to the auditor.
- Indicate and **document** the **continuing appropriateness of management's representations**.
- **Reduce** the **possibility** of **misunderstanding** concerning the matters that are the subject of the representations.
- **Complement** the **other auditing procedures** by **corroborating** the information discovered in performing those procedures.
- **Obtain evidence** concerning management's **future plans** and **intentions**, e.g., when refinancing debt or discontinuing a line of business.

b. 1. The representation letter should be addressed **to the auditor** and dated no earlier than **the date of the auditor's report**.

2. The letter should be signed by **members of management** whom the auditor believes are **responsible for and knowledgeable**, directly or through others in the organization, about the matters covered by the representation. Their refusal to sign the letter would constitute a **limitation on the scope** of the audit sufficient to preclude an unqualified opinion and affect the auditor's ability to **rely on other management representations**.

c. Obtaining a management representation letter does **not relieve an auditor** of any other responsibility for planning or performing an audit. Accordingly, an auditor should still perform all the usual tests to corroborate representations made by management.

Response #2: Research (1 point)

Paragraph Reference Answer: AU 315.22

Guidance: AU 315.22 states, "If the client refuses to inform the predecessor auditor or if the successor auditor is not satisfied with the resolution of the matter, the successor auditor should evaluate (a) possible implications on the current engagement and (b) whether to resign from the engagement. Furthermore, the successor auditor may wish to consult with his or her legal counsel in determining an appropriate course of further action."

(6244)

Solution 24-8

Response #1: Communication (9 points)

a. The factors Kent should consider in the process of selecting Park include

- Park's **professional certification**, license, or other recognition of Park's competence.
- Park's **reputation** and standing in the view of Park's **peers** and others familiar with Park's capability or performance.
- Park's **relationship**, if any, to Davidson Corporation.

b. The understanding among Kent, Park, and Davidson's management as to the nature of the work to be performed by Park should cover

- The **objectives and scope** of Park's work.
- Park's representations as to Park's relationship, if any, to Davidson.
- The **methods** or **assumptions** to be **used**.
- A comparison of the methods or assumptions to be used with those used in the preceding period.
- Park's **understanding** of Kent's **corroborative use of Park's findings**.

- The form and content of Park's report that would enable Kent to evaluate Park's findings.

c. Kent **may refer to Park in the auditor's report** if Kent decides to issue an unqualified opinion, only if it will facilitate an understanding of the reason for an explanatory paragraph.

d. Kent **may refer** to Park in the auditor's report if Kent decides to **issue other than an unqualified opinion** as a result of Park's findings. Reference is permitted if it will facilitate an understanding of the reason for the modification.

Response #2: Research (1 point)

Paragraph Reference Answer: AU 334.04

Guidance: AU 334.04 states, "An audit performed in accordance with generally accepted auditing standards cannot be expected to provide assurance that all related party transactions will be discovered. Nevertheless, during the course of his audit, the auditor should be aware of the possible existence of material related party transactions that could affect the financial statements and of common ownership or management control relationships for which FASB ASC 850-10-50 requires disclosure. Many of the procedures outlined in the following paragraphs are normally performed in an audit in accordance with generally accepted auditing standards, even if the auditor has no reason to suspect that related party transactions or control relationships exist. Other audit procedures set forth in this section are specifically directed to related party transactions."

(6245)

Solution 24-9

Response #1: Communication (9 points)

The omissions, ambiguities, and inappropriate statements and terminology in Brown's letter are as follows:

1. The **action** that Consolidated **intends to take** concerning each suit (for example, to contest the matter vigorously, to seek an out-of-court settlement, or to an appeal an adverse decision) is omitted.

2. A **description of the progress** of each case to date is omitted.

3. An **evaluation** of the **likelihood of an unfavorable outcome** of each case is omitted.

4. An **estimate,** if one can be made, of the **amount or range of potential loss** of each case is omitted.

5. The various **other pending or threatened litigation** on which Young was consulted is not identified and included.

6. The **unasserted claims and assessments** probable of assertion that have a reasonable possibility of an unfavorable outcome are not identified.

7. Consolidated's understanding of Young's responsibility to advise Consolidated concerning the **disclosure of unasserted possible claims or assessments** is omitted.

8. **Materiality** (or the limits of materiality) is not addressed.

9. The reference to a **limitation** on Young's response **due to confidentiality is inappropriate**.

10. Young is not requested to identify the nature of and **reasons for any limited response**.

11. **Young is not requested to include matters that existed after December 31, Year 5**, up to the date of Young's response.

12. The **date** by which Young's **response is needed** is not indicated.

13. The reference to Young's **response possibly being quoted or referred** to in the financial statements is inappropriate.

14. **Vague terminology** such as "slight" and "some chance" is included where "remote" and "possible" are more appropriate.

15. There is **no inquiry about** any unpaid or **unbilled charges**, services, or disbursements.

Response #2: Research (1 point)

Paragraph Reference Answer: AU 333.04

Guidance: AU 333.04 states, "If a representation made by management is contradicted by other audit evidence, the auditor should investigate the circumstances and consider the reliability of the representation made. Based on the circumstances, the auditor should consider whether his or her reliance on management's representations relating to other aspects of the financial statements is appropriate and justified."

(6246)

Solution 24-10

Response #1: Communication (9 points)

The audit procedures Temple should apply to identify Ford's related party relationships and transactions include the following:

- Evaluate the company's procedures for **identifying and properly reporting** related party relationships and transactions.
- **Request** from management the **names of all related parties** and inquire whether there were any transactions with these parties during the period.
- **Review tax returns** and filings with other regulatory agencies for the names of related parties.
- Determine the **names of all pension plans** and other trusts and the names of their officers and trustees.
- Review **stock certificate book** to identify the stockholders.
- Review material investment transactions to determine whether the investments created **related party relationships**.
- Review the **minutes of board of directors' meetings**.
- Review **conflict-of-interest statements** obtained by the company from its management.
- Review the **extent and nature of business transacted with major customers, suppliers, borrowers, and lenders**.
- Consider whether transactions are occurring, but are not being given proper accounting recognition, e.g., **personal use** of company vehicles, **interest-free loans**, etc.
- Review accounting records for **large, unusual, or nonrecurring transactions** or balances, paying particular attention to transactions recognized at or near the end of the reporting period.
- **Review confirmations of compensating balance arrangements** for indications that balances are or were maintained for or by related parties.
- Review **invoices from law firms** that have performed services for the company for indications of the existence of related party relationships or transactions.
- Review **confirmations of loans receivable and payable** for indications of **guarantees**, and determine their nature and the relationships, if any, of the guarantors to the reporting entity.

Response #2: Research (1 point)

Paragraph Reference Answer: AU 333.10

Guidance: AU 333.10 states, "If current management was not present during all periods covered by

the auditor's report, the auditor should nevertheless obtain written representations from current management on all such periods. The specific written representations obtained by the auditor will depend on the circumstances of the engagement and the nature and basis of presentation of the financial statements. As discussed in paragraph .08, management's representations may be limited to matters that are considered either individually or collectively material to the financial statements."

(6247)

Solution 24-11

Response #1: Communication (9 points)

The substantive audit procedures that Young should apply when testing for loss contingencies relating to litigation, claims, and assessments include the following:

- **Read minutes** of meetings of stockholders, directors, and committees.
- **Read contracts, loan agreements, leases**, and other documents.
- Read **correspondence with taxing** and other governmental **agencies**.
- Read **correspondence with insurance** and bonding **companies**.
- Read **confirmation replies** for information concerning guarantees.
- **Discuss with management** the entity's **policies and procedures** for identifying, evaluating, and accounting for litigation, claims, and assessments.
- **Obtain from management** or inside general counsel a **description and evaluation of litigation, claims, and assessments**.
- Obtain **written assurance from management** that the financial statements include all accruals and disclosures required by Statement of Financial Accounting Standards No. 5.
- **Examine documents** in the client's possession concerning litigation, claims, or assessments, including correspondence from lawyers.
- Obtain an analysis of **professional fee expenses and review supporting invoices** for indications of contingencies.
- Request the client's management to prepare for transmittal a **letter of inquiry to** those **lawyers** consulted by the client concerning litigation, claims, and assessments.
- **Compare the lawyer's response to the items in the letter of inquiry** to the description and evaluation of litigation, claims, and assessments obtained from management.
- Determine that the financial statements include **proper accruals and disclosures** of the contingencies.

Response #2: Research (1 point)

Paragraph Reference Answer: AU 316.23

Guidance: AU 316.23 states, "For entities that have an internal audit function, the auditor also should inquire of appropriate internal audit personnel about their views about the risks of fraud, whether they have performed any procedures to identify or detect fraud during the year, whether management has satisfactorily responded to any findings resulting from these procedures, and whether the internal auditors have knowledge of any fraud or suspected fraud."

(3033)

Solution 24-12

Response #1: Risk Factors (1 point)

Answer: B

Redesigning the company's accounting policies and procedures introduces many changes that affect the financial statements; therefore, the auditor will need to focus more attention in this area to determine the reasons underlying these changes and whether s/he agrees with them.

Response #2: Ratios (1 point)

1. 3.42

The current ratio equals current assets divided by current liabilities (85,280,000/24,965,000).

2. 13.77%

Return on equity equals net income divided by average stockholder's equity. Editor's Note: Be careful to follow directions. This problem specifies that for turnover ratios, year-end balances should be used (13,815,000 / 100,315,000).

Response #3: Analytical Results (4 points)

. 1. E

Days sales in accounts receivable equals 360 days divided by receivables turnover. Receivables turnover equals net credit sales divided by average net receivables. If a larger percentage of sales occurred during the last month of the year, average receivables would increase which would then decrease receivables turnover, thereby increasing days sales in accounts receivable.

2. B

Operating profit margin equals operating profit divided by total sales revenue. Operating profit equals gross profit minus operating expenses. Therefore, if operating expenses increase at a higher rate than sales revenue, then operating profit would decrease more than sales revenue would increase, thereby decreasing operating profit margin.

Response #4: Substantive Tests (3 points)

1. A

Performing tests of subsequent cash receipts after the balance sheet date would help verify the existence of accounts receivable since they should have been paid by then if they were valid balances. False accounts receivable would not be paid.

2. E

Performing shipping cut-off procedures would help determine that the inventory balance is accurately stated because to include inventory that was shipped before the end of the year would overstate the inventory balance.

Response #5: Communication (5 points)

Expected response should include:

Before a CPA firm that was engaged to audit an entity's financial statements might agree to change the engagement to a review, the firm should consider the reason given for the entity's request. A change in circumstances that affects the entity's requirement for an audit or a misunderstanding concerning the nature of an audit would ordinarily be considered a reasonable basis for requesting the change. However, if the auditing procedures are substantially complete or the cost to complete such procedures is relatively insignificant, the firm should consider the propriety of accepting a change in the engagement.

Response #6: Research (1 point)

Paragraph Reference Answer: AU 508.44

"The auditor is not required to prepare a basic financial statement (for example, a statement of cash flows for one or more periods) and include it in the report if the company's management declines to present the statement. Accordingly, in these cases, the auditor should ordinarily qualify the report in the following manner:

Independent Auditor's Report

We have audited the accompanying balance sheets of X Company as of December 31, 20X2 and 20X1, and the related statements of income and retained earnings for the years then ended. These financial statements are the responsibility of the Company's management. Our responsibility is to express an opinion on these financial statements based on our audit.

[*Same second paragraph as the standard report.*]

The Company declined to present a statement of cash flows for the years ended December 31, 20X2 and 20X1. Presentation of such statement summarizing the Company's operating, investing, and financing activities is required by accounting principles generally accepted in the United States of America.

In our opinion, except that the omission of a statement of cash flows results in an incomplete presentation as explained in the preceding paragraph, the financial statements referred to above present fairly, in all material respects, the financial position of X Company as of December 31, 20X2 and 20X1, and the results of its operations for the years then ended in conformity with accounting principles generally accepted in the United States of America."

(8169)

CHAPTER 25

AUDIT PROGRAMS

CHAPTER 25

AUDIT PROGRAMS

I. **Substantive Procedures (AU 318, SAS 110 continued)**

A. **Overview**
Substantive procedures, or tests, are designed to detect material misstatements at the relevant assertion level; they include tests of details of classes of transactions, account balances, and disclosures as well as analytical procedures. Substantive procedures should be designed to be responsive to the assessment of the risks of material misstatement with the objective of obtaining sufficient appropriate audit evidence to achieve the planned level of assurance at the relevant assertion level.

  1. **Required** Due to the judgment involved in the auditor's risk assessment and inherent limitations in internal control, the auditor should design and perform substantive procedures for all relevant assertions related to each material class of transactions, account balance, and disclosure.

  2. **Specific Procedures Required** The following audit procedures related to the financial statement reporting process are required in all audits:

     a. Agreeing the financial statements, including their accompanying notes, to the underlying accounting records.

     b. Examining material journal entries and other adjustments made during the course of preparing the financial statements. The nature and extent of these procedures depend on the nature and complexity of the entity's financial reporting system and the assessed risks of material misstatement.

  3. **Significant Risks** The auditor should perform substantive procedures that are specifically responsive to significant risks identified in the auditor's risk assessment process as needing special audit consideration. For example, if the auditor determines that management is under pressure to meet earnings expectations, there may be a risk that management is inflating sales by improperly recognizing revenue related to sales agreements with terms that preclude revenue recognition or by invoicing sales before shipment. In these circumstances, the auditor may, for example, design external written confirmation requests not only to confirm outstanding amounts, but also to confirm the details of the sales agreements, including date, any rights of return, and delivery terms. Also, the auditor may find it effective to supplement such external written confirmations with inquiries of nonfinancial personnel in the entity regarding any changes in sales agreements and delivery terms.

B. **Nature**
The auditor should plan substantive procedures to be responsive to the planned level of detection risk. In some cases, analytics may be sufficient to reduce the planned level of detection risk to an acceptably low level, for example, when the auditor's risk assessment has been reduced by obtaining audit evidence from testing the operating effectiveness of controls. On the other hand, the auditor may determine that tests of details only are appropriate, or that a combination of analytics and tests of details is most responsive to the assessed risks. The determination of which substantive procedures are most appropriate to obtain the planned level of detection risk is affected by whether the auditor has obtained audit evidence about the operating effectiveness of controls to reduce control risk.

Exhibit 1 ▶ Substantive Tests Mnemonic

C	Confirm
O	Observe
R	Retrace (Trace)
V	Vouch
A	Analytics
I	Inquire
R	Recompute

1. **Tests of Details** Tests of details are ordinarily more appropriate to obtain audit evidence regarding certain relevant assertions about account balances. The auditor should design tests of details responsive to the assessed risk with the objective of obtaining sufficient appropriate audit evidence to achieve the planned level of assurance at the relevant assertion level.

   a. **Tests of Transactions** These tests are performed to determine whether the entity's transactions are recorded and summarized correctly in the accounting records. Many of these tests can be performed simultaneously with the tests of controls (i.e., dual-purpose tests).

   b. **Tests of Balances** These tests are concerned primarily with monetary misstatements in the account balances. Tests of balances relate to individual accounts, whereas the tests of transactions relate to the different transaction cycles.

2. **Analytical Procedures** Analytics generally are more applicable to large volumes of transactions that tend to be predictable over time. The following matters should be considered when designing substantive analytical procedures:

   a. The suitability of using substantive analytical procedures, given the assertions.

   b. The reliability of the data (internal or external) from which the expectation of recorded amounts or ratios is developed. The auditor should consider testing the controls, if any, over the entity's preparation of information to be used. Alternatively, the auditor may consider whether the information was subjected to audit testing in the current or prior period.

   c. Whether the expectation is sufficiently precise to identify the possibility of a material misstatement at the desired level of assurance.

   d. The amount of any difference in recorded amounts from expected values that is acceptable.

C. Timing

1. **Interim Testing** When substantive procedures are performed at an interim date, the auditor should perform further substantive procedures or a combination of substantive procedures and tests of controls covering the remaining period to provide a reasonable basis for extending the audit conclusions to the end of the period. Interim testing increases the risk that misstatements existing at the period end will not be detected. This risk increases as the length of the remaining period increases.

   a. **Factors to Consider** In considering whether to perform substantive procedures at an interim date, the auditor should consider such factors as:

      (1) The control environment and other relevant controls

       (2)   The availability of information at a later date that is necessary for the auditor's procedures

       (3)   The objective of the substantive procedure

       (4)   The assessed risk of material misstatement (RMM)

       (5)   The nature of the class of transactions or account balance and relevant assertions

       (6)   The auditor's ability to reduce the risk that misstatements existing at the end of the period will not be detected

    b.   **Misstatements** If misstatements are detected at the interim date, the auditor should consider modifying the risk assessment and the planned nature, timing, or extent of audit procedures covering the remaining period. The auditor may determine that it is necessary to extend or reperform the original procedure at the balance-sheet date.

    c.   **Remaining Period** The auditor may compare and reconcile ending balances with balances at the interim date to identify amounts that appear unusual, investigate such amounts, and perform substantive procedures to test the remaining period. When planning to perform analytics with respect to the remaining period, the auditor should consider whether the amount, relative significance, and composition of an ending balance are reasonably predictable. The auditor also should consider whether the entity's procedures for analysis, adjustment, and cutoff of such balances at interim dates are appropriate. Furthermore, the auditor should consider whether the financial reporting system will provide sufficient information to permit investigation of: (1) significant unusual transactions or entries; (2) other causes of significant fluctuations, or expected fluctuations that did not occur; and (3) changes in the composition of classes of transactions or account balances.

  2.   **Period End** To best address certain identified risks of material misstatement, such as the risk of fraudulent financial reporting, the auditor may need to perform substantive procedures at or near the end of the reporting period. Procedures to extend audit conclusions from an interim date to the period-end may not be effective.

  3.   **Prior Period** Substantive audit evidence from a prior audit is not sufficient for reducing detection risk to an acceptably low level in the current audit. In order for such evidence to be used in the current period as substantive audit evidence, the audit evidence and the related subject matter must not change fundamentally. The auditor must perform procedures to establish the continuing relevance of the audit evidence. An example of substantive audit evidence obtained in a prior period that may be relevant in the current period is audit evidence substantiating the purchase cost of a building.

  4.   **Coordination of Procedures** In planning the timing of procedures, the auditor should consider the coordination of related audit procedures. This includes, for example: (a) coordinating the audit procedures applied to related party transactions and balances; (b) coordinating the testing of interrelated accounts and accounting cutoffs; and (c) maintaining temporary audit control over assets that are readily negotiable and simultaneously testing such assets.

D. **Extent**

As the risk of material misstatement increases, the acceptable level of detection risk decreases; this means, the extent of substantive procedures must increase. Therefore, if the auditor has obtained satisfactory evidence regarding the operating effectiveness of controls to reduce the risk of material misstatement, substantive tests may be reduced as the acceptable level of detection risk increases.

E.   **Review of Audit Evidence**

Exhibit 2 ▶ Audit Evidence Review Mnemonic

C	Calculations by auditor
A	Analytics
D	Documents (authoritative)
S	Subsequent events
C	Client statements
R	Records (subsidiary)
I	Internal control
P	Physical evidence
T	Third party statements

1.   **Calculations by Auditor**   For example, the auditor may recompute a tax liability or depreciation. In addition to verifying the amount in the financial records, this procedure also contributes to the auditor's understanding of the summarization of the data in the financial statements.

2.   **Analytics**   The interrelationships among the various data are investigated to provide evidence of reasonable presentation in the financial statements. For example, the auditor may examine the ratio of interest expense to long-term debt, the ratio of accounts receivable to sales, and the gross profit ratios for a period of several years. Alternatively, the auditor may match several associated accounts and audit the data simultaneously (e.g., purchases and accounts payable, accounts receivable and sales).

3.   **Authoritative Documents**   Documents such as vendor's invoices, time cards, receiving reports, and purchase orders provide support for recording transactions in journals and are used to authorize transactions.

   a.   **Preparation**   In general, documents prepared by third parties are a better form of evidence than those prepared by the client.

   b.   **Circulation**   In general, documents used by third parties are a better form of evidence than those used only by the client.

   c.   **Internal Control**   Authoritative documents prepared under strong internal control are generally considered better evidence than those prepared under weak internal control.

4.   **Subsequent Events**   The occurrence of events subsequent to the financial statement date is especially important evidence regarding cutoff work on year-end balances. An important use of subsequent evidence is the search for unrecorded liabilities. In analyzing the cash disbursements made after the year-end, the auditor is looking for items that were a liability at year-end but that were not recorded and disclosed in the financial statements.

Exhibit 3 ▶ Subsequent Events Discovery Mnemonic

M	Management representation letter
I	Inquiry
R	Read minutes / interim financial statements
A	Asset / liability valuation
C	Cutoff
L	Legal letters

5. **Client's Statements** The auditor frequently must rely on statements made by the client. The client's explanations must be evaluated as to the treatment of various items and as to the reasoning that supports certain judgmental decisions.

6. **Subsidiary Records** Subsidiary records add to the audit evidence supporting the financial statement generation process. Subsidiary ledgers for accounts receivable, inventory, and fixed assets are examples of this type of evidence.

7. **Internal Control** Can be thought of as a form of audit evidence because the auditor considers internal control in reaching conclusions concerning the fairness of the financial statements. The strength of internal control affects the nature, timing, and extent of the procedures that will be performed. Therefore, under strong internal control, the auditor may require less audit evidence than under weak internal control.

8. **Physical Evidence** Examples include counting cash, counting inventory, and observing fixed assets such as buildings and machines.

9. **Third-Party Statements** Statements by third parties are strong types of evidence because they are prepared by independent parties. Examples include accounts receivable confirmations, confirmations from insurance brokers concerning the status of various insurance policies, confirmations of the number of shares outstanding from registrars, and confirmations of account balances by banks.

II. Standardized Audit Procedures

A. General Audit Procedures
The following are frequently used audit procedures. Because they are in general form, each procedure in an audit program should specify the account balance or transaction to which it applies (e.g., vouch sales journal entries to the bills of lading).

1. Obtain an understanding of the entity and its environment, including internal control to assess the risk of material misstatement in order to ascertain the nature, timing, and extent of further audit procedures to be applied.

2. Evaluate whether transactions are properly recorded in conformity with GAAP.

3. Reconcile detail records and data with the general ledger.

4. Confirm and observe for proper segregation of duties in actual practice.

5. Test posting from the journals to the ledgers.

6. Compare an account's beginning balance with the ending balance from the previous period.

7. Scan the accounts for unusual items.

8. Investigate unusual items.

9. Test for proper authorizations.

10. Vouch (i.e., examine) source documents.

11. Inquire about significant accounts and events.

12. Test for adequate disclosures.

13. Foot and cross-foot.

14. Test for interrelationships between certain accounts and between certain amounts (i.e., perform analytics).

15. Recalculate significant figures.

16. Review cutoff dates.

17. Examine subsequent events.

18. Make inquiries of client personnel.

19. Obtain written representations from management.

20. Read the minutes of the board of directors' meetings and committee meetings of the board.

21. Make inquiries of the client's attorney.

Exhibit 4 ▶ Standardized Audit Procedures Mnemonic

T	TRACING	Follow transaction from supporting documentation to accounting records
R	RECONCILE	Account for difference between two amounts
A	ANALYZE	Search for unexpected trends or the lack of expected deviations
F	FOOT	Recompute column totals within financial statements and individual accounts
I	INSPECT	Physically confirm the existence of assets such as stock certificates
C	CONFIRM	Confirmation of certain account balances with third parties
C	CONSIDER	Entity & its environment, including internal control
I	INQUIRE	Make inquiries of client management and employees
V	VOUCHING	Examine documentation that supports entries in the accounting records
I	INVESTIGATE	Look for cause of detected fraud discovered in testing
C	COUNT	Physical count of inventories on hand and fixed assets owned
S	SUBSEQUENT EVENTS	Events occurring after the year-end that may have an effect on the financial statements

B. Guidelines for Tracing & Vouching
Exam questions frequently require determination of the purpose of tracing or vouching given documents through the accounting process.

1. **Tracing From Source Documents to Ledgers** Provides evidence of completeness (i.e., all transactions are recorded and the ledger accounts are not understated). This is indicated by the upward arrow in Exhibit 5.

2. **Vouching From Ledgers to Source Documents** Provides evidence of existence or occurrence (i.e., all transactions summarized in the ledgers actually occurred, the ledgers contain no unsupported entries, and ledger balances are not overstated). This is indicated by the downward arrow in Exhibit 5.

Exhibit 5 ▶ Tracing & Vouching Guidelines

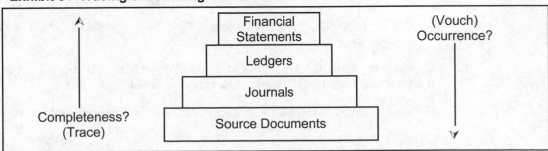

C.   **Fair Value Measurements & Disclosures (AU 328, SAS 101)**

1.   **Overview** SAS 101, *Auditing Fair Value Measurements & Disclosures*, provides guidance for auditing financial statement components and related disclosures that are required by GAAP to be measured at fair value. Fair value measurements (FVM) may occur both when a transaction is initially recorded and later for changes in value. In the absence of observable market prices, GAAP requires fair value to be based on the best information available. The estimation of fair value may be achieved through the use of a valuation method.

2.   **Management Responsibilities** Management is responsible for making the FVM and disclosures included in the financial statements. This includes:

a.   Establishing an accounting and financial reporting process for determining FVM and disclosures

b.   Selecting and preparing the valuation method

c.   Identifying and supporting the significant underlying assumptions used

d.   Ensuring both the presentation and disclosures are in accordance with GAAP

3.   **Obtaining an Understanding of Entity's Process & Assessing Risk** The auditor should obtain an understanding of the entity's process for determining FVM and disclosures and of the relevant controls sufficient to assess the risk of material misstatement. S/he should then develop an effective audit approach, i.e., determine the nature, timing, and extent of the audit procedures. Generally, more complex FVM requirements impose a greater risk of material misstatement. When obtaining this understanding, an auditor may consider:

a.   Controls over the process

b.   Expertise and experience of the people involved

c.   Role of information technology

d.   Types of accounts or transactions requiring FVM or disclosures

e.   Extent of the reliance on a service organization to either provide the measurement or the data that supports it

f.   Extent to which specialists are used

g.   Significant assumptions (including the process to develop and apply them) and related supporting documentation

h.   Process to monitor changes in assumptions

i.   Integrity of change controls and security procedures for valuation models and relevant information systems, including approval processes

j.   Controls over the consistency, timeliness, and reliability of the data used in valuation models

4.   **Conformity With GAAP** The auditor should evaluate whether the FVM and disclosures in the financial statements are in conformity with GAAP.

a.   If relevant, the auditor should evaluate management's intent and ability to carry out specific courses of action. The auditor may consider:

(1)   Management's past history of carrying out its stated intentions with respect to assets or liabilities

(2)   Written plans and other documentation, for example, budgets or minutes

(3)   Management's stated reasons for the selection of a particular course of action

(4)   Management's ability to carry out a particular course of action given the entity's economic circumstances or contractual commitments or restraints

b.   When a valuation method is used (because there are no observable market prices), the auditor should evaluate its appropriateness. This would involve a discussion with management about their rationale for selecting the valuation method. The auditor considers:

    (1)   Whether management has sufficiently evaluated and appropriately applied the criteria, if any, provided by GAAP to support the selected method

    (2)   Whether the valuation method is appropriate given the nature of the item being valued and in relation to the business, industry, and environment of the entity

    (3)   In cases where management considered methods with a wide range of values, how they investigated the reasons for the differences

c.   The auditor should evaluate whether the entity's method for determining FVM is consistently applied, and if so, whether the consistency is appropriate considering possible changes in the environment or accounting principles.

5.   **Engaging a Specialist** The auditor may have the ability to perform the audit related to fair values or may decide to use a specialist. If a specialist is to be used, the auditor should consider whether the specialist's understanding of the definition of fair value and the method s/he will use is consistent with those of management and is in conformity with GAAP. The auditor should follow the guidance in AU 336, *Using the Work of a Specialist,* (see Chapter 24) to obtain an understanding of the assumptions and the methods used by the specialist and if s/he considers the findings to be unreasonable, should apply additional procedures.

6.   **Audit Procedures & Evaluation of Results** FVM can vary widely and can be associated with very different levels of risk of material misstatement, thus audit procedures can vary significantly in nature, timing, and extent. Substantive tests may involve (a) testing management's significant assumptions, the valuation model, and the underlying data; (b) developing independent fair value estimates for corroborative purposes; or (c) reviewing subsequent events and transactions.

The auditor should evaluate the sufficiency and appropriateness of the FVM audit evidence obtained as well as its consistency with other audit evidence. The auditor's evaluation of whether the FVM and disclosures are in conformity with GAAP is performed in the context of the financial statements taken as a whole.

7.   **Testing Management's Significant Assumptions, the Valuation Model & the Underlying Data**

a.   The auditor evaluates whether (1) management's assumptions are reasonable and reflect, or are not inconsistent with, market information; (2) the FVM was determined using the appropriate model; and (3) management used relevant information that was reasonably available at the time.

b.   Where applicable, the auditor should evaluate whether the significant assumptions used by management, taken individually or as a whole, provide a reasonable basis for the FMV and disclosures in the financial statements. Assumptions are frequently interdependent and therefore need to be internally consistent.

    c.   Management must exercise judgment to identify the assumptions that are significant. The auditor focuses on the significant assumptions identified by management. Generally, significant assumptions cover matters that materially affect the FVM and may include those that are:

        (1)   Sensitive to variation or uncertainty in amount or nature

        (2)   Susceptible to misapplication or bias

    d.   To be considered reasonable, assumptions need to be reliable and consistent with:

        (1)   The general economic environment, the economic environment of the specific industry, and the entity's economic circumstances

        (2)   Existing market information

        (3)   The plans of the entity, including what management expects will be the outcome of specific objectives and strategies

        (4)   If appropriate, assumptions made in prior periods

        (5)   Experience of, or previous conditions experienced by, the entity to the extent currently applicable

        (6)   Other matters related to the financial statements (e.g., assumptions about other accounting estimates)

        (7)   If applicable, the risk associated with cash flows, including the potential variability in the amount and timing of the cash flows and the related effect on the discount rate

    e.   **Valuation Model** For items valued using a valuation model, the auditor is not an appraiser, i.e., s/he does substitute her/his judgment for that of management. The auditor reviews the model and evaluates its reasonableness and appropriateness.

    f.   **Data** The auditor tests the data to evaluate whether it is accurate, complete and relevant; and whether the FVM has been properly determined using such data and management's assumptions.

8.   **Developing independent Fair Value Estimates for Corroborative Purposes** When performing substantive procedures, the auditor may make an independent estimate to corroborate FVM, either using management's assumptions or the auditor's own. In the latter case, the auditor should still take management's assumptions into account. The understanding of management's assumptions helps to ensure that the auditor's independent estimate includes consideration of all significant variables. It also helps the auditor to evaluate any significant difference between the two estimates.

9.   **Reviewing Subsequent Events & Transactions** Events and transactions that occur after the balance sheet date but before the date of the auditor's report may provide audit evidence regarding management's FVM as of the balance sheet date. When using a subsequent event or transaction to substantiate a FVM, the auditor considers only those events or transactions that reflect circumstances existing at the balance sheet date.

10.   **Disclosures** Disclosure of fair value information is an important aspect of financial statements. Often fair value disclosure is required because of the relevance to users in the evaluation of the entity's performance and financial position. The auditor obtains sufficient appropriate evidence that the method of estimation and significant assumptions used are adequately disclosed in accordance with GAAP. If an item contains a high degree of measurement uncertainty, the auditor assesses whether the disclosures are sufficient to inform users of such uncertainty.

11. **Management Representations** The auditor generally should obtain written representations from management regarding the reasonableness of significant assumptions, including whether they appropriately reflect management's intent and ability to carry out specific courses of action where relevant to the use of FVM or disclosures. Management representations about fair values may include representations about:

   a. The appropriateness of the measurement methods, including related assumptions, used by management in determining fair value and the consistency in application of the methods.

   b. The completeness and adequacy of disclosures related to fair values.

   c. Whether subsequent events require adjustment to the FVM and disclosures included in the financial statements.

12. **Communication With Those Charged With Governance** The auditor should determine that those charged with governance are informed about the process used by management in formulating particularly sensitive accounting estimates, including FMV estimates, and about the basis for the auditor's conclusions regarding the reasonableness of those estimates. For example, the auditor should consider communicating the:

   a. Nature of significant assumptions used in FVM

   b. Degree of subjectivity involved in the development of the assumptions

   c. Relative materiality of the items being measured at fair value to the statements as a whole

   The auditor should follow the guidance in AU 380, *The Auditor's Communication With Those Charged With Governance*, as to the nature and form of the communication. (See Chapter 22.)

III. Audit Programs

A. Cash
The audit procedures in Exhibit 6 generally are performed during the audit of cash accounts to obtain supporting evidence of the objectives.

1. **Audit Objectives' Focus** To ensure (a) there are adequate internal control policies and procedures over cash, (b) all cash that should be in the custody of the client is (existence), (c) all of the cash in custody of the client is recorded properly (completeness), and (d) the cash in the custody of the client is disclosed properly in the financial statements.

2. **Subfunctions** Subfunctions for cash include (a) accounts receivable, (b) accounts payable, (c) cash sales, and (d) general ledger accounting.

3. **Kiting** This is the practice whereby an employee who is embezzling funds makes a transfer of funds from a bank account in one bank to a bank account in another bank near the end of the period. The transfer is effected through the use of a check and, therefore, does not show up as a withdrawal from the first bank until the check clears. It is listed as a deposit in transit on the receiving bank's books but not as an outstanding check on the disbursing bank's books. As a result, the overall cash balance is temporarily overstated at the balance sheet date and the embezzlement is not detected.

Example 1 ▶ Kiting

Allen Richards is the bookkeeper for Diversified Inc. Diversified has two bank accounts— one in the First Federal Bank and another in the Fourth National Bank. On a hot tip from Allen's investment broker, Allen writes himself a $5,000 check on the First Federal account, makes no entry, and purchases stock in STCG Inc. Shortly thereafter, STCG Inc. is subjected to SEC investigation and all trading in its stock is frozen. As the end of the year nears, Allen's predicament remains unchanged. To cover the defalcation, Allen writes a $5,000 check on the Fourth National account on December 31 and deposits it in the First Federal account on the same day. Furthermore, he makes no entry in the cash disbursements journal and fails to list the check as outstanding on the year-end bank reconciliation. The check will not show up as a decrease in the Fourth National account until it clears, so that account will still reflect the same account balance without the check deduction, and the First Bank will reflect the $5,000 deposited as of December 31. The money "appears" to be in both accounts, when in reality, only due to the delay in transaction posting, it is not.

Exhibit 6 ▶ Sample Program for Cash

Procedures	Assertions*
1. Prepare proof of cash—to ascertain that all recorded receipts have been deposited in the bank	Existence
2. Account for all check numbers—to determine whether there are any missing or outstanding checks that might cause the cash balance to be overstated	Completeness
3. Obtain and review or prepare a year-end bank reconciliation—to accurately determine the client's actual cash position at the close of the period	Completeness
4. Obtain a bank cutoff statement directly from the bank—to ascertain whether the items on the year-end reconciliation have cleared the bank and, therefore, were valid. Bank cutoff statements generally are requested for one to two weeks after year-end. After finishing this procedure, the cutoff bank statement is given to the client. This procedure is useful for detecting kiting between account balances.	Completeness Cutoff
5. Investigate any checks made to cash or bearer—to determine the propriety of the disbursement	Rights & Obligations
6. Trace a sample of entries in the cash receipts journal to the A/R subsidiary ledger, duplicate deposit ticket, and general ledger—to determine whether the cash is stated accurately	Valuation & Allocation Completeness
7. Simultaneously count all cash on hand—to ensure that no cash is counted more than once (coordinate with count of marketable securities on hand)	Existence
8 Investigate NSF checks and other debit memos—because these may be an indication of the covering up of a cash shortage	Existence
9. Prepare a schedule of bank transfers around year-end—to help detect kiting	Existence
10. Confirm the existence of year-end bank balances of the following:	Existence Rights & Obligations
a. Amounts on deposit	
b. Direct liabilities	
c. Contingent liabilities on notes discounted	

d.   Other direct or contingent liabilities

e.   Other security agreements

11. Determine If any cash is restricted—so that the restricted balance is classified properly on the balance sheet, and requirements of compensating balance agreements are disclosed properly

All Presentation &
Disclosure Assertions

---

* Note that many procedures may test multiple assertions. This program is not intended to be a complete presentation. See Chapter 24 for details on assertions.

B.   Accounts Receivable & Sales

The procedures (and the purpose behind each procedure) in Exhibit 7 generally are performed during the audit of accounts receivable and sales to obtain supporting evidence of the objectives.

1.   **Audit Objectives' Focus** To ascertain: (a) adequate internal control policies and procedures exist; (b) all sales and receivables that should be recorded are properly recorded (completeness); (c) only sales and receivables that should be recorded are recorded (existence); and (d) accounts receivable are presented at approximate realizable value

2.   **Subfunctions** After the audit objectives for an audit area are specified, they should be broken into subfunctions. For accounts receivable and sales, possible subfunctions include (a) credit granting, (b) billing, (c) shipping, (d) cash receipts, (e) detailed ledger bookkeeping, and (f) general ledger accounting

3.   **Broad Outline of Audit Program for Accounts Receivable & Sales**

a.   **Interim Work** Possibilities include (1) obtaining an understanding of the internal control (may include walking through a transaction, inquiry, and observation), and (2) performing tests of controls as to operating effectiveness

b.   **Year-End Work: Sales** (1) Analytics (including ratio and trend analysis), (2) review sales cutoff and consignment sales, and (3) review sales returns and allowances and sales discounts

c.   **Year-End Work: Accounts Receivable** (1) Review aged trial balance, (2) confirm accounts receivable by positive and/or negative confirmations, and (3) review the bad debts allowance and expense

4.   **Confirmation of Accounts Receivable (AU 330, SAS 67)** Confirmation of accounts receivable is a generally accepted auditing procedure (although not a standard). Therefore, the procedure is optional; however, if the procedure is not performed, the auditor must document the reason.

a.   **Auditor's Responsibility** Confirmation requests always should be mailed by the auditor. In addition, the auditor's firm should receive all requests directly. These procedures diminish the possibility that the confirmation requests could be altered by the client, either during the mailing process or upon receipt.

b.   **Extent & Method of Confirmation** The extent and method of confirmation is determined by the auditor after considering (1) the effectiveness of internal control; (2) the possibility of disputes, inaccuracies, and fraud in the accounts; (3) the expected degree of cooperation by the debtor; (4) the probability that the debtor will be able to confirm the amounts involved; and (5) the materiality of the amounts involved. A combination of the two forms may be appropriate, with the positive form used for large balances and the negative form for small balances.

c.   **Subject of Confirmation** Confirmations may deal with the account balance or with individual items. The latter are useful when the customer may not be in a position to confirm the total account balance owed to the client. This occurs frequently when sales or contracts are made with governmental agencies.

d. **Positive Form of Confirmation Request** Requests a response concerning whether or not the customer is in agreement with the client's records. A positive request also may be blank, requesting the recipient to indicate balances and furnish other information. Use of the blank form provides a greater degree of assurance about the information confirmed because some respondents may sign a "completed" confirmation without verifying it. However, because the blank form requires more effort on the part of the recipient, there may be a lower response rate.

The positive form is preferable when individual account balances are relatively large or when there is reason to believe that a substantial number of the accounts may be disputed or that errors and/or fraud exist.

- **Nonresponse** Generally, nonresponse requires the use of follow-up requests such as additional mailings or telephone calls. In cases where there is still no response to requests dealing with significant accounts, alternative procedures should be used to obtain adequate evidence. These additional procedures may involve the examination of documents such as subsequent cash receipts, sales invoices, and shipping documents.

e. **Negative Form of Confirmation Request** Requests a response only in cases where the customer disagrees with the stated balance.

The negative form is useful when the assessed level of control risk is low, when a large number of small balances are involved, and when the auditor has no reason to believe the persons receiving the requests are unlikely to give them consideration.

- **Nonresponse** An inherent weakness in the negative form is that a nonresponse does not necessarily mean that the balance is accurate. Rather, a nonresponse may have nothing to do with the correctness or incorrectness of the balance. The response form may simply have not been returned by the debtor or may have been lost enroute from the debtor to the auditor.

5. **Lapping** This is one of the most common types of fraud. It involves the delay in the recording of a cash receipt in order to cover up an existing shortage in the actual cash on hand. Lapping is made possible through either bad internal control (i.e., having the same employee handle both the cash and the accounts receivable records) or collusion. In order to detect a lapping scheme, the auditor must compare the name, amounts, and dates shown on the customers' remittance advices with entries in the cash receipts journal and the related deposit slips.

Example 2 ▶ Lapping

Georgia Thomas is the bookkeeper for Farley Fabrics (a retail cloth distributor), and her duties consist of receiving the checks from the customers and recording the payments in the A/R subsidiary ledger. On January 8th, Georgia hears the president talk about a one-time purchase of a unique fabric by Colin's Casuals. She also hears that Colin's is going to make a $640 purchase. The next day, Colin's Casuals submits its order for that $640 of fabric. With all of this in mind, Georgia embezzles $640 of that day's payments received from Mama's Moo Moos and Jabba's Jammies (both of whom are regular customers of Farley). Georgia makes no entries in the accounts. Five days later, Colin's Casuals pays its bill, and Georgia credits the payments to Mama's and Jabba's accounts. Colin does no more business with Farley and, at the end of the year, Georgia writes off Colin's receivable as uncollectible.

Exhibit 7 ▶ Sample Program for A/R & Sales

Procedures	Assertions*
1. Compare a sample of shipping documents to the related sales invoices—to discover orders that have been shipped, but not billed	Completeness
2. Reconcile a sample of cash register tapes and sales tickets with the sales journals—so that evidence is gathered that shows that all sales have been recorded, and recorded accurately	Completeness Accuracy
3. Perform analytics—for example, a gross profit test, to determine that all sales have been recorded and classified correctly; investigate any unexpected fluctuations	Completeness Classification
4. Review sales discount procedures and documentation—to determine that discounts were granted only for payments received within the discount period	Accuracy
5. Vouch debits in individual A/R accounts to sales invoices—to determine whether the sales actually occurred	Occurrence Rights & Obligations
6. Review sales and receipts occurring near year-end—to ascertain that such transactions were recorded in the proper time period and were valid transactions	Cutoff Occurrence
7. Test foot the sales journal and reconcile with postings to the general ledger—to find out if the sales figures were brought forward accurately	Accuracy
8. Vouch debit entries in the allowance for doubtful accounts to individual accounts and original write-off authorizations—so that it can be determined that such write-offs were reflected properly in the accounts and were authorized	Valuation & Allocation
9. Prepare or obtain an aged A/R schedule—to (a) help identify accounts that should be written off, (b) determine the reasonableness of the bad-debt expense and allowance for doubtful accounts, and (c) aid the confirmation of A/R	Valuation & Allocation
10. Recalculate and review bad-debt expense and allowance—for reasonableness of expense and adequacy of the allowance	Valuation & Allocation
11. Examine cash receipts after the balance sheet date—to provide evidence of collectibility at the balance sheet date	Valuation & Allocation
12. Confirm A/R on a test basis—to verify the existence and accuracy of the account balances and that the receivables are the rights of the company	Existence Accuracy Rights & Obligations
13. Examine all aspects of a sample of sales transactions—to determine whether the internal control procedures are being applied properly (i.e., perform tests of controls directed toward operating effectiveness); this procedure includes the following: a. Comparing the sales invoice with the customer's purchase order b. Checking for proper credit approval c. Comparing prices on sales invoice with those on price list; ascertaining the propriety of discounts granted to purchasers d. Recomputing extensions and footings	Occurrence Accuracy

> e. Checking the recording in the sales journal and the posting of the sale in the A/R subsidiary ledger
>
> 14. Review loan agreements—for pledging of accounts and agreements, for any factoring of accounts, and for disclosure purposes
>
> All Presentation & Disclosure Assertions

* Note that many procedures may test multiple assertions. This program is not intended to be a complete presentation. See Chapter 24 for details on assertions.

C. Inventory

The audit procedures in Exhibit 8 typically are performed during the audit of the inventory account to obtain supporting evidence of the objectives.

1. **Audit Objectives' Focus** To ascertain (a) the inventory exists and the client owns it (existence and rights), (b) it is priced correctly, (c) the quantities shown are reasonable (rights), (d) the computations used to arrive at the inventory dollar amounts are accurate (valuation), and (e) there is adequate disclosure in the financial statements

2. **Subfunctions** Subfunctions for inventory include (a) purchasing, (b) receiving, (c) storing, (d) processing, (e) shipping, (f) detailed bookkeeping, and (g) general ledger accounting

3. **Evidence for Inventories (AU 331)** The observation of the taking of the inventory is a generally accepted auditing procedure (although not a standard). Therefore, if an observation is not performed, the auditor must document the reason.

   a. **Periodic Inventory** When the client determines its inventory quantities entirely by means of a physical count at or near the balance sheet date, the auditor ordinarily must be present at the count. The auditor should use suitable observations, tests, and inquiries to become satisfied that the method of accounting for inventory is effective and that the client's claims as to the quantities and physical condition are reliable.

   b. **Perpetual Inventory System** When a good perpetual inventory system is maintained in which the client periodically compares the inventory records with the physical counts, the auditor should observe the counting and comparing. However, this can be done either during the period (assuming an adequate system of internal control over inventory and the assessed level of control risk is low) or at or after the end of the period.

   c. **Advanced Methods** Some companies have developed highly effective inventory methods (using statistical sampling) that make annual counts of each item of inventory unnecessary. In these cases, the auditor must be present at such partial countings as considered necessary. The auditor also must be satisfied that the inventory method will produce results that are comparable to those that would be obtained by an annual count of physical inventory. If the inventory plan is based on statistical sampling, the auditor must be satisfied that the plan has statistical validity and is properly applied, and that the resulting precision and reliability are statistically reasonable.

   d. **Sufficient Audit Evidence** Tests of the accounting records are not sufficient evidence as to current inventories. Rather, the auditor always will have to make or observe some physical counts of the inventory, apply appropriate tests to the intervening transactions, and review any client counts and procedures relating to the physical inventory.

   e. **Auditor Has Not Audited Prior Inventories** When auditing financial statements covering the current period and one or more periods for which the auditor has not observed or made some physical counts of prior inventories, the auditor must be satisfied as to the prior period's inventory through the results of appropriate tests. These tests might include tests of prior transactions, review of prior record counts, and gross profit tests. An example of this type of situation would be the first audit of a new client who has beginning inventory.

f. **Inventories Held in Public Warehouses** In some cases, inventories are held in public warehouses or by other outside custodians. In these situations, direct written confirmation from the custodian is acceptable when the inventory is not material. When the amounts are substantial, relative to current or total assets, the auditor should undertake one or more of the following procedures: (1) test the owner's control procedures for investigating the warehouse and evaluating its performance; (2) obtain an independent accountant's report on the warehouse's control procedures relevant to custody of goods and, if applicable, pledging of receipts; (3) apply alternative procedures at the warehouse to gain reasonable assurance that information received from the warehouse is reliable; (4) observe physical counts wherever reasonable and practicable; and finally (5) obtain confirmations from lenders in cases where warehouse receipts have been pledged as collateral.

g. **Outside Inventory-Taking Firm (AU 9508)** Some companies (e.g., retail stores, hospitals, and automobile dealers) use outside firms of nonaccountants who specialize in the taking of physical inventories to count, list, price, and subsequently compute the total dollar amount of the inventory. While the use of an outside firm ordinarily will reduce the work, it is not, by itself, a satisfactory substitute for the auditor's observation or taking of physical counts. In this situation, the auditor's primary concern will be to evaluate the effectiveness of the outside firm's procedures. Therefore, the auditor would (1) examine its inventory program, (2) observe its procedures and controls, (3) make or observe some physical counts of the inventory, (4) recompute calculations of the submitted inventory on a test basis, and (5) apply appropriate tests to the intervening transactions.

Exhibit 8 ▶ Sample Program for Inventory

Procedures	Assertions*
1. Account for the numerical sequence of inventory purchase requisitions—to ascertain that none are missing, thereby helping to assure that no unauthorized purchases were made	Completeness
2. Trace a sample of receiving reports for inventory to the perpetual inventory records—to determine that all shipments were reflected properly in the accounts; (this cutoff test must be performed at the inventory observation date and at the balance sheet date, if different)	Completeness Cutoff
3. Perform analytics on cost of goods sold—to determine if significant fluctuations exist that would necessitate an audit investigation; perform procedures to test turnover and compare gross margin of current year with that of prior year to test for overstatement or understatement	Completeness
4. Account for inventory tags and count sheets—to verify the inventory has been accounted for completely	Completeness
5. Trace test counts of inventory items from the floor to the client's inventory listing—to ensure all items of inventory have been counted and included in the total inventory balance	Completeness
6. Vouch a sample of inventory requisitions to customer or department order—so that evidence is obtained that all requisitions are valid	Rights & Obligations
7. Review purchase and sales cutoffs—to ascertain that ending inventory is valued properly and that the inventory transactions are recorded in the proper time period	Cutoff Rights & Obligations
8. Review inventory on consignment (as both consignee and consignor)—to determine the inventory actually owned by the client	Rights & Obligations

9. Confirm inventory held at public warehouses and with third parties—to identify other inventory actually owned by the client	Rights & Obligations Existence
10. Test pricing method used by the client—so that the proper inventory value is attained	Valuation & Allocation
11. Apply lower-of-cost-or-market rule—so that the proper inventory value and any losses are recognized and disclosed	Valuation & Allocation
12. Perform analytics—such as, gross profit percentage calculations, inventory turnover ratios, and number of days sales in inventory ratio analysis	Valuation & Allocation

In addition, inventory audit procedures for a manufacturing client could include the following:

13. Test cost accumulation process—so that the ending inventory and cost-of-goods-sold are valued properly	Valuation & Allocation
14. Review the overhead allocations and rates—for accuracy when compared with actual experience	Valuation & Allocation
15. Vouch a sample of additions to perpetual inventory to supporting receiving reports—to assure that the recorded inventory actually was received	Existence
16. Physical inventory: observe the physical count—to become satisfied that the counting methods are effective and the client's representations are reliable	Existence
17. Physical inventory: trace client's physical counts to perpetual records and inventory sheets—to test the completeness of perpetual records	Completeness
18. Physical inventory: vouch the validity of the perpetual records and inventory sheets against the physical count—to determine that items in perpetual records exist and quantities are correct	Existence
19. Physical inventory: test inventory sheet and perpetual record computation for clerical accuracy—thereby helping to ascertain that the inventory is valued properly and quantities are correct	Valuation & Allocation
20. Physical inventory: make random test counts—to assure that the counts made by the client are accurate; test counts of inventory items also should be traced to client's inventory sheets and to client's final inventory compilation report	Existence
21. Review purchase and sales commitments—to determine whether there is a need to accrue a loss and disclose its relevant facts	Completeness of Disclosures
22. Determine whether any inventory has been pledged—to assure that such facts are disclosed properly in the financial statements	All Presentation & Disclosure Assertions

* Note that many procedures may test multiple assertions. This program is not intended to be a complete presentation. See Chapter 24 for details on assertions.

D. Fixed Assets

The procedures in Exhibit 9 normally are performed during the audit of fixed assets to obtain supporting evidence of the objectives.

1. **Audit Objectives' Focus** To (a) ascertain the adequacy of internal control policies and procedures over fixed assets, (b) verify the existence and ownership of the fixed assets, and (c) ascertain the adequacy of valuation and disclosure of the fixed assets in the financial statements

2. **Subfunctions** Subfunctions for fixed assets include (a) depreciation, (b) financing, (c) detailed ledger bookkeeping, and (d) general ledger accounting

Exhibit 9 ▶ Sample Program for Fixed Assets

Procedures	Assertions*
1. Trace from fixed assets to the property, plant and equipment subsidiary ledger—to determine that the assets are recorded	Completeness
2. Obtain or prepare an analysis of the repair and maintenance expense account—to consider if any items should be classified as capital expenditures	Classification
3. Review rental revenue and property tax expense—by obtaining a map of rented and leased property; this procedure will help determine the accuracy of the rental revenue and tax expense accounts by exposing all the client's real property, thereby enabling a thorough evaluation	Accuracy
4. Verify the client's ownership of the assets—by examining titles to the fixed assets	Rights & Obligations
5. Review lease agreements—for determining whether assets should be capitalized	Classification
6. Reconcile the property, plant and equipment subsidiary ledger with the general ledger—to determine that the accounting for property, plant and equipment transactions was consistent	Valuation & Allocation
7. Recalculate the accounting for retirements of fixed assets	Valuation & Allocation
8. Review depreciation methods—for consistency with prior periods	Valuation & Allocation
9. Review useful lives—for appropriateness and consistency with prior periods	Valuation & Allocation
10. Recalculate depreciation computations	Valuation & Allocation
11. Vouch from the property, plant and equipment subsidiary ledger to the fixed assets—to determine that the assets actually exist	Existence
12. Vouch acquisitions to purchase orders or contracts approved by appropriate personnel	Existence
13. Review loan agreements—to verify any loans collateralized by property or equipment for proper disclosure	All Presentation & Disclosure Assertions

* Note that many procedures may test multiple assertions. This program is not intended to be a complete presentation. See Chapter 24 for details on assertions.

E. Investments

The audit procedures in Exhibit 10 generally are performed during the audit of long-term investments to obtain supporting evidence of the objectives.

1. **Audit Objectives' Focus** To (a) ascertain the adequacy of internal control policies and procedures over long-term investments; (b) ascertain whether the investments are accounted for in conformity with GAAP; (c) ascertain the adequacy of financial statement disclosure of such investments; (d) determine whether a loss in value of such investments should be considered as temporary or permanent; and (e) obtain evidence as to the existence of securities by inspection and/or confirmation

2. **Subfunctions** Subfunctions for long-term investments include (a) financing, (b) cash, (c) detailed ledger bookkeeping, and (d) general ledger accounting.

3. **Evidence for Long-Term Investments** The auditor is concerned with gathering sufficient appropriate audit evidence pertaining to the existence, ownership, and cost of long-term investments, as well as their carrying amounts, or valuation, on the balance sheet.

a. Evidence of the existence, ownership, and cost of long-term investments can be obtained from the accounting records and documents of the investor. In the case of securities, such evidence can be corroborated through inspection or, when appropriate, confirmation from an independent custodian. In the case of loans, bonds, and similar debt obligations, evidence should be corroborated through written confirmation from the debtor or trustee.

b. Evidence of the carrying amount of long-term investments and income and losses attributable to such investments can be obtained from the following sources:

(1) **Audited Financial Statements** Generally provide sufficient audit evidence, when the statements have been audited by an independent auditor, regarding equity in underlying net assets and results of operation of investee, as well as corroboration of investments in bonds and other debt instruments.

(2) **Unaudited Financial Statements** Provide insufficient information. The investor's auditor may utilize the investee's auditor to apply auditing procedures to unaudited statements, thereby obtaining sufficient evidence.

(3) **Market Quotations** If the market is reasonably broad and active, such quotations ordinarily constitute sufficient appropriate audit evidence as to the current market value of unrestricted securities.

(4) **Published Dividend Records** These provide the strongest evidence supporting dividends earned on marketable equity securities.

Exhibit 10 ▶ Sample Program for Investments

Procedures	Assertions*
1. Obtain or prepare an account analysis for the long-term investment and related revenue or loss accounts—allows the auditor to:	Accuracy Completeness
a. Establish the accuracy of the individual debits and credits occurring during the year, and	
b. Prove the validity of the year-end balance in the accounts	
2. Perform analytics—by comparing dividends, interest and other investment income with those of prior years to ascertain the reasonableness of the completeness of recorded investment income, calculate the percentage of accrued investment income to total investments and estimate total accrued income based on current investments	Completeness
3. Verify purchases and sales of securities during the year and for a short period subsequent to the balance sheet date—allows the auditor to determine whether all of the securities are accounted for in the accounting records	Completeness Rights & Obligations
4. Investigate method of accounting for equity securities	Valuation & Allocation
5. Determine FMV of securities on balance sheet date	Valuation & Allocation
6. Verify the interest earned on bonds—by recomputing the interest earned on the basis of the face amount, interest rate, and period held	Valuation & Allocation

7. Examine financial statements of investee companies—to determine gains and losses from investments in equity securities, as well as the carrying amounts of securities accounted for under the equity method	Valuation & Allocation
8. Test calculations of premium and discount amortization for accuracy	Valuation & Allocation Accuracy
9. Impairment—must consider management's evaluation relating to the existence of an other-than-temporary impairment	Valuation & Allocation
10. Inspection—inspect securities on hand and compare serial numbers with those shown in previous year's working papers; will help identify any undisclosed sales or purchases of investments; coordinate with cash count to prevent substitution	Existence
11. Obtain confirmation of securities from third-party custodian—to provide evidence as to the existence of such investments	Existence
12. Evaluate—evaluate whether management's stated intent to buy and hold an investment is supported by actual activities and the entity's ability to do so	Classification
13. Examine financial presentation of long-term investments—to determine whether GAAP is followed	Classification & Understandability Presentation Accuracy & Valuation
14. Inquiry—inquire of management and review loan documents as to possible pledging of securities for appropriate disclosure purposes	All Presentation & Disclosure Assertions

* Note that many procedures may test multiple assertions. This program is not intended to be a complete presentation. See Chapter 24 for details on assertions.

4. **Classification** The auditor must determine whether investments are accounted for in conformity with GAAP. Some investments require cost or equity methods of accounting. Some entities follow specialized industry accounting policies. The auditor normally obtains written management representations concerning the proper classification of securities. The procedures that auditors perform to obtain audit evidence concerning investments vary depending on the types of investments involved and the assessment of audit risk for a particular engagement.

5. **Valuation** The auditor should be aware that GAAP requires the use of several possible methods including cost, equity, or fair value. For the vast majority of instruments, GAAP calls for the fair value valuation model. Also, GAAP may call for recognition of gains and/or losses prior to realization.

   a. The accounting model will differ depending on the type of security, the nature of the transaction, management's objectives related to the security, and the type of entity.

   b. When quoted prices are not readily available, a significant amount of judgment will be needed to evaluate the sufficiency of the audit evidence properly for the valuation assertion. For securities which are not subject to mark-to-market accounting, there is the additional issue of determining whether an impairment loss exists which should be recognized. This involves judgment because the auditor is compelled to make a determination as to whether a loss is considered to be other than temporary which necessitates an estimation of the outcome of future events.

F. **Accounts Payable, Purchases & Other Liabilities**
   The audit procedures in Exhibit 11 commonly are performed during the audit of the A/P, purchasing, and other liability accounts to obtain supporting evidence of the objectives.

1. **Audit Objectives' Focus** To ensure: (a) there are adequate internal control policies and procedures over payables and purchases; (b) all transactions that should be recorded are recorded (completeness); (c) those transactions that are recorded are recorded properly (valuation); and (d) the financial statement presentation is adequate (disclosure and obligation)

2. **Subfunctions** Subfunctions for payables and purchases include (a) purchasing, (b) receiving, (c) payment, (d) detailed ledger bookkeeping, and (e) general ledger accounting

Exhibit 11 ▶ Sample Program for Short-Term Liabilities

Procedures	Assertions*
1. Perform search for unrecorded liabilities—to ascertain that all payables have been recorded in the proper period; performed, at the balance sheet date, in the following areas:	Completeness Cutoff Classification
a. Unmatched invoices and unbilled receiving reports	
b. Significant payments subsequent to the end of the period may indicate liabilities that existed at the end of the period	
c. Invoices received after the end of the period may have been for goods received at, or before, the end of the period	
d. Customer deposits recorded as credits to A/R	
e. Unbilled professional fees at the end of the period under audit	
f. Perform inventory receiving cutoff test	
2. Perform analytics—to assess the reasonableness of balances; compare the average number of days purchases in accounts payable at the end of the current year to prior years; compare purchases divided by payables to payables divided by total current liabilities for the current and prior years; compare payables and purchases to budgeted or forecasted amounts	Completeness
3. Vouch the paid check and invoice from the vendor to the receiving report—to determine if any payments were made for goods that were not received	Existence
4. Review the cutoff of purchases, returns, and disbursements—to determine that transactions are recorded in the proper periods	Cutoff
5. Recalculate the extensions and footings on customer invoices—to determine whether such invoices were priced and computed accurately	Accuracy Valuation & Allocation
6. Trace vendor invoices to voucher register and checks to check register—to determine that all payables and related disbursements were recorded properly	Valuation & Allocation
7. Foot voucher register and trace to general ledger—to substantiate the entries in the general ledger	Valuation & Allocation
8. Reclassify debit balances as receivables and review for collectibility	Valuation & Allocation
9. Recalculate other (accrued) liabilities—to test computations for reasonableness and consistent treatment when compared to prior years; examples include property and income taxes, commissions, profit-sharing and pension plans, and warranties	Valuation & Allocation

Procedures	Assertions
10. Vouch purchase requisitions of a sample of purchase orders—to determine if any unrequested purchases were made	Existence
11. Confirm A/P balances with vendors—although not a generally accepted audit procedure, confirm in cases of suspected fraud, sloppy or missing records, or suspected understatements	Completeness
12. Inspect copies of notes and other agreements	Existence
13. Review purchase commitments—to determine whether there are any losses to be accrued and/or disclosed	Completeness

* Note that many procedures may test multiple assertions. This program is not intended to be a complete presentation. See Chapter 24 for details on assertions.

G.   Payroll

The audit procedures in Exhibit 12 usually are performed during the audit of the payroll accounts to obtain supporting evidence of the objectives.

1.   Audit Objectives' Focus To (a) ascertain the adequacy of internal control over payroll, (b) verify that all employees included in the payroll actually exist and work for the client (existence), (c) verify the accuracy of the payroll computations (valuation), and (d) ascertain the adequacy of disclosure in the financial statements.

2.   Subfunctions Subfunctions for payroll include (a) personnel, (b) production, (c) detailed ledger bookkeeping, and (d) general ledger accounting.

Exhibit 12 ▶ Sample Program for Payroll

Procedures	Assertions*
1. Review time reports and piecework or commission records—to determine that such reports and records agree with production records	Completeness
2. Examine payroll cutoff—to determine that wages were reported in the proper time period	Cutoff
3. Review accounting for unclaimed wages—to ascertain that they are being classified properly	Classification Rights & Obligations
4. Verify payroll deductions—to ascertain that they are computed appropriately and that they agree with withholding authorizations	Valuation & Allocation
5. Analyze officers' compensation—to determine that salaries agree with contracts, minutes of directors' meeting, or other authorization	Rights & Obligations
6. Recompute payroll register—to determine its accuracy	Accuracy Valuation & Allocation
7. Vouch items from the payroll register to employee time cards—to verify employees worked the number of hours for which pay was computed	Occurrence
8. Observe the use of time clocks by employees—to be assured that each employee punches only one time card	Valuation & Allocation Occurrence
9. Review the results of audits of related pension and profit-sharing plans	Valuation & Allocation

10. Perform analytics—to determine reasonableness of balances; calculate ratios to determine whether accounts relate to each other in the manner expected; if relationships vary significantly from expected results, additional substantive tests of account balances may be necessary; compare payroll expenses with prior periods and investigate differences to determine the accuracy and validity of the expense	Valuation & Allocation Accuracy
11. Review payroll checks and bank reconciliations—to determine that all checks were cashed	Existence
12. Review the payroll register—to determine if all payroll transactions were recorded	Completeness
13. Examine personnel records—to determine that a name, salary rate, and job position all exist for each employee on the payroll	Existence
14. On a surprise basis, observe the distribution of paychecks—to determine that every name on the company payroll is that of a bona fide employee presently working	Existence
15. Review related tax expense and liability, unemployment insurance, and other payroll deduction accounts—to determine accuracy and proper classification in the financial statements	Accuracy & Valuation Classification

* Note that many procedures may test multiple assertions. This program is not intended to be a complete presentation. See Chapter 24 for details on assertions.

H. Long-Term Liabilities

The audit procedures in Exhibit 13 normally are performed during the audit of long-term liabilities to obtain supporting evidence of the objectives.

1. **Audit Objectives' Focus** To (a) ascertain the adequacy of internal control policies and procedures over long-term liabilities; (b) verify that all long-term liabilities are recorded properly (existence and obligation); (c) verify that interest expense is computed correctly and that other contractual obligations are satisfied (valuation); and (d) ascertain the adequacy of disclosure of long-term liabilities in the financial statements

2. **Subfunctions** Subfunctions for long-term liabilities include (a) financing, (b) fixed assets, (c) cash, (d) detailed ledger bookkeeping, and (e) general ledger accounting.

Exhibit 13 ▶ Sample Program for Long-Term Liabilities

Procedures	Assertions*
1. Obtain or prepare an account analysis for the long-term debt, discount, premium, and related interest accounts—allows the auditor to:	Accuracy Completeness
a. Verify the payment or other disposition of the debt listed as outstanding at the beginning of the period	
b. Establish the accuracy of the individual debits and credits occurring during the year	
c. Prove the validity of the year-end balance in the accounts	
2. Perform analytics—compare current amortization amounts to prior actual and current budget amounts; compare current interest costs to prior actual and current budget amounts; compare current and noncurrent debt obligations to prior actual and current budget amounts	Completeness
3. Review bank confirmation—for indication of loans and other commitments, including any unrecorded debt	Completeness Rights & Obligations
4. Review cutoff—to determine that transactions recorded at the end of the year are recorded in the proper period	Cutoff
5. Verify interest computations and amortization of premiums and/or discounts—to determine whether such amounts were disclosed properly and accurately; also aids in the discovery of undisclosed liabilities	Valuation & Allocation Accuracy Completeness
6. Confirm with creditor the transactions of the period and compliance with the contractual provisions—provides evidence that the transactions actually occurred and that the transactions were carried out properly (e.g., deposits into a sinking fund)	Occurrence Rights & Obligations
7. Review contractual provisions and supporting documents of long-term debt—to determine that details of the debt instruments correspond to those in the account analysis and that such details are disclosed accurately in the financial statements; supporting documents include note and loan agreements, bond indentures, and lease agreements	All Presentation & Disclosure Assertions

* Note that many procedures may test multiple assertions. This program is not intended to be a complete presentation. See Chapter 24 for details on assertions.

I. **Stockholders' Equity**

The audit procedures in Exhibit 14 normally are performed during the audit of stockholders' equity to obtain supporting evidence of the objectives.

   1. **Audit Objectives' Focus** To (a) ascertain the adequacy of internal control over stock transactions, stock certificates, receipts and payments; (b) verify that the transactions are authorized properly and comply with applicable regulations; (c) verify that the transactions are recorded in conformity with GAAP; and (d) ascertain the adequacy of disclosure of stockholders' equity in the financial statements

   2. **Subfunctions** Subfunctions for stockholders' equity include (a) financing, (b) cash, (c) detailed ledger bookkeeping, and (d) general ledger accounting.

Exhibit 14 ▶ Sample Program for Stockholders' Equity

Procedures	Assertions*
1. Obtain or prepare an account analysis for all accounts—to outline the historical picture of corporate capital and any changes to corporate capital	Completeness
2. Account for all certificate numbers—to determine that no unauthorized securities were issued during the period	Completeness
3. Perform analytics—by computing the return on stockholders' equity, the book value per share, and the dividend payout ratio and comparing them to those of prior years; compare current year dividend amounts and balances for common and preferred stock and additional paid-in capital to those of prior years	Completeness
4. Vouch all retirements of securities—to ascertain that no certificates were reissued fraudulently	Rights & Obligations
5. Review compliance with stock option plans and other restrictions on capital stocks—allows the auditor to do the following:	All Presentations & Disclosure Assertions
a. Determine the adequacy of disclosure with respect to these arrangements	
b. Verify the number of shares issued during the year through conversion or exercise of convertible stocks and bonds, stock options, and stock warrants	
c. Ascertain whether the shares held in reserve exceed the shares authorized, but unissued	
d. Determine that the call provisions of preferred stock are carried out accurately	
6. Review minutes of board of directors' meetings—to verify that stock and dividend transactions have been authorized properly	Rights & Obligations
7. Account for all proceeds from security issues—to determine whether the transactions were accounted for in accordance with underwriting contracts, state stock issuance permits, and SEC registration statements	Valuation & Allocation
8. Analyze treasury stock transactions—to determine that such transactions were authorized properly and recorded in conformity with GAAP	Accuracy Valuation & Allocation
9. Reconcile subsidiary ledger with general ledger control account—to establish the amount of outstanding stock and to rule out the possibility of an over-issuance of shares	Valuation & Allocation
10. Reconcile dividend distributions and verify dividend calculations—to ascertain the accurate dividend amount and to discover any declared, but yet unpaid, dividends	Accuracy Completeness
11. Confirm shares outstanding with registrar—to ascertain whether the corporate records are accurate and that stock is issued in accordance with the authorization of the board of directors and the articles of incorporation	Accuracy Existence
12. Analyze the retained earnings account—to determine whether it is disclosed accurately in the financial statements, and determine the amount of any restrictions on retained earnings that result from loans, other agreements, or state law	All Presentation & Disclosure Assertions

---

13. Analyze prior-period adjustments—to ascertain whether they are valid and are treated properly in the financial statements and determine the amount of any restrictions on retained earnings that result from loans, other agreements, or state law

All Presentation & Disclosure Assertions

---

* Note that many procedures may test multiple assertions. This program is not intended to be a complete presentation. See Chapter 24 for details on assertions.

J.   Accounting Estimates (AU 342, SAS 57)

1.   **Audit Objectives' Focus** To determine if (a) all accounting estimates that could be material to the financial statements have been developed, (b) the estimates are reasonable, and (c) the estimates are in conformity with GAAP and are disclosed properly

   a.   Accounting estimates are used when the measurement of some amounts or the valuations of some accounts is uncertain pending the outcome of future events.

   b.   Estimates also are used when relevant data concerning events that have occurred already cannot be accumulated on a timely, cost-effective basis.

2.   **Developing Accounting Estimates** Management is responsible for establishing the process for preparing accounting estimates. Generally this consists of:

   a.   Identifying situations that require accounting estimates

   b.   Identifying relevant factors

   c.   Accumulating relevant, sufficient, and reliable data on which to base the estimate

   d.   Developing assumptions based on management's judgment of the most likely circumstances and events

   e.   Determining estimated amounts based on the assumptions

   f.   Determining the estimate is presented in conformity with applicable accounting principles and that disclosure is adequate

3.   **Internal Control** Internal control may reduce the risk of material misstatements of accounting estimates. Some relevant features of internal control include:

   a.   Management communication of the need for proper accounting estimates

   b.   Accumulation of relevant, sufficient, and reliable data on which to base an accounting estimate

   c.   Preparation of estimates by qualified personnel

   d.   Adequate review and approval of accounting estimates by appropriate levels of authority

   e.   Comparison of prior accounting estimates with subsequent results to assess the reliability of the process used to develop estimates

   f.   Consideration by management of whether the resulting accounting estimate is consistent with the operational plans of the entity

4.   **Evaluating Accounting Estimates** The auditor must evaluate the reasonableness of accounting estimates and consider them with an attitude of professional skepticism. The auditor should develop an independent expectation of the estimate based on knowledge of the entity and its industry.

    a.   In evaluating the reasonableness of an estimate, the auditor normally concentrates on key factors and assumptions that are

        (1)   Significant to the accounting estimate

        (2)   Sensitive to variations

        (3)   Deviations from historical patterns

        (4)   Subjective and susceptible to misstatement and bias

    b.   To determine whether management has identified all accounting estimates that could be material to the financial statements, the auditor should evaluate information regarding the following: changes made or planned in the entity's business; changes in the method of accumulating information; litigation, claims, and assessments; minutes of meetings; and regulatory or examination reports.

    c.   The auditor should understand how management develops estimates and the historical experience of the entity in making past estimates. Management's process of developing accounting estimates should be reviewed and tested. The auditor should consider performing the following procedures:

        (1)   Identify controls over the preparation of accounting estimates and supporting data that may be useful in the evaluation.

        (2)   Identify the sources of data and factors that management used and consider whether such data and factors are relevant, reliable, and sufficient for the purpose.

        (3)   Evaluate whether the assumptions are consistent with each other, the supporting data, historical data, and industry data.

        (4)   Consider whether changes in business or industry may cause other factors to become significant.

        (5)   Consider whether there are additional factors that should be evaluated.

        (6)   Evaluate historical data used to develop assumptions to assess whether data is comparable and consistent with data of the period being audited.

CHAPTER 25—AUDIT PROGRAMS

Problem 25-1 MULTIPLE CHOICE QUESTIONS (128 to 160 minutes)

1. The objective of tests of details of transactions performed as substantive tests is to
a. Comply with generally accepted auditing standards
b. Attain assurance about the reliability of the accounting system
c. Detect material misstatements in the financial statements
d. Evaluate whether management's policies and procedures operated effectively
(11/95, AUD, #51, 5998)

2. Which of the following procedures would an auditor least likely perform before the balance sheet date?
a. Confirmation of accounts payable
b. Observation of merchandise inventory
c. Assessment of control risk
d. Identification of related parties
(5/95, AUD, #73, 5691)

3. An auditor confirmed accounts receivable as of an interim date, and all confirmations were returned and appeared reasonable. Which of the following additional procedures most likely should be performed at year-end?
a. Send confirmations for all new customer balances incurred from the interim date to year-end
b. Resend confirmations for any significant customer balances remaining at year-end
c. Review supporting documents for new large balances occurring after the interim date, and evaluate any significant changes in balances at year-end
d. Review cash collections subsequent to the interim date and the year-end
(R/05, AUD, #45, 7840)

4. An auditor plans to apply substantive tests to the details of asset and liability accounts as of an interim date rather than as of the balance sheet date. The auditor should be aware that this practice
a. Eliminates the use of certain statistical sampling methods that would otherwise be available
b. Presumes that the auditor will reperform the tests as of the balance sheet date
c. Should be especially considered when there are rapidly changing economic conditions
d. Potentially increases the risk that errors that exist at the balance sheet date will not be detected
(R/06, AUD, #8, 8126)

5. Which of the following procedures would an auditor most likely perform in obtaining evidence about subsequent events?
a. Determine that changes in employee pay rates after year-end were properly authorized
b. Recompute depreciation charges for plant assets sold after year-end
c. Investigate changes in long-term debt occurring after year-end
d. Inquire about payroll checks that were recorded before year-end but cashed after year-end
(5/95, AUD, #65, amended, 5683)

6. An auditor compared the current year gross margin with the prior year gross margin to determine if cost of sales is reasonable. What type of audit procedure was performed?
a. Test of transactions
b. Analytical procedures
c. Test of controls
d. Test of details
(R/06, AUD, #22, 8140)

7. Which of the following procedures would an auditor most likely perform in auditing the statement of cash flows?
a. Compare the amounts included in the statement of cash flows to similar amounts in the prior year's statement of cash flows
b. Reconcile the cutoff bank statements to verify the accuracy of the year-end bank balances
c. Vouch all bank transfers for the last week of the year and first week of the subsequent year
d. Reconcile the amounts included in the statement of cash flows to the other financial statements' balances and amounts
(5/95, AUD, #56, 5674)

8. In testing the existence assertion for an asset, an auditor ordinarily works from the
a. Financial statements to the potentially unrecorded items
b. Potentially unrecorded items to the financial statements
c. Accounting records to the supporting evidence
d. Supporting evidence to the accounting records
(11/90, AUD, #17, 0136)

9. In determining whether transactions have been recorded, the direction of the audit testing should be from the
a. General ledger balances
b. Adjusted trial balance
c. Original source documents
d. General journal entries
(5/95, AUD, #57, 5675)

10. Tracing copies of computer-prepared sales invoices to copies of the corresponding computer-prepared shipping documents provides evidence that
a. Shipments to customers were properly billed.
b. Entries in the accounts receivable subsidiary ledger were for sales actually shipped.
c. Sales billed to customers were actually shipped.
d. No duplicate shipments to customers were made. (R/06, AUD, #27, 8145)

11. On receiving a client's bank cutoff statement, an auditor most likely would trace
a. Prior year checks listed in the cutoff statement to the year-end outstanding checklist
b. Deposits in transit listed in the cutoff statement to the year-end bank reconciliation
c. Checks dated after year-end listed in the cutoff statement to the year-end outstanding checklist
d. Deposits recorded in the cash receipts journal after year-end to the cutoff statement
(R/02, AUD, #8, 7098)

12. The usefulness of the standard bank confirmation request may be limited because the bank employee who completes the form may
a. Not believe that the bank is obligated to verify confidential information to a third party
b. Sign and return the form without inspecting the accuracy of the client's bank reconciliation
c. Not have access to the client's cutoff bank statement
d. Be unaware of all the financial relationships that the bank has with the client
(11/95, AUD, #45, 5992)

13. Which of the following characteristics most likely would be indicative of check kiting?
a. High turnover of employees who have access to cash
b. Many large checks that are recorded on Mondays
c. Low average balance compared to high level of deposits
d. Frequent ATM checking account withdrawals
(R/02, AUD, #17, 7107)

14. An auditor most likely would limit substantive audit tests of sales transactions when control risk is assessed as low for the occurrence assertion concerning sales transactions and the auditor has already gathered evidence supporting
a. Opening and closing inventory balances
b. Cash receipts and accounts receivable
c. Shipping and receiving activities
d. Cutoffs of sales and purchases
(11/95, AUD, #46, 5993)

15. An auditor observed that a client mails monthly statements to customers. Subsequently, the auditor reviewed evidence of follow-up on the errors reported by the customers. This test of controls most likely was performed to support management's financial statement assertion(s) of

	Classification and understandability	Rights and obligations
a.	Yes	Yes
b.	Yes	No
c.	No	Yes
d.	No	No

(R/02, AUD, #11, amended, 7101)

16. Which of the following internal control procedures most likely would deter lapping of collections from customers?
a. Independent internal verification of dates of entry in the cash receipts journal with dates of daily cash summaries
b. Authorization of write-offs of uncollectible accounts by a supervisor independent of credit approval
c. Segregation of duties between receiving cash and posting the accounts receivable ledger
d. Supervisory comparison of the daily cash summary with the sum of the cash receipts journal entries (5/93, AUD, #14, 3910)

17. An auditor suspects that a client's cashier is misappropriating cash receipts for personal use by lapping customer checks received in the mail. In attempting to uncover this embezzlement scheme, the auditor most likely would compare the
a. Dates checks are deposited per bank statements with the dates remittance credits are recorded.
b. Daily cash summaries with the sums of the cash receipts journal entries.
c. Individual bank deposit slips with the details of the monthly bank statements.
d. Dates uncollectible accounts are authorized to be written off with the dates the write-offs are actually recorded. (11/95, AUD, #28, 5975)

18. In evaluating the adequacy of the allowance for doubtful accounts, an auditor most likely reviews the entity's aging of receivables to support management's financial statement assertion of
a. Existence
b. Valuation and allocation
c. Completeness
d. Rights and obligations
(5/93, AUD, #29, amended, 3925)

19. An auditor discovered that a client's accounts receivable turnover is substantially lower for the current year than for the prior year. This may indicate that
a. Fictitious credit sales have been recorded during the year.
b. Employees have stolen inventory just before the year-end.
c. The client recently tightened its credit-granting policies.
d. An employee has been lapping receivables in both years. (R/02, AUD, #19, 7109)

20. Which of the following most likely would be detected by an auditor's review of a client's sales cutoff?
a. Shipments lacking sales invoices and shipping documents
b. Excessive write-offs of accounts receivable
c. Unrecorded sales at year-end
d. Lapping of year-end accounts receivable
(5/92, AUD, #25, 2778)

21. An auditor selects a sample from the file of shipping documents to determine whether invoices were prepared. This test is performed to satisfy the audit objective of
a. Accuracy
b. Completeness
c. Existence
d. Control (Editors, 7494)

22. Under which of the following circumstances would the use of the blank form of confirmations of accounts receivable most likely be preferable to positive confirmations?
a. The recipients are likely to sign the confirmations without devoting proper attention to them.
b. Subsequent cash receipts are unusually difficult to verify.
c. Analytical procedures indicate that few exceptions are expected.
d. The combined assessed level of inherent risk and control risk is low. (11/98, AUD, #23, 6714)

23. When an auditor does not receive replies to positive requests for year-end accounts receivable confirmations, the auditor most likely would
a. Inspect the allowance account to verify whether the accounts were subsequently written off
b. Increase the assessed level of detection risk for the valuation and completeness assertions
c. Ask the client to contact the customers to request that the confirmations be returned
d. Increase the assessed level of inherent risk for the revenue cycle (5/95, AUD, #46, 5664)

24. Which of the following statements would an auditor most likely add to the negative form of confirmation of accounts receivable to encourage timely consideration by the recipients?
a. "This is not a request for payment; remittances should not be sent to our auditors in the enclosed envelope."
b. "Report any differences on the enclosed statement directly to our auditors; no reply is necessary if this amount agrees with your records."
c. "If you do not report an differences within 15 days, it will be assumed that this statement is correct."
d. "The following invoices have been selected for confirmation and represent amounts that are overdue." (R/99, AUD, #19, 6835)

25. Which of the following strategies most likely could improve the response rate of the confirmation of accounts receivable?
a. Including a list of items or invoices that constitute the account balance
b. Restricting the selection of accounts to be confirmed to those customers with relatively large balances
c. Requesting customers to respond to the confirmation requests directly to the auditor by fax or e-mail
d. Notifying the recipients that second requests will be mailed if they fail to respond in a timely manner (R/00, AUD, #11, 6936)

26. In confirming accounts receivable, an auditor decided to confirm customers' account balances rather than individual invoices. Which of the following most likely would be included with the client's confirmation letter?
a. An auditor-prepared letter explaining that a non-response may cause an inference that the account balance is correct
b. A client-prepared letter reminding the customer that a nonresponse will cause a second request to be sent
c. An auditor-prepared letter requesting the customer to supply missing and incorrect information directly to the auditor
d. A client-prepared statement of account showing the details of the customer's account balance
(R/99, AUD, #18, 6834)

27. In auditing accounts receivable, the negative form of confirmation request most likely would be used when
a. The total recorded amount of accounts receivable is immaterial to the financial statements taken as a whole.
b. Response rates in prior years to properly designed positive confirmation requests were inadequate.
c. Recipients are likely to return positive confirmation requests without verifying the accuracy of the information.
d. The combined assessed level of inherent risk and control risk relative to accounts receivable is low.
(11/97, AUD, #19, 6582)

28. An independent auditor asked a client's internal auditor to assist in preparing a standard financial institution confirmation request for a payroll account that had been closed during the year under audit. After the internal auditor prepared the form, the controller signed it and mailed it to the bank. What was the major flaw in this procedure?
a. The internal auditor did not sign the form.
b. The form was mailed by the controller.
c. The form was prepared by the internal auditor.
d. The account was closed, so the balance was zero. (R/05, AUD, 0087A, #5, 7800)

29. To measure how effectively an entity employs its resources, an auditor calculates inventory turnover by dividing average inventory into
a. Net sales
b. Cost of goods sold
c. Operating income
d. Gross sales (11/95, AUD, #42, 5989)

30. While observing a client's annual physical inventory, an auditor recorded test counts for several items and noticed that certain test counts were higher than the recorded quantities in the client's perpetual records. This situation could be the result of the client's failure to record
a. Purchase discounts
b. Purchase returns
c. Sales
d. Sales returns (5/95, AUD, #52, 5670)

31. When auditing inventories, an auditor would least likely verify that
a. The financial statement presentation of inventories is appropriate.
b. Damaged goods and obsolete items have been properly accounted for.
c. All inventory owned by the client is on hand at the time of the count.
d. The client has used proper inventory pricing.
(5/93, AUD, #28, 7495)

32. An auditor most likely would inspect loan agreements under which an entity's inventories are pledged to support management's financial statement assertion of
a. Completeness of disclosures
b. Valuation of inventory
c. Existence of inventory
d. Completeness of inventory
(5/95, AUD, #40, amended, 5658)

33. A client maintains perpetual inventory records in both quantities and dollars. If the assessed level of control risk is high, an auditor would probably
a. Increase the extent of tests of controls of the inventory cycle
b. Request the client to schedule the physical inventory count at the end of the year
c. Insist that the client perform physical counts of inventory items several times during the year
d. Apply gross profit tests to ascertain the reasonableness of the physical counts
(11/94, AUD, #58, 5131)

34. Which of the following audit procedures probably would provide the most reliable evidence concerning the entity's assertion of rights and obligations related to inventories?
a. Inspect the open purchase order file for significant commitments that should be considered for disclosure
b. Inspect agreements to determine whether any inventory is pledged as collateral or subject to any liens
c. Select the last few shipping advices used before the physical count and determine whether the shipments were recorded as sales
d. Trace test counts noted during the entity's physical count to the entity's summarization of quantities (5/92, AUD, #17, amended, 2770)

35. Which of the following auditing procedures most likely would provide assurance about a manufacturing entity's inventory valuation?
a. Testing the entity's computation of standard overhead rates
b. Obtaining confirmation of inventories pledged under loan agreements
c. Reviewing shipping and receiving cutoff procedures for inventories
d. Tracing test counts to the entity's inventory listing (11/94, AUD, #48, 5121)

36. To gain assurance that all inventory items in a client's inventory listing schedule are valid, an auditor most likely would trace
a. Inventory tags noted during the auditor's observation to items listed in the inventory listing schedule
b. Inventory tags noted during the auditor's observation to items listed in receiving reports and vendors' invoices
c. Items listed in the inventory listing schedule to inventory tags and the auditor's recorded count sheets
d. Items listed in receiving reports and vendors' invoices to the inventory listing schedule
(5/95, AUD, #53, 5671)

37. An auditor selected items for test counts while observing a client's physical inventory. The auditor then traced the test counts to the client's inventory listing. This procedure most likely obtained evidence concerning management's assertion of
a. Rights and obligations
b. Completeness
c. Existence
d. Valuation   (5/94, AUD, #41, amended, 4706)

38. Which of the following procedures would an auditor most likely perform to obtain assurance that slow-moving and obsolete items included in inventories are properly identified?
a. Testing shipping and receiving cutoff procedures
b. Confirming inventories at locations outside the entity's premises
c. Examining an analysis of inventory turnover
d. Tracing inventory observation test counts to perpetual listings   (R/05, AUD, #9, 7804)

39. In auditing a manufacturing entity, which of the following procedures would an auditor least likely perform to determine whether slow-moving, defective, and obsolete items included in inventory are properly identified?
a. Test the computation of standard overhead rates
b. Tour the manufacturing plant or production facility
c. Compare inventory balances to anticipated sales volume
d. Review inventory experience and trends
(R/06, AUD, #34, 8152)

40. An auditor analyzes repairs and maintenance accounts primarily to obtain evidence in support of the audit assertion that all
a. Noncapitalizable expenditures for repairs and maintenance have been recorded in the proper period.
b. Expenditures for property and equipment have been recorded in the proper period.
c. Noncapitalizable expenditures for repairs and maintenance have been properly charged to expense.
d. Expenditures for property and equipment have not been charged to expense.
(11/94, AUD, #62, 5135)

41. Which of the following explanations most likely would satisfy an auditor who questions management about significant debits to the accumulated depreciation accounts?
a. The estimated remaining useful lives of plant assets were revised upward.
b. Plant assets were retired during the year.
c. The prior year's depreciation expense was erroneously understated.
d. Overhead allocations were revised at year-end.
(11/95, AUD, #49, 5996)

42. In auditing intangible assets, an auditor most likely would review or recompute amortization and determine whether the amortization period is reasonable in support of management's financial statement assertion of
a. Valuation and allocation
b. Existence
c. Completeness
d. Rights and obligations
(5/95, AUD, #41, amended, 5659)

43. An auditor usually tests the reasonableness of dividend income from investments in publicly-held companies by computing the amounts that should have been received by referring to
a. Dividend record books produced by investment advisory services
b. Stock indentures published by corporate transfer agents
c. Stock ledgers maintained by independent registrars
d. Annual audited financial statements issued by the investee companies (11/96, AUD, #11, 6363)

44. In testing long-term investments, an auditor ordinarily would use analytical procedures to ascertain the reasonableness of the
a. Completeness of recorded investment income
b. Classification between current and noncurrent portfolios
c. Valuation of marketable equity securities
d. Existence of unrealized gains or losses in the portfolio (5/93, AUD, #31, 3927)

45. In establishing the existence and ownership of a long-term investment in the form of publicly-traded stock, an auditor should inspect the securities or
a. Correspond with the investee company to verify the number of shares owned
b. Inspect the audited financial statements of the investee company
c. Confirm the number of shares owned that are held by an independent custodian
d. Determine that the investment is carried at the fair market value
(11/94, AUD, #49, amended, 5122)

46. When a client engages in transactions involving derivatives, the auditor should
a. Develop an understanding of the economic substance of each derivative
b. Confirm with the client's broker whether the derivatives are for trading purposes
c. Notify the audit committee about the risks involved in derivative transactions
d. Add an explanatory paragraph to the auditor's report describing the risks associated with each derivative (R/06, AUD, #13, 8131)

47. An auditor usually determines whether dividend income from publicly-held investments is reasonable by computing the amounts that should have been received by referring to
a. Stock ledgers maintained by independent registrars
b. Dividend records on file with the SEC
c. Records produced by investment services
d. Minutes of the investee's board of directors
(R/06, AUD, #17, 8135)

48. An auditor's inquiries of management disclosed that the entity recently invested in a series of energy derivatives to hedge against the risks associated with fluctuating oil prices. Under these circumstances, the auditor should
a. Perform analytical procedures to determine if the derivatives are properly valued
b. Examine the contracts for possible risk exposure and the need to recognize losses
c. Confirm the marketability of the derivatives with a commodity specialist
d. Document the derivatives in the auditor's communication with the audit committee
(R/06, AUD, #30, 8148)

49. Which of the following procedures would an auditor most likely perform in searching for unrecorded liabilities?
a. Trace a sample of accounts payable entries recorded just before year-end to the unmatched receiving report file
b. Compare a sample of purchase orders issued just after year-end with the year-end accounts payable trial balance
c. Vouch a sample of cash disbursements recorded just after year-end to receiving reports and vendor invoices
d. Scan the cash disbursements entries recorded just before year-end for indications of unusual transactions (11/95, AUD, #47, 5994)

50. An auditor traced a sample of purchase orders and the related receiving reports to the purchases journal and the cash disbursements journal. The purpose of this substantive audit procedure most likely was to
a. Identify unusually large purchases that should be investigated further
b. Verify that cash disbursements were for goods actually received
c. Determine that purchases were properly recorded
d. Test whether payments were for goods actually ordered (11/95, AUD, #48, 5995)

51. Which of the following is a substantive test that an auditor most likely would perform to verify the existence and valuation of recorded accounts payable?
a. Investigating the open purchase order file to ascertain that prenumbered purchase orders are used and accounted for
b. Receiving the client's mail, unopened, for a reasonable period of time after the year-end to search for unrecorded vendor's invoices
c. Vouching selected entries in the accounts payable subsidiary ledger to purchase orders and receiving reports
d. Confirming accounts payable balances with known suppliers who have zero balances
(5/93, AUD, #36, 3932)

52. An auditor suspects that certain client employees are ordering merchandise for themselves over the Internet without recording the purchase or receipt of the merchandise. When vendors' invoices arrive, one of the employees approves the invoices for payment. After the invoices are paid, the employee destroys the invoices and the related vouchers. In gathering evidence regarding the fraud, the auditor most likely would select items for testing from the file of all
a. Cash disbursements
b. Approved vouchers
c. Receiving reports
d. Vendors' invoices   (R/01, AUD, #4, 7019)

53. To determine whether accounts payable are complete, an auditor performs a test to verify that all merchandise received is recorded. The population of documents for this test consists of all
a. Payment vouchers
b. Receiving reports
c. Purchase requisitions
d. Vendor's invoices   (11/93, AUD, #26, 4263)

54. An auditor most likely would extend substantive tests of payroll when
a. Payroll is extensively audited by the state government.
b. Payroll expense is substantially higher than in the prior year.
c. Overpayments are discovered in performing tests of details.
d. Employees complain to management about too much overtime.   (5/94, AUD, #49, 4714)

55. An auditor vouched data for a sample of employees in a payroll register to approved clock card data to provide assurance that
a. Payments to employees are computed at authorized rates.
b. Employees work the number of hours for which they are paid.
c. Segregation of duties exists between the preparation and distribution of the payroll.
d. Internal controls relating to unclaimed payroll checks are operating effectively.
(5/95, AUD, #37, 5655)

56. When control risk is assessed as low for assertions related to payroll, substantive tests of payroll balances most likely would be limited to applying analytical procedures and
a. Observing the distribution of paychecks
b. Footing and cross-footing the payroll register
c. Inspecting payroll tax returns
d. Recalculating payroll accruals
(5/95, AUD, #54, 5672)

57. In auditing long-term bonds payable, an auditor most likely would
a. Perform analytical procedures on the bond premium and discount accounts
b. Examine documentation of assets purchased with bond proceeds for liens
c. Compare interest expense with the bonds payable amount for reasonableness
d. Confirm the existence of individual bondholders at year-end   (11/94, AUD, #60, 5133)

58. In auditing a client's retained earnings account, an auditor should determine whether there are any restrictions on retained earnings that result from loans, agreements, or state law. This procedure is designed to corroborate management's financial statement assertion of
a. Valuation and allocation
b. Occurrence
c. Completeness of disclosures
d. Rights and obligations
(11/98, AUD, #22, amended, 6713)

59. The primary responsibility of a bank acting as registrar of capital stock is to
a. Ascertain that dividends declared do not exceed the statutory amount allowable in the state of incorporation
b. Account for stock certificates by comparing the total shares outstanding to the total in the shareholders subsidiary ledger
c. Act as an independent third party between the board of directors and outside investors concerning mergers, acquisitions, and the sale of treasury stock
d. Verify that stock is issued in accordance with the authorization of the board of directors and the articles of incorporation   (5/91, AUD, #32, 0133)

60. An auditor usually obtains evidence of stockholders' equity transactions by reviewing the entity's
a. Minutes of board of directors meetings
b. Transfer agent's records
c. Canceled stock certificates
d. Treasury stock certificate book
(R/99, AUD, #21, 6837)

61. When a company's stock record books are maintained by an outside registrar or transfer agent, the auditor should obtain confirmation from the registrar or transfer agent concerning the
a. Amount of dividends paid to related parties
b. Expected proceeds from stock subscriptions receivable
c. Number of shares issued and outstanding
d. Proper authorization of stock rights and warrants
(R/06, AUD, #2, 8120)

62. Which of the following procedures most likely would assist an auditor in determining whether management has identified all accounting estimates that could be material to the financial statements?
a. Inquire about the existence of related party transactions
b. Determine whether accounting estimates deviate from historical patterns
c. Confirm inventories at locations outside the entity
d. Review the lawyer's letter for information about litigation   (R/02, AUD, #4, 7094)

63. In evaluating the reasonableness of an entity's accounting estimates, an auditor normally would be concerned about assumptions that are
a. Susceptible to bias
b. Consistent with prior periods
c. Insensitive to variations
d. Similar to industry guidelines
(5/97, AUD, #6, 6395)

64. In evaluating an entity's accounting estimates, one of the auditor's objectives is to determine whether the estimates are
a. Prepared in a satisfactory control environment
b. Consistent with industry guidelines
c. Based on verifiable objective assumptions
d. Reasonable in the circumstances
(R/06, AUD, #48, 8166)

Problem 25-2 ADDITIONAL MULTIPLE CHOICE QUESTIONS (58 to 73 minutes)

65. In which of the following circumstances is substantive testing of accounts receivable before the balance sheet date most appropriate?
a. The client has a new sales incentive program in place.
b. Internal controls during the remaining period are effective.
c. There is a high turnover of senior management.
d. It is a first engagement of a new client.
(R/07, AUD, #26, 8398)

66. Before applying principal substantive tests to an entity's accounts receivable at an interim date, an auditor should
a. Consider the likelihood of assessing the risk of incorrect rejection too low
b. Project sampling risk at the maximum for tests covering the remaining period
c. Ascertain that accounts receivable are immaterial to the financial statements
d. Assess the difficulty in controlling the incremental audit risk   (R/07, AUD, #41, 8413)

67. The primary purpose of sending a standard confirmation request to financial institutions with which the client has done business during the year is to
a. Detect kiting activities that may otherwise not be discovered
b. Corroborate information regarding deposit and loan balances
c. Provide the data necessary to prepare a proof of cash
d. Request information about contingent liabilities and secured transactions (5/93, AUD, #34, 3930)

68. Which of the following cash transfers results in a misstatement of cash at December 31, 20X1?

Bank Transfer Schedule			
Disbursement Date		Receipt Date	
per books	per bank	per books	per bank
a. 12/31/X1	01/05/X2	12/31/X1	01/04/X2
b. 01/04/X2	01/11/X2	01/04/X2	01/04/X2
c. 12/31/X1	01/04/X2	12/31/X1	12/31/X1
d. 01/04/X2	01/05/X2	12/31/X1	01/04/X2

(R/07, AUD, #8, 8380)

69. An auditor most likely would review an entity's periodic accounting for the numerical sequence of shipping documents and invoices to support management's financial statement assertion of
a. Occurrence
b. Rights and obligations
c. Valuation and allocation
d. Completeness (5/93, AUD, #27, amended, 3923)

70. Which of the following audit procedures would an auditor most likely perform to test controls relating to management's assertion concerning the completeness of sales transactions?
a. Verify that extensions and footings on the entity's sales invoices and monthly customer statements have been recomputed
b. Inspect the entity's reports of prenumbered shipping documents that have not been recorded in the sales journal
c. Compare the invoiced prices on prenumbered sales invoices to the entity's authorized price list
d. Inquire about the entity's credit granting policies and the consistent application of credit checks
(5/94, AUD, #27, 4692)

71. An auditor's purpose in reviewing credit ratings of customers with delinquent accounts receivable most likely is to obtain evidence concerning management's assertions about
a. Valuation and allocation
b. Classification and understandability
c. Existence
d. Rights and obligations
(11/94, AUD, #50, amended, 5123)

72. To reduce the risks associated with accepting e-mail responses to requests for confirmation of accounts receivable, an auditor most likely would
a. Request the senders to mail the original forms to the auditor
b. Examine subsequent cash receipts for the accounts in question
c. Consider the e-mail responses to the confirmations to be exceptions
d. Mail second requests to the e-mail respondents
(5/98, AUD, #12, 6629)

73. Hemp, CPA, is auditing the financial statements of a small rural municipality. The receivable balances represent residents' delinquent real estate taxes. Internal control at the municipality is weak. To determine the existence of the accounts receivable balances at the balance sheet date, Hemp would most likely
a. Send positive confirmation requests
b. Send negative confirmation requests
c. Inspect the internal records such as copies of the tax invoices that were mailed to the residents
d. Examine evidence of subsequent cash receipts
(Editors, 0178)

74. An auditor decides to use the blank form of accounts receivable confirmation rather than the positive form. The auditor should be aware that the blank form may be less efficient because
a. Subsequent cash receipts need to be verified.
b. Statistical sampling may not be used.
c. A higher assessed level of detection risk is required.
d. More nonresponses are likely to occur.
(R/03, AUD, #18, 7640)

75. The confirmation of customers' accounts receivable rarely provides reliable evidence about the completeness assertion because
a. Many customers merely sign and return the confirmation without verifying its details.
b. Recipients usually respond only if they disagree with the information on the request.
c. Customers may not be inclined to report understatement errors in their accounts.
d. Auditors typically select many accounts with low recorded balances to be confirmed.
(11/95, AUD, #39, 5986)

76. Which of the following statements is correct concerning the use of negative confirmation requests?
a. Unreturned negative confirmation requests rarely provide significant explicit evidence.
b. Negative confirmation requests are effective when detection risk is low.
c. Unreturned negative confirmation requests indicate that alternative procedures are necessary.
d. Negative confirmation requests are effective when understatements of account balances are suspected. (5/95, AUD, #45, 5663)

77. Which of the following strategies most likely could improve the response rate of the confirmations of accounts receivable?
a. Restrict the selection of accounts to be confirmed to those customers with large balances
b. Include a list of items or invoices that constitute the customers' account balances
c. Explain to customers that discrepancies will be investigated by an independent third party
d. Ask customers to respond to the confirmation requests directly to the auditor by fax
(R/07, AUD, #35, 8407)

78. An auditor most likely would make inquiries of production and sales personnel concerning possible obsolete or slow-moving inventory to support management's financial statement assertion of
a. Valuation and allocation
b. Rights and obligations
c. Existence
d. Classification and understandability
(5/95, AUD, #43, amended, 5661)

79. To obtain assurance that all inventory items in a client's inventory listing are valid, an auditor most likely would trace
a. Inventory tags noted during the auditor's observation to items listed in receiving reports and vendors' invoices
b. Items listed in receiving reports and vendors' invoices to the inventory listing
c. Inventory tags noted during the auditor's observation to items in the inventory listing
d. Items in the inventory listing to inventory tags and the auditor's recorded count sheets
(R/07, AUD, #46, 8418)

80. When there are numerous property and equipment transactions during the year, an auditor who plans to assess control risk at a low level usually performs
a. Analytical procedures for property and equipment balances at the end of the year
b. Analytical procedures for current year property and equipment transactions
c. Tests of controls and limited tests of current year property and equipment transactions
d. Tests of controls and extensive tests of property and equipment balances at the end of the year
(11/95, AUD, #27, amended, 5974)

81. A weakness of internal control over recording retirements of equipment may cause an auditor to
a. Inspect certain items of equipment in the plant and trace those items to the accounting records
b. Review the subsidiary ledger to ascertain whether depreciation was taken on each item of equipment during the year
c. Trace additions to the "other assets" account to search for equipment that is still on hand but no longer being used
d. Select certain items of equipment from the accounting records and locate them in the plant
(11/95, AUD, #34, 5981)

82. An auditor's principal objective in analyzing repairs and maintenance expense accounts is to
a. Determine that all obsolete property, plant, and equipment assets were written off before the year-end
b. Verify that all recorded property, plant, and equipment assets actually exist
c. Discover expenditures that were expensed but should have been capitalized
d. Identify property, plant, and equipment assets that cannot be repaired and should be written off
(R/07, AUD, #19, 8391)

83. An analysis of which of the following accounts would best aid in verifying that all fixed assets have been capitalized?
a. Cash
b. Depreciation expense
c. Property tax expense
d. Repairs and maintenance
(R/07, AUD, #28, 8400)

84. To satisfy the valuation assertion when auditing an investment accounted for by the equity method, an auditor most likely would
a. Inspect the stock certificates evidencing the investment
b. Examine the audited financial statements of the investee company
c. Review the broker's advice or canceled check for the investment's acquisition
d. Obtain market quotations from financial newspapers or periodicals   (11/91, AUD, #44, 2312)

85. In confirming with an outside agent, such as a financial institution, that the agent is holding investment securities in the client's name, an auditor most likely gathers evidence in support of management's financial statement assertions of existence and
a. Valuation and allocation
b. Rights and obligations
c. Completeness
d. Classification and understandability
          (5/95, AUD, #44, amended, 5662)

86. In establishing the existence and ownership of long-term investments in the form of publicly-traded stock, an auditor most likely would inspect the securities or
a. Correspond with the investee company to verify the number of shares owned
b. Confirm the number of shares owned that are held by an independent custodian
c. Apply analytical procedures to the dividend income and investments accounts
d. Inspect the cash receipts journal for amounts that could represent the sale of securities
          (R/07, AUD, #37, 8409)

87. In auditing accounts payable, an auditor's procedures most likely would focus primarily on management's assertion of
a. Existence
b. Classification and understandability
c. Completeness
d. Valuation and allocation
          (11/93, AUD, #37, amended, 4274)

88. Cooper, CPA, performs a test to determine whether all merchandise for which the client was billed was received. The population for this test consists of all
a. Merchandise received
b. Vendors' invoices
c. Receiving reports
d. Canceled checks   (Editors, 0195)

89. When using confirmations to provide evidence about the completeness assertion for accounts payable, the two most appropriate populations most likely would be
a. Vendors with zero balances in the accounts payable subsidiary ledger
b. Vendors with whom the entity has previously done business
c. Amounts recorded in the accounts payable subsidiary ledger
d. Payees of checks drawn in the month after the year-end
e. Invoices filed in the entity's open invoice file
          (11/94, AUD, #53, amended, 5126)

90. An auditor reviews the reconciliation of payroll tax forms that a client is responsible for filing in order to
a. Verify that payroll taxes are deducted from employees' gross pay
b. Determine whether internal control activities are operating effectively
c. Uncover fictitious employees who are receiving payroll checks
d. Identify potential liabilities for unpaid payroll taxes
          (R/02, AUD, #14, 7104)

91. An auditor's program to examine long-term debt most likely would include steps that require
a. Comparing the carrying amount of the debt to its year-end market value
b. Correlating interest expense recorded for the period with outstanding debt
c. Verifying the existence of the holders of the debt by direct confirmation
d. Inspecting the accounts payable subsidiary ledger for unrecorded long-term debt
          (5/91, AUD, #8, 0127)

92. In performing tests concerning the granting of stock options, an auditor should
a. Confirm the transaction with the Secretary of State in the state of incorporation
b. Verify the existence of option holders in the entity's payroll records or stock ledgers
c. Determine that sufficient treasury stock is available to cover any new stock issued
d. Trace the authorization for the transaction to a vote of the board of directors
          (11/94, AUD, #61, 5134)

93. Which of the following procedures would an auditor ordinarily perform first in evaluating the reasonableness of management's accounting estimates?

a. Review transactions occurring prior to the completion of fieldwork that indicate variations from expectations

b. Compare independent expectations with recorded estimates to assess management's process

c. Obtain an understanding of how management developed its estimates

d. Analyze historical data used in developing assumptions to determine whether the process is consistent   (R/05, AUD, #26, 7821)

SIMULATIONS

Problem 25-3 (20 to 30 minutes)

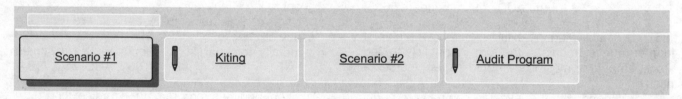

The information below was taken from the bank transfer schedule prepared during the audit of Fox Co.'s financial statements for the year ended December 31, Year 1. All checks are dated and issued on December 30, Year 1.

Check	Bank Accounts		Disbursement Date		Receipt Date	
No.	From	To	Per Books	Per Bank	Per Books	Per Bank
1	National	Federal	Dec. 30	Jan. 4	Dec. 30	Jan. 3
2	County	State	Jan. 3	Jan. 2	Dec. 30	Dec. 31
3	Federal	American	Dec. 31	Jan. 3	Jan. 2	Jan. 2
4	State	Republic	Jan. 2	Jan. 2	Jan. 2	Dec. 31

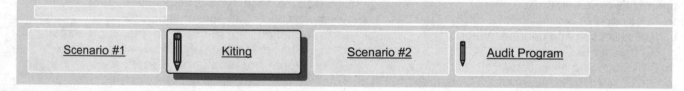

1. Which two checks might indicate kiting?
2. Which two checks illustrate deposits/transfers in transit at December 31, Year 1?

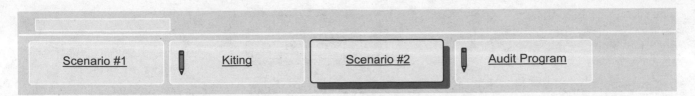

MLG Company's auditor received directly from the banks, confirmations and cutoff statements with related checks and deposit tickets for MLG's three general-purpose bank accounts. The auditor determined that internal control over cash was satisfactory and control risk could be assessed at below the maximum level. The proper cutoff of external cash receipts and disbursements was established. No bank accounts were opened or closed during the year.

Prepare the audit program of substantive procedures to verify MLG's bank balances. Ignore any other cash accounts.

What authoritative reference discusses the qualitative aspects of misstatements that an auditor should consider when misstatements are discovered in samples during substantive tests?

Paragraph Reference Answer: _____

(5/92, AUD, #27, amended, 2780)

Problem 25-4 (15 to 25 minutes)

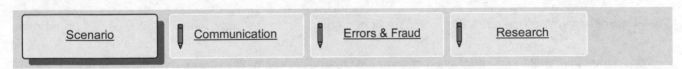

King, CPA, is auditing the financial statements of Cycle Co., an entity that has receivables from customers, which have arisen from the sale of goods in the normal course of business. King is aware that the confirmation of accounts receivable is generally accepted auditing procedure.

In designing confirmation requests, what factors are likely to affect King's assessment of the reliability of confirmations that King sends?

The following items represent possible errors and fraud that an auditor suspects are present. The accompanying List of Auditing Procedures represents procedures that the auditor would consider performing to gather evidence concerning possible errors and fraud. For each item, select one or two procedures, as indicated, that the auditor most likely would perform to gather evidence in support of that item.

_____ *Possible Errors and Fraud* _____

1. The auditor suspects that a kiting scheme exists because an accounting department employee who can issue and record checks seems to be leading an unusually luxurious lifestyle. (Select only 1 procedure)

2. The auditor suspects that the controller wrote several checks and recorded the cash disbursements just before the year-end but did not mail the checks until after the first week of the subsequent year. (Select only 1 procedure)

3. The entity borrowed funds from a financial institution. Although the transaction was properly recorded, the auditor suspects that the loan created a lien on the entity's real estate that is not disclosed in its financial statements. (Select only 1 procedure)

4. The auditor discovered an unusually large receivable from one of the entity's new customers. The auditor suspects that the receivable may be fictitious because the auditor has never heard of the customer and because the auditor's initial attempt to confirm the receivable has been ignored by the customer. (Select only 2 procedures)

5. The auditor suspects that fictitious employees have been placed on the payroll by the entity's payroll supervisor, who has access to payroll records and to the paychecks. (Select only 1 procedure)

6. The auditor suspects that selected employees of the entity received unauthorized raises from the entity's payroll supervisor, who has access to payroll records. (Select only 1 procedure)

_____ *List of Auditing Procedures* _____

A. Compare the details of the cash receipts journal entries with the details of the corresponding daily deposit slips.

B. Scan the debits to the fixed asset accounts and vouch selected amounts to vendors' invoices and management authorization.

C. Perform analytical procedures that compare documented authorized pay rates to the entity's budget and forecast.

D. Obtain the cutoff bank statement and compare the cleared checks to the year-end bank reconciliation.

E. Prepare a bank transfer schedule.

F. Inspect the entity's deeds to its real estate.

G. Make inquiries of the entity's attorney concerning the details of real estate transactions.

H. Confirm the terms of borrowing arrangements with the lender.

I. Examine selected equipment repair orders and supporting documentation to determine the propriety of the charges.

J. Send requests to confirm the entity's accounts receivable on a surprise basis at an interim date.

K. Send a second request for confirmation of the receivable to the customer and make inquiries of a reputable credit agency concerning the customer's creditworthiness.

L. Examine the entity's shipping documents to verify that the merchandise that produced the receivable was actually sent to the customer.

M. Inspect the entity's correspondence files for indications of customer disputes or for evidence that certain shipments were on consignment.

N. Perform edit checks of data on the payroll transaction tapes.

O. Inspect payroll check endorsements for similar handwriting.

P. Observe payroll check distribution on a surprise basis.

Q. Vouch data in the payroll register to documented authorized pay rates in the human resources department's files.

R. Reconcile the payroll checking account and determine if there were unusual time lags between the issuance and payment of payroll checks.

S. Inspect the file of prenumbered vouchers for consecutive numbering and proper approval by an appropriate employee.

T. Determine that the details of selected prenumbered vouchers match the related vendor's invoices.

U. Examine the supporting purchase orders and receiving reports for selected paid vouchers.

Scenario	Communication	Errors & Fraud	Research

What authoritative reference provides examples of subsequent events that require disclosure, but not adjustment, to financial statements?

Paragraph Reference Answer: _____

(5/94, AUD, #5, amended, 6248)

Problem 25-5 (20 to 30 minutes)

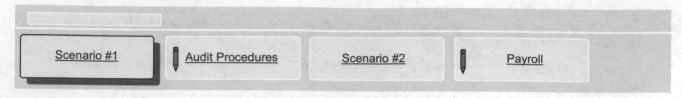

American Manufacturers, Inc.
Long-Term Debt
October 31, Year 01

Lender	Interest rate	Payment terms	Collateral	Balance 10/31/X0	Current year borrowings	Current year reductions	Balance 10/31/X1	Interest paid to	Accrued interest payable 10/31/X1	Comments
▲ First National Bank	10%	Interest only on last day of each quarter; principal due in full on 9/30/03.	Manufacturing equipment	500,000 ■	200,000 ◆ 3/31/01	(100,000) ✪ 6/30/01	600,000 √	9/30/01	5,000 ✖	[1]
▲ Second State Bank	9%	$10,000 principal plus interest due on the 1st of each month; due in full on 1/1/04.	First mortgage on production facilities	380,000 ■	0	(110,000) ✚	270,000 √★	9/30/01	2,025 ✖	[2]
▲ Third Savings & Loan	12%	$5,000 principal plus interest due on the 15th of each month; due in full on 10/15/03	Second mortgage on production facilities	180,000 ■	0	(60,000)	120,000 ★★	10/15/01	600	[3]
▲ A. Clark, majority stockholder	0%	Due in full 10/31/03.	Unsecured	700,000 ■	0	(200,000) 10/28/01	500,000 √		0	[4]
				1,760,000	200,000	(470,000)	1,490,000 ●		7,625 ●	

[1] First National confirms that interest payments are current and agrees with account balance.
[2] Monthly payment for $12,025 was mailed on 11/3/01; Second State agrees with account balance.
[3] Third Savings & Loan claims 10/15/01 payment wasn't received as of 11/5/01; adjusting entry proposed to increase accrued interest payable.
[4] Borrowed additional $200,000 from Clark on 11/5/01; need to investigate reborrowing just after year-end and consider imputed interest on 0% stockholder loan.

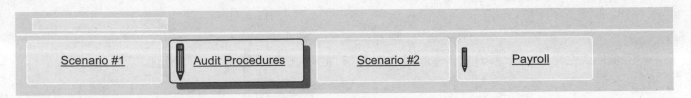

The items to be answered represent tick marks (symbols) that indicate procedures performed or comments documented in auditing the *Long-term Debt* account of American Manufacturers, Inc.

Select, from the accompanying lists of procedures/comments, the procedure/comment that the auditor most likely performed/documented at each point of the audit where a tick mark was made on the working papers. Select only one procedure/comment for each item. Assume that the working papers foot and cross-foot.

List of Procedures/Comments

A. Confirmed, without exception.

B. Confirmed, with exception.

C. Traced amount to prior year's working papers.

D. Traced amount to current year's trial balance and general ledger.

E. Does not recompute correctly.

F. Tested reasonableness of calculations.

G. Agreed to canceled checks and lender's monthly statements.

H. Agreed to canceled check and board of directors' authorization.

I. Agreed interest rate, terms, and collateral to note & loan agreement.

J. Agreed to loan agreement, validated bank deposit ticket, and board of directors' authorization.

K. Reclassification entry proposed for current portion of long-term debt.

Items to Be Answered

1. ▲
2. ▪
3. ◆
4. ✪
5. ✚
6. √
7. ★
8. ✳
9. ●
10. ✕

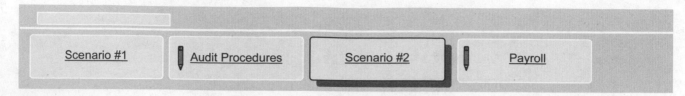

Bell, CPA, was engaged to audit the financial statements of Kent Company, a continuing audit client. Bell is about to audit Kent's Payroll transactions. Kent uses an in-house payroll department to compute payroll data, and prepare and distribute payroll checks.

During the planning process, Bell determined that the inherent risk of overstatement of payroll expense is high. In addition, Bell obtained an understanding of internal control and assessed control risk at the maximum level for payroll-related assertions.

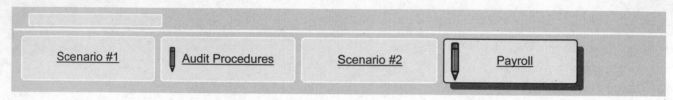

Describe the audit procedures Bell should consider performing in the audit of Kent's payroll transactions to address the risk of overstatement. Do not discuss Kent's internal control structure.

What authoritative reference provides guidance when the auditor detects misstatements in classes of transactions or account balances at an interim date?

Paragraph Reference Answer: _____

(11/97, AUD, #2, amended, 6249)

Problem 25-6 (20 to 30 minutes)

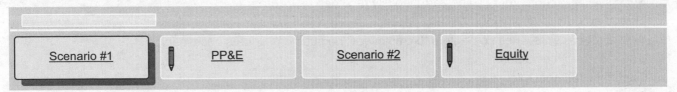

| Scenario #1 | | PP&E | | Scenario #2 | | Equity |

American Manufacturers, Inc.
Property, Plant, & Equipment and Accumulated Depreciation
October 31, Year 01

Property, Plant, & Equipment

Account	Balance 10/31/00		Additions		Disposals		Other		Balance 10/31/01	
Lane	650,000	➢	70,000	↕	0		0	⊗	720,000	→
Buildings	3,270,000	➢	230,000	✓	0		(30,000)		3,470,000	→
Equipment	1,750,000	➢	90,000	<	(12,000)	↔	0		1,828,000	→
Fixtures	850,000	➢	200,000	✓	0		30,000	⊗	1,080,000	→
	6,520,000		590,000		(12,000)		0		7,098,000	

Accumulated Depreciation

Account	Depreciation Rate	Method	Balance 10/31/00		Provision		Disposal		Balance 10/31/01	
Land										
Buildings	5%	S/L	1,144,500	➢	168,500	↵	0		1,313,000	→
Equipment	10%	S/L	700,000	➢	179,500	↵	(12,000)		867,500	→
Fixtures	15%	S/L	510,000	➢	144,750	↵	0		654,750	→
			2,354,500		492,750		(12,000)		2,835,250	

| Scenario #1 | | PP&E | | Scenario #2 | | Equity |

The items to be answered represent tick marks (symbols) that indicate procedures performed or comments documented in auditing the Property, plant, and equipment and Accumulated depreciation accounts of American Manufacturers, Inc. During the year under audit, American Manufacturers purchased new computers directly from wholesalers and constructed an addition to one of its buildings. The company's employees also refurbished the fixtures of several older buildings.

Select, from the accompanying lists of procedures/comments, the procedure/comment that the auditor most likely performed/documented at each point of the audit where a tick mark was made on the working papers. Select only one procedure/comment for each item. Assume that the working papers foot and cross-foot.

List of Procedures/Comments

A. Does not recompute correctly.
B. Tested reasonableness of calculation.
C. Traced amount to current year's trial balance and general ledger.

D. Reclassification entry for fixtures erroneously recorded as buildings.

E. Reclassification entry for buildings erroneously recorded as fixtures.

F. Traced amount to prior year's working papers.

G. Sold six fully-depreciated computers to employees; no audit procedures necessary.

H. Confirmed, with exception.

I. Confirmed, without exception.

J. Examined supporting vendors' invoices, canceled checks, asset subsidiary ledger and board of directors' minutes of meetings authorizing transactions.

K. Examined supporting work orders and engineers' reports, canceled checks, asset subsidiary ledger, and board of directors' minutes of meetings authorizing transactions.

L. Examined supporting deed and purchase contract, canceled checks, asset subsidiary ledger, and board of directors' minutes of meeting authorizing transactions.

___Items to Be Answered___

1. ➢

2. ↕

3. ✓

4. ∠

5. ↔

6. ⊗

7. →

8. ↵

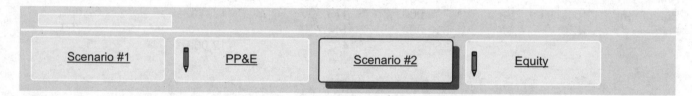

Jones, CPA, the continuing auditor of Sussex, Inc., is beginning the audit of the common stock and treasury stock accounts. Jones has decided to assess control risk at the maximum level.

Sussex has no par, has no stated value common stock, and acts as its own registrar and transfer agent. During the past year Sussex both issued and reacquired shares of its own common stock, some of which the company still owned at year-end. Additional common stock transactions occurred among the shareholders during the year.

Common stock transactions can be traced to individual shareholders' accounts in a subsidiary ledger and to a stock certificate book. The company has not paid any cash or stock dividends. There are no other classes of stock, stock rights, warrants, or option plans.

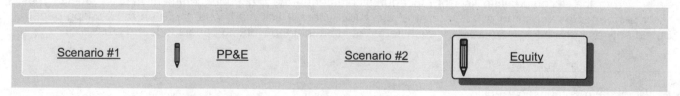

What substantive audit procedures should Jones apply in examining the common stock and treasury stock accounts?

What authoritative reference provides guidance regarding when an auditor should obtain an updating representation letter from management?

Paragraph Reference Answer: _____

(11/97, AUD, #2, amended, 6250)

Problem 25-7 (20 to 30 minutes)

King, CPA, is auditing the financial statements of Cycle Co., an entity that has receivables from customers, which have arisen from the sale of goods in the normal course of business. King is aware that the confirmation of accounts receivable is generally accepted auditing procedure.

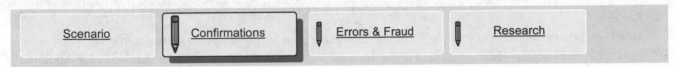

a. Under what circumstances could King justify omitting the confirmation of Cycle's accounts receivable?

b. What alternative procedures would King consider performing when replies to positive confirmation requests are not received?

The following items represent possible errors and fraud that an auditor suspects are present. The accompanying *List of Auditing Procedures* represents procedures that the auditor would consider performing to gather evidence concerning possible errors and fraud. For each item, select one or two procedures, as indicated, that the auditor most likely would perform to gather evidence in support of that item.

_____Possible Errors and Fraud_____

1. The entity's cash receipts of the first few days of the subsequent year were properly deposited in its general operating account after the year-end. However, the auditor suspects that the entity recorded the cash receipts in its books during the last week of the year under audit. (Select only 1 procedure)

2. The auditor suspects that vouchers were prepared and processed by an accounting department employee for merchandise that was neither ordered nor received by the entity. (Select only 1 procedure)

3. The details of invoices for equipment repairs were not clearly identified or explained to the accounting department employees. The auditor suspects that the bookkeeper incorrectly recorded the repairs as fixed assets. (Select only 1 procedure)

4. The auditor suspects that a lapping scheme exists because an accounting department employee who has access to cash receipts also maintains the accounts receivable ledger and refuses to take any vacation or sick days. (Select only 2 procedures)

Possible Errors and Fraud (contd.)

5. The auditor suspects that the entity is inappropriately increasing the cash reported on its balance sheet by drawing a check on one account and not recording it as an outstanding check on that account, and simultaneously recording it as a deposit in a second account. (Select only 1 procedure)

6. The auditor suspects that the entity's controller has overstated sales and accounts receivable by recording fictitious sales to regular customers in the entity's books. (Select only 2 procedures)

List of Auditing Procedures

A. Compare the details of the cash receipts journal entries with the details of the corresponding daily deposit slips.

B. Scan the debits to the fixed asset accounts and vouch selected amounts to vendors' invoices and management authorization.

C. Perform analytical procedures that compare documented authorized pay rates to the entity's budget and forecast.

D. Obtain the cutoff bank statement and compare the cleared checks to the year-end bank reconciliation.

E. Prepare a bank transfer schedule.

F. Inspect the entity's deeds to its real estate.

G. Make inquiries of the entity's attorney concerning the details of real estate transactions.

H. Confirm the terms of borrowing arrangements with the lender.

I. Examine selected equipment repair orders and supporting documentation to determine the propriety of the charges.

J. Send requests to confirm the entity's accounts receivable on a surprise basis at an interim date.

K. Send a second request for confirmation of the receivable to the customer and make inquiries of a reputable credit agency concerning the customer's creditworthiness.

L. Examine the entity's shipping documents to verify that the merchandise that produced the receivable was actually sent to the customer.

M. Inspect the entity's correspondence files for indications of customer disputes or for evidence that certain shipments were on consignment.

N. Perform edit checks of data on the payroll transaction tapes.

O. Inspect payroll check endorsements for similar handwriting.

P. Observe payroll check distribution on a surprise basis.

Q. Vouch data in the payroll register to documented authorized pay rates in the human resources department's files.

R. Reconcile the payroll checking account and determine if there were unusual time lags between the issuance and payment of payroll checks.

S. Inspect the file of prenumbered vouchers for consecutive numbering and proper approval by an appropriate employee.

T. Determine that the details of selected prenumbered vouchers match the related vendor's invoices.

U. Examine the supporting purchase orders and receiving reports for selected paid vouchers.

Scenario		Confirmations		Errors & Fraud		Research

What authoritative reference provides guidance as to whether an auditor may use the work of a specialist who has a relationship with the client?

Paragraph Reference Answer: _____

(5/97, AUD, #2, amended, 6400)

Problem 25-8 (25 to 35 minutes)

Miller, CPA, is engaged to audit the financial statements of Superior Wholesaling for the year ended December 31, 20X1. Miller obtained and documented an understanding of Superior's internal control relating to accounts receivable and assessed risk of material misstatement relating to accounts receivable as high. Miller requested and obtained from Superior an aged accounts receivable schedule listing the total amount owed by each customer as of December 31, 20X1, and sent positive confirmation requests to a sample of the customers. Subsequently, Miller tested the accuracy of the aged accounts receivable schedule. Miller has asked Adler, the staff assistant assigned to the engagement, to follow up on the eight returned confirmations* that appear on the following two pages. Assume that each confirmation is material if the potential misstatement is projected to the population.

Superior Wholesaling, Inc
123 Commercial Blvd.
Anytown, USA

January 15, 20X2

Atom Co.
362 Main Street   Confirm # 11
Anytown, USA

Dear *C. L. Adams*:

Our auditor, Miller, CPA, is currently auditing our financial statements. To facilitate this audit, please confirm the balance due us as of December 31, 20X1, which is shown on our records as *$15,000*. Indicate in the space below whether this is in agreement with your records. If there are exceptions, please provide any information that will assist the auditor in reconciling the difference

Please mail your reply directly to Miller, CPA. A stamped, self-addressed envelope is enclosed for your convenience.

Sincerely

J. Blake

J. Blake, Controller
Superior Wholesaling, Inc.

To Miller, CPA:

The amount shown above is correct as of December 31, 20X1, except as follows:

Yes, we ordered $15,000 worth of merchandise from Superior in November. However, we mailed Superior a check for $15,000 on 12/18/X1.

Name *C. L. Adams*   Position *Accounting Mgr.*
Date *1/22/X2*

Note to files: Blake indicates that the check was received and deposited on 12/28/X1, but posted to the wrong customer's account.

C. Miller

Superior Wholesaling, Inc
123 Commercial Blvd.
Anytown, USA

January 15, 20X2

Baker Co.
18 Lakeview Drive   Confirm # 28
Central City, USA

Dear *S. Brown*: ... *$25,000*. ...

To Miller, CPA:

The amount shown above is correct as of December 31, 20X1, except as follows:

Sure we ordered $25,000 of merchandise on Oct. 10, 20X1, but Superior was out-of-stock until recently. They back-ordered the goods and we finally received them on Jan. 6, 20X2.

Name *S. Brown*   Position *A/P Supervisor*
Date *Jan. 18, 20X2*

---

* The portion of the confirmation form after the greeting and ending with "J. Blake, Controller, Superior Wholesaling, Inc." is abbreviated for all but the first confirmation, # 11. In the illustration, the repetitive material has been replaced with the balance to be confirmed by Superior Wholesaling's customers. Aside from this value, this section of these forms did not differ from the first confirmation, #11.

Superior Wholesaling, Inc
123 Commercial Blvd.
Anytown, USA

January 15, 20X2

Clark Retailing
35 Lincoln Avenue   *Confirm # 34*
Jackson, USA

Dear *J. P. Cummings*: ... *$32,000*. ...

To Miller, CPA:

The amount shown above is correct as of December 31, 20X1, except as follows:

We received $24,000 of goods on consignment from
Superior on 12/10/X1, but they're not sold yet!

Name   *J. Cummings*   Position   *President*
Date   *1/19/X2*

Superior Wholesaling, Inc
123 Commercial Blvd.
Anytown, USA

January 15, 20X2

Delta Outlet Stores, Inc.   *Confirm # 41*
Sunshine Mall.
River City, USA

Dear *R. Dunn*: ... *$45,000*. ...

To Miller, CPA:

The amount shown above is correct as of December 31, 20X1, except as follows:

No way! Superior promised these goods in 10 days
on Dec. 2nd. When we didn't receive them, I
canceled the order on Dec. 12th. General
Wholesaling shipped us similar goods overnight!

Name *R. Dunn*   Position   *General Manager*
Date   *Jan. 18th*

Superior Wholesaling, Inc
123 Commercial Blvd.
Anytown, USA

January 15, 20X2

Eagle Distributors
2700 Ocean Shore Blvd.   *Confirm # 58*
Ocean City, USA

Dear *I. Eagle*: ... *$59,000*. ...

To Miller, CPA:

The amount shown above is correct as of December 31, 20X1, except as follows:

I use an accounts payable voucher system by
individual invoice. I can't verify $59,000, but
Superior is one of my regular suppliers. I am sure I
probably owe them something.

Name   *I. Eagle*   Position   *Accounting Mgr.*
Date   *1-20-X2*

Superior Wholesaling, Inc
123 Commercial Blvd.
Anytown, USA

January 15, 20X2

Franklin Co.   *Confirm # 67*
17 United Street
Industry City, USA

Dear *S. Brown*: ... *$65,000*. ...

To Miller, CPA:

The amount shown above is correct as of December 1, 20X1, except as follows:

Name   Position
Date

Note to files: This confirmation was returned by
the postal service as "return to sender—no such
address at this location."

C. Miller

```
┌─────────────────────────────────────┐   ┌─────────────────────────────────────┐
│        Superior Wholesaling, Inc     │   │        Superior Wholesaling, Inc     │
│          123 Commercial Blvd.        │   │          123 Commercial Blvd.        │
│             Anytown, USA             │   │             Anytown, USA             │
│                                      │   │                                      │
│              January 15, 20X2        │   │              January 15, 20X2        │
│  Grove Retailing                     │   │  Hall Enterprises, Inc.              │
│  3838 Curtis Blvd.     Confirm # 71  │   │  55 Green St.          Confirm # 86  │
│  Union Center, USA                   │   │  Grant City, USA                     │
│                                      │   │                                      │
│  Dear H. Gates: ... $75,000. ...     │   │  Dear K. Hines: ... $80,000. ...     │
│                                      │   │                                      │
│  To Miller, CPA:                     │   │  To Miller, CPA:                     │
│      The amount shown above is       │   │      The amount shown above is       │
│  correct as of December 31, 20X1,    │   │  correct as of December 31, 20X1,    │
│  except as follows:                  │   │  except as follows:                  │
│                                      │   │                                      │
│  Our records show that a check for   │   │  Mailed that check for full amount   │
│  $75,000 was mailed on 12/27/X1.     │   │  on 1-3-X2, merchandise was only     │
│                                      │   │  received on 12-23-X1.               │
│  Name H. Gates   Position Controller │   │  Name K. Hines   Position Accountant │
│  Date 1/22/X2                        │   │  Date                                │
└─────────────────────────────────────┘   └─────────────────────────────────────┘
```

Scenario	✏ Confirmations	✏ Research

a. Describe the procedure(s), if any, that Adler should perform to resolve each of the eight confirmations that were returned. Assume that Superior will record any necessary adjusting entries and that Adler will verify that they are appropriate.

b. Assume that Miller sent second requests for accounts receivable balances initially selected for confirmation for which no responses were received. Describe the alternative substantive procedures that Miller should consider applying to the accounts receivable selected for confirmation for which no responses were received to Miller's second requests. Assume that these accounts receivable in the aggregate, when projected as misstatements to the population, would affect Miller's decision about whether the financial statements are materially misstated.

c. In addition to performing the confirmation procedures and alternative procedures described in requirements a. and b. and the procedures described in the scenario, what additional substantive procedures should Miller consider performing to complete the audit of Superior's accounts receivable and related allowances? Assume that all accounts receivable are trade receivables.

Scenario	✏ Confirmations	✏ Research

What authoritative reference provides guidance on the procedures an auditor might perform to obtain evidence regarding investments in securities valued at cost?

Paragraph Reference Answer: _____

(5/97, AUD, #3, amended, 6401)

Problem 25-9 (15 to 25 minutes)

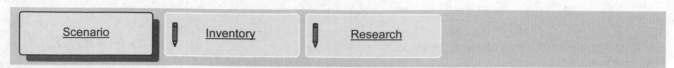

The purpose of all auditing procedures is to gather sufficient appropriate audit evidence for an auditor to form an opinion regarding the financial statements taken as a whole.

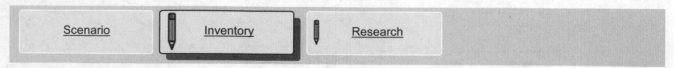

a. In addition to the example below, identify and describe five means or techniques of gathering audit evidence used to evaluate a client's inventory balance.

Technique	Description
Observation	An auditor watches the performance of some function, such as a client's annual inventory count.

b. Identify the four general assertions regarding a client's inventory balance and describe one different substantive auditing procedure for each assertion. Use the format illustrated below.

Assertion	Substantive Auditing Procedure

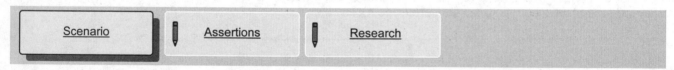

What authoritative reference provides guidance on auditing inventories held by outside custodians?

Paragraph Reference Answer: _____

(11/88, AUD, #5, amended, 6402)

Problem 25-10 (15 to 25 minutes)

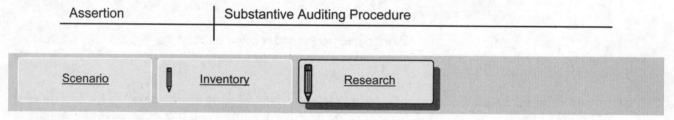

Larkin, CPA, has been engaged to audit the financial statements of Vernon Distributors, Inc., a continuing audit client, for the year ended September 30, Year 1. After obtaining an understanding of Vernon's internal control, Larkin assessed the risk of material misstatement as high for all financial statement assertions concerning investments. Larkin determined that Vernon is unable to exercise significant influence over any investee and none are related parties.

Larkin obtained from Vernon detailed analyses of its investments in domestic securities showing:

- The classification between trading, available-for-sale, and held-to-maturity portfolios;
- A description of each security, including the interest rate and maturity date of bonds and par value and dividend rate on stocks;

- A notation of the location of each security, either in the Treasurer's safe or held by an independent custodian;
- The number of shares of stock or face amount of bonds held at the beginning and end of the year;
- The beginning and ending balances at cost and at market, and the unamortized premium or discount on bonds;
- Additions to and sales from the portfolios for the year, including date, number of shares, face amount of bonds, cost, proceeds, and realized gain or loss;
- Valuation allowances at the beginning and end of the year and changes therein;
- Accrued investment income for each investment at the beginning and end of the year, and income earned and collected during the year.

Larkin then prepared the following partial audit program of substantive auditing procedures:

1. Foot and cross-foot the analyses.

2. Trace the ending totals to the general ledger and financial statements.

3. Trace the beginning balances to the prior year's working papers.

4. Obtain positive confirmation as of the balance sheet date of the investments held by any independent custodian.

5. Determine that income from investments has been properly recorded as accrued or collected by reference to published sources, by computation, and by tracing to recorded amounts.

6. For investments in nonpublic entities, compare carrying value to information in the most recently available audited financial statements.

7. Determine that all transfers between trading and available-for-sale portfolios have been properly authorized and recorded.

8. Determine that any other-than-temporary decline in the price of an investment has been properly recorded.

a. Identify the primary financial statement assertion relative to investments that would be addressed by each of the procedures #4 through #8 and describe the primary audit objective of performing those procedures. Use the format illustrated below.

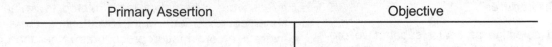

Primary Assertion	Objective

b. Describe three additional substantive auditing procedures Larkin should consider in auditing Vernon's investments.

What authoritative reference requires auditors to implement procedures to prevent unauthorized access to audit documentation?

Paragraph Reference Answer: _____

(11/91, AUD, #4, amended, 6403)

Problem 25-11 (25 to 35 minutes)

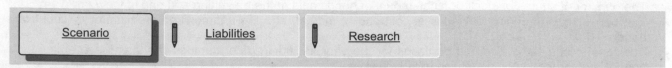

Cook, CPA, is auditing the financial statements of DollarMart, a local retailer of clothes, appliances, sporting goods, and electronics. During prior years' audits of DollarMart, Cook noticed that management was less concerned about the timely recording of expenses and liabilities than revenues and assets. As a result, very little of DollarMart's internal control resources were expended in assuring an accurate and timely recording of accounts payable. Cook also believes that DollarMart's management may be motivated to delay recording its liabilities at year-end, so Cook is approaching the search for unrecorded liabilities with caution.

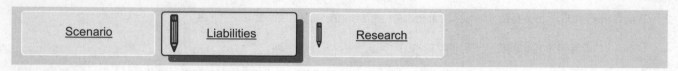

a. What substantive auditing procedures would Cook most likely consider performing in searching for DollarMart's unrecorded liabilities?

b. How would the nature, timing, and extent of Cook's substantive auditing procedures most likely be affected by DollarMart's deficient control environment?

What authoritative reference provides guidance regarding whether it is an auditor's responsibility to design audit procedures *solely* to identify conditions and events that indicate that there could be substantial doubt about an entity's ability to continue as a going concern?

Paragraph Reference Answer: _____

(5/96, AUD, #3, amended, 6404)

Solution 25-1 MULTIPLE CHOICE ANSWERS

Substantive Procedures

1. (c) In selecting particular substantive procedures to achieve audit objectives, an auditor considers, among other things, the risk of material misstatement of the financial statements. Omitting a test of details of transactions in some situations would not be a violation of auditing standards. Attaining assurance about the reliability of the accounting system and evaluating whether management's policies and procedures operated effectively are objectives of tests of controls. (5998)

2. (a) While the confirmation of accounts receivable and the other answer options are common audit procedures, confirmation of accounts *payable* is an extended procedure and usually occurs under unusual conditions. The greater the combined level of risk, the greater the assurance that the auditor needs from substantive tests related to a financial statement assertion. In these situations, the auditor might use confirmation procedures rather than or in conjunction with tests directed toward documents or parties within the entity. In a low risk situation, review of post balance sheet date payments to vendors may adequately substantiate the accounts payable balance. (5691)

3. (c) The lack of misstatements at the interim date would not cause the auditor to increase the assessment of control risk. The auditor most likely would review supporting documents for new large balances and evaluate significant changes in year-end balances. Without an increase in the assessment of control risk, additional extensive procedures, such as sending confirmations to new customers and reviewing subsequent cash collections are unlikely. If the auditor planned to resend confirmations for

any customer balances remaining at year-end when interim confirmations returned from these same customers appeared reasonable, it is unlikely that the auditor would plan to confirm accounts receivable as of an interim date. (7840)

4. (d) Applying principal substantive tests to the details of an asset or liability account as of an interim date rather than as of the balance sheet date potentially increases the risk that misstatements that may exist at the balance sheet date will not be detected by the auditor. Performing substantive tests at an interim date does not eliminate the use of any sampling techniques. The auditor would only need to consider reperforming substantive tests, as of the balance sheet date, if misstatements are detected at the interim date. Asset and liability accounts should be examined as of the balance sheet date if there are rapidly changing economic conditions. (8126)

5. (c) The auditor should perform other auditing procedures with respect to the period after the balance sheet date for the purpose of ascertaining the occurrence of subsequent events that may require adjustment or disclosure including investigating changes in long-term debt after year-end. Other procedures are applied to transactions occurring after the balance sheet date for the purpose of assurance that proper cutoffs have been made, and for the purpose of obtaining information to aid in the evaluation of the assets and liabilities as of the balance sheet date. Answers (a), (b), and (d) would not provide evidence about subsequent events as (a) is a test of controls and (b) and (d) are not common procedures. (5683)

6. (b) Analytics involve comparisons of recorded amounts, or ratios developed from recorded amounts, to expectations developed by the auditor. The auditor develops expectations by identifying relationships that reasonably are expected to exist from understanding the client and the industry in which the client operates. In this case, the auditor expected the current year's gross margin to be comparable to the prior year's gross margin. Tests of transactions are test of details that involves other types of procedures such as tracing and vouching to determine whether transactions were recorded correctly. Tests of controls evaluate the effectiveness of the design and operation of policies and procedures in preventing or detecting material misstatements. (8140)

7. (d) A reconciliation between the amounts included in the cash flow statement and other financial statements would be a procedure the auditor would perform because the cash flow statement amounts are a result of the transactions reflected in and the changes in balances on the other financial statements. Relationships between current year and prior year amounts due do not necessarily exist as can be expected on the balance sheet and income statement. This procedure would provide more audit evidence in the overall review stage of the audit for the balance sheet and income statement. Answer (b) is a procedure an auditor would perform in auditing the cash balance on the balance sheet. Answer (c) is a procedure the auditor would perform in auditing the cash balance on the balance sheet. (5674)

8. (c) In testing the existence assertion for an asset, the auditor would start with the accounting records themselves to determine that the assets recorded on the client's books do exist. Further evidence of the asset existence would then be found in the supporting evidence. (0136)

9. (c) To determine whether transactions have been recorded (completeness), procedures include tracing from supporting documentation (original source documents) to accounting records. Testing from general ledger balances, the adjusted trial balance, and general journal entries (vouching) would provide evidence of existence or occurrence. (5675)

10. (c) Vouching from sales invoices to copies of the corresponding shipping document provides evidence that sales billed to customers were actually shipped (occurrence). Tracing from the shipping documents to the corresponding sales invoices would provide evidence that shipments to customers were properly billed and that no duplicate shipments were made (completeness). Vouching from the accounts receivable subsidiary ledger to the shipping documents would provide evidence that those entries were actually shipped and are valid (occurrence). (8145)

Cash

11. (a) An auditor compares prior year checks listed in the cutoff statement compared to the year-end outstanding checklist to make sure that all year-end outstanding checks were handled correctly on the bank reconciliation. Deposits in transit are listed on the bank reconciliation, not on the cutoff statements; once on the cutoff statement, they cease to be in transit. Checks dated after year-end in the cutoff statement should not be on the year-end outstanding checklist; by definition, they were not outstanding at year-end. Checks and deposits dated after year-end merely provide information about liabilities or assets available at year-end. (7098)

12. (d) The AICPA Standard Form to Confirm Account Balance Information With Financial

Institutions is designed to substantiate information that is stated on the confirmation request; the form is not designed to provide assurance that information about accounts not listed on the form will be reported. The bank employee completing the form may be unaware of all the financial relationships that the client has with the bank and the request may not ask specifically about all the financial relationships, thus the usefulness of the confirmation in providing evidence for financial statement assertions may be limited. Responding to bank confirmation requests is a normal activity for a bank. It would be unlikely that a bank employee would not believe that the bank is obligated to verify confidential information to the third party, especially as the confirmation request is signed by the client authorizing the bank to release the information to the auditor. The bank would not have access to the client's bank reconciliation and thus would not inspect its accuracy. The bank does have access to the client's cutoff bank statements, but that information is not used by the bank to confirm year-end balances. (5992)

13. (c) One would expect a high account balance with a high deposit level. A kiting scheme involves drawing a check on one account to inflate the balance in another; it usually requires careful attention by a trusted perpetrator who is familiar with the operation, and especially, knows the time for checks to clear. This would tend not to be the situation with high turnover. An ATM withdrawal is posted quickly, reducing the time lag necessary for kiting. Kiting would not tend to produce large checks on any one particular day of the week, unless the perpetrator had an unusual work pattern. (7107)

A/R & Sales

14. (b) When the auditor has already gathered evidence supporting cash receipts and accounts receivable, the same evidence would support sales. Thus, having already gathered this evidence and having assessed control risk as low for the existence or occurrence assertion regarding sales transactions, the auditor most likely would conclude that s/he has substantial evidence for sales and would limit substantive tests of sales transactions. Evidence supporting opening and closing inventory balances, shipping and receiving activities, and cutoffs of sales and purchases would give only limited information regarding sales. (5993)

15. (c) This procedure helps ensure that the accounts receivable (a right to payment) amount is correct, but not that it is reported or disclosed appropriately and clearly. Classification and understandability is an assertion about presentation and disclosure. (7101)

16. (c) The segregation of custody and reporting is an important internal control that is most likely to deter a lapping scheme. Authorization of write-offs by a supervisor is a good control but would not in itself prevent an employee from misappropriating accounts receivable collections because the supervisor is unfamiliar with the accounts, as indicated in the question, and would, therefore, not be aware of customers who are delinquent in their payments. Answers (a) and (d) are examples of good internal controls but would not by themselves uncover a lapping scheme. (3910)

17. (a) Lapping involves the theft of one customer's payment and subsequently crediting the customer with payment made by another customer. Future remittances may be deposited but would be credited to the account from which funds were stolen, thus comparison of remittance dates would detect the scheme. Answers (b), (c), and (d) occur after the theft and would not show differences to pursue. (5975)

18. (b) Valuation and allocation is the assertion that assets, liabilities, and equity interests are included in the financial statements at appropriate amounts and any resulting valuation or allocation adjustments are appropriately recorded. Answer (a) deals with whether assets, liabilities, or equity interests exist at a given date. Answer (c) deals with whether all transactions, accounts, and disclosures that should be presented in the financial statements are so included. Answer (d) deals with whether assets are the rights of the entity and liabilities are the obligations of the entity. (3925)

19. (a) A/R turnover is the number of times that the A/R balance is collected during the year. Fictitious sales increase A/R, but leave collections the same, so A/R turnover decreases. A/R turnover would be unaffected by current inventory levels. Tightening credit-granting policies would tend to increase A/R turnover. Lapping receivables in two years would result in both years' receivables being misstated, but unless the volume of lapped amounts changed, turnover would not be affected. (7109)

20. (c) In general, cutoff tests are used to detect unrecorded transactions at the end of the period. In this question, the auditor would most likely detect unrecorded sales for the year by reviewing a sales cutoff to determine that sales were recorded in the period in which title to the goods passed to the customer. Such a review would not reveal shipments lacking invoices, excessive write-offs of accounts receivable, or lapping of year-end accounts receivable. (2778)

21. (b) This test is performed to satisfy the audit objective of completeness. The primary purpose of this objective is to establish whether all transactions that should have been recorded by the client are included in the accounts. (7494)

A/R Confirmations

22. (a) Blank A/R confirmations request that the customers supply the amount owed, if any. By having the customers provide the information, the auditor increases the likelihood that customers did examine their records. Positive confirmations have the amount that the customers owe provided by the client, typically invoice-by-invoice. The invoice-by-invoice form simplifies verifying subsequent cash receipts as compared to a single sum owed. Negative confirmations request the customer to return the confirmation, with corrections, only if their records differ. They usually are used if the combined assessed level of inherent risk and control risk is low, i.e., if few exceptions are expected. (6714)

23. (c) Nonresponse to positive requests for accounts receivable confirmations generally requires the use of follow-up requests, such as additional mailings or telephone calls. It is appropriate that the auditor ask the client to contact the customers. In cases where there is still no response to requests dealing with significant accounts, alternative procedures should be used to obtain adequate evidence. These additional procedures may involve the examination of documents such as subsequent cash receipts, sales invoices, and shipping documents. While nonresponse increases risks associated with the audit, it is the auditor's responsibility to apply alternative procedures to keep the risks within acceptable levels. (5664)

24. (c) Answer (c) clearly states the consequences of the client's customer's actions and informs the customer of the deadline. Answer (b) omits any indication of a deadline. While informing the client's customers that the confirmation request is not a payment request may be included in the letter, it only informs the client's customers what not to do—rather than the desired action. Amounts on A/R confirmation requests represent all owed amounts, not just those that are overdue. (6835)

25. (a) Providing additional information may make the task of confirming debts appear easier to the client's customers' employees, resulting in a response getting prepared and approved, rather than indefinitely waiting in a stack for a supervisor to examine and then approve. Customers with large balances may have the worse response rate. The use of fax or e-mail may impact the response time,

but probably not the response rate. The threat of a second request will probably have no more positive impact than the first request had, and may annoy the client's customers. (6936)

26. (d) The client prepares account confirmation requests. To maintain customer goodwill, an indication that a non-response will cause a second request should be avoided. A non-response to a positive confirmation request generates further inquires, not an assumption that a balance is correct. (6834)

27. (d) Negative confirmations are used when the auditor can tolerate a high level of detection risk, i.e., when the combined assessed level of inherent risk and control risk relative to accounts receivable is low. Negative confirmations provide less persuasive evidence than positive confirmations because the auditor is unable to determine if a lack of response is due to customer agreement or lack of delivery of the request for confirmation, etc. If the total recorded amount of accounts receivable is immaterial to the financial statement taken as a whole, confirmations of any kind would be unlikely. If response rates in prior years were inadequate, the auditor is more likely to consider other procedures rather than a type of confirmation for which response rates cannot be determined. If recipients are likely to return positive confirmations requests without verifying the accuracy of the information, it is unlikely they would have greater inclination to verify the accuracy of the information for negative confirmations. (6582)

28. (b) Confirmation requests always should be mailed by the auditor and be returned directly to the auditor's place of business. This is to diminish the possibility that the confirmation request could be altered by the client, either during the mailing process or upon receipt. The internal auditor need not sign the form. It is not inappropriate to get confirmations for closed accounts. The internal auditor may prepare confirmation requests. (7800)

Inventory

29. (b) The formula for inventory turnover is cost of goods sold divided by average inventory. Cost of goods sold includes only inventory related expenses and thus is the best value to use to compare to average inventory to calculate inventory turnover. Net sales, operating income, and gross sales are all based on the prices charged the customers, not the actual costs to the company for the goods that were sold, and thus are not as closely related to the costs associated with inventory. (5989)

30. (d) Physical counts of inventory items higher than the recorded quantities in perpetual inventory records could be the result of the failure to record sales returns in the books when sales return items were returned to inventory. Failure to record purchase discounts would have nothing to do with the recorded quantities in the records. Failure to record purchase returns and sales would result in the physical counts being lower than the quantities in the perpetual records. (5670)

31. (c) When auditing inventory, the auditor needs to obtain evidence supporting management's assertions about presentation and disclosure, answer (a), and valuation, answers (b) and (d). It would not be unusual for the client to have inventory out on consignment or held in a warehouse beyond the client's premises. Also, some of the inventory items could be in transit at the inventory date. The auditor needs to obtain confirmation or perform other auditing procedures to support management's assertions as to the existence and valuation of these assets, but the assets would not necessarily need to be on hand. (7495)

32. (a) The valuation, existence, and completeness of the inventory are not in question. The inventory is collateral for a loan; disclosure is the issue. (5658)

33. (b) Normally, when perpetual inventory records are well-kept and physical count comparisons are made on a regular basis, an auditor may perform inventory observation during or after the end of the period being audited. An auditor would probably request that the physical inventory count be done at year-end if the auditor does not have much confidence in the ability of the internal controls to detect errors when control risk is high. (5131)

34. (b) Inspecting agreements to determine whether any inventory is pledged as collateral or subject to any liens would provide the accountant with evidence concerning the assertions about rights and obligations which deal with whether assets are the rights of the entity and liabilities are the obligations of the entity. (2770)

35. (a) The procedure in answer (a) helps provide assurance about valuation of inventory. The procedures in answers (b), (c), and (d) provide assurance regarding existence. (5121)

36. (c) To gain assurance that all items in a client's inventory listing schedule are valid, an auditor most likely would trace items listed in the listing schedule to inventory tags and the auditor's recorded count sheets. To trace the inventory tags to the listing schedule and to trace items listed in receiving reports and vendors' invoices to the listing schedule would provide assurance that all the inventory items are on the schedule, but would not give assurance that all of the items on the schedule are valid; some items on the schedule may not exist. Tracing tags to receiving reports and vendors' invoices does not involve the inventory listing schedule and thus does not provide any assurances related to the listing schedule. (5671)

37. (b) Assertions about completeness deal with whether all transactions, accounts, and disclosures that should be presented in the financial statements are so included. By tracing from the inventory floor to the records, the auditor is checking for completeness. Answer (a) would deal with the rights to the inventory which would be evidenced by vendor invoices. Answer (c) would be tested by vouching or going from the inventory list to the floor to identify the assets are in existence. Answer (d) would be tested by multiplying the inventory count of an item by its cost based on a vendor's invoice. (4706)

38. (c) Inventory turnover ratios measure the speed with which inventory is purchased or made and subsequently sold. Slow-moving and obsolete items have low turnover ratios. Slow-moving and obsolete items are unlikely to be shipped or received. Existence at locations outside the entity's premises occurs with slow-moving, obsolete, and current items. Slow-moving, obsolete, and current items may all be traced easily to inventory observation test counts to perpetual listings. (7804)

39. (a) Testing the computation of standard overhead rates would not help identify any slow-moving, defective, or obsolete inventory. While touring the plant or production facility, the auditor may actually see these types of items. In comparing inventory balances to anticipated sales volume and reviewing inventory experience and trends, the auditor may become aware of an excessive inventory balance that may indicate that these types of items have not been properly accounted for. (8152)

Fixed Assets

40. (d) The repairs and maintenance expense accounts are analyzed by an auditor in obtaining evidence regarding the completeness of fixed assets, since there is the possibility that items were expensed that should have been capitalized. (5135)

41. (b) When plant assets are retired, the accumulated depreciation account is debited for the amount of depreciation that has been recorded for those assets, which could be a satisfactory

explanation for significant debits to this account. When the estimated remaining useful life of a plant asset is revised upward, the calculation for current and future depreciation is revised to reflect the new estimate of remaining useful life; accumulated depreciation is not affected. If the prior year's depreciation expense was erroneously understated, a correction would require a credit, not a debit, to accumulated depreciation. Revisions in overhead allocations would not affect the accumulated depreciation accounts. (5996)

42. (a) Amortization allocates the cost of the intangible to the periods in which the benefit is received and yields an appropriate valuation of the intangible in those periods. Amortization is not relevant to the existence, completeness, or rights and obligations assertions. (5659)

Investments

43. (a) Investment advisory services have an interest in having accurate records of dividends and are ordinarily independent of the audit client. Stock indentures and stock ledgers may not have dividend records. Annual audited investee financial statements may not be timely available. (6363)

44. (a) Analytical tests as a source of information for developing expectations include analysis of the relationships among elements of financial information within the period. The reasonableness of answers (b), (c), and (d) cannot be analytically determined due to the nature of the assertions. (3927)

45. (c) In the case of investments in the form of securities (such as stocks, bonds, and notes), existence and ownership can be corroborated by inspection of the securities, or by written confirmation from an independent custodian of securities on deposit, pledged, or in safekeeping. Shares owned and signed over to new owners or purchased from other investors would not always be made known to the issuing company on a timely basis. Inspecting the financial statements of the investee company would not indicate the number of shares owned and who the owners are. Answer (d) would provide evidence about the valuation assertion. (5122)

46. (a) The auditor will need to understand the economic substance of each derivative in order to evaluate the application of GAAP. The client's broker would not be knowledgeable about management's classification of derivatives. The audit committee should already be aware of the risks involved in derivative transactions. The risks associated with each derivative would not be appropriate to include in the auditor's report. (8131)

47. (c) Published dividend records provide the strongest evidence supporting dividends earned on publicly-held investments. Answers (a), (b), and (d) are not common procedures. (8135)

48. (b) The auditor is required to design procedures to obtain reasonable assurance of detecting misstatements of assertions about derivatives and securities. When designing such procedures, the auditor should consider the inherent risk and control risk for these assertions. Analytical procedures would not provide sufficient evidence to determine the valuation of any investment. The auditor does not need to confirm the marketability of a derivative nor inform the audit committee of them. (8148)

A/P, Purchases & Other Liabilities

49. (c) In searching for unrecorded liabilities, the auditor would most likely vouch a sample of cash disbursements recorded just after year-end to receiving reports and vendor invoices to ascertain that payables had been recorded in the proper period. Tracing a sample of accounts payable entries recorded just after (not just before) year-end to the year-end unmatched receiving report file, comparing a sample of purchase orders issued just before (not just after) year-end with the year-end accounts payable, and scanning the cash disbursements entries recorded just after (not just before) year-end for indications of unusual transactions may also aid in the detection of unrecorded liabilities. (5994)

50. (c) Tracing a sample of purchase orders and the related receiving reports to the purchases journal and the cash disbursements journal provides evidence to determine that purchases were properly recorded. Although during this audit procedure the auditor might identify unusually large purchases that should be investigated further, this would not be the prevailing purpose of this substantive audit procedure. To verify that cash disbursements were for goods actually received would require vouching from the cash disbursements journal to the receiving reports. To test whether payments were for goods actually ordered would require vouching from the cash disbursements journal to the purchase orders. (5995)

51. (c) In order to verify the existence and valuation of the accounts payable account, the auditor should go to the source documents. These would include purchase orders and receiving reports. Answer (a) pertains to the completeness assertion and whether or not management has included all obligations in the account. Answer (b) is not a standard auditing procedure but deals with determining whether management has included all obligations for

the rights and obligations assertions in the account. Answer (d) also pertains to determining whether or not there are any unrecorded obligations of the company not recorded in the account. (3932)

52. (a) When internal control dictates that each cash disbursement be accompanied by an approved voucher and supported by a prenumbered purchase order and a prenumbered receiving report, the auditor would select items for testing from the population of all cash disbursements (canceled checks). If the auditor were to consider populations made up of all approved vouchers, receiving reports, or invoices, the canceled checks that did not have supporting documentation would not be discovered. (7019)

53. (b) To verify that all merchandise received is recorded, the auditor would trace from the receiving reports to the related records. Payment vouchers, purchase requisitions, and vendor's invoices would not provide evidence that the related merchandise was actually received. (4263)

Payroll

54. (c) Finding overpayments while performing tests of details may cause the auditor to increase the assessed risk of material misstatement. Generally, as the risk of material misstatement increases, the acceptable level of detection risk decreases; this means, the extent of substantive procedures must increase. Answer (a), (b), and (d) do not necessarily increase the risk of material misstatement. (4714)

55. (b) To test for the appropriate number of hours worked, the auditor examines clock card data. To test for answer (a), the auditor checks personnel records. To test for answers (c) and (d), the auditor uses inquiries and observation. (5655)

56. (d) Substantive tests of payroll balances when control risk is assessed as low most likely would be limited to applying analytical procedures and recalculating payroll accruals to assure the accuracy of the payroll liabilities. Observing the distribution of paychecks, recomputing the payroll register and inspecting payroll tax returns would be of greater importance if control risk related to payroll was assessed as high. In such a case, these procedures would be required to assure the accuracy and other assertions related to payroll accounts. (5672)

Long-Term Liabilities

57. (c) One of the audit objectives of long-term liabilities is to verify that interest expense is correctly computed and that other contractual obligations are satisfied. The auditor would most likely compare interest expense with the bonds payable amount to see if it is reasonable, and thereby test valuation. This could also aid discovery of undisclosed liabilities. (5133)

Stockholders' Equity

58. (c) Restrictions on retained earnings should be disclosed in the financial statements. Restrictions would not impact the valuation, allocation, or occurrence of retained earnings. Rights and obligations pertain to assets and liabilities, not retained earnings. (6713)

59. (d) The primary responsibility of a registrar of capital stock is to verify that securities are properly issued, recorded, and transferred. (0133)

60. (a) One of the auditor's objectives in the examination of owners' equity is to determine that all transactions during the year affecting owners' equity accounts were properly authorized and recorded. In the case of a corporation, changes in capital stock accounts should receive formal advance approval by the board of directors. A transfer agent's records show detail about the owners of the stock, and do not focus on the total outstanding. Canceled stock certificates and a treasury stock certificate book are less reliable than the minutes, as they would be updated only after the transaction is complete. (6837)

61. (c) The auditor will need to confirm the shares issued and outstanding with the registrar to ascertain whether the corporate records are accurate and that stock is issued in accordance with the authorization of the board of directors and the articles of incorporation. Confirming the amount of dividends paid to related parties is not a common procedure. The auditor would obtain confirmations from subscribers to determine the expected proceeds from stock subscriptions receivable. Proper authorization of stock rights and warrants would be verified through reading the minutes of the board of directors' meetings. (8120)

Accounting Estimates

62. (d) Inquiries about related party transactions and inventories at external locations are not focused on accounting estimates. Accounting estimates appropriately change with changes in circumstances; further, determining deviation from historical patterns doesn't indicate that all accounting estimates are identified. Unresolved litigation is a frequent reason for accounting estimates, due to the uncertainty in the litigation outcome. (7094)

63. (a) Assumptions that are susceptible to bias provide an opportunity for the overstatement of assets and income and understatement of liabilities. Assumptions that meet the criteria of the other answers offer less scope for creative accounting.

(6395)

64. (d) The auditor's objectives in evaluating an entity's accounting estimates are to ensure (1) all accounting estimates that could be material to the financial statements have been developed, (2) the estimates are reasonable, and (3) the estimates are in conformity with GAAP and are disclosed properly.

(8166)

Solution 25-2 ADDITIONAL MULTIPLE CHOICE ANSWERS

Substantive Procedures

65. (b) The higher the risk of material misstatement, the more effective it may be to perform substantive procedures nearer to, or at, the period end. If the auditor performs test of controls or substantive procedures at an interim date, the auditor needs to consider the additional evidence for the reminder of the period, including the control environment. Effective internal controls allow the auditor greater confidence in such evidence than ineffective controls. A new sales incentive program may provide increased motivation for employees to inflate sales numbers, and hence, accounts receivable; any new program provides increased potential for errors or fraud. A high turnover of senior management is a risk factor of fraud due to fraudulent financial reporting. A first engagement of a new client tends to increase the risk that something will be overlooked due to the unfamiliarity with the client's operations. Editor's Note: While one could argue that interim testing of A/R would be appropriate for a new client, in order that audit staff have additional time to investigate unusual items and, if significant issues are found, more time for management and the auditor to address such issues; however, the examiners instruct candidates to select the best answer. (8398)

66. (d) When substantive procedures are performed at an interim date, the auditor should perform further substantive procedures or a combination of substantive procedures and tests of controls covering the remaining period to provide a reasonable basis for extending the audit conclusions to the end of the period. Interim testing increases the risk that misstatements existing at the period end will not be detected. Evaluations of inappropriate assessments of risk would not be a factor in deciding whether interim testing would be appropriate. Sampling risk need not necessarily be projected at the maximum for tests covering the remaining period. Whether or not substantive tests of accounts receivable may be performed at an interim date does not hinge on whether the balance is material to the financial statements. (8413)

Cash

67. (b) When audit evidence can be obtained from independent sources outside an entity, it provides greater assurance of reliability for the purposes of an independent audit than that secured solely within the entity. Answers (a), (c), and (d) represent audit procedures that may be performed and evidence that can be obtained as a by-product of receiving the standard confirmation; however, they do not represent the primary purpose for obtaining the confirmation. (3930)

68. (d) This bank transfer results in an overstatement of cash at December 31. The receipt of the transfer was recorded in the books on December 31, thus increasing that bank account's cash balance on that date. However, the disbursement of the transfer was not recorded in the books until January 4; thus, that bank account's cash balance was not decreased until after the financial statement date. The bank transfers indicated in answers (a), (b), and (c) do not result in a misstatement of cash. The books recorded the disbursement and receipt of each of these bank transfers in the same fiscal year.

(8380)

A/R & Sales

69. (d) Assertions about completeness deal with whether all transactions, accounts, and disclosures that should be presented in the financial statements are included. Periodically accounting for the numerical sequence of documents and invoices helps ensure that all entries affecting those accounts have been recognized and posted. Answer (a) deals with whether recorded transactions have actually occurred and pertain to the entity. Answer (b) deals with whether assets are the rights of the entity and liabilities are the obligations of the entity. Answer (c) deals with whether assets, liabilities, and equity interests have been included in the financial statements at appropriate amounts. (3923)

70. (b) Assertions about completeness deal with whether all transactions, assets, liabilities,

equity interests and disclosures that should be presented in the financial statements are included. Inspecting the entity's reports of prenumbered shipping documents that have not been recorded in the sales journal will help the auditor determine whether all transactions have been accounted for. Answer (a) is a clerical test for accuracy. Answer (c) relates to management's assertion of accuracy and valuation. Answer (d) is a test of controls for authorization of credit prior to the sale being approved.

(4692)

71. (a) Valuation and allocation deal with whether assets, liabilities, and equity interests are included in financial statements at appropriate amounts. If the bad debt allowance account is too low, net accounts receivable would be too high, and the assets would, therefore, be overstated. (5123)

A/R Confirmations

72. (a) The original forms are the (signed) evidence that the auditor first sought. A/R confirmations are more timely and complete evidence than subsequent cash receipts. Accounts may not be paid rapidly or in single payments. Considering e-mail responses as exceptions is unreasonably harsh. Second requests generally would gain the same response as the first requests. (6629)

73. (a) The positive (confirmation) form is preferable when individual account balances are relatively large or when there is reason to believe that there may be a substantial number of accounts in dispute or with errors or fraud. In this case, errors or fraud are likely since internal controls are weak. Negative confirmations are used when the assessed level of control risk is low. With weak internal controls, the auditor needs to obtain third party verification. (0178)

74. (d) Blank confirmations merely ask for a balance owed, whereas regular positive confirmations include the amount that the customer owes provided by the client, either listed by invoice or as a single sum. Providing additional information may make the task of confirming debts appear easier to the client's customers' employees, resulting in a response getting prepared and approved, rather than indefinitely waiting in stacks for a supervisor to assign, examine, and then approve. (7640)

75. (c) The A/R and sales audit objective related to the completeness assertion is to ascertain that all sales and receivables that should be recorded are properly recorded. Customers may not be inclined to report understatement errors in their accounts, and thus not all the sales and receivables

that should be recorded are necessarily recorded. It is not as likely that customers will merely sign and return the confirmation without verifying its details; the accounts they are verifying represent liabilities to them. It is more likely that the customers will not return forms. A nonresponse could mean that the intended recipient did not receive the request, has misplaced or not processed the request, or has returned the request but it was delayed or lost in transit. Auditors typically confirm few accounts with low recorded balances and a high percentage of accounts with large balances. (5986)

76. (a) Unreturned negative confirmations do not provide explicit evidence. Negative confirmations may be effective when the combined assessed level of inherent and control risk is low. Alternative procedures are used for unreturned positive confirmations. The auditor would be more likely to use positive confirmations, which provide more persuasive evidence, if understatements are suspected.

(5663)

77. (b) By including a list of items or invoices that constitute the customers' account balances, the auditor makes it easier for the customers to respond, irrespective of how the customers' records are organized; this tends to increase the response rate. Neither restricting the selection of accounts to be confirmed to those customers with large balances nor explaining to customers that discrepancies will be investigated by an independent third party will likely have much impact on the response rate. (Furthermore; most customers understand that an auditor is independent and is the one investigating discrepancies.) If anything, asking customers to respond to the request by fax may slow or decrease the response rate, as this may be cumbersome for some customers. (8407)

Inventory

78. (a) The cost of obsolete or slow-moving inventory may have to be written down; this affects the valuation assertion. Rights, obligations, existence, classification, and understandability are not affected by obsolete or slow-moving items. (5661)

79. (d) To test that all items in the inventory listing are valid, the auditor would work from the inventory listing to the tags. An auditor would be unlikely to work directly from inventory tags to receiving reports and vendor invoices, or vice versa, without an intermediate step—as these documents don't reference each other, this process would be awkward; moreover, neither of these procedures would test the items in the inventory listing. Working from inventory tags to the inventory listing tests that

all items on tags are included in the inventory listing (completeness). (8418)

Fixed Assets

80. (c) The auditor should perform tests of controls when the auditor's risk assessment includes an expectation of the operating effectiveness of controls (control risk is low) or when substantive procedures alone do not provide sufficient appropriate audit evidence. Regardless of the audit approach selected, the auditor should design and perform substantive procedures for all relevant assertions related to each material class of transactions, account balance, and disclosure because effective internal controls generally reduce, but do not eliminate, risk of material misstatement, tests of controls reduce, but do not eliminate, the need for substantive procedures.

(5974)

81. (d) A weakness in internal control over recording retirements of equipment most likely would result in assets that have been retired continuing to be carried in the accounting records. Tracing from the records to the actual assets would be an audit procedure designed to detect such errors. Tracing equipment in the plant to the accounting records would only provide evidence about equipment not yet retired. Depreciation is applied to assets carried on the books and thus depreciation would continue to be taken on retired equipment erroneously still on the books. A review of depreciation would not of itself indicate that certain equipment had been retired. Additions to the "other assets" account would be newly acquired other assets rather than retired equipment and would not likely give any evidence about retired equipment. (5981)

82. (c) By reviewing the repairs and maintenance expense accounts, an auditor may uncover transactions that involve assets that should be capitalized rather than expensed. The repairs and maintenance expense accounts are not involved in the write-off of obsolete assets. Property, plant and equipment (PP&E) that cannot be repaired would not tend to involve transactions in the repairs and maintenance expense accounts either. To verify that all recorded PP&E assets exist, an auditor would tend to inspect the assets themselves against the listings in the PP&E accounts, rather than review expense accounts. (8391)

83. (d) By reviewing the repairs and maintenance expense accounts, an auditor may uncover transactions that involve assets that should be capitalized rather than expensed. Analysis of depreciation expense accounts would not reveal the existence of assets that should be capitalized, but

are not; all entries to these accounts are due to assets being capitalized already. It is less likely that an asset would be involved in the calculation of property tax and yet not be capitalized than it is that an asset would be expensed in the repair and maintenance account; if the entity prepares a property tax report, it probably would be prepared based on the listing of capital assets. (8400)

Investments

84. (b) The valuation assertion for an investment accounted for by the equity method can generally be satisfied by referring to the audited financial statements of the investee company. (2312)

85. (b) An auditor confirms with an outside agent that the agent is holding investment securities in the client's name to support the existence and rights and obligations assertions. The auditor would check valuation with a listing of market values. Completeness would not be confirmed, as an entity might have more than one agent or have some securities in transit. Classification and understandability is an assertion about presentation and disclosure and would depend, in part, on the nature of the securities, not that they are being held. (5662)

86. (b) Confirmation from a third-party custodian provides evidence as to the existence and ownership of securities. In the event of a sale close to the period end, an investee company might not yet be aware of a sale unrecorded in the audit client books; further, if the investment is held by a custodian, the investee company might not realize the audit client has an ownership interest. In the event of a sale close to the period end, analytics applied to the dividend income and investment accounts would not necessarily detect an unrecorded sale. A sale of stolen securities most likely would not appear in the cash receipts journal. (8409)

A/P, Purchases & Other Liabilities

87. (c) Completeness deals with whether all transactions, assets, liabilities, and equity interests that should have been recorded have been recorded. Completeness also pertains to whether all disclosures that should have been included in the financial statements have been included. Because liabilities have the inherent risk of being understated, substantive tests and tests of controls are directed towards determining that all liabilities of the company as of the balance sheet date are properly included.

(4274)

88. (b) The objective of the auditor's test is to determine whether all merchandise for which the

client was billed was received. The population for this test consists of all vendor's invoices (bills for merchandise). The auditor would select a sample of vendor's invoices and then trace them to supporting receiving reports to assure that the merchandise for which the client was billed was received. (0195)

89. (a, b) In performing a search for unrecorded liabilities, one procedure performed is to send requests of confirmation of zero liabilities to previous vendors or vendors with zero balances in the accounts payable subsidiary ledger. These liabilities would be tend to be unrecorded, if they did exist. Requesting confirmations of payees of checks drawn just after year-end provides evidence of timing, not completeness. (5126)

Payroll

90. (d) When reviewing payroll tax form reconciliations, an auditor is concerned with unrecorded liabilities. Analytics or review of the calculation process would be better to determine accuracy in the deductions calculation. The effective operation of internal control is determined by tests of controls. Observing check distribution, rather than reconciling tax forms, would bring fictitious employees to light. (7104)

Long-Term Liabilities

91. (b) An auditor's program to examine long-term debt should include a step where the auditor reconciles interest expense with debt outstanding during the year (period). This step would provide information as to the completeness and valuation of the account balance. The auditor is not concerned with the year-end market value of the debt. The auditor would not verify the existence of the holders of the debt by direct confirmation. Outstanding balances, terms, and conditions are confirmed with the credit grantor or independent trustee. The search for unrecorded liabilities would generally be made by scanning cash disbursements made in the period following the balance sheet date. Also, the accounts payable subsidiary ledger would not likely provide evidence as to long-term liabilities. (0127)

Stockholders' Equity

92. (d) One of the primary objectives in testing related to Stockholders' Equity and Capital accounts is to verify that capital transactions are appropriately authorized and approved. The granting of stock options would require board of director approval because it could affect the number of shares outstanding. (5134)

Accounting Estimates

93. (c) Of the answer options, the auditor first would learn how management developed its estimates. Then, the auditor would compare the current process to previous estimate development to gain evidence regarding consistency. After evaluating management's estimate process, the auditor considers whether there are factors that the auditor's estimates failed to take into account. Then, the auditor would be ready to compare management's and the auditor's estimates. Reviewing variations from expectations may occur after the period end, when the client finishes its preaudit financial statements, while the other answer options could commence at an interim date. (7821)

PERFORMANCE BY SUBTOPICS

Each category below parallels a subtopic covered in Chapter 25. Record the number and percentage of questions you correctly answered in each subtopic area.

Substantive Procedures			Cash			A/R & Sales			A/R Confirmations		
Question #	Correct	√	Question #	Correct	√	Question #	Correct	√	Question #	Correct	√
1			11			14			22		
2			12			15			23		
3			13			16			24		
4			# Questions	3		17			25		
5						18			26		
6			# Correct			19			27		
7			% Correct			20			28		
8						21			# Questions	7	
9						# Questions	8				
10									# Correct		
# Questions	10					# Correct			% Correct		
						% Correct					
# Correct											
% Correct											

Inventory				Investments				Payroll				Stockholders' Equity		
Question #	Correct	√		Question #	Correct	√		Question #	Correct	√		Question #	Correct	√
29				43				54				58		
30				44				55				59		
31				45				56				60		
32				46				# Questions	3			61		
33				47								# Questions	4	
34				48				# Correct						
35				# Questions	6			% Correct				# Correct		
36												% Correct		
37				# Correct				**Long-Term Liabilities**						
38				% Correct				Question #	Correct	√		**Accounting Estimates**		
39								57				Question #	Correct	√
# Questions	11			**A/P, Purchases & Other Liabilities**				# Questions	1			62		
				Question #	Correct	√						63		
# Correct				49				# Correct				64		
% Correct				50				% Correct				# Questions	3	
				51										
Fixed Assets				52								# Correct		
Question #	Correct	√		53								% Correct		
40				# Questions	5									
41														
42				# Correct										
# Questions	3			% Correct										
# Correct														
% Correct														

SIMULATION SOLUTIONS

Solution 25-3

Response #1: Kiting (2 points)

1. 2, 4

The term kiting refers to the practice of transferring cash between or among various bank accounts, with recording of the cash receipt (deposit) being made on a timely basis, while the recording of the disbursement (withdrawal) is delayed. Thus, for a period of time, the amount of the check could appear in two different accounts simultaneously. In this question, note that the receipt of check #2 was recorded (per the books) at 12/30, while the disbursement was not recorded (per the books) until 1/3. Also, note that check #4 (written from State Bank) was received by the bank on 12/31 but was not recorded on the Fox Co.'s books until 1/2.

2. 1, 3

Deposits/transfers in transit refer to checks which have been recorded on the entity's books but have not yet cleared the bank. In this question, note that checks #1 and #3 were disbursed (per books) at the end of December, but were not received by the bank until early January.

Response #2: Audit Program (7 points)

The auditor should:

- **Review answers to questions on confirmation requests** to determine proper recognition in accounting records and the necessity for financial statement disclosure.
- Make inquiries as to compensating balances and restrictions.
- **Obtain copies** of the **bank reconciliations** as of the balance sheet date, and
- **Trace** the adjusted book balances to the general ledger balances.
- Compare the bank balances to the **opening balances on the cutoff bank statements.**
- Compare the bank balances to the **balances on the confirmations.**
- Trace amounts of **deposits in transit** to the cutoff bank statements and ascertain whether the **time lags** are reasonable.
- Verify the **clerical accuracy** of the reconciliations.
- Obtain explanation for **unusual reconciling items,** including checks drawn to "bearer," "cash," and related parties.
- Trace checks dated prior to the **end of the period** that were returned with the cutoff statements to the **list of outstanding checks.**
- **Investigate outstanding checks** that did not clear with the cutoff bank statements.

- **Examine a sample of checks** for payee, amount, date, authorized signatures, and endorsements to determine any irregularities from company policy or accounting records.
- **Prepare a bank transfer schedule** from a review of the cash receipts and disbursements journals, bank statements, and related paid checks for the last few days before and the first few days after the year-end, and
- Review the schedule to determine that the deposit and disbursement of each transfer is **recorded in the proper period.**
- **Trace incomplete transfers** to the schedule of outstanding checks and deposits in transit.

Response #3: Research (1 point)

Paragraph Reference Answer: AU 350.27

Guidance: AU 350.27 states, "In addition to the evaluation of the frequency and amounts of monetary misstatements, consideration should be given to the qualitative aspects of the misstatements. These include (a) the nature and cause of misstatements, such as whether they are differences in principle or in application, are errors or are caused by fraud, or are due to misunderstanding of instructions or to carelessness, and (b) the possible relationship of the misstatements to other phases of the audit. The discovery of fraud ordinarily requires a broader consideration of possible implications than does the discovery of an error."

(2780)

Solution 25-4

Response #1: Communication (4 points)

Among the factors likely to affect the **reliability of confirmations** that King sends is King's decision in choosing the confirmation form. Some positive forms **request agreement or disagreement with information stated** on the form; other positive forms, known as **blank forms,** request the respondent to **fill in the balance or furnish other information;** **negative forms request** a response **only if there is disagreement** with the information stated on the request.

King's prior experience with Cycle or similar clients is also likely to affect reliability because King probably would have **prior knowledge** of the **expected confirmation response rates,** inaccurate **information on prior years' confirmations,** and **misstatements identified during prior audits.**

The **nature of the information** being confirmed may affect the **competence of the evidence** obtained as well as the response rate. For example, Cycle's **customers' accounting systems** may permit confirmation of individual transactions, but not account balances, or vice versa.

Additionally, King's sending of each confirmation request to the **proper respondent** will likely provide meaningful and appropriate evidence. Each request should be sent to a person who King believes is **knowledgeable about the information** to be confirmed.

Response #2: Errors & Fraud (5 points)

1. E

Preparing a bank transfer schedule would permit the auditor to determine whether a kiting scheme exists.

2. D

Obtaining a cutoff bank statement and comparing the cleared checks to the year-end bank reconciliation would provide some evidence that checks were not mailed until after the first week of the subsequent year.

3. H

Confirming loan terms with a lender would reveal that lender's lien on the real estate.

4. K, L

Sending a second confirmation request and making inquiries of a reputable credit agency would provide evidence of the customer's existence and credit worthiness. Examining the shipping documents assists the auditor to determine whether merchandise was actually shipped to the customer.

5. P

A surprise observation of the distribution of payroll checks would provide evidence that the new employees exist and are currently working.

6. Q

Vouching data in the payroll register to authorized pay rates in the human resource files would permit the auditor to determine whether rate increases are properly authorized.

Response #3: Research (1 point)

Paragraph Reference Answer: AU 560.06

Guidance: AU 560.06 states, "Examples of events of the second type that require disclosure to the financial statements (but should not result in adjustment) are: a. Sale of a bond or capital stock issue; b. Purchase of a business; c. Settlement of litigation when the event giving rise to the claim took place subsequent to the balance-sheet date; d. Loss of plant or inventories as a result of fire or flood; e. Losses on receivables resulting from conditions (such as a customer's major casualty) arising subsequent to the balance-sheet date."

(6248)

Solution 25-5

Response #1: Audit Procedures (6 points)

1. I

A mark next to the lenders' names is most likely to indicate that the information in the next 3 columns is accurate. This mark is unlikely to relate to a dollar balance as it is not positioned closely to any numbers.

2. C

Material beginning balances are generally traced to the prior year's working papers.

3. J

Increased borrowings should be processed with the board of directors' authorization, should correspond to the loan agreement, and their disposition should be traceable. These are all items of interest to an auditor.

4. H

As the loan to First National Bank has the principal due in Year 03, any payment before that date would have specific authorization by board of directors. The auditor would also likely examine the canceled check(s) associated with this transfer.

5. G

The repayments did not agree to the board of directors (BOD) authorization. [Assume the BOD authorized payment of the full $120,000 ($10,000 × 12 months), based on the terms of the loan.] Confirmation of receipt of the $110,000 is obtained from the monthly statement that the bank issues. The auditor also would likely examine the canceled check(s) associated with this transfer.

6. A

The comments column shows that two of the three lenders with this mark in the ending balance column agrees with the account balance. The third doesn't show a dispute about the amount. The lender without this mark does have a comment about a dispute.

7. K

This mark is next to the two loans that have required payments of due in the next year.

8. B

This mark is next to the one loan that has a dispute between the lender and the audit client.

9. D

The total long-term debt and the total accrued interest payable are likely to be entire, separate accounts in the trial balance and general ledger. It is reasonable to trace accounts to the current year financial statements (via the trial balance etc.) after examining them.

10. F

It is normal for the auditor to recompute interest accruals and check the reasonableness of the client's interest accrual.

Response #2: Payroll (3 points)

Bell should consider performing the following procedures in the audit of Kent's payroll transactions:

Select a **sample of payments to employees** from the **payroll register** and compare each selected transaction to the related documents and records examining

- Evidence in support of **authorization of rate** of pay.
- Evidence in support of **time** on which compensation was based, such as approved **time cards or attendance records**.
- Evidence in support of proper **authorization** of payroll **withholdings**.
- Evidence in support of payments, such as **canceled payroll checks**.
- Evidence in support of **account distribution**.
- The **clerical accuracy** of the transaction.
- The entry to the employee's records used to **summarize employee compensation** for payroll reporting purposes.

Obtain the **payroll register** for a selected period and

- Test the **arithmetical accuracy** of the payroll register.
- Determine whether **payroll** was **approved** in accordance with management's prescribed procedures.
- **Trace totals per the register** to postings in the general ledger.
- **Observe the distribution** of payroll checks.
- Review the accounting for **unclaimed wages**.
- **Observe a sample of employees** in the performance of their duties.
- Perform **analytical procedures**.

Response #3: Research (1 point)

Paragraph Reference Answer: AU 318.63

Guidance: AU 318.63 states, "If misstatements are detected in classes of transactions or account balances at an interim date, the auditor should consider modifying the related assessment of risk and the planned nature, timing, or extent of the substantive procedures covering the remaining period that relate to such classes of transactions or account balances, or the auditor may extend or may repeat such audit procedures at the period end."

(6249)

Solution 25-6

Response #1: PP&E (5 points)

1. F

Material beginning balances are generally traced to the prior year's working papers.

2. L

Documentation for additions to PP&E generally is examined in an audit. Deeds and purchase contracts would be appropriate documents to examine for a land purchase.

3. K

Documentation for additions to PP&E generally is examined in an audit. Work orders and engineers' reports would be appropriate documents to examine for constructed assets.

4. J

Documentation for additions to PP&E generally is examined in an audit. Vendors' invoices would be appropriate documents to examine for purchased assets.

5. G

As the disposals are fully depreciated and of relatively small amount, procedures may not be necessary.

6. D

An amount is removed from buildings and added to fixtures, but the net for PP&E is zero.

7. C

The individual categories of PP&E and accumulated depreciation are likely to be entire, separate accounts in the trial balance and general ledger. It is reasonable to trace accounts to the current year financial statements (via the trial balance etc.) after auditing them.

8. B

The provision for accumulated depreciation can be easily checked against the PP&E accounts, as the rate and method for each category is known.

Response #2: Equity (4 points)

The substantive audit procedures that Jones should apply in examining the common stock and treasury stock accounts are as follows:

- **Review the corporate charter** to verify details of the common stock such as authorized shares, par value, etc.
- **Obtain** or prepare an **analysis of changes** in common stock and treasury stock accounts.
- **Compare opening balances** with prior year's working papers.
- **Foot the total shares outstanding** in the stockholders' ledger and stock certificate book.
- Determine **authorization for common stock issuances and treasury stock transactions** by inspecting the minutes of the board of directors' meetings.
- **Verify capital stock issuances** by examining supporting documentation and tracing entries into the records.
- **Verify treasury stock transactions** by examining supporting documentation and tracing entries into the records.
- **Examine all certificates canceled** during the year.
- **Inspect all treasury stock certificates** owned by the client.
- **Reconcile** the details of the individual certificates in the stock certificate book with the individual shareholders' accounts in the stockholders' ledger.
- **Compare** the totals in the stockholders' ledger and the stock certificate book to the balance sheet presentation.
- **Recompute** the weighted average number of shares outstanding.
- **Compare** the **financial statement presentation** and disclosure with generally accepted accounting principles.
- Determine the existence of, and proper accounting for, common stock and treasury stock **transactions occurring since year-end.**
- **Obtain written representations** concerning common and treasury stock in the client representation letter.

Response #3: Research (1 point)

Paragraph Reference Answer: AU 333.12

Guidance: AU 333.12 states, "There are circumstances in which an auditor should obtain updating representation letters from management. If a predecessor auditor is requested by a former client to reissue (or consent to the reuse of) his or her report on the financial statements of a prior period, and those financial statements are to be presented on a comparative basis with audited financial statements of a subsequent period, the predecessor auditor should obtain an updating representation letter from the management of the former client. Also, when performing subsequent events procedures in connection with filings under the Securities Act of 1933, the auditor should obtain certain written representations. The updating management representation letter should state (a) whether any information has come to management's attention that would cause them to believe that any of the previous representations should be modified, and (b) whether any events have occurred subsequent to the balance-sheet date of the latest financial statements reported on by the auditor that would require adjustment to or disclosure in those financial statements."

(6250)

Solution 25-7

Response #1: Confirmations (4 points)

a. Although there is a presumption that King will request the confirmation of Cycle's accounts receivable, King could justify omitting this procedure if Cycle's accounts receivable are **immaterial to its financial statements**. King could also justify omitting this procedure if the **expected response rates** to properly designed confirmation requests **will be inadequate,** or if **responses will be unreliable**. In these circumstances, King may determine that the use of confirmations would be **ineffective**.

Additionally, King could justify omitting the confirmation of Cycle's accounts receivable if King's **combined assessed level of inherent** and **control risk** (or risk of material misstatement) is low and the **assessed level, in conjunction** with the **evidence** expected to be **provided by analytical procedures** or other **substantive tests of details**, is **sufficient to reduce audit risk** to an **acceptably low level** for the applicable financial assertions.

b. The nature of the alternative procedures King would apply when replies to positive confirmation request are not received varies according to the account and assertion in question. Possible alternative procedures include **examining subsequent cash receipts,** and **matching** such **receipts with the actual items being paid**. King would also consider **inspecting Cycle's shipping documents or invoices,** or Cycle's **customers' purchase orders** on file. **Inspecting correspondence** between Cycle and its customers could provide additional evidence. King may also establish the existence of Cycle's customers by **reference to credit sources** such as Dun & Bradstreet.

Response #2: Errors & Fraud (5 points)

1. A

Comparing the details of the cash receipts journal entries with the corresponding daily deposit slips would permit the auditor to determine whether the receipts were properly recorded.

2. U

Examining the purchase orders and receiving reports for selected vouchers would permit the auditor to determine whether the merchandise was ordered and received by the entity.

3. B

Vouching fixed asset accounts debits to the vendors' invoices would permit the auditor to determine whether equipment repairs had been misclassified as fixed assets.

4. A, J

Comparing the details of cash receipts journal entries with the corresponding daily deposit slips and confirming the entity's accounts receivable on a surprise basis would permit the auditor to determine whether a lapping scheme exists.

5. E

Preparing a bank transfer schedule would permit the auditor to determine whether cash is being inappropriately increased by drawing an unrecorded check on one account and simultaneously recording a deposit in a second account.

6. J, L

Confirming the entity's accounts receivable on a surprise basis would permit the auditor to determine whether sales to those customers were genuine. Examining the shipping documents would permit the auditor to determine whether merchandise was actually shipped to those customers.

Response #3: Research (1 point)

Paragraph Reference Answer: AU 336.11

Guidance: AU 336.11 states, "When a specialist does not have a relationship with the client, the specialist's work usually will provide the auditor with greater assurance of reliability. However, the work of a specialist who has a relationship with the client may be acceptable under certain circumstances. If the specialist has a relationship with the client, the auditor should assess the risk that the specialist's objectivity might be impaired. If the auditor believes the relationship might impair the specialist's objectivity, the auditor should perform additional procedures with respect to some or all of the specialist's assumptions, methods, or findings to determine that the findings are not unreasonable or should engage another specialist for that purpose.

(6400)

Solution 25-8

Response #1: Confirmations (9 points)

a. Confirmation #11—Atom. Adler should determine that Superior received and deposited Atom's check on December 28, 20X1, by **examining supporting documentation**, e.g., the entry in the cash receipts journal and either Superior's deposit ticket or its bank statement. Adler should also determine the account to which the check was recorded and **why** it was not credited to Atom's account.

Confirmation #28—Baker. Adler should **examine the terms of the sale and the shipping documents**, especially whether the sale/shipment was to be FOB shipping point or FOB destination and the date the goods were shipped to Baker, to **verify** when the **criteria for revenue recognition were met**.

Confirmation #34—Clark. Adler should read Superior's correspondence files for evidence concerning the **terms of the shipment** to Clark to determine whether the criteria for revenue recognition were met.

Confirmation #41—Delta. Adler should investigate whether the merchandise was ever shipped to Delta and, if so, whether the sale was ever consummated, or whether the merchandise was returned, or whether Superior expects it to be returned.

Confirmation #58—Eagle. Adler should send a **second request** to Eagle providing the individual invoice numbers and amounts or attaching copies of the individual unpaid invoices that Eagle's accounts payable voucher system can verify. In the alternative, Adler should examine shipping documents and subsequent cash receipts.

Confirmation #67—Franklin. Adler should determine Franklin's correct address and send a **second request.**

Confirmation #71—Grove. Adler should **determine when the check was received** and where it was recorded by examining Superior's cash receipts records, bank statements, and accounts receivable detail.

Confirmation #86—Hall. No additional procedures are necessary to resolve this confirmation request, although Adler may want to **trace the cash receipt** to verify that Hall's check was actually received, deposited, and credited to Hall's account in January 20X2.

b. When replies to positive confirmation requests have not been received, Miller should apply alternative substantive procedures to the nonresponding accounts receivable. Miller most likely would **examine subsequent cash receipts** for the accounts that have been paid. This would include matching such receipts with the actual items being paid. In addition, especially for receivables that have not been paid, Miller should **inspect shipping documents** or other client documentation (e.g. sales invoices, customers' purchase orders, etc.) that may provide evidence for the existence assertion. Miller should also consider reading any correspondence in Superior's files that may indicate disagreements with its customers about the amounts billed or the terms of the sales. In addition, Miller may consider **contacting a reputable credit agency** to verify the existence of customers who are new to the client or who Miller may be unfamiliar with.

c. The additional substantive procedures that Miller should consider performing to complete the audit of Superior's accounts receivable and related allowances include the following:

- **Test the cutoff** of sales, cash receipts, and sales returns and allowances.
- **Evaluate the reasonableness** of all allowances against receivables.
- **Perform analytical procedures** for accounts receivable, such as sales returns and allowances to sales, bad debt expense to net credit sales, accounts receivable turnover, and days' sales in receivables.
- **Determine that** Superior's revenue recognition **policies are appropriate**, including policies for consignment sales.
- **Review activity after the balance sheet date for** unusual transactions, such as large sales returns.
- Determine whether any accounts receivable are **pledged or factored**.

Determine that the **presentation and disclosure** of accounts receivable and related allowances are in conformity with generally accepted accounting principles.

Response #2: Research (1 point)

Paragraph Reference Answer: AU 332.27

Guidance: AU 332.27 states, "*Valuation Based on Cost*. Procedures to obtain evidence about the cost of securities may include inspection of documentation of the purchase price, confirmation with the issuer or holder, and testing discount or premium amortization, either by recomputation or analytical procedures. The auditor should evaluate management's conclusion about the need to recognize an impairment loss for a decline in the security's fair value below its cost that is other than temporary."

(6401)

Solution 25-9

Response #1: Inventory (9 points)

a. The means or techniques of gathering audit evidence, in addition to the example, are as follows:

Technique	Description
Inquiry	An auditor **questions** client personnel about events and conditions, such as obsolete inventory.
Confirmation	An auditor obtains **acknowledgments** in writing from third parties of transactions or balances, such as inventory in public warehouses or on consignment.
Calculation or Recomputation	An auditor **recomputes** certain amounts, such as the multiplication of quantity times price to determine inventory amounts.
Analysis	An auditor **combines amounts in meaningful ways** to allow the application of audit judgment, such as the determination of whether a proper inventory cutoff was performed.
Inspection	An auditor **examines** documents relating to transactions and balances, such as shipping and receiving records to establish ownership of inventory.
Comparison	An auditor **relates two or more amounts**, such as inventory cost in perpetual inventory records to costs as shown on vendor invoices as part of the evaluation of whether inventory is priced at the lower of cost or market.

b. Substantive auditing procedures that would satisfy the four general assertions regarding a client's inventory balance include the following (one different procedure required for each assertion):

Assertion	Substantive Auditing Procedure
1. Existence	• **Observe physical inventory** counts. • **Obtain confirmation** of inventories at locations outside the entity. • **Test inventory transactions between a preliminary physical inventory date** and the balance sheet date. • **Review perpetual inventory records**, production records, and purchasing records for indications of current activity. • **Compare inventories** with a current sales catalog and subsequent sales and delivery reports. • Use the work of specialists to **corroborate the nature of specialized products**.
2. Completeness	• **Observe physical inventory counts**. • Apply **analytical procedures** to the relationship of inventory balances to recent purchasing, production, and sales activities. • Test shipping and receiving **cutoff** procedures. • **Obtain confirmation** of inventories at locations outside the entity. • **Trace test counts** recorded during the physical inventory observation to the inventory listing. • **Account for all inventory tags** and count sheets used in recording the physical inventory counts. • Test the **clerical accuracy of inventory listings**. • **Reconcile physical counts to perpetual records** and general ledger balances and investigate significant fluctuations.
3. Rights and Obligations	• **Observe** physical inventory counts. • Obtain **confirmation of inventory** at **locations outside the entity**. • Examine **paid vendors' invoices, consignment agreements**, and **contracts**. • Test **shipping and receiving cutoff** procedures.
4. Valuation and Allocation	• Examine **paid vendors' invoices**. • Review **direct labor rates**. • **Test the computation** of standard overhead rates. • Examine **analyses** of purchasing and manufacturing **standard cost variances**. • Examine an **analysis of inventory turn-over**. • Review **industry experience and trends**. • Apply analytical procedures to the relationship of **inventory balances to anticipated sales volume**. • **Tour** the plant. • Inquire of production and sales personnel concerning possible **excess or obsolete inventory** items. • Review current market value quotations. • Obtain **current market value** quotations. • Examine **sales after year-end and open purchase order** commitments.

Response #2: Research (1 point)

Paragraph Reference Answer: AU 331.14

Guidance: AU 331.14 states, "If inventories are in the hands of public warehouses or other outside custodians, the auditor ordinarily would obtain direct confirmation in writing from the custodian. If such inventories represent a significant proportion of current or total assets, to obtain reasonable assurance with respect to their existence, the auditor should apply one or more of the following procedures as he considers necessary in the circumstances. a. Test the owner's procedures for investigating the warehouseman and evaluating the warehouseman's performance. b. Obtain an independent accountant's report on the warehouseman's control procedures relevant to custody of goods and, if applicable, pledging of receipts, or apply alternative procedures at the warehouse to gain reasonable assurance that information received from the warehouseman is reliable. c. Observe physical counts of the goods, if practicable and reasonable. d. If warehouse receipts have been pledged as collateral, confirm with lenders pertinent details of the pledged receipts (on a test basis, if appropriate)."

(6402)

Solution 25-10

Response #1: Assertions (9 points)

a.

Primary Assertion	Objective
4. **Existence**	To determine that the custodian **holds the securities** as identified in the confirmation.
5. **Completeness**	To determine that **all income and related collections** from the investments are properly **recorded**.
6. **Valuation and allocation**	To determine that the **market or other value** of the investments is **fairly stated**.
7. **Classification and understandability**	To determine that the financial statement **presentation and disclosure** of investments is in **conformity** with generally accepted accounting principles **consistently applied**.
8. **Valuation and allocation**	To determine that the **market or other value** of the investments is **fairly stated** and the **loss** is properly **recognized and recorded**.

b. Larkin should consider applying the following additional substantive auditing procedures in auditing Vernon's investments:

- **Inspect** securities on hand in the presence of the custodian.
- **Examine supporting evidence** (broker's advices, etc.) for transactions between the balance sheet date and the inspection date.
- Obtain **confirmation** from the issuers or trustees for investments in nonpublic entities.
- **Examine** contractual **terms** of debt securities and preferred stock.
- Determine that sales and purchases were properly **approved** by the Board of Directors or its designee.
- **Examine** broker's advices in support of transactions or **confirm transactions** with broker.
- Determine that **gains and losses** on dispositions have been **properly computed.**
- **Trace** payments for purchases to canceled checks, and proceeds from sales to entries in the cash receipts journal.
- Determine that the **amortization** of premium and discount on bonds has been properly computed.
- **Determine** that **market value** for trading, available-for-sale, and held-to-maturity portfolios has been properly computed by tracing quoted market prices to competent published or other sources.
- **Compute the unrealized** gains and losses on trading, available-for-sale, and held-to-maturity portfolios for marketable equity securities.
- Determine that the unrealized **gains and losses** on the trading and available-for-sale portfolios have been **properly classified** in the income statement, and the unrealized gains and losses on the held-to-maturity portfolio have been properly classified in the equity section of the balance sheet.
- **Ascertain whether** any investments are pledged as collateral or encumbered by liens, and, if so, are properly **disclosed**.

Response #2: Research (1 point)

Paragraph Reference Answer: AU 339.34

Guidance: AU 339.34 states, "Whether audit documentation is in paper, electronic, or other media, the integrity, accessibility, and retrievability of the underlying data may be compromised if the documentation could be altered, added to, or deleted without the auditor's knowledge, or could be permanently lost or damaged. Accordingly, the auditor should apply appropriate and reasonable controls for audit documentation to: a. Clearly determine when and by whom audit documentation was created, changed, or reviewed; b. Protect the integrity of the information at all stages of the audit, especially when the information is shared within the audit team or transmitted to other parties via electronic means; c. Prevent unauthorized changes to the documentation; and d. Allow access to the documentation by the audit team and other authorized parties as necessary to properly discharge their responsibilities."

(6403)

Solution 25-11

Response #1: Liabilities (9 points)

a. In searching for DollarMart's unrecorded liabilities, Cook most likely would **review** DollarMart's **cash disbursements journal near the conclusion of fieldwork for checks written after year-end** and examine the supporting documentation, such as receiving reports and vendors' invoices, for selected disbursements to determine that the related accounts payable were properly recorded and to **verify the cutoff** of DollarMart's receipt of inventory. Alternatively, Cook could review DollarMart's voucher register for selected transactions similarly recorded shortly after year-end and examine the supporting detail to identify items that should have been recorded at the balance sheet date, but were not.

Cook most likely would consider examining files of receiving reports and comparing them to recorded accounts payable entries. This would assist Cook in **searching for significant merchandise received before year-end** to verify DollarMart's schedule of merchandise received but not yet billed. Cook may also consider **inspecting** DollarMart's files of **unprocessed vendors' invoices,** vendors' statements, and outstanding purchase orders, and comparing them with the receiving records and accounts payable entries for unrecorded liabilities.

Although confirmations are usually not the best source of evidence for unrecorded accounts payable, Cook may consider confirming selected **accounts payable** with vendors, including regular suppliers showing small or zero balances at year-end.

Cook most likely would consider performing **analytical procedures** such as comparing gross margin, purchases, or certain expense account balances with those of the prior year to identify any large changes that should be investigated because they may represent unrecorded liabilities.

Additionally, Cook may tailor the **management representation letter** to impress upon DollarMart the need to be concerned about unrecorded accounts payable.

b. Cook most likely would perform more **substantive auditing procedures** at year-end because of DollarMart's deficient control environment. For example, Cook would be more likely to confirm DollarMart's accounts payable. Tests would most likely be performed **further into the subsequent year** and at a **lower dollar value or materiality level** than otherwise.

Response #2: Research (1 point)

Paragraph Reference Answer: AU 341.05

Guidance: AU 341.05 states, "It is not necessary to design audit procedures solely to identify conditions and events that, when considered in the aggregate, indicate there could be substantial doubt about the entity's ability to continue as a going concern for a reasonable period of time. The results of auditing procedures designed and performed to achieve other audit objectives should be sufficient for that purpose. The following are examples of procedures that may identify such conditions and events: Analytical procedures; Review of subsequent events; Review of compliance with the terms of debt and loan agreements; Reading of minutes of meetings of stockholders, board of directors, and important committees of the board; Inquiry of an entity's legal counsel about litigation, claims, and assessments; [and] Confirmation with related and third parties of the details of arrangements to provide or maintain financial support."

(6404)

BOARDS OF ACCOUNTANCY

Certified public accountants are licensed to practice by the individual boards of accountancy of the states and territories (jurisdictions) of the United States. The exam is one component of the licensing process. An application form to sit for the exam should be requested from your individual board or its designated agent (exam administrator)—some jurisdictions arrange for an exam administrator, such as CPA Examination Services, a division of NASBA, to handle the review of applications, collection of fees, etc.

IT IS EXTREMELY IMPORTANT THAT YOU COMPLETE THE APPLICATION FORM CORRECTLY AND RETURN IT BEFORE THE DEADLINE. Errors may result in the delay of approval or rejection of your application. Be sure to enclose all required materials. Requirements vary as to education, experience and other matters, as do cutoff dates to apply to receive approval in time to sit for a particular testing window. If you have not already done so, take a moment to call or visit the Web site of the appropriate board for specific and current requirements.

PAY SPECIAL ATTENTION TO THE FORM OF YOUR NAME ON YOUR APPLICATION. YOUR APPLICATION INFORMATION WILL BE USED TO GENERATE YOUR NTS AND THE ORDER AND SPELLING OF YOUR NAME ON YOUR **NTS** MUST EXACTLY MATCH YOUR **2 IDs—THE 3 ITEMS YOU MUST BRING TO THE TEST CENTER IN ORDER TO BE ADMITTED**.

It may be possible to sit for the exam outside of your jurisdiction. Candidates wishing to do so should also contact the board of accountancy in the jurisdiction where they plan to be certified. NASBA has links (www.nasba.org) to all of the board sites.

See the *Practical Advice* appendix for more information regarding the exam.

CHAPTER 26

AUDIT SAMPLING

CHAPTER 26

AUDIT SAMPLING

I. Overview

A. Definition

AU 350 defines audit sampling as the application of an audit procedure to less than 100 percent of the items within an account balance or class of transactions (the population) with the intent of drawing conclusions about the population based on the results of the sample. The third standard of fieldwork requires sufficient appropriate audit evidence to be obtained through audit procedures to afford a reasonable basis for an opinion on the financial statements. The use of sampling relates to this standard. There are two general approaches to audit sampling: statistical and nonstatistical. Both require the auditor to use professional judgment.

1. **Effective** The underlying principle of sampling is that the results of a sample yield information about the population from which the sample was taken. Sampling, therefore, can be looked upon as an effective and efficient method of gathering audit evidence.

2. **Efficient** Without sampling procedures, an auditor would examine every item comprising an account balance or every transaction occurring within a class of transactions. The cost would (a) be prohibitive due to the amount of time required to perform the examination and (b) far outweigh the benefit obtained. Sampling provides the auditor with a means of obtaining information, but at a much lower cost.

3. **Sufficient** The sufficiency of audit evidence is determined by the size and design of an audit sample (among other factors).

   a. **Size** Depends on both the objectives and efficiency of the sample.

   b. **Design** Relates to the efficiency of the sample; for example, one sample is more efficient than another if it achieves the same objectives with a smaller sample size.

4. **Appropriate** The appropriateness of audit evidence is determined by auditor judgment—not the design and evaluation of an audit sample.

B. Types of Sampling

1. **Attributes Sampling** In the auditor's consideration of internal control, tests are performed on the client's internal control policies and procedures in order to determine the degree to which the client's employees have complied (i.e., tests of controls). These tests involve the determination of the rate of occurrence of some characteristic (i.e., attribute), in a population. The attribute of interest is frequently a deviation from the particular control procedure. Thus, the auditor takes a sample from the population, computes the deviation rate in the sample, and draws conclusions about the true population deviation rate.

2. **Variables Sampling** In performing the tests of details of transactions and account balances (i.e., substantive tests), the auditor is concerned with the dollar amounts reported in the financial statements. Thus, the auditor draws a sample from the population of interest, determines the proper dollar value of the items sampled, and makes inferences, based upon projection of the sample results to the population, about the fairness of the amounts reported in the financial statements.

3. **Dual-Purpose Sampling** In some circumstances, the auditor may design a test that will be used for dual purposes—tests of controls and substantive testing. A dual-purpose sample is

a sample that is designed to both test the operating effectiveness of an identified control and test whether the recorded monetary amounts of a transaction are correct.

a. **Low Risk Factor** Generally, the auditor who plans to use this type of sample believes that there is an acceptably low risk that the rate of deviations from prescribed internal controls in the population is greater than the tolerable rate.

b. **Size** The size of the sample should be the larger of the samples that would have been designed for the two separate purposes.

C. Uncertainty

The concept of a *reasonable basis for an opinion* suggests some degree of uncertainty or audit risk. The theory of sampling is well established in auditing practice because it is unusual to find instances where 100 percent of the items need to be examined for each account balance and class of transactions.

1. **Circumstances** There are some situations in which the surrounding factors do not justify the acceptance of any amount of sampling risk, and, therefore, *all* related data is examined.

2. **Audit Risk** The uncertainty inherent in applying audit procedures is referred to as audit risk. Audit risk involves uncertainties due to both sampling and nonsampling risks.

a. **Sampling Risk** Sampling risk results from the possibility that if a test is restricted to a sample, the conclusions reached may be different than the conclusions that would have resulted if the entire population was examined. The smaller the sample size is, the greater the sampling risk becomes; thus sampling risk varies inversely with sample size.

b. **Nonsampling Risk** Nonsampling risk includes all aspects of audit risk not due to sampling. Nonsampling risk can be reduced by adequate planning and supervision of audit work and adherence to quality control standards. Examples of nonsampling risks include:

(1) Failure to select appropriate audit procedures for a given objective.

(2) Failure to recognize misstatements, thus making a procedure ineffective.

D. Assessing Sampling Risk

The judgment of the auditor should be used to assess sampling risk.

1. **Audit Risk Model** Because the acceptable level of audit risk is a matter of professional judgment, the audit risk model is not intended to be a mathematical formula including all factors that may influence the determination of audit risk. However, the model may be useful for planning appropriate risk levels for audit procedures to achieve the desired audit risk.

Exhibit 1 ▶ Audit Risk Model

$$AR = RMM \times DR \text{ or } AR = (IR \times CR) \times (AP \times TD)$$

AR = The allowable **audit risk** that monetary misstatements equal to tolerable misstatements might remain undetected for the account balance or class of transactions and related assertions after the auditor has completed all audit procedures deemed necessary.

RMM = The risk (consisting of inherent risk and control risk) that the relevant assertions related to balances, classes, or disclosures contain misstatements that could be material to the financial statements when aggregated with other misstatements.

IR = **Inherent risk** is the susceptibility of an assertion to a material misstatement assuming there are no related internal control policies or procedures.

CR = **Control risk** is the risk that material misstatements that could occur in an assertion will not be prevented or detected on a timely basis by the entity's internal control policies and procedures.

DR	=	The risk that the auditor will not detect a material misstatement that exists in an assertion.
AP	=	The auditor's assessment of the risk that **analytical procedures** and other relevant substantive test will not detect misstatements that could occur in an assertion equal to tolerable misstatement, given that such misstatements are not detected by internal controls.
TD	=	The allowable risk of incorrect acceptance that **tests of details** will not detect misstatements equal to tolerable misstatement, given that such misstatements are not detected by internal controls or analytical procedures and other relevant substantive procedures.

2. **Subjective Assessments** The auditor can compute TD mathematically, if the auditor first assigns an acceptable audit risk (AR) and subjectively quantifies the risk of material misstatement (RMM) and the risk that analytical procedures and other relevant substantive test will not detect misstatements (AP). To compute TD, the model must be restated as TD = AR/(RMM × AP).

Example 1 ▶ Audit Risk Model Use

Assume the auditor is planning a sampling application to test a client's accounts receivable voucher register. If AR = .05 and the auditor has subjectively assessed RMM and AP equal to 50% and 30%, respectively, then the auditor can use the model to compute an appropriate level of risk of incorrect acceptance (sampling risk).

$$TD = AR/(RMM \times AP)$$
$$TD = 0.05/(0.5 \times 0.3)$$
$$TD = 0.33 \text{ (or 33\%)}$$

3. **Tests of Internal Control** The auditor is concerned with two aspects of sampling risk while performing tests of controls.

    a. **Risk of Assessing Control Risk Too Low** The risk that the assessed level of control risk based on the sample is less than the true operating effectiveness of the internal control policy or procedure.

    b. **Risk of Assessing Control Risk Too High** The risk that the assessed level of control risk based on the sample is greater than the true operating effectiveness of the internal control policy or procedure.

Exhibit 2 ▶ Risk for Tests of Control Procedures

	Client's Control Risk Is	
Auditor's Assessment of Control Risk Is	Less Than Maximum	Maximum
Less than Maximum Level	Correct Decision (1)	Incorrect Decision (2)
Maximum Level	Incorrect Decision (3)	Correct Decision (4)

(2)   Assessing Control Risk Too Low (effectiveness)
(3)   Assessing Control Risk Too High (efficiency)

4. **Substantive Tests of Details** The auditor is concerned with two aspects of sampling risk while performing substantive tests.

Exhibit 3 ▶ Risk for Substantive Tests

Indication of Sample Results	Client's Book Value Is	
	Fairly Stated	Not Fairly Stated
Accept Book Value	Correct Decision (5)	Incorrect Decision (6)
Reject Book Value	Incorrect Decision (7)	Correct Decision (8)

(6) Incorrect Acceptance (effectiveness)
(7) Incorrect Rejection (efficiency)

a. **Risk of Incorrect Acceptance (Beta Risk)** The risk that the sample supports the conclusion that the recorded account balance is not misstated materially, when in fact, it is misstated materially.

b. **Risk of Incorrect Rejection (Alpha Risk)** The risk that the sample supports the conclusion that the recorded account balance is misstated materially, when in fact, it is not misstated materially.

5. **Efficiency & Effectiveness** The risk of incorrect rejection and the risk of assessing control risk too high relate to the efficiency of the audit. Thus, if the auditor assesses control risk too high, additional substantive tests will be performed beyond what is necessary. The risk of incorrect acceptance and the risk of assessing control risk too low relate to the effectiveness of the audit in the detection of existing material misstatements. This potentially could result in materially misstated financial statements from not expanding substantive audit tests to a necessary level.

E. **Sample Selection**
Items for sampling should be chosen in such a way that the sample can be representative of the population. The auditor should ensure that all items have an opportunity to be selected. Commonly used selection procedures include: haphazard sampling, random sampling, systematic sampling, stratified sampling, block sampling, and probability-proportional-to-size sampling. Note that block sampling does not meet the requirements for a representative sample.

F. **Tests of Internal Controls**
Sampling applies to tests of controls when the auditor needs to decide whether a rate of deviation is equal to or less than a tolerable rate. However, sampling does not apply to risk assessment procedures performed to obtain an understanding of internal control. Furthermore, sampling concepts may not apply to some tests of controls such as the following: (1) tests of automated application controls (generally these are tested only once or a few times when effective IT general controls are present); (2) analyses of controls for determining appropriate segregation of duties or other analyses that do not examine documentary evidence of performance; (3) tests of certain documented controls or analyses of the effectiveness of security and access controls; or (4) tests directed toward obtaining audit evidence about the operation of the control environment or accounting system.

1. **Planning Sample** The auditor should take the following judgmental factors into consideration when planning samples for tests of controls:

a. **Relationship** The relationship of the sample to the objective of the test of controls.

b. **Tolerable Rate of Deviations** The maximum, or tolerable, rate of deviations from prescribed internal control policies and procedures that would support the auditor's assessed level of control risk. The tolerable rate is assessed by considering the relationship of procedural deviations to (1) the assessed level of control risk and (2) the degree of assurance desired by the auditor related to the audit evidence in the sample.

c. **Allowable Risk** The auditor's allowable risk of assessing control risk too low. When the degree of assurance desired by the sample is high, the auditor should allow for a low level of sampling risk (that is, the risk of assessing control risk too low).

d. **Characteristics** Characteristics of the population, that is, the items comprising the account balance or class of transactions of interest

e. **Size** The auditor uses professional judgment to relate the following factors in determining a sample size for a test of controls: (1) the tolerable rate of deviation from the tested control, (2) the likely rate of deviations, and (3) the allowable risk of assessing control risk too low.

2. **Performance & Evaluation** In performing audit procedures on items included in a sample and in evaluating sample results, the auditor should repeat the same steps that are outlined for substantive testing. However, for tests of controls, if the auditor is unable to perform all tests on a selected item, it is considered a deviation. If the auditor concludes that the sample results do not support the assessed level of control risk for an assertion, the auditor should reevaluate the nature, timing, and extent of substantive procedures based on a revised consideration of the assessed level of control risk.

G. **Substantive Tests of Details**

1. **Planning Sample** The auditor should consider the audit objectives to be achieved and decide on the procedure(s) to be applied that will achieve those objectives. The auditor should consider the following factors in planning a sample for a substantive test of details:

a. **Relationship** The relationship of the sample to the relevant audit objectives, i.e., the population being sampled should be appropriate for the audit objective.

b. **Materiality** Preliminary judgments of materiality levels

c. **Allowable Risk** Auditor's allowable risk of incorrect acceptance

d. **Characteristics** Characteristics of the population, that is, the items comprising the account balance or class of transactions of interest. The auditor may be able to reduce the needed sample size by separating the population into relatively homogenous groups on the basis of some characteristic related to the specific audit objective. (For example, dividing accounts receivable into several groups based on the size of the individual account balances.)

e. **Tolerable Misstatement** How much monetary misstatement in the related account balance may exist when combined with misstatements that may be found in other tests without causing the financial statements to be misstated materially. This is called the tolerable misstatement or tolerable error for the sample. Tolerable misstatement should usually be set for a particular audit procedure at less than financial statement materiality so that when the results of all audit procedures are aggregated, the required overall assurance will be attained.

f. **Size** The required sample size for a test of details is influenced by (1) the tolerable misstatement and expected misstatement, (2) the audit risk, (3) the characteristics of the population, (4) the assessed risk of material misstatement (RMM), and (5) the assessed risk for other substantive procedures related to the same assertion. Statistical sampling involves the use of tables or formulas to compute sample sizes based on these factors while nonstatistical sample sizes depend on the auditor's professional judgment in relating these factors.

2. **Performance** Procedures that are appropriate to the particular audit objective should be applied to each sample item. If certain selected sample items cannot be examined, the auditor's treatment of these unexpected items will depend upon their effect on the auditor's evaluation of the sample. If the auditor's evaluation of the sample results would not be altered by considering those unexamined items to be misstated, it is not necessary to examine the items. However, if considering those unexamined items to be misstated would lead to a conclusion that the balance or class contains material misstatements, the auditor should consider alternative procedures, and should consider whether the inability to examine the items has implications in relation to (a) assessing the risks of material misstatement due to fraud, (b) the assessed level of control risk the auditor expects to be supported, or (c) the degree of reliance on management representations.

3. **Evaluation** The auditor compares total projected misstatement with the tolerable misstatement.

    a. **Judgment** The auditor's judgment is a necessary factor in this evaluation for both statistical and nonstatistical sampling.

    b. **Quality** In addition to the evaluation of the frequency and amounts of monetary misstatements, consideration should be given to the qualitative aspects of the misstatements. Specifically, the auditor considers the nature and cause of the misstatement and the possible relationship of the misstatement to other phases of the audit.

    c. **Aggregate** When the auditor evaluates whether the financial statements taken as a whole may be misstated materially, projected misstatement results for all audit sampling applications and all known misstatements from nonsampling applications should be considered in the aggregate along with other relevant audit evidence.

H. Statistical Sampling

Statistical sampling is based on the assumption that, within a given confidence level and allowance for sampling risk, a randomly selected sample of items from a population will reflect the same characteristics that occur in the population. Therefore, auditors may draw valid conclusions based on data derived from a relatively small sample of the total population.

1. **Similarities** Both statistical and nonstatistical sampling involve examining less than the whole body of data to express a conclusion about the total body of data. Both methods involve audit judgment in planning and performing a sampling procedure and evaluating the results of the sample. Both provide sufficient appropriate audit evidence. Also, the audit procedures involved in examining the selected items in a sample generally do not depend on the sampling approach used.

2. **Distinguishing Feature** A properly designed nonstatistical sampling application can provide results that are as effective as those from a properly designed statistical sampling application. The distinguishing feature of statistical sampling methods as opposed to nonstatistical methods is that the user is able to provide a mathematical measurement of the degree of uncertainty that results from examining only part of a population. That is, statistical sampling allows an auditor to measure sampling risk.

3. **Sampling Approach** Statistical or nonstatistical approaches can provide sufficient audit evidence. The auditor must choose between statistical and nonstatistical sampling. This choice primarily is a cost/benefit consideration.

    a. **Selection** Because either can provide sufficient audit evidence, the auditor chooses between statistical or nonstatistical sampling after considering their relative cost and effectiveness in the specific situation.

      b.   **Advantages** Statistical sampling helps to (1) design efficient samples, (2) measure the sufficiency of audit evidence, and (3) evaluate sample results.

4.   **Risks** If audit sampling (either nonstatistical or statistical) is used, some sampling risk is always present. One benefit of statistical sampling is that it uses the laws of probability to measure sampling risk.

5.   **Sample Sizes** Another benefit of statistical sampling is that it provides a model for determining sample size while explicitly recognizing relevant factors such as the risk of assessing control risk too low, tolerable misstatement, and the expected population deviation rate. With nonstatistical sampling, on the other hand, the auditor implicitly recognizes the relevant factors while determining the sample size based on her/his own judgment and experience.

6.   **Costs** Statistical sampling might involve additional costs for (1) training auditors, (2) designing individual samples to meet the statistical requirements, and (3) selecting the items to be examined. For example, if the individual balances comprising an account balance to be tested are not maintained in an organized pattern, it might not be cost effective for an auditor to select items in a way that would satisfy the requirements of a properly designed statistical sample.

II. Classical Sample Selection Methods

A.   **Judgmental (Haphazard) Sampling**
The auditor uses professional judgment to decide how many and which items should be included in the sample. (i.e., the items included in the sample are selected without any conscious bias and without any special reason for including or omitting items from the sample).

1.   **Description** It does **not** consist of sampling units selected in a careless manner; rather, the sample is selected in a manner the auditor expects to be representative of the population. For example, the auditor decides to select 100 accounts from a population of 1,000 accounts based on the auditor's judgment as to how many and which specific accounts should be included in the sample.

2.   **Use** While haphazard sampling is useful for nonstatistical sampling, it is not used for statistical sampling because it does not allow measurement of the probability of selecting the combination of sampling units.

B.   **Random Number Sampling**
The auditor may select a random sample by matching random numbers generated by a computer or selected from a random number table with, for example, document numbers. With this method, every item in the population has the same probability of being selected as every other item in the population, and every sample has the same probability of being selected as every other sample of the same size.

1.   **Replacement** With random number and other sample selection methods, the auditor may sample with or without replacement (i.e., with or without replacing an item in the population after its value or attribute has been selected). Sampling with replacement may result in the appearance of a particular item in the sample more than once. In practice, auditors generally choose the without replacement approach.

2.   **Use** This approach is useful for both statistical and nonstatistical sampling.

C.   **Systematic Sampling**
For this method, the auditor determines a uniform interval by dividing the number of physical units in the population by the sample size. A random number is selected as a starting point for the first interval, and one item is selected throughout the population at each of the uniform intervals from the starting point (every nth item). For example, if the auditor wishes to select 100 items from a population of 20,000 items, the uniform interval is every 200th item. First the auditor selects a

random starting point (a random number from 1 to 200) and then selects every 200th item from the random start, including the random start item.

1. **Description** Because a random start is used, the systematic method provides a sample that allows every sampling unit in the population an equal chance of being selected. If the population is arranged randomly, systematic selection essentially is the same as random number selection. However, unlike random number sampling, this method may not always give every possible combination of sampling units the same probability of being selected. For example, a population of employees on a payroll for a construction company might be organized by teams, each team consisting of a crew leader and nine other workers. A selection of every tenth employee will list either every crew leader or no crew leaders, depending on the random start. No combination would include both crew leaders and other employees. In these circumstances, the auditor may consider using a different sample selection method such as random selection or making a systematic selection with multiple starts. For example, in the case related to payroll cited above, the auditor could use an interval of 50 rather than 10. This would require that the auditor select 5 different random starting points and move through the population 5 different times.

2. **Use** This method is useful for both statistical and nonstatistical sampling.

D. **Stratified Sampling**

The population is divided into groups, called strata, according to some common characteristic, and then random sampling is applied to each stratum. For example, the auditor may divide the client's accounts receivable into three strata—those with balances of $2,000 and above, those with balances between $500 and $2,000, and those with balances of $500 and below. The auditor might positively confirm the whole population of accounts with balances of $2,000 and above, positively confirm a random sample of the accounts with balances between $500 and $2,000, and negatively confirm a random sample of those accounts with balances of $500 and below. The primary objective of stratified sampling is to decrease the effect of variance in the total population thereby reducing sample size.

1. **Mean-Per-Unit** The mean-per-unit (MPU) method is a classical variables sampling technique that uses the sample average to project the total population dollar value by multiplying the sample average by the number of items in the population. A smaller sample size can be obtained by stratifying a highly variable population into segments. These segments then will have a minimum of variability within segments and variability between segments will be eliminated. As a result, the total sample size of all combined segments will be less. This is accomplished without a loss of reliability or precision. Therefore, stratified MPU sampling may be more efficient than unstratified MPU because it usually produces an estimate having the desired level of precision, with a smaller sample size.

2. **Use** This approach can be used for both statistical and nonstatistical sampling. It is particularly useful in reducing the overall sample size when the auditor is using the MPU approach on populations that include sampling units (such as individual customer receivable balances) that have a wide range of dollar values.

E. **Block Sampling**

A block sample consists of selecting contiguous transactions. For example, a block sample from a population of all vouchers processed for the year 20X8 might be all vouchers processed on February 3, May 17, and July 19, 20X8. This sample includes only three sampling units out of 250 business days because the sampling unit, in this case, is a period of time rather than an individual transaction. A sample with so few blocks generally is not adequate to reach a reasonable audit conclusion. Although a block sample might be designed with enough blocks to minimize this limitation, using such samples might be inefficient. If an auditor decides to use a block sample, special care should be exercised to control sampling risk in designing that sample. Block sampling should not be used with statistical sampling approaches. Block sampling is often used to evaluate changes in control procedures by examining all transactions at that time.

III. Attributes Sampling

A. Operating Effectiveness of Internal Control Policies & Procedures

The attribute of interest normally is a control procedure. For example, the auditor may be concerned with estimating the percentage of purchase orders that do not have proper authorization.

1. **Deviation Rate** In performing tests of controls, the auditor frequently is interested in determining the rate of deviation from prescribed internal control policies and procedures. The sampling plan generally used in this situation is attribute sampling.

    Tests of Controls → Attribute Sampling → Deviation Rate

2. **Impact** A weakness in internal control does not necessarily mean that there will be a misstatement in the financial statements. If a material misstatement occurs and is not detected by internal controls or substantive tests, only then will the financial statements be misstated.

3. **Tolerable Rate** The auditor should determine the maximum rate of deviations from the prescribed internal control policy and procedure that s/he would be willing to accept without altering the planned assessed level of control risk. This is referred to as the tolerable rate.

B. Methods

1. **Sequential Sampling** The sample is selected in several steps, with each step conditional on the results of previous steps.

2. **Attribute Estimation Method** A sample is selected and its attribute error rate is determined. This rate serves as an estimate of the error rate in the population and allows the auditor to make statistical statements about the population attribute error rate.

3. **Acceptance Sampling Method** A special case of estimation of attributes. An acceptance sampling table, which utilizes the population size, sample size, and number of errors found in the sample, is used to make a statistical statement that the error rate in the population is not greater than a specified error rate. For example, based on sample results, an auditor may obtain 95 percent confidence that the actual error rate in the population does not exceed 8 percent.

4. **Discovery Sampling Method** A special case of acceptance sampling. The objective is to attain a specified level of confidence that if the error rate in the population is at least a certain percentage the sample will include at least one instance of failure to comply with the control procedure being audited. For example, discovery sampling can be used to determine how large a sample needs to be for the auditor to have 95 percent confidence that, if the error rate in the population is 1 percent or higher, the auditor's sample will include at least one example of an error. What if a sample of the determined size is selected and no error found? The auditor then has 95 percent confidence that the error rate in the population is less than 1 percent.

    • Discovery sampling frequently is used when the auditor expects an extremely low error rate, usually zero. It often is used in testing for critical problems such as forgery. If a forgery is found, the auditor would discontinue sampling and investigate further.

C. Steps

The following general steps are appropriate for attributes sampling in tests of compliance with prescribed internal control procedures:

1. **Determine Objective** In a compliance test of control procedures, the objective is to compare the actual deviation rate to the tolerable rate. It should be remembered that the purpose of the test is to provide reasonable assurance that internal controls are operating in an effective manner.

2. **Determine Tolerable Rate** This is the maximum rate of deviations from the prescribed internal control procedure (i.e., maximum misstatement rate) that the auditor is willing to accept without altering the assessment of control risk on the particular internal control procedure and is a judgmental decision. Therefore, the tolerable rate is a function of both the expected level of control risk and the degree of assurance desired. Thus, an increase in the tolerable rate would allow a reduction in sample size. If, after performing the sampling application, the auditor finds that the rate of deviations from the prescribed control procedure is close to or exceeds the tolerable rate, the auditor normally would decide that there is an unacceptably high risk that the deviation rate for the population exceeds the tolerable rate. In such cases, the auditor should consider modifying the assessed level of control risk.

3. **Determine Confidence (Reliability) Level** This is a judgmental decision that quantifies the level of sampling risk that the auditor is willing to accept. The auditor's willingness to accept sampling risk is determined, to a large extent, by the nature of the other tests that the auditor intends to perform that would complement the test of controls.

4. **Determine Expected Population Deviation Rate** This is the expected rate of occurrence of deviations from the prescribed internal control procedure (i.e., the expected error rate). The expected population deviation rate should not exceed the tolerable rate. If prior to testing, the auditor believes that the actual deviation rate is higher than the tolerable rate, the auditor generally omits testing of that control procedure and either seeks to obtain assurance by testing other relevant internal controls, or assesses control risk at the maximum level for the related financial statement assertion. The auditor estimates the expected population deviation rate, considering such factors as results of the prior years' tests and the overall control environment. Prior years' results should be considered in light of changes in the entity's internal controls and changes in personnel.

5. **Consider Effect of Population Size** When a sample is small in relation to the population, the population size has little or no effect on the determination of an appropriate sample size. If the sample size is greater than 10 percent of the population size, which rarely is the case, a finite population correction factor may be used. However, the finite population correction factor tends to decrease the sample size. Therefore, most auditors ignore the factor because any error in sample size that results will be on the conservative side.

6. **Determine Method of Selecting Sample** The sample should be representative of the population, and all items should have a chance of being selected. The various methods for selecting samples are discussed in Section III.B.

7. **Compute Sample Size** Sample sizes can be computed by the use of formulas, computer software, and sample size tables. Consideration should be given to the following when determining sample size:

   a. **Assessing Control Risk Too Low** As discussed earlier, there is an inverse relationship between the risk of assessing control risk too low and sample size.

   b. **Tolerable Deviation Rate** The maximum rate of deviation from a prescribed control policy or procedure that the auditor is willing to accept without modifying the planned level of control risk.

Exhibit 4 ▶ Sample Size When Other Factors Are Changed

Increase in	Effect on Sample Size
Population	Slight increase for increased populations, generally little or no effect
Tolerable rate	Decrease
Expected deviation rate	Increase

When Sample Size Is Changed	
Sample Size	Increase in
Decrease	Risk of assessing control risk too low

Table 1 ▶ Tolerable Rate

Expected Population Deviation Rate	5% Risk of Assessing Control Risk Too Low (with number of expected errors in parentheses)										
	2%	3%	4%	5%	6%	7%	8%	9%	10%	15%	20%
0.00%	149(0)	99(0)	74(0)	59(0)	49(0)	42(0)	36(0)	32(0)	29(0)	19(0)	14(0)
.25	236(1)	157(1)	117(1)	93(1)	78(1)	66(1)	58(1)	51(1)	46(1)	30(1)	22(1)
.50	*	157(1)	117(1)	93(1)	78(1)	66(1)	58(1)	51(1)	46(1)	30(1)	22(1)
.75	*	208(2)	117(1)	93(1)	78(1)	66(1)	58(1)	51(1)	46(1)	30(1)	22(1)
1.00	*	*	156(2)	93(1)	78(1)	66(1)	58(1)	51(1)	46(1)	30(1)	22(1)
1.25	*	*	156(2)	124(2)	78(1)	66(1)	58(1)	51(1)	46(1)	30(1)	22(1)
1.50	*	*	192(3)	124(2)	103(2)	66(1)	58(1)	51(1)	46(1)	30(1)	22(1)
1.75	*	*	227(4)	153(3)	103(2)	88(2)	77(2)	51(1)	46(1)	30(1)	22(1)
2.00	*	*	*	181(4)	127(3)	88(2)	77(2)	68(2)	46(1)	30(1)	22(1)
2.25	*	*	*	208(5)	127(3)	88(2)	77(2)	68(2)	61(2)	30(1)	22(1)
2.50	*	*	*	*	150(4)	109(3)	77(2)	68(2)	61(2)	30(1)	22(1)
2.75	*	*	*	*	173(5)	109(3)	95(3)	68(2)	61(2)	30(1)	22(1)
3.00	*	*	*	*	195(6)	129(4)	95(3)	84(3)	61(2)	30(1)	22(1)
3.25	*	*	*	*	*	148(5)	112(4)	84(3)	61(2)	30(1)	22(1)
3.50	*	*	*	*	*	167(6)	112(4)	84(3)	76(3)	40(2)	22(1)
3.75	*	*	*	*	*	185(7)	129(5)	100(4)	76(3)	40(2)	22(1)
4.00	*	*	*	*	*	*	146(6)	100(4)	89(4)	40(2)	22(1)
5.00	*	*	*	*	*	*	*	158(8)	116(6)	40(2)	30(2)
6.00	*	*	*	*	*	*	*	*	179(11)	50(3)	30(2)
7.00	*	*	*	*	*	*	*	*	*	68(5)	37(3)

* Sample size is too large to be cost-effective for most audit applications.

NOTE: This table assumes a large population.

Example 2 ▶ Use of Table 1 to Determine Sample Size

The auditor would like to assess control risk at below the maximum level. In this case, in order to do this, the auditor must have 95% confidence that the actual population deviation rate (i.e., the percentage of vouchers that are paid without being approved) is not greater than 6%. Therefore, the tolerable rate is 6%; i.e., the auditor will be able to assess control risk at below the maximum level as long as the auditor can conclude with 95% confidence that not more than 6% of the unpaid vouchers lack approval. Based on the error rate observed in last year's sample, the auditor expects a population deviation rate of only 1.50% this year. Using Table 1, 103 vouchers should be examined to yield the desired confidence about the population error rate.

8. **Select & Audit Sample Items** Audit procedures should be applied to the items in the sample to determine deviations from the prescribed control procedures previously identified. Deviations should be grouped according to whether they are occurring with some regularity or are isolated events. In cases where selected items cannot be examined, they should be counted as deviations from control procedures. This occurs, for example, when documentation used

to test for the procedures has been misplaced, lost, or destroyed. A voided item generally would be replaced by another randomly selected item, if it was voided properly.

9. **Evaluate Sample Results** The results of the sample must be analyzed in order to make an inference about the population error rate. This can be done by formula, but most often is accomplished by tables or computer programs based on the appropriate formula.

Table 2 ▶ Actual Number of Deviations Found

Sample Size	Statistical Sample Results Evaluation Upper Limit at 5% of Assessing Control Risk Too Low										
	0	1	2	3	4	5	6	7	8	9	10
25	11.3	17.6	*	*	*	*	*	*	*	*	*
30	9.5	14.9	19.6	*	*	*	*	*	*	*	*
35	8.3	12.9	17.0	*	*	*	*	*	*	*	*
40	7.3	11.4	15.0	18.3	*	*	*	*	*	*	*
45	6.5	10.2	13.4	16.4	19.2	*	*	*	*	*	*
50	5.9	9.2	12.1	14.8	17.4	19.9	*	*	*	*	*
55	5.4	8.4	11.1	13.5	15.9	18.2	*	*	*	*	*
60	4.9	7.7	10.2	12.5	14.7	16.8	18.8	*	*	*	*
65	4.6	7.1	9.4	11.5	13.6	15.5	17.4	19.3	*	*	*
70	4.2	6.6	8.8	10.8	12.6	14.5	16.3	18.0	19.7	*	*
75	4.0	6.2	8.2	10.1	11.8	13.6	15.2	16.9	18.5	20.0	*
80	3.7	5.8	7.7	9.5	11.1	12.7	14.3	15.9	17.4	18.9	*
90	3.3	5.2	6.9	8.4	9.9	11.4	12.8	14.2	15.5	16.8	18.2
100	3.0	4.7	6.2	7.6	9.0	10.3	11.5	12.8	14.0	15.2	16.4
125	2.4	3.8	5.0	6.1	7.2	8.3	9.3	10.3	11.3	12.3	13.2
150	2.0	3.2	4.2	5.1	6.0	6.9	7.8	8.6	9.5	10.3	11.1
200	1.5	2.4	3.2	3.9	4.6	5.2	5.9	6.5	7.2	7.8	8.4

* Over 20 percent

NOTE: This table presents upper limits as percentages. This table assumes a large population.

a. The first step in the evaluation of the results is tabulating the number of deviations found and comparing this to the number of deviations expected to occur using the sample size determined from the above table. The expected number of deviations is the parenthetical number found next to each sample size. In cases where the deviations found are less than the number that would be expected (the parenthetical number), it can be assumed that the risk of assessing control risk too low and the allowance for sampling risk is not more than the tolerable rate.

b. When the actual deviations are more than those that would be expected according to the parenthetical number in Table 1, the auditor can calculate the maximum deviation rate in the population using a table similar to Table 2. Table 2 is for evaluating sample results for a 5 percent risk of assessing control risk too low or a 95 percent confidence level.

c. No one table can accommodate an evaluation of every possible size and number of deviations, and the auditor often will need to use other references to find appropriate tables. In cases where a particular sample size does not appear in a table, it is a good idea to be conservative by using the next smaller sample size shown.

Example 3 ▶ Table 2 Use

Only one error is discovered from the 103 sample items selected in Example 2. Use of Table 2, reveals that there is no corresponding sample size for 103 items, so the next lowest (100 sample size) is used. The intersection of the sample size and the number of deviations found reveals the maximum population deviation rate in this case is 4.7%. This maximum population deviation rate is less than the tolerable rate of 6%, so it can be concluded that within a 95% reliability level, the control is functioning as required.

10. **Reach Overall Conclusion** The auditor uses professional judgment to reach an overall conclusion about the effect of the evaluation of the test of controls on the nature, timing, and extent of planned substantive tests. If the sample results, along with other relevant audit evidence, support the assessed level of control risk, the auditor generally does not need to modify planned substantive tests. If the sample results do not support the assessed level of control risk, the auditor ordinarily either would perform tests of controls on other relevant internal controls for which control risk can be assessed at below the maximum level, or assess control risk at a higher, or the maximum, level and modify the nature, timing, and/or extent of substantive testing. In addition to the evaluation of the frequency and amounts of monetary misstatements, consideration should be given to the qualitative aspects of the misstatements. These would include the nature and cause of the misstatements. For example, were there differences in principle or applications or differences due to misunderstanding of instructions or carelessness? Also, consideration should be given to the possible relationship of the misstatements to other phases of the audit.

11. **Document Sampling Procedure** Documentation might include such items as follows: (a) a description of the prescribed control procedure being tested; (b) the objectives of the test, including the relationship to planned substantive testing; (c) the definition of the population and sampling unit; (d) the definition of the deviation condition (i.e., what is considered a deviation from prescribed internal control policies and procedures); (e) the rationale for the confidence level, the tolerable rate, and the expected population deviation rate used in the application; (f) the method of sample size determination; (g) the method of sample selection; (h) a description of the sampling procedure performed and a listing of compliance deviations identified in the sample; and (i) the evaluation of the sample and a summary of the overall conclusion.

IV. Classical Variables Sampling

A. Substantive Tests of Details

The auditor performs substantive tests either to detect misstatements or to obtain evidence about the validity and propriety of the accounting treatment of transactions and balances. In substantive testing, the auditor is interested primarily in dollar amounts. An example of a substantive test is the use of a sample from the accounts receivable subsidiary ledger to estimate the balance in the control account. The traditional method of performing substantive tests of details is by variables sampling.

Substantive Tests → Variables Sampling → Dollar Amount

B. Methods

1. **Simple Extension (Mean-Per-Unit Approach)** A method of estimating variables in which the auditor finds the average audited value for the items in the sample and then estimates the population value by multiplying the average sample value by the size of the population. For example, if the mean of a sample of 50 accounts is calculated to be $100 and there are 1,000 accounts in the population, the total value of the 1,000 accounts would be estimated at $100,000 [i.e., ($100 per account) × (1,000 accounts)] plus or minus an allowance for sampling error that is determined statistically. Note that the auditor needs to know the audited values of the items in the sample but does not need to know their book values.

2. **Difference Estimation** The auditor first finds the average difference between the audited value and the book value of the items in the sample. This average difference is then multiplied by the size of the population in order to estimate the difference between the book value of the population and its actual value. For example, if the average difference between the book value and audited value for each account in a sample of 100 accounts is $10 and if there are 10,000 accounts in the population, the auditor will estimate that there is a $100,000 difference between the book value of the population and the actual value (i.e., $10 × 10,000 accounts) plus or minus an allowance for sampling risk that is determined statistically. The interval, so determined, then is compared against the precision required (i.e., against the amount of acceptable difference) in order to decide if the account appears to be stated reasonably.

3. **Ratio Method** The auditor uses sample results to estimate the ratio of audited value to book value. This ratio then is applied to the population to estimate the actual value. Ratio estimation should be used when each population item has a book value, an audited value may be ascertained for each sample item, and differences occur frequently. For example, if the auditor finds that the average ratio of audited value to book value for the sample is 1.05 and if the book value for the population is $100,000, the actual value for the population can be estimated to be $105,000 (i.e., 1.05 × $100,000) plus or minus an allowance for sampling risk.

C. **Steps**
The following general steps are appropriate in substantive tests of details:

1. **Determine Objectives** It is important for the auditor to specify the purpose of the test because this will determine the population of the test. For example, the purpose may be to prove the existence of an account balance or to show that the account is complete.

2. **Define Population** The auditor must match the objectives of the test to the appropriate population. The population is made up of the account balances or class of transactions of interest to the auditor. Defining the population involves consideration of the individual sampling units of the entire population, whether the entire population is available to be picked, and the identification of those items that are individually significant. Those items that are individually significant may be accounts that are large enough to exceed the level of tolerable deviation by themselves. These would not be included in the population available for sampling, but should be tested separately.

3. **Determine Confidence Level** The confidence level for the auditor's substantive tests generally will vary inversely with the assessed level of control risk (i.e., the stronger the internal control is judged to be, the lower the assessed level of control risk, thereby affecting the extent of substantive tests). The confidence level for a particular substantive test is a matter of judgment, but the auditor should consider the overall confidence level in making the determination. This confidence level is related to the auditor's assessment of sampling risk.

4. **Determine Expected Standard Deviation of Population, or Expected Amount of Misstatement Directly in Dollar Value** This also is a matter of judgment, frequently based on the prior year's audit or on the results of a small pilot sample. As expected misstatement increases, a larger sample size is required.

5. **Determine Tolerable Misstatement** The tolerable misstatement is the maximum monetary misstatement that may exist when combined with misstatements that may be found in other tests without causing the financial statements to be misstated materially. This is a judgmental value which should relate closely to the auditor's preliminary estimates of materiality levels. As tolerable misstatement increases, sample size decreases.

6. **Select Method of Audit Sampling** These can be either statistical or nonstatistical. If statistical sampling is used, either PPS or classical variables techniques would be used.

7. **Determine Sample Size** Compute the sample size by using a sample size table, formula, or software. The sample size formula for substantive testing is illustrated in Exhibit 5.

Exhibit 5 ▶ Substantive Testing Sample Size Formula

$$n = \frac{c^2 \times s^2 \times N^2}{A^2} = \frac{c^2 \times s^2}{a^2}$$

Where:

n = Size of the sample

c = Confidence (reliability) coefficient; this is the number of standard deviations that corresponds to the selected confidence level.

s = Standard deviation of the population (usually the standard deviation of a small pilot sample or the standard deviation found in previous years)

N = Size of the population

A = Population allowance for sampling error (tolerable misstatement less expected amount of misstatement)

a = Allowance for sampling error per population item

Exhibit 6 ▶ Summary of Sampling Factor Relationships

Decrease in	Effect on Sample Size
Confidence (reliability) coefficient	Decrease
Tolerable misstatement	Increase
Expected standard deviation of the population	Decrease

Sample Size	Decrease in
Increase	Risk-Incorrect Acceptance
Increase	Risk-Incorrect Rejection

8. **Inspection** Select and audit the sample items.

Example 4 ▶ Sample Size

An auditor wishes to apply statistical sampling as part of substantive testing of the accounts receivable control account. The account has a book value of $500,000 and is composed of 5,000 individual accounts. The auditor determines that 90% confidence is necessary in the results of substantive testing for this account. The auditor sets total allowance for sampling error (precision) at $40,000. Next, the auditor takes a small pilot sample in order to estimate the standard deviation of the population. The pilot sample has a standard deviation of $40. The number of standard deviations corresponding to 90% for a normal distribution is 1.64.

N	=	5,000	A	=	$40,000
c	=	1.64	s	=	$40
a	=	$40,000/5,000 = $8			

Required: Calculate the sample size.

Solution: Substituting the information into the sample size formula and solving the equation gives the following:

$$n = \frac{(1.64)^2 \, (\$40)^2}{(\$8)^2} = 67.24 \approx 68 \text{ accounts}$$

> The auditor should take a random sample of 68 accounts from the population of 5,000 accounts receivable in order to have 90% confidence that the inference based on the sample results will be within $40,000 of the true (actual) value of accounts receivable. That is, if a population of 5,000 accounts actually has a standard deviation of $40, 90% of the possible samples of 68 accounts will yield estimates that are within $40,000 of the actual value of accounts receivable.

9. **Evaluate Sample Results** The auditor computes the actual sampling error (precision) and confidence level attained by the sample.

   a. Estimate the population value (multiply the sample mean by the population size).

   b. Compute the actual sampling error (i.e., precision) by solving the sample size formula for A.

   $$A = \frac{c \times s \times N}{\sqrt{n}}$$

   c. Compute the actual confidence level by solving the sample size formula for c.

   $$c = \frac{A \times \sqrt{n}}{s \times N}$$

Example 5 ▶ Computation of Sampling Error

The auditor selects a sample of 68 accounts as described in Example 4. The auditor would audit these accounts to determine the actual value of each account, then compute the average audited balance. Assume that the average audited balance is $95 per account. The estimated population value is $475,000 ($95 × 5,000 accounts). If the standard deviation of the sample is assumed to be $40, we can compute the actual sampling error (precision) as follows:

$$A = \frac{c \times s \times N}{\sqrt{n}} = \frac{(1.64)\ (\$40)\ (5,000)}{\sqrt{68}} = \$39,775 \approx \$40,000$$

And the confidence level coefficient as follows:

$$c = \frac{A \times \sqrt{n}}{s \times N} = \frac{\$40,000 \times \sqrt{68}}{(\$40)\ (5,000)} = 1.649 \approx 1.65$$

The auditor can rely on the results of the test, with 90% confidence, yielding an estimated value for accounts receivable that differs from the true value by no more than $40,000.

10. **Reach Overall Conclusion** The auditor should project the results of the sample to the population from which the sample was taken before evaluating the results of the sample. The client may adjust the book value of the account to correct the misstatements actually found in the sample and any misstatements discovered in any 100 percent-examined items. The total projected misstatement after the book value has been adjusted should be compared with the tolerable misstatement. If the auditor considers the projected misstatement unacceptable, the auditor should take appropriate action (for example, performing other substantive tests on the account). Note that the auditor also considers the qualitative aspects of misstatements (i.e., misstatements in amount vs. misapplication of accounting principle, or errors vs. fraud) in reaching an overall conclusion.

11. **Document Sampling Procedure** Documentation might include the following: (a) the objectives of the test and a description of other audit procedures related to those objectives; (b) the definition of the population and the sampling unit, including how the auditor considered completeness of the population; (c) the definition of a misstatement; (d) the rationale for the risk

of incorrect acceptance, the risk of incorrect rejection, the tolerable misstatement, and the expected population deviation amount used in the application; (e) the audit sampling technique used; (f) the method of sample selection; (g) a description of the performance of the sampling procedure and a listing of misstatements identified in the sample; and (h) the evaluation of the sample and a summary of the overall conclusion.

V. Probability-Proportional-to-Size Sampling

A. Distinguishing Features

Probability-proportional-to-size sampling (PPS) is a form of variables sampling that uses attribute sampling theory for substantive testing. The sampling unit is not an individual account or transaction, but an individual dollar in an account balance (or another logical unit). PPS sampling has two unique properties.

1. **Stratification** The audit population is stratified automatically by monetary value.

2. **Overstatements** Larger dollar amounts have a higher probability of being selected. Therefore, overstatements are more likely to be detected than understatements. Hence, PPS sampling is most appropriate when an auditor desires testing for material overstatements. PPS sampling is ineffective in searching for unrecorded items. (The probability of an item being selected is directly proportional to its recorded dollar value.)

Example 6 ▶ PPS Sampling

X Co.'s account receivable balance is $2,000,000	The population is 2,000,000
Customer Y has a balance of $120,000	The sampling unit is 1

Required: Figure the probability that Customer Y has of being selected.

Solution: Customer Y has a 6% chance of being selected (120,000 / 2,000,000 = 6%).

3. **Select Sample Items** Systematic sampling selection is used most often. Audit procedures then are employed to determine the value of each sample item.

4. **Sample Size** Sample sizes in low-error environments tend to be relatively small because their approach does not use standard deviations (which tend to be large in most credit environments) in determining sample size.

5. **Other Advantages** This method also reduces audit work because several dollars selected will appear in the same sample item (for example, a customer's account balance) and, therefore, the same audit procedures often determine the audited value of more than one sample item. Also, this approach does not require a high number of errors to be observed in the sample for the results to be statistically valid, as is the case with Difference Estimation and Ratio Estimation.

B. Disadvantages

An understatement is less likely to be discovered than an overstatement because those accounts with higher dollar values have a greater chance of being selected. Therefore, PPS sampling generally is considered inappropriate for liability accounts. Also, special consideration must be given to zero and negative balance accounts which usually are excluded from the PPS sample. A third disadvantage occurs when the population has a high expected misstatement rate; the auditor then must obtain sample sizes larger than those required by classical variables sampling.

C. Determining Sample Size

Requires that the auditor determine a reliability factor for overstatement errors, a tolerable rate, and an expected error rate.

1. **Reliability Factor for Overstatement Errors** Can be determined from tables after specifying the expected number of overstatement errors and the risk of incorrect acceptance. The

auditor controls the risk of incorrect acceptance by specifying the risk level for the sampling plan. As PPS sampling is most appropriate when no errors are expected, zero is the appropriate estimate for the number of overstatement errors. The risk of incorrect acceptance is a matter of professional judgment; with PPS sampling, it represents an auditor's risk that book value is not overstated materially when material monetary overstatements exist.

Table 3 ▶ Reliability Factors for Errors of Overstatement

Number of Over-statement Errors	Risk of Incorrect Acceptance								
	1%	5%	10%	15%	20%	25%	30%	37%	50%
0	4.61	3.00	2.31	1.90	1.61	1.39	1.21	1.00	.70
1	6.64	4.75	3.89	3.38	3.00	2.70	2.44	2.14	1.68
2	8.41	6.30	5.33	4.72	4.28	3.93	3.62	3.25	2.68
3	10.05	7.76	6.69	6.02	5.52	5.11	4.77	4.34	3.68
4	11.61	9.16	8.00	7.27	6.73	6.28	5.90	5.43	4.68
5	13.11	10.52	9.28	8.50	7.91	7.43	7.01	6.49	5.68
6	14.57	11.85	10.54	9.71	9.08	8.56	8.12	7.56	6.67
7	16.00	13.15	11.78	10.90	10.24	9.69	9.21	8.63	7.67
8	17.41	14.44	13.00	12.08	11.38	10.81	10.31	9.68	8.67
9	18.79	15.71	14.21	13.25	12.52	11.92	11.39	10.74	9.67
10	20.15	16.97	15.41	14.42	13.66	13.02	12.47	11.79	10.67
11	21.49	18.21	16.60	15.57	14.78	14.13	13.55	12.84	11.67
12	22.83	19.45	17.79	16.72	15.90	15.22	14.63	13.89	12.67
13	24.14	20.67	18.96	17.86	17.02	16.32	15.70	14.93	13.67
14	25.45	21.89	20.13	19.00	18.13	17.40	16.77	15.97	14.67
15	26.75	23.10	21.30	20.13	19.24	18.49	17.84	17.02	15.67
16	28.03	24.31	22.46	21.26	20.34	19.58	18.90	18.06	16.67
17	29.31	25.50	23.61	22.39	21.44	20.66	19.97	19.10	17.67
18	30.59	26.70	24.76	23.51	22.54	21.74	21.03	20.14	18.67
19	31.85	27.88	25.91	24.63	23.64	22.81	22.09	21.18	19.67
20	33.11	29.07	27.05	25.74	24.73	23.89	23.15	22.22	20.67

Example 7 ▶ Table 3 Use

The auditor's risk of incorrect acceptance for Co. X is 5% and the number of overstatement errors is 0. The reliability factor for errors of overstatement is 3.00.

2. **Tolerable Rate** The tolerable rate (or tolerable error) is the maximum monetary error that may exist in an account balance without causing the financial statements to be misstated materially. Thus, tolerable error in PPS sampling is related closely to the auditor's planned level of materiality. The sampling interval and the sample size can be determined using the formulas in Exhibit 7.

Exhibit 7 ▶ PPS Sampling Interval & Sample Size

$$n = \frac{c^2 \times s^2 \times N^2}{A^2} = \frac{c^2 \times s^2}{a^2}$$

$$Sampling\ Interval = \frac{Tolerable\ Misstatement}{Reliability\ Factor\ for\ the\ Error\ of\ Overstatement}$$

$$Sampling\ Size = \frac{Population}{Sampling\ Interval}$$

Example 8 ▶ Sampling Interval & Sample Size

Using the same assumptions as Example 7, the population is 2,000,000 and the tolerable misstatement is $60,000.

Required: Figure the sampling interval and the sample size.

Solution: The sampling interval is $20,000. (60,000 / 3.00 = 20,000)

The sample size is 100. (2,000,000 / 20,000 = 100)

3. **Expected Error Rate** If some errors are expected, the sample interval can be computed by determining the expected error rate. In cases where the expected error rate is not shown on the table, the auditor would use the sample size for the next higher percentage. If the tolerable rate percentage is not found it would be appropriate to select the sample size for the next smaller percentage shown. This follows the accounting convention of conservatism.

Exhibit 8 ▶ PPS Expected Error Rate

$$n = \frac{c^2 \times s^2 \times N^2}{A^2} = \frac{c^2 \times s^2}{a^2}$$

$$Expected\ Error\ Rate = \frac{Expected\ Misstatements}{Population}$$

Example 9 ▶ Sampling Interval & Sample Size

Using the same assumptions as Example 7, we determine that the expected misstatement for Co. X is $10,000 based on our prior experience with the client. The population is 2,000,000. Our expected error rate is .005 (10,000 / 2,000,000 = .005). The tolerable rate has been determined to be 3%. (This example is unrelated to Example 8.)

Required: Figure the sampling interval and the sample size.

Solution: Using Table 1, our sample size is 157.

The sampling interval is then computed by dividing the population by the sample size. (2,000,000 / 157 = 12,739)

D. **Evaluate Sample Results**
Misstatements from the sample should be projected to the population to calculate an allowance for sampling risk. This allowance for sampling risk is a calculation with an incremental allowance for projected errors (misstatements). If the sample contains less than 100 percent errors, the formula for determining the upper limit is as in Exhibit 9.

Exhibit 9 ▶ PPS Upper Limit for Misstatements

Upper limit for errors (misstatements)	=	Projected errors (misstatements)	+	Basic precision	+	Incremental allowance for projected errors (misstatements)

1. **Upper Limit for Misstatements** The upper limit on misstatement is calculated by adding the projected misstatement, the basic precision, and the incremental allowance for projected errors.

    a. Projected misstatements are calculated for each sample item depending on whether the recorded book value is less than or greater than the sampling interval. If less than, the difference between the recorded value and the audited value is divided by the recorded value to arrive at a percentage error known as tainting. The projected misstatement is the tainting percentage multiplied by the sampling interval.

b. Basic precision is calculated by multiplying the reliability factor by the sampling interval.

c. An incremental allowance for projected misstatement is calculated using only those errors in logical units less than the sampling interval. These are ranked from highest to lowest (in terms of tainting percentage), considering the incremental changes in reliability factors for the actual number of errors found.

2. Comparison Finishing the evaluation procedure involves comparing the upper limit on errors to the previously estimated tolerable error. If the upper limit on misstatements is less than the tolerable misstatement, such as above, it can be concluded that the total population is not misstated by an amount greater than the originally estimated tolerable misstatement, at the specified risk of incorrect acceptance.

a. If the upper limit on misstatements is greater than the tolerable misstatement, then the sample results do not support the conclusion that the population is not misstated by more than the tolerable misstatement. This may occur if the population was not represented by the sample, the sample was too small due to an excessively low expectation of misstatement, or if the population itself was misstated.

b. In cases where the recorded book value is greater than the sampling interval, the projected misstatement is equal to the actual error.

c. If no errors are found, both the projected errors and the incremental allowance for projected errors would be zero. Therefore, the auditor could conclude that the recorded amount of accounts is not overstated by more than the tolerable error estimated earlier because the only factor with a value other than zero would be the basic precision.

Example 10 ▶ Evaluating Sample Results

Audit procedures reveal four errors. The projected misstatement total is calculated first, followed by the other two components of the upper limits, precision, and the incremental allowance for projected misstatement.

a. Projected Misstatement:

(1)	(2)	(3)	(4)	(5)
Book value	Audited value	Tainting % (1) − (2) / (1)	Sampling interval	Projected error (3) × (4)
$ 500	$ 450	0.10	$12,739	$1,274
11,000	10,340	0.06	12,739	764
5,700	5,625	0.013	12,739	166
25,350	23,350	—	—	2,000
				$4,204

b. Basic precision: 3 × $12,739 = $38,217

c.   Incremental allowance:

(1) Projected error	(2) Reliability factor (from table)	(3) Incremental change in reliability factor (from table) (increment–1)	(4) Incremental allowance (3) × (1)
$1,274	4.75	0.75 [1]	$ 956
764	6.30	0.55 [2]	420
166	7.76	0.46 [3]	76
			$1,452

[1] 4.75 – 3.00 – 1.00 = 0.75   [2] 6.30 – 4.75 – 1.00 = 0.55   [3] 7.76 – 6.30 – 1.00 = 0.46

d.   Overall conclusion:

Projected misstatement	$ 4,204
Precision	38,217
Incremental allowance	1,452
Upper limit	$43,873

In this example, it can be concluded that the audited sample supports the conclusion that the population is not misstated by more than the tolerable misstatement.

VI. Appendix: Sampling Terms

allowance for sampling error (precision; sampling error) A measure of the closeness of a sample estimate to the corresponding population characteristic for a specified sampling risk.

alpha risk See risk of incorrect rejection and risk of assessing control risk too high.

attribute Any characteristic that is either present or absent. In tests of controls directed toward operating effectiveness, the presence or absence of evidence of the application of a specified internal control policy or procedure is sometimes referred to as an attribute.

attributes sampling A statistical procedure based on estimating whether the rate of occurrence of a particular attribute in a population exceeds a tolerable rate.

audit sampling The application of an audit procedure to less than 100 percent of the items within an account balance or class of transactions for the purpose of evaluating some characteristic of the balance or class.

beta risk See risk of incorrect acceptance and risk of assessing control risk too low.

block sample (cluster sample) A sample consisting of contiguous transactions.

classical variables sampling A sampling approach that measures sampling risk using the variation of the underlying characteristic of interest. This approach includes methods such as mean-per-unit, ratio estimation, and difference estimation.

confidence level (reliability level) The complement of the applicable sampling risk (see risk of incorrect acceptance, risk of assessing control risk too low, risk of incorrect rejection, and risk of assessing control risk too high). In practice, the confidence level is often set equal to the complement of the risk of incorrect rejection (i.e., to the complement of the alpha risk).

difference estimation A classical variables sampling technique that uses the total difference between audited values and individual book values to estimate the total dollar error in a population and an allowance for sampling error.

dollar-unit sampling See probability-proportional-to-size sampling.

expected population deviation rate An anticipation of the deviation rate in the entire population. It is used in determining an appropriate sample size for an attributes sample.

haphazard sample A sample consisting of sampling units selected by the auditor without any special reason for including or omitting particular items.

mean-per-unit method A classical variables sampling technique that uses the sample average to project the total population dollar value by multiplying the sample average by the number of items in the population.

nonsampling risk All aspects of audit risk not due to sampling.

nonstatistical sampling A sampling technique for which the auditor considers sampling risk in evaluating an audit sample without using statistical theory to measure that risk.

population (field; universe) The items comprising the account balance or class of transactions, or a portion of that balance or class of interest. The population excludes individually significant items of which the auditor has decided to examine 100 percent or other items that will be tested separately.

precision See allowance for sampling errors.

probability-proportional-to-size (PPS) sampling (Dollar-unit sampling; CMA sampling) A variables sampling procedure that uses attributes theory to express a projection of the error in a population in dollar amounts.

random sample A sample drawn so that every combination of the same number of items in the population has an equal probability of selection.

ratio estimation A classical variables sampling technique that uses the ratio of audited values to book values in the sample to estimate the total dollar value of the population and an allowance for sampling error.

reliability level See confidence level.

risk of assessing control risk too high The risk that the assessed level of control risk based on the sample is greater than the true operating effectiveness of the internal control policies or procedures.

risk of assessing control risk too low The risk that the assessed level of control risk based on the sample is less than the true operating effectiveness of the internal control policies or procedures.

risk of incorrect acceptance (beta risk; type II misstatement) The risk that the sample supports the conclusion that the recorded account balance is not materially misstated when it is, in fact, materially misstated.

risk of incorrect rejection (alpha risk; type I misstatement) The risk that the sample supports the conclusion that the recorded account balance is materially misstated when, in fact, it is not.

sample Items selected from a population to reach a conclusion about the population.

sampling risk The risk that the auditor's conclusion based on a sample may be different from the conclusion the auditor would reach if the test were applied in the same way to the entire population. For tests of controls, sampling risk is the risk of assessing control risk too high or too low. For substantive testing, sampling risk is the risk of incorrect acceptance or rejection.

sequential sampling A sampling plan for which the sample is selected in several steps, with each step conditional on the results of the previous steps.

standard deviation A measure of the dispersion among the respective values of a particular characteristic as measured for all items in the population for which a sample estimate is developed.

statistical sampling Audit sampling that uses the laws of probability for selecting and evaluating a sample from a population for the purpose of reaching a conclusion about the population.

stratification Division of the population into relatively homogeneous groups.

systematic sampling A method of drawing a sample in which every nth item is drawn from one or more random starts.

tolerable misstatement An estimate of the maximum monetary misstatement that may exist in an account balance or class of transactions when combined with misstatements that may be found in other tests without causing the financial statements to be materially misstated.

tolerable rate The maximum population rate of deviations from a prescribed control procedure that the auditor will tolerate without modifying the nature, timing, or extent of substantive testing.

variables sampling Statistical sampling that reaches a conclusion on the monetary amounts of a population.

CHAPTER 26—AUDIT SAMPLING

Problem 26-1 MULTIPLE CHOICE QUESTIONS (62 to 78 minutes)

1. Which of the following courses of action would an auditor most likely follow in planning a sample of cash disbursements if the auditor is aware of several unusually large cash disbursements?
a. Set the tolerable rate of deviation at a lower level than originally planned
b. Stratify the cash disbursements population so that the unusually large disbursements are selected
c. Increase the sample size to reduce the effect of the unusually large disbursements
d. Continue to draw new samples until all the unusually large disbursements appear in the sample
(11/94, AUD, #55, 5128)

2. In confirming a client's accounts receivable in prior years, an auditor found that there were many differences between the recorded account balances and the confirmation replies. These differences, which were not misstatements, required substantial time to resolve. In defining the sampling unit for the current year's audit, the auditor most likely would choose
a. Individual overdue balances
b. Individual invoices
c. Small account balances
d. Large account balances (5/95, AUD, #49, 5667)

3. An auditor is determining the sample size for an inventory observation using mean-per-unit estimation, which is a variables sampling plan. To calculate the required sample size, the auditor usually determines the

	Variability in the dollar amounts of inventory items	Risk of incorrect acceptance
a.	Yes	Yes
b.	Yes	No
c.	No	Yes
d.	No	No

(R/99, AUD, #20, 6836)

4. The risk of incorrect acceptance and the likelihood of assessing control risk too low relate to the
a. Allowable risk of tolerable misstatement
b. Preliminary estimates of materiality levels
c. Efficiency of the audit
d. Effectiveness of the audit
(11/95, AUD, #19, 5966)

5. An auditor may decide to increase the risk of incorrect rejection when
a. Increased reliability from the sample is desired.
b. Many differences (audit value minus recorded value) are expected.
c. Initial sample results do not support the planned level of control risk.
d. The cost and effort of selecting additional sample items is low. (11/92, AUD, #38, 2972)

6. The diagram below depicts an auditor's estimated maximum deviation rate compared with the tolerable rate, and also depicts the true population deviation rate compared with the tolerable rate.

Auditor's estimate based on sample results	True state of population	
	Deviation rate is less than tolerable rate	Deviation rate exceeds tolerable rate
Maximum deviation rate is less than tolerable rate	I.	III.
Maximum deviation rate exceeds tolerable rate	II.	IV.

As a result of tests of controls, the auditor assesses control risk too low and thereby decreases substantive testing. This is illustrated by situation
a. I
b. II
c. III
d. IV (11/95, AUD, #17, 5964)

7. As a result of tests of controls, an auditor assessed control risk too low and decreased substantive testing. This assessment occurred because the true deviation rate in the population was
a. Less than the risk of assessing control risk too low, based on the auditor's sample
b. Less than the deviation rate in the auditor's sample
c. More than the risk of assessing control risk too low, based on the auditor's sample
d. More than the deviation rate in the auditor's sample (5/95, AUD, #28, 5646)

8. An advantage of statistical sampling over non-statistical sampling is that statistical sampling helps an auditor to
a. Eliminate the risk of nonsampling errors
b. Reduce the level of audit risk and materiality to a relatively low amount
c. Measure the sufficiency of the audit evidence obtained
d. Minimize the failure to detect errors and fraud
(11/95, AUD, #44, amended, 5991)

9. In statistical sampling methods used in substantive testing, an auditor most likely would stratify a population into meaningful groups if
a. Probability proportional to size (PPS) sampling is used.
b. The population has highly variable recorded amounts.
c. The auditor's estimated tolerable misstatement is extremely small.
d. The standard deviation of recorded amounts is relatively small. (5/95, AUD, #50, 5668)

10. Using statistical sampling to assist in verifying the year-end accounts payable balance, an auditor has accumulated the following data:

	Number of accounts	Book balance	Balance determined by the auditor
Population	4,100	$5,000,000	?
Sample	200	$ 125,000	$150,000

Using the ratio estimation technique, the auditor's estimate of year-end accounts payable balance would be
a. $6,150,000
b. $6,000,000
c. $5,125,000
d. $5,050,000 (Editors, 7496)

11. The expected population deviation rate of client billing misstatements is 2%. The auditor has established a tolerable rate of 3%. In the review of client invoices the auditor should use
a. Stratified sampling
b. Discovery sampling
c. Variable sampling
d. Attribute sampling (Editors, 0266)

12. Which of the following sampling methods would be used to estimate a numerical measurement of a population, such as a dollar value?
a. Attributes sampling
b. Stop-or-go sampling
c. Variables sampling
d. Random-number sampling
(11/94, AUD, #54, 5127)

Items 13 and 14 are based on the following:

An auditor desired to test credit approval on 10,000 sales invoices processed during the year. The auditor designed a statistical sample that would provide 1% risk of assessing control risk too low (99% confidence) that not more than 7% of the sales invoices lacked approval. The auditor estimated from previous experience that about 2½% of the sales invoices lacked approval. A sample of 200 invoices was examined and 7 of them were lacking approval. The auditor then determined the achieved upper precision limit to be 8%.

13. In the evaluation of this sample, the auditor decided to increase the level of the preliminary assessment of control risk because the
a. Tolerable rate (7%) was less than the achieved upper precision limit (8%)
b. Expected deviation rate (7%) was more than the percentage of errors in the sample (3½%)
c. Expected deviation rate (2½%) was less than the tolerable rate (7%)
d. Achieved upper precision limit (8%) was more than the percentage of errors in the sample (3½%) (11/90, AUD, #59, amended, 0250)

14. The allowance for sampling risk was
a. 5½%
b. 4½%
c. 3½%
d. 1% (11/90, AUD, #60, 0251)

15. What is an auditor's evaluation of a statistical sample for attributes when a test of 50 documents results in 3 deviations if tolerable rate is 7%, the expected population deviation rate is 5%, and the allowance for sampling risk is 2%?
a. Modify the planned assessed level of control risk because the tolerable rate plus the allowance for sampling risk exceeds the expected population deviation rate
b. Accept the sample results as support for the planned assessed level of control risk because the sample deviation rate plus the allowance for sampling risk exceeds the tolerable rate
c. Accept the sample results as support for the planned assessed level of control risk because the tolerable rate less the allowance for sampling risk equals the expected population deviation rate
d. Modify the planned assessed level of control risk because the sample deviation rate plus the allowance for sampling risk exceeds the tolerable rate
(5/92, AUD, #54, 2807)

16. An auditor who uses statistical sampling for attributes in testing internal controls should reduce the planned reliance on a prescribed control when the
a. Sample rate of deviation plus the allowance for sampling risk equals the tolerable rate.
b. Sample rate of deviation is less than the expected rate of deviation used in planning the sample.
c. Tolerable rate less the allowance for sampling risk exceeds the sample rate of deviation.
d. Sample rate of deviation plus the allowance for sampling risk exceeds the tolerable rate.
(11/95, AUD, #25, 5972)

17. Which of the following statements is correct about the sample size in statistical sampling when testing internal controls?
a. The auditor should consider the tolerable rate of deviation from the controls being tested in determining sample size.
b. As the likely rate of deviation decreases, the auditor should increase the planned sample size.
c. The allowable risk of assessing control risk too low has **no** effect on the planned sample size.
d. Of all the factors to be considered, the population size has the greatest effect on the sample size. (R/06, AUD, #16, 8134)

18. Which of the following statements is correct concerning statistical sampling in tests of controls?
a. As the population size increases, the sample size should increase proportionately.
b. Deviations from specific internal control procedures at a given rate ordinarily result in misstatements at a lower rate.
c. There is an inverse relationship between the expected population deviation rate and the sample size.
d. In determining tolerable rate, an auditor considers detection risk and the sample size.
(11/94, AUD, #27, 5100)

19. An auditor established a $60,000 tolerable misstatement for an asset with an account balance of $1,000,000. The auditor selected a sample of every twentieth item from the population that represented the asset account balance and discovered overstatements of $3,700 and understatements of $200. Under these circumstances, the auditor most likely would conclude that
a. There is an unacceptably high risk that the actual misstatements in the population exceed the tolerable misstatement because the total projected misstatement is more than the tolerable misstatement.
b. There is an unacceptably high risk that the tolerable misstatement exceeds the sum of actual overstatements and understatements.
c. The asset account is fairly stated because the total projected misstatement is less than the tolerable misstatement.
d. The asset account is fairly stated because the tolerable misstatement exceeds the net of projected actual overstatements and understatements. (R/00, AUD, #13, 6938)

20. The likelihood of assessing control risk too high is the risk that the sample selected to test controls
a. Does not support the auditor's planned assessed level of control risk when the true operating effectiveness of internal control justifies such an assessment
b. Contains misstatements that could be material to the financial statements when aggregated with misstatements in other account balances or transactions classes
c. Contains proportionately fewer monetary errors or deviations from prescribed internal control structure policies or procedures than exist in the balance or class as a whole
d. Does not support the tolerable error for some or all of management's assertions
(11/94, AUD, #33, amended, 5106)

21. For which of the following audit tests would an auditor most likely use attribute sampling?
a. Selecting accounts receivable for confirmation of account balances
b. Inspecting employee time cards for proper approval by supervisors
c. Making an independent estimate of the amount of a LIFO inventory
d. Examining invoices in support of the valuation of fixed asset additions (5/96, AUD, #4, 6236)

22. An auditor is selecting vouchers for testing an entity's internal control activities related to the proper approval of vouchers before checks are prepared. The auditor is matching random numbers with voucher numbers to determine which vouchers to inspect. If a random number matches a voided voucher, that voucher ordinarily would be replaced by another voucher in the random sample if the voided voucher
a. Cannot be located in the voucher file
b. Represents a dollar amount that is material
c. Indicates a deviation from the prescribed activity
d. Has been properly voided

(R/03, AUD, #14, 7636)

23. Samples to test internal control procedures are intended to provide a basis for an auditor to conclude whether
a. The control procedures are operating effectively.
b. The financial statements are materially misstated.
c. The risk of incorrect acceptance is too high.
d. Materiality for planning purposes is at a sufficiently low level.

(5/91, AUD, #40, amended, 0246)

24. An auditor should consider the tolerable rate of deviation when determining the number of check requests to select for a test to obtain assurance that all check requests have been properly authorized. The auditor should also consider

	The average dollar value of the check requests	The allowable risk of assessing control risk too low
a.	Yes	Yes
b.	Yes	No
c.	No	Yes
d.	No	No

(R/99, AUD, #17, 6833)

25. Which of the following most likely would be an advantage in using classical variables sampling rather than probability-proportional-to-size (PPS) sampling?
a. An estimate of the standard deviation of the population's recorded amounts is not required.
b. The auditor rarely needs the assistance of a computer program to design an efficient sample.
c. Inclusion of zero and negative balances generally does not require special design considerations.
d. Any amount that is individually significant is automatically identified and selected.

(5/93, AUD, #43, 3939)

26. When using classical variables sampling for estimation, an auditor normally evaluates the sampling results by calculating the possible error in either direction. This statistical concept is known as
a. Precision
b. Reliability
c. Projected error
d. Standard deviation

(5/91, AUD, #18, 0244)

27. The use of the ratio estimation sampling technique is most effective when
a. The calculated audit amounts are approximately proportional to the client's book amounts
b. A relatively small number of differences exist in the population
c. Estimating populations whose records consist of quantities, but not book values
d. Large overstatement differences and large understatement differences exist in the population

(5/95, AUD, #51, 5669)

28. When planning a sample for a substantive test of details, an auditor should consider tolerable misstatement for the sample. This consideration should
a. Be related to the auditor's business risk
b. Not be adjusted for qualitative factors
c. Be related to the auditor's determination of materiality
d. Not be changed during the audit process

(5/90, AUD, #51, amended, 0255)

29. In a probability-proportional-to-size sample with a sampling interval of $10,000, an auditor discovered that a selected account receivable with a recorded amount of $5,000 had an audited amount of $4,000. If this were the only misstatement discovered by the auditor, the projected misstatement of this sample would be
a. $ 1,000
b. $ 2,000
c. $ 5,000
d. $10,000

(R/00, AUD, #10, 6935)

30. Hill has decided to use probability-proportional-to-size (PPS) sampling, sometimes called dollar-unit sampling, in the audit of a client's accounts receivable balances. Hill plans to use the following PPS sampling table:

TABLE
Reliability Factors for Errors of Overstatement

Number of overstatement misstatements	Risk of incorrect acceptance				
	1%	5%	10%	15%	20%
0	4.61	3.00	2.31	1.90	1.61
1	6.64	4.75	3.89	3.38	3.00
2	8.41	6.30	5.33	4.72	4.28
3	10.05	7.76	6.69	6.02	5.52
4	11.61	9.16	8.00	7.27	6.73

Additional Information:

Tolerable misstatement (net of effect of expected misstatement)	$ 48,000
Risk of incorrect acceptance	20%
Number of misstatements allowed	1
Recorded amount of accounts receivable	$480,000
Number of accounts	360

What sample size should Hill use?
a. 120
b. 108
c. 60
d. 30 (Editors, 7497)

31. Which of the following statements is correct concerning probability-proportional-to-size (PPS) sampling, also known as dollar-unit sampling?
a. The sampling distribution should approximate the normal distribution.
b. Overstated units have a lower probability of sample selection than units that are understated.
c. The auditor controls the risk of incorrect acceptance by specifying that risk level for the sampling plan.
d. The sampling interval is calculated by dividing the number of physical units in the population by the sample size. (5/91, AUD, #17, 0243)

Problem 26-2 ADDITIONAL MULTIPLE CHOICE QUESTIONS (24 to 30 minutes)

32. Given random selection, the same sample size, and the same precision requirement for the testing of two unequal populations, the risk of assessing control risk too low on the smaller population is
a. Higher than assessing control risk too low for the larger population
b. Indeterminate relative to assessing control risk too low for the larger population
c. Lower than assessing control risk too low for the larger population
d. The same as assessing control risk too low for the larger population (Editors, 7498)

33. An auditor may use a systematic sampling technique with a start at any randomly selected item when performing a test of controls with respect to control over cash receipts. The biggest disadvantage of this type of sampling is that the items in the population
a. Must be systematically replaced in the population after sampling
b. May occur in a systematic pattern, thus destroying the sample randomness
c. Must be recorded in a systematic pattern before the sample can be drawn
d. May systematically occur more than once in the sample (Editors, 0267)

34. While performing a test of details during an audit, an auditor determined that the sample results supported the conclusion that the recorded account balance was materially misstated. It was, in fact, not materially misstated. This situation illustrates the risk of
a. Assessing control risk too high
b. Assessing control risk too low
c. Incorrect rejection
d. Incorrect acceptance   (5/94, AUD, #43, 4708)

35. As a result of tests of controls, an auditor assesses control risk too high. This incorrect assessment most likely occurred because
a. Control risk based on the auditor's sample is less than the true operating effectiveness of the client's control activity.
b. The auditor believes that the control activity relates to the client's assertions when, in fact, it does not.
c. The auditor believes that the control activity will reduce the extent of substantive testing when, in fact, it will not.
d. Control risk based on the auditor's sample is greater than the true operating effectiveness of the client's control activity.
(R/07, AUD, #21, 8393)

36. Which of the following statements is correct concerning the auditor's use of statistical sampling?
a. An auditor needs to estimate the dollar amount of the standard deviation of the population to use classical variables sampling.
b. The selection of zero balances usually does not require special sample design considerations when using PPS sampling.
c. A classical variables sample needs to be designed with special considerations to include negative balances in the sample.
d. An assumption of PPS sampling is that the underlying accounting population is normally distributed.   (Editors, 0265)

37. A principal advantage of statistical methods of attribute sampling over nonstatistical methods is that they provide a scientific basis for planning the
a. Risk of assessing control risk too low
b. Expected population deviation rate
c. Tolerable rate
d. Sample size   (Editors, 0260)

38. Which of the following factors is (are) considered in determining the sample size for a test of controls?

	Expected deviation rate	Tolerable deviation rate
a.	Yes	Yes
b.	No	No
c.	No	Yes
d.	Yes	No

(11/95, AUD, #33, 5980)

39. In determining the number of documents to select for a test to obtain assurance that all sales returns have been properly authorized, an auditor should consider the tolerable rate of deviation from the control activity. The auditor should also consider

I. The likely rate of deviations
II. The allowable risk of assessing control risk too high

a. I only
b. II only
c. Both I and II
d. Either I or II   (11/97, AUD, #16, amended, 6579)

40. In performing tests of controls over authorization of cash disbursements, which of the following statistical sampling methods would be most appropriate?
a. Variables
b. Stratified
c. Ratio
d. Attributes   (5/93, AUD, #25, 3921)

41. For which of the following audit tests would a CPA most likely use attribute sampling?
a. Identifying entries posted to incorrect accounts
b. Estimating the amount in an expense account
c. Evaluating the reasonableness of depreciation expense
d. Selecting receivables for confirmation of account balances   (R/07, AUD, #34, 8406)

42. An auditor examining inventory most likely would use variables sampling rather than attributes sampling to
a. Identify whether inventory items are properly priced
b. Estimate whether the dollar amount of inventory is reasonable
c. Discover whether misstatements exist in inventory records
d. Determine whether discounts for inventory are properly recorded
(R/05, AUD, 0380A, #21, 7816)

43. Which of the following characteristics most likely would be an advantage of using classical variables sampling rather than probability-proportional-to-size (PPS) sampling?

a. The selection of negative balances requires **no** special design considerations.

b. The sampling process can begin before the complete population is available.

c. The auditor need **not** consider the preliminary judgments about materiality.

d. The sample will result in a smaller sample size if few errors are expected. (R/07, AUD, #32, 8404)

SIMULATIONS

Problem 26-3 (15 to 25 minutes)

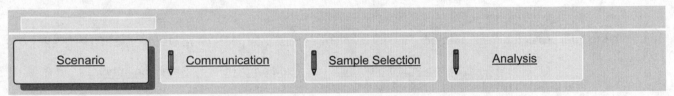

Edwards has decided to use probability-proportional-to-size (PPS) sampling, sometimes called dollar-unit sampling, in the audit of a client's accounts receivable balance. Few, if any, misstatements of account balance overstatement are expected. Edwards plans to use the following PPS sampling table.

TABLE
Reliability Factors for Errors of Overstatement

Number of overstatements misstatements	Risk of incorrect acceptance				
	1%	5%	10%	15%	20%
0	4.61	3.00	2.31	1.90	1.61
1	6.64	4.75	3.89	3.38	3.00
2	8.41	6.30	5.33	4.72	4.28
3	10.05	7.76	6.69	6.02	5.52
4	11.61	9.16	8.00	7.27	6.73

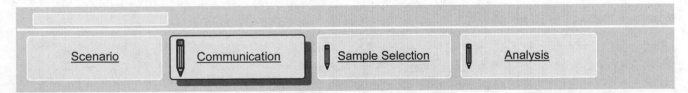

Identify the advantages of using PPS sampling over classical variables sampling.

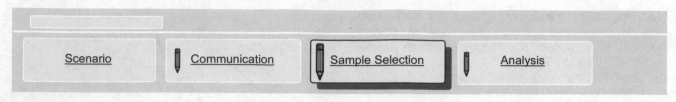

Calculate the sampling interval and the sample size Edwards should use given the following information:

Tolerable misstatement	$ 15,000
Risk of incorrect acceptance	5%
Number of misstatements allowed	0
Recorded amount of accounts receivable	$300,000

Calculate the total projected misstatement if the following three misstatements were discovered in a PPS sample:

	Recorded amount	Audit amount	Sampling interval
1st misstatement	$ 400	$ 320	$1,000
2nd misstatement	500	0	1,000
3rd misstatement	3,000	2,000	1,000

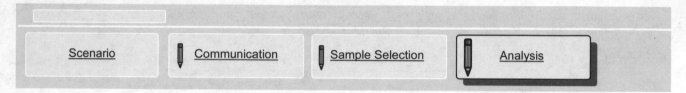

What authoritative reference provides guidance to an auditor on choosing between statistical and non-statistical sampling?

Paragraph Reference Answer: _____

(5/87, AUD, #3, amended, 9030)

Problem 26-4 (15 to 25 minutes)

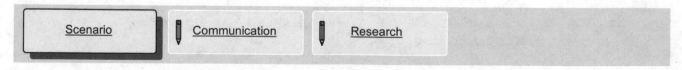

Baker, CPA, was engaged to audit Mill Company's financial statements. After obtaining an understanding of Mill's internal control structure, Baker decided to obtain audit evidence about the effectiveness of both the design and operation of the policies and procedures that may support a low assessed level of control risk concerning Mill's shipping and billing functions. During the prior years' audits Baker used nonstatistical sampling but for the current year Baker used a statistical sample in the tests of controls to eliminate the need for judgment.

Baker wanted to assess control risk at a low level, so a tolerable rate of deviation or acceptable upper precision limit (UPL) of 20% was established. To estimate the population deviation rate and the achieved UPL, Baker decided to apply a discovery sampling technique of attribute sampling that would use a population expected error rate of 3% for the 8,000 shipping documents, and decided to defer consideration of allowable risk of assessing control risk too low (risk of overreliance) until evaluating the sample results. Baker used the tolerable rate, the population size, and the expected population error rate to determine that a sample size of 80 would be sufficient. When it was subsequently determined that the actual population was about 10,000 shipping documents, Baker increased the sample size to 100.

Baker's objective was to ascertain whether Mill's shipments had been properly billed. Baker took a sample of 100 invoices by selecting the first 25 invoices from the first month of each quarter. Baker then compared the invoices to the corresponding prenumbered shipping documents.

When Baker tested the sample, eight errors were discovered. Additionally, one shipment that should have been billed at $10,443 was actually billed at $10,434. Baker considered this $9 to be immaterial and did not count it as an error.

In evaluating the sample results Baker made the initial determination that a reliability level of 95% (risk of assessing control risk too low 5%) was desired and, using the appropriate statistical sampling table, determined that for eight observed deviations from a sample size of 100, the achieved UPL was 14%. Baker then calculated the allowance for sampling risk to be 5%, the difference between the actual sample deviation rate (8%) and the expected error rate (3%). Baker reasoned that the actual sample deviation rate (8%) plus the allowance for sampling risk (5%) was less than the achieved UPL (14%); therefore, the sample supported a low level of control risk.

Describe each incorrect assumption, statement, and inappropriate application of attribute sampling in Baker's procedures.

What authoritative reference illustrates reference to sampling in an auditor's standard report on an audit of historical financial statements?

Paragraph Reference Answer: _____

(11/91, AUD, #5, amended, 3041)

Problem 26-5 (15 to 25 minutes)

Sampling for attributes is often used to allow an auditor to reach a conclusion concerning a rate of occurrence in a population. A common use in auditing is to test the rate of deviation from a prescribed internal control policy or procedure to determine whether planned assessed level of control risk is appropriate.

a. When an auditor samples for attributes, identify the factors that should influence the auditor's judgment concerning the determination of

1. Acceptable level of risk of assessing control risk too low,
2. Tolerable deviation rate, and
3. Expected population deviation rate.

b. State the effect on sample size of an increase in each of the following factors, assuming all other factors are held constant:

1. Acceptable level of risk of assessing control risk too low,
2. Tolerable deviation rate, and
3. Expected population deviation rate.

c. Evaluate the sample results of a test for attributes if authorizations are found to be missing on 7 check requests out of a sample of 100 tested. The population consists of 2,500 check requests, the tolerable deviation rate is 8%, and the acceptable level of risk of assessing control risk too low is low.

d. How may the use of statistical sampling assist the auditor in evaluating the sample results described in c., above?

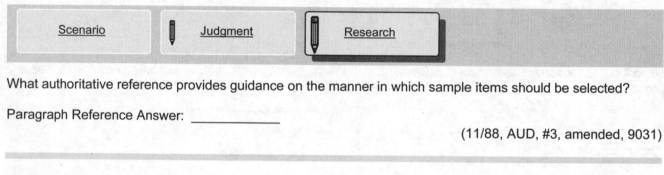

What authoritative reference provides guidance on the manner in which sample items should be selected?

Paragraph Reference Answer: _____

(11/88, AUD, #3, amended, 9031)

Problem 26-6 (15 to 25 minutes)

Smith, CPA, has decided to assess control risk at below the maximum level for an audit client's internal controls affecting receivables. Smith plans to use sampling to obtain substantive evidence concerning the reasonableness of the client's accounts receivable balances. Smith has identified the first few steps in an outline of the sampling plan as follows:

1. Determine the audit objectives of the test.
2. Define the population.
3. Define the sampling unit.
4. Consider the completeness of the population.
5. Identify individually significant items.

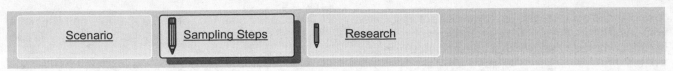

Identify the remaining steps which Smith should include in the outline of the sampling plan. Illustrations and examples need not be provided.

What authoritative reference provides guidance when an auditor chooses to design a sample that will be used for both testing the operating effectiveness of an identified control and testing whether the recorded monetary amount of transactions is correct?

Paragraph Reference Answer: _____

(5/86, AUD, #5, amended 9032)

Solution 26-1 MULTIPLE CHOICE ANSWERS

Audit Sampling

1. (b) In planning a sample of cash disbursements, if the auditor is aware of several unusually large cash disbursements, the auditor will most likely stratify the sample to include the unusually large disbursements. By stratifying the sample, the auditor will decrease the effect of the variances in the total population, and, therefore, be able to reduce the number of items in the sample. (5128)

2. (b) It is easiest to reconcile differences and for customers to research the auditor's questions on an individual invoice level. The designation of a sampling unit depends on the type of applied auditing procedures. The auditor considers which sampling unit leads to the most efficient and effective application, given the circumstances. In the case of a high number of expected differences in amounts for accounts receivable confirmations, if the auditor selects the customer balance as a sampling unit, the auditor may need to test each individual transaction supporting that balance in the event of a contradictory report from the customer. (5667)

3. (a) With the mean-per-unit method, stratification of a highly variable population into segments allows an auditor to use a smaller sample size. Thus, variability in the dollar amounts of inventory items is considered. The risk of incorrect assessment has an inverse relationship with sample size. (6836)

4. (d) The risk of incorrect acceptance and the risk of assessing control risk too low relate to the effectiveness of an audit in detecting an existing material misstatement. If the auditor incorrectly accepts an account as being materially accurate or incorrectly concludes that control risk is below the maximum, additional procedures that may detect this incorrect conclusion are either eliminated or reduced and the audit would prove ineffective in detecting misstatements. Answers (a) and (b) are incorrect because of an inappropriate combination of terms. In (a), risk should relate to exceeding tolerable misstatement levels. In (b), materiality is judged, not estimated, and related to tolerable misstatement. Audit efficiency is related to the risk of incorrect rejection or the risk of assessing control risk as too high. (5966)

5. (d) The risk of incorrect rejection is the risk that the auditor will conclude that an account balance is materially misstated when, in fact, it is not. When this error occurs, the auditor will generally extend her/his audit procedures and would eventually discover that the original conclusion of a material misstatement was incorrect. The cost of this mistake is the cost of the additional procedures that were necessary to discover that the original conclusion was erroneous. If, however, the cost and effort of those additional procedures is low, the auditor may well decide to use a high risk of incorrect rejection because doing so will reduce original sample size. If the desired results are achieved with the original small sample, overall audit cost will be lowered. If an incorrect rejection occurs, however, the incremental cost incurred would not be excessive. An increase in the desired reliability would likely result in a decrease (not increase) in the risk of incorrect rejection. The number of differences expected should have no bearing on the risk of incorrect rejection specified. The

"risk of incorrect rejection" is not a concept associated with tests of controls. "Risk of underreliance" would be the corresponding risk that is associated with control testing. (2972)

6. (c) When the auditor's estimate based on the sample results indicates that the maximum deviation rate is less than the tolerable rate and the true state of the population shows that the deviation rate exceeds the tolerable rate, the auditor assesses control risk too low and does not plan sufficient substantive testing. Answer (b) is an example of the auditor assessing control risk higher than necessary and, thereby increasing substantive testing. Answer (a) and (d) represent correct audit decisions regarding controls and planned substantive evidence. (5964)

7. (d) If the sample deviation rate is lower than the true deviation rate in the population, the auditor mistakenly assesses control risk too low. The result is that detection risk is allowed to rise too high and substantive testing is decreased. (5646)

Statistical Sampling

8. (c) Both statistical and nonstatistical sampling plans can provide sufficient audit evidence if properly applied. The distinguishing feature of statistical sampling methods as opposed to nonstatistical methods is that the user is able to provide a mathematical measurement of the degree of uncertainty that results from examining only part of a population. Statistical sampling, as well as nonstatistical sampling, is subject to nonsampling errors (procedural mistakes or human error). Both methods of sampling may be used to reduce audit risk, but neither would affect the level of materiality. Both can be used to reduce the risk of failing to detect errors and fraud, which is the risk of incorrect acceptance. (5991)

9. (b) Stratified sampling can be particularly useful in reducing the overall sample size on populations that have a wide range of dollar values (or highly variable recorded amounts). The primary objective is to decrease the effect of variance in the total population, thereby reducing sample size. PPS sampling insures items with large amounts all make it into the sample, but not by stratifying the population. The estimated tolerable misstatement and standard deviation are irrelevant to a decision to stratify. (5668)

10. (b) Under the ratio estimation technique, the auditor uses sample results to estimate the ratio of audited value to book value. The ratio is then applied to the population book value to estimate the audited value of the population. The sample "audited value/book value" ratio equals 1.2:1 ($150,000 ÷ $125,000). When this ratio is applied to the popula-

tion book balance of $5,000,000, an estimated $6,000,000 audited value results. (7496)

11. (d) Attribute sampling provides evidence of the rate of occurrence of a specified characteristic in a population at auditor-specified levels of precision and reliability. Variable sampling is used by the auditor to estimate the total dollar amount of a population at auditor-specified levels of precision and reliability. Discovery sampling is a form of attribute sampling that is designed to locate at least one exception if the rate of occurrence in the population is at or above a specified rate. This method is used to search for critical occurrences that may indicate the existence of an irregularity, and is appropriate when the expected occurrence rate is quite low (usually near zero) and the auditor wants a sample that will provide a specified chance to observe one occurrence. Answer (a) is incorrect, as the population is not divided into groups according to a common characteristic. (0266)

12. (c) Substantive tests of details are performed by the auditor to either detect misstatements or obtain evidence about the validity and propriety of the accounting treatment of transactions and balances. In substantive testing, the auditor is primarily interested in dollar amounts, and the traditional method of performing substantive tests is by variables sampling. (5127)

13. (a) The auditor would increase the preliminary assessment of control risk because the achieved upper precision limit of 8% (sample error rate plus an allowance for sampling risk) exceeded the tolerable error rate of 7% (determined by professional judgment). Therefore, the results of the test did not allow the auditor to conclude with 99% confidence that the error rate in the population did not exceed 7%. All other answers describe comparisons that are meaningless. (0250)

14. (b) The allowance for sampling risk is the difference between the observed sample rate and the achieved upper precision limit. The observed sample rate was 3.5% (7/200). Therefore, the allowance for sampling risk would be 4.5% (8% – 3.5%). (0251)

15. (d) The auditor should modify her/his planned assessed level of control risk when the sample deviation rate plus the allowance for sampling risk exceeds the tolerable rate. In this question, the deviation rate of 6% (3 deviations among 50 documents) plus the allowance for sampling risk of 2% is greater than the given tolerable rate of 7%. (2807)

16. (d) When the sample rate of deviation plus the allowance for sampling risk, which is the upper deviation limit, exceeds the tolerable rate, the sample results do not support the assessed level of control

risk and the auditor should reduce the planned reliance on a prescribed control. Answers (a), (b), and (c) represent results that support planned reliance. (5972)

17. (a) An increase in the tolerable rate of deviation would allow a reduction in sample size. As the likely deviation rate decreases, the auditor may **decrease** the planned sample size. The allowable risk of assessing control risk too low has an inverse effect on the sample size. Of all the factors to be considered, the population size has the **least** effect on the sample size. (8134)

Attributes Sampling

18. (b) Deviations from pertinent control procedures at a given rate ordinarily would be expected to result in misstatements at a lower rate. The sufficiency of audit sample sizes is determined by factors such as the assessments of control risk, inherent risk, and risk for other substantive tests related to a given assertion. Population size is not a determining factor. The relationship between the expected population deviation rate and sample size is direct, not inverse. In determining tolerable rate, an auditor should consider control risk and the degree of assurance desired by the audit evidence. (5100)

19. (a) The net of projected actual misstatements [($3,700 − $200) × 20 =] is $70,000, which is larger than the tolerable misstatement of $60,000. If the tolerable misstatement exceeds the sum of actual overstatements and understatements, the auditor may consider the account fairly stated. (6938)

20. (a) The risk of assessing control risk *too high* is the risk that the assessed level of control risk based on the sample is greater than the true operating effectiveness of the control structure policy or procedure. Answer (b) is incorrect because fewer errors or deviations would be discovered; therefore, the auditor would not identify those misstatements. Answer (c) is incorrect because the true operating effectiveness of internal control would not support such an assessment; the auditor would find fewer errors or deviations. Answer (d) is incorrect because the sample would support the tolerable error for misstatements because the sample would reveal fewer errors or deviations than exist in the balance or class of transactions. (5106)

21. (b) In performing tests of controls, the auditor is frequently interested in determining the rate of deviation from prescribed internal control policies and procedures. The sampling plan generally used in this situation is attribute sampling. (6236)

22. (d) In an auditor's test of transactions, if a random number matches the number of a voided voucher, that voucher ordinarily should be replaced by another voucher in the random sample if the voucher has been properly voided. The voucher would be counted as an error and would not be replaced if it could not be located or constituted a deviation. The materiality of the dollar amount is irrelevant because the focus in a test of controls is whether or not procedures are properly performed, not the dollar value of the transaction being tested. (7636)

23. (a) Rather than using the sample to estimate an unknown, the auditor's objective is generally to corroborate the accuracy of certain client data, such as data about account balances or classes of transactions, or to evaluate the internal accounting controls over the processing of data. Thus, the auditor is concerned with whether the control procedures are operating effectively. Answers (b) and (c) relate to substantive tests rather than to tests of controls. Materiality is based on the auditor's judgment, not on sampling procedures. (0246)

24. (c) Check authorization is an internal control. In tests of internal controls, the auditor is determining the rate of occurrence of a deviation from the control procedure, not testing the dollar amounts reported in the financial statements. The allowable risk of assessing control risk too low affects the degree of assurance desired by the auditor. If a high degree of assurance is sought, sampling risk must be low. Sample size and risk are inversely related. (6833)

Variables Sampling

25. (c) A disadvantage of PPS sampling to classical variables sampling is that special consideration must be given to zero and negative balance accounts because they are usually excluded from the PPS sample. Answers (a), (b), and (d) are advantages of PPS sampling. (3939)

26. (a) In classical variables sampling for estimation, precision represents the range within which the sample result is expected to be accurate. Hence, it provides a calculation of the maximum acceptable error in either direction. Reliability varies inversely with the assessed level of control risk and is a measure of the probability the sample result will fall within the precision range as mentioned above. Projected error is the anticipated deviation rate, based on the sample, in the entire population. The standard deviation is a measure of the dispersion among the relative values of a particular characteristic. (0244)

27. (a) The use of the ratio estimation sampling technique is most effective when the calculated audit amounts are approximately proportional to the client's book amounts. The auditor uses sample results to estimate the ratio of audited value to book value, which is then applied to the population to estimate the actual value. Ratio estimation should be used when each population item *has a book value,* an audited value may be ascertained for each sample item, and *differences occur frequently.* Large overstatement or understatement differences would reduce the effectiveness of this technique. (5669)

28. (c) Tolerable misstatement is a planning concept and is related to the auditor's determination of materiality for planning the financial statement audit in such a way that tolerable misstatement, combined for all of the tests in the entire audit, does not exceed materiality for the financial statements. Materiality judgments (tolerable misstatements) are not affected by the auditor's business risk. Judgments about materiality (tolerable misstatements) are subjective and do involve consideration of qualitative as well as quantitative factors and ordinarily will change during the process of conducting an audit as the auditor develops new evidence. (0255)

PPS Sampling

29. (b) Book value less audit value divided by book value is the tainting percentage (($5,000 − $4,000) / $5,000 = 0.2). The tainting percentage times the sampling interval is the projected error ($0.2 \times \$10,000 = \$2,000$). The sum of all the projected errors is the projected misstatement; there was only one error in this sample. (6935)

30. (d) This is one of several approaches that can be used to determine sample size when errors are expected, but it is the only approach possible with the information given. (7497)

$$\text{Sampling Interval} = \frac{\text{Tolerable Misstatement}}{\text{Reliability Factor for Misstatement of Overstatement}}$$

$$= \frac{\$48,000}{3.00} = \$16,000$$

$$\text{Sample Size} = \frac{\text{Recorded Amount}}{\text{Sample Interval}}$$

$$= \frac{\$480,000}{\$16,000} = 30$$

31. (c) In PPS sampling, the auditor achieves control over the risk of incorrect acceptance by specifying the level of risk the auditor is willing to assume. PPS sampling does not require direct consideration of the standard deviation of dollar amounts to determine the appropriate sample. The book value of the unit determines how probable it is that it will be included in the sample, not whether it is over or understated. The sampling interval is calculated by dividing the book value of the population by the sample size. (0243)

Solution 26-2 ADDITIONAL MULTIPLE CHOICE ANSWERS

Audit Sampling

32. (c) The risk of assessing control risk too low is the risk that the assessed level of control risk based on the sample is less than the true operating effectiveness of the control. All things being equal, a sample taken from a smaller population will be more representative of the population than a sample of the same size taken from a larger population. Thus, the risk that the sample taken from the smaller population will yield a result different from the result obtained had the entire population been examined, is *lower* than such a risk inherent in sampling from a larger population. (7498)

33. (b) When using the systematic sampling technique, the auditor determines a uniform interval by dividing the number of physical units in the population by the sample size. A random number is selected as a starting point for the first interval, and one item is selected throughout the population at each of the uniform intervals from the starting point. The randomness of the sample can be destroyed if the items in the population occur in a systematic pattern. For example, a population of employees on a payroll for a construction company might be organized by teams; each team consists of a crew leader and nine other workers. A selection of every tenth employee will list either every crew leader or no crew leaders, depending on the random start. No combination would include both crew leaders and other employees. (0267)

34. (c) The risk of incorrect rejection is the risk that the sample supports the conclusion that the recorded account balance is materially misstated when it is not materially misstated. The risk of assessing control risk too high is the risk that the assessed level of control risk based on the sample is greater than the true operating effectiveness of the control. The risk of assessing control risk too low is just the opposite. The risk of incorrect acceptance is the risk that the sample supports the conclusion that

the recorded account balance is not materially misstated when it is materially misstated. (4708)

35. (d) The risk of assessing control risk too high is the risk that the assessed level of control risk based on the sample is greater than the true operating effectiveness of the control. If a control activity is unrelated to the client's assertions, the assessment could have been either too low or too high. The auditor's decisions reduce the extent of substantive testing, not the control activity itself. (8393)

Statistical Sampling

36. (a) The factors affecting sample size when using classical variables sampling are (1) desired precision, (2) desired sample reliability, (3) variability among item values in the population (the estimate of the population's standard deviation) and (4) population size. PPS is a non-parametric method that does not assume a normal distribution. PPS plans require special design to deal with negative balances and zero balances because sample selection is based on the *cumulative sum* of dollars of the population. Negative figures distort the cumulative sum and zero balances would not be considered without special adjustments in a PPS plan. Classical variables techniques are unaffected by either zero balances or negative balances. (0265)

37. (d) The principal advantage of statistical over nonstatistical sampling methods is that statistical methods provide a model for determining sample size while explicitly recognizing relevant factors (e.g. risk of assessing control risk too low, tolerable rate, and expected deviation rate). In nonstatistical sampling, the auditor implicitly recognizes the relevant factors while determining the sample size based on his or her own judgment and experience. 0260)

Attributes Sampling

38. (a) Both the expected (likely) deviation rate and the tolerable deviation rate are considerations in determining the sample size for a test of controls. (5980)

39. (a) When determining sample size, the auditor gives consideration to assessing control risk

too low and the tolerable deviation rate. The "allowable risk of assessing control risk too high" is a distracter. (6579)

40. (d) When performing tests of controls, the auditor is looking for the deviation rate from established control procedures set by the client. Thus, the auditor performs attributes sampling procedures. Answers (a) and (c) represent substantive sampling procedures. Answer (b) describes a selection method that is not relevant to attribute sampling. (3921)

41. (a) Attributes sampling involves the determination of the rate of occurrence of some characteristic (attribute) in a population. In an audit, the attribute of interest is frequently a deviation from a particular control procedure. Identifying entries posted to incorrect accounts is an example of testing compliance with the use of correct accounts. In estimating the amount in an expense account, evaluating the reasonableness of depreciation expense, and selecting receivables for confirmation of balances, a CPA is testing for dollar amounts which would involve variables sampling. (8406)

Variables Sampling

42. (b) Generally, variables sampling involves the determining of proper dollar value of the sampled items and makes inferences about the fairness of the amounts reported in the financial statements. Variables sampling typically involves deciding whether the dollar value of an account is reasonable. Generally, attributes sampling involves the determination of the rate of occurrence of some characteristic in a population. Proper prices, the number of misstatements, or proper recording are attributes. (7816)

43. (a) Special consideration must be given to zero and negative balance accounts which usually are excluded from a probability proportional to size (PPS) sample. For both classical variables sampling and PPS sampling, the sampling process may begin before the complete population is available and the auditor must consider the preliminary judgments about materiality. If few errors are expected, the sample will result in a smaller sample size using PPS sampling than if classical variables sampling is used. (8404)

PERFORMANCE BY SUBTOPICS

Each category below parallels a subtopic covered in Chapter 26. Record the number and percentage of questions you correctly answered in each subtopic area.

Audit Sampling

Question #	Correct	√
1		
2		
3		
4		
5		
6		
7		
# Questions	7	
# Correct		
% Correct		

Statistical Sampling

Question #	Correct	√
8		
9		
10		
11		
12		
13		
14		
15		
16		
17		
# Questions	10	
# Correct		
% Correct		

Attributes Sampling

Question #	Correct	√
18		
19		
20		
21		
22		
23		
24		
# Questions	7	
# Correct		
% Correct		

Variables Sampling

Question #	Correct	√
25		
26		
27		
28		
# Questions	4	
# Correct		
% Correct		

PPS Sampling

Question #	Correct	√
29		
30		
31		
# Questions	3	
# Correct		
% Correct		

SIMULATION SOLUTIONS

Solution 26-3

Response #1: Communication (3 points)

The advantages of PPS sampling over classical variables sampling are as follows:

- PPS sampling is generally **easier to use** than classical variables sampling.
- **Size** of a PPS sample is **not based on the estimated variation** of audited amounts.
- PPS sampling automatically results in a **stratified sample.**
- Individually significant items are **automatically identified.**
- If no misstatements are expected, PPS sampling will usually result in a **smaller sample** size than classical variables sampling.
- A PPS sample can be **easily designed** and sample selection can begin **before the complete population is available.**

Response #2: Sample Selection (3 points)

$$\text{Sampling Interval} = \frac{\textit{Tolerable Misstatement}}{\textit{Reliability Factor for Misstatement of Overstatement}}$$

$$= \frac{\$15,000}{3.00} = \$5,000$$

$$\text{Sample Size} = \frac{\textit{Recorded Amount}}{\textit{Sample Interval}}$$

$$= \frac{\$300,000}{\$5,000} = 60$$

Response #3: Analysis (3 points)

	Recorded amount	Audit amount	Tainting	Sampling interval	Projected misstatement
1st misstatement	$ 400	$ 320	20%	$1,000	$ 200
2nd misstatement	500	0	100%	1,000	1,000
3rd misstatement	3,000	2,500	*	1,000	500
Total projected misstatement					$1,700

* The recorded amount is greater than the sampling interval; therefore, the **projected misstatement equals the actual misstatement.**

Response #4: Research (1 point)

Paragraph Reference Answer: AU 350.46

Guidance: AU 350.46 states, "Statistical sampling helps the auditor (a) to design an efficient sample, (b) to measure the sufficiency of the audit evidence obtained, and (c) to evaluate the sample results. By using statistical theory, the auditor can quantify sampling risk to assist himself in limiting it to a level he considers acceptable. However, statistical sampling involves additional costs of training auditors, designing individual samples to meet the statistical requirements, and selecting the items to be examined. Because either nonstatistical or statistical sampling can provide sufficient audit evidence, the auditor chooses between them after considering their relative cost and effectiveness in the circumstances."

(9030)

Solution 26-4

Response #1: Communication (9 points)

1.   Statistical sampling **does not eliminate the need for professional judgment.**

2.   The **tolerable rate of deviation** or acceptable upper precision limit (UPL) is **too high (20%)** if Baker plans to assess control risk at a **low level (substantial reliance).**

3.   **Discovery sampling** is **not an appropriate sampling technique** in this attribute sampling application.

4.   The sampling technique employed is **not discovery sampling**.

5.   The **increase** in the **population size** has **little or no effect** on determining sample size.

6.   Baker failed to consider the **allowable risk** of assessing control risk too low **(risk of overreliance)** in **determining the sample size.**

7.   The population from which the sample was chosen (invoices) was an **incorrect population.**

8.   The sample selected was **not randomly selected.**

9.   Baker failed to consider the difference of an immaterial amount to be an **error.**

10. The **allowance for sampling risk** was **incorrectly calculated.**

11. Baker's reasoning concerning the decision that the sample **supported a low assessed level of control risk** was **erroneous.**

Response #2: Research (1 point)

Paragraph Reference Answer: AU 508.08

Guidance: AU 508.08 states, "The auditor's standard report identifies the financial statements audited in an opening (introductory) paragraph, describes the nature of an audit in a scope paragraph, and expresses the auditor's opinion in a separate opinion paragraph. The basic elements of the report are the following: (a) A title that includes the word *independent;* (b) A statement that the financial statements identified in the report were audited; (c) A statement that the financial statements are the responsibility of the Company's management and that the auditor's responsibility is to express an opinion on the financial statements based on his or her audit; (d) A statement that the audit was conducted in accordance with generally accepted auditing standards and an identification of the United States of America as the country of origin of those standards (for example, auditing standards generally accepted in the United States of America or U.S. generally accepted auditing standards); (e) A statement that those standards require that the auditor plan and perform the audit to obtain reasonable assurance about whether the financial statements are free of material misstatement; [and] (f) **A statement that an audit includes—(1) Examining, on a test basis, evidence supporting the amounts and disclosures in the financial statements;** (2) Assessing the accounting principles used and significant estimates made by management; [and] (3) Evaluating the overall financial statement presentation...."

Editor note: The reference to sampling is the phrase "on a test basis."

(3041)

Solution 26-5

Response #1: Judgment (9 points)

a.   1.   In determining an **acceptable level of risk of assessing control risk too low,** an auditor should consider the **importance** of the control to be tested in determining the **extent** to which substantive tests will be **restricted** and the **planned assessed level of control risk.**

2.   In determining the **tolerable deviation rate,** an auditor should consider the planned assessed level of control risk for the controls to be tested and how **materially** the financial statements would be affected if the control does not function properly. For example, **how likely** is the control to **prevent** or **detect material misstatements.**

3.   In determining the expected population deviation rate, an auditor should consider the results of prior years' tests, the overall control environment, or utilize a preliminary sample.

b.   1.   There is a decrease in sample size if the acceptable level of risk of assessing control risk too low is increased.

2.   There is a **decrease** in sample size if the **tolerable deviation rate** is **increased.**

3.   There is an **increase** in sample size if the **population deviation rate** is **increased.**

c.   For a **low risk of assessing control risk too low** it assessed level of control risk as the calculated **estimate of the population deviation rate** identified in the sample (7%) **approaches the tolerable**

deviation rate (8%). This is because there may be an **unacceptably high sampling risk** that these sample results could have occurred with an **actual population deviation rate higher than the tolerable deviation rate.**

d.   If statistical sampling is used, an allowance for sampling risk can be calculated. If the **calculated estimate of the population deviation rate** plus the allowance for sampling risk is **greater than the tolerable deviation rate,** the sample results should be interpreted as not supporting the assessed level of control risk for the control.

Response #2: Research (1 point)

Paragraph Reference Answer: AU 350.24

Guidance: AU 350.24 states, "Sample items should be selected in such a way that the sample can be expected to be representative of the population. Therefore, all items in the population should have an opportunity to be selected. For example, haphazard and random-based selection of items represents two means of obtaining such samples."

(9031)

Solution 26-6

Response #1: Sampling Steps (9 points)

The remaining steps are as follows:

6.   Treat the individually significant items as a **separate population.**

7.   **Choose** an audit **sampling technique.**

8.   **Determine** the **sample size,** giving consideration for—

a.   **Variations** within the population.

b.   **Acceptable level of risk.**

c.   **Tolerable misstatement.**

d.   **Expected** amount of misstatement.

e.   **Population size.**

9.   Determine the **method** of selecting a representative sample.

10. **Select** the sample items.

11. **Apply** appropriate audit procedures to the sample items.

12. **Evaluate** the sample **results.**

a.   **Project** the misstatement to the population and consider sampling risk.

b.   Consider the **qualitative** aspects of misstatements and reach an overall conclusion.

13. **Document** the sampling procedure.

Response #2: Research (1 point)

Paragraph Reference Answer: AU 350.44

Guidance: AU 350.44 states, "In some circumstances the auditor may design a sample that will be used for dual purposes: testing the operating effectiveness of an identified control and testing whether the recorded monetary amount of transactions is correct. In general, an auditor planning to use a dual-purpose sample would have made a preliminary assessment that there is an acceptably low risk that the rate of deviations from the prescribed control in the population exceeds the tolerable rate. For example, an auditor designing a test of control over entries in the voucher register may plan a related substantive procedure at a risk level that anticipates a particular assessed level of control risk. The size of a sample designed for dual purposes should be the larger of the samples that would otherwise have been designed for the two separate purposes. In evaluating such tests, deviations from the prescribed control and monetary misstatements should be evaluated separately using the risk levels applicable for the respective purposes. The absence of monetary misstatements detected in a sample does not necessarily imply that related controls are effective; however, misstatements that the auditor detects by performing substantive procedures should be considered by the auditor as a possible indication of a control failure when assessing the operating effectiveness of related controls."

(9032)

CHAPTER 27

AUDITING IT SYSTEMS

CHAPTER 27

AUDITING IT SYSTEMS

I. IT-Based Systems

A. Electronic Data Processing (EDP)
An IT-based, or EDP-based, system includes (1) hardware, (2) software, (3) documentation, (4) personnel, (5) data, and (6) controls. There can be significant differences between IT-based activities and non-IT activities.

1. Considerations

a. **Documentation** Many control procedures in IT systems do not leave documentary evidence of performance.

b. **Electronic Information** Files and records are usually in machine-readable form and cannot be read without using a computer.

c. **Reduced Human Involvement** Computers may obscure errors that a human would notice while handling the transaction.

d. **Reliability** IT systems are more reliable than manual systems because all of the data are subjected to the same controls. Manual systems are subject to human error on a random basis. Computer processing virtually eliminates computational errors associated with manual processing.

e. **Knowledge** An auditor may need specialized IT knowledge to perform an audit.

f. **Difficulty of Change** It is harder to change an IT system once it is implemented than it is to change a manual system. Therefore, the auditor will want to become familiar with a new IT system at an early stage of the development process so that the auditor can anticipate possible future audit problems.

2. Processing Methodology

a. **Transaction Processing Modes** Transactions may be processed either in batches or online.

(1) **Batch Processing** Transactions to be processed are accumulated in groups (batches) before processing and are then processed as a batch. Batch processing frequently involves sequential access to the data files. For example, a company may accumulate a day's charge sales before processing them against the master file during the night. Before they are processed, the transactions would be sorted into the order of the records on the master file. One disadvantage of batch processing is that, because of the time delays, errors may not be detected immediately. The file updating process is most efficient when the transaction file has been sorted into the same order as the master file. There are four basic steps in the process of updating a batch of records in a master file that is kept on a magnetic disk. First, a transaction enters the CPU. Second, the record to be updated is read from its location on the disk into the CPU. Third, the record is updated in the CPU. Fourth, the updated record is written onto the disk in the same location as the original record. The result is that the original record is replaced by the updated record. This results in the original record being erased.

(2) **Online Processing** Transactions are processed and the file is updated as the transactions occur. Online processing usually involves files that can be accessed directly. For example, a cash register terminal may update the inventory file automatically when a sale is made.

(3) **Real-Time Processing** An online system is operating in real time if the data is processed fast enough to get the response back in time to influence the process. For example, an airline reservation system is an online, real-time (OLRT) system because the customer receives reservations after waiting only a few moments.

(4) **Integrated System** All files affected by a transaction are updated in one transaction-processing run, rather than having a separate run for each file. For example, in an integrated system, a sales transaction may update the sales summary file, the accounts receivable master file, and the inventory file during one processing run.

b. **Processing External to Client** While many companies have their own equipment to do their processing within the company (i.e., in-house), others utilize outside processors. Several common arrangements are as follows:

(1) **Block Time** Client rents a certain block of computer time from an outside party. For example, a company may rent time from a bank that does not utilize its computer system 24 hours per day.

(2) **Time-Sharing** A number of users share a computer system. Each may have a terminal that it can use to access a CPU located outside of the client. Each user can access the system whenever it wishes.

(3) **Service Bureau** An outside organization that provides a wide range of data processing services for a fee.

3. **Development & Implementation** A CPA sometimes becomes involved in the development and implementation of a computer-based application system. The CPA may do the work or may work with client personnel (systems analysts, programmers, etc.). The development and implementation process involves the following phases:

a. **Systems Analysis (Feasibility Study)** The system's overall objectives and requirements are clearly determined. The existing system then is studied to see if it is meeting them adequately. Broad alternative approaches also are considered.

b. **Systems Design** In general systems design, the alternative approaches are evaluated in more detail and a specific proposal is developed for implementing the alternative that is felt to be best. In detailed systems design, the recommended system is designed in detail. This includes designing files, determining resource requirements, and developing plans for the following phases.

c. **Program Specifications & Implementation Planning** Detailed specifications are developed for the computer programs that will be required, and plans are made for testing the program and implementing the system. This involves (1) hardware installation; (2) coding and debugging programs; (3) training users; (4) systems testing; and (5) conversion and volume testing. Coding and debugging involves programmers writing and testing the required programs. In systems testing, the system is tested thoroughly. The results of the tests are compared with the specifications and requirements of the system to determine whether it does what it is supposed to do. Conversion is done from the old system to the new system. This involves such things as converting and verifying files and data. Conversion may involve parallel processing (i.e., parallel operations) in which the old system and the new system are run at the same time with the actual data for the period and the results compared. This checks the new system and avoids disaster if the new system fails the first time it is used. Volume testing involves testing the capacity of the system to handle expected volumes of information and transactions.

d. **Implementation** The system is released to the user.

e. **Monitoring** Once the system is operating routinely, it is reviewed to be sure it is attaining the original objectives set for it, and to correct any problems.

B. **Client Documentation**

Documentation is an important aspect of control and communication. It generally provides (1) an understanding of the system's objectives, concepts, and output, (2) a source of information for systems analysts and programmers when involved in program maintenance and revision, (3) information that is needed for a supervisory review, (4) a basis for training new personnel, (5) a means of communicating common information, (6) a source of information about accounting controls, and (7) a source of information that will aid in providing continuity in the event experienced personnel leave. If reliable documentation is not available, the auditor must find other sources of information. There are several types of documentation.

Exhibit 1 ▶ IT System Documentation Mnemonic

O	Operations documentation
P	Problem definition documentation
S	Systems documentation
O	Operator documentation
U	User documentation
P	Program documentation

1. **Problem Definition Documentation** Permits the auditor to gain a general understanding of the system without having to become involved in the details of the programs. Contents include the following:

a. Description of the reasons for implementing the system

b. Description of the operations performed by the system

c. Project proposals

d. Evidence of approval of the system and subsequent changes (for example, a particular individual may have to sign a form to indicate these)

e. A listing of the assignment of project responsibilities

2. **Systems Documentation** Provides sufficient information to trace accounting data from its original entry to system output. Contents include the following:

a. A description of the system

b. A systems flowchart shows the flow of data through the system and the interrelationships between the processing steps and computer runs.

c. Input descriptions

d. Output descriptions

e. File descriptions

f.   Descriptions of controls

g.   Copies of authorizations and their effective dates for systems changes that have been implemented

3.   **Program Documentation**   Primarily used by systems analysts and programmers to provide a control over program corrections and revisions. However, it may be useful to the auditor to determine the current status of a program. Contents include the following:

a.   Brief description of the program

b.   Program flowchart, decision table, or detailed logic narrative

    (1)   **Program Flowchart**   Shows the steps followed by the program in processing the data

    (2)   **Decision Table**   This describes a portion of the logic used in the program. Although it is not always used, it can replace or supplement the program flowchart.

    (3)   **Detailed Logic Narrative**   Narrative description of the logic followed by a program

c.   Source statements (i.e., a listing of the program instructions) or parameter listings

d.   List of control features

e.   Detailed description of file formats and record layouts

f.   Table of code values used to indicate processing requirements

g.   Record of program changes, authorizations, and effective dates

h.   Input and output formats

i.   Operating instructions

j.   Descriptions of any special features

4.   **Operations Documentation**   Information provided to the computer operator; it can be used by the auditor to obtain an understanding of the functions performed by the operator and to determine how data is processed; contents include the following:

a.   A brief description of the program

b.   Description of the inputs and outputs that are required (e.g., the forms used)

c.   Sequence of cards, tapes, disks, and other files

d.   Setup instructions and operating system requirements

e.   Operating notes listing program messages, halts, and action necessary to signal the end of jobs

f.   Control procedures to be performed by operations

g.   Recovery and restart procedures (to be used for hardware or software malfunctions)

h.   Estimated normal and maximum run time

i. Instructions to the operator in the event of an emergency

5. **User Documentation** This is a description of the input required for processing and an output listing. The auditor may use it to gain an understanding of the functions performed by the user and the general flow of information. Contents include a description of the system, description of the input and output, list of control procedures and an indication of the position of the person performing the procedures, error correction procedures, cutoff procedures for submitting the data to the IT department, and a description of how the user department should check reports for accuracy.

6. **Operator Documentation** Documentation should be prepared that will indicate the jobs run and any operator interaction.

   a. **Daily Computer Log** This may be prepared manually by the computer operator. It indicates the jobs run, the time required, who ran them, etc.

   b. **Console Log** This is a listing of all interactions between the console and the CPU. Prepared by the computer as messages are entered from the console, it can be a valuable control for detecting unauthorized intervention of the computer operator during the running of a program. It also shows how the operator responded to processing problems.

II. Effects of IT-Based Systems on Audits

A. Engagement Planning
An auditor's objectives do not change when auditing the financial statements of a company using an IT system. The ultimate objective is still to express an opinion on the fairness of presentation of the financial statements. While the audit objectives do not change, the audit procedures used to accomplish them may change. The auditor should consider the following matters:

1. **Extent** The extent to which the computer is used in each significant accounting application.

2. **Complexity** The complexity of the entity's computer operations, including the use of an outside service center.

3. **Organization** The organizational structure of the computer processing activities.

4. **Availability of Data** Some data may only be available for a limited time.

5. **Analytics** An additional factor in the use of analytics is the increased availability of data that is used by management. Such computer-prepared data and analyses, although not necessarily a part of the basic accounting records, may be valuable sources of information (e.g., budget and variance information).

6. **CAAT** The use of computer-assisted audit techniques (CAAT) to increase the efficiency of performing audit procedures. If specific skills are needed, and a specialist is used, the auditor should have sufficient computer-related knowledge to (a) communicate the objectives of the other professional's work; (b) evaluate whether the specified procedures will meet the auditor's objectives; and (c) evaluate the results of the procedures applied as they relate to the nature, timing, and extent of other planned audit procedures. The auditor's responsibilities with respect to using such a professional are equivalent to those for other assistants.

B. Consideration of IT Controls

1. **Only Reasonable Assurance** All internal control systems, regardless of how well designed, face certain inherent limitations which make the achievement of absolute assurance an impossibility. In an IT system, errors can occur in designing, maintaining, or monitoring automated controls. For example, IT personnel may not understand how an IT system processes sales transactions which could result in incorrect changes to the system which processes

sales for a new product line. Additionally, errors can occur in the use of the information produced by the IT system.

2.   **Basic Concepts** The characteristics that distinguish computer processing from manual processing include the following:

   a.   **Transaction Trails** Some computer systems are designed so that a complete transaction trail that is useful for audit purposes might exist for only a short period of time or only in computer-readable form. This trail is used to monitor the system, answer queries, and deter fraud.

   b.   **Uniform Processing of Transactions** Computer processing uniformly subjects like transactions to the same processing instructions. Consequently, computer processing virtually eliminates the occurrence of clerical error normally associated with manual processing. Conversely, errors will result in all like transactions being processed incorrectly.

   c.   **Segregation of Functions** Many internal control procedures once performed by separate individuals in manual systems may be concentrated in systems that use computer processing. Therefore, an individual who has access to the computer may be in a position to perform incompatible functions. As a result, other control procedures may be necessary in computer systems to achieve the control objectives ordinarily accomplished by segregation of functions in manual systems.

   d.   **Potential for Errors & Fraud** Decreased human involvement in handling transactions processed by computers can reduce the potential for observing errors and fraud. Errors or fraud occurring during the design or changing of application programs can remain undetected for long periods of time.

   e.   **Potential for Increased Management Supervision** Computer systems offer management a wide variety of analytical tools that may be used to review and supervise the operations of the company. The availability of these additional controls may serve to enhance the entire internal control structure on which the auditor may wish to assess control risk at below the maximum level. For example, comparisons by management of budget to actual results and the response by management to unusual fluctuations indicate management's monitoring of the ongoing operations as a prevention of unfavorable crisis situations.

   f.   **Initiation or Subsequent Execution of Transactions by Computer** The authorization of "automatic" transactions or procedures might not be documented in the same way as those initiated in a manual accounting system, and management's authorization of those transactions may be implicit in its acceptance of the design of the computer system.

   g.   **Dependence of Other Controls on Controls Over Computer Processing** Computer processing may produce reports and other output that are used in performing manual control procedures. The effectiveness of these manual control procedures can be dependent on the effectiveness of controls over the completeness and accuracy of computer processing.

3.   **Accounting Control Procedures** Internal accounting control procedures sometimes are defined by classifying control procedures into two types: general and application control procedures.

   a.   **General Controls** Those controls that relate to all or many computerized accounting applications and often include control over the development, modification, and maintenance of computer programs and control over the use of and changes to data maintained on computer files. When an auditor anticipates assessing control risk at a low level, the auditor would focus initially on these general controls.

    b.   **Application Controls** Those controls that relate to specific computerized accounting applications, i.e., input, processing, and output controls for an accounts payable application.

4.   **Review of Internal Control** Due to the increased concentration of functions within the computer processing operation, the auditor's concern over the interdependence of control procedures is generally greater than it is in a manual system. In fact, application controls often are dependent upon general controls. Accordingly, it may be more efficient to review the design of general controls before reviewing the specific application controls.

C.   **Audit Evidence**
The auditor can use either manual audit procedures, computer-assisted audit techniques, or a combination of both to obtain sufficient appropriate audit evidence.

1.   **Substantive Procedures Only** During the risk assessment process, the auditor may determine that it is not possible or practicable to reduce detection risk at the relevant assertion level to an acceptably low level with audit evidence obtained from substantive procedures alone. In these circumstances, the auditor should perform tests of controls to obtain audit evidence about the operating effectiveness of relevant controls. For example, the auditor may find it impossible to design effective substantive procedures that by themselves provide sufficient appropriate audit evidence when an entity uses IT to conduct its business and no documentation of transactions is produced or maintained, other than through the IT system.

2.   **Information Availability** Sometimes information and corroborating audit evidence are available in electronic form only. Source documents (purchase orders, bills of lading, invoices, and checks) may be in the form of electronic messages. Certain electronic evidence might not be accessible after a specified period of time if files are changed, unless backup files are created. The auditor should consider the time when information is available in determining the nature, timing, and extent of substantive tests and tests of controls.

    a.   **Electronic Data Interchange (EDI)** With EDI, an entity and its customers or vendors conduct business electronically. EDI transactions must be formatted using uniform standards, and transmitted such that they are both secure and private. Purchasing, shipping, billing, cash receipt, and cash disbursement functions may be achieved through electronic exchanges, ordinarily without paper documents.

    b.   **Image Processing** With image processing systems, paper documents are scanned into electronic images for electronic storage and retrieval. The entity might keep paper documents only for a limited time after this conversion.

3.   **Internal Consistency** Auditors test accounting information by analysis and review, retracing, recalculation, and reconciliation. By performing these procedures, auditors may evaluate the internal consistency of information. Normally, internally consistent information provides evidence about the fairness of financial statement presentations.

4.   **Data Mining** Data mining (also known as relationship mapping, data interrogation, or knowledge discovery) is the distillation of previously unknown information from raw data. The largest strength of data mining is identification of unexpected relationships. Manual review may be inefficient for entities with a high number of transactions. Data mining is used for many purposes (streamlining operations, marketing analysis), although this discussion focuses on auditing. Data mining tools can assist auditors to perceive patterns in mountainous databases in a timely manner. By quickly discovering a fraudulent scheme, auditors could prevent future fraud and facilitate asset recovery.

Exhibit 2 ▶ Fraud Profile Examples for Accounts Payable

Vendor records that list more than one payment address. (Vendors may have multiple branches, or payments to a legitimate vendor may have been redirected fraudulently.)

Vendor records showing only post office box addresses. (While payments are frequently sent to lock boxes, usually there is one address—for instance, shipping or purchasing—that is a street address.)

In a large organization, records for one vendor showing the same authorized signer on every check and/or the same receiving clerk accepting every delivery connected with that vendor. (In an organization with several possible signers and receiving clerks for any given transaction, this circumstance is an unlikely coincidence.)

Matching employee and vendor addresses. (It is rare that an employee's home-based business is a legitimate vendor.)

Mailing addresses that are shared by vendors. (Several false vendors may share the same address or payments may be redirected to the same address for a perpetrator's convenience.)

Payments close to payment-review thresholds. (Management review is not necessary up to the threshold. Employees may aim to commit fraud for the largest amount possible per transaction.)

Invoice numbers from the same vendor that are close in sequence. (Legitimate vendors typically have many customers.)

a. A data-mining tool is like a sieve, allowing an auditor to sift through large amounts of data quickly, providing an overview of an entity. These preliminary procedures can be performed on entire populations, instead of relatively small samples. Auditors analyze identified questionable relationships, allowing them to devote more time to examining relationships that appear characteristic of error or fraud.

b. For example, a bank may have the same employees who authorized a loan to a debtor named Jones being named on checks drawn on the account that Jones opened with the loan proceeds. This coincidence might escape manual detection and yet warrant extra auditor scrutiny.

c. Analysis tools also can highlight individual transactions that fit a fraud profile. A fraud profile is a summary of expected data characteristics that an auditor expects to find in a particular type of fraudulent transaction, based on an understanding of a given entity's internal control weaknesses. Not all transactions fitting a fraud profile are necessarily fraudulent, but an auditor may increase audit efficiency by selecting transactions to examine based on a fraud profile.

5. **Electronic vs. Paper Evidence** The term electronic evidence relates to information that is transmitted, processed, maintained, and/or accessed by electronic means (e.g., using a computer, scanner, sensor, and/or magnetic media). Many of the issues related to electronic evidence also are applicable to evidence in the form of computer-printed documents and reports, particularly if there is no way to review or validate the printed information independently. The attributes of audit evidence (paper versus electronic) are:

a. **Difficulty of Alteration** Easily-altered evidence lacks credibility and has reduced value to the auditor. Paper evidence is difficult to alter without detection. An auditor has a reasonable likelihood of detecting significant alterations that have been made to paper documents. This quality provides auditors with some assurance that the evidence represents original information. Alterations due to the operation of a IT system may not be detected, unless specifically-designed tests are performed.

b. ***Prima Facie* Credibility** Credibility of evidence is enhanced when the source of the evidence is independent in relation to the client and the auditor has the ability to corroborate that evidence. Paper documents (e.g., incoming purchase orders) usually have a high degree of credibility. However, a purchase order transmitted electronically from a customer derives its credibility primarily from the controls within the electronic environment. A fraudulent or altered electronic purchase order exhibits no apparent difference, compared to a valid purchase order, when extracted from the electronic environment of the entity.

c. **Completeness of Documents** Appropriate audit evidence includes the essential terms of a transaction so that an auditor can verify the validity of the transaction. Paper evidence typically includes all of the essential terms of a transaction. Paper evidence also includes information regarding other parties to the transaction (e.g., customer name and address, or preferred shipping methods), on the face of the document. Work on the completeness assertion for paper documents often includes review of acknowledgments of data entry and postings. An electronic environment may mask this evidence with codes or by cross-references to other data files that may not be visible to the users of the data.

d. **Evidence of Approvals** Approvals integrated into the evidence add to the completeness of the evidence. Paper documents typically show approvals on their face. For example, incoming purchase orders may have marketing department price approvals and credit department approvals written on the face of each original document. The same treatment may apply to electronic approvals by integrating approvals into the electronic record. Electronic elements may require additional interpretation.

e. **Ease of Use** This factor relates to evaluating and understanding evidence. Auditors use traditional paper evidence without additional tools or expert analysis. Electronic evidence often requires extraction of the desired data by an auditor knowledgeable in electronic data extraction techniques or through use of a specialist.

f. **Clarity** Appropriate audit evidence should allow the same conclusions to be drawn by different auditors performing the same tasks. The nature of electronic evidence is not always clear.

D. **Fundamental Change**

Auditors may need to consider the implications of IT in evaluating any of the five components of internal control as they relate to the achievement of the entity's objectives. For example, in today's business world, it is not uncommon to find entities which have complex, highly integrated IT systems that share data and that are used to support all aspects of the entity's financial reporting, operations, and compliance objectives. As enterprise resource planning (ERP) systems become more comprehensive and more widely in use, this issue becomes more prevalent—even for small and mid-sized entities. The use of IT often changes the fundamental manner in which transactions are initiated, recorded, processed, and reported from paper-based systems that rely primarily on manual controls to electronic systems using a combination of manual and automated controls.

1. **Manual** In a manual system, an entity uses manual procedures and records in paper format (e.g., to enter sales orders, authorize credit, prepare shipping reports and invoices, and maintain accounts receivable records). Controls in a "traditional" system also are manual, and may include procedures such as approvals and reviews of activities, and reconciliations and follow-up of reconciling items. Manual controls are performed by people, and therefore pose specific risks to the entity's internal control. Manual controls may be less reliable than automated controls because they can be more easily bypassed, ignored, or overridden; they are also more prone to errors and mistakes. Therefore, consistent application of a manual control cannot be assumed. However, manual controls may be more appropriate when judgment is required, such as in the following circumstances:

a. Large, unusual, or nonrecurring transactions

b. Circumstances where misstatements are difficult to define, anticipate, or predict

c. In changing circumstances that require a control response outside the scope of an existing automated control

d. In monitoring the effectiveness of automated controls

2. **Automated** Alternatively, an entity may have complex IT systems that use automated procedures to initiate, record, process, and report transactions, in which case records in electronic format replace paper documents such as purchase orders, invoices, and shipping documents. Controls in systems that use IT consist of a combination of automated controls (e.g., controls embedded in computer programs) and manual controls. Further, manual controls may be independent of the IT system and may use information produced by the IT system, or may be limited to monitoring the effective functioning of the system and the automated controls and handling exceptions. An entity's mix of manual and automated controls varies with the nature and complexity of the entity's use of IT.

3. **Benefits** An IT environment provides benefits to the auditor related to effectiveness and efficiency because it enables the entity to perform the following:

a. Consistently apply predefined business rules and perform complex calculations in processing large volumes of transactions or data

b. Enhance the timeliness, availability, and accuracy of information

c. Facilitate the additional analysis of information

d. Enhance the ability to monitor the performance of the entity's activities and its policies and procedures

e. Reduce the risk that controls will be circumvented, especially if controls over changes to the IT system are effective

4. **Risks** Some of the risks that an auditor faces when working within an IT environment include the following:

a. Overreliance on information provided by the IT system that could be incorrectly processing data or consistently processing inaccurate data

b. Unauthorized access to data that may result in destruction of data or improper changes to data including the recording of unauthorized or nonexistent transactions or inaccurate recording of transactions

c. Unauthorized changes to computer programs

d. Failure to make necessary changes to computer programs

e. Inappropriate manual intervention

f. Potential loss of data

E. Procedures
In understanding a reporting entity's financial reporting process, the auditor must understand procedures utilized for entering transaction totals into the general ledger, procedures utilized for initiating, recording, and processing journal entries in the general ledger (both standard and nonstandard journal entries), and procedures utilized for recording recurring and nonrecurring adjustments to financial statements that are not reflected in formal journal entries (e.g., consolidating adjustments, report combinations, and reclassifications).

F.   **Tests of Controls**

1.   **Design** In designing tests of controls, the auditor should consider indirect controls on which direct controls depend. For example, the auditor should consider controls related to the accuracy and completeness of information when other controls depend on that information to operate effectively.

2.   **Automated Controls** Due to the inherent consistency of IT processing, audit evidence concerning the implementation of an automated application control combined with audit evidence concerning the operating effectiveness of general IT controls, particularly security and change controls, may provide substantial audit evidence about the operating effectiveness of the application control.

3.   **No Tests of Controls** When the auditor is not performing tests of controls, the auditor needs to be satisfied that performing substantive tests alone would be effective in restricting detection risk to an acceptable level. For example, the auditor may determine that performing substantive tests alone would be effective and more efficient than performing tests of controls for assertions related to fixed assets and to long-term debt in an entity where a limited number of transactions are related to those financial statement elements and when the auditor can readily obtain corroborating evidence in the form of documents and confirmations.

4.   **Combined With Substantive Tests** In complex situations—especially where there is a large volume of transactions processed within the complex IT environment—the auditor may determine that performing tests of controls for certain assertions would be effective and more efficient than performing only substantive tests. Alternatively, the auditor may determine that it is not practical or even possible to restrict detection risk to an acceptable level by performing only substantive tests. In making the determination as to whether tests of controls are mandatory, factors an auditor considers include the following:

    a.   The nature of the financial statement assertion

    b.   The volume of transactions or data related to the financial statement assertion

    c.   The nature and complexity of the systems, including the use of IT, by which the entity processes and controls information supporting the financial statement assertions

    d.   The nature of the available audit evidence, including audit evidence that is available only in electronic form

5.   **Examples** Examples of situations where the auditor may determine that tests of controls are necessary include the following:

    a.   An entity that conducts business using a system in which the computer initiates orders for goods based on predetermined rules and pays the related payables based on electronic information in transactions regarding receipt of goods. No other documentation of orders or goods received is produced or maintained.

    b.   An entity that provides electronic services to customers (e.g., an Internet service provider or a telephone company) and uses computer applications to log services provided to users, initiate bills for the services, process the billing transactions, and automatically record such amounts in electronic accounting records that are used to produce the financial statements.

G.   **Special Systems**

1.   **Online, Real-Time (OLRT) Systems** Because of the technical complexity of OLRT systems, the auditor will need more technical expertise to consider internal control. Care also must be exercised not to disrupt the system. Techniques such as test data (integrated test

facility) and tagging may be used. Generalized audit software may be used to perform substantive tests on the data files.

2. **Personal Computer Systems** The basic control and audit considerations in a small computer environment are the same as those in a larger and more complex IT system. However, the specific procedures the auditor uses needs to be adapted to fit the personal computer environment. The number of records that can be stored in a minicomputer system is limited, so audit trails often are retained for a limited period of time. Therefore, the auditor must plan the audit steps to take place when sufficient supporting information is available.

   a. **Segregation of Functions** Often, segregation of functions within the IT department and between the IT department and user departments does not exist to a significant extent in a small business system. Users even may perform IT functions. The most desirable segregation controls in this environment would include (1) segregation between data entry and processing and (2) segregation between IT and user transaction authorization. The auditor should assist management in identifying and implementing alternative or compensating controls where separation of functions does not exist. When the auditor finds weaknesses in segregation, the audit program generally should include more substantive tests.

   b. **System Design & Documentation** Users should be involved in the selection of both hardware and software because the choice of software in small systems is influenced by the hardware. Although access to program documentation should be limited, it is difficult to enforce in many small computer environments where the data processing group is small. Regardless, there may be times when the auditor may not be able to rely upon the documentation in such an environment.

   c. **File Conversion & System Testing** Frequently, an organization's initial IT applications include the use of a small business computer system. File conversion and system testing are particularly important in these initial applications and, therefore, should influence the auditor in the audit. Before relying on the contents of converted files, the auditor should evaluate the controls used to ensure against lost or distorted data during conversion. If the auditor determines that sufficient user system testing has not been performed by the client, the auditor should perform procedures that will allow for sufficient testing of the system.

   d. **Hardware Control** Limiting access to computer hardware is difficult in the small computer environment. Often, these systems lack controls that would prevent access to the actual hardware. Such a situation may cause the auditor to reduce reliance on stored data records. However, good application controls usually can compensate for problems caused by the absence or ineffectiveness of hardware controls.

   e. **Software Control** All program changes should be authorized, tested, and documented. However, in some small data processing environments, the auditor will not be able to rely on program change controls. Thus, the auditor may find it appropriate to obtain a copy of the original software directly from the manufacturer. It is also important to control disks with stored data when not in use. Files should be copied or backed up to ensure against loss of data. The use of hard disk drives calls for access protection with the use of passwords, IDs, and the like.

   f. **Application Controls** Many of the protection controls available in large systems to prohibit file manipulation or processing errors are not available in minicomputer systems.

      (1) Limit (reasonableness) checks generally are not adapted to specific situations because most small system software is purchased off the shelf.

    (2)   The auditor should look for the existence of external labels on software. Review of the client's storage and use procedures is also appropriate.

    (3)   Most data is **not** converted into machine-readable form before input into the personal computer system. This should cause the auditor to be more concerned with data input controls and less concerned with data conversion controls.

    (4)   In small organizations or situations that generally characterize these environments, there is usually less movement of data between departments. Also, data processing personnel are familiar with system output users. Therefore, the auditor may be concerned less with controls over movement of data between departments and the distribution of output to authorized users than if the auditor was in a large IT environment.

  g.   **Small IT Environment Audit Impact** In a small environment, many of the computer personnel functions are combined for a small number of employees. In these situations, two key functions that should be segregated are the applications programmer and the operator. When these functions are not segregated, fraud can be perpetrated and concealed because the programmer knows exactly what the IT system is capable of performing.

3.   **Distributed Systems** Distributed systems are a network of remote computer sites where small computers are connected to the main computer system. Access at each location should be well controlled and audited separately to verify the integrity of the data processed. Also, because users may have both authorization and recording duties, compensating controls should exist for this lack of segregation of duties.

4.   **Service Center (Service Bureau)** Certain controls are particularly important because of the nature of the client-IT service center relationship.

Exhibit 3 ▶ IT Service Center Controls Mnemonic

T	Transmission
E	Error correction
A	Audit trail
M	Master file changes
O	Output
S	Security

  a.   **Transmission** Document counts, hash totals, financial totals, etc., may be used to control the transmission of data to and from the client's office.

  b.   **Error Correction** Client should receive an error listing that identifies all of the errors that occurred in the system. Correction, review, and approval procedures should be established and used.

  c.   **Audit Trail** An audit trail must be maintained. This may be done through proper filing and sequencing of original transaction documents, and also through periodic printouts of journal and ledger balances.

  d.   **Master File Changes** Printout of all master file changes should be sent to the client. Control counts of master file records and control totals of items within master file records may be used.

  e.   **Output** Output must be restricted to the client. An output distribution list (indicating who should receive the output) and control tests on samples of output may be used.

    f.   **Security** Service center must have adequate controls to protect the client's data (while being stored and during processing). Further, there must be adequate reconstruction procedures so that the client's data files can be reconstructed (i.e., recreated) if all or part of them are destroyed. A service center sometimes hires a CPA to issue a report on its internal control and security. An auditor whose client uses the service center may rely on this report, or if the auditor feels it is inadequate, the auditor may visit the service center to observe the operations.

    5.   **Time-Sharing Systems** Audit considerations are primarily the same as discussed for online, real-time systems. Additionally, the auditor may decide to visit the time-sharing center to review its controls if the auditor (a) feels that a large amount of the client's important financial data is processed there and (b) is not able to determine from other sources (such as a review by another auditor) the quality of the center's control and compliance procedures.

III. General Controls (GC)

A. Organization & Operation Controls

    1.   **GC 1:**   Segregation of functions between the IT department and users

    2.   **GC 2:**   Provision for general authorization over the execution of transactions (prohibiting the IT department from initiating or authorizing transactions)

    3.   **GC 3:**   Part of proper internal control is the segregation of functions within the IT department. Among the various functions that should be segregated are the following:

Exhibit 4 ▶ IT Department Functions Segregation Mnemonic

C	Control group	Responsible for internal control within IT department
O	Operators	Convert data into machine readable form
P	Programmer	Develops and writes the computer programs; responsible for debugging of programs; writes the run manual
A	Analyst	Designs the overall system and prepares the system flowchart
L	Librarian	Keeps track of program and file use; maintains storage of all data and backups; controls access to programs

    a.   **Input Preparation** Process of converting the input data into machine-readable form. Input methods include key-to-tape (i.e., keying the information directly onto the magnetic tape), key-to-disk, and optical character recognition (OCR).

    b.   **Computer Operations** Computer operators physically run the equipment. This includes loading (i.e., entering) the program and data into the computer at the correct time, mounting tapes and disks on the appropriate tape and disk drives, and dealing with problems that occur during processing.

    c.   **Programming**

        (1)   Applications programmers write, test, and debug the application programs from the specifications provided by the systems analyst.

        (2)   Systems programmers implement, modify, and debug the software necessary to make the hardware operate.

    d.   **Systems Analysis** Systems analysts investigate a business system and decide how the computer can be applied. This includes designing the system, deciding what the programs will do, and determining how the outputs should appear.

    e.   Librarians Librarians provide control over the various programs, data tapes, disks, and documentation (manuals, etc.) when they are not in use; also, librarians are responsible for restricting access to IT materials to authorized personnel only. Library-control software may be used in some systems to keep control over programs, data, etc., that is kept online.

    f.   Data Integrity Data must be safeguarded for maximum control. To this end, users are given passwords or IDs to ensure that only authorized persons can access selected data. These passwords and IDs are changed frequently to further ensure the integrity of the system and its data. Passwords can be used to limit access to the entire system and to limit what the individual can access and/or change once in the system.

    g.   Database Administrator The database administrator is responsible for maintaining the database and restricting its access to authorized personnel.

B.   Systems Development & Documentation Controls
A weakness in systems development and documentation controls means that an auditor usually will have to spend more time in order to understand the system and evaluate the controls. Because application controls often are dependent on the quality of general controls, the absence of effective system development controls may weaken the accounting application controls.

    1.   **GC 4:**   The procedures for system design, including the acquisition of software packages, should require active participation by representatives of the users and, as appropriate, the accounting department and internal auditors.

    2.   **GC 5:**   Each system should have written specifications that are reviewed and approved by an appropriate level of management and users in applicable departments.

    3.   **GC 6:**   Systems testing should be a joint effort of users and IT personnel and should include both the manual and computerized phases of the system.

    4.   **GC 7:**   Final approval should be obtained prior to placing a new system into operation.

    5.   **GC 8:**   All master file and transaction file conversions should be controlled to prevent unauthorized changes and to provide accurate and complete results.

    6.   **GC 9:**   After a new system has been placed in operation, all program changes should be approved before implementation to determine whether they have been authorized, tested, and documented.

    7.   **GC 10:**   Management should require various levels of documentation and establish formal procedures to define the system at appropriate levels of detail.

C.   Hardware & Systems Software Controls
Hardware controls are controls that are built into the computer. A weakness in hardware and systems software controls may affect the auditor's assessed level of control risk.

    1.   **Parity Bit (Redundant Character Check)** In odd parity, an odd number of magnetized dots (on tape, disk, etc.) always should represent each character. When recording data, the computer automatically checks this. Then, when reading the data, the computer checks to see if there is still an odd number. In even parity, an even number of magnetized dots is used to represent each character. For example, the use of a parity bit probably would discover a distortion caused by dust on a tape or a distortion caused by sending data over telephone lines.

    2.   **Echo Check** CPU sends a signal to activate an input or output device in a certain manner. The device then sends a signal back to verify activation. The CPU then compares the signals.

3. **Hardware Check** Computer checks to make sure the equipment is functioning properly. For example, periodically the computer may search for circuits that are going bad.

4. **Boundary Protection** Keeps several files or programs separate when they share a common storage. For example, in time-sharing, several users may share primary storage. Boundary protection would prevent their data and/or programs from becoming mixed and the different users from accessing each other's data.

5. **GC 11:** The control features inherent in the computer hardware, operating system, and other supporting software should be utilized to the maximum possible extent to provide control over operations and to detect and report hardware malfunctions.

6. **GC 12:** Systems software should be subjected to the same control procedures as those applied to the installation of, and changes to, application programs.

D. Access Controls
A weakness in access controls increases the opportunity for unauthorized modifications of files and programs and misuse of the system; thereby decreasing the integrity of the system.

1. **Physical Access Controls** Only authorized personnel should have access to the facilities housing IT equipment, files and documentation.

2. **Electronic Access Controls** Access control software and other sophisticated devices are available to limit system access.

3. **GC 13:** Access to program documentation should be limited to those persons who require it in the performance of their duties.

4. **GC 14:** Access to data files and programs should be limited to those individuals authorized to process or maintain particular systems.

5. **GC 15:** Access to computer hardware should be limited to authorized individuals.

E. Data & Procedural Controls
Serious weaknesses in data and procedural controls can affect the auditor's assessment of control risk when establishing the scope of the substantive testing.

1. **File Labels**

   a. **External Labels** Human-readable labels attached to the outside of a secondary storage device, indicating the name of the file, expiration date, etc.

   b. **Internal Labels** Labels in machine-readable form.

   (1) **Header Label** Appears at the beginning of the file and contains such information as the file name, identification number, and the tape reel number.

   (2) **Trailer Label** Appears at the end of the file and contains such information as a count of the number of the records in the file and an end-of-file code.

2. **File Protection Ring:** A plastic ring that must be attached to a reel of magnetic tape before the tape drive will write on the tape. Writing on magnetic tape automatically erases the data already there, so the file protection ring guards against the inadvertent erasure of the information on the tape.

3. **File Protection Plans**

   a. **Duplicate Files** The most important data files are duplicated and the duplicates are safely stored away from the computer center.

b. **Disk Reconstruction Plan** In updating a record in a disk file, the record is read from the disk into the CPU, altered, and then written back to its previous location on the disk, thereby erasing the preupdated record. Therefore, a "disk dump" is used in which a copy of the contents of the disk is made on magnetic tape periodically, say each morning. Then, as the day's transactions are processed against the disk file, copies of the transactions are recorded on another tape. If it becomes necessary to reconstruct the disk file at any time during the day, the old file can be read from the tape to the disk and reupdated with the transactions from the transaction tape.

c. **Grandparent-Parent-Child (or Vice Versa) Retention Concept** This is also known as Grandfather-Father-Son Retention. The master file is updated at the end of each day by the day's transaction file, illustrated in Exhibit 5. After updating on Thursday, the Thursday updated master file (TUMF) is the child, the Wednesday updated master file (WUMF) is the parent, and the Tuesday updated master file (TSUMF) is the grandparent. These three files plus Wednesday's and Thursday's transaction files (WTF and TTF, respectively) are retained. If there is a problem during Friday's update run, the TUMF can be regenerated by running the copy of the WUMF with Thursday's transaction file. If necessary the WUMF could be reconstructed by processing TSUMF with Wednesday's transaction file. Once updating is completed on Friday, Friday's updated master file (FUMF) becomes the child, TUMF becomes the parent and WUMF becomes the grandparent. Therefore, at that time, TSUMF and Wednesday's transaction file can be erased.

Exhibit 5 ▶ Grandparent-Parent-Child Retention Concept

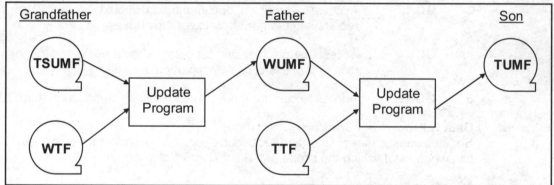

4. **Physical Safeguards**

a. **Proper Physical Environment** Consider extreme temperature, humidity, dust, etc.

b. **Environment Free From Possibility of Disasters** Includes proper fireproofing and locating the computer in a safe place (for example, not in the basement if there is a danger of flooding).

c. **Backup Facilities** Arrangements should be made to use other equipment in the case of disasters or other serious problems. Backup arrangements are frequently made with service bureaus or with computer installations of subsidiaries. Backup facilities are referred to as "hot" or "cold" sites, depending on their state of readiness.

d. **Control Access to Computer Room** Only authorized personnel should have access. For example, computer operators would be authorized to be in the computer room, but programmers would not be. Further, there should be at least two people in the computer room at all times. A weakness in internal control exists when a client uses microcomputers, because these computers rarely are isolated in a limited-access location and operators may remove hardware and software components and modify them at home more readily.

5. **GC 16:** A control function should be responsible for receiving all data to be processed, for ensuring that all data are recorded, for following up on errors detected during processing to see that the transactions are corrected and resubmitted by the proper party, and for verifying the proper distribution of output.

6. **GC 17:** A written manual of systems and procedures should be prepared for all computer operations and should provide for management's general or specific authorizations to process transactions.

7. **GC 18:** Internal auditors or an other independent group within an organization should review and evaluate proposed systems at critical stages of development.

8. **GC 19:** On a continuing basis, internal auditors or an other independent group within an organization should review and test computer processing activities.

IV. Application Controls (AC)

A. Input Controls

Input controls are designed to provide reasonable assurance that data received by IT have been authorized, converted into machine sensible form, and identified properly. Further, they assure that data have not been lost, suppressed, added, duplicated, or otherwise changed improperly. Basic categories of input to be controlled are (1) transaction entry, (2) file maintenance transactions (e.g., changing sales prices on a product master file), (3) inquiry transactions (e.g., how many units of a particular inventory item are on hand), and (4) error correction transactions.

1. **AC 1:** Only properly authorized and approved input, prepared in accordance with management's general or specific authorization, should be accepted for processing by IT.

2. **AC 2:** The system should verify all significant codes used to record data.

3. **AC 3:** Conversion of data into machine-sensible form should be controlled.

4. **Common Errors in Conversion** Keying errors and the losing or dropping of records.

5. **Input Control Techniques**

   a. **Control Totals** A total is computed and then recomputed at a later time. The totals are compared and should be the same. Control totals can be used as input, processing, and output controls.

      (1) **Financial Total** This has financial meaning in addition to being a control. For example, the dollar amount of accounts receivable to be updated can be compared with a computer-generated total of the dollar amount of updates read from the tape.

      (2) **Hash Total** This has meaning only as a control. For example, a total of the account numbers of those accounts that should have been updated can be compared with a computer-generated total of those account numbers actually entered.

      (3) **Record Count (Document Count)** This is a count of the number of transactions processed. For example, the computer can be programmed to print the total number of A/R records actually inputted.

   b. **Computer Editing** Computers can be programmed to perform a wide range of edit tests (i.e., edit checks) on records as they are being entered into the system. If a particular record does not meet the test, it is not processed. Edit tests include the following:

(1)   **Limit (Reasonableness) Test** A particular field of an input transaction record is checked to be sure it is not greater (or smaller) than a prespecified amount, or that it is within a prespecified range of acceptable values. For example, "hours worked" on a payroll record may be checked to be sure it does not exceed 50 hours in one week.

(2)   **Valid Field and/or Character Test** The particular field is examined to be sure it is of the proper size and composition. For example, if a customer account number should be numeric digits appearing in the first 7 spaces of the record, the first 7 spaces can be examined to be sure that there are numbers there.

(3)   **Valid Number or Code Test** Verifies that a particular number or code is one of those that is recognized by the system. For example, if a company has 5 retail outlets and records sales by using a location code of 1-5, the computer can check to be sure the code digit on the transaction record is a 1, 2, 3, 4, or 5.

(4)   **Sequence Check** If the input records should be in some particular sequence, the computer can be programmed to verify the sequence. For example, after sorting, the day's transaction file that is being entered should be in ascending order by customer account number.

(5)   **Missing Data Test** This verifies that all of the data fields actually contain data. For example, a point-of-sale terminal may be programmed not to accept a transaction unless the clerk has entered 10 pieces of required data.

(6)   **Valid Transaction Test** There are only a certain number of transaction types that would be expected for most files, so the computer can be programmed to verify that a particular transaction is an appropriate type for a particular file. For example, in the case of inventory, the only valid transaction may be to debit the inventory account when inventory is added and credit the account when inventory is taken away.

(7)   **Valid Combination of Fields** This is a check to be sure a certain combination of fields is reasonable. For example, a large retail outlet may program its computer to check the reasonableness of the product code field and the quantity-sold field. This would disclose a clerical error that resulted in a sale being entered for 11 television sets when only 1 was sold; i.e., it is not reasonable that one retail customer would purchase 11 television sets.

(8)   **Check Digit (Self-Checking Digit)** This is a digit (determined according to a prespecified mathematical routine) that is added to the same place in a piece of numeric data to permit the numeric data to be checked for accuracy during input, processing, or output. For example, a customer account number may be 1234. A check digit could be formed by adding the first and third digits and using the sum. The sum of the two digits is 4 (i.e., 1 + 3), so the check digit is 4. It is added to the end of the number that is assigned to the customer. The new customer account number becomes 12344. The computer can be programmed to verify the check digit at appropriate times. For instance, if the number is accidentally entered as 13244, the check digit would not match and the transaction would not be accepted. In practice, the mathematical routine generally is more complex than the one illustrated here.

(9)   **Valid Sign Test** A particular field can be checked to be sure it has the proper sign. For example, the quantity received in an inventory record should not be negative.

c.   **Error Log (Error Listing)** This is a computer-prepared list of those transactions that were not processed because of some error condition (e.g., an invalid customer account number). When an error is encountered, the usual procedure is for the computer to not process the erroneous transaction, but to skip it and continue processing the valid transactions rather than to halt processing altogether. A control function should be responsible for following up on errors detected during processing to see that the transactions are corrected and resubmitted by the proper party. This control function ideally should be delegated to a special IT control group that is independent from system analysis, programming, and operation.

6. **AC 4:**   Movement of data between one processing step and another, or between departments, should be controlled.

7. **AC 5:**   The correction of all errors detected by the application system and the resubmission of corrected transactions should be reviewed and controlled.

B. **Processing Controls**
    Many input controls are also valid processing controls.

    1. **AC 6:**   Control totals should be produced and reconciled with input control totals.

    2. **AC 7:**   Controls should prevent processing the wrong file, detect errors in file manipulation, and highlight operator-caused errors.

    3. **AC 8:**   Limit and reasonableness checks should be incorporated within programs.

    4. **AC 9:**   Run-to-run controls should be verified at appropriate points in the processing cycle.

C. **Output Controls**
    Primarily balancing, visual scanning or verification, and distribution.

    1. **AC 10:**   Output control totals should be reconciled with input and processing controls.

    2. **AC 11:**   Output should be scanned and tested by comparison to original source documents.

    3. **AC 12:**   Systems output should be distributed only to authorized users.

D. **Audit Effect of Weakness in Application Controls**
    This must be considered in relation to the particular application and to the total audit. Controls in the categories of input, processing, and output must be considered in relation to each other; i.e., a strong control in processing may compensate for a weakness in input.

V. **General Auditing Approaches**

A. **Around (Without) the Computer**
    The computer is treated as a "black box" that is ignored for all practical purposes. The auditor concentrates on input and output; i.e., if the inputs are correct and the outputs are correct, what went on within the computer also must be correct. The auditor does **not** test or directly examine the computer program, nor use the computer to perform the tests. Rather, the auditor relies on computer-prepared documents and printouts, which provide a visible audit trail that can be used in performing the audit procedures.

    1. **Type of System** Auditing around the computer is appropriate for simple systems that provide extensive printouts of processing, i.e., systems that provide a good audit trail.

    2. **Testing of Controls** Extensive use is made of the error listing (error log) to verify the existence and functioning of the control procedures. For example, if the error listing shows that a payroll transaction was not processed because the "hours-worked" field exceeded the limit allowed, the auditor has evidence that the limit test exists and is functioning. The auditor also

will trace transactions from the source documents (for example, a sales slip) through processing to their final place in the accounts and reports. Note that while computer-generated output is being used, the computer is not being used as an audit tool.

3. **Substantive Testing** The computer-prepared output is used as a basis for substantive testing. For example, the auditor may select a sample of accounts receivable to be confirmed from a computer-prepared listing of all the individual accounts receivable.

B. **Through (With) the Computer**
    The computer is used to perform tests of controls and substantive testing. The auditor places emphasis on the input data and the processing of the data. While output is not ignored, the auditor reasons that if the input is correct and the processing is correct, then the output must be correct. As a system becomes more complex, more processing is done within the computer and more data files are kept only in machine-readable form. This causes the audit trail to disappear. When this happens, auditing through the computer is really the only alternative open to the auditor. The following techniques are available to the auditor:

Exhibit 6 ▶ Auditing Through Computer Mnemonic

W	Writing own program
E	Embedded audit modules
T	Tagging
C	Client-prepared program
U	Utility programs (utility routines)
P	Program comparison
T	Test data (test deck)
R	Review of program logic
I	Integrated test facility (ITF, minicompany approach)
P	Parallel simulation
P	Program tracing

1. **Writing Own Program** The auditor writes a program for the specific substantive test to be performed. The major drawback is the time and effort required to get the program operational.

2. **Embedded Audit Modules** Sections of program code are included in the client's application program to collect audit data for the auditor. For example, at the auditor's direction, a file may be created of all sales transactions that are for more than $100. This monitors the client's system as transactions are actually processed. It can be hard to install once the application program is operational. Thus, it may be most efficiently included during system design.

3. **Tagging** Selected transactions are "tagged" (i.e., specially marked) at the auditor's direction. Then, as they are processed, additional documentation is generated so that the auditor can see how the transactions are handled as they are processed, i.e., it allows the auditor to examine the transactions at the intermediate steps in processing that normally are done within the computer but not displayed.

4. **Client-Prepared Program** Often the internal audit staff has programs to do the same things the auditor would like to do. Therefore, the auditor may be able to use the programs. However, first the auditor must test them to make sure that they do what they are supposed to do and that their integrity can be relied on.

5. **Utility Programs (Utility Routines)** Standard programs are furnished by the computer manufacturer for performing common data processing functions such as (a) changing the media a file is stored on (e.g., tape-to-disk, disk-to-tape, tape-to-paper), (b) modifying the data by changing or deleting records within a file, (c) creating or destroying a file, (d) changing the name or password of a file, (e) printing the contents of a file so it may be inspected visually, (f) sorting a file, and (g) merging two or more files. Utility programs may be more technical than GAS (see V., C.). Therefore, the auditor may have to be more technically proficient with IT to use them efficiently. The auditor also must be sure the utility program has not been altered. Consideration should be given as to whether the use of a utility routine will decrease the audit time or if GAS may be more appropriate.

6. **Program Comparison** The auditor-controlled copy of the program is compared with the program the client is using currently (usually done on a surprise basis). The idea behind this technique is that the comparison will disclose unauthorized changes made in the program. While the auditor may do this manually, there is software available to do it. A major drawback is the problem of the auditor maintaining a current copy of the program. Routine maintenance (updating) by programmers may mean that the auditor's copy does not agree with the copy being used, and it is the auditor's copy that is wrong.

7. **Test Data (Test Deck)** The auditor prepares a series of fictitious transactions (test data), some of which are valid and some of which contain errors that should be detected by the controls the auditor wants to test. The auditor uses the client's programs to process the test data and then examines the output to check processing, including the computer-prepared error listing.

    a. For example, if the payroll program is not supposed to process payroll data for employees whose employee time cards indicate they have worked more than 60 hours per week, the auditor's test data would contain at least one time card with more than 60 hours worked on it. If the control is working, the particular transaction should not be processed but should appear on the computer-prepared error listing.

    b. There are at least three potential problems with using test data: (1) Care must be exercised to prevent the fictitious data from becoming part of the client's real data files. (2) Time and care are required to prepare the test data so that it will test for the things that could go wrong and that are of interest to the auditor. (3) The auditor must take steps to make sure that the program being tested (i.e., the program testing the fictitious data) is the one that actually is used in routine processing.

8. **Review of Program Logic** The auditor reviews the application program's documentation, including the flowcharts and possibly the program listing, to obtain a sufficient understanding of the logic of the program in order to evaluate it. This may be time consuming. Unless the auditor specifically believes there is a logic error in the program, other audit techniques probably will be more efficient.

9. **Integrated Test Facility (ITF), Minicompany Approach** The auditor creates a fictitious entity within the client's actual data files. The fictitious data then is processed for the entity as part of the client's regular data processing. For example, if the auditor wants to test the accounts receivable update program, the auditor could create a fictitious customer's account receivable in the client's actual accounts receivable master file. During the period under audit, the auditor occasionally would introduce transactions for the fictitious customer. For instance, the "customer" would make credit purchases, would overpay the account, would not pay the account, would make purchase returns, etc. These transactions would be processed as part of the client's normal processing. The auditor knows what effect the various transactions should have on the accounts receivable, so the auditor can check the status of the account at any time to verify that transactions are being processed correctly, i.e., that the application programs are working as they should.

    a.   **Advantage Over Test Data** Two of the main advantages of ITF over the use of test data are that the auditor introduces fictitious data throughout the period (approaches continuous auditing) and it is processed along with the client's other "live" (i.e., actual) data.

    b.   **Problems** Several potential problems relating to the use of ITF are as follows:

        (1)   The data is part of the client's data files, so it accidentally may be included in the financial statements and reports that are prepared. To avoid this, the auditor may wish to introduce reversing entries to reverse the effects of the fictitious transactions (for example, to remove the "sales" made to the fictitious customer from the sales account) or the auditor may have the statement preparation program modified to skip the fictitious account when preparing the financial statements. Or, the auditor may decide to use small dollar amounts so that even if they are not removed, they will not have a material effect.

        (2)   Time, effort, and skill are required to make the fictitious entity operational and make sure the transactions processed against it will test the conditions and controls of interest to the auditor.

        (3)   There is also the problem of secrecy because the auditor's confidence in the technique will decrease if the client's data preparation and computer operations personnel know that the entity is fictitious and that the transactions for it are being introduced by the auditor in order to audit compliance.

10.   **Parallel Simulation** Once the auditor has checked a program, the auditor must determine that the client continues to use it. Parallel simulation involves processing actual client data through an auditor's software program, possibly using the client's computer. After processing the data, the auditor compares the output with output obtained from the client. Two techniques that can be used to help the auditor verify that the program being used for routine processing is the one that has been checked are as follows:

    a.   **Controlled Processing** The auditor observes (i.e., controls) an actual processing run and compares the results against those expected.

    b.   **Controlled Reprocessing** The auditor tests a program and keeps a copy of the program. At some future point in time, the auditor has the client use the auditor's control copy of the program to process some actual transactions. The results are compared with those from the client's routine processing run. For example, the auditor may have a control copy of the payroll program. The auditor would select the time cards and payroll data for several employees and have them processed using the control copy. The auditor would then compare the results of gross pay, net pay, withholding, etc., from the program with those that were attained by the payroll program the client had just used. A major problem is for the auditor to keep the control copy of the program current.

11.   **Tracing (Program Tracing, Tracing Software)** This prints a listing of the program instructions (steps) that were executed in processing a transaction. The auditor must be familiar with the programming language in which the client's application program is written. Even then, it may be time consuming to follow through the program listing.

C.   **Generalized Audit Software (GAS)**

This is a set of programs or routines (i.e., a software package) specifically designed to perform certain data processing functions that are useful to the auditor. The auditor can use GAS on the data files of a variety of clients. The auditor only need describe the organization of each client's files to GAS briefly, rather than write computer programs. Also known as General Purpose Audit Software or General Purpose Computer Audit Software, this is the computer-assisted audit technique used most prevalently.

1. **Reasons**

   a. **Use of Large Variety of Data** Much of a client's data is retained only in machine-readable form. GAS makes it possible for the auditor to access the data, analyze it, and present the results in a meaningful and convenient form.

   b. **Effectively Deal With Large Quantities of Data** GAS lets the auditor examine more data in more detail. For example, given an insurance company that has a policy file maintained on disk, the auditor can use GAS to perform mathematical tests on each of the policy records in the file. If auditing the file manually, the auditor could examine only a sample of the policies.

   c. **Lessens Dependence on Client Personnel** The auditor can do much of the computerized testing; i.e., the auditor does not need to rely as much on client personnel.

   d. **Economy** GAS produces economies in the audit while increasing audit quality.

   e. **Access to Data** GAS enables the auditor to gain access and test information stored in the client's files without having to acquire a complete understanding of the client's IT system.

2. **Audit Tasks Performed by GAS** While the exact procedures performed will vary among software packages, audit software is used to accomplish six basic types of audit tasks.

   a. **Examining Records for Quality, Completeness, Consistency & Correctness** GAS can be instructed to scan the records in a file and print those that are exceptions to auditor-specified criteria. Examples include (1) reviewing accounts receivable balances for amounts that are over the credit limit, (2) reviewing inventory quantities for negative or unreasonably large balances, (3) reviewing payroll files for terminated employees, and (4) reviewing bank demand deposit files for unusually large deposits or withdrawals.

   b. **Testing Calculations & Making Computations** GAS can test the accuracy of mathematical computations and can perform quantitative analyses to evaluate the reasonableness of client representations. Examples include (1) recalculating the extensions of inventory items, depreciation amounts, the accuracy of sales discounts, and interest, and (2) determining the accuracy of the net pay computations for employees.

   c. **Comparing Data on Separate Files** GAS can be used to determine if identical information on separate files agrees. Examples include (1) comparing changes in accounts receivable balances between two dates with details of sales and cash receipts on transaction files, (2) comparing payroll details with personnel records, and (3) comparing current and prior-period inventory files to assist in locating obsolete or slow-moving items.

   d. **Selecting, Printing & Analyzing Audit Samples** GAS can select statistical samples (random, stratified, etc.), print the items for the auditor's working papers or on special confirmation forms, and then, when the results are known (for example, when the confirmations are returned), analyze the data statistically. Examples include (1) select and print accounts receivable confirmations, (2) select inventory items for observation, and (3) select fixed asset additions for vouching.

   e. **Summarizing or Resequencing Data & Performing Analyses** GAS can reformat and aggregate data in a variety of ways. Examples include (1) refooting account files, (2) testing accounts receivable aging, (3) preparing general ledger trial balances, (4) summarizing inventory turnover statistics for obsolescence analysis, and (5) resequencing inventory items by location to facilitate physical observations.

f.   **Comparing Data Obtained Through Other Audit Procedures With Company Records** Manually gathered audit evidence can be converted to machine-readable form and then GAS can compare it to other machine-readable data. Examples include (1) comparison of inventory test counts with perpetual records and (2) comparison of creditor statements with accounts payable files.

Example 1 ▶ Potential Applications of GAS in Audit of Inventory

1. Determine the inventory items that should be reduced for quick sale, according to company policy.

2. Merge last year's inventory file with this year's and list those items that have unit costs of more than $100 that have increased by more than 10 percent.

3. Test for quantities on hand in excess of units sold during a period and list possible obsolete inventory items.

4. Select a sample of inventory items for a physical count and reconcile to the perpetual records.

5. Scan the sequence of inventory tag numbers and print a list of any missing numbers.

6. Select a random sample of inventory items for price testing and test the price.

7. Perform a net-realizable value test on year-end inventory quantities, using unit selling price data, and list any items where inventory cost exceeds net realizable value.

Example 2 ▶ Potential Applications of GAS in Audit of Accounts Receivable

1. Select and list accounts according to auditor-defined past-due conditions (e.g., over $5,000 and more than 90 days past-due).

2. List a random sample of past-due accounts to use in determining if follow-up procedures conform to company policy.

3. Select a sample of customer accounts for confirmation and have the computer print the confirmation requests.

4. Determine if the accounts receivable master file balance agrees with the general ledger and independently prove a company-prepared aging of accounts.

5. Match subsequent cash collections with accounts receivable records and independently age receivables not yet paid several weeks after the trial balance date.

6. Compare amounts due from individual customers with their approved credit limits and print a list of customers with balances in excess of their authorized amounts.

7. Print, for review and follow-up, a list of accounts for which collection efforts have been temporarily suspended.

3.   **Feasibility** When deciding whether to use GAS, the auditor should consider the following:

a.   **Nature of the Audit Area & Audit Approach** In some cases, the use of GAS may be the only feasible approach to attain the audit objective, for example, in complex systems with invisible audit trails. Additionally, the client may support or oppose the use of GAS.

b.   **Significance of Audit Effort & Timing** GAS may permit the auditor to complete an audit procedure quicker than any other alternative.

c.   **Availability of Data** Some data is available only in machine-readable form. Other data is not in machine-readable form and therefore, would have to be converted before GAS could be applied to it.

d. **Availability of Qualified Staff Personnel** Does the auditor or staff possess the necessary technical expertise to use GAS on the system being audited? For example, an auditor may be experienced in using GAS on relatively simple systems, but not on complex systems.

e. **Economic Considerations** While GAS can accomplish many things for the auditor, it has costs associated with its use such as staff hours, technical review hours, and mechanical assistance hours.

4. **Planning GAS Applications** The following steps should be followed in planning:

a. Set the objectives of the GAS application.

b. Determine the reports and other output requirements.

c. Review the content, accessibility, etc., of client data files.

d. Identify client personnel who may provide administrative or technical assistance.

e. Determine the need for equipment and supplies.

f. Determine the degree of audit control needed so that the auditor will have confidence that the GAS is processed correctly.

g. Prepare application budgets and timetables.

5. **Steps in Using GAS** The auditor goes through a series of steps in applying GAS.

a. **Determine Routines** Determine the specific GAS routines to be used and the particular order in which to use them for the particular application. The auditor does not have to use all of the routines available. Any routine can be used as many times as the auditor wishes.

b. **Complete Coding Sheets** The auditor describes the routines to use, the order in which to use them, the client's system, and data files to GAS.

c. **Processing** The GAS, the auditor's instructions, and the client's data files are entered into a computer and processed. The auditor should maintain physical control over the GAS (i.e., it should be kept in the auditor's possession) and should be present when it is run. The auditor should also be present to receive the output directly from the computer.

d. **Use Output** The auditor uses the GAS output in the audit.

6. **Statistical Sampling** Computer programs have been developed to assist the auditor in planning and evaluating sampling procedures. These programs overcome the limitations of tables and perform calculations, such as a standard deviation computation, that are difficult and time consuming to perform manually.

a. **Flexibility** Computer programs are flexible. For example, they can calculate sample sizes for different sampling techniques. They can help the auditor select a random sample. They can evaluate samples covering single or multiple locations and can offer many more options for the auditor's planning considerations. These programs generally have built-in controls over human errors. For example, programs can be designed to include controls to identify unreasonable input.

b. **Documentation** The printed output generally is written in nontechnical language that can be understood easily by an auditor. The printout can be included in the auditor's working papers as documentation of the sampling procedure.

c. **Programs** Programs offered by vendors generally are developed by vendors, by third parties for the vendor, or by CPA firms. In selecting a program, the auditor should obtain reasonable assurance that the program is suitable. The auditor should determine whether the statistical theory used to develop the program is appropriate for the auditor's purpose. It is important for the auditor to test a program adequately before use or to determine that the vendor did so. Statistical sampling software should contain basic control features that, for example, reject negative numbers where inapplicable or alert the auditor to inappropriately high risk levels or tolerable rates.

VI. Appendix: IT Terms

ad hoc **report** Nonstandardized report composed when the need arises. Frequently developed by users, rather than programmers with extensive training, for limited use.

application program Designed to perform the processing of a specific application. For example, an accounts receivable update program is an application program that processes accounts receivable data to update the accounts receivable master file.

bit A binary digit (0 or 1, on or off, etc.), representing the smallest unit of data possible.

byte A group of bits that represents a single character, whether alphabetic or numeric.

characters Letters, numbers, and special symbols (e.g., periods, commas, and hyphens).

central processing unit (CPU, mainframe) Primary hardware component. The actual processing of data occurs in the CPU. It contains primary storage, a control unit, and an arithmetic/logic unit.

> **primary storage (main memory)** Portion of the CPU that holds the program, data, and results (intermediate and final) during processing; therefore, this includes only temporary storage. The primary storage contains the data and program steps that are being processed by the CPU and is divided into RAM (random-access memory) and ROM (read-only memory).

> **control unit** Portion of the CPU that controls and directs the operations of the computer. It interprets the instructions from the program and directs the computer system to carry them out.

> **arithmetic/logic unit** Portion of the CPU that has special circuitry for performing arithmetic calculations and logical operations. This may be combined with the control unit.

cold site Location where equipment and power is available in the event of disaster at the primary location, but requiring considerable effort to get an operational system functioning. (Compare to hot site.)

collaborative computing applications (groupware, shareware) A program that allows several people to have access to the same information and attempts to track the authors of changes.

CPA SysTrust An attestation service developed in part by the AICPA, that is designed to provide assurance on whether a system's controls are operating effectively and allow the system to function reliably.

CPA WebTrust A symbol appearing on a Web site that indicates that the organization meets joint Canadian Institute of Chartered Accountants and AICPA business practice disclosures, transaction integrity, and information protection criteria.

database A structured set of interrelated files combined to eliminate redundancy of data items within the files and to establish logical connections between data items. For example, within personnel and payroll files, some of the data in the two records will be the same; in a database system, these files would be combined to eliminate the redundant data.

database management system (DBMS) A set of programs (software) that manages the database (i.e., creates, accesses, and maintains the database).

decision tables Decision tables emphasize the relationships among conditions and actions, and present decision choices. Decision tables often supplement systems flowcharts.

decode Convert data from an encoded state to its original form.

digital signature Encryption feature used to authenticate the originator of a document and insure that the message is intact.

disaster recovery Restoration of data and business function after loss.

document management Electronic document storage and retrieval.

downtime Time when the computer is not functioning. This may be scheduled or unscheduled.

edit Refers to the addition, deletion, and/or rearrangement of data. **Input editing** refers to editing before processing and **output editing** refers to editing after processing.

electronic commerce (e-commerce) Business via the Internet, including EDI.

electronic data interchange (EDI) Electronic communication among entities such as financial institutions and customer-vendor partners (typically involving order placement, invoicing, and payment and may involve inventory monitoring and automatic restocking). ANSI X12 is a domestic EDI format. EDIFACT is an international EDI format.

electronic document submission Submission of documents such as federal tax returns and securities reports in electronic form, usually over the Internet.

e-mail Electronic messages, typically delivered through the Internet. The messages may have attached files, including documents and programs.

encode, encrypt Scrambling data to prevent unauthorized use.

enterprise resource planning software Large multimodule applications that manage a business' different aspects, from traditional accounting to inventory management and advanced planning and forecasting.

extranet A password-protected intranet, usually for established vendors and customers. (Compare to internet.)

field Group of related characters. For example, a customer name.

file Group of related records. For example, a customer file. (Also see master file and transaction file.)

firewall Software designed to prevent unauthorized access to data by separating one segment from another.

gateway Software or hardware that links two or more computer networks.

groupware A program designed to allow several people to work on a single project. While this allows for greater flexibility, there is a loss of accountability. (Also see collaborative computing applications.)

hardware maintenance Involves equipment service. Routine service is scheduled. Unscheduled maintenance arises when there are unanticipated problems.

heuristic In computing, the adjective *heuristic* signifies *able to change;* it is used to describe a computer program that can modify itself in response to the user, for example, a spell check program.

hot site Location where a functioning system is planned for use with minimal preparation in the event of a disaster at the primary work location. (Compare to cold site.)

input/output devices Devices for transferring data in and out of the CPU. Examples include:

bar code reader An input device to scan bar codes, such as universal product codes on merchandise.

keyboard Typewriterlike device to allow the user to type information into the computer.

magnetic ink character recognition (MICR) Sensing information recorded in special magnetized ink. MICR is commonly used by the banking industry for check processing.

magnetic tape reader A device to sense information recorded as magnetized spots on magnetic tape (e.g., the magnetic strips used on credit cards and ATM cards).

modem A device to allow users to transfer files over telephone lines to distant computers.

monitor, screen A televisionlike screen to display information, providing feedback to the user.

mouse, trackball A pointing device to manipulate representations displayed on a screen.

optical character recognition (OCR) scanner A device to sense printed information through the use of light-sensitive devices.

printer A device to produce output on paper, including invoices and checks.

Internet A network of networks. The Internet is a public network of many networks. (Compare to intranet.)

intranet A network generally restricted to employee access. LANs are typically intranets. (Compare to internet and extranet.)

inventory control system A system that tracks the quantity of inventory bought and sold.

library program (library routine) Programs that are frequently used by other programs. They are kept within the system and "called up" whenever necessary. One example is generating random numbers.

local area network (LAN) A network of computers within a small area (i.e., a building) to transmit information electronically and share files and peripheral equipment among members (compare to wide area network).

management information system (MIS) An information system within an organization that provides management with the information needed for planning and control. This involves an integration of the functions of gathering and analyzing data, and reporting (i.e., communicating) the results to management in a meaningful form.

mapping Converting data between application format and a standard format, such as EDI.

master file Contains relatively permanent data. For example, an accounts receivable master file would contain a record for each customer and each record would include fields for customer number, name, address, credit limit, amount owed, etc. (Compare to transaction file.)

network An arrangement of computers to allow users access to common data, hardware, and/or software.

operating system (OS) Manages the coordinating and scheduling of various application programs and computer functions. Examples include the following:

multiprocessing Allows the execution of two or more programs at the same time and requires the utilization of more than one CPU.

multiprogramming A program is processed until some type of input or output is needed. The OS then delegates the process to a piece of peripheral equipment, and the CPU begins executing other programs. Processing speed is enhanced considerably, making it appear as if more than one program is being processed concurrently, while utilizing only one CPU.

virtual storage The OS divides a program into segments (called pages) and brings only sections of the program into memory as needed to execute the instructions. This saves memory and processing cost because the majority of the program remains in less expensive secondary storage.

pass (run) A complete cycle of input, processing, and output in the execution of a computer program.

patch Addition of a new part to a program. It may be added to correct or update a program. For example, if a new government regulation affecting withholding tax becomes effective, a patch may be added to the payroll program to provide for this. A patch may also be added for a fraudulent purpose. For example, an employee might insert a patch into a payroll program to print an extra check.

peripheral equipment Equipment that is **not** part of the CPU but that may be placed under the control of the CPU, i.e., which may be accessed directly by the CPU. Input/output devices and secondary storage devices are peripheral equipment.

point-of-sale (POS) system A system that records goods sold and figures the amount due at the cash register, frequently also verifying credit cards or checks.

program Set of instructions that the computer follows to accomplish a specified task (e.g., accounts receivable update program, inventory management program, and payroll program).

program maintenance Refers to making changes in the program in order to keep it current and functioning properly. For example, maintenance of the payroll program may involve modifying it because of changes in the social security law or to provide for a greater number of employees.

record Group of related fields. For example, a customer record would include ID number, name, address, etc.

router Switches that transfer incoming messages to outgoing links via the most efficient route possible, for example, over the Internet.

secondary storage Devices external to the CPU that store data.

> **disk, diskette** Randomly accessible data is represented in concentric circles called "tracks." A magnetic disk is a platter coated on both sides with a material on which data can be represented as magnetized dots according to a predetermined code. Diskettes are more common than disks, as they hold more data. Still more data can be stored on CDs (also called laser disks). A disk drive is used to read data from the disk into the CPU and to write data from the CPU onto the disk. A hard drive is more permanently fixed than a disk or diskette, with faster retrieval. Disks are usually more easily moved than a hard drive.

> **magnetic tape** Plastic tape that is coated with a material on which data can be represented as magnetized dots according to a predetermined code. It resembles audio tape.

> **off-line storage** Not in direct communication with the CPU. Human intervention is needed for the data to be processed. For example, a disk must be inserted in a disk drive before it can be accessed.

> **online storage** In direct communication with the CPU without human intervention. For example, a hard drive ordinarily is accessed by the CPU without human intervention.

> **randomly accessible (direct access)** Data records can be accessed directly. Disks are an example. For example, if the customer records are stored in a file on a disk, the disk drive could go directly to a specific customer's record without having to read any of the other customer records.

> **sequentially accessible** Requires the reading of all data between the starting point and the information sought. Magnetic tape is sequentially accessible. For example, if alphabetized records are

on magnetic tape and none are read, most of the tape must be read to get to a specific customer's data.

self-service applications Software that allows customers to provide much of their own customer service.

software Programs, routines, documentation, manuals, etc., that make it possible for the computer system to operate and process data. (Compare to hardware.)

systems programs (supervisory programs) Perform the functions of coordinating and controlling the overall operation of the computer system.

telecommuting Working outside of a traditional office, remaining connected by the Internet, phone, etc. Usually implies a office in the employee's home, although a sales agent or insurance adjuster might also work from a vehicle and/or customer sites.

transaction (detail) file Contains current, temporary data. A transaction file is used to update a master file. For example, the day's charge sales would be accumulated on a transaction file that would be used to update the accounts receivable master file during an update run.

Trojan horse A seemingly legitimate program that operates in an unauthorized manner, usually causing damage.

universal in-box A system to collect email and voice mail in one "place," accessible by either regular phone or computer.

utility program (utility routine) Standard program for performing routine functions, e.g., sorting and merging.

value-added network (VAN) A network service that provides additional services beyond mere connections to the Internet, particularly services enabling EDI.

video conference Real-time meeting over the Internet.

virus A program that replicates and attaches itself to other programs. The effects of a virus can be a merely annoying message or malicious activity, such as reformatting a hard drive or flooding an e-mail system.

virus hoax An e-mail message with a false warning. Its originator tries to get it circulated as widely as possible.

voice mail A system that records, directs, stores, and replays telephone messages.

web crawler A program used to search the World Wide Web for files meeting user criteria.

wide area network (WAN) A computer network encompassing a large area (i.e., citywide or globally) to transmit information electronically and share files among members (typically companywide only). (Compare to local area network).

CHAPTER 27—AUDITING IT SYSTEMS

Problem 27-1 MULTIPLE CHOICE QUESTIONS (66 to 83 minutes)

1. Which of the following computer documentations would an auditor most likely utilize in obtaining an understanding of internal control?
a. Systems flowcharts
b. Record counts
c. Program listings
d. Record layouts
(5/90, AUD, #27, amended, 0278)

2. One of the major problems in an IT system is that incompatible functions may be performed by the same individual. One compensating control for this is the use of
a. Echo checks
b. A self-checking digit system
c. Computer-generated hash totals
d. A computer log
e. Source code comparison (Editors, 0297)

3. Which of the following strategies would a CPA most likely consider in auditing an entity that processes most of its financial data only in electronic form, such as a paperless system?
a. Continuous monitoring and analysis of transaction processing with an embedded audit module
b. Increased reliance on internal control activities that emphasize the segregation of duties
c. Verification of encrypted digital certificates used to monitor the authorization of transactions
d. Extensive testing of firewall boundaries that restrict the recording of outside network traffic
(R/99, AUD, #23, 6839)

4. A retail entity uses electronic data interchange (EDI) in executing and recording most of its purchase transactions. The entity's auditor recognizes that the documentation of the transactions will be retained for only a short period of time. To compensate for this limitation, the auditor most likely would
a. Increase the sample of EDI transactions to be selected for cutoff tests
b. Perform tests several times during the year, rather than only at year end
c. Plan to make a 100% count of the entity's inventory at or near the year end
d. Decrease the assessed level of control risk for the existence or occurrence assertion
(R/00, AUD, #9, 6934)

5. Which of the following is an engagement attribute for an audit of an entity that processes most of its financial data in electronic form without any paper documentation?
a. Discrete phases of planning, interim, and year-end fieldwork
b. Increased effort to search for evidence of management fraud
c. Performance of audit tests on a continuous basis
d. Increased emphasis on the completeness assertion (R/99, AUD, #22, 6838)

6. An auditor anticipates assessing control risk at a low level in a computerized environment. Under these circumstances, on which of the following procedures would the auditor initially focus?
a. Programmed control procedures
b. Application control procedures
c. Output control procedures
d. General control procedures
(5/92, AUD, #36, 2789)

7. Which of the following is an example of how specific internal controls in a database environment may differ from controls in a nondatabase environment?
a. Controls should exist to ensure that users have access to and can update only the data elements that they have been authorized to access.
b. Controls over data sharing by diverse users within an entity should be the same for every user.
c. The employee who manages the computer hardware should also develop and debug the computer programs.
d. Controls can provide assurance that all processed transactions are authorized, but cannot verify that all authorized transactions are processed. (R/00, AUD, #8, 6933)

8. Misstatements in a batch computer system caused by incorrect programs or data may **not** be detected immediately because
a. Errors in some transactions may cause rejection of other transactions in the batch.
b. The identification of errors in input data typically is not part of the program.
c. There are time delays in processing transactions in a batch system.
d. The processing of transactions in a batch system is not uniform. (11/94, AUD, #37, 5110)

9. Which of the following most likely represents a significant deficiency in internal control?

a. The systems programmer designs systems for computerized applications and maintains output controls.

b. The systems analyst reviews applications of data processing and maintains systems documentation.

c. The control clerk establishes control over data received by the IT department and reconciles control totals after processing.

d. The accounts payable clerk prepares data for computer processing and enters the data into the computer. (Editors, 2304)

10. When evaluating internal control of an entity that processes sales transactions on the Internet, an auditor would be most concerned about the

a. Lack of sales invoice documents as an audit trail

b. Potential for computer disruptions in recording sales

c. Inability to establish an integrated test facility

d. Frequency of archiving and data retention (R/99, AUD, #10, 6826)

11. Which of the following statements is correct concerning internal control in an electronic data interchange (EDI) system?

a. Preventive controls generally are more important than detective controls in EDI systems.

b. Control objectives for EDI systems generally are different from the objectives for other information systems.

c. Internal controls in EDI systems rarely permit control risk to be assessed at below the maximum.

d. Internal controls related to the segregation of duties generally are the most important controls in EDI systems. (R/99, AUD, #11, 6827)

12. In an environment that is highly automated, an auditor determines that it is not possible to reduce detection risk solely by substantive tests of transactions. Under these circumstances, the auditor most likely would

a. Perform tests of controls to support a lower level of assessed control risk

b. Increase the sample size to reduce sampling risk and detection risk

c. Adjust the materiality level and consider the effect on inherent risk

d. Apply analytical procedures and consider the effect on control risk (R/05, AUD, #44, 7839)

13. Which of the following is **not** a major reason for maintaining an audit trail for a computer system?

a. Deterrent to fraud

b. Monitoring purposes

c. Analytical procedures

d. Query answering (11/91, AUD, #24, 2292)

14. Which of the following is an essential element of the audit trail in an electronic data interchange (EDI) system?

a. Disaster recovery plans that ensure proper back-up of files

b. Encrypted hash totals that authenticate messages

c. Activity logs that indicate failed transactions

d. Hardware security modules that store sensitive data (R/99, AUD, #13, 6829)

15. Which of the following activities most likely would detect whether payroll data were altered during processing?

a. Monitor authorized distribution of data control sheets

b. Use test data to verify the performance of edit routines

c. Examine source documents for approval by supervisors

d. Segregate duties between approval of hardware and software specifications (R/00, AUD, #14, 6939)

16. An auditor would most likely be concerned with which of the following controls in a distributed data processing system?

a. Hardware controls

b. Systems documentation controls

c. Access controls

d. Disaster recovery controls (5/91, AUD, #16, 0273)

17. To obtain evidence that on-line access controls are properly functioning, an auditor most likely would

a. Create checkpoints at periodic intervals after live data processing to test for unauthorized use of the system

b. Examine the transaction log to discover whether any transactions were lost or entered twice due to a system malfunction

c. Enter invalid identification numbers or passwords to ascertain whether the system rejects them

d. Vouch a random sample of processed transactions to assure proper authorization (5/93, AUD, #41, 3937)

18. Which of the following would an auditor ordinarily consider the greatest risk regarding an entity's use of electronic data interchange (EDI)?
a. Authorization of EDI transactions
b. Duplication of EDI transmissions
c. Improper distribution of EDI transactions
d. Elimination of paper documents

(6/99, AUD, #3, 6850)

19. Which of the following controls is a processing control designed to ensure the reliability and accuracy of data processing?

	Limit test	Validity check test
a.	Yes	Yes
b.	No	No
c.	No	Yes
d.	Yes	No

(11/94, AUD, #38, 5111)

Items 20 and 21 are based on the following:

Invoice #	Product	Quantity	Unit price
201	F10	150	$ 5.00
202	G15	200	$10.00
203	H20	250	$25.00
204	K35	300	$30.00

20. Which of the following numbers represents the record count?
a. 1
b. 4
c. 810
d. 900

(5/98, AUD, #3, 6620)

21. Which of the following most likely represents a hash total?
a. FGHK80
b. 4
c. 204
d. 810

(5/98, AUD, #4, 6621)

22. When an auditor tests a computerized accounting system, which of the following is true of the test data approach?
a. Several transactions of each type must be tested.
b. Test data are processed by the client's computer programs under the auditor's control.
c. Test data must consist of all possible valid and invalid conditions.
d. The program tested is different from the program used throughout the year by the client.

(5/95, AUD, #72, 5690)

23. Which of the following is the primary reason that many auditors hesitate to use embedded audit modules?
a. Embedded audit modules cannot be protected from computer viruses.
b. Auditors are required to monitor embedded audit modules continuously to obtain valid results.
c. Embedded audit modules can easily be modified through management tampering.
d. Auditors are required to be involved in the system design of the application to be monitored.

(R/02, AUD, #20, 7110)

24. What **two** selections are crucial to achieving audit efficiency and effectiveness with a personal computer?
a. The appropriate audit tasks for personal computer applications
b. The appropriate software to perform the selected audit tasks
c. Audit procedures that are generally applicable to several clients in a specific industry
d. Client data that can be accessed by the auditor's personal computer

(Editors, 7499)

Item 25 is based on the following flowchart:

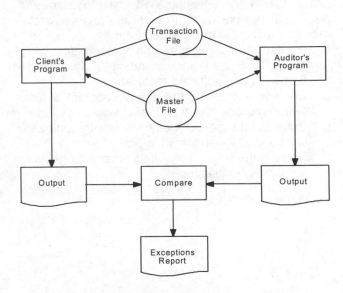

25. The preceding flowchart depicts
a. Program code checking
b. Parallel simulation
c. Controlled reprocessing
d. Integrated test facility

(Editors, 0308)

26. An auditor most likely would test for the presence of unauthorized IT program changes by running
a. A program with test data
b. A check digit verification program
c. A source code comparison program
d. A program that computes control totals
(11/92, AUD, #37, amended, 2971)

27. Which of the following computer-assisted auditing techniques allows fictitious and real transactions to be processed together without client operating personnel being aware of the testing process?
a. Integrated test facility
b. Input controls matrix
c. Parallel simulation
d. Data entry monitor (11/94, AUD, #70, 5143)

28. Which of the following computer-assisted auditing techniques processes client input data on a controlled program under the auditor's control to test controls in the computer system?
a. Test data
b. Review of program logic
c. Integrated test facility
d. Parallel simulation (R/01, AUD, #17, 7032)

29. A primary advantage of using generalized audit software packages to audit the financial statements of a client is that the auditor may
a. Access information stored on computer files while having a limited understanding of the client's hardware and software features
b. Consider increasing the use of substantive tests of transactions in place of analytical procedures
c. Substantiate the accuracy of data through self-checking digits and hash totals
d. Reduce the level of required tests of controls to a relatively small amount
(11/95, AUD, #52, amended, 5999)

30. When conducting fieldwork for a physical inventory, an auditor **cannot** perform which of the following steps using a generalized audit software package?
a. Observing inventory
b. Selecting sample items of inventory
c. Analyzing data resulting from inventory
d. Recalculating balances in inventory reports
(R/06, AUD, #49, 8167)

31. Using personal computers in auditing may affect the methods used to review the work of staff assistants because
a. Supervisory personnel may not have an understanding of the capabilities and limitations of personal computers.
b. Working paper documentation may not contain readily observable details of calculations.
c. Documenting the supervisory review may require assistance of management services personnel.
d. The audit fieldwork standards for supervision may differ. (Editors, 0196)

32. Which of the following is a term for an attest engagement in which a CPA assesses a client's commercial Internet site for predefined criteria that are designed to measure transaction integrity, information protection, and disclosure of business practices?
a. ElectroNet
b. EDIFACT
c. TechSafe
d. WebTrust (R/99, AUD, #2, 6818)

33. Which of the following is a professional engagement that a CPA may perform to provide assurance on a system's reliability?
a. MAS AssurAbility
b. CPA WebMaster
c. MAS AttestSure
d. CPA SysTrust (R/06, AUD, #10, 8128)

Problem 27-2 ADDITIONAL MULTIPLE CHOICE QUESTIONS (44 to 55 minutes)

34. A retailing entity uses the Internet to execute and record its purchase transactions. The entity's auditor recognizes that the documentation of details of transactions will be retained for only a short period of time. To compensate for this limitation, the auditor most likely would
a. Compare a sample of paid vendors' invoices to the receiving records at year end
b. Plan for a large measure of tolerable misstatement in substantive tests
c. Perform tests several times during the year, rather than only at year end
d. Increase the sample of transactions to be selected for cutoff tests   (R/07, AUD, #2, 8374)

35. Which of the following would most likely be a weakness in internal control of a client that utilizes microcomputers rather than a larger computer system?
a. Employee collusion possibilities are increased because microcomputers from one vendor can process the programs of a system from a different vendor.
b. The microcomputer operators may be able to remove hardware and software components and modify them at home.
c. Programming errors result in all similar transactions being processed incorrectly when those transactions are processed under the same conditions.
d. Certain transactions may be automatically initiated by the microcomputers and management's authorization of these transactions may be implicit in its acceptance of the system design.
(Editors, 7500)

36. Which of the following statements most likely represents a disadvantage for an entity that keeps microcomputer-prepared data files rather than manually prepared files?
a. Attention is focused on the accuracy of the programming process rather than errors in individual transactions.
b. It is usually easier for unauthorized persons to access and alter the files.
c. Random error associated with processing similar transactions in different ways is usually greater.
d. It is usually more difficult to compare recorded accountability with physical count of assets.
(5/94, AUD, #16, 4681)

37. Which of the following characteristics distinguishes computer processing from manual processing?
a. Computer processing virtually eliminates the occurrence of computational error normally associated with manual processing.
b. The potential for systematic error is ordinarily greater in manual processing than in computerized processing.
c. Errors or fraud in computer processing will be detected soon after their occurrences.
d. Most computer systems are designed so that transaction trails useful for audit purposes do not exist.   (Editors, 0289)

38. Which of the following control procedures most likely could prevent IT personnel from modifying programs to bypass programmed controls?
a. Periodic management review of computer utilization reports and systems documentation
b. Segregation of duties within IT for computer programming and computer operations
c. Participation of user department personnel in designing and approving new systems
d. Physical security of IT facilities in limiting access to IT equipment
(11/95, AUD, #14, amended, 5961)

39. When an accounting application is processed by computer, an auditor cannot verify the reliable operation of programmed control procedures by
a. Constructing a processing system for accounting applications and processing actual data from throughout the period through both the client's program and the auditor's program
b. Manually comparing detail transaction files used by an edit program to the program's generated error listings to determine that errors were properly identified by the edit program
c. Manually reperforming, as of a point in time, the processing of input data and comparing the simulated results to the actual results
d. Periodically submitting auditor-prepared test data to the same computer process and evaluating the results   (Editors, 0279)

40. A client that recently installed a new accounts payable system assigned employees a user identification code (UIC) and a separate password. Each UIC is a person's name, and the individual's password is the same as the UIC. Users are not required to change their passwords at initial log-in nor do passwords ever expire. Which of the following statements does not reflect a limitation of the client's computer-access control?
a. Employees can easily guess fellow employees' passwords.
b. Employees are not required to change passwords.
c. Employees can circumvent procedures to segregate duties.
d. Employees are not required to take regular vacations. (R/05, AUD, #42, 7837)

41. Matthews Corp. has changed from a system of recording time worked on clock cards to a computerized payroll system in which employees record time in and out with magnetic cards. The EDP system automatically updates all payroll records. Because of this change
a. A generalized computer audit program must be used.
b. Part of the audit trail is altered.
c. Transactions must be processed in batches.
d. The potential for payroll-related fraud is diminished. (Editors, 0296)

42. An auditor who is testing IT controls in a payroll system would most likely use test data that contain conditions such as
a. Deductions not authorized by employees
b. Overtime not approved by supervisors
c. Payroll checks with unauthorized signatures
d. Time tickets with invalid job numbers
(Editors, 0286)

43. In a computerized payroll system environment, an auditor would be least likely to use test data to test controls related to
a. Missing employee numbers
b. Proper approval of overtime by supervisors
c. Time tickets with invalid job numbers
d. Agreement of hours per clock cards with hours on time tickets (5/91, AUD, #31, 0049)

44. Which of the following is usually a benefit of using electronic funds transfer for international cash transactions?
a. Improvement of the audit trail for cash receipts and disbursements
b. Creation of self-monitoring access controls
c. Reduction of the frequency of data entry errors
d. Off-site storage of source documents for cash transactions (R/99, AUD, #8, 6824)

45. Which of the following statements is correct concerning the security of messages in an electronic data interchange (EDI) system?
a. When the confidentiality of data is the primary risk, message authentication is the preferred control rather than encryption.
b. Encryption performed by physically secure hardware devices is more secure than encryption performed by software.
c. Message authentication in EDI systems performs the same function as segregation of duties in other information systems.
d. Security at the transaction phase in EDI systems is not necessary because problems at that level will usually be identified by the service provider.
(R/99, AUD, #12, 6828)

46. The completeness of IT-generated sales figures can be tested by comparing the number of items listed on the daily sales report with the number of items billed on the actual invoices. This process uses
a. Check digits
b. Control totals
c. Process tracing data
d. Validity tests (Editors, 0292)

47. An IT input control is designed to ensure that
a. Only authorized personnel have access to the computer area.
b. Machine processing is accurate.
c. Data received for processing are properly authorized and converted to machine readable form.
d. Electronic data processing has been performed as intended for the particular application.
(Editors, 0306)

48. A customer intended to order 100 units of product Z96014, but incorrectly ordered nonexistent product Z96015. Which of the following controls most likely would detect this error?
a. Check digit verification
b. Record count
c. Hash total
d. Redundant data check (5/98, AUD, #5, 6622)

49. Which of the following input controls is a numeric value computed to provide assurance that the original value has not been altered in construction or transmission?
a. Hash total
b. Parity check
c. Encryption
d. Check digit (5/98, AUD, #8, 6625)

50. An auditor would least likely use computer software to
a. Construct parallel simulations
b. Access client data files
c. Prepare spreadsheets
d. Assess IT control risk

(5/93, AUD, #40, amended, 3936)

51. Processing data through the use of simulated files provides an auditor with information about the operating effectiveness of control policies and procedures. One of the techniques involved in this approach makes use of
a. Controlled reprocessing
b. An integrated test facility
c. Input validation
d. Program code checking

(11/92, AUD, #36, 2970)

52. An auditor who wishes to capture an entity's data as transactions are processed and continuously test the entity's computerized information system most likely would use which of the following techniques?
a. Snapshot application
b. Embedded audit module
c. Integrated data check
d. Test data generator   (R/01, AUD, #15, 7030)

53. In parallel simulation, actual client data are reprocessed using an auditor software program. An advantage of using parallel simulation, instead of performing tests of controls without a computer, is that
a. The test includes all types of transaction errors and exceptions that may be encountered.
b. The client's computer personnel do not know when the data are being tested.
c. There is no risk of creating potentially material errors in the client's data.
d. The size of the sample can be greatly expanded at relatively little additional cost.

(R/05, AUD, #17, 7812)

54. When an auditor tests the internal controls of a computerized accounting system, which of the following is true of the test data approach?
a. Test data are coded to a dummy subsidiary so they can be extracted from the system under actual operating conditions.
b. Test data programs need not be tailor-made by the auditor for each client's computer applications.
c. Test data programs usually consist of all possible valid and invalid conditions regarding compliance with internal controls.
d. Test data are processed with the client's computer and the results are compared with the auditor's predetermined results.

(R/07, AUD, #17, 8389)

55. When companies use information technology (IT) extensively, evidence may be available only in electronic form. What is an auditor's best course of action in such situations?
a. Assess the control risk as high
b. Use audit software to perform analytical procedures
c. Use generalized audit software to extract evidence from client databases
d. Perform limited tests of controls over electronic data   (R/07, AUD, #29, 8401)

SIMULATIONS

Problem 27-3 (15 to 25 minutes)

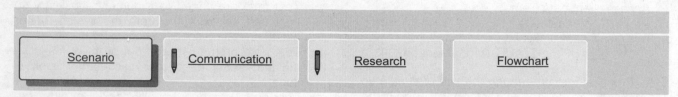

Software has been developed to improve the efficiency and effectiveness of the audit. Electronic spreadsheets and other software packages are available to aid in the performance of audit procedures otherwise performed manually.

Describe the potential benefits to an auditor of using software in an audit as compared to performing an audit without the use of a computer.

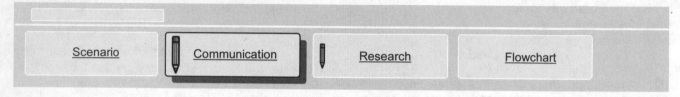

What authoritative reference provides guidance for when the auditor should complete the assembly of the final audit file?

Paragraph Reference Answer: _____

Scenario	✎ Communication	✎ Research	Flowchart

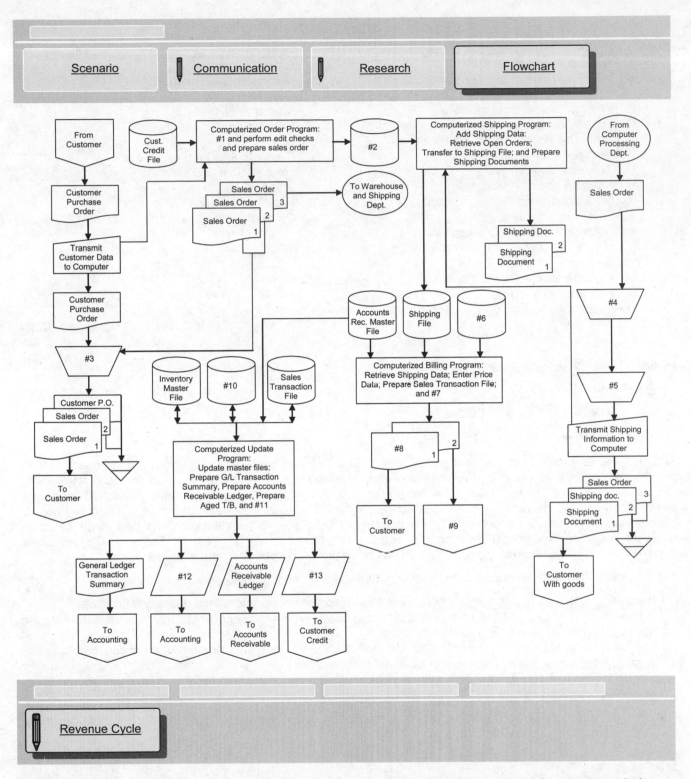

✎ Revenue Cycle

The accompanying flowchart depicts part of a client's revenue cycle. Some of the flowchart symbols are labeled to indicate control procedures and records. For each symbol labeled 1 through 13, select one response from the answer list below.

Answer List

Operations and control procedures	*Documents, journals, ledgers, and files*
A. Enter shipping data	P. Shipping document
B. Verify agreement of sales order and shipping document	Q. General ledger master file
	R. General journal
C. Write off accounts receivable	S. Master price file
D. To warehouse and shipping department	T. Sales journal
E. Authorize account receivable write-off	U. Sales invoice
F. Prepare aged trial balance	V. Cash receipts journal
G. To sales department	W. Uncollectible accounts file
H. Release goods for shipment	X. Shipping file
I. To accounts receivable department	Y. Aged trial balance
J. Enter price data	Z. Open order file
K. Determine that customer exists	
L. Match customer purchase order with sales order	
M. Perform customer credit check	
N. Prepare sales journal	
O. Prepare sales invoice	

(11/93, AUD, #2, amended, 9033)

Problem 27-4 (20 to 25 minutes)

Brown, CPA, is auditing the financial statements of Big Z Wholesaling, Inc., a continuing audit client, for the year ended January 31, Year 2. Brown issued an unqualified opinion on the prior year's financial statements. On January 5, Year 2, Brown observed the tagging and counting of Big Z's physical inventory and made appropriate test counts. All inventory is purchased for resale and located in a single warehouse. These test counts have been recorded on a computer file. As in prior years, Big Z gave Brown two computer files. One file represents the perpetual inventory (FIFO) records for the year ended January 31, Year 2. The other file represents the January 5 physical inventory count. Brown has appropriate computerized audit software.

The perpetual inventory file contains the following information in item number sequence:

(1) Beginning balances at February 1, Year 1; item number, item description, total quantity, and prices.
(2) For each item purchased during the year: date received, receiving report number, vendor, item number, item description, quantity, and total dollar amount.
(3) For each item sold during the year: date shipped, invoice number, item number, item description, quantity shipped, and dollar amount of the cost removed from inventory.
(4) For each item adjusted for physical inventory count differences: date, item number, item descriptions, quantity, and dollar amount.

The physical inventory file contains the following information in item number sequence: tag number, item number, item description, and count quantity.

Describe the substantive auditing procedures Brown may consider performing with computerized audit software using Big Z's two computer files and Brown's computer file of test counts. The substantive auditing procedures described may indicate the reports to be printed out for Brown's follow-up by subsequent application of manual procedures. Do not describe subsequent manual auditing procedures. Group the procedures by those using (1) the perpetual inventory file and (2) the physical inventory and test count files.

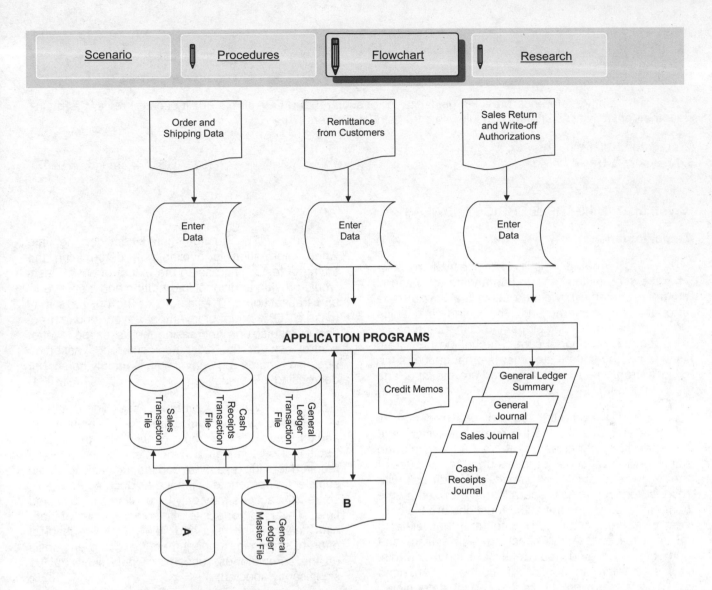

Based on the accompanying flowchart of a client's revenue cycle, what do the symbols marked A and B most likely represent?

Answer List

- A. Accounts receivable master file
- B. Cash disbursements transaction file
- C. Customer checks
- D. Customer orders
- E. Receiving reports
- F. Receiving report file
- G. Remittance advice file
- H. Sales invoices

Scenario	✎ Procedures	✎ Flowchart	✎ Research

What authoritative reference provides guidance for ensuring that a CPA firm's quality control reviewers maintain their objectivity when they consult with engagement partners?

Paragraph Reference Answer: _____

(5/92, AUD, #4, amended, 6297)

Solution 27-1 MULTIPLE CHOICE ANSWERS

Documentation

1. (a) An auditor is likely to use systems flowcharts in obtaining an understanding of internal control. Systems flowcharts show the flow of data through the system and the interrelationships between the processing steps and computer runs. A record count is an input control technique. Program listings are the source statements or language of the client's programs. Record layouts are the input and output formats. (0278)

2. (d) A computer log provides evidence as to which employees used the computer system and the operations performed by them. As a result, the computer log will protect against unauthorized use of the IT system, and it will provide an audit trail with respect to incompatible operations performed by the same individual. Incompatible functions are the concern of general controls, i.e., controls that relate to all IT activities. A self-checking digit system and computer-generated hash totals are input controls, i.e., they relate to application controls. An echo check is a hardware control aimed at determining whether the computer is operating properly. It has no effect on the control over incompatible functions. A source code comparison could fail to bring errors to light, as the system could be processing incorrect data in the prescribed manner. (0297)

Planning

3. (a) When a client processes financial data in electronic form without a paper trail, the auditor may need to audit on a more continuous basis to obtain sufficient, appropriate evidence because documentation for some transactions may only be available for a limited time. An embedded audit module can facilitate this "continuous" auditing. If anything, an auditor may rely less on internal control activities that emphasize the segregation of duties. Digital certificate verification and testing of firewall boundaries are more concerned with security than internal control. (6839)

4. (b) The auditor should consider the time when information is available in determining the timing of tests. Increasing the extent of cut-off tests would provide additional information about only year-end transactions. The nature of the business may make a 100% count of inventory at year end impractical or insufficient. Increasing the assessed level of control risk for the existence/occurrence assertion because records are unavailable is unduly harsh, but decreasing it is unjustified. (6934)

5. (c) When a client processes financial data in electronic form without paper documentation, the auditor may audit on a more continuous basis than a traditional system, as a convenience, and may be required to audit on a more continuous basis to obtain sufficient, appropriate evidence as documentation for some transactions may only be available for a limited time. This is the opposite of discrete phases of planning, interim, and year-end fieldwork. The level of effort to search for management fraud and emphasis on the completeness assertion would likely not be significantly affected. (6838)

6. (d) When an auditor anticipates assessing control risk at a low level in a computerized environment, generally, the auditor would initially focus on general control procedures, which are those controls that relate to all or many computerized accounting activities and often include control over the development, modification, and maintenance of computer programs and control over the use of and changes to data maintained on computer files. (2789)

Internal Control

7. (a) Controls in a database environment can be very specific as to which elements of a record can be accessed or changed, resulting in a more detailed set of authorizations. [Note: The examiners say to select the best answer.] Controls over data sharing should be appropriate for each user, usually resulting in diverse controls. Preferably, hardware management and software development are segregated. The relationship between authorization and processing

usually is the same within a database and a non-database environment.   (6933)

8.   (c)   There are time delays when data is processed in batches, so errors may not be detected immediately. The identification of errors in input data would be identified through various means such as the use of batch totals and normally would be part of the program. The processing of transactions in a batch system is uniform.   (5110)

9.   (a)   A weakness in internal control exists where an individual is in a position to both perpetrate and conceal an error or fraud. Hence, a systems programmer should not be given any control over the review or distribution of the output of the IT system.
                                                              (2304)

10.   (b)   Computer disruptions could destroy the only record of an online transaction. By their nature, sales transactions processed on the Internet don't involve sales invoice documents. Integrated test facilities, archiving, and data retention are issues that arise whether sales are on the Internet or entered into a computer system by the entity.   (6826)

11.   (a)   Preventive controls are generally more important than detective controls in EDI systems because of the speed with which goods and services are delivered. Objectives remain the same as for other information systems. Internal controls in EDI systems must be strong to minimize losses. Segregation of duties is not as important as protection of assets in an EDI system.   (6827)

Evidence

12.   (a)   When the auditor has determined that it is not possible or practicable to reduce the detection risks at the relevant assertion level to an acceptably low level with audit evidence obtained only from substantive procedures, s/he should perform tests of controls to obtain audit evidence about their operating effectiveness. The auditor may find it impossible to design effective substantive procedures that by themselves provide sufficient appropriate audit evidence at the relevant assertion level when an entity conducts its business using information technology (IT) and no documentation of transactions is produced or maintained, other than through the IT system. Increasing the sample size for substantive tests in this circumstance would be ineffective as the question states that it is not possible to reduce detection risk solely by substantive tests of transactions. Changing the materiality level would be inappropriate. Further, changing the materiality level does not have an effect on inherent risk, which is the susceptibility of an assertion to

misstatement without any internal controls. Analytics performed by the auditor do not have an effect on control risk, which is the risk that the entity's internal controls will not detect material misstatements in the financial statements.   (7839)

13.   (c)   Analytical procedures involve the analysis of the plausible relationship among both financial and nonfinancial data. A lack of an accounting audit trail for a computer system would not preclude the auditor from performing analytical procedures. The purpose of an audit trail would be to monitor the system, answer queries, and deter fraud.   (2292)

14.   (c)   Logs with failed transactions are examined to determine whether the corrected transactions were eventually executed and to detect attempts of unauthorized system use. Proper file backup is a recovery issue. Message authentication and hardware security modules are security issues.   (6829)

15.   (b)   With test data, the auditor can readily compare actual results to anticipated results. Monitoring distribution wouldn't detect data alteration. Source documents could be correctly approved and data could be later altered in processing without impact on the source documents. Segregation of duties discourages fraud, but not unintentional mistakes. Further, approval of hardware and software specifications are not necessarily the most critical functions to segregate in the IT area.   (6939)

General Controls

16.   (c)   A distributed data processing system is one in which many different users have access to the main computer through various computer locations. Thus, access controls, which restrict access to the main computer, are necessary to maintain a strong internal control structure, because those with access to the computer are in a position to perform incompatible functions. Hardware controls, systems documentation controls, and disaster recovery controls would not be as important in assessing control risk and would not likely present unusual problems in a distributed system.   (0273)

17.   (c)   Password controls, used in restricting access to computers, are designed to preclude access capabilities of those employees whose regular functions are incompatible with computer use. To obtain evidence that user identification and password controls are functioning as designed, an auditor would most likely examine a sample of invalid passwords or numbers to determine whether the computer is recognizing the invalid passwords and rejecting access. Answer (a) checks the level of authorization an employee has once within the

system rather than access to the online system. Answer (b) is a procedure for determining the completeness of transaction processing. Answer (d) does not address whether the online access is being limited or circumvented. (3937)

Application Controls

18. (c) Improper transactions, regardless of the media, are usually the greatest risk. Appropriate authorization of EDI transactions doesn't present a risk. Duplication of EDI transactions would likely be found by one of the involved parties upon reconciliation. Elimination of paper documents is a goal of EDI. (6850)

19. (a) Computers can be programmed to perform a wide range of edit tasks on records as they are being inputted into the system. If a particular record does not meet the test, it would not be processed. Edit tests include limit tests, validity check tests, check digit tests, etc. (5111)

20. (b) A record count is a count of the number of records in a batch or file or similar group. (6620)

21. (d) A hash total is a numeric total with meaning only as a control. Because of the alpha characters in the product codes, a hash total cannot be derived from product codes without a conversion of letters into numeric amounts. Totals of quantities have meaning beyond a control. (6621)

CAAT

22. (b) In the test data approach to testing a computerized accounting system, test data are processed by the client's computer programs under the auditor's control. The auditor will determine how many transactions and what types of transactions to test which may or may not include several transactions of each type. The auditor need not include test data for all possible valid and invalid conditions. The object is to test the client's program that is used throughout the year and the auditor must take steps to make sure that the program being tested is the one that is actually used in routine processing; thus, a different program would not be tested. (5690)

23. (d) Embedded audit modules can be difficult to install once the application program is operational, but efficiently included during system design. Embedded audit modules can be protected from viruses as well as other applications. Sporadic or occasional monitoring of embedded audit modules can produce valid results. Management tampering can modify other applications as easily as embedded audit modules. (7110)

24. (a, b) Two responses are required for full point value. Personal computers may be used to prepare trial balances, to perform analytical procedures, for automated working papers, word processing, and graphics, among other uses. With the appropriate software, applied to the appropriate audit tasks, personal computers can improve audit efficiency and effectiveness. (7499)

25. (b) In parallel simulation, the auditor compares the results of the client's processing with results obtained by using the client's input and files and the auditor's own program. In program code checking, the auditor reviews the client's program documentation, including a narrative description and the source code. An integrated test facility includes processing of dummy records with the client's records using the client's program. In controlled reprocessing, the auditor maintains control over the reprocessing of previously processed results using a version of the program the auditor has tested and compares the computer output of the original processing and reprocessing. (0308)

26. (c) A source code comparison program could be used to compare the original code written for a specific program to the current code in use for that program. Thus, it would make note of any differences in the program from the time it was originally written. Test data would generally be used to test the output of the program but would provide no evidence as to whether the program code had been changed. A check digit program involves the use of a digit that is added to the end of a piece of numeric data to permit the data to be checked for accuracy during input, processing, or output. Control totals are totals computed at different times in the computer process and are used as input, processing, and output controls. They would not provide evidence as to whether any changes were made to the original program code. (2971)

27. (a) An integrated test facility (ITF) processes fictitious data with real data in order to test computer controls; client personnel are unaware of the testing. An input control matrix documents controls and their presence. Parallel simulation processes client input data on an auditor-controlled program to test controls; test data is not utilized. The term "data entry monitor" is not commonly used. (5143)

28. (d) Parallel simulation processes actual client data through an auditor-controlled program. Test data and integrated test facilities run fictitious data through the client's programs. A review of program logic does not test any data. (7032)

Generalized Audit Software

29. (a) One of the reasons for using generalized audit software (GAS) is that it enables the auditor to gain access and test information stored in the client's files without having to acquire a complete understanding of the client's IT system. Although the use of GAS enables the auditor to deal more effectively with large quantities of data and produces economies in the audit while increasing the quality of the audit, it cannot replace analytical procedures. Self-checking digits and hash totals are controls in the client system. Reducing the level of required tests of controls to a relatively small amount is the result of assessing control risk and applying preliminary tests of controls, not a result of using a GAS package. (5999)

30. (a) While the exact procedures performed will vary among software packages, generalized audit software is used to accomplish six basic types of audit tasks: (1) examining records for quality, completeness, consistency and correctness; (2) testing calculations and making computations; (3) comparing data on separate files; (4) selecting, printing and analyzing audit samples; (5) summarizing or resequencing data and performing analyses; and (6) comparing data obtained through other audit procedures with company records. (8167)

31. (b) Working paper documentation may not contain readily observable details of calculations because these calculations would be performed by the computer. If supervisory personnel do not have an understanding of the capabilities and limitations of personal computers, the auditor should seek the assistance of a professional possessing such skills, who may be either on the auditor's staff or an outside professional. The auditor's responsibilities with respect to using such a professional are equivalent to those for other assistants. The audit fieldwork standards for supervision do not differ when personal computers are used in an audit. (0196)

Definitions

32. (d) The CPA WebTrust symbol on a web site indicates that the organization meets AICPA business practice disclosures, transaction integrity, and information protection criteria. A specially trained and licensed CPA reviews compliance with these criteria every 90 days. EDIFACT is an international EDI format. (ANSI X12 is a domestic EDI format.) ElectroNet and TechSafe are not widely used terms. (6818)

33. (d) CPA SysTrust is an attestation service developed in part by the AICPA, that is designed to provide assurance on whether a system's controls are operating effectively and allow the system to function reliably. Answers (a), (b), and (c) are nonsense answer choices. (8128)

Solution 27-2 ADDITIONAL MULTIPLE CHOICE ANSWERS

Planning

34. (c) When documentation is only retained for a short period of time, the auditor most likely would compensate for this limitation by performing tests several times during the year, rather than only at year-end. (8374)

Internal Control

35. (b) Both large computer systems and microcomputers are vulnerable to employee collusion and programming errors. Microcomputer hardware and software could more readily be removed from a place of business than large computer systems. (7500)

36. (b) Many internal control procedures once performed by separate individuals in manual systems may be concentrated in systems that use computer processing. Therefore, an individual who has access to the computer may be in a position to perform incompatible functions. Answers (a) and (c) are false statements. Detailed ledger accounts may be maintained as easily with microcomputer data files as with manually prepared files. (4681)

37. (a) An advantage of computer processing is that it virtually eliminates computational errors. Errors or fraud are not detected more quickly when computer processing is used. The potential for systematic errors is greater in computer processing than in manual processing. Transaction trails useful for audit purposes are created but the data may be available for only a short period of time. (0289)

38. (b) A control procedure for preventing employees from modifying programs to bypass programmed controls is to segregate the functions of programming and computer operations. Answers (a), (c), and (d) are all appropriate IT controls but by themselves would not prevent IT employees from modifying programs. (5961)

39. (c) The auditor would not be able to verify the reliable operation of programmed control procedures by the reperformance of the processing of the *client's* input data through the *client's* computer program as it would produce the same output as that created by the client. The auditor would be able to verify the reliable operation of control procedures when s/he is submitting auditor-prepared test data to the client's computer process, submitting actual data to the auditor's computer program, or utilizing an edit program, as these would allow the auditor to make comparisons between the client's expected output, using the client's data and computer program, and the auditor's expected results using auditor-prepared data, the auditor's computer program, and the auditor's edit program. (0279)

General Controls

40. (d) The question asks for a response that is not a limitation of the computer-access control. While not requiring employees to take regular vacations is a poor practice from an internal control standpoint, it does not reflect a limitation of the *computer-access* control. The ability to guess fellow employees' passwords easily, the lack of a requirement to change passwords, and the ability to circumvent procedures to segregate duties reflect limitations of the computer-access controls. (7837)

Evidence

41. (b) When time clock cards are used, they constitute a form of physical evidence that can be examined in determining the proper amount of wage expense. By changing to an IT system, part of the audit trail is altered—although not necessarily destroyed. The IT system can be audited in numerous ways that don't require the use of a generalized audit program. The potential for payroll fraud may or may not change depending on the internal controls incorporated into the new payroll system. The system automatically updates the payroll records whenever anyone punches in or out. Batch processing is eliminated in this system. (0296)

42. (d) An auditor testing IT controls in a payroll system would most likely use test data containing time tickets with invalid job numbers. The computer should be programmed to compare job numbers on the time tickets with a list of valid, authorized job numbers. Answers (a) and (b) relate to preparation of data before it enters the IT system. Answer (c) relates to controls after data processing has taken place. (0286)

43. (b) Proper approval of overtime would most likely be made by inspection of the related documents and reports to assess whether the authorization policy was applied. The computerized system would be unable to make such a judgment. The computerized payroll system could be utilized to test controls related to missing employee numbers, time tickets with invalid job numbers, and agreement of hours per clock cards with hours on time tickets. (0049)

Application Controls

44. (c) With EDI, information is entered into a system once and transmitted to other parties. These other parties do not have to re-enter the information into their systems, eliminating an opportunity for errors to occur. Using EDI, audit trails typically are less clear, if anything. Creation of self-monitoring access controls and off-site storage of source documents for cash transactions could occur with or without EDI. (6824)

45. (b) Physically secure hardware devices are less likely to be compromised than software. Message authentication provides assurance about messages' sources. Encryption provides assurance about privacy. Message authentication performs similarly to control duties in non-IT systems, but not the segregation of duties aspect. Service providers usually do not provide security at the transaction level. (6828)

46. (b) The use of control totals is an example of a processing control which is designed to provide reasonable assurances that EDP has been performed as intended for the particular application, i.e., that all transactions are processed as authorized, that no authorized transactions were omitted, and that no unauthorized transactions were added. A *check digit* is a number that is added at the end of a numerical entry to check its accuracy. A *validity test,* is designed to ensure that only data meeting specific criteria are allowed. Answer (c) apparently refers to "tagging" of data, a technique used by auditors to follow a transaction through the processing cycle. (0292)

47. (c) Input controls are designed to provide reasonable assurance that data received by IT have been properly authorized, converted into machine readable form and identified as well as that data has not been lost, added, duplicated, or otherwise improperly changed. Answer (a) describes an access control. Answer (b) describes an output control. Answer (d) describes a processing control. (0306)

48. (a) A check digit is a digit that is appended to a piece of numeric data following a pre-specified routine. A record count is a count of the number of

records in a batch or file or similar group. A hash total is a numeric total with meaning only as a control. A redundant data check would check one piece of data against another, not the elements of a product code label against each other. (6622)

49. (d) A check digit is a digit that is appended to a piece of numeric data following a pre-specified routine. A hash total is a numeric total with meaning only as a control. A parity check is an extra bit attached to the end of a string of bits to detect errors resulting from electronic interference when transmitting the string. Encryption is the conversion of a message into a coded message. (6625)

CAAT

50. (d) After obtaining an understanding of the client's IT controls, the auditor must assess control risk for the IT portion of the client's internal control. Assessing control risk is the process of evaluating the effectiveness of an entity's internal control policies and procedures in preventing or detecting material misstatements in the financial statements. Procedures to judge the effectiveness of internal control design would include inquiries, observations, and inspections. One would not need computer software to accomplish this task. Gaining access to client data files, preparing spreadsheets, and constructing parallel simulations would all make use of computer software. (3936)

51. (b) Processing data through the use of simulated files makes use of an integrated test facility. Using this method, the auditor creates a fictitious entity within the client's actual data files. The auditor then processes fictitious data for the entity as part of the client's regular data processing. Controlled reprocessing involves the processing of the client's actual data through the auditor's controlled copy of the client's program. Input validation is concerned only that the inputted data is accurate. Program code checking involves analysis of the client's actual program. (2970)

52. (b) Embedded audit modules are coded into a client's application to collect data for the auditor. Integrated data checks and test data generators involve auditor-controlled fictitious data. Snapshot applications capture screen images. (7030)

53. (d) Compared to auditing without a computer, the size of the sample can be greatly expanded at little cost using a computer. Parallel simulation might not include all types of transaction errors and exceptions that may be encountered. Using parallel simulation is no guarantee that the client's personnel are unaware that the data is being tested. As there is little risk of creating material errors in the client's data with a non-computer audit procedure, this hardly can be said to be an advantage of parallel simulation using a computer over not using a computer at all. (7812)

54. (d) In the test data approach to testing a computerized accounting system, test data are processed by the client's computer programs under the auditor's control. No dummy subsidiary is involved. Test data must be customized to each audit. The auditor need not include test data for all possible valid and invalid conditions. (8389)

Generalized Audit Software

55. (c) Generalized audit software (GAS) makes it possible for an auditor to access data in electronic form; typical GAS will analyze data and present results in a meaningful and convenient form. Assessing control risk as high may result in unnecessary additional audit procedures; an IT system may have strong internal control, and consequently, low control risk. Analytics cannot be performed if the information is available only in electronic form and there is no means to access it. If data is available only in electronic form, tests of controls over that data likely should be extensive, rather than limited. (8401)

PERFORMANCE BY SUBTOPICS

Each category below parallels a subtopic covered in Chapter 27. Record the number and percentage of questions you correctly answered in each subtopic area.

Documentation

Question #	Correct	√
1		
2		
# Questions	2	
# Correct		
% Correct		

Planning

Question #	Correct	√
3		
4		
5		
6		
# Questions	4	
# Correct		
% Correct		

Internal Control

Question #	Correct	√
7		
8		
9		
10		
11		
# Questions	5	
# Correct		
% Correct		

Evidence

Question #	Correct	√
12		
13		
14		
15		
# Questions	4	
# Correct		
% Correct		

General Controls

Question #	Correct	√
16		
17		
# Questions	2	
# Correct		
% Correct		

Application Controls

Question #	Correct	√
18		
19		
20		
21		
# Questions	4	
# Correct		
% Correct		

CAAT

Question #	Correct	√
22		
23		
24		
25		
26		
27		
28		
# Questions	7	
# Correct		
% Correct		

Generalized Audit Software

Question #	Correct	√
29		
30		
31		
# Questions	3	
# Correct		
% Correct		

Definitions

Question #	Correct	√
32		
33		
# Questions	2	
# Correct		
% Correct		

SIMULATION SOLUTIONS

Solution 27-3

Response #1: Communication (6 points)

The potential benefits to an auditor of using software in an audit as compared to performing an audit without the use of a computer include the following:

1. **Time** may be **saved** by eliminating manual footing, cross-footing, and other routine calculations.

2. **Calculations,** comparisons, and other data manipulations are **more accurately performed**.

3. **Analytical procedures** calculations may be **more efficiently performed.**

4. The **scope** of analytical procedures may be **broadened**.

5. Audit **sampling** may be **facilitated**.

6. Potential **weaknesses** in a client's internal control structure may be more readily **identified**.

7. Preparation and **revision of flowcharts** depicting the flow of financial transactions in a client's structure may be **facilitated**.

8. **Working papers** may be easily **stored** and accessed.

9. **Graphics capabilities** may allow the auditor to generate, display, and evaluate various financial and nonfinancial relationships graphically.

10. Engagement-management information such as **time budgets** and the monitoring of **actual time vs. budgeted amounts** may be more easily generated and analyzed.

11. **Customized working papers** may be developed with greater ease.

12. **Standardized audit correspondence,** such as engagement letters, client representation letters, and attorney letters **may be stored and easily modified**.

13. **Supervisory-review time** may be **reduced**.

14. Staff morale and productivity may be improved by reducing the time spent on clerical tasks.

15. **Client's personnel may not need to manually prepare** as many **schedules** and otherwise spend as much time assisting the auditor.

16. Computer-generated working papers are generally more **legible** and consistent.

Paragraph Reference Answer: AU 339.27

Guidance: AU 339.27 states, "The auditor should complete the assembly of the final audit file on a timely basis, but within 60 days following the report release date (documentation completion date). Statutes, regulations, or the audit firm's quality control policies may specify a shorter period of time in which this assembly process should be completed."

1. M

Before preparing a sales order, the computer processing department should perform a credit check to determine that the sale will be made to a creditworthy customer. This information may be obtained from the customer credit file or from outside sources.

2. Z

Once the sales order has been prepared, it will be recorded and placed in the open order file.

3. L

This manual operation represents the process of matching customer purchase orders with sales orders for agreement.

4. B

This manual operation represents matching the shipping document with the sales order for agreement.

5. H

Once the shipping document and sales order have been matched, the goods will be released for shipment.

6. S

In order to prepare the customer bill, the computerized billing program will retrieve the shipping data from the shipping file and enter the price data from the master price file.

7. O

Once the shipping data and price data have been retrieved and the sale to the customer generated, the sales invoice will be prepared.

8. U

This document represents the duplicate copy sales invoice generated by the computerized billing program.

9. I

One copy of the sales invoice will be sent to the customer, and one will be sent to the accounts receivable department as support for the entry to the accounts receivable ledger—to be held until remittance is made by the customer.

10. Q

The computer processing department will (daily, weekly, or monthly) update the master files, such as the accounts receivable ledger, the inventory master file, the sales transaction file, and the general ledger master file.

11. N

The computer processing department will prepare, based upon the update program, an accounts receivable ledger, an aged trial balance, a general ledger transaction summary, and a sales journal.

12. T

This output function represents the sales journal which was generated by the computerized update program for the day, week, or month, depending upon the frequency of report generation established by management.

13. Y

This output report represents the aged trial balance generated by the computerized update program, which combined information from the general ledger master file, the sales transaction file, and the inventory master file.

(9033)

Solution 27-4

The **substantive auditing procedures** Brown may consider performing include the following:

Using the perpetual inventory file,

- **Recalculate the beginning and ending balances** (prices × quantities), foot, and print out a report to be used to reconcile the totals with the general ledger (or agree beginning balance with the prior year's working papers).

- **Calculate the quantity balances** as of the physical inventory date **for comparison to** the **physical inventory file**. (Alternatively, update the physical inventory file for purchases and sales from January 6 to January 31, Year 2, for comparison to the perpetual inventory at January 31, Year 2.)
- Select and print out a **sample of items received and shipped** for the periods (a) before and after January 5 and 31, Year 2, **for cut-off testing,** (b) between January 5 and January 31, Year 2, **for vouching or analytical procedures,** and (c) prior to January 5, Year 2, **for tests of details** or analytical procedures.
- Compare quantities sold during the year to quantities on hand at year end. Print out a **report of items for which turnover is less than expected.** (Alternatively, calculate the number of days' sales in inventory for selected items.)
- **Select items** noted as possibly **unsalable** or **obsolete** during the physical inventory observation and print out information about purchases and sales for further consideration.
- **Recalculate** the prices used to value the year-end FIFO inventory by matching prices and quantities to the most recent purchases.
- Select a **sample** of **items for comparison** to **current sales prices**.
- **Identify** and print out **unusual transactions**. (These are transactions other than purchases or sales for the year, or physical inventory adjustments as of January 5, Year 2.)
- **Recalculate the ending inventory** (or selected items) by taking the beginning balances plus purchases, less sales, (quantities and/or amounts) and print out the differences.
- **Recalculate the cost of sales** for selected items sold during the year.

Using the physical inventory and test count files,

- **Account for all inventory tag numbers** used and print out a report of missing or duplicate numbers for follow-up.
- **Search for tag numbers** noted during the physical inventory observation as being **voided or not used**.
- **Compare the physical inventory file to the file of test counts** and print out a report of differences for auditor follow-up.
- **Combine the quantities** for each item appearing on more than one inventory tag number for comparison to the perpetual file.
- **Compare** the **quantities** on the file to the calculated quantity balances on the perpetual inventory file as of January 5, Year 2. (Alternatively,

compare the physical inventory file updated to year end to the perpetual inventory file.)
- **Calculate the quantities and dollar amounts of the book-to-physical adjustments** for each item and the total adjustment. Print out a report to reconcile the total adjustment to the adjustment recorded in the general ledger before the year end.
- Using the calculated book-to-physical adjustments for each item, **compare the quantities and dollar amounts of each adjustment to the perpetual inventory file** as of January 5, Year 2, and print out a report of differences for follow-up.

Response #2: Flowchart (2 points)

1. A

This symbol represents a file. In the revenue cycle application process, the most likely output among the choices given is an accounts receivable master file, especially since there is a cash receipts transaction file. A remittance file (G) is not typically a separately constructed file. Answers F and B are not part of the revenue cycle.

2. H

This symbol represents some sort of printed output. Sales invoices are the most likely output from the system at this point. The customer orders would most likely be at the beginning of the revenue cycle. Receiving reports are not part of the revenue cycle. Customer checks are not created by the system but are received from the customer.

Response #3: Research (1 point)

Paragraph Reference Answer: QC 10.96

Guidance: QC 10.96 states, "The engagement partner may consult the engagement quality control reviewer at any stage during the engagement, for example, to establish that a judgment made by the engagement partner will be acceptable to the engagement quality control reviewer. Such consultation need not impair the engagement quality control reviewer's eligibility to perform the role. However, when the nature and extent of the consultations become significant, the reviewer's objectivity may be impaired unless both the engagement team and the reviewer are careful to maintain the reviewer's objectivity."

(6297)

Using Audio Tutor to Study

Actively listen to the audio lectures, taking notes if convenient. If you are strong in a topic, your audio review and question drill may be sufficient. If your strength is moderate in a topic, you might find that reading the related text before listening to the audio lectures is helpful. If you are weak in a topic, one successful strategy is to listen to the audio lectures, read the book, and then listen to the audio lectures again. Even strong candidates find that listening to the audio lectures again a few weeks after their first exposure increases their retention.

The Audio Tutor lectures have similar content as the Hot•Spot™, Intensive™, and online video lectures, but they are not exactly the same. Audio Tutor and this book have topics arranged in essentially the same chapters, although material might be organized differently within the chapters.

STUDY TIP: STANDARD AUDIT REPORT

The editors recommend that candidates memorize the standard audit report **word for word** because audit report questions frequently appear on the CPA exam. Learning the modifications for various situations is considerably easier than learning dozens of reports. These modifications are summarized in Exhibit 26, *Conditions Requiring Modification of Report.*

FAQ

This question frequently is asked by candidates, but not necessarily the examiners. For a more complete discussion, see the related material in the text and explanations to questions.

Q: Why is it that one place in Chapter 28 says that an opinion may be given on one financial statement and a disclaimer of opinion or adverse opinion given on the rest of the financial statements, but another place in Chapter 28 says that "piecemeal opinions" may not be given?

A: An auditor may have an unqualified opinion on the balance sheet and a disclaimer of opinion on the income statement. These statements are at the same level. The balance sheet is not part of the income statement. "Multiple opinions" is as a good term for this circumstance as any other.

If an auditor disclaims an opinion on the income statement and then gives an opinion on the revenues in the income statement, this might overshadow the disclaimer of opinion on the income statement. The difference from the above situation is that the revenues are part of the income statement. This situation commonly is described by the term "piecemeal opinion."

CHAPTER 28

REPORTS ON AUDITED FINANCIAL STATEMENTS

CHAPTER 28

REPORTS ON AUDITED FINANCIAL STATEMENTS

I. **Reporting Standards**

A. **Adherence to GAAP**

1. **Definitions**

a. **GAAP** Generally accepted accounting principles (GAAP) is a technical accounting term that:

(1) Encompasses the conventions, rules, and procedures that define accepted accounting practice at a particular time

(2) Includes broad guidelines as well as detailed practices and procedures

b. **GAAP Hierarchy** GAAP hierarchy identifies the sources of accounting principles and the framework for selecting principles to be used in the preparation of financial statements.

2. **First Standard of Reporting**

Exhibit 1 ▶ The First Standard of Reporting

The auditor must state in the auditor's report whether the financial statements are presented in accordance with generally accepted accounting principles (GAAP).

Editor note: An identification of the country of origin of those generally accepted accounting principles is also required.

The American Institute of Certified Public Accountants' (AICPA) Code of Professional Conduct (ET 203) provides that an unqualified opinion should not be expressed if the financial statements contain a material departure from accounting principles promulgated by bodies they have designated unless, due to unusual circumstances, adherence to the principles would make the statements misleading. Therefore, ET 203 implies that application of officially established accounting principles results in the fair presentation of financial position, results of operations, and cash flows in conformity with GAAP.

3. **Professional Judgment** Professional judgment determines which accounting principles should be used in any situation. The auditor's judgment should be applied within the framework of GAAP.

The auditor's opinion that financial statements present fairly an entity's financial position, results of operations, and cash flows in conformity with GAAP should be based on the auditor's judgment as to whether the

a. Accounting principles selected and applied have general acceptance;

b. Accounting principles are appropriate in the circumstances;

c. Financial statements, including the related notes, are informative of matters that may affect their use, understanding, and interpretation;

d. Information presented in the financial statements is classified and summarized in a reasonable manner, that is, neither too detailed nor too condensed; and

e. Financial statements reflect the underlying transactions and events in a manner that presents the financial position, results of operations, and cash flows stated within a range of acceptable limits that are reasonable and practicable to attain in financial statements.

4. **Sources of GAAP** The AICPA is authorized under ET 203 to designate bodies to establish accounting principles. These designated bodies and their respective accounting principles are:

    a. **FASB** The Financial Accounting Standards Board (FASB) with respect to the *FASB Accounting Standards Codification™* (ASC or Codification). (The ASC is the single source of accounting principles for nongovernmental entities.)

    b. **GASB** The Governmental Accounting Standards Board (GASB), with respect to Statements of Governmental Accounting Standards issued in July 1984 and thereafter. (The GASB establishes accounting principles for state and local governmental entities.)

    c. **FASAB** Federal Accounting Standards Advisory Board (FASAB), with respect to Statements of Federal Accounting Standards adopted and issued in March 1993 and subsequently. (The FASAB establishes accounting principles for federal government entities.)

5. **Nongovernmental GAAP** On July 1, 2009, the *FASB Accounting Standards Codification™* became the single official source of authoritative U.S. generally accepted accounting principles (GAAP) for public and nonpublic nongovernmental entities, superseding existing FASB, AICPA, EITF, and related literature. The Codification does not change GAAP; it presents it in an organized and easily accessible new structure. It reorganizes the thousands of U.S. GAAP pronouncements into approximately 90 accounting topics. Also included is relevant SEC guidance that follows the same topical structure.

    a. **GAAP Hierarchy** With the Codification, only two levels of U.S. GAAP exist:

        (1) Authoritative represented by the Codification

        (2) Nonauthoritative represented by all other literature

        Sources of nonauthoritative accounting guidance and literature include, for example, practices that are widely recognized and prevalent either generally or in the industry, FASB Concepts Statements, AICPA Issues Papers, International Financial Reporting Standards of the International Accounting Standards Board (IASB), pronouncements of professional associations or regulatory agencies, Technical Information Service Inquiries and Replies included in AICPA Technical Practice Aids, and accounting textbooks, handbooks, and articles.

    Editor note: The Public Company Accounting Oversight Board (PCAOB) has removed the GAAP hierarchy from its adopted interim standards (AU 411). The PCAOB believes the hierarchy should reside in the accounting rather than the auditing standards and further, because the FASB has incorporated the hierarchy in its Codification, it is no longer needed in the auditing standards.

    b. **Content** The Codification includes all previous level A—D GAAP issued by a standard setter, including pronouncements issued by the FASB, EITF, the Accounting Standards Executive Committee (AcSEC), the APB, etc. The source of material used by the Codification is from the "as amended" versions of accounting standards, and as such, the Codification does not identify any documents that only amended other standards.

The Codification will contain content from new standards not yet fully effective for all entities—this content will be labeled as such and appear specially marked.

For reference by public companies, the Codification also includes Securities and Exchange Commission (SEC) content (displayed separately below the related topical content). Content contained in the SEC sections of the Codification is provided for convenience and related only to SEC registrants. The SEC sections are not the authoritative sources of such content and do not contain the entire population of SEC rules, regulations, interpretive releases, and staff guidance.

    c.   **Unspecified Treatment** If the guidance for a transaction or event is not specified within a source of authoritative GAAP for that entity, an entity shall first consider accounting principles for *similar* transactions or events within a source of authoritative GAAP for that entity and then consider nonauthoritative guidance from other sources. The appropriateness of other sources of accounting guidance depends on its relevance to particular circumstances, the specificity of the guidance, the general recognition of the issuer or author as an authority, and the extent of its use in practice. An entity shall not follow the accounting treatment specified in accounting guidance for *similar* transactions or events in cases in which those accounting principles either prohibit the application of the accounting treatment to the particular transaction or event or indicate that the accounting treatment should not be applied by analogy.

6.   **State & Local Governments GAAP Hierarchy** The hierarchy for sources of GAAP for state and local government entities is composed of four categories, or levels of authority, as follows.

    a.   Level one: consists of GASB Statements and Interpretations, as well as AICPA and FASB pronouncements made applicable to state and local governmental entities by GASB Statements or Interpretations.

    b.   Level two: consists of GASB Technical Bulletins and when cleared by the GASB, AICPA Statements of Position and Industry Auditing and Accounting Guides, to the extent the AICPA makes these latter documents applicable to state and local government entities.

    c.   Level three: consists of AICPA Practice Bulletins to the extent these bulletins are made applicable to state and local governmental entities and cleared by the GASB. Also included are consensus positions of a group of accountants organized by the GASB that attempt to reach consensus positions on accounting issues applicable to state and local governmental entities.

    d.   Level four: consists of questions and answers published by the GASB staff, as well as practices that are widely recognized and prevalent in state and local government.

7.   **Federal Government GAAP Hierarchy** The hierarchy for sources of GAAP for federal government units is also composed of four categories, or levels of authority. These are:

    a.   Level one: consists of Federal Accounting Standards Advisory Board (FASAB) Statements and Interpretations, as well as AICPA and FASB pronouncements made applicable to federal governmental entities by FASAB Statements or Interpretations.

    b.   Level two: consists of FASAB Technical Bulletins and, if specifically made applicable to federal entities by the AICPA and cleared by the FASAB, AICPA Industry Audit and Accounting Guides and AICPA SOP.

    c.   Level three: consists of AICPA Practice Bulletins, if specifically made applicable to federal governmental entities and cleared by the FASAB, as well as Technical Releases of the Accounting and Auditing Policy Committee of the FASAB.

       d.   Level four: includes implementation guides published by the FASAB staff, as well as practices that are widely recognized and prevalent in the federal government.

8.   **Conflicts / Unspecified Treatment (Governmental Entities)**

       a.   **Conflicts** If there is a conflict between accounting principles relevant to the circumstances from sources in different categories, the auditor should follow the treatment specified by the source in the higher category. For example, category (B) should be followed before categories (C) or (D).

       b.   **Unspecified Treatment** If the accounting treatment of a transaction or event is not specified by a pronouncement covered by ET 203 or another source of established accounting principles, the auditor should consider other accounting literature. The appropriateness of other accounting literature depends on its relevance to particular circumstances, the specificity of the guidance, and the general recognition of the issuer or author as an authority.

Exhibit 2 ▶ Governmental GAAP Hierarchy

State and Local Governments	Federal Governmental Units
CATEGORY A (LEVEL ONE)	
GASB Statements	FASAB Statements
GASB Interpretations	FASAB Interpretations
AICPA and FASB Pronouncements if made applicable to state and local governments by GASB Statements or Interpretations	AICPA and FASB pronouncements made applicable to federal governmental entities by FASAB Statements or Interpretations
CATEGORY B (LEVEL TWO)	
GASB Technical Bulletins	FASAB Technical Bulletins
AICPA Industry Audit and Accounting Guides and Statements of Position*	AICPA Industry Audit and Accounting Guides and AICPA SOP**
CATEGORY C (LEVEL THREE)	
GASB EITF Consensuses (not yet organized by GASB)	AICPA Practice Bulletins**
AICPA Practice Bulletins*	Technical Releases of the Accounting and Auditing Policy Committee of the FASAB
CATEGORY D (LEVEL FOUR)	
"Qs and As" published by GASB staff	Implementation guides published by the FASAB staff
Prevalent practice	Practices that are widely recognized and prevalent in the federal government
* If made applicable to state and local governments by AICPA	**If specifically made applicable to federal governmental entities and cleared by the FASAB.

B.   Consistency (AU 420)

Exhibit 3 ▶ The Second Standard of Reporting—the Consistency Standard

> The auditor must identify in the auditor's report those circumstances in which such principles [GAAP] have not been consistently observed in the current period in relation to the preceding period.

1.   **Consistency Is Implied in Standard Report** Consistency in application of accounting principles is implied in the standard auditor's report, i.e., *if satisfied*, the auditor does **not** refer to consistency in the audit report.

2.   **Objective of Consistency Standard** The objective of the second standard of reporting is to provide assurance that if comparability has been materially affected by changes in accounting principles that it will be reported appropriately by the auditor.

3.   **Explanatory Paragraph Required** If there has been a change in accounting principles or in their method of application that has a material effect on the comparability of the company's financial statements (and the auditor determines it has been handled appropriately), the auditor should refer to the change in an explanatory paragraph in the report. The explanatory paragraph (**following** the opinion paragraph) should identify the nature of the change and make reference to the note in the financial statements that describes the change. This is not a qualification of the audit opinion hence the auditor's concurrence with the change is implied in the report.

Editor Note: According to the guidance (PCAOB AS 6) for issuers (public companies), both a change in accounting principle *and an adjustment to correct a misstatement (error) in previously issued financial statements* are matters relating to consistency that the auditor should recognize in the audit report if they have a material effect on the financial statements. Note that this makes the evaluation of consistency for issuers broader than the second standard of reporting because it includes *errors not involving an accounting principle*. Additionally, the explanatory paragraph added to audit reports of issuers must clearly indicate whether an adjustment to previously issued financial statements was due to a change in accounting principal or the correction of a misstatement.

4.   **Accounting Changes Affecting Consistency** The following are accounting changes that affect consistency and if evaluated by the auditor as having been handled appropriately, require the addition of an explanatory paragraph (**following** the opinion paragraph) to the auditor's report.

Editor note: If the auditor finds that an accounting change is not justified or has not been made according to GAAP (the new principle is not GAAP; the method of accounting for the effect of the change is not GAAP, or disclosure is inadequate) the change should be treated as a departure from GAAP, resulting in either a qualified for adverse opinion.

a.   **Change in Accounting Principle** A change in accounting principle arises (1) from the use of a generally accepted accounting principle that is different from the one previously used (both apply and are GAAP); (2) when the accounting principle formerly used is no longer GAAP; or (3) from the use of a different method of applying a generally accepted accounting principle.

The standard setters make special note that the following cases involve changes in principles:

(1)   **Change in Reporting Entity** A change in reporting entity **not** resulting from a transaction or event.

A change in reporting entity that *does* result from a transaction or event, such as the creation, cessation, or complete or partial purchase or disposition of a subsidiary or other business unit, does *not* require recognition in the auditor's report.

(2) Changes in Presentation of Cash Flows An entity should disclose its policy for determining which items are treated as cash equivalents. Any change to that policy is a change in accounting principle that is reported by restating financial statements for earlier years presented for comparative purposes.

(3) Investment Accounted for by the Equity Method If a company's financial statements contain an investment accounted for by the equity method, the auditor's evaluation of consistency should include consideration of the investee. If the investee makes a change in accounting principle that is material to the investing company's financial statements, the auditor should add an explanatory paragraph (following the opinion paragraph) to the auditor's report.

b. Correction of an Error in Principle This involves changing from an accounting principle that is not generally accepted to one that is generally accepted (including correcting a mistake in the application of a principle).

Editor note: Although guidance for both issuers and nonissuers consider this a consistency issue, PCAOB AS 6 categorizes it as the correction of a misstatement, thus it must be identified as a misstatement in the explanatory paragraph of an audit report for an issuer.

c. Change in Principle Inseparable From Change in Estimate When the effect of a change in accounting estimate is inseparable from the effect of a related change in accounting principle, although the *accounting* for the change is handled as a change in estimate, a change in principle is involved.

5. Changes *Not* Affecting Consistency The following changes do **not** affect consistency *if no element of accounting principles or their application is involved*. Therefore, they do **not** require recognition in the auditor's report. *However, if material, they may require disclosure in the financial statements and the opinion must be qualified or adverse if disclosure is inadequate.*

a. Changes in Accounting Estimates Accounting estimates will be changed as circumstances change. Estimates such as expected salvage values and service lives of fixed assets are a normal part of doing business.

b. Error Correction That Does Not Involve an Accounting Principle This is the correction of an error in previously issued financial statements that resulted from mathematical mistakes, oversight, or misuse of facts.

c. Changes in Classification & Reclassification These are changes in classifications made in previously issued financial statements to enhance comparability with current financial statements.

Editor note: PCAOB AS 6 includes expanded guidance for auditors of issuers concerning the evaluation of whether such reclassifications involve corrections of material misstatements or changes in accounting principles. For example, if items were incorrectly classified in previously issued financial statements, the reclassification should be recognized in the auditor's report as the correction of a misstatement.

d. Substantially Different Transactions or Events A consistency problem does not arise when the use of a different accounting principle is required because the transactions and events being processed are clearly different from those in the previous period.

    e.   **Current Change Expected to Have a Material Future Effect** A consistency problem does not arise when an accounting change does not affect the current year's financial statements but is expected to have a substantial effect in later years. (It should be disclosed in the notes to the financial statements whenever the statements of the period of change are presented.)

6.   **Current Year** When reporting only on the current period's financial statements, the auditor should obtain sufficient appropriate audit evidence about the consistency of the application of accounting principles even though the prior period financial statements are not presented.

    When the auditor has not audited the financial statements of the preceding year, the auditor should adopt procedures that are practicable and reasonable in the circumstances to be assured that the accounting principles are consistent between the current and the preceding year.

7.   **Multiple Years** When reporting on the financial statements of two or more years that are presented for comparative purposes, the auditor should report on a lack of consistency between the years. The auditor should also report on a lack of consistency between the years and the year prior to the earliest year presented.

Exhibit 4 ▶ Matters Affecting Comparability of Financial Statements

Do they affect consistency? (require recognition in the auditor's report by the addition of an explanatory paragraph **following** the opinion paragraph)	**Yes**	**No**
Change in accounting principle or method of applying it	√	
Change in reporting entity		
Not resulting from a transaction or event	√	
Resulting from a transaction or event		√
Changes in presentation of cash flows	√	
Investment accounted for by the equity method; investee makes a change in accounting principle	√	
Correction of an error in principle	√	
Misstatement in previously issued financial statements—**not** involving a principle		
Nonissuer		√
Issuer (public entity)	√	
Change in principle inseparable from a change in estimate	√	
Change in accounting estimate		√
Changes in classification and reclassification		√
Different events & transactions from previously issued financial statements		√
Changes expected to have a material future effect, but no substantial effect on current financial statements		√

C. **Adequacy of Disclosure in Financial Statements (AU 431)**

Exhibit 5 ▸ The Third Standard of Reporting

> When the auditor determines that informative disclosures are not reasonably adequate, the auditor must so state in the auditor's report.

1. **Material Matters** Financial statements presented in conformity with GAAP must contain adequate disclosure of material matters. Adequate disclosure includes the form, arrangement, and content of the statements and notes, including the terminology used, amount of detail, classification of items, and the bases of amounts set forth. In determining whether a particular matter should be disclosed, the auditor should consider the circumstances and facts that the auditor is aware of at the time.

   a. Failure by management to include information required by GAAP in the financial statements will result in the auditor expressing a qualified or adverse opinion on the statements.

   b. If practicable, the auditor should provide the information in the report, unless its omission from the report is sanctioned by a specific SAS. "Practicable" means that the information can reasonably be obtained from the client's accounts and records, and that providing it in the report does **not** require the auditor to assume the position of *preparer* of financial information. For instance, an auditor is **not** expected to provide a basic financial statement or segment information omitted by management.

2. **Confidential Information** In conducting an audit of financial statements and in other areas of work with the client, the auditor uses confidential information provided by the client. Thus, the auditor should **not** disclose—without management's consent—information **not** required to be disclosed in financial statements to comply with GAAP.

D. **Association With Financial Statements**

The objective of the fourth standard is to prevent any misinterpretation of the degree of responsibility which the auditor is assuming when her/his name is associated with financial statements. Reference to the financial statements taken as a whole applies equally to a complete set of financial statements and to an individual financial statement, such as a balance sheet, and also applies to the current period as well as any prior periods that are presented on a comparative basis. Thus, an auditor may express one opinion on a balance sheet and another opinion or disclaim an opinion on an income statement, if circumstances warrant.

Exhibit 6 ▸ The Fourth Standard of Reporting

> The auditor must either express an opinion regarding the financial statements, taken as a whole, or state that an opinion cannot be expressed, in the auditor's report. When the auditor cannot express an overall opinion, the auditor should state the reasons therefor in the auditor's report. In all cases where an auditor's name is associated with financial statements, the auditor should clearly indicate the character of the auditor's work, if any, and the degree of responsibility the auditor is taking, in the auditor's report.

1. **Piecemeal Opinions** Piecemeal opinions are expressions of opinion on certain identified items (e.g. specific accounts) in the financial statements. Piecemeal opinions should **not** be expressed when the auditor has disclaimed an opinion or has expressed an adverse opinion on the financial statements taken as a whole because piecemeal opinions tend to overshadow or contradict a disclaimer of opinion or an adverse opinion.

2. **Certain Identified Items** An auditor is able to express an opinion on one or more certain identified items of a financial statement, provided that the identified items and the scope of the related audit are **not** intended to encompass so many elements as to constitute a major portion of the financial statements. For example, an auditor may be able to express an

opinion on an entity's accounts receivable balance even if the auditor disclaimed an opinion on the financial statements taken as a whole. However, the report on the certain identified item should be restricted to specific parties and presented separately from the report on the financial statements. (See Chapter 30 for further explanation.)

II. Types of Opinions (AU 508)

A. Unqualified Opinion, Standard Report
The standard report is issued when the auditor feels the financial statements fairly present, in all material respects, the financial position, results of operations, and cash flows in conformity with U.S. GAAP (including adequate disclosure). The audit must have been conducted in accordance with U.S. GAAS.

Editor note: Auditors of public companies (issuers) must state that the audit was conducted in accordance with the standards of the Public Company Accounting Oversight Board (United States) rather than GAAS. An auditor must also include the city and state (or city and country, in the case of non-U.S. auditors) from which the auditor's report has been issued.

Exhibit 7 ▶ Necessary Conditions for Unqualified Opinion, Standard Report

1. No departures from U.S. GAAP.
2. Disclosures in financial statements (notes to the financial statements) are adequate and complete.
3. No unusual uncertainties (contingencies) surrounding the financial statements.
4. No scope limitations.
5. GAAP must be consistently followed between periods.
6. Independent auditor.

B. Unqualified Opinion, Explanatory Language Added to Auditor's Report
Certain circumstances, while **not** affecting the auditor's unqualified opinion on the financial statements, may require that the auditor add an explanatory paragraph (or other explanatory language) to the report. Explanatory language would be added when part of the audit is performed by other independent auditors; or when a change in consistency, a material uncertainty, or substantial doubt about the entity's ability to continue as a going concern exists; or when the auditor wants to emphasize a matter.

C. Qualified Opinion
States that the financial statements present fairly, in all material respects, the results of operations, financial position, and cash flows in conformity with GAAP "except for" the effects of the matter to which the qualification relates. A qualification may exist due to a scope limitation.

D. Adverse Opinion
Expressed when, in the auditor's judgment, the financial statements, taken as a whole, do **not** fairly present the financial position, results of operations, or cash flows in conformity with GAAP.

E. Disclaimer of Opinion
States that the auditor does **not** express an opinion on the financial statements, typically due to the lack of independence or scope limitations.

III. Unqualified Opinions & the Standard Report (AU 508 continued)

A. Implications of the Standard Report
The auditor's standard report states that the financial statements present fairly, in all material respects, an entity's financial position, results of operations, and cash flows in conformity with U.S. GAAP. The auditor may express this opinion only when an audit conducted according to U.S. GAAS

has been completed and the necessary conditions are met. The auditor's standard report identifies the financial statements audited in an opening, introductory paragraph, describes the nature of an audit in a scope paragraph, and expresses the auditor's opinion in a separate opinion paragraph. The country of the origin of the GAAS and GAAP should be specified.

B. Components of the Standard Report
The basic elements of the report include the following:

1. **Title** A title that includes the word "independent."

2. **Address** Addressed to the company, to its board of directors, or to its stockholders (**not to management**). If the auditor is retained to audit the financial statements of a company that is **not** the auditor's client, the report would be addressed to the client and **not** to the directors or stockholders of the company being audited.

3. **Introductory Paragraph**

    a. A statement that identifies the financial statements that were audited.

    b. A statement that the financial statements are the responsibility of the company's management and that the auditor's responsibility is to express an opinion on the financial statements based on the audit.

4. **Scope Paragraph**

    a. A statement that the audit was conducted in accordance with U.S. GAAS.

    b. A statement that GAAS requires that the auditor plan and perform the audit to obtain reasonable assurance about whether the financial statements are free of material misstatement.

    c. Statements that an audit includes:

        (1) Examining, on a test basis, evidence supporting the amounts and disclosures in the financial statements.

        (2) Assessing the accounting principles used and significant estimates made by management.

        (3) Evaluating the overall financial statement presentation.

    d. A statement that the auditor believes that the audit provides a reasonable basis for the auditor's opinion.

5. **Opinion Paragraph** An opinion as to whether the financial statements present fairly, in all material respects, the financial position of the company as of the balance sheet date and the results of its operations and its cash flows for the period then ended in conformity with U.S. GAAP.

6. **Signature** The manual or printed signature of the auditor's firm.

7. **Date** The date of the report should be no earlier than the date on which the auditor has obtained sufficient appropriate audit evidence to support the opinion.

Exhibit 8 ▶ The Form of the Auditor's Standard Report for a Single Year

<u>Independent Auditor's Report</u>

Address (The title and address should be included in all letters, but is not reproduced in all subsequent exhibits.)

(Introductory paragraph)

We have audited the accompanying balance sheet of X Company as of December 31, 20XX, and the related statements of income, retained earnings, and cash flows for the year then ended. These financial statements are the responsibility of the Company's management. Our responsibility is to express an opinion on these financial statements based on our audit.

(Scope paragraph)

We conducted our audit in accordance with U.S. generally accepted auditing standards. Those standards require that we plan and perform the audit to obtain reasonable assurance about whether the financial statements are free of material misstatement. An audit includes examining, on a test basis, evidence supporting the amounts and disclosures in the financial statements. An audit also includes assessing the accounting principles used and significant estimates made by management, as well as evaluating the overall financial statement presentation. We believe that our audit provides a reasonable basis for our opinion.

(Opinion paragraph)

In our opinion, the financial statements referred to above present fairly, in all material respects, the financial position of X Company as of (at) December 31, 20XX, and the results of its operations and its cash flows for the year then ended in conformity with U.S. generally accepted accounting principles.

Signature & Date (These should be included in all letters, but are not reproduced in all subsequent exhibits.)

C.   **Additional Explanatory Language**

There are certain circumstances which, while **not** affecting the auditor's unqualified opinion, may require that the auditor add explanatory language to the standard report. These circumstances include the following:

1.   **Part of Audit Performed by Other Independent Auditors (AU 543)** Sometimes the auditor will be in a position where other independent auditors have audited the financial statements of subsidiaries, divisions, branches, components, or investments that are included in the financial statements the auditor is auditing. The auditor must first decide whether s/he has participated sufficiently to be the principal auditor (i.e., to report on the financial statements).

Exhibit 9 ▶ Report Indicating Division of Responsibility

<u>Independent Auditor's Report</u>

(Introductory paragraph)

We have audited the consolidated balance sheets of ABC Company as of December 31, 20X2 and 20X1, and the related consolidated statements of income, retained earnings, and cash flows for the years then ended. These financial statements are the responsibility of the company's management. Our responsibility is to express an opinion on these financial statements based on our audits. We did not audit the financial statements of B Company, a wholly owned subsidiary, which statements reflect total assets of $_____ and $_____ as of December 31, 20X2 and 20X1, respectively, and total revenues of $_____ and $_____ for the years then ended. Those statements were audited by other auditors whose report has been furnished to us, and our opinion, insofar as it relates to the amounts included for B Company, is based solely on the report of other auditors.

(Scope paragraph)

We conducted our audits in accordance with U.S. generally accepted auditing standards. Those standards require that we plan and perform the audit to obtain reasonable assurance about whether the financial statements are free of material misstatements. An audit includes examining on a test basis, evidence supporting the amounts and disclosures in the financial statements. An audit also includes assessing the accounting principles used and significant estimates made by management, as well as evaluating the overall financial statements presentation. We believe that our audits and other auditors' reports provide a reasonable basis for our opinion.

(Opinion paragraph)

In our opinion, based on our audits and other auditors' reports, the consolidated financial statements referred to above present fairly, in all material respects, the financial position of ABC Company as of December 31, 20X2 and 20X1, and the results of its operations and its cash flows for the years then ended in conformity with U.S. generally accepted accounting principles.

---

a. **Whether to Make Reference to Other Auditor** As principal auditor, the auditor must decide whether to take responsibility for the work of the other auditor as it relates to the expression of an opinion. If the principal auditor does **not** assume this responsibility, the principal auditor should make reference to the other auditor's examination and clearly indicate the division of responsibility in the audit report.

   (1) **Decision Not to Make Reference** The principal auditor must be satisfied of the other auditor's independence, professional reputation, and the quality and scope of the audit performed. This position is usually appropriate when (a) the other auditor is an associated or correspondent firm, (b) the other auditor was retained by the principal auditor, (c) the principal auditor takes steps necessary to be satisfied with the other auditor's work, or (d) the other auditor audited an immaterial portion of the financial statements.

   (2) **Decision to Make Reference** The principal auditor's report should clearly indicate, in the introductory, scope, and opinion paragraphs, the division of responsibility between the portion of the financial statements covered by the principal auditor's own audit and that covered by the audit of the other auditor. The portion examined by the other auditor should be indicated (e.g., dollar amounts or percentages of total assets, total revenues, etc.). The other auditor may be named only if (a) the other auditor has given permission, and (b) the other auditor's report is included.

b. **Other Procedures** Regardless of whether or not reference is made, the principal auditor should inquire as to the professional reputation and independence of the other auditors and should attempt to achieve a proper coordination of their activities.

2. **Justifiable Departure From Promulgated Accounting Principle (Ethics Rule 203)** In the rare circumstance where the auditor can demonstrate that, due to unusual circumstances, the financial statements would be misleading if promulgated GAAP were applied, the auditor must describe the departure, its approximate effects, if practicable, and the reasons why compliance would result in a misleading statement. In this situation, it is appropriate for the auditor to express an unqualified opinion on the financial statements with an explanatory paragraph.

3. **Lack of Consistency** The auditor's standard report implies that the accounting principles have been consistently applied between periods. In these cases, the auditor should **not** refer to consistency in the report. If there has been a change affecting consistency, the auditor should refer to the change in an explanatory paragraph of the report. The explanatory

paragraph, **following** the opinion paragraph, should identify the nature of the change and refer the reader to the note in the financial statements that discusses the change in detail. An unqualified opinion would be expressed. The auditor's concurrence with a change is implicit unless the auditor takes exception to the change.

Exhibit 10 ▶ Change in Accounting Principle (following opinion paragraph)

> As discussed in Note X to the financial statements, the Company changed its method of accounting for long-term contracts in 20X1.

4. **Uncertainties** A matter involving an uncertainty is one that is expected to be resolved at a future date when sufficient appropriate audit evidence concerning its outcome should become available. In some instances, the outcome of future events may affect the financial statements.

Exhibit 11 ▶ Uncertainty: Explanatory Paragraph (following opinion paragraph)

> As discussed in Note X to the financial statements, the Company is a defendant in a lawsuit alleging infringement of certain patent rights and claiming royalties and punitive damages. The Company has filed a counteraction, and preliminary hearings and discovery proceedings on both actions are in progress. The ultimate outcome of the litigation cannot presently be determined. Accordingly, no provision for any liability that may result upon adjudication has been made in the accompanying financial statements.

a. **Evaluation** Management may not always be able to estimate the effect of such events, so the auditor must consider the likelihood of a material loss resulting from the resolution of the uncertainty.

    (1) **Remote Likelihood of Material Loss** In this case, the auditor would **not** add an explanatory paragraph to the report because of the matter.

    (2) **Probable Chance of Material Loss** If management is unable to provide a reasonable estimate of the amount or range of a material probable loss, the auditor should consider adding an explanatory paragraph to the report. This is **not**, however, a substitute for accrual if a reasonable estimate is available. If management makes a reasonable accrual for the potential loss, the auditor would decide whether an explanatory paragraph would be appropriate depending upon the materiality of the loss and the likelihood of its occurrence.

    (3) **Reasonable Possibility of Material Loss** When the chance of material loss is more than remote but less than probable, in deciding whether to add an explanatory paragraph, the auditor would consider the magnitude by which the amount of the potential loss exceeds the auditor's judgment about materiality and the likelihood of its occurrence.

b. **Need For Explanatory Paragraph** As long as any matter is disclosed sufficiently in the notes to the financial statements, an auditor may add an explanatory paragraph to the auditor's report. Emphasis paragraphs are never required; they may be added solely at the auditor's discretion. If a material uncertainty affects the financial statements, an auditor can disclaim an opinion.

c. **Location** If the auditor concludes that an explanatory paragraph is warranted, it should be included **following** the opinion paragraph. The explanatory paragraph should include a description of the matter giving rise to the uncertainty and should indicate that its outcome cannot be determined. The separate paragraph may be shortened by making reference to financial statement notes. No reference should be made to the uncertainty in the introductory, scope, or opinion paragraphs. If, however, the uncertainty is **not** properly accounted for or disclosed, the auditor should issue a qualified or adverse opinion.

5. **Going Concern Questions** The audit report should include an explanatory paragraph **following** the opinion paragraph if the auditor concludes that substantial doubt about the entity's ability to continue as a going concern does exist. If the auditor concludes that the entity's disclosures regarding its ability to continue as a going concern for a reasonable time are inadequate, misleading, or depart from GAAP, a qualified or an adverse opinion should be issued. This paragraph should **not** include any conditional language.

Exhibit 12 ▶ Going Concern Uncertainty: Explanatory Paragraph (following opinion paragraph)

The accompanying financial statements have been prepared assuming that the Company will continue as a going concern. As discussed in Note X to the financial statements, the Company has suffered recurring losses from operations and has a net capital deficiency, raising substantial doubt about its ability to continue as a going concern. Management's plans in regard to these matters are also described in Note X. The financial statements do not include any adjustments that might result from the outcome of this uncertainty.

---

6. **Emphasis of a Matter** The auditor may wish to emphasize a matter regarding the financial statements even though the auditor intends to express an unqualified opinion. For example, the auditor may wish to emphasize that the entity is a component of a larger business enterprise or that it has had significant transactions with related parties. The auditor may wish to mention an important subsequent event. This should be presented in a separate paragraph in the auditor's report with an unqualified opinion.

IV. Departures From Unqualified Opinions (AU 508 continued)

A. Qualified Opinions

When the auditor expresses a qualified opinion, the auditor should disclose all of the substantive reasons in one or more separate explanatory paragraph(s) **preceding** the opinion paragraph of the report. A qualified opinion should include the word *except* or *exception* in a phrase such as *except for* or *with the exception of.* Phrases such as *subject to* and *with the foregoing explanation* are **not** clear or forceful enough and should **not** be used.

1. **Scope Limitations** Restrictions on the scope of an audit, whether imposed by the client or by circumstances, may require the auditor to express a qualified opinion. The decision depends upon the auditor's assessment of the importance of the omitted procedure(s) in relation to the financial statements. When a significant scope limitation is imposed by the client, the auditor normally would disclaim an opinion on the financial statements.

Exhibit 13 ▶ Scope Limitations

<u>Independent Auditor's Report</u>

(Same first paragraph as the standard report)

Except as discussed in the following paragraph, we conducted our audits in accordance with U.S. generally accepted auditing standards. Those standards require that we plan and perform the audit to obtain reasonable assurance about whether the financial statements are free of material misstatement. An audit includes examining, on a test basis, evidence supporting the amounts and disclosures in the financial statements. An audit also includes assessing the accounting principles used and significant estimates made by management, as well as evaluating the overall financial statement presentation. We believe that our audits provide a reasonable basis for our opinion.

We were unable to obtain audited financial statements supporting the Company's investment in a foreign affiliate stated at $_____ and $_____ at December 31, 20X2 and 20X1, respectively, or its equity in earnings of that affiliate of $_____ and $_____, which is included in net income for the years then ended as described in Note X to the financial statements; nor were we able to satisfy ourselves as to the carrying value of the investment in the foreign affiliate or the equity in its earnings by other auditing procedures.

In our opinion, except for the effects of such adjustments, if any, as might have been determined to be necessary had we been able to examine evidence regarding the foreign affiliate investment and earnings, the financial statements referred to in the first paragraph above present fairly, in all material respects, the financial position of X Company as of December 31, 20X2 and 20X1, and the results of its operations and its cash flows for the years then ended in conformity with U.S. generally accepted accounting principles.

a. **Qualified Opinion** If a qualified opinion is expressed, the reasons should be explained in the audit report in an explanatory paragraph (preceding the opinion paragraph) and referred to in both the scope and opinion paragraphs. The wording in the opinion paragraph should indicate that the qualification pertains to the possible effects on the financial statements and **not** to the scope limitation itself.

b. **Scope Limitation Examples**

   (1) The auditor is unable to observe physical inventories or apply alternative procedures to verify their balances.

   (2) The client refuses to permit its attorney to furnish information requested in a letter of audit inquiry.

c. **Limited Reporting Engagements** The auditor is **not** precluded from reporting on only one of the basic financial statements and not the others. A scope limitation would **not** exist if the auditor is able to apply all the procedures to the one financial statement the auditor considers necessary. Such engagements involve limited reporting objectives.

2. **Departure From GAAP**

   Exhibit 14 ▶ Departure From GAAP

   <u>Independent Auditor's Report</u>

   (Same first and second paragraphs as the standard report)

   The company has excluded, from property and debt in the accompanying balance sheets, certain lease obligations that, in our opinion, should be capitalized in order to conform with generally accepted accounting principles. If these lease obligations were capitalized, property would be increased by $_____ and $_____, long-term debt by $_____ and $_____, and retained earnings by $_____ and $_____ as of December 31, 20X2 and 20X1, respectively. Additionally, net income would be increased (decreased) by $_____ and $_____, and earnings per share would be increased (decreased) by $_____ and $_____, respectively, for the years then ended.

   In our opinion, except for the effects of not capitalizing certain lease obligations as discussed in the preceding paragraph, the financial statements referred to above present fairly, in all material respects, the financial position of X Company as of December 31, 20X2 and 20X1, and the results of its operations and its cash flows for the years then ended in conformity with U.S. generally accepted accounting principles.

   a. When financial statements are materially affected by a departure from GAAP, the auditor should express a qualified or an adverse opinion. Materiality, significance of an item to the entity, pervasiveness of the misstatement, and the effect of the misstatement on the financial statements as a whole, must be considered in deciding whether to express a qualified or an adverse opinion.

b.   When the auditor expresses a qualified opinion, the auditor should disclose, in a separate explanatory paragraph(s) **preceding** the opinion paragraph, the substantive reasons that have led the auditor to conclude that there is a departure from GAAP. The opinion paragraph should include appropriate qualifying language and should refer to the explanatory paragraph(s). The explanatory paragraph(s) also should disclose the principal effects of the matter on the financial position, results of operations and cash flows, if practicable. If the effects cannot be determined, the report should so state.

3.   **Inadequate Disclosure**

a.   If information that is essential for a fair presentation of financial statements in conformity with GAAP is **not** disclosed in the financial statements or accompanying notes, the auditor should express a qualified or an adverse opinion, and should provide the information in the report if practicable, unless its omission from the auditor's report is recognized as appropriate by a specific SAS.

Exhibit 15 ▶ Report Qualified for Inadequate Disclosure

Independent Auditor's Report

(Same first and second paragraphs as the standard report)

The Company's financial statements do not disclose (describe the nature of the omitted disclosures). In our opinion, disclosure of this information is required by U.S. generally accepted accounting principles.

In our opinion, except for the omission of the information discussed in the preceding paragraph,...

---

b.   The auditor is **not** required to prepare a basic financial statement and include it in the report if the company's management declines to present the statement. In the case of, for example, the omission of a cash flow statement, a qualified opinion would be appropriate, with an explanatory paragraph added **preceding** the opinion paragraph.

Exhibit 16 ▶ Report Qualified: Lacking Basic Financial Statement

---

Independent Auditor's Report

We have audited the accompanying balance sheets of X Company as of December 31, 20X2 and 20X1, and the related statements of income and retained earnings for the years then ended. These financial statements are the responsibility of the Company's management. Our responsibility is to express an opinion on these financial statements based on our audit.

(Same second paragraph as the standard report)

The Company declined to present a statement of cash flows for the years ended December 31, 20X2 and 20X1. Presentation of such statement summarizing the Company's operating, investing, and financing activities is required by U.S. generally accepted accounting principles.

In our opinion, except that the omission of a statement of cash flows results in an incomplete presentation as explained in the preceding paragraph, the financial statements referred to above present fairly, in all material respects, the financial position of X Company as of December 31, 20X2 and 20X1, and the results of its operations for the years then ended in conformity with U.S. generally accepted accounting principles.

---

4. Accounting Changes The auditor should evaluate a change in accounting principle to be satisfied that (a) the newly adopted accounting principle is a generally accepted accounting principle, (b) the method of accounting for the effect of the change is in conformity with GAAP, and (c) management's justification for the change is reasonable. If a change in accounting principle does **not** meet these conditions, the auditor should express a qualified opinion, or if the effect of the change is sufficiently material, an adverse opinion should be expressed.

Exhibit 17 ▶ Report Qualified: Accounting Change Not Justified by Management

> Independent Auditor's Report
>
> (Same first and second paragraphs as the standard report)
>
> As disclosed in Note X to the financial statements, the Company adopted, in 20X2, the first-in, first-out method of accounting for its inventories, whereas it previously used the last-in, first-out method. Although use of the first-in, first-out method is in conformity with generally accepted accounting principles, in our opinion, the Company has not provided reasonable justification for making this change as required by generally accepted accounting principles.
>
> In our opinion, except for the change in accounting principle discussed in the preceding paragraph, the financial statements referred to above present fairly, in all material respects, the financial position of X Company as of December 31, 20X2 and 20X1, and the results of its operations and its cash flows for the years then ended in conformity with U.S. generally accepted accounting principles.

B. Adverse Opinions

State that financial statements do **not** present fairly the financial position, the results of operations, or cash flows in conformity with GAAP.

Exhibit 18 ▶ Adverse Opinion

> Independent Auditor's Report
>
> (Same first and second paragraphs as the standard report)
>
> As discussed in Note X to the financial statements, the Company carries its property, plant and equipment accounts at appraisal values, and provides depreciation on the basis of such values. Further, the Company does not provide for income taxes with respect to differences between financial income and taxable income arising because of the use, for income tax purposes, of the installment method of reporting gross profit from certain types of sales. Generally accepted accounting principles require that property, plant, and equipment be stated at an amount not in excess of cost, reduced by depreciation based on such amount, and that deferred income taxes be provided.
>
> Because of the departures from generally accepted accounting principles identified above, as of December 31, 20X2 and 20X1, inventories have been increased $_____ and $_____ by inclusion in manufacturing overhead of depreciation in excess of that based on cost; property, plant, and equipment, less accumulated depreciation, is carried at $_____ and $_____ in excess of an amount based on the cost to the Company; and deferred income taxes of $_____ and $_____ have not been recorded, resulting in an increase of $_____ and $_____ in retained earnings and in appraisal surplus of $_____ and $_____, respectively. For the years ended December 31, 20X2 and 20X1, cost of goods sold has been increased $_____ and $_____, respectively, because of the effects of the depreciation accounting referred to above and deferred income taxes of $_____ and $_____ have not been provided, resulting in an increase in net income of $_____ and $_____, respectively.

> In our opinion, because of the effects of the matters discussed in the preceding paragraphs, the financial statements referred to above do not present fairly, in conformity with U.S. generally accepted accounting principles, the financial position of X Company as of December 31, 20X2 and 20X1, or the results of its operations or its cash flows for the years then ended.

1. **Explanatory Paragraph** The auditor should disclose in a separate explanatory paragraph(s) **preceding** the opinion paragraph of the report (a) all the substantive reasons for the adverse opinion, and (b) the principal effects of the subject matter of the adverse opinion on financial position, results of operations, and cash flows, if practicable. If the effects are not reasonably determinable, the report should so state.

2. **Opinion Paragraph** The opinion paragraph should include a direct reference to a separate paragraph that discloses the basis for the adverse opinion.

C. **Disclaimer of Opinion**
States that the auditor does **not** express an opinion on the financial statements. It is appropriate when the auditor has **not** performed an audit sufficient in scope to enable the auditor to form an opinion on the financial statements.

Exhibit 19 ▶ Disclaimer of Opinion Due to Scope Limitation

> <u>Independent Auditor's Report</u>
>
> We were engaged to audit the accompanying balance sheets of X Company as of December 31, 20X2 and 20X1, and the related statements of income, retained earnings, and cash flows for the years then ended. These financial statements are the responsibility of the Company's management.
>
> [Second (scope) paragraph of standard report should be omitted.]
>
> The Company did not make a count of its physical inventory in 20X2 or 20X1, stated in the accompanying financial statements at $_____ as of December 31, 20X2, and at $_____ as of December 31, 20X1. Further, evidence supporting the cost of property and equipment acquired prior to December 31, 20X1, is no longer available. The Company's records do not permit the application of other auditing procedures to inventories or property and equipment.
>
> The Company did not take physical inventories and we were not able to apply other auditing procedures to satisfy ourselves as to inventory quantities and the cost of property and equipment, thus, the scope of our work was not sufficient to enable us to express, and we do not express, an opinion on these financial statements.

1. **Scope Limitation** If a scope limitation is the reason for the disclaimer, the auditor should indicate in a separate paragraph the reasons for the scope limitation. The auditor should state that the scope of the audit was not sufficient to warrant the expression of an opinion, but the auditor should **not** identify the procedures that were performed nor include the paragraph describing the characteristics of an audit (that is, the scope paragraph).

2. **Material Departures** A disclaimer of opinion should **not** be expressed when the auditor believes, on the basis of the audit, that there are material departures from GAAP.

V. **Reports on Comparative Financial Statements (AU 508 continued)**

A. **Standard Report**
An auditor's standard report covers statements of the current period and those of one or more prior periods that are presented on a comparative basis. Therefore, a continuing auditor, an auditor who has audited the current period's financial statements and those of one or more immediately preceding periods, will update the report (re-express an opinion) on the individual financial statements of those prior periods. The updated opinion may differ from that previously given if circumstances warrant a change. During the audit of the current period financial statements, the auditor should be

alert for circumstances or events that affect the prior period financial statements. Generally, the date of the report should be no earlier than the date on which the auditor has obtained sufficient appropriate audit evidence to support the opinion.

Exhibit 20 ▶ Auditor's Standard Report: Comparative Financial Statements

---

<u>Independent Auditor's Report</u>

We have audited the accompanying balance sheets of X Company as of December 31, 20X2 and 20X1, and the related statements of income, retained earnings, and cash flows for the years then ended. These financial statements are the responsibility of the Company's management. Our responsibility is to express an opinion on these financial statements based on our audits.

We conducted our audits in accordance with U.S. generally accepted auditing standards. Those standards require that we plan and perform the audit to obtain reasonable assurance about whether the financial statements are free of material misstatement. An audit includes examining, on a test basis, evidence supporting the amounts and disclosures in the financial statements. An audit also includes assessing the accounting principles used and significant estimates made by management, as well as evaluating the overall financial statement presentation. We believe that our audits provide a reasonable basis for our opinion.

In our opinion, the financial statements referred to above present fairly, in all material respects, the financial position of X Company as of December 31, 20X2 and 20X1, and the results of its operations and its cash flows for the years then ended in conformity with U.S. generally accepted accounting principles.

B.   Differing Opinions

The auditor's report on the comparative statements applies to the individual financial statements that are presented. Therefore, the same type of opinion is **not** required (qualified, unqualified, etc.) on all of the statements. When it is **not** the same, the auditor should (1) disclose all of the substantive reasons for the modified opinion (or for disclaiming an opinion) in a separate explanatory paragraph of the report, and (2) in the opinion paragraph, include an appropriate modification (or disclaimer of opinion) along with a reference to the explanation.

Exhibit 21 ▶ Differing Opinions

<u>Independent Auditor's Report</u>

(Same first and second paragraphs as the standard report)

The Company has excluded, from property and debt in the accompanying 20X2 balance sheet, certain lease obligations that were entered into in 20X2 which, in our opinion, should be capitalized in order to conform with U.S. generally accepted accounting principles. If these lease obligations were capitalized, property would be increased by $_____, long-term debt by $_____, and retained earnings by $_____ as of December 31, 20X2, and net income and earnings per share would be increased (decreased) by $_____ and $_____, respectively, for the year then ended.

In our opinion, except for the effects on the 20X2 financial statements of not capitalizing certain lease obligations as described in the preceding paragraph, the financial statements referred to above present fairly, in all material respects, the financial position of ABC Company as of December 31, 20X2 and 20X1, and the results of its operations and its cash flows for the years then ended in conformity with U.S. generally accepted accounting principles.

C.   Subsequent Restatement of Prior Period Statements to Conform With GAAP

If the auditor, during the current audit, becomes aware of circumstances or events that affect the financial statements of a prior period, the auditor should consider such matters when updating the report.

Exhibit 22 ▶ Changed Opinion

<u>Independent Auditor's Report</u>

(Same first and second paragraphs as the standard report)

In our report dated March 1, 20X2, we expressed an opinion that the 20X1 financial statements did not fairly present financial position, results of operations, and cash flows in conformity with generally accepted accounting principles because of two departures from such principles: (1) the Company carried its property, plant and equipment at appraisal values, and provided for depreciation on the basis of such values, and (2) the Company did not provide for deferred income taxes with respect to differences between income for financial reporting purposes and taxable income. As described in Note X, the Company has changed its method of accounting for these items and restated its 20X1 financial statements to conform with generally accepted accounting principles. Accordingly, our present opinion on the 20X1 financial statements, as presented herein, is different from that expressed in our previous report.

In our opinion, the financial statements referred to above present fairly, in all material respects, the financial position of X Company as of December 31, 20X2 and 20X1, and the results of its operations and its cash flows for the years then ended in conformity with U.S. generally accepted accounting principles.

---

1. **Unqualified Opinion** If an auditor previously had qualified the opinion on the financial statements of a prior period because of a departure from GAAP, and the prior period financial statements are restated in the current period to conform with GAAP, the updated report of the prior period should indicate that the statements have been restated and should express an unqualified opinion with respect to the restated financial statements.

2. **Different Opinion From Previous** If the auditor decides to express a different opinion than that previously expressed, the auditor should disclose all the substantive reasons for the different opinion in a separate explanatory paragraph(s) **preceding** the opinion paragraph of the report. The explanatory paragraph should disclose (a) the date of the auditor's previous report, (b) the type of opinion previously expressed, (c) the circumstances or events that caused the auditor to express a different opinion, and (d) that the auditor's updated opinion on the financial statements of the prior period is different from the auditor's previous opinion on those statements.

D. **Report of Predecessor Auditor**

1. **Reissued** The predecessor auditor should consider whether the opinion previously issued on the financial statements of the prior period is still appropriate. This should include (a) reading the financial statements of the current period, (b) comparing the statements reported on with those that are being presented for comparative purposes, (c) obtaining a letter of representation from the successor auditor as to whether the successor's audit found anything that might have a material effect on (or require disclosure in) the prior period's statements, and (d) obtaining an updating representation letter from management.

   a. **Procedures** If the predecessor becomes aware of circumstances that may affect the predecessor's own previous opinion, the predecessor should inquire about the event and may want to perform tests such as reviewing the working papers of the successor auditor in regard to the matter. The predecessor must then decide whether to revise the opinion.

   b. **Report** When the predecessor reissues the report, the predecessor should use the same date as that of the predecessor's own previous report to avoid any implication that the predecessor examined any records, transactions, or events after that date. The predecessor should **not** refer to the work or report of the successor auditor. If the predecessor revises the report or if the financial statements are restated, the report should be dual dated.

2. **Not Presented** If the financial statements of a prior period are presented for comparative purposes, but the report of the predecessor auditor is **not** presented, the successor auditor should modify the introductory paragraph of the report to indicate (a) that another auditor audited the prior period financial statements, (b) the date of the predecessor's report, (c) the type of report issued by the predecessor auditor, and (d) if the report was other than standard, and the substantive reasons therefore.

Exhibit 23 ▶ Report When Predecessor's Report Is Not Presented

> We have audited the balance sheet of ABC Company as of December 31, 20X2, and the related statements of income, retained earnings, and cash flows for the year then ended. These financial statements are the responsibility of the Company's management. Our responsibility is to express an opinion on these financial statements based on our audit. The financial statements of ABC Company as of December 31, 20X1, were audited by other auditors whose report dated March 31, 20X2, expressed an unqualified opinion on those statements.
>
> (Same second paragraph as the standard report)
>
> In our opinion, the 20X2 financial statements referred to above present fairly, in all material respects, the financial position of ABC Company as of December 31, 20X2, and the results of its operations and its cash flows for the year then ended in conformity with U.S. generally accepted accounting principles.

a. If the predecessor auditor's opinion was other than a standard report, the successor auditor should describe the nature of and the reasons for the report modifications.

Exhibit 24 ▶ Predecessor Auditor's Report Not Standard

> ...were audited by other auditors whose report, dated March 1, 20X2, on those statements included an explanatory paragraph that described the litigation discussed in Note X to the financial statements.

b. If the financial statements of the prior period have been restated, the introductory paragraph should indicate that a predecessor auditor reported on the financial statements of the prior period before restatement. In addition, if the successor auditor applies sufficient procedures to satisfy the appropriateness of the restatement adjustments, the successor may also state this in the report.

Exhibit 25 ▶ Prior Period Is Restated

> We also audited the adjustments described in Note X that were applied to restate the 20X1 financial statements. In our opinion, such adjustments are appropriate and have been properly applied.

VI. Summary of Various Audit Opinions & Corresponding Reports

A. Unqualified
When all of the necessary conditions for an unqualified opinion are met and none of the following situations exist, the auditor may issue a standard report.

1. **Part of Audit Performed by Other Auditor**

   a. **Principal Auditor Takes Responsibility for Other Auditor's Work** Standard report issued.

   b. **Principal Auditor Does Not Take Responsibility for Other Auditor's Work** Make reference to other auditor and clearly indicate division of responsibility (do **not** name unless other gives permission and other's report is included). Introductory, scope, and opinion paragraphs should all be changed to reflect this. (**No** explanatory paragraph.)

2. **Justifiable Departure From GAAP (rare)** Add explanatory paragraph. Describe departure, approximate effects, and reasons why compliance would result in a misleading statement.

3. **Uncertainties**

   a. **Remote** Standard report issued.

   b. **Probable** Explanatory paragraph if **not** estimable; if estimable, management should accrue, or this would be a departure from GAAP (resulting in a qualified or adverse opinion).

4. **Doubt About Ability to Continue as a Going Concern** Explanatory paragraph.

5. **Lack of Consistency**

   a. **Material** Explanatory paragraph added.

   b. **Immaterial** Standard report issued.

6. **Emphasis of a Matter** Explanatory paragraph added. When an explanatory paragraph is necessary and it doesn't impact the opinion, it should be placed **after** the opinion paragraph.

B. **Qualified**
An explanatory paragraph is added **preceding** the opinion paragraph; words such as *except for* or *with the exception of* are used.

1. **Scope Limitation** If significant, disclaim; otherwise, explanatory paragraph **preceding** opinion paragraph added and referred to in scope and opinion paragraphs. This does **not** refer the reader to the notes to the financial statements for details.

2. **Material Departure From GAAP** Qualified or adverse depending on materiality, significance of item to entity, pervasiveness of misstatement, and effect of misstatement on statements taken as a whole. If qualified, explanatory paragraph added **preceding** opinion paragraph and referred to in opinion.

3. **Inadequate Disclosure—Qualified or Adverse** Explanatory paragraph added and referred to in opinion.

4. **Inappropriate Accounting Changes—Qualified or Adverse** Explanatory paragraph **preceding** opinion paragraph added and referred to in opinion.

C. **Adverse**
Explanatory paragraph **preceding** opinion paragraph. Explanatory paragraph added and referred to in adverse opinion.

D. **Disclaimer**
Explanatory paragraph **preceding** "opinion" paragraph. If a scope limitation, scope paragraph omitted, explanatory paragraph added and referred to in the disclaimer of opinion paragraph.

E. **Comparative**

1. **Qualified Prior Year, Standard in Current Year** Explanatory paragraph **preceding** opinion, referred to in opinion paragraph: "except for..."

2. **Qualified Prior Year, Change Made in Current Year to Conform to GAAP** Explanatory paragraph **preceding** opinion, standard opinion paragraph.

F.   Predecessor Auditor
If predecessor report is **not** presented with comparative statements, modify introductory paragraph, no change to scope paragraph, and only express opinion on audited (current year, by successor) statements.

Exhibit 26 ▶ Conditions Requiring Modification of Report

Reasons for Modification*	Opinion Expressed	Explanatory Paragraph	Opinion Paragraph
GAAP Departure	Qualified or Adverse	**Before** opinion paragraph to explain the departure and amount(s)	**Modified** to provide qualifying language and refer to explanatory paragraph(s)
Inadequate Disclosure	Qualified or Adverse	**Before** opinion paragraph to explain missing disclosure	**Modified** to provide qualifying language and refer to explanatory paragraph(s)
Scope Limitation	Qualified or Disclaimer	**Before** opinion paragraph to explain scope limitation and potential monetary effects	**Modified** to provide qualifying language or to provide disclaimer**
Uncertainty	Unqualified (disclaimer is allowed)	**After** opinion paragraph to describe uncertainty and refer reader to the note in the financial statements***	**Not** modified
Going Concern Uncertainty	Unqualified (disclaimer is allowed)	**After** opinion paragraph to describe going concern using wording "substantial doubt" about entity's ability to continue as a going concern and refer reader to the note in the financial statements	**Not** modified
Consistency Violation (if properly accounted for and disclosed, if not, treat as GAAP departure)	Unqualified	**After** opinion paragraph describing accounting GAAP departure change and referring reader to the note in the financial statements	**Not** modified
Emphasis of a Matter	Unqualified	**After** opinion paragraph describing matter and referring reader to the note in the financial statements	**Not** modified
Reliance on Another Auditor	Unqualified	Division of responsibility indicated in introductory paragraph including significance of portion of entity done by other auditor	**Modified** to refer to other auditor
Changed Opinion on Prior Period Information	Unqualified	**Before** opinion paragraph to describe reason for different opinion	**Not** modified

NOTE: When **not** qualifying an opinion, an explanatory paragraph generally (but not always) comes **after** the opinion paragraph (which is **not** modified). When the opinion is other than unqualified and an explanatory paragraph is included, it comes **before** the opinion.

---

*   Assuming item is material
**   Qualified opinion requires modification of second paragraph (using "except for" language). Disclaimer requires modification of introductory paragraph and the second (scope) paragraph is NOT included.
*** This explanatory paragraph is optional.

VII. Timing Issues

A.   Dating the Auditor's Report (AU 530)

1.   **General Rule** The date of the report should be no earlier than the date on which the auditor has obtained sufficient appropriate audit evidence to support the opinion. Sufficient evidence includes evidence that the audit documentation has been reviewed and that the entity's financial statements, including disclosures, have been prepared and that management has

asserted that it has taken responsibility for them. This will ordinarily result in a report date that is close to the report release date. The auditor does **not** have responsibility to make any inquiries or to conduct any audit procedures after this date (with the exception of filings under the Securities Act of 1933).

2. **Subsequent Events**

    a. **Adjustment** If the auditor becomes aware of an event requiring adjustment (Type I subsequent event) of the financial statements that occurred after the date of the audit report but before it is issued, the statements should be adjusted or the opinion should be qualified. If the adjustment is made without any disclosure in the financial statements, the auditor's original report date is still used. If the adjustment is made and disclosed in the financial statements, or if the audit report is qualified due to lack of adjustment, the auditor may dual date the report by using the original report date except for the subsequent event which is dated later.

    b. **Disclosure** The auditor may become aware of a new event requiring disclosure (Type II subsequent event) (such as a lawsuit filed after the balance sheet date but before the financial statements are issued.) If disclosure is **not** made, the audit opinion would be qualified. If disclosure is made, the auditor may dual date the report. If dual dating is used, the responsibility for any events that occurred after the report date is limited to the particular subsequent event that is dual dated. If the auditor chooses, the later date may be used for the entire report. However, the auditor's responsibility for events occurring after the original report date will then extend to the later date.

3. **Reissuance** When an auditor reissues a report, the original report date should be used. This implies that there has been no audit past this date. When events that occurred subsequent to the date of the report require modification of the statements or the opinion, a dual date is appropriate. If events that occurred subsequent to the date of the report only require disclosure in the financial statements, the events may be disclosed in a note to the statements and the date of the original report may be used.

B. **Subsequent Events (AU 560)**
Subsequent events are events or transactions having a material effect on the financial statements that occur after the balance sheet date, but before the date the financial statements are issued.

1. **Types**

    a. **Require Adjustment** Subsequent events that provide additional evidence about conditions that existed at the date of the balance sheet and affect the estimates used in preparing the financial statements require adjustment of the financial statements. Examples include a loss on an uncollectible trade account because a customer went bankrupt shortly after the end of the period (this indicates that the customer's financial position at the balance sheet date was not adequate to meet obligations), and the settlement of litigation for an amount different from the amount recorded in the accounts (as long as the reason for the litigation occurred prior to the balance sheet date).

    b. **Require Only Disclosure** Subsequent events that provide evidence about conditions that did **not** exist at the balance sheet date but arose after that date, do **not** require adjustment of the financial statements. The conditions should be disclosed if their disclosure is required to keep the financial statements from being misleading. In some cases, *pro forma* statements may be prepared. Occasionally, the auditor may decide to include an explanatory paragraph in the report to draw the attention of the reader to the event. Examples of events requiring disclosure (but **not** adjustment) include (a) sale of a bond or capital stock issue, (b) purchase of a business, (c) settlement of litigation arising from events that occurred subsequent to the balance sheet date, (d) loss of plant or inventories as a result of a fire or flood, and (e) losses on receivables resulting from conditions that arose after the balance sheet date (such as a customer's major casualty loss).

2. **Reissuance of Financial Statements** Events that occur between the time of the original issuance of the statements and the time of reissuance of the statements (for example, in reports filed with a regulatory agency) should **not** result in an adjustment of the financial statements unless the adjustment would meet the criteria for the correction of an error or the criteria for prior period adjustments.

3. **Auditing Procedures in Subsequent Period** The subsequent period extends from the balance sheet date to the date of the auditor's report.

    a. Certain audit procedures should be performed after the balance sheet date to assure a proper cutoff and to evaluate the balances of certain asset and liability accounts.

    b. Additional auditing procedures should be applied to the period after the balance sheet date to identify subsequent events that may require adjustment or disclosure. These generally include (1) reading the latest interim financial statements and comparing them with the financial statements being reported on, (2) discussing with management the existence of substantial contingent liabilities, any significant change in stockholders' equity items, the current status of financial statement items that were accounted for on a tentative basis, and the existence of any unusual adjustments made after the balance sheet date, (3) reading the minutes of the board of directors' and stockholders' meetings, (4) inquiring of the client's legal counsel about litigation, claims, and assessments, (5) obtaining a letter of representation from management, dated as of the date of the auditor's report, as to whether any subsequent events occurred that would require adjustment to or disclosure in the statements, and (6) making any additional inquiries and performing any procedures that are considered necessary by the auditor.

C. **Subsequent Discovery of Facts Existing at Date of Auditor's Report (AU 561)**
The auditor may, after the date of the report, become aware of facts that existed at that date and that might have affected the report had the auditor been aware of them.

1. **Responsibility** The auditor does **not** have any obligation to perform auditing procedures or make inquiries after the report date unless the auditor becomes aware of this type of information. When the auditor becomes aware of information that relates to financial statements previously reported on by the auditor, but that was **not** known at the date of the report, and that is of such a nature and from such a source that the auditor would have investigated it, had the auditor been aware of it during the audit, the auditor should, as soon as practicable, determine whether the information is reliable and whether the facts existed at the date of the report.

    a. The auditor should discuss the matter with the appropriate level of the client's management, and request cooperation in the investigation into the matter.

    b. The auditor should consult an attorney when encountering these circumstances because of legal implications that may be involved, including the confidentiality of auditor-client communications.

2. **Preventing Future Reliance on Report** When the subsequently discovered information is found both to be reliable and to have existed at the report date, the auditor should take action if the nature and effect of the matter are such that the report would have been affected by the information had it been known, and such that the auditor believes there are persons currently relying on, or likely to rely on, the financial statements. To prevent future reliance on the report, the auditor should advise the client to make appropriate disclosure of the newly discovered information, and the effect of the facts to the persons relying on, or likely to rely on, the statements.

a. **Client Cooperates** If the client cooperates, the method used will depend on the circumstances.

   (1) **Revise & Reissue** The statements should be revised and reissued if the effect of the subsequently discovered information can be determined promptly. The reasons for the revision usually will be described in a note to the statements and referred to in the auditor's report.

   (2) **Statements of a Subsequent Period** If the issuance of financial statements and the auditor's report for a subsequent period is imminent, appropriate revision can be made in such statements.

   (3) **Notification by Client** If the effect on the statements cannot be determined promptly, but it appears the statements will be revised after investigation, the client should notify persons who are relying (or are likely to rely) on the statements and report that they should not do so, and that revised statements and the report will be issued when the investigation is complete.

b. **Client Does Not Cooperate** If the client does **not** cooperate, the auditor should notify the board of directors that unless the client cooperates, the auditor will (1) notify the client that the auditor's report cannot be associated with the financial statements, (2) notify regulatory agencies that the auditor's report should not be relied upon, and (3) notify each person that the auditor knows is relying on the statements and report that they should no longer do so.

3. **Disclosure to Other Parties**

a. When the auditor must make a disclosure and the auditor has been able to make a satisfactory investigation and determine that the information is reliable, the disclosure should include a description of the nature of the subsequently acquired information and describe the effect of the information on the financial statements and the report. The disclosure should be as factual and precise as possible, but it should **not** contain any comment on the conduct or motive of any person.

b. When the auditor has been prevented from making a satisfactory investigation, the auditor need **not** provide detailed information but can indicate that additional information, that the client has not helped substantiate, has come to the auditor's attention, and if true, the auditor believes the report should no longer be relied upon. No such disclosure should be made unless the auditor believes that the financial statements are likely to be misleading.

D. **Consideration of Omitted Procedures After Report Date (AU 390)**
The auditor may conclude, after the date of the report, that one or more auditing procedures considered necessary at that date were omitted from the audit, even though there is **no** indication that the financial statements are not fairly presented in conformity with GAAP or another comprehensive basis of accounting.

1. **Responsibility** Although the auditor does **not** have any responsibility to perform a retrospective review of the work performed, the omission of a necessary auditing procedure may be disclosed when the reports and working papers relating to the engagement are subjected to post-issuance review (e.g., a firm's internal inspection program or peer review).

2. **Assessment** Upon concluding that a necessary auditing procedure has been omitted, the auditor should assess the importance of the omitted procedure to the auditor's present ability to support a previously expressed opinion regarding the financial statements in question. This assessment can be aided by (a) reviewing the working papers, (b) discussing the audit circumstances with engagement personnel and others, and (c) reevaluating the overall scope

of the audit. The results of other procedures that were applied may tend to compensate for, or make less important, the omitted procedure.

3.   **Course of Action** If the auditor concludes that the omission of the necessary procedure impairs the present ability to support the previously expressed opinion, and the auditor believes that there are persons currently relying, or likely to rely, on the report, the auditor should proceed as follows:

    a.   **Previously Omitted Procedures Can Be Applied** The auditor should promptly apply the omitted procedure(s) or alternative procedures that would provide a satisfactory basis for the auditor's opinion. If, as a result, the auditor becomes aware of facts existing at the date of the report that would have affected that report had the auditor been aware of them, then the auditor should take steps to prevent future reliance on the report.

    b.   **Previously Omitted Procedures Can Not Be Applied** The auditor should consult an attorney to determine an appropriate course of action concerning responsibilities to the client, regulatory authorities, if any, having jurisdiction over the client, and persons relying, or likely to rely, on the report.

VIII.   Association With Financial Statements (AU 504, SAS 26)

A.   Association
The fourth standard of reporting seeks to avoid any misunderstanding as to the responsibility the accountant is assuming when her/his name is associated with financial statements. The objective is to provide reporting guidance to a CPA who is associated with the audited or unaudited financial statements of a public entity or with the audited financial statements of a nonpublic entity. [Statements on Standards for Accounting and Review Services (SSARS) apply to the unaudited financial statements of a nonpublic entity.]

Exhibit 27 ▶ The Fourth Standard of Reporting

> "…In all cases where an auditor's name is associated with financial statements, the auditor should clearly indicate the character of the auditor's work, if any, and the degree of responsibility the auditor is taking in the auditor's report."

1.   The CPA is associated with an entity's financial statements when the CPA (1) has agreed to the use of her/his name in a report, document, or written communication that contains the financial statements and/or (2) submits financial statements that the CPA has prepared (or assisted in preparing) to the client or to others (even if the CPA does not append her/his name to the financial statements).

2.   Association does **not** occur when the CPA prepares data, such as tax returns, solely for submission to taxing authorities because these do **not** constitute financial statements.

B.   Disclaimer of Opinion on Unaudited Financial Statements
When associated with a **public** entity's financial statements that the CPA has **not** audited **or** reviewed, the CPA should issue the disclaimer shown in Exhibit 28. Note that this disclaimer is different from a disclaimer of opinion due to a scope limitation discussed earlier.

Exhibit 28 ▶ Disclaimer

> The accompanying balance sheet of X Company as of December 31, 20X1, and the related statements of income, retained earnings, and cash flows for the year then ended were not audited by us and, accordingly, we do not express an opinion on them.

1.   **Location** Disclaimer may accompany, or may be placed directly on, the unaudited financial statements.

2. **Markings** Each page of the statement should be marked as *unaudited*.

3. **Responsibility** CPA's only responsibility is to read the financial statements for obvious material misstatements.

4. **Procedures** The CPA should **not** describe any procedures that may have been applied, because to do so might give the impression that the CPA audited or reviewed the financial statements.

5. **Inclusion of Name** When a CPA learns that a client who is a public entity plans to include the CPA's name in a client-prepared written communication that will contain financial statements that the CPA has **not** audited or reviewed, the CPA should ask (a) that her/his name **not** be used or (b) that the client clearly mark the financial statements as *unaudited* and that a notation be made that the auditor does **not** express an opinion on them. If the client refuses, the CPA may need to consult legal counsel as to appropriate actions.

C. **Disclaimer of Opinion on Unaudited OCBOA Financial Statements**

Exhibit 29 ▶ OCBOA Financial Statements

> The accompanying statement of assets and liabilities resulting from cash transactions of XYZ Corporation as of December 31, 20X1, and the related statement of revenues collected and expenses paid during the year then ended were not audited by us and, accordingly, we do not express an opinion on them.

1. **Modification of Disclaimer** The unaudited disclaimer applies except that the identification of the financial statements should be modified to conform to SAS 62, *Special Reports.*

2. **Note to Financial Statements** Should describe the difference between the basis of presentation and GAAP. The monetary effect of such differences does **not** need to be stated.

D. **Disclaimer of Opinion When CPA Is Not Independent**
The Second General Standard requires independence in mental attitude. The CPA cannot be in accordance with GAAS if the CPA is **not** independent, so the CPA should disclaim an opinion and clearly state that s/he is not independent (the CPA should **not** give the reasons for this lack of independence).

Exhibit 30 ▶ Lack of Independence

> We are not independent with respect to XYZ Company, and the accompanying balance sheet as of December 31, 20X1, and the related statements of income, retained earnings, and cash flows for the year then ended were not audited by us and, accordingly, we do not express an opinion on them.

1. **Nonpublic Entity** The CPA should follow SSARS when the financial statements are those of a nonpublic entity.

2. **Public Entity** Paragraphs 1. through 2. of C., above, should be followed except that the disclaimer should be modified so that it clearly indicates the CPA is **not** independent. The reasons for lack of independence should **not** be described.

E. **Modified Disclaimer**
If the CPA feels the unaudited financial statements do not conform to GAAP (which includes adequate disclosure), the CPA should ask the client to revise the statements. If the client refuses, the CPA should describe the departure in a disclaimer by (1) specifically referring to the nature of the departure and (2) if practicable, stating the effects of the departure on the financial statements or including the information that is needed in order to provide adequate disclosure.

1. **Indeterminable or Impracticable** If the effects of the departure cannot be reasonably determined, the CPA should state this in the disclaimer. In the case of inadequate disclosure, it may not be practicable for the CPA to include the omitted disclosures in the disclaimer.

2. **Withdrawal** If the client refuses to revise the statements or accept the disclaimer describing the departure, the CPA should refuse to be associated with the statements. The CPA may find it necessary to withdraw from the engagement.

3. **Negative Assurance** The CPA should **not** include statements in the disclaimer that would give negative assurance except as specifically permitted by the AICPA. (One permissible area is letters for underwriters.)

F. **Comparative Financial Statements**

1. **Documents Filed With the SEC** Unaudited financial statements presented in comparative form with audited financial statements should be clearly marked "unaudited." The auditor's report should **not** refer to the unaudited statements.

2. **Documents Other Than Those Filed With SEC** The unaudited financial statements should be clearly marked to indicate they have **not** been audited and either (a) the report on the prior period should be reissued or (b) the current period's report should contain a separate paragraph that describes the responsibility assumed for the financial statements of the prior period. In either case, the CPA should consider any information that has come to her/his attention during the CPA's current engagement that would help in evaluating the current form and presentation of the prior period information.

   a. **Current Period Financial Statements Unaudited, Prior Period Financial Statements Audited** If a separate paragraph is to be used, it should state (1) the prior period's statements were previously audited, (2) the date of the previous report, (3) the type of opinion that was previously expressed, (4) if it was **not** unqualified, the substantive reasons for this, and (5) that no auditing procedures have been performed after the date of the previous report.

   Exhibit 31 ▶ Prior Audited, Current Unaudited

   > The financial statements for the year ended December 31, 20X1, were audited by us (other accountants) and we (they) expressed an unqualified opinion on them in our (their) report dated March 1, 20X2, but we (they) have not performed any auditing procedures since that date.

   b. **Prior Period Financial Statements Were Not Audited** If a separate paragraph is to be used, it should (1) state the service that was performed in the prior period, (2) state the date of the report on that service, (3) describe any material modifications noted in that report, and (4) state that the scope of the service was less than that of an audit and, therefore, does **not** provide a basis for the expression of an opinion on the financial statements taken as a whole. When the financial statements are those of a public entity, the separate paragraph should include a disclaimer of opinion or a description of a review. When the prior period statements are for a nonpublic entity and were compiled or reviewed, the separate paragraph should contain an appropriate description of the compilation or review. The unaudited financial statements should be clearly marked to indicate their status.

Exhibit 32 ▶ Review Performed on Prior Period Financial Statements & Current Year's Statements Audited

> The 20X1 financial statements were reviewed by us (other accountants) and our (their) report thereon, dated March 1, 20X2, stated we (they) were not aware of any material modifications that should be made to those statements for them to be in conformity with generally accepted accounting principles. However, a review is substantially less in scope than an audit and does not provide a basis for the expression of an opinion on the financial statements taken as a whole.

Exhibit 33 ▶ Compiled Prior Period Financial Statements

> The 20X1 financial statements were compiled by us (other accountants) and our (their) report thereon, dated March 1, 20X2, stated we (they) did not audit or review those financial statements and, accordingly, express no opinion or other form of assurance on them.

IX. Consideration of Entity's Ability to Continue as Going Concern (AU 341, SAS 59)

A. Responsibility

Continuation of an entity as a going concern is assumed in financial reporting in the absence of significant information to the contrary. The auditor is responsible for evaluating information gathered during the audit to determine whether there is substantial doubt about the entity's ability to continue as a going concern for a reasonable period of time. A reasonable period of time is defined as a period **not** to exceed one year from the date of the financial statements.

1. **Scope** The auditor's evaluation is based on knowledge of events and relevant conditions that exist at or have occurred prior to the date of the auditor's report.

2. **Nature** Key information to be considered includes the entity's inability to meet its obligations in a timely manner without substantial disposal of assets outside the normal course of business, restructuring of debt, externally forced revisions of operations, or similar actions. Some examples of nonfinancial factors include the possible loss of key personnel, suppliers, and/or major customers.

3. **Future** The auditor is **not** expected to predict future conditions or events. If an entity ceases to exist within a year of receiving an audit report which does **not** refer to substantial doubt about the entity's ability to continue as a going concern, it does **not** necessarily indicate an inadequate performance by the auditor. The absence of a reference to substantial doubt should **not** be interpreted as an assurance of the entity's ability to continue as a going concern.

B. Audit Procedures

Audit procedures do **not** need to be designed specifically to identify conditions and events that, when considered in the aggregate, may indicate substantial doubt about the entity's ability to continue as a going concern. The results of auditing procedures designed and performed to achieve other audit objectives should be sufficient for that purpose. The following are examples of procedures that may identify such conditions and events:

1. Analytics

2. Review of subsequent events

3. Review of compliance with the terms of debt and loan agreements

4. Reading of minutes of meetings of stockholders, board of directors, and major committees of the board

5.   Inquiry of an entity's legal counsel about litigation, claims, and assessments

6.   Confirmation with related and third parties of the details of arrangements to provide or maintain financial support

C.   Indications

Procedures such as those listed above may identify conditions and events that, when considered in the aggregate, indicate that substantial doubt may exist. Such conditions and events include the following:

1.   **Negative Trends**   For example, working capital deficiencies, recurring operating losses, negative cash flows from operating activities, or adverse key financial ratios.

2.   **Other Indications of Possible Financial Difficulties**   For example, default on loan or similar agreements, arrearages in dividends, denial of usual trade credit from suppliers, restructuring of debt, noncompliance with statutory capital requirements, need to seek new sources or methods of financing, or to dispose of substantial assets.

3.   **Internal Matters**   For example, work stoppages or other labor difficulties, substantial dependence on the success of a particular project, uneconomic long-term commitments, or need to significantly revise operations.

4.   **External Matters That Have Occurred**   For example, legal proceedings, legislation, or similar matters that might jeopardize an entity's ability to operate; loss of a key franchise, license, or patent; loss of a principal customer or supplier; or uninsured or underinsured catastrophe such as a drought, earthquake, or flood.

D.   Conclusions

If, after completing the audit, the auditor finds that conditions and events exist that, when considered in the aggregate, indicate that there could be substantial doubt about the entity's ability to continue as a going concern for a reasonable period of time, the following steps should be taken:

1.   **Mitigating Factors**   The auditor should obtain any additional information available about the conditions and events or about mitigating factors including management's plans.

2.   **Management Plans**   The auditor must consider management's plans in order to evaluate the likelihood of successful implementation. The auditor should obtain information about the plans and decide whether it is likely the adverse effects will be mitigated for a reasonable period of time and that such plans can be implemented effectively. The auditor's consideration relating to management's plans may include the following:

a.   **Dispose of Assets**

(1)   Restrictions on disposal of assets, such as covenants limiting such transactions in loan or similar agreements or encumbrances against assets

(2)   Apparent marketability of assets that management plans to sell

(3)   Possible direct or indirect effects of disposal of assets

b.   **Borrow Money or Restructure Debt**

(1)   Availability of debt financing, including existing or committed credit arrangements, such as lines of credit or arrangements for factoring receivables or sale-leaseback of assets

(2)   Existing or committed arrangements to restructure or subordinate debt or to guarantee loans to the entity

       (3)   Existing restrictions on additional borrowing or the sufficiency of available collateral

    c.   **Reduce or Delay Expenditures**

       (1)   Apparent feasibility of plans to reduce overhead or administrative expenditures, to postpone maintenance or research and development projects, or to lease rather than purchase assets

       (2)   Possible direct or indirect effects of reduced or delayed expenditures

    d.   **Increase Ownership Equity**

       (1)   Apparent feasibility of plans to increase ownership equity, including existing or committed arrangements to raise additional capital

       (2)   Existing or committed arrangements to reduce current dividend requirements or to accelerate cash distributions from affiliates or other investors

    e.   **Prospective Financial Information** When prospective financial information is significant to management's plans, the auditor should request management to provide that information and should consider the adequacy of support for significant assumptions underlying that information. The auditor should give particular attention to assumptions that are (1) material to the prospective financial statements, (2) especially sensitive or susceptible to change, or (3) inconsistent with historical trends. The auditor's consideration should include reading the information and the underlying assumptions, comparing the prospective information in prior periods with actual results, and comparing prospective information for the current period with actual results to date.

3.   **Disclosure of Doubt** The auditor should consider the adequacy of the disclosure of the doubt about the entity's ability to continue and include an explanatory paragraph **following** the opinion paragraph in the audit report. If the auditor concludes that substantial doubt about the entity's ability to continue as a going concern exists, the auditor must consider disclosure of the conditions or events in the financial statements. Information that might be disclosed include the following:

    a.   Pertinent conditions and events giving rise to the assessment of substantial doubt about the entity's ability to continue as a going concern for a reasonable period of time

    b.   The possible effects of such conditions and events

    c.   Management's evaluation of the significance of those conditions and events and any mitigating factors

    d.   Possible discontinuance of operations

    e.   Management's plans (including relevant prospective financial information)

    f.   Information about the recoverability or classification of recorded asset amounts or the amounts or classification of liabilities

4.   **Disclosure of Trigger** If the auditor concludes that substantial doubt does **not** exist, the auditor should consider the disclosure of the information that triggered concern about the entity's ability to continue as a going concern for a reasonable period of time and outline mitigating circumstances, including management's plans.

E.   **Audit Report**

The audit report should include an explanatory paragraph **following** the opinion paragraph if the auditor concludes that substantial doubt about the entity's ability to continue as a going concern does exist. If the auditor concludes that the entity's disclosures regarding its ability to continue as a going concern for a reasonable time are inadequate, misleading, or a departure from GAAP, a qualified or an adverse opinion should be issued. The use of conditional language regarding the entity's ability to continue as a going concern is prohibited.

1. **Inappropriate Statement** "If XYZ Company is unable to renegotiate the labor contract, there may be substantial doubt about XYZ Company's ability to continue as a going concern."

2. **Appropriate Statement** "The accompanying financial statements have been prepared assuming that the Company will continue as a going concern. As discussed in Note X to the financial statements, the Company has suffered recurring losses from operations and has a net capital deficiency that raise substantial doubt about its ability to continue as a going concern. Management's plans in regard to these matters are also described in Note X. The financial statements do not include any adjustments that might result from the outcome of this uncertainty."

F. **Comparison With Prior Financial Statements**
Substantial doubt about an entity's ability to continue as a going concern that arose in the current period should **not** affect the auditor's report on the financial statements of prior periods used for comparison with current financial statements. If substantial doubt existed in the prior period, but has been alleviated in the current period, the explanatory paragraph **following** the opinion paragraph in the auditor's report should **not** be repeated.

G. **Communications**
The auditor should communicate with those charged with governance if s/he concludes that there is substantial doubt about the entity's ability to continue as a going concern for a reasonable period of time after s/he considers identified conditions and events in the aggregate as well as management's plans. This communication should include:

1. The nature of the events or conditions identified

2. The possible effect on the financial statements and the adequacy of related disclosures in the financial statements

3. The effects on the auditor's report

H. **Documentation**
The auditor should document:

1. The conditions or events that led the auditor to believe that there is substantial doubt about the entity's ability to continue as a going concern for a reasonable period of time.

2. The elements of management's plans that the auditor considered to be particularly significant to overcoming the adverse effects of the conditions or events.

3. The auditing procedures performed and evidence obtained to evaluate the significant elements of management's plans.

4. The auditor's conclusion as to whether substantial doubt about the entity's ability to continue as a going concern for a reasonable period of time remains or is alleviated. If substantial doubt remains, the auditor also should document the possible effects of the conditions or events on the financial statements and the adequacy of the related disclosures. If substantial doubt is alleviated, the auditor also should document the conclusion as to the need for disclosure of the principal conditions and events that initially caused the auditor to believe there was substantial doubt.

5. The auditor's conclusion as to whether s/he should include an explanatory paragraph in the audit report. If disclosures with respect to an entity's ability to continue as a going concern are inadequate, the auditor also should document the conclusion as to whether to express a

qualified or adverse opinion for the resultant departure from generally accepted accounting principles.

X. Other Information in Documents Containing Audited Financial Statements (AU 550)

A. Applicability

Applies to (1) annual reports for owners of the company, annual reports of charitable organizations that are distributed to the public, and annual reports filed with regulatory authorities under the Securities Exchange Act of 1934 or (2) other documents the auditor devotes attention to at the client's request. This section does **not** apply to reports filed under the Securities Act of 1933 or to other information on which the auditor is engaged to express an opinion.

B. Responsibilities

Auditors' responsibility does **not** extend beyond the financial information that has been identified in the report. The auditor has **no** obligation to perform any procedures to corroborate other information that is contained in documents (e.g., annual report) that contain the financial statements the auditor is reporting on. However, the auditor should read the information and consider whether there appear to be any material inconsistencies between the other data (or its presentation) and the financial statements.

1. **Inconsistency** When the auditor concludes that a material inconsistency exists, the auditor must decide whether the financial statements, the report, or both require revision. If the auditor decides that they do not, but that the other information does require revision, the client should be requested to revise the other information. If the client refuses, the auditor should consider revising the report to describe the material inconsistency, withholding the use of the report in the document, and, possibly, withdrawing from the engagement.

2. **Misstatement** While reading the other information, the auditor may become aware of information the auditor believes is a material misstatement of fact although it is **not** a material inconsistency. The matter should be discussed with the client. If the auditor continues to feel there is a material misstatement, the auditor should propose that the client consult with some other party such as its legal counsel. If the auditor still is not satisfied, consideration should be given to notifying the client of these views in writing and consulting with legal counsel.

3. **Optional Reporting** An auditor has the option to issue a report providing an opinion, in relation to the basic financial statements taken as a whole, on supplementary information and other information that has been subjected to the auditing procedures applied in the audit of those basic financial statements.

4. **Web Sites** Electronic sites on public computer networks (for instance, the SEC's EDGAR system or the World Wide Web area of the Internet) are a means of information distribution and are **not** documents under AU 550 criteria. Entities may include annual reports and general company information (press releases, promotional material, et cetera). The auditor is **not** required to read other information on these sites or to consider its consistency with the audited financial statements.

XI. Required Supplementary Information (AU 558, SAS 52)

A. Applicability

Some FASB and GASB requirements call for supplementary information outside of the basic financial statements. SAS 52 applies to an audit conducted according to GAAS of financial statements that are included in a document that should contain such information. It does **not** apply if the auditor has been engaged to audit the supplementary information.

1. **Procedures Applied** Although **not** required to do so, a company may decide voluntarily to include supplementary information the FASB or the GASB requires of others in a document of its own that contains audited financial statements. In this situation, SAS 52 applies unless (a) the client clearly indicates that the auditor has **not** applied the procedures that are

contained in this Statement or (b) the auditor includes a disclaimer on the information in the report on the audited financial statements.

2. **Procedures Not Applied** *Other Information in Documents Containing Audited Financial Statements* (AU 550, SAS 8), applies when the information is included voluntarily, but the auditor does **not** apply the procedures described in SAS 52.

3. **Optional Reporting** An auditor has the option to issue a report providing an opinion, in relation to the basic financial statements taken as a whole, on supplementary information and other information that has been subjected to the auditing procedures applied in the audit of those basic financial statements.

4. **Information Outside of Financial Statements** While GAAS does **not** require the auditor to audit information that is outside the basic financial statements, the auditor's responsibility with respect to this information depends on the information and the documents in which they appear. For example, SAS 8 applies to other information that is included in annual reports but **not** required by the FASB.

B. **Required by FASB or GASB**

This information is unique from other types of information presented outside of the basic financial statements because (1) the FASB or the GASB consider the information to be an essential part of financial reporting and (2) guidelines for measuring and presenting the information are established. Therefore, the auditor should apply certain limited procedures to the supplementary information. Any deficiencies in, or omission of, such information should be reported.

1. **Procedures** The auditor should first consider whether the FASB or the GASB requires supplementary information in the circumstances. If so, the auditor ordinarily should:

    a. Inquire of management about the methods used in preparing the information. This includes (1) whether FASB or GASB prescribed guidelines were followed in measuring and presenting the information, (2) whether there has been a change (from the prior period) in the methods used in measuring and presenting the information (and if so, the reasons why), and (3) any significant assumptions or interpretations that underlie the measurement or presentation.

    b. Compare the information for consistency with (1) the responses management gives to inquiries, (2) the audited financial statements, and (3) other knowledge that was obtained during the audit engagement.

    c. Consider whether representations in the supplementary information required by the FASB or the GASB should be included in specific written representations from management gathered per SAS 85, *Management Representations.*

    d. Apply additional procedures if prescribed by other Statements for specific types of supplementary information required by the FASB or GASB.

    e. Make additional inquiries if the auditor feels the information gathered through the foregoing procedures may not meet the guidelines.

2. **Circumstances That Require Reporting** The auditor usually will **not** refer to the supplementary information or to the auditor's limited procedures in the audit report, because the auditor has **not** audited the information and it is **not** a required part of the basic financial statements. Additional paragraphs that might be included in the auditor's report are presented below.

    a. **Explanatory Paragraph** An explanatory paragraph should be added to the report if (1) supplementary information required by the FASB or GASB is omitted (the auditor does **not** need to present the information), (2) the auditor feels that the measurement or presentation is materially different from that prescribed by the FASB or GASB, (3) the auditor cannot complete the prescribed procedures, or (4) the auditor is unable to remove substantial doubts about whether the supplementary information conforms to prescribed guidelines.

Exhibit 34 ▶ Omission of Required Supplementary Information

The (Company or Government Unit) has not presented (describe the supplementary information required by the FASB or GASB in the circumstances) that the (Financial or Governmental) Accounting Standards Board has determined is necessary to supplement, although not required to be part of, the basic financial statements.

Exhibit 35 ▶ Material Departures From Guidelines

The (specifically identify the supplementary information) on page XX is not a required part of the basic financial statements, and we did not audit and do not express an opinion on such information. However, we have applied certain limited procedures, which consisted principally of inquiries of management regarding the methods of measurement and presentation of the supplementary information. As a result of such limited procedures, we believe that the (specifically identify the supplementary information) is not in conformity with guidelines established by the Financial (or Governmental) Accounting Standards Board because (describe the material departure[s] from the FASB or GASB guidelines).

Exhibit 36 ▶ Prescribed Procedures Not Completed

The (specifically identify the supplementary information) on page XX is not a required part of the basic financial statements, and we did not audit and do not express an opinion on such information. Further, we were unable to apply to the information certain procedures prescribed by professional standards because (state the reasons).

b. **Effect on Opinion** The occurrence of any of these four circumstances will **not** affect the auditor's opinion on the basic financial statements because the supplementary information does **not** affect the standards that apply to the basic statements.

c. **Facts Known to the Auditor** Even if the auditor cannot complete the prescribed procedures, the auditor may feel that the supplementary information has not been properly measured and/or presented. In this case, the auditor should suggest appropriate revision and, if not revised, the auditor should describe the nature of any material departure(s) in the audit report.

d. **Client Disclosure** The auditor should expand the report to include a disclaimer on the supplementary information if the client includes statements with the supplementary information that the auditor performed some procedures on the information, but fails to state that an opinion is not expressed by the auditor on the information.

e. **Presentation of Supplementary Information** Generally, supplementary information required by the FASB or GASB should be presented distinct from the audited financial statements and should be identified separately from other information outside of the financial statements (which is **not** required by the FASB or GASB).

- If management chooses to include the supplementary information in the basic financial statements, the information should be clearly marked as unaudited. If it is **not** so marked, the audit report should be expanded to include a disclaimer on the supplementary information.

CHAPTER 28—REPORTS ON AUDITED FINANCIAL STATEMENTS

Problem 28-1 MULTIPLE CHOICE QUESTIONS (174 to 218 minutes)

1. When issuing an unqualified opinion, the auditor who evaluates the audit findings should be satisfied that the
a. Amount of known misstatement is documented in the management representation letter.
b. Estimate of the total likely misstatement is less than a material amount.
c. Amount of known misstatement is acknowledged and recorded by the client.
d. Estimate of the total likely misstatement includes the adjusting entries already recorded by the client. (11/98, AUD, #21, 6712)

2. The fourth standard of reporting requires the auditor's report to contain either an expression of opinion regarding the financial statements taken as a whole or an assertion to the effect that an opinion cannot be expressed. The objective of the fourth standard is to prevent
a. An auditor from expressing different opinions on each of the basic financial statements
b. Restrictions on the scope of the audit, whether imposed by the client or by the inability to obtain evidence
c. Misinterpretations regarding the degree of responsibility the auditor is assuming
d. An auditor from reporting on one basic financial statement and not the others (11/95, AUD, #68, 6015)

3. Field is an employee of Gold Enterprises. Hardy, CPA, is asked to express an opinion on Field's profit participation in Gold's net income. Hardy may accept this engagement only if
a. Hardy also audits Gold's complete financial statements.
b. Gold's financial statements are prepared in conformity with GAAP.
c. Hardy's report is available for distribution to Gold's other employees.
d. Field owns controlling interest in Gold. (11/95, AUD, #83, 6030)

4. When single-year financial statements are presented, an auditor ordinarily would express an unqualified opinion in an unmodified report if the
a. Auditor is unable to obtain audited financial statements supporting the entity's investment in a foreign affiliate.
b. Entity declines to present a statement of cash flows with its balance sheet and related statements of income and retained earnings.
c. Auditor wishes to emphasize an accounting matter affecting the comparability of the financial statements with those of the prior year.
d. Prior year's financial statements were audited by another CPA whose report, which expressed an unqualified opinion, is not presented. (5/94, AUD, #74, 4739)

5. If a company issues financial statements that purport to present its financial position and results of operations but omits the statement of cash flows, the auditor ordinarily will express a(an)
a. Disclaimer of opinion
b. Qualified opinion
c. Review report
d. Unqualified opinion with a separate explanatory paragraph (5/93, AUD, #46, amended, 3942)

6. Restrictions imposed by a client prohibit the observation of physical inventories, which account for 35% of all assets. Alternative audit procedures cannot be applied, although the auditor was able to examine satisfactory evidence for all other items in the financial statements. The auditor should issue a(an)
a. "Except for" qualified opinion
b. Unqualified opinion with an explanation in the scope paragraph
c. Unqualified opinion with a separate explanatory paragraph
d. Disclaimer of opinion (Editors, 7501)

7. In which of the following circumstances would an auditor not express an unqualified opinion?
a. There has been a material change between periods in accounting principles.
b. Quarterly financial data required by the SEC has been omitted.
c. The auditor wishes to emphasize an unusually important subsequent event.
d. The auditor is unable to obtain audited financial statements of a consolidated investee. (11/95, AUD, #69, 6016)

8. An explanatory paragraph following the opinion paragraph of an auditor's report describes an uncertainty as follows:

As discussed in Note X to the financial statements, the Company is a defendant in a lawsuit alleging infringement of certain patent rights and claiming damages. Discovery proceedings are in progress. The ultimate outcome of the litigation cannot presently be determined. Accordingly, no provision for any liability that may result upon adjudication has been made in the accompanying financial statements.

What type of opinion should the auditor express under these circumstances?
a. Adverse
b. Qualified due to a scope limitation
c. Qualified due to a GAAP violation
d. Unqualified   (11/95, AUD, #70, 6017)

9. Park, CPA, was engaged to audit the financial statements of Tech Co., a new client, for the year ended December 31, Year 1. Park obtained sufficient audit evidence for all of Tech's financial statement items except Tech's opening inventory. Due to inadequate financial records, Park could not verify Tech's January 1, Year 1, inventory balances. Park's opinion on Tech's Year 1 financial statements most likely will be

	Balance sheet	*Income statement*
a.	Disclaimer	Disclaimer
b.	Unqualified	Disclaimer
c.	Disclaimer	Adverse
d.	Unqualified	Adverse

            (5/94, AUD, #76, amended, 4741)

10. In which of the following situations would an auditor ordinarily choose between expressing a qualified opinion or an adverse opinion?
a. The auditor did not observe the entity's physical inventory and is unable to become satisfied about its balance by other auditing procedures.
b. Conditions that cause the auditor to have substantial doubt about the entity's ability to continue as a going concern are inadequately disclosed.
c. There has been a change in accounting principles that has a material effect on the comparability of the entity's financial statements.
d. The auditor is unable to apply necessary procedures concerning an investor's share of an investee's earnings recognized on the equity method.   (R/00, AUD, #17, 6942)

11. An auditor most likely would express an unqualified opinion and would **not** add explanatory language to the report if the auditor
a. Wishes to emphasize that the entity had significant transactions with related parties
b. Concurs with the entity's change in its method of accounting for inventory
c. Discovers that required supplementary information has been omitted
d. Believes that there is a remote likelihood of a material loss resulting from an uncertainty
            (11/95, AUD, #64, amended, 6011)

12. If a client makes a change in accounting principle that is inseparable from the effect of a change in estimate, this material event should be accounted for as a change in
a. Estimate and the auditor would report a consistency exception
b. Estimate and the auditor would not modify the report
c. Principle and the auditor would report a consistency exception
d. Principle and the auditor would not modify the report   (Editors, 7502)

13. Which of the following statements is a basic element of the auditor's standard report?
a. The disclosures provide reasonable assurance that the financial statements are free of material misstatement.
b. The financial statements are consistent with those of the prior period.
c. An audit includes assessing significant estimates made by management.
d. The auditor evaluated the overall internal control.
            (11/95, AUD, #62, amended, 6009)

14. The existence of audit risk is recognized by the statement in the auditor's standard report that the
a. Auditor is responsible for expressing an opinion on the financial statements, which are the responsibility of management.
b. Financial statements are presented fairly, in all material respects, in conformity with GAAP.
c. Audit includes examining, on a test basis, evidence supporting the amounts and disclosures in the financial statements.
d. Auditor obtains reasonable assurance about whether the financial statements are free of material misstatement.   (11/94, AUD, #9, 5082)

15. An auditor's responsibility to express an opinion on the financial statements is
a. Explicitly represented in the opinion paragraph of the auditor's standard report
b. Explicitly represented in the opening paragraph of the auditor's standard report
c. Explicitly represented in the scope paragraph of the auditor's standard report
d. Implicitly represented in the auditor's standard report   (5/92, AUD, #11, amended, 7503)

16. For an entity that does **not** receive governmental financial assistance, an auditor's standard report on financial statements generally would **not** refer to
a. Significant estimates made by management
b. The entity's internal control
c. Management's responsibility for the financial statements
d. An assessment of the entity's accounting principles   (5/94, AUD, #71, amended, 4736)

17. Which paragraphs of an auditor's standard report on financial statements should refer to generally accepted auditing standards (GAAS) and generally accepted accounting principles (GAAP) in which paragraphs?

	GAAS	GAAP
a.	Opening	Scope
b.	Scope	Scope
c.	Scope	Opinion
d.	Opening	Opinion

(5/94, AUD, #77, 4742)

18. March, CPA, is engaged by Monday Corp., a client, to audit the financial statements of Wall Corp., a company that is not March's client. Monday expects to present Wall's audited financial statements with March's auditor's report to 1st Federal Bank to obtain financing in Monday's attempt to purchase Wall. In these circumstances, March's auditor's report would usually be addressed to
a. Monday Corp., the client that engaged March
b. Wall Corp., the entity audited by March
c. 1st Federal Bank
d. Both Monday Corp. and 1st Federal Bank
(11/95, AUD, #78, 6025)

19. A CPA's standard report on audited financial statements would be inappropriate if it referred to
a. Management's responsibility for the financial statements
b. An assessment of the entity's accounting principles
c. Significant estimates made by management
d. The CPA's assessment of sampling risk factors
(R/06, AUD, #47, 8165)

20. In which of the following circumstances would an auditor most likely add an explanatory paragraph to the standard report while not affecting the auditor's unqualified opinion?
a. The auditor is asked to report on the balance sheet, but not on the other basic financial statements.
b. There is substantial doubt about the entity's ability to continue as a going concern.
c. Management's estimates of the effects of future events are unreasonable.
d. Certain transactions cannot be tested because of management's records retention policy.
(5/93, AUD, #47, 3943)

21. An auditor would express an unqualified opinion with an explanatory paragraph added to the auditor's report for

	An unjustified accounting change	A material weakness in internal control
a.	Yes	Yes
b.	Yes	No
c.	No	Yes
d.	No	No

(11/95, AUD, #65, amended, 6012)

22. In which of the following situations would an auditor ordinarily issue an unqualified audit opinion without an explanatory paragraph?
a. The auditor wishes to emphasize that the entity had significant related party transactions.
b. The auditor decides to make reference to the report of another auditor as a basis, in part, for the auditor's opinion.
c. The entity issues financial statements that present financial position and results of operations, but omits the statement of cash flows.
d. The auditor has substantial doubt about the entity's ability to continue as a going concern, but the circumstances are fully disclosed in the financial statements.   (11/90, AUD, #6, 0324)

23. Which of the following procedures would the principal auditor most likely perform after deciding to make reference to another CPA who audited a subsidiary of the entity?
a. Review the working papers and the audit programs of the other CPA
b. Visit the other CPA and discuss the results of the other CPA's audit procedures
c. Make inquiries about the professional reputation and independence of the other CPA
d. Determine that the other CPA has a sufficient understanding of the subsidiary's internal control
(R/99, AUD, #15, 6831)

24. The introductory paragraph of an auditor's report contains the following sentences:

We did not audit the financial statements of EZ Inc., a wholly-owned subsidiary, which statements reflect total assets and revenues constituting 27 percent and 29 percent, respectively, of the related consolidated totals. Those statements were audited by other auditors whose report has been furnished to us, and our opinion, insofar as it relates to the amounts included for EZ Inc., is based solely on the report of the other auditors.

These sentences
a. Indicate a division of responsibility
b. Assume responsibility for the other auditor
c. Are an improper form of reporting
d. Require a departure from an unqualified opinion
(11/95, AUD, #77, amended, 6024)

25. Pell, CPA, decides to serve as principal auditor in the audit of the financial statements of Tech Consolidated, Inc. Smith, CPA, audits one of Tech's subsidiaries. In which situation(s) should Pell make reference to Smith's audit?

I. Pell reviews Smith's working papers and assumes responsibility for Smith's work, but expresses a qualified opinion on Tech's financial statements.
II. Pell is unable to review Smith's working papers; however, Pell's inquiries indicate that Smith has an excellent reputation for professional competence and integrity.

a. I only
b. II only
c. Both I and II
d. Neither I nor II
(5/97, AUD, #5, 6394)

26. Delta Life Insurance Co. prepares its financial statements on an accounting basis insurance companies use pursuant to the rules of a state insurance commission. If Wall, CPA, Delta's auditor, discovers that the statements are **not** suitably titled, Wall should
a. Disclose any reservations in an explanatory paragraph and qualify the opinion
b. Apply to the state insurance commission for an advisory opinion
c. Issue a special statutory basis report that clearly disclaims any opinion
d. Explain in the notes to the financial statements the terminology used (5/93, AUD, #57, 3953)

27. When financial statements contain a departure from GAAP because, due to unusual circumstances, the statements would otherwise be misleading, the auditor should explain the unusual circumstances in a separate paragraph and express an opinion that is
a. Unqualified
b. Qualified
c. Qualified or adverse, depending on materiality
d. Adverse (5/94, AUD, #75, amended, 4740)

28. The following explanatory paragraph was included in an auditor's report to indicate a lack of consistency:

"As discussed in note T to the financial statements, the company changed its method of accounting for long-term contracts in Year 2."

How should the auditor report on this matter if the auditor concurred with the change?

Type of opinion	Location of explanatory paragraph
a. Unqualified	Before opinion paragraph
b. Unqualified	After opinion paragraph
c. Qualified	Before opinion paragraph
d. Qualified	After opinion paragraph

(11/91, AUD, #18, amended, 2286)

29. For which of the following events would an auditor issue a report that omits any reference to consistency?
a. A change in the method of accounting for inventories
b. A change from an accounting principle that is not generally accepted to one that is generally accepted
c. A change in the useful life used to calculate the provision for depreciation expense
d. Management's lack of reasonable justification for a change in accounting principle
(11/96, AUD, #15, 6367)

30. When an entity changes its method of accounting for income taxes, which has a material effect on comparability, the auditor should refer to the change in an explanatory paragraph added to the auditor's report. This paragraph should identify the nature of the change and
a. Explain why the change is justified under generally accepted accounting principles
b. Describe the cumulative effect of the change on the audited financial statements
c. State the auditor's explicit concurrence with or opposition to the change
d. Refer to the financial statement note that discusses the change in detail
(5/93, AUD, #49, 3945)

31. In the first audit of a client, an auditor was not able to gather sufficient evidence about the consistent application of accounting principles between the current and the prior year, as well as the amounts of assets or liabilities at the beginning of the current year. This was due to the client's record retention policies. If the amounts in question could materially affect current operating results, the auditor would

a. Be unable to express an opinion on the current year's results of operations and cash flows
b. Express a qualified opinion on the financial statements because of a client-imposed scope limitation
c. Withdraw from the engagement and refuse to be associated with the financial statements
d. Specifically state that the financial statements are not comparable to the prior year due to an uncertainty   (5/98, AUD, #15, 6632)

32. When there has been a change in accounting principles, but the effect of the change on the comparability of the financial statements is not material, the auditor should

a. Refer to the change in an explanatory paragraph
b. Explicitly concur that the change is preferred
c. Not refer to consistency in the auditor's report
d. Refer to the change in the opinion paragraph   (5/94, AUD, #73, 4738)

33. Management believes and the auditor is satisfied that the chance of a material loss resulting from the resolution of a lawsuit is more than remote but less than probable. Which of the following matters should the auditor consider in deciding whether to add an explanatory paragraph?

	Likelihood that the loss is closer to probable than remote	Magnitude by which the loss exceeds the auditor's materiality
a.	Yes	Yes
b.	Yes	No
c.	No	Yes
d.	No	No

(11/93, AUD, #47, 4284)

34. Management believes and the auditor is satisfied that a material loss probably will occur when pending litigation is resolved. Management is unable to make a reasonable estimate of the amount or range of the potential loss, but fully discloses the situation in the notes to the financial statements. If management does not make an accrual in the financial statements, the auditor

a. May express a qualified opinion due to a scope limitation
b. Must express a qualified opinion due to a scope limitation
c. May express an unqualified opinion with an explanatory paragraph
d. Must express an unqualified opinion with an explanatory paragraph   (5/94, AUD, #86, amended, 4751)

35. An auditor includes a separate paragraph in an otherwise unmodified report to emphasize that the entity being reported on had significant transactions with related parties. The inclusion of this separate paragraph

a. Is considered an "except for" qualification of the opinion
b. Violates generally accepted auditing standards if this information is already disclosed in the notes to the financial statements
c. Necessitates a revision of the opinion paragraph to include the phrase "with the foregoing explanation"
d. Is appropriate and would not negate the unqualified opinion   (5/94, AUD, #69, 4734)

36. Which of the following phrases should be included in the opinion paragraph when an auditor expresses a qualified opinion?

	When read in conjunction with Note X	With the foregoing explanation
a.	Yes	No
b.	No	Yes
c.	Yes	Yes
d.	No	No

(11/92, AUD, #46, 2980)

37. An auditor may not issue a qualified opinion when

a. An accounting principle at variance with GAAP is used.
b. The auditor lacks independence with respect to the audited entity.
c. A scope limitation prevents the auditor from completing an important audit procedure.
d. The auditor's report refers to the work of a specialist.   (11/95, AUD, #63, 6010)

38. When qualifying an opinion because of an insufficiency of audit evidence, an auditor should refer to the situation in the

	Opening (introductory) paragraph	Scope paragraph
a.	No	No
b.	Yes	No
c.	Yes	Yes
d.	No	Yes

(5/94, AUD, #88, 4753)

39. An auditor may reasonably issue an "except for" qualified opinion for a(an)

	Scope limitation	Unjustified accounting change
a.	Yes	No
b.	No	Yes
c.	Yes	Yes
d.	No	No

(11/91, AUD, #16, 2284)

40. An auditor decides to issue a qualified opinion on an entity's financial statements because a major inadequacy in its computerized accounting records prevents the auditor from applying necessary procedures. The opinion paragraph of the auditor's report should state that the qualification pertains to
a. A client-imposed scope limitation
b. A departure from generally accepted auditing standards
c. The possible effects on the financial statements
d. Inadequate disclosure of necessary information

(11/93, AUD, #49, 4286)

41. When qualifying an opinion because of an insufficiency of audit evidence, an auditor should refer to the situation in the

	Scope paragraph	Notes to the financial statements
a.	Yes	Yes
b.	Yes	No
c.	No	Yes
d.	No	No

(R/02, AUD, #10, 7100)

42. Due to a scope limitation, an auditor disclaimed an opinion on the financial statements taken as a whole, but the auditor's report included a statement that the current asset portion of the entity's balance sheet was fairly stated. The inclusion of this statement is
a. Not appropriate because it may tend to over-shadow the auditor's disclaimer of opinion
b. Not appropriate because the auditor is prohibited from reporting on only one basic financial statement
c. Appropriate provided the auditor's scope paragraph adequately describes the scope limitation
d. Appropriate provided the statement is in a separate paragraph preceding the disclaimer of opinion paragraph

(5/94, AUD, #72, 4737)

43. Harris, CPA, has been asked to audit and report on the balance sheet of Fox Co., but not on the statements of income, retained earnings, or cash flows. Harris will have access to all information underlying the basic financial statements. Under these circumstances, Harris may
a. Not accept the engagement because it would constitute a violation of the profession's ethical standards
b. Not accept the engagement because it would be tantamount to rendering a piecemeal opinion
c. Accept the engagement because such engagements merely involve limited reporting objectives
d. Accept the engagement but should disclaim an opinion because of an inability to apply the procedures considered necessary

(11/95, AUD, #61, 6008)

44. A limitation on the scope of an audit sufficient to preclude an unqualified opinion will usually result when management
a. Is unable to obtain audited financial statements supporting the entity's investment in a foreign subsidiary
b. Refuses to disclose in the notes to the financial statements related party transactions authorized by the board of directors
c. Does not sign an engagement letter specifying the responsibilities of both the entity and the auditor
d. Fails to correct a significant deficiency communicated to the audit committee after the prior year's audit

(5/93, AUD, #56, amended, 3952)

45. When a qualified opinion results from a limitation on the scope of the audit, the situation should be described in an explanatory paragraph
a. Preceding the opinion paragraph and referred to only in the scope paragraph of the auditor's report
b. Following the opinion paragraph and referred to in both the scope and opinion paragraphs of the auditor's report
c. Following the opinion paragraph and referred to only in the scope paragraph of the auditor's report
d. Preceding the opinion paragraph and referred to in both the scope and opinion paragraphs of the auditor's report   (5/90, AUD, #22, 0340)

46. Which of the following phrases would an auditor most likely include in the auditor's report when expressing a qualified opinion because of inadequate disclosure?
a. Subject to the departure from generally accepted accounting principles, as described above
b. With the foregoing explanation of these omitted disclosures
c. Except for the omission of the information discussed in the preceding paragraph
d. Does not present fairly in all material respects
                              (11/95, AUD, #71, 6018)

47. When an auditor qualifies an opinion because of inadequate disclosure, the auditor should describe the nature of the omission in a separate explanatory paragraph and modify the

	Introductory paragraph	Scope paragraph	Opinion paragraph
a.	Yes	No	No
b.	Yes	Yes	No
c.	No	Yes	Yes
d.	No	No	Yes

(5/91, AUD, #46, 0317)

48. In which of the following circumstances would an auditor be most likely to express an adverse opinion?
a. The chief executive officer refuses the auditor access to minutes of board of directors' meetings.
b. Tests of controls show that the entity's internal control structure is so poor that it cannot be relied upon.
c. The financial statements are not in conformity with GAAP regarding the capitalization of leases.
d. Information comes to the auditor's attention that raises substantial doubt about the entity's ability to continue as a going concern.
                              (5/94, AUD, #87, 4752)

49. An auditor most likely would issue a disclaimer of opinion because of
a. Inadequate disclosure of material information
b. The omission of the statement of cash flows
c. A material departure from generally accepted accounting principles
d. Management's refusal to furnish written representations   (5/91, AUD, #53, 0319)

50. Please select **two** responses. When comparative financial statements are presented, the fourth standard of reporting, which refers to financial statements *taken as a whole*, should be considered to apply to the financial statements of
a. The current period
b. One period immediately preceding the current period
c. One period immediately preceding the earliest periods presented
d. Periods presented other than the current period
e. No other periods   (Editors, 7504)

51. A registration statement filed with the SEC contains the reports of two independent auditors on their audits of financial statements for different periods. The predecessor auditor who audited the prior period financial statements generally should obtain a letter of representation from the
a. Successor independent auditor
b. Client's audit committee
c. Principal underwriter
d. Securities and Exchange Commission
                              (11/95, AUD, #86, 6033)

52. A former client requests a predecessor auditor to reissue an audit report on a prior period's financial statements. The financial statements are not restated and the report is not revised. What date(s) should the predecessor auditor use in the reissued report?
a. The date of the prior period report
b. The date of the client's request
c. The dual dates
d. The date of reissue   (Editors, 0352)

53. The predecessor auditor, who is satisfied after properly communicating with the successor auditor, has reissued a report because the audit client desires comparative financial statements. The predecessor auditor's report should make
a. Reference to the report of the successor auditor only in the scope paragraph
b. Reference to the work of the successor auditor in the scope and opinion paragraphs
c. Reference to both the work and the report of the successor auditor only in the opinion paragraph
d. No reference to the report or the work of the successor auditor   (5/90, AUD, #13, 0334)

54. Comparative financial statements include the prior year's statements that were audited by a predecessor auditor whose report is not presented. If the predecessor's report was unqualified, the successor should

a. Add an explanatory paragraph that expresses only limited assurance concerning the fair presentation of the prior year's financial statements

b. Express an opinion only on the current year's financial statements and make no reference to the prior year's financial statements

c. Indicate in the auditor's report that the predecessor auditor expressed an unqualified opinion on the prior year's financial statements

d. Obtain a letter of representations from the predecessor auditor concerning any matters that might affect the successor's opinion

(R/03, AUD, #13, 7635)

55. An auditor issued an audit report that was dual dated for a subsequent event occurring after the original report date but before issuance of the auditor's report. The auditor's responsibility for events occurring subsequent to the original report date was

a. Limited to include only events occurring up to the date of the last subsequent event referenced

b. Limited to the specific event referenced

c. Extended to subsequent events occurring through the date of issuance of the report

d. Extended to include all events occurring since the original report date

(11/94, AUD, #67, amended, 5140)

56. In May Year 3, an auditor reissues the auditor's report on the Year 1 financial statements at a continuing client's request. The Year 1 financial statements are not restated and the auditor does not revise the wording of the report. The auditor should

a. Dual date the reissued report

b. Use the release date of the reissued report

c. Use the current-period auditor's report date on the reissued report

d. Use the original report date on the reissued report (5/94, AUD, #66, amended, 4731)

57. Samson, CPA, obtained sufficient appropriate audit evidence to support an opinion on Coco's December 31, Year 1, financial statements on March 6, Year 2. A subsequent event requiring adjustment to the Year 1 financial statements occurred on April 10, Year 2, and came to Samson's attention on April 24, Year 2. If the adjustment is made without disclosure of the event, Samson's report ordinarily should be dated

a. March 6, Year 2

b. April 10, Year 2

c. April 24, Year 2

d. Using dual dating (Editors, 2765)

58. On February 25, a CPA issued an auditor's report expressing an unqualified opinion on financial statements for the year ended January 31. On March 2, the CPA learned that on February 11 the entity incurred a material loss on an uncollectible trade receivable as a result of the deteriorating financial condition of the entity's principal customer that led to the customer's bankruptcy. Management then refused to adjust the financial statements for this subsequent event. The CPA determined that the information is reliable and that there are creditors currently relying on the financial statements. The CPA's next course of action most likely would be to

a. Notify the entity's creditors that the financial statements and the related auditor's report should no longer be relied on

b. Notify each member of the entity's board of directors about management's refusal to adjust the financial statements

c. Issue revised financial statements and distribute them to each creditor known to be relying on the financial statements

d. Issue a revised auditor's report and distribute it to each creditor known to be relying on the financial statements (R/99, AUD, #32, 6848)

59. Which of the following procedures would an auditor most likely perform to obtain evidence about the occurrence of subsequent events?

a. Confirming a sample of material accounts receivable established after year-end

b. Comparing the financial statements being reported on with those of the prior period

c. Investigating personnel changes in the accounting department occurring after year-end

d. Inquiring as to whether any unusual adjustments were made after year-end

(11/95, AUD, #56, 6003)

60. Zero Corp. suffered a loss that would have a material effect on its financial statements on an uncollectible trade account receivable due to a customer's bankruptcy. This occurred suddenly due to a natural disaster ten days after Zero's balance sheet date, but one month before the issuance of the financial statements and the auditor's report. Under these circumstances,

	The financial statements should be adjusted	The event requires financial statement disclosure, but no adjustment	The auditor's report should be modified for a lack of consistency
a.	Yes	No	No
b.	Yes	No	Yes
c.	No	Yes	Yes
d.	No	Yes	No

(5/94, AUD, #53, 4718)

61. A client acquired 25% of its outstanding capital stock after year-end and prior to the audit report date. The auditor should
a. Advise management to adjust the balance sheet to reflect the acquisition
b. Disclose the acquisition in the opinion paragraph of the auditor's report
c. Advise management to disclose the acquisition in the notes to the financial statements
d. Issue pro forma financial statements giving effect to the acquisition as if it had occurred at year-end (Editors, 0372)

62. An auditor is concerned with completing various phases of the audit after the balance-sheet date. This "subsequent period" extends to the date of the
a. Final review of the audit working papers
b. Delivery of the auditor's report to the client
c. Public issuance of the financial statements
d. Auditor's report (Editors, 0381)

63. Which of the following events occurring after the issuance of an auditor's report most likely would cause the auditor to make further inquiries about the previously issued financial statements?
a. A lawsuit is resolved that is explained in a separate paragraph of the prior year's auditor's report.
b. New information is discovered concerning undisclosed related party transactions of the prior year.
c. A technological development occurs that affects the entity's ability to continue as a going concern.
d. The entity sells a subsidiary that accounts for 35% of the entity's consolidated sales. (R/05, AUD, #24, 7819)

64. After issuing a report, an auditor has **no** obligation to make continuing inquiries or perform other procedures concerning the audited financial statements, unless
a. Information, which existed at the report date and may affect the report, comes to the auditor's attention.
b. Management of the entity requests the auditor to reissue the auditor's report.
c. Information about an event that occurred after the audit report date comes to the auditor's attention.
d. Final determinations or resolutions are made of contingencies that had been disclosed in the financial statements. (11/91, AUD, #20, amended, 2288)

65. Subsequent to the issuance of an auditor's report, the auditor became aware of facts existing at the report date that would have affected the report had the auditor then been aware of such facts. After determining that the information is reliable, the auditor should next
a. Determine whether there are persons relying or likely to rely on the financial statements who would attach importance to the information
b. Request that management disclose the newly discovered information by issuing revised financial statements
c. Give public notice that the auditor is no longer associated with financial statements
d. Issue revised pro forma financial statements taking into consideration the newly discovered information (11/94, AUD, #89, amended, 5162)

66. On March 15, Year 2, Kent, CPA, issued an unqualified opinion on a client's audited financial statements for the year ended December 31, Year 1. On May 4, Year 2, Kent's internal inspection program disclosed that engagement personnel failed to observe the client's physical inventory. Omission of this procedure impairs Kent's present ability to support the unqualified opinion. If the stockholders are currently relying on the opinion, Kent should first
a. Advise management to disclose to the stockholders that Kent's unqualified opinion should not be relied on
b. Undertake to apply alternative procedures that would provide a satisfactory basis for the unqualified opinion
c. Compensate for the omitted procedure by performing tests of controls to reduce audit risk to a sufficiently low level
d. Reissue the auditor's report and add an explanatory paragraph describing the departure from generally accepted auditing standards (5/94, AUD, #70, amended, 4735)

67. An auditor concludes that an audit procedure considered necessary at the time of the audit had been omitted. The auditor should assess the importance of the omitted procedure to the ability to support the previously expressed opinion. Which of the following would be **least** helpful in making that assessment?
a. A discussion with the client about whether there are persons relying on the auditor's report
b. A discussion of the circumstances with engagement personnel
c. A reevaluation of the overall scope of the audit
d. A review of the other audit procedures that were applied that might compensate for the one omitted (Editors, 0371)

68. An auditor is considering whether the omission of a substantive procedure considered necessary at the time of an audit may impair the auditor's present ability to support the previously expressed opinion. The auditor need **not** apply the omitted procedure if the
a. Financial statements and auditor's report were not distributed beyond management and the board of directors.
b. Auditor's previously expressed opinion was qualified because of a departure from GAAP.
c. Results of other procedures that were applied tend to compensate for the procedure omitted.
d. Omission is due to unreasonable delays by client personnel in providing data on a timely basis.
(5/95, AUD, #85, 5703)

69. An auditor concludes that a substantive auditing procedure considered necessary during the prior period's audit was omitted. Which of the following factors would most likely cause the auditor promptly to apply the omitted procedure?
a. There are no alternative procedures available to provide the same evidence as the omitted procedure.
b. The omission of the procedure impairs the auditor's present ability to support the previously expressed opinion.
c. The source documents needed to perform the omitted procedure are still available.
d. The auditor's opinion on the prior period's financial statements was unqualified.
(5/92, AUD, #33, 2786)

70. When an independent CPA assists in preparing the financial statements of a publicly held entity, but has **not** audited or reviewed them, the CPA should issue a disclaimer of opinion. In such situations, the CPA has **no** responsibility to apply any procedures beyond
a. Ascertaining whether the financial statements are in conformity with generally accepted accounting principles
b. Determining whether management has elected to omit substantially all required disclosures
c. Documenting that the client's internal control is not being relied on
d. Reading the financial statements for obvious material misstatements
(5/92, AUD, #2, amended, 2755)

71. When an independent CPA is associated with the financial statements of a publicly held entity but has **not** audited or reviewed such statements, the appropriate form of report to be issued must include a (an)
a. Regulation S-X exemption
b. Report on pro forma financial statements
c. Unaudited association report
d. Disclaimer of opinion   (11/94, AUD, #76, 5149)

72. If an accountant concludes that unaudited financial statements on which the accountant is disclaiming an opinion also lack adequate disclosure, the accountant should suggest appropriate revision. If the client does **not** accept the accountant's suggestion, the accountant should
a. Issue an adverse opinion and describe the appropriate revision in the report
b. Accept the client's inaction because the statements are unaudited and the accountant has disclaimed an opinion
c. Describe the appropriate revision to the financial statements in the accountant's disclaimer of opinion
d. Make reference to the appropriate revision and issue a modified report expressing limited assurance   (Editors, 7505)

73. Which of the following procedures most likely would assist an auditor in identifying conditions and events that may indicate substantial doubt about an entity's ability to continue as a going concern?
a. Performing cutoff tests of sales transactions with customers with long-standing receivable balances
b. Evaluating the entity's procedures for identifying and recording related party transactions
c. Inspecting title documents to verify whether any real property is pledged as collateral
d. Inquiring of the entity's legal counsel about litigation, claims, and assessments
(R/06, AUD, #35, 8153)

74. After considering an entity's negative trends and financial difficulties, an auditor has substantial doubt about the entity's ability to continue as a going concern. The auditor's considerations relating to management's plans for dealing with the adverse effects of these conditions most likely would include management's plans to
a. Increase current dividend distributions
b. Reduce existing lines of credit
c. Increase ownership equity
d. Purchase assets formerly leased
(R/01, AUD, #11, 7026)

75. When an auditor concludes there is substantial doubt about a continuing audit client's ability to continue as a going concern for a reasonable period of time, the auditor's responsibility is to
a. Issue a qualified or adverse opinion, depending upon materiality, due to the possible effects on the financial statements
b. Consider the adequacy of disclosure about the client's possible inability to continue as a going concern
c. Report to the client's audit committee that management's accounting estimates may need to be adjusted
d. Reissue the prior year's auditor's report and add an explanatory paragraph that specifically refers to "substantial doubt" and "going concern"
(5/94, AUD, #62, 4727)

76. An auditor concludes that there is substantial doubt about an entity's ability to continue as a going concern for a reasonable period of time. If the entity's financial statements adequately disclose its financial difficulties, the auditor's report is required to include an explanatory paragraph that specifically uses the phrase(s)

	"Reasonable period of time, not to exceed one year"	"Going concern"
a.	Yes	Yes
b.	Yes	No
c.	No	Yes
d.	No	No

(5/98, AUD, #14, 6631)

77. Mead, CPA, had substantial doubt about Tech Co.'s ability to continue as a going concern when reporting on Tech's audited financial statements for the year ended June 30, Year 1. That doubt has been removed in Year 2. What is Mead's reporting responsibility if Tech is representing its financial statements for the year ended June 30, Year 2, on a comparative basis with those of Year 1?
a. The explanatory paragraph included in the Year 1 auditor's report should not be repeated.
b. The explanatory paragraph included in the Year 1 auditor's report should be repeated in its entirety.
c. A different explanatory paragraph describing Mead's reasons for the removal of doubt should be included.
d. A different explanatory paragraph describing Tech's plans for financial recovery should be included. (11/95, AUD, #73, amended, 6020)

78. Which of the following statements is correct with respect to the auditor's consideration of an entity's ability to continue as a going concern?
a. The auditor's workpapers must include audit evidence which provides assurance that the entity will continue as a going concern.
b. If there is absence of reference to substantial doubt in the auditor's report, this should be viewed as assurance as to an entity's ability to continue as a going concern.
c. It is not necessary for the auditor to design audit procedures solely to identify conditions and events that, when considered in the aggregate, indicate there could be substantial doubt about the entity's ability to continue as a going concern for a reasonable period of time.
d. The auditor has a responsibility to evaluate whether there is substantial doubt about the entity's ability to continue as a going concern for a reasonable period of time, not to exceed the date of the financial statements being audited.
(Editors, 7506)

79. Which of the following auditing procedures most likely would assist an auditor in identifying conditions and events that may indicate substantial doubt about an entity's ability to continue as a going concern?
a. Inspecting title documents to verify whether any assets are pledged as collateral
b. Confirming with third parties the details of arrangements to maintain financial support
c. Reconciling the cash balance per books with the cutoff bank statement and the bank confirmation
d. Comparing the entity's depreciation and asset capitalization policies to other entities in the industry (5/94, AUD, #55, 4720)

80. An auditor believes that there is substantial doubt about an entity's ability to continue as a going concern for a reasonable period of time. In evaluating the entity's plans for dealing with the adverse effects of future conditions and events, the auditor most likely would consider, as a mitigating factor, the entity's plans to
a. Repurchase the entity's stock at a price below its book value
b. Issue stock options to key executives
c. Lease rather than purchase operating facilities
d. Accelerate the due date of an existing mortgage
(R/06, AUD, #11, 8129)

81. When an auditor has substantial doubt about an entity's ability to continue as a going concern because of the probable discontinuance of operations, the auditor most likely would express a qualified opinion if

a. The effects of the adverse financial conditions likely will cause a bankruptcy filing.
b. Information about the entity's ability to continue as a going concern is not disclosed.
c. Management has no plans to reduce or delay future expenditures.
d. Negative trends and recurring operating losses appear to be irreversible.
(R/06, AUD, #5, 8123)

82. Which of the following conditions or events most likely would cause an auditor to have substantial doubt about an entity's ability to continue as a going concern?
a. Significant related party transactions are pervasive.
b. Usual trade credit from suppliers is denied.
c. Arrearages in preferred stock dividends are paid.
d. Restrictions on the disposal of principal assets are present. (5/98, AUD, #13, 6630)

83. An auditor concludes that there is a material inconsistency in the other information in an annual report to shareholders containing audited financial statements. If the auditor concludes that the financial statements do **not** require revision, but the client refuses to revise or eliminate the material inconsistency, the auditor may
a. Revise the auditor's report to include a separate explanatory paragraph describing the material inconsistency
b. Issue an "except for" qualified opinion after discussing the matter with the client's board of directors
c. Consider the matter closed, since the other information is not in the audited financial statements
d. Disclaim an opinion on the financial statements after explaining the material inconsistency in a separate explanatory paragraph
(11/94, AUD, #86, 5159)

84. Investment and property schedules are presented for purposes of additional analysis in an auditor-submitted document. The schedules are not required parts of the basic financial statements, but accompany the basic financial statements. When reporting on such additional information, the measurement of materiality is the
a. Same as that used in forming an opinion on the basic financial statements taken as a whole
b. Lesser of the individual schedule of investments or schedule of property taken by itself
c. Greater of the individual schedule of investments or schedule of property taken by itself
d. Combined total of both the individual schedules of investments and property taken as a whole
(5/94, AUD, #63, 4728)

85. An auditor concludes that there is a material inconsistency in the other information in an annual report to shareholders containing audited financial statements. The auditor believes that the financial statements do not require revision, but the client is unwilling to revise or eliminate the material inconsistency in the other information. Under these circumstances, what action would the auditor most likely take?
a. Consider the situation closed because the other information is not in the audited financial statements
b. Issue an "except for" qualified opinion after discussing the matter with the client's audit committee
c. Disclaim an opinion on the financial statements after explaining the material inconsistency in a separate explanatory paragraph
d. Revise the auditor's report to include a separate explanatory paragraph describing the material inconsistency (R/06, AUD, #29, 8147)

86. If management declines to present supplementary information required by the Governmental Accounting Standards Board (GASB), the auditor should issue a(an)
a. Adverse opinion
b. Qualified opinion with an explanatory paragraph
c. Unqualified opinion
d. Unqualified opinion with an additional explanatory paragraph (5/90, AUD, #25, 0399)

87. What is an auditor's responsibility for supplementary information, such as the disclosure of pension information, which is outside the basic financial statements but required by the GASB?
a. The auditor should apply substantive tests of transactions to the supplementary information and verify its conformity with the GASB requirement.
b. The auditor should apply certain limited procedures to the supplementary information and report deficiencies in, or omissions of, such information.
c. The auditor's only responsibility for the supplementary information is to determine that such information has **not** been omitted.
d. The auditor has **no** responsibility for such supplementary information as long as it is outside the basic financial statements.

(R/03, AUD, #20, 7642)

Problem 28-2 ADDITIONAL MULTIPLE CHOICE QUESTIONS (46 to 58 minutes)

88. The first standard of reporting requires that the auditor state in the auditor's report whether the financial statements are presented in accordance with generally accepted accounting principles. This should be construed to require
a. A statement of fact by the auditor
b. An implied measure of fairness
c. An objective measure of compliance
d. An opinion by the auditor (Editors, 7507)

89. In which of the following situations would an auditor ordinarily choose between expressing an "except for" qualified opinion or an adverse opinion?
a. The auditor did not observe the entity's physical inventory and is unable to become satisfied as to its balance by other auditing procedures.
b. The financial statements fail to disclose information that is required by generally accepted accounting principles.
c. The auditor is asked to report only on the entity's balance sheet and not on the other basic financial statements.
d. Events disclosed in the financial statements cause the auditor to have substantial doubt about the entity's ability to continue as a going concern.
(5/93, AUD, #58, 3954)

90. Digit Co. uses the FIFO method of costing for its international subsidiary's inventory and LIFO for its domestic inventory. Under these circumstances, the auditor's report on Digit's financial statements should express an
a. Unqualified opinion
b. Opinion qualified because of a lack of consistency
c. Opinion qualified because of a departure from GAAP
d. Adverse opinion (11/95, AUD, #67, 6014)

91. An auditor concludes that a client's illegal act, which has a material effect on the financial statements, has not been properly accounted for or disclosed. Depending on the materiality of the effect on the financial statements, the auditor should express either a(an)
a. Adverse opinion or a disclaimer of opinion
b. Qualified opinion or an adverse opinion
c. Disclaimer of opinion or an unqualified opinion with a separate explanatory paragraph
d. Unqualified opinion with a separate explanatory paragraph or a qualified opinion
(5/95, AUD, #13, 5631)

92. Which of the following representations does an auditor make explicitly and which implicitly when issuing an unqualified opinion?

	Conformity with GAAP	Adequacy of disclosure
a.	Implicitly	Implicitly
b.	Explicitly	Explicitly
c.	Implicitly	Explicitly
d.	Explicitly	Implicitly

(Editors, 0363)

93. Eagle Company's financial statements contain a departure from generally accepted accounting principles because, due to unusual circumstances, the statements would otherwise be misleading. The auditor should express an opinion that is
a. Unqualified but not mention the departure in the auditor's report
b. Unqualified and describe the departure in a separate paragraph
c. Qualified and describe the departure in a separate paragraph
d. Qualified or adverse, depending on materiality, and describe the departure in a separate paragraph (11/90, AUD, #12, 0329)

94. In the first audit of a new client, an auditor was able to extend auditing procedures to gather sufficient evidence about consistency. Under these circumstances, the auditor should
a. Not report on the client's income statement
b. Not refer to consistency in the auditor's report
c. State that the consistency standard does not apply
d. State that the accounting principles have been applied consistently   (11/95, AUD, #74, 6021)

95. A limitation on the scope of an audit sufficient to preclude an unqualified opinion will usually result when management
a. States that the financial statements are not intended to be presented in conformity with generally accepted accounting principles
b. Presents financial statements that are prepared in accordance with the cash receipts and disbursements basis of accounting
c. Does not make the minutes of the board of directors' meetings available to the auditor
d. Asks the auditor to report on the balance sheet and not on the other basic financial statements
(Editors, 0345)

96. When disclaiming an opinion due to a client-imposed scope limitation, an auditor should indicate in a separate paragraph why the audit did not comply with generally accepted auditing standards. The auditor should also omit the

	Scope paragraph	Opinion paragraph
a.	No	Yes
b.	Yes	Yes
c.	No	No
d.	Yes	No

(11/93, AUD, #46, 4283)

97. Restrictions imposed by a retail entity that is a new client prevent an auditor from observing any physical inventories. These inventories account for 40% of the entity's assets. Alternative auditing procedures cannot be applied due to the nature of the entity's records. Under these circumstances, the auditor should express a(an)
a. Disclaimer of opinion
b. Qualified opinion
c. Adverse opinion
d. Unqualified opinion with an explanatory paragraph   (R/03, AUD, #19, 7641)

98. Under which of the following circumstances would a disclaimer of opinion **not** be appropriate?
a. The auditor is unable to determine the amounts associated with an employee fraud scheme.
b. Management does not provide reasonable justification for a change in accounting principles.
c. The client refuses to permit the auditor to confirm certain accounts receivable or apply alternative procedures to verify their balances.
d. The chief executive officer is unwilling to sign the management representation letter.
(11/95, AUD, #66, 6013)

99. Jewel, CPA, audited Infinite Co.'s prior year financial statements. These statements are presented with those of the current year for comparative purposes without Jewel's auditor's report, which expressed a qualified opinion. In drafting the current year's auditor's report, Crain, CPA, the successor auditor, should

I. Not name Jewel as the predecessor auditor
II. Indicate the type of report issued by Jewel
III. Indicate the substantive reasons for Jewel's qualification

a. I only
b. I and II only
c. II and III only
d. I, II, and III   (11/95, AUD, #76, 6023)

100. The auditor's report should be dated no earlier than when the auditor has
a. Delivered the report to the client
b. Completed the review of the working papers
c. Obtained sufficient appropriate audit evidence to support the opinion
d. Completed the fieldwork   (Editors, 0386)

101. On August 13, a CPA obtained sufficient appropriate audit evidence to support an opinion on a client's financial statements for the year ended June 30. On August 27, an event came to the CPA's attention that should be disclosed in the notes to the financial statements. The event was properly disclosed by the entity, but the CPA decided not to dual date the auditor's report and dated the report August 27. Under these circumstances, the CPA was taking responsibility for
a. All subsequent events that occurred through August 27
b. Only the specific subsequent event disclosed by the entity
c. All subsequent events that occurred through August 13 and the specific subsequent event disclosed by the entity
d. Only the subsequent events that occurred through August 13
(R/03, AUD, #3, amended, 7625)

102. Which of the following procedures would an auditor most likely perform in obtaining evidence about subsequent events?
a. Examine a sample of transactions that occurred since the year-end to verify the effectiveness of computer controls
b. Inquire of management whether there have been significant changes in working capital since the year-end
c. Recompute depreciation charges for plant assets sold for substantial gains since the year-end
d. Reperform the tests of controls that indicated significant deficiencies in the operation of internal control　　　　　　　(R/05, AUD, #23, 7818)

103. Six months after issuing an unqualified opinion on audited financial statements, an auditor discovered that the engagement personnel failed to confirm several of the client's material accounts receivable balances. The auditor should first
a. Request the permission of the client to undertake the confirmation of accounts receivable
b. Perform alternative procedures to provide a satisfactory basis for the unqualified opinion
c. Assess the importance of the omitted procedures to the auditor's ability to support the previously expressed opinion
d. Inquire whether there are persons currently relying, or likely to rely, on the unqualified opinion
　　　　　　　(11/90, AUD, #35, 0332)

104. On February 9, Brown, CPA, expressed an unqualified opinion on the financial statements of Web Co. On October 9, during a peer review of Brown's practice, the reviewer informed Brown that engagement personnel failed to perform a search for subsequent events for the Web engagement. Brown should first
a. Request Web's permission to perform substantive procedures that would provide a satisfactory basis for the opinion
b. Inquire of Web whether there are persons currently relying, or likely to rely, on the financial statements
c. Take no additional action because subsequent events have no effect on the financial statements that were reported on
d. Assess the importance of the omitted procedures to Brown's present ability to support the opinion　　　　　　　(R/05, AUD, #28, 7823)

105. Which of the following audit procedures most likely would assist an auditor in identifying conditions and events that may indicate substantial doubt about an entity's ability to continue as a going concern?
a. Reading the minutes of meetings of the stockholders and the board of directors
b. Comparing the market value of property to amounts owed on the property
c. Reviewing lease agreements to determine whether leased assets should be capitalized
d. Inspecting title documents to verify whether any assets are pledged as collateral
　　　　　　　(R/05, AUD, #12, 7807)

106. Which of the following conditions or events most likely would cause an auditor to have substantial doubt about an entity's ability to continue as a going concern?
a. Cash flows from operating activities are negative
b. Research and development projects are postponed
c. Significant related party transactions are pervasive
d. Stock dividends replace annual cash dividends
　　　　　　　(11/94, AUD, #71, 5144)

107. Kane, CPA, concludes that there is substantial doubt about Lima Co.'s ability to continue as a going concern for a reasonable period of time. If Lima's financial statements adequately disclose its financial difficulties, Kane's auditor's report is required to include an explanatory paragraph that specifically uses the phrase(s)

	"Possible discontinuance of operations"	"Reasonable period of time, not to exceed one year"
a.	Yes	Yes
b.	Yes	No
c.	No	Yes
d.	No	No

　　　　　　　(11/95, AUD, #72, 6019)

108. When audited financial statements are presented in a client's document containing other information, the auditor should
a. Perform inquiry and analytical procedures to ascertain whether the other information is reasonable
b. Add an explanatory paragraph to the auditor's report without changing the opinion on the financial statements
c. Perform the appropriate substantive auditing procedures to corroborate the other information
d. Read the other information to determine that it is consistent with the audited financial statements
　　　　　　　(11/92, AUD, #57, 2991)

109. An auditor reads the letter of transmittal accompanying a county's comprehensive annual financial report and identifies a material inconsistency with the financial statements. The auditor determines that the financial statements do not require revision. Which of the following actions should the auditor take?

a. Request that the client revise the letter of transmittal
b. Include an explanatory paragraph in the auditor's report
c. Consider withdrawing from the engagement
d. Request a client representation letter acknowledging the inconsistency (R/07, AUD, #27, 8399)

110. An auditor determines that the entity is presenting certain supplementary financial disclosures of pension information that are required by the GASB. Under these circumstances, the auditor should

a. Add an explanatory paragraph to the auditor's report that refers to the required supplementary information
b. State that the audit is not being performed in accordance with generally accepted auditing standards
c. Document in the working papers that the required supplementary information is presented, but should not apply any procedures to the information
d. Compare the required supplementary information for consistency with the audited financial statements (R/07, AUD, #14, 8386)

SIMULATIONS

Problem 28-3 (20 to 30 minutes)

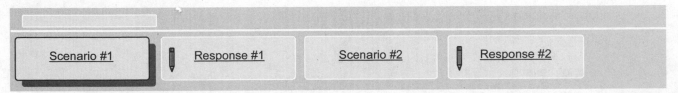

- The auditor is independent.
- The auditor previously expressed an unqualified opinion on the prior year's financial statements.
- Only single-year (not comparative) statements are presented for the current year.
- The conditions for an unqualified opinion exist unless contradicted in the factual situations.
- The conditions stated in the factual situations are material.
- No report modifications are to be made except in response to the factual situation.

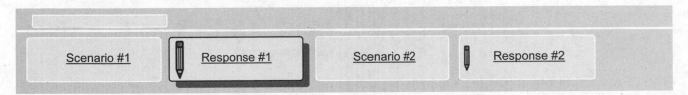

The following items present various independent factual situations an auditor might encounter in conducting an audit. The list represents the types of opinions the auditor ordinarily would issue. For each situation, select one response. Select, as the **best** answer for each item, the action the auditor normally would take based on Scenario #1.

1. In auditing the long-term investments account, an auditor is unable to obtain audited financial statements for an investee located in a foreign country. The auditor concludes that sufficient appropriate audit evidence regarding this investment cannot be obtained.

2. Due to recurring operating losses and working capital deficiencies, an auditor has substantial doubt about an entity's ability to continue as a going concern for a reasonable period of time. However, the financial statement disclosures concerning these matters are adequate.

3. A principal auditor decides to take responsibility for the work of another CPA who audited a wholly owned subsidiary of the entity and issued an unqualified opinion. The total assets and revenues of the subsidiary represent 17% and 18%, respectively, of the total assets and revenues of the entity being audited.

4. An entity issues financial statements that present financial position and results of operations but omits the related statement of cash flows. Management discloses in the notes to the financial statements that it does not believe the statement of cash flows to be a useful financial statement.

5. An entity changes its method of inventory pricing from LIFO to FIFO. The auditor concurs with the change although it has a material effect on the comparability of the entity's financial statements.

6. An entity is a defendant in a lawsuit alleging infringement of certain patent rights. However, the ultimate outcome of the litigation cannot be reasonably estimated by management. The auditor believes there is a reasonable possibility of a significant material loss, but the lawsuit is adequately disclosed in the notes to the financial statements.

7. An entity discloses in the notes to the financial statements certain lease obligations. The auditor believes that the failure to capitalize these leases is a departure from generally accepted accounting principles.

Types of Opinions

A. An "except for" qualified opinion.

B. An unqualified opinion.

C. An adverse opinion.

D. A disclaimer of opinion.

E. Either an "except for" qualified opinion or an adverse opinion.

F. Either a disclaimer of opinion or an "except for" qualified opinion.

G. Either an adverse opinion or a disclaimer of opinion.

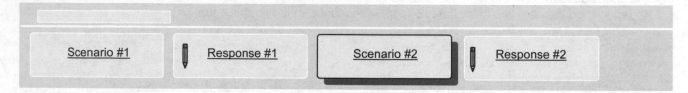

Post, CPA, accepted an engagement to audit the financial statements of General Co., a new client. General is a publicly held retailing entity that recently replaced its operating management. In the course of applying auditing procedures, Post discovered that General's financial statements may be materially misstated due to the existence of fraud.

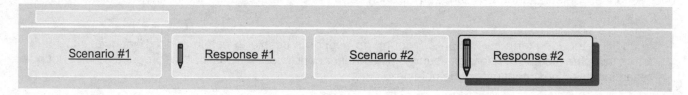

a. Describe Post's responsibilities on the circumstances described in Scenario #2.

b. Describe Post's responsibilities for reporting on General's financial statements and other communications if Post is precluded from applying necessary procedures in searching for fraud.

What authoritative reference provides guidance as to what is considered a comprehensive basis of accounting other than generally accepted accounting principles?

Paragraph Reference Answer: _____

(5/92, AUD, #61-67, part A, amended, 7543)

Problem 28-4 (20 to 30 minutes)

Webb & Weber, CPAs, audited the consolidated financial statements of Quest Co. and all but one of its subsidiaries for the year ended September 30, Year 1, and expressed a qualified opinion because Quest capitalized certain research and development expenditures that should have been expensed.

Webb & Weber also audited Quest's consolidated financial statements and all but one of its subsidiaries for the year ended September 30, Year 2. These consolidated financial statements are being presented on a comparative basis with those of the prior year and an unqualified opinion is being expressed.

Webb, the engagement partner, instructed Perry, an assistant on the engagement, to draft the auditor's report on November 4, Year 2, the date of completion of the audit. In drafting the report on page 15, Perry considered the following:

- In preparing its Year 2 financial statements, Quest changed its method of accounting for research and development costs and properly expensed these amounts. Quest also restated its Year 1 financial statements to conform with GAAP. Consequently, Webb & Weber's present opinion on the Year 1 financial statements is different (unqualified) from the opinion expressed on November 5, Year 1.

- Hill & Hall, CPAs, audited the financial statements of Biotherm, Inc., a consolidated subsidiary of Quest, for the years ended September 30, Year 2 and Year 1. The subsidiary's financial statements reflect total assets constituting 23% and 22% at September 30, Year 2 and Year 1, respectively, and total revenues constituting 21% and 20% in Year 2 and Year 1, respectively, of the consolidated totals. Hill & Hall expressed an unqualified opinion each year and furnished Webb & Weber with a copy of each year's auditor's report. Webb & Weber have decided not to assume responsibility for the work of Hill & Hall insofar as it relates to the expression of an opinion on the consolidated financial statements taken as a whole because of the materiality of Biotherm's financial statements to the consolidated financial statements. Hill & Hall's report will not be presented together with that of Webb & Weber.

- Quest is the subject of a grand jury investigation into possible violations of federal antitrust laws and possible related crimes. Related civil class actions are pending. This is adequately disclosed in Note 12 to Quest's consolidated financial statements. Because of the early stage of the investigation, the ultimate outcome of these matters cannot presently be determined. Therefore, no provision for any liability that may result has been recorded.

- Quest experienced a net loss in Year 2 and is currently in default under substantially all of its debt agreements. Management's plans in regard to these matters are adequately disclosed in Note 14 to Quest's consolidated financial statements, although the financial statements do not include any adjustments that might result from the outcome of this uncertainty. These matters raise substantial doubt about Quest's ability to continue as a going concern.

Webb reviewed Perry's draft and indicated *(in Webb's Review Notes)* that there were many deficiencies in Perry's draft.

Independent Auditor's Report

We have audited the consolidated financial statements of Quest Co. and subsidiaries as of September 30, Year 2 and Year 1, and the related consolidated statements of income, changes in stockholders' equity, and cash flows for the years then ended. These financial statements are the responsibility of the Company's management. Our responsibility is to express an opinion on these financial statements based on our audits. We did not audit the financial statements of Biotherm, Inc., a wholly-owned subsidiary, which statements reflect total assets constituting 23% and 22% at September 30, Year 2 and Year 1, respectively, and total revenues constituting 21% and 20% in Year 2 and Year 1, respectively, of the consolidated totals. Those statements were audited by Hill & Hall, CPAs, whose reports have been furnished to us, and our opinion, insofar as it relates to the amounts included for Biotherm, Inc., is based solely on their reports.

We conducted our audits in accordance with generally accepted auditing standards. Those standards require that we plan and perform the audit to obtain reasonable assurance about whether the financial statements are free of material misstatement. An audit includes examining, on a test basis, evidence supporting the amounts and disclosures in the financial statement. An audit also includes assessing the accounting principles used, as well as assessing control risk. We believe that our audits provide a reasonable basis for our opinion.

In our previous report dated November 5, Year 1, we expressed a qualified opinion that, except for the effects on the Year 1 financial statements of not expensing certain research and development costs, the Year 1 financial statements present fairly, in all material respects, the financial position of Quest Co. and subsidiaries as of September 30, Year 1, and the results of its operations and its cash flows for the year then ended in conformity with generally accepted accounting principles. As described in Note 10, the Company has changed its method of accounting for these items and restated its Year 1 financial statements to conform with generally accepted accounting principles. Accordingly, our present opinion on the Year 1 financial statements, as presented herein, is different from that expressed in our previous report.

In our opinion, based on our audits and the reports of the other auditors, the consolidated financial statements referred to above present fairly, in all material respects, the financial position of Quest Co. as of September 30, Year 2 and Year 1, in conformity with generally accepted accounting principles, except for the uncertainty, which is discussed in Note 12 to the consolidated financial statements.

The accompanying consolidated financial statements have been prepared assuming that the Company will continue in existence for a reasonable period of time. As discussed in Note 14 to the consolidated financial statements, the Company suffered a net loss in Year 2 and is currently in default under substantially all of its debt agreements. Management's plans in regard to these matters are also described in Note 14. The consolidated financial statements do not include any adjustments that might result from the outcome of this uncertainty.

Webb & Weber, CPAs
November 4, Year 2

The following items represent the deficiencies noted by Webb. For each deficiency based on Scenario #1, indicate whether

W.   Webb's review note is correct.
P.   Perry's draft is correct.
B.   Both Webb's review note and Perry's draft are incorrect.

Webb's Review Notes

1. The reference to the subsidiary, Biotherm, and the magnitude of its financial statements should be in the scope paragraph rather than in the opening (introductory) paragraph.

2. The other independent auditors, Hill & Hall, should be named in the scope paragraph rather than in the opening (introductory) paragraph.

3. The reference in the scope paragraph to "the financial statements are free of material misstatement" should be followed by the phrase "whether caused by error or fraud."

4. The required reference in the scope paragraph to assessing "significant estimates made by management" has been omitted.

5. The reference in the scope paragraph to "assessing control risk" is inappropriate and should be omitted from the report.

6. The required reference in the scope paragraph to "evaluating the overall financial statement presentation" has been omitted.

7. A separate explanatory paragraph describing the grand jury investigation into possible violations of federal antitrust laws is required to be placed between the scope and opinion paragraphs.

8. The reference in the first explanatory paragraph (between the scope and opinion paragraphs) to the qualified opinion on the Year 1 financial statements is not properly placed. It should be placed in the opinion paragraph.

The CPA firm of May & Marty has audited the consolidated financial statements of BGI Corporation. May & Marty performed the audit of the parent company and all subsidiaries except for BGI-Western Corporation, which was audited by the CPA firm of Dey & Dee. BGI-Western constituted approximately 10% of the consolidated assets and 6% of the consolidated revenue.

Dey & Dee issued an unqualified opinion on the financial statements of BGI-Western. May & Marty will be issuing an unqualified opinion on the consolidated financial statements of BGI.

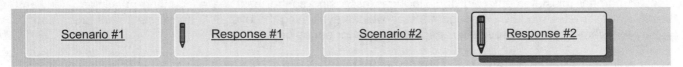

Based on Scenario #2, what procedures should May & Marty consider performing with respect to Dey & Dee's audit of BGI-Western's financial statements that will be appropriate whether or not reference is to be made to the other auditors?

(11/98, AUD, #2, amended, 6717)

Problem 28-5 (15 to 25 minutes)

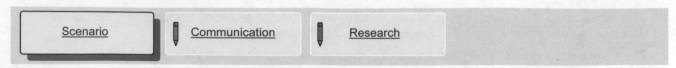

The auditor's report below was drafted by Miller, a staff accountant of Pell & Pell, CPAs, at the completion of the audit of the consolidated financial statements of Bond Co. for the year ended July 31, Year 2. The report was submitted to the engagement partner who reviewed the audit working papers and properly concluded that an unqualified opinion should be issued. In drafting the report, Miller considered the following:

- Bond's consolidated financial statements for the year ended July 31, Year 1, are to be presented for comparative purposes. Pell previously audited these statements and appropriately rendered an unmodified report.
- Bond has suffered recurring losses from operations and has adequately disclosed these losses and management's plans concerning the losses in a note to the consolidated financial statements. Although Bond has prepared the financial statements assuming it will continue as a going concern, Miller has substantial doubt about Bond's ability to continue as a going concern.
- Smith & Smith, CPAs, audited the financial statements of BC Services, Inc., a consolidated subsidiary of Bond, for the year ended July 31, Year 2. The subsidiary's financial statements reflected total assets and revenues of 15% and 18%, respectively, of the consolidated totals. Smith expressed an unqualified opinion and furnished Miller with a copy of the auditor's report. Smith also granted permission to present the report together with the principal auditor's report. Miller decided not to present Smith's report with that of Pell, but instead to make reference to Smith.

Independent Auditor's Report

We have audited the consolidated balance sheets of Bond Co. and subsidiaries as of July 31, Year 2, and Year 1, and the related consolidated statements of income and retained earnings for the years then ended. Our responsibility is to express an opinion on these financial statements based on our audits. We did not audit the financial statements of BC Services, Inc., a wholly-owned subsidiary. Those statements were audited by Smith & Smith, CPAs, whose report has been furnished to us, and our opinion, insofar as it relates to the amounts included for BC Services, Inc., is based solely on the report of Smith & Smith.

We conducted our audits in accordance with generally accepted auditing standards. Those standards require that we plan and perform the audit to obtain reasonable assurance about whether the financial statements are free of material misstatement. An audit includes assessing control risk, the accounting principles used, and significant estimates made by management, as well as evaluating the overall financial statement presentation. We believe that our audits provide a reasonable basis for our opinion.

In our opinion, based on our audits and the report of Smith & Smith, CPAs, the consolidated financial statements referred to above present fairly, in all material respects except for the matter discussed below, the financial position of Bond Co. as of July 31, Year 2, and Year 1, and the results of its operations for the years then ended.

The accompanying consolidated financial statements have been prepared with the disclosure in Note 13 that the company has suffered recurring losses from operations. Management's plans in regard to those matters are also discussed in Note 13. The financial statements do not include any adjustments that might result from the outcome of this uncertainty.

Pell & Pell, CPAs
November 4, Year 2

Identify the deficiencies in the auditor's report as drafted by Miller. Group the deficiencies by paragraph and in the order in which the deficiencies appear. Do not redraft the report.

What authoritative reference defines the term "generally accepted accounting principles?"

Paragraph Reference Answer: _____

(11/93, AUD, #3, amended, 6718)

Problem 28-6 (20 to 30 minutes)

- The auditor is independent.
- The auditor previously expressed an unqualified opinion on the prior year's financial statements.
- Only single-year (not comparative) statements are presented for the current year.
- The conditions for an unqualified opinion exist unless contradicted in the factual situations.
- The conditions stated in the factual situations are material.
- No report modifications are to be made except in response to the factual situation.

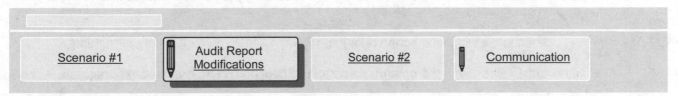

The following items present various independent factual situations an auditor might encounter in conducting an audit. The list represents the report modifications (if any) that would be necessary. For each situation, select one response. Select, as the **best** answer for each item, the action the auditor normally would take, based on Scenario #1.

1. In auditing the long-term investments account, an auditor is unable to obtain audited financial statements for an investee located in a foreign country. The auditor concludes that sufficient appropriate audit evidence regarding this investment cannot be obtained.

2. Due to recurring operating losses and working capital deficiencies, an auditor has substantial doubt about an entity's ability to continue as a going concern for a reasonable period of time. However, the financial statement disclosures concerning these matters are adequate.

3. A principal auditor decides to take responsibility for the work of another CPA who audited a wholly owned subsidiary of the entity and issued an unqualified opinion. The total assets and revenues of the subsidiary represent 17% and 18%, respectively, of the total assets and revenues of the entity being audited.

4. An entity issues financial statements that present financial position and results of operations but omits the related statement of cash flows. Management discloses in the notes to the financial statements that it does not believe the statement of cash flows to be a useful financial statement.

5. An entity changes its method of inventory pricing from LIFO to FIFO. The auditor concurs with the change although it has a material effect on the comparability of the entity's financial statements.

6. An entity is a defendant in a lawsuit alleging infringement of certain patent rights. However, the ultimate outcome of the litigation cannot be reasonably estimated by management. The auditor believes there is a reasonable possibility of a significant material loss, but the lawsuit is adequately disclosed in the notes to the financial statements.

7. An entity discloses in the notes to the financial statements certain lease obligations. The auditor believes that the failure to capitalize these leases is a departure from generally accepted accounting principles.

Report Modifications

A. Describe the circumstances in an explanatory paragraph **preceding** the opinion paragraph **without modifying** the three standard paragraphs.

B. Describe the circumstances in an explanatory paragraph **following** the opinion paragraph **without modifying** the three standard paragraphs.

C. Describe the circumstances in an explanatory paragraph **preceding** the opinion paragraph and **modify** the opinion paragraph.

D. Describe the circumstances in an explanatory paragraph **following** the opinion paragraph and **modify** the opinion paragraph.

E. Describe the circumstances in an explanatory paragraph **preceding** the opinion paragraph and **modify** the scope and opinion paragraphs.

F. Describe the circumstances in an explanatory paragraph **following** the opinion paragraph and **modify** the scope and opinion paragraphs.

G. Describe the circumstances within the **scope** paragraph without adding an explanatory paragraph.

H. Describe the circumstances within the **opinion** paragraph without adding an explanatory paragraph.

I. Describe the circumstances within the **scope** and **opinion** paragraphs without adding an explanatory paragraph.

J. Issue the **standard** auditor's report **without modification.**

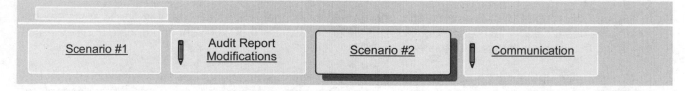

Post, CPA, accepted an engagement to audit the financial statements of General Co., a new client. General is a publicly held retailing entity that recently replaced its operating management. In the course of applying auditing procedures, Post discovered that General's financial statements may be materially misstated due to the existence of fraud.

a. Describe Post's responsibilities for reporting on General's financial statements and other communications if Post concludes that General's financial statements are materially affected by fraud.

b. Describe the circumstances in which Post may have a duty to disclose fraud to third parties outside General's management and its audit committee.

What authoritative reference provides guidance on an engagement to report on only one basic financial statement, but not the others, when the auditor's access to information and application of procedures is not limited in scope?

Paragraph Reference Answer: _____

(5/92, AUD, 61-67, part B, amended, 6719

Problem 28-7 (15 to 25 minutes)

The auditors' report below was drafted by Moore, a staff accountant of Tyler & Tyler, CPAs, at the completion of the audit of the financial statements of Park Publishing Co., Inc., for the year ended September 30, Year 2. The report was submitted to the engagement partner who reviewed the audit working papers and properly concluded that an unqualified opinion should be issued. In drafting the report, Moore considered the following:

• During fiscal year Year 2, Park changed its depreciation method. The engagement partner concurred with this change in accounting principle and its justification and Moore included an explanatory paragraph in the auditor's report.

• The Year 2 financial statements are affected by an uncertainty concerning a lawsuit, the outcome of which cannot presently be estimated. Moore has included an explanatory paragraph in the auditors' report.

• The financial statements for the year ended September 30, Year 1, are to be presented for comparative purposes. Tyler & Tyler previously audited these statements and expressed an unqualified opinion.

<u>Independent Auditors' Report</u>

To the Board of Directors of Park Publishing Co., Inc.:

We have audited the accompanying balance sheets of Park Publishing Co., Inc. as of September 30, Year 2, and Year 1, and the related statements of income and cash flows for the years then ended. These financial statements are the responsibility of the company's management.

We conducted our audits in accordance with generally accepted auditing standards. Those standards require that we plan and perform the audit to obtain reasonable assurance about whether the financial statements are fairly presented. An audit includes examining, on a test basis, evidence supporting the amounts and disclosures in the financial statements. An audit also includes assessing significant estimates made by management, as well as evaluating the overall financial statement presentation. We believe that our audits provide a basis for determining whether any material modifications should be made to the accompanying financial statements.

As discussed in Note X to the financial statements, the company changed its method of computing depreciation in fiscal Year 2.

In our opinion, except for the accounting change, with which we concur, the financial statements referred to above present fairly, in all material respects, the financial position of Park Publishing Co., Inc. as of September 30, Year 2, and the results of its operations and its cash flows for the year then ended in conformity with generally accepted accounting principles.

As discussed in Note Y to the financial statements, the company is a defendant in a lawsuit alleging infringement of certain copyrights. The company has filed a counteraction, and preliminary hearings on both actions are in progress. Accordingly, any provision for liability is subject to adjudication of this matter.

Tyler & Tyler, CPAs
November 5, Year 2

Identify the deficiencies in the auditors' report as drafted by Moore. Group the deficiencies by paragraph and in the order in which the deficiencies appear. Do not redraft the report.

What authoritative reference provides guidance for an engagement partner's competency requirements that should be included in a CPA firm's quality control system's policies?

Paragraph Reference Answer: _____

(11/92, AUD, #3, amended, 6720)

Problem 28-8 (15 to 25 minutes)

Green, CPA, is auditing the financial statements of Taylor Corporation for the year ended December 31, Year 1. Green plans to complete the audit and sign the auditor's report about May 10, Year 2. Green is concerned about events and transactions occurring after December 31, Year 1 that may affect the Year 1 financial statements.

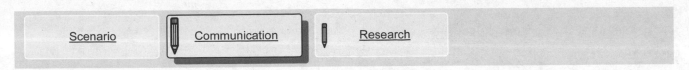

a. What are the general types of subsequent events that require Green's consideration and evaluation?

b. What are the auditing procedures Green should consider performing to gather evidence concerning subsequent events?

What authoritative reference provides guidance when an auditor decides to make reference to the report of another auditor as a basis, in part, for her/his opinion regarding *where* s/he should disclose this fact in her/his report?

Paragraph Reference Answer: _____

(5/90, AUD, #4, amended, 6721)

Problem 28-9 (15 to 25 minutes)

On September 30, Year 2, White & Co., CPAs, was engaged to audit the consolidated financial statements of National Motors, Inc. for the year ended December 31, Year 2. The consolidated financial statements of National had not been audited the prior year. National's inadequate inventory records precluded White from forming an opinion as to the proper or consistent application of generally accepted accounting principles to inventory balances on January 1, Year 2. Therefore, White decided not to express an opinion on the results of operations for the year ended December 31, Year 2. National elected not to present comparative financial statements.

Rapid Parts Company, a consolidated subsidiary of National, was audited for the year ended December 31, Year 2, by Green & Co., CPAs. Green obtained sufficient appropriate audit evidence to support their opinion on February 28, Year 3, and submitted an unqualified opinion on Rapid's financial statements on March 7, Year 3. Rapid's statements reflect total assets and revenues constituting 22% and 25%, respectively, of the consolidated totals of National. White decided not to assume responsibility for the work of Green. Green's report on Rapid does not accompany National's consolidated statements.

White obtained sufficient appropriate audit evidence to support their opinion on March 28, Year 3, and submitted its auditor's report to National on April 4, Year 3.

Prepare White and Company's auditor's report on the consolidated financial statements of National Motors, Inc.

Scenario	✎	Report	✎	Research

What authoritative reference describes how to determine the due date for a CPA firm's initial peer review?

Paragraph Reference Answer: _____

(11/86, AUD, #5, amended, 6722)

Problem 28-10 (20 to 30 minutes)

Scenario #1	✎	Response #1	Scenario #2	✎	Response #2

Webb & Weber, CPAs, audited the consolidated financial statements of Quest Co. and all but one of its subsidiaries for the year ended September 30, Year 1, and expressed a qualified opinion because Quest capitalized certain research and development expenditures that should have been expensed.

Webb & Weber also audited Quest's consolidated financial statements and all but one of its subsidiaries for the year ended September 30, Year 2. These consolidated financial statements are being presented on a comparative basis with those of the prior year and an unqualified opinion is being expressed.

Webb, the engagement partner, instructed Perry, an assistant on the engagement, to draft the auditor's report on November 4, Year 2, the date of completion of the audit. In drafting the report on page 15, Perry considered the following:

- In preparing its Year 2 financial statements, Quest changed its method of accounting for research and development costs and properly expensed these amounts. Quest also restated its Year 1 financial statements to conform with GAAP. Consequently, Webb & Weber's present opinion on the Year 1 financial statements is different (unqualified) from the opinion expressed on November 5, Year 1.

- Hill & Hall, CPAs, audited the financial statements of Biotherm, Inc., a consolidated subsidiary of Quest, for the years ended September 30, Year 2 and Year 1. The subsidiary's financial statements reflect total assets constituting 23% and 22% at September 30, Year 2 and Year 1, respectively, and total revenues constituting 21% and 20% in Year 2 and Year 1, respectively, of the consolidated totals. Hill & Hall expressed an unqualified opinion each year and furnished Webb & Weber with a copy of each year's auditor's report. Webb & Weber have decided not to assume responsibility for the work of Hill & Hall insofar as it relates to the expression of an opinion on the consolidated financial statements taken as a whole because of the materiality of Biotherm's financial statements to the consolidated financial statements. Hill & Hall's report will not be presented together with that of Webb & Weber.

- Quest is the subject of a grand jury investigation into possible violations of federal antitrust laws and possible related crimes. Related civil class actions are pending. This is adequately disclosed in Note 12 to Quest's consolidated financial statements. Because of the early stage of the investigation, the ultimate outcome of these matters cannot presently be determined. Therefore, no provision for any liability that may result has been recorded.

- Quest experienced a net loss in Year 2 and is currently in default under substantially all of its debt agreements. Management's plans in regard to these matters are adequately disclosed in Note 14 to Quest's consolidated financial statements, although the financial statements do not include any adjustments that might result from the outcome of this uncertainty. These matters raise substantial doubt about Quest's ability to continue as a going concern.

Webb reviewed Perry's draft and indicated (in Webb's Review Notes) that there were many deficiencies in Perry's draft.

Independent Auditor's Report

We have audited the consolidated financial statements of Quest Co. and subsidiaries as of September 30, Year 2 and Year 1, and the related consolidated statements of income, changes in stockholders' equity, and cash flows for the years then ended. These financial statements are the responsibility of the Company's management. Our responsibility is to express an opinion on these financial statements based on our audits. We did not audit the financial statements of Biotherm, Inc., a wholly-owned subsidiary, which statements reflect total assets constituting 23% and 22% at September 30, Year 2 and Year 1, respectively, and total revenues constituting 21% and 20% in Year 2 and Year 1, respectively, of the consolidated totals. Those statements were audited by Hill & Hall, CPAs, whose reports have been furnished to us, and our opinion, insofar as it relates to the amounts included for Biotherm, Inc., is based solely on their reports.

We conducted our audits in accordance with generally accepted auditing standards. Those standards require that we plan and perform the audit to obtain reasonable assurance about whether the financial statements are free of material misstatement. An audit includes examining, on a test basis, evidence supporting the amounts and disclosures in the financial statement. An audit also includes assessing the accounting principles used, as well as assessing control risk. We believe that our audits provide a reasonable basis for our opinion.

In our opinion, based on our audits and the reports of the other auditors, the consolidated financial statements referred to above present fairly, in all material respects, the financial position of Quest Co. as of September 30, Year 2 and Year 1, in conformity with generally accepted accounting principles, except for the uncertainty, which is discussed in Note 12 to the consolidated financial statements.

The accompanying consolidated financial statements have been prepared assuming that the Company will continue in existence for a reasonable period of time. As discussed in Note 14 to the consolidated financial statements, the Company suffered a net loss in Year 2 and is currently in default under substantially all of its debt agreements. Management's plans in regard to these matters are also described in Note 14. The consolidated financial statements do not include any adjustments that might result from the outcome of this uncertainty.

Webb & Weber, CPAs
November 4, Year 2

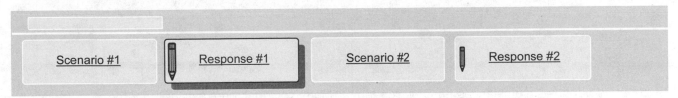

The following items represent the deficiencies noted by Webb. For each deficiency, indicate whether

W. Webb's review note is correct.
P. Perry's draft is correct.
B. Both Webb's review note and Perry's draft are incorrect.

Webb's Review Notes

1. The reference in the first explanatory paragraph (between the scope and opinion paragraphs) to Note 10 does not express our concurrence with Quest's change in accounting principle. Our concurrence should be specifically expressed in this paragraph.

2. The reference to the other auditors in the opinion paragraph is incomplete. It should specifically include the words "unqualified opinion" to describe the type of opinion expressed by Hill & Hall.

3. The opinion paragraph should extend the auditor's opinion beyond financial position to include the results of Quest's operations and its changes in stockholders' equity.

4. The reference to the uncertainty in the opinion paragraph is incomplete. It should describe the nature of the uncertainty as pertaining to the grand jury investigation into possible violations of federal antitrust laws.

5. The explanatory paragraph following the opinion paragraph does not include the term "substantial doubt." This term is required to be used in this paragraph under these circumstances.

6. The explanatory paragraph following the opinion paragraph does not include the term "going concern." This term is required to be used in this paragraph under these circumstances.

7. The explanatory paragraph following the opinion paragraph includes an inappropriate statement that "the consolidated financial statements do not include any adjustments that might result from the outcome of this uncertainty." This statement is misleading and should be omitted.

8. The auditor's report is not correctly dated. It should be dual dated because of Note 12, the grand jury investigation, and also because of Note 14, the going concern uncertainty.

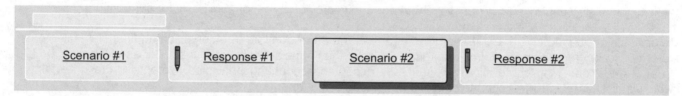

The CPA firm of May & Marty has audited the consolidated financial statements of BGI Corporation. May & Marty performed the audit of the parent company and all subsidiaries except for BGI-Western Corporation, which was audited by the CPA firm of Dey & Dee. BGI-Western constituted approximately 10% of the consolidated assets and 6% of the consolidated revenue.

Dey & Dee issued an unqualified opinion on the financial statements of BGI-Western. May & Marty will be issuing an unqualified opinion on the consolidated financial statements of BGI.

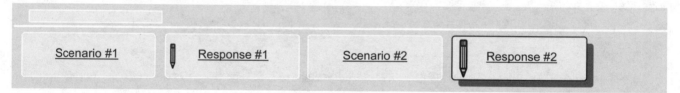

Describe the various circumstances under which May & Marty could take responsibility for the work of Dey & Dee and make no reference to Dey & Dee's audit of BGI-Western in May & Marty's auditor's report on the consolidated financial statements of BGI.

What authoritative reference provides guidance regarding the date used when a continuing auditor reissues a report on audited financial statements after the date of the original report?

Paragraph Reference Answer: _____

(11/98, AUD, #2 partial, amended, 6723)

Problem 28-11 (15 to 25 minutes)

On November 19, Year 1, Wall, CPA, was engaged to audit the financial statements of Trendy Auto Imports, Inc. for the year ended December 31, Year 1. Wall is considering Trendy's ability to continue as a going concern.

a. Describe Wall's basic responsibility in considering Trendy's ability to continue as a going concern.

b. Describe the audit procedures Wall most likely would perform to identify conditions and events that may indicate that Trendy has a going concern problem.

c. Describe the management plans that Wall should consider that could mitigate the adverse effects of Trendy's financial difficulties if Wall identified conditions and events that indicated a potential going concern problem.

What authoritative reference provides guidance to an auditor issuing a single combined report covering both a presentation that requires a restriction on use and a presentation that ordinarily requires no such restriction?

Paragraph Reference Answer: _____

(5/95, AUD, #5, amended, 6724)

Solution 28-1 MULTIPLE CHOICE ANSWERS

Reporting Standards

1. **(b)** An unqualified opinion should be issued only when the auditor is satisfied that the financial statements present fairly, in all material respects, the financial position of the entity as of the balance sheet date and the results of its operations and its cash flows in conformity with GAAP. Documentation, acknowledgment, or recording of the amount of known misstatements are insufficient to accomplish this goal. Adjusting entries already recorded by the client would correct misstatements, not be a part of the total misstatement. (6712)

2. **(c)** The objective of the fourth reporting standard is to prevent misinterpretation of the degree of responsibility the auditor is assuming when associated with financial statements. The auditor may express different opinions on the statements presented. Material scope restrictions result in a qualification or disclaimer of opinion. An auditor is not precluded from reporting on only one of the basic financial statements and not the others. (6015)

3. **(a)** If the specified item is based upon an entity's net income, the auditor should have audited the complete financial statements to express an opinion on the specified item. Hardy could express an opinion even if Gold's financial statements are not prepared in conformity with GAAP or if Field does not own controlling interest in Gold. There is no requirement that Hardy's report be available for distribution to Gold's other employees; such disclosure might actually conflict with client confidentiality requirements. Also see the text discussion of piecemeal opinions. (6030)

Types of Opinions

4. **(d)** Since single-year financial statements are presented, an auditor need not modify her/his report to indicate that the prior year statements were

audited by other auditors. The inability to obtain audited financial statements supporting an entity's investment in a foreign affiliate represents a scope limitation resulting in a qualified opinion or a disclaimer of opinion. The entity's omission of the statement of cash flows would result in a qualified opinion. While emphasis of a matter does not preclude the issuance of an unqualified opinion, the report must be modified to include a separate paragraph discussing the matter. (4739)

5. (b) If a company issues financial statements that purport to present financial position and results of operations but *omits the related statement of cash flows*, the auditor will normally issue a *qualified opinion*. (3942)

6. (d) When restrictions that significantly limit the scope of the audit are imposed by the client, ordinarily the auditor should disclaim an opinion on the financial statements. (7501)

7. (d) The inability to obtain audited financial statements of a consolidated investee represents a scope limitation resulting in a qualified opinion or a disclaimer of opinion. The circumstances in answers (a), (b), and (c) may require an explanatory paragraph, but they do not preclude an unqualified opinion. (6016)

8. (d) If, after considering the existing conditions and available evidence, the auditor concludes that sufficient audit evidence supports management's assertions about the nature of a matter involving an uncertainty an unqualified opinion is ordinarily appropriate. When an explanatory paragraph does not affect an opinion, it comes after the opinion paragraph. (6017)

9. (b) The auditor may express differing opinions on the balance sheet and income statement. The opinion on the balance sheet is unqualified because the ending inventory is fairly stated. The opinion on the income statement is a disclaimer because of an inability to obtain sufficient audit evidence (a scope limitation) regarding cost of goods sold (because beginning inventory has a significant impact on cost of goods sold). (4741)

10. (b) When inadequately disclosed conditions exist that cause an auditor to have substantial doubt about the entity's ability to continue as a going concern, the statements are not in accordance with GAAP. An adverse opinion generally is not an option when a scope limitation is present. An inability to apply procedures (including not observing physical inventory) is a scope limitation. A change in accounting principles, if adequately disclosed, would not result in an adverse opinion. (6942)

11. (d) If, after considering the existing conditions and available evidence, the auditor concludes that sufficient audit evidence supports management's assertions about the nature of a matter involving an uncertainty, an unqualified opinion is ordinarily appropriate. Answers (a), (b), and (c) would be appropriate for mention in explanatory language to an auditor's standard report. When an entity has a change in accounting principle, the auditor should refer to the change in an explanatory paragraph even if the auditor concurs with the change. Without this, the report implies consistency. (6011)

12. (a) The effect of a change in accounting principle may be inseparable from the effect of a change in estimate. Although the accounting for such a change is the same as that accorded a change only in estimate, a change in principle is involved. Accordingly, this type of change requires recognition in the auditor's report through the addition of an explanatory paragraph. (7502)

Standard Report

13. (c) The scope paragraph of an auditor's standard report includes a statement that an audit also includes assessing the accounting principles used and significant estimates made by management, as well as evaluating the overall financial statement presentation. Answers (a) and (d) are not mentioned in the report. Consistency is only mentioned when it is absent and requires explanatory language be added to the standard report **after** the opinion paragraph. (6009)

14. (d) The statement that the auditor obtains reasonable assurance about whether the financial statements are free of material misstatement recognizes the existence of audit risk. Answers (a), (b), and (c) do not recognize the existence of audit risk. (5082)

15. (b) The basic elements of the introductory paragraph of the auditor's standard report are a statement that financial statements identified in the report were audited and a statement that the financial statements are the responsibility of the company's management and that the auditor's responsibility is to express an opinion on the financial statements based on the audit. (7503)

16. (b) The basic elements of the standard audit report on financial statements do not include a reference to the entity's internal control. The other answers are included in the report. (4736)

17. (c) GAAS is referred to in the scope paragraph; GAAP is referred to in the opinion paragraph. (4742)

18. (a) If the auditor is engaged to audit the financial statements of a company that is not the auditor's client, the report should be addressed to the client and not to the directors or stockholders of the company being audited. (6025)

19. (d) A CPA's assessment of sampling risk factors should not be referred to in an audit report. Management's responsibility for the financial statements is always mentioned in the introductory paragraph. "An audit also includes assessing the accounting principles used and significant estimates made by management..." is stated in the scope paragraph. (8165)

Explanatory Language

20. (b) An explanatory paragraph may be added to the standard report because of a matter involving the uncertainty as to an entity's ability to continue as a going concern. The other answers are examples of when a qualified or adverse opinion or a disclaimer of an opinion should be issued. (3943)

21. (d) A material unjustified accounting change would require that the auditor express a qualified or adverse opinion on the financial statements. If one or more material weaknesses in internal control exist, the auditor would express an adverse opinion on internal control over financial reporting. (6012)

22. (b) If reference is made to the report of another auditor as a basis, in part, for the opinion, this divided responsibility is indicated in the introductory, scope, and opinion paragraphs of the report. In some circumstances, the auditor may wish to emphasize a matter regarding the financial statements, but nevertheless intends to express an unqualified opinion. For example, he may wish to emphasize that the entity has had significant transactions with related parties. Such explanatory information should be presented in a separate paragraph (**following** the opinion paragraph) of the auditor's report. If a company issues financial statements that purport to present financial position and results of operations but omits the related statement of cash flows, the auditor will normally conclude that the omission requires qualification of his opinion. An explanatory paragraph would be added **before** the opinion paragraph. If the auditor concludes that substantial doubt about the entity's ability to continue as a going concern for a reasonable period of time remains, the audit report should include an explanatory paragraph (**following** the opinion paragraph) to reflect that conclusion. (0324)

Another Auditor

23. (c) When the principal auditor makes reference to another auditor, the principal auditor doesn't assume responsibility for the other auditor's work. At a minimum, the principal auditor should inquire about the professional reputation and independence of the other CPA. Reviewing the other CPA's working papers, discussing the results of the other CPA's procedures, and determining that the other CPA has a sufficient understanding of the subsidiary's internal control are beyond the principal auditor's minimum duties. (6831)

24. (a) When the auditor decides to make reference to the report of another auditor as a basis, in part, for her/his opinion, s/he should disclose this fact in the introductory paragraph of her/his report and should refer to the report of the other auditor in expressing her/his opinion. These references indicate division of responsibility for performance of the audit. (6024)

25. (b) Situation I is incorrect because Pell is satisfied and assumes responsibility for the work of the Smith. If the principal auditor is able to satisfy her/himself as to the independence and professional reputation of the other auditor, s/he may be able to express an opinion on the financial statements taken as a whole without making reference in the report to the audit of the other auditor. Only situation II is correct because Pell cannot review the workpapers, therefore cannot assume responsibility; thus, Pell should make reference to Smith's audit in the audit report. (6394)

Departure From GAAP

26. (a) If the auditor believes that the financial statements are not suitably titled, the auditor should disclose these reservations in an explanatory paragraph of the report and qualify the opinion. The auditor should not rely on someone else for her/his opinion. The opinion should be qualified; a disclaimer of opinion would be inappropriate under these circumstances. Terms such as balance sheet, statement of financial position, statement of income, statement of operations, and statement of cash flows or similar titles are generally understood to be applicable only to financial statements that are intended to present financial position, results of operations, or cash flows in conformity with GAAP. Therefore, explanatory language in the notes to the financial statements is insufficient. (3953)

27. (a) If the financial statements contain a departure from the GAAP and the auditor can demonstrate that due to unusual circumstances the financial statements would otherwise have been misleading, the auditor can express an unqualified opinion (with respect to the conformity of the financial statements with GAAP) if a separate paragraph is added to the report describing the departure, its approximate effects, if practicable, and the reasons why compliance with the principle would result in a misleading statement. (4740)

Consistency

28. (b) If there has been a change in accounting principles or in the method of their application that has a material effect on the comparability of the company's financial statements, the auditor should refer to the change in an explanatory paragraph of the report. Such explanatory paragraph (**following the opinion paragraph**) should identify the nature of the change and refer the reader to the note in the financial statements that discusses the change in detail. The lack of consistency would not require that the auditor qualify the opinion if the auditor concurs with the change. (2286)

29. (c) Consistency is only mentioned when it is absent in the financial statements. A change in the useful life used to calculate the provision for depreciation expense is merely a change in estimate and does not require comment by the auditor. The other three answer options would require explanations regarding consistency. (6367)

30. (d) If there has been a change in accounting principles or in the method of their application that has a material effect on the comparability of the company's financial statements, the auditor should refer to the change in an explanatory paragraph, identify the nature of the change, and refer the reader to the note in the financial statements that discussed the change in detail. The justification of the change should not be given, the justification is implied by the statement in the auditor's report that the financial statements are presented fairly. The auditor would not describe the effect of the change in the audit report nor her/his concurrence because this is also implied in the auditor's opinion. (3945)

31. (a) An auditor must disclaim an opinion if unable to gather sufficient evidence. (6632)

32. (c) An auditor would not refer to consistency in the auditor's report if no change in accounting principles or in the method of their application had occurred or if the effect of a change on comparability of the financial statements was not material. (4738)

Uncertainty

33. (a) Both the likelihood that the loss is closer to probable than remote and its materiality would be factors in deciding whether to add an explanatory paragraph. The more likely its occurrence and the greater its magnitude, the more likely an auditor would be to add a paragraph. (4284)

34. (c) If management determines that a reasonable estimate cannot be made and the auditor concludes that sufficient audit evidence supports management's analysis of the nature of the uncertainty and its disclosure in the financial statements, an unqualified opinion is ordinarily appropriate. The situation described is not due to a scope limitation—it's an uncertainty. An uncertainty is not a circumstance that requires an explanatory paragraph. (4751)

Emphasis

35. (d) In some circumstances, the auditor may wish to emphasize a matter regarding the financial statements, but intends to express an unqualified opinion. Examples of matters the auditor may wish to emphasize include that the entity has had significant transactions with related parties; that the entity is a component of a larger business enterprise; unusually important subsequent events; or accounting matters, other than those involving a changes in accounting principles, affecting the comparability of the financial statements with those of the preceding period. As just explained, these circumstances would not require an "except for" qualified report. The information may be included in the emphasis paragraph and the notes to the financial statements. Typically, more detail regarding the matter is provided in the notes to the financial statements. Phrases such as "with the foregoing explanation" should not be used in the opinion paragraph if an emphasis paragraph is included in the auditor's report. (4734)

Qualified Opinion

36. (d) Neither phrase should be used when the auditor is expressing a qualified opinion. Phrases such as *subject to* and *with the foregoing explanation* are not clear or forceful enough and should not be used. Because accompanying notes are part of

the financial statements, wording such as *fairly presented, in all material respects, when read in conjunction with Note 1* is likely to be misunderstood and should not be used. (2980)

37. (b) A CPA cannot be in accordance with GAAS if the CPA is not independent, so the CPA must disclaim an opinion and should state specifically that s/he is not independent. A qualified opinion may be issued when there is a material departure from GAAP. When there are scope limitations, the auditor should qualify or disclaim an opinion. Reference may be made to the work of a specialist when there is a departure from an unqualified opinion and such reference will help to clarify the reason for the qualification. (6010)

38. (d) In a qualified opinion resulting from a scope limitation, the scope and opinion paragraphs are modified and an explanatory paragraph is added **preceding** the opinion paragraph. The introductory paragraph is the same as in a standard unqualified report. (4753)

39. (c) Restrictions on the scope of an audit, whether imposed by the client or by circumstances, such as the timing of procedures, the inability to obtain sufficient appropriate audit evidence, or an inadequacy in the accounting records, may require the auditor to qualify the opinion or to disclaim an opinion. If management has not provided reasonable justification for a change in accounting principle, the auditor should express a qualified opinion or, if the effect of the change is sufficiently material, the auditor should express an adverse opinion on the financial statements. (2284)

40. (c) When an auditor qualifies an opinion because of a scope limitation, the opinion paragraph should indicate that the qualification pertains to the possible effects on the financial statements rather than to the scope limitation itself. Reference in the opinion paragraph to a client-imposed scope limitation or to Inadequate disclosure of necessary information are examples of incorrectly basing the exception on the restriction. The auditor was unable to apply audit procedures; s/he did not depart from GAAS. (4286)

Scope Limitation

41. (b) When qualifying an opinion because of insufficiency of audit evidence, an auditor refers to the situation in the scope and opinion paragraphs and includes an explanatory paragraph **before** the opinion paragraph. It is inappropriate to include a description of the scope of the audit in a note to the financial statements (which are the responsibility of management) because the auditor, not management, is responsible for the scope of the audit. (7100)

42. (a) Piecemeal opinions (expressions of opinion as to certain identified items in financial statements) should not be expressed when the auditor has disclaimed an opinion because piecemeal opinions tend to overshadow or contradict a disclaimer of opinion. The auditor may issue an audit report on only one basic financial statement; this is a limited reporting engagement and does not involve scope limitations if the auditor's access to information is not limited and the auditor is able to apply all necessary procedures. When disclaiming an opinion due to a scope limitation, the scope paragraph is omitted from the audit report. The inclusion of the statement is inappropriate in any paragraph of an audit report that disclaims an opinion. (4737)

43. (c) An auditor is not precluded from reporting on only one of the basic financial statements and not the others. A scope limitation would not exist if the auditor's access to information is not limited and the auditor is able to apply all the procedures the auditor considers necessary. Such engagements involve limited reporting objectives. Nothing in the question's scenario indicates a violation of professional ethics or an inability to apply necessary procedures. A piecemeal opinion is an opinion on specific elements of the financial statements when the auditor has disclaimed an opinion or expressed an adverse opinion on the statements as a whole and is unacceptable. (6008)

44. (a) The auditor can determine that the expression of an unqualified opinion is appropriate only if the audit has been conducted in accordance with GAAS and if the auditor has, therefore, been able to apply all the procedures necessary in the circumstances. Restrictions on the scope of work, the inability to obtain sufficient appropriate audit evidence or an inadequacy in the accounting records may require the auditor to qualify or disclaim an opinion. An unqualified opinion may be issued in the circumstances in answer (b), but an explanatory paragraph and language would be added to the report stating that disclosures required by GAAP have not been presented. Engagement letters are for documenting an understanding with the client. If management refused to sign it, the engagement would be rejected. Significant deficiencies and management's decisions concerning costs to be incurred and related benefits are the responsibility of management. Failure to correct significant deficiencies does not create a scope limitation; however it is the auditor's responsibility to communicate existing significant deficiencies until they are corrected. (3952)

45. (d) When a qualified opinion results from a limitation on the scope of the audit or an insufficiency of audit evidence, the situation should be described in an explanatory paragraph **preceding** the opinion paragraph and referred to in both the scope and opinion paragraphs of the auditor's report. (0340)

Inadequate Disclosure

46. (c) The language generally used in this circumstance is *except for the omission of the information discussed in the preceding paragraph. Subject to* and w*ith the foregoing explanation* are unacceptable language because they are not clear or forceful enough. The language in answer (d) is for an adverse opinion. (6018)

47. (d) The opinion paragraph should be modified. The scope and introductory paragraphs are not affected. (0317)

Adverse Opinion

48. (c) If the financial statements are not in conformity with GAAP and the departure has a material, pervasive effect, an adverse opinion is appropriate. A client-imposed restriction to the auditor's access to the minutes of the board of directors' meetings is a scope limitation and could result in a qualified opinion or more likely, a disclaimer of an opinion. An internal control structure that cannot be relied on will result in expanding substantive tests or determining that the entity is not auditable. Substantial doubt about the entity's ability to continue as a going concern will result in the addition of an explanatory paragraph (**following** the opinion paragraph) to the standard unqualified report assuming the entity's disclosure of the situation is adequate. (4752)

Disclaimer of Opinion

49. (d) Management's refusal to furnish written representations constitutes a scope limitation that is sufficient to preclude an unqualified opinion and is ordinarily sufficient to cause an auditor to disclaim an opinion or withdraw from the engagement. The other answers are all departures from GAAP and would resulting a qualified or an adverse opinion. (0319)

Comparative Financial Statements

50. (a, d) Reference in the fourth reporting standard to the financial statements *taken as a whole* applies not only to the financial statements of the current period, but also to those of one or more prior periods that are presented on a comparative basis with those of the current period. (7504)

51. (a) The letter of representation should be obtained from the successor independent auditor. An auditor who has audited the financial statements for prior periods, but has not audited the statements for the most recent audited period included in the registration statement has a responsibility relating to events subsequent to the date of the prior period financial statements, and extending to the effective date, that bear materially on the prior period financial statements on which s/he reported. Generally he should obtain a letter of representation from the successor independent auditor regarding whether her/his audit (including the procedures with respect to subsequent events) revealed any matters that might have a material effect on the financial statements reported on by the predecessor auditor or would require disclosure. (6033)

52. (a) The date of the prior period report should be used. A predecessor auditor's knowledge of the current affairs of his/her former client is obviously limited in the absence of a continuing relationship. Consequently, when reissuing a report on prior period financial statements, a predecessor auditor should use the date of her/his previous report to avoid any implication that s/he has examined any records, transactions, or events after that date. If the predecessor auditor revises her/his report or if the financial statements are restated, s/he should dual date the report. (0352)

53. (d) A predecessor auditor who reissues a report because the audit client desires comparative statements should not refer in her/his reissued report to the report or work of the successor auditor. (0334)

54. (c) If the financial statements of a prior period have been audited by a predecessor auditor whose standard report is not presented, the successor auditor should indicate in the *introductory* paragraph of her/ his report that the financial statements of the prior period were audited by another auditor, the date of the predecessor's report, and that an unqualified opinion was expressed. If the predecessor's report was other than a standard (unqualified) report, the nature of and reasons for the explanatory paragraph that was part of the predecessor's report or the predecessor's opinion qualification should also be included in the *introductory* paragraph of the successor's report. An explanatory paragraph is not required and no assurance on the prior year's statements is given. The predecessor auditor's knowledge of the current affairs of a former client is obviously limited so a letter of representation

as described in answer "d" is nonsensical. If the predecessor's report was reissued (not the case here), the predecessor auditor would obtain a letter from the successor auditor as to whether the successor's audit revealed any issues that might materially affect the prior year's financial statements.

(7635)

Dating

55. (b) When using dual dating, the auditor's responsibility for events occurring subsequent to the original report date is limited to the specific event disclosed. (5140)

56. (d) Use of the original report date in a reissued report removes any implication that records, transactions, or events after that date have been examined or reviewed. (4731)

57. (a) When the financial statements are adjusted without disclosure for a subsequent event that occurs after the date of the independent auditor's report but before its issuance, the report should ordinarily be dated no earlier than when the auditor has obtained sufficient appropriate audit evidence to support the opinion. If adjustment *and* disclosure are made or if adjustment is not made (and the auditor qualifies his/her opinion), the auditor can either dual date or use the later date (of the subsequent event). If the later date is used, the auditor's responsibility for subsequent events extends to this date and thus s/he should extend / perform "subsequent period" audit procedures to that date. (2765)

Subsequent Events

58. (b) Informing third parties is appropriate only when the audit committee (a committee of the board of directors) fails to take appropriate action.

(6848)

59. (d) One of the auditor's procedures to determine the occurrence of subsequent events that may require adjustment or disclosure is asking management if any unusual adjustments were made after year-end. Confirming a sample of accounts receivable established after year-end is usually done to determine if proper cutoff was made. Comparison between the current and the prior year financial statements is unlikely to uncover evidence about the occurrence of subsequent events—rather a comparison of the current statements to the latest interim statements and an analysis those interim statements should be done. Investigating personnel changes in the accounting department occurring after year-end would be more likely when possible misconduct, rather than a subsequent event, is being considered.

(6003)

60. (d) Two types of subsequent events require consideration by management and evaluation by the auditor. This is an example of the second type which does not result in adjustment of the current financial statements because the condition did not exist at the balance sheet date. However, as it is described as "material", it should be disclosed to keep the current financial statements from being misleading. Consistency refers to changes in accounting principles or adjustments to correct misstatements rather than the occurrence of subsequent events.

(4718)

61. (c) This is an example of a type II subsequent event which do not result in adjustment of the current financial statements because the condition did not exist at the balance sheet date. However, because of its nature, the auditor should advise management to disclose it in the notes to the current financial statements so they are not misleading. The opinion paragraph should not be modified—the auditor may include an explanatory paragraph if s/he wishes to emphasize it by directing attention to the disclosure in the notes to the financial statements. Management, not the auditor, is responsible for issuing the financial statements (and *pro forma* financial statements), including appropriate disclosures. (0372)

62. (d) This "subsequent period" extends to the date of the auditor's report. (0381)

Subsequent Discovery of Facts

63. (b) Management represents that it has informed the auditor of all related parties in its representation letter to the auditor and that it has disclosed all material related party transactions in financial statements by claiming those statements to be in accordance with GAAP. To discover that related party transactions existed at the date of the audit report that the auditor did not know about calls into question either the thoroughness of the audit or management's integrity. The postreport resolution of a lawsuit properly reported in the financial statements, technological advancements, and subsidiary sales occurring after the date of the auditor's report generally require no action by the auditor. (7819)

64. (a) After the date of the report, the auditor has no obligation to make any further or continuing inquiry or perform any other auditing procedures with respect to the audited financial statements covered by that report, unless new information which may affect the report becomes known by the auditor.

(2288)

65. (a) After determining that information regarding subsequent discovery of facts is reliable, the auditor next determines if people are relying on the information who would believe the information is important. (5162)

Consideration of Omitted Procedures

66. (b) If the auditor concludes that the omission of a procedure considered necessary at the time of the audit in the circumstances then existing impairs her/his present ability to support the previously expressed opinion regarding the financial statements, and the auditor believes there are persons currently relying on the report, s/he should promptly undertake to apply the omitted procedure or alternative procedures that would provide a satisfactory basis for the opinion. Answer (a) is a procedure to be followed when the auditor determines, after attempting to perform procedures, that an unqualified opinion is inappropriate. Answer (c) would not be feasible and would not eliminate the need to perform some auditing procedures beyond tests of controls. Answer (d) would not be an alternative in any situation. (4735)

67. (a) When an auditor concludes that an audit procedure considered necessary has been omitted, the first concern should be to determine whether the previously issued opinion can still be supported. A review of the working papers, discussion of the circumstances with engagement personnel and others, and a reevaluation of the overall scope of the audit may be helpful in making this assessment. If the opinion can still be supported, no further action is necessary. Otherwise, if the auditor believes there are persons relying on the report, then the auditor must promptly undertake the omitted procedures or alternative procedures. A determination of whether or not there are persons relying on the report would provide no evidence to the auditor in assessing the importance of the omitted procedure. (0371)

68. (c) The results of other procedures that were applied during the audit may tend to compensate for the one omitted or make its omission less important. The distribution of the report, the type of the opinion, or client delays do not reduce the auditor's responsibility to perform omitted procedures if the auditor's present ability to support the previously expressed opinion is impaired. (5703)

69. (b) If the auditor concludes that the omission of a procedure considered necessary at the time of the audit in the circumstances then existing impairs her/his present ability to support her/his previously expressed opinion regarding the financial statements taken as a whole, and s/he believes there are persons currently relying, or likely to rely, on the report, s/he should promptly undertake to apply the omitted procedure or alternative procedures that would provide a satisfactory basis for her/his opinion. (2786)

Association With Financial Statements

70. (d) When an accountant is associated with the financial statements of a public entity, but has not audited or reviewed them and thus disclaims an opinion, s/he has no responsibility to apply any procedures beyond reading the financial statements for obvious material misstatements. (2755)

71. (d) A disclaimer of opinion is the appropriate report in this situation. (5149)

72. (c) If the accountant concludes that the unaudited financial statements on which s/he is disclaiming an opinion are not in conformity with GAAP in that they do not include adequate disclosure, s/he should suggest appropriate revision; failing that, s/he should describe the departure in the disclaimer of opinion. This description should refer specifically to the lack of disclosure and include the necessary information for adequate disclosure. The auditor cannot accept the client's inaction. When a disclaimer of opinion is appropriate, it cannot be replaced with another type of opinion. (7505)

Going Concern

73. (d) The entity's legal counsel may provide information about the probability of litigation, claims, and assessments that could possibly cause the company to cease to exist. The procedures in answers (a), (b), and (c) would not provide evidence of an entity's inability to continue as a going concern. Performing cutoff tests provides evidence about whether account balances are stated accurately. Evaluating procedures concerning related party transactions would provide evidence of proper disclosure of such transactions. Real property pledged as collateral does not necessarily indicate a cause for concern. (8153)

74. (c) In this situation, an auditor's consideration of management's plans may include plans to dispose of assets, restructure debt, reduce expenditures, and increase ownership equity. (7026)

75. (b) When the auditor concludes there is substantial doubt about the entity's ability to continue as a going concern for a reasonable period of time, the auditor should consider the possible effects on the financial statements and the adequacy of the

related disclosure. The auditor would not issue a qualified or adverse opinion unless the auditor concludes that the entity's disclosure with respect to the ability to continue as a going concern is inadequate. The auditor may report such adjustments to the audit committee; however, further action is required to deal specifically with the going concern issue, regardless of the changes to any accounting estimates. Substantial doubt about the entity's ability to continue as a going concern for a reasonable period of time that arose in the current period does not imply that a basis for such doubt existed in the prior period and should not affect the auditor's report on the financial statements of the prior period presented on a comparative basis. (4727)

76. (c) The terms *substantial doubt* and *going concern* are required. (6631)

77. (a) If substantial doubt about the entity's ability to continue as a going concern existed at the date of prior period financial statements that are presented on a comparative basis, and that doubt has been removed in the current period, the explanatory paragraph included in the auditor's report (following the opinion paragraph) should not be repeated. A different explanatory paragraph is not required. (6020)

78. (c) It is not necessary to design audit procedures *solely* to identify conditions and events that, when considered in the aggregate, indicate there could be substantial doubt about the entity's ability to continue as a going concern for a reasonable period of time. The results of auditing procedures designed and performed to achieve other audit objectives should be sufficient for that purpose. There is no requirement that the auditor's workpapers include evidence which provides assurance that the entity will continue as a going concern. The fact that the entity may cease to exist as a going concern subsequent to receiving a report from the auditor that does not refer to substantial doubt, even within one year following the date of the financial statements, does not, in itself, indicate inadequate performance by the auditor. Accordingly, the absence of reference to substantial doubt in an auditor's report should not be viewed as providing assurance as to an entity's ability to continue as a going concern. (The auditor is not responsible for predicting future conditions or events.) *A reasonable period of time* is defined as not to exceed one year *beyond* the date of the financial statements. (7506)

79. (b) Confirmation with related and third parties of the details of arrangements to provide or maintain financial support is an audit procedure which may identify conditions and events that may indicate substantial doubt about the entity's ability to continue as a going concern. Pledging assets as collateral does not indicate an inability to continue as a going concern. The other two auditing procedures described ("c" and "d") would not provide evidence about an entity's ability to continue as a going concern. (4720)

80. (c) Possible plans to mitigate the adverse effects of future conditions and events may include: *reducing* or *delaying* expenditures such as leasing instead of purchasing operating facilities; *increasing* ownership equity; and borrowing money or restructuring debt. Issuing stock options would only cost the company money if they were exercised rather than mitigate the situation. (8129)

81. (b) Going concern issues alone do not affect an unqualified opinion. However, if the auditor concludes that the entity's disclosures regarding its ability to continue as a going concern are inadequate, misleading, or depart from GAAP, a qualified or an adverse opinion should be issued. Answers (a) and (d) are conditions that cause doubt about an entity's ability to continue as a going concern. Management does not need to have plans to reduce or delay future expenditures; this also may be a cause for concern, but does not require a qualified opinion. (8123)

82. (b) Denial of usual trade credit from suppliers may drive a business into bankruptcy, even if it wasn't floundering previously. As suppliers have the conflicting goals of selling as much as possible, but extending credit only to creditworthy customers, they remain cognizant of the recent payment history of their debtors. Related party transactions and restrictions on the disposal of assets are commonly encountered in healthy businesses. The payment of arrearages in preferred stock dividends are generally made only when "surplus" money is available. (6630)

Other Information in Documents Containing Audited Financial Statements

83. (a) One of the auditor's alternatives in this situation is to include an explanatory paragraph in her/his report describing the material inconsistency. The addition of this paragraph would not affect the auditor's opinion. The auditor may also decide to withhold the use of her/his report in the document or withdraw from the engagement—the auditor should

not consider the matter closed. A qualified opinion of a disclaimer of opinion would not be appropriate.
(5159)

84. (a) When reporting on additional information included in auditor-submitted documents, the measurement of materiality is the same as that used in forming an opinion on the basic financial statements taken as a whole. Accordingly, the auditor need not apply procedures as extensive as would be necessary to express an opinion on the information taken by itself. (4728)

85. (d) When the auditor concludes that a material inconsistency exists, the auditor must decide whether the financial statements, the report, or both require revision. If the auditor decides that they do not, but that the other information does require revision, the client should be requested to revise the other information. If the client refuses, the auditor should consider revising the report to describe the material inconsistency, withholding the use of the report in the document, and, possibly, withdrawing from the engagement. (8147)

Required Supplementary Information

86. (d) Because the required supplementary information does not change the standards of financial accounting and reporting used for the preparation of the entity's basic financial statements, the auditor's opinion on the fairness of presentation of such financial statements in conformity with GAAP is not affected. Then auditor should issue an unqualified opinion with an additional explanatory paragraph. (0399)

87. (b) Required supplementary information differs from other types of information outside the basic financial statements because the FASB, GASB or FASAB considers the information an essential part of the financial reporting of certain entities and because authoritative guidelines for the measurement and presentation of the information have been established. Accordingly, the auditor should apply certain limited procedures to required supplementary information and should report deficiencies in, or the omission of, such information. (7642)

Solution 28-2 ADDITIONAL MULTIPLE CHOICE ANSWERS

Reporting Standards

88. (d) The first reporting standard is construed to require an opinion by the auditor as to whether the financial statements are presented in accordance with GAAP rather than a statement of fact. The auditor must also judge whether the financial statements are presented fairly within the framework of GAAP, not some implied measure of fairness. The audit report contains the auditor's *subjective* opinion concerning the financial statement presentation.
(7507)

Types of Opinions

89. (b) When financial statements are materially affected by a departure from GAAP and the auditor has audited the statements in accordance with GAAS, the auditor should express a qualified or an adverse opinion. Answer (a) describes a scope limitation which would ordinarily result in a qualified opinion or a disclaimer of opinion. Answer (c) describes a limited reporting engagement and could result in any of the reporting opinions. Answer (d) is an example of a situation where the auditor is required to add an explanatory paragraph to an unqualified opinion (as long as adequate disclosure is made) or may disclaim an opinion. (3954)

90. (a) The auditor's standard report implies that the auditor is satisfied that the statements are consistent with respect to GAAP, and such principles have been consistently applied between periods. Use of different cost principles for different inventories is not inherently inconsistent. (6014)

91. (b) Whenever an auditor concludes that an illegal act has a material effect on the financial statements, and the act has not been properly accounted for or disclosed, the auditor should express a qualified or an adverse opinion, depending on the materiality of the effect on the statements. An unqualified opinion with an explanatory paragraph is not appropriate. A disclaimer of opinion generally would be appropriate if the auditor is precluded by the client from obtaining sufficient appropriate audit evidence to determine if such an illegal act has occurred or is likely to have occurred—this is not the case described. (5631)

Standard Report

92. (d) An unqualified opinion states that the financial statements present fairly, in all material respects, the financial position, results of operations, and cash flows in conformity with GAAP. Disclosure, per the third standard of reporting, is not explicitly mentioned unless it is found to be inadequate.
(0363)

Departure From GAAP

93.   (b)   Rule 203 of the AICPA Code of Professional Conduct requires members to follow GAAP whenever possible. However, if the statements contain a departure from GAAP and it can be shown that due to unusual circumstances the financial statements would otherwise be misleading, the member can comply with the rule by describing the departure, its approximate effects, if practicable, and the reasons why compliance with the principle would result in a misleading statement. This should be done in a separate paragraph, or paragraphs, of the auditor's report, and it is appropriate for an unqualified opinion to be expressed.   (0329)

Consistency

94.   (b)   In this case, the auditor was able to extend auditing procedures to gather sufficient evidence about consistency, so an unqualified opinion can be expressed and there should be no reference to consistency in the auditor's report. Per the second reporting standard, the standard report *implies* that the auditor is satisfied that the comparability of financial statements between periods has not been materially affected by changes in accounting principles and that such principles have been consistently applied. There is no reason to exclude the income statement. The consistency standard does apply in first-year audits. When the independent auditor has not audited the financial statements of a company for the preceding year, the auditor should adopt procedures that are practicable and reasonable in the circumstances to assure the auditor that the accounting principles employed are consistent between the current and the preceding year. When adequate records have been maintained by the client, it is usually practicable to gather sufficient appropriate audit evidence about consistency.

(6021)

Scope Limitation

95.   (c)   When restrictions that significantly limit the scope of the audit are imposed by the client, ordinarily the auditor should disclaim an opinion on the financial statements. The auditor should review the minutes of board of director's meetings for information about material transactions authorized or discussed at the meetings. Answer (a) contemplates a departure from GAAP, not a scope limitation. The auditor is not precluded from reporting on financial statements prepared in accordance with the cash receipts and disbursements basis of accounting. Answer (b) is simply an example of an other comprehensive basis of accounting and would require a special report. The auditor is not precluded from

reporting on one basic financial statement and not on the others. This is a limited reporting engagement and does not involve a scope limitation if the auditor's access to information underlying the basic financial statements is not limited and if s/he is able to apply all necessary procedures.   (0345)

96.   (d)   When disclaiming an opinion because of a scope limitation, the auditor should not identify the procedures that were performed nor include the paragraph describing the characteristics of an audit, i.e., the scope paragraph; to do so may tend to overshadow the disclaimer. The disclaimer of opinion paragraph replaces the opinion paragraph.

(4283)

97.   (a)   A disclaimer is appropriate when the auditor has not performed an audit sufficient in scope to enable her/him to form an opinion on the financial statements. The only viable alternative answer would be a qualified opinion; however, common restrictions on the scope of the audit include those applying to the observation of physical inventories and the confirmation of accounts receivable by direct communication with debtors. Restrictions on the application of these or other audit procedures to important elements of the financial statements require the auditor to decide whether s/he has examined sufficient appropriate audit evidence to permit her/him to express an unqualified or qualified opinion, or whether s/he should disclaim an opinion. When restrictions that significantly limit the scope of the audit are imposed by the client, ordinarily the auditor should disclaim an opinion on the financial statements. Inventories that account for 40% of a retail entity's assets are sufficiently significant to warrant a disclaimer.   (7641)

Disclaimer of Opinion

98.   (b)   An unjustified accounting change would require that the auditor express a qualified or adverse opinion. Answers (a), (b), and (c) represent various restrictions of the scope of the audit. A restriction of the scope of the audit, whether imposed by the client or circumstances, may require the auditor to express a qualified opinion or a disclaimer of opinion.   (6013)

Comparative Financial Statements

99.   (d)   If the financial statements of a prior period have been audited by a predecessor auditor whose report is not presented, the successor auditor should indicate in the introductory paragraph of the report that the financial statements of the prior period were audited by another auditor, the date of that report, the type of report issued by the predecessor auditor, and if the report was other than a

standard report, the substantive reasons therefor. The successor auditor should not name the predecessor auditor in the report. (6023)

Dating

100. (c)   The auditor's report should not be dated earlier than the date on which the auditor has obtained sufficient appropriate audit evidence to support the opinion. (0386)

101. (a)   The auditor may use *dual dating,* for example, February 16, 20__, except for Note __, as to which the date is March 1, 20__, or may date the report as of the later date. In the former instance, the responsibility for events occurring subsequent to the original report date is limited to the specific event referred to in the note (or otherwise disclosed). In the latter instance, the independent auditor's responsibility for subsequent events extends to the date of the report. (7625)

Subsequent Events

102. (b)   Certain procedures are performed after the balance sheet date: (1) check for proper cutoff; (2) confirm balances that were unknown until after the balance sheet date; and (3) obtain a management representation letter. Although other procedures are performed if warranted, additional procedures generally include inquiries and reading interim statements and minutes of meetings. Examining internal controls in the next fiscal period and recomputing amounts applicable to the next fiscal period typically are beyond the scope of this work. If tests of controls indicate significant deficiencies in internal controls, those tests are unlikely to be performed again. (7818)

Consideration of Omitted Procedures

103. (c)   When the auditor concludes that an auditing procedure considered necessary at the time of the audit in the circumstances then existing was omitted from her/his audit of financial statements, s/he should assess the importance of the omitted procedure to her/his present ability to support her/his previously expressed opinion regarding those financial statements taken as a whole. Answers (a), (b), and (d) are steps that can be performed after the required assessment. (0332)

104. (d)   Upon concluding that an auditing procedure was omitted, the auditor should first assess the importance of the omitted procedure to the auditor's present ability to support the previously expressed opinion. Procedures that were performed may compensate for the omitted procedure. If the auditor can support the previously expressed opinion without the omitted procedure, further procedures are unnecessary. If the auditor's ability to support the previously expressed opinion is impaired and the auditor believes there are persons currently relying, or likely to rely, on the report, the auditor should apply the omitted procedures or alternative procedures. The auditor, not management, determines whether there are persons currently relying, or likely to rely, on the report. (7823)

Going Concern

105. (a)   The minutes of meetings of stockholders and the board of directors are likely to contain clear indications of doubts about the entity's ability to continue as a going concern. Comparisons of market value of property and related loans don't focus on the financial condition of the entity as a whole; many assets—such as relationships with customers and suppliers—are very valuable, and yet do not appear on the balance sheet. Lease agreements rarely highlight financial distress. Assets often are pledged as collateral by entities in strong financial condition. (7807)

106. (a)   Negative cash flows from operating activities is an example of a condition that, when considered with other events, may indicate there is substantial doubt about an entity's ability to continue as a going concern. (5144)

107. (d)   The terms substantial doubt and going concern should be used in a phrase similar to substantial doubt about its ability to continue as a going concern. Neither phrase given as an answer alternative is required. (6019)

Other Information in Documents Containing Audited Financial Statements

108. (d)   The auditor's responsibility with respect to information in a document does not extend beyond the financial information identified in her/his report, and the auditor has no obligation to perform any procedures to corroborate other information contained in a document. However, s/he should read the other information and consider whether such information, or the manner of its presentation, is materially inconsistent with information, or the manner of its presentation, appearing in the financial statements. The auditor has no obligation to perform inquiry, analytical procedures, or other substantive auditing procedures to corroborate other information in a document. An explanatory paragraph would only be considered if the auditor concludes that there is a material inconsistency in the other information, and the other

information is not revised to eliminate the material inconsistency. (2991)

109. (a) The auditor first requests the client to revise the other information. Only if the client refuses would the auditor consider revising the report to describe the material inconsistency, withholding the use of the report in the document, or possibly, withdrawing from the engagement. A representation letter acknowledging the inconsistency would not adequately protect the public interest; thus, this option would never be appropriate resolution of such an issue. (8399)

Required Supplementary information

110. (d) Required supplementary information (RSI) differs from other types of information outside the basic financial statements because the GASB considers the information an essential part of the financial reporting of certain entities and because authoritative guidelines for the measurement and presentation of the information have been established. Accordingly, the auditor should apply certain limited procedures to RSI and should report deficiencies in, or the omission of, such information. One of the procedures the auditor ordinarily should apply is to compare the RSI for consistency with audited statements. Because the RSI is not audited and is not a required part of the basic financial statements, the auditor need not add an explanatory paragraph to the report on the audited financial statements to refer to the RSI or to her/his limited procedures, as long as the auditor is able to apply the procedures needed to determine that the RSI is presented appropriately. The objective of an audit of financial statements in accordance with generally accepted auditing standards is the expression of an opinion on such statements. The auditor has no responsibility to *audit* information outside the basic financial statements in accordance with generally accepted auditing standards. However, as described above, the auditor does have certain responsibilities with respect to information outside the financial statements. (8386)

PERFORMANCE BY SUBTOPICS

Each category below parallels a subtopic covered in Chapter 28. Record the number and percentage of questions you correctly answered in each subtopic area.

Reporting Standards

Question #	Correct	√
1		
2		
3		
# Questions	3	
# Correct		
% Correct		

Types of Opinions

Question #	Correct	√
4		
5		
6		
7		
8		
9		
10		
11		
12		
# Questions	9	
# Correct		
% Correct		

Standard Report

Question #	Correct	√
13		
14		
15		
16		
17		
18		
19		
# Questions	7	
# Correct		
% Correct		

Explanatory Language

Question #	Correct	√
20		
21		
22		
# Questions	3	
# Correct		
% Correct		

Another Auditor

Question #	Correct	√
23		
24		
25		
# Questions	3	
# Correct		
% Correct		

Departure From GAAP

Question #	Correct	√
26		
27		
# Questions	2	
# Correct		
% Correct		

Consistency

Question #	Correct	√
28		
29		
30		
31		
32		
# Questions	5	
# Correct		
% Correct		

Uncertainty

Question #	Correct	√
33		
34		
# Questions	2	
# Correct		
% Correct		

Emphasis

Question #	Correct	√
35		
# Questions	1	
# Correct		
% Correct		

Qualified Opinion

Question #	Correct	√
36		
37		
38		
39		
40		
# Questions	5	
# Correct		
% Correct		

Scope Limitation

Question #	Correct	√
41		
42		
43		
44		
45		
# Questions	5	
# Correct		
% Correct		

Inadequate Disclosure

Question #	Correct	√
46		
47		
# Questions	2	
# Correct		
% Correct		

Adverse Opinion

Question #	Correct	√
48		
# Questions	1	
# Correct		
% Correct		

Disclaimer of Opinion

Question #	Correct	√
49		
# Questions	1	
# Correct		
% Correct		

Comparative Financial Statements

Question #	Correct	√
50		
51		
52		
53		
54		
# Questions	5	
# Correct		
% Correct		

Dating

Question #	Correct	√
55		
56		
57		
# Questions	3	
# Correct		
% Correct		

Subsequent Events

Question #	Correct	√
58		
59		
60		
61		
62		
# Questions	5	
# Correct		
% Correct		

Subsequent Discovery of Facts

Question #	Correct	√
63		
64		
65		
# Questions	3	
# Correct		
% Correct		

Consideration of Omitted Procedures

Question #	Correct	√
66		
67		
68		
69		
# Questions	4	
# Correct		
% Correct		

Association With Financial Statements

Question #	Correct	√
70		
71		
72		
# Questions	3	
# Correct		
% Correct		

Going Concern

Question #	Correct	√
73		
74		
75		
76		
77		
78		
79		
80		
81		
82		
# Questions	10	
# Correct		
% Correct		

Other Information in Documents Containing Audited Financial Statements

Question #	Correct	√
83		
84		
85		
# Questions	3	
# Correct		
% Correct		

Required Supplementary Information

Question #	Correct	√
86		
87		
# Questions	2	
# Correct		
% Correct		

SIMULATION SOLUTIONS

Solution 28-3

Response #1: Types of Opinions (5 points)

1. F

Restrictions on the scope of an auditor's audit, whether imposed by the client or by the circumstances, such as an inability to obtain sufficient appropriate audit evidence, or an inadequacy in the accounting records, may require the auditor to qualify her/his opinion or to disclaim an opinion. Further, a common scope restriction involves accounting for long-term investments when the auditor has not been able to obtain audited financial statements of an investee.

2. B

A substantial doubt about an entity's ability to continue as a going concern is one of the circumstances which does not affect the auditor's unqualified opinion, but does require the addition of an explanatory paragraph *after* the opinion paragraph.

3. B

If the principal auditor is able to satisfy her/himself as to the independence and professional reputation of the other auditor and takes steps considered appropriate to satisfy her/himself as to the audit performed by the other auditor, s/he may express an unqualified opinion on the financial statements taken as a whole.

4. A

The auditor is not required to prepare a basic financial statement and include it in her/his report if the company's management declines to present the statement. Accordingly, the auditor should issue an "except for" qualified opinion.

5. B

Since the auditor concurs with the change in accounting principle, s/he does not take exception to the change in expressing her/his opinion as to fair presentation of the financial statements in conformity with generally accepted accounting principles. Therefore, the auditor may express an unqualified opinion.

6. B

If, after considering existing conditions and available evidence, the auditor concludes that sufficient audit evidence supports management's assertions about an uncertainty and its presentation or disclosure, an unqualified opinion ordinarily is appropriate.

7. E

When financial statements are materially affected by a departure from generally accepted accounting principles and the auditor has audited the statements in accordance with generally accepted auditing standards, s/he should express a qualified or an adverse opinion. Factors to consider when deciding whether to issue either of these two opinions include the dollar magnitude of the effect, the qualitative and quantitative aspects of the departure, the pervasiveness of the misstatement, and the effects on the other financial statements.

Response #2: Reporting Fraud (4 points)

a. If Post discovers that General's financial statements may be materially misstated due to the **existence of fraud**, Post should consider the **implications** for other aspects of the audit and discuss the matter and approach to further investigation with an **appropriate level of management that is at least one level above those involved** with the fraud. Post should also attempt to obtain sufficient appropriate audit evidence to determine whether, in fact, material fraud exist and, if so, their effect. Post may suggest that General **consult with its legal counsel** on matters concerning questions of law.

b. If Post is precluded from applying necessary procedures, Post should **disclaim or qualify** the financial statements and communicate these findings to General's audit committee or its board of directors.

Response #3: Research (1 point)

Paragraph Reference Answer: AU 623.04

Guidance: AU 623.04 states, "For purposes of this section, a comprehensive basis of accounting other than generally accepted accounting principles is one of the following—(a) A basis of accounting that the reporting entity uses to comply with the requirements or financial reporting provisions of a governmental regulatory agency to whose jurisdiction the entity is subject. An example is a basis of accounting insurance companies use pursuant to the rules of a state insurance commission; (b) A basis of accounting that the reporting entity uses or expects to use to file its income tax return for the period covered by the financial statements; (c) The cash receipts and disbursements basis of accounting, and modifications of the cash basis having substantial support, such as recording depreciation on fixed assets or accruing income taxes; [or] (d) A definite set of criteria having substantial support that is applied to all material items appearing in financial statements, such as the price-level basis of accounting. Unless one of the foregoing descriptions applies, reporting under the provisions of paragraph .05 is not permitted."

(7543)

Solution 28-4

Response #1: Report Deficiencies (5 points)

1. P

A division of responsibility is indicated in the introductory paragraph including the significance of the portion of the entity audited by another auditor. Either the amount or the percentage of total assets and revenues that are reflected in the subsidiary's statements are adequate.

2. B

A division of responsibility is indicated in the introductory paragraph including the significance of the portion of the entity audited by another auditor. The scope and opinion paragraphs are also modified to refer to the other auditor.

3. P

The phrase, "whether caused by error or fraud," is not part of the standard auditor's report.

4. W

The phrase, "significant estimates made by management," is included in the scope paragraph of the standard report.

5. W

Control risk is not mentioned in the standard report on financial statements. The scenario did not describe this as an audit of ICFR that was integrated with an audit of financial statements.

6. W

The phrase, "evaluating the overall financial statement presentation" is included in the scope paragraph of the standard report.

7. P

As the investigation is adequately disclosed in the notes to the financial statements, it need not be mentioned in the auditor's report. If the auditor wanted to emphasize this matter and yet still issue an unqualified opinion, the auditor would mention it in an explanatory paragraph following the opinion paragraph.

8. P

If an auditor had previously qualified the opinion on the financial statements of a prior period because of a departure from GAAP, and the prior period financial statements are restated in the current period, the updating report should indicate that the statements have been restated in a paragraph preceding the opinion paragraph.

Response #2: Other Auditors (4 points)

In order for May & Marty to satisfy itself about the independence and professional reputation of Dey & Dee and assure itself that there has been coordination of activities between the two auditors in order to achieve a proper review of matters affecting consolidation, May & Marty, whether or not it makes reference to Dey & Dee's audit, should consider performing the following procedures:

Make **inquiries about the professional reputation** and standing of Dey & Dee to one or more of the following:

- AICPA, applicable state society of CPAs, and/or local chapter.
- Other appropriate sources such as other practitioners, bankers, and other credit grantors.

Obtain a representation from Dey & Dee that it is independent under the requirements of the AICPA and, if appropriate, the requirements of the SEC. Ascertain through **communication with Dey & Dee that**

- Dey & Dee is aware that the **BGI-Western financial statements are to be included** in the BGI consolidated financial statements on which May & Marty will report, and that **Dey & Dee's report will be relied upon** by May & Marty.
- Dey & Dee is familiar with GAAP and GAAS and will conduct its audit in accordance therewith.
- Dey & Dee has **knowledge of the relevant financial reporting requirements** for statements and schedules to be filed with regulatory agencies such as the SEC, if appropriate.
- A **review will be made of matters affecting elimination of intercompany transactions and accounts** and, if appropriate in the circumstances, the uniformity of accounting practices among components included in the financial statements.

(6717)

Solution 28-5

Deficiencies in Miller's draft are as follows:

Within the opening (introductory) paragraph

- The **statement of cash flows** is not identified in this paragraph or in the opinion paragraph.
- The financial statements are not stated to be the **responsibility of management**.
- The magnitude of the portion of the consolidated financial statements audited by the **other auditors** is not disclosed.
- Smith **may not be named** in this paragraph or in the opinion paragraph unless Smith's report is presented together with Pell's report.

Within the second (scope) paragraph

- The statement "An audit includes examining, on a test basis, evidence supporting the amounts and disclosures in the financial statements" is omitted.
- It is inappropriate to state that an audit includes "assessing control risk."
- Reference to the audit of the other auditors as part of the basis for the opinion is omitted.

Within the third (opinion) paragraph

- Use of the phrase **"except for the matter discussed below"** is inappropriate.
- Reference to **"conformity with generally accepted accounting principles"** is omitted.

Within the fourth (explanatory) paragraph

- The terms **"substantial doubt"** and **"going concern"** are omitted.

Paragraph Reference Answer: AU 411.02

Guidance: AU 411.02 states, "The first standard of reporting requires an auditor who has audited financial statements in accordance with generally accepted auditing standards to state in the auditor's report whether the statements are presented in conformity with generally accepted accounting principles. The phrase "generally accepted accounting principles" is a technical accounting term that encompasses the conventions, rules, and procedures necessary to define accepted accounting practice at a particular time. It includes not only broad guidelines of general application, but also detailed practices and procedures. Those conventions, rules, and procedures provide a standard by which to measure financial presentations."

(6718)

Solution 28-6

1. E

When a qualified opinion results from a limitation on the scope of the audit or an insufficiency of audit evidence, the situation should be described in an explanatory paragraph preceding the opinion paragraph and referred to in both the scope and opinion paragraphs of the auditor's report.

2. B

If, after considering identified conditions and events and management's plans, the auditor concludes that substantial doubt about the entity's ability to continue as a going concern for a reasonable period of time remains, the audit report should include an explanatory paragraph (following the opinion paragraph) to reflect that conclusion. Inadequate disclosure with respect to an entity's ability to continue as a going concern is a departure from GAAP, resulting in either an "except for" qualified opinion or an adverse opinion. In this case, however, because it was concluded that financial statement disclosures were adequate, an unqualified opinion with an explanatory paragraph is appropriate.

3. J

If the auditor decides that it is appropriate for her/him to serve as the principal auditor, s/he must then decide whether to make reference in her/his report to the audit performed by another auditor. If the principal auditor decides to assume responsibility for the work of the other auditor insofar as that work relates to the principal auditor's expression of an opinion taken as a whole, no reference should be made to the other auditor's work or report.

4. C

The auditor is not required to prepare a basic financial statement and include it in her/his report if the company's management declines to present the statement. Accordingly, the auditor should issue an "except for" qualified opinion. The circumstances surrounding the qualification are to be reported in a separate paragraph preceding the opinion paragraph. The opinion paragraph should then be modified using the appropriate "except for" wording, making reference to the separate explanatory paragraph.

5. B

Changes in accounting principle having a material effect on the financial statements require recognition in the independent auditor's report through the addition of an explanatory paragraph (following the opinion paragraph). Such explanatory paragraph should identify the nature of the change and refer the reader to the note in the financial statements that discusses the change in detail.

6. J

Circumstances that may require the auditor to add an explanatory paragraph to a standard report, while not precluding an unqualified opinion, do not include an uncertainty. An emphasis paragraph may be added. However, emphasis paragraphs are never required; they may be added solely at the auditor's discretion.

7. C

The auditor should disclose, in a separate explanatory paragraph preceding the opinion paragraph, all the substantive reasons for a departure from generally accepted accounting principles and that the opinion paragraph should include appropriate qualifying language.

Response #2: Communication (4 points)

a. If Post concludes that General's financial statements **are materially affected** by fraud, Post should insist that the **financial statements be revised** and, if they are not, express a **qualified** or an **adverse** opinion on the financial statements, disclosing all the substantive reasons for such an opinion. Additionally, Post should adequately inform General's audit committee or its board of directors about the fraud.

b. Post may have a duty to disclose fraud to **third parties** outside General's management and its audit committee in the following circumstances:

- When General reports an auditor change under the appropriate securities law.
- When a successor auditor appropriately makes inquiries of a predecessor auditor.
- When responding to a subpoena.
- When communicating with a funding or other specified agency, as required for entities that receive financial assistance from a government agency.

Response #3: Research (1 point)

Paragraph Reference Answer: AU 508.33

Guidance: AU 508.33 states, "*Limited reporting engagements.* The auditor may be asked to report on one basic financial statement and not on the others. For example, he or she may be asked to report on the balance sheet and not on the statements of income, retained earnings or cash flows. These engagements do not involve scope limitations if the auditor's access to information underlying the basic financial statements is not limited and if the auditor applies all the procedures he considers necessary in the circumstances; rather, such engagements involve limited reporting objectives."

(6719)

Solution 28-7

Response #1: Deficiencies: Uncertainty & Accounting Change (9 points)

Deficiencies in the auditors' report are as follows:

First (Introductory) Paragraph

1. The **statement of retained earnings** is not identified.
2. The auditor's **responsibility to express an opinion** is omitted.

Second (Scope) Paragraph

3. The auditor obtains reasonable assurance about whether the financial statements are **"free of material misstatement,"** not **"fairly presented."**
4. The auditors' **assessment of the accounting principles** used is omitted.
5. An audit provides a **"reasonable basis for an opinion,"** not a "basis for determining whether any material modifications should be made."

Third (First Explanatory) Paragraph

6. An explanatory paragraph added to the report to describe a change in accounting principle (lack of consistency) should **follow the opinion paragraph**, not precede it.

Fourth (Opinion) Paragraph

7. The phrase **"except for" should not be used**.
8. The auditor's **concurrence** with the change in accounting principles **is implicit** and should **not be mentioned**.
9. **Reference to the prior year's** financial statements is omitted.

Fifth (Second Explanatory) Paragraph

10. The **fact that the outcome** of the lawsuit **cannot presently be estimated is omitted**.

11. It is inappropriate to state that **"provision for any liability is subject to adjudication"** because the report is **ambiguous** as to whether a liability has been recorded.

Response #2: Research (1 point)

Paragraph Reference Answer: QC 10.45

Guidance: QC 10.45 states, "In practice, the competency requirements necessary for the engagement partner are broad and varied in both their nature and number. Required competencies include the following, as well as other competencies as necessary in the circumstances.

- Understanding of the role of a system of quality control and the Code of Professional Conduct. An understanding of the role of a firm's system of quality control and the AICPA's Code of Professional Conduct, both of which play critical roles in assuring the integrity of the various kinds of reports.
- Understanding of the service to be performed. An understanding of the performance, supervision, and reporting aspects of the engagement. This understanding is usually gained through actual participation under appropriate supervision in that type of engagement.
- Technical proficiency. An understanding of the applicable professional standards including those standards directly related to the industry in which a client operates and the kinds of transactions in which a client engages.
- Familiarity with the industry. An understanding of the industry in which a client operates, to the extent required by professional standards applicable to the kind of service being performed. In performing an audit or review of financial statements, this understanding would include an industry's organization and operating characteristics sufficient to identify areas of high or unusual risk associated with an engagement and to evaluate the reasonableness of industry-specific estimates.
- Professional judgment. Skills that indicate sound professional judgment. In performing engagements covered by this section, such skills would typically include the ability to exercise professional skepticism and identify areas requiring special consideration including, for example, the evaluation of the reasonableness of estimates and representations made by management and

the determination of the kind of report appropriate in the circumstances.

- Understanding the organization's information technology systems. A sufficient understanding of how the organization is dependent on or enabled by information technologies and the manner in which the information systems are used to record and maintain financial information, to determine when involvement of an IT professional is necessary for an audit engagement."

(6720)

Solution 28-8

Response #1: Subsequent Events (9 points)

a. The first type of subsequent event includes those events that provide **additional evidence concerning conditions that existed at the balance sheet date** and affect the estimates inherent in the process of preparing financial statements. This type of subsequent event **requires that the financial statements** be adjusted for any changes in estimates resulting from the use of such additional evidence.

The second type of subsequent event consists of those events that provide evidence concerning conditions that did not exist at the balance sheet date but arose subsequent to that date. These events should not result in adjustment to the financial statements but may be such that disclosure is required to keep the financial statements from being misleading.

b. The auditing procedures Green should consider performing to gather evidence concerning subsequent events include the following:

- **Compare** the latest available **interim statements** with the financial statements being audited.
- Ascertain whether the **interim statements were prepared on the same basis** as the audited financial statements.
- Inquire whether any **contingent liabilities or commitments** existed at the balance sheet date or the date of inquiry.
- **Inquire** whether there was any significant **change** in the capital stock, long-term debt, or working capital to the date of inquiry.
- **Inquire** about the current status of **items** in the audited financial statements that were accounted for on the basis of **tentative, preliminary, or inconclusive data**.
- Inquire about any unusual adjustments made since the balance sheet date.
- **Read or inquire about** the **minutes** of meetings of stockholders or the board of directors.

- Inquire of the client's **legal counsel** concerning litigation, claims, and assessments.
- Obtain a **management representation letter**, dated as of the date of Green's report, as to whether any subsequent events would require adjustment or disclosure.
- Make such **additional inquiries or perform such additional procedures** Green considers necessary and appropriate.

Response #2: Research (1 point)

Paragraph Reference Answer: AU 508.12

Guidance: AU 508.12 states, "When the auditor decides to make reference to the report of another auditor as a basis, in part, for his or her opinion, he or she should disclose this fact in the introductory paragraph of his or her report and should refer to the report of the other auditor in expressing his or her opinion. These references indicate division of responsibility for performance of the audit."

(6721)

Solution 28-9

Response #1: Audit Report (9 points)

To the Board of Directors of National Motors, Inc.:

We have audited the consolidated balance sheet of National Motors, Inc. and subsidiaries as of December 31, Year 2, and the related consolidated statements of income, retained earnings, and cash flows for the year then ended. These financial statements are the responsibility of the Company's management. Our responsibility is to express an opinion on these financial statements based on our audit. **We did not audit** the financial statements of Rapid Parts Company, a consolidated subsidiary, which statements reflect total assets and revenues constituting 22 percent and 25 percent, respectively, of the related consolidated totals. **Those statements were audited by other auditors** whose report has been furnished to us, and **our opinion,** insofar as it relates to the amounts included for Rapid Parts Company, **is based solely upon the report of the other auditors**.

Except as explained in the following paragraph, we conducted our audit in accordance with generally accepted auditing standards. Those standards require that we plan and perform the audit to obtain **reasonable assurance** about whether the financial statements are free of material misstatement. An audit includes **examining, on a test basis, evidence supporting** the amounts and disclosures in the financial statements. An audit also includes **assessing the accounting principles** used and **significant** estimates made by management, as well as evaluating the overall financial statement presentation. **We believe that our audits and the report of other auditors provide a reasonable basis for our opinion**.

We did not observe the taking of the physical inventory as of December 31, Year 1, since that date was prior to our appointment as auditors for National Motors, Inc. and we were unable to satisfy ourselves regarding inventory quantities by means of other auditing procedures. Inventory amounts as of December 31, Year 1, enter into the determination of net income and cash flows for the year ended December 31, Year 2.

Because of the matter discussed in the **preceding paragraph**, the **scope** of our work was **not sufficient** to enable us to express, and we do not express, an opinion on the results of operations and cash flows for the year ended December 31, Year 2.

In our opinion, based on our audit and the report of the other auditors, **the balance sheet referred to above presents fairly**, in all material respects, the financial position of National Motors, Inc. and subsidiaries as of December 31, Year 2, in conformity with generally accepted accounting principles.

White & Co.
March 28, Year 3

Response #2: Research (1 point)

Paragraph Reference Answer: PR 100.13

Guidance: PR 100.13 states, "A firm's due date for its initial peer review is 18 months from the date it enrolled in the program or should have enrolled, whichever date is earlier (see interpretations)."

(6722)

Solution 28-10

Response #1: Report Deficiencies (5 points)

1. P

Concurrence with a change in accounting principle is implicit and need not be explicitly stated. If management does not provide reasonable justification for a change, the auditor's opinion would be qualified.

2. P

Such a reference is not required.

3. B

The opinion paragraph should extend the auditor's opinion beyond the statement of financial position to include the results of operations and cash flows, not changes in stockholders' equity.

4. B

SAS 79 removes the requirement for an uncertainties paragraph in an auditor's report. If an uncertainty is mentioned, it should be in a paragraph following the opinion paragraphs and include a description of the matter giving rise to the uncertainty and should indicate that its outcome cannot be determined. No reference should be made to the uncertainty in the introductory, scope, or opinion paragraphs.

5. W

If the auditor concludes that substantial doubt about the entity's ability to continue as a going concern exists, the term "substantial doubt" is required to be used in an explanatory paragraph.

6. W

If the auditor concludes that substantial doubt about the entity's ability to continue as a going concern exists, the term "going concern" is required to be used in an explanatory paragraph.

7. P

This sentence is the last sentence in the standard going concern uncertainty paragraph.

8. P

Auditors use dual dates when subsequent events, not going concern uncertainties, are mentioned.

Response #2: Other Auditors (4 points)

May & Marty could adopt the position of not making reference to Dey & Dee's audit of BGI-Western if May & Marty is able to satisfy itself about the **independence** and **professional reputation** of Dey & Dee and takes **steps** it considers **appropriate** to satisfy itself as to Dey & Dee's audit of BGI-Western. Ordinarily, May & Marty would be able to adopt the position of not making reference to Dey & Dee's audit when any one of the following conditions exists:

- **Dey & Dee is an associate or correspondent firm** and its work is acceptable to May & Marty based on May & Marty's knowledge of the professional standards and competence of Dey & Dee; or

- **Dey & Dee is retained by May & Marty** and the work is performed under May & Marty's guidance and control; or

- **May & Marty takes steps it considers necessary to satisfy itself as to Dey & Dee's audit**. Such steps may include a visit to Dey and Dee to discuss Dey and Dee's audit procedures or a review of Dey and Dee's audit programs and/or working papers. In addition, May and Marty is satisfied about the reasonableness of the statements of BGI-Western for purposes of inclusion in BGI's consolidated financial statements; or

- **BGI-Western's financial statements are not a material part** of BGI's consolidated financial statements.

Response #3: Research (1 point)

Paragraph Reference Answer: AU 530.06

Guidance: AU 530.06 states, "An independent auditor may reissue his report on financial statements contained in annual reports filed with the Securities and Exchange Commission or other regulatory agencies or in a document he submits to his client or to others that contains information in addition to the client's basic financial statements subsequent to the date of his original report on the basic financial statements. An independent auditor may also be requested by his client to furnish additional copies of a previously issued report. Use of the original report date in a reissued report removes any implication that records, transactions, or events after that date have been examined or reviewed. In such cases, the independent auditor has no responsibility to make further investigation or inquiry as to events which may have occurred during the period between the original report date and the date of the release of additional reports. However, see section 711 as to an auditor's responsibility when his report is included in a registration statement filed under the Securities Act of 1933 and see section 508.70-.73, for the predecessor auditor's responsibility when reissuing or consenting to the reuse of a report previously issued on the financial statements of a prior period."

(6723)

Solution 28-11

Response #1: Going Concern (9 points)

a. Wall has a responsibility to evaluate whether there is substantial doubt about Trendy's ability to continue as a going concern for a **reasonable period of time, not to exceed one year** beyond the date of Trendy's audited financial statements. This evaluation is based on Wall's knowledge of **conditions and** events that exist at, or have **occurred before**, the date of the audit report.

b. While it is not necessary that Wall design specific audit procedures solely to identify conditions and events that may indicate Trendy's has a going concern problem, Wall most likely would perform **analytical procedures** to identify ratios and patterns indicative of present and future financial difficulties.

Wall most likely would review any debt and **loan agreements** to ascertain whether Trendy is complying with their terms. Additionally, if there are any **agreements with stockholders or creditors** to provide or maintain financial support, confirmation of the details of these arrangements would be appropriate.

Wall's **review of subsequent events** near the completion of fieldwork also would produce evidence about Trendy's financial difficulties. Wall would especially focus on **reading the minutes of the directors' meetings, inquiring** of Trendy's legal counsel concerning litigation, and reading the **latest interim financial statements**.

c. Wall should **consider** any **management plans** to increase sales, reduce costs, or dispose of assets that could mitigate the adverse effects of Trendy's financial difficulties. The **marketability** of the assets, any **restrictions** on their disposal and the possible **operational effects** of their disposal should be considered in evaluating whether such plans can be effectively implemented.

If management plans to borrow money or restructure its debts, Wall should consider several factors including the **availability of financing**, the **possibility of restructuring** or subordinating debt, the effects of **existing borrowing restrictions**, and the **sufficiency of collateral**.

Wall should evaluate any management plans to **reduce or delay expenditures**, such as overhead or administrative expenditures. The **postponement** of maintenance and R&D, and the leasing of assets ordinarily purchased also may be feasible.

Wall also should consider any plans to **increase ownership equity and raise capital**. Arrangements to **reduce current dividend requirements** or accelerate cash distributions from subsidiaries or cash infusions from investors also may be possible.

Response #2: Research (1 point)

Paragraph Reference Answer: AU 532.12

Guidance: AU 532.12 states, "If an auditor issues a single combined report covering both (a) subject matter or presentations that require a restriction on use to specified parties and (b) subject matter or presentations that ordinarily do not require such a restriction, the use of such a single combined report should be restricted to the specified parties."

(6724)

Testing Windows

There are four exam windows each year; the first one starts in January. Generally, a candidate can take any or all sections (in any order) during any testing window, but check your board's requirements. A candidate may not take the same exam section more than once during any one testing window. Between windows, during the third month of each quarter, the exam is not given. Exam sites typically are open Monday through Friday; some are also open on Saturday.

Testing Windows		No Testing
January	February	March
April	May	June
July	August	September
October	November	December

CHANGE ALERTS

PCAOB AS 6, *Evaluating Consistency of Financial Statements* (issued 9/2008)

In September 2008, the Securities and Exchange Commission (SEC) approved the Public Company Accounting Oversight Board (PCAOB) Auditing Standard (AS) 6, *Evaluating Consistency of Financial Statements.* AS 6 supersedes the PCAOB's adopted interim standards AU 420, *Consistency of Application of Generally Accepted Accounting Principles* and AU 9420, *Consistency of Application of Generally Accepted Accounting Principles: Auditing Interpretations of Section 420.* It is effective November 15, 2008.

This statement is eligible to be tested beginning with the July-August 2009 exam window.

PCAOB AS 7, *Engagement Quality Review* (issue date pending SEC approval)

In July 2009, the PCAOB adopted AS 7, *Engagement Quality Review* (EQR). AS 7, **subject to SEC approval**, will become effective for EQRs of audits and interim reviews for fiscal years beginning on or after December 15, 2009 and will supersede the PCAOB's existing concurring partner review requirement. When this volume went to press, AS 7 had not been approved by the SEC. Visit the standards section of the PCAOB's Web site (www.pcaob.org) to check its status and confirm its effective date

If approved by the SEC with its current effective date and without early adoption permitted, this statement is eligible to be tested beginning with the July-August 2010 exam window.

STUDY TIPS

Government Auditing

Candidates studying governmental auditing should realize that the applicability of AU 801, *Compliance Auditing Considerations in Audits of Governmental Entities and Recipients of Governmental Financial Assistance* and governmental auditing guidance overlap. AU 801 is the AICPA's guidance. *Government Auditing Standards* and OMB Circular A-133, *Audits of States, Local Governments, and Non-Profit Organizations,* are issued by the federal government. (*Government Auditing Standards* are also referred to as the "Yellow Book" because they were published in a book with a yellow cover. Currently, the complete text is available at www.gao.gov/new.items/d07731g.pdf on the U.S. Government Accountability Office's Web site.

PCAOB Standards

PCAOB requirements tend to be similar to GAAS in nature, but generally more stringent. PCAOB standards are in addition to GAAS requirements. The editors recommend that candidates thoroughly review GAAS first, and then review PCAOB standards once GAAS are well understood.

CHAPTER 29

OTHER AUDITING STANDARDS

CHAPTER 29

OTHER AUDITING STANDARDS

I. Government Auditing

A. **Compliance Auditing Considerations in Governmental Audits (AU 801)**
Federal, state, and local governments supply financial assistance to other entities, including non-profit entities and business enterprises. These entities are primary recipients, subrecipients, or beneficiaries. This financial assistance may be grants of assets, loans, loan guarantees, or interest-rate subsidies. By accepting such assistance, accepting entities may be subject to laws and regulations that may have a direct and material effect on amounts in their financial statements.

1. **Applicability** AU 801 is applicable when an auditor is engaged to audit a government entity under GAAS and engaged to test and report on compliance with laws and regulations under *Government Auditing Standards* (the "Yellow Book") or in other circumstances involving governmental financial assistance, such as single (or organization-wide) audits or program-specific audits under certain federal or state audit regulations. *Governmental Auditing Standards,* often referred to as generally accepted government auditing standards (GAGAS), are issued by the U.S. Government Accountability Office (GAO) and apply to audits of government entities, programs, activities, and functions as well as audits of government assistance received by nongovernmental organizations (including contractors and nonprofit entities).

2. **Management Responsibilities** Management is responsible for ensuring that an entity complies with applicable laws and regulations. This includes identifying applicable laws and regulations and establishing internal controls to provide reasonable assurance of compliance.

3. **Auditor's Responsibilities** The auditor must design an audit to provide reasonable assurance that the financial statements are free of material misstatements resulting from violations of laws and regulations that have a direct and material effect on the determination of financial statement amounts.

4. **Auditor's Procedures** The auditor should obtain an understanding of the possible effects of laws and regulations that have a direct and material effect on the determination of amounts in an entity's financial statements. The auditor should determine whether management has identified these applicable laws and regulations. To accomplish this, the auditor may perform the following procedures:

    a. Consider knowledge obtained in prior years' audits.

    b. Discuss laws and regulations with the entity's chief financial officer, legal counsel, or grant administrators.

    c. Obtain written management representations regarding the completeness of management's identification.

    d. Review any directly related agreements, such as those related to grants and loans.

    e. Review the minutes of meetings of the governing board of a governmental entity for the enactment of applicable laws and regulations.

    f. Inquire of the appropriate audit oversight organization about the laws and regulations applicable to entities within its jurisdiction, including statutes and uniform reporting requirements.

g.   Review information about compliance requirements and state and local policies and procedures.

5.   **Misstatements** GAGAS require the auditor to design the audit to provide reasonable assurance of detecting material misstatements resulting from noncompliance with provisions of contracts or grant agreements that have a direct and material effect on the financial statements.

6.   **Additional GAGAS Requirements** For financial audits, GAGAS prescribe fieldwork and reporting standards beyond those required by GAAS. The general standards of GAGAS relate to ethics, independence, auditor's professional competence and judgment, and quality control.

7.   **Characteristics** The audits of recipients of federal financial assistance in accordance with federal audit regulations vary, but generally the auditor:

a.   Conducts the audit in accordance with GAAS and GAGAS

b.   Obtains and documents an understanding of internal control established to ensure compliance with the laws and regulations applicable to the federal award; in some instances, federal audit regulations mandate a test of controls to evaluate the effectiveness of the design and operation of the policies and procedures in preventing or detecting material noncompliance

c.   Issues a report on the consideration of internal control

d.   Determines and reports on whether the federal award has been administered in accordance with applicable laws and regulations (compliance requirements)

8.   **Financial Assistance Recipients** A recipient of a federal award may be subject to a single (or organization-wide) audit or to a program-specific audit. In planning the audit, the auditor should determine and consider the specific federal audit requirements applicable to the engagement, including the issuance of additional reports. Federal audit regulations for both single and program-specific audits typically require consideration of internal control beyond that typically required by GAAS and GAGAS as well as an evaluation as to whether applicable compliance requirements have been met.

a.   **Compliance Requirements** The U.S. Office of Management and Budget's (OMB) Compliance Supplements outline general and specific requirements for many federal programs awarded to state and local governments and nonprofit entities and suggest audit procedures to test compliance. General requirements apply to most federal financial assistance programs; they involve national policy. Specific requirements, typically established by statutory and regulatory requirements, apply to some federal programs. Specific requirements also may be included in grant agreements or contracts. For program-specific audits, federal agency audit guides identify general and specific requirements as well as suggested audit procedures.

b.   **Audit Requirements** The auditor must determine whether the recipient complied with applicable general and specific requirements. The level of assurance and report form vary depending on the particular agency's or program's requirements.

9.   **Evaluation** In evaluating whether an entity has complied with laws and regulations that, if not complied with, could have a material effect on each major federal award program, the auditor should consider the effect of identified instances of noncompliance on each such program.

a.   In doing so, the auditor should consider:

(1)   The frequency of noncompliance identified in the audit.

(2)   The adequacy of the primary recipient's system of monitoring subrecipients and the possible effect on the program of any noncompliance identified by the primary recipient or the auditors of the subrecipients.

(3)   Whether any instances of noncompliance identified in the audit resulted in "questioned costs," and if so, whether questioned costs are material to the program.

b.   Regardless of the auditor's overall opinion on compliance, regulations may require a report of any instance of noncompliance found and any related known questioned costs. Different federal agencies have different definitions of *questioned costs*. *Likely questioned costs* are the auditor's best estimate of total costs questioned for each major federal financial assistance program. *Known questioned costs* are questioned costs that are identified specifically.

c.   The auditor also must consider whether identified instances of noncompliance affect the opinion on the entity's financial statements.

10.   **Communication** Management is responsible for obtaining audits in accordance with legal, regulatory, or contractual requirements. If an auditor becomes aware that the entity is subject to an audit requirement beyond the terms of the engagement during a GAAS audit, the auditor should communicate to management and the audit committee that a GAAS audit may be insufficient. If this communication is oral, the auditor should document the communication in the working papers. Also, the auditor should consider the client's actions in this matter in relationship to the financial statement audit.

B.   **Governmental Auditing Standards (2007 Revision)**
GAGAS apply to audits and attestation engagements of government entities, programs, activities, and functions and of government assistance administered by nongovernmental organizations (including nonprofit entities and business enterprises). The ethical principles that provide the overall framework for application of GAGAS and thus guide the work of auditors are (1) the public interest; (2) integrity; (3) objectivity; (4) proper use of government information, resources, and position; and (5) professional behavior. The concept of accountability underlies decision makers' need to know whether (1) resources are managed properly and used in compliance with laws and regulations; (2) programs achieve their objectives and desired outcomes; (3) services are provided effectively, efficiently, economically, ethically, and equitably; and (4) managers are held accountable for their use of public resources. Auditors may use GAGAS in conjunction with professional standards issued by other authoritative bodies and may cite their use in their reports.

1.   **Professional Requirements** GAGAS identify professional requirements with specific language (consistent with SAS 102) to indicate the degree of responsibility imposed on auditors and audit organizations. The two categories of requirements are: *unconditional requirements* (in which the words *must* or is *required* are used) and *presumptively mandatory requirements* (in which the word *should* is used). Explanatory material intended to provide guidance or to be descriptive rather than required is also included in the standards in which the words *may, might* and *could* are used.

2.   **Engagement Types**

a.   **Financial Audits** Financial audits are concerned primarily with providing reasonable assurance as to whether financial statements are presented fairly in all material respects in conformity with GAAP or with an other comprehensive basis of accounting (OCBOA). Other objectives include providing special reports for portions of financial statements; reviewing interim financial information; issuing letters for underwriters and certain other requesting parties; reporting on the controls over transaction processing by service organizations; and auditing compliance with regulations relating to federal award expenditures and other government financial assistance in conjunction with a financial statement audit.

b. **Attestation Engagements** Attestation engagements concern examining, reviewing or performing agreed-upon procedures on a subject matter or an assertion about a subject matter and reporting on the results. They may be concerned with either financial or nonfinancial matters and may provide different levels of assurance about the subject matter or assertion depending on the user's needs.

c. **Performance Audits** Performance audits provide assurance or conclusions based on an evaluation of sufficient, appropriate evidence to assess program performance against stated criteria. Their objectives include assessments of program effectiveness, economy and efficiency; internal control; compliance; and prospective analyses.

3. **General Standards** These general standards apply to financial audits, attestation engagements and performance audits in accordance with GAGAS.

a. **Independence** In all matters relating to the audit work, the audit organization and the individual auditor, whether government or public, must be free from personal, external, and organizational impairments to independence, and must avoid the appearance of such impairments of independence. GAGAS do not provide standards for other services, thus auditors must not report that nonaudit services were conducted in accordance with GAGAS. Audit organizations need to ensure that their independence is not impaired by any nonaudit services they provide.

b. **Professional Judgment** Auditors must use professional judgment in planning and performing audits and attestation engagements and in reporting the results.

c. **Competence** The staff assigned to perform the audit or attestation engagement must collectively possess adequate professional competence for the tasks required.

d. **Quality Control** Each audit organization performing audits or attestation engagements in accordance with GAGAS must:

(1) Establish a system of quality control that is designed to provide the audit organization with reasonable assurance that the organization and its personnel comply with professional standards and applicable legal and regulatory requirements

(2) Have an external peer review at least once every 3 years; external audit organizations should make their most recent peer review report publicly available; internal audit organizations should share the report with those charged with governance; government audit organizations should communicate the results of their reviews and availability of the report with appropriate oversight bodies

4. **Standards Common to GAGAS Engagements** The following standards apply to financial audits, attestation engagements, and performance audits conducted in accordance with GAGAS. In detail, there are variations among them; however, to the depth of this coverage, these standards are very similar.

a. **Documentation** Documentation must contain sufficient information to enable an experienced auditor with no previous connection to the engagement to obtain a clear understanding of the work performed and ascertain that the evidence supports the auditors' significant judgments and conclusions. Documentation must be complete before auditors issue their reports.

b. **Reporting Compliance With GAGAS** Reports should state that the engagements were performed in accordance with GAGAS.

c. **Reporting Officials' Views** If the auditors' report on the engagement discloses deficiencies in internal control, fraud, illegal acts, violations of provisions of contracts or grant agreements, or abuse, auditors should obtain and report the views of responsible officials concerning the findings, conclusions, and recommendations, as well as planned corrective actions. Auditors should also include in the report an evaluation of the comments.

d. **Reporting Confidential or Sensitive Information** If certain pertinent information is prohibited from public disclosure or is excluded from a report due to the confidential or sensitive nature of the information, auditors should disclose in the report that certain information has been omitted and the reason or other circumstances that makes the omission necessary. When audit organizations are subject to public records laws, auditors should determine whether public records laws could impact the availability of classified or limited-official-use reports and determine whether other means of communicating with management and those charged with governance would be more appropriate.

e. **Report Issuance & Distribution** If the subject of the audit involves material that is classified for security purposes or contains confidential or sensitive information, auditors may limit the report distribution. Auditors should document any limitation on report distribution. Distribution of reports depends on the relationship of the auditors to the audited organization and the nature of the information contained in the report.

5. **Standards Common to Financial Audits & Attestation Engagements** The following standards apply to financial audits and attestation engagements in accordance with GAGAS. To the depth of this coverage, these standards are similar for both types of engagements.

a. **Communication During Planning** Auditors should communicate their understanding of the services to be performed for each engagement, in writing to management, those charged with governance, and to the individuals contracting for or requesting the audit or engagement.

b. **Results of Previous Engagements** Auditors should evaluate whether the entity has taken appropriate corrective action to address findings and recommendations from previous engagements that could have a material effect on the financial statements or the subject matter.

c. **Elements of Findings** The elements needed for a finding depend on the particular audit or engagement objectives. Thus, a finding or set of findings is complete to the extent that the objectives are satisfied. When deficiencies are identified auditors should plan and perform procedures to develop the elements of a finding to achieve those objectives.

d. **Reporting Internal Control Deficiencies, Fraud, Illegal Acts, Violations & Abuse** For all financial audit and attestation engagements, auditors must report, as applicable to the engagement objectives, all instances of fraud and illegal acts unless clearly inconsequential and violations of provisions of contracts or grant agreements and abuse that could have a material effect on the financial statements or the subject matter of the engagement. When auditors detect violations of provisions of contracts or grant agreements or abuse that have an effect on the financial statements or the subject matter that is less than material but more than inconsequential, they should communicate those findings in writing to entity officials. Also, auditors should report significant deficiencies and material weaknesses in internal control.

6. **Financial Audit Standards** GAGAS incorporate the AICPA fieldwork and reporting standards and the related SASs unless specifically excluded or modified by GAGAS and outline the following additional fieldwork and reporting standards for financial audits performed in accordance with GAGAS.

a. **Communication During Planning** Auditors should communicate in writing the nature of planned work and level of assurance to be provided related to internal control over financial reporting and compliance with laws, regulations, and provisions of contracts or grant agreements and any potential restriction on the auditors' reports, in order to reduce the chance of any misunderstanding.

b. **Detecting Misstatements Resulting From Violations or Abuse** Auditors should design the audit to provide reasonable assurance of detecting misstatements resulting from violations of provisions of contracts or grant agreements that could have a direct and material effect on the determination of financial statement amounts or other financial data significant to the audit objectives. If specific information comes to the auditors' attention that provides evidence of such possible violations, the auditors should apply procedures to ascertain whether such violations have, or are likely to have, occurred. Likewise, if during the course of the audit, auditors become aware of abuse that could be quantitatively or qualitatively material to the financial statements, auditors should apply audit procedures to ascertain the potential effect.

c. **Reporting on Internal Control & Compliance** When providing an opinion or a disclaimer on financial statements, auditors must also report on internal control over financial reporting and on compliance with laws, regulations, and provisions of contracts or grant agreements. Auditors should include either in the same or in separate report(s) a description of the scope of this testing of internal control. If the auditor issues separate reports, the auditors' report on financial statements should include in a reference to these separate reports that these reports are an integral part of a GAGAS audit and important for assessing the results of the audit. Auditors should state in these reports whether the tests they performed provided sufficient, appropriate evidence to support an opinion on the effectiveness of internal control over financial reporting and on compliance with laws, regulations, and provisions of contracts or grant agreements.

d. **Communicating Significant Matters** Due to the public interest in the operations of government entities and entities that receive or administer government awards, in GAGAS audits there may be situations in which certain types of information in addition to the examples presented in AICPA standards would help facilitate the readers' understanding of the financial statements and the auditors' report. The determination of whether to include such information is a matter of professional judgment.

e. **Restated Financial Statements** Auditors should advise management to make appropriate disclosures when the auditors become aware that it is likely that previously issued financial statements are materially misstated. Auditors also should evaluate the timeliness and appropriateness of management's disclosure and actions to determine and correct misstatements; report on restated financial statements; and report directly to appropriate officials when the audited entity does not take the necessary steps.

7. **Attestation Engagement Standards** GAGAS incorporate the AICPA general attestation standard on criteria, its fieldwork and reporting standards for attestation engagements plus the Statements on Standards for Attestation Engagements (SSAEs), unless specifically excluded or modified by GAGAS, as well as outline additional government attestation standards. Of course, the GAGAS general standards also apply.

a. **Communication During Planning** Auditors should obtain written acknowledgment or other evidence of the entity's responsibilities for the subject matter or the written assertion as it relates to the objectives of the engagement. Auditors should communicate the nature, timing, and extent of planned testing and reporting; the level of assurance the auditor will provide; and any potential restriction on the auditors' reports, in order to reduce the chance of any misunderstanding.

b. **Internal Control** In planning examination-level attestation engagements, auditors should obtain a sufficient understanding of internal control that is material to the subject matter or assertion to plan the engagement and design procedures to achieve the engagement objectives.

c. **Detecting Fraud, Illegal Acts, Violations & Abuse** If auditors become aware of abuse that could be quantitatively or qualitatively material, auditors should apply procedures specifically directed to ascertain the potential effect on the subject matter or other data significant to the engagement objectives.

    (1) **Examination** In planning, auditors should design the engagement to provide reasonable assurance of detecting fraud, illegal acts, or violations of provisions of contracts or grant agreements that could have a material effect on the subject matter of the attestation engagement.

    (2) **Review or Agreed-Upon Procedures** If during the course of the engagement, information comes to the auditors' attention indicating that fraud, illegal acts, or violations of provisions of contracts or grant agreements that could have a material effect on the subject matter may have occurred, auditors should perform procedures as necessary to determine if fraud, illegal acts, or violations of provisions of contracts or grant agreements are likely to have occurred and, if so, determine their effect on the results of the attestation engagement.

8. **Performance Audit Standards**

a. **Planning & Supervision** Work must be planned adequately and staff must be supervised properly. In planning the audit, auditors should assess significance and audit risk and apply these assessments in defining the audit objectives and the scope and methodology to address those objectives. Auditors must plan the audit to reduce audit risk to an appropriate level for the auditors to provide reasonable assurance that the evidence is sufficient and appropriate to support the auditors' findings and conclusions. Auditors must prepare a written audit plan for each audit.

b. **Evidence** Sufficient, appropriate evidence must be obtained to provide a reasonable basis for the auditor's findings and conclusions.

c. **Form** Auditors must prepare audit reports communicating the results of each audit. Auditors should use a form of the audit report that is appropriate for its intended use and is in writing or in another retrievable form.

d. **Report Contents** The report should include the objectives, scope, and methodology; and the audit results, including findings, conclusions, and recommendations, as appropriate.

e. **Report Quality Elements** The report should be as timely, complete, accurate, objective, convincing, clear, and concise as the subject permits.

C. **Single Audit Act**
OMB Circular A-133, *Audits of States, Local Governments, and Nonprofit Organizations,* sets forth requirements for audits in accordance with the Single Audit Act and the Single Audit Act Amendments of 1996.

1. **Threshold** The amount of federal awards expended by a nonfederal entity (as opposed to receipts) within a fiscal year determines whether an entity meets the threshold. The threshold is $500,000.

a. Entities that expend total federal awards equal to or in excess the threshold in a fiscal year require an audit performed in accordance with the Single Audit Act and OMB Circular A-133. Those that equal or exceed the threshold, but receive awards under only one program, have the option of having an audit performed in accordance with A-133 or having an audit made of the one program.

b. Institutions expending less than the threshold annually in federal awards are exempt from federal audit requirements, but records must be available for review by appropriate officials of the grantor agency or sub-granting agency.

2. **Compliance Reporting** Compliance should be tested for those requirements that relate to the allowability of program expenditures as well as the eligibility of the individual or groups to which federal award is provided. The auditor should test and report on the following matters pertaining to compliance with laws and regulations:

    a. Laws and regulations that may have a material effect on the financial statements.

    b. General requirements applicable to federal financial assistance.

    c. Specific requirements that may have a material effect on each major program, as defined by the Single Audit Act.

    d. Certain laws and regulations applicable to nonmajor federal award programs.

3. **Compliance Requirements** OMB Circular A-133 identifies compliance requirements. For each federal program, the auditor reports whether there are audit findings for each of 14 types of compliance requirements and the total amount of questioned costs.

    a. **Activities Allowed or Unallowed** Specifies the types of goods or services entities may purchase with financial assistance.

    b. **Allowable Costs/Cost Principles** Prescribes the direct and indirect costs allowable for federal reimbursement.

    c. **Cash Management** Requires recipients of federal award to minimize the time lapsed between receipt and disbursement of that assistance.

    d. **Davis-Bacon Act** Requires that laborers working on federally financed construction projects be paid a wage not less than the prevailing regional wage established by the Secretary of Labor.

    e. **Eligibility** Specifies the characteristics of individuals or groups to whom entities may give financial assistance.

    f. **Equipment and Real Property Management**

    g. **Matching, Level of Effort, Earmarking** Specifies amounts entities should contribute from their own resources toward projects for which financial assistance is provided.

    h. **Period of Availability of Federal Funds**

    i. **Procurement and Suspension and Debarment**

    j. **Program Income**

    k. **Real Property Acquisition and Relocation Assistance** Prescribes how real property should be acquired with federal awards and how recipients must help relocate people displaced when that property is acquired.

    l. **Reporting** Specifies reports entities must file in addition to those required by the general requirements.

    m. **Subrecipient Monitoring**

    n. **Special Tests and Provisions** Other provisions for which federal agencies have determined noncompliance could materially affect the program (for example, some programs require recipients to hold public hearings on the proposed use of federal awards; other programs set a deadline for the expenditure of federal awards).

4. **Management Responsibilities** Management is required to prepare a schedule of major and nonmajor federal award programs.

5. **Materiality** In auditing an entity's compliance with requirements governing each major federal award program in accordance with the Single Audit Act, the auditor considers materiality in relation to each program. (This differs from audits in accordance with GAAS.)

6. **Risk** OMB Circular A-133 prescribes a risk-based approach to determine major programs, requiring the auditor to consider a combination of materiality, internal control, and other factors in determining whether a program must be tested as major. It also allows federal agencies to designate certain programs as major, requiring the auditor to test them as major, even though they may not satisfy the risk-based criteria. The auditor must perform procedures that assess inherent and control risk and restrict detection risk. The auditor must obtain an understanding of internal control over federal programs sufficient to plan the audit to support a low assessed level of control risk for major programs.

   a. **Inherent Risk** In assessing inherent risk, the auditor considers the results of any procedures performed as part of the audit of the financial statements, and of any tests of compliance with the general requirements.

   b. **Detection Risk** In determining an acceptable level of detection risk, the auditor considers the level to which s/he seeks to restrict audit risk related to the major federal award program and the assessed levels of inherent risk and control risk.

   c. **Cluster of Programs** A cluster of programs is a group of closely related programs that share common compliance requirements. The auditor must consider a cluster of programs as one program for determining major programs, with some exceptions.

7. **Consistency With Financial Statements** Auditors must determine whether financial reports and claims for advances and reimbursement contain information supported by the records from which the basic financial statements were prepared, and that amounts claimed or used for matching purposes were determined in accordance with OMB Circulars A-87 and A-102.

8. **Noncompliance** To evaluate the effects of questioned costs on the opinion on compliance properly, the best estimate of total costs questioned for each major federal award program is considered, not just those questioned costs that were identified specifically. The auditor must report any instances of noncompliance found and resulting questioned costs.

9. **Subrecipients** In a single year, if a primary recipient passes $25,000 or more of federal award through to a subrecipient, that primary recipient becomes responsible for determining that the assistance is spent in accordance with applicable laws and regulations. The primary recipient should:

   a. Determine that subrecipients met the audit requirements of OMB Circular A-133, if applicable.

   b. Determine if the assistance was spent in accordance with applicable laws and regulations.

   c. Ensure that corrective action is taken within six months after receipt of a report that identifies instances of noncompliance.

   d. Consider the need for an adjustment to the records of the primary recipient.

   e. Require each subrecipient to permit independent auditors to have access to their records and financial statements as necessary to comply with OMB Circular A-133.

10. **Nonmajor Programs** The Single Audit Act requires that "transactions selected from federal assistance programs, other than major federal assistance programs, ...shall be tested for compliance with federal laws and regulations that apply to such transactions."

11. **Reporting** The auditor must summarize the results of the audit concerning internal control, financial statements, and compliance with laws and regulations. The audit report must be issued within 9 months after the entity's year-end.

   a. Auditees and recipient entities must complete their respective parts of a data collection form. This form states whether the audit was completed in accordance with Circular A-133 and provides information about the entity, its federal programs, and the results of the audit.

   b. Auditors must report findings and questioned costs in a single schedule, using prescribed criteria for reporting. The schedule of findings and questioned costs must include a summary of the auditor's results, the auditor's findings relating to the financial statements, and findings and questioned costs for federal awards.

   c. Recipient entities must prepare a summary schedule of prior audit findings. Auditees must report the status of all audit findings included in the prior audit's schedule of findings and questioned costs relative to federal awards.

12. **Conflict of Interest** The same auditor may not prepare the indirect cost proposal or cost allocation plan when indirect costs exceed $1,000,000 in the prior year. The auditor should not audit her/his own work.

D. **Other Compliance Auditing Responsibilities**

1. **Program-Specific Audits** The Single Audit Act and OMB Circular A-133 permit certain recipients of federal awards to have program-specific audits. When engaged to conduct such an audit, the auditor should first obtain an understanding of the audit requirements for that particular program from an agreement with the grantor agency, from an audit guide published by the grantor agency, or through contact with the grantor agency.

2. **Compliance Testing** An auditor may be engaged to test and report on compliance with laws and regulations other than those previously discussed.

   a. **Procedures** Auditors should consider performing the following procedures:

      (1) Inquire of management about additional compliance auditing requirements applicable to the entity.

      (2) Inquire of the office of the state or local auditor or other appropriate audit oversight organization about audit requirements applicable to the entity.

      (3) Review information about governmental audit requirements available from state societies of CPAs or associations of governments.

   b. **Noncompliance** When the audit of an entity's compliance with requirements governing a major federal award program detects noncompliance with those requirements that the auditor believes have a material effect on the program, the auditor should express a qualified or adverse opinion.

II. **Sarbanes-Oxley Act of 2002**

A. **Public Company Accounting Oversight Board (PCAOB)**
The Sarbanes-Oxley Act of 2002 established the PCAOB and charged it with the responsibility of overseeing the audit firms of public companies. The Securities and Exchange Commission (SEC)

has oversight and enforcement authority over the PCAOB. The term "public companies" refers to issuers of publicly traded securities.

1. **Responsibilities** The PCAOB's duties include registering public accounting firms; establishing auditing, quality control, ethics, independence and other standards relating to public company audits; conducting inspections, investigations and disciplinary proceedings of registered accounting firms; and enforcing compliance with the Act.

2. **Registration** Public accounting firms that perform or participate in the performance of audits of public companies, or their subsidiaries, must be registered with the PCAOB; registrations must be updated annually.

3. **Interim Guidance** The PCAOB adopted interim (or transitional) professional standards of auditing, attestation, independence, quality control, and ethics issued by the AICPA that were in existence on April 16, 2003. In doing so, the PCAOB adopted the existing body of audit and attest literature as its interim standards. Each of the interim standards set forth remain in effect until modified or superseded, either by PCAOB action approved by the SEC, or by SEC action.

4. **SEC-Approved PCAOB Standards** The SEC approves auditing standards (AS) adopted by the PCAOB. These are discussed in the following sections of this chapter.

B. **Prohibited Services**
The Sarbanes-Oxley Act of 2002 prohibits any registered public accounting firm from providing the following nonaudit services to its audit clients that are issuers of publicly traded securities: (1) bookkeeping or other services related to the accounting records of financial statements of the audit client; (2) financial information system design and implementation; (3) appraisal or valuation services, fairness opinions, or contribution-in-kind reports; (4) actuarial services; (5) internal audit outsourcing services; (6) management functions or human resources; (7) broker, dealer, investment advisor, or investment banking services; (8) legal services and expert services unrelated to the audit; and (9) any other service that the Board determines, by regulation, is impermissible. A CPA may perform these services for clients that are issuers of public securities, if the CPA does not audit that client also. An auditor may perform other nonaudit services not listed above, such as tax preparation services, for audit clients that are issuers of public securities only with advance approval from the audit committee.

C. **Rotation**
The Sarbanes-Oxley Act of 2002 prohibits a registered public accounting firm from providing audit services to an issuer if the lead audit partner, or the audit partner responsible for reviewing the audit, has performed audit services for that issuer in each of the five previous fiscal years of that issuer.

D. **Conflicts of Interest**
It is prohibited for a firm to provide audit services to an issuer if the issuer's CEO, controller, CFO, CAO, or other person serving in an equivalent capacity, was employed in the audit firm and participated in the audit of that issuer during the previous fiscal year of that issuer.

E. **Audit Committee Responsibilities**
In addition to normal responsibilities, the Sarbanes-Oxley Act of 2002 requires that audit committees be directly responsible for appointing, compensating and overseeing the external audit firm. This includes resolving any disagreements between the external auditor and management. Audit committees are also responsible for preapproving any allowed nonaudit services. If these permissible nonaudit services are related to internal control over financial reporting, the registered public accounting firm must provide, in writing, to the audit committee a description of the scope of the service and discuss with the audit committee the potential effects of the service on the independence of the firm. The firm must then document this discussion.

III. PCAOB Audit Documentation Standards

A. Report Reference
PCAOB AS 1 requires auditors' reports on engagements conducted in accordance with the PCAOB's standards to include a reference that the engagement was performed in accordance with the standards of the PCAOB, rather than U.S. GAAS.

B. Audit Documentation
PCAOB AS 3, *Audit Documentation,* presents many of the same requirements as SAS 103 (Chapter 24) with the exception of the following major differences:

1. Documentation Completion Date The auditor should complete the final audit file within 45 days following the report release date.

2. Retention Workpapers must be retained for 7 years from the report release date.

3. Significant Findings or Issues In addition to SAS 103 requirements pertaining to significant findings or issues, PCAOB AS 3 requires that all significant findings or issues be identified in an *engagement completion document.* This document may include all information necessary to understand the significant findings/issues or it may consist of cross-references to the supporting audit documentation.

4. Workpapers of Other Auditors All supporting documentation prepared by other auditors must be retained by or accessible to the office issuing the auditor's report. In addition, the following specific documentation must be obtained, reviewed and retained by the office issuing the audit report (unless reference is made to the other auditor):

a. An engagement completion document including any cross-referenced documentation

b. A list of significant fraud risk factors and results of related audit procedures

c. Sufficient information concerning significant findings/issues that contradict or are inconsistent with final conclusions

d. Any findings affecting the consolidating or combining of accounts in the consolidated financial statements

e. Sufficient information to show that financial statement amounts audited by the other auditor reconcile to the information underlying the consolidated financial statements

f. A schedule of audit adjustments including descriptions of the nature and cause of each misstatement

g. All significant deficiencies and material weaknesses with a clear distinction between the two

h. Management representation letters

i. All matters to be communicated to the audit committee

IV. Audit of Internal Control Over Financial Reporting (ICFR)

A. Overview
PCAOB AS 5, *An Audit of Internal Control Over Financial Reporting That Is Integrated with An Audit of Financial Statements,* is applicable to audits of a company (an issuer of securities) subject to the reporting requirements of the Securities Exchange Act of 1934. It establishes requirements and provides guidance for auditors engaged to audit management's assessment of the effectiveness of ICFR that is integrated with an audit of the financial statements. Effective ICFR provides

reasonable assurance that the financial reporting process and the preparation of the financial statements are reliable for external purposes.

B.   Auditor's Objective in an Audit of ICFR
The objective of the auditor for this type of engagement is to express an opinion on the effectiveness of the company's ICFR as of a point in time and taken as a whole. To express an opinion as of a point in time, the auditor must obtain evidence that ICFR has operated effectively for a sufficient period of time which may be less than the period covered by the company's financial statements. To express an opinion on ICFR as a whole, the auditor must obtain evidence about the effectiveness of selected controls over *all* relevant assertions. This involves testing the design and operating effectiveness of controls that in most cases would **not** be required if *only* expressing an opinion on the financial statements. During an audit of financial statements, when the auditor's risk assessment of specific financial statement assertions includes an expectation of the operating effectiveness of the relevant controls, evidence must be obtained that these controls were effective for a particular time (or throughout the period) upon which s/he plans to rely on them. The auditor's risk assessment, during a financial statement audit, would ordinarily **not** include an expectation of the operating effectiveness of controls for *all* relevant assertions.

1.   **Material Weaknesses** If one or more material weaknesses exist, a company's ICFR is not effective. Therefore, the auditor must plan and perform the audit to obtain evidence that is sufficient to obtain reasonable assurance about whether material weaknesses exist as of the date of management's assessment. There may be a material weakness in ICFR even when financial statements are not materially misstated. Indicators of material weaknesses include:

a.   Identification of fraud, whether or not material, on the part of senior management

b.   Restatement of previously issued financial statements to reflect the correction of a material misstatement

c.   Auditor identification of a material misstatement of current period financial statements that would not have been detected by the company's ICFR

d.   Ineffective oversight by the company's audit committee of external financial reporting and ICFR

2.   **Standards & Criteria** The three GAAS general standards are applicable to an audit of ICFR. PCAOB AS 5 establishes the applicable fieldwork and reporting standards. The auditor should use the same appropriate, established control framework to perform an audit of ICFR as the company's management uses in its annual evaluation of the effectiveness of ICFR.

C.   Definitions
This standard defines the following terms:

1.   **Control Objective** "A *control objective* provides a specific target against which to evaluate the effectiveness of controls. A control objective for internal control over financial reporting generally relates to a relevant assertion and states a criterion for evaluating whether the company's control procedures in a specific area provide reasonable assurance that a misstatement or omission in that relevant assertion is prevented or detected by controls on a timely basis."

2.   **Deficiency** "A *deficiency* in internal control over financial reporting exists when the design or operation of a control does not allow management or employees, in the normal course of performing their assigned functions, to prevent or detect misstatements on a timely basis.

a.   A deficiency *in design* exists when

(1)   A control necessary to meet the control objective is missing or

(2) An existing control is not properly designed so that, even if the control operates as designed, the control objective would not be met.

b. A deficiency in *operation* exists when a properly designed control does not operate as designed, or when the person performing the control does not possess the necessary authority or competence to perform the control effectively."

3. **Financial Statements & Related Disclosures** "*Financial statements and related disclosures* refers to a company's financial statements and notes to the financial statements as presented in accordance with generally accepted accounting principles (GAAP). References to financial statements and related disclosures do not extend to the preparation of management's discussion and analysis or other similar financial information presented outside a company's GAAP-basis financial statements and notes."

4. **Internal Control Over Financial Reporting** "*Internal control over financial reporting* is a process designed by, or under the supervision of, the company's principal executive and principal financial officers, or persons performing similar functions, and effected by the company's board of directors, management, and other personnel, to provide reasonable assurance regarding the reliability of financial reporting and preparation of financial statements for external purposes in accordance with GAAP and includes those policies and procedures that:

   a. Pertain to the maintenance of records that, in reasonable detail, accurately and fairly reflect the transactions and dispositions of the assets of the company;

   b. Provide reasonable assurance that transactions are recorded as necessary to permit preparation of financial statements in accordance with generally accepted accounting principles, and that receipts and expenditures of the company are being made only in accordance with authorizations of management and directors of the company; and

   c. Provide reasonable assurance regarding prevention or timely detection of unauthorized acquisition, use, or disposition of the company assets that could have a material effect on the financial statements.

   Note: The auditor's procedures as part of either the audit of internal control over financial reporting or the audit of the financial statements are not part of a company's internal control over financial reporting.

   Note: Internal control over financial reporting has inherent limitations. Internal control over financial reporting is a process that involves human diligence and compliance and is subject to lapses in judgment and breakdowns resulting from human failures. Internal control over financial reporting also can be circumvented by collusion or improper management override. Because of such limitations, there is a risk that material misstatements will not be prevented or detected on a timely basis by internal control over financial reporting. However, these inherent limitations are known features of the financial reporting process. Therefore, it is possible to design into the process safeguards to reduce, though not eliminate, this risk."

5. **Management's Assessment** "*Management assessment* is the assessment described in Item 308(a)(3) of Regulations S-B and S-K that is included in management's annual report on internal control over financial reporting." It is described therein as "Management's assessment of the effectiveness of the registrant's internal control over financial reporting as of the end of the registrant's most recent fiscal year, including a statement as to whether or not internal control over financial reporting is effective. This discussion must include disclosure of any material weakness in the registrant's internal control over financial reporting identified by management. Management is not permitted to conclude that the registrant's internal control over financial reporting is effective if there are one or more material weaknesses in the registrant's internal control over financial reporting;…"

6. **Material Weakness** "A *material weakness* is a deficiency, or a combination of deficiencies, in internal control over financial reporting, such that there is a reasonable possibility that a material misstatement of the company's annual or interim financial statements will not be prevented or detected on a timely basis.

   Note: There is a reasonable possibility of an event, as used in this standard, when the likelihood of the event is either 'reasonably possible' or 'probable,' as those terms are used in Financial Accounting Standards Board Statement No. 5, *Accounting for Contingencies* ('FAS 5')." Reasonably possible is defined therein as "...more than remote but less than likely." Probable is defined therein as "...likely to occur."

7. **Preventive or Detective Controls** "Controls over financial reporting may be preventive controls or detective controls. Effective internal control over financial reporting often includes a combination of preventive and detective controls.

   a. Preventive controls have the objective of preventing errors or fraud that could result in a misstatement of the financial statements from occurring.

   b. Detective controls have the objective of detecting errors or fraud that has already occurred that could result in a misstatement of the financial statements."

8. **Relevant Assertion** "A *relevant assertion* is a financial statement assertion that has a reasonable possibility of containing a misstatement or misstatements that would cause the financial statements to be materially misstated. The determination of whether an assertion is a relevant assertion is based on inherent risk, without regard to the effect of controls."

9. **Significant Account or Disclosure** "An account or disclosure is a *significant account or disclosure* if there is a reasonable possibility that the account or disclosure could contain a misstatement that, individually or when aggregated with others, has a material effect on the financial statements, considering the risks of both overstatement and understatement. The determination of whether an account or disclosure is significant is based on inherent risk, without regard to the effect of controls."

10. **Significant Deficiency** "A *significant deficiency* is a deficiency, or a combination of deficiencies, in internal control over financial reporting that is less severe than a material weakness, yet important enough to merit attention by those responsible for oversight of the company's financial reporting."

D. **Integrating Audits of ICFR & Financial Statements**
Although an audit of ICFR and an audit of financial statements have distinct objectives, the auditor must plan an integrated approach and perform the work so that the objectives of both are achieved.

1. **Test of Controls** The tests of controls should be designed to simultaneously meet the objectives of both audits—to obtain sufficient evidence to support both the auditor's opinion on ICFR as of year-end and the auditor's control risk assessments during the audit of financial statements. During an audit of the financial statements, when making a determination of the effectiveness of controls to assess control risk, the auditor should consider the results of the additional tests of controls that were performed in order to express an opinion on ICFR. Likewise, during an audit of ICFR, the results of any additional tests of controls performed to support the opinion of the financial statements should be considered. And although the absence of misstatements verified by substantive procedures in an audit of financial statements is no substitute for the direct testing of controls required by an audit of ICFR. However, their absence should be taken into consideration by the auditor when making risk assessments that underlie the decisions about the testing needed to determine the effectiveness of controls in an audit of ICFR.

2. **Substantive Procedures** Although some procedures performed in an audit of ICFR may reduce the work needed during an audit of financial statements, the auditor must perform

substantive procedures for all relevant assertions. This requirement for an audit of financial statements is **not** diminished by the procedures performed during an audit of ICFR.

E.   Planning

1.   Audit Procedure Considerations The following matters should be considered to determine if and if so, how, they will impact the auditor's procedures and risk assessment.

a.   Previous Engagements Knowledge of the company's ICFR obtained during previous engagements

b.   Industry Issues Industry issues such as financial reporting practices, economic conditions, laws and regulations, and technological changes

c.   Company-Specific Issues Company-specific issues such as its organization; operating system characteristics and degree of complexity; capital structure; ongoing legal or regulatory matters; any recent changes in the company and its operations or its ICFR; and public information about the company that is relevant to the evaluation of the likelihood of material financial statement misstatements and the effectiveness of its ICFR

d.   Auditor's Preliminary Judgments The auditor's preliminary judgments about the effectiveness of ICFR; and materiality, risk, and other factors related to the identification of material weaknesses

e.   Auditor's Client Acceptance & Retention Evaluation Consideration of any risks analyzed as part of the auditor's client acceptance and retention evaluation

f.   Identified Control Deficiencies Control deficiencies previously communicated to the audit committee or management

g.   Other Available Evidence Type and extent of available other evidence that is relevant to the effectiveness of the company's ICFR

2.   Role of Risk Assessment The assessment of risk affects all the auditor's decisions. In assessing risk, the auditor should focus on the areas of highest risk—there is no need to test controls when their failure would not result in the reasonable possibility of a material misstatement to the financial statements. The risk that a company's ICFR will fail to prevent or detect a misstatement caused by fraud is usually greater than the risk that it will fail to prevent or detect an error.

3.   Scaling the Audit The audit should be adjusted to fit the size and complexity of the company. Smaller and/or less complex companies may address the risks of misstatement and the needed controls differently than more complex companies.

4.   Risk of Fraud & Management Override When selecting controls to test, the auditor should consider whether the company's controls sufficiently address the risk of material misstatement due to fraud and management override of other controls.

5.   Using the Work of Others Assistance can be obtained from internal auditors, other company personnel and third parties. The auditor's decision to use others and the extent to use them should be based on an evaluation of their competence and objectivity. The auditor should also consider the risk associated with the control being tested—the higher the risk, the more important it becomes for the auditor to perform the work.

6.   Materiality The standard directs the auditor of ICFR to use the same guidance for materiality considerations used in planning an audit of financial statements.

F.   Selection of Controls to Test
The auditor should use a "top-down" approach to identify risks and select controls. The auditor should begin at the financial statement level and gain an understanding of the overall risks to ICFR. Then the auditor should evaluate the entity-level controls. Next, s/he should identify the significant accounts and disclosures and their relevant assertions. The auditor should then verify her/his understanding of the risks in the company's processes and select for testing those controls that sufficiently address the assessed risk of misstatement to each relevant assertion.

1.   **Entity-Level Controls** Entity-level controls that are important to the auditor's determination of the effectiveness of the company's ICFR must be tested. Depending on their nature and precision, the degree of effectiveness of the entity-level controls can impact both the selection of other controls to be tested as well as the nature, timing and extent of the testing of other controls. The entity-level controls include:

a.   Controls related to the control environment

b.   Controls over management override of other controls

c.   The company's risk assessment processes

d.   Centralized processing and controls, including shared service environments

e.   Controls to monitor results of operations

f.   Controls to monitor other controls, including activities of the internal audit function, the audit committee, and self-assessment programs

g.   Controls over the period-end financial reporting process

h.   Policies that address significant business control and risk management practices

2.   **Assessment of Control Environment** The auditor must determine whether management's philosophy and operating style promote effective ICFR by reflecting their sound integrity and ethical values. The auditor must also determine if the board or audit committee understands and exercises oversight responsibility over ICFR.

3.   **Evaluation of Period-End Financial Reporting Process** The period-end financial reporting process evaluation by the auditor should include assessing:

a.   Inputs, procedures performed, and outputs of the processes the company uses to produce its annual and quarterly financial statements

b.   Types of adjusting and consolidating entries

c.   Effect of and the degree to which information technology (IT) is used

d.   Who participates from management

e.   Locations involved

f.   Nature and extent of the oversight by management, the board of directors, and the audit committee

4.   **Identification of Significant Accounts & Disclosures & Their Relevant Assertions** The auditor should evaluate both the qualitative and quantitative risk factors related to the financial statement line items and disclosures in order to identify significant accounts and disclosures and their relevant assertions. These risk factors are the same for both an audit of ICFR and an audit of the financial statements as are the significant accounts and disclosures and their relevant assertions—however for various reasons, the audit of financial statements may also

involve performing substantive procedures on items that are not identified as part of this significant group. The components of an account or disclosure might be subject to different risks and thus may require different controls to address these separate risks. As part of this process, the auditor should also determine the likely sources of potential misstatements that would cause the financial statements to be materially misstated. The auditor should reflect on scenarios of what could go wrong.

5. **Multiple Locations or Business Units** Tests should only be performed at locations that present a reasonable possibility of material misstatement to the consolidated financial statements. For other locations or business units, the testing of entity-level controls may be sufficient to provide the needed assurance. Entities that are acquired on or before the date of management's assessment and operations that are accounted for as discontinued operations on the date of management's assessment should be included in the auditor's considerations. Testing of controls over the reporting of equity method investments would ordinarily **not** extend to the investee's controls.

6. **Understanding Likely Sources of Misstatement** The auditor should continue to develop a further understanding of the likely sources of misstatement which s/he started while identifying significant accounts and disclosures and their relevant assertions.

   a. **Auditor's Objectives** The auditor's objectives are to:

      (1) Understand the flow of transactions (including the effect of IT) related to the relevant assertions, including how these transactions are initiated, authorized, processed, and recorded

      (2) Confirm that all the points within the company's processes at which a material (individually or combined with other misstatements) misstatement could arise have been identified

      (3) Identify the controls that management has implemented over the prevention or timely detection of unauthorized acquisition, use, or disposition of the company's assets that could result in a material misstatement of the financial statements

   b. **Procedures** The procedures used to achieve these objectives should either be performed by the auditor or under her/his direct supervision due to the degree of judgment required.

   c. **Walk-Throughs** An effective method to achieve these objectives is to perform walk-throughs. The auditor follows a transaction from its origin to its reflection in the financial statements, step-by-step, using the same documents and information technology that a company's personnel use. Walk-throughs usually involve a combination of procedures, including inquiry, observation, inspections of documentation and reperformance.

7. **Selection of Controls** The decision for selection is based on whether a control by itself (or in combination with other controls) sufficiently addresses the assessed risk of misstatement to a given relevant assertion. It is not necessary to test all the controls that address an assertion.

G. **Testing Controls**

1. **Testing Design Effectiveness** The auditor should test the design of a control by determining whether the control, if performed correctly by persons with the necessary authority and competence, meets the company's control objectives and can be expected to prevent or detect errors or fraud that could result in material misstatements in the financial statements. Walk-throughs that include inquiries of appropriate people, observation of the company's operations, and inspection of documentation will usually suffice.

2. **Testing Operating Effectiveness** The auditor should test the operating effectiveness of a control by determining if the control is operating as designed and confirming that it is being performed by a person with the necessary authority and competence. Procedures for this test would include reperformance of the control in addition to inquiries of appropriate people, observation of the company's operations, and inspection of documentation.

3. **Evidence to Be Obtained** The evidence obtained is dependent on the nature, timing, and extent of audit procedures performed. Generally, more evidence is required to support the conclusion that a control is operating effectively than is needed when a control is deemed ineffective. The auditor should increase the amount of evidence gathered as the risk associated with a control increases. The following factors affect the risk associated with a control:

    a. The nature and materiality of misstatements that the control is intended to prevent or detect

    b. The inherent risk associated with the related account(s) and assertion(s)

    c. Whether there have been changes in the volume or nature of transactions that might adversely affect control design or operating effectiveness

    d. Whether the account has a history of errors

    e. The effectiveness of entity-level controls, especially controls that monitor other controls

    f. The nature of the control and the frequency with which it operates

    g. The degree to which the control relies on the effectiveness of other controls

    h. The competence of the personnel who perform the control or monitor its performance and whether there have been changes in these key personnel

    i. Whether the control relies on performance by an individual or is automated, i.e., an automated control would generally be expected to be lower risk if relevant information technology general controls are effective

    j. The complexity of the control and the significance of the judgments that must be made in connection with its operation

4. **Deviations From Controls** When deviations from controls are discovered, the auditor should determine the impact on the assessment of the risk associated with the control, the evidence being gathered, and the operating effectiveness of the control. Any *one* control does not necessarily have to operate without any deviation to be considered effective because effective ICFR does not provide *absolute* assurance.

5. **Special Considerations to Reduce Testing for Subsequent Years' Audits** The auditor should incorporate knowledge gained in prior years' audits of ICFR into the determination of the nature, timing, and extent of audit procedures selected to test controls.

    a. **Risk Factors** After taking into account various risk factors, the additional information provided in subsequent years' audits may allow the auditor to assess the risk as lower than in the first year and thus reduce the testing in the subsequent audits. The factors affecting the risk associated with a control in subsequent years' audits includes those listed in the previous "Evidence to Be Obtained" section of this topic plus the following factors:

        (1) The nature, timing, and extent of procedures performed in previous audits

        (2) The results of the previous years' testing of the control

        (3)   Whether there have been changes in the control or the process in which it operates since the previous audit

    b.   **Benchmarking** The standard specifically allows the use of a benchmarking strategy (establishment of a baseline) under certain conditions for automated (IT) application controls in subsequent years' audits because of their inherent reliability. If the auditor is able to obtain evidence that general controls over program changes, access to programs, and computer operations are effective and continue to be tested; and that there have been no changes to the automated application controls since they were last tested, the auditor may conclude that the automated application controls continue to be effective.

6.   **Vary the Testing** The auditor should vary the nature, timing, and extent of the testing of controls from one year to another to allow for changes in circumstances as well as to make the audit unpredictable.

7.   **Service Organizations** The relevant concepts in AU 324, *Service Organizations,* (concerning a company that obtains services from another organization that are part of the company's information system) are applicable to ICFR audits. If, as described in AU 324, the services provided are part of the company's information system, then it follows that they are part of the information and communications component of the company's ICFR. Thus, the auditor should include the activities of the service organization in the determination of what evidence is needed to support her/his opinion. The auditor should gain an understanding of both the controls of the service organization that are relevant to the company's internal control and the controls of the company over the activities of the service organization. Then the auditor should obtain evidence that the relevant controls are operating effectively. The auditor may use a service auditor's report on controls placed in operation and tests of operating effectiveness if s/he judges that the report provides sufficient evidence and is satisfied as to the professional reputation, competence and independence of the service auditor. However, the auditor should **not** refer to the service auditor's report in her/his opinion of ICFR.

8.   **Superseded Controls** Sometimes management changes controls during the period being audited. The auditor must use professional judgment to determine if testing of the superseded controls is needed.

H.   **Evaluating Identified Deficiencies**

1.   **Severity of the Deficiency** The auditor must determine if each control deficiency identified, either individually or in combination, is a material weakness as of the date of management's assessment by evaluating its severity. However, the auditor is **not** required to search for deficiencies that do not constitute a material weakness. The severity of a deficiency is dependent on whether there is a reasonable possibility that the company's controls will fail to prevent or detect a misstatement and the magnitude of the potential misstatement. Severity is not dependent on whether a misstatement has actually occurred. What matters is the lack of effectiveness of a company's controls, i.e., if there is a reasonable possibility that a deficiency, or a combination of deficiencies, will result in a misstatement of an account balance or disclosure.

2.   **Prudent Official Standard** The auditor should set and use a *prudent official* standard to help evaluate the severity of a deficiency, or combination of deficiencies. To do so, the auditor must determine the level of detail and degree of assurance that would satisfy prudent officials in the conduct of their own affairs that they have reasonable assurance that transactions are recorded as necessary to permit the preparation of financial statements in conformity with GAAP. If this standard is not met, the auditor should consider the deficiency, or combination of deficiencies, to be an indicator of a material weakness.

3.   **Compensating Controls** The auditor should consider the effect of compensating controls when determining if a deficiency, or combination of deficiencies, constitutes a material weakness. The compensating control should be judged effective enough to prevent or detect a misstatement that could be material in order to be considered to have a mitigating effect.

I.   **Management's Written Representations**
The standard refers the auditor to AU 333, *Management Representations,* for further guidance on the management representation letter such as who should sign it, the period it covers, and when to obtain an updated letter as these are the same as for an audit of the financial statements. The auditor should obtain the following written representations from management:

1.   Acknowledgment of management's responsibility for establishing and maintaining effective ICFR

2.   Statement that management has performed an evaluation and made an assessment of the effectiveness of the company's ICFR and specifying the control criteria

3.   Statement that management did not use the auditor's procedures performed during either the audit of ICFR or the financial statements as part of the basis for management's assessment of the effectiveness of the company's ICFR

4.   Statement of management's conclusion, as set forth in its assessment, about the effectiveness of the company's ICFR based on the control criteria as of a specified date

5.   Statement that management disclosed to the auditor all deficiencies in the design or operation of ICFR identified as part of management's evaluation, including separately disclosing all such deficiencies that it believes to be significant deficiencies or material weaknesses in ICFR

6.   Description of any fraud resulting in a material misstatement to the company's financial statements and any other fraud that involves senior management or management or other employees who have a significant role in the company's ICFR

7.   Statement of whether control deficiencies identified and communicated to the audit committee during previous engagements have been resolved, and specifically identifying any that have not

8.   Statement whether there were, subsequent to the date being reported on, any changes in ICFR or other factors that might significantly affect ICFR, including any corrective actions taken by management with regard to significant deficiencies and material weaknesses

J.   **Communications**

1.   **Ineffective Oversight** In the case where the auditor concludes that oversight by the company's audit committee of external financial reporting and ICFR is ineffective, the auditor must communicate that conclusion, in writing, to the board of directors.

2.   **Material Weaknesses** The auditor must communicate, in writing, to management and the audit committee all material weaknesses identified during the audit. This should be done prior to the issuance of the audit report on ICFR. If a material weakness has **not** been included in management's assessment, the auditor should also communicate this fact, in writing, to the audit committee.

3.   **Significant Deficiencies** The auditor must also communicate, in writing, all significant deficiencies to the audit committee.

4.   **Deficiencies** The auditor should communicate, in writing, all deficiencies in ICFR to management of which s/he is *aware*—the auditor is **not** required to perform procedures that are sufficient to identify *all* control deficiencies. The audit committee should be informed by the auditor when this communication to management has been made.

5. **Scope Limitation** If the auditor concludes that s/he cannot express an opinion because there has been a scope limitation, the auditor should communicate, in writing, to management and the audit committee that the audit of ICFR cannot be completed. See the "Disclaiming an Opinion or Withdrawing From the Engagement" section of this topic for further information.

6. **Material Misstatement in Additional Information Included With Management's Report** If the auditor determines that the other information included with management's annual report on ICFR contains a material misstatement of fact and if after a discussion with management, management does not remedy it, the auditor should communicate her/his concerns, in writing, to management and the audit committee. See the "Report Modifications" section of this topic for additional information.

7. **Fraud & Illegal Acts** The standard refers the auditor to AU 316, *Consideration of Fraud in a Financial Statement Audit,* AU 317, *Illegal Acts by Clients,* and §10A of the Securities Exchange Act of 1934 for guidance regarding the auditor's responsibilities if s/he becomes aware of fraud or possible illegal acts.

8. **Management's Annual Certification is Misstated** The standard refers the auditor to AU 722, *Interim Financial Information,* for guidance as to communication responsibilities in this instance. See the "Report Modifications" section of this topic and Chapter 30 of the textbook for additional information on interim financial information.

9. **Auditor Disagrees With Management's Exclusion of Certain Entities** The auditor may disagree with management's application of the SEC's criteria for exclusion of certain entities from the assessment of ICFR or find their disclosure of the exclusion inadequate. The standard refers the auditor to AU 722, *Interim Financial Information,* for guidance as to communication responsibilities in this instance. See the "Report Modifications" section of this topic and Chapter 30 of the textbook for additional information on interim financial information.

K. **Reporting**

1. **Forming an Opinion** The auditor should form an opinion of the effectiveness of ICFR after considering the evidence obtained from all sources. In addition to the evidence from the auditor's testing of controls and identification of control deficiencies, this would include misstatements identified during the financial statement audit and the evidence in current reports on ICFR issued by internal auditors or others. The auditor should **not** issue a report stating that no deficiencies exist because an audit of ICFR does not provide assurance that all deficiencies less severe than a material weakness have been identified.

2. **Required Elements of Audit Report** The following must be included in the auditor's report on ICFR:

   a. A title that includes the word *independent*

   b. A statement that management is responsible for maintaining effective ICFR and for assessing the effectiveness of ICFR

   c. An identification of management's report on internal control

   d. A statement that the auditor's responsibility is to express an opinion on the company's ICFR based on her/his audit

   e. A definition of ICFR as stated in paragraph A5 of the standard (see the "Definitions" section of this topic)

   f. A statement that the audit was conducted in accordance with the standards of the PCAOB (United States)

g. A statement that the standards of the PCAOB require that the auditor plan and perform the audit to obtain reasonable assurance about whether effective ICFR was maintained in all material respects

h. A statement that an audit includes obtaining an understanding of ICFR, assessing the risk that a material weakness exists, testing and evaluating the design and operating effectiveness of internal control based on the assessed risk, and performing such other procedures as the auditor considered necessary in the circumstances

i. A statement that the auditor believes the audit provides a reasonable basis for her/his opinion

j. A paragraph stating that because of inherent limitations, ICFR may not prevent or detect misstatements and that projections of any evaluation of effectiveness to future periods are subject to the risk that controls may become inadequate because of changes in conditions, or that the degree of compliance with the policies or procedures may deteriorate

k. The auditor's opinion on whether the company maintained, in all material respects, effective ICFR as of the specified date, based on the control criteria

l. The manual or printed signature of the auditor's firm

m. The city, and state (or city and country, in the case of non-U.S. auditors) from which the auditor's report has been issued

n. The date of the audit report

3. **Separate or Combined Reports** The auditor may choose to issue separate reports on the company's financial statements and ICFR or to issue a combined report containing both opinions. If the auditor issues separate reports, a separate paragraph should be added to each report that cross-references the other report, giving the date and nature of its opinion. The reference in the financial statement report to the ICFR report should also identify the control criteria on which the ICFR opinion is based.

4. **Date of Report** The auditor should date the audit report(s) no earlier than the date on which the auditor has obtained sufficient competent evidence to support the auditor's opinion. If separate reports on the financial statements and ICFR are issued, the date of the reports should be the same, as the auditor cannot audit ICFR without also auditing the financial statements.

5. **Audit Report on ICFR Included With Filings Under Federal Securities Statutes** AU 711, *Filings Under Federal Securities Statutes,* is applicable when the auditor's report is included in registration statements, proxy statements, or periodic reports filed under federal securities statutes.

6. **Report Modifications** The auditor should modify the report if any of the following conditions exist:

a. **Elements of Management's Annual Report on ICFR Are Incomplete or Improperly Presented** After forming an opinion on the effectiveness of ICFR, the auditor should review management's presentation on the elements that is required by the SEC to be included in the company's annual report on ICFR. If the auditor determines that any of these elements are incomplete or not properly presented the auditor should add an explanatory paragraph that describes the reasons why the auditor found management's report unsatisfactory.

b. **Scope Limitation** See the "Disclaiming an Opinion or Withdrawing From the Engagement" section of this topic.

c. **Auditor Decides to Refer to the Report of Other Auditors** When another auditor has audited the financial statements and ICFR of one or more components of a company, the auditor needs to determine whether s/he may serve as the principal auditor and use the work and reports of another auditor as a basis, in part, for her/his opinion on ICFR. The standard states that AU 543, *Part of Audit Performed by Other Independent Auditors,* is applicable to this determination by the auditor. If the auditor decides that s/he should be the principal auditor of the financial statements, then s/he must also be the principal auditor for ICFR. The principal auditor's decision whether to make reference in the report on ICFR to the audit of ICFR performed by another auditor is similar to the same decision for financial reporting, so again, AU 543 is applicable. When the auditor decides to make this reference, the auditor should refer to the report of the other auditor when describing the scope of the audit and when expressing the opinion.

d. **Other Information in Management's Annual Report on ICFR** If the additional information included by management appears to be part of management's annual report on ICFR, then the auditor should disclaim an opinion on the other information. If the auditor determines that the other information contains a material misstatement of fact and if after a discussion with management, management does not remedy it, the auditor should communicate her/his concerns, in writing, to management and the audit committee. This standard also refers the auditor to AU 317, *Illegal Acts by Clients,* and §10A of the Securities Exchange Act of 1934 for further direction because in some circumstances additional action may be required.

e. **Management's Annual Certification Is Misstated** The standard refers the auditor to AU 722, *Interim Financial Information,* for guidance as to communication requirements if matters come to her/his attention that convince her/him that modifications to the disclosures about changes in ICFR are needed for the annual certifications to be accurate and to be in compliance with either the requirements of §302 of Sarbanes-Oxley Act of 2002 or Securities Exchange Act rules for any interim period. If management and the audit committee fail to respond satisfactorily, the auditor (in addition to the requirements described in AU 722) should add an explanatory paragraph to her/his report on ICFR which explains the reasons s/he believes management's disclosures should be modified.

f. **Assessment of ICFR Excludes Certain Entities** The SEC allows management to limit its assessment of ICFR by excluding certain entities and the auditor may choose to do likewise. This situation is **not** considered a scope limitation. However, the auditor should include, either in an additional explanatory paragraph or as part of the scope paragraph in her/his report, a disclosure similar to management's concerning the exclusion of an entity from both the scope of management's assessment and the auditor's audit of ICFR. If the auditor considers management's application of the SEC's exclusion criteria to be unreasonable or management's disclosure inadequate, the auditor should follow the guidance in paragraphs 29 through 32 of AU 722, *Interim Financial Information,* as to communication requirements. In addition, the auditor should add in explanatory paragraph to her/his report on ICFR which describes the reasons why the auditor believes management's disclosures should be modified.

g. **Subsequent Events** The auditor may obtain knowledge about subsequent events with respect to conditions that did *not* exist at the date of the assessment, but arose subsequent to that date and before issuance of the auditor's report and had a material effect on the company's ICFR. The auditor should add an explanatory paragraph to her/his report describing the event and its effects or a reference to the disclosure in management's report. (If the effect cannot be determined, the auditor should disclaim an opinion. For additional information see the "Subsequent Events" section of this topic.)

7. **Adverse Opinion** If there are one or more material weaknesses, the auditor must express an adverse opinion on the company's ICFR unless the scope of the audit has been limited. (The auditor must either withdraw from the engagement or disclaim an opinion if there are restrictions on the scope of the engagement. See the "Disclaiming an Opinion or Withdrawing From the Engagement" section of this topic.)

   a. **Disclosure** The auditor should include a disclosure in the report as to whether the opinion on the financial statements was affected by the adverse opinion on ICFR.

   b. **Material Weakness** An adverse opinion report resulting from a material weakness must include the definition of a material weakness (see the "Definitions" section of this topic per paragraph A7 of the standard). The remaining modifications to the report and required actions depend on if and if so, how, the material weakness was also included in management's assessment.

      (1) When a material weakness was identified and was included in management's assessment, the report must include a statement that a material weakness was identified and an identification of the material weakness described in management's assessment. If the auditor finds that the disclosure is not fairly presented in all material respects, the auditor's report should describe this conclusion and the information needed to fairly describe the material weakness.

      (2) When a material weakness was identified, but was **not** included in management's assessment the following items must be included in the auditor's report:

         (a) A statement that a material weakness was identified, but not included in management's assessment

         (b) A description of the material weakness that includes specific information about its nature plus the actual and potential effect on the financial statements issued during its existence

         (c) Additionally, the auditor should communicate, in writing, to the audit committee that the material weakness was not identified or disclosed in management's assessment.

8. **Disclaiming an Opinion or Withdrawing From the Engagement**

   a. **Scope Limitation** The auditor may not form an opinion on the effectiveness of ICFR if there have been restrictions on the scope of the auditor's work to the degree that the auditor was unable to apply the procedures necessary under the circumstances. If there has been such a scope limitation the auditor is required to disclaim an opinion or withdraw from the engagement. One example of a scope limitation is when the auditor is unable to obtain written representations from management. In this case, the auditor should also consider the effects of management's refusal on her/his ability to rely on other representations made by management, including those made in conjunction with the audit of the financial statements. The auditor may issue a disclaimer as soon as s/he determines that a scope limitation will prevent the attainment of evidence sufficient to gain the reasonable assurance needed to express an opinion. No additional work is required by the auditor at this point. The report date is the date that the auditor has gained sufficient competent evidence to support the representations contained in her/his report. The auditor should communicate, in writing, to management and the audit committee that s/he is unable to satisfactorily complete the audit of ICFR. When disclaiming an opinion due to a scope limitation, the auditor's report should:

      (1) Include a statement that the scope of the audit was not sufficient to warrant the expression of an opinion

(2) Include a separate paragraph(s) that gives the substantive reasons for the disclaimer

(3) **Not** identify the procedures that were performed **nor** include the description of the characteristics of an audit of ICFR to avoid overshadowing the disclaimer

(4) Include a description of any material weakness that was identified in the company's ICFR (if the auditor was able to conclude it existed based on the limited procedures applied); this should include specifics about the nature of the material weakness and its actual and potential effect on the presentation of the company's financial statements issued during the existence of the material weakness—this description should conform to the requirements in paragraph 91 of the standard for the issuance of an adverse opinion due to a material weakness (covered in the previous "Adverse Opinion" section of this topic); the definition of the term material weakness per "Appendix A" of the standard (paragraph A7; see the "Definitions" section of this topic) should also be included

b. **Effect of Subsequent Event Not Determinable** The auditor should disclaim an opinion when s/he cannot determine the effect that a subsequent event (with respect to conditions that existed at the date of the assessment) had on a company's ICFR. For additional information see the "Subsequent Events" section of this topic.

L. **Subsequent Events**

1. **Procedures to Identify Subsequent Events** Changes in ICFR or other factors that have a material impact on ICFR may occur subsequent to the date that ICFR is being audited but before the date of the auditor's report. AU 560, *Subsequent Events,* provides direction on subsequent events for a financial statement audit that may also be helpful during an audit of ICFR. As previously covered, the auditor should attain written representations from management relating to subsequent events. The auditor should review, for this subsequent period, the following:

a. Internal audit reports

b. Other independent auditor reports of deficiencies in internal control

c. Regulatory agency reports on the company's ICFR

d. Information about the company's ICFR obtained via other engagements.

2. **When the Subsequent Event Became Known or Arose** *Before* **the Issuance of the Auditor's Report:**

a. **And** *Did* **Exist As of the Date of Management's Assessment** If the auditor becomes aware of subsequent events that materially and adversely affect ICFR as of the date of the assessment, the auditor should issue an adverse opinion. If management's assessment states that ICFR is effective, the auditor should follow the guidance described previously under "Adverse Opinion" in this topic. If the auditor cannot determine the effect of the event on the company's ICFR, the auditor should disclaim an opinion.

b. **And Did** *Not* **Exist As of Date of Management's Assessment** The auditor may become aware of a subsequent event with respect to conditions that did **not** exist as of the date specified in management's assessment, but arose subsequent to that date and before issuance of the auditor's report. If the subsequent event had a material effect on ICFR, the auditor should add an explanatory paragraph to her/his report that either describes the event and its effect or includes a referral to the disclosure in management's report.

3. **When the Subsequent Event Became Known *After* the Issuance of the Auditor's Report**
If after the auditor issues the report, s/he becomes aware of a subsequent event that existed as of the report date and that might have affected her/his opinion, the auditor should follow the guidance in AU 561, *Subsequent Discovery of Facts Existing at the Date of the Auditor's Report.*

V. Reporting on Whether a Previously Reported Material Weakness Continues to Exist

A. Overview
PCAOB AS 4, *Reporting on Whether a Previously Reported Material Weakness Continues to Exist,* applies when an auditor is engaged to report on whether a previously reported material weakness in ICFR continues to exist as of a date specified by management. A *previously reported material weakness* means a material weakness that was described previously in an auditor's report on ICFR as required by PCAOB AS 5. The PCAOB does not require this type of engagement. The auditor may report on more than one previously reported material weakness in a single engagement.

B. Conditions
There may be certain material weaknesses that are not suitable for this type of engagement; that is, if identifying *all* stated control objectives affected by the material weakness is difficult, then the material weakness should be addressed, instead, in the annual audit of ICFR. The following conditions must all be met for an auditor to complete this type of engagement:

1. Management has accepted responsibility for the effectiveness of ICFR.

2. Management has evaluated the effectiveness of the specific control(s) using the same stated control objectives and control criteria it used for its most recent annual assessment of ICFR.

3. Management has asserted that the specific control(s) identified is/are effective in achieving the stated control objective.

4. Management has supported its assertion with sufficient evidence, including documentation.

5. Management has presented a written report that will accompany the audit report that contains all required elements.

C. Opinion
In order to render an unqualified opinion, the auditor must have (1) obtained evidence about the design and operating effectiveness of the specifically identified controls, (2) determined that the material weakness no longer exists, and (3) determined that there were no scope limitations. If a scope limitation exists, the auditor is required to either disclaim an opinion or withdraw from the engagement. A qualified opinion is not allowed.

D. Material Weakness Continues to Exist
If an auditor determines that a material weakness continues to exist, the following should be considered:

1. If the auditor issues a report, it must state that the material weakness continues to exist as of the date specified by management.

2. If the auditor does not issue a report (which is not required), s/he must communicate to the audit committee, in writing, her/his conclusion that the material weakness continues to exist. If another material weakness is discovered during the engagement, it must also be communicated to the audit committee in writing.

3. The auditor must consider the conclusion that the material weakness continues to exist as part of her/his evaluation of management's quarterly disclosures about ICFR, as required by PCAOB AS 5.

4. If an auditor is engaged to report on two previously reported material weaknesses and only one of them continues to exist, the auditor can report in either of two ways: (1) the auditor can issue one report that contains two different opinions on each material weakness; or (2) the auditor can issue a report that contains a single opinion on the material weakness that no longer exists if management modifies its assertion to address only that material weakness. The auditor will still need to communicate in writing to the audit committee, the conclusion regarding the second material weakness that continues to exist.

VI. Evaluating Consistency of Financial Statements

A.   Consistency & the Auditor's Report

1. **Objective of AS 6** PCAOB Auditing Standard (AS) 6 establishes requirements and provides direction for the auditor's evaluation of the consistency of the financial statements, including changes to previously issued financial statements, and the effect of that evaluation on the auditor's report on the financial statements.

2. **Comparability of Financial Statements Between Periods** To identify consistency matters that might affect the report, the auditor should evaluate whether the comparability of the financial statements between periods has been materially affected by changes in accounting principles or by material adjustments to previously issued financial statements for the relevant periods.

3. **Periods to Evaluate** The periods covered in the auditor's evaluation of consistency depend on the periods covered by the auditor's report on the financial statements. When reporting only on the current period, the auditor should evaluate whether the current period financial statements are consistent with those of the preceding period. When reporting on two or more periods, the auditor should evaluate consistency between such periods and the consistency of such periods with the period prior thereto if such prior period is presented with the financial statements being reported upon.

4. **Recognition in Audit Report** The auditor should recognize the following matters relating to the consistency of the company's financial statements in the auditor's report if those matters have a material effect on the financial statements.

    a. A change in accounting principle

    b. An adjustment to correct a misstatement in previously issued financial statements

    An explanatory paragraph should be added, following the opinion paragraph, as discussed in the following topics.

B.   Change in Accounting Principle

1. **Definition** A change in accounting principle is a change from one generally accepted accounting principle to another generally accepted accounting principle when

    (a)   There are two or more generally accepted accounting principles that apply

    (b)   The accounting principle formerly used is no longer generally accepted

    (c)   A change in the method of applying an accounting principle has occurred

2. **Change in Accounting Estimate Effected by a Change in Accounting Principle** The auditor should evaluate and report on a change in accounting estimate effected by a change in accounting principle like other changes in accounting principles.

3. **Change in Reporting Entity** The auditor should recognize a change in the reporting entity like other changes in accounting principles unless the change in reporting entity results from

a transaction or event. (A change in reporting entity that results from a transaction or event, such as the creation, cessation, or complete or partial purchase or disposition of a subsidiary or other business unit does not require recognition in the auditor's report.)

4. **Investee's Change in Accounting Principle** If a company's financial statements contain an investment accounted for by the equity method, the auditor's evaluation of consistency should include consideration of the investee. If the investee makes a change in accounting principle that is material to the investing company's financial statements, the auditor should add an explanatory paragraph (following the opinion paragraph) to the auditor's report.

5. **Auditor's Evaluation** The auditor should evaluate a change in accounting principle to determine whether

   a. The newly adopted accounting principle is a generally accepted accounting principle

   b. The method of accounting for the effect of the change is in conformity with generally accepted accounting principles

   c. The disclosures related to the accounting change are adequate

   d. The company has justified that the alternative accounting principle is preferable

   Editor note: If the above criteria are not met, the auditor should consider the matter to be a departure from GAAP and, if the effect of the change in accounting principle is material, issue a qualified or adverse opinion.

6. **Explanatory Paragraph** If the auditor concludes that the above criteria have been met, the auditor should add an explanatory paragraph to the auditor's report, through the addition of an explanatory paragraph **following** the opinion paragraph. The explanatory paragraph should include identification of the nature of the change and a reference to the note disclosure describing the change.

   a. **Adoption of a New Pronouncement Example**
   "As discussed in Note X to the financial statements, the company has changed its method of accounting for [*describe accounting method change*] in [*year(s) of financial statements that reflect the accounting method change*] due to the adoption of [*name of accounting pronouncement*]."

   b. **Change in Accounting Principle Not Involving a New Pronouncement Example**
   "As discussed in Note X to the financial statements, the company has elected to change its method of accounting for [*describe accounting method change*] in [*year(s) of financial statements that reflect the accounting method change*]."

   c. **Report Recognition Periods Required** The explanatory paragraph relating to a change in accounting principle should be included in reports on financial statements in the year of the change and in subsequent years until the new accounting principle is applied in all periods presented. If the accounting change is accounted for by retrospective application to the financial statements of all prior periods presented, the additional paragraph is needed only in the year of the change.

C. **Correction of a Material Misstatement in Previously Issued Financial Statements**

1. **Explanatory Paragraph** The correction of a material misstatement in previously issued financial statements should be recognized in the auditor's report through the addition of an explanatory paragraph **following** the opinion paragraph. The explanatory paragraph should include the following.

   a. A statement that the previously issued financial statements have been restated for the correction of a misstatement in the respective period

        b.   A reference to the company's disclosure of the correction of the misstatement.

        c.   **Example**
               "As discussed in Note X to the financial statements, the 20X2 financial statements have been restated to correct a misstatement."

    2.   **Report Recognition Periods Required** This type of explanatory paragraph in the auditor's report should be included in reports on financial statements when the related financial statements are restated to correct the prior material misstatement. The paragraph need not be repeated in subsequent years

Editor note: A change from an accounting principle that is not generally accepted to one that is generally accepted is a correction of a misstatement.

D.   **Change in Classification**
Changes in classification in previously issued financial statements do **not** require recognition in the auditor's report, unless the change represents the correction of a material misstatement or a change in accounting principle. Accordingly, the auditor should evaluate a material change in financial statement classification and the related disclosure to determine whether such a change also is a change in accounting principle or a correction of a material misstatement. For example, certain reclassifications in previously issued financial statements, such as reclassifications of debt from long-term to short-term or reclassifications of cash flows from the operating activities category to the financing activities category, might occur because those items were incorrectly classified in the previously issued financial statements. In such situations, the reclassification also is the correction of a misstatement.

VII.   **Interim Financial Information**

    A.   **Overview**

        1.   **Objective** The objective of the guidance covered by the PCAOB's adopted and amended AU 722, *Interim Financial Information*, is to provide the CPA with a basis for communicating whether material modifications are needed to make the information conform with GAAP.

        2.   **Period Covered** The term *interim financial information* means financial information or statements covering a period less than a full year or for a 12-month period ending on a date other than the entity's fiscal year end.

        3.   **SEC Filing Requirements** The Securities and Exchange Commission (SEC) requires a registrant to engage an independent accountant to review the registrant's interim financial information, in accordance with AU 722, before the registrant files its quarterly report on Form 10-Q or Form 10-QSB. The SEC also requires management, with the participation of the principal executive and financial officers (the certifying officers) to make certain quarterly and annual certifications with respect to the company's internal control over financial reporting. Although AU 722 does not require an accountant to issue a written report on a review of interim financial information, the SEC requires that an accountant's review report be filed with the interim financial information if, in any filing, the entity states that the interim financial information has been reviewed by an independent public accountant

        4.   **Review vs. Audit** The objective of a review of interim financial information differs significantly from that of an audit conducted in accordance with GAAP. A review of interim financial information does not provide a basis for expressing an opinion about whether the financial statements are presented fairly, in all material respects, in conformity with generally accepted accounting principles. A review consists principally of performing analytical procedures and making inquiries of persons responsible for financial and accounting matters, and does not contemplate (*a*) tests of accounting records through inspection, observation, or confirmation; (*b*) tests of controls to evaluate their effectiveness; (*c*) obtaining corroborating evidence in response to inquiries; or (*d*) performing certain other procedures ordinarily performed in an audit. A review may bring to the accountant's attention significant matters affecting the interim financial information, but it does not provide assurance that the accountant will become aware of all significant matters that would be identified in an audit Also, a review is not designed to provide assurance on internal control or to identify significant deficiencies. However, the accountant is responsible for communicating with the audit committee or others with equivalent authority or responsibility, regarding any significant deficiencies that come to her/his attention

The auditor's responsibility as it relates to management's quarterly certifications on internal control over financial reporting is also different from the auditor's responsibility as it relates to management's annual assessment of internal control over financial reporting. The auditor should perform limited procedures quarterly to provide a basis for determining whether s/he has become aware of any material modifications that, in the auditor's judgment, should be made to the disclosures about changes in internal control over financial reporting.

B.   Procedures

    1.   Inquiries & Other Review Procedures

        a.   Reading Minutes Reading the available minutes of meetings of stockholders, directors, and appropriate committees, and inquiring about matters dealt with at meetings for which minutes are not available, to identify matters that may affect the interim financial information.

        b.   Obtaining Reports From Other Accountants Obtaining reports from other accountants, if any, who have been engaged to perform a review of the interim financial information of significant components of the reporting entity, its subsidiaries, or its other investees, or inquiring of those accountants if reports have not been issued.

        c.   Inquiring of Members of Management Inquiring of members of management who have responsibility for financial and accounting matters concerning

            (1) Whether the interim financial information has been prepared in conformity with generally accepted accounting principles consistently applied.

            (2) Unusual or complex situations that may have an effect on the interim financial information.

            (3) Significant transactions occurring or recognized in the last several days of the interim period.

            (4) The status of uncorrected misstatements identified during the previous audit and interim review (that is, whether adjustments had been recorded subsequent to the prior audit or interim period and, if so, the amounts recorded and period in which such adjustments were recorded).

            (5) Matters about which questions have arisen in the course of applying the review procedures.

            (6) Events subsequent to the date of the interim financial information that could have a material effect on the presentation of such information.

            (7) Their knowledge of any fraud or suspected fraud affecting the entity involving (a) management, (b) employees who have significant roles in internal control, or (c) others where the fraud could have a material effect on the financial statements.

(8) Whether they are aware of allegations of fraud or suspected fraud affecting the entity, for example, received in communications from employees, former employees, analysts, regulators, short sellers, or others.

(9) Significant journal entries and other adjustments.

(10) Communications from regulatory agencies.

(11) Significant deficiencies, including material weaknesses, in the design or operation of internal controls which could adversely affect the issuer's ability to record, process, summarize, and report financial data.

d. **Accounting Records** Obtaining evidence that the interim financial information agrees or reconciles with the accounting records. For example, the accountant may compare the interim financial information to

(1) The accounting records, such as the general ledger

(2) A consolidating schedule derived from the accounting records

(3) Other supporting data in the entity's records

In addition, the accountant should consider inquiring of management as to the reliability of the records to which the interim financial information was compared or reconciled.

e. **Reading Interim Financial Information** To determine whether it conforms to GAAP.

f. **Other Information** Reading other information that accompanies the interim financial information and is contained in reports (to consider whether such information or the manner of its presentation is materially inconsistent with the interim financial information)

(1) To holders of securities or beneficial interests

(2) Filed with regulatory authorities under the Securities Exchange Act of 1934 (such as Form 10-Q or 10-QSB)

If the accountant concludes that there is a material inconsistency, or becomes aware of information that s/he believes is a material misstatement of fact, the action taken will depend on her/his judgment in the particular circumstances.

g. **Management's Quarterly Certifications About Internal Control** Evaluating management's quarterly certifications about internal control over financial reporting by performing the following procedures:

(1) Inquiring of management about significant changes in the design or operation of internal control over financial reporting as it relates to the preparation of annual as well as interim financial information that could have occurred subsequent to the preceding annual audit or prior review of interim financial information

(2) Evaluating the implications of misstatements identified by the auditor as part of the auditor's other interim review procedures as they relate to effective internal control over financial reporting

(3) Determining, through a combination of observation and inquiry, whether any change in internal control over financial reporting has materially affected, or is reasonably likely to materially affect, the company's internal control over financial reporting

h.   **Analytics** Applied to interim financial information to provide a basis for inquiring about unusual items. These procedures consist of

    (1) Comparing the financial information with the immediately preceding interim period and with the corresponding previous period(s)

    (2) Comparing actual results with anticipated results

    (3) Studying the relationships of those elements that can be expected to conform to predictable patterns. The CPA should consider the types of matters that required accounting adjustments in the preceding year or quarters.

i.   **Obtaining Written Representations** From management, concerning management's responsibility for the financial information, completeness of the minutes, subsequent events, etc.

2.   **Required Procedures** AU 722 specifically requires the following procedures:

a.   **Disaggregated Comparison** Comparing disaggregated revenue data, for example, comparing revenue reported by month and by product line or business segment for the current interim period with that of comparable prior periods.

b.   **Reconciliation** Obtaining evidence that the interim financial information agrees or reconciles with the accounting records.

c.   **Fraud Inquiry** Inquiring of members of management who have responsibility for financial and accounting matters as to their knowledge of any fraud or suspected fraud affecting the entity, and whether they are aware of allegations of fraud or suspected fraud, affecting the entity received in communications from employees, former employees, analysts, regulators, short sellers, or others.

If the auditor becomes aware of information indicating that fraud or an illegal act has or may have occurred, the auditor must also determine her/his responsibilities under AU sec. 316, *Consideration of Fraud in a Financial Statement Audit*, AU sec. 317, *Illegal Acts by Clients*, and Section 10A of the Securities Exchange Act of 1934.

3.   **Timing** Performing some of the work before the end of the interim period (a) usually permits the work to be carried out more efficiently, and (b) permits early consideration of accounting matters that affect the interim financial information.

4.   **Extent** The extent to which the CPA applies procedures depends on the accountant's knowledge of changes in accounting practices or in the nature or volume of business activity; inquiry concerning litigation, claims, and assessments; questions raised in performing other procedures; and modification of review procedures.

5.   **Understanding With Client** AU 722 requires an accountant to establish an understanding with her/his client regarding the services to be performed in an engagement to review interim financial information. This understanding is usually in the form of an engagement letter that includes: a general description of the procedures; a statement that the procedures are substantially less in scope than an audit performed in accordance with GAAS; an explanation that the financial information is the responsibility of the company's management; and a description of the form of the report, if any.

6.   **Knowledge of the Entity's Business & It's Internal Control** AU 722 requires that, for an accountant to perform a review of interim financial information, there must exist a sufficient knowledge of the client's business and internal control policies and procedures as they relate to the preparation of both annual and interim financial information to: (a) identify types of potential material misstatements in the interim financial information and consider the likelihood of their occurrence; and (b) select the inquiries and analytics that will provide the

accountant with a basis for reporting whether material modifications should be made for such information to conform with GAAP.

7. **Subsequent Events** Subsequent discovery of facts that existed at the date of the auditor's report should be handled in accordance with AU 561.

8. **Quality of Principles & Estimates** AU 722 requires an auditor to discuss the quality of accounting principles and accounting estimates, but limited to the impact of transactions, events, and changes considered in performing review procedures. The auditor should attempt a discussion with those charged with governance prior to filing the Form 10-Q. The discussion should occur before the filing or as soon thereafter as practicable.

C. **Communications to Management, Audit Committees & Others**
As a result of conducting a review of interim financial information, the accountant may become aware of matters that cause her/him to believe that

1. Material modification should be made to the interim financial information for it to conform with generally accepted accounting principles

2. Modification to the disclosures about changes in internal control over financial reporting is necessary for the certifications to be accurate and to comply with the requirements of Section 302 of the Act and Securities Exchange Act Rule 13a-14(a) or 15d-14(a), whichever applies

3. The entity filed the Form 10-Q or Form 10-QSB before the completion of the review

In such circumstances, the accountant should communicate the matter(s) to the appropriate level of management as soon as practicable.

When conducting a review of interim financial information, the accountant may become aware of matters relating to internal control that may be of interest to the audit committee. Matters that should be reported to the audit committee are referred to as significant deficiencies. A significant deficiency is a deficiency, or a combination of deficiencies, in internal control over financial reporting, that is less severe than a material weakness yet important enough to merit attention by those responsible for oversight of the company's financial reporting.

D. **Report**
The report should consist of: (1) a statement that the review conformed to the standards for a review of interim financial information; (2) an identification of the information reviewed; (3) a description of the procedures for a review; (4) a statement that the scope of a review is substantially less than that of an audit and that an opinion on the financial statements, taken as a whole, is **not** expressed; and (5) a statement as to whether the CPA is aware of any material modifications needed to make the financial information conform with GAAP.

1. **Report Form** The report is addressed to the company, its board of directors, or its stockholders and is dated as of the completion of the review. Each page of the interim financial information should be clearly marked "unaudited." The CPA may use and make reference to the report of another accountant, such reference indicates a division of responsibility for performing the review.

Exhibit 1 ▶ Report on Interim Financial Information

> We have reviewed the accompanying (describe the information or statement reviewed) of ABC Company and consolidated subsidiaries as of September 30, 20X1, and for the three-month and nine-month periods then ended. These financial statements (information) are (is) the responsibility of the company's management.
>
> We conducted our review in accordance with standards established by the American Institute of Certified Public Accountants. A review of interim financial information consists principally of applying analytical procedures to financial data, and making inquiries of persons responsible for financial and accounting matters. It is substantially less in scope than an audit conducted in accordance with U.S. generally accepted auditing standards, the objective of which is the expression of an opinion regarding the financial statements taken as a whole. Accordingly, we do not express such an opinion.
>
> Based on our review, we are not aware of any material modifications that should be made to the accompanying financial (information or statements) for them (it) to be in conformity with U.S. generally accepted accounting principles.

2. **Modification of CPA's Report** Neither an uncertainty **nor** a lack of consistency in applying accounting principles would result in a modified report as long as the matters are disclosed adequately in the interim financial information or statements. However, a modification is required if a change in accounting principle is **not** in conformity with GAAP.

    a. **Departure From GAAP** Report should be modified when the interim financial information is affected materially by a departure from GAAP. The nature of the departure and, if practicable, its effects should be disclosed.

Exhibit 2▶ Departure From GAAP

> (Explanatory third paragraph)
>
> Based on information furnished to us by management, we believe that the Company has excluded from property and debt in the accompanying balance sheet certain lease obligations that should be capitalized to conform with generally accepted accounting principles. This information indicates that if these lease obligations were capitalized at September 30, 20X1, property would be increased by \$_____, long-term debt by \$_____, and net income and earnings per share would be increased (decreased) by \$_____, \$_____, \$_____, and \$_____, respectively, for the three-month and nine-month periods then ended.
>
> (Concluding paragraph)
>
> Based on our review, with the exception of the matter(s) described in the preceding paragraph(s), we are not aware of any material modifications that should be made to the accompanying financial (information or statements) for them (it) to be in conformity with U.S. generally accepted accounting principles.

    b. **Inadequate Disclosure** Report should be modified and, if practicable, the needed information should be included.

Exhibit 3 ▶ Inadequate Disclosure

> (Explanatory third paragraph)
>
> Management has informed us that the Company is presently contesting deficiencies in federal income taxes proposed by the Internal Revenue Service for the years 20X1 through 20X3 in the aggregate amount of approximately $_____, and that the extent of the company's liability, if any, and the effect on the accompanying (information or statements) are (is) not determinable at this time. The (information or statements) fail to disclose these matters, which we believe are required to be disclosed in conformity with generally accepted accounting principles.
>
> (Concluding paragraph)
>
> Based on our review, with the exception of the matter(s) described in the preceding paragraph(s), we are not aware of any material modifications that should be made to the accompanying financial (information or statements) for them (it) to be in conformity with U.S. generally accepted accounting principles.

E.   Presented in Note to Audited Financial Statements
SEC Regulation S-K requires some companies to include a note containing selected quarterly financial information in their audited financial statements. In addition, other companies may choose to do so. If the quarterly data is presented voluntarily, the auditor should review it or the auditor should expand the report to state the data has not been reviewed. The interim financial information is **not** required by GAAP and has not been audited; therefore, the auditor ordinarily will **not** modify the report on the audited financial statements to refer to the quarterly data.

1.   **Omission** If the CPA has audited the annual financial statements for which the quarterly information required by Regulation S-K is presented, the CPA should review the quarterly information. If unable to perform such review, the report on the audited financial statements may need to be modified. If the quarterly data either has been omitted **or** has not been reviewed, the auditor's report on the annual statements should be modified.

2.   **Other** The auditor's report also should be expanded when the following occurs: the interim financial information is not marked "unaudited;" the interim information is presented voluntarily, but has not been reviewed and is not appropriately marked as such; the interim information does not conform to GAAP; or the information, although reviewed, fails to indicate that a review is substantially less in scope than an audit performed per GAAS.

VIII. Engagement Quality Review (PCAOB AS 7, Subject to the Approval of the SEC)

   A.   Overview

   1.   **Applicability of Standard** An engagement quality review and concurring approval of issuance are required for each audit engagement and for each engagement to review interim financial information conducted pursuant to the standards of the PCAOB.

   2.   **Objective** The objective of the engagement quality reviewer is to perform an evaluation of the significant judgments made by the engagement team and the related conclusions reached in forming the overall conclusion on the engagement and in preparing the engagement report, if a report is to be issued, in order to determine whether to provide concurring approval of issuance.

   B.   Qualifications of an Engagement Quality Reviewer

   1.   The engagement quality reviewer must be an associated person of a registered public accounting firm. An engagement quality reviewer from the firm that issues the engagement report (or communicates an engagement conclusion, if no report is issued) must be a partner or another individual in an equivalent position. The engagement quality reviewer may also be an individual from outside the firm.

2. An engagement quality reviewer must have competence, independence, integrity, and objectivity.

    a. **Competence** The engagement quality reviewer must possess the level of knowledge and competence related to accounting, auditing, and financial reporting required to serve as the engagement partner on the engagement under review.

    b. **Independence, Integrity & Objectivity** The engagement quality reviewer must be independent of the company, perform the engagement quality review with integrity, and maintain objectivity in performing the review.

3. **Objectivity** To maintain objectivity, the engagement quality reviewer and others who assist the reviewer should not make decisions on behalf of the engagement team or assume any of the responsibilities of the engagement team. The engagement partner remains responsible for the engagement and its performance, notwithstanding the involvement of the engagement quality reviewer and others who assist the reviewer.

4. The person who served as the engagement partner during either of the two audits preceding the audit subject to the engagement quality review may not be the engagement quality reviewer. Registered firms that qualify for the exemption under Rule 2-01(c)(6)(ii) of Regulation S-X, 17 C.F.R. §210.2-01(c)(6)(ii), are exempt from the requirement in this paragraph.

C. **Engagement Quality Review for an Audit**

1. **Process** In an audit engagement, the engagement quality reviewer should evaluate the significant judgments made by the engagement team and the related conclusions reached in forming the overall conclusion on the engagement and in preparing the engagement report. To evaluate such judgments and conclusions, the engagement quality reviewer should (1) hold discussions with the engagement partner and other members of the engagement team, and (2) review documentation. The engagement quality reviewer should:

    a. Evaluate the significant judgments that relate to engagement planning, including

        (1) The consideration of the firm's recent engagement experience with the company and risks identified in connection with the firm's client acceptance and retention process

        (2) The consideration of the company's business, recent significant activities, and related financial reporting issues and risks

        (3) The judgments made about materiality and the effect of those judgments on the engagement strategy

    b. Evaluate the engagement team's assessment of, and audit responses to

        (1) Significant risks identified by the engagement team, including fraud risks

        (2) Other significant risks identified by the engagement quality reviewer through performance of the procedures required by this standard

    c. Evaluate the significant judgments made about (1) the materiality and disposition of corrected and uncorrected identified misstatements and (2) the severity and disposition of identified control deficiencies.

    d. Review the engagement team's evaluation of the firm's independence in relation to the engagement.

e. Review the engagement completion document and confirm with the engagement partner that there are no significant unresolved matters.

f. Review the financial statements, management's report on internal control, and the related engagement report.

g. Read other information in documents containing the financial statements to be filed with the SEC and evaluate whether the engagement team has taken appropriate action with respect to any material inconsistencies with the financial statements or material misstatements of fact of which the engagement quality reviewer is aware.

h. Based on the procedures required by this standard, evaluate whether appropriate consultations have taken place on difficult or contentious matters. Review the documentation, including conclusions, of such consultations.

i. Based on the procedures required by this standard, evaluate whether appropriate matters have been communicated, or identified for communication, to the audit committee, management, and other parties, such as regulatory bodies.

2. **Evaluation of Engagement Documentation** The engagement quality reviewer should evaluate whether the engagement documentation that s/he reviewed when performing the procedures described above

a. Indicates that the engagement team responded appropriately to significant risks

b. Supports the conclusions reached by the engagement team with respect to the matters reviewed

3. **Concurring Approval of Issuance** The engagement quality reviewer may provide concurring approval of issuance only if, after performing with due professional care the review required by this standard, s/he is not aware of a significant engagement deficiency. The firm may grant permission to the client to use the engagement report only after the engagement quality reviewer provides concurring approval of issuance.

D. **Engagement Quality Review for a Review of Interim Financial Information**

1. **Process** The engagement quality reviewer should evaluate the significant judgments made by the engagement team and the related conclusions reached in forming the overall conclusion on the engagement and in preparing the engagement report, if a report is to be issued. To evaluate such judgments and conclusions, the engagement quality reviewer should, to the extent necessary to satisfy the requirements described below: (1) hold discussions with the engagement partner and other members of the engagement team, and (2) review documentation. The engagement quality reviewer should

a. Evaluate the significant judgments that relate to engagement planning, including the consideration of

(1) The firm's recent engagement experience with the company and risks identified in connection with the firm's client acceptance and retention process

(2) The company's business, recent significant activities, and related financial reporting issues and risks

(3) The nature of identified risks of material misstatement due to fraud

b. Evaluate the significant judgments made about (1) the materiality and disposition of corrected and uncorrected identified misstatements and (2) any material modifications that should be made to the disclosures about changes in internal control over financial reporting.

c. Perform the procedures described in paragraphs C 1 d. and e. above.

d. Review the interim financial information for all periods presented and for the immediately preceding interim period, management's disclosure for the period under review, if any, about changes in internal control over financial reporting, and the related engagement report, if a report is to be issued.

e. Read other information in documents containing interim financial information to be filed with the SEC and evaluate whether the engagement team has taken appropriate action with respect to material inconsistencies with the interim financial information or material misstatements of fact of which the engagement quality reviewer is aware.

f. Perform the procedures in C1 h. and i. above.

2. **Evaluation of Engagement Documentation** The engagement quality reviewer should evaluate whether the engagement documentation that s/he reviewed when performing the required procedures supports the conclusions reached by the engagement team with respect to the matters reviewed.

3. **Concurring Approval of Issuance** The engagement quality reviewer may provide concurring approval of issuance only if, after performing with due professional care the review required by this standard, s/he is not aware of a significant engagement deficiency. In a review of interim financial information, the firm may grant permission to the client to use the engagement report (or communicate an engagement conclusion to its client, if no report is issued) only after the engagement quality reviewer provides concurring approval of issuance.

E. **Documentation of Engagement Quality Review**
Documentation of an engagement quality review should contain sufficient information to enable an experienced auditor, having no previous connection with the engagement, to understand the procedures performed by the engagement quality reviewer, and others who assisted the reviewer, to comply with the provisions of this standard, including information that identifies:

1. The engagement quality reviewer, and others who assisted the reviewer

2. The documents reviewed by the engagement quality reviewer, and others who assisted the reviewer

3. The date the engagement quality reviewer provided concurring approval of issuance or, if no concurring approval of issuance was provided, the reasons for not providing the approval

Documentation of an engagement quality review should be included in the engagement documentation. The requirements related to retention of and subsequent changes to audit documentation in PCAOB Auditing Standard No. 3, *Audit Documentation*, apply with respect to the documentation of the engagement quality review.

CPA Exam Week Checklist

What to pack if you are traveling (staying overnight) to take the exam:

1. CPA exam registration material

2. Hotel confirmation

3. Cash and/or a major credit card

4. Alarm clock—Don't rely on a hotel wake-up call

5. Comfortable clothing that can be layered to suit varying temperatures

6. A watch

7. Appropriate review materials, pencils, erasers, and pencil sharpener.

8. Healthy snack foods

Evenings before exam sections:

1. Read through your Bisk Education chapter outlines.

2. Eat lightly and monitor your intake of alcohol and caffeine. Get a good night's rest.

3. Do not try to cram. A brief review of your notes will help to focus your attention on important points and remind you that you are well prepared, but too much cramming can undermine your self-confidence. If you have reviewed conscientiously, you are already well prepared for the CPA exam.

The morning of each exam section:

1. Eat a satisfying breakfast. It will be several hours before your next meal. Eat enough to ward off hunger, but not so much that you feel uncomfortable.

2. Dress appropriately.

3. Arrive at the exam center thirty minutes early. Check in as soon as you are allowed to do so.

More helpful exam information is included in the **Practical Advice** appendix in this volume.

Editor's note: Carefully read the section "Step 4: Take Your Examination" in the AICPA's *The Uniform CPA Examination Candidate Bulletin / Information for Applicants*. This section contains a long list of items you are **not** allowed to bring into the testing room and other important requirements and restrictions. Don't assume that it will be what you expect. **For example, some of the prohibited items are:**
*   Watch (The exam's computer screen displays the time remaining to complete the exam.)
*   Pen / pencil (The testing center will provide scratch paper and pencils.)
*   Pencil sharpener
*   Eraser
*   Food or beverage
*   Purse / Wallet (You will be assigned a small storage locker with a key.)
This section of the bulletin further states: "In addition, jackets and sweaters are also prohibited; however, if you require a separate sweater or a jacket due to room temperature, it must be worn at all times."

CHAPTER 29—OTHER AUDITING STANDARDS

Problem 29-1 MULTIPLE CHOICE QUESTIONS (46 to 58 minutes)

1. Although the scope of audits of recipients of federal financial assistance in accordance with federal audit regulations varies, these audits generally have which of the following elements in common?
a. The auditor is to determine whether the federal financial assistance has been administered in accordance with applicable laws and regulations.
b. The materiality levels are lower and are determined by the government entities that provided the federal financial assistance to the recipient.
c. The auditor should obtain written management representations that the recipient's internal auditors will report their findings objectively without fear of political repercussion.
d. The auditor is required to express both positive and negative assurance that illegal acts that could have a material effect on the recipient's financial statements are disclosed to the inspector general. (5/98, AUD, #1, 7597)

2. The scope of audits of recipients of federal financial assistance in accordance with federal audit regulations varies. Which of the following elements do these audits have in common?
a. The auditor is required to disclose all situations and transactions that could be indicative of fraud, abuse, and illegal acts to the federal inspector general.
b. The materiality levels are higher and are determined by the government entities that provide the federal financial assistance to the recipients.
c. The auditor is required to document an understanding of internal control established to ensure compliance with the applicable laws and regulations.
d. The accounts should be 100% verified by substantive tests because certain statistical sampling applications are **not** permitted.
(R/06, AUD, #31, 8149)

3. In reporting under *Government Auditing Standards,* an auditor most likely would be required to report a falsification of accounting records directly to a federal inspector general when the falsification is
a. Discovered after the auditor's report has been made available to the federal inspector general and to the public
b. Reported by the auditor to the audit committee as a significant deficiency in internal control
c. Voluntarily disclosed to the auditor by low-level personnel as a result of the auditor's inquiries
d. Communicated by the auditor to the auditee and the auditee fails to make a required report of the matter (R/99, AUD, #31, 6847)

4. An auditor was engaged to conduct a performance audit of a governmental entity in accordance with *Government Auditing Standards.* These standards do **not** require, as part of this auditor's report
a. A statement of the audit objectives and a description of the audit scope
b. Indications or instances of illegal acts that could result in criminal prosecution discovered during the audit
c. The pertinent views of the entity's responsible officials concerning the auditor's findings
d. A concurrent opinion on the financial statements taken as a whole (11/94, AUD, #90, 5163)

5. Which of the following is a documentation requirement that an auditor should follow when auditing in accordance with *Government Auditing Standards?*
a. The auditor should obtain written representations from management acknowledging responsibility for correcting instances of fraud, abuse, and waste.
b. The auditor's working papers should contain sufficient information so that supplementary oral explanations are **not** required.
c. The auditor's working papers should contain a caveat that all instances of material errors and fraud may **not** be identified.
d. The auditor should document the procedures that assure discovery of all illegal acts and contingent liabilities resulting from noncompliance.
(11/93, AUD, #44, amended, 4281)

6. An auditor notes significant deficiencies in a financial statement audit conducted in accordance with *Government Auditing Standards*. In reporting on internal control, the auditor should state that
a. Expressing an opinion on the entity's financial statements provides **no** assurance on internal control.
b. The auditor obtained an understanding of the design of relevant policies and procedures, and determined whether they have been placed in operation.
c. The specified government funding or legislative body is responsible for reviewing internal control as a condition of continued funding.
d. The auditor has **not** determined whether any of the significant deficiencies described in the report are so severe as to be material weaknesses. (5/94, AUD, #85, amended, 4750)

7. For financial statement audits, generally accepted government auditing standards (GAGAS) incorporate the *Statements on Auditing Standards* (SAS) that are issued by the AICPA. GAGAS prescribe additional standards on

	Direct reporting of illegal acts	*Reporting on internal controls*
a.	Yes	Yes
b.	Yes	No
c.	No	Yes
d.	No	No

(R/03, AUD, #4, 7626)

8. The GAO standards of reporting for governmental financial audits incorporate the AICPA standards of reporting and prescribe supplemental standards to satisfy the unique needs of governmental audits. Which of the following is a supplemental reporting standard for governmental financial audits?
a. Auditors should report the scope of their testing of compliance with laws and regulations and of internal controls.
b. Material indications of illegal acts should be reported in a document distributed only to the entity's senior officials.
c. All changes in the audit program from the prior year should be reported to the entity's audit committee.
d. Any privileged or confidential information discovered should be reported to the organization that arranged for the audit. (R/06, AUD, #3, 8121)

9. When auditing an entity's financial statements in accordance with *Government Auditing Standards* (the "Yellow Book"), an auditor is required to report on

I. Recommendations for actions to improve operations
II. The scope of the auditor's tests of compliance with laws and regulations

a. I only
b. II only
c. Both I and II
d. Neither I nor II (R/00, AUD, #19, 6944)

10. Wolf is auditing an entity's compliance with requirements governing a major federal financial assistance program in accordance with *Government Auditing Standards*. Wolf detected noncompliance with requirements that have a material effect on the program. Wolf's report on compliance should express
a. No assurance on the compliance tests
b. An adverse or disclaimer of opinion
c. A qualified or adverse opinion
d. Reasonable assurance on the compliance tests
(11/94, AUD, #85, amended, 5158)

11. The auditor's report on internal controls and compliance with laws and regulations in accordance with *Government Auditing Standards* (the "Yellow Book"), is required to include

I. The scope of the auditor's testing of internal controls
II. Uncorrected misstatements that were determined by management to be immaterial

a. I only
b. II only
c. Both I and II
d. Neither I nor II (R/02, AUD, #16, 7106)

12. Hill, CPA, is auditing the financial statements of Helping Hand, a not-for-profit organization that receives financial assistance from governmental agencies. To detect misstatements in Helping Hand's financial statements resulting from violations of laws and regulations, Hill should focus on violations that
a. Could result in criminal prosecution against the organization
b. Involve significant deficiencies to be communicated to the organization's trustees and the funding agencies
c. Have a direct and material effect on the amounts in the organization's financial statements
d. Demonstrate the existence of material weaknesses in the organization's internal control
(11/92, AUD, #56, amended, 2990)

13. Tell, CPA, is auditing the financial statements of Youth Services Co. (YSC), a not-for-profit organization, in accordance with *Government Auditing Standards*. Tell's report on YSC's compliance with laws and regulations is required to contain statements of

	Positive assurance	*Negative assurance*
a.	Yes	Yes
b.	Yes	No
c.	No	Yes
d.	No	No

(5/93, AUD, #60, 3956)

14. In auditing compliance with requirements governing major federal financial assistance programs under the Single Audit Act, the auditor's consideration of materiality differs from materiality under generally accepted auditing standards. Under the Single Audit Act, materiality is
a. Calculated in relation to the financial statements taken as a whole
b. Determined separately for each major federal financial assistance program
c. Decided in conjunction with the auditor's risk assessment
d. Ignored, because all account balances, regardless of size, are fully tested

(11/95, AUD, #89, 6036)

15. Which of the following statements is correct concerning the Sarbanes-Oxley Act of 2002 and publicly-traded audit clients?
a. The lead engagement and reviewing audit partners must change every seven years.
b. An audit firm may not perform an audit for a client whose controller was previously employed by the audit firm and participated in the audit of the client within the client's previous fiscal year.
c. The audit firm may not also provide tax services to an audit client.
d. The audit firm may also provide tax services to an audit client without the preapproval of the audit committee. (Editors, 8065)

16. Under the Sarbanes-Oxley Act of 2002, a registered public accounting firm may perform which of the following services with pre-approval from the audit committee for an audit client that is a publicly-traded company?
a. Internal audit outsourcing services
b. Tax services
c. Bookkeeping services
d. Financial information systems design

(Editors, 8063)

17. The Sarbanes-Oxley Act of 2002 requires audit committees to be directly responsible for which of the following activities?

	Hiring Auditor	Negotiating Fees	Overseeing Audit Work
a.	Yes	No	Yes
b.	Yes	Yes	No
c.	No	Yes	Yes
d.	Yes	Yes	Yes

(Editors, 8064)

18. The Public Company Accounting Oversight Board (PCAOB) uses the term *internal control over financial reporting* to describe a process that does **not** include which of the following?
a. Procedures performed by the auditor
b. Procedures that pertain to the maintenance of reasonably detailed records that accurately and fairly reflect the transactions and dispositions of the company's assets
c. Procedures that provide reasonable assurance that transactions are recorded as necessary to permit preparation of the financial statements in accordance with GAAP and that receipts and expenditures are made only in accordance with company management and director authorization
d. Procedures that provide reasonable assurance regarding prevention or timely detection of unauthorized acquisition, use, or disposition of company assets that could have a material effect on the financial statements (Editors, 7938)

19. The standards of the Public Company Accounting Oversight Board (PCAOB) recognize that a public company's internal control over financial reporting cannot provide absolute assurance of achieving financial reporting objectives due to inherent limitations. Which of the following is **not** such an inherent limitation?
a. Breakdowns from human failures
b. Circumvention by collusion
c. Improper management override
d. Lack of controls over information technology
e Lapses in judgment (Editors, 7941)

20. Which of the following statements apply to an audit of internal control over financial reporting conducted in accordance with the standards of the Public Company Accounting Oversight Board (PCAOB)?

I. The auditor should consider the effect of compensating controls in assessing whether the objectives of internal control over financial reporting have been achieved.
II. While management is responsible for the company's internal control, the auditor should also assess the effectiveness of the board of directors' and audit committee's oversight as part of evaluating the control environment.

a. I only
b. II only
c. Both I and II
d. Neither I nor II   (Editors, 7943)

21. Mammoth Co. plans to present comparative financial statements for the years ended December 31, year 5, and year 6, respectively. Brown, CPA, audited Mammoth's financial statements for both years and plans to report on the comparative financial statements on March 1, year 7. Brown's audit is subject to the requirements of the Public Company Accounting Oversight Board (PCAOB). Mammoth's current management team was not present until January 1, year 6. What period of time should be covered by Mammoth's management representation letter?
a. January 1, year 5, through December 31, year 6
b. January 1, year 5, through March 1, year 7
c. January 1, year 6, through December 31, year 6
d. January 1, year 6, through March 1, year 7
                                (Editors, 7944)

22. Which of the following requirements must an auditor meet to express an opinion on a public company's effectiveness of internal control over financial reporting as of a point in time and taken as a whole?

I. The auditor must obtain evidence that internal control over financial reporting has operated effectively for the entire period covered by the company's financial statements.
II. The auditor must test the design and operating effectiveness of controls that the auditor ordinarily would **not** test if expressing an opinion only on the financial statements.

a. I only
b. II only
c. Both I and II
d. Neither I nor II   (Editors, 7945)

23. Wale Company plans to present comparative financial statements for the years ended December 31, year 7, and year 8, respectively. Dauphin, CPA, audited Wale's financial statements for both years and plans to report on the comparative financial statements on March 1, year 9. Dauphin's audit is subject to the requirements of the Public Company Accounting Oversight Board (PCAOB). What time is covered by Dauphin's opinion on internal control over financial reporting (ICFR)?
a. The end of Year 7 and the end of Year 8
b. The end of Year 8
c. Year 7 and Year 8
d. Year 8   (Editors, 7947)

Problem 29-2 ADDITIONAL MULTIPLE CHOICE QUESTIONS (34 to 43 minutes)

24. When auditing an entity's financial statements in accordance with *Government Auditing Standards* (the "Yellow Book"), an auditor is required to report on

I. Noteworthy accomplishments of the program
II. The scope of the auditor's testing of internal controls

a. I only
b. II only
c. Both I and II
d. Neither I nor II   (R/00, AUD, #18, 6943)

25. Because of the pervasive effects of laws and regulations on the financial statements of governmental units, an auditor may consider obtaining written management representations acknowledging that management has
a. Identified and disclosed all laws and regulations that have a direct and material effect on its financial statements
b. Implemented internal control policies and procedures designed to detect all illegal acts
c. Expressed both positive and negative assurance to the auditor that the entity complied with all laws and regulations
d. Employed internal auditors who can report their findings, opinions, and conclusions objectively without fear of political repercussion
                    (5/94, AUD, #84, amended, 4749)

26. In performing a financial statement audit in accordance with *Government Auditing Standards,* an auditor is required to report on the entity's compliance with laws and regulations. This report should

a. State that compliance with laws and regulations is the responsibility of the entity's management
b. Describe the laws and regulations that the entity must comply with
c. Provide an opinion on overall compliance with laws and regulations
d. Indicate that the auditor does **not** possess legal skills and **cannot** make legal judgments
(11/93, AUD, #58, 4295)

27. In auditing a not-for-profit entity that receives governmental financial assistance, the auditor has a responsibility to

a. Issue a separate report that describes the expected benefits and related costs of the auditor's suggested changes to the entity's internal control
b. Render an opinion concerning the entity's continued eligibility for the governmental financial assistance
c. Notify the governmental agency providing the financial assistance that the audit is **not** designed to provide any assurance of detecting errors and fraud
d. Assess whether management has identified laws and regulations that have a direct and material effect on the entity's financial statements
(11/95, AUD, #88, amended, 6035)

28. Reporting on internal control under *Government Auditing Standards* differs from reporting under generally accepted auditing standards in that *Government Auditing Standards* requires a

a. Statement of positive assurance that internal control procedures designed to detect material errors and fraud were tested
b. Written report describing each significant deficiency observed including identification of those considered material weaknesses
c. Statement of negative assurance that internal control procedures **not** tested have an immaterial effect on the entity's financial statements
d. Written report describing the entity's internal control procedures specifically designed to prevent fraud, abuse, and illegal acts
(5/93, AUD, #24, amended, 3920)

29. In an audit in accordance with *Government Auditing Standards,* an auditor is required to report on the auditor's tests of the entity's compliance with applicable laws and regulations. This requirement is satisfied by designing the audit to provide

a. Positive assurance that the internal control policies and procedures tested by the auditor are operating as prescribed
b. Reasonable assurance of detecting misstatements that are material to the financial statements
c. Negative assurance that significant deficiencies communicated during the audit do **not** prevent the auditor from expressing an opinion
d. Limited assurance that the internal controls designed by management will prevent or detect errors, fraud, and illegal acts
(5/92, AUD, #32, amended, 2785)

30. In reporting on compliance with laws and regulations during a financial statement audit in accordance with *Government Auditing Standards,* an auditor should include in the auditor's report

a. A statement of assurance that all controls over fraud and illegal acts were tested
b. Material instances of fraud and illegal acts that were discovered
c. The materiality criteria used by the auditor in considering whether instances of noncompliance were significant
d. An opinion on whether compliance with laws and regulations affected the entity's goals and objectives
(5/95, AUD, #89, 5707)

31. Which of the following bodies promulgates standards for audits of federal financial assistance recipients?

a. Governmental Accounting Standards Board
b. Financial Accounting Standards Board
c. Governmental Auditing Standards Board
d. Government Accountability Office (Editors, 7513)

32. Which of the following statements is a standard applicable to financial statement audits in accordance with *Government Auditing Standards* (the "Yellow Book")?

a. An auditor should report on the scope of the auditor's testing of compliance with laws and regulations.
b. An auditor should assess whether the entity has reportable measures of economy and efficiency that are valid and reliable.
c. An auditor should report recommendations for actions to correct problems and improve operations.
d. An auditor should determine the extent to which the entity's programs achieve the desired results.
(R/99, AUD, #28, 6844)

33. Which of the following statements is a standard applicable to financial statement audits in accordance with *Government Auditing Standards* (the "Yellow Book")?
a. An auditor should report on the scope of the auditor's testing of internal controls.
b. All instances of abuse, waste, and mismanagement should be reported to the audit committee.
c. An auditor should report the views of responsible officials concerning the auditor's findings.
d. Internal control activities designed to detect or prevent fraud should be reported to the inspector general. (R/99, AUD, #29, 6845)

34. An enterprise engaged a CPA to audit its financial statements in accordance with *Government Auditing Standards* (the "Yellow Book") because of the provisions of government grant funding agreements. Under these circumstances, the CPA is required to report on the enterprise's internal controls either in the report on the financial statements or in
a. The report on the performance audit
b. The notes to the financial statements
c. A letter to the government funding agency
d. A separate report (R/07, AUD, #13, 8385)

35. Reporting standards for financial audits under *Government Auditing Standards* (the "Yellow Book") differ from reporting under generally accepted auditing standards in that *Government Auditing Standards* require the auditor to
a. Provide positive assurance that control activities regarding segregation of duties are consistent with the entity's control objectives
b. Present the results of the auditor's tests of controls
c. Provide negative assurance that the auditor discovered **no** evidence of intentional override of internal controls
d. Describe the scope of the auditor's principal substantive tests (R/07, AUD, #45, 8417)

36. In an audit of internal control over financial reporting conducted in accordance with the standards of the Public Company Accounting Oversight Board (PCAOB), the auditor must communicate in writing to the audit committee
a. Significant deficiencies only
b. Material weaknesses only
c. All deficiencies in internal control over financial reporting
d. Significant deficiencies and material weaknesses (Editors, 7949)

37. What does the Public Company Accounting Oversight Board (PCAOB) call a deficiency of internal control over financial reporting (ICFR) such that there is a reasonable possibility that a material misstatement of the company's annual or interim financial statements will not be prevented or detected on a timely basis?
a. Control deficiency
b. Material deficiency
c. Material weakness
d. Significant deficiency (Editors, 7950)

38. The conceptual definition of materiality that applies to an audit of a public company's internal control over financial reporting includes which of the following considerations?

	Qualitative	Quantitative
a.	Yes	Yes
b.	Yes	No
c.	No	Yes
d.	No	No (Editors, 7951)

39. In an audit of internal control over financial reporting conducted in accordance with the standards of the Public Company Accounting Oversight Board (PCAOB), which procedure is insufficient by itself to test the effectiveness of a control?
a. Inquiries of appropriate personnel
b. Inspection of relevant documents
c. Observation of operations
d. Reperformance of the control procedure (Editors, 7953)

40. Which of the following statements is **false** in regard to an audit of internal control over financial reporting conducted in accordance with the standards of the Public Company Accounting Oversight Board (PCAOB)?
a. The auditor may rely upon the judgments of others regarding the sufficiency of evidence.
b. The auditor may use the work of others to alter the nature, timing, or extent of the work that the auditor performs.
c. The extent to which the auditor may use the work of others depends on their objectivity.
d. As the risk associated with a control increases, the need for the auditor to perform her/his own work on the control increases. (Editors, 7954)

SIMULATION

Problem 29-3 (50 to 60 minutes)

Toxic Waste Disposal Co., Inc. (TWD), a continuing audit client, has engaged your firm to audit its financial statements for the year ended July 31, Year 5, in accordance with *Government Auditing Standards.* TWD is a nonprofit organization that contracts with municipal governments to remove environmental wastes. TWD receives grants and fees from various state and municipal governments as well as grants from several federal government agencies. Accordingly, the auditors' reports are to be submitted by TWD to the granting government agencies, which make the reports available for public inspection.

You are considering audit risk at the financial statement level in planning the audit of TWD's financial statements for the year ended July 31, Year 5. Audit risk at the financial statement level is influenced by the risk of material misstatements, which may be indicated by a combination of factors related to management, the industry, and the entity.

Based only on the information given below, indicate whether each of the following factors would most likely increase audit risk (I), decrease audit risk (D), or have no effect on audit risk (N).

1. The internal auditor reports to the controller.

2. The accounting department has experienced a high rate of turnover of key personnel.

3. TWD's bank has a loan officer who meets regularly with TWD's CEO and controller to monitor TWD's financial performance.

4. TWD's employees are paid biweekly.

5. Your firm has audited TWD for five years.

6. During Year 5, litigation filed against TWD in Year 1 alleging that TWD discharged pollutants into state waterways was dropped by the state. Loss contingency disclosures that TWD included in prior years' financial statements are being removed for the Year 1 financial statements.

7. During July, TWD completed a barter transaction with a municipality. TWD removed waste from a municipally-owned site and acquired title to another contaminated site at below market price. TWD intends to service this new site in Year 6.

8. During July, TWD increased its casualty insurance coverage on several pieces of sophisticated machinery from historical cost to replacement cost.

9. Inquiries about the substantial increase in revenue TWD recorded in the fourth quarter of Year 5 disclosed a new policy. TWD guaranteed to several municipalities that it would refund the federal and state funding paid to TWD if any municipality fails federal or state site clean-up inspection in Year 6.

TWD's management has asked you to issue the auditor's report by September 1, Year 5. There is not sufficient time to perform all of the necessary fieldwork in August, but there will be time to perform most of the fieldwork as of an interim date, May 31. For the accounts to be tested at the interim date, substantive tests covering the transactions of the final two months of the year will need to be performed. This will be necessary to extend your conclusions to the year end.

In a memo to the audit team, describe the factors that should be considered before applying substantive tests to TWD's balance sheet accounts at May 31.

The auditors' separate report on compliance with laws and regulations that was drafted by a staff accountant of your firm at the completion of the engagement contained the statements below. It was submitted to the engagement partner who reviewed matters thoroughly and properly concluded that no material instances of noncompliance were identified. For each of the statements below, indicate whether each is an appropriate (A) or inappropriate (I) element within the report on compliance with laws and regulations.

1. A statement that the audit was conducted in accordance with generally accepted auditing standards and with *Government Auditing Standards* issued by the Comptroller General of the United States.

2. A statement that the auditors' procedures included tests of compliance.

3. A statement that the standards require the auditors to plan and to perform the audit to detect all instances of noncompliance with applicable laws and regulations.

4. A statement that management is responsible for compliance with laws, regulations, contracts, and grants.

5. A statement that the auditors' objective was to provide an opinion on compliance with the provisions of laws and regulations equivalent to that to be expressed on the financial statements.

6. A statement of positive assurance that the results of the tests indicate that, with respect to the items tested, the entity complied, in all material respects, with the provisions of laws, regulations, contracts, and grants.

7. A statement of negative assurance that, with respect to items tested, nothing came to the auditors' attention that caused the auditors to believe that the entity had not complied, in all material respects, with the provisions of laws, regulations, contracts, and grants.

8. A statement that the report is intended only for the information of the specific legislative or regulatory bodies, and that this restriction is intended to limit the distribution of the report.

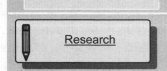

Research

What authoritative reference provides guidance on the objectives of a CPA firm's quality control system's policies and procedures for documentation of consultations with other professionals that involve complex, unusual, unfamiliar, difficult, or contentious matters?

Paragraph Reference Answer: _____

(5/94, AUD, #3, amended, 8066)

Solution 29-1 MULTIPLE CHOICE ANSWERS

GAGAS—Responsibilities

1. (a)   The auditor must design the audit to provide reasonable assurance that the financial statements are free of material misstatements resulting from violations of law and regulations that have a direct and material effect on the determination of financial statement amounts. Materiality levels are determined by the auditor in relation to an entity's federal programs. An auditor generally does not obtain representations regarding internal auditors' reports. An auditor usually does not express assurance on disclosures to an inspector general. (7597)

2. (c)   All audits of recipients of federal financial assistance require the auditor to obtain and document an understanding of internal control established to ensure compliance with the laws and regulations applicable to the federal award.   (8149)

3. (d)   Generally, the auditor need report a falsification of accounting records only to the audit committee (or equivalent). If auditors have communicated such irregularities or illegal acts to the auditee, and it fails to report them, then the auditors should communicate their awareness of that failure to the auditee's governing body. If the auditee does not make the required report as soon as practicable after the auditors' communication with its governing body, then the auditors should report the irregularities or illegal acts directly to the external party specified.   (6847)

4. (d)   *Governmental Auditing Standards* do not require an opinion on the financial statements taken as a whole, when the engagement is a *performance* audit. GAGAS does require a statement of the audit scope, indications of illegal acts discovered during the audit, and—if the auditor's report on the engagement discloses deficiencies in internal control, fraud, illegal acts, violations of contracts or grant agreement provisions, or abuse—the views of the responsible officials concerning the auditor's findings in the auditor's report.   (5163)

5. (b)   Included in the fieldwork standards of supplemental working paper requirements for financial audits is the statement that working papers should contain sufficient information so that supplementary oral explanations are not required. Written representations from management are not required. The auditor's work papers should include positive statements about the procedures applied and the results of those procedures; thus, there is no requirement that the working papers contain a caveat statement. An audit does not ensure that all illegal acts and contingent liabilities resulting from noncompliance will be discovered by the auditor.   (4281)

GAGAS—Internal Control

6. (b)   The auditor should obtain a sufficient understanding by performing risk assessment procedures to evaluate the design of controls relevant to an audit of financial statements and to determine whether they have been implemented. This includes governmental audits. GAGAS requires that the auditor include in their report on the financial statements either a description of the scope of the auditors' testing of internal control and the results of those tests or an opinion, if sufficient work was performed; or reference to the separate report(s) containing that information. GAGAS requires that auditors identify those significant deficiencies that are individually or in the aggregate considered to be material weaknesses.   (4750)

7. (a)   According to GAGAS, when providing an opinion or a disclaimer on financial statements, auditors should include in their report on the financial statements either a description of the scope of the auditors' testing of internal control over financial

reporting and compliance with laws, regulations, and provisions of contracts or grant agreements and the results of those tests or an opinion, if sufficient work was performed; or reference to the separate report(s) containing that information. In some circumstances, auditors should report fraud and illegal acts directly to parties external to the audited entity. (7626)

8. (a) In addition to GAAS, GAGAS require auditors to include in their report either a description of the scope of the auditors' testing of internal control over financial reporting and compliance with laws, regulations, and provisions of contracts or grant agreements and the results of those tests or, if sufficient work was performed, an opinion; or a reference to the separate report(s) containing that information. In some circumstances, auditors must report illegal acts directly to parties external to the audited entity. Auditors are not required to disclose all changes in the audit program. Certain privileged or confidential information may be prohibited from disclosure; the report should state the nature of the omitted information and the requirement that makes the omission necessary. (8121)

GAGAS—Compliance

9. (b) In an audit in accordance with GAGAS, an auditor is required to report on the auditor's test of the entity's compliance with applicable laws and regulations. Among the basic elements of such a report is a statement that the standards require that the auditor plan and perform the audit to obtain reasonable assurance about whether the financial statements are free of material misstatement. Recommendations for actions to improve operations are a side-benefit of an audit and are not required. (6944)

10. (c) When an auditor detects noncompliance with requirements that have a material effect on a program, the auditor should express a qualified or adverse opinion. A disclaimer is appropriate only when an audit has not been completed. Reasonable assurance on tests is implicit, not explicit. (5158)

11. (a) GAGAS require that the auditor include in their report on the financial statements either a description of the scope of the auditors' testing of internal control and the results of those tests or an opinion, if sufficient work was performed; or reference to the separate report(s) containing that information. Material misstatements in the financial statements impact the audit report, not the report on internal control. Uncorrected misstatements that are immaterial have no impact on the audit report or the report on internal control. (7106)

12. (c) Due to their acceptance of financial assistance from government agencies, not-for-profit organizations may be subject to laws and regulations. The audit should be designed to give reasonable assurance that the financial statements are free of misstatements resulting from violations of laws and regulations that have a direct and material effect on the determination of financial statement amounts. The audit should not be restricted to the consideration of violations that result in the conditions described in (a), (b), and (d). (2990)

13. (a) Reports on compliance with laws and regulations, in accordance with GAGAS, should contain positive assurance consisting of a statement by the auditor that the tested items were in compliance with applicable laws and regulations, and negative assurance stating that nothing came to the auditor's attention as a result of specified procedures that caused the auditor to believe the untested items were not in compliance with applicable laws and regulations. (3956)

14. (b) In auditing an entity's compliance with requirements governing each major federal financial assistance program in accordance with the Single Audit Act, the auditor considers materiality in relation to each program. (6036)

Sarbanes-Oxley Act of 2002

15. (b) It is prohibited for a firm to provide audit services to an issuer if the issuer's CEO, controller, CFO, CAO, or other person serving in the equivalent capacity, was employed in the audit firm and participated in the audit of that issuer during the one-year fiscal period prior to the current audit. The Sarbanes-Oxley Act of 2002 also prohibits a registered public accounting firm from providing audit services to an issuer if the lead audit partner, or the audit partner responsible for reviewing the audit, has performed audit services for that issuer in each of the five previous fiscal years. An auditor may perform other services, such as tax preparation services, for audit clients that are issuers of public securities only with advance approval from the audit committee. (8065)

16. (b) The Sarbanes-Oxley Act of 2002 prohibits any registered public accounting firm from providing bookkeeping, financial information system design, and internal audit outsourcing services as well as many other non-audit services to a publicly-traded audit client. A firm may, however, perform tax services, for a publicly-traded audit client only with the advance approval of the audit committee. (8063)

17. (d) The Sarbanes-Oxley Act of 2002 requires that audit committees be directly responsible for appointing, compensating and overseeing the external audit firm. (8064)

PCAOB

18. (a) An auditor's procedures performed during either an audit of ICFR or an audit of financial statements are not part of a company's internal control over financial reporting (ICFR). The term *internal control over financial reporting* is defined as a process designed by, or under the supervision of, the company's principal executive and principal financial officers, or persons performing similar functions, and effected by the company's board of directors, management, and other personnel, to provide reasonable assurance regarding the reliability of financial reporting and the preparation of financial statements for external purposes in accordance with GAAP. Answers b, c, and d describe what its policies and procedures pertain to or provide. (7938)

19. (d) Lack of information technology (IT) controls is not an inherent limitation of internal control. Controls may be programmed into IT systems. All of the other answer alternatives are examples of the inherent limitations of ICFR. (7941)

20. (c) The auditor should consider the effect of compensating controls when determining if a deficiency constitutes a material weakness. The compensating control should be judged effective enough to prevent or detect a material misstatement in order to be considered to have a mitigating effect. Ineffective oversight by the audit committee of the company's external financial reporting and internal control over financial reporting (ICFR) should be

regarded as an indication of a material weakness in ICFR. (7943)

21. (b) Issues such as who should sign the letter, the period to be covered by the letter, and when an updated letter should be obtained are the same as in a financial statement audit under GAAS. If comparative financial statements are reported on, the written representations obtained at the completion of the most recent audit should address all periods being reported on. The representations should be made as of the date of the auditor's report. If current management was not present during all periods covered by the auditor's report, the auditor should nevertheless obtain written representations from current management on all such periods. (7944)

22. (b) To express an opinion on ICFR effectiveness as of a *point in time,* the auditor should obtain evidence that ICFR has operated effectively for a sufficient period of time, which may be less than the entire period covered by the company's financial statements. To express an opinion on ICFR effectiveness *taken as a whole,* the auditor must obtain evidence about the effectiveness of controls over all relevant assertions. This requires the auditor to test the design and operating effectiveness of controls that the auditor ordinarily would not test if expressing an opinion only on the financial statements. (7945)

23. (b) The auditor's opinion on ICFR is as of a specified date rather than a period of time. When the auditor elects to issue a combined report, the audit opinion will address multiple periods for the financial statements presented, but only the end of the most recent fiscal year for the effectiveness of ICFR. (7947)

Solution 29-2 ADDITIONAL MULTIPLE CHOICE ANSWERS

GAGAS

24. (b) GAGAS require a written report on the consideration of internal control in all audits; whereas GAAS require communication only when the auditor has noted significant deficiencies. Reporting on program accomplishments is not required of the auditor. (6943)

25. (a) The auditor should assess whether management has identified laws and regulations that have a direct and material effect on the determination of amounts in the entity's financial statements. The auditor may consider obtaining written representation from management regarding the completeness of management's identification of applicable laws and

regulations. The items in (b), (c) and (d) are not required. (4749)

26. (a) The basic elements of a report on compliance should include a statement that management is responsible for compliance with laws, regulations, contracts, and grants. The items in (b), (c) and (d) are not required. (4295)

27. (d) The auditor, when auditing a nonprofit organization that receives governmental financial assistance should assess whether management has identified laws and regulations that have a direct and material effect on the entity's financial statements. (6035)

28. (b) GAGAS require a written report on the consideration of internal control in all audits; whereas GAAS require communication only when the auditor has noted significant deficiencies. The auditor is not required to report on the description of the entity's internal control procedures. The auditor should not issue the representations in answer (c) or give positive assurance because of the potential for misinterpretation of the limited degree of assurance associated with the auditor's written report representing that no significant deficiencies were noted. (3920)

29. (b) In an audit in accordance with GAGAS, an auditor is required to report on the entity's compliance with applicable laws and regulations. The standards require that the auditor plan and perform the audit to obtain reasonable assurance about whether the financial statements are free of material misstatement. Answers (a), (c), and (d) relate to internal control; the auditor does not give any form of assurance on the entity's internal control in this type of audit. (2785)

30. (b) AICPA standards and GAGAS require auditors to address the effect fraud or illegal acts may have on the audit report and to determine that the audit committee or others with equivalent authority and responsibility are adequately informed about the fraud or illegal acts. GAGAS further require that this information be in writing and also include reporting on significant violations of provisions of contracts or grant agreements and significant abuse. Therefore, when auditors conclude, on the basis of evidence obtained, that fraud, an illegal act, a significant violation of a contract or grant agreement, or significant abuse either has occurred or is likely to have occurred, they should include in their audit report the relevant information. Answer (c) is the second best answer; GAGAS require auditors to place their findings in proper perspective and identify the condition, criteria, cause, and effect of noncompliance. There is no requirement that all controls be tested. Answer (d) is not required in a financial statement audit. (5707)

31. (d) The standards for audits of federally assisted programs may be found in the publication of the U.S. Government Accountability Office (GAO) entitled *Government Auditing Standards*. The Governmental Accounting Standards Board (GASB) establishes financial accounting principles for state and local government entities. The Financial Accounting Standards Board (FASB) establishes GAAP. The Governmental Auditing Standards Board does not exist. (7513)

32. (a) The auditor must report on the scope of tests of compliance with laws and regulations. An auditor may report recommendations to correct problems and improve operations, but this is not the purpose of an audit. The auditor expresses an opinion on whether the information is correct; users of the report determine whether the measures of economy and efficiency are valid and reliable as well as the extent to which programs achieve the desired results. (6844)

33. (a) The auditor must summarize the audit results concerning internal control, financial statements, and compliance with laws and regulations. Immaterial amounts are not necessarily reported to the audit committee. Officials may report their own views—it is the auditor's duty to do so only if the auditor's report on the engagement discloses deficiencies in internal control, fraud, illegal acts, violations of provisions of contracts or grant agreements, or abuse. A report on all internal control activities designed to detect or prevent fraud is far more than need be reported to the inspector general or other parties. (6845)

34. (d) *Government Auditing Standards* require that when providing an opinion or a disclaimer on financial statements, auditors must also report on internal control over financial reporting and on compliance with laws, regulations, and provisions of contracts or grant agreements. Auditors should include either in the same or in a separate report(s) a description of the scope of the auditors' testing of internal control over financial reporting and compliance with laws, regulations, and provisions of contracts or grant agreements. An auditor sends a letter to a funding agency in certain circumstances; while the auditor may include this information in such a letter, the auditor still must include this information in an audit report. (8385)

35. (b) When providing an opinion or a disclaimer of opinion on financial statements in accordance with GAGAS, the audit must include in the report either a description of the scope of the auditor's testing of internal control over financial reporting and compliance with laws, regulations, and contractual provisions and the results of those tests (negative assurance) or, if sufficient work was performed, an opinion (positive assurance); or refer to a separate report containing that information. The auditor does not necessarily assure that no evidence of intentional override of controls was found. The auditor doesn't report the scope of the principal substantive tests. (8417)

PCAOB

36. (d)   The auditor must communicate, in writing, to the audit committee, all significant deficiencies and material weaknesses identified during the audit.   (7949)

37. (c)   A *material weakness* is a deficiency of internal control over financial reporting such that there is a reasonable possibility that a material misstatement of the company's annual or interim financial statements will not be prevented or detected on a timely basis. A significant deficiency is a deficiency that is less severe than a material weakness; yet important enough to merit attention by those responsible for oversight of the company's financial reporting. A control deficiency exists when the design or operation of a control does not allow management or employees, in the normal course of performing their assigned functions, to prevent or detect misstatements on a timely basis. The PCAOB standards don't use the term material deficiency.   (7950)

38. (a)   In planning the audit of ICFR, the auditor should use the same materiality considerations used in planning the audit of a entity's annual financial statements. Materiality judgments are made in the light of surrounding circumstances and necessarily involve both quantitative and qualitative considerations.   (7951)

39. (a)   Inquiry alone does not provide sufficient evidence to support a conclusion about the effectiveness of a control. Some tests, by their nature, provide greater evidence than others. The following tests that an auditor might perform are listed in the order of least to most evidence that they ordinarily produce: inquiry, observation, inspection of relevant documentation, and reperformance of a control. Auditors normally use a mix of these procedures.   (7953)

40. (a)   Judgments about evidence sufficiency and other factors affecting the opinion must be the auditor's. The other statements are true.   (7954)

PERFORMANCE BY SUBTOPICS

Each category below parallels a subtopic covered in Chapter 29. Record the number and percentage of questions you correctly answered in each subtopic area.

GAGAS—Responsibilities

Question #	Correct	√
1		
2		
3		
4		
5		
# Questions	5	
# Correct		
% Correct		

GAGAS—Internal Control

Question #	Correct	√
6		
7		
8		
# Questions	3	
# Correct		
% Correct		

GAGAS—Compliance

Question #	Correct	√
9		
10		
11		
12		
13		
14		
# Questions	6	
# Correct		
% Correct		

Sarbanes-Oxley Act of 2002

Question #	Correct	√
15		
16		
17		
# Questions	3	
# Correct		
% Correct		

PCAOB

Question #	Correct	√
18		
19		
20		
21		
22		
23		
# Questions	6	
# Correct		
% Correct		

SIMULATION SOLUTION

Solution 29-3

Response #1: Audit Risk (4 points)

1. I

Audit risk is increased when the internal auditors report to the person they are evaluating (i.e., controller).

2. I

High turnover of accounting personnel increases the potential for errors due to poorly trained personnel and, thus, increases audit risk.

3. D

The monitoring of financial performance decreases audit risk.

4. N

The pay period has no effect on audit risk since it has no effect on the possibility for error or fraud.

5. D

Audit risk is decreased due to familiarity with the audit history, client industry, and client procedures.

6. D

The settlement of a contingency reduces audit risk.

7. I

Difficult-to-audit transactions, such as the barter transaction, increase audit risk.

8. N

The increase in casualty insurance coverage has no effect on the possibility of errors and fraud and, therefore, does not effect audit risk.

9. I

The guarantee represents a loss contingency which could result in revenue not being realized. Therefore, audit risk is increased.

Response #2: Communication (6 points)

Expected response should include:

Before applying principal substantive tests to balance sheet accounts at May 31, Year 5, the interim date, the following factors should be considered:

- The **control environment** and other **relevant controls**;
- Whether the financial reporting system will provide **sufficient information** to **permit investigation** of: (1) **significant unusual transactions** or **entries**; (2) other causes of **significant fluctuations**, or **expected fluctuations** that did not occur; and (3) changes in the **composition** of classes of transactions or account balances when needed;
- The **objectives** of the **substantive procedures**;
- The **assessed risk of material misstatement**;
- The **nature** of the **account balances** and **relevant assertions**;
- The auditor's **ability** to **reduce** the **risk** that **misstatements existing** at the **end** of the **period** will not be **detected**;
- Whether the **amount**, **relative significance**, and **composition** of an **ending balance** are reasonably **predictable**;
- Whether the entity's procedures for **analysis**, **adjustment**, and **cutoff** of balances at **interim dates** are **appropriate.**

Response #3: Report (4 points)

1. A

2. A

3. I

The auditors are required to plan and perform the audit to provide reasonable assurance of detecting instances of noncompliance having a direct and material effect on the financial statements, not all instances of noncompliance.

4. A

5. I

Rendering an opinion is a higher level of reporting than the positive and negative assurance required by Government Auditing Standards.

6. A

7. I

Negative assurance applies to items not tested.

8. I

GAGAS requires that, unless restricted by law or regulation, copies of the reports should be made available for public inspection.

Response #4: Research (1 point)

Paragraph Reference Answer: QC 10.77

Guidance: QC 10.77 states, "Documentation of consultations with other professionals that involve complex, unusual, unfamiliar, difficult, or contentious matters that is sufficiently complete and detailed contributes to an understanding of:

• The issue on which consultation was sought; and
• The results of the consultation, including any decisions made, the basis for those decisions, and how they were implemented."

(8066)

CHANGE ALERT

SAS 116 (AU 722), *Interim Financial Information* **(issued 2/2009)**

In February 2009, the Auditing Standards Board of the American Institute of Certified Public Accountants issued Statement on Auditing Standards (SAS) 116, *Interim Financial Information*. It is effective for reviews of interim financial information for interim periods beginning after December 15, 2009. Early application is permitted.

SAS 116 amends AU 722 to better accommodate reviews of interim financial information of nonissuers performed for a broader range of purposes. Additionally, it removes guidance of reviews of interim financial information for public companies (issuers) because guidance for issuers appropriately resides in the Public Company Accounting Oversight Board's auditing standards.

This statement would apply when the interim financial information is intended to provide a periodic update to year-end reporting and the following conditions are met. (If these conditions are *not* met, reviews of interim financial information of nonissuers should be performed in accordance with Statements on Standards for Accounting and Review Services—SSARS).

- The entity's latest annual financial statements have been audited by the accountant or a predecessor;

- The accountant has been engaged to audit the entity's current year financial statements, or the accountant audited the entity's latest annual financial statements and expects to be engaged to audit the current year financial statements;

- The client prepares its interim financial information in accordance with the same financial reporting framework as that used to prepare the annual financial statements; and

- If the interim financial information is condensed information, all of the following conditions are met:

  - The condensed interim financial information purports to conform with an appropriate financial reporting framework, which includes appropriate form and content of interim financial statements;

  - The condensed interim financial information includes a note that the financial information does not represent complete financial statements and should be read in conjunction with the entity's latest annual audited financial statements.

  - The condensed interim financial information accompanies the entity's latest audited annual financial statements or such audited annual financial statements are made readily available by the entity.

This statement is eligible to be tested beginning in the October-November 2009 exam window.

CHAPTER 30

OTHER TYPES OF REPORTS

CHAPTER 30

OTHER TYPES OF REPORTS

I. **Information Accompanying Basic Financial Statements in Auditor-Submitted Documents**

A. **Overview**

AU 551 provides guidance on reporting when the auditor submits to a client, or others, a document containing information in addition to the basic financial statements and the audit report.

Exhibit 1 ▶ Auditor's Report Guidelines Mnemonic

A	**Audit** made to form opinion on financial statements taken as whole
S	**State** (or disclaim) opinion as to whether accompanying information is fairly stated in all material respects in relation to basic financial statements taken as a whole
A	**Accompanying** information not a required part of financial statements
I	**Identify** accompanying information
R	**Report** on accompanying information may be added to standard audit report or may appear in separate auditor-submitted document

1. **Nature** Such information (**not** required by GAAP) includes additional details or explanations of items in or related to the basic financial statements, consolidating information, historical summaries of items extracted from the basic financial statements, statistical data, and other material, some of which may be from sources outside the accounting system or the entity.

2. **Exempt From Guidance** AU 551 does **not** apply when the client merely includes other information (that the auditor has not been engaged to report upon) in a document containing the basic financial statements and the auditor's standard report. In this instance, the auditor must read the information to ensure that it is consistent with the audited financial statements (SAS 8). Only if there is an inconsistency must the auditor report on other information (exception reporting). SAS 8, 29, and 52 do not indicate whether an auditor may issue a report providing an opinion, in relation to the basic financial statements taken as a whole, on supplementary information and other information that has been subjected to the auditing procedures applied in the audit of those basic financial statements. SAS 98 clarifies that such reporting is allowed.

B. **Objectives**

The objectives of the auditor's report on information accompanying the basic financial statements are the same as the report on the basic financial statements (i.e., to describe the character of the work and the degree of responsibility, if any, the auditor is taking).

1. **Guidelines** The report on the accompanying information may be added to the auditor's standard report on the basic financial statements or may appear separately in the auditor-submitted document.

   a. The report should: (1) state that the audit has been made for the purpose of forming an opinion on the basic financial statements taken as a whole; (2) identify the accompanying information, by descriptive title or page number of the document; and (3) state that the accompanying information is presented for purposes of additional analysis and is not a required part of the basic financial statements.

   b. The report should include either an opinion on whether the accompanying information is stated fairly in all material respects in relation to the basic financial statements taken as a whole or a disclaimer of opinion, depending on whether the information was subject to the auditing procedures applied in the audit of the basic financial statements. The auditor may express an opinion on a portion of the accompanying information and disclaim an opinion on the remainder.

2. **Materiality** The purpose of an audit is to provide an opinion on the fairness of the basic financial statements *taken as a whole.* If the auditor expresses an opinion on the additional accompanying information, the same materiality level used for the financial statements is used. Accordingly, the auditor does not need to apply additional procedures on the additional information taken by itself.

3. **Misstatements** If the auditor believes that the additional information is materially misstated, in relation to the financial statements, the auditor should discuss it with management and propose a revision. If the client does not agree, the auditor should either: (a) modify the report on the accompanying information and describe the misstatement; or (b) refuse to include the information in the document.

Exhibit 2 ▶ Auditing Procedures Performed on Accompanying Information

> Our audit was conducted for the purpose of forming an opinion on the basic financial statements taken as a whole. The (identify accompanying information) is presented for purposes of additional analysis and is not a required part of the basic financial statements. Such information has been subjected to the auditing procedures applied in the audit of the basic financial statements and, in our opinion, is fairly stated in all material respects in relation to the basic financial statements taken as a whole.

Exhibit 3 ▶ Disclaimer on Accompanying Information

> Our audit was conducted for the purpose of forming an opinion on the basic financial statements taken as a whole. The (identify accompanying information) is presented for purposes of additional analysis and is not a required part of the basic financial statements. Such information has not been subjected to the auditing procedures applied in the audit of the basic financial statements, and, accordingly, we express no opinion on it.

C. Effects of Report

If the auditor modifies the report on the basic financial statements, the auditor should consider the effects on any related accompanying information (see Exhibit 4). When the auditor expresses an adverse opinion or disclaims an opinion on the basic financial statements, the auditor should disclaim an opinion on all accompanying information.

Exhibit 4 ▶ Reporting on Accompanying Information to Which a Qualification in the Auditor's Report on the Basic Financial Statements Applies

> Our audit was made for the purpose of forming an opinion on the basic financial statements taken as a whole. The schedules of investments (page 7), property (page 8) and other assets (page 9) as of December 31, 20X1, are presented for purposes of additional analysis and are not a required part of the basic financial statements. The information in such schedules has been subjected to the auditing procedures applied in the audit of the basic financial statements, and, in our opinion, except for the effects on the schedule of investments of not accounting for the investments in certain companies by the equity method as explained in the third paragraph of this report, such information is fairly stated in all material respects in relation to the basic financial statements taken as a whole.

D. Required Supplementary Information (RSI)

When supplementary information required by the FASB or GASB is presented outside the basic financial statements in an auditor-submitted document, the auditor should disclaim an opinion on the information unless s/he has been engaged to audit and express an opinion on it.

Exhibit 5 ▶ Disclaimer on RSI Presented Outside the Basic Statements

> The (identify the supplementary information) on page XX is not a required part of the basic financial statements but is supplementary information required by the (Financial or Governmental) Accounting Standards Board. We have applied certain limited procedures, which consisted principally of inquiries of management regarding the methods of measurement and presentation of the supplementary information. However, we did not audit the information, and express no opinion on it.

- The auditor's report should be expanded if RSI is omitted, the auditor has concluded that the measurement or presentation of RSI departs materially from guidelines prescribed by the FASB or GASB, the auditor is unable to remove substantial doubts about whether the RSI conforms to prescribed guidelines, or the auditor is unable to complete the procedures prescribed by SAS 52.

E. Consolidating Information

1. Consolidated Statements Only An auditor may be engaged to provide an opinion on consolidated financial statements on which consolidating information also is provided (e.g., the individual amounts making up the consolidated totals). The auditor must be satisfied that the consolidating information is identified suitably.

Exhibit 6 ▶ Consolidating Information Not Separately Audited

> Our audit was conducted for the purpose of forming an opinion on the consolidated financial statements taken as a whole. The consolidating information is presented for purposes of additional analysis of the consolidated financial statements rather than to present the financial position, results of operations, and cash flows of the individual companies. The consolidating information has been subjected to the auditing procedures applied in the audit of the consolidated financial statements, and, in our opinion, is fairly stated in all material respects in relation to the consolidated financial statements taken as a whole.

2. Consolidated Statements & Separate Statements An auditor may be engaged to form an opinion on both the consolidated statements and the separate statements of the components of a consolidated group. In this case, the auditor's responsibility with respect to the separate financial statements is the same as the responsibility for the consolidated statements.

II. Special Reports (AU 623, SAS 62)

A. Special Purpose Reports
Auditor's reports that apply only to (1) financial statements prepared in conformity with OCBOA; (2) specified elements, accounts, or items of a financial statement; (3) compliance with aspects of contractual agreements or regulatory requirements related to audited financial statements; (4) financial presentations to comply with contractual agreements or regulatory provisions that result in either incomplete presentations or a presentation that is not in conformity with GAAP or OCBOA; or (5) financial information presented in prescribed forms or schedules that require a prescribed form of auditor's report.

B. Reports on Financial Statements Prepared in Conformity With OCBOA
GAAS applies whenever an auditor conducts an audit of and reports on any financial statement.

Exhibit 7 ▶ Auditor's Report on Cash Basis Financial Statements

<u>Independent Auditor's Report*</u>

We have audited the accompanying statements of assets and liabilities arising from cash transactions of XYZ Company as of December 31, 20X2 and 20X1, and the related statements of revenue collected and expenses paid for the years then ended. These financial statements are the responsibility of the company's management. Our responsibility is to express an opinion on these financial statements based on our audits.

We conducted our audits in accordance with U.S. generally accepted auditing standards. Those standards require that we plan and perform the audit to obtain reasonable assurance about whether the financial statements are free of material misstatement. An audit includes examining, on a test basis, evidence supporting the amounts and disclosures in the financial statements. An audit also includes assessing the accounting principles used and significant estimates made by management, as well as evaluating the overall financial statement presentation. We believe that our audits provide a reasonable basis for our opinion.

As described in Note X, these financial statements were prepared on the basis of cash receipts and disbursements, which is a comprehensive basis of accounting other than generally accepted accounting principles.

In our opinion, the financial statements referred to above present fairly, in all material respects, the assets and liabilities arising from cash transactions of XYZ Company as of December 31, 20X2 and 20X1, and the revenue collected and expenses paid during the years then ended, on the basis of accounting described in Note X.

* This report should be addressed, signed, and dated as previously discussed. For the sake of brevity, these elements are omitted from this and most other exhibits of reports in this chapter.

1.   **OCBOA**   A comprehensive basis other than GAAP is (a) a basis that is used to comply with the requirements or financial provisions of a government regulatory agency, but only for filing with that agency (e.g., state insurance commission rules for insurance companies); (b) a basis used (or expected to be used) for filing the client's income tax return for the period covered by the financial statements; (c) the cash receipts and disbursements basis (including modifications to cash basis that have substantial support); and (d) a definite set of criteria having substantial support that is applied to all material financial statement items, (e.g., price-level basis of accounting).

2.   **Statement Titles**   "Balance sheet," "statement of financial position," "statement of income," "statement of operations," "statement of cash flows," etc., apply only to statements prepared in conformity with GAAP. Suitable titles should be given to financial statements prepared in conformity with a comprehensive basis of accounting other than GAAP. For example, an appropriate title for a cash basis financial statement might be "statement of assets and liabilities arising from cash transactions," and an appropriate title for a financial statement prepared on a statutory basis might be "statement of income—statutory basis."

   a.   **Same**   Elements the same as the standard audit report are: (1) a title that includes the word "independent"; (2) paragraph one, an introductory paragraph; (3) paragraph two, a scope paragraph; (4) the firm's signature; and (5) a date.

   b.   **Paragraph Three**   States: (1) the basis of presentation, and refers to the note that describes the basis, and (2) that the basis of presentation is a comprehensive basis of accounting other than GAAP.

   c.   **Paragraph Four**   Expresses the auditor's opinion on the financial statements in accordance with the OCBOA basis.

   d.   **Restrictive Paragraph**   This paragraph is used when the financial statements are prepared in conformity with the requirements of a government regulatory agency. It states that the distribution of the report is restricted to those within the entity and for filing with the regulatory agency.

e. **Financial Statement Titles** The auditor should disclose reservations in an explanatory paragraph of the report and qualify the opinion in cases where the auditor believes the financial statements are not titled appropriately.

C. **Reports on Specified Elements, Accounts, or Items of a Financial Statement**
Examples include rentals, royalties, a profit participation, or a provision for income taxes.

Exhibit 8 ▶ Report Relating to Royalties

Independent Auditor's Report

We have audited the accompanying schedule of royalties applicable to engine production of the Q Division of XYZ Corporation for the year ended December 31, 20X2, under the terms of a license agreement dated May 14, 20X0, between ABC Company and XYZ Corporation. This schedule is the responsibility of XYZ Corporation's management. Our responsibility is to express an opinion on this schedule based on our audit.

We conducted our audit in accordance with U.S. generally accepted auditing standards. Those standards require that we plan and perform the audit to obtain reasonable assurance about whether the schedule of royalties is free of material misstatement. An audit includes examining, on a test basis, evidence supporting the amounts and disclosures in the schedule. An audit also includes assessing the accounting principles used and significant estimates made by management, as well as evaluating the overall schedule presentation. We believe that our audit provides a reasonable basis for our opinion.

We have been informed that, under XYZ Corporation's interpretation of the agreement referred to in the first paragraph, royalties were based on the number of engines produced after giving effect to a reduction for production retirements that were scrapped, but without a reduction for field returns that were scrapped, even though the field returns were replaced with new engines without charge to customers.

In our opinion, the schedule of royalties referred to above presents fairly, in all material respects, the number of engines produced by the Q Division of XYZ Corporation during the year ended December 31, 20X2, and the amount of royalties applicable thereto, under the license agreement referred to above.

This report is intended solely for the information and use of the boards of directors and management of XYZ Corporation and ABC Company and should not be used for any other purpose.

---

1. **GAAS** The ten GAAS are applicable with the exception of the first standard of reporting which is applicable only when the specified elements, accounts, or items are intended to be presented in conformity with GAAP.

2. **Materiality** An engagement to express an opinion on one or more specified elements, accounts, or items may be undertaken as a separate engagement or in conjunction with an audit of the financial statements. An opinion is being expressed on each of the specified elements, accounts, or items encompassed by the auditor's report, so materiality must be related to each of the specified elements, accounts, or items. Therefore, the audit will usually be more extensive in regard to the element, account, or item than it would be if the only objective were to express an opinion on the financial statements taken as a whole. The auditor must consider any interrelationships among the specified elements, accounts, or items being reported on and other items in the financial statements.

3. **Piecemeal Opinion** When the auditor has expressed an adverse opinion or disclaimed an opinion on the financial statements taken as a whole, the auditor should **not** report on specified elements, accounts, or items that are included in those statements if the effect is to express a piecemeal opinion. The auditor is able to report on one or more specified elements,

accounts, or items provided that a major portion of the financial statements is not involved. This report should be presented separately from the report on the financial statements.

D.   Reports on Compliance With Aspects of Contractual Agreements or Regulatory Requirements Related to Audited Financial Statements
Contractual agreements sometimes require entities to furnish compliance reports prepared by independent auditors (e.g., a loan agreement may contain provisions relating to payments made to a sinking fund and maintenance of a specified current ratio).

Exhibit 9 ▶ Compliance With Contractual Provisions Given in a Separate Report

---

We have audited, in accordance with auditing standards generally accepted in the United States of America, the balance sheet of XYZ Company as of December 31, 20X2, and the related statements of income, retained earnings, and cash flows for the year then ended, and have issued our report thereon dated February 16, 20X3.

In connection with our audit, nothing came to our attention that caused us to believe that the company failed to comply with the terms, covenants, provisions or conditions of Sections XX to XX, inclusive, of the Indenture dated July 21, 20X0, with ABC Bank. However, it should be noted that our audit was not directed primarily toward obtaining knowledge of such noncompliance.

This report is intended solely for the information and use of the board of directors and management of XYZ Company and ABC Bank and is not intended to be and should not be used by anyone other than those specified parties.

---

1.   **Negative Assurance** The auditor normally gives negative assurance regarding compliance with agreements. This may be done by using a separate report or it may be added to the report accompanying the financial statements. Negative assurance should be given only when the auditor has audited the financial statements to which the agreements or requirements relate and the report's use will be restricted to the named parties.

2.   **Report** The auditor's report includes the following:

    a.   **Title, Signature & Date** A title that includes the word "independent."

    b.   **Paragraph One** The financial statements were audited in accordance with GAAS and includes the date of the auditor's report on those financial statements. Any departure from the standard report should also be disclosed.

    c.   **Paragraph Two** A reference to the specific covenants or paragraphs of the agreement, provides negative assurance relative to the compliance with the applicable covenants insofar as they relate to accounting matters, and specifies that the negative assurance is being given in connection with the audit of the financial statements.

    d.   **Paragraph Three** A description and source of significant interpretations, if any, made by the company's management relating to the provisions of a relevant agreement.

    e.   **Paragraph Four** Restricts the use of the report to those within the entity and the parties to the contract or agreement or for filing with the regulatory agency.

E.   Incomplete Presentation Otherwise in Conformity With GAAP or OCBOA
This might include a situation where a buy-sell agreement requires that assets and liabilities be presented in accordance with GAAP, but it only includes those items that will be sold and transferred under the agreement rather than all the entity's assets and liabilities. This situation constitutes a financial statement in the limited circumstances addressed by SAS 62.

1.   **Presentation** The presentation should be titled appropriately so that no confusion exists (terms such as *balance sheet, income statement, statement of cash flows,* should **not** be

used). Disclosures should be made similar to those provided in a complete set of financial statements.

2. **Materiality** Materiality is in relation to the presentation taken as a whole.

3. **Report** The audit report includes an introductory paragraph, a scope paragraph, an explanatory paragraph, an opinion paragraph, and a paragraph restricting the use of the report.

   a. The introductory paragraph identifies the financial information being reported on and states the responsibilities of management and the auditor.

   b. The explanatory paragraph (1) explains what the financial presentation is intended to present and refers the reader to a note that describes the basis of the financial presentation, and (2) states that the financial presentation is not intended to be a complete set of financial information in accordance with GAAP.

F. **Statements Prepared on a Prescribed Basis Not in Conformity With GAAP or OCBOA**
An auditor can be associated with financial statements using specified reporting requirements. For example, a loan application may call for financial statements, with the inventory to be valued at sales price; or in an acquisition agreement, the financial statements may request that fixed assets and inventories be measured at their liquidation values.

1. **Materiality** The auditor considers the adequacy of the disclosures associated with the financial statements. Materiality is considered at the financial statement level.

2. **Report** The auditor's report includes the following:

   a. A responsibility paragraph

   b. A scope paragraph

   c. An explanatory paragraph similar to an incomplete presentation otherwise in conformity with GAAP

   d. A paragraph that includes a description and the source of significant interpretations made by management

   e. An opinion paragraph

   f. A paragraph restricting the distribution of the report

G. **Financial Information Presented in Prescribed Forms or Schedules**
Regulatory bodies, government agencies, and others sometimes use printed forms or schedules that prescribe the form of the auditor's report. A problem arises if the prescribed report does not conform to the applicable professional reporting standards of the public accounting profession (e.g., calling for assertions that are not consistent with the auditor's function).

1. **Procedures** Insertion of additional wording can make some report forms acceptable; other report forms require complete revision.

2. **Assertions** If a printed report calls for an assertion the auditor believes is not justified, the auditor should either reword the form or attach a separate report.

III. **Letters for Underwriters**

A. **Filings Under Federal Securities Statutes (AU 711, SAS 37)**
The financial representations contained in documents filed with the SEC are the responsibility and representations of management. However, the Securities Act of 1933 imposes responsibility on an

auditor for false or misleading financial statements (or for omissions that make them misleading) in an effective registration statement prepared or certified by the CPA.

1. **Auditor's Defense** The auditor must prove that (a) there were reasonable grounds to believe (and the auditor did believe) that the statements in the registration statement were true and that there was no omission of a material fact at the date of the registration statement or (b) that the part of the registration statement that is in question did not fairly represent the auditor's statement as an expert or was not fairly copied or extracted from the report or valuation.

   - **Reasonableness Standard** The standard of reasonableness is that standard which would be used by a prudent person in the management of her/his own property.

2. **Date** The auditor's responsibility extends to the effective date of the registration statement.

3. **Use of Name** The auditor should be sure her/his name is not used in a way that may indicate that the auditor's responsibility is greater than it really is.

4. **Subsequent Events Procedures in 1933 Act Filings** The auditor should extend subsequent event procedures from the date of the report to the effective date of the registration statement. The auditor can rely, for the most part, on inquiries of responsible officials and employees. The auditor should perform the auditing procedures used to assess the existence of subsequent events (e.g., inquiry of management, reading of minutes, etc.) and, in addition, should (a) read the entire prospectus and other pertinent portions of the registration statement, and (b) obtain written confirmation from officers and other executives regarding subsequent events that have a material effect on the audited financial statements included in the registration statement or which require disclosure in order to keep the statements from being misleading.

5. **Response to Subsequent Events & Subsequently Discovered Facts** If the auditor discovers either (a) subsequent events requiring adjustment or disclosure or (b) facts existing at the time of the report which might have affected the report had the auditor known about them, the auditor should do the following:

   a. Ask management to revise the statements and/or add the required disclosures.

   b. If management refuses, the auditor should modify the report accordingly and consider obtaining advice from legal counsel.

6. **Reports Based on a Review of Interim Financial Information** The SEC requires that when a report based on a review of interim financial information is presented or incorporated in a registration statement by reference, a clarification should be made that the review report is not a "report" or "part" of the registration statement within the meaning of Sections 7 and 11 of the Securities Act of 1933.

7. **Two or More Auditors** A registration statement filed with the SEC may contain the reports of two or more auditors for different periods. An auditor who has not audited the financial statements for the most recent period has a responsibility for events that have a material effect on the financial statements the auditor reported on that occurred during the period running from the date of the report until the effective date of the registration statement. The auditor generally should (a) read the pertinent portions of the prospectus and registration statement and (b) obtain a letter of representation from the successor auditor about subsequent events which the successor has become aware.

B. **Letters for Underwriters & Certain Other Requesting Parties (AU 634)**
   AU 634 provides guidance to accountants for reporting on the results of and performing engagements to issue letters for underwriters and certain other requesting parties, commonly referred to as comfort letters, in connection with financial statements and financial statement schedules contained in registration statements filed with the SEC under the Securities Act of 1933. Comfort letters

are not required under the Act, and copies are not filed with the SEC. It is nonetheless a common condition of an underwriting agreement in connection with the offering for sale of securities registered with the SEC under the Act that the accountants are to furnish a comfort letter.

1. **Purpose** Section 11 of the Act provides that underwriters, among others, could be liable if any part of a registration statement contains material omissions or misstatements. The Act also provides for an affirmative defense for underwriters if it can be demonstrated that, after an investigation, the underwriter has reasonable grounds to believe that there were no material omissions or misstatements. An accountant's issuance of a comfort letter is one procedure used to establish that an underwriter has conducted a reasonable investigation.

2. **Representations** Using a statutory due diligence defense under Section 11 of the Act, a comfort letter may be addressed to parties other than a named underwriter, only when a law firm or attorney for the requesting party issues a written opinion to the accountants that states that such party has a due diligence defense under Section 11 of the Act. AU 634 precludes the accountant from providing a comfort letter if an appropriate representation letter is not provided. An attorney's letter indicating that a party "may" be deemed to be an underwriter, or has liability substantially equivalent to that of an underwriter under the securities laws, would not meet this requirement. If the requesting party, in a securities offering registered pursuant to the Act, other than a named underwriter, cannot provide such a letter, s/he must provide a representation letter for the accountant to provide her/him with a comfort letter. The letter should be addressed to the accountants, signed by the requesting party, and contain a due diligence process paragraph.

Exhibit 10 ▶ Representation Letter Excerpt

> This review process, applied to the information relating to the issuer, is substantially consistent with the due diligence review process that we would perform if this placement of securities were being registered pursuant to the Securities Act of 1933. We are knowledgeable with respect to the due diligence review process that would be performed if this placement of securities were being registered pursuant to the Act.

3. **Limitations** In requesting comfort letters, underwriters generally are seeking assistance on matters of importance to them. They wish to perform a "reasonable investigation," as a defense against possible claims under Section 11, of financial and accounting data that has not been "expertized." Accountants normally are willing to assist underwriters, but the assistance accountants can provide by way of comfort letters is subject to limitations. One limitation is that independent accountants properly can comment in their professional capacity only on matters to which their professional expertise is substantially relevant. Another limitation is that procedures short of an audit, such as those contemplated in a comfort letter, provide the accountants with a basis for expressing, at the most, negative assurance.

4. **Draft** Because the underwriter will expect the accountants to furnish a comfort letter of a scope to be specified in the underwriting agreement, a draft of that agreement should be furnished to the accountants so that they can indicate whether they will be able to furnish a letter in acceptable form. It is a desirable practice for the accountants, promptly after they have received the draft of the agreement, to prepare a draft of the form of the letter they expect to furnish. The draft should deal with all matters to be covered in the final letter.

5. **Prohibited** Accountants should not comment on matters merely because they are capable of reading, counting, measuring, or performing other functions that might be applicable. Examples of matters that, unless subjected to the controls over financial reporting, should not be commented on by accountants include the square footage of facilities and backlog information. Accountants should not comment on tables, statistics, and other financial information relating to an unaudited period, unless they have obtained knowledge of the client's internal control over financial reporting (comparable to that obtained during an audit). In addition, accountants should not comment on information subject to legal interpretation.

6. **Additional Letters** Accountants may not issue any additional letters or reports to the under-writer or the other requesting parties, in connection with the offering or placement of securities, in which the accountants comment on items for which commenting is otherwise precluded by AU 634, such as square footage of facilities.

7. **Format & Content**

    a. **Permissible Topics** Generally, accountants may comment only with respect to infor-mation (1) obtained from accounting records that are subject to the entity's controls over financial reporting and that is expressed in dollars (or percentages derived from such dollar amounts), or (2) derived directly from accounting records by analysis or computation. Accountants also may comment on quantitative information that has been obtained from an accounting record, if the information is subject to the same controls over financial reporting as the dollar amounts. Permissible topics include the following:

        (1) The independence of the accountants.

        (2) Whether the audited financial statements and financial statement schedules included in the registration statement comply as to form in all material respects with the applicable accounting requirements of the Act and the related pub-lished rules and regulations.

        (3) Unaudited financial statements, condensed interim financial information, capsule financial information, pro forma financial information, financial forecasts, and changes in selected financial statement items during a period subsequent to the date and period of the latest registration statement.

        (4) Tables, statistics, and other financial information included in the registration statement.

        (5) Negative assurance as to whether certain nonfinancial statement information complies as to form with Regulation S-K, if the information is (a) derived from the accounting records subject to the entity's controls over financial reporting and (b) capable of evaluation against SEC criteria. Accountants may perform procedures and report findings with respect to conformity with Regulation S-K.

    b. **Date** The letter ordinarily is dated on or shortly before the date on which the registra-tion statement becomes effective.

    c. **Addressee** The letter should not be addressed or given to any parties other than the client and the named underwriter, broker-dealer, financial intermediary, or buyer or seller. The appropriate addressee is the intermediary who has negotiated the agree-ment with the client, and with whom the accountants will deal in discussions regarding the scope and sufficiency of the letter.

    d. **Explanatory Paragraph** When the report on the audited financial statements and financial statement schedules included in the registration statement departs from the standard report, the accountants should refer to that fact in the comfort letter and dis-cuss the subject matter of the paragraph.

    e. **Reiterate Audit Opinion** The underwriter occasionally requests the accountants to repeat in the comfort letter their report on the audited financial statements included in the registration statement. Because of the special significance of the date of the accountants' report, the accountants should **not** repeat their opinion. The underwriter sometimes requests negative assurance regarding the accountants' report. Because accountants have a statutory responsibility with respect to their opinion as of the effec-tive date of a registration statement, and because the additional significance, if any, of negative assurance is unclear and such assurance may therefore give rise to misunderstanding, accountants should **not** give negative assurance.

f.   **Optional**   Accountants may refer (in the introductory paragraphs of the comfort letter) to the fact that they have issued reports on (1) condensed financial statements that are derived from audited financial statements; (2) selected financial data; (3) interim financial information; (4) pro forma financial information; (5) a financial forecast; and (6) management's discussion and analysis.   Any optional references should be to previously-issued accountants' reports.   If the reports were not included (or incorporated by reference) in the registration statement, they may be attached to the comfort letter.   The accountants should not repeat previously-issued reports, otherwise imply that they are reporting as of the date of the comfort letter, or imply that they assume responsibility for the sufficiency of the procedures for the underwriter's purposes.   For certain information on which they have reported, accountants may agree to comment regarding compliance with SEC criteria.   Accountants should not mention reports issued in accordance with SAS 112, *Communicating Internal Control Related Matters Identified in an Audit,* or any restricted-use reports issued in connection with procedures performed on the client's internal control in accordance with AT 501.

g.   *Pro Forma* **Information**   Accountants should **not** comment in a comfort letter on *pro forma* financial information unless they have an appropriate level of knowledge of the accounting and financial reporting practices of the entity.   This ordinarily would have been obtained by the accountant's audit or review of historical financial statements of the entity for the most recent annual or interim period for which the pro forma financial information is presented.

h.   **Compliance**   Accountants may be requested to express an opinion on whether the financial statements covered by their report comply as to form with the pertinent SEC accounting requirements.   Accountants may provide positive assurance on compliance as to form with SEC requirements only with respect to those rules and regulations applicable to the form and content of financial statements and financial statement schedules that they have audited.   Accountants are limited to providing negative assurance on compliance as to form on unaudited statements or schedules.   If there is a material departure from SEC criteria, it must be disclosed.

Exhibit 11 ▶ Sample Paragraph Regarding Compliance With SEC Criteria

> In our opinion (include the phrase *except as disclosed in the registration statement,* if applicable) the (*identify the financial statements and financial statement schedules*) audited by us and included (incorporated by reference) in the registration statement comply as to form in all material respects with the applicable accounting requirements of the Act and the related rules and regulations adopted by the SEC.

8.   **Subsequently Discovered Matters**   Accountants who discover matters that are not mentioned in the draft letter, that may require mention in the final comfort letter, (e.g., changes, increases, or decreases in specified items not disclosed in the registration statement) will need to discuss them with their client so that consideration can be given to whether disclosure should be made in the registration statement.   If disclosure is not to be made, the accountants should inform the client that the matters will be mentioned in the comfort letter and should suggest that the underwriter be informed promptly.

IV.   Service Organizations (AU 324)

A.   Overview

AU 324 provides guidance on the factors an independent auditor considers when auditing the financial statements of an entity that uses a service organization to process transactions.   It also provides guidance for independent auditors who issue reports on the processing of transactions by a service organization for use by other auditors.

1. **User Organization** The entity that has engaged a service organization and whose financial statements are being audited.

2. **Service Organization** The entity (or a segment of that entity) that provides services to the user organization. Services provided could include the processing of payroll information for other companies or the processing of checks and daily paperwork for banks.

B. **Service Auditor**
The service auditor reports on the processing of transactions by a service organization. The service auditor is responsible for the representations in her/his report and for exercising due care in the application of procedures that support those representations. The service auditor's work should be performed in accordance with the general standards and relevant fieldwork and reporting standards. AU 324 clarifies that a service auditor should inquire of management regarding subsequent events.

1. **Independence** The service auditor should be independent from the service organization. However, the service auditor is **not** required to be independent with regard to each client, or user, organization.

2. **Engagement** The type of engagement to be performed and report to be prepared should be established by the service organization. A service auditor's report on a service organization's description of the controls that may be relevant to a user organization's internal control. The service auditor may issue either of the following types of reports:

    a. **Reports on Controls Placed in Operation** The auditor reports on whether the controls were (1) suitably designed to achieve specified objectives and (2) placed in operation as of a specific date.

    b. **Reports on Controls Placed in Operation & Tests of Operating Effectiveness** Like the report previously discussed, the auditor reports on whether such controls were (1) suitably designed to achieve specified objectives and (2) placed in operation as of a specific date. The auditor also reports on whether the controls that were tested were operating with sufficient effectiveness to provide reasonable, but not absolute, assurance that the related objectives were achieved during the period specified.

3. **Format & Content of Special-Purpose Reports** A report expressing an opinion on a description of controls placed in operation at a service organization should contain the following:

    a. A specific reference to the applications, services, products or other aspects of the service organization covered.

    b. Identification of the party specifying the objectives and of the parties for whom the report is intended.

    c. A description of the scope and nature of the service auditor's procedures.

    d. An indication that the purpose of the service auditor's engagement was to obtain reasonable assurance about whether the service organization's description presents fairly, in all material respects, the aspects of the service organization's controls that may be relevant to a user organization's internal control; that the controls were suitably designed to achieve specified control objectives; and that such controls had been placed in operation as of a specific date.

    e. A disclaimer of opinion on the operating effectiveness of the controls.

    f. The service auditor's opinion on whether the description presents fairly, in all material respects, the relevant aspects of the service organization's policies and procedures that had been placed in operation as of a specific date and whether, in the service auditor's opinion, the policies and procedures were suitably designed to provide reasonable assurance that the specified objectives would be achieved if those controls were complied with satisfactorily.

g. A statement of the inherent limitations of the potential effectiveness of the policies and procedures at the service organization and of the risk of projecting to future periods any evaluation of the description.

Exhibit 12 ▶ Report on Internal Controls at Service Organization

To XYZ Service Organization:

We have examined the accompanying description of the _____ application of XYZ Service Organization. Our examination included procedures to obtain reasonable assurance about whether (1) the accompanying description presents fairly, in all material respects, the aspects of XYZ Service Organization's controls that may be relevant to a user organization's internal control, (2) the internal controls included in the description were suitably designed to achieve the objectives specified in the description, if those controls were complied with satisfactorily, and (3) such controls had been placed in operation as of _____. The objectives were specified by _____. Our examination was performed in accordance with standards established by the American Institute of Certified Public Accountants and included those procedures we considered necessary in the circumstances to obtain a reasonable basis for rendering our opinion.

We did not perform procedures to determine the operating effectiveness of controls for any period. Accordingly, we express no opinion on the operating effectiveness of any aspects of XYZ Service Organization's controls, individually or in the aggregate.

In our opinion, the accompanying description of the aforementioned application presents fairly, in all material respects, the relevant aspects of XYZ Service Organization's controls that had been placed in operation as of _____. Also, in our opinion, the controls, as described, are suitably designed to provide reasonable assurance that the specified objectives would be achieved if the described controls were complied with satisfactorily.

The description of controls at XYZ Service Organization is as of _____ and any projection of such information to the future is subject to the risk that, because of change, the description may no longer portray the system in existence. The potential effectiveness of specific controls at the Service Organization is subject to inherent limitations and, accordingly, errors or fraud may occur and not be detected. Furthermore, the projection of any conclusions, based on our findings, to future periods is subject to the risk that changes may alter the validity of such conclusions.

This report is intended solely for use by the management of XYZ Service Organization, its customers, and the independent auditors of its customers.

C. User Auditor

The user auditor reports on the financial statements of the user organization. The explicit addition of service organizations to the audit planning requirement clarifies the auditor's responsibility to understand all controls relevant to a financial statement audit. The auditor should obtain an understanding of each of the five components of an entity's internal control (control environment, etc.) sufficient to plan the audit. SAS 88 states that this understanding may encompass controls placed in operation by the entity and by service organizations whose services are part of the entity's information system.

1. Client's System Under SAS 88, a service organization's services are part of an entity's information system if they affect any of the following: (a) how the entity's transactions are initiated; (b) the accounting records, supporting information, and specific accounts in the financial statements involved in the processing and reporting of the entity's transactions; (c) the processing involved from the initiation of the transactions to their inclusion in the financial statements, including electronic means used to transmit, process, maintain, and access information; and (d) the financial reporting process used to prepare the entity's financial statements, including significant accounting estimates and disclosures.

2. **Significance** SAS 88 notes that the significance of the service organization's controls to those of the user organization depends on the services provided by the service organization in two primary areas: (a) the nature and materiality of the transactions it processes for the user organization, and (b) the degree of interaction between its activities and those of the user organization.

3. **Reputation** In considering whether the service auditor's report is satisfactory for her/his purposes, the user auditor should make inquiries concerning the service auditor's professional reputation.

4. **Additional Procedures** If the user auditor believes that the service auditor's report may not be sufficient to meet her/his objectives, the user auditor may supplement her/his understanding of the service auditor's procedures and conclusions by discussing with the service auditor the scope and results of the service auditor's work. If the user auditor believes it is necessary, s/he may contact the service organization, through the user organization, to request that the service auditor perform agreed-upon procedures at the service organization, or the user auditor may perform such procedures.

5. **Reference** The user auditor should not make reference to the service auditor's report as a basis for her/his own opinion on the user organization's financial statements.

V. Interim Financial Information (AU 722)

A. Overview

1. **Definitions**

    a. **Interim Financial Information** *Interim financial information* means financial information or statements covering a period less than a full year or for a 12-month period ending on a date other than the entity's fiscal year-end. Interim financial information may be condensed or in the form of a complete set of financial statements.

    b. **Applicable Financial Reporting Framework** *Applicable financial reporting framework* means a set of criteria used to determine measurement, recognition, presentation, and disclosure of all material items appearing in the financial statements; for example, U.S. GAAP, International Financial Reporting Standards or comprehensive bases of accounting other than GAAP.

3. **Modified GAAS** The three general standards of GAAS are applicable to reviews of interim financial information conducted in accordance with AU 722, *Interim Financial Information*. AU 722 provides guidance on the application of the fieldwork and reporting standards to a review of interim financial information, to the extent those standards are relevant.

4. **Applicability**
    AU 722 is applicable to the review of interim financial information of nonissuers. (Guidance for the review of public companies' interim financial information resides in the auditing standards of the Public Company Accounting Oversight Board.) An accountant may conduct, in accordance with AU 722, a review of interim financial information if the following conditions are met.

    Editor note: These conditions are an acknowledgement of the difference between a review performed by an accountant with an audit base of knowledge versus that performed by an accountant who is not the entity's auditor. Further, when these conditions are met, generally the review engagement is intended to provide a periodic update to the year-end reporting and is considered an extension of the annual audit. Thus, the standard setters decided the requirements and guidance should reside in the auditing literature. Accordingly, if these conditions are *not* met, reviews of interim financial information of nonissuers should be performed in accordance with Statements on Standards for Accounting and Review Services (SSARS).

a. The entity's latest annual financial statements have been audited by the accountant or a predecessor.

b. The accountant has been engaged to audit the entity's current year financial statements, or the accountant audited the entity's latest annual financial statements and expects to be engaged to audit the current year financial statements.

c. The client prepares its interim financial information in accordance with the same financial reporting framework as that used to prepare the annual financial statements.

d. If the interim financial information is condensed information, all of the following conditions are met:

   (1) The condensed interim financial information purports to conform with an appropriate financial reporting framework, which includes appropriate form and content of interim financial statements.

   (2) The condensed interim financial information includes a note that the financial information does not represent complete financial statements and should be read in conjunction with the entity's latest annual audited financial statements.

   (3) The condensed interim financial information accompanies the entity's latest audited annual financial statements or such audited annual financial statements are made readily available by the entity.

5. **Condition for Engagement Acceptance** Prior to accepting the engagement, the accountant should assess management's ability to acknowledge their responsibility to establish and maintain controls that are sufficient to provide a reasonable basis for the preparation of reliable interim financial information in accordance with the applicable financial reporting framework. If management does not have the ability to make such an acknowledgement of its responsibility, the independent accountant should not accept the engagement.

6. **Establishing an Understanding With the Client**
    The understanding established with the client should be documented in a written communication. It should include:

    a. **Objectives** The objective of a review of interim financial information is to provide the accountant with a basis for communicating whether there are any material modifications that should be made to the interim financial information for it to conform with the applicable financial reporting framework

    A review includes obtaining sufficient knowledge of the entity's business and its internal control as it relates to the preparation of both annual and interim financial information to

    (1) Identify the types of potential material misstatements in the interim financial information and consider the likelihood of their occurrence.

    (2) Select the inquiries and analytical procedures that will provide the accountant with a basis for communicating whether the accountant is aware of any material modifications that should be made to the interim financial information for it to conform with the applicable financial reporting framework.

b. **Limitations**

    (1) A review does **not** provide a basis for expressing an opinion about whether the financial information is presented fairly, in all material respects, in conformity with the applicable financial reporting framework.

    (2) A review does not provide assurance that the accountant will become aware of all significant matters that would be identified in an audit.

    (3) A review is not designed to provide assurance on internal control or to identify significant deficiencies and material weaknesses in internal control; however, the accountant is responsible for communicating to management and those charged with governance any significant deficiencies or material weaknesses in internal control that the accountant identified.

c. **Management's Responsibilities**

    (1) The entity's interim financial information

    (2) Establishing and maintaining effective internal control over financial reporting

    (3) Identifying and ensuring that the entity complies with the laws and regulations applicable to its activities

    (4) Making all financial records and related information available to the accountant

    (5) Providing the accountant, at the conclusion of the engagement, with a letter confirming certain representations made during the review

    (6) Adjusting the interim financial information to correct material misstatements— Although a review of interim financial information is not designed to obtain reasonable assurance that the interim financial information is free from material misstatement, management also is responsible for affirming in its representation letter to the accountant that the effects of any uncorrected misstatements aggregated by the accountant during the current engagement and pertaining to the current-year period(s) under review are immaterial, both individually and in the aggregate, to the interim financial information taken as a whole.

d. **Accountant's Responsibilities**

    (1) Conducting the review in accordance with AICPA standards

    (2) Performing analytical procedures and making inquiries of persons responsible for financial and accounting matters;

    (3) A review is substantially less in scope than an audit conducted in accordance with auditing standards generally accepted in the United States of America, the objective of which is the expression of an opinion regarding the financial information taken as a whole. Accordingly, the accountant will not express an opinion on the interim financial information

e. **Form of the Communication** The understanding with the client should include whether the expected form of the communication upon completion of the engagement, is to be written or oral.

f. **Report Required to Be Included If Accountant Associated With Review** A statement should also be included in the understanding that if the entity states in any report, document, or written communication containing the interim financial information that the information has been reviewed by the accountant or makes other reference to the accountant's association, that the accountant's review report will be included in the document.

8. **Knowledge of the Entity's Business & It's Internal Control** The accountant must have a sufficient knowledge of the client's business and internal control to

   a. Identify types of potential material misstatements in the interim financial information and consider the likelihood of their occurrence

   b. Select the inquiries and analytics that will provide the accountant with a basis for reporting whether material modifications should be made for such information to conform with the applicable financial reporting framework.

B. **Procedures**

1. **Analytical Procedures & Related Inquiries** The accountant should apply analytical procedures to the interim financial information to identify and provide a basis for inquiry about the relationships and individual items that appear to be unusual and that may indicate a material misstatement. This should include comparing

   a. Interim financial information with comparable information for the immediately preceding interim period, if applicable, and with the corresponding period(s) in the previous year

   b. Plausible relationships among both financial and, where relevant, nonfinancial information

   c. Recorded amounts, or ratios developed from recorded amounts, to expectations developed by the accountant

   d. Disaggregated revenue data

   Expectations developed by the accountant in performing analytical procedures in connection with a review of interim financial information ordinarily are less precise than those developed in an audit. Also, in a review the accountant ordinarily is not required to corroborate management's responses with other evidence. However, the accountant should consider the reasonableness and consistency of management's responses in light of the results of other review procedures and the accountant's knowledge of the entity's business and its internal control.

2. **Other Procedures & Inquires** The following are inquiries the accountant should make and other review procedures the accountant should perform when conducting a review of interim financial information. If, as a result, the accountant believes that the interim financial information may not be in conformity with the applicable financial reporting framework in all material respects, the accountant should make additional inquiries or perform other procedures.

   a. Reading the available minutes of meetings of stockholders, directors, and appropriate committees, and inquiring about matters dealt with at meetings for which minutes are not available, to identify matters that may affect the interim financial information.

   b. Obtaining reports from other accountants, if any, who have been engaged to perform a review of the interim financial information of significant components of the reporting entity, its subsidiaries, or its other investees, or inquiring of those accountants if reports have not been issued.

   c. Inquiring of members of management who have responsibility for financial and accounting matters concerning:

(1) Whether the interim financial information has been prepared in conformity with the applicable financial reporting framework consistently applied

(2) Unusual or complex situations that may have an effect on the interim financial information

(3) Significant transactions occurring or recognized in the last several days of the interim period

(4) The status of uncorrected misstatements identified during the previous audit and interim review

(5) Matters about which questions have arisen in the course of applying the review procedures

(6) Events subsequent to the date of the interim financial information that could have a material effect on the presentation of such information

(7) Their knowledge of any fraud or suspected fraud affecting the entity involving management, employees who have significant roles in internal control, or others where the fraud could have a material effect on the financial information

(8) Whether they are aware of allegations of fraud or suspected fraud affecting the entity

(9) Significant journal entries and other adjustments

(10) Communications from regulatory agencies

(11) Significant deficiencies, including material weaknesses, in the design or operation of internal control as it relates to the preparation of both annual and interim financial information

d. Obtaining evidence that the interim financial information agrees or reconciles with the accounting records

e. Reading the interim financial information to consider whether, based on the results of the review procedures performed and other information that has come to the accountant's attention, the information to be reported conforms with the applicable financial reporting framework

f. Reading other information in documents containing the interim financial information to consider whether such information or the manner of its presentation is materially inconsistent with the interim financial information.

3. **Written Management Representations** Written representations from management should be obtained for all interim financial information presented and for all periods covered by the review.

4. **Evaluation of Results of Procedures** Misstatements identified by the accountant or brought to the accountant's attention, including inadequate disclosure, should be evaluated individually and in the aggregate to determine whether material modification should be made to the interim financial information for it to conform with the applicable financial reporting framework.

The accountant should use her/his professional judgment in evaluating the materiality of any likely misstatements that the entity has not corrected. The accountant should consider matters such as (a) the nature, cause and amount of the misstatements; (b) whether the misstatements originated in the preceding year or interim periods of the current year;

(c) materiality judgments made in conjunction with the current or prior year's annual audit; and (d) the potential effect of the misstatements on future interim or annual periods.

C.   Communications to Management & Those Charged With Governance

1.   **Material Modification**   If the accountant determines that a material modification should be made to the interim financial information for it to conform with the applicable financial reporting framework, the accountant should communicate this to the appropriate level of management as soon as practicable.   If management does not respond appropriately, the accountant should inform those charged with governance as soon as practicable.   If done orally, the communication should be documented.   If those charged with governance do not respond appropriately, the accountant should evaluate whether to resign from the engagement and as the entity's auditor, in which case consultation with an attorney may be advisable.

2.   **Fraud or Illegal Acts**   Possible fraud or illegal acts discovered should be brought to the attention of the appropriate level of management.   If a matter involves possible fraud on the part of senior management or the fraud results in a material misstatement, the accountant should communicate directly with those charged with governance.

3.   **Significant Deficiencies or Material Weaknesses in Internal Control**   Significant deficiencies or material weaknesses in internal control discovered should be communicated to management and those charged with governance.

D.   Report on Review of Interim Financial Information
Although this section generally does not require an accountant to issue a written report on a review of interim financial information, an accountant's review report should accompany the interim financial information if, in a report; document; or written communication containing the reviewed interim financial information, the entity states that the interim financial information has been reviewed by an independent public accountant or makes other reference to the accountant's association.   In other situations, the accountant may determine it appropriate to issue a written report to address the risk that a user of interim financial information may associate the accountant with the interim financial information and, in the absence of a review report, inappropriately assume a higher level of assurance than that obtained,

Each page of the interim financial information should be clearly marked as unaudited.   The report should contain these elements:

a.   A title that includes the word independent.

b.   A statement that the interim financial information identified in the report was reviewed.

c.   A statement that the interim financial information is the responsibility of the entity's management.

d.   A statement that the review of interim financial information was conducted in accordance with standards established by the AICPA.

e.   A description of the procedures for a review of interim financial information.

f.   A statement that a review of interim financial information is substantially less in scope than an audit conducted in accordance with auditing standards generally accepted in the United States, the objective of which is an expression of an opinion regarding the financial information taken as a whole, and accordingly, no such opinion is expressed.

g.   A statement about whether the accountant is aware of any material modifications that should be made to the accompanying interim financial information for it to conform with the applicable financial reporting framework. The statement should include an identification of the country of origin of those accounting principles (for example, accounting principles generally accepted in the United States of America or U.S. generally accepted accounting principles).

h.   The manual or printed signature of the accountant's firm.

i.   The date of the review report. (Generally, the report should be dated as of the date of completion of the review procedures.)

VI. Reporting on Condensed Financial Statements & Selected Financial Data (AU 552)

A.   Condensed Financial Statements
AU 552 provides guidance on reporting in a client-prepared document on condensed financial statements derived from audited financial statements of a public entity that are required to be filed with a regulatory agency. Condensed financial statements are presented in considerably less detail than statements presented in conformity with GAAP. Therefore, they should be read in conjunction with the entity's most recent complete financial statements.

Exhibit 13 ▶ Condensed Financial Statements With Audited Financial Statements

We have audited, in accordance with U.S. generally accepted auditing standards, the consolidated balance sheet of X Company and subsidiaries as of December 31, 20X0, and the related consolidated statements of income, retained earnings, and cash flows for the year then ended (not presented herein); and in our report dated February 15, 20X1, we expressed an unqualified opinion on those consolidated financial statements.

In our opinion, the information set forth in the accompanying condensed consolidated financial statements is fairly stated, in all material respects, in relation to the consolidated financial statements from which it has been derived.

1.   Not GAAP Because condensed financial statements do not constitute a fair presentation of financial position, results of operations, and cash flows in conformity with GAAP, an auditor engaged to report on such statements should not report in the same manner as an auditor reporting on the complete financial statements from which the condensed statements are derived.

2.   Report The report on condensed financial statements that are derived from financial statements that the auditor has audited should indicate the following:

a.   That the auditor has audited and expressed an opinion on the complete financial statements

b.   The date of the auditor's report on the complete financial statements, thereby removing any implication that records, transactions, or events after that date have been audited

c.   The type of opinion expressed

d.   Whether, in the auditor's opinion, the information set forth in the condensed financial statements is fairly stated in all material respects in relation to the complete financial statements from which it has been derived

3.   Optional Reporting If a client makes a statement in a client-prepared document that both names the auditor and states that condensed financial statements have been derived from audited financial statements, the auditor is **not** required to report on the condensed financial statements provided that they are included in a document that either contains the audited financial statements or incorporates such statements by reference to information filed with a regulatory agency.

a.   If such a statement is included in a client-prepared document of a public entity, and that document neither contains the audited financial statements nor incorporates such statements by reference, the auditor should request the client to either delete the auditor's name from the document or include the auditor's report on the condensed financial statements as described in 2., above.

b. If the client does not comply with the auditor's request, the auditor should consider other appropriate actions, such as consulting legal counsel.

4. **Comparative Statements** Condensed financial statements derived from audited financial statements of a public entity may be presented on a comparative basis with interim financial information as of a subsequent date that is accompanied by the auditor's review report. In such a case, the auditor should report on the condensed financial statements of each period in a manner appropriate for the type of service rendered in each period.

B. Selected Financial Data

AU 552 also provides guidance for selected financial data that are derived from audited financial statements and are presented in a document that either includes audited financial statements or incorporates such statements by reference to information filed with a regulatory agency.

Exhibit 14 ▶ Selected Financial Data With Audited Financial Statements

We have audited the accompanying consolidated balance sheets of ABC Company and subsidiaries as of December 31, 20X2 and 20X1, and the related consolidated statements of income, retained earnings, and cash flows for each of the three years in the period ended December 31, 20X2. These financial statements are the responsibility of the company's management. Our responsibility is to express an opinion on these financial statements based on our audits.

We conducted our audits in accordance with U.S. generally accepted auditing standards. Those standards require that we plan and perform the audit to obtain reasonable assurance about whether the financial statements are free of material misstatement. An audit includes examining, on a test basis, evidence supporting the amounts and disclosures in the financial statements. An audit also includes assessing the accounting principles used and significant estimates made by management, as well as evaluating the overall financial statement presentation. We believe that our audits provided a reasonable basis for our opinion.

In our opinion, the consolidated financial statements referred to above present fairly, in all material respects, the financial position of the ABC Company and subsidiaries as of December 31, 20X2 and 20X1, and the results of its operations and their cash flows for each of the three years in the period ended December 31, 20X2, in conformity with U.S. generally accepted accounting principles.

We have also previously audited, in accordance with U.S. generally accepted auditing standards, the consolidated balance sheets as of December 31, 20X3, 20X2, and 20X1, and the related consolidated statements of income, retained earnings, and cash flows for the years ended December 31, 20X2 and 20X1 (none of which are presented herein); and we expressed unqualified opinions on those consolidated financial statements.

In our opinion, the information set forth in the selected financial data for each of the five years in the period ended December 31, 20X2, appearing on page XX is fairly stated in all material respects in relation to the consolidated financial statements from which it has been derived.

1. **SEC Requirements** Selected financial data are not a required part of the basic financial statements, and the entity's management is responsible for determining the specific selected financial data to be presented. However, certain reports must include, for each of the last five fiscal years, selected financial data in accordance with SEC Regulation S-K. (There is no SEC requirement for the auditor to report on such selected financial data.)

2. **Limit Report Scope** If the auditor is engaged to report on the selected financial data, the report should be limited to data that are derived from financial statements audited by that auditor.

     a.   If the selected data includes both data derived from audited statements and other information (such as the number of employees or square footage of facilities), the report should identify specifically the data on which the auditor is reporting and should indicate the same items as mentioned in A.2., above.

     b.   The auditor is not precluded from expressing an opinion on one or more of the specified elements, accounts, or items of a financial statement in accordance with the provisions of SAS 62, *Special Reports.*

     c.   If the selected financial data are derived from financial statements that were audited by another independent auditor, the report on the selected financial data should state so, and the auditor should not express an opinion on that data.

3.   **Optional Reporting** In situations where the client names the independent auditor in a client-prepared document and states that the selected financial data are derived from financial statements audited by the named auditor, the auditor is not required to report on the selected financial data provided that the document either contains audited financial statements or incorporates such statements by reference to information filed with a regulatory agency.

     a.   If the client document is lacking these characteristics, the auditor should either:

          (1)   Request that neither the auditor's name nor reference to the auditor be associated with the information.

          (2)   Disclaim an opinion on the selected information and request that the disclaimer be included in the document.

     b.   If the client does not comply, the client should be advised that there is no consent to either the use of the auditor's name or the reference to the auditor, and the auditor should consider a consultation with legal counsel.

VII. Reports on Application of Accounting Principles (AU 625)

A.   **General**
AU 625 outlines the required procedures for accountants in public practice who report or give either written or oral advice (either to management of an entity or to intermediaries such as lenders, major suppliers, underwriters, or regulatory agencies) on the following:

1.   The application of accounting principles to specific completed or uncompleted transactions

2.   The type of opinion that may be rendered on an entity's financial statements

3.   The application of accounting principles to factual or circumstantial hypothetical transactions

B.   **Exceptions**
Exceptions include engagements to report on financial statements, assist in litigation involving accounting matters, provide expert testimony in accounting-related litigation, give advice to another accountant in public practice, and communications such as position papers. Position papers include newsletters, articles, speeches or lectures, and text of speeches or lectures. Position papers do not include communications intended to provide guidance on the application of accounting principles to a specific transaction.

C.   **Procedures**
The accountant should be capable of making reasonable professional judgments. The general standards of training and due care must be followed. The work must be planned adequately and assistants must be supervised properly. Sufficient information must be gathered to provide a reasonable basis for a professional judgment. Prior to making a judgment, the accountant should (1) obtain an understanding of the form and substance of the transactions involved; (2) review applicable generally accepted accounting principles; (3) perform research to ascertain and consider the

existence of creditable precedents or analogies; and (4) consult with other professionals or experts, if necessary.

1. **Hypothetical Transaction** AU 625 prohibits an accountant in public practice (a reporting accountant) from issuing a written report on the application of accounting principles or the type of opinion that may be expressed on financial statements not involving facts and circumstances of a specific entity and transaction, in other words, a hypothetical transaction.

2. **Management** Rather than arranging the engagement through, or inquiring of, a principal or intermediary, the accountant contacts the entity's management.

D. **Reporting Standards**
AU 625 does not prohibit oral reports. It is as applicable to oral advice as to a written report, if the reporting accountant believes the principal to a transaction intends to use the advice as an important factor in decision making.

1. **Type of Opinion** When preparing the report and the included opinion, the accountant should consider the requester of the report, the circumstances under which the request is made, the purpose of the request, and the intended use of the report.

    a. The reporting accountant (one who has been engaged to give advice) has the responsibility to consult with the continuing accountant who prepares or audits the financial statements to determine the form and substance of transactions, how the management applied accounting principles to similar transactions, if management disputes the method of accounting recommended by the continuing accountant, and if the continuing accountant has reached a different conclusion on the application of accounting principles or type of opinion.

    b. The responsibilities of the continuing accountant to respond to the reporting accountant are the same as the responsibilities of a predecessor auditor to a successor auditor.

2. **Address** The accountant's written report is addressed to the requesting entity and ordinarily includes identification of the specific entity and the country of origin of the appropriate accounting principles.

3. **Description** The first part of the report should describe the engagement.

    a. Include a brief description of the nature of the engagement and state that the engagement was performed in accordance with acceptable AICPA standards.

    b. Describe the transactions, relevant facts, circumstances, assumptions, and sources of information. This includes identifying principals to specific transactions, describing hypothetical transactions, describing nonspecific principals such as Company A and Company B.

    c. Describe the appropriate accounting principles or the type of opinion, and the reasons for the reporting accountant's conclusion.

4. **Concluding Comments** The report should state that (a) responsibility for proper accounting rests with the preparers of the financial statements who should consult with their continuing accountants; and (b) any difference in the facts, circumstances, or assumptions presented may change the report.

5. **Restrictions** The accountant's written report includes a final paragraph stating the following restrictions: (a) a restriction of the report for the information and use of specified parties; (b) identification of the specified parties; and (c) a statement that the report is not intended to be, and should not be, used by other than the specified parties.

Exhibit 15 ▶ Report on Application of Accounting Principles or Type of Opinion

---

(Introduction)

We have been engaged to report on the appropriate application of accounting principles generally accepted in [country of origin of such principles] to the specific transaction described below. This report is being issued to the ABC Company for assistance in evaluating accounting principles for the described specific transaction. Our engagement has been conducted in accordance with standards established by the American Institute of Certified Public Accountants.

(Description of transaction)

The facts, circumstances, and assumptions relevant to the specific transaction as provided to us by the management of ABC Company are as follows: [text describing transaction].

(Appropriate accounting principles)

[Text discussing generally accepted accounting principles]

(Concluding comments)

The ultimate responsibility for the decision on the appropriate application of accounting principles generally accepted in [country of origin of such principles] for an actual transaction rests with the preparers of financial statements, who should consult with their continuing accountants. Our judgment on the appropriate application of accounting principles generally accepted in [country of origin of such principles] for the described specific transaction is based solely on the facts provided to us as described above. Should these facts and circumstances differ, our conclusion may change.

(Restricted Use)

This report is intended solely for the information and use of the board of directors and management of ABC Company and is not intended to be, and should not be, used by anyone other than those specified parties.

VIII. Reporting on Financial Statements Prepared for Use in Other Countries (AU 534)

A. Applicability
AU 534 provides guidelines for an independent auditor engaged to report on financial statements of a U.S. entity for use outside the United States, given the following conditions:

1. **Foreign GAAP** Financial statements are prepared in conformity with GAAP of another country.

2. **U.S. Entity** The entity is organized or domiciled in the U.S.

3. **U.S. Auditor** The auditor practices in the United States.

B. Purpose of Statements
Such financial statements may be prepared, for example, when: (1) the statements will be included in the financial statements of a non-U.S. parent; (2) the entity has substantial non-U.S. investors; and (3) capital is to be raised in another country.

C. General & Fieldwork Standards
The auditor should comply with the general and fieldwork standards of U.S. GAAS. However, the U.S. procedures may need to be modified to apply when there are differences between accounting principles generally accepted in the other country and U.S. GAAP.

1.   **Examples**

    a.   **Valuation** Accounting principles generally accepted in another country may require that certain assets be revalued to adjust for the effects of inflation—in which case, the auditor should perform procedures to test the revaluation adjustments.

    b.   **Recognition** Another country's accounting principles may not require or permit recognition of deferred taxes—consequently, procedures for testing deferred tax balances would not be applicable.

2.   **Auditor's Understanding & Knowledge** The auditor should understand the accounting principles and auditing standards generally accepted in the other country and the legal responsibilities involved.

    a.   **References** The auditor may obtain such knowledge by reading the applicable statutes, professional literature, and codification of accounting principles and auditing standards generally accepted in that country. The auditor should consider consulting with persons having expertise in the accounting principles and auditing standards of the other country.

    b.   **No GAAP** If the accounting principles of another country are not established with sufficient authority or by general acceptance, the auditor may report on the financial statements if both the following criteria are met:

        (1)   The auditor judges the client's principles and practices to be appropriate.

        (2)   The client's principles and practices are disclosed in a clear and comprehensive manner.

    c.   **International Standards** The International Accounting Standards established by the International Accounting Standards Committee may be used.

D.   Reporting Standards
The auditor may prepare either a U.S.-style or foreign-style report, or both.

1.   **Modified U.S. Report** A U.S.-style report that is modified to the accounting principles is preferred. Recall that the standard U.S.-style report includes that the U.S. GAAP is used.

> **Exhibit 16 ▶ Financial Statements Prepared in Conformity With Accounting Principles Generally Accepted in Another Country in a U.S.-Style Report**
>
> We have audited the balance sheet of the International Company as of December 31, 20X1, and the related statements of income, retained earnings, and cash flows for the year then ended, which, as described in Note X, have been prepared on the basis of accounting principles generally accepted in (name of country). These financial statements are the responsibility of the Company's management. Our responsibility is to express an opinion on these financial statements based on our audit.
>
> We conducted our audit in accordance with auditing standards generally accepted in the United States (and in [name of country]). U.S. standards require that we plan and perform the audit to obtain reasonable assurance about whether the financial statements are free of material misstatement. An audit includes examining, on a test basis, evidence supporting the amounts and disclosures in the financial statements. An audit also includes assessing the accounting principles used and significant estimates made by management, as well as evaluating the overall financial statement presentation. We believe that our audit provides a reasonable basis for our opinion.
>
> In our opinion, the financial statements referred to above present fairly, in all material respects, the financial position of the International Company at December 31, 20X1, and the results of its operations and cash flows for the year then ended, in conformity with accounting principles generally accepted in (name of country).

a. The report should include (in addition to standard required items) the following:

 (1) A reference to the note to the financial statements that describes the basis of preparation, including the nationality of the accounting principles.

 (2) A note that says the audit was made in accordance with GAAS and the auditing standards of the other country, if appropriate.

b. Although the report is intended for use only outside the U.S., this is not intended to preclude limited use of the financial statements to parties (such as banks) within the U.S. that deal directly with the entity.

2. **Foreign Report** The standard report of another country may be used, provided that the following is evident:

a. The standard report is used by auditors in the other country, given similar circumstances.

b. The auditor understands the meaning and implications of the report with respect to different customs and different word interpretations.

c. The auditor is in the position to make the attestations contained in the report.

d. When using a standard report of a foreign country that is similar to the one used in the U.S., the country name should be added to the report to avoid erroneous interpretation due to a different custom or culture.

3. **Dual Report** Use of both a U.S.-style and a foreign-style report also is allowed. The auditor should include a note such as the one in Exhibit 17.

Exhibit 17 ▸ Note Describing Differences Between U.S. & Foreign GAAP

We also have reported separately on the financial statements of International Company for the same period presented in conformity with accounting principles generally accepted in (name of country). (The significant differences between the accounting principles accepted in [name of country] and those generally accepted in the United States are summarized in Note X.)

IX. Restricting Use of Audit Report (AU 532)

A. Applicability
AU 532, *Restricting the Use of an Auditor's Report,* provides guidance in determining whether an engagement necessitates a restricted-use report and the language to use. AU 532 is **not** applicable to reports issued under the provisions of AU 324, *Service Organizations,* or AU 634, *Letters for Underwriters and Certain Other Requesting Parties.*

B. Guidance
General use signifies that the report is not restricted to specified parties. Auditor's reports on financial statements prepared in accordance with GAAP or certain bases of accounting other than GAAP ordinarily are **not** restricted as to use. (However, nothing in AU 532 precludes an auditor from restricting the use of any report.) *Restricted use* signifies that reports are intended only for specified parties. Reports are restricted as to use for a variety of reasons, including the purpose of the report, the nature of the procedures or assumptions used, and its potential for being misunderstood when taken out of context.

1. **Restrictions** Auditors should restrict the use of a report when the:

a. Subject matter of the report is based on criteria contained in contractual agreements or regulatory provisions **not** in accordance with GAAP or OCBOA. This type of report is restricted as to use because it is based on assumptions or criteria developed for and directed only to the parties to the agreement or regulatory agencies responsible for the provisions. Auditors can exercise professional judgment as to whether to add others as specified parties to this type of restricted-use report.

b. Report is a by-product of an audit of financial statements. The use of a by-product report is restricted because as it is not the primary objective of the engagement, the potential for misunderstanding exists due to the limited degree of assurance associated with it—because generally only limited procedures were directed toward its subject matter. Auditors should **not** add other parties (other than management, those charged with governance, other internal users, specified regulatory agencies, or contractual parties) as specified parties.

2. **Combined Report** If an auditor issues a single combined report covering subject matter that requires a restriction on use as well as material that is not restricted, the combined report is a restricted-use report.

3. **Distribution** Auditors are not responsible for their client's distribution of their reports; however, they should consider informing their clients about a restricted-use report's limited distribution, i.e., that the reports are not intended for distribution to nonspecified parties.

4. **Report Language** An auditor's restricted-use report should contain a separate paragraph at the end of the report that includes:

a. A statement that the report is intended solely for the information and use of the specified parties

b. An identification of the specified parties

c. A statement that the report is not intended to be and should not be used by anyone other than the specified parties

---

CHAPTER 30—OTHER TYPES OF REPORTS

Problem 30-1 MULTIPLE CHOICE QUESTIONS (58 to 73 minutes)

1. What is an auditor's reporting responsibility concerning information accompanying the basic financial statements in an auditor-submitted document?
a. The auditor should report on all the accompanying information included in the document.
b. The auditor should report on the accompanying information only if the auditor participated in its preparation.
c. The auditor should report on the accompanying information only if the auditor did **not** participate in its preparation.
d. The auditor should report on the accompanying information only if it contains obvious material misstatements. (5/98, AUD, #16, 6633)

2. Information accompanying the basic financial statements in an auditor-submitted document should **not** include which **two** of the following?
a. An analysis of inventory by location
b. A statement that the allowance for doubtful accounts is adequate
c. An analysis of revenue by product line
d. A statement that the depreciable life of a new asset is 20 years
e. A statement that the auditor is not aware of any material modifications that should be made to the accompanying information in order for them to be in conformity with U.S. generally accepted accounting principles (Editors, 7509)

3. If information accompanying the basic financial statements in an auditor-submitted document has been subjected to auditing procedures, the auditor may include in the auditor's report on the financial statements an opinion that the accompanying information is fairly stated in
a. Accordance with generally accepted auditing standards
b. Conformity with generally accepted accounting principles
c. All material respects in relation to the basic financial statements taken as a whole
d. Accordance with attestation standards expressing a conclusion about management's assertions (5/95, AUD, #87, 5705)

4. An accountant who is **not** independent of a client is precluded from issuing a
a. Report on consulting services
b. Compilation report on historical financial statements
c. Compilation report on prospective financial statements
d. Special report on compliance with contractual agreements (11/90, AUD, #37, 0393)

5. Helpful Co., a nonprofit entity, prepared its financial statements on an accounting basis prescribed by a regulatory agency solely for filing with that agency. Green audited the financial statements in accordance with generally accepted auditing standards and concluded that the financial statements were fairly presented on the prescribed basis. Green should issue a
a. Qualified opinion
b. Standard three paragraph report with reference to footnote disclosure
c. Disclaimer of opinion
d. Special report (11/91, AUD, #17, 2285)

6. An auditor's report on financial statements prepared on the cash receipts and disbursements basis of accounting should include all of the following **except**
a. A reference to the note to the financial statements that describes the cash receipts and disbursements basis of accounting
b. A statement that the cash receipts and disbursements basis of accounting is **not** a comprehensive basis of accounting
c. An opinion as to whether the financial statements are presented fairly in conformity with the cash receipts and disbursements basis of accounting
d. A statement that the audit was conducted in accordance with generally accepted auditing standards (5/95, AUD, #82, 5700)

7. An accountant may accept an engagement to apply agreed-upon procedures that are not sufficient to express an opinion on one or more specified accounts or items of a financial statement provided that

a. The accountant's report does not enumerate the procedures performed.
b. The accountant is also the entity's continuing auditor.
c. Use of the accountant's report is restricted.
d. The financial statements are prepared in conformity with a comprehensive basis of accounting other than generally accepted accounting principles. (Editors, 2933)

8. When an auditor reports on financial statements prepared on an entity's income tax basis, the auditor's report should

a. Disclaim an opinion on whether the statements were examined in accordance with generally accepted auditing standards
b. Not express an opinion on whether the statements are presented in conformity with the comprehensive basis of accounting used
c. Include an explanation of how the results of operations differ from the cash receipts and disbursements basis of accounting
d. State that the basis of presentation is a comprehensive basis of accounting other than GAAP (5/94, AUD, #83, 4748)

9. An auditor is engaged to report on selected financial data that are included in a client-prepared document containing audited financial statements. Under these circumstances, the report on the selected data should

a. Be limited to data derived from the audited financial statements
b. Be distributed only to senior management and the board of directors
c. State that the presentation is a comprehensive basis of accounting other than GAAP
d. Indicate that the data are **not** fairly stated in all material respects (11/95, AUD, #87, 6034)

10. Comfort letters ordinarily are

	Addressed to the client's	Signed by the client's
a.	Audit committee	Independent auditor
b.	Underwriter of securities	Senior management
c.	Audit committee	Senior management
d.	Underwriter of securities	Independent auditor

(R/07, AUD, #15, 8387)

11. When an accountant issues to an underwriter a comfort letter containing comments on data that have **not** been audited, the underwriter most likely will receive

a. Negative assurance on capsule information
b. Positive assurance on supplementary disclosures
c. A limited opinion on "pro forma" financial statements
d. A disclaimer on prospective financial statements (5/92, AUD, #8, 2761)

12. Which of the following statements is correct concerning letters for underwriters, commonly referred to as comfort letters?

a. Letters for underwriters are required by the Securities Act of 1933 for the initial public sale of registered securities.
b. Letters for underwriters typically give negative assurance on unaudited interim financial information.
c. Letters for underwriters usually are included in the registration statement accompanying a prospectus.
d. Letters for underwriters ordinarily update auditors' opinions on the prior year's financial statements. (5/95, AUD, #86, 5704)

13. When an independent accountant's report based on a review of interim financial information is presented in a registration statement, a prospectus should include a statement about the accountant's involvement. This statement should clarify that the

a. Accountant is **not** an "expert" within the meaning of the Securities Act of 1933.
b. Accountant's review report is **not** a "part" of the registration statement within the meaning of the Securities Act of 1933.
c. Accountant performed only limited auditing procedures on the interim financial statements.
d. Accountant's review was performed in accordance with standards established by the American Institute of CPAs. (5/90, AUD, #24, 0398)

14. The Securities and Exchange Commission has authority to
a. Require a change of auditors of governmental entities after a given period of years as a means of ensuring auditor independence
b. Deny lack of privity as a defense in third-party actions for gross negligence against the auditors of public companies
c. Determine accounting principles for the purpose of financial reporting by companies offering securities to the public
d. Prescribe specific auditing procedures to detect fraud concerning inventories and accounts receivable of companies engaged in interstate commerce   (Editors, 7510)

15. Comfort letters ordinarily are signed by the client's
a. Independent auditor
b. Underwriter of securities
c. Audit committee
d. Senior management   (11/92, AUD, #58, 2992)

16. Dunn, CPA, is auditing the financial statements of Taft Co. Taft uses Quick Service Center (QSC) to process its payroll. Price, CPA, is expressing an opinion on a description of the controls placed in operation at QSC regarding the processing of its customers' payroll transactions. Dunn expects to consider the effects of Price's report on the Taft engagement. Price's report should contain a (an)
a. Description of the scope and nature of Price's procedures
b. Statement that Dunn may assess control risk based on Price's report
c. Assertion that Price assumes **no** responsibility to determine whether QSC's controls are suitably designed
d. Opinion on the operating effectiveness of QSC's internal controls   (R/01, AUD, #16, 7031)

17. Payroll Data Co. (PDC) processes payroll transactions for a retailer. Cook, CPA, is engaged to express an opinion on a description of PDC's internal controls placed in operation as of a specific date. These controls are relevant to the retailer's internal control, so Cook's report may be useful in providing the retailer's independent auditor with information necessary to plan a financial statement audit. Cook's report should
a. Contain a warning that misstatements may occur and not be detected
b. State whether PDC's controls were suitably designed to achieve the retailer's objectives
c. Identify PDC's controls relevant to specific financial statement assertions
d. Disclose Cook's assessed level of control risk for PDC   (R/99, AUD, #30, amended, 6846)

18. Select **two** responses. Lake, CPA, is auditing the financial statements of Gill Co. Gill uses the EDP Service Center, Inc. to process its payroll transactions. EDP's financial statements are audited by Cope, CPA, who recently issued a report on EDP's internal control. Lake is considering Cope's report on EDP's internal control in assessing control risk on the Gill engagement. What is Lake's responsibility concerning making reference to Cope as a basis, in part, for Lake's own opinion?
a. Lake may refer to Cope only if Lake is satisfied as to Cope's professional reputation and independence.
b. Lake may refer to Cope only if Lake relies on Cope's report in restricting the extent of substantive tests.
c. Lake may refer to Cope only if Lake's report indicates the division of responsibility.
d. Lake may not refer to Cope under the circumstances above.
e. Lake should make inquires concerning Cope's professional reputation.
f. Lake should make inquires concerning Cope's objectivity.   (5/94, AUD, #36, amended, 4701)

19. The objective of a review of interim financial information of a nonissuer is to provide an accountant with a basis for reporting whether
a. Material modifications should be made to conform with the applicable financial reporting framework
b. A reasonable basis exists for expressing an updated opinion regarding the financial statements that were previously audited
c. Condensed financial statements or *pro forma* financial information should be included in a registration statement
d. The financial information is presented fairly in accordance with generally accepted accounting principles   (5/95, AUD, #83, amended, 5701)

20. Which of the following procedures ordinarily should be applied when an independent accountant conducts a review of interim financial information of a nonissuer?
a. Verify changes in key account balances
b. Read the minutes of the board of directors' meeting
c. Inspect the open purchase order file
d. Perform cutoff tests for cash receipts and disbursements   (11/92, AUD, #51, 2985)

21. Which of the following circumstances requires modification of the accountant's report on a review of interim financial information of a nonissuer?

	An uncertainty	Inadequate disclosure
a.	No	No
b.	Yes	Yes
c.	Yes	No
d.	No	Yes (Editors, 0410)

22. An auditor may report on condensed financial statements that are derived from complete financial statements if the
a. Condensed financial statements are distributed to stockholders along with the complete financial statements.
b. Auditor describes the additional procedures performed on the condensed financial statements.
c. Condensed financial statements are presented in comparative form with the prior year's condensed financial statements.
d. Auditor indicates whether the information in the condensed financial statements is fairly stated in all material respects in relation to the complete financial statements from which it has been derived. (5/98, AUD, #17, amended, 6634)

23. In the standard report on condensed financial statements that are derived from a public entity's audited financial statements, a CPA should indicate that the
a. Condensed financial statements are prepared in conformity with another comprehensive basis of accounting.
b. CPA has audited and expressed an opinion on the complete financial statements.
c. Condensed financial statements are **not** fairly presented in all material respects.
d. CPA expresses limited assurance that the financial statements conform with GAAP.
(11/94, AUD, #87, 5160)

24. A CPA is permitted to accept a separate engagement (**not** in conjunction with an audit of financial statements) to audit an entity's schedule of

	Accounts receivable	Royalties
a.	Yes	Yes
b.	Yes	No
c.	No	Yes
d.	No	No

(11/93, AUD, #56, 7694)

25. An auditor may express an opinion on an entity's accounts receivable balance even if the auditor has disclaimed an opinion on the financial statements taken as a whole provided the
a. Report on the accounts receivable discloses the reason for the disclaimer of opinion on the financial statements.
b. Distribution of the report on the accounts receivable is restricted to internal use only.
c. Auditor also reports on the current asset portion of the entity's balance sheet.
d. Report on the accounts receivable is presented separately from the disclaimer of opinion on the financial statements. (5/96, AUD, #8, 6240)

26. In connection with a proposal to obtain a new audit client, a CPA in public practice is asked to prepare a report on the application of accounting principles to a specific transaction. The CPA's report should include a statement that
a. The engagement was performed in accordance with Statements on Standards for Accounting and Review Services.
b. Responsibility for the proper accounting treatment rests with the preparers of the financial statements.
c. The evaluation of the application of accounting principles is hypothetical and may not be used for opinion-shopping.
d. The report is based solely on communications with a specified intermediary, if that is the case.
(R/00, AUD, #20, amended, 6945)

27. The financial statements of KCP America, a U.S. entity, are prepared for inclusion in the consolidated financial statements of its non-U.S. parent. These financial statements are prepared in conformity with the accounting principles generally accepted in the parent's country and are for use only in that country. How may KCP America's auditor report on these financial statements?

I. A U.S.-style report (unmodified)
II. A U.S.-style report modified to report on the accounting principles of the parent's country
III. The report form of the parent's country

	I	II	III
a.	Yes	No	No
b.	No	Yes	No
c.	Yes	No	Yes
d.	No	Yes	Yes (5/91, AUD, #49, 0389)

28. Before reporting on the financial statements of a U.S. entity that have been prepared in conformity with another country's accounting principles, an auditor practicing in the U.S. should
a. Understand the accounting principles generally accepted in the other country
b. Be certified by the appropriate auditing or accountancy board of the other country
c. Notify management that the auditor is required to disclaim an opinion on the financial statements
d. Receive a waiver from the auditor's state board of accountancy to perform the engagement
(11/94, AUD, #88, 5161)

29. A U.S. entity prepares its financial statements in conformity with accounting principles generally accepted in another country. These financial statements will be included in the consolidated financial statements of its non-U.S. parent. Before reporting on the financial statements of the U.S. entity, the auditor practicing in the U.S. should
a. Notify management of the U.S. entity that the auditor is required to disclaim an opinion on the financial statements
b. Receive a waiver to report on the U.S. entity from the appropriate accountancy authority in the other country
c. Obtain written representations from management of the U.S. entity regarding the purpose and uses of the financial statements
d. Communicate with the auditor of the non-U.S. parent regarding the level of assurance to be provided
(R/03, AUD, #17, 7639)

SIMULATION

Problem 30-2 (15 to 25 minutes)

The auditor's report below was drafted by a staff accountant of Baker and Baker, CPAs, at the completion of the audit of the comparative financial statements of Ocean Shore Partnership for the years ended December 31, Year 2 and Year 1. Ocean Shores prepares its financial statements on the income tax basis of accounting. The report was submitted to the engagement partner who reviewed matters thoroughly and properly concluded that an unqualified opinion should be expressed.

Auditor's Report

We have audited the accompanying statements of assets, liabilities, and capital—income tax basis of Ocean Shore Partnership as of December 31, Year 2 and Year 1, and the related statements of revenue and expenses—income tax basis and changes in partners' capital accounts—income tax basis for the years then ended.

We conducted our audits in accordance with standards established by the American Institute of Certified Public Accountants. Those standards require that we plan and perform the audit to obtain reasonable assurance about whether the financial statements are free of material misstatement. An audit includes examining, on a test basis, evidence supporting the amounts and disclosures in the financial statements. An audit also includes assessing the accounting principles used as well as evaluating the overall financial statement presentation.

As described in Note A, these financial statements were prepared on the basis of accounting the Partnership uses for income tax purposes. Accordingly, these financial statements are not designed for those who do not have access to the Partnership's tax returns.

In our opinion, the financial statements referred to above present fairly, in all material respects, the assets, liabilities, and capital of Ocean Shore Partnership as of December 31, Year 2 and Year 1, and its revenue and expenses and changes in partners' capital accounts for the years then ended, in conformity with generally accepted accounting principles applied on a consistent basis.

Baker and Baker, CPAs
April 3, Year 3

Identify the deficiencies contained in the auditors' report as drafted by the staff accountant. Group the deficiencies by paragraph, where applicable. Do not redraft the report.

What authoritative reference provides guidance on who a comfort letter may be addressed to?

Paragraph Reference Answer: _____

(5/91, AUD, #2, amended, 6636)

Solution 30-1 MULTIPLE CHOICE ANSWERS

Accompanying Information

1. (a) Note that this question concerns an *auditor*-submitted document. The auditor's report on information accompanying the basic financial statements describes the character of the work and the degree of responsibility that the auditor is taking. (6633)

2. (b, e) Information accompanying the basic financial statements (BFS) in an auditor-submitted document is presented outside the BFS and is not considered necessary for presentation of financial position, results of operations, or cash flows in conformity with GAAP. Such information includes additional details or explanations of items in or related to the basic financial statements [see answers (a), (c), and (d) for examples]. The adequacy of the allowance for doubtful accounts is implied and is not necessary as additional information. As the information accompanying the BFS is not considered necessary for presentation of financial position, results of operations, or cash flows in conformity with U.S. GAAP, a statement that the auditor is not aware of any material modifications necessary to bring them in conformity with GAAP would tend to confuse the reader, and hence, should be avoided. (7509)

3. (c) The report should include either an opinion on whether the accompanying information is fairly stated in all material respects in relation to the basic financial statements taken as a whole, or a disclaimer of opinion. The auditor's opinion is on whether the statements are fairly stated in conformity with GAAP, not GAAS. The auditor's opinion on fair presentation in conformity with GAAP relates to the basic financial statements and does not extend to the accompanying information. The auditor does not express a conclusion on management's assertions in the report. Attestation standards relate to a different engagement. (5705)

Special Reports

4. (d) Entities may be required by contractual agreements, such as certain bond indentures and loan agreements, or by regulatory agencies to furnish compliance reports by independent auditors. A lack of independence would not preclude an accountant from issuing compilation reports or a report on consulting services. (0393)

5. (d) Special reports include those that are related to financial statements prepared on an accounting basis prescribed by a regulatory agency solely for filing with that agency. (2285)

6. (b) The cash receipts and disbursements schedule is merely a comprehensive basis of accounting other than GAAP (OCBOA). The auditor's report should include a paragraph that refers to the note to the financial statements that describes the basis of accounting. The report should include a paragraph that expresses the auditor's opinion on whether the financial statements are presented fairly. The report should include a paragraph that states that the audit was conducted in accordance with GAAS. (5700)

7. (c) The accountant's report in this circumstance should include, a statement of restrictions on the use of the report because it is intended to be used solely by the specified users. If the report is a

matter of public record, the report should state so and also state, "its distribution is not limited." (2933)

8. (d) The auditor's report should include a paragraph that refers to the note to the financial statements that describes the basis of accounting. The auditor utilized GAAS in the examination; thus, there is no need for a disclaimer. Answer (b) is incorrect because an opinion is presented. The auditor is not required to include the explanation described in answer (c). (4748)

9. (a) An auditor's report on information accompanying the basic financial statements (BFS) should include either an opinion on whether the accompanying information is fairly stated in all material respects in relation to the BFS taken as a whole or as a disclaimer of opinion. The report should be limited to data that are derived from financial statements audited by that auditor. There is no restriction on the distribution. The basis of accounting is not necessarily other than GAAP. The data generally are indicated as fairly stated in all material respects.
(6034)

Letters for Underwriters

10. (d) In connection with audited financial statements and schedules included in a registration statement to be filed with the SEC, underwriters may request accountants to provide them with a comfort letter. The comfort letter is addressed to the underwriter and signed by the auditor. (8387)

11. (a) When an accountant issues to an underwriter a comfort letter containing comments on data that have not been audited, the underwriter most likely will receive negative assurance on capsule information. Negative assurance should not be given, with respect to capsule information, unless the accountants have obtained knowledge of the client's internal control policies and procedures relating to the preparation of financial statements. This problem gave no indication that such knowledge was not obtained. (2761)

12. (b) A typical comfort letter includes a statement regarding the accountant's independence, an opinion regarding whether the audited financial information included or incorporated by reference complies to the Securities Act of 1933, negative assurance on unaudited condensed interim financial information included or incorporated by reference, and negative assurance on whether there has been any later changes in specified accounts in the financial statement items included in the registration statement. Comfort letters are not required under the Act and copies are not filed with the SEC. Comfort

letters ordinarily express an opinion regarding the audited financial statements' compliance with the Act, which is not an "update" of the audit opinion.
(5704)

13. (b) The Securities and Exchange Commission requires that, when an independent accountant's report based on a review of interim financial information is presented or incorporated by reference in a registration statement, a prospectus that includes a statement about the independent accountant's involvement should clarify that her/his review report is not a report or part of the registration statement within the meaning of Sections 7 and 11 of the Securities Act of 1933. (0398)

14. (c) The SEC has the authority to prescribe the accounting and reporting requirements for companies under its jurisdiction. However, the SEC has looked to the private sector for leadership in establishing and improving accounting principles and standards through the FASB. The SEC does not prescribe specific auditing procedures for companies involved in interstate commerce, deny lack of privity as a defense in third-party actions, or require a change of auditors of governmental entities. (7510)

15. (a) In connection with audited financial statements and schedules included in a registration statement to be filed with the SEC, a client may request the services of an independent auditor. One of these services is the issuance of comfort letters for underwriters. The underwriter of securities receives the comfort letter. The client and senior management do not sign the comfort letter. (2992)

Service Organizations

16. (a) A special-purpose report expressing an opinion on controls at a service organization should include a description of the scope and nature of the auditor's procedures. (7031)

17. (a) Cook was engaged to express an opinion on a description of internal controls, not on the operating effectiveness of those controls. Evaluating whether the controls are suitably designed to achieve PDC's client's objectives, identifying control relevant to PDC's client's assertions, or assessing a level of control risk are beyond the scope of this engagement.
(6846)

18. (d, e) The user auditor should not make reference to the report of the service auditor as a basis, for his or her own opinion. The user auditor should make inquires concerning the service auditor's professional reputation. The user auditor should make

his or her own judgment as to the service auditor's objectivity. (4701)

Interim Financial Information

19. (a) The objective of a review of interim financial information is to provide the accountant with a basis for reporting whether material modifications should be made for such information to conform with the applicable financial reporting framework. Only the financial information under current review should be reported on. The review objective is to provide the accountant with a basis for reporting whether material modifications should be made, not whether condensed statements or *pro forma* information should be included. In a review, the accountant supplies only limited assurance and would not provide an opinion stating the financial information is presented fairly. (5701)

20. (b) The procedures for a review of interim financial information should include reading the minutes of meetings of stockholders, board of directors, and committees of the board of directors to identify actions that may affect the interim financial information. Answers (a), (c), and (d) are not among the procedures normally applied in a review of interim financial information. (2985)

21. (d) The accountant's report on a review of interim financial information should be modified for departures from the applicable financial reporting framework, which include inadequate disclosure and changes in accounting principles that are not in conformity with the applicable financial reporting framework. The existence of an uncertainty or a lack of consistency in the application of accounting principles affecting interim financial information would not require the accountant to include an additional paragraph in the report, provided that the interim financial information appropriately discloses such matters. (0410)

Condensed Statements & Selected Data

22. (d) The auditor's report on condensed financial statements (CFS) derived from financial statements that s/he has audited should indicate (1) that the auditor has audited and expressed an opinion on the complete financial statements; (2) the date of the auditor's report on the complete financial statements; (3) the type of opinion expressed; and (4) whether, in the auditor's opinion, the information set forth in the CFS is fairly stated in all material respects in relation to the complete financial statements from which it has been derived. The statements need not be distributed to stockholders merely because an auditor reports on them. The auditor

generally does not describe procedures performed on the CFS. CFS need not be presented in comparison to another year's statements. (6634)

23. (b) The auditor's report on condensed financial statements that are derived from financial statements that s/he has audited should indicate that the auditor has audited and expressed an opinion on the complete financial statements, the date of the auditor's report on the complete financial statements, the type of opinion expressed, and whether, in the auditor's opinion, the information set forth in the condensed financial statements is fairly stated in all material respects in relation to the complete financial statements from which it has been derived. (5160)

24. (a) An engagement to express an opinion on one or more specified elements, accounts, or items of a financial statement may be undertaken either as a separate engagement or in conjunction with an audit of financial statements. (7694)

25. (d) The auditor should not express an opinion on specified elements, accounts, or items included in financial statements on which the auditor has expressed an adverse opinion or disclaimed an opinion based on an audit, if such reporting would be tantamount to expressing a piecemeal opinion on the financial statements. However, an auditor would be able to express an opinion on one or more specified elements provided the matters were not intended to and did not encompass so many elements as to constitute a major portion of the financial statements. However, the report on the specified element(s) should be presented separately from the report on the financial statements of the entity. (6240)

Accounting Principles

26. (b) The CPA's report should include a statement that the responsibility for the proper accounting treatment rests with the preparers of the financial statements, who should consult with their continuing accountant, i.e., the accountant who has been engaged to report on the financial statements. The report should also state the engagement was conducted in accordance with standards established by the AICPA; not in accordance with SSARS. There should not be a statement in the report that the application of accounting principles is hypothetical—the CPA should not undertake an engagement to provide a report on the application of accounting principles to a hypothetical transaction. Nor should the CPA accept an engagement to prepare a report based solely on communications with an intermediary. (6945)

For Use in Other Countries

27. (d)   If financial statements prepared in conformity with accounting principles generally accepted in another country are prepared for use *only* outside the United States, the auditor may report using either a U.S.-style report modified to report on the accounting principles of another country, or if appropriate, the report form of the other country. An unmodified U.S.-style report would be inappropriate in this situation.   (0389)

28. (a)   The auditor must understand the accounting principles of the other country. The auditor does not have to be certified in the other country, disclaim an opinion, or receive a waiver from a board of accountancy.   (5161)

29. (c)   A U.S. entity ordinarily prepares financial statements for use in the United States in conformity with accounting principles generally accepted in the United States, but it may also prepare financial statements that are intended for use outside the United States and are prepared in conformity with accounting principles generally accepted in another country. Before reporting on financial statements prepared in conformity with the accounting principles of another country, the auditor should have a clear understanding of, and obtain written representations from management regarding, the purpose and uses of such financial statements.   (7639)

PERFORMANCE BY SUBTOPICS

Each category below parallels a subtopic covered in Chapter 30. Record the number and percentage of questions you correctly answered in each subtopic area.

Accompanying Information

Question #	Correct	√
1		
2		
3		
# Questions	3	
# Correct		
% Correct		

Special Reports

Question #	Correct	√
4		
5		
6		
7		
8		
9		
# Questions	6	
# Correct		
% Correct		

Letters for Underwriters

Question #	Correct	√
10		
11		
12		
13		
14		
15		
# Questions	6	
# Correct		
% Correct		

Service Organizations

Question #	Correct	√
16		
17		
18		
# Questions	3	
# Correct		
% Correct		

Interim Financial Information

Question #	Correct	√
19		
20		
21		
# Questions	3	
# Correct		
% Correct		

Condensed Statements & Selected Data

Question #	Correct	√
22		
23		
24		
25		
# Questions	4	
# Correct		
% Correct		

Accounting Principles

Question #	Correct	√
26		
# Questions	1	
# Correct		
% Correct		

For Use in Other Countries

Question #	Correct	√
27		
28		
29		
# Questions	3	
# Correct		
% Correct		

SIMULATION SOLUTION

Solution 30-2

Report: Income Tax Basis Report (9 points)

The auditors' report contains the following deficiencies:

1. "**Independent**" is omitted from the title of the auditors' report.

Introductory paragraph

2. **Management's responsibility** for the financial statements is omitted.

3. The auditors' **responsibility** to **express** an **opinion** on the financial statements is omitted.

Scope paragraph

4. "**Generally accepted auditing standards**" should be referred to, not standards established by the AICPA.

5. Reference to assessing "**significant estimates made by management**" is omitted.

6. The concluding statement that the auditors "**believe that our audits provide a reasonable basis for our opinion**" is omitted.

Explanatory paragraph

7. Reference to the **income tax basis** of accounting as "a comprehensive basis of accounting other than generally accepted accounting principles" is omitted.

8. The statement that the financial statements are "not designed for those who do not have access to the Partnership tax returns" is **inappropriate.**

Opinion paragraph

9. "**The income tax basis of accounting described in Note A**" should be referred to, not "generally accepted accounting principles."

10. There should be **no reference to consistency unless** the accounting principles **have not been applied consistently.**

Research: Research (1 point)

Paragraph Reference Answer: AU 634.25

Guidance: AU 634.25 states, "The letter should not be addressed or given to any parties other than the client and the named underwriters, broker-dealer, financial intermediary or buyer or seller. The appropriate addressee is the intermediary who has negotiated the agreement with the client, and with whom the accountants will deal in discussions regarding the scope and sufficiency of the letter. When a comfort letter is furnished to other accountants, it should be addressed in accordance with the guidance in this paragraph and copies should be furnished to the principal accountants and their client."

(6636)

Wondering how to find
20 hours a week for study time?

Robert Monette used this method to find 20 hours a week to study while working 40 hours a week. (Ask a customer service representative about a copy of Bob's demo video.) Notice how this plan leaves most of the weekend free, ensuring time for you to take care of yourself, spend time with your family, meet with friends, and in general, take care of your other commitments.

Lunch hours, Monday through Friday	5 hours
Three hours, after work, Monday through Thursday	12 hours
Three hours, Saturday morning	3 hours
Sunday, total break from studying	0 hours
Weekly total	20 hours

This plan may work for you, or it may not. Consider Bob's plan and adapt it to your situation. For example, perhaps you prefer to study an hour before work Tuesday through Thursday, and relax on Saturday as well as Sunday.

Also consider how you use time. Listening to audio lectures could transform an hour of radio listening into an hour of study time. Do you have a 30-minute commute to and from work? That could add up to 5 hours in a work week. Do you jog three times a week? That could be study time as well as exercise time.

Remember, with the techniques and information in your material,

A passing score is well within reach!

———————————

CHANGE ALERTS

SSAE 15 (AT 501), *Examination of an Entity's Internal Control Over Financial Reporting That Is Integrated With an Audit of Its Financial Statements* **(issued 10/08)**

In October 2008, the Auditing Standards Board of the American Institute of Certified Public Accountants issued Statement on Standards for Attestation Engagements (SSAE) 15, *An Examination of an Entity's Internal Control Over Financial Reporting That Is Integrated With an Audit of Its Financial Statements.* It is effective for integrated audits for periods ending on or after December 15, 2008. Earlier implementation is permitted.

AT 501, the section of the authoritative guidance that covers SSAE 15, establishes requirements and provides guidance for the performance of an examination of a nonissuer's internal control over financial reporting that is integrated with an audit of financial statements. It supersedes section AT 501A, *Reporting on an Entity's Internal Control Over Financial Reporting.* The new statement was issued to align the definitions and related guidance for evaluating deficiencies in internal control with Public Company Accounting Oversight Board Auditing Standard 5, *An Audit of Internal Control Over Financial Reporting That is Integrated with an Audit of Financial Statements.*

This statement is eligible to be tested beginning with the April-May 2009 exam window.

SSARS 18 (AR 100), *Applicability of Statements on Standards for Accounting and Review Services* **(issued 2/09)**

In February 2009, the Accounting and Review Services Committee of the AICPA issued Statement of Standards for Accounting and Review Services (SSARS) 18, *Applicability of Statements on Standards for Accounting and Review Services.* It is effective for compilations and reviews of financial statements for periods beginning after December 15, 2009. Early application is permitted.

SSARS 18, was issued at the same time as Statement on Auditing Standards 116 (AU 722), *Interim Financial Information*, to revise the applicability of the SSARS (amend AR 100) so that the SSARS do not apply when the provisions of AU 722 apply. The reasoning being that guidance for auditors performing reviews of interim financial information should be in the auditing literature (SAS), not in the SSARS because of the difference between a review performed by an accountant with an audit base of knowledge versus that performed by an accountant who is not the entity's auditor.

Reviews of *interim* financial information should be performed in accordance with AU 722 (not the SSARS) when the following conditions are met:

- The entity's latest annual financial statements have been audited by the accountant or a predecessor;

- The accountant has been engaged to audit the entity's current year financial statements, or the accountant audited the entity's latest annual financial statements and expects to be engaged to audit the current year financial statements; and

- The client prepares its interim financial information in accordance with the same financial reporting framework as that used to prepare the annual financial statements.

This statement is eligible to be tested beginning with the October-November 2009 exam window.

CHAPTER 31

OTHER PROFESSIONAL SERVICES

CHAPTER 31

OTHER PROFESSIONAL SERVICES

I. Compilations & Reviews (AR 100)

A. Authoritative Guidance

Statements on Standards for Accounting and Review Services (SSARS) apply when a CPA is associated with the unaudited financial statements of a nonissuer. The CPA should not submit unaudited financial statements to a client or third party unless the CPA has at least complied with the provisions that apply to a compilation.

Reviews of *interim* financial information should be performed in accordance with AU 722 (not the SSARS) when the following conditions are met:

- The entity's latest annual financial statements have been audited by the accountant or a predecessor;

- The accountant has been engaged to audit the entity's current year financial statements, or the accountant audited the entity's latest annual financial statements and expects to be engaged to audit the current year financial statements; and

- The client prepares its interim financial information in accordance with the same financial reporting framework as that used to prepare the annual financial statements.

This is in acknowledgement of the difference between a review performed by an accountant with an audit base of knowledge versus that performed by an accountant who is not the entity's auditor. Further, if the above conditions are met, generally the review engagement to provide limited assurance on interim financial reporting is intended to provide a periodic update to the year-end reporting and is considered an extension of the annual audit. Thus, the standard setters decided the requirements and guidance should reside in the auditing literature.

1. Authoritative Guidance Hierarchy

    a. SSARS SSARS are issued by a senior technical committee, the Accounting and Review Services Committee (ARSC) of the AICPA and provide performance and reporting standards for compilations and reviews. A CPA must perform a compilation or review of a nonissuer in accordance with SSARS. Professional judgment must sometimes be used in the application of SSARS.

    b. Interpretative Publications Interpretative publications provide guidance on the application of SSARS. They consist of Interpretations of SSARSs, appendices to the SSARSs, compilation and review guidance included in AICPA *Audit and Accounting Guides* and Statements of Position. CPAs should be aware of interpretive publications to the extent that they are applicable to specific engagements. Interpretations are not as authoritative as the SSARS—they are recommendations, not standards—however a CPA should be prepared to justify a departure from an Interpretation if the quality of their work is questioned.

    c. Other Publications Other compilation and review publications have no authoritative status, however they may be helpful. Other publications include AICPA compilation and review publications not listed above; the AICPA annual *Compilation and Review Alert;* compilation and review articles in the *Journal of Accountancy, The CPA Letter,* and other professional journals; and other instruction materials.

2. **Definitions**

    a. **Issuer** "An issuer is defined in section 3 of the Securities Exchange Act of 1934 [15 U.S.C. 78c], the securities of which are registered under section 12 of that Act (15 U.S.C. 78l), or that is required to file reports under section 15(d) (15 U.S.C. 78o(d)), or that files or has filed a registration statement that has not yet become effective under the Securities Act of 1933 (15 U.S.C. 77a et seq.), and that it has not withdrawn."

    The Securities Exchange Act of 1934 states: "The term '**issuer**' means any person who issues or proposes to issue any security; ..."

    b. **Nonissuer** "All entities except for those defined as issuers."

    c. **Professional Requirements** The SSARSs use two categories of professional requirements, identified by specific terms to describe the degree of responsibility they impose on CPAs—*unconditional requirements and presumptively mandatory requirements*—which are defined in a fashion similar to the same terms in SAS 102. (See Chapter 21.)

    d. **Those Charged With Governance** "The person(s) with responsibility for overseeing the strategic direction of the entity and obligations related to the accountability of the entity. This includes overseeing the financial reporting process. In some cases, those charged with governance are responsible for approving the entity's financial statements (in other cases, management has this responsibility). In some entities, governance is a collective responsibility that may be carried out by a board of directors, a committee of the board of directors, a committee of management, partners, equivalent persons, or some combination thereof. Those charged with governance are specifically excluded from management, unless they perform management functions as defined below."

    e. **Management** "The person(s) responsible for achieving the objectives of the entity and who have the authority to establish policies and make decisions by which those objectives are to be pursued. Management is responsible for the financial statements, including designing, implementing, and maintaining effective internal control over financial reporting."

    f. **Third Party** "All persons, including those charged with governance, except for those members of management as defined above."

    g. **Financial Statement** A presentation of financial data (balance sheet, income statement, etc.), including accompanying notes, in accordance with GAAP or OCBOA. AR §100 excludes financial forecasts and projections as well as financial presentations included in tax returns from this definition.

    h. **Compilation of Financial Statements** Presenting information in the form of financial statements that is the representation of management without undertaking to express any assurance on the statements.

    i. **Review of Financial Statements** Performing inquiries and analytics to provide a reasonable basis for the CPA to express limited assurance that there are no material modifications that need to be made to the financial statements in order for them to be in conformity with GAAP or, if applicable, with some other comprehensive basis of accounting. The CPA may need to perform a compilation and/or other accounting services to review the financial statements.

        (1) **Review vs. Compilation** The objective of a review is to express limited assurance. A compilation does not involve any level of assurance.

        (2) **Review vs. Audit** An audit provides a reasonable basis (assurance) for expression of an opinion on the financial statements taken as a whole. A review

expresses only limited assurance and does not involve obtaining an understanding of internal control, assessing fraud risk, or other procedures ordinarily performed in an audit.

3. **More Than One Service** Whenever a CPA performs more than one level of service (e.g., a compilation and a review, or a review and an audit), the CPA should issue the report for the highest level of service rendered.

4. **Use of CPA's Name** A CPA's name should not appear in documents or written communications containing unaudited financial statements of a nonissuer unless the CPA has compiled or reviewed them in compliance with the SSARSs, or there is a clear indication that the CPA has not compiled or reviewed the statements and the CPA assumes no responsibility for them. A CPA could indicate this as follows: "The accompanying balance sheet of X Company as of December 31, 20X1, the related statements of income, and cash flows for the year then ended were not audited, reviewed, or compiled by us and, accordingly, we do not express an opinion or any other form of assurance on them." If a CPA becomes aware that her/his name has been used improperly, the client should be advised that the use of the CPA's name is inappropriate and the CPA should consider consulting an attorney.

5. **Understanding With the Client** A CPA should reach an understanding, preferably in writing, with the client as to the services to be performed. An engagement letter is recommended. (However, if the engagement is to *compile* financial statements **not** expected to be used by a third party, a written communication—a report or engagement letter—is required. See "Documentation When Not Expected to Be Used by a Third Party" in this chapter under "Compilation of Financial Statements.") It should include a description of the nature and limitations of the services to be performed as well as a description of the report (if a report is to be issued). The understanding should also include that although the engagement cannot be relied upon to disclose errors, fraud or illegal acts, that the CPA will inform the appropriate level of management of any material errors and any evidence or information that fraud or illegal acts *may* have occurred (unless they are inconsequential) of which the CPA becomes aware.

6. **Limited Reporting Engagement** The CPA is **not** precluded from issuing a compilation or review report on one financial statement and not on the others. However, in a *review* engagement, this is allowable only if the scope of the inquiry and analytical procedures has not been restricted.

B. **Compilation of Financial Statements**

1. **Objective** "The objective of a compilation engagement is to present in the form of financial statements, information that is the representation of management (owners) without undertaking to express any assurance on the financial statements."

2. **Performance Requirements** These performance requirements are applicable to a compilation of financial statements whenever a CPA is engaged to report on compiled financial statements; submits financial statements to a client that are or reasonably might be expected to be used by a third party; or submits financial statements to a client that are **not** expected to be used by a third party.

   a. **Knowledge of Accounting Principles & Industry Practices** To compile financial statements that are appropriate in form for a particular industry, a CPA should understand the accounting principles and practices of that industry. The CPA has a responsibility to obtain the required level of knowledge. This does not prevent a CPA from accepting an engagement for an entity in an industry in which the CPA has no previous experience as long as the CPA can acquire it through AICPA industry guides, industry publications, talking with other practitioners, etc.

b. **Knowledge About Client** A CPA should possess a general understanding of the nature of the client's business transactions, the form of its accounting records, the stated qualifications of its accounting personnel, the accounting basis used for the financial statements, and the form and content of the financial statements. This knowledge usually is acquired through experience with the client or inquiry of the client's personnel. Based on this understanding, the CPA can determine whether it will be necessary to perform other accounting services (such as assisting with adjusting entries) in order to perform the compilation.

c. **Check-Over** Before submission, the CPA should read the financial statements to determine if they appear to be appropriate in form and free from obvious material errors (mistakes in the compilation of the financial statements). This would encompass detection of math errors, misapplication of accounting principles, inadequate disclosures, etc.

d. **Procedures Not Required** A compilation does not include performing inquiries, analytical procedures or other procedures performed in a review. Also, a compilation (and a review, for that matter) does not consider obtaining an understanding of an entity's internal control structure; assessing fraud risk; and other tests of accounting records or procedures performed during an audit to obtain sufficient appropriate audit evidence.

e. **Financial Statements Materially Misstated Due to Fraud or Illegal Acts** Although the CPA is not required to perform any procedures to verify information supplied by the client, s/he may become aware of information that leads s/he to believe that the financial statements are materially misstated due to fraud or illegal acts that may have occurred. The CPA should consider the effects of these matters on her/his compilation report. The CPA should request that management consider the effects on the financial statements and provide revised information. If management refuses, the CPA should withdraw from the engagement.

3. **Reporting** When a CPA is engaged to report on complied financial statements or submits financial statements that are reasonably expected to be used by a third party, the statements should be accompanied by a report.

a. **Basic Elements of the Report** The basic elements are listed below. Any other procedures that the CPA may have performed should **not** be described.

(1) A statement that a compilation has been performed in accordance with SSARS issued by the AICPA

(2) A statement that a compilation is limited to presenting in the form of financial statements information that is the representation of management

(3) A statement that the financial statements have not been audited or reviewed and, accordingly, the CPA does not express an opinion or any other form of assurance on them

(4) A signature of the accounting firm or the CPA

(5) The date of the report, which should be the date of the completion of the compilation

Exhibit 1 ▶ Standard Compilation Report

> I (We) have compiled the accompanying balance sheet of XYZ Company as of December 31, 20X0, and the related statements of income, retained earnings, and cash flows for the year then ended, in accordance with Statements on Standards for Accounting and Review Services issued by the American Institute of Certified Public Accountants.
>
> A compilation is limited to presenting, in the form of financial statements, information that is the representation of management (owners). I (We) have not audited or reviewed the accompanying financial statements and, accordingly, do not express an opinion or any other form of assurance on them.

b. **Financial Statements Referenced to the Report** Each page of the financial statements should include a reference, such as "See Accountant's Compilation Report."

c. **Emphasis of a Matter** As long as it is disclosed in the financial statements, a CPA may, at her/his discretion, include explanatory information in a separate paragraph in the compilation report to emphasize a matter.

d. **Independence Not Required** A CPA may issue a report on compiled financial statements for an entity with respect to which the CPA is not independent.

(1) The lack of independence should be specifically disclosed by adding a statement to the last paragraph of the report: "I am (we are) not independent with respect to XYZ Company."

(2) The reason for the lack of independence should **not** be described.

e. **Financial Statements That Omit Substantially All Disclosures** A CPA may be requested to compile financial statements that omit substantially all disclosures required by GAAP or OCBOA. This is permissible as long as the omission is clearly indicated in the report and the intent is not to mislead anyone who might reasonably be expected to use the financial statements. Note: A CPA cannot issue a *review* report on financial statements that omits substantially all disclosures required (by GAAP or OCBOA).

Exhibit 2 ▶ Substantially All Disclosures Omitted Paragraph

> Management has elected to omit substantially all the disclosures required by U.S. generally accepted accounting principles. If the omitted disclosures were included in the financial statements, they might influence the user's conclusions about the company's financial position, results of operations, and cash flows. Accordingly, these financial statements are not designed for those who are not informed about such matters.

(1) **Emphasis of a Matter Caution** An emphasis of a matter paragraph should not be used in lieu of management disclosures, therefore a CPA should not include such a paragraph in her/his report on financial statements that omit substantially all disclosures.

(2) **Inclusion of Selected Disclosures** If the client wants to include disclosures on only a few matters in the form of notes to the financial statements, such disclosures should be labeled, for example, "Selected Information—Substantially All Disclosures Required by Generally Accepted Accounting Principles Are Not Included." In this case, an emphasis of a matter paragraph may be included in the CPA's compilation report as long as the matter discussed is disclosed in the selected information.

(3) **Disclosure of OCBOA Basis** If compiled financial statements omit substantially all disclosures with no reference to basis, but are otherwise in conformity with OCBOA, the basis should be disclosed in the CPA's report.

4. **Documentation When Not Expected to Be Used by a Third Party** When a CPA submits compiled financial statements to a client that are not expected to used by a third party, the CPA should either issue a report as described above or document the understanding with their client with an engagement letter, preferably signed by management. If an understanding cannot be established, the CPA should decline the engagement.

a. **Elements of the Documentation of the Understanding** The documentation of the understanding should include these statements or descriptions:

(1) The nature and limitations of the services to be performed

(2) A compilation is limited to presenting in the form of financial statements information that is the representation of management

(3) The financial statements will not be audited or reviewed

(4) No opinion or any other form of assurance on the financial statements will be provided

(5) Management has knowledge about the nature of the procedures applied and the basis of accounting and assumptions used in the preparation of the financial statements

(6) Acknowledgment of management's representation and agreement that the financial statements are not to be used by third parties

(7) The engagement cannot be relied upon to disclose errors, fraud, or illegal acts

And if applicable, the following matters should also be addressed:

(8) Material departures from GAAP or OCBOA may exist and the effects of those departures, if any, on the financial statement may not be disclosed

(9) Substantially all disclosures required by GAAP or OCBOA may be omitted

(10) Lack of independence

(11) Refer to supplementary information

b. **Restricted to Management's Use**

(1) Each page of the financial statements should include a reference, such as "Restricted for Management's Use Only."

(2) If the CPA learns that the financial statements have been distributed to third parties, the CPA should:

(a) Request that the client have the statements returned

(b) If the client doesn't cooperate in a timely fashion, the CPA should notify the third parties that the financial statements are not intended for their use, preferably in consultation with an attorney

C. **Review of Financial Statements**

1. **Objective** The objective of a review engagement is to express limited assurance that there are no material modifications that should be made to the financial statements in order for the statements to be in conformity with GAAP or OCBOA.

2. **Performance Requirements** In order to obtain a reasonable basis for this expression of limited assurance, the CPA must perform analytical procedures, make inquiries of management, and obtain representations from management for all financial statements and periods covered by the CPA's review report. In some situations, it may be appropriate to make inquires of other company personnel as well.

   a. **Knowledge About the Client and Its Industry** Knowledge of the accounting principles and practices of the client's industry and an understanding of the client's business is needed so that the CPA can determine and apply appropriate inquiries and analytics. This does not prevent a CPA from accepting a review engagement for an entity in an industry in which the CPA has no previous experience as long as the CPA can acquire it through AICPA industry guides, industry publications, talking with other practitioners, etc. The CPA's understanding of the client's business should include a general understanding of the entity's organization, its operating characteristics, and the nature of its assets, liabilities, revenues, and expenses. This understanding also involves a general knowledge of the entity's production, distribution, and compensation methods; types of products and services; the various locations where the entity operates; and material transactions with related parties. This knowledge usually is acquired through experience with the client or its industry and inquiry of the client's personnel.

   b. **Analytical Procedures** A CPA must apply analytical procedures to the financial statements in order to identify unusual items that may indicate material misstatements. The expectations developed by the performance of analytical procedures are not as encompassing as in an audit. Nor, as in an audit, is the CPA required to corroborate management's responses. However, in a review, a CPA should consider the reasonableness and consistency of management's responses.

   c. **Inquiries to Financial Management** The CPA must make inquires of management; these are inquiries that s/he should consider making of financial management.

      (1) Whether the financial statements have been prepared in conformity with GAAP consistently applied

      (2) The client's accounting principles and practices and the methods followed in applying them and procedures for recording, classifying, and summarizing transactions, and accumulating information for disclosure in the financial statements

      (3) Unusual or complex situations that may have an effect on the financial statements

      (4) Significant transactions occurring or recognized near the end of the reporting period

      (5) The status of uncorrected misstatements identified during the previous engagement

      (6) Questions that have arisen in the course of applying the review procedures

      (7) Events subsequent to the date of the financial statements that could have a material effect on the financial statements

(8) Their knowledge of any fraud or suspected fraud affecting the entity involving management or others where the fraud could have a material effect on the financial statements

(9) Significant journal entries and other adjustments

(10) Communications from regulatory agencies

d. **Other Inquiries & Review Procedures** The CPA should also consider making these inquiries or performing these procedures:

(1) Inquiries concerning actions taken at meetings of stockholders, board of directors, committees of the board of directors, or comparable meetings that may affect the financial statements

(2) Reading the financial statements to consider whether the financial statements appear to conform with GAAP

(3) Obtaining reports from other accountants, if any, who have been engaged to audit or review the financial statements of significant components of the entity, its subsidiaries and other investees

e. **Management Representations** The CPA must obtain representations from management for all financial statements and periods covered by the CPA's review report. Exactly which representations are needed will depend on the circumstances.

(1) Specific representations regarding a review of GAAP financial statements should address the following:

(a) Management's acknowledgment of its responsibility for the fair presentation in the financial statements of financial position, results of operations, and cash flows in conformity with generally accepted accounting principles

(b) Management's belief that the financial statements are fairly presented in conformity with generally accepted accounting principles

(c) Management's acknowledgement of its responsibility to prevent and detect fraud

(d) Knowledge of any fraud or suspected fraud affecting the entity involving management or others where the fraud could have a material effect on the financial statements, including any communications received from employees, former employees, or others

(e) Management's full and truthful response to all inquiries

(f) Completeness of information

(g) Information concerning subsequent events

(2) **Date of Management Representations** The letter should be dated the date that the client presents and signs the letter—ordinarily the date of the CPA's review report which is the date of the completion of the CPA's review procedures. In no event should this date be prior to the date of the CPA's review report.

(3) **Address** The letter should be addressed to the CPA.

(4) **Signature(s)** The letter should be signed by members of management that the CPA believes to be knowledgeable about and responsible for the matters covered. Current management must provide the representations for all periods covered by the financial statements and the CPA's review report even if they were not present for all periods.

(5) **Updating Management Representations**

(a) Triggers for Requesting an Update

The CPA should obtain an updated management representation letter when:

(i) A predecessor accountant is requested by a former client to reissue her/his report on the financial statements of a prior period, and those financial statements are to be presented on a comparative basis with reviewed financial statements of a subsequent period, the predecessor accountant should obtain an updating representation letter from the management of the former client

Examples of when a CPA should *consider* obtaining an updated management representation letter include when:

(ii) There is a significant delay between the date of the letter (the date of the completion of the accountant's review procedures and thus the date of her/his review report) and the *release* of the CPA's review report

(iii) A material subsequent event occurs after the completion of the CPA's review procedures and receipt of the original representation letter, but before the release of the CPA's review report

(b) **Elements of the Update** The updated management representation letter should state:

(i) Whether any information has come to management's attention that would cause management to believe that any of the previous representations should be modified

(ii) Whether any subsequent events require adjustment to or disclosure in the financial statements

f. **Modification of Review Procedures as a Result of Other Services Performed** Information about an entity obtained from an audit, compilation, or other accounting services may result in the modification of review procedures. However, this modification would not reduce the degree of responsibility the CPA has with respect to the reviewed financial statements.

g. **Procedures Not Required** A review does not consider obtaining an understanding of the entity's internal control; assessing fraud risk, or other tests of the accounting records or procedures performed during an audit to obtain sufficient appropriate audit evidence.

h. **Incomplete Review** During the performance of these review procedures the CPA may become aware that the information s/he is collecting is unsatisfactory due to errors, or to fraud or illegal acts that may have occurred. The CPA should request that management consider the effects on the financial statements and likewise, the CPA should consider the effect on her/his review report. If the CPA believes the financial statements are materially misstated, s/he should perform the further procedures needed to attain limited assurance that no material modifications are needed to bring the financial statements into conformity with GAAP or OCBOA. (Also see "Departures from GAAP" in this chapter under "Reporting Issues Common to Compilations & Reviews.") If the CPA is unable to do this or if the client does not provide a management representation letter the review will be incomplete and so a review report cannot be issued. The CPA should then consider if it is appropriate to issue a compilation report (See the information under "Change of Engagement Type" in this chapter).

    i.   **Documentation of Review Procedures & Conclusions Reached** Because of differing circumstances, it is not possible to specify the form or content of the documentation that a CPA should prepare for each engagement; however, documentation should include any findings and issues that, in the judgment of the CPA, are significant. At a minimum, documentation should include the following:

        (1)   Matters covered in the CPA's inquiries

        (2)   Analytical procedures performed, including:

            (a)   Recorded amounts or ratios developed from recorded amounts

            (b)   Associated expectations, including factors considered in developing expectations

            (c)   Results of the comparisons of the expectations to the recorded amounts or ratios

        (3)   Description and the results of additional procedures performed in response to significant unexpected differences that arise in the performance of analytics

        (4)   Unusual matters that the CPA considered while performing the review procedures, including the disposition of these matters

        (5)   Communications (oral and written) to the appropriate level of management regarding fraud or illegal acts that came to the CPA's attention

        (6)   Management representation letter

    j.   **Other Means of Support for Review Report** A CPA is not precluded from supporting her/his review report by other means *in addition* to review documentation. This could include:

        (1)   Written information from the files of other engagements or quality control activities

        (2)   Oral explanations, limited to situations to supplement or clarify documentation; not as the principle support for work performed or conclusions reached

3.   **Reporting** Financial statements reviewed by a CPA should be accompanied by a report.

    a.   **Independence Required** Unlike a compilation, the CPA must be independent to perform a review of financial statements.

    b.   **Basic Elements of the Report** The basic elements are listed below. Any other procedures that the CPA may have performed should **not** be described.

        (1)   A statement that a review has been performed in accordance with SSARS issued by the AICPA

(2) A statement that all information included in the financial statements is the representation of the management (owners) of the entity

(3) A statement that a review consists principally of inquiries of company personnel and analytical procedures applied to financial data

(4) A statement that a review is substantially less in scope than an audit, the objective of which is the expression of an opinion regarding the financial statements taken as a whole and, accordingly, no such opinion is expressed

(5) A statement that the accountant is not aware of any material modifications that should be made to the financial statements in order for them to be in conformity with GAAP, other than those modifications, if any, indicated in the report

(6) A signature of the accounting firm or the accountant (manual, stamped, electronic, or typed)

(7) The date of the report, which should be the date of the completion of the review procedures

Exhibit 3 ▶ Standard Review Report

I (We) have reviewed the accompanying balance sheet of XYZ Company as of December 31, 20X0, and the related statements of income, retained earnings, and cash flows for the year then ended, in accordance with Statements on Standards for Accounting and Review Services issued by the American Institute of Certified Public Accountants. All information included in these financial statements is the representation of the management (owners) of XYZ Company.

A review consists principally of inquiries of company personnel and analytical procedures applied to financial data. It is substantially less in scope than an audit in accordance with U.S. generally accepted auditing standards, the objective of which is the expression of an opinion regarding the financial statements taken as a whole. Accordingly, I (we) do not express such an opinion.

Based on my (our) review, I am (we are) not aware of any material modifications that should be made to the accompanying financial statements in order for them to be in conformity with U.S. generally accepted accounting principles.

(c) **Financial Statements Referenced to the Report** Each page of the financial statements should include a reference, such as "See Accountant's Review Report."

(d) **Emphasis of a Matter** As long as it is disclosed in the financial statements, a CPA may, at her/his discretion, include explanatory information in a separate paragraph in the review report to emphasize a matter.

D. Reporting Issues Common to Compilations & Reviews

Please see both of the previous topics for reporting issues specific to either a compilation or a review engagement.

1. **Departures From GAAP** If a CPA becomes aware of a departure from GAAP that is material to the financial statements and the statements are not revised, s/he must determine if modification to the standard report is adequate to disclose the departure. Note: Normally, neither an uncertainty (including an uncertainty about an entity's ability to continue as a going concern) nor an inconsistency in application of accounting principles would be cause for the modification of a CPA's standard report as long as the financial statements included appropriate disclosure.

a. **When Modification of the Report is Appropriate** The departure should be disclosed in a separate paragraph of the report. The effect on the financial statements should be described if a determination has been made by management or is known as a result of the CPA's procedures. If this is not the case, the CPA is not required to determine them; however the CPA must state in her/his report that such a determination has not been made.

Exhibit 4 ▶ Compilation Report That Discloses Departures From GAAP

<same title and introductory paragraph as the standard compilation report>

A compilation is limited to presenting, in the form of financial statements, information that is the representation of management (owners). I (We) have not audited or reviewed the accompanying financial statements and, accordingly, do not express an opinion or any other form of assurance on them. However, I (we) did become aware of a departure (certain departures) from U.S. generally accepted accounting principles that is (are) described in the following paragraph(s).

(Separate paragraph)

As disclosed in note X to the financial statements, generally accepted accounting principles require that land be stated at cost. Management has informed me (us) that the company has stated its land at appraised value and that, if generally accepted accounting principles had been followed, the land account and stockholders' equity would have been decreased by $500,000.

or

A statement of cash flows for the year ended December 31, 20X0, has not been presented. Generally accepted accounting principles require that such a statement be presented when financial statements purport to present financial position and results of operations. (**NOTE:** The first paragraph should be modified accordingly when a statement of cash flows is not presented.)

Exhibit 5 ▶ Review Report That Discloses Departures From GAAP

<same title and introductory paragraph as the standard review report>

<same scope paragraph as the standard review report>

Based on my (our) review, with the exception of the matter(s) described in the following paragraph(s), I am (we are) not aware of any material modifications that should be made to the accompanying financial statements in order for them to be in conformity with U.S. generally accepted accounting principles.

(Separate paragraph)

As disclosed in note X to the financial statements, generally accepted accounting principles require that inventory cost consists of material, labor, and overhead. Management has informed me (us) that the inventory of finished goods and work in process is stated in the accompanying financial statements at material and labor cost only, and that the effects of this departure from generally accepted accounting principles on financial position, results of operations, and cash flows have not been determined.

or

> As disclosed in note X to the financial statements, the company has adopted (description of newly adopted method), whereas it previously used (description of previous method). Although the (description of newly adopted method) is in conformity with generally accepted accounting principles, the company does not appear to have reasonable justification for making a change as required by Statement of Financial Accounting Standards No. 154, *Accounting Changes and Error Corrections.*

    b.   **When Modification of the Report is Not Appropriate** The CPA should withdraw from the engagement (and provide no further services with respect to those financial statements) if s/he determines that modification to the standard report is not adequate to disclose the deficiencies in the financial statements, taken as a whole. It may also be advisable for the CPA to consult with her/his attorney.

2.   **Restriction of Report to Specified Parties** A CPA should restrict the use of a report to specified parties when the subject matter of her/his report or the presentation being reported on is based on measurement or disclosure criteria contained in contractual agreements or regulatory provisions that are not in conformity with GAAP or OCBOA. The restriction is needed because the reports could be misunderstood by those who are not adequately informed of the basis, assumptions, or purpose of the presentation. These reports are termed *restricted use* whileas reports on financial statements prepared in conformity with GAAP or OCBOA are termed *general use.*

    a.   **Combined Reports** If a CPA issues a single report that covers both restricted and general use subject matter or presentations, then the combined report should be restricted.

    b.   **Report Language** A separate paragraph should be added at the end of the CPA's report for a restricted-use report.

        Exhibit 6 ▶ Sample Restricted-Use Compilation or Review Report Paragraph

> This report is intended solely for the information and use of (the specified parties) and is not intended to be and should not be used by anyone other than these specified parties.

3.   **Going Concern Issues** A CPA may become aware that there may be an uncertainty about an entity's ability to continue as a going concern for a reasonable period of time, not to exceed one year beyond the date of the financial statements. The CPA should ask management to consider the possible effects on the financial statements. The CPA should then consider the reasonableness of management's conclusions (as well as the adequacy of the related disclosures, if applicable). If the CPA determines that management's conclusions are unreasonable or the related disclosures are inadequate (if applicable), then s/he should follow the guidance described above regarding departures from GAAP.

4.   **Subsequent Events** During the performance of procedures or after the date of the CPA's report but before its release, a CPA may become aware of a subsequent event that has a material effect on the financial statements. In either case, the CPA should follow the same guidance described above for going concern issues.

5.   **Subsequent Discovery of Facts Existing at Date of Report** After the date of a compilation or review report, the CPA may become aware that facts may have existed at that date that, had the CPA been aware of them, might have caused the CPA to believe that the information the client supplied was incorrect, incomplete, or otherwise unsatisfactory. The CPA would be advised to consult with an attorney and insurance provider. SAS 1 provides guidance to help determine the course of action—allowing for differences between the CPA's engagement and an audit. For example, if the information is actionable, in respect to a compilation engagement, the CPA would attempt to obtain additional or revised information from the client. And in respect to a review engagement, the CPA would perform additional procedures needed. Also the SSARS note that if the client does not cooperate, that although a compilation report does not express any form of assurance on the financial statements, the CPA should in nearly all cases, in the absence of notification of third party users by the client, notify them when s/he knows that the financial statements should be revised. Note: Although, the reference to SAS 1 is no longer included in the SSARS (it was eliminated along with other similar references by SSARS 15 in consideration of those not familiar with auditing literature—see the Change Alert at the beginning of this chapter), obviously the reference is still viable for CPA exam candidates. This topic is covered in Chapter 28 of this text, under "Timing Issues."

6. **Supplementary Information** In cases where the basic financial statements are accompanied by information that is presented for purposes of supplementary analysis, the CPA should indicate clearly the responsibility, if any, that the CPA is taking with respect to the information.

    a. **Review** In the review report (or in a separate report), the CPA may indicate that the supplementary information was subjected to the same review procedures as the financial statements and the CPA is not aware of any material modifications that should be made to it. Alternatively, the CPA may indicate that the data are presented only for supplementary purposes and has not been subjected to the review procedures applied to the financial statements, but was compiled from information that is the representation of management (and no opinion or any other form of assurance is given).

    b. **Compilation** The compilation report should include the supplementary data when the CPA has compiled the supplementary information to be presented with the basic financial statements. SSARS 9 explicitly allows reporting separately on supplementary information in a compilation engagement, consistent with the guidance in connection with a review engagement.

E. **Change in Engagement Type**
    Before an audit [or review] engagement has been completed, the client may ask the CPA to change the engagement to a review [or a compilation]. In reaching a decision, the CPA should consider: (1) the client's reason for making the request (especially if either the client or circumstances have imposed a restriction on the scope of the audit or review), (2) the amount of effort needed to complete the audit [review], and (3) the estimated additional cost to complete the audit [review].

    1. **Reasonable Basis for Changing** A change in the circumstances that caused the client to require an audit (or review) or a misunderstanding concerning the nature of an audit, review, or compilation usually would be considered acceptable reasons for changing. For example, the client's bank may have decided to accept reviewed financial statements in place of audited financial statements.

    2. **Unreasonable Basis for Changing** When procedures are substantially complete or there is a relatively insignificant cost to complete the engagement, the CPA should consider the propriety of changing the engagement carefully.

    3. **Restriction on Engagement Scope** The CPA should consider whether the information affected by the scope restriction may be incorrect, incomplete, or otherwise unsatisfactory. When the CPA has been engaged to audit an entity's financial statements, the CPA ordinarily would be precluded from issuing a review or a compilation report when the client has prohibited correspondence with the client's legal counsel. If in an audit or a review engagement a client does not provide the CPA with a signed representation letter, the CPA would be precluded from issuing a review report on the financial statements and ordinarily would be precluded from issuing a compilation report on the financial statements.

4. **Report** When the CPA decides that a change in engagement is appropriate and the requirements for a compilation or a review have been met, the CPA should issue an appropriate compilation or review report. It should not include any reference to the original engagement, any auditing or review procedures that may have been performed, or any scope limitations that resulted in the changed engagement.

F. **Prescribed Forms (AR 300)**
A prescribed form is any standard preprinted form designed or adopted by the body to which it is to be submitted, for example, forms used by industry trade associations, credit agencies, banks, and governmental and regulatory bodies other than those concerned with the sale or trading of securities. A form designed or adopted by the entity whose financial statements are to be compiled is **not** considered to be a prescribed form.

Exhibit 7 ▶ Compilation Report for Prescribed Form

I (We) have compiled the [identification of financial statements, including period covered and name of entity] included in the accompanying prescribed form in accordance with Statements on Standards for Accounting and Review Services issued by the American Institute of Certified Public Accountants.

My (Our) compilation was limited to presenting in the form prescribed by (name of body) information that is the representation of management (owners). I (We) have not audited or reviewed the financial statements referred to above and, accordingly, do not express an opinion or any other form of assurance on them.

These financial statements (including related disclosures) are presented in accordance with the requirements of [name of body], which differ from U.S. generally accepted accounting principles. Accordingly, these financial statements are not designed for those who are not informed about such differences.

---

1. **Applicability** AR 300 provides for an alternative form of standard compilation report when the prescribed form or related instructions call for departure from GAAP by specifying a measurement principle not in conformity with GAAP or by failing to request the disclosures required by GAAP. AR 300 also provides additional guidance applicable to reports on financial statements included in a prescribed form.

2. **Presumption** There is a presumption that the information required by a prescribed form is sufficient to meet the needs of the body that designed or adopted the form and that there is no need for that body to be advised of departures from GAAP required by the prescribed form or related instructions. Therefore, without a requirement or a request for a review report on the financial statements included in a prescribed form, the following form of standard compilation report may be used when the unaudited financial statements of a **nonpublic** entity are included in a prescribed form that calls for a departure from GAAP.

3. **Departures From GAAP** If the CPA becomes aware of a departure from GAAP other than departures that may be called for by the prescribed form or related instructions, the CPA should follow the guidance in SSARS 1 regarding such departures. The sentence introducing the separate paragraph of the report disclosing the departure might read as follows: "However, I did become aware of a departure from generally accepted accounting principles that is not called for by the prescribed form or related instructions, as described in the following paragraph."

4. **Departures From Other Requirements** If the CPA becomes aware of a departure from the requirements of the prescribed form or related instructions, the CPA considers that departure as the equivalent of a departure from GAAP in determining its effect on the CPA's report.

5. **Preprinted Form Not Conforming With SSARS** The CPA should not sign a preprinted report form that does not conform with the guidance in SSARS 3 or SSARS 1 (as amended)

whichever is applicable. In such circumstances, the CPA should append an appropriate report to the prescribed form.

G.   Personal Financial Statements (AR 600)
SSARS 6 allows a CPA to submit a written personal financial plan containing unaudited personal financial statements to a client without complying with the amended requirements of SSARS 1 when certain conditions exist.

Exhibit 8 ▶ Personal Financial Statement Report Excerpt

> The accompanying Statement of Financial Condition of X, as of December 31, 20X0, was prepared solely to help you develop your personal financial plan. Accordingly, it may be incomplete or contain other departures from generally accepted accounting principles and should not be used to obtain credit or for any purposes other than developing your financial plan. We have not audited, reviewed, or compiled the statement.

1.   **Requirements** The CPA must establish an understanding with the client that the financial statements will be used solely to assist the client and the client's advisers to develop the client's personal financial goals and objectives, and will not be used to obtain credit or for any purposes other than developing these goals and objectives. Nothing must come to the CPA's attention during the engagement that contradicts this understanding.

2.   **Report** A CPA using the exemption provided by SSARS 6 should issue a written report.

H.   Plain Paper Financial Statements
SSARS 8 provides communication and performance requirements for unaudited financial statements submitted to a client in three circumstances, when the accountant: (1) is engaged to report on compiled financial statements; (2) submits financial statements to a client that are, or reasonably might be expected to be, used by a third party; or (3) submits financial statements to a client where there is no expectation that the statements will be used by third parties. The requirements for the first and second situations basically are the same as under SSARS 1. SSARS 8 gives practitioners **reporting** alternatives, not **performance** alternatives. In any financial statement compilation, practitioners must meet the same performance standards. SSARS 8 has a report alternative (which basically follows SSARS 1) and it has a no-report alternative. Practitioners may reach an agreement with the client that the statements are only for the client's internal use (the statements will not be distributed to other parties) and document that agreement in an engagement letter. In this case, practitioners may elect the no-report alternative.

1.   **Without Report** SSARS 8 allows an accountant submitting unaudited financial statements to a client that are not expected to be used by a third party to either (a) issue a compilation report in accordance with the reporting requirements, or (b) **document** an understanding with the entity through the use of an engagement letter, preferably signed by management, regarding the services performed and the limitations on the use of those financial statements. A written communication is required, if the engagement is to compile financial statements under this alternative.

2.   **Reliance** A CPA may rely on management's representation that the statements will be used only internally, without further inquiry, unless information comes to her/his attention that contradicts management's representation.

3.   **Combination** A CPA may adopt the no-report alternative for interim financial statements and use the report alternative for annual financial statements.

4.   **Improper Distribution** Upon becoming aware that financial statements were distributed to third parties, the CPA should request that the client have the statements returned. If the client does not do so within a reasonable time period, the CPA should notify known third parties that the statements are not intended for their use, in consultation with an attorney.

I. **Communications Between Predecessor & Successor Accountants (AR 400)**
    SSARS 4, as amended by SSARS 9, provides guidance to a successor accountant who decides to communicate with a predecessor accountant regarding an engagement to compile or review the financial statements of a **nonpublic** entity. SSARS 9 emphasizes that the successor should remain cognizant that the predecessor and the client may have disagreed about significant matters.

   1. **Successor Accountant** SSARS 9 defines a successor accountant as an accountant who is either considering accepting a client's invitation to make a proposal for an engagement to compile or review financial statements or who has accepted such an engagement.

   2. **Predecessor Accountant** SSARS 9 defines a predecessor accountant as an accountant who either has (a) reported on the most recently compiled or reviewed financial statements or was engaged to perform, but did not complete, such a review or compilation, or (b) resigned, declined to accept another engagement, or been notified that her/his services have been or may be terminated.

   3. **Optional** A successor is not required to communicate with a predecessor in connection with a compilation or review engagement, but may decide to do so, for example, when circumstances such as the following exist: the information obtained about the prospective client and its management and principals is limited or appears to require special attention, the change in accountants takes place substantially after the end of the accounting period, or there have been frequent changes in accountants.

       a. SSARS 9 removes the requirement that the predecessor accountant respond to a successor accountant's inquiries, even in ordinary circumstances.

       b. SSARS 9 clarifies that the successor accountant would make inquires of the predecessor to obtain information useful in deciding whether to accept the engagement.

   4. **Client Consent** Except as permitted by the AICPA Rules of Conduct, a CPA is precluded from disclosing any confidential information obtained during a professional engagement without the consent of the client. A successor should obtain specific consent from a prospective client to make inquires of a predecessor. A successor should inquire about reasons for a client's refusal or limitation on the predecessor's response and consider the implications of such a refusal or limitation.

   5. **Content** The successor accountant's inquires should be specific and reasonable regarding matters that would assist the successor in evaluating whether to accept the client, including knowledge of any relevant fraud or illegal acts and the predecessor's understanding of the reason for changing accountants. When the successor decides to communicate with the predecessor, inquiries may be oral or written and ordinarily include inquiries concerning the following: (a) information that might bear on the integrity of management; (b) the predecessor's understanding of the reason for the change of accountants; and (c) disagreements with management about accounting principles or the necessity for the performance of certain procedures and the cooperation of management in providing additional or revised information, if necessary.

   6. **Response** The predecessor should respond promptly and fully, on the basis of known facts, when the predecessor receives inquiries described above, as distinguished from other inquiries. The predecessor may decide, due to potential litigation or other unusual circumstances, not to respond fully to the successor's inquiries. If the predecessor decides not to respond fully, the predecessor should indicate that her/his response is limited. The successor should consider the reasons for, and implications of, such a response in connection with acceptance of the engagement.

   7. **Other Inquiries** The successor may wish to make other inquiries of the predecessor to facilitate the conduct of the engagement. Examples of such inquiries include questions about prior periods regarding the following: (a) inadequacies noted in the entity's underlying finan-

cial data; (b) the necessity to perform other accounting services; and (c) areas that have required an inordinate amount of time in prior periods.

    a.   **Work Papers** A successor also may wish to obtain access to the predecessor's working papers. In these circumstances, the successor should request the client to authorize the predecessor to allow such access. Ordinarily, the predecessor should provide the successor access to working papers relating to matters of continuing accounting significance and those related to contingencies. Valid business reasons (including, but not limited to, unpaid fees) may lead the predecessor to decide not to allow access to the working papers. The predecessor may decide to reach an understanding about the use of work papers with the successor, possibly including written communication from the successor.

    b.   **Reference** The successor should not refer to the report or work of a predecessor in her/his own report, except as specifically permitted by SSARS 2, SSARS 11, or SAS 26 regarding the financial statements of a prior period.

8.   **Prior Financial Statements Require Revision** If the successor becomes aware of information that causes her/him to question whether there should be revisions to financial statements included in the predecessor's reports and the client refuses to communicate with the predecessor, the successor should consider the implications for the current engagement, including whether resignation from the engagement or consultation with legal counsel is appropriate.

J.   **Compilations of Presentations Other Than Financial Statements**
Prior to SSARS 13, *Compilation of Specified Elements, Accounts, or Items of a Financial Statement,* and SSARS 14, *Compilation of Pro Forma Financial Information,* the SSARSs provided guidance only when the CPA compiled or reviewed financial statements. By definition, presentations of financial statement elements and *pro forma* financial information are not financial statements; as such, the SSARSs were not applicable to these compilations. SSARS 13 and 14 are applicable to compilation engagements only (not to review or audit engagements).

1.   **All Items Other Than Financial Statements** For this coverage, an "item" refers to either *pro forma* financial information (including the summary of significant assumptions) or a specified element (or specified elements) of financial statements.

    a.   **Association** If a CPA prepares or assists a client in preparing an item, the CPA should consider how the presentation will be used. Essentially, the CPA should consider the potential of being associated with the item and the likelihood that the user may inappropriately infer (through that association) an unintended level of assurance. If the CPA believes that s/he will be associated with the item, s/he should consider issuing a compilation report so that a user will not infer a level of assurance that does not exist.

    b.   **Understanding** The CPA should establish an understanding of the engagement with the client (preferably in writing) regarding the services to be performed. The understanding should include a description of the nature and limitations of the services to be performed and a description of the report. The understanding also should include the following:

        (1)   The engagement cannot be relied upon to disclose errors, fraud, or illegal acts.

        (2)   The CPA will inform the appropriate level of management of any material errors, of any evidence or information that comes to the CPA's attention during the engagement that fraud or an illegal act may have occurred. The CPA need not report any matters regarding illegal acts that may have occurred that are clearly inconsequential and may reach agreement in advance with the entity on the nature of any these type matters to be communicated.

    c.   **Minimum Requirements** The CPA should read the compiled item and consider whether the information appears to be appropriate in form and free of obvious material errors.

    d.   **Independence** A CPA is not precluded from issuing a compilation report on an item when s/he is not independent with respect to the reporting entity. The CPA should add a one-sentence paragraph to the compilation report indicating the lack of independence.

    e.   **Report** The CPA must adhere to the compilation performance requirements contained in SSARS 1 (as amended). SSARS 13 is not intended to preclude a CPA from preparing (or assisting in the preparation of) one or more financial statement elements and submitting these specified elements, accounts, or items to the client without the issuance of a compilation report, unless the CPA has been engaged to compile the specified elements. SSARS 14 is not intended to preclude a CPA from preparing (or assisting in the preparation of) *pro forma* financial information and submitting the *pro forma* financial information to the client without the issuance of a compilation report, unless CPA has been engaged to compile the *pro forma* information.

2.   **Financial Statements Elements** Examples of elements include schedules of rents/royalties, schedules of fixed assets, schedules of receivables, etc.

Exhibit 9 ▶ Sample Compilation Report on an Accounts Receivable Schedule

> We have compiled the accompanying schedule of accounts receivable of Glynn Company as of December 31, 2005, in accordance with Statements on Standards for Accounting and Review Services issued by the American Institute of Certified Public Accountants.
>
> A compilation is limited to presenting financial information that is the representation of management (owners). We have not audited or reviewed the accompanying schedule of accounts receivable and, accordingly, do not express an opinion or any other form of assurance on it.

3.   *Pro Forma* **Financial Information** An engagement to compile *pro forma* financial information may be undertaken as a separate engagement or in conjunction with a compilation of financial statements. The CPA's compilation or review report or the auditor's report on the historical financial statements should be included (or incorporated by reference) in the document containing the *pro forma* financial information. If the presentation does not include all applicable disclosures, a paragraph highlighting that circumstance should be added to the accountant's compilation report.

Exhibit 10 ▶ Sample Compilation Report on *Pro Forma* Financial Information

> We have compiled the accompanying *pro forma* financial information as of and for the year ended December 31, 2005, reflecting the business combination of the Company and Glynn Company in accordance with Statements on Standards for Accounting and Review Services issued by the American Institute of Certified Public Accountants. The historical condensed financial statements are derived from the historical unaudited financial statements of Cohen Company, which were compiled by us, and of Glynn Company, which were compiled by other accountants.
>
> A compilation is limited to presenting *pro forma* financial information that is the representation of management (owners). We have not audited or reviewed the accompanying *pro forma* financial information and, accordingly, do not express an opinion or any other form of assurance on it.

The objective of this *pro forma* financial information is to show what the significant effects on the historical financial information might have been had the transaction (or event) occurred at an earlier date. However, the *pro forma* financial information is not necessarily indicative of the results of operations or related effects on financial position that would have been attained had the above-mentioned transaction (or event) actually occurred earlier.

Exhibit 11 ▶ Sample Paragraph Highlighting Omitted Disclosures (*Pro Forma* Compilation)

Management has elected to omit all of the disclosures ordinarily included in *pro forma* financial information. The omitted disclosures might have added significant information regarding the company's *pro forma* financial position and results of operations. Accordingly, this *pro forma* financial information is not designed for those who are not informed about such matters.

a. **Nature** Examples of *pro forma* financial information include presentations showing the effects of transactions such as: (1) business combinations, (2) changes in capitalization of the reporting entity, (3) dispositions of significant business components, and (4) changes in the form of business organization or status of the reporting entity as an autonomous entity.

b. **Presentation** *Pro forma* financial information should be labeled to distinguish it from historical financial information. The presentation should describe the transaction (or event) that is reflected in the *pro forma* financial information, the source of the historical financial information on which it is based, the significant assumptions used in developing the *pro forma* adjustments, and any significant uncertainties about those assumptions. The presentation also should indicate that the *pro forma* financial information should be read in conjunction with the related historical financial information and that the *pro forma* financial information is not necessarily indicative of the results (such as financial position and results of operations, as applicable) that would have been attained had the transaction (or event) actually taken place earlier.

c. **Historical Financial Statements** The CPA may agree to compile *pro forma* financial information if the document that contains the *pro forma* financial information includes (or incorporates by reference) complete historical financial statements of the reporting entity for the most recent year (or for the preceding year if financial statements for the most recent year are not yet available) and, if *pro forma* financial information is presented for an interim period, the document also includes (or incorporates by reference) historical interim financial information for that period (which may be presented in condensed form).

d. **Business Combination** In the case of a business combination, the document should include (or incorporate by reference) the appropriate historical financial information for the significant constituent parts of the combined entity. Additionally, the historical financial statements of the entity (or, in the case of a business combination, of each significant constituent part of the combined entity) on which the *pro forma* financial information is based must have been compiled, reviewed, or audited.

II. Compilation & Review of Comparative Financial Statements (AR 200)

A. Overview

Comparative financial statements (CFS) are financial statements of two or more periods which are presented in a columnar format. SSARS 2 applies when reporting on comparative financial statements of a nonpublic entity when the financial statements of one or more periods presented have been compiled or reviewed per SSARS 1. The CPA should issue an appropriate report that covers each of the periods presented in the comparative financial statements.

1. **Common Report Elements** The same common report elements required for compilation and review reports on financial statements of a single period are applicable to comparative financial statements.

2. **Continuing Accountant** An accountant engaged to audit, review, or compile the current period's financial statements and has audited, reviewed, or compiled those of one or more consecutive periods immediately prior to the current period.

3. **Updated Report** Issued by the continuing accountant. It takes into account information the continuing accountant becomes aware of during the current engagement. In it, the continuing accountant will either reexpress the previous conclusion on the prior-period statements or, in some cases, express a different conclusion on the prior-period statements as of the date of the continuing CPA's current report.

4. **Reissued Report** Issued after the date of the original report, but bearing the same date as the original report. If it must be revised because of the effects of specific events, it should be dual-dated, using the original date and a separate date that applies to the effects of such events.

5. **Separate Pages** It is permissible for the client to include client-prepared financial statements of some periods that have not been audited, reviewed, or compiled by the CPA on separate pages of a document containing financial statements on which the CPA has issued an audit, review, or compilation report, provided that they are accompanied by an indication from the client that the CPA has not audited, reviewed, or compiled those statements and, therefore, the CPA does not assume any responsibility for them.

6. **Columnar Format** If the CPA becomes aware that, within the CFS, the client has included in a columnar format some information the CPA has not audited, reviewed, or compiled and some that the CPA has, and the report on the latter or the CPA's name is included in the documents containing the CFS, the CPA should advise the client that this is inappropriate. The CPA should consider appropriate action, including consultation with legal counsel.

7. **Modified Report** When financial statements are presented for comparative purposes in columnar form, the CPA may issue an unmodified report on some statements and a modified report on others.

8. **Omission of Disclosures** Statements that omit substantially all disclosures are not comparable to financial statements that include such disclosures. Therefore, the CPA should not issue a report on CFS when statements for some, but not all, of the periods presented omit substantially all required disclosures.

9. **Change of Status (Public/Nonpublic Entity)** A question arises as to whether SAS or SSARS applies when the status of an entity changes. For example, a company is a public entity in the current period, but was a nonpublic entity in the prior period.

    a. **Current Status** The current status of the entity governs when the CPA is reporting on comparative financial statements for either interim or annual periods. If a previously issued report is not appropriate for the current status of the entity, it should **not** be reissued or referred to in the report on the current-period statements.

    b. **Public** It is not appropriate to reissue or refer to the compilation or review report on the prior-period financial statements if the entity is a public entity in the current period but was a nonpublic entity in the prior period (SAS should be followed).

    c. **Nonpublic** If an entity is currently nonpublic and an unaudited disclaimer was issued for the prior period, the disclaimer should not be reissued or referred to in the report on the current statements.

B. Continuing Accountant's Standard Report
Form depends on the level of service (compilation or review) provided with respect to the financial statements presented.

1. **Same or Higher Level of Service in Current Period** The continuing CPA should update the report on the financial statements of a prior period that are presented with those of the current period when the CPA (a) compiled the prior-period statements and the current-period statements, (b) compiled the prior-period statements and reviewed the current statements, or (c) reviewed the prior-period statements and the current-period statements.

Exhibit 12 ▶ Review Each Period

I (We) have reviewed the accompanying balance sheets of XYZ Company as of December 31, 20X2 and 20X1, and the related statements of income, retained earnings, and cash flows for the years then ended, in accordance with Statements on Standards for Accounting and Review Services issued by the American Institute of Certified Public Accountants. All information included in these financial statements is the representation of the management (owners) of XYZ Company.

A review consists principally of inquiries of company personnel and analytical procedures applied to financial data. It is substantially less in scope than an audit in accordance with U.S. generally accepted auditing standards, the objective of which is the expression of an opinion regarding the financial statements taken as a whole. Accordingly, I (we) do not express such an opinion.

Based on my (our) reviews, I am (we are) not aware of any material modifications that should be made to the accompanying financial statements in order for them to be in conformity with U.S. generally accepted accounting principles.

Exhibit 13 ▶ Compilation Each Period

I (We) have compiled the accompanying balance sheets of XYZ Company as of December 31, 20X2 and 20X1 and the related statements of income, retained earnings, and cash flows for the years then ended, in accordance with Statements on Standards for Accounting and Review Services issued by the American Institute of Certified Public Accountants.

A compilation is limited to presenting, in the form of financial statements, information that is the representation of management (owners). I (We) have not audited or reviewed the accompanying financial statements and, accordingly, do not express an opinion or any other form of assurance on them.

Exhibit 14 ▶ Review in Current Period & Compilation in Prior Period

I (We) have reviewed the accompanying balance sheet of XYZ Company as of December 31, 20X2, and the related statements of income, retained earnings, and cash flows for the year then ended, in accordance with Statements on Standards for Accounting and Review Services issued by the American Institute of Certified Public Accountants. All information included in these financial statements is the representation of the management (owners) of XYZ Company.

A review consists principally of inquiries of company personnel and analytical procedures applied to financial data. It is substantially less in scope than an audit in accordance with U.S. generally accepted auditing standards, the objective of which is the expression of an opinion regarding the financial statements taken as a whole. Accordingly, I (we) do not express such an opinion.

Based on my (our) review, I am (we are) not aware of any material modifications that should be made to the 20X2 financial statements in order for them to be in conformity with U.S. generally accepted accounting principles.

> The accompanying 20X1 financial statements of XYZ Company were compiled by me (us). A compilation is limited to presenting, in the form of financial statements, information that is the representation of management (owners). I (We) have not audited or reviewed the 20X1 financial statements and, accordingly, do not express an opinion or any other form of assurance on them.

2. **Lower Level of Service in Current Period** A continuing CPA who has compiled the current-period financial statements and previously reviewed those of the prior period(s) presented for comparative purposes should either issue a compilation report or a combined report. Alternatively, the CPA may separately present the compilation report on the current statements and the review report on the prior period. Both versions of this report should contain a statement that the auditor has not performed any procedures pertaining to the review after the original date of the review report.

Exhibit 15 ▶ Descriptive Paragraph for Compilation Report When Prior-Period Financial Statements Were Reviewed

> The accompanying 20X1 financial statements of XYZ Company were previously reviewed by me (us) and my (our) report dated March 1, 20X2, stated that I was (we were) not aware of any material modifications that should be made to those statements in order for them to be in conformity with U.S. generally accepted accounting principles. I (We) have not performed any procedures in connection with that review engagement after the date of my (our) report on the 20X1 financial statements.

   a. **Compilation Report** The auditor includes, in the compilation report on the current-period financial statements, a paragraph that describes the responsibility the auditor is assuming for the prior-period statements. The description should include the date of the original report.

   b. **Combined Report** The auditor may combine the compilation report on the current-period financial statements with the reissued review report on the prior-period financial statements.

C. **Continuing Accountant's Changed Reference to Departure From GAAP**
Circumstances or events may come to the CPA's attention during the current engagement which affect the prior-period financial statements that are presented (including the adequacy of their disclosure). If the CPA's report on the comparative statements includes a changed reference to a departure from GAAP, a separate explanatory paragraph is included in the report indicating the date of the CPA's previous report, the circumstances or events that caused the CPA to refer to the change and, when applicable, that the prior-period financial statements have been changed.

   • **Changed Reference** Includes a reference that is different from the one made in the previous report, the removal of a prior reference, or the inclusion of a new reference.

Exhibit 16 ▶ Explanatory Paragraph for Changed Reference to GAAP Departure

> In my (our) previous (compilation) (review) report dated March 1, 20X2, on the 20X1 financial statements, I (we) referred to a departure from generally accepted accounting principles because the company carried its land at appraised values. However, as disclosed in note X, the company has restated its 20X1 financial statements to reflect its land at cost in conformity with U.S. generally accepted accounting principles.

D. **Predecessor's Compilation or Review Report**
At the client's request, a predecessor CPA may reissue the compilation or review report on the prior-period financial statements.

Exhibit 17 ▶ Additional Paragraph for Predecessor Compilation

> The 20X1 financial statements of XYZ Company were compiled by other accountants whose report, dated February 1, 20X2, stated that they did not express an opinion or any other form of assurance on those statements.

Exhibit 18 ▶ Additional Paragraph for Predecessor Review

> The 20X1 financial statements of XYZ Company were reviewed by other accountants whose report, dated March 1, 20X2, stated that they were not aware of any material modifications that should be made to those statements in order for them to be in conformity with U.S. generally accepted accounting principles.

1. **Predecessor's Report Not Presented** When a predecessor CPA has compiled or reviewed the financial statements of a prior period (that are presented for comparative purposes) but does not reissue the compilation or review report, the successor CPA should either: (a) perform a compilation, review, or audit of the prior-period financial statements and issue an appropriate report, or (b) include an additional paragraph(s) in the report on the current-period financial statements that makes reference to the predecessor's report on the prior-period financial statements.

   a. **Making Reference to Predecessor's Report** The additional paragraph(s) should include: (1) a statement that another accountant compiled or reviewed the prior-period financial statements (the predecessor should not be named); (2) the date of the predecessor's report; (3) a description of the standard form of disclaimer or limited assurance that appeared in the report; and (4) a description of any modifications that were made to the standard report and of any paragraphs that were included to emphasize a matter(s) in the financial statements.

   b. **Predecessor's Name** SSARS 11 stipulates that the successor accountant should not name the predecessor accountant; however, a successor accountant may name the predecessor accountant if the predecessor accountant's practice was acquired by, or merged with, that of the successor accountant.

2. **Predecessor's Report Reissued** A predecessor considers whether the report on the prior-period financial statements is still appropriate before the predecessor reissues it. In this regard, the predecessor should consider (a) the current form and manner of presentation of the prior-period financial statements, (b) subsequent events that the predecessor was not aware of at the time of the original report, and (c) if there are any changes in the financial statements that would require the predecessor to either add or delete modifications to the standard report. The predecessor should not refer to the successor's letter or report in the reissued report.

   a. **Minimal Procedures** Before reissuance of the compilation or review report of a prior period, the predecessor should (1) read the current-period financial statements and the report of the successor CPA; (2) compare the prior-period financial statements with those that were issued previously and with those of the current period; and (3) obtain a letter from the successor indicating whether any matters came to her/his attention which, in the successor's opinion, might have a material effect on the prior-period statements, including disclosures. The predecessor should obtain a written statement from the former client that states the information currently acquired and its effect on the prior-period financial statements and, if applicable, includes an expression of the former client's understanding of the information's effect on the predecessor's reissued report.

   b. **Additional Procedures** If the predecessor becomes aware of information that may affect the financial statements of the prior period and/or the report on them, the predecessor should make inquiries or perform analytics similar to the ones the predecessor would have performed at the date of the report on the prior-period statements had the predecessor been aware of the information, and perform any other necessary procedures. Examples include discussion with the successor and/or review of the successor's workpapers on the matter.

c. **Date** The date of the previous report should be used when reissuing a report. This avoids any connotation that the predecessor performed any procedures (other than those in a. and b., above) after that date. Dual-dating is appropriate if the predecessor revised the report or if the financial statements are restated (e.g., "March 15, 20X1 except for note X, as to which the date is March 31, 20X2").

d. **Limitation** The predecessor should not reissue the report if the predecessor is unable to complete the procedures described in a., b., and c., above. The predecessor may want to consult legal counsel in deciding the appropriate course of action.

3. **Changed Prior-Period Financial Statements** Either the predecessor or the successor may report on prior-period financial statements that have been changed. It is possible that the restatement may be for reasons other than a change in accounting principles or their application, e.g., a revision to correct an error. In this case, as long as the financial statements adequately disclose the matter, the CPA may decide to include an explanatory paragraph in the report, concerning the restatement. SSARS 12 allows the successor accountant the alternative of reporting on the restatement adjustment while indicating that a predecessor accountant reported on the financial statements of the prior period before restatement.

a. **Predecessor** When reporting, the predecessor should adhere to D.2., above.

b. **Successor** When reporting, the successor should comply with SSARS 1 (or perform an audit). The successor should not refer to the predecessor's previously issued report in the successor's report.

E. **Reporting When One Period Is Audited**

1. **Current-Period Financial Statements Audited** SASs apply when reporting on comparative financial statements in which the current-period statements have been audited and those for one or more prior periods have been compiled or reviewed. AU 504.15 states that when unaudited financial statements are presented in comparative form with audited financial statements, the financial statements that have not been audited should be marked clearly to indicate their status and either (a) the report on the prior period should be reissued or (b) the report on the current period should include, as a separate paragraph, an appropriate description of the responsibility assumed for the unaudited financial statements.

2. **Prior-Period Financial Statements Audited** When a nonpublic entity's current-period financial statements have been compiled or reviewed and the prior-period statements (presented for comparative purposes) have been audited, an appropriate compilation or review report should be issued on the current-period statements. In addition, either the prior-period report should be reissued or a separate paragraph should be added to the current-period's report. If a separate paragraph is used, it should describe the responsibility the CPA is assuming for the financial statements of the prior period. Specifically, a separate paragraph should indicate: (a) that the prior-period's financial statements were audited previously; (b) the date of the previous report; (c) the type of opinion that was expressed previously; (d) if the previous opinion was not unqualified, the substantive reasons for this; and (e) that no auditing procedures have been performed since the date of the previous report.

Exhibit 19 ▶ Prior-Period Financial Statements Audited Separate Paragraph

> The financial statements for the year ended December 31, 20X1, were audited by us (other accountants) and we (they) expressed an unqualified opinion on them in our (their) report date March 1, 20X2, but we (they) have not performed any auditing procedures since that date.

F. **Reporting on Financial Statements That Previously Did Not Omit Disclosures**
Even though a CPA may have compiled, reviewed, or audited financial statements that did not omit substantially all required disclosures, the CPA may later be asked to compile financial statements for the same period that **do** omit substantially all the disclosures required by GAAP so that the statements can be presented in comparative financial statements. In this case, the CPA may report on these statements as long as an additional paragraph is included in the report that indicates the nature of the previous service and the date of the previous report.

Exhibit 20 ▶ Prior-Period Statements Omitting Substantially All Disclosures Compiled From Previously Reviewed Statements

> I (We) have compiled the accompanying balance sheet of XYZ Company as of December 31, 20X2, and the related statements of income, retained earnings, and cash flows for the year then ended, in accordance with Statements on Standards for Accounting and Review Services issued by the American Institute of Certified Public Accountants.
>
> A compilation is limited to presenting, in the form of financial statements, information that is the representation of management (owners). I (We) have not audited or reviewed the accompanying financial statements and, accordingly, do not express an opinion or any other form of assurance on them.
>
> Management has elected to omit substantially all the disclosures required by U.S. generally accepted accounting principles. If the omitted disclosures were included in the financial statements, they might influence the user's conclusions about the company's financial position, results of operations, and cash flows. Accordingly, these financial statements are not designed for those who are not informed about such matters.
>
> The accompanying 20X1 financial statements were compiled by me (us) from financial statements that did not omit substantially all the disclosures required by U.S. generally accepted accounting principles and that I (we) previously reviewed as indicated in my (our) report dated March 1, 20X2.

III. Overview of Attestation Standards (AT 101)

A. **Attestation Engagements**
Statements on Standards for Attestation Engagements (SSAE) 10 defines an attest engagement as one in which a CPA in public practice (or practitioner) is engaged to, or does, issue an **examination, review,** or **agreed-upon procedures** report on subject matter or an assertion about subject matter that is the responsibility of another party. In our coverage, guidelines for AT 101 are applicable to all attest engagements, unless otherwise stated; guidelines in other sections are applicable only to the subject matter in that particular section, unless otherwise stated.

1. **Practitioner** Throughout this discussion of attest standards, unless otherwise stated, the terms "CPA" and "practitioner" signify an independent CPA in public practice.

2. **Degrees of Responsibility** SSAE 13 (AT 20) defines two kinds of requirements that describe the practitioner's degrees of responsibility.

a. **Unconditional Requirements** The practitioner is required to comply with an unconditional requirement in all cases in which the requirement applies. The words must or is required indicate an unconditional requirement.

b.   **Presumptively Mandatory Requirements** The practitioner is also required to comply with a presumptively mandatory requirement in all cases in which the requirement applies. However, in rare circumstances, the practitioner may depart from such a requirement provided the practitioner documents the justification in the workpapers and the alternative procedures performed to achieve the objectives of that requirement. The word should indicates a presumptively mandatory requirement.

3.   **Other Engagements** When the practitioner performs an attest engagement for a government and agrees to follow specified governmental standards, the practitioner must follow those standards in addition to SSAE standards. An attest engagement may be part of a larger engagement, for example, a feasibility study or business acquisition study that includes an examination of prospective financial information. In such circumstances, these standards apply only to the attest portion of the engagement. Any report issued by a practitioner under other professional standards should be clearly distinguishable from attest reports.

4.   **Inapplicable Engagements** A CPA may perform several services outside the scope of the attestation standards, including engagements: (a) performed in accordance with SAS, (b) performed in accordance with SSARS, (c) performed in accordance with SSCS, (d) client advocacy engagements (e.g., as before the IRS), and (e) tax advice and return preparation services.

5.   **Subject Matter** The subject matter of an attest engagement may take many forms, including: (a) historical or prospective performance or condition (e.g., historical or prospective financial information, performance measurements, backlog data); (b) physical characteristics (e.g., descriptions, square footage of facilities); (c) historical events (e.g., the market price of products or services at a specific time); (d) analyses (e.g., break-even analyses, target profit levels); (e) systems and processes (e.g., internal control); and (f) behavior (e.g., corporate governance, compliance with laws and regulations, human resource practices).

6.   **Written Assertion** An assertion is any declaration(s) about whether subject matter is based on, or in conformity with, selected criteria. A CPA may attest to a written assertion or directly on the subject matter. In either situation, the CPA typically obtains a written assertion in an examination or a review engagement. A written assertion may be presented to the CPA in several ways, including: a narrative description, a schedule, or as part of a representation letter which clearly identifies what is being presented and the point in time or period of time covered. Without a written assertion, the CPA still may report on the subject matter; however, the CPA needs to exercise caution and ensure that interested parties clearly understand the subject matter in question, including restricting use of the report, when appropriate.

7.   **Subsequent Events** Subsequent events are defined by AT 101 in the same manner as for audits. While the practitioner has no responsibility to detect subsequent events, the practitioner should inquire of the responsible party (and the client, if different) as to whether they are aware of any subsequent events through the report date. The representation letter ordinarily contains a representation about subsequent events. The practitioner may later become aware of conditions that existed at that date that might have affected the report had the practitioner been aware of them. In this situation, the practitioner considers the guidance in the auditing standards (AU 561).

8.   **Quality Control Standards** Attest standards relate to the conduct of individual engagements; quality control standards relate to the conduct of a firm's attest practice as a whole. Attestation standards and quality control standards are related and the quality control policies and procedures that a firm adopts may affect both the conduct of individual attest engagements and the conduct of a firm's attest practice. SSAE 12 clarifies that although an effective quality control system is conducive to compliance with attestation standards, deficiencies in, or noncompliance with, a firm's quality control system do not, in and of themselves, indicate that an engagement was not performed in accordance with the applicable professional standards.

B.   Responsible Party
The CPA attests to either a written assertion or subject matter that is the representation of a responsible party. The responsible party is the person or persons who are responsible for the subject matter. The responsible party may be the management of the client entity or it may be another party (such as the management of an entity seeking to sell a property to the client).

1.   **No Responsible Party** Due to the nature of the subject matter, there may be no obvious responsible party. In that situation, a party who has a reasonable basis for making a written assertion about the subject matter becomes the responsible party. Practitioners may be engaged to gather information to enable the responsible party to evaluate the subject matter in connection with providing a written assertion. Regardless of the procedures performed by the CPA, the responsible party must accept responsibility for the assertion and the subject matter and must not base that assertion solely on procedures performed by the CPA. Because of the CPA's attest role, the CPA may **not** assume the role of the responsible party in an attest engagement.

2.   **Prerequisite** The identification of a responsible party is a prerequisite for an attest engagement. A CPA may accept an engagement to perform an examination, a review, or an agreed-upon procedures engagement on subject matter or a written assertion provided that **one** of the following conditions is met:

   a.   The party wishing to engage the CPA is responsible for the subject matter, or has a reasonable basis for providing a written assertion about the subject matter if the nature of the subject matter is such that a responsible party does not otherwise exist.

   b.   The party wishing to engage the CPA is not responsible for the subject matter but is able to (or have a third party who is responsible for the subject matter) provide the CPA with evidence of the third party's responsibility for the subject matter.

3.   **Acknowledgment** The CPA should obtain written acknowledgment or other evidence of the responsible party's responsibility for the subject matter or the written assertion, as it relates to the engagement. The responsible party can acknowledge that responsibility in a number of ways including in an engagement letter, a representation letter, the presentation of the subject matter, or a written assertion. If the CPA is not able to obtain direct written acknowledgment, the CPA should obtain other evidence of the responsible party's responsibility for the subject matter (e.g., by reference to legislation, regulation, or contract).

C.   General Standards
Note that three of the five general standards parallel the three auditing general standards.

1.   **Training** The practitioner must have adequate technical training and proficiency to perform the attestation engagement.

2.   **Knowledge** The practitioner must have adequate knowledge in the subject matter. The CPA may use specialists, provided that the CPA has enough knowledge of the subject matter (1) to communicate to the specialist the objectives of the work, and (2) to evaluate the specialist's work to determine if the objectives were achieved.

3.   **Criteria** The practitioner must have reason to believe that the subject matter is capable of evaluation against criteria that are suitable and available to users. Suitable criteria must be objective, measurable, complete, and relevant.

   a.   Criteria promulgated by a body designated by Council under the AICPA Code of Professional Conduct are considered suitable criteria by definition. Criteria issued by regulatory agencies and other bodies of experts that follow due-process procedures also are considered suitable. Criteria issued by industry associations or other groups should be examined critically for suitability. Such criteria should be described clearly in the presentation.

    b.   Competent persons using the same or similar criteria ordinarily should be able to obtain materially similar estimates or measurements. However, competent persons will not always reach the same conclusions because: (1) measurements often require exercise of considerable professional judgment, and (2) a slightly different evaluation of the facts could yield a significant difference in the conclusion.

    c.   Criteria may be available to users in several ways. If criteria availability is limited, the practitioner's report must be restricted to those who have access.

  4.   **Independence** The practitioner must maintain independence in mental attitude in all matters relating to the engagement.

  5.   **Due Professional Care** The practitioner must exercise due professional care in the planning and performance of the engagement and the preparation of the report.

D.   **Fieldwork Standards**
Note that these two standards are similar to two of the three auditing fieldwork standards.

  1.   **Planning & Supervision** The practitioner must adequately plan the work and must properly supervise any assistants. An understanding with the client as to the services to be performed must be reached.

  2.   **Evidence** The practitioner must obtain sufficient evidence to provide a reasonable basis for the conclusion that is expressed in the report.

    a.   **Documentation** The quantity, type, and content of workpapers will vary with the situation. (An examination will require more evidence than a review.) A CPA prepares and retains workpapers during attest engagements that are appropriate to the situation and the CPA's needs. (The guidance regarding attest workpapers is similar to that for audit workpapers.) Workpapers should be sufficient to document that: (1) work was adequately planned and supervised; and (2) the CPA obtained evidential matter providing a reasonable basis for the conclusion expressed in the CPA's report.

    b.   **Representations** If the client or responsible party refuses to furnish appropriate written representations, the CPA should consider the effects of this refusal on her/his ability to rely on other representations. If the representation letter is necessary evidence for reporting, this refusal constitutes a scope limitation on the examination sufficient to require a qualified opinion, a disclaimer of an opinion, or withdrawal from the engagement.

E.   **Reporting Standards**
SSAE 10 provides for three types of attestation engagements: examinations, reviews, and applications of agreed-upon procedures. Reports on examination or review engagements may be used by the general public. Use of reports on agreed-upon procedures are restricted to the use of parties who have agreed to the specified procedures.

  1.   **Identification** The practitioner must identify the subject matter or the assertion being reported on and state the character of the engagement in the report. If the attestation is on an assertion, the assertion must accompany, or be restated within, the CPA's report. The statement of the character of an attest engagement designed to result in a general-use report (i.e., an examination or a review) includes two elements: (a) a description of the nature and scope of the work performed, and (b) a reference to the professional (AICPA) standards governing the engagement.

  2.   **Conclusion** The practitioner must state the practitioner's conclusion about the subject matter or the assertion in relation to the criteria against which the subject matter was evaluated in the report.

a. **Misstatements** If deviations from the criteria or material misstatements exist, the practitioner should modify the report, directly expressing an opinion on the subject matter, rather than the assertion.

b. **Materiality** The CPA should consider the idea of materiality in applying this standard. Materiality is determined by the relative size of a misstated or omitted fact, rather than by its absolute amount. Materiality would consider whether a reasonable person relying on the presentation of assertions would be influenced by the inclusion or correction of an individual assertion.

c. **Use** General-use attest reports are limited to two levels of assurance: one based on a reduction of attestation risk to an appropriately low level (an "examination") and the other based on a reduction of attestation risk to a moderate level (a "review").

   (1) **Examinations** A practitioner selects, from all available procedures, any combination that restricts attest risk to an appropriately low level. A conclusion is expressed in the form of a **positive** opinion.

   (2) **Reviews** Procedures typically are limited to inquiries and analytical procedures. The conclusion is expressed in the form of **limited** assurance.

3. **Reservations** The practitioner must state all of the practitioner's significant reservations about the engagement subject matter and, if applicable, the assertion related thereto in the report.

   a. **Unresolved Problem** "Reservations about the engagement" refers to any unresolved problem the CPA had in complying with the standards and guidance applicable to attestation services or procedures agreed to by the specified parties. An unqualified conclusion should not be expressed if the CPA has been unable to apply all the procedures considered necessary to comply with attestation standards.

   b. **Scope Restrictions** Restrictions on the scope of the engagement, whether imposed by the client or by other circumstances, may require the CPA to qualify the report, to disclaim any assurance, or to withdraw from the engagement. The decision as to the appropriate course of action depends on the effect of the omitted procedure(s) on the CPA's ability to express assurance on the presentation of assertions. When restrictions that significantly limit the scope of the engagement are imposed by the client, the CPA generally should either withdraw from the engagement or disclaim any assurance on the subject matter, assertions, or presentation. An incomplete **review** engagement requires the CPA to withdraw.

4. **Restrictions** AT 101 does **not** prohibit a practitioner from restricting the use of any report. The fourth standard of reporting is as follows: The practitioner must state in the report that the report is intended solely for the information and use of the specified parties under the following circumstances:

   • When the criteria used to evaluate the subject matter are determined by the practitioner to be appropriate only for a limited number of parties who either participated in their establishment or can be presumed to have an adequate understanding of the criteria

   • When the criteria used to evaluate the subject matter are available only to specified parties

   • When reporting on subject matter and a written assertion has not been provided by the responsible party

   • When the report is on an attestation engagement to apply agreed-upon procedures to the subject matter

When a report is restricted as to use, it contains a separate final paragraph that includes the following types of statements: (a) indicate the report is intended solely for the use of the specified parties, (b) identify the specified parties, and (c) indicate the report is not intended to be, and should not be, used by anyone other than the specified parties.

5. **Other Information in Client-Prepared Document** The client may publish documents containing information in addition to the practitioner's attest report and the related assertion. This guidance is inapplicable if the practitioner or another practitioner is engaged to issue an opinion on the other information or when the other information appears in a registration statement filed under the Securities Act of 1933.

   a. The practitioner's responsibility doesn't extend beyond the information identified in the practitioner's report or by the report of another practitioner. The practitioner should read the other information in the document and consider whether it, or the manner of its presentation, is materially inconsistent with the information appearing in the practitioner's report.

   b. If the practitioner is aware of inconsistencies with the other information, either the practitioner's report or the other information should be revised. If the practitioner believes the other information must be changed, and it is not, the practitioner should consider other actions: adding an explanatory paragraph to the practitioner's report, withholding the use of the report in the document, or withdrawal.

   c. If the practitioner is aware of an apparent material misstatement of fact in the other information, the practitioner should discuss such concerns with the client. If a valid basis for concern remains, the practitioner should propose the client consult with another party whose advice may be useful (for example, legal counsel). If a valid basis for concern remains after discussion, the practitioner should consider consulting legal counsel and notifying the client's management and audit committee of the practitioner's views.

6. **Common Report Components** Standard reports for examinations and reviews share some elements:

   a. **Title** The title includes the word *independent.*

   b. **Responsible Party's Responsibility** A statement that the *subject matter* [or, assertion] is the responsible party's responsibility.

   c. **Identification** An identification of the *subject matter* [or, assertion] and the responsible party. When reporting on the assertion, if the assertion doesn't accompany the practitioner's report, the first paragraph of the report also contains a statement of the assertion.

   d. **Restriction** A statement restricting the report use to specified parties under the following situations:

      (1) **Suitability** When the practitioner determines the criteria used to evaluate the subject matter are appropriate only for a limited number of parties who either participated in criteria development or can be inferred to have an adequate understanding of the criteria.

      (2) **Availability** When the criteria used to evaluate the subject matter are available only to specified parties.

      (3) **Written Assertion** When a written assertion was not provided by the responsible party.

   e. **Signature & Date** The practitioner's manual or printed signature. The date of the completion of the procedures.

F.   Examinations

Examinations represent the highest level of assurance. When CPAs are engaged to express an opinion as the result of an attestation engagement, they should state clearly whether: (1) management's assertion is presented (or fairly stated), in all material respects, based on (or in conformity with) the established/stated criteria, or (2) the subject matter of the assertion is based on (or in conformity with) the established or stated criteria in all material respects. SSAE 10 doesn't prohibit a practitioner from examining the assertion and providing an opinion on the subject matter.

Exhibit 21 ▶ Examination Report on Subject Matter

> We have examined the [identify the subject matter—for example, the accompanying schedule of investment returns of X Company for the year ended December 31, 20X1]. X Company's management is responsible for the schedule of investment returns. Our responsibility is to express an opinion based on our examination.
>
> Our examination was made in accordance with attestation standards established by the American Institute of Certified Public Accountants and, accordingly, included examining, on a test basis, evidence supporting [identify the subject matter—for example, X Company's schedule of investment returns] and performing such other procedures as we considered necessary in the circumstances. We believe our examination provides a reasonable basis for our opinion.
>
> [Additional paragraph(s) may be added to emphasize certain matters relating to the attest engagement or the subject matter.]
>
> In our opinion, the schedule referred to above presents, in all material respects, [identify the subject matter—for example, the schedule of investment returns of X Company for the year ended December 31, 20X1] in conformity with [identify established or stated criteria—for example, the ABC criteria set forth in Note 1].

1.   **Modifications**   Reports expressing a positive opinion on the reliability of an assertion may be qualified or modified for an aspect of the subject matter, assertion, or the engagement. In addition, examination reports may emphasize certain matters relating to the attest engagement, subject matter, or assertion. Remember, if deviations from the criteria or material misstatements exist, the practitioner should modify the report, directly expressing an opinion on the **subject matter,** rather than the **assertion.**

2.   **Report Components**   The practitioner reports on either the subject matter or the assertion. The practitioner's examination report includes the following:

a.   **Responsibility**   A statement that the practitioner's responsibility is to express an opinion on the *subject matter* [or, assertion] based on the practitioner's examination.

b.   **Standards**   A statement that the examination was performed in accordance with attestation standards established by the AICPA, and, accordingly, included procedures that the practitioner considered necessary in the situation.

c.   **Basis**   A statement that the practitioner believes the examination provides a reasonable basis for her/his opinion.

d.   **Conclusion**   The practitioner's opinion on whether the *subject matter is based on (or in conformity with)* [or, the assertion is presented (or fairly stated) based on] the criteria in all material respects.

G.   Reviews

A review report provides **limited** assurance. The CPA's report states whether any information came to the CPA's attention on the basis of the work performed that indicates that the subject matter is materially misstated or divergent from criteria; or that assertions are **not** presented in all material respects in conformity with criteria. The report: (1) indicates that the work performed was less in scope than an examination, (2) disclaims a positive opinion on the assertions, and (3) contains a statement of limitations on the use of the report when it has been prepared in conformity with specified criteria that have been agreed upon by the specified parties because it is intended solely for specified parties. The practitioner reports on either the subject matter or the assertion. The practitioner's review report includes the following:

1. **Standards** A statement that the review was performed in accordance with attestation standards established by the AICPA.

2. **Disclaimer** A statement that a review is substantially less in scope than an examination, the objective of which is an expression of an opinion on the subject matter [or, assertion], and accordingly, no such opinion is expressed.

3. **Conclusion** A statement about whether the practitioner is aware of any material modifications that should be made to the *subject matter in order for it to be based on (or in conformity with), in all material respects,* [or, assertion in order for it to be presented (or fairly stated) in all material respects, based on (or in conformity with)] the criteria, other than those modifications, if any, indicated in the practitioner's report.

Exhibit 22 ▶ Restricted Review Report

We have reviewed management's assertion that [identify the assertion—for example, the accompanying schedule of investment returns of XYZ Company for the year ended December 31, 20X1, is presented in accordance with the ABC criteria referred to in Note 1]. XYZ Company's management is responsible for the schedule of investment returns.

Our review was conducted in accordance with attestation standards established by the American Institute of Certified Public Accountants. A review is substantially less in scope than an examination, the objective of which is the expression of an opinion on management's assertion. Accordingly, we do not express such an opinion.

[Additional paragraph(s) may be added to emphasize certain matters.]

Based on our review, nothing came to our attention that caused us to believe that management's assertion referred to above is not fairly stated, in all material respects, based on [identify the criteria—for example, the ABC criteria referred to in the investment management agreement between XYZ Company and DEF Investment Managers, dated November 15, 20X1].

This report is intended solely for the information and use of XYZ Company and [identify other specified parties—for example, DEF Investment Managers] and is not intended to be and should not be used by anyone other than these specified parties.

IV. **Guidance for Particular Attest Engagements**

A. **Agreed-Upon Procedures (AT 201)**
An agreed-upon procedures engagement is one in which a practitioner is engaged to issue a report of findings based on specific procedures performed on subject matter. A client engages the practitioner to assist specified parties in evaluating subject matter or an assertion as a result of needs of specified parties. The specified parties and the practitioner agree upon procedures to be performed by the practitioner that the specified parties believe are appropriate. The nature, timing and extent of procedures may vary widely. The specified parties assume responsibility for the sufficiency of the procedures since they best understand their own needs. The practitioner does not provide an opinion or negative assurance. Instead, the practitioner's report on agreed-upon procedures should be in the form of procedures and findings. A practitioner's report on such engagements should indicate clearly that its use is **restricted** to those specified parties. A written assertion is **not** required for engagements covered by AT 201, unless required by another attest standard section. (See Exhibit 23)

1. **Required Conditions for Engagements** To satisfy the agreement and responsibility requirements enumerated here, the practitioner ordinarily communicates directly with, and obtains affirming acknowledgments from, each specified party. If there is no such communication, the

practitioner may find other procedures adequate, such as: (a) comparing proposed procedures to written requirements from specified parties; (b) discussing procedures with appropriate representatives of specified parties; or (c) reviewing relevant contracts with, or correspondence from, specified parties.

a. **Responsibility** The specified parties take responsibility for the adequacy of the procedures for their purpose, plus a party responsible for the subject matter (either the client or third party, see AT 101 coverage) exists.

b. **Agreement** The specified parties and the practitioner agree upon procedures to be performed and the criteria to be used in the determination of findings.

c. **Suitability** The specific subject matter is subject to reasonably consistent measurement. The procedures are expected to result in reasonably consistent findings using the criteria. Evidential matter related to the specific subject matter is expected to exist to provide a reasonable basis for expressing findings in the practitioner's report.

d. **Materiality** Where applicable, the practitioner and the specified parties agree on any materiality limits; these are described in the practitioner's report.

e. **Use** Use of the report is restricted to the specified parties.

f. **Disclosure** For engagements involving prospective financial information, prospective financial statements include a summary of significant assumptions.

2. **Nature** The requirements of the attest standards, except the second reporting standard, are applicable. A management representation letter is optional.

a. **Specialist** The specified parties and the practitioner must agree explicitly on the involvement of a specialist.

b. **Internal Auditors & Other Personnel** The agreed-upon procedures are to be performed entirely by the practitioner and any assisting specialists; however, internal auditors or other client personnel may prepare schedules or provide other information for the practitioner's use in performing the procedures.

3. **Findings** The practitioner reports all findings from applying the agreed-upon procedures. The concept of materiality is inapplicable unless the specified parties and the practitioner have established a definition of materiality.

4. **Report Components** In addition to elements listed in paragraph III., E., 6., the practitioner's report contains the following:

a. **Nature** An identification of the character of the engagement.

b. **Responsibility** A statement that the sufficiency of the procedures is solely the specified parties' responsibility. A disclaimer of responsibility on the part of the practitioner for the sufficiency of the procedures.

c. **Description** A list of, or reference to, the procedures performed and related findings.

d. **Materiality** Where applicable, a description of any agreed-upon materiality limits.

e. **Disclaimer** A statement that the practitioner did not conduct an examination of the subject matter, the objective of which would be the expression of an opinion on the subject matter, and a statement that if the practitioner had performed additional procedures, other matters might have come to her/his attention that would have been reported.

f. **Restriction** A statement restricting the report use because it is intended solely for the use of specified parties (see the fourth reporting standard).

g. **Limitations** Where applicable, reservations or restrictions concerning procedures or findings.

h. **Prospective Financial Information** Where applicable, items required by AT 301.

i. **Specialist** Where applicable, a description of the assistance provided by a specialist.

Exhibit 23 ▶ Report on Agreed-Upon Procedures

To the Board of Directors and Management of ABC, Inc.

We have performed the procedures enumerated below, which were agreed to by the board of directors and management of ABC Inc., solely to assist you in connection with the proposed acquisition of XYZ Company as of December 31, 20X1. XYZ Company is responsible for its cash and accounts receivable records. This agreed-upon procedures engagement was performed in accordance with standards established by the American Institute of Certified Public Accountants. The sufficiency of these procedures is solely the responsibility of the parties specified in this report. Consequently, we make no representation regarding the sufficiency of the procedures described below either for the purpose for which this report has been requested or for any other purpose.

The procedures and associated findings are as follows:

(1) We reconciled cash on deposit with the following banks to the balances in the respective general ledger accounts and obtained confirmation of the related balances from the banks.

Bank	Balance Per General Ledger
First National Bank	$ 5,000
DEF State Bank	13,776
Sun Trust Company—regular account	86,912
Sun Trust Company—payroll account	5,000

(2) We obtained an aged trial balance of the accounts receivable subsidiary records; traced the age and amounts of approximately 10 percent of the accounts to the accounts receivable ledger; and added the trial balance and compared the total with the balance in the general ledger control account. We mailed requests for positive confirmation of balances to 150 customers. The differences disclosed in confirmation replies were minor in amount and nature and we reconciled them to our satisfaction. The results are summarized as follows:

	Accounts Receivable Aging and Confirmation Results		
	Account Balance	Requested	Received
Current:	$156,000	$ 76,000	$ 65,000
Past due:			
Less than one month	60,000	30,000	19,000
One to three months	36,000	18,000	10,000
Over three months	48,000	48,000	8,000
	$300,000	$172,000	$102,000

We were not engaged to, and did not, perform an audit, the objective of which would be the expression of an opinion on the cash and accounts receivable of XYZ Company. Accordingly, we do not express such an opinion. Had we performed additional procedures, other matters might have come to our attention that would have been reported to you.

This report is intended solely for the use of the board of directors and management of ABC, Inc., and is not intended to be, and should not be, used by anyone other than these specified parties.

5. **Explanatory Language** The practitioner may include explanations about issues such as the following: (a) disclosures of stipulated facts, assumptions, or interpretations used in applying procedures; (b) condition of records, controls, or data; (c) a statement that the practitioner has no responsibility to update the report.

6. **Scope Limitations** When the situation imposes restrictions on the performance of procedures, the practitioner should obtain agreement from the specified parties to modify the agreed-upon procedures, describe any restrictions in the report, or withdraw from the engagement.

7. **Additional Specified Parties** After completing an engagement, a practitioner may add another party as a specified party, considering such factors as used in determining the original specified parties. If the report is reissued, the practitioner does not change the date.

8. **Outside Knowledge** The practitioner need not perform additional procedures, but if a matter comes to the practitioner's attention that significantly contradicts the subject matter, the practitioner should include this matter in the report.

9. **Request to Change Engagement Type** If the practitioner concludes, based on professional judgment, that there is reasonable justification to change the engagement, and provided the practitioner complies with the standards applicable to that engagement, the practitioner issues the report appropriate to the new engagement type. This report should not include reference to either the original engagement or performance limitations that resulted in a different engagement. If the original engagement procedures are substantially complete or the effort to do so is relatively insignificant, the practitioner should evaluate the propriety of an engagement change.

10. **Combined Reports** The reports on applying agreed-upon procedures may be combined with reports on other services, provided the types of services can be distinguished clearly and applicable guidance for each service is followed.

B. **Financial Forecasts & Projections (AT 301)**
    AT 301 establishes guidance concerning performance and reporting for engagements to examine, compile, or apply agreed-upon procedures to prospective financial statements (PFS).

    1. **Applicability** The guidance applies to a CPA who submits (to the client or others) PFS that the CPA has assembled or assisted in assembling, or reports on PFS, if such statements are (or reasonably might be) expected to be used by a third party. In deciding whether the PFS are (or reasonably might be) expected to be used by a third party, the CPA may rely on either the written or oral representation of the responsible party, unless contradictory information comes to her/his attention. An exception to this guidance exists for litigation support services, because the practitioner's work is subject to detailed analysis and challenge by parties to the dispute. This exception is inapplicable when either all third parties do not have opportunity for analysis and challenge or if the practitioner is engaged specifically to issue a report on PFS.

    2. **Preparation** The practitioner's work may not be described as including *preparation* of the PFS. The practitioner may assist the responsible party in identifying assumptions, gathering information, or assembling the statements. The responsible party still has sole responsibility for the preparation and presentation of the PFS, because the PFS are dependent on the responsible party's actions, plans, and assumptions. A practitioner may prepare a financial analysis, including collecting information, forming assumptions, and assembling a presentation. Such an analysis is inappropriate for general use and is not a forecast or projection. If the responsible party reviews and adopts the assumptions and presentation, or bases assumptions and a presentation on the analysis, the practitioner may perform an AT 301 engagement and issue a report appropriate for general use.

3. **Definitions**

a. **Prospective Financial Statements (PFS)** Either financial forecasts or financial projections that include summaries of significant assumptions and accounting policies (does not include *pro forma* financial statements or partial presentations).

b. **Partial Presentation** A presentation of prospective financial information omitting required elements of PFS.

c. **Financial Forecast** PFS that present, to the best of the responsible party's knowledge and belief, an entity's expected financial position, results of operations, and cash flows. A financial forecast may be expressed in specific monetary amounts as a single-point estimate of forecasted results or as a range, where the responsible party selects key assumptions to form a range within which it reasonably expects, to the best of its knowledge and belief, the item or items subject to the assumptions actually to fall.

d. **Financial Projection** PFS that present, to the best of the responsible party's knowledge and belief, given one or more hypothetical assumptions, an entity's expected financial position, results of operations, and cash flows. A financial projection sometimes is prepared to present one or more hypothetical courses of action for evaluation. It answers the question, "What would happen if...?" A financial projection is based on the responsible party's assumptions reflecting conditions it expects would exist and the course of action it expects would be taken, given one or more hypothetical assumptions. It may also contain a range.

e. **Entity** Any unit, existing or to be formed, for which financial statements could be prepared in conformity with GAAP or OCBOA.

f. **Hypothetical Assumption** An assumption used in a financial projection to present a condition or course of action that is not necessarily expected to occur, but is consistent with the purpose of the projection.

g. **Responsible Party** The person or persons who are responsible for the assumptions underlying the prospective financial statements, usually management. It can be persons outside the entity who currently do not have authority to direct operations.

h. **Assembly** Processing related to the presentation of prospective financial statements.

i. **Key Factors** The significant matters on which an entity's future results are expected to depend. Key factors are the bases for assumptions.

j. **Materiality** Materiality is a concept that is judged in the light of the expected range of reasonableness of the information. Users should not expect prospective information to be as precise as historical information.

4. **Uses of PFS**

a. **General Use** Refers to the use of PFS by persons with whom the responsible party is not negotiating directly. Since users are unable to ask questions of the responsible party, the presentation most useful to them is one that portrays, to the best of the responsible party's knowledge and belief, the expected results. Only a financial forecast is appropriate for general use.

b. **Limited Use** Refers to the use of PFS by the responsible party alone or by the responsible party and third parties with whom the responsible party is negotiating directly. Third-party recipients of PFS intended for limited use can ask questions of the responsible party and directly negotiate terms with it. Any type of PFS that would be useful in the circumstances normally is appropriate for limited use. The presentation may be a financial forecast **or** a financial projection.

5. **Partial Presentations** The practitioner's procedures in an engagement connected with a partial presentation is affected by the nature of the information presented. The scope for an examination or compilation of some partial presentations may be similar to that for the examination or compilation of a presentation of PFS. Reports on partial presentations of both forecasted and projected information should include a description of any limitations of the usefulness of the presentation.

6. **Common Report Elements** Standard reports for the three engagements share some elements: (a) a caveat that the prospective results might **not** be achieved; (b) a statement that the CPA assumes no responsibility to update the report for events and circumstances occurring after the date of the report; (c) the practitioner's signature; and (d) the date of the completion of the CPA's procedures.

7. **Compilation of PFS** A compilation of PFS involves (a) assembling, to the extent necessary, the PFS based on the responsible party's assumptions, (b) performing the required compilation procedures, including reading the statements and considering whether they are appropriate and are presented in conformity with AICPA presentation guidelines, and (c) issuing a compilation report. Independence is **not** necessary for a compilation engagement.

    a. **Limited Procedures** A compilation is not intended to provide assurance on the PFS or the assumptions underlying such statements. Because of the limited nature of the CPA's procedures, a compilation does not provide assurance that the CPA will become aware of significant matters that might be disclosed by more extensive procedures.

    b. **Assumptions** Since this summary is essential to the reader's understanding of PFS, the CPA should not compile PFS that exclude disclosure of the summary of significant assumptions. Also, the CPA should not compile a financial projection that omits (1) an identification of the hypothetical assumptions or (2) a description of the limitations on the usefulness of the presentation.

    c. **Obviously Inappropriate** The practitioner should consider when representations or other information appear to be obviously inappropriate, incomplete, etc., and if so, should attempt to clarify the matter. If the matter is not clarified, the practitioner ordinarily withdraws from the engagement.

8. **Compilation Reports** In addition to the previously discussed elements, the standard compilation report includes: (a) identification of the PFS presented by the responsible party; (b) a statement that the CPA has compiled the PFS in accordance with attestation standards established by the AICPA; and (c) a statement that a compilation is limited in scope and does not enable the CPA to express an opinion or any other form of assurance on the PFS or the assumptions.

Exhibit 24 ▶ Compilation Report on a Forecast (Projection)

We have compiled the accompanying *forecasted* [projected] balance sheet, statements of income, retained earnings, and cash flows of XYZ Company as of December 31, 20X1, and for the year then ending, in accordance with standards established by the American Institute of Certified Public Accountants. [The accompanying projection and this report were prepared for the information and use of (state special purpose, for example, "the DEF National Bank for the purpose of negotiating a loan to expand XYZ Company's plant").]

A compilation is limited to presenting in the form of a forecast [projection] information that is the representation of management and does not include evaluation of the support for the assumptions underlying the projection. We have not examined the forecast [projection] and, accordingly, do not express an opinion or any other form of assurance on the accompanying statements or assumptions. Furthermore, [even if (describe hypothetical assumption, for example, "the loan is granted and the plant is expanded,")] there will usually be differences between the forecasted [projected] and actual results, because events and circumstances frequently do not occur as expected, and those differences may be material. We have no responsibility to update this report for events and circumstances occurring after the date of this report.

<Additional paragraph for a projection report>

The accompanying projection and this report are intended solely for the information and use of (identify specified parties, for example, "XYZ Company and DEF National Bank") and is not intended to be and should not be used by anyone other than these specified parties.

a. **Projection Presentation** The practitioner's report should include a separate paragraph that describes the limitations on the usefulness of the presentation.

b. **Range** When the PFS contain a range, the practitioner's report also should include a separate paragraph that states that the responsible party has elected to portray the expected results of one or more assumptions as a range.

Exhibit 25 ▶ Separate Paragraph for Forecast Containing Range

As described in the summary of significant assumptions, management of XYZ company has elected to portray forecasted [describe financial statement element or elements for which the expected results of one or more assumptions fall within a range, and identify the assumptions expected to fall within a range, for example, "revenue at the amounts $X,XXX and $Y,YYY, which is predicated upon occupancy rates of XX percent and YY percent of available apartments,"] rather than as a single point estimate. Accordingly, the accompanying forecast presents forecasted financial position, results of operations, and cash flows [describe one or more assumptions expected to fall within a range, for example, "at such occupancy rates"]. However, there is no assurance that the actual results will fall within the range [describe one or more assumptions expected to fall within a range, for example, "occupancy rates"] presented.

c. **Emphasis** In some circumstances, a CPA may wish to expand the report to emphasize a matter regarding the PFSs. Such information may be presented in a separate paragraph of the CPA's report. However, the CPA should exercise care that emphasizing such a matter does not give the impression that the CPA is expressing assurance or expanding the degree of responsibility the CPA is taking regarding such information.

d. **Historical Financial Information** PFS may be included in a document that also includes historical financial statements (HFS) with a related practitioner's report. Additionally, HFS may be summarized and presented with PFS for comparative purposes.

Exhibit 26 ▶ Paragraph for Forecast Presented With Historical Information

The historical financial statements for the year ended December 31, 20X1, and our report thereon are set forth on pages XX-YY of this document.

e. **Independence** A CPA may compile PFS for an entity with respect to which a CPA is not independent. In such circumstances, the CPA should disclose this lack specifically; however, the reason for the lack is not described. When the CPA is not independent, the CPA should include the following after the last paragraph, "We are not independent with respect to XYZ Company."

    f.   **Omitted Information**   An entity may request a CPA to compile PFS that contain presentation deficiencies or omit disclosures other than those relating to significant assumptions. The CPA may compile such PFS provided the deficiency or omission is indicated clearly in the report and is not, to the CPA's knowledge, undertaken with the intention of misleading those who reasonably might be expected to use such statements. In particular, if the PFS are presented in conformity with OCBOA and do not disclose the basis of accounting, the basis should be disclosed in the CPA's report.

Exhibit 27 ▶ Paragraph for Forecast With Omitted Information

Management has elected to omit the summary of significant accounting policies required by the guidelines for presentation of a forecast established by the American Institute of Certified Public Accountants. If the omitted disclosures were included in the forecast, they might influence the user's conclusions about the Company's financial position, results of operations, and cash flows for the forecast period. Accordingly, this forecast is not designed for those who are not informed about such matters.

9.   **Examination of PFS**   An examination of PFS is a professional service that involves (a) evaluating the preparation of the PFS, (b) evaluating the support underlying the assumptions, (c) evaluating the presentation of the PFS for conformity with AICPA presentation guidelines, and (d) issuing an examination report. The practitioner follows the general, fieldwork, and reporting standards outlined in AT 101 as applicable to examination engagements.

10.   **Examination Reports**   As a result of the examination, the CPA has a basis for reporting on whether, in the CPA's opinion, (a) the assumptions provide a reasonable basis for the responsible party's forecast or projection, given the hypothetical assumptions, and (b) whether the PFS are presented in accordance with AICPA guidelines.

    a.   **Standard Report**   In addition to the previously listed elements, the CPA's standard report on an examination of PFS includes the following: (1) an identification of the PFS presented; (2) a statement that the practitioner's responsibility is to express an opinion on the PFS based on an examination; (3) a brief description of the nature of an examination of PFS; and (4) the CPA's opinion that the PFS are presented in accordance with AICPA presentation guidelines and that the underlying assumptions provide a reasonable basis for the forecast (or projection, given the hypothetical assumptions).

    b.   **Projection**   When a CPA examines a projection, the CPA's opinion regarding the assumptions should be conditioned on the hypothetical assumptions; that is, the CPA should express an opinion on whether the assumptions provide a reasonable basis for the projection given the hypothetical assumptions. Also, the report should include a separate paragraph that limits the use to specified parties.

Exhibit 28 ▶ Standard Report on Examination of Forecast (Projection)

We have examined the accompanying forecasted [projected] balance sheet, statements of income, retained earnings, and cash flows of XYZ Company as of December 31, 20X1, and for the year then ending. XYZ Company is responsible for the forecast [projection]. Our responsibility is to express an opinion on the forecast [projection] based on our examination.

Our examination was made in accordance with attestation standards established by the American Institute of Certified Public Accountants and, accordingly, included such procedures as we considered necessary to evaluate both the assumptions used by management and the preparation and presentation of the forecast [projection]. We believe our examination provides a reasonable basis for our opinion.

<Opinion paragraph for a forecast report>

In our opinion, the accompanying forecast is presented in conformity with guidelines for presentation of a forecast established by the American Institute of Certified Public Accountants, and the underlying assumptions provide a reasonable basis for management's forecast. However, there will usually be differences between the forecasted and actual results, because events and circumstances frequently do not occur as expected, and those differences may be material. We have no responsibility to update this report for events and circumstances occurring after the date of this report.

<Opinion paragraph for a projection report>

In our opinion, the accompanying projection is presented in conformity with guidelines for presentation of a projection established by the American Institute of Certified Public Accountants, and the underlying assumptions provide a reasonable basis for management's projection [describe the hypothetical assumption, for example, "assuming the granting of the requested loan to expand XYZ Company's plant as described in the summary of significant assumptions."]. However, even if [describe hypothetical assumption, for example, "the loan is granted and the plant is expanded,"] there will usually be differences between the projected and actual results, because events and circumstances frequently do not occur as expected, and those differences may be material. We have no responsibility to update this report for events and circumstances occurring after the date of this report.

<Additional paragraph for a projection report>

The accompanying projection and this report were prepared for [identify specified parties, for example, "XYZ Company and DEF National Bank"] and are not intended to be and should not be used by anyone other than these specified parties.

---

c.   **Range** Ranges should be handled as discussed for compilations.

d.   **Historical Financial Information** Comparative historical financial information is handled as discussed for a compilation.

e.   **Emphasis** The practitioner may wish to emphasize a matter regarding the PFS, but issue an unqualified opinion. The practitioner may present other information and comments, such as explanatory comments or other informative material, in a separate paragraph of the report.

f.   **Evaluation Based in Part on Report of Another Accountant** When the principal practitioner decides to refer to the report of another CPA as a basis, in part, for the principal's own opinion, the principal practitioner should disclose that fact in stating the scope of the examination and refer to the report of the other CPA in expressing the opinion. Such a reference indicates the division of responsibility for the performance of the examination.

g.   **Part of Larger Engagement** When the practitioner's examination of PFS is part of a larger engagement, for example, a financial feasibility study or business acquisition study, it is appropriate to expand the report on the examination of the PFS to describe the entire engagement.

h.   **Qualified Opinion** In a qualified report, the CPA states, in a separate paragraph, all the substantive reasons for modifying the opinion, and describes the departure from AICPA presentation guidelines. The opinion includes the words "except" or "exception" as the qualifying language and refers to the separate explanatory paragraph.

Exhibit 29 ▶ Qualifying Language for Forecast (Examination Report)

> The forecast does not disclose the significant accounting policies. Disclosure of such policies is required by guidelines for presentation of a forecast established by the American Institute of Certified Public Accountants.
>
> In our opinion, except for the omission of the disclosure of the significant accounting policies as discussed in the preceding paragraph, the accompanying forecast is presented in conformity with...

i. **Adverse Opinion** In an adverse opinion, the CPA states, in a separate paragraph, all the substantive reasons for the adverse opinion. The opinion should state that the presentation is not in conformity with presentation guidelines and should refer to the explanatory paragraph. When applicable, the opinion paragraph also should state that, in the accountant's opinion, the assumptions do not provide a reasonable basis for the prospective financial statements.

(1) If the presentation, including the summary of significant assumptions, fails to disclose assumptions that, at the time, appear to be significant, the CPA should describe the assumptions in the report and issue an adverse opinion.

(2) The CPA should not examine a presentation that omits all disclosures of assumptions. Also, the CPA should not examine a financial projection that omits: (a) an identification of the hypothetical assumptions or (b) a description of the limitations on the usefulness of the presentation.

Exhibit 30 ▶ Adverse Opinion for Forecast (Examination Report)

> We have examined the accompanying forecasted balance sheet, statements of income, retained earnings, and cash flows of XYZ Company as of December 31, 20X1, and for the year then ending. XYZ Company is responsible for the forecast. Our responsibility is to express an opinion on the forecast based on our examination.
>
> Our examination was made in accordance with attestation standards established by the American Institute of Certified Public Accountants and, accordingly, included such procedures as we considered necessary to evaluate both the assumptions used by management and the preparation and presentation of the forecast. We believe our examination provides a reasonable basis for our opinion.
>
> As discussed under the caption "Sales" in the summary of significant forecast assumptions, the forecasted sales include, among other things, revenue from the Company's federal defense contracts continuing at the current level. The Company's present federal defense contracts will expire in March 20X1. No new contracts have been signed and no negotiations are under way for new federal defense contracts. Furthermore, the federal government has entered into contracts with another company to supply the items being manufactured under the Company's present contracts.
>
> In our opinion, the accompanying forecast is not presented in conformity with guidelines for presentation of a financial forecast established by the American Institute of Certified Public Accountants because management's assumptions, as discussed in the preceding paragraph, do not provide a reasonable basis for management's forecast. We have no responsibility to update this report for events or circumstances occurring after the date of this report.

j. **Disclaimer of Opinion** In a disclaimer of opinion, the CPA's report should indicate, in a separate paragraph, the respects in which the examination did not comply with standards for an examination. The CPA should state that the scope of the examination was not sufficient to enable an opinion to be expressed concerning the presentation or the underlying assumptions, and the CPA's disclaimer of opinion should include a direct reference to the explanatory paragraph. When there is a scope limitation and the CPA also believes there are material departures from the presentation guidelines, those departures should be described in the CPA's report.

Exhibit 31 ▶ Disclaimer of Opinion for Forecast (Examination Report)

We were engaged to examine the accompanying forecasted balance sheet, statements of income, retained earnings, and cash flows of XYZ Company as of December 31, 20X1, and for the year then ending. XYZ Company is responsible for the forecast.

As discussed under the caption "Income From Investee" in the summary of significant forecast assumptions, the forecast includes income from an equity investee constituting 23 percent of forecasted net income, which is management's estimate of the Company's share of the investee's income to be accrued for 20X1. The investee has not prepared a forecast for the year ending December 31, 20X1, and we were therefore unable to obtain suitable support for this assumption.

Because, as described in the preceding paragraph, we are unable to evaluate management's assumption regarding income from an equity investee and other assumptions that depend thereon, we express no opinion concerning the presentation of or the assumptions underlying the accompanying forecast. We have no responsibility to update this report for events and circumstances occurring after the date of this report.

11. **Agreed-Upon Procedures**

a. **Standards** The guidance in AT 101 (including general, fieldwork, and reporting standards) and AT 201 applies to engagements to apply agreed-upon procedures to PFS. This includes the extent of procedures and agreement among the parties regarding the procedures.

b. **Conditions** A practitioner may accept an engagement to apply agreed-upon procedures to PFS provided that: (1) the practitioner is independent; (2) the practitioner and the specified users agree upon the procedures and criteria; (3) the specified users take responsibility for the sufficiency of the agreed-upon procedures for their purposes; (4) the PFS include a summary of significant assumptions; (5) the PFS are subject to reasonably consistent evaluation against criteria that are suitable and available to the specified parties; (6) the procedures are expected to result in reasonably consistent findings using the criteria; (7) evidential matter related to the PFS is expected to exist to provide a reasonable basis for expressing the findings in the practitioner's report; (8) where applicable, the practitioner and the specified user agree on any materiality limits for reporting purposes; and (9) use of the report is restricted to the specified parties.

12. **Reports on Results of Applying Agreed-Upon Procedures** When the CPA reports on the results of applying agreed-upon procedures, the CPA should **not** express any form of **negative** assurance on the PFS. In addition to the previously discussed elements, the practitioner's report **must** include: (a) a title that includes the word *independent;* (b) identification of the specified parties; (c) reference to the PFS and the character of the engagement; (d) a statement that the procedures performed were those agreed to by the specified parties identified in the report; (e) identification of the responsible party and a statement that the PFS are the responsible party's responsibility; (f) a statement that the engagement was conducted in accordance with attestation standards established by the AICPA; (g) a statement that the sufficiency of the procedures is solely the responsibility of the specified parties and a disclaimer of responsibility for the sufficiency of those procedures; (h) a list of (or reference to) procedures performed and related findings; (i) where applicable, a description of any

agreed-upon materiality limits; (j) a statement that the practitioner was not engaged to and did not conduct an examination of PFS; (k) a disclaimer of opinion on whether the presentation of the PFS is in conformity with AICPA presentation guidelines and on whether the underlying assumptions provide a reasonable basis for the forecast or a reasonable basis for the projection given the hypothetical assumptions; (l) a statement that if the practitioner had performed additional procedures, other matters might have come to her/his attention that would have been reported; (m) a restriction on the use of the report, because it is intended to be used solely by the specified parties, and should not be used by others; (n) where applicable, reservations or restrictions concerning procedures or findings; and (o) where applicable, a description of assistance provided by a specialist.

C.   *Pro Forma* **Financial Information (AT 401)**

Pro forma financial information is used to show what the significant effects on historical financial information *might have been* if a consummated or proposed transaction or event had occurred at an earlier date. *Pro forma* financial information generally is used to show the effects of transactions such as a business combination, a change in capitalization, the disposition of a significant portion of a business, a change in the form of business organization, or the proposed sale of securities and the application of proceeds. Engagements to report on an examination or review of *pro forma* financial information are covered by AT 101 and AT 401. When *pro forma* financial information is presented outside the basic financial statements but within the same document, and the CPA is not engaged to report on the *pro forma* financial information, the CPA's responsibilities are described in SAS 8, *Other Information in Documents Containing Audited Financial Statements* (AU 550), and in SAS 37, *Filings Under Federal Securities Statutes* (AU 711).

1.   **Requirements** A CPA may agree to report on an examination or a review of *pro forma* financial information if the following conditions are met.

    a.   *Pro forma* adjustments should be based on management's assumptions and should consider all significant effects directly attributable to the transaction or event. The transaction or event reflected in the *pro forma* information should be described, as well as the source of the historical information upon which it is based, the significant assumptions used, and any significant uncertainties about those assumptions. The presentation should indicate that the *pro forma* information should be read in conjunction with the historical data. The presentation also should state that the *pro forma* financial information does not necessarily indicate the results that would have been attained had the transaction actually taken place earlier.

    b.   The document containing *pro forma* information includes (or incorporates by reference), complete historical financial statements (HFS) of the entity for the most recent year, or for the preceding year, if financial statements for the most recent year are not yet available. Interim *pro forma* financial information must include (or incorporate by reference), historical interim financial information, which may be condensed, for that period. In the case of a business combination, the document must include (or incorporate by reference) the appropriate historical financial information for the significant constituent parts of the combined entity.

    c.   The HFS of the entity (or, of each significant constituent part of the combined entity) on which the *pro forma* financial information is based must have been audited or reviewed. The practitioner's attestation risk relating to the *pro forma* financial information is affected by the scope of the engagement providing the practitioner with assurance about the underlying historical financial information to which the *pro forma* adjustments are applied.

       (1)   The level of assurance given by the CPA on the *pro forma* financial information is limited to the lowest level of assurance provided on the underlying HFS of any significant constituent part of the combined entity. For example, if the underlying HFS of each significant constituent part of the combined entity have been audited at year-end **and** reviewed at an interim date, the CPA may

perform an examination or a review of the *pro forma* financial information at year-end, **but** is limited to performing a review of the *pro forma* financial information at the interim date.

(2) The practitioner must have an appropriate level of knowledge of the accounting and financial reporting practices of each significant constituent part of the combined entity.

2. **Examination Objective** Examination procedures applied to *pro forma* financial information are to provide reasonable assurance as to whether the following exists: (a) management's assumptions provide a reasonable basis for presenting the significant effects directly attributable to the underlying transaction or event; (b) the related *pro forma* adjustments give appropriate effect to those assumptions; and (c) the *pro forma* column reflects the proper application of those adjustments to the HFS.

3. **Review Objective** Review procedures are to provide negative assurance as to whether any information came to the CPA's attention to cause a belief that: (a) management's assumptions do **not** provide a reasonable basis for presenting the significant effects directly attributable to the transaction or event; (b) the related *pro forma* adjustments do **not** give appropriate effect to those assumptions; and (c) the related *pro forma* column does **not** reflect the proper application of those adjustments to the HFS.

4. **Procedures** The procedures the CPA applies to the assumptions and *pro forma* adjustments for either an examination or a review engagement, other than those applied to the HFS, are as follows:

    a. Obtain an understanding of the underlying transaction or event, for example, by reading relevant contracts and minutes of meetings of the board of directors, and by making inquiries of appropriate officials.

    b. Obtain a level of knowledge of each significant constituent part of the combined entity in a business combination. Matters to consider include accounting principles and financial reporting practices followed, transactions between the entities, and material contingencies.

    c. Discuss with management its assumptions regarding the effects of the transaction or event.

    d. Evaluate whether *pro forma* adjustments are included for all significant effects directly attributable to the transaction or event.

    e. Obtain sufficient evidence in support of adjustments. The evidence required to support the level of assurance given is a matter of professional judgment. The CPA typically would obtain more evidence in an examination engagement than in a review engagement. Examples of evidence are purchase, merger, or exchange agreements; appraisal reports; debt agreements; employment agreements; actions of the board of directors; and existing or proposed legislation or regulatory actions.

    f. Evaluate whether management's assumptions that underlie the *pro forma* adjustments are presented in a sufficiently clear and comprehensive manner. Also, evaluate whether the *pro forma* adjustments are consistent with each other and with the data used to develop them.

    g. Determine that computations of *pro forma* adjustments are mathematically correct, and that the *pro forma* column reflects the proper application of those adjustments to the HFS.

h. Obtain written representations from management acknowledging responsibility for the assumptions used in determining the *pro forma* adjustments and concerning management's belief that: (1) the assumptions provide a reasonable basis for presenting all the significant effects directly attributable to the transaction or event; (2) the related *pro forma* adjustments give appropriate effect to those assumptions; (3) the *pro forma* column reflects the proper application of those adjustments to the historical financial statements; and (4) the significant effects directly attributable to the transaction or event are appropriately disclosed in the *pro forma* financial information.

i. Read the *pro forma* financial information and evaluate whether: (1) the underlying transaction or event, the *pro forma* adjustments, the significant assumptions, and the significant uncertainties, if any, about those assumptions have been appropriately described; and (2) the source of the historical financial information on which the *pro forma* financial information is based has been appropriately identified.

5. Report The report on *pro forma* financial information may be added to the CPA's report on historical financial information, or it may appear separately.

Exhibit 32 ▶ Report on Examination of *Pro Forma* Financial Information

We have examined the *pro forma* adjustments reflecting the transaction [or event] described in Note 1 and the application of those adjustments to the historical amounts in [the assembly of] the accompanying *pro forma* condensed balance sheet of X Company as of December 31, 20X1, and the *pro forma* condensed statement of income for the year then ended. The historical condensed financial statements are derived from the historical financial statements of X Company, which were audited by us, and of Y Company, which were audited by other accountants, appearing elsewhere herein [or incorporated by reference]. Such *pro forma* adjustments are based upon management's assumptions described in Note 2. X Company's management is responsible for the *pro forma* financial statements. Our responsibility is to express an opinion on the *pro forma* financial information based on our examination.

Our examination was made in accordance with attestation standards established by the American Institute of Certified Public Accountants and, accordingly, included such procedures as we considered necessary under the circumstances. We believe our examination provides a reasonable basis for our opinion.

The objective of this *pro forma* financial information is to show what the significant effects on the historical financial information might have been had the transaction [or event] occurred at an earlier date. However, the *pro forma* condensed financial statements are not necessarily indicative of the results of operations or related effects on financial position that would have been attained had the above-mentioned transaction [or event] occurred earlier.

[Additional paragraph(s) may be added to emphasize certain matters relating to the engagement.]

In our opinion, management's assumptions provide a reasonable basis for presenting the significant efforts directly attributable to the above-mentioned transaction [or event] described in Note 1, the related *pro forma* adjustments give appropriate effect to those assumptions, and the *pro forma* column reflects the proper application of those adjustments to the historical financial statement amounts in the *pro forma* condensed balance sheet as of December 31, 20X1, and the *pro forma* condensed statement of income for the year then ended.

a. Contents In addition to the previously listed items, a report on *pro forma* financial information includes the following:

(1) Limitation A separate paragraph explaining the objective of *pro forma* financial information and its limitations.

(2) **Reference** A reference to the financial statements from which the historical financial information is derived and any modification in the practitioner's report on the historical financial information.

(3) **Date** The practitioner's report on *pro forma* financial information should be dated as of the completion of the appropriate procedures. If the reports are combined and the date of completion of the procedures for the examination or review of the *pro forma* financial information is **after** the date of completion of the fieldwork for the audit or review of the historical financial information, the combined report should be dual-dated.

b. **Modifications** Restrictions on the scope of the engagement, significant uncertainties about the assumptions that could affect the transaction or event materially, reservations about the propriety of the assumptions and the conformity of the presentation with those assumptions (including inadequate disclosure of significant matters), or other reservations may require the CPA to qualify the opinion, render an adverse opinion, disclaim an opinion, or withdraw from the engagement. The CPA should disclose **all** substantive reasons for **any** report modifications. Uncertainty as to whether the transaction or event will be consummated ordinarily would not require a report modification.

c. **Examination** In addition to the previously listed elements, an examination report also includes the following:

(1) **Reference** A statement that the historical financial statements were audited.

(2) **Responsibility** A statement that the practitioner's responsibility is to express an opinion on the *pro forma* financial information based on her/his examination.

(3) **Standards** A statement that the examination was made in accordance with attestation standards established by the AICPA, and accordingly, included such procedures as the practitioner considered necessary in the circumstances.

(4) **Basis** A statement that the practitioner believes the examination provides a reasonable basis for her/his opinion.

(5) **Opinion** The practitioner's opinion as to whether management's assumptions provide a reasonable basis for presenting the significant effects directly attributable to the transaction or event, whether the related *pro forma* adjustments give appropriate effect to those assumptions, and whether the *pro forma* column reflects the proper application of those adjustments to the historical financial statements.

d. **Review** In addition to the previously listed elements, a review report also includes the following:

Exhibit 33 ▶ Report on Review of *Pro Forma* Financial Information

We have reviewed the *pro forma* adjustments reflecting the transaction [or event] described in Note 1 and the application of those adjustments to the historical amounts in [the assembly of] the accompanying *pro forma* condensed balance sheet of X Company as of March 31, 20X2, and the *pro forma* condensed statement of income for the three months then ended. These historical condensed financial statements are derived from the historical unaudited financial statements of X Company, which were reviewed by us, and of Y Company, which were reviewed by other accountants, appearing elsewhere herein [or incorporated by reference]. Such *pro forma* adjustments are based on management's assumptions as described in Note 2. X Company's management is responsible for the *pro forma* financial statements.

Our review was conducted in accordance with attestation standards established by the American Institute of Certified Public Accountants. A review is substantially less in scope than an examination, the objective of which is the expression of an opinion on management's assumptions, the *pro forma* adjustments, and the application of those adjustments to historical financial information. Accordingly, we do not express such an opinion.

<Same third paragraph as in an examination report.>

[Additional paragraph(s) may be added to emphasize certain matters relating to the engagement.]

Based on our review, nothing came to our attention that caused us to believe that management's assumptions do not provide a reasonable basis for presenting the significant effects directly attributable to the above-mentioned transaction [or event] described in Note 1, that the related *pro forma* adjustments do not give appropriate effect to those assumptions, or that the *pro forma* column does not reflect the proper application of those adjustments to the historical financial statement amounts in the *pro forma* condensed balance sheet as of March 31, 20X2, and the *pro forma* condensed statement of income for the three months then ended.

(1) **Reference** A statement as to whether the historical financial statements were audited or reviewed.

(2) **Disclaimer** A statement that a review is substantially less in scope than an examination, the objective of which is the expression of an opinion on the *pro forma* financial information, and accordingly, the practitioner does not express such an opinion.

(3) **Conclusion** The practitioner's conclusion as to whether any information came to the CPA's attention to cause a belief that management's assumptions do not provide a reasonable basis for presenting the significant effects directly attributable to the transaction or event, or that the related *pro forma* adjustments do not give appropriate effect to those assumptions, or that the *pro forma* column does not reflect the proper application of those adjustments to the historical financial statements.

D. **Examination of Internal Control Over Financial Reporting (AT 501)**
AT 501 establishes requirements and provides guidance for the performance of an examination of a nonissuer's internal control over financial reporting (internal control) that is integrated with an audit of financial statements. (An auditor should **not** accept an engagement to *review* an entity's internal control or a written assertion thereon.) It aligns the definitions and related guidance for evaluating deficiencies in internal control with PCAOB AS 5, *An Audit of Internal Control Over Financial Reporting That is Integrated with an Audit of Financial Statements.*

1. **Applicability** AT 501 does **not** provide guidance for the following engagements:

a. As covered under AT 101, *Attest Engagements:*

(1) Examining the suitability of design of an entity's internal control

(2) Examining controls over the effectiveness and efficiency of operations

b. Performance of agreed-upon procedures on controls covered under AT 201, *Agreed-Upon Procedures Engagements*

c. Examining controls over compliance with laws and regulations covered under AT 601, *Compliance Attestation*

    d.   Reporting on controls at a service organization covered under AU 334, *Service Organizations*

2.   **Objective** The auditor's objective is to form an opinion on the effectiveness of an entity's internal control as of a point in time and taken as a whole. To express an opinion as of a point in time, the auditor should obtain evidence that internal control has operated effectively for a sufficient period of time which may be less than the period covered by the company's financial statements. To express an opinion on internal control taken as a whole, the auditor should obtain evidence about the effectiveness of selected controls over *all* relevant assertions. This involves testing the design and operating effectiveness of controls that in most cases would **not** be required if *only* expressing an opinion on the financial statements.

    a.   **Material Weaknesses** If one or more material weaknesses exist, an entity's internal control *cannot* be considered effective, thus the auditor must obtain sufficient appropriate evidence to obtain reasonable assurance about whether material weaknesses exist as of the date specified in management's assertion. There may be a material weakness in internal control even when financial statements are **not** materially misstated. An auditor is **not** required to search for deficiencies that are less severe than a material weakness.

    b.   **Standards and Criteria** An auditor should comply with the general, fieldwork, and reporting attestation standards required for all attestation engagements and the specific requirements covered in this statement. An auditor should use the same suitable and available criteria to perform an examination as management uses for its evaluation.

3.   **Definitions**

    a.   **Control Objective** The aim or purpose of specified controls. Control objectives ordinarily address the risks that the controls are intended to mitigate. In the context of internal control, a control objective generally relates to a relevant assertion for a significant account or disclosure and addresses the risk that the controls in a specific area will not provide reasonable assurance that a misstatement or omission in that relevant assertion is prevented, or detected and corrected on a timely basis.

    b.   **Deficiency** A deficiency in internal control exists when the design or operation of a control does not allow management or employees, in the normal course of performing their assigned functions, to prevent, or detect and correct misstatements on a timely basis.

        (1)   A deficiency in *design* exists when

            (a)   A control necessary to meet the control objective is missing or

            (b)   An existing control is not properly designed so that, even if the control operates as designed, the control objective would not be met.

        (2)   A deficiency in *operation* exists when a properly designed control does not operate as designed, or when the person performing the control does not possess the necessary authority or competence to perform the control effectively.

    c.   **Detective Control** A control that has the objective of detecting and correcting errors or fraud that have already occurred that could result in a misstatement of the financial statements.

    d.   **Financial Statements and Related Disclosures** An entity's financial statements and notes to the financial statements as presented in accordance with the applicable financial reporting framework. References to financial statements and related disclosures do **not** extend to the preparation of other financial information presented outside an entity's basic financial statements and notes.

e. **Internal Control Over Financial Reporting** A process effected by those charged with governance, management, and other personnel, designed to provide reasonable assurance regarding the preparation of reliable financial statements for external purposes in accordance with the applicable financial reporting framework and includes those policies and procedures that

(1) Pertain to the maintenance of records that, in reasonable detail, accurately and fairly reflect the transactions and dispositions of the assets of an entity

(2) Provide reasonable assurance that transactions are recorded as necessary to permit preparation of financial statements in accordance with the applicable financial reporting framework, and that receipts and expenditures of an entity are being made only in accordance with authorizations of management and those charged with governance

(3) Provide reasonable assurance regarding prevention, or timely detection and correction of unauthorized acquisition, use, or disposition of an entity's assets that could have a material effect on the financial statements

Note: Internal control has *inherent limitations.* Internal control is a process that involves human diligence and compliance and is subject to lapses in judgment and breakdowns resulting from human failures. Internal control also can be circumvented by collusion or improper management override. Because of such limitations, there is a risk that material misstatements will not be prevented, or detected and corrected on a timely basis by internal control. However, these inherent limitations are known aspects of the financial reporting process.

f. **Management's Assertion** Management's conclusion about the effectiveness of an entity's internal control that is included in management's report on internal control.

g. **Material Weakness** A deficiency, or a combination of deficiencies, in internal control such that there is a *reasonable possibility* (per the FASB's definition regarding accounting for contingencies) that a material misstatement of an entity's financial statements will not be prevented, or detected and corrected on a timely basis.

h. **Preventive Control** A control that has the objective of preventing errors or fraud that could result in a misstatement of the financial statements.

i. **Relevant Assertion** A financial statement assertion that has a reasonable possibility of containing a misstatement or misstatements that would cause the financial statements to be materially misstated. The determination of whether an assertion is a relevant assertion is made without regard to the effect of controls.

j. **Significant Account or Disclosure** An account balance or disclosure that has a reasonable possibility that it could contain a misstatement that, individually or when aggregated with others, has a material effect on the financial statements, considering the risks of both overstatement and understatement. The determination of whether an account balance or disclosure is a significant account or disclosure is made without regard to the effect of controls.

k. **Significant Deficiency** A deficiency, or a combination of deficiencies, in internal control that is less severe than a material weakness, yet important enough to merit attention by those charged with governance.

4. **Required Conditions for Performance of Examination**

a. Management accepts responsibility for the effectiveness of the entity's internal control.

    b.   Management evaluates the effectiveness of the entity's internal control using suitable and available criteria.

    c.   Management supports its assertion about the effectiveness of the entity's internal control with sufficient appropriate evidence. This includes documentation of the controls and their objectives and evidence of monitoring activities.

    d.   Management provides its assertion about the effectiveness of the entity's internal control in a report that accompanies the auditor's report.

5.   **Integrating the Examination With the Financial Statement Audit**

    a.   **Significant Accounts and Disclosures and Their Relevant Assertions** The significant accounts and disclosures and their relevant assertions and the risk factors used to identify them are the same in the examination of internal control (examination) as in an audit of financial statements (audit).

    b.   **Tests of Controls** The tests of controls should be designed to achieve the objectives of both engagements simultaneously, i.e., to obtain sufficient appropriate evidence to support the auditor's opinion on internal control as well as the auditor's risk assessment for purposes of the audit. As previously mentioned, for the purposes of the audit, the auditor is **not** required to test the controls of *all* relevant assertions as is required in the examination. Consideration of the results of the additional tests of controls performed for the purposes of the examination may affect the auditor's decisions about the nature, timing and extent of substantive procedures and further tests of controls for the purposes of the audit. Obviously, this would be particularly true if deficiencies were identified in the examination.

    c.   **Substantive Procedures** Likewise, the results of substantive procedures performed for purposes of the audit should be evaluated to determine their effect on the auditor's risk assessments regarding the testing necessary to form a conclusion about the effectiveness of a control in the examination. Results of substantive tests of particular interest include those related to fraud, illegal acts, related party transactions, and those that detect misstatements or indicate management bias in making accounting estimates or selecting accounting principles.

    d.   **Period End Reporting Process** As part of the examination, the auditor should evaluate the procedures that make up the period end reporting process because of its importance to financial reporting and the integrated approach.

    e.   **Risk Assessment and Materiality** The same materiality should be used for planning and performing both engagements and the same risk assessment process supports both.

    f.   **Fraud Risk Assessment** The results of the fraud risk assessment for the purposes the audit should be incorporated into the examination. The auditor should consider whether the identified risks due to fraud and inappropriate management override of other controls are sufficiently addressed by the internal control system.

    g.   ***As of* Date or Period Covered** The date specified in management's assertion (the *as of* date of the examination) should correspond to the balance sheet date of the period covered by the financial statements. If management chooses an *as of* date for the examination that is different than the end of the entity's fiscal year, the examination and the audit should still be integrated. If the auditor is engaged to examine the effectiveness of internal control for a period of time (rather than an *as of* date), the examination should be integrated with an audit that covers the same period.

    h.   **Auditor's Report Date** Because the examination is integrated with the audit, the dates of the reports should be the same.

6. **Planning**

   a. **Role of Risk Assessment** Risk assessment underlies all phases of the examination process. Obviously, the auditor should focus on areas with the highest risk. It is **not** necessary to test controls that, even if deficient, do not present a reasonable possibility of a material misstatement to the financial statements. The auditor should bear in mind that an entity's internal control is *less* likely to prevent or detect and correct a misstatement caused by fraud than one due to error. Additionally, the size and complexity of an organization affects the auditor's risk assessment, allowing scaling of the examination for smaller and/or less complex entities.

   b. **Using the Work of Others** In an examination, the auditor may use the work of others within the entity (in addition to internal auditors) and third parties. The auditor should consider their objectivity and competence in the same manner as that of internal auditors for purposes of the audit. As the risk associated with a control increases, so does the need for the auditor to perform the work.

   c. **Control Environment** The auditor should evaluate the control environment because of its importance to effective internal control.

7. **Selection of Controls to Test** The auditor should use a top-down approach, starting with the financial statements and then focusing on the entity-level controls; working down to the identification of the significant accounts, disclosures and their relevant assertions that present a reasonable possibility of material misstatement of the financial statements. The auditor can then select the controls that sufficiently address the assessed risk of material misstatement to each relevant assertion.

8. **Testing Controls** As the risk associated with a control increases, the evidence the auditor should obtain also increases. As previously mentioned, the auditor is expressing an opinion on internal control *taken as whole*. The risk-based approach allows the auditor to vary the amount of evidence obtained for individual controls.

   In order of *least* evidence produced to most, these are the tests an auditor might perform: inquiry, observation, inspection of documentation, recalculation, and reperformance of a control. Inquiry alone does **not** provide sufficient appropriate evidence to support a conclusion about the effectiveness of a control. The quality of evidence is enhanced by testing controls over a longer period of time and closer to the *as of* date of the examination.

   a. **Design Effectiveness** Walk-throughs (following a transaction from origination through the entity's processes until it is reflected in the financial statements, using the same documents and information technology that entity personnel use) are usually sufficient to evaluate design effectiveness.

   b. **Operating Effectiveness** Procedures include a mix of inquiry, observation, inspection of documentation, recalculation, and reperformance of the control. Because only reasonable rather than absolute assurance is provided by effective internal control, an individual control does **not** have to operate without any deviation to be considered effective.

9. **Evaluation of Identified Deficiencies**

   a. **Severity** The auditor should evaluate the severity of each deficiency to determine whether it, individually or in combination, is a material weakness. The severity does **not** depend on whether a misstatement actually occurred. A compensating control can limit the severity of a deficiency and prevent it from being a material weakness. Severity depends on

      (1) The magnitude of the potential misstatement

      (2)   Whether there is a reasonable possibility that the entity's controls will fail to prevent, or detect and correct a misstatement

  b.   **Indicators of a Material Weakness**

      (1)   Identification of fraud, whether or not material, on the part of senior management

      (2)   Restatement of previously issued financial statements to reflect the correction of a material misstatement due to error or fraud

      (3)   Identification by the auditor of a material misstatement of financial statements under audit in circumstances that indicate that the misstatement would not have been detected and corrected by the entity's internal control

      (4)   Ineffective oversight of the entity's financial reporting and internal control by those charged with governance

  c.   **Prudent Official Standard** If a determination is made that a deficiency is **not** a material weakness, the auditor should consider whether prudent officials, having knowledge of the same facts and circumstances, would likely reach the same conclusion.

10. **Evaluation of Management's Report** The auditor should determine if management's report appropriately includes the following:

  a.   A statement regarding management's responsibility for internal control

  b.   A description of the subject matter of the examination

  c.   An identification of the criteria against which internal control is measured

  d.   Management's assertion about the effectiveness of internal control

  e.   A description of the material weaknesses, if any

  f.   The date as of which management's assertion is made

11. **Management's Written Representations** The auditor should obtain representations from management:

  a.   Acknowledging management's responsibility for establishing and maintaining effective internal control

  b.   Stating that management has performed an evaluation of the effectiveness of the entity's internal control and specifying the control criteria

  c.   Stating that management did not use the auditor's procedures performed during the integrated audit as part of the basis for management's assertion

  d.   Stating management's assertion about the effectiveness of the entity's internal control based on the control criteria as of a specified date

  e.   Stating that management has disclosed to the auditor all deficiencies in the design or operation of internal control, including separately disclosing to the auditor all such deficiencies that it believes to be significant deficiencies or material weaknesses in internal control

  f.   Describing any fraud resulting in a material misstatement to the entity's financial statements and any other fraud that does not result in a material misstatement to the entity's financial statements, but involves senior management or management or other employees who have a significant role in the entity's internal control

g. Stating whether the significant deficiencies and material weaknesses identified and communicated to management and those charged with governance during previous engagements have been resolved and specifically identifying any that have not

h. Stating whether there were, subsequent to the date being reported on, any changes in internal control or other factors that might significantly affect internal control, including any corrective actions taken by management with regard to significant deficiencies and material weaknesses

12. **Communications**

a. Significant deficiencies and material weaknesses should be communicated, in writing by the auditor's report release date, to the entity's management and those charged with governance, including those previously communicated, but **not** remediated. In the case where the nature of some matters directs their early communication, even if such significant deficiencies or material weaknesses are remediated during the audit, they should still be included in this formal written communication. (At the time of their initial early communication, they are not required to be in writing.)

b. If the auditor concludes that the oversight of the entity's financial reporting and internal control by the entity's audit committee (or similar subgroup) is inadequate, the auditor should communicate this, in writing by the auditor's report release date, to the board of directors (or similar governing body if one exists).

c. The auditor should also communicate to management, in writing, all identified deficiencies which are not significant deficiencies or material weaknesses, no later than 60 days following the report release date and inform those charged with governance when this communication has been made. As previously mentioned, the auditor is **not** required to search for deficiencies that are less severe than a material weakness, thus this communication would only include deficiencies of which the auditor is *aware.*

d. If one or more material weaknesses are identified which are **not** disclosed or identified in management's report, the auditor should communicate this, in writing, to those charged with governance.

e. If the auditor cannot express an opinion because there has been a limitation on the scope of the examination, the auditor should communicate, in writing, to management and those charged with governance that the examination cannot be satisfactorily completed.

f. If the auditor concludes that additional information contained in management's report contains a material misstatement of fact that management refuses to revise, the auditor should notify management and those charged with governance, in writing, of the auditor's views.

13. **Reporting on Internal Control**

a. The auditor's report on an examination should include these elements:

(1) A title that includes the word *independent*

(2) A statement that management is responsible for maintaining effective internal control and for evaluating the effectiveness of internal control

(3) An identification of management's assertion on internal control that accompanies the auditor's report, including a reference to management's report

(4) A statement that the auditor's responsibility is to express an opinion on the entity's internal control (or on management's assertion) based on the auditor's examination

(5) A statement that the examination was conducted in accordance with attestation standards established by the American Institute of Certified Public Accountants

(6) A statement that such standards require that the auditor plan and perform the examination to obtain reasonable assurance about whether effective internal control was maintained in all material respects

Editor's note: An examination provides the same level of assurance as an audit.

(7) A statement that an examination includes obtaining an understanding of internal control, assessing the risk that a material weakness exists, testing and evaluating the design and operating effectiveness of internal control based on the assessed risk, and performing such other procedures as the auditor considers necessary in the circumstances

(8) A statement that the auditor believes the examination provides a reasonable basis for the auditor's opinion

(9) A definition of internal control (the auditor should use the same description of the entity's internal control as management uses in its report)

(10) A paragraph stating that, because of inherent limitations, internal control may not prevent, or detect and correct misstatements and that projections of any evaluation of effectiveness to future periods are subject to the risk that controls may become inadequate because of changes in conditions, or that the degree of compliance with the policies or procedures may deteriorate

(11) The auditor's opinion on whether the entity maintained, in all material respects, effective internal control as of the specified date, based on the control criteria; **or,** the auditor's opinion on whether *management's assertion* about the effectiveness of the entity's internal control as of the specified date is fairly stated, in all material respects, based on the control criteria

(12) The manual or printed signature of the auditor's firm

(13) The date of the report which should be no earlier than the date on which the auditor has obtained sufficient appropriate evidence to support the auditor's opinion.

b. The auditor should **not** issue a report stating that **no** deficiencies were identified.

c. The auditor should **not** issue a report indicating that **no** material weaknesses were identified.

d. The auditor may issue a combined report or separate reports on the entity's financial statements and on internal control.

e. **Report Modifications**

(1) **Defects in Management's Report** If the elements of management's report are incomplete or improperly presented and management refuses to revise their report, the auditor should add an explanatory paragraph to the auditor's report describing the reasons for this determination.

(2) **Opinion Based, in Part, on the Report of Another Auditor** When the auditor has examined the internal control of one or more components of an entity, the auditor should determine whether to serve as the principal auditor and use the work and report of another auditor as the basis, in part, for the her/his own opinion. The standard states that AU 543, *Part of Audit Performed by Other Independent Auditors,* is applicable to this determination by the auditor. When the auditor decides to make reference to the report of another auditor, the scope and opinion paragraphs of the principal auditor's report should be modified accordingly.

(3) **Additional Information in Management's Report** If management's report includes additional information (beyond the elements previously described) that appear to be part of management's report, the auditor should add an explanatory paragraph as the last paragraph in the auditor's report that disclaims an opinion on the additional information. If the auditor believes the additional information contains a material misstatement of fact the auditor should refer to the guidance in AT 101 on the same issue with information contained in a client-prepared document containing a practitioner's attest report. In some instances, the auditor may also need to apply the guidance in AU 317, *Illegal Acts by Clients.*

(4) **Subsequent Event** If the auditor obtains knowledge about conditions that did **not** exist at the date specified in management's assertion, but arose subsequent to that date and before the release of the auditor's report that had a material effect on the entity's internal control, the auditor should include an explanatory paragraph in the auditor's report that describes the event and its effects or refers the reader to the same information in management's report.

f. **Adverse Opinion** If there is more than one material weakness, the auditor should express an adverse opinion. (This also applies when the auditor discovers a material weakness subsequent to the *as of* date of the examination, but before the date of the auditor's report that existed as of the date in management's assertion and whose effect on internal control can be determined. If this type of subsequently discovered material weakness's effect cannot be determined, the auditor should disclaim an opinion.) Under these circumstances, the auditor is prohibited from expressing an opinion on management's assertion and should report *directly* on the effectiveness of internal control. (See the eleventh element of the auditor's report.) The auditor should determine the effect of an adverse opinion on the auditor's opinion on the financial statements and disclose whether the auditor's opinion on the financial statements was affected by the material weakness. This adverse report on internal control should include

(1) A definition of material weakness

(2) A statement that one or more material weaknesses have been identified and an identification of the material weaknesses described in management's report; the auditor's report does **not** need to include a description of the material weaknesses *as long as* each material weakness is included and fairly presented in all material respects in management's report

(3) If management's report does **not** include a fair presentation of all material weaknesses, the auditor's report should include

(a) A statement that one or more material weaknesses have been identified and not included in management's report

> (b) A description of all such material weaknesses which contains specific information about the nature of each, and its actual and potential effect on the presentation of the entity's financial statements
>
> (c) In the case where one or more material weaknesses have been included in management's report, but not fairly presented, the auditor's report should state this conclusion and include the information needed for a fair presentation

g. Disclaimer of Opinion or Withdrawal From an Engagement

> (1) Management's refusal to furnish an assertion about the effectiveness of the entity's internal control in a report that accompanies the auditor's report should cause the auditor to withdraw from the engagement. If a law or regulation prohibits the auditor's withdrawal, the auditor should disclaim an opinion on internal control.
>
> (2) If there are restrictions on the scope of an engagement, for example, if management refuses to provide written representations, the auditor should either withdraw from the engagement or disclaim an opinion. The auditor may issue the disclaimer of opinion as soon as the auditor concludes that the scope limitation will prevent the auditor from obtaining the reasonable assurance necessary to express an opinion. No additional work is required.
>
> (3) The auditor should disclaim an opinion when the auditor discovers a material weakness subsequent to the *as of* date of the examination, but before the date of the auditor's report that existed as of the date in management's assertion and whose effect on internal control can**not** be determined. (If its effect can be determined, the auditor should issue an adverse opinion.)
>
> (4) A disclaimer of opinion should include
>
> > (a) A statement that the auditor does not express an opinion on the effectiveness of internal control
> >
> > (b) In a separate paragraph or paragraphs, an explanation that includes the substantive reasons for the disclaimer
> >
> > (c) The auditor should **not** identify the procedures that were performed **nor** include the statements describing the characteristics of an examination
> >
> > (d) If the limited procedures performed allowed the auditor to conclude that one or more material weaknesses exist, the auditor's report should also include the definition of a material weakness and a description of any material weakness identified that includes specific information about the nature of any material weakness and its actual and potential effect on the entity's financial statements. The auditor should also determine the effect the material weakness has on the auditor's opinion of the financial statements and should disclose whether the auditor's opinion was affected by the material weaknesses.

E. Compliance Attestation (AT 601)

AT 601 provides guidance for engagements related to an entity's compliance with requirements of specified laws, regulations, rules, contracts, or grants, as well as the effectiveness of an entity's internal control (IC) over compliance with specified requirements. The subject matter may be financial or nonfinancial compliance requirements. IC over compliance may include parts of (but is not the same as) IC over financial reporting. An attest engagement must comply with the general, fieldwork, and reporting standards delineated in AT 101 as well as specific standards established in AT 601.

1. **Appropriate Engagements** CPAs may be engaged to perform agreed-upon procedures to assist users in evaluating compliance with specified requirements (or related assertions) and/or the effectiveness of an entity's IC over compliance. These engagements also are subject to the requirements of AT 201. CPAs also may be engaged to **examine,** but **not** review, an entity's compliance with specified requirements, or related written assertions. CPAs may provide nonattest services connected with compliance; these services adhere to professional consulting standards, rather than SSAE 10.

2. **Responsibilities** The responsible party is responsible for ensuring that the entity complies with the requirements applicable to its activities.

3. **Conditions for Engagement Performance** For both types of engagements, the responsible party must accept responsibility for the entity's compliance with specified requirements and the effectiveness of IC over compliance, and provide a written assertion about compliance with specified requirements or IC over compliance in either: (a) a separate report to accompany the practitioner's report; or (b) a representation letter to the practitioner.

   a. **Agreed-Upon Procedures** The responsible party evaluates compliance with specified requirements or the effectiveness of the entity's IC over compliance.

   b. **Examinations** The responsible party evaluates compliance with specified requirements, and sufficient evidential matter exists, or could be developed, to support that evaluation.

4. **Written Assertion** In an examination, the responsible party's refusal to provide a written assertion requires the practitioner to withdraw unless the engagement is mandated legally. In that case, the practitioner must either express an adverse opinion in a restricted-use report or disclaim an opinion. In an agreed-upon procedures engagement where the client is the responsible party, absence of a written assertion requires the practitioner to withdraw, unless the engagement is mandated legally. In an agreed-upon procedures engagement where the client is not the responsible party, absence of a written assertion does not force the practitioner to withdraw, but the practitioner should consider the effects of the refusal on the engagement and report.

5. **Representations** When the practitioner's client is not the responsible party, the practitioner also may obtain written representations from the client. A responsible party's refusal to provide a written representation letter is a limitation on the scope of an examination or agreed-upon procedures engagement sufficient to preclude an unqualified opinion. Based on the nature of the representations not received or the refusal, the practitioner may determine that a qualified opinion is appropriate. When the practitioner's client is the responsible party, the refusal constitutes a limitation on the engagement scope sufficient to require the practitioner to withdraw. When the practitioner's client is not the responsible party, the practitioner is not required to withdraw. The practitioner should consider the effects of the responsible party's refusal on her/his ability to rely on other representations by the responsible party.

6. **Modifications** The practitioner modifies the report if: (a) material noncompliance with specified requirements exists; (b) a restriction on the engagement scope exists; or (c) the practitioner refers to another practitioner's report as the basis, in part, for the report.

7. **Agreed-Upon Procedures Engagement** The objective of this engagement is to present specific findings to assist users in evaluating an entity's assertion about compliance with specified requirements or about the effectiveness of an entity's IC over compliance based on procedures agreed-upon by the report users. The CPA's procedures generally may be as limited or as extensive as the specified parties desire as long as the specified users participate in establishing the procedures to be performed, and take responsibility for the adequacy of such procedures for their purposes. Prior to performing procedures, the practitioner should obtain an understanding of the specified compliance requirements.

Exhibit 35 ▶ Standard Report on Agreed-Upon Compliance Procedures

<u>Independent Accountant's Report</u>

We have performed the procedures enumerated below, which were agreed to by [list specified parties], solely to assist the specified parties in evaluating W Company's internal control over compliance with [list specified compliance requirements] during the three months ending December 31, 20X1. Management is responsible for W Company's compliance with those requirements. This agreed-upon procedures engagement was conducted in accordance with attestation standards established by the American Institute of Certified Public Accountants. The sufficiency of the procedures is solely the responsibility of those parties specified in this report. Consequently, we make no representation regarding the sufficiency of the procedures described below either for the purpose for which this report has been requested or for any other purpose.

[List the procedures performed and related findings.]

We were not engaged to and did not conduct an examination, the objective of which would be the expression of an opinion on compliance. Accordingly, we do not express such an opinion. Had we performed additional procedures, other matters might have come to our attention that would have been reported to you.

This report is intended solely for the information and use of [list or refer to specified parties] and is not intended to be and should not be used by anyone other than these specified parties.

a. When a situation imposes restrictions on the engagement scope, the practitioner attempts to obtain agreement to modify the procedures. If such agreement is not obtained, the practitioner should describe the restrictions in the report or withdraw from the engagement.

b. The practitioner has no obligation to perform beyond the agreed-upon procedures and no responsibility to perform procedures to detect noncompliance in the subsequent period, beyond obtaining the responsible party's representation about noncompliance in the subsequent period (the period starting at the end of the period addressed by the practitioner's report and ending on the date of completion of the procedures, also the report date). However, if noncompliance is found by other means or in the subsequent period, it typically is reported.

c. If the practitioner is engaged to report on both compliance with specified requirements and the effectiveness of IC over compliance, the practitioner may issue one report.

d. The practitioner's report should **not** provide negative assurance about whether management's assertion is fairly stated.

8. **Examination Engagement** The objective of an examination is to express an opinion on an entity's compliance with specified requirements (or related assertion) based on specified criteria. To express such an opinion, the practitioner accumulates sufficient evidence regarding the entity's compliance with specified requirements, thereby limiting attestation risk to an appropriately low level. Among other procedures, the practitioner considers subsequent events. The practitioner considers issues that parallel those in a financial statement audit, but the perspective may be different. Some of these issues are risk, materiality, planning, professional skepticism, relevant internal controls and internal audit functions, use of specialists, and obtaining sufficient evidence.

Exhibit 36 ▶ Standard Report on Examination of Compliance

<u>Independent Accountant's Report</u>

We have examined W Company's internal control over compliance with [list specified compliance requirements] during the three months ending December 31, 20X1. W Company's management is responsible for W Company's compliance with those requirements. Our responsibility is to express an opinion on W Company's compliance based on our examination.

Our examination was conducted in accordance with attestation standards established by the American Institute of Certified Public Accountants and, accordingly, included examining, on a test basis, evidence about W Company's compliance with those requirements and performing such other procedures as we considered necessary in the circumstances. We believe that our examination provides a reasonable basis for our opinion. Our examination does not provide a legal determination on W Company's compliance with specified requirements.

In our opinion, W Company complied, in all material respects, with the aforementioned requirements for the three months ended December 31, 20X1.

F.   Management's Discussion & Analysis (AT 701)
Management is responsible for MD&A preparation. AT 701 provides specific guidance to CPAs related to the performance of an attest engagement with respect to MD&A prepared pursuant to Securities and Exchange Commission (SEC) regulations. This guidance does not change an auditor's responsibility in a financial statement audit, or apply to situations where CPAs provide recommendations rather than assurance. (SAS 8 requires an auditor to read the MD&A and consider whether it is materially inconsistent with information appearing in the financial statements.) A practitioner engaged to examine or review MD&A complies with AT 101 plus the specific standards in AT 701. A practitioner engaged to perform agreed-upon procedures on MD&A follows the guidance in AT 201.

1.   Objectives The objective is to report on MD&A taken as a whole. An **examination** of MD&A provides users with an independent opinion regarding whether: (a) the presentation meets SEC criteria, (b) the historical financial information is derived accurately from the financial statements, and (c) the underlying information and assumptions provide a reasonable basis for the disclosures contained therein. A **review** of MD&A provides users and preparers with negative assurance concerning such matters.

2.   Engagement Acceptance A CPA may perform an examination or review of MD&A for an annual period, an interim period, or a combined annual and interim period. A base knowledge of the entity gained through a financial statement audit is necessary to provide the CPA with sufficient knowledge to evaluate the results of procedures. For nonpublic entities, the CPA also must receive a written assertion from management that MD&A was prepared using SEC criteria.

a.   Annual Period A CPA may accept an engagement to examine or review MD&A of an entity for an annual period, provided the practitioner audits the financial statements for at least the latest period to which MD&A relates and the financial statements for the other periods covered by MD&A have been audited.

b.   Review of Interim Period A CPA may accept an engagement to review MD&A for an interim period provided that MD&A for the most recent fiscal year has been (or will be) examined or reviewed (by either the CPA or a predecessor) and the CPA performs either an audit of the interim financial statements or a review for either of the following:

(1)   Public Entity A review of the financial statements for the related comparative interim periods and issues a review report in accordance with SAS 100.

        (2)   **Nonpublic Entity** A review of either (a) the financial statements for the related interim periods under SSARSs and issues a review report, or (b) the related condensed interim financial information in accordance with SAS 100 and issues a review report, and such information is accompanied by complete financial statements for the most recent audited fiscal year.

    c.   **Predecessor** If a predecessor audited prior-period financial statements, the successor CPA must acquire sufficient knowledge of the entity and apply appropriate procedures relating to prior years included in the MD&A presentation.

3.   **Scope** The practitioner considers the following as well as historical financial information:

    a.   *Pro Forma* **Information** The guidance in AT 401 when performing procedures with respect to any *pro forma* information, even if MD&A indicates that certain information is derived from unaudited financial statements.

    b.   **External Information** For example, debt ratings of a rating agency.

    c.   **Forward-Looking Information** Tested only for the purpose of expressing an opinion or providing limited assurance on MD&A taken as a whole. The CPA considers whether cautionary language concerning achievability is included.

    d.   **Voluntary Information** When the entity includes other information in MD&A required by other SEC regulations, the CPA also considers those other SEC criteria in subjecting such information to procedures.

4.   **Engagement Procedures** The CPA obtains an understanding of the SEC criteria for MD&A and management's MD&A preparation method; plans the engagement; considers materiality; considers relevant portions of the entity's internal control; considers subsequent events; and obtains appropriate written representations from management. The misstatement of an individual assertion is material if the magnitude of the misstatement (individually or aggregated) is such that a reasonable person would be influenced by its correction. A practitioner also considers whether management (and any assistants) has appropriate knowledge of rules and regulations of the SEC to prepare MD&A.

    a.   **Examination** The CPA obtains sufficient evidence, including testing completeness, and forms an opinion consistent with examination objectives. The CPA considers the results of financial statement audits for the periods covered by MD&A, including the possible impact on the examination engagement scope of a modified auditor's report.

    b.   **Review** Procedures generally are limited to inquiries and analytics concerning factors that have a material effect on financial condition, results of operations, and cash flows. The CPA also forms a conclusion consistent with review objectives.

5.   **Examination Performance** The CPA applies procedures to obtain reasonable assurance of detecting material misstatements. In a financial statement audit, the auditor applies procedures to some information included in MD&A. Because the objective of an audit is different from that of an examination of MD&A, additional procedures typically are performed in an examination.

6.   **Review Performance** The CPA develops an overall strategy for analytics and inquiries. The CPA considers factors such as matters affecting the entity's industry; matters relating to the entity's business; the types of relevant information that management reports to external analysts; the extent of management's knowledge of, and experience with, SEC criteria for MD&A; if the entity is a nonpublic entity, the intended use of MD&A; matters identified during other engagements; and, the nature of complex or subjective matters that may require special skill or knowledge.

7. **Reports** A report on a examination or review of MD&A includes the date of the completion of the CPA's procedures, which should not precede the date of the audit (or review) report on the latest historical financial statements covered by the MD&A. If the entity is a **non-public** entity, the following sentence is added to the beginning of the explanatory paragraph: "Although W Company is not subject to the rules and regulations of the Securities and Exchange Commission, the accompanying Management's Discussion and Analysis is intended to be a presentation in accordance with the rules and regulations adopted by the Securities and Exchange Commission."

Exhibit 37 ▶ Standard Report on Examination of MD&A

<u>Independent Accountant's Report</u>

We have examined W Company's Management's Discussion and Analysis taken as a whole, included [incorporated by reference] in the company's [insert description of registration statement or document]. Management is responsible for the preparation of the company's Management's Discussion and Analysis, pursuant to rules and regulations adopted by the Securities and Exchange Commission. Our responsibility is to express an opinion on the presentation based on our examination. We have audited, in accordance with auditing standards generally accepted in the United States of America, the financial statements of W Company as of December 31, 20X2 and 20X1, and for each of the years in the three-year periods ended December 31, 20X2, and in our report dated March 31, 20X3, we expressed an unqualified opinion on those financial statements.

The preparation of Management's Discussion and Analysis requires management to interpret the criteria, make determinations as to the relevancy of information to be included, and make estimates and assumptions that affect reported information. Management's Discussion and Analysis includes information regarding the estimated future impact of transactions and events that have occurred or are expected to occur, expected sources of liquidity and capital resources, operating trends, commitments, and uncertainties. Actual results in the future may differ materially from management's present assessment of this information because events and circumstances frequently do not occur as expected.

Our examination of Management's Discussion and Analysis was conducted in accordance with attestation standards established by the American Institute of Certified Public Accountants and, accordingly, included examining, on a test basis, evidence supporting the historical amounts and disclosures in the presentation. An examination also includes assessing the significant determinations made by management as to the relevancy of information to be included and the estimates and assumptions that affect reported information. We believe that our examination provides a reasonable basis for our opinion.

In our opinion, the company's presentation of Management's Discussion and Analysis includes, in all material respects, the required elements of the rules and regulations adopted by the Securities and Exchange Commission; the historical financial amounts included therein have been accurately derived, in all material respects, from the company's financial statements; and the underlying information, determinations, estimates, and assumptions of the company provide a reasonable basis for the disclosures contained therein.

Exhibit 38 ▶ Standard Report on Review of MD&A

<u>Independent Accountant's Report</u>

We have reviewed W Company's Management's Discussion and Analysis taken as a whole, included [incorporated by reference] in the company's [insert description of registration statement or document]. Management is responsible for the preparation of the company's Management's Discussion and Analysis, pursuant to rules and regulations adopted by the Securities and Exchange Commission. We have audited, in accordance with auditing standards generally accepted in the United States of America, the financial statements of W Company as of December 31, 20X2 and 20X1, and for each of the years in the three-year periods ended December 31, 20X2, and in our report dated March 31, 20X3, we expressed an unqualified opinion on those financial statements.

We conducted our review of Management's Discussion and Analysis in accordance with attestation standards established by the American Institute of Certified Public Accountants. A review of Management's Discussion and Analysis consists principally of applying analytical procedures and making inquiries of persons responsible for financial, accounting, and operational matters. It is substantially less in scope than an examination, the objective of which is the expression of an opinion on the presentation. Accordingly, we do not express such an opinion.

<Same explanatory paragraph as in an examination report>

Based on our review, nothing came to our attention that caused us to believe that the company's presentation of Management's Discussion and Analysis does not include, in all material respects, the required elements of the rules and regulations adopted by the Securities and Exchange Commission; that the historical financial amounts included therein have not been accurately derived, in all material respects, from the company's financial statements; or that the underlying information, determinations, estimates, and assumptions of the company do not provide a reasonable basis for the disclosures contained therein.

This report is intended solely for the information and use of [list or refer to specified parties] and is not intended to be and should not be used by anyone other than the specified parties.

---

8. **Review Presentation** In order for a CPA to issue a report on a review of MD&A, the financial statements for the periods covered by MD&A and the related auditor's or practitioner's report(s) should accompany MD&A (or be incorporated by reference to information filed with a regulatory agency). There are additional requirements in the following circumstances:

    a. **Interim Periods** The comparative financial statements for the most recent annual period and the related MD&A should accompany the interim MD&A (or be incorporated by reference). Generally, this requirement is satisfied by a public entity that has filed its annual financial statements and MD&A in its annual Form 10-K.

    b. **Nonpublic Entity** The MD&A should include a statement that it was prepared using SEC criteria or a separate written assertion should accompany MD&A.

CHAPTER 31—OTHER PROFESSIONAL SERVICES

Problem 31-1 MULTIPLE CHOICE QUESTIONS (106 to 133 minutes)

1. An accountant who had begun an audit of the financial statements of a nonissuer was asked to change the engagement to a review because of a restriction on the scope of the audit. If there is reasonable justification for the change, the accountant's review report should include reference to the

	Scope limitation that caused the changed engagement	Original engagement that was agreed to
a.	Yes	No
b.	No	Yes
c.	No	No
d.	Yes	Yes

(11/94, AUD, #78, amended, 5151)

2. In reviewing the financial statements of a nonissuer, an accountant is required to modify the standard review report for which of the following matters?

	Inability to assess the risk of material misstatement due to fraud	Discovery of significant deficiencies in the design of the entity's internal control
a.	Yes	Yes
b.	Yes	No
c.	No	Yes
d.	No	No

(R/01, AUD, #8, amended, 7023)

3 May an accountant accept an engagement to compile or review the financial statements of a not-for-profit entity if the accountant is unfamiliar with the specialized industry accounting principles, but plans to obtain the required level of knowledge before compiling or reviewing the financial statements?

	Compilation	Review
a.	No	No
b.	Yes	No
c.	No	Yes
d.	Yes	Yes

(5/94, AUD, #46, 4711)

4. If requested to perform a review engagement for a nonissuer in which an accountant has an immaterial direct financial interest, the accountant is
a. Not independent and, therefore, may not be associated with the financial statements
b. Not independent and, therefore, may not issue a review report
c. Not independent and, therefore, may issue a review report, but may not issue an auditor's opinion
d. Independent because the financial interest is immaterial and, therefore, may issue a review report   (5/95, AUD, #20, amended, 5638)

5. An accountant should perform analytical procedures during an engagement to

	Compile a nonissuer's financial statements	Review a nonissuer's financial statements
a.	No	No
b.	Yes	Yes
c.	Yes	No
d.	No	Yes

(5/94, AUD, #59, amended, 4724)

6. Which of the following procedures is usually the first step in reviewing the financial statements of a nonissuer?
a. Make preliminary judgments about risk and materiality to determine the scope and nature of the procedures to be performed
b. Obtain a general understanding of the entity's organization, its operating characteristics, and its products or services
c. Assess the risk of material misstatement arising from fraudulent financial reporting and the misappropriation of assets
d. Perform a preliminary assessment of the operating efficiency of the entity's internal control activities   (R/06, AUD, #33, amended, 8151)

7. A CPA is required to comply with the provisions of *Statements on Standards for Accounting and Review Services* when

	Processing financial data for clients of other CPA firms	Consulting on accounting matters
a.	Yes	Yes
b.	Yes	No
c.	No	Yes
d.	No	No

(11/93, AUD, #12, 4249)

8. An accountant is required to comply with the provisions of *Statements on Standards for Accounting and Review Services* when

I. Reproducing client-prepared financial statements, without modification, as an accommodation to a client
II. Preparing standard monthly journal entries for depreciation and expiration of prepaid expenses

a. I only
b. II only
c. Both I and II
d. Neither I nor II   (5/96, AUD, #1, 6233)

9. When engaged to compile the financial statements of a nonissuer, an accountant is required to possess a level of knowledge of the entity's accounting principles and practices. This requirement most likely will include obtaining a general understanding of the
a. Stated qualifications of the entity's accounting personnel
b. Design of the entity's internal controls placed in operation
c. Risk factors relating to misstatements arising from illegal acts
d. Internal control awareness of the entity's senior management   (R/99, AUD, #7, amended, 6823)

10. Miller, CPA, is engaged to compile the financial statements of Web Co., a nonissuer, in conformity with the income tax basis of accounting. If Web's financial statements do not disclose the basis of accounting used, Miller should
a. Disclose the basis of accounting in the accountant's compilation report
b. Clearly label each page "Distribution Restricted—Material Modifications Required"
c. Issue a special report describing the effect of the incomplete presentation
d. Withdraw from the engagement and provide no further services to Web
         (11/94, AUD, #81, amended, 5154)

11. An accountant may compile a nonissuer's financial statements that omit all of the disclosures required by GAAP only if the omission is

I. Clearly indicated in the accountant's report
II. Not undertaken with the intention of misleading the financial statement users

a. I only
b. II only
c. Both I and II
d. Either I or II   (5/94, AUD, #79, amended, 4744)

12. Compiled financial statements should be accompanied by a report stating that
a. A compilation is substantially less in scope than a review or an audit in accordance with generally accepted auditing standards.
b. The accountant does not express an opinion but expresses only limited assurance on the compiled financial statements.
c. A compilation is limited to presenting in the form of financial statements information that is the representation of management.
d. The accountant has compiled the financial statements in accordance with standards established by the Auditing Standards Board.
         (5/94, AUD, #78, 4743)

13. Which of the following representations does an accountant make implicitly when issuing the standard report for the compilation of a nonissuer's financial statements?
a. The accountant is independent with respect to the entity.
b. The financial statements have not been audited.
c. A compilation consists principally of inquiries and analytical procedures.
d. The accountant does not express any assurance on the financial statements.
         (11/93, AUD, #54, amended, 4291)

14. An accountant has compiled the financial statements of a nonissuer in accordance with Statements on Standards for Accounting and Review Services (SSARS). Does SSARS require that the compilation report be printed on the accountant's letterhead and that the report be manually signed by the accountant?

	Printed on the accountant's letterhead	Manually signed by the accountant
a.	Yes	Yes
b.	Yes	No
c.	No	Yes
d.	No	No

         (R/99, AUD, #1, amended, 6817)

15. Financial statements of a nonissuer compiled without audit or review by an accountant should be accompanied by a report stating that
a. The scope of the accountant's procedures has not been restricted in testing the financial information that is the representation of management.
b. The accountant assessed the accounting principles used and significant estimates made by management.
c. The accountant does not express an opinion or any other form of assurance on the financial statements.
d. A compilation consists principally of inquiries of entity personnel and analytical procedures applied to financial data.
(11/95, AUD, #80, amended, 6027)

16. Compiled financial statements should be accompanied by an accountant's report stating that
a. A compilation includes assessing the accounting principles used and significant management estimates, as well as evaluating the overall financial statement presentation.
b. The accountant compiled the financial statements in accordance with *Statements on Standards for Accounting and Review Services.*
c. A compilation is substantially less in scope than an audit in accordance with GAAS, the objective of which is the expression of an opinion.
d. The accountant is not aware of any material modifications that should be made to the financial statements to conform with GAAP.
(5/95, AUD, #78, 5696)

17. An accountant's standard report issued after compiling the financial statements of a nonissuer should state that
a. I am **not** aware of any material modifications that should be made to the accompanying financial statements.
b. A compilation consists principally of inquiries of company personnel and analytical procedures.
c. A compilation is limited to presenting in the form of financial statements information that is the representation of management.
d. A compilation is substantially **less** in scope than an audit in accordance with GAAS, the objective of which is the expression of an opinion.
(R/06, AUD, #36, amended, 8154)

18. What type of analytical procedure would an auditor most likely use in developing relationships among balance sheet accounts when reviewing the financial statements of a nonissuer?
a. Trend analysis
b. Regression analysis
c. Ratio analysis
d. Risk analysis (5/95, AUD, #74, amended, 5692)

19. Which of the following should be the first step in reviewing the financial statements of a nonissuer?
a. Comparing the financial statements with statements for comparable prior periods and with anticipated results
b. Completing a series of inquiries concerning the entity's procedures for recording, classifying, and summarizing transactions
c. Obtaining a general understanding of the entity's organization, its operating characteristics, and its products or services
d. Applying analytical procedures designed to identify relationships and individual items that appear to be unusual (R/05, AUD, #13, amended, 7808)

20. Which of the following procedures should an accountant perform during an engagement to review the financial statements of a nonissuer?
a. Communicating significant deficiencies discovered during the assessment of control risk
b. Obtaining a representation letter from members of management
c. Sending bank confirmation letters to the entity's financial institutions
d. Examining cash disbursements in the subsequent period for unrecorded liabilities
(11/94, AUD, #75, amended, 5148)

21. When performing an engagement to review a nonissuer's financial statements, an accountant most likely would
a. Obtain an understanding of the entity's internal control
b. Limit the distribution of the accountant's report
c. Confirm a sample of significant accounts receivable balances
d. Ask about actions taken at board of directors' meetings (R/05, AUD, #8, amended, 7803)

22. Each page of a nonissuer's financial statements reviewed by an accountant should include the following reference:
a. See Accompanying Accountant's Footnotes
b. Reviewed, **No** Material Modifications Required
c. See Accountant's Review Report
d. Reviewed, No Accountant's Assurance Expressed (5/95, AUD, #81, amended, 5699)

23. Baker, CPA, was engaged to review the financial statements of Hall Co., a nonissuer. During the engagement Baker uncovered a complex scheme involving client illegal acts and fraud that materially affect Hall's financial statements. If Baker believes that modification of the standard review report is not adequate to indicate the deficiencies in the financial statements, Baker should
a. Disclaim an opinion
b. Issue an adverse opinion
c. Withdraw from the engagement
d. Issue a qualified opinion
(5/95, AUD, #80, amended, 5698)

24. Which of the following would be used on a review engagement?
a. Examination of board minutes
b. Confirmation of cash and accounts receivable
c. Comparison of current-year to prior-year account balances
d. Recalculation of depreciation expense
(R/06, AUD, #50, 8168)

25. During an engagement to review the financial statements of a nonissuer, an accountant becomes aware that several leases that should be capitalized are not capitalized. The accountant considers these leases to be material to the financial statements. The accountant decides to modify the standard review report because management will not capitalize the leases. Under these circumstances, the accountant should
a. Issue an adverse opinion because of the departure from GAAP
b. Express no assurance of any kind on the entity's financial statements
c. Emphasize that the financial statements are for limited use only
d. Disclose the departure from GAAP in a separate paragraph of the accountant's report
(5/96, AUD, #7, amended, 6239)

26. Select **two** responses. The standard report issued by an accountant after reviewing the financial statements of a nonissuer states that
a. A review includes assessing the accounting principles used and significant estimates made by management.
b. A review includes examining, on a test basis, evidence supporting the amounts and disclosures in the financial statements.
c. The engagement was performed in accordance with Statements on Standards for Accounting and Review Services issued by the American Institute of Certified Public Accountants.
d. The accountant is not aware of any material modifications that should be made to the financial statements.
e. The accountant does not express an opinion or any other form of assurance on the financial statements. (11/92, AUD, #53, amended, 2987)

27. Moore, CPA, has been asked to issue a review report on the balance sheet of Dover Co., a nonissuer. Moore will not be reporting on Dover's statements of income, retained earnings, and cash flows. Moore may issue the review report provided the
a. Balance sheet is presented in a prescribed form of an industry trade association.
b. Scope of the inquiry and analytical procedures has not been restricted.
c. Balance sheet is not to be used to obtain credit or distributed to creditors.
d. Specialized accounting principles and practices of Dover's industry are disclosed.
(5/95, AUD, #79, amended, 5697)

28. An accountant is asked to issue a review report on the balance sheet, but not on other related statements. The scope of the inquiry and analytical procedures has not been restricted, but the client failed to provide a representation letter. Which of the following should the accountant issue under these circumstances?
a. Review report with a qualification
b. Review report with a disclaimer
c. Review report and footnote exceptions
d. Compilation report with the client's consent
(R/05, AUD, #49, 7844)

29. Financial statements of a nonissuer that have been reviewed by an accountant should be accompanied by a report stating that a review
a. Provides only limited assurance that the financial statements are fairly presented
b. Includes examining, on a test basis, information that is the representation of management
c. Consists principally of inquiries of company personnel and analytical procedures applied to financial data
d. Does not contemplate obtaining corroborating evidential matter or applying certain other procedures ordinarily performed during an audit
(11/95, AUD, #79, 6026)

30. Financial Information is presented in a printed form that prescribes the wording of the independent auditor's report. The form is not acceptable to the auditor because the form calls for statements that are inconsistent with the auditor's responsibility. Under these circumstances, the auditor most likely would
a. Withdraw from the engagement
b. Reword the form or attach a separate report
c. Express a qualified opinion with an explanation
d. Limit distribution of the report to the party who designed the form (11/96, AUD, #16, 6368)

31. Kell engaged March, CPA, to submit to Kell a written personal financial plan containing unaudited personal financial statements. March anticipates omitting certain disclosures required by GAAP because the engagement's sole purpose is to assist Kell in developing a personal financial plan. For March to be exempt from complying with the requirements of SSARS 1, *Compilation and Review of Financial Statements,* Kell is required to agree that the
a. Financial statements will not be presented in comparative form with those of the prior period.
b. Omitted disclosures required by GAAP are not material.
c. Financial statements will not be disclosed to a non-CPA financial planner.
d. Financial statements will not be used to obtain credit. (5/95, AUD, #21, 5639)

32. Must a CPA in public practice be independent in fact and appearance when providing the following services?

	Compilation of personal financial statements	Preparation of a tax return	Compilation of a financial forecast
a.	No	No	No
b.	No	No	Yes
c.	Yes	No	No
d.	No	Yes	No

(5/92, AUD, #56, 2809)

33. Clark, CPA, compiled and properly reported on the financial statements of Green Co., a nonissuer, for the year ended March 31, year 1. These financial statements omitted substantially all disclosures required by generally accepted accounting principles (GAAP). Green asked Clark to compile the statements for the year ended March 31, year 2, and to include all GAAP disclosures for year 2 statements only, but otherwise present both years' financial statements in comparative form. What is Clark's responsibility concerning the proposed engagement?
a. Clark may **not** report on the comparative financial statements because the year 1 statements are **not** comparable to the year 2 statements that include the GAAP disclosures.
b. Clark may report on the comparative financial statements provided Clark updates the report on the year 1 statements that do **not** include the GAAP disclosures.
c. Clark may report on the comparative financial statements provided an explanatory paragraph is added to Clark's report on the comparative financial statements.
d. Clark may report on the comparative financial statements provided the year 1 statements do not contain any obvious material misstatements.
(5/92, AUD, #4, amended, 2757)

34. Gole, CPA, is engaged to review the year 4 financial statements of North Co., a nonissuer. Previously, Gole audited North's year 3 financial statements and expressed an unqualified opinion. Gole decides to include a separate paragraph in the year 4 review report because North plans to present comparative financial statements for year 4 and year 3. This separate paragraph should indicate that

a. The year 4 review report is intended solely for the information of management and the board of directors.
b. There are justifiable reasons for changing the level of service from an audit to a review.
c. No auditing procedures were performed after the date of the year 3 auditor's report.
d. The year 3 auditor's report may no longer be relied on.   (11/94, AUD, #79, amended, 5152)

35. A nonissuer engaged a CPA to determine whether the client's Web sites meet defined criteria for standard business practices and controls over transaction integrity and information protection. In performing this engagement, the CPA should comply with the provisions of
a. Statements on Assurance Standards
b. Statements on Standards for Attestation Engagements
c. Statements on Standards for Management Consulting Services
d. Statements on Auditing Standards
          (R/99, AUD, #3, amended, 6819)

36. A CPA is required to comply with the provisions of *Statements on Standards for Attestation Engagements* (SSAE) when engaged to
a. Report on financial statements that the CPA generated through the use of computer software
b. Review management's discussion and analysis (MD&A) prepared pursuant to rules and regulations adopted by the SEC
c. Provide the client with a financial statement format that does **not** include dollar amounts
d. Audit financial statements that the client prepared for use in another country
          (R/02, AUD, #13, 7103)

37. Which of the following activities would most likely be considered an attestation engagement?
a. Consulting with management representatives of a firm to provide advice
b. Issuing a report about a firm's compliance with laws and regulations
c. Advocating a client's position on tax matters that are being reviewed by the IRS
d. Preparing a client's tax returns
          (R/05, AUD, #40, 7835)

38. Which of the following is a conceptual difference between the attestation standards and generally accepted auditing standards?
a. The attestation standards provide a framework for the attest function beyond historical financial statements.
b. The requirement that the practitioner be independent in mental attitude is omitted from the attestation standards.
c. The attestation standards do not permit an attest engagement to be part of a business acquisition study or a feasibility study.
d. None of the standards of fieldwork in generally accepted auditing standards are included in the attestation standards.   (5/94, AUD, #10, 4675)

39. Negative assurance may be expressed when an accountant is requested to report on the

I. Results of applying agreed-upon procedures to an account within unaudited financial statements
II. Compilation of prospective financial statements

a. I only
b. II only
c. Both I and II
d. Neither I nor II   (Editors, 0430)

40. Which of the following is **not** an attestation standard?
a. The practitioner must obtain sufficient evidence to provide a reasonable basis for the conclusion that is expressed in the report.
b. The practitioner must identify the subject matter or the assertion being reported on and state the character of the engagement in the report.
c. The practitioner must adequately plan the work and must properly supervise any assistants.
d. A sufficient understanding of internal control shall be obtained to plan the engagement.
          (5/93, AUD, #4, amended, 3900)

41. An accountant's standard report on a compilation of a projection should **not** include a
a. Statement that a compilation of a projection is limited in scope
b. Disclaimer of responsibility to update the report for events occurring after the report's date
c. Statement that the accountant expresses only limited assurance that the results may be achieved
d. Caveat that the prospective results may not be achieved   (11/93, AUD, #57, amended, 4294)

42. An accountant may accept an engagement to apply agreed-upon procedures to prospective financial statements provided that
a. Use of the report is restricted to the specified users.
b. The prospective financial statements are also examined.
c. Responsibility for the adequacy of the procedures performed is taken by the accountant.
d. Negative assurance is expressed on the prospective financial statements taken as a whole.
(11/94, AUD, #23, amended, 5096)

43. When an accountant examines a financial forecast that fails to disclose several significant assumptions used to prepare the forecast, the accountant should describe the assumptions in the accountant's report and issue a(an)
a. Unqualified opinion with a separate explanatory paragraph
b. "Subject to" qualified opinion
c. "Except for" qualified opinion
d. Adverse opinion (Editors, 0432)

44. When a CPA examines a client's projected financial statements, the CPA's report should
a. Explain the principal differences between historical and projected financial statements
b. State that the CPA performed procedures to evaluate management's assumptions
c. Refer to the CPA's auditor's report on the historical financial statements
d. Include the CPA's opinion on the client's ability to continue as a going concern
(R/02, AUD, #1, 7091)

45. When an accountant compiles a financial forecast, the accountant's report should include a(an)
a. Explanation of the differences between a financial forecast and a financial projection
b. Caveat that the prospective results of the financial forecast may **not** be achieved
c. Statement that the accountant's responsibility to update the report is limited to one year
d. Disclaimer of opinion on the reliability of the entity's internal controls (R/06, AUD, #32, 8150)

46. Which of the following conditions is necessary for an auditor to accept an engagement to examine the design and operating effectiveness of a nonissuer's internal control over financial reporting that is integrated with an audit of financial statements?
a. The auditor anticipates relying on the entity's internal control in a financial statement audit.
b. Management provides its assertion about the effectiveness of internal control in a report that accompanies the auditor's report.
c. The auditor is a continuing auditor who previously has audited the entity's financial statements.
d. Management agrees not to present the auditor's report in a general-use document to stockholders. (11/94, AUD, #18, amended, 5091)

47. In reporting on a nonissuer's internal control over financial reporting, an auditor should include a paragraph that describes the
a. Documentary evidence regarding the control environment factors
b. Changes in internal control since the prior report
c. Potential benefits from the auditor's suggested improvements
d. Inherent limitations of any internal control structure (5/95, AUD, #84, amended, 5702)

48. Brown, CPA, has accepted an engagement to examine the effectiveness of internal control over financial reporting of Crow Company (a nonissuer). Crow Company's written assertion about the effectiveness of internal control should be presented

I. In a separate report that will accompany Brown's report
II. In a representation letter to Brown

a. Neither I nor II
b. Either I or II
c. I only
d. II only (11/95, AUD, #36, amended, 5983)

49. How do the scope, procedures, and objective of an engagement to examine the design and operating effectiveness of an entity's internal control over financial reporting compare to those for obtaining an understanding of internal control and assessing control risk as part of an audit?

	Scope	Procedures	Objective
a.	Similar	Different	Similar
b.	Different	Similar	Similar
c.	Different	Different	Different
d.	Different	Similar	Different

(5/90, AUD, #40, amended, 0400)

50. Mill, CPA, was engaged by a group of royalty recipients to apply agreed-upon procedures to financial data supplied by Modern Co. regarding Modern's written assertion about its compliance with contractual requirements to pay royalties. Mill's report on these agreed-upon procedures should contain a (an)
a. Disclaimer of opinion about the fair presentation of Modern's financial statements
b. List of the procedures performed (or reference thereto) and Mill's findings
c. Opinion about the effectiveness of Modern's internal control activities concerning royalty payments
d. Acknowledgment that the sufficiency of the procedures is solely Mill's responsibility

(R/01, AUD, #13, 7028)

51. A CPA's report on agreed-upon procedures related to management's assertion about an entity's compliance with specified requirements should contain
a. A statement of restrictions on the use of the report
b. An opinion about whether management's assertion is fairly stated
c. Negative assurance that control risk has not been assessed
d. An acknowledgment of responsibility for the sufficiency of the procedures

(11/95, AUD, #81, 6028)

52. A practitioner's report on agreed-upon procedures that is in the form of procedures and findings should contain
a. Negative assurance that the procedures did **not** necessarily disclose all reportable conditions
b. An acknowledgment of the practitioner's responsibility for the sufficiency of the procedures
c. A statement of restrictions on the use of the report
d. A disclaimer of opinion on the entity's financial statements

(R/06, AUD, #14, 8132)

53. An accountant's report on a review of pro forma financial information should include a
a. Statement that the entity's internal control was not relied on in the review
b. Disclaimer of opinion on the financial statements from which the pro forma financial information is derived
c. Caveat that it is uncertain whether the transaction or event reflected in the pro forma financial information will ever occur
d. Reference to the financial statements from which the historical financial information is derived

(5/94, AUD, #68, amended, 4733)

Problem 31-2 ADDITIONAL MULTIPLE CHOICE QUESTIONS (76 to 95 minutes)

54. The authoritative body designated to promulgate standards concerning an accountant's association with unaudited financial statements of an entity that is **not** required to file financial statements with an agency regulating the issuance of the entity's securities is the
a. Financial Accounting Standards Board
b. Government Accountability Office
c. Accounting and Review Services Committee
d. Auditing Standards Board

(11/90, AUD, #40, 0006)

55. Which of the following statements is correct concerning both an engagement to compile or to review a nonissuer's financial statements?
a. The accountant should obtain a written management representation letter.
b. The accountant must be independent in fact and appearance.
c. The accountant expresses **no** assurance on the financial statements.
d. The accountant does **not** contemplate obtaining an understanding of internal control.

(11/91, AUD, #59, amended, 2327)

56. When providing limited assurance that the financial statements of a nonissuer require no material modifications to be in accordance with generally accepted accounting principles, the accountant should
a. Assess the risk that a material misstatement could occur in a financial statement assertion
b. Confirm with the entity's lawyer that material loss contingencies are disclosed
c. Understand the accounting principles of the industry in which the entity operates
d. Develop audit programs to determine whether the entity's financial statements are fairly presented

(5/95, AUD, #58, amended, 5676)

57. Under which of the following circumstances would an accountant most likely conclude that it is necessary to withdraw from an engagement to review a nonissuer's financial statements?

a. The entity does **not** have reasonable justification for making a change in accounting principle.

b. The entity prepares its financial statements on the income tax basis of accounting.

c. The entity requests the accountant to report only on the balance sheet, and not on the other financial statements.

d. The entity declines to provide the accountant with a signed representation letter.
(R/03, AUD, #5, amended, 7627)

58. *Statements on Standards for Accounting and Review Services* (SSARS) require an accountant to report when the accountant has

a. Typed client-prepared financial statements, without modification, as an accommodation to the client

b. Provided a client with a financial statement format that does **not** include dollar amounts, to be used by the client in preparing financial statements

c. Proposed correcting journal entries to be recorded by the client that change client-prepared financial statements

d. Generated, through the use of computer software, financial statements prepared in accordance with a comprehensive basis of accounting other than GAAP   (11/94, AUD, #22, 5095)

59. *Statements on Standards for Accounting and Review Services* establish standards and procedures for which of the following engagements?

a. Assisting in adjusting the books of account for a partnership

b. Reviewing interim financial data required to be filed with the SEC

c. Processing financial data for clients of other accounting firms

d. Compiling an individual's personal financial statement to be used to obtain a mortgage
(11/91, AUD, #13, 2281)

60. Which of the following describes how the objective of a review of financial statements differs from the objective of a compilation engagement?

a. The primary objective of a review engagement is to test the completeness of the financial statements prepared, but a compilation tests for reasonableness.

b. The primary objective of a review engagement is to provide positive assurance that the financial statements are fairly presented, but a compilation provides **no** such assurance.

c. In a review engagement, accountants provide limited assurance, but a compilation expresses **no** assurance.

d. In a review engagement, accountants provide reasonable or positive assurance that the financial statements are fairly presented, but a compilation provides limited assurance.
(R/07, AUD, #9, 8381)

61. Which of the following procedures is ordinarily performed by an accountant in a compilation engagement of a nonissuer?

a. Reading the financial statements to consider whether they are free of obvious mistakes in the application of accounting principles

b. Obtaining written representations from management indicating that the compiled financial statements will not be used to obtain credit

c. Making inquiries of management concerning actions taken at meetings of the stockholders and the board of directors

d. Applying analytical procedures designed to corroborate management's assertions that are embodied in the financial statement components
(5/95, AUD, #75, amended, 5693)

62. When compiling the financial statements of a nonissuer, an accountant should

a. Review agreements with financial institutions for restrictions on cash balances

b. Understand the accounting principles and practices of the entity's industry

c. Inquire of key personnel concerning related parties and subsequent events

d. Perform ratio analyses of the financial data of comparable prior periods
(11/92, AUD, #44, amended, 2978)

63. How does an accountant make the following representations when issuing the standard report for the compilation of a nonissuer's financial statements?

	The financial statements have not been audited	The accountant has compiled the financial statements
a.	Implicitly	Implicitly
b.	Explicitly	Explicitly
c.	Implicitly	Explicitly
d.	Explicitly	Implicitly

(11/91, AUD, #26, amended, 2294)

64. When an accountant is engaged to compile a nonissuer's financial statements that omit substantially all disclosures required by GAAP, the accountant should indicate in the compilation report that the financial statements are
a. Not designed for those who are uninformed about the omitted disclosures
b. Prepared in conformity with a comprehensive basis of accounting other than GAAP
c. Not compiled in accordance with Statements on Standards for Accounting and Review Services
d. Special-purpose financial statements that are not comparable to those of prior periods

(11/94, AUD, #82, amended, 5155)

65. An accountant had begun to audit the financial statements of a nonissuer. Which of the following circumstances most likely would be considered a reasonable basis for agreeing to the entity's request to change the engagement to a compilation?
a. The entity's management does **not** provide the accountant with a signed representation letter.
b. The accountant is prohibited from corresponding with the entity's legal counsel.
c. The entity's principal creditors **no** longer require the entity to furnish audited financial statements.
d. The accountant is prevented from examining the minutes of the board of directors' meetings.

(R/05, AUD, #27, amended, 7822)

66. Which of the following procedures is **not** usually performed by the accountant during a review engagement of a nonissuer?
a. Inquiring about actions taken at meetings of the board of directors that may affect the financial statements
b. Issuing a report stating that the review was performed in accordance with standards established by the AICPA
c. Reading the financial statements to consider whether they conform with generally accepted accounting principles
d. Communicating any material weaknesses discovered during the consideration of internal control

(11/92, AUD, #45, amended, 2979)

67. Which of the following inquiry or analytical procedures ordinarily is performed in an engagement to review a nonissuer's financial statements?
a. Analytical procedures designed to test the accounting records by obtaining corroborating evidential matter
b. Inquiries concerning the entity's procedures for recording and summarizing transactions
c. Analytical procedures designed to test management's assertions regarding continued existence
d. Inquiries of the entity's attorney concerning contingent liabilities

(11/92, AUD, #43, amended, 2977)

68. Which of the following procedures would an accountant **least** likely perform during an engagement to review the financial statements of a nonissuer?
a. Observing the safeguards over access to and use of assets and records
b. Comparing the financial statements with anticipated results in budgets and forecasts
c. Inquiring of management about actions taken at the board of directors' meetings
d. Studying the relationships of financial statement elements expected to conform to predictable patterns

(11/94, AUD, #74, amended, 5147)

69. An accountant has been engaged to review a nonissuer's financial statements that contain several departures from GAAP. If the financial statements are **not** revised and modification of the standard review report is **not** adequate to indicate the deficiencies, the accountant should
a. Withdraw from the engagement and provide no further services concerning these financial statements
b. Inform management that the engagement can proceed only if distribution of the accountant's report is restricted to internal users
c. Determine the effects of the departures from GAAP and issue a special report on the financial statements
d. Issue a modified review report provided the entity agrees that the financial statements will not be used to obtain credit

(11/94, AUD, #20, amended, 5093)

70. Which of the following procedures is usually performed by the accountant in a review engagement of a nonissuer?
a. Sending a letter of inquiry to the entity's lawyer
b. Comparing the financial statements with statements for comparable prior periods
c. Confirmation of receivables
d. Communicating significant deficiencies discovered during the study of internal control

(5/92, AUD, #34, amended, 2787)

71. An accountant has been asked to issue a review report on the balance sheet of a nonissuer without reporting on the related statements of income, retained earnings, and cash flows. The accountant may issue the requested review report only if

a. The balance sheet is **not** to be used to obtain credit or distributed to the entity's creditors.
b. The balance sheet is part of a comprehensive personal financial plan developed to assist the entity.
c. There have been **no** material changes during the year in the entity's accounting principles.
d. The scope of the accountant's inquiry and analytical procedures has **not** been restricted.
(R/05, AUD, #30, amended, 7825)

72. Which of the following statements is correct regarding a review engagement of a nonissuer's financial statements performed in accordance with the Statements on Standards for Accounting and Review Services (SSARS)?

a. An accountant must establish an understanding with the client in an engagement letter.
b. An accountant must obtain an understanding of the client's internal control when performing a review.
c. A review provides an accountant with a basis for expressing limited assurance on the financial statements.
d. A review report contains an accountant's opinion of the financial statements taken as a whole.
(R/07, AUD, #6, amended, 8378)

73. Which of the following procedures does a CPA normally perform first in a review engagement in accordance with Statements on Standards for Accounting and Review Services (SSARS)?

a. Inquiry regarding the client's principles and practices and the method of applying them
b. Inquiry concerning the effectiveness of the client's system of internal control
c. Inquiry to identify transactions between related parties and management
d. Inquiry of the client's professional advisors, including bankers, insurance agents, and consultants (R/07, AUD, #7, 8379)

74. The standard report issued by an accountant after reviewing the financial statements of a nonissuer should state that

a. A review is limited to presenting in the form of financial statements information that is the representation of management.
b. A review consists of inquiries of company personnel and analytical procedures applied to financial data.
c. The accountant does **not** express an opinion or any other form of assurance on the financial statements.
d. The accountant did **not** obtain an understanding of the entity's internal control or assess fraud risk. (R/07, AUD, #38, amended, 8410)

75. While auditing the financial statements of a nonissuer, a CPA was requested to change the engagement to a review in accordance with Statements on Standards for Accounting and Review Services (SSARS) because of a scope limitation. If the CPA believes the client's request is reasonable, the CPA's review report should

I. Refer to the scope limitation that caused the change
II. Describe the auditing procedures that have already been applied

a. I only
b. II only
c. Both I and II
d. Neither I nor II (R/07, AUD, #44, amended, 8416)

76. When unaudited financial statements are presented in comparative form with audited financial statements in a document filed with the Securities and Exchange Commission, such statements should be

	Marked as "unaudited"	Withheld until audited	Referred to in the auditor's report
a.	Yes	No	No
b.	Yes	No	Yes
c.	No	Yes	Yes
d.	No	Yes	No

(11/93, AUD, #50, 4287)

77. When unaudited financial statements of a nonissuer are presented in comparative form with audited financial statements in the subsequent year, the unaudited financial statements should be clearly marked to indicate their status and

I. The report on the unaudited financial statements should be reissued.
II. The report on the audited financial statements should include a separate paragraph describing the responsibility assumed for the unaudited financial statements.

a. I only
b. II only
c. Both I and II
d. Either I or II   (5/94, AUD, #89, amended, 4754)

78. A CPA in public practice is required to comply with the provisions of the Statements on Standards for Attestation Engagements (SSAE) when

	Testifying as an expert witness in accounting and auditing matters given stipulated facts	Compiling a client's financial projection that presents a hypothetical course of action
a.	Yes	Yes
b.	Yes	No
c.	No	Yes
d.	No	No

(R/01, AUD, #1, 7016)

79. Which of the following professional services would be considered an attestation engagement?
a. Advocating on behalf of a client about trust tax matters under review by the Internal Revenue Service
b. Providing financial analysis, planning, and capital acquisition services as a part-time, in-house controller
c. Advising management in the selection of a computer system to meet business needs
d. Preparing the income statement and balance sheet for one year in the future based on client expectations and predictions

(R/05, AUD, #43, 7838)

80. An accountant has been engaged to examine pro forma adjustments that show the effects on previously audited historical financial statements due to a proposed disposition of a significant portion of an entity's business. Other than the procedures previously applied to the historical financial statements, the accountant is required to

	Reevaluate the entity's internal control over financial reporting	Determine that the computations of the pro forma adjustments are mathematically correct
a.	Yes	Yes
b.	Yes	No
c.	No	Yes
d.	No	No

(R/03, AUD, #6, 7628)

81. Which of the following procedures would be most effective in reducing attestation risk?
a. Discussion with responsible individuals
b. Examination of evidence
c. Inquiries of senior management
d. Analytical procedures   (R/07, AUD, #4, 8376)

82. A CPA is engaged to examine management's assertion that the entity's schedule of investment returns is presented in accordance with specific criteria. In performing this engagement, the CPA should comply with the provisions of
a. Statements on Standards for Accounting and Review Services (SSARS)
b. Statements on Auditing Standards (SAS)
c. Statements on Standards for Consulting Services (SSCS)
d. Statements on Standards for Attestation Engagements (SSAE)   (R/07, AUD, #43, 8415)

83. Which of the following is a prospective financial statement for general use upon which an accountant may appropriately report?
a. Pro forma financial statement
b. Partial presentation
c. Financial projection
d. Financial forecast   (Editors, 7511)

84. When an accountant examines projected financial statements, the accountant's report should include a separate paragraph that
a. Restricts the use of the report because it is intended to be used solely by specified parties
b. Provides an explanation of the differences between an examination and an audit
c. States that the accountant is responsible for events and circumstances up to one year after the report's date
d. Disclaims an opinion on whether the assumptions provide a reasonable basis for the projection
(11/95, AUD, #82, amended, 6029)

85. Which of the following statements concerning prospective financial statements is correct?
a. Only a financial forecast would normally be appropriate for limited use.
b. Only a financial projection would normally be appropriate for general use.
c. Any type of prospective financial statement would normally be appropriate for limited use.
d. Any type of prospective financial statement would normally be appropriate for general use.
(5/90, AUD, #23, 0424)

86. An accountant's compilation report on a financial forecast should include a statement that
a. The forecast should be read only in conjunction with the audited historical financial statements.
b. The accountant expresses only limited assurance on the forecasted statements and their assumptions.
c. There will usually be differences between the forecasted and actual results.
d. The hypothetical assumptions used in the forecast are reasonable in the circumstances.
(11/94, AUD, #83, 5156)

87. Accepting an engagement to examine an entity's financial projection most likely would be appropriate if the projection were to be used by
a. All employees who work for the entity
b. Potential stockholders who request a prospectus or a registration statement
c. All stockholders of record as of the report date
d. A bank with which the entity is negotiating for a loan (5/94, AUD, #14, amended, 4679)

88. An examination of a financial forecast is a professional service that involves
a. Compiling or assembling a financial forecast that is based on management's assumptions
b. Evaluating the preparation of a financial forecast and the support underlying management's assumptions
c. Assuming responsibility to update management on key events for one year after the report's date
d. Limiting the distribution of the accountant's report to management and the board of directors
(5/95, AUD, #22, amended, 5640)

89. An accountant's standard report on a compilation of a projection should not include a statement that
a. There will usually be differences between the forecasted and actual results.
b. The hypothetical assumptions used in the projection are reasonable in the circumstances.
c. The accountant has no responsibility to update the report for future events and circumstances.
d. The compilation of a projection is limited in scope. (R/05, AUD, #19, 7814)

90. When an accountant compiles projected financial statements, the accountant's report should include a separate paragraph that
a. Explains the difference between a compilation and a review
b. Documents the assessment of the risk of material misstatement due to fraud
c. Expresses limited assurance that the actual results may be within the projected range
d. Describes the limitations on the projection's usefulness (R/07, AUD, #39, 8411)

91. An accountant may accept an engagement to apply agreed-upon procedures to prospective financial statements provided the
a. Provisions of Statements on Standards for Accounting and Review Services (SSARS) are followed.
b. Accountant also examines the prospective financial statements.
c. Distribution of the report is restricted to the specified users.
d. The accountant takes responsibility for the adequacy of the procedures performed.
(R/07, AUD, #49, 8421)

SIMULATIONS

Problem 31-3 (15 to 25 minutes)

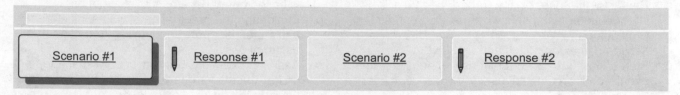

Wallace & Wallace, CPAs, audited the financial statements of West Co., a nonissuer, for the year ended September 30, year 1, and expressed an unqualified opinion. For the year ended September 30, year 2, West issued comparative financial statements. Wallace & Wallace reviewed West's year 2 financial statements and Gordon, an assistant on the engagement, drafted the accountant's review report below. Martin, the engagement supervisor, decided not to reissue the prior year's auditor's report, but instructed Gordon to include a separate paragraph in the current year's review report describing the responsibility assumed for the prior year's audited financial statements.

Martin reviewed Gordon's draft and indicated that there were many deficiencies in Gordon's draft.

Accountant's Review Report

We have reviewed the accompanying balance sheet of West Company as of September 30, year 2, and the related statements of income and cash flows for the year then ended, in accordance with standards issued by the American Institute of Certified Public Accountants. All information included in these financial statements is the representation of the management of West Company. Our responsibility is to express limited assurance on these financial statements based on our review.

A review consists principally of inquiries of company personnel and analytical procedures applied to financial data. A review also includes assessing the accounting principles used and significant estimates made by management, as well as evaluating the overall financial statement presentation.

Based on our review, we are not aware of any material modifications that should be made to the accompanying financial statements. Accordingly, the accompanying financial statements have been prepared assuming that the company will continue as a going concern. Furthermore, we have no responsibility to update this report for events and circumstances occurring after the date of this report.

The financial statements for the year ended September 30, year 1, were audited by us and we expressed an unqualified opinion on them in our report dated November 7, year 1, but we have not performed any auditing procedures since that date. In our opinion, the financial statements referred to above are presented fairly, in all material respects, for the year then ended in conformity with generally accepted accounting principles.

Wallace & Wallace, CPAs
November 6, year 2

Each of the following items represents a deficiency noted by Martin. For each deficiency, indicate whether Martin is correct and Gordon is incorrect (M); Gordon is correct and Martin is incorrect (G); or both Martin and Gordon are incorrect (B).

1. There should be a reference to the prior year's audited financial statements in the first (introductory) paragraph.

2. All of the current year's basic financial statements are not properly identified in the first (introductory) paragraph.

3. The standards referred to in the first (introductory) paragraph should not be standards issued by the American Institute of Certified Public Accountants, but should be standards for the compilation and review of financial statements.

4. The accountant's responsibility to express limited assurance on the financial statements, mentioned in the first (introductory) paragraph, should be in the second (scope) paragraph.

5. There should be a reference to the prior year's audited financial statements in the second (scope) paragraph.

6. There should be a comparison of the scope of a review to an audit in the second (scope) paragraph.

7. There should be no reference to "assessing the accounting principles used," "significant estimates made by management," and "evaluating the overall financial statement presentation" in the second (scope) paragraph.

8. There should be a statement that no opinion is expressed on the current year's financial statements in the second (scope) paragraph.

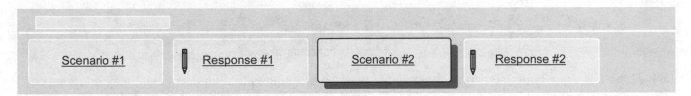

Hart, CPA, has been engaged to perform an examination of Unidyne Co.'s internal control over financial reporting that is integrated with an audit of its financial statements. Unidyne is a nonissuer.

In planning and performing this attest engagement

a. How should Hart determine the appropriate level of materiality?

b. How does the level of risk associated with a control affect what Hart should take into consideration when deciding whether and how to use the work of others?

What authoritative reference provides guidance for the date of a practitioner's report on agreed-upon procedures?

Paragraph Reference Answer: _____

(11/96, AUD, #2, amended, 6370)

Problem 31-4 (15 to 25 minutes)

An accountant is sometimes called on by clients to report on or assemble prospective financial statements for use by third parties.

1.   Identify the types of engagements that an accountant may perform under the circumstances in the scenario.

2.   Explain the difference between "general use" of and "limited use" of prospective financial statements.

3.   Explain what types of prospective financial statements are appropriate for "general use" and what types are appropriate for "limited use."

Each of the following items represents a series of unrelated procedures that an accountant may consider performing in separate engagements to review the financial statements of a nonissuer (a review) and to compile the financial statements of a nonissuer (a compilation). Select, as the best answer for each item, whether the procedure is required (R) or not required (N) for both review and compilation engagements. Make two selections for each procedure.

1.   The accountant should establish an understanding with the entity regarding the nature and limitations of the services to be performed.

2.   The accountant should make inquiries concerning actions taken at the board of directors' meetings.

3.   The accountant, as the entity's successor accountant, should communicate with the predecessor accountant to obtain access to the predecessor's working papers.

4.   The accountant should obtain a level of knowledge of the accounting principles and practices of the entity's industry.

5. The accountant should obtain an understanding of the entity's internal control structure.

6. The accountant should perform analytical procedures designed to identify relationships that appear to be unusual.

7. The accountant should make an assessment of the fraud risk.

What authoritative reference requires a practitioner to prohibit the use of his or her name in connection with a financial projection distributed to parties not negotiating directly with the party responsible for the projection?

Paragraph Reference Answer: _____

(11/95, AUD, #91, amended, 6054)

Problem 31-5 (15 to 25 minutes)

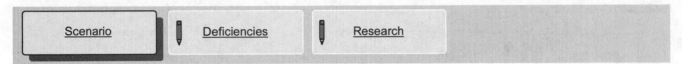

The following report was drafted on October 25, year 1, by Major, CPA, at the completion of the engagement to compile the financial statements of Ajax Company for the year ended September 30, year 1. Ajax is a nonissuer in which Major's child has a material direct financial interest. Ajax decided to omit substantially all of the disclosures required by generally accepted accounting principles because the financial statements will be for management's use only. The statement of cash flows was also omitted because management does not believe it to be a useful financial statement.

To the Board of Directors of Ajax Company:

I have compiled the accompanying financial statements of Ajax Company as of September 30, year 1, and for the year then ended. I planned and performed the compilation to obtain limited assurance about whether the financial statements are free of material misstatements.

A compilation is limited to presenting information in the form of financial statements. It is substantially less in scope than an audit in accordance with generally accepted auditing standards, the objective of which is the expression of an opinion regarding the financial statements taken as a whole. I have not audited the accompanying financial statements and, accordingly, do not express any opinion on them.

Management has elected to omit substantially all of the disclosures required by generally accepted accounting principles. If the omitted disclosures were included in the financial statements, they might influence the user's conclusions about the Company's financial position, results of operations, and changes in financial position.

I am not independent with respect to Ajax Company. This lack of independence is due to my child's ownership of a material direct financial interest in Ajax Company.

This report is intended solely for the information and use of the Board of Directors and management of Ajax Company and should not be used for any other purpose.

Major, CPA

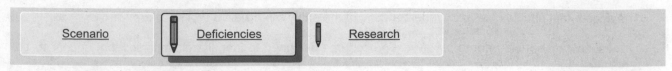

Identify the deficiencies contained in Major's report on the compiled financial statements. Group the deficiencies by paragraph where applicable. Do not redraft the report.

What authoritative reference provides guidance on reporting when an accountant is engaged to compile financial statements that omit substantially all the disclosures required by GAAP, including disclosures that might appear in the body of the financial statements?

Paragraph Reference Answer: _____

(11/90, AUD, #5, amended, 3069)

Problem 31-6 (15 to 25 minutes)

An accountant is sometimes called on by clients to report on or assemble prospective financial statements for use by third parties.

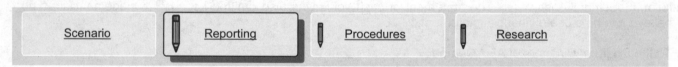

Describe the contents of the accountant's standard report on a compilation of a financial projection.

Each of the following items represents a series of unrelated procedures that an accountant may consider performing in separate engagements to review the financial statements of a nonissuer (a review) and to compile the financial statements of a nonissuer (a compilation). Select, as the best answer for each item, whether the procedure is required (R) or not required (N) for both review and compilation engagements. Make two selections for each procedure.

1. The accountant should send a letter of inquiry to the entity's attorney to corroborate the information furnished by management concerning litigation.

2. The accountant should obtain a management representation letter from the entity.

3. The accountant should compare recorded amounts, or ratios developed from recorded amounts, to expectations developed by the accountant.

4.   The accountant should communicate to the entity's senior management illegal employee acts discovered by the accountant that are clearly inconsequential.

5.   The accountant should make inquiries about events subsequent to the date of the financial statements that would have a material effect on the financial statements.

6.   The accountant should modify the accountant's report if there is a change in accounting principles that is adequately disclosed.

7.   The accountant should submit a hard copy of the financial statements and accountant's report when the financial statements and accountant's report are submitted on a computer disk.

8.   The accountant should perform specific procedures to evaluate whether there is substantial doubt about the entity's ability to continue as a going concern.

What authoritative reference provides guidance for an accountant issuing a compilation report when the accountant in question is not independent?

Paragraph Reference Answer: _____

(11/95, AUD, #98, amended, 6060)

Problem 31-7 (15 to 25 minutes)

Wallace & Wallace, CPAs, audited the financial statements of West Co., a nonissuer, for the year ended September 30, year 1, and expressed an unqualified opinion. For the year ended September 30, year 2, West issued comparative financial statements. Wallace & Wallace reviewed West's year 2 financial statements and Gordon, an assistant on the engagement, drafted the accountant's review report below. Martin, the engagement supervisor, decided not to reissue the prior year's auditor's report, but instructed Gordon to include a separate paragraph in the current year's review report describing the responsibility assumed for the prior year's audited financial statements.

Martin reviewed Gordon's draft and indicated that there were many deficiencies in Gordon's draft.

Accountant's Review Report

We have reviewed the accompanying balance sheet of West Company as of September 30, year 2, and the related statements of income and cash flows for the year then ended, in accordance with standards issued by the American Institute of Certified Public Accountants. All information included in these financial statements is the representation of the management of West Company. Our responsibility is to express limited assurance on these financial statements based on our review.

A review consists principally of inquiries of company personnel and analytical procedures applied to financial data. A review also includes assessing the accounting principles used and significant estimates made by management, as well as evaluating the overall financial statement presentation.

Based on our review, we are not aware of any material modifications that should be made to the accompanying financial statements. Accordingly, the accompanying financial statements have been prepared assuming that the company will continue as a going concern. Furthermore, we have no responsibility to update this report for events and circumstances occurring after the date of this report.

The financial statements for the year ended September 30, year 1, were audited by us and we expressed an unqualified opinion on them in our report dated November 7, year 1, but we have not performed any auditing procedures since that date. In our opinion, the financial statements referred to above are presented fairly, in all material respects, for the year then ended in conformity with generally accepted accounting principles.

Wallace & Wallace, CPAs
November 6, year 2

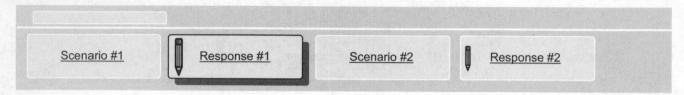

Each of the following items represents a deficiency noted by Martin. For each deficiency, indicate whether Martin is correct and Gordon is incorrect (M); Gordon is correct and Martin is incorrect (G); or both Martin and Gordon are incorrect (B).

1. There should be a reference to "conformity with generally accepted accounting principles" in the third paragraph.

2. There should be a reference to consistency in the third paragraph.

3. There should be a restriction on the distribution of the accountant's review report in the third paragraph.

4. The reference to "going concern" in the third paragraph should be in the second (scope) paragraph.

5. The accountant's lack of responsibility to update the report in the third paragraph should be in the second (scope) paragraph.

6. There should be no mention of the type of opinion expressed on the prior year's audited financial statements in the fourth (separate) paragraph.

7. All of the prior year's basic financial statements are not properly identified in the fourth (separate) paragraph.

8. The reference in the fourth (separate) paragraph to the fair presentation of the prior year's audited financial statements in accordance with generally accepted accounting principles should be omitted.

9. The report should be dual dated to indicate the date of the prior year's auditor's report.

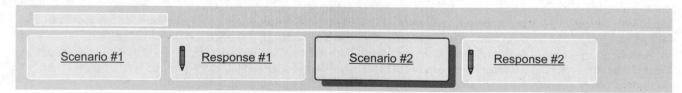

Hart, CPA, has been approached by Unidyne Co. to accept an attest engagement to perform an examination of the design and operating effectiveness of Unidyne's internal control over financial reporting that is integrated with an audit of its financial statements.

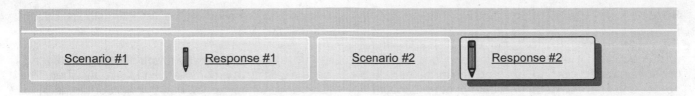

a. In order for Hart to perform an examination of Unidyne's internal control, one of the conditions that management must meet is the support of its assertion about the effectiveness of Unidyne's internal control with sufficient appropriate evidence. Describe how management should provide this evidence Also describe the other conditions that must be met by management to allow Hart to perform the examination.

b. Describe the other types of attest services that Hart may provide and any, if any, that are specifically **not** permitted in connection with Unidyne's internal control.

What authoritative reference provides guidance for an integrated audit on the dating of an auditor's report on the examination of internal control over financial reporting in relation to the dating of the report on the financial statements?

Paragraph Reference Answer: _____

(5/95, AUD, #4, amended, 6160)

Solution 31-1 MULTIPLE CHOICE ANSWERS

Compilations & Reviews

1. (c) When there is reasonable justification to change the engagement because of scope restrictions, the report should not include reference to the original engagement, any auditing procedures that were performed, or the scope limitation. (5151)

2. (d) In a review under SSARS guidance, a CPA is not expected to obtain an understanding of an entity's internal control or assess fraud risk. (7023)

3. (d) For a compilation or review engagement, the requirement that the CPA possess a level of knowledge of the accounting principles and practices of the industry in which the entity operates does not prevent a CPA from accepting a compilation or review engagement for an entity. However, it does place upon the CPA a responsibility to obtain the required level of knowledge. (4711)

4. (b) An accountant is precluded from issuing a review report on the financial statements of an entity with respect to which the auditor is not independent. Judgments about independence should be guided by the AICPA Code of Professional Conduct.

Rule 101 states that independence is considered impaired if there is *any* direct or material indirect financial interest. (5638)

5. (d) For a financial statement compilation, the accountant is not required to make inquiries or perform other procedures to verify, corroborate, or review information supplied by the entity. A financial statement review involves performing inquiries and analytics that provide a reasonable basis for expressing limited assurance that there are no material modifications that should be made to the statements in order for them to be in conformity with GAAP. (4724)

6. (b) Obtaining a general understanding of the entity's organization, operating characteristics, and products or services allows the accountant to plan the engagement effectively. Without a general understanding of the entity, the accountant would not be able to: make preliminary judgments about risk and materiality; assess the risk of material misstatement; or assess the operating efficiency of the entity's internal control. (8151)

SSARS

7. (d) The SSARS do not establish standards or procedures for other accounting services such as consulting on accounting, tax, and similar matters, or processing financial data for clients of other accounting firms. (4249)

8. (d) The SSARS provide performance and reporting standards for compilations and reviews. The SSARS define compilations of financial statements as presenting in the form of financial statements information that is the representation of management (owners) without undertaking to express any assurance on the statements. Reviews are defined as a service, the objective of which is to express limited assurance that there are no material modifications that should be made to the statements for them to be in conformity with GAAP or, if applicable, with an other comprehensive basis of accounting (OCBOA). Answer I is incorrect because merely reproducing client-prepared financial statements without modification is merely making a copy of the financial statements; this does not meet the definition of a compilation or a review. Answer II is incorrect because preparing standard monthly journal entries also does not meet the definition of a compilation or a review as described above. (6233)

Compilation Engagements

9. (a) To compile financial statements, the accountant should possess a general understanding of the nature of the entity's business transactions, the form of its accounting records, and the stated qualifications of its accounting personnel. Generally, a financial statement compilation is limited to presenting information that is the representation of management in the form of financial statements without undertaking to express any assurance on the statements. Generally, internal control is not considered in a compilation. (6823)

10. (a) If financial statements which are compiled in conformity with OCBOA do not include disclosure of the basis, the accountant must disclose the basis. Answers (b), (c), and (d) are not options mentioned in the Standards. (5154)

11. (c) Both provisions are required by the SSARS. (4744)

Compilation Reports

12. (c) The components of a compilation report include the requirements noted in answer (c). Answer (a) is incorrect because it refers to GAAS. By using the term "limited assurance," answer (b) is referring to a review. The AICPA establishes the standards. (4743)

13. (a) An accountant would discuss independence explicitly in a compilation report only when s/he *lacks* independence. When the accountant is independent, it is implicit. Financial statements compiled by an accountant should be accompanied by a report stating that the financial statements have not been audited or reviewed and, accordingly, the accountant does not express an opinion or any other form of assurance on them; thus, answers (b) and (d) are *explicitly* stated. Inquiry and analytics are performed during a review engagement, but generally not in a compilation engagement. (4291)

14. (d) There is no requirement that a compilation report be printed on letterhead or that it be signed manually. (6817)

15. (c) Financial statements compiled without audit or review should be accompanied by a report stating that the accountant does not express an opinion or any other form of assurance on the financial statements. One of the elements of a compilation report is a statement that the statements have not been audited or reviewed and, therefore, no opinion or other form of assurance is expressed on them. No reference to testing the financial information or to assessing the principles and estimates used is made in the report. Testing the information supplied is not required in a compilation. A *review* consists primarily of inquiries of entity personnel and analytics. (6027)

16. (b) The compilation report should include a statement that a compilation has been performed in accordance with Statements on Standards for Accounting and Review Services issued by the American Institute of Certified Public Accountants. A compilation does not include the assessments and evaluations in answer (a). Answers (c) and (d) are both items that should be in a review report, but not in a compilation report. (5696)

17. (c) A compilation report should state that a compilation is limited to presenting, in the form of financial statements, information that is the representation of management. Answers (a), (b), and (d) pertain to a review, not a compilation. (8154)

Review Engagements

18. (c) In reviewing the financial statements of a nonissuer, the auditor would most likely use ratio analysis as an analytic for developing relationships among balance sheet accounts. Ratios are useful in evaluating an entity's solvency. Ratio analysis that includes relationships between income statement

and balance sheet accounts are useful in evaluating operational efficiency and profitability. Ratio analysis provides an indication of the firm's financial strengths and weaknesses. (5692)

19. (c) Obtaining a general understanding of the entity's organization, operating characteristics, and products or services allows the accountant to plan the engagement effectively. Without a general understanding of the entity, the accountant would not be able to: anticipate results; develop appropriate questions about procedures for recording, classifying, and summarizing transactions; or determine whether relationships and individual items appear unusual. (7808)

20. (b) Obtaining a management representation letter is required by the SSARS. The procedures in the other answer alternatives are not required. (5148)

21. (d) In an engagement to review a nonissuer's financial statements, a CPA uses inquiry and analytics to provide a basis for expressing limited assurance that the financial statements to do not contain material deviation from GAAP or OCBOA. Inquiries about actions taken at board of directors' meetings falls within this scope. A review of a nonissuer's financial statements does not require the CPA to obtain an understanding of internal control, assess control risk, or test account records. A review report is appropriate for general use. (7803)

22. (c) Each page of the financial statements reviewed by the accountant should include a reference, such as "See Accountant's Review Report." (5699)

23. (c) When the accountant believes that modification of the standard report is not adequate to indicate the deficiencies in the financial statements as a whole, the accountant should withdraw from the compilation or review engagement. (5698)

24. (c) Review engagement procedures generally are limited to inquiries and analytics. Comparison of current-year to prior-year account balances is an analytical procedure. Answers (a), (b), and (d) are audit procedures. (8168)

Review Reports

25. (d) When a departure from GAAP is in the financial statements, if the financial statements are not revised, the accountant should consider whether modification of her/his standard report is adequate to disclose the departure. If the accountant concludes that modification of the standard report is appropriate,

the departure should be disclosed in a separate paragraph. The other answers are irrelevant to this circumstance. Answer (a) is appropriate to an audit. (6239)

26. (c, d) The standard report for a financial statement review should include a statement that the accountant is not aware of any material modifications that should be made to the financial statements in order for them to be in conformity with generally accepted accounting principles, other than those modifications, if any, indicated in the report and that a review consists principally of inquiries of company personnel and analytical procedures applied to financial data. A review report does not express an opinion, but it does indicate limited assurance. The first two alternatives include procedures that would be performed in an audit, not a review. (2987)

27. (b) The CPA may issue the review report on just the balance sheet if the scope of her/his inquiry and analytical procedures has not been restricted. The other answers are not requirements. (5697)

28. (d) Failure by the client's management to provide a representation letter covering all of the periods under review precludes the completion of a review. The accountant may issue a compilation report as an accountant is not required to verify, corroborate, or review information supplied for a compilation. (7844)

29. (c) Financial statements reviewed by an accountant should be accompanied by a report stating that a review consists primarily of inquiries of company personnel and analytical procedures applied to the financial data. The other answers are not review report elements. 6026)

Prescribed Forms

30. (b) When a printed report form calls upon an independent auditor to make a statement that s/he is not justified in making, the auditor should reword the form or attach a separate report. (6368)

Personal Financial Statements

31. (d) One condition of exemption from SSARS 1 is an understanding with the client that the financial statements will not be used to obtain credit. The statements may be presented in comparative form and in conformity with GAAP or OCBOA. The certification of the user financial planner is irrelevant to the issuance of the report. (5639)

32. (a) A CPA need not be independent to perform compilation services or prepare tax returns. (2809)

Comparative Financial Statements

33. (a) Compiled financial statements that omit substantially all of the disclosures required by GAAP are not comparable to financial statements that include such disclosures. Accordingly, the accountant should not issue a report on the comparative financial statements when statements for one or more, but not all, of the periods presented omit substantially all of the disclosures required by GAAP. (2757)

34. (c) When the current period financial statements of a nonissuer have been compiled or reviewed and those of the prior period have been audited, the accountant should issue an appropriate compilation or review report on the current period financial statements and **either** the report on the prior period should be reissued **or** the report on the current period should include as a separate paragraph an appropriate description of the responsibility assumed for the financial statements of the prior period. In the latter case, the separate paragraph should indicate (a) that the financial statements of the prior period were audited previously, (b) the date of the previous report, (c) the type of opinion expressed previously, (d) if the opinion was other than unqualified, the substantive reasons therefor, and (e) that *no auditing procedures were performed after the date of the previous report.* (5152)

Attestation Standards

35. (b) Attestation engagements involve the issuance of a report on a subject matter or an assertion about a subject matter that is the responsibility of another party. Statements on Auditing Standards apply to financial statement audits of nonissuers. The other two alternatives do not exist. (6819)

36. (b) An attest engagement is one in which a CPA in public practice (or practitioner) is engaged to, or does, issue an examination, review, or agreed-upon procedures report on subject matter or an assertion about subject matter that is the responsibility of another party. Reports on financial statements are subject to the guidance of Statements on Auditing Standards (SAS) and Statements on Standards for Accounting & Review Services (SSARS). Supplying a client with a blank financial statement format is a service exempt from SAS and SSARS; SSAEs do not apply to financial statements. (7103)

37. (b) An attest engagement is one in which a CPA in public practice is engaged to issue an examination, review, or agreed-upon procedures report on subject matter or an assertion about subject matter that is the responsibility of another party. AT 600 established guidance concerning attest engagements on an entity's compliance with requirements of specified laws, regulations, rules, contracts, etc. AT 100 specifically lists, as engagements to which attest standards are inapplicable, engagements performed in accordance with Statements on Standards for Consulting Services, client advocacy engagements, and tax return preparation services. (7835)

38. (a) The attestation standards provide guidance and establish a broad framework for a variety of attest services than include providing assurance on representations that are not limited to historical financial statements and are in forms other than the positive opinion. The fourth general attestation standard requires that the practitioner maintain independence in mental attitude in all matters relating to the engagement. An attest engagement may be part of a larger engagement, such as a feasibility study, that may include an examination of prospective financial information. The two attestation fieldwork standards are very similar to the first and third standards of fieldwork for audits. (4675)

39. (d) Neither I nor II. In an agreed-upon procedures engagement, the practitioner should **not** provide negative assurance about whether the subject matter or the assertion is fairly stated based on the criteria. Compilation engagements do not provide *any* type of assurance. (0430)

40. (d) A sufficient understanding of internal control for planning an engagement is not an attestation standard. The other answer alternatives are attestation standards. Answer *a* is the second standard of fieldwork; answer *b* is the first standard of reporting; and answer *c* is the first standard of fieldwork. (3900)

Financial Forecasts & Projections

41. (c) The practitioner's standard report on a compilation of prospective financial statements should include a statement that a compilation is limited in scope and does not enable the practitioner to express an opinion *or any other form of assurance* on the prospective financial statements or the assumptions; a statement that the practitioner assumes no responsibility to update the report for events and circumstances occurring after the date of the report; and a caveat that the prospective results may not be achieved. It should also include an identification of the prospective financial statements

presented by the responsible party and a statement that the practitioner compiled the prospective financial statements in accordance with attestation standards established by the AICPA. (4294)

42. (a) A practitioner may perform an agreed-upon procedures attestation engagement on prospective financial statements provided that use of the report is to be restricted to the specified parties. SSAE 10 merely requires the subject matter to be subject to reasonably consistent estimation or measurement. Responsibility for adequacy for the procedures performed is taken by the specified users, not the accountant. The practitioner should not provide negative assurance. (5096)

43. (d) When a CPA examines a financial forecast that fails to disclose several assumptions that appear to be significant, the CPA should describe the assumptions in the report and issue an adverse opinion. (0432)

44. (b) When a CPA examines a projection, the CPA should express an opinion on whether the assumptions provide a reasonable basis for the projection given the hypothetical assumptions. The standard report includes the following in the scope paragraph, "...included such procedures as we considered necessary to evaluate both the assumptions used by management and the preparation and presentation of the projection." (7091)

45. (b) A standard compilation report of prospective financial statements requires a caveat that the prospective results may not be achieved. An explanation of the difference between a financial forecast and a financial projection is not needed. The practitioner assumes no responsibility to update the report for events and circumstances occurring after the date of the report. A compilation does not consider the entity's internal controls. (8150)

Reporting on Internal Control

46. (b) An auditor may perform an examination of internal control only if (1) management provides its assertion about the effectiveness of the entity's internal control in a report that accompanies the auditor's report; (2) management accepts responsibility for the effectiveness of the entity's internal control; (3) management evaluates the effectiveness of the entity's internal control using suitable and available criteria; and (4) management supports its assertion about the effectiveness of the entity's internal control with sufficient appropriate evidence. The other alternatives are not required conditions for acceptance of the engagement. (5091)

47. (d) A paragraph describing the inherent limitations of any internal control structure is one of required elements of the auditor's report on the examination of internal control. The other alternatives are not required elements. (5702)

48. (c) Management must present its written assertion about the effectiveness of the entity's internal control in a report that accompanies the auditor's report. (5983)

49. (d) Although the examination of an entity's internal control over financial reporting should be integrated with the audit of financial statements, the two engagements have different objectives and generally differ in scope. However, the procedures are similar in nature. (0400)

Other Attestation Engagements

50. (b) A list of or reference to procedures performed, and related findings, are required elements of a report on agreed-upon procedures. No references to fairness of presentation, effectiveness of internal control, or acknowledgement of sufficiency of procedures are required. (7028)

51. (a) A report on an engagement consisting of applying agreed-upon procedures should include *a statement of restrictions on the use of the report* because it is intended to be used solely by the specified parties. In an agreed-upon procedures engagement, the practitioner does not provide an opinion; instead the report should be presented in the form of procedures and findings. Negative assurance is not allowed. The sufficiency of the procedures is solely the responsibility of the specified parties who agreed to those procedures; the practitioner should disclaim responsibility for the sufficiency of the procedures. (6028)

52. (c) In an agreed-upon procedures engagement, a client engages the practitioner to assist specified parties in evaluating subject matter or an assertion as a result of needs of the specified parties. The specified parties and the practitioner agree upon procedures to be performed by the practitioner that the specified parties believe are appropriate. Therefore, the specified parties assume responsibility for the sufficiency of the procedures since they best understand their own needs. The practitioner does not provide an opinion or negative assurance. Instead, the practitioner's report on agreed-upon procedures should be in the form of procedures and findings. A practitioner's report on such engagements should indicate clearly that its use is restricted to those specified parties. (8132)

53. (d) The practitioner's report on pro forma financial information should include reference to the financial statements from which the historical financial information is derived. The statement in answer (a) should not be made in any review engagement. Answer (b) is incorrect because the report on pro forma information is a different engagement from reporting on the financial statements from which the pro forma information was derived; thus, the practitioner would not issue an opinion or disclaimer of opinion on those statements. No reference to

uncertainty should be made as that is assumed, based upon the nature of the engagement, and the accountant need only provide a conclusion as to whether any information came to her/his attention to cause her/him to believe management's assumptions do not provide a reasonable basis for the effects directly attributable to the transaction or event or that the pro forma column does not reflect the proper application of those adjustments to the historical financial statements. (4733)

Solution 31-2 ADDITIONAL MULTIPLE CHOICE ANSWERS

Compilations & Reviews

54. (c) SSARS are issued by the AICPA Accounting and Review Services Committee, the senior technical committee of the institute designated to issue pronouncements in connection with the unaudited financial statements or other unaudited financial information of a nonissuer. (0006)

55. (d) Neither a review nor a compilation engagement contemplates obtaining an understanding of internal control or assessing fraud risk; testing of accounting records and of responses to inquiries by obtaining sufficient appropriate audit evidence; and certain other procedures ordinarily performed during an audit. (2327)

56. (c) In a review of financial statements, where the CPA expresses limited assurance that the financial statements do not contain material deviations from GAAP, the accountant is required to obtain a knowledge of the accounting principles and practices of the industry in which the entity operates. This is required so that the CPA can determine and apply proper inquiry and analytics. The CPA does not need to apply the procedures listed in the other answers for a review. (5676)

57. (d) CPA to must obtain a representation letter from management to complete a review. If a CPA becomes aware of a departure from GAAP (such as a lack of justification for a change in accounting principles) in the financial statements, the CPA should consider whether the departure can be adequately disclosed by modifying the standard report. If it can, a separate paragraph should be used to disclose the departure. An accountant may review financial statements prepared in accordance with a basis of accounting other than GAAP, such as the income tax basis. A CPA may issue a review report on one financial statement and not on other related financial statements if the scope of her/his inquiries and analytical procedures has not been restricted. (7627)

SSARS

58. (d) The CPA must, at a minimum, comply with the provisions applicable to a compilation when submitting unaudited financial statements of a issuer. Submission of financial statement is defined as presenting to the client financial statements the accountant has generated, either manually or through the use of computer software. Answers (a), (b), and (c) are services that do not constitute the submission of financial statements. (5095)

59. (d) An engagement to *compile an individual's personal financial statements to be used to obtain a mortgage* must be performed in compliance with the SSARS. Personal financial statements that are included in a written personal financial plan prepared by an accountant are exempt from the SSARS if they will not be used to obtain credit or for any other purpose than developing the client's personal financial goals. (2281)

60. (c) The objective of a review differs significantly from the objective of a compilation. The inquiry and analytical procedures performed in a review should provide the accountant with a reasonable basis for expressing limited assurance that there are no material modifications that should be made to the financial statements. No expression of assurance is contemplated in a compilation. (8381)

Compilations

61. (a) Before submission, the accountant should read the compiled financial statements and consider whether such financial statements appear to be appropriate in form and free from obvious material errors. In this context, the term *error* refers to mistakes in the compilation of financial statements, including arithmetical or clerical mistakes, and mistakes in the application of accounting principles, including inadequate disclosure. A representation letter from members of management usually is not

obtained in a compilation engagement. Inquiry of management concerning actions taken at meetings of the stockholders and the board of directors is a procedure normally used in a review engagement, and is not necessary in a compilation engagement. The accountant is not required to make inquiries or perform other procedures to verify, corroborate, or review information supplied by the entity. (5693)

62. (b)   The accountant should possess a level of knowledge of the accounting principles and practices of the industry in which the entity operates that will enable the accountant to compile financial statements that are appropriate in form for an entity operating in that industry. Answers (a), (c), and (d) represent procedures beyond the scope of a compilation. (2978)

63. (b)   Financial statements compiled without audit or review by an accountant should be accompanied by a report stating that—(1) A compilation has been performed in accordance with Statements on Standards for Accounting and Review Services issued by the American Institute of Certified Public Accountants. (2) A compilation is limited to presenting in the form of financial statements information that is the representation of management (owners). (3) The financial statements have not been audited or reviewed and, accordingly, the accountant does not express an opinion or any other form of assurance on them. (2294)

64. (a)   When compiled financial statements omit substantially all disclosures, the accountant should indicate this in the report. The SSARS include the following as an example of an appropriate additional paragraph: "Management has elected to omit substantially all the disclosures (and the statement of cash flows) required by generally accepted accounting principles. If the omitted disclosures and statement were included in the financial statements, they might influence the user's conclusions about the company's financial position, results of operations, and cash flows. Accordingly, these financial statements are *not designed for those who are not informed about such matters*." The accountant must conclude that the omission was not made with the intention of misleading those who might reasonably be expected to use such financial statements. Answer *b*, indicating that the statements are prepared in conformity with OCBOA is an inappropriate remedy for the omission of disclosures required by GAAP. However, it should be noted that if financial statements compiled in conformity with a comprehensive basis of accounting other than GAAP do not include disclosure of the *basis* of accounting used, the basis should be disclosed in the accountant's

report. Answers *c* and *d* are not acceptable statements for inclusion in the report. (5155)

65. (c)   Before an audit engagement has been completed, the client may ask the CPA to change the engagement to a compilation. In reaching a decision, the CPA should consider the client's reasons for making the request, especially if either the client or circumstance have imposed a restriction on the scope of the audit. A change in the circumstances that caused the client to require an audit usually is considered an acceptable reason for change of an audit to a review or compilation engagement. The CPA should consider whether the information affected by the scope restriction may be incorrect, incomplete, or otherwise unsatisfactory. When correspondence with the client's legal counsel is prohibited in an audit engagement, the CPA ordinarily is prohibited from issuing a compilation report as well as an audit report. (7822)

Reviews

66. (d)   A review does *not* contemplate obtaining an understanding of the internal control or assessing control risk, tests of accounting records and of responses to inquiries by obtaining sufficient appropriate audit evidence, and certain other procedures ordinarily performed during an audit. Answers (a), (b), and (c) are usually performed by the accountant in a review engagement of a nonissuer. (2979)

67. (b)   Procedures ordinarily performed during a review of a nonissuer's financial statements include inquiries concerning the entity's procedures for recording and summarizing transactions. Practitioners would not be concerned with corroborating evidential matter, management's assertions concerning continued existence, or the entity's attorney's opinion concerning contingent liabilities. (2977)

68. (a)   Procedures for conducting a review of financial statements generally are limited to analytical procedures and inquiries. The practitioner does not need to observe internal controls. (5147)

69. (a)   If the accountant believes that modification of the standard report is not adequate to indicate the deficiencies in the financial statements taken as a whole, the accountant should withdraw from the compilation or review engagement and not provide any further services regarding those financial statements. The accountant would follow the procedures in answer (c) if modification of the standard report was considered adequate. (5093)

70. (b) In a review engagement, the accountant must apply analytical procedures to the financial statements. The purpose of analytical procedures is to identify and provide a basis for inquiry about the relationships and individual items that appear to be unusual and that may indicate a material misstatement. Analytical procedures may include *comparison of the financial statements with statements for comparable prior period(s)*; comparing current financial information with anticipated results, such as budgets or forecasts; comparing current financial information with relevant nonfinancial information; comparing ratios and indicators for the current period with expectations based on prior periods; comparing ratios and indicators for the current period with those of entities in the same industry; comparing relationships among elements in the current financial information with corresponding relationships in the financial information of prior periods. Answers a, and c are procedures that should be performed in an *audit,* rather than a review engagement. A review engagement does not include a study of the entity's internal control. (2787)

71. (d) An accountant is not precluded from issuing a compilation or review report on one financial statement and not on the others. (7825)

72. (c) A review provides an accountant with a basis for expressing limited assurance on the financial statements. The accountant should establish an understanding with the entity, preferably in writing, regarding the services to be performed, but an engagement letter is not required. A review does not contemplate obtaining an understanding of internal control. A review does not provide the basis for the expression of an opinion of the financial statements taken as a whole. (8378)

73. (a) A review provides an accountant with a basis for expressing limited assurance on financial statements. Inquiries should be made regarding the client's principles and practices, including the methods used in applying them. In performing a review, it is not intended that the CPA will obtain an understanding of internal control; assess fraud risk; test accounting records; or other procedures normally performed during an audit (such as identifying related party transactions). (8379)

74. (b) The standard review report mentions that a review consists of inquiries of company personnel and analytics applied to financial data. A compilation is limited to presenting, in the form of financial statements, information that is the representation of management. In a review, a CPA expresses limited assurance on the financial statements. While a CPA generally does not obtain an

understanding of the entity's internal control or assess fraud risk in a financial statement review, it is not mentioned in the standard review report of a nonissuer. (8410)

75. (d) When the CPA decides that a change in engagement is appropriate and the requirements of the new engagement type are met, the CPA should issue an appropriate report, without including any reference to the original engagement, any auditing procedures that may have been performed, or any scope limitations that resulted in the changed engagement. (8416)

Comparative Financial Statements

76. (a) When unaudited financial statements are presented in comparative form with audited financial statements in documents filed with the Securities and Exchange Commission, such statements should be clearly marked as "unaudited" but not referred to in the auditor's report. (4287)

77. (d) Either reissuance or reference in a separate paragraph is acceptable. (4754)

Attestation Standards

78. (c) SSAE do not apply to client advocacy engagements, but they do apply to engagements to examine, compile, or apply agreed-upon procedures to financial forecasts and projections. (7016)

79. (d) The SSAEs provide guidance concerning attest engagements on prospective financial statements. The other alternatives would not be considered attest engagements. (7838)

80. (c) Other than the procedures applied to the historical financial statements, the procedures the practitioner should apply to the assumptions and pro forma adjustments for either an examination or a review engagement include the determination that computations of pro forma adjustments are mathematically correct and that the pro forma column reflects the proper application of those adjustments to the historical financial statements. However, the practitioner is not required to reevaluate the entity's internal control over financial reporting. (7628)

81. (b) Examination of evidence is the most effective procedure. In the hierarchy of available attest procedures, those that involve search and verification (for example, inspection, confirmation, or observation), particularly when using independent sources outside the entity, are generally more effective in restricting attestation risk than those involving internal inquires and comparisons of internal information (for example, analytical procedures and

discussions with individuals responsible for the subject matter or the assertion). (8376)

82. (d) SSAE apply when a CPA in public practice is engaged to issue an examination, review, or agreed-upon procedures report on subject matter or an assertion about subject matter that is the responsibility of another party. SSARS apply to compilations and reviews of financial statements. SAS apply to audits to financial statements. SSCS apply to consulting engagements. (8415)

Financial Forecasts & Projections

83. (d) Prospective financial statements are for either *general use* or *limited use*. *General use* of prospective financial statements refers to use of the statements by persons with whom the responsible party is not negotiating directly, for example, in an offering statement of an entity's debt or equity interests. Because recipients of prospective financial statements distributed for general use are unable to ask the responsible party directly about the presentation, the presentation most useful to them is one that portrays, to the best of the responsible party's knowledge and belief, the expected results. Thus, only a *financial forecast* is appropriate for general use. (7511)

84. (a) The report should contain a separate paragraph that restricts the use of the report because it is intended to be used solely by specified parties. The report does not provide an explanation of the differences between an examination and an audit. The accountant is not responsible for events occurring after the date of the report. The standard report contains the practitioner's opinion that the prospective financial statements are presented in conformity with AICPA presentation guidelines and that the underlying assumptions provide a reasonable basis for the forecast or a reasonable basis for the projection given the hypothetical assumptions. (6029)

85. (c) Any type of prospective financial statements that would be useful in the circumstances would normally be appropriate for limited use. Thus, the presentation may be a financial forecast or a financial projection. Only the financial forecast is appropriate for general use. (0424)

86. (c) The standard report in includes a statement that there will usually be differences between the forecasted and actual results. The items in answers (a), (b), and (d) are not in the standard report. (5156)

87. (d) A projection, since it is not meant for general use, would be inappropriate for all stockholders of record and employees, as it would be unreasonable to expect these groups to be familiar with the basis of the projection or to be involved closely with those preparing it. (4679)

88. (b) An examination of prospective financial statements...involves evaluating the preparation of the prospective financial statements, evaluating the support underlying the assumptions, evaluating the presentation of the prospective financial statements for conformity with AICPA presentation guidelines, and issuing an examination report. This service does not include compiling the forecast, or assuming responsibility to update management on key events afterwards. The report may be for general use, in which case the distribution need not be limited. (5640)

89. (b) A report on a compilation of a financial projection must include a statement that a compilation is limited in scope and does not enable the accountant to express an opinion or any other form of assurance on the prospective financial statements or the assumptions. As a compilation report should provide no assurance, a statement that that the assumptions used are reasonable is inappropriate. Reports for all types of engagements involving financial projections must include a caveat that the prospective results may not be achieved and a statement that the accountant assumes no responsibility to update the report for events and circumstances occurring after the date of the report. (7814)

90. (d) An accountant's report on a compilation of projected financial statements should include a description of the limitations on the projection's usefulness. It does not express an opinion or any other form of assurance, nor does it mention fraud or the difference between a compilation and a review. (8411)

91. (c) Among other things, a report on the results of applying agreed-upon procedures to financial forecasts and projections must include a restriction on the use of the report. The Statements on Standards for Attestation Engagements (SSAE) apply to engagements to apply agreed-upon procedures to prospective financial statements, not SSARS. A CPA may perform agreed-upon procedures without examining or compiling the related prospective financial statements. The client must accept responsibility for the adequacy of the procedures performed in an agreed-upon procedures engagement. (8421)

PERFORMANCE BY SUBTOPICS

Each category below parallels a subtopic covered in Chapter 31. Record the number and percentage of questions you correctly answered in each subtopic area.

Compilations & Reviews

Question #	Correct	√
1		
2		
3		
4		
5		
6		
# Questions	6	

\# Correct _____
% Correct _____

SSARS

Question #	Correct	√
7		
8		
# Questions	2	

\# Correct _____
% Correct _____

Compilation Engagements

Question #	Correct	√
9		
10		
11		
# Questions	3	

\# Correct _____
% Correct _____

Compilation Reports

Question #	Correct	√
12		
13		
14		
15		
16		
17		
# Questions	6	

\# Correct _____
% Correct _____

Review Engagements

Question #	Correct	√
18		
19		
20		
21		
22		
23		
24		
# Questions	7	

\# Correct _____
% Correct _____

Review Reports

Question #	Correct	√
25		
26		
27		
28		
29		
# Questions	5	

\# Correct _____
% Correct _____

Prescribed Forms

Question #	Correct	√
30		
# Questions	1	

\# Correct _____
% Correct _____

Personal Financial Statements

Question #	Correct	√
31		
32		
# Questions	2	

\# Correct _____
% Correct _____

Comparative Financial Statements

Question #	Correct	√
33		
34		
# Questions	2	

\# Correct _____
% Correct _____

Attestation Standards

Question #	Correct	√
35		
36		
37		
38		
39		
40		
# Questions	6	

\# Correct _____
% Correct _____

Financial Forecasts & Projections

Question #	Correct	√
41		
42		
43		
44		
45		
# Questions	5	

\# Correct _____
% Correct _____

Reporting on Internal Control

Question #	Correct	√
46		
47		
48		
49		
# Questions	4	

\# Correct _____
% Correct _____

Other Attestation Engagements

Question #	Correct	√
50		
51		
52		
53		
# Questions	4	

\# Correct _____
% Correct _____

SIMULATION SOLUTIONS

Solution 31-3

Response #1: Review Report (5 points)

1.   G

Gordon is correct. The first paragraph of the report should not include a reference to the prior year's audited financial statements. The standard review report should be issued on the current-period statements and the prior-period report should be reissued or a separate paragraph should be added to the current-period report.

2.   M

Martin is correct. The statement of retained earnings should be listed in the first paragraph.

3.   B

Both are incorrect. The review should be conducted in accordance with Statements on Standards for Accounting and Review Services which are issued by the AICPA.

4.   B

Both are incorrect. The statement, "Our responsibility is to express limited assurance on these financial statements based on our review" should be omitted. The standard review report does not express an opinion on the financial statements.

5. G

Gordon is correct. The prior year's audited financial statements should not be referred to in the second paragraph of the review report. Either the prior-period report should be reissued or a separate paragraph should be added to the current-period report.

6. M

Martin is correct. The second paragraph of the review report should include the following comparison of the scope of a review to an audit, "It is substantially less in scope than an audit in accordance with generally accepted auditing standards, the objective of which is the expression of an opinion regarding the financial statements taken as a whole."

7. M

Martin is correct. There should be no reference to "assessing the accounting principles used," "significant estimates made by management," or "evaluating the overall financial statement presentation," since these statements are not part of the standard review report.

8. M

Martin is correct. The scope paragraph should include the statement, "Accordingly, we do not express such an opinion."

Response #2: ICFR (4 points)

a. Hart should use the **same materiality** used in planning and performing the **audit** of the entity's **financial statements**.

b. First, to determine the extent to which the work of others may be used, Hart should assess their competence and objectivity. As the **risk associated with a control decreases**, the necessary **level of competence and objectivity decreases** as well. As the **risk associated with a control increases**, the **need for Hart to perform the work on the control increases**. For example, for controls that address specific fraud risks, use of the work of others would be limited, if it could be used at all.

Response #3: Research (1 point)

Paragraph Reference Answer: AT 201.34

Guidance: AT 201.34 states, "The date of completion of the agreed-upon procedures should be used as the date of the practitioner's report."

(6370)

Solution 31-4

Response #1: Financial Projections (4 points)

1. An accountant who reports on or assembles **prospective financial statements for use by third parties** should perform any one of three engagements. The accountant may **compile**, **examine**, or **apply agreed-upon procedures** to the prospective financial statements.

2. **"General use"** of prospective financial statements refers to use of the statements by persons (creditors, stockholders, etc.) with whom the **responsible party** (management) is **not negotiating directly**. **"Limited use"** of prospective financial statements refers to the use of prospective financial statements by the **responsible party and third parties** with whom the responsible party is **negotiating directly**.

3. Only a **financial forecast is appropriate for general use**, but any type of prospective financial statements (either a financial forecast or a financial projection) would normally be appropriate for **limited use**.

Response #2: Engagement Requirements (5 points)

1. R, R

AR 100.05 states, "The accountant should establish an understanding with the entity, preferably in writing, regarding the services to be performed." AR 100.05 applies to both reviews and compilations.

2. R, N

AR 100.38, applicable to reviews, lists several procedures that ordinarily are performed in a review, including "Inquiries concerning actions taken at meetings of stockholders, board of directors, committees of the board of directors, or comparable meetings that may affect the financial statements." AR 100.10, applicable to compilations, indicates that the accountant is not required to make inquiries about information supplied by the client.

3. N, N

AR 400.08 states, "The successor accountant also may wish to review the predecessor's working papers." This step is not required in either a review or a compilation.

4. R, R

AR 100.08, applicable to compilations, states, "The accountant should possess a level of knowledge of the accounting principles and practices of the industry in which the entity operates that will enable him or her to compile financial statements that are appropriate in form for an entity operating in that industry." AR 100.33, applicable to reviews, states a similar, but more comprehensive, requirement than for a compilation.

5. N, N

AR 100.32 states, "A review does not contemplate obtaining an understanding of the entity's internal control structure; assessing fraud risk; tests of accounting records...." A compilation engagement is even more narrow in scope than a review (AR 100.12).

6. R, N

AR 100.36 describes such analytics for a review. AR 100.12 states that, for compilations, the accountant is not required to perform such procedures.

7. N, N

According to AR 100.32, a review does not contemplate assessing fraud risk. A compilation is even more narrow in scope than a review (AR 100.12).

Response #3: Research (1 point)

Paragraph Reference Answer: AT 301.11

Guidance: AT 301.11 states, "Because a financial projection is not appropriate for general use, a practitioner should not consent to the use of his or her name in conjunction with a financial projection that he or she believes will be distributed to those who will not be negotiating directly with the responsible party, for example, in an offering statement of an entity's debt or equity interests, unless the projection is used to supplement a financial forecast."

(6054)

Solution 31-5

Response #1: Compilation Report (9 points)

Deficiencies in the report on the compiled financial statements are as follows:

Within the first paragraph:

- The financial statements are **not properly identified**.
- **Statements on Standards for Accounting and Review Services** issued by the AICPA should be referred to.
- The expression **"to obtain limited assurance"** should not be used.

Within the second paragraph:

- The information is not stated to be the **representation of management**.
- The phrase **"less in scope than an audit"** is **inappropriate**.
- Reference to the **financial statements not being reviewed** is omitted.
- Reference to **"any other form of assurance"** is omitted.

Within the third paragraph:

- Reference to the omission of the statement of cash flows is omitted.
- There should be a statement that the financial statements are not designed for those uninformed about the omitted disclosures.
- It is inappropriate to refer to changes in financial position.

Within the fourth paragraph:

- The reason for the accountant's **lack of independence** should not be described.

Inclusion of the **fifth paragraph is inappropriate**.

The accountant's compilation report is **not dated** October 25, year 1.

Response #2: Research (1 point)

Paragraph Reference Answer: AR 100.19

Guidance: AR 100.19 states, "An entity may request an accountant to compile financial statements that omit substantially all the disclosures required by GAAP, including disclosures that might appear in the body of the financial statements. (As previously noted, reference to GAAP in this Section includes, where applicable, OCBOA.) The accountant may compile such financial statements provided the omission of substantially all disclosures is clearly indicated in the report and is not, to his or her knowledge, undertaken with the intention of misleading those who might reasonably be expected to use such financial statements. When the entity wishes to include disclosures about only a few matters in the form of notes to such financial statements, such disclosures should be labeled 'Selected Information—Substantially All Disclosures Required by Generally Accepted Accounting Principles Are Not Included.'"

(3069)

Solution 31-6

Response #1: Financial Projections (4 points)

The accountant's standard report on a compilation of a financial projection should include

- An **identification** of the **projection** presented by the responsible party.
- A statement that the accountant has **compiled** the **projection in accordance with standards established by the AICPA**.
- A separate paragraph that describes the **limitations** on the **use of the presentation**.
- A statement that a compilation is limited in **scope** and **does not enable** the accountant to **express an opinion** or any other **form of assurance** on the **projection** or the **assumptions**.
- A caveat that the **prospective results may not be achieved**.
- A statement that the **accountant assumes no responsibility to update** the report for events and circumstances occurring after the date of the report.

Response #2: Engagement Requirements (5 points)

1. N, N

AR 100.38 indicates various inquiries appropriate to a review. A letter of inquiry to the entity's attorney is not included. A compilation engagement is even more narrow in scope than a review (AR 100.10).

2. R, N

AR 100.39 states that the accountant is required to obtain a written representation from members of management in a review engagement. AR 100.10, applicable to a compilation, states that an "accountant is not required to make inquiries or perform other procedures to verify, corroborate, or review information supplied by the entity."

3. R, N

AR 100.36, applicable to reviews, states that analytical procedures such as this are required.

4. N, N

AR 100.84 states, "When evidence comes to the accountant's attention during the performance of compilation or review procedures that fraud or an illegal act may have occurred, that matter should be brought to the attention of the appropriate level of management. The accountant need **not** report matters regarding illegal acts that are clearly inconsequential...."

5. R, N

AR 100.38 states that a review includes "Inquires to members of management who have responsibility for financial and accounting matters concerning... events subsequent to the date of the financial statements that could have a material effect on the financial statements." A compilation does not require inquiries about subsequent events. (AR 100.10)

6. N, N

As long as the change is appropriate and is appropriately disclosed in the financial statements, there is no requirement to alter the report for a compilation or review.

7. N, N

There is no professional requirement that the accountant submit a hard copy of financial statements or the accountant's report for a review or a compilation.

8. N, N

AR 100.69 states that during the performance of compilation or review procedures, evidence *may* come to the accountant's attention indicating there may be an uncertainty about the entity's ability to continue as a going concern. Specific procedures for the evaluation of an entity's ability to continue as a going concern are not required for either type of engagement.

Response #3: Research (1 point)

Paragraph Reference Answer: AR 100.23

Guidance: AR 100.23 states, "An accountant is not precluded from issuing a report with respect to a compilation of financial statements for an entity with respect to which the accountant is not independent. If the accountant is not independent, he or she should specifically disclose the lack of independence. However, the reason for the lack of independence should not be described. When the accountant is not independent, the following should be included as the last paragraph of the report: I am (we are) not independent with respect to XYZ Company." (6060)

Solution 31-7

Response #1: Review Report (5 points)

1. M

Martin is correct. The third paragraph should include a reference to "conformity with generally accepted accounting principles."

2. G

Gordon is correct. The standard review report does not refer to consistency.

3. G

Gordon is correct. The standard review report does not contain a restriction on distribution.

4. B

Both are incorrect. The standard review report does not contain a reference to a "going concern."

5. B

Both are incorrect. The statement regarding responsibility to update the report should be omitted.

6. G

Gordon is correct. The fourth paragraph should describe the responsibility the CPA is assuming for the financial statements of the prior period. Specifically, it should indicate (1) that the prior-period's financial statements were audited previously; (2) the date of the previous report; (3) the type of opinion that was previously expressed and (4) that no auditing procedures have been performed since the date of the previous report.

7. G

Gordon is correct. A list of the basic financial statements is not required in the fourth paragraph.

8. M

Martin is correct. The reference in the fourth paragraph to the fair presentation of the prior year's audited financial statements in accordance with generally accepted accounting principles should be omitted.

9. G

Gordon is correct. The report should be dated as of the completion of the inquiry and analytical procedures; the report should not be dual dated. The fourth paragraph correctly indicates the date of the audit report for the prior year's financial statements.

Response #2: Internal Control (4 points)

a. Management must **identify and document the controls and related objectives**. This documentation is the basis for management's assertion about the effectiveness of internal control. It provides evidence that the identified controls can be **communicated to the employees responsible for performing the controls** and such performance can be **monitored and evaluated** by the company on an **ongoing basis**. Any **deficiencies identified** should be **reported and corrected**.

Hart may perform the examination of internal control only if Unidyne's management meets certain conditions. **Management** must: (1) **accept responsibility** for the effectiveness of the company's internal control; (2) **evaluate** the effectiveness of the company's internal control using **suitable and available criteria**; (3) **support its assertion** about the effectiveness of the company's internal control with **sufficient appropriate evidence** (as discussed in the preceding paragraph); and (4) **provide its assertion** about the effectiveness of the company's internal control **in a report that accompanies the Hart's report**.

b. Other attest services (separate from an examination of an entity's ICFR that is integrated with an audit of its financial statements) involving internal control include engagements to (1) examine the **suitability of design** of an entity's internal control; (2) examine controls over the **effectiveness and efficiency of operations**; (3) examine controls over **compliance with laws and regulations**; and (4) **report on controls at a service organization**.

Hart should **not accept an engagement to review an entity's internal control or a written assertion thereon**.

Response #3: Research (1 point)

Paragraph Reference Answer: AT 501.110

Guidance: AT 501.110 states, "The auditor should date the report no earlier than the date on which the auditor has obtained sufficient appropriate evidence to support the auditor's opinion. Because the examination of internal control is integrated with the audit of the financial statements, the dates of the reports should be the same. " (6160)

APPENDIX A
PRACTICE EXAM

Editor's Note: There is only one practice (or final) examination. Do not take this exam until you are ready for it. If you did not mark the answers on the diagnostic exam, it can be used as a second "final" exam.

Testlet 1 MULTIPLE-CHOICE QUESTIONS (60 to 75 minutes)

1. To exercise due professional care an auditor should
a. Attain the proper balance of professional experience and formal education
b. Design the audit to detect all instances of illegal acts
c. Critically review the judgment exercised by those assisting in the audit
d. Examine all available corroborating evidence supporting management's assertions   (8945)

2. A CPA establishes quality control policies and procedures for deciding whether to accept a new client or continue to perform services for a current client. One of the main purposes for establishing such policies and procedures is
a. To enable the auditor to attest to the integrity or reliability of a client
b. To comply with the quality control standards established by regulatory bodies
c. To lessen the exposure to litigation resulting from failure to detect fraud in client financial statements
d. To minimize the likelihood of association with clients whose management lacks integrity   (8946)

3. Prior to the acceptance of an audit engagement with a client who has terminated the services of the predecessor auditor, the CPA should
a. Contact the predecessor auditor without advising the prospective client and request a complete report of the circumstances leading to the termination, with the understanding that all information disclosed will be kept confidential
b. Accept the engagement without contacting the predecessor auditor since the CPA can include audit procedures to verify the reason given by the client for the termination
c. Not communicate with the predecessor auditor because this would violate the confidential relationship between auditor and client
d. Advise the client of the intention to contact the predecessor auditor and request permission for the contact   (8947)

4. An auditor's engagement letter should include
a. Management's acknowledgment of its responsibility for maintaining effective internal control
b. The auditor's preliminary assessment of the risk factors relating to misstatements arising from fraudulent financial reporting
c. A reminder that management is responsible for illegal acts committed by employees
d. A request for permission to contact the client's lawyer for assistance in identifying litigation, claims, and assessments   (7093)

5. Holding other planning considerations equal, a decrease in the amount of misstatements in a class of transactions that an auditor could tolerate most likely would cause the auditor to
a. Apply the planned substantive tests prior to the balance sheet date
b. Perform the planned auditing procedures closer to the balance sheet date
c. Increase the assessed level of control risk for relevant financial statement assertions
d. Decrease the extent of auditing procedures to be applied to the class of transactions   (6574)

6. The senior auditor responsible for coordinating the fieldwork usually schedules a pre-audit conference with the audit team primarily to
a. Give guidance to the staff regarding both technical and personnel aspects of the audit
b. Provide an opportunity to document staff disagreements regarding technical issues
c. Establish the need for using the work of specialists and internal auditors
d. Discuss staff suggestions concerning the establishment and maintenance of time budgets   (5077)

7. Which of the following statements is **not** correct about materiality?
a. The concept of materiality recognizes that some matters are important for fair presentation of financial statements in conformity with GAAP, while other matters are **not** important.
b. An auditor considers materiality for planning purposes in terms of the largest aggregate level of misstatements that could be material to any one of the financial statements.
c. An auditor's consideration of materiality is influenced by the auditor's perception of the needs of a reasonable person who will rely on the financial statements.
d. Materiality judgments are made in light of surrounding circumstances and necessarily involve both quantitative and qualitative judgments.

(5084)

8. Which of the following statements best describes the auditor's responsibility regarding the detection of material errors and fraud?
a. The auditor is responsible for the failure to detect material errors and fraud only when such failure results from the nonapplication of generally accepted accounting principles.
b. Extended auditing procedures are required to detect material errors and fraud if the audit indicates that they may exist.
c. The auditor is responsible for the failure to detect material errors and fraud only when the auditor fails to confirm receivables or observe inventories.
d. Extended auditing procedures are required to detect unrecorded transactions even if there is no evidence that material errors and fraud may exist.

(8948)

9. Which of the following relatively small misstatements most likely could have a material effect on an entity's financial statements?
a. An illegal payment to a foreign official that was **not** recorded
b. A piece of obsolete office equipment that was **not** retired
c. A petty cash fund disbursement that was **not** properly authorized
d. An uncollectible account receivable that was **not** written off

(5627)

10. Morris, CPA, suspects that a pervasive scheme of illegal bribes exists throughout the operations of Worldwide Import-Export Inc., a new audit client. Morris notified the audit committee and Worldwide's legal counsel, but neither could assist Morris in determining whether the amounts involved were material to the financial statements or whether senior management was involved in the scheme. Under these circumstances, Morris should
a. Express an unqualified opinion with a separate explanatory paragraph
b. Disclaim an opinion on the financial statements
c. Express an adverse opinion of the financial statements
d. Issue a special report regarding the illegal bribes

(0165)

11. Management's attitude toward aggressive financial reporting and its emphasis on meeting projected profit goals most likely would significantly influence an entity's control environment when
a. External policies established by parties outside the entity affect its accounting practices.
b. Management is dominated by one individual who is also a shareholder.
c. Internal auditors have direct access to the board of directors and the entity's management.
d. The audit committee is active in overseeing the entity's financial reporting policies.

(6390)

12. The objective of tests of details of transactions performed as tests of controls is to
a. Monitor the design and use of entity documents such as prenumbered shipping forms
b. Determine whether internal controls have been implemented
c. Detect material misstatements in the account balances of the financial statements
d. Evaluate whether internal control procedures operated effectively

(5115)

13. In the consideration of an entity's internal control, the auditor is basically concerned that the controls provide reasonable assurance that
a. Operational efficiency has been achieved in accordance with management plans.
b. Errors and fraud have been prevented or detected.
c. Management **cannot** override the controls.
d. Controls have **not** been circumvented by collusion.

(7488)

14. Which one of the following would the auditor consider to be an incompatible operation if the cashier receives remittances from the mailroom?
a. The cashier posts the receipts to the accounts receivable subsidiary ledger cards.
b. The cashier makes the daily deposit at a local bank.
c. The cashier prepares the daily deposit.
d. The cashier endorses the checks. (8949)

15. Sound internal control policies and procedures dictate that defective merchandise returned by customers should be presented to the
a. Inventory control clerk
b. Sales clerk
c. Purchasing clerk
d. Receiving clerk (8950)

16. A significant deficiency in internal control exists when
a. The design or operation of a control does not allow management or employees, in the normal course of performing their assigned functions, to be able to prevent, or detect and correct misstatements on a timely basis.
b. The person performing the control does not possess the necessary authority or competence to perform the control effectively.
c. There is a deficiency, or a combination of deficiencies, that is less severe than a material weakness, yet important enough to merit attention by those charged with governance.
d. The auditor finds evidence that a misstatement of the financial statements actually occurred as a direct result of a missing control. (Editors, 9036)

17. Which of the following statements is correct concerning control deficiencies in an audit?
a. An auditor is required to search for control deficiencies during an audit.
b. All significant deficiencies are also considered to be material weaknesses.
c. An auditor may communicate deficiencies during an audit or after the audit's completion.
d. An auditor may report that no significant deficiencies were noted during an audit. (5656)

18. While substantive tests may support the accuracy of underlying records, these tests frequently provide no affirmative evidence of segregation of duties because
a. Substantive tests rarely guarantee the accuracy of the records if only a sample of the transactions has been tested.
b. The records may be accurate even though they are maintained by persons having incompatible functions.
c. Substantive tests relate to the entire period under audit, but tests of control ordinarily are confined to the period during which the auditor is on the client's premises.
d. Many computerized procedures leave no audit trail of who performed them, so substantive tests may necessarily be limited to inquiries and observation of office personnel. (8951)

19. Which of the following circumstances most likely would cause an auditor to suspect that material misstatements exist in a client's financial statements?
a. The assumptions used in developing the prior year's accounting estimates have changed.
b. Differences between reconciliations of control accounts and subsidiary records are not investigated.
c. Negative confirmation requests yield fewer responses than in the prior year's audit.
d. Management consults with another CPA firm about complex accounting matters. (7097)

20. For audits of financial statements made in accordance with generally accepted auditing standards, the use of analytical procedures is required to some extent

	As a substantive test	In the final review stage
a.	Yes	Yes
b.	Yes	No
c.	No	Yes
d.	No	No	(8952)

21. The auditor notices significant fluctuations in key elements of the company's financial statements. If management is unable to provide an acceptable explanation, the auditor should
a. Consider the matter a scope limitation
b. Perform additional audit procedures to investigate the matter further
c. Intensify the audit with the expectation of detecting management fraud
d. Withdraw from the engagement   (8953)

22. A written representation from a client's management which, among other matters, acknowledges responsibility for the fair presentation of financial statements, should normally be signed by the
a. Chief executive officer and the chief financial officer
b. Chief financial officer and the chairman of the board of directors
c. Chairman of the audit committee of the board of directors
d. Chief executive officer, the chairman of the board of directors, and the client's lawyer   (8954)

23. The auditor is most likely to seek information from the plant manager with respect to the
a. Adequacy of the provision for uncollectible accounts
b. Appropriateness of physical inventory observation procedures
c. Existence of obsolete machinery
d. Deferral of procurement of certain necessary insurance coverage   (8955)

24. Analytical procedures used in the overall review stage of an audit generally include
a. Gathering evidence concerning account balances that have **not** changed from the prior year
b. Retesting control procedures that appeared to be ineffective during the assessment of control risk
c. Considering unusual or unexpected account balances that were **not** previously identified
d. Performing tests of transactions to corroborate management's financial statement assertions   (5665)

25. Which of the following factors would **least** likely affect the quantity and content of an auditor's working papers?
a. The condition of the client's records
b. The assessed level of control risk
c. The nature of the auditor's report
d. The content of the representation letter   (5146)

26. After issuing a report an auditor concludes that an auditing procedure considered necessary at the time of the audit was omitted from the audit. The auditor should first
a. Undertake to apply the omitted procedure or alternative procedures that would provide a satisfactory basis for the auditor's opinion
b. Assess the importance of the omitted procedure to the auditor's ability to support the opinion expressed on the financial statements taken as a whole
c. Notify the audit committee or the board of director's that the auditor's opinion can **no** longer be relied upon
d. Review the results of other procedures that were applied to compensate for the one omitted or to make its omission less important   (8956)

27. The auditor concludes that there is a material inconsistency in the other information in an annual report to shareholders containing audited financial statements. If the client refuses to revise or eliminate the material inconsistency, the auditor should
a. Revise the auditor's report to include a separate explanatory paragraph describing the material inconsistency
b. Consult with a party whose advice might influence the client, such as the client's legal counsel
c. Issue a qualified opinion after discussing the matter with the client's board of directors
d. Consider the matter closed since the other information is **not** in the audited financial statements   (8957)

28. An auditor would be most likely to consider expressing a qualified opinion if the client's financial statements include a footnote on related party transactions that
a. Lists the amounts due from related parties including the terms and manner of settlement
b. Discloses compensating balance arrangements maintained for the benefit of related parties
c. Represents that certain transactions with related parties were consummated on terms equally as favorable as would have been obtained in transactions with unrelated parties
d. Presents the dollar volume of related party transactions and the effects of any change in the method of establishing terms from that of the prior period   (8958)

29. Which of the following is a documentation requirement that an auditor should follow when auditing in accordance with *Government Auditing Standards?*
a. The auditor should obtain written representations from management acknowledging responsibility for correcting instances of fraud, abuse, and waste.
b. The auditor's working papers should contain sufficient information so that supplementary oral explanations are **not** required.
c. The auditor's working papers should contain a caveat that all instances of material errors and fraud may **not** be identified.
d. The auditor should document the procedures that assure discovery of all illegal acts and contingent liabilities resulting from noncompliance. (4281)

30. When auditing an entity's financial statements in accordance with *Government Auditing Standards,* an auditor should prepare a written report on the auditor's
a. Identification of the causes of performance problems and recommendations for actions to improve operations
b. Understanding of internal control and assessment of control risk
c. Field work and procedures that substantiated the auditor's specific findings and conclusions
d. Opinion on the entity's attainment of the goals and objectives specified by applicable laws and regulations (4282)

Testlet 2 MULTIPLE-CHOICE QUESTIONS (60 to 75 minutes)

1. Which of the following factors most likely would cause an auditor to question the integrity of management?
a. Management has an aggressive attitude toward financial reporting and meeting profit goals.
b. Audit tests detect material fraud that was known to management, but **not** disclosed to the auditor.
c. Managerial decisions are dominated by one person who is also a stockholder.
d. Weaknesses in internal control reported to the audit committee are not corrected by management. (7631)

2. In developing a preliminary audit strategy, an auditor should consider
a. Whether the allowance for sampling risk exceeds the achieved upper precision limit
b. Findings from substantive tests performed at interim dates
c. Whether the inquiry of the client's attorney identifies any litigation, claims, or assessments **not** disclosed in the financial statements
d. The potential risks of material misstatement (2276)

3. In planning an audit, the auditor's knowledge about the design of relevant internal control policies and procedures should be used to
a. Identify the types of potential misstatements that could occur
b. Assess the operational efficiency of the internal control structure
c. Determine whether controls have been circumvented by collusion
d. Document the assessed level of control risk (5951)

4. Management philosophy and operating style most likely would have a significant influence on an entity's control environment when
a. The internal auditor reports directly to management.
b. Management is dominated by one individual.
c. Accurate management job descriptions delineate specific duties.
d. The audit committee actively oversees the financial reporting process. (5954)

5. Inherent risk and control risk differ from detection risk in that they
a. Arise from the misapplication of auditing procedures
b. May be assessed in either quantitative or nonquantitative terms
c. Exist independently of the financial statement audit
d. Can be changed at the auditor's discretion (5081)

6. A weakness in internal control over recording retirements of equipment may cause an auditor to
a. Trace additions to the "other assets" account to search for equipment that is still on hand but **no** longer being used
b. Select certain items of equipment from the accounting records and locate them in the plant
c. Review the subsidiary ledger to ascertain whether depreciation was taken on each item of equipment during the year
d. Inspect certain items of equipment in the plant and trace those items to the accounting records (0081)

7. Independent internal verification of inventory occurs when employees who
a. Issue raw materials obtain material requisitions for each issue and prepare daily totals of materials issued.
b. Compare records of goods on hand with physical quantities do **not** maintain the records or have custody of the inventory.
c. Are independent of issuing production orders update records from completed job cost sheets and production cost reports on a timely basis.
d. Obtain receipts for the transfer of completed work to finished goods prepare a completed production report. (0089)

8. A client erroneously recorded a large purchase twice. Which of the following internal control measures would be most likely to detect this error in a timely and efficient manner?
a. Footing the purchases journal
b. Reconciling vendors' monthly statements with subsidiary payable ledger accounts
c. Tracing totals from the purchases journal to the ledger accounts
d. Sending written quarterly confirmations to all vendors (8959)

9. An internal control questionnaire indicates that an approved receiving report is required to accompany every check request for payment of merchandise. Which of the following procedures provides the greatest assurance that this control is operating effectively?
a. Select and examine canceled checks and ascertain that the related receiving reports are dated **no** earlier than the checks
b. Select and examine canceled checks and ascertain that the related receiving reports are dated **no** later than the checks
c. Select and examine receiving reports and ascertain that the related canceled checks are dated **no** earlier than the receiving reports
d. Select and examine receiving reports and ascertain that the related canceled checks are dated **no** later than the receiving reports (8960)

10. To improve accountability for fixed asset retirements, management most likely would implement a system of internal control that includes
a. Continuous analysis of the repairs and maintenance account
b. Periodic inquiry of plant executives by internal auditors as to whether any plant assets have been retired
c. Continuous utilization of serially numbered retirement work orders
d. Periodic inspection of insurance policies by the internal auditors (8961)

11. In assessing the objectivity of internal auditors, an independent auditor should
a. Evaluate the quality control program in effect for the internal auditors
b. Examine documentary evidence of the work performed by the internal auditors
c. Test a sample of the transactions and balances that the internal auditors examined
d. Determine the organizational level to which the internal auditors report (5950)

12. In designing written audit programs, an auditor should establish specific audit objectives that relate primarily to the
a. Timing of audit procedures
b. Cost-benefit of gathering evidence
c. Selected audit techniques
d. Financial statement assertions (4673)

13. The auditor will most likely perform extensive tests for possible understatement of
a. Revenues
b. Assets
c. Liabilities
d. Capital (8962)

14. Which of the following factors would **least** influence an auditor's consideration of the reliability of data for purposes of analytical procedures?
a. Whether the data were processed in an IT system or in a manual accounting system
b. Whether sources within the entity were independent of those who are responsible for the amount being audited
c. Whether the data were subjected to audit testing in the current or prior year
d. Whether the data were obtained from independent sources outside the entity or from sources within the entity (0151)

15. The date of the management representation letter should be as of the date of the
a. Balance sheet
b. Latest interim financial information
c. Auditor's report
d. Latest related party transaction (5685)

16. Which of the following statements extracted from a client's lawyer's letter concerning litigation, claims, and assessments most likely would cause the auditor to request clarification?
a. "I believe that the possible liability to the company is nominal in amount"
b. "I believe that the action can be settled for less than the damages claimed"
c. "I believe that the plaintiff's case against the company is without merit"
d. "I believe that the company will be able to defend this action successfully" (6364)

17. An auditor's working papers serve mainly to
a. Provide the principal support for the auditor's report
b. Satisfy the auditor's responsibilities concerning the Code of Professional Conduct
c. Monitor the effectiveness of the CPA firm's quality control procedures
d. Document the level of independence maintained by the auditor (5689)

18. "There have been no communications from regulatory agencies concerning noncompliance with, or deficiencies in, financial reporting practices that could have a material effect on the financial statements." The foregoing passage is most likely from a
a. Report on internal control
b. Special report
c. Management representation letter
d. Letter for underwriters (6397)

19. To be effective, analytical procedures in the overall review stage of an audit engagement should be performed by
a. The staff accountant who performed the substantive auditing procedures
b. The managing partner who has responsibility for all audit engagements at that practice office
c. A manager or partner who has a comprehensive knowledge of the client's business and industry
d. The CPA firm's quality control manager or partner who has responsibility for the firm's peer review program (7025)

20. In the confirmation of accounts receivable, the auditor would most likely
a. Request confirmation of a sample of the inactive accounts
b. Seek to obtain positive confirmations for at least 50% of the total dollar amount of the receivables
c. Require confirmation of all receivables from agencies of the federal government
d. Require that confirmation requests be sent within one month of the fiscal year-end (8963)

21. Which of the following might be detected by an auditor's review of the client's sales cut-off?
a. Excessive goods returned for credit
b. Unrecorded sales discounts
c. Lapping of year-end accounts receivable
d. Inflated sales for the year (8964)

22. Which of the following is not one of the independent auditor's objectives regarding the examination of inventories?
a. Verifying that inventory counted is owned by the client
b. Verifying that the client has used proper inventory pricing
c. Ascertaining the physical quantities of inventory on hand
d. Verifying that all inventory owned by the client is on hand at the time of the count (8965)

23. When an auditor is unable to inspect and count a client's investment securities until after the balance sheet date, the bank where the securities are held in a safe deposit box should be asked to
a. Verify any differences between the contents of the box and the balances in the client's subsidiary ledger
b. Provide a list of securities added and removed from the box between the balance sheet date and the date of the security count
c. Confirm that there has been **no** access to the box between the balance sheet date and the date of the security count
d. Count the securities in the box so the auditor will have an independent direct verification (8966)

24. The accounts payable department receives the purchase order form to accomplish all of the following **except**
a. Compare invoice price to purchase order price
b. Ensure the purchase had been properly authorized
c. Ensure the goods had been received by the party requesting the goods
d. Compare quantity ordered to quantity purchased (8967)

25. Which of the following auditing procedures most likely would provide assurance about a manufacturing entity's inventory valuation?
a. Testing the entity's computation of standard overhead rates
b. Obtaining confirmation of inventories pledged under loan agreements
c. Reviewing shipping and receiving cutoff procedures for inventories
d. Tracing test counts to the entity's inventory listing (5121)

26. An auditor analyzes repairs and maintenance accounts primarily to obtain evidence in support of the audit assertion that all
a. Noncapitalizable expenditures for repairs and maintenance have been recorded in the proper period.
b. Expenditures for property and equipment have been recorded in the proper period.
c. Noncapitalizable expenditures for repairs and maintenance have been properly charged to expense.
d. Expenditures for property and equipment have **not** been charged to expense. (5135)

27. When qualifying an opinion because of an insufficiency of audit evidence, an auditor should refer to the situation in the

	Scope paragraph	Notes to the financial statements
a.	Yes	Yes
b.	Yes	No
c.	No	Yes
d.	No	No (7100)

28. When using the work of a specialist, the auditor may make reference to and identify the specialist in the auditor's report if the
a. Auditor decides to express a qualified opinion.
b. Specialist's reputation or professional certification is being emphasized.
c. Auditor wishes to indicate a division of responsibility.
d. Specialist's work provides the auditor greater assurance of reliability. (8968)

29. When comparative financial statements are presented but the predecessor auditor's report is **not** presented, the current auditor should do which of the following in the audit report?
a. Disclaim an opinion on the prior year's financial statements
b. Identify the predecessor auditor who audited the financial statements of the prior year
c. Make **no** comment with respect to the predecessor audit
d. Indicate the type of opinion expressed by the predecessor auditor (8969)

30. An accountant who is **not** independent of a client is precluded from issuing a
a. Report on consulting services
b. Compilation report on historical financial statements
c. Compilation report on prospective financial statements
d. Special report on compliance with contractual agreements (0393)

Testlet 3 MULTIPLE-CHOICE QUESTIONS (60 to 75 minutes)

1. Which of the following is intended to detect deviations from prescribed Accounting Department procedures?
a. Substantive tests specified by a standardized audit program
b. Tests of controls designed specifically for the client
c. Analytical procedures as designed in the industry audit guide
d. Computerized analytical procedures tailored for the configuration of IT equipment in use (8970)

2. The auditor would **least** likely be concerned about internal control as it relates to
a. Land and buildings
b. Common stock
c. Shareholder meetings
d. Minutes of board of directors meetings (8971)

3. The permanent file section of the working papers that is kept for each audit client most likely contains
a. Review notes pertaining to questions and comments regarding the audit work performed
b. A schedule of time spent on the engagement by each individual auditor
c. Correspondence with the client's legal counsel concerning pending litigation
d. Narrative descriptions of the client's accounting procedures and internal control structure (8972)

4. An auditor decides to use the blank form of accounts receivable confirmation rather than the positive form. The auditor should be aware that the blank form may be **less** efficient because
a. Subsequent cash receipts need to be verified.
b. Statistical sampling may **not** be used.
c. A higher assessed level of detection risk is required.
d. More nonresponses are likely to occur. (7640)

5. The diagram below depicts an auditor's estimated maximum deviation rate compared with the tolerable rate, and also depicts the true population deviation rate compared with the tolerable rate.

Auditor's estimate based on sample results	True state of population	
	Deviation rate is less than tolerable rate	Deviation rate exceeds tolerable rate
Maximum deviation rate is less than tolerable rate	I.	III.
Maximum deviation rate exceeds tolerable rate	II.	IV.

As a result of tests of controls, the auditor assesses control risk too low and thereby decreases substantive testing. This is illustrated by situation
a. I
b. II
c. III
d. IV (5964)

6. In performing tests of controls over authorization of cash disbursements, which of the following statistical sampling methods would be most appropriate?
a. Variables
b. Stratified
c. Ratio
d. Attributes (3921)

7. In a probability-proportional-to-size sample with a sampling interval of $10,000, an auditor discovered that a selected account receivable with a recorded amount of $5,000 had an audited amount of $4,000. If this were the only misstatement discovered by the auditor, the projected misstatement of this sample would be
a. $ 1,000
b. $ 2,000
c. $ 5,000
d. $10,000 (6935)

8. The theoretical distribution of means from all possible samples of a given size is a normal distribution and this distribution is the basis for statistical sampling. Which of the following statements is **not** true with respect to the sampling distribution of sample means?
a. Approximately 68% of the sample means will be within one standard deviation of the mean for the normal distribution.
b. The distribution is defined in terms of its mean and its standard error of the mean.
c. An auditor can be approximately 95% confident that the mean for a sample is within two standard deviations of the population mean.
d. The items drawn in an auditor's sample will have a normal distribution. (8973)

9. Camela Department Stores has a fully integrated IT accounting system and is planning to issue credit cards to creditworthy customers. To strengthen internal control by making it difficult for one to create a valid customer account number, the company's independent auditor has suggested the inclusion of a check digit which should be placed
a. At the beginning of a valid account number, only
b. In the middle of a valid account number, only
c. At the end of a valid account number, only
d. Consistently in any position (8974)

10. Processing data through the use of simulated files provides an auditor with information about the operating effectiveness of control policies and procedures. One of the techniques involved in this approach makes use of
a. Controlled reprocessing
b. An integrated test facility
c. Input validation
d. Program code checking   (2970)

11. Which of the following strategies would a CPA most likely consider in auditing an entity that processes most of its financial data only in electronic form, such as a paperless system?
a. Continuous monitoring and analysis of transaction processing with an embedded audit module
b. Increased reliance on internal control activities that emphasize the segregation of duties
c. Verification of encrypted digital certificates used to monitor the authorization of transactions
d. Extensive testing of firewall boundaries that restrict the recording of outside network traffic
                                                       (6839)

12. Which of the following procedures would the principal auditor most likely perform after deciding to make reference to another CPA who audited a subsidiary of the entity?
a. Review the working papers and the audit programs of the other CPA
b. Visit the other CPA and discuss the results of the other CPA's audit procedures
c. Make inquiries about the professional reputation and independence of the other CPA
d. Determine that the other CPA has a sufficient understanding of the subsidiary's internal control
                                                       (6831)

13. Harris, CPA, has been asked to audit and report on the balance sheet of Fox Co. but not on the statements of income, retained earnings, or cash flows. Harris will have access to all information underlying the basic financial statements. Under these circumstances, Harris may
a. Not accept the engagement because it would constitute a violation of the profession's ethical standards
b. Not accept the engagement because it would be tantamount to rendering a piecemeal opinion
c. Accept the engagement because such engagements merely involve limited reporting objectives
d. Accept the engagement but should disclaim an opinion because of an inability to apply the procedures considered necessary   (6008)

14. Which of the following subsequent events will be **least** likely to result in an adjustment to the financial statements?
a. Culmination of events affecting the realization of accounts receivable owned as of the balance sheet date
b. Culmination of events affecting the realization of inventories owned as of the balance sheet date
c. Material changes in the settlement of liabilities which were estimated as of the balance sheet date
d. Material changes in the quoted market prices of listed investment securities since the balance sheet date   (8975)

15. When an auditor concludes there is substantial doubt about a continuing audit client's ability to continue as a going concern for a reasonable period of time, the auditor's responsibility is to
a. Issue a qualified or adverse opinion, depending upon materiality, due to the possible effects on the financial statements
b. Consider the adequacy of disclosure about the client's possible inability to continue as a going concern
c. Report to the client's audit committee that management's accounting estimates may need to be adjusted
d. Reissue the prior year's auditor's report and add an explanatory paragraph that specifically refers to "substantial doubt" and "going concern" (4727)

16. In an audit of internal control over financial reporting conducted in accordance with the standards of the Public Company Accounting Oversight Board (PCAOB), which procedure is insufficient by itself to test the effectiveness of a control?
a. Inquiries of appropriate personnel
b. Inspection of relevant documents
c. Observation of operations
d. Reperformance of the control procedure
                                             (Editors, 7953)

17. What does the Public Company Accounting Oversight Board (PCAOB) call a deficiency of internal control over financial reporting (ICFR) such that there is a reasonable possibility that a material misstatement of the company's annual or interim financial statements will not be prevented or detected on a timely basis?
a. Control deficiency
b. Material deficiency
c. Material weakness
d. Significant deficiency   (Editors, 7950)

18. The objective of a review of interim financial information for a nonissuer is to provide the accountant with a basis for communicating whether
a. A reasonable basis exists for expressing an updated opinion regarding the financial statements that were previously audited.
b. Material modifications should be made to conform with the applicable financial reporting framework.
c. The financial statements are presented fairly in accordance with standards of interim reporting.
d. The financial statements are presented fairly in conformity with the applicable financial reporting framework. (8976)

19. An auditor's report on financial statements prepared on the cash receipts and disbursements basis of accounting should include all of the following **except**
a. A reference to the note to the financial statements that describes the cash receipts and disbursements basis of accounting
b. A statement that the cash receipts and disbursements basis of accounting is **not** a comprehensive basis of accounting
c. An opinion as to whether the financial statements are presented fairly in conformity with the cash receipts and disbursements basis of accounting
d. A statement that the audit was conducted in accordance with generally accepted auditing standards (5700)

20. An auditor's report issued in connection with which of the following is generally not considered to be a special report?
a. Compliance with aspects of contractual agreements unrelated to audited financial statements
b. Specified elements, accounts, or items of a financial statement presented in a document
c. Financial statements prepared in accordance with an entity's income tax basis
d. Financial information presented in a prescribed schedule that requires a prescribed form of auditor's report (8977)

21. If requested to perform a review engagement for a nonpublic entity in which an accountant has an immaterial direct financial interest, the accountant is
a. Not independent and, therefore, may **not** be associated with the financial statements
b. Not independent and, therefore, may **not** issue a review report
c. Not independent and, therefore, may issue a review report, but may **not** issue an auditor's opinion
d. Independent because the financial interest is immaterial and, therefore, may issue a review report (5638)

22. When engaged to compile the financial statements of a nonpublic entity, an accountant is required to possess a level of knowledge of the entity's accounting principles and practices. This requirement most likely will include obtaining a general understanding of the
a. Stated qualifications of the entity's accounting personnel
b. Design of the entity's internal controls placed in operation
c. Risk factors relating to misstatements arising from illegal acts
d. Internal control awareness of the entity's senior management (6823)

23. Brown, CPA, has accepted an engagement to examine the effectiveness of internal control over financial reporting of Crow Company (a nonissuer). Crow Company's written assertion about the effectiveness of internal control should be presented

I. In a separate report that will accompany Brown's report
II. In a representation letter to Brown

a. Neither I nor II
b. Either I or II
c. I only
d. II only (11/95, AUD, #36, amended, 5983)

24. Which of the following statements is correct concerning both an engagement to compile and an engagement to review a nonpublic entity's financial statements?
a. The accountant should obtain a written management representation letter.
b. The accountant must be independent in fact and appearance.
c. The accountant expresses **no** assurance on the financial statements.
d. The accountant does **not** contemplate obtaining an understanding of internal control. (2327)

25. Which of the following procedures is **not** usually performed by the accountant during a review engagement of a nonissuer?
a. Inquiring about actions taken at meetings of the board of directors that may affect the financial statements
b. Issuing a report stating that the review was performed in accordance with standards established by the AICPA
c. Reading the financial statements to consider whether they conform with generally accepted accounting principles
d. Communicating any material weaknesses discovered during the consideration of internal control (2979)

26. Which of the following procedures is usually performed by the accountant in a review engagement of a nonpublic entity?
a. Sending a letter of inquiry to the entity's lawyer
b. Comparing the financial statements with statements for comparable prior periods
c. Confirming a significant percentage of receivables by direct communication with debtors
d. Communicating significant deficiencies discovered during the study of internal control (2787)

27. Which of the following inquiry or analytical procedures ordinarily is performed in an engagement to review a nonpublic entity's financial statements?
a. Analytical procedures designed to test the accounting records by obtaining corroborating evidential matter
b. Inquiries concerning the entity's procedures for recording and summarizing transactions
c. Analytical procedures designed to test management's assertions regarding continued existence
d. Inquiries of the entity's attorney concerning contingent liabilities (2977)

28. Which one of the following is generally more important in a review than in a compilation?
a. Determining the accounting basis on which the financial statements are to be presented
b. Gaining familiarity with industry accounting principles and practices
c. Obtaining a signed engagement letter
d. Obtaining a signed representation letter (8978)

29. When an accountant examines projected financial statements, the accountant's report should include a separate paragraph that
a. Describes the limitations on the usefulness of the presentation
b. Provides an explanation of the differences between an examination and an audit
c. States that the accountant is responsible for events and circumstances up to one year after the report's date
d. Disclaims an opinion on whether the assumptions provide a reasonable basis for the projection (6029)

30. When an accountant compiles projected financial statements, the accountant's report should include a separate paragraph that
a. Describes the differences between a projection and a forecast
b. Identifies the accounting principles used by management
c. Expresses limited assurance that the actual results may be within the projection's range
d. Describes the limitations on the projection's usefulness (8979)

SIMULATIONS

Testlet 4 (40 to 50 minutes)

| Company Profile | Audit Risk | Confirmations | Resources |

The year under audit is year 2.

Company

Aquatic Jet Products, Inc. is a manufacturer of jet boats and personal watercraft, with headquarters in northern Florida. Personal watercraft are manufactured at the Florida facility. The company's jet boats are manufactured at a facility in Mexico. Finished goods are sold primarily to independent marine stores throughout the United States.

The company, in its ninth year of operations, has experienced two years of declining sales after a period of rapid growth. The overall market demand for watercraft has also declined and many competitors have filed for bankruptcy in recent years. Tough new federal emissions regulations further threaten industry profitability.

Business Projection

Eager to revive the company's profitability, the board of directors has implemented several new changes, starting with the hiring of a new CEO, lured away from a major competitor. The new CEO is optimistic and ambitious and has set a goal of a 25% increase in sales for year 2. To help achieve this goal, the CEO has changed the sales staff's compensation from salaried to commission-based.

Unhappy with past sales performance, the CEO plans to terminate relationships with several retail customers and identify new outlets for distribution of its product lines. To further protect its bottom line, the board of directors has also restructured the CFO's compensation package, to include a substantial bonus based on the company's net profits. The company's bank, wary of declining trends, has placed strict new covenants on the company's renewed line-of-credit.

Auditors

This is the second year that the company has engaged your firm to perform the annual audit of its financial statements. The prior audit firm is upset that they have lost the audit. However, they indicate that no disagreements with management have previously occurred. You learn that a senior accountant from the prior audit firm has taken an accounting position with the company.

The CFO gives your audit team a tour of the Florida facility. During the tour, you note that parts of the facility may require repair. You also note that the finished watercraft inventory is kept in an open lot outside the facility. The CFO explains that due to its rural location, the company has not had any problems with theft of its products. The CFO comments on the collegiality of the workforce. However, in your tour of the office, you overhear two clerical employees complaining about their rate of pay.

Other Issues

During the year, the company uncovered an embezzlement by the payroll clerk. According to the CFO, the clerk's scheme was to add hours to her timesheet after approval, during processing of the timecards. While the accounting department is not required to take vacations, the company was fortunate to discover the theft while the employee was out sick for two days. The CFO indicates that while this discovery was unexpected, the company is confident that this was an isolated occurrence.

Based on the information in the Company Profile, indicate by checking the appropriate box next to each item whether or not the item would most likely increase audit risk.

PROFILE INFORMATION	Increased audit risk?	
	Yes	No
A. Finished goods are sold primarily to independent marine stores throughout the United States.		
B. Tough new federal emissions regulations further threaten industry profitability.		
C. The company's bank, wary of declining trends, has placed strict new covenants on the company's renewed line-of-credit.		
D. The prior audit firm is upset that they have lost the audit.		
E. A senior accountant from the prior audit firm has taken an accounting position with the company.		
F. Finished watercraft inventory is kept in an open lot outside the Florida facility.		
G. In your tour of the office, you overhear two clerical employees complaining about their rate of pay.		

As part of the fieldwork on this engagement, the auditor obtained and documented an understanding of the company's internal controls relating to accounts receivable and assessed control risk related to accounts receivable at the maximum level. Susan, the staff person assigned to the engagement, requested and obtained from the company an aged accounts receivable schedule listing the total amount owed by each customer as of December 31, year 2, and sent positive confirmation requests to a sample of the company customers. Review Susan's comments on each of the following confirmations and determine the best conclusion and/or follow-up procedures for each item.

⟶

Confirmation letters can be found under the RESOURCES tab. Assume that all confirmations received have been appropriately signed, unless otherwise noted. For each customer in the table below, review the relevant confirmation letter and the comments at the bottom of each. Then select the procedure that should be followed to clear the exception, if one exists. Choose only one procedure per confirmation. A procedure may be used once, more than once, or not at all.

Customer	Conclusion/procedure
A. Performance Marine Sales, Inc.	
B. West Coast Ski Center, Inc.	
C. Fish & Ski World, Inc.	
D. NC Boating Center, Inc.	

Selection List

1. Send a second request for confirmation to the customer.	4. Verify that additional invoices noted on confirmation pertain to the subsequent year.
2. Exception noted; propose adjustment and request that the controller post it to the accounting records.	5. Not an exception, no further audit work deemed necessary.
3. Verify by examining subsequent cash collections and/or shipping documents	6. Not an exception, no adjustment necessary. Determine the sufficiency of allowance for doubtful accounts

| Company Profile | Audit Risk | Confirmations | Resources |

Confirmation Letters

February 1, year 3

Performance Marine Sales, Inc.
1284 River Road
Louisville, Kentucky 40059

Re: Balance at December 31, year 2 - $267,000

Dear Sirs:

As of December 31, year 2, our records indicate your balance with our company as the amount listed above. Please complete and sign the bottom portion of this letter and return the entire letter to our auditors, JS LLP, P.O. Box 100, Orlando, Florida 32806.

A stamped, self-addressed envelope is enclosed for your convenience.

Sincerely,

_____
Aquatic Jet Products, Inc.

The above balance is   ☐ Correct

               ☒ Incorrect (show amount) *$325,000*

If incorrect, please provide information that could help to reconcile your account.

| Response: We placed an order for $58,000 on December 26, year 2. |

| Signature | Title | Date |

Susan's note to file:

| Per discussion with the controller, the order for $58,000 was shipped f.o.b. shipping point on December 30, year 2, and was received by the customer on January 3, year 3. Therefore, no entry has been made to record the sale in year 2. |

February 1, year 3

West Coast Ski Center, Inc.
163 Tide Avenue
Monterey, California 93940

Re: Balance at December 31, year 2 - $414,000

Dear Sirs:

As of December 31, year 2, our records indicate your balance with our company as the amount listed above. Please complete and sign the bottom portion of this letter and return the entire letter to our auditors, JS LLP, P.O. Box 100, Orlando, Florida 32806.

A stamped, self-addressed envelope is enclosed for your convenience.

Sincerely,

_____
Aquatic Jet Products, Inc.

The above balance is   ☐ Correct

               ☒ Incorrect (show amount) *$320,000*

If incorrect, please provide information that could help to reconcile your account.

| Response: We made a payment of $94,000 on December 12, year 2. |

| Signature | Title | Date |

Susan's note to file:

| Per discussion with the controller, the company received the payment of $94,000 on December 15, year 2, and posted it to "Other Income." |

February 1, year 3

Fish & Ski World, Inc.
5660 Ocean Blvd
Port Arkansas, Texas 78373

Re: Balance at December 31, year 2 - $72,000

Dear Sirs:

As of December 31, year 2, our records indicate your balance with our company as the amount listed above. Please complete and sign the bottom portion of this letter and return the entire letter to our auditors, JS LLP, P.O. Box 100, Orlando, Florida 32806.

A stamped, self-addressed envelope is enclosed for your convenience.

Sincerely,

_____
Aquatic Jet Products, Inc.

- -

The above balance is ☐ Correct

☒ Incorrect
(show amount) _$163,000_

If incorrect, please provide information that could help to reconcile your account.

Response: Per our records, the following invoices are outstanding:
Invoice #4212 $72,000
Invoice #4593 $66,000
Invoice #4738 $25,000

Signature	Title	Date

Susan's note to file:

Invoices #4593 and 4738 are not on the A/R aging report at December 31, year 2.

February 1, year 3

NC Boating Center Inc.
110 Windward Blvd
Tierra Verde, Florida 33715

Re: Balance at December 31, year 2 - $239,000

Dear Sirs:

As of December 31, year 2, our records indicate your balance with our company as the amount listed above. Please complete and sign the bottom portion of this letter and return the entire letter to our auditors, JS LLP, P.O. Box 100, Orlando, Florida 32806.

A stamped, self-addressed envelope is enclosed for your convenience.

Sincerely,

_____
Aquatic Jet Products, Inc.

- -

The above balance is ☐ Correct

☐ Incorrect
(show amount) $_____

If incorrect, please provide information that could help to reconcile your account.

Response: We cannot determine the balance due at December 31, year 2.

Signature	Title	Date

Susan's note to file:

No amount was confirmed on the response letter.

For each of the potential December 31, year 2, sales cutoff problems listed below, select the appropriate adjustment for year 2 from the list provided. Each item in the list may be used once, more than once, or not at all.

Potential cutoff problem	Adjustment
A. The company shipped merchandise (f.o.b. destination) to a customer on December 29, year 2, and recorded the sale but not the relief of inventory. The customer received the merchandise on December 31, year 2.	
B. The company shipped merchandise (f.o.b. shipping point) on December 3, year 2, to a customer, and recorded the sale and relief of inventory. The customer, unhappy with the merchandise, returned the goods on December 29, year 2. The company records the following entry upon receipt of the goods: Inventory (dr.), Cost of Sales (cr.)	
C. The company shipped merchandise to a consignee on December 16, year 2, and did not record the transaction. The consignee returned the merchandise on December 28, year 2. Upon receipt of the goods, the company made the following entry: Inventory (dr.), Sales (cr.)	
D. The company shipped merchandise (f.o.b. shipping point) on December 29, year 2, and recorded relief of inventory, but not the sale, on that date. The customer has not received the merchandise and the company has not recorded the sale as of January 3, year 3.	

Selection List

1. No adjustment necessary.	6. Accounts Receivable (dr.) Inventory (cr.)
2. Accounts Receivable (dr.) Sales (cr.)	7. Sales (dr.) Accounts Receivable (cr.) Inventory (dr.) Cost of Sales (cr.)
3. Sales (dr.) Accounts Receivable (cr.)	8. Sales (dr.) Inventory (cr.)
4. Inventory (dr.) Cost of Sales (cr.)	9. Accounts Receivable (dr.) Sales (cr.) Cost of Sales (dr.) Inventory (cr.)
5. Cost of Sales (dr.) Inventory (cr.)	10. Sales (dr.) Cost of Sales (cr.)

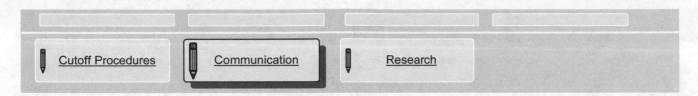

Based on the Company Profile, discuss how the company's discovery of an embezzlement by an accounting department employee might affect your fraud risk assessment, and indicate two fieldwork procedures your firm might utilize to satisfy itself that the extent of the theft has been properly identified in this particular situation.

REMINDER: On the actual exam your response will be graded for both technical content and writing skills. Technical content will be evaluated for information that is helpful to the intended reader and clearly relevant to the issue. Writing skills will be evaluated for development, organization, and the appropriate expression of ideas in professional correspondence. Use a standard business memo or letter format with a clear beginning, middle, and end. Do not convey information in the form of a table, bullet point list, or other abbreviated presentation.

During the course of your audit of the company for year 2, you identify that the company had purchase transactions with Risotto, LLC. You also determine that Risotto, LLC is owned by the CEO and vice president of the company. The purchases accounted for 28% of materials purchases for the year. Management has declined to disclose the related-party transactions in the footnotes. This is the only item that the auditor wishes to consider for the report on financial statements. What is the citation that gives an example of a report that addresses this finding?

Paragraph Reference Answer: _____

(R/07, AUD, #51, 8423)

Testlet 5 (25 to 35 minutes)

Field, CPA, is auditing the financial statements of Miller Mailorder, Inc. (MMI) for the year ended January 31, 20X1. Field has compiled a list of possible errors and fraud that may result in the misstatement of MMI's financial statements.

For each possible error and fraud listed, select one internal control procedure from the answer list that, if properly designed and implemented, most likely could assist MMI in preventing or detecting the errors and fraud.

<u>Possible Errors & Fraud</u>

1. Customers' checks are received for less than the customers' full account balances, but the customers' full account balances are credited.

2. Customers' checks are misappropriated before being forwarded to the cashier for deposit.

3. Customers' checks are credited to incorrect customer accounts.

4. Different customer accounts are each credited for the same cash receipt.

5. Customers' checks are properly credited to customer accounts and are properly deposited, but errors are made in recording receipts in the cash receipts journal.

6. Customers' checks are misappropriated after being forwarded to the cashier for deposit.

7. Invalid transactions granting credit for sales returns are recorded.

<u>Internal Control Procedures</u>

A. Shipping clerks compare goods received from the warehouse with the details on the shipping documents.

B. Approved sales orders are required for goods to be released from the warehouse.

C. Monthly statements are mailed to all customers with outstanding balances.

D. Shipping clerks compare goods received from the warehouse with approved sales orders.

E. Customer orders are compared with the inventory master file to determine whether items ordered are in stock.

F. Daily sales summaries are compared with control totals of invoices.

G. Shipping documents are compared with sales invoices when goods are shipped.

H. Sales invoices are compared with the master price file.

I. Customer orders are compared with an approved customer list.

J. Sales orders are prepared for each customer order.

K. Control amounts posted to the accounts receivable ledger are compared with control totals of invoices.

L. Sales invoices are compared with shipping documents and approved customer orders before invoices are mailed.

M. Prenumbered credit memos are used for granting credit for goods returned.

N. Goods returned for credit are approved by the supervisor of the sales department.

O. Remittance advices are separated from the checks in the mailroom and forwarded to the accounting department.

P. Total amounts posted to the accounts receivable ledger from remittance advices are compared with the validated bank deposit slip.

Q. The cashier examines each check for proper endorsement.

R. Validated deposit slips are compared with the cashier's daily cash summaries.

S. An employee, other than the bookkeeper, periodically prepares a bank reconciliation.

T. Sales returns are approved by the same employee who issues receiving reports evidencing actual return of goods.

An auditor is required to obtain a sufficient understanding of each of the components of an entity's internal control. This is necessary to plan the audit of the entity's financial statements and to assess the risk of material misstatement. What are an auditor's documentation requirements concerning the understanding of an entity's internal control?

What authoritative reference requires a user auditor to make inquires regarding a service auditor's professional reputation when considering whether to use the service auditor's report?

Paragraph Reference Answer: _____ (5732)

Testlet 1 MULTIPLE-CHOICE ANSWERS

Chapter 21: Standards & Related Topics

1. (c) Exercise of due care requires critical review at every level of supervision of the work done and the judgment exercised by those assisting in the audit. Answers (a), (b), and (d) do not relate to critical review. (8945)

2. (d) Policies and procedures should be established for deciding whether to accept or continue a client relationship in order to minimize the likelihood of association with a client whose management lacks integrity. Establishing such procedures does not imply that a firm vouches for the integrity or reliability of a client. The failure to detect fraud in client financial statements will result in exposure to litigation regardless of quality control (QC) policies and procedures; however, the existence of QC procedures reduces the likelihood of not detecting such fraud. (8946)

3. (d) The successor auditor should explain to her/his prospective client the need to make an inquiry of the predecessor and should request permission to do so. The predecessor should be contacted prior to final engagement acceptance. The predecessor may communicate with the successor provided that the client grants permission; such communication does not violate the auditor-client confidentiality. (8947)

Chapter 22: Planning

4. (a) An understanding with the client regarding an audit of the financial statements generally includes a statement that management is responsible for establishing and maintaining effective internal control over financial reporting. An engagement letter should document this understanding. At the point at which an engagement letter usually is sent, the auditor typically has not performed any assessment of risk factors relating to misstatements arising from any circumstances. Management's liability for employee acts is irrelevant to audit engagement terms. It is appropriate for the client to understand the auditor will request permission to contact the client's lawyer for assistance in identifying litigation, claims, and assessments; however, this permission

typically is requested separately from the engagement letter. (7093)

5. (b) If an auditor must decrease detection risk, the auditor should change the nature, extent, or timing of audit procedures. Performing procedures closer to the balance sheet date allows less opportunity for misstatements due to roll-forward adjustments to the auditor's interim work. An increase in the assessed level of control risk will cause a decrease in the amount of misstatements that an auditor can tolerate. A decrease in the tolerable amount of misstatements would increase, not decrease, the extent of auditing procedures. (6574)

6. (a) In a preaudit conference, a senior auditor would most likely discuss the technical and personnel aspects of a job. Feedback from the staff would occur later. Establishing the need for specialists and the use of internal auditors is done during the planning stage. Answer (b) is done during field-work. (5077)

7. (b) The auditor must determine a materiality level for the financial statements **taken as a whole.** The concept of materiality recognizes that some matters affect the fair presentation of financial statements, while others do not. Materiality judgments involve both quantitative and qualitative considerations. In making the assessment of materiality, an auditor should consider the needs of a reasonable person who would rely on the financial statements. (5084)

8. (b) The auditor has a responsibility to plan and perform the audit to obtain reasonable assurance about whether the financial statements are free of material misstatements, whether caused by error or fraud. The auditor satisfies this responsibility by exercising due care in the performance of procedures appropriate under the circumstances. If procedures indicate that material errors or fraud may exist, the auditor should extend procedures. (8948)

9. (a) The auditor should consider the implications of an illegal act in relation to other aspects of the audit, particularly the reliability of representations of management. A relatively small misstatement of unretired fixed assets, improperly authorized petty cash fund disbursement, or uncollectible account receivable that was not written off have less impact on the financial statements taken as a whole and, by themselves, do not tend to place doubt on the integrity of management. (5627)

10. (b) When an auditor is unable to conclude whether the financial statements are materially misstated due to an illegal act, s/he should disclaim an opinion or issue a qualified opinion. (0165)

Chapter 23: Internal Control

11. (b) The control environment reflects the overall attitude, awareness, and actions of the board of directors, management, owners and others concerning the importance of control and its emphasis in the entity. If management is dominated by one individual who is also a shareholder, aggressive reporting and the achievement of profit goals may be overemphasized to the detriment of proper reporting. Answers (a), (c), and (d) represent examples of positive control environment influences. (6390)

12. (d) The auditor may design a test of controls to be performed concurrently with a test of details on the same transaction. The objective of tests of controls is to evaluate whether a control operated effectively. Answer (a) would be a substantive test rather than a test of controls. Determining whether internal controls have been implemented is an objective of obtaining an understanding of an entity's internal control. Answer (c) is the objective of substantive procedures. (5115)

13. (b) The auditor's primary consideration is whether, and how, a specific control prevents, or detects and corrects, material misstatements in relevant assertions related to classes of transactions, account balances, or disclosures. An auditor is usually concerned with the operating effectiveness of controls as apposed to operating efficiency. Answers (c) and (d) are inherent limitations of internal control. (7488)

14. (a) Incompatible functions are those that place any person in a position to both perpetrate and conceal errors or fraud in the normal course of his or her duties. An employee who has access to assets and the accounting records related to those assets performs incompatible functions. The cashier performs incompatible functions if s/he can both receive remittances and post the receipts to the accounts receivable subsidiary ledger. Answers (b), (c), and (d) are all functions normally performed by the cashier. (8949)

15. (d) Sound control procedures dictate that an employee should not perform incompatible functions. Thus, all incoming shipments, including customer returns, should be processed by receiving department personnel. A receiving clerk should inspect the merchandise and prepare a receiving report. This employee should not have control over the inventory records because that would enable her/him to divert merchandise without recording it. (8950)

16. (c) A significant deficiency is a deficiency in internal control, or combination of deficiencies in internal control, that is less severe than a material weakness, yet important enough to merit attention by those charged with governance. Answer (a) is the definition of a deficiency in internal control. Answer (b) describes one of the conditions for a deficiency in the operation of a control to exist (the other condition is when a properly designed control does not operate as designed). Answer (d) is false; the severity of a deficiency in internal control (taken into consideration by the auditor in the determination of whether a deficiency is either a significant deficiency or a material weakness) does not depend on whether a misstatement actually occurred. (9036)

17. (c) The required written communication is best made by the report release date, but should be made no later than 60 days after the report release date. However, the auditor may decide to communicate certain identified significant deficiencies and material weaknesses during the audit. Such early communication is not required to be in writing. However, regardless of how the early communication is delivered, the auditor must communicate all significant deficiencies and material weaknesses in writing to management and those charged with governance. The auditor is not obligated to search for control deficiencies. All material weaknesses are significant deficiencies, but not all significant deficiencies are material weaknesses. An auditor is prohibited from reporting that no significant deficiencies were identified because of the potential for misinterpretation. (5656)

Chapter 24: Evidence & Procedures

18. (b) The primary purpose of substantive tests is to determine the validity of the accounting for transactions, or, conversely, errors. Substantive tests may support the accuracy of records, but they frequently provide no affirmative evidence of segregation of duties because the records may be accurate even though they are maintained by persons having incompatible functions. *Tests of controls* provide evidence of segregation of duties since the primary purpose of these tests is to determine how policies or procedures are applied, the consistency with which they were applied, and by whom they were applied. (8951)

19. (b) Unreconciled differences between control and subsidiary accounts indicate a disregard for common accounting safeguards. Assumptions used in developing estimates should change with changing circumstances. A lower response rate for negative confirmation requests indicates fewer customer account misstatements. Consultation with a CPA firm about complex accounting matters often indicates conscientious accounting. (7097)

20. (c) Analytics should be applied to some extent to assist the auditor in planning the procedures to be performed and as an overall review in the final review stage. (8952)

21. (b) If management is unable to provide an acceptable explanation of significant fluctuations, the auditor should perform additional procedures to investigate those fluctuations further. A scope limitation would only result if, after applying all the procedures considered necessary, the auditor is not able to explain the significant fluctuations. The existence of fluctuations does not necessarily indicate fraud. The auditor should consider withdrawal from an engagement if her/his audit indicates fraud or illegal acts by clients; mere discovery of significant fluctuations does not provide the auditor with enough evidence of such problems. (8953)

22. (a) The written representation letter should be signed by members of management who the auditor believes are responsible for and knowledgeable, directly or through others in the organization, about the matters covered by the representations. Normally, the chief executive officer and chief financial officer should sign the letter. (8954)

23. (c) The plant manager has a thorough knowledge of factory operations. This knowledge includes an awareness of the productive capability of the plant machinery, as well as new machinery on the market. As a result, s/he would know whether a particular machine is obsolete. The plant manager has no contact with accounts receivable and, thus, is not in a position to know about the adequacy of the provision for uncollectible accounts. The auditor determines the appropriateness of inventory observation procedures. The plant manager would be helpful in identifying the location of inventory. The plant manager is not responsible for procuring necessary insurance coverage and, therefore, would not be aware that such procurement was deferred. (8955)

24. (c) The objective of analytical procedures used in the overall review stage of the audit is to assist the auditor in assessing the conclusions reached and in the evaluation of the overall financial statement presentation. The overall review would generally include reading the financial statements and notes and considering unusual or unexpected balances or relationships that were not previously identified. The other options are done before the overall review stage. (5665)

25. (d) The matters noted in answers (a), (b), and (c) would all have a significant impact on the quantity and content of the auditor's working papers. While the content of the representation letter may affect the quantity and content of the auditor's work papers, the effect is minimal. (5146)

Chapter 28: Reports on Audited Financial Statements

26. (b) The omission of a procedure that was considered necessary at the time of the audit does not necessarily imply that the original opinion is faulty, or that not enough procedures were performed. Thus, the auditor should first assess the importance of the omitted procedure to her/his present ability to support the previously expressed opinion. The results of other procedures originally applied or the results of subsequent audits may provide evidence for the original audit opinion. If, at this point, the auditor concludes that the omitted procedure is indeed necessary to support the opinion, then s/he should undertake to apply the omitted or an alternative procedure. (8956)

27. (a) If the other information is not revised to eliminate the material inconsistency, the auditor should consider other actions such as revising her/his report to include an explanatory paragraph describing the material inconsistency. An auditor should never consult with a client's legal counsel without first obtaining the client's permission. Issuing a qualified opinion would be misleading since the financial statements are presented fairly. (8957)

28. (c) It is difficult to substantiate representations that a related-party transaction was consummated on terms equivalent to those that prevail in arm's-length transactions. Thus, if a footnote includes such a representation, the auditor should express a qualified or adverse opinion because of a departure from GAAP. Answers (a), (b), and (d) are all appropriate disclosures with respect to related-party transactions. (8958)

Chapter 29: Other Auditing Standards

29. (b) Included in the fieldwork standards of supplemental working paper requirements for financial audits is the statement that working papers should contain sufficient information so that supplementary oral explanations are not required. Written representations from management are not required. An audit does not ensure that all illegal acts and contingent liabilities resulting from noncompliance will be discovered by the auditor. The auditor's workpapers should include positive statements about the procedures applied and the results of those procedures; thus, there is no requirement that the working papers contain a caveat statement. (4281)

30. (b) In accordance with *Government Auditing Standards,* an auditor must also report on internal control over financial reporting and on compliance with laws, regulations, and provisions of contracts or grant agreements when providing an opinion or a disclaimer on financial statements. Answer (a) represents procedures to be reported in a performance audit. Specific procedures performed are not included in the auditor's report. The auditor provides an opinion on the fairness of the presentation of the financial statements taken as a whole rather than an opinion on an entity's attainment of goals and objectives. (4282)

Testlet 2 MULTIPLE-CHOICE ANSWERS

Chapter 22: Planning

1. (b) As management signs a representation letter that includes a statement that all known fraud has been reported to the auditor, if an auditor discovers fraud known to management, but undisclosed to the auditor, the auditor has evidence that management has lied regarding audit information at least once. This impairs reliance on other management statements. While an aggressive attitude toward meeting profit goals is suggestive of incentive and management decision dominated by one person may provide opportunity to commit fraud, they are not as important as actual known management deception. Some weaknesses in internal control may be knowingly left uncorrected due to cost-benefit considerations. (7631)

2. (d) In planning the scope of the audit, the auditor should consider, among other matters, the effect of the assessed risk of material misstatement at the overall financial statement level. When the auditor is developing a preliminary audit strategy, the auditor has not performed sampling procedures, interim tests, nor inquiry of the client's attorney. (2276)

Chapter 23: Internal Control

3. (a) The auditor should use the knowledge obtained in evaluating the design and implementation of controls to identify types of potential misstatements; consider factors that affect the risks of material misstatement; and design tests of controls, when applicable, and substantive procedures. (5951)

4. (b)   Management philosophy and operating style will influence the control environment of any company, but when management is dominated by one or a few individuals the influence will be become significant. The internal auditor reporting directly to management would impact the monitoring component of internal control. Accurate management job descriptions delineating specific duties would impact the control activities component of internal control. The audit committee actively overseeing the financial reporting process would help decrease the influence that management's philosophy and operating style would have on the control environment. (5954)

5. (c)   Inherent risk and control risk are present whether or not an audit is done. Detection risk is the risk that a material misstatement is present, and it is not detected during the audit. All three components of audit risk may be assessed in quantitative or qualitative terms. None of these types of risk arise from the misapplication of auditing standards; they are present in any audit. Inherent risk and control risk cannot be changed at the auditor's discretion; the auditor can only change the *assessment* of the level of inherent and control risk. (5081)

6. (b)   The auditor may test controls over the recording of retirements by tracing certain items of equipment from the accounting records and locating them in the plant to make sure that they have not been retired. The "other assets" account has nothing to do with the recording of retired fixed assets. Tracing from the plant assets to the books does not consider assets which may appear on the books even though they have been retired. If retired equipment was not removed from the records, the related depreciation calculation would not reveal its retirement. (0081)

7. (b)   Incompatible functions are those that place any person in a position to both perpetrate and conceal errors or fraud in the normal course of her/his duties. A well-designed plan of organization separates the duties of *authorization, recordkeeping, and custody* of assets. Answers (a) and (d) do not separate custody and recordkeeping. Answer (c) does not provide verification of inventory. (0089)

8. (b)   By reconciling vendors' monthly statements with the subsidiary payable ledger accounts, the error would be corrected in at most a month's time. Footing the purchases journal only verifies its mathematical accuracy. Answer (c) is incorrect because the erroneous purchase amount in the purchases journal was originally carried through from the client's ledger accounts. Vendors might not confirm the fact that the client is overstating its liability for purchases. (8959)

9. (b)   The requirement is to determine the best test of controls for a procedure that calls for an approved receiving report to accompany every check. This control can be tested by selecting canceled checks and ascertaining that the related receiving reports are dated no later than the check. (In addition, the auditor probably would want to ascertain that the check amounts correspond to the price of the goods received.) If the auditor selects receiving reports (rather than checks) to test the control, s/he will not become aware of instances of checks with no related receiving report. (8960)

10. (c)   Continuous utilization of serially numbered retirement orders provides assurance that the authorized retirements were in fact reflected in the accounting records. Analysis of repair and maintenance accounts provides assurance that capitalizable expenditures are not expensed. Periodic inquiry of plant executives is not an effective procedure because such executives might not be aware of fixed asset retirements. Periodic inspection of insurance policies by internal auditors improves insurance expense accountability, but some fixed assets may not be insured, nor would the retirement of assets always be indicated in insurance policies. (8961)

Chapter 24: Evidence & Procedures

11. (d)   When assessing the internal auditor's objectivity, the auditor should obtain information about the organizational status of the internal auditor including the organizational level to which the internal auditor reports. Answers (a), (b), and (c) indicate competency, not objectivity. (5950)

12. (d)   Once the audit strategy has been established, the auditor is able to start the development of a more detailed audit plan to address the various matters identified in the audit strategy, taking into account the need to achieve the audit objectives. The audit program should include a description of the nature, timing, and extent of planned further audit procedures at the relevant assertion level for each material class of transactions, account balance, and disclosure. Answers (a), (b), and (c) are all considerations of the substantive and analytical procedures necessary to satisfy the audit objectives. (4673)

13. (c)   The financial statements are the representations of management, who would like the financial position of the entity to appear as sound as possible. Thus, the auditor is concerned with possible *overstatements* of revenues, income, assets, and capital. Conversely, the auditor is concerned

with the possible *understatement* of any losses, expenses, and liabilities. (8962)

14. (a) Whether the data were processed in an IT system or in a manual accounting system generally would not influence the auditor's consideration of the reliability of data for purposes of analytics. Factors that do influence the reliability of data include whether the data was obtained from independent sources outside the entity or from sources within the entity; whether sources within the entity were independent of those who are responsible for the amount being audited; whether the data was developed under a reliable system with adequate controls; whether the data was subjected to audit testing in the current or prior year; and whether the expectations were developed using data from a variety of sources. (0151)

15. (c) The management representation letter should be dated as of the date of the auditor's report. (5685)

16. (b) The response in answer (b) is vague and probably would need clarification. The other answer options indicate that the client probably doesn't have any material liability concerning the matters discussed. (6364)

17. (a) Audit documentation provides the principal support for the representation in the auditor's report that the auditor performed the audit in accordance with generally accepted auditing standards; and provides the principal support for the opinion expressed regarding the financial information or the assertion to the effect that an opinion cannot be expressed. (5689)

18. (c) Whether there have been communications from regulatory agencies concerning noncompliance with or deficiencies in financial reporting practices should be addressed in a management representation letter. A report on internal control or another special report generally would not discuss communications from other entities. Letters for underwriters concentrate on financial statements more than internal control. (6397)

19. (c) Understanding financial relationships is essential to evaluating the results of analytics, and usually requires knowledge of the client and of the industry. (7025)

Chapter 25: Audit Programs

20. (a) By requesting confirmation of a sample of inactive accounts, the auditor seeks to determine the accuracy of records relating to those accounts.

Due to their inactive nature, defalcations could occur in these accounts, e.g., through lapping or an improper write-off. The cost of obtaining positive confirmations for at least 50% of the total dollar value of receivables generally would outweigh the benefits derived from such confirmations. The auditor does not treat receivables from federal agencies differently than other receivables, i.e., they are also subject to selective testing. Receivable confirmations can be sent as of any date. (8963)

21. (d) The main objective of the sales cutoff test is to determine that sales are recorded in the proper period. The auditor would test for excessive sales returns and discounts from a sample encompassing the entire period, not just the year-end. Lapping of A/R would be detected by tracing payments received to postings in the appropriate receivable subsidiary ledger. (8964)

22. (d) It is common practice for inventory to be sold on consignment. It is not necessary for consigned inventory to be on hand at the time of the count. However, the auditor should perform procedures to verify the existence and amount of consigned inventory. Answers (a), (b), and (c) are all audit objectives regarding inventory examination. (8965)

23. (c) The bank should be asked to confirm that there has been no access to the box between the balance sheet date and the date of the security count. If the client had access to the box between those dates, the auditor should obtain from the client a list of items added or removed, so as to reconcile the securities on hand on the count date to the securities in the subsidiary ledger on the balance sheet date. The auditor should test the list of securities added or removed by tracing them to brokers' documents indicating security transactions. Procedures in answers (a) and (d) should be performed by the auditor, not by bank staff. In general, evidential matter is more persuasive when directly obtained by the auditor than when obtained from third parties. Banks normally don't keep lists of safe deposit box contents. (8966)

24. (c) The A/P department receives the vendor's invoice with quantities, descriptions, and prices of purchases. A copy of the purchase order enables the A/P department to (1) compare the invoice and purchase order price, (2) ensure that the purchase was authorized, and (3) compare the quantity ordered and purchased. The A/P copy of the purchase order will not ensure that the goods were received by the party requesting the goods. (8967)

25. (a)   The procedure in answer (a) helps provide assurance about valuation of inventory. The procedures in answers (b), (c), and (d) provide assurance regarding existence.   (5121)

26. (d)   The repairs and maintenance expense accounts are analyzed by an auditor in obtaining evidence regarding the completeness of fixed assets, since there is the possibility that items were expensed that should have been capitalized.   (5135)

Chapter 28: Reports on Audited Financial Statements

27. (b)   When qualifying an opinion because of insufficiency of audit evidence, an auditor refers to the situation in the scope and opinion paragraphs and includes an explanatory paragraph before the opinion paragraph. Management is responsible for the financial statements, including the notes; an auditor merely recommends changes.   (7100)

28. (a)   If the auditor decides to depart from an unqualified opinion as a result of the report or findings of a specialist, reference to and identification of the specialist may be made in the auditor's report if the auditor believes such reference will facilitate an understanding of the reason for the departure.
                    (8968)

29. (d)   The current auditor should indicate in the introductory paragraph of her/his report (1) that the financial statements of the prior period were audited by another auditor, (2) the date of the prior report, (3) the type of report issued by the predecessor auditor, and (4) the reasons for any report other than a standard report. The current auditor expresses an opinion in the opinion paragraph only on the period which s/he audited. The current auditor does not disclaim or express an opinion on the prior-period statements. The successor should not name the predecessor in her/his report unless the predecessor's practice was acquired by, or merged with, that of the successor.   (8969)

Chapter 30: Other Types of Reports

30. (d)   Entities may be required by contractual agreements, such as certain bond indentures and loan agreements, or by regulatory agencies to furnish compliance reports by independent auditors. A lack of independence would not preclude an accountant from issuing compilation reports or a report on consulting services.   (0393)

Testlet 3 MULTIPLE-CHOICE ANSWERS

Chapter 23: Internal Control

1. (b)   Tests of controls are designed to obtain evidence about the operating effectiveness of internal controls. Deviations from prescribed procedures would be evidence of ineffectiveness. Answers (a), (c), and (d) are substantive tests (tests of details and analytics) performed *to detect* material misstatements in the account balance, transaction class, and disclosure components of financial statements.
                    (8970)

2. (c)   The independent auditor is concerned primarily with those policies and procedures that are relevant to the audit. Generally, controls that are relevant to the audit pertain to an entity's objective of preparing financial statements for external purposes that are fairly presented in conformity with GAAP. Controls over land and buildings and common stock are of primary concern to the auditor because they relate directly to financial statement assertions. Control over meetings of shareholders and the minutes of BOD meetings are in the nature of administrative controls. Although these controls are of secondary

concern to the auditor, the controls over the minutes of BOD meetings are more important than those over shareholder meetings because they relate **directly** to transaction authorization. Shareholder meetings have only an indirect impact on such authorization.
                    (8971)

Chapter 24: Evidence & Procedures

3. (d)   The permanent file (as indicated by its name) contains client information that is **not** likely to change annually. This information should be updated periodically and is often a basis for preliminary design of the current year's engagement. Descriptions of the client's procedures and controls are types of information found in this file. The types of information listed in answers (a), (b), and (c) mainly affect only the current year's engagement and so they likely are found in the current, not the permanent, file.   (8972)

Chapter 25: Audit Programs

4. (d)   Blank confirmations merely ask for a balance owed, whereas regular positive confirmations include the amount that the customer owes

provided by the client, either listed by invoice or as a single sum. Providing additional information may make the task of confirming debts appear easier to the client's customers' employees, resulting in a response getting prepared and approved, rather than indefinitely waiting in stacks for a supervisor to assign, examine, and then approve. (7640)

Chapter 26: Audit Sampling

5. (c) When the auditor's estimate based on the sample results indicates that the maximum deviation rate is less than the tolerable rate and the true state of the population shows that the deviation rate exceeds the tolerable rate, the auditor assesses control risk too low and does not plan sufficient substantive testing. Answer (b) is an example of the auditor assessing control risk higher than necessary and, thereby having excessive substantive testing. Answers (a) and (d) represent correct audit decisions regarding controls and planned substantive evidence. (5964)

6. (d) When performing tests of controls, the auditor is looking for the deviation rate from established control procedures set by the client. Thus, the auditor performs attributes sampling procedures. Answers (a) and (c) represent substantive sampling procedures. Answer (b) describes a selection method that is not relevant to attribute sampling. (3921)

7. (b) Book value less audit value divided by book value is the tainting percentage. [($5,000 − $4,000) / $5,000 = 0.2] The tainting percentage times the sampling interval is the projected error. 0.2 × $10,000 = $2,000 The sum of all the projected errors is the projected misstatement; there was only one error in this sample. (6935)

8. (d) Upon repeated random samples of a given size from a population, the distribution of the means of those samples will be a normal distribution. The mean of the distribution is equal to the population mean and the standard error of the mean of the distribution equals the population standard deviation divided by the square root of the sample size. Approximately 68% and 95% of the sample means will be within one and two standard deviations, respectively, of the mean of the distribution. All of these characteristics relate to the distribution of sample means that results from repeated samples of a given size from a population. However, the distribution of the items drawn by the auditor in a particular sample may take any form; such a sample does not necessarily have a normal distribution. (8973)

Chapter 27: Auditing IT Systems

9. (d) A check digit is a redundant digit added to a code or ID number for validation purposes. It may be inserted into any position as long as it is inserted consistently. One may recompute the check digit to determine whether a number is valid. (8974)

10. (b) Processing data through the use of simulated files makes use of an integrated test facility. Using this method, the auditor creates a fictitious entity within the client's actual data files. S/he then processes fictitious data for the entity as part of the client's regular data processing. Controlled reprocessing involves the processing of the client's actual data through the auditor's controlled copy of the client's program. Input validation is concerned only that the inputted data is accurate. Program code checking involves analysis of the client's actual program. (2970)

11. (a) When a client processes financial data in electronic form without paper documentation, the auditor may audit on a more continuous basis than a traditional system, as a convenience, and may be required to audit on a more continuous basis to obtain sufficient, competent evidence as documentation for some transactions may be available only for a limited time. An embedded audit module can facilitate this continuous auditing. If anything, an auditor may rely less on controls that emphasize segregation of duties. Digital certificate verification and testing of firewall boundaries are more concerned with security than internal control. (6839)

Chapter 28: Reports on Audited Financial Statements

12. (c) When the principal auditor makes reference to another auditor, the principal auditor doesn't assume responsibility for the other auditor's work. At a minimum, the principal auditor should inquire about the professional reputation and independence of the other CPA. Reviewing the other CPA's work papers, discussing the results of the other CPA's procedures, and determining that the other CPA has a sufficient understanding of the subsidiary's controls are beyond the minimum requirements. (6831)

13. (c) An auditor is not precluded from reporting on only one of the basic financial statements and not the others. A scope limitation would not exist if the auditor is able to apply all the procedures the auditor considers necessary. Such engagements involve limited reporting objectives. Acceptance of the engagement is not a violation of the profession's ethical standards, as the work can be expected to be accomplished. A *piecemeal opinion* is an opinion on

specific elements of the financial statements when the auditor has disclaimed an opinion on the statements as a whole and is unacceptable. A disclaimer of opinion would be unnecessary because Harris will have access to all information underlying the basic financial statements and, thus, could apply all the procedures s/he considers necessary. (6008)

14. (d) Subsequent events such as changes in the quoted market prices of securities ordinarily should not result in adjustment of the financial statements because such changes typically reflect a concurrent evaluation of new conditions. Statements typically are adjusted for subsequent events that provide additional evidence with respect to conditions that existed at the balance sheet date and affect estimates inherent in the preparation process. Answers (a), (b), and (c) are subsequent events that typically result in adjustments to the statements, because they are conditions that existed at the balance sheet date. (8975)

15. (b) When...the auditor concludes there is substantial doubt about the entity's ability to continue as a going concern for a reasonable period of time, the auditor should consider the possible effects on the financial statements and the adequacy of the related disclosure. The auditor would issue a qualified or adverse opinion if the auditor concludes that the entity's disclosure with respect to the ability to continue as a going concern is inadequate. The auditor may report adjustments to the audit committee, however, further action is required to deal specifically with the going concern issue, regardless of changes to accounting estimates. Substantial doubt about the entity's ability to continue as a going concern for a reasonable period of time that arose in the current period does not imply that a basis for such doubt existed in the prior period and should not affect the auditor's report on the prior-period statements presented on a comparative basis. (4727)

16. (a) Inquiry alone does not provide sufficient evidence to support a conclusion about the effectiveness of a control. Some tests, by their nature, provide greater evidence than others. The following tests that an auditor might perform are listed in the order of least to most evidence that they ordinarily produce: inquiry, observation, inspection of relevant documentation, and reperformance of a control. Auditors normally use a mix of these procedures. (7953)

Chapter 29: Other Auditing Standards

17. (c) A *material weakness* is a deficiency of internal control over financial reporting such that there is a reasonable possibility that a material

misstatement of the company's annual or interim financial statements will not be prevented or detected on a timely basis. A significant deficiency is a deficiency that is less severe than a material weakness; yet important enough to merit attention by those responsible for oversight of the company's financial reporting. A control deficiency exists when the design or operation of a control does not allow management or employees, in the normal course of performing their assigned functions, to prevent or detect misstatements on a timely basis. The PCAOB standards don't use the term material deficiency. (7950)

Chapter 30: Other Types of Reports

18. (b) The objective of a review of interim financial information is to provide the accountant with a basis for communicating whether there are any material modifications that should be made to the interim financial information for it to conform with the applicable financial reporting framework. (8976)

19. (b) The cash receipts and disbursements schedule is merely a comprehensive basis of accounting other than GAAP (OCBOA). The auditor's report should include a paragraph that refers to the note to the financial statements that describes the basis of accounting. The report should include a paragraph that expresses the auditor's opinion on whether the financial statements are presented fairly. The report should include a paragraph that states that the audit was conducted in accordance with GAAS. (5700)

20. (a) Special reports include auditors' reports issued in connection with (1) financial statements that are prepared in conformity with a comprehensive basis of accounting other than GAAP, (2) specified elements, accounts, or items of a financial statement, (3) compliance with aspects of contractual agreements or regulatory requirements related to audited financial statements, (4) financial presentations to comply with contractual agreements or regulatory provisions, and (5) financial information presented in prescribed forms or schedules that require a prescribed form of auditor's report. A report issued in connection with compliance with aspects of contractual agreements *unrelated* to audited statements is not considered to be a special report. (8977)

Chapter 31: Other Professional Services

21. (b) An accountant is precluded from issuing a review report on the financial statement of an entity with respect to which s/he is not independent. Rule 101 of the AICPA Code of Professional Conduct

states that independence is deemed impaired if there is *any* direct or material indirect financial interest. (5638)

22. (a) To compile financial statements, the accountant should possess a general understanding of the nature of the entity's business transactions, the form of its accounting records, and the stated qualifications of its accounting personnel. Generally, a financial statement compilation is limited to presenting information that is the representation of management in the form of financial statements without undertaking to express any assurance on the statements. Generally, internal control is not considered in a compilation. (6823)

23. (c) Management must present its written assertion about the effectiveness of the entity's internal control in a report that accompanies the auditor's report. (5983)

24. (d) Neither a review nor a compilation engagement contemplates obtaining an understanding of internal control or assessing control risk; testing of accounting records and of responses to inquiries by obtaining corroborating evidential matter; and certain other procedures ordinarily performed during an audit. (2327)

25. (d) A review does *not* contemplate obtaining an understanding of the internal control or assessing control risk, tests of accounting records and of responses to inquiries by obtaining corroborating evidential matter, and certain other procedures ordinarily performed during an audit. Answers (a), (b), and (c) are usually performed by the accountant in a review engagement of a nonpublic entity. (2979)

26. (b) An accountant's review procedures will include inquiry and analytical procedures. Analytics are designed to identify relationships and individual items that appear to be unusual, and consist of (1) comparison of the financial statements with statements for comparable prior period(s), (2) comparison of the statements with anticipated results, if available, and (3) study of the relationships of the elements of the statements that would be expected to conform with a predictable pattern based on the entity's experience. Answers (a), (c), and (d) are procedures that should be performed in an audit. (2787)

27. (b) Procedures ordinarily performed during a review of a nonpublic entity's financial statements include inquiries concerning the entity's procedures for recording and summarizing transactions. They are not concerned with corroborating evidential matter, management's assertions concerning continued existence, or the entity's attorney's opinion concerning contingent liabilities. (2977)

28. (d) In a compilation, the accountant presents, in the form of financial statements, information that is management's representation. No expression of assurance is contemplated in a compilation. In a review, an accountant makes inquiries and performs analytics that should provide a reasonable basis for expressing limited assurance that there are no material modifications that should be made to the statements. Because of the level of responsibility in a review, the accountant must obtain a management representation letter. Answers (a), (b), and (c) each list one of the prerequisites for performing either a compilation or a review. (8978)

29. (a) The report has a separate paragraph describing the limitations on the presentation use. The report does not provide an explanation of differences between an examination and an audit. The accountant is not responsible for events occurring after the report date. The standard report contains the phrase, "In our opinion, the underlying assumptions provide a reasonable basis for management's projection." (6029)

30. (d) When a CPA compiles projected financial statements, the accountant's report should include a separate paragraph that describes limitations on the presentation's usefulness. (8979)

PERFORMANCE BY TOPICS

The practice examination questions corresponding to each chapter of the Auditing & Attestation text are listed below. The number preceding the colon is the testlet number; the number after the colon is the question number. To assess your preparedness for the CPA exam, record the number and percentage of questions you correctly answered in each CSO area. The point distribution of the multiple choice questions approximates that of the CPA exam.

Chapter 21:
Standards &
Related Topics

Question #	Correct	√
1:1		
1:2		
1:3		
# Questions	3	
# Correct		
% Correct		

Chapter 22: Planning

Question #	Correct	√
1:4		
1:5		
1:6		
1:7		
1:8		
1:9		
1:10		
2:1		
2:2		
# Questions	9	
# Correct		
% Correct		

Chapter 23:
Internal Control

Question #	Correct	√
1:11		
1:12		
1:13		
1:14		
1:15		
1:16		
1:17		
2:3		
2:4		
2:5		
2:6		
2:7		
2:8		
2:9		
2:10		
3:1		
3:2		
# Questions	17	
# Correct		
% Correct		

Chapter 24:
Evidence & Procedures

Question #	Correct	√
1:18		
1:19		
1:20		
1:21		
1:22		
1:23		
1:24		
1:25		
2:11		
2:12		
2:13		
2:14		
2:15		
2:16		
2:17		
2:18		
2:19		
3:3		
# Questions	18	
# Correct		
% Correct		

Chapter 25:
Audit Programs

Question #	Correct	√
2:20		
2:21		
2:22		
2:23		
2:24		
2:25		
2:26		
3:4		
# Questions	8	
# Correct		
% Correct		

Chapter 26:
Audit Sampling

Question #	Correct	√
3:5		
3:6		
3:7		
3:8		
# Questions	4	
# Correct		
% Correct		

Chapter 27:
Auditing IT Systems

Question #	Correct	√
3:9		
3:10		
3:11		
# Questions	3	
# Correct		
% Correct		

Chapter 28:
Reports on Audited
Financial Statements

Question #	Correct	√
1:26		
1:27		
1:28		
2:27		
2:28		
2:29		
3:12		
3:13		
3:14		
3:15		
3:16		
# Questions	11	
# Correct		
% Correct		

Chapter 29:
Other Auditing Standards

Question #	Correct	√
1:29		
1:30		
3:17		
# Questions	3	
# Correct		
% Correct		

Chapter 30:
Other Types of Reports

Question #	Correct	√
2:30		
3:18		
3:19		
3:20		
# Questions	4	
# Correct		
% Correct		

Chapter 31:
Other Professional
Services

Question #	Correct	√
3:21		
3:22		
3:23		
3:24		
3:25		
3:26		
3:27		
3:28		
3:29		
3:30		
# Questions	10	
# Correct		
% Correct		

PERFORMANCE BY CONTENT SPECIFICATION

The practice examination questions corresponding to the AICPA content specification are listed below. To assess your preparedness for the CPA exam, record the number and percentage of questions you correctly answered in each CSO area. The point distribution of the multiple choice questions approximates that of the CPA exam.

CSO I Plan the engagement, evaluate the prospective client and engagement, decide whether to accept or continue the client and the engagement, and enter into an agreement with the client (22%–28%)

Question #	Correct √
1:1	
1:2	
1:3	
1:4	
1:5	
1:6	
1:7	
1:11	
2:1	
2:2	
2:3	
2:5	
2:6	
2:11	
2:12	
3:5	
3:12	
3:13	
3:18	
3:21	
3:22	
3:23	

\# Questions   22

\# Correct   _____
% Correct   _____

CSO II Consider internal control in both manual and computerized environments (12%–18%)

Question #	Correct √
1:12	
1:13	
1:14	
1:15	
2:4	
2:7	
2:8	
2:9	
2:10	
3:1	
3:2	
3:6	
3:9	
3:10	

\# Questions   14

\# Correct   _____
% Correct   _____

CSO III Obtain and document information to form a basis for conclusions (32%–38%)

Question #	Correct √
1:8	
1:9	
1:16	
1:18	
1:19	
1:20	
1:21	
1:22	
1:23	
1:26	
2:13	
2:14	
2:15	
2:16	
2:20	
2:21	
2:22	
2:23	
2:24	
2:25	
2:26	
3:4	
3:7	
3:8	
3:11	
3:14	
3:17	
3:24	
3:25	
3:26	
3:27	
3:28	

\# Questions   32

\# Correct   _____
% Correct   _____

CSO IV Review the engagement to provide reasonable assurance that objectives are achieved and evaluate information obtained to reach and to document engagement conclusions (8%–12%)

Question #	Correct √
1:24	
1:25	
1:29	
2:17	
2:18	
2:19	
3:3	
3:15	
3:16	

\# Questions   9

\# Correct   _____
% Correct   _____

CSO V Prepare communications to satisfy engagement objectives (12%–18%)

Question #	Correct √
1:10	
1:17	
1:27	
1:28	
1:30	
2:27	
2:28	
2:29	
2:30	
3:19	
3:20	
3:29	
3:30	

\# Questions   13

\# Correct   _____
% Correct   _____

SIMULATION SOLUTIONS

Testlet 4

Response #1: Audit Risk (7 points)

A. No

The sale of finished goods to independent marine stores throughout the United States is not likely to increase audit risk. This is an example of a customary business practice.

B. Yes

Tough new federal emissions regulations that further threaten industry profitability is an example of a change in the company's regulatory environment. A risk that relates to the regulatory environment in which the company operates is a pervasive risk that affects many of the financial statement assertions in many accounts.

C. Yes

The auditor will need to focus more attention on the strict new covenants on the Company's renewed line-of-credit to determine whether there have been any violations and whether they need to be disclosed in the financial statements.

D. No

The information in the company profile indicated that no disagreements with management had occurred with the prior audit firm.

E. No

A senior accountant from the prior audit firm taking a position with the firm is not likely to increase audit risk.

F. Yes

The company's practice of storing finished watercraft inventory in an open lot increases the risk of theft.

G. No

The overheard conversation about dissatisfaction with pay rates is not, in and of itself, an occurrence that is likely to increase audit risk. However, dissatisfaction with their employer is often cited by employees as a reason for committing fraud and theft. In situations like this, the auditor must exercise professional judgment to determine if the degree of dissatisfaction of employees detected is great enough to increase audit risk.

Response #2: Confirmations (6 points)

A. 2

The client should record the sale and relief of inventory because the title passed to the client's customer when the merchandise (order for $58,000) was delivered to the common carrier (f.o.b. shipping point) on December 30, year 2.

B. 2

The client should adjust the accounting records by debiting "Other Income" and crediting "Accounts Receivable".

C. 4

The auditor must confirm that the additional invoices (nos. 4593 and 4738) listed by the client's customer on the confirmation pertain to the subsequent year. If they do, it is not an exception and no adjustment to the accounting records is needed.

D. 3

The auditor should perform the additional audit procedures described, i.e., examining subsequent cash receipts and/or shipping documents to confirm the accounting records are correct. As an alternative (not included on this particular simulation's selection list) the auditor could decide to send a second confirmation request providing the individual invoice numbers and amounts or attaching copies of the individual unpaid invoices if in her/his judgment this would help the client's customer with the verification.

Response #3: Cutoff Procedures (6 points)

A. 5

The only adjustment needed is for the client to record the relief of inventory because the title passed to the client's customer when it received the merchandise from the common carrier (f.o.b. destination point) on December 31, year 2. The client has already recorded the sale.

B. 3

The only adjustment needed is for the client to reduce "sales" (dr.) and "accounts receivable" (cr.) for the merchandise that was returned on December 29, year 2. The client has already made the entry to include the merchandise in the inventory account.

C.   8

Merchandise out on consignment remains the property of the consignor, in this case, the client. The client handled the shipment correctly by **not** recording a sale or relief of inventory. However, they did not handle the subsequent return/receipt of the merchandise from the consignee correctly. The client needs to make an adjustment to reverse the entry it made, i.e., debit "Accounts Receivable" and credit "Inventory."

D.   2

The only adjustment needed is for the client to record the sale because the title passed to the client's customer when the merchandise was delivered to the common carrier (f.o.b. shipping point) on December 29, year 2. The client has already recorded the relief of inventory.

Response #4: Communication (10 points)

To: Partner-in-Charge

From: Senior Auditor

Re: Fraud Risk Assessment, Annual Audit of
             Aquatic Jet Products, Inc.

During the year, the client discovered that a payroll clerk committed fraud by adding hours to her timesheet after approval, during processing of the timecards. The accounting department is not required to take vacations; however, the client was fortunate to discover the theft while the employee was out sick for two days. I have discussed the matter with the CFO and he informed me that the company feels that this was an isolated occurrence.

I recommend increasing our fraud risk assessment due to the presence of at least two **fraud risk factors**. First, management has not strengthened the company's internal control structure by **requiring the accounting department to take vacations** even though the **discovery of the theft while the employee was out sick demonstrated the effectiveness of such a control**. Additionally, I observed that the **finished watercraft inventory is kept in an open lot** outside the facility. The CFO explained that due to its rural location, the company has not had any problems with theft of it products. Both of these examples may indicate a **disregard by management for the need for reducing the risks related to misappropriation of assets**. Second, as described above, a payroll clerk was able to add hours to her timesheet after approval, demonstrating that a **lack of adequate controls provided the opportunity to commit fraud**.

To respond to this increase in our assessment of fraud, I recommend that we perform **additional procedures** to satisfy ourselves that the extent of the theft has been properly identified. We should **interview other employees in the payroll department to obtain their insights about the risk** and **how controls address the risk**. We should also **increase the number of entries in the payroll register to be vouched** to source documents (time cards and approved timesheets) and **traced** from the same source documents to the payroll register.

Response #5: Research (1 point)

Paragraph Reference Answer: AU 508.42

Independent Auditor's Report

[Same first and second paragraphs as the standard report]

The Company's financial statements do not disclose [describe the nature of the omitted information that it is not practicable to present in the auditor's report]. In our opinion, disclosure of this information is required by accounting principles generally accepted in the United States of America.

In our opinion, except for the omission of the information discussed in the preceding paragraph…

(8423)

Testlet 5

Response #1: Errors & Fraud (5 points)

1.   P

The company would be able to detect errors in postings to customer accounts by placing certain control procedures in place. For example, by comparing the validated bank deposit slip total to the A/R posting total for the day, a difference in the amount posted from the remittance advices to the A/R ledger and the amount of checks actually received and deposited would be discovered.

2.   C

Mailing monthly statements to all customers with outstanding balances would most likely detect customers' checks that are misappropriated before being forwarded to the cashier for deposit. The customers would be billed for invoices already paid and would let MMI know.

3.   C

The company should implement control procedures to detect errors in postings to customer accounts. For example, mailing monthly statements to all customers with outstanding balances would detect errors as customers who had paid (but receive statements indicating a balance due) most likely would call the company to report the error.

4.   P

By comparing the A/R postings to the validated deposit slip total, the difference resulting from posting one cash receipt remittance advice amount to two accounts in the A/R ledger would be detected.

5.   S

Errors made in recording receipts in the cash receipts journal would most likely be detected if bank statements are reconciled periodically as the deposit amounts on the bank statements would be compared to the receipts as listed in the cash receipts journal. For internal control purposes, the person preparing the bank reconciliation should be someone other than the bookkeeper who is preparing the cash receipts journal.

6.   P

The company should implement control procedures to prevent customer checks from being misappropriated before being deposited by the cashier. One procedure would compare the total amount posted to the accounts receivable ledger from the remittance advice to the validated deposit slip. Differences may indicate misappropriation of checks because they were not deposited or were deposited to incorrect bank accounts.

7.   N

To prevent invalid transactions granting credit for sales returns from being recorded, control procedures should be implemented to require proper authorization of any sales returns. Authorization by the sales department supervisor would be appropriate, especially as this supervisor's goals are generally higher sales, and thus, s/he would not likely have a motivation for approving invalid sales returns.

Response #2: Communication (4 points)

The auditor should **document** the following regarding the **understanding** of **internal control:** (a) **key elements** of the understanding obtained regarding the **five components** of internal control; (b) the **sources** of **information** from which the understanding was obtained; and (c) the **risk assessment procedures** performed.

Response #3: Research (1 point)

Paragraph Reference Answer: AU 324.18

Guidance: AU 324.18 states, "In considering whether the service auditor's report is satisfactory for his or her purposes, the user auditor should make inquiries concerning the service auditor's professional reputation. Appropriate sources of information concerning the professional reputation of the service auditor are discussed in section 543, *Part of Audit Performed by Other Independent Auditors,* paragraph 10a."

(5732)

What Is Eligible to Be Tested?

Accounting and auditing pronouncements are eligible to be tested on the CPA Examination in the testing window beginning six months after a pronouncement's *effective* date, unless early application is permitted. When early application is permitted, a new pronouncement may be tested in the window beginning 6 months after the *issue* date. In this case, *both* the previous and the new pronouncements can be tested until the previous pronouncement has been superseded.

APPENDIX B
PRACTICAL ADVICE

Your first step toward an effective review program is to carefully read the material in this appendix. It will provide you with essential information that will help you succeed on the exam. This material will assist you in organizing an efficient study plan and will demonstrate effective techniques and strategies for taking the exam.

SECTION ONE: GENERAL COMMENTS ON THE EXAM

OVERVIEW

The difficulty and comprehensiveness of the exam is a well-known fact to all candidates. However, success on the exam is a reasonable, attainable goal. You should keep this point in mind as you study this appendix and develop your study plan. A positive attitude toward the exam, combined with determination and discipline, will enhance your opportunity to pass.

Purpose of the Exam

The exam is designed as a licensing requirement to measure the technical competence of candidates. Although licensing occurs at the state or territory level (usually by a board of accountancy), the exam is uniform at all sites and has national acceptance. Passing the exam in one jurisdiction generally allows a candidate to obtain a reciprocal certificate or license in another jurisdiction if they meet that jurisdiction's requirements.

Boards of accountancy also rely upon other means to ensure that candidates possess the necessary technical and character attributes, including interviews, letters of reference, affidavits of employment, ethics exams, and educational requirements. Each board's contact information is listed in this section of the *Practical Advice* appendix and on the Web site (www.nasba.org) of the National Association of the State Boards of Accountancy (NASBA).

The exam is essentially an academic exam that tests the breadth of material covered by good accounting curricula. It emphasizes the body of knowledge required for the practice of public accounting. It is to your advantage to take the exam as soon as possible after completing the formal education requirements.

We recommend that most candidates study for two exam sections at once because there are synergies to be gained. All sections of the exam share some common subjects (particularly Financial Accounting & Reporting and Auditing & Attestation); so as you study for one section, you are also studying, in part, for the others. This advice may not apply to all candidates. Some candidates with full-time jobs and other responsibilities may find that studying for just one exam section at a time is best for them.

Exam "Partners"

The exam is offered jointly by three organizations on behalf of the boards of accountancy. (See the "Boards of Accountancy" topic of this section; although the boards are not directly involved in *offering* the exam, they play a critical role in the process.) The AICPA is responsible for developing and scoring the exam. NASBA's role in the process is to operate as a gateway to the exam for all candidates via its maintenance of a national candidate database. (NASBA was created to serve as a forum to enhance the effectiveness of its members—the boards of accountancy.) Prometric is responsible for delivery of the exam. (Prometric is a commercial testing center that operates a network of computer-based test centers.) Candidates schedule their exam appointments directly with Prometric after they receive their notice to schedule (NTS).

Exam Sections

The exam has four sections:

1. **Financial Accounting & Reporting (FAR)**—This section covers knowledge of generally accepted accounting principles and their application for business enterprises, government entities, and not-for-profit organizations. (**4 hours**)

2. **Auditing & Attestation (AUD)**—This section covers knowledge and application of auditing procedures; generally accepted auditing standards; and other standards and procedures for other types of engagements. (**4½ hours**)

3. **Regulation (REG)**—This section covers knowledge and application of federal taxation; ethics; professional and legal responsibilities; and business law. (**3 hours**)

4. **Business Environment & Concepts (BEC)**—This section covers knowledge and application of general business environment and concepts underlying the business reasons for and accounting implications of business transactions. (**2½ hours**)

Computer-Based Testing (CBT) / Tutorial and Sample Tests

The exam is offered only in English and only in a CBT format. The AICPA provides a tutorial and sample tests for the CBT on their exam Web site (www.cpa-exam.org). You must review these before the exam because neither is available at the test centers. The AICPA recommends reviewing the tutorial before the sample tests. Exposure to both will allow you to become familiar with how to navigate through the exam, gain exposure to the exam's directions, and preview its content. The time you spend with these materials will prevent you from losing any points on the exam due to unfamiliarity with the CBT system. The simulations use both a word processor and a spreadsheet program that are similar, but not identical to commercial applications. Even if you are completely comfortable with commercial applications, you may find it unsettling to encounter different or missing functionalities on your exam day. View the tutorial and take the sample tests at least a month before taking the exam and then again a week before the exam.

Exam Availability—Testing Windows

There are four exam windows each year; the first one starts in January. Generally, a candidate can take any or all sections (in any order) during any testing window, but check your board's requirements. **A candidate may not take the same exam section more than once during any one testing window.** Between windows, during the third month of each quarter, the exam is not given. Exam sites typically are open Monday through Friday; some are also open on Saturday.

Testing Windows		No Testing
January	February	March
April	May	June
July	August	September
October	November	December

Scoring

Generally, boards report scores on a scale of 0-99, with 75 as a passing score. Each exam section is scored separately. (There are no minimum score requirements—scores on one exam section do not affect credit on other exam sections.) All responses except those to written communication exercises are scored electronically—a combination of human graders and electronic scoring is used to score those responses. You receive credit for correct responses. **You are not penalized for incorrect responses.**

Scores are approved and released to candidates by boards of accountancy. (Prometric, the AICPA, or NASBA do not provide score information to candidates.)

Time Limit for Passing All Four Sections

Typically, candidates must pass all four sections within a rolling 18-month period to retain credit. Candidates should check with their board of accountancy.

Reference Materials

All the material you need to review to pass the exam is in your Bisk Education *CPA Comprehensive Exam Review* texts. However, if you would like more detailed coverage in any area; you can consult the actual authoritative literature. Individual copies of recent pronouncements are available from the FASB, AICPA, SEC, etc. To order materials from the FASB or AICPA contact:

FASB Order Department
P.O. Box 5116
Norwalk, CT 06856-5116
Telephone (800) 748-0659
fasbpubs.stores.yahoo.net

AICPA/ CPA2Biz Service Center
220 Leigh Farm Road
Durham, NC 27707-8110
Telephone (888) 777-7077
www.cpa2biz.org

The AICPA offers candidates with their NTS a **free** six-month subscription to some of the databases of authoritative literature used in the FAR and AUD sections of the exam. Visit the AICPA's exam Web site (www.cpa-exam.org) for more information and to subscribe.

BOARDS OF ACCOUNTANCY

Application Form

Certified public accountants are licensed to practice by the individual boards of accountancy of the states and territories (jurisdictions) of the United States. The exam is one component of the licensing process. An application form to sit for the exam should be requested from your individual board or its designated agent (exam administrator)—some jurisdictions arrange for an exam administrator, such as CPA Examination Services, a division of NASBA, to handle the review of applications, collection of fees, etc.

IT IS EXTREMELY IMPORTANT THAT YOU COMPLETE THE APPLICATION FORM CORRECTLY AND RETURN IT BEFORE THE DEADLINE. Errors may result in the delay of approval or rejection of your application. Be sure to enclose all required materials. Requirements vary as to education, experience and other matters, as do cutoff dates to apply to receive approval in time to sit for a particular testing window. If you have not already done so, take a moment to call or visit the Web site of the appropriate board for specific and current requirements. (See the "Contacting Your Board" topic within this section.)

PAY SPECIAL ATTENTION TO THE FORM OF YOUR NAME ON YOUR APPLICATION. YOUR APPLICATION INFORMATION WILL BE USED TO GENERATE YOUR NTS AND THE ORDER AND SPELLING OF YOUR NAME ON YOUR **NTS** MUST EXACTLY MATCH YOUR **2 IDs**—THE 3 ITEMS YOU MUST BRING TO THE TEST CENTER IN ORDER TO BE ADMITTED. (See the "Notice to Schedule (NTS) & IDs" topic within this section.)

It may be possible to sit for the exam outside of your jurisdiction. Candidates wishing to do so should also contact the board of accountancy in the jurisdiction where they plan to be certified. NASBA has links (www.nasba.org) to all of the board sites.

Contacting Your Board

CPA Examination Services, a division of NASBA, administers the exam for the jurisdictions listed below. Contact CPA Examination Services at **(800) CPA-EXAM (272-3926)** or **www.nasba.org**.

AK	CO	CT	DE	FL	GA	HI	IN	IA	KS	LA	ME	MA	MI	MN	MO
MT	NE	NH	NJ	NM	NY	OH	PA	PR	RI	SC	TN	UT	VT	WI	

Castle Worldwide, Inc. at (800) 655-4845 or www.castleworldwide.com/wboa administers the exam for the **Washington** State Board of Accountancy.

These are the telephone numbers for the other boards that administer the exam themselves.

AL	(334)-242-5700	KY	(502)-595-3037	SD	(605) 367-5770
AZ	(602)-364-0804	MD	(410)-230-6224	TX	(512) 305-7800
AR	(501)-682-1520	MS	(601)-354-7320	VI	(340) 773-2226
CA	(916)-263-3680	NV	(775)-786-0231	VA	(804)-367-8505
DC	(202)-442-4333	NC	(919)-733-4222	WV	(304) 558-3557
GU	(671)-647-0813	ND	(800)-532-5904	WY	(307) 777-7551
ID	(208)-334-2490	OK	(405)-521-2397		
IL	(217)-531-0950	OR	(503)-378-4181		

The Web sites for the boards that administer the exam themselves are listed below. These addresses and the preceding telephone numbers are subject to change without notice.

AL	www.asbpa.alabama.gov/	NV	www.nvaccountancy.com/
AZ	www.accountancy.state.az.us/	NC	www.nccpaboard.gov/
AR	www.arkansas.gov/asbpa/	ND	www.nd.gov/ndsba/
CA	www.dca.ca.gov/cba/	OK	www.ok.gov/oab_web/
DC	www.vue.com/dc/accountancy/	OR	www.oregon.gov/BOA/
GU	www.guamboa.org/	SD	www.state.sd.us/dol/boards/accountancy/
ID	www.isba.idaho.gov/	TX	www.tsbpa.state.tx.us/
IL	www.ilboa.org/	VI	www.dlca.gov.vi/
KY	cpa.ky.gov/	VA	www.boa.virginia.gov/
MD	www.dllr.state.md.us/license/occprof/account.html	WV	www.wvboacc.org/
MS	www.msbpa.state.ms.us/	WY	cpaboard.state.wy.us/

THE UNIFORM CPA EXAMINATION PROCESS

The information presented here is intended to give candidates an overall idea of what the exam will be like. It is **not** intended to take the place of *The Uniform CPA Examination Candidate Bulletin: Information for Applicants* (Candidate Bulletin). The Candidate Bulletin will provide you with more detailed instructions and information. Read it. (At the test center you will be required to attest to the fact that you have had the opportunity to read it and that you agree to all its terms and conditions.) The Candidate Bulletin is available on the AICPA's exam Web site (www.cpa-exam.org) and NASBA's (www.nasba.org).

This information is as accurate as possible; however, circumstances are subject to change after this text goes to press. Candidates should check to confirm they have the most recent Candidate Bulletin 45 days before their exam.

In addition to understanding the basic process as described in the Candidate Bulletin, you need to know your board of accountancy's requirements for each step in the exam process.

Registration

To sit for the exam, candidates must apply to the appropriate board of accountancy or its exam administrator. (Some boards contract with an exam administrator to handle candidate applications.) Once a board or its exam administrator determines that a candidate is eligible to sit for the exam, they inform NASBA and NASBA adds the candidate to its database. With a national database, NASBA is able to ensure that no candidate can sit for the same exam section more than once during a single exam window. NASBA then sends Prometric a NTS. When you receive your NTS (from whom you receive your NTS varies by jurisdiction), you can make your appointment to sit for the exam with Prometric. You should verify the accuracy of your NTS before making your appointment—see the "Notice to Schedule (NTS) & IDs" topic within this section.

Special Testing Accommodations

Special accommodations must be requested as part of the application process. (Ordinarily, candidates may not bring anything into the testing room—including prescription medications.) Check with your board or its exam administrator and give them your information to request their approval. If approved, the type of accommodation needed will be sent to NASBA. NASBA will ensure that the information is included on your NTS and sent to Prometric. When you receive your NTS, if the accommodations are not correct, you will need to contact your board again. Changes to special accommodations cannot be made by Prometric.

Notice to Schedule (NTS) & IDs

When you receive your NTS, verify that all the information is correct and make sure that your name as it appears on the NTS **exactly** matches your name on the IDs you will be using to check in at the testing center. If your name on your NTS is different in any way (the order or spelling) from your IDs, you will not be permitted to test. If any information on your NTS is incorrect or your name doesn't match your IDs, immediately contact your board or its exam administrator to request a correction.

See the Candidate Bulletin to review a list of examples of acceptable forms of identification. You must have **two forms of identification. One of them must contain a recent photograph. Both must bear your signature. Neither can be expired.**

If you do not present acceptable identification, you will not be allowed to take the exam and you will forfeit all fees for that section.

Fees

Boards or their exam administrators inform candidates of the amount and types of fees as well as the timing for their payment. The rules vary by jurisdiction. You may be required to pay all or some of the application and exam fees when you submit your application. You may be instructed to pay portions of the fees to different entities.

It is best not to apply for a section of the exam until you are ready to take it because refunds of fees are usually not available—check with your board or its exam administrator regarding their specific refund policy. Generally, if you fail to make an appointment during the period your NTS is valid or need to cancel your appointment and do not wish to reschedule it, you will not receive a refund or a credit. Nor will you receive a refund or a credit if you fail to appear for your appointment at the test center or give less than 24 hours notice for a cancellation. In either case, you will have to reapply for the exam and pay the fees again.

Scheduling Your Exam Appointment

If taking the exam on a particular day is important to you, it is advisable to schedule it at least 45 days in advance. **No appointment can be made fewer than 5 days in advance of a desired test date**. Your NTS will have an expiration date which is set by your board. After the expiration date, you must reapply and pay the fees again. Candidates may select any available date during the open window. Candidates may schedule, confirm, reschedule, or cancel an exam appointment or change its location as well as find their preferred testing location online at **www.prometric.com/cpa** or by calling **(800) 580-9648**. See the Candidate Bulletin for deadlines and fees associated with changes to appointments—depending on when you notify Prometric of a change or cancellation, you may be required to pay a rescheduling fee or you may forfeit the exam fees.

Refer to the Candidate Bulletin for additional information about scheduling your appointment. If you are planning on taking the exam in Guam, the Candidate Bulletin has specific instructions that are different from those for all other locations.

Candidates with special testing accommodations preapproved by their board or exam administrator (indicated on their NTS) **must schedule at least 10 days in advance** of the desired date and must call

(800) 967-1139 to schedule their appointment. If you need to make any changes to your appointment you should use this same number. If you use a teletypewriter, call (800) 529-3590.

Checking In on Exam Day

Candidates must arrive 30 minutes before their scheduled appointment to allow enough time for check-in and seating procedures. (If you arrive late you may be denied permission to test and you will not receive a refund.) You will not be admitted without your **NTS** and **2 acceptable forms of identification** and you will forfeit all fees for that exam section. A digital photograph of your face will be taken. Your ID will be scanned and swiped in a magnetic strip and barcode reader and biometrics will be used to capture your fingerprint. You will be given a key to a *small* locker for storage of a few belongings such as your purse/wallet and cell phone because you are not allowed to take these items into the testing room. Pencils and scratch paper will be given to you.

Testing Room Regulations

In addition to the security measures surrounding your identification there are very strict rules in place for the testing room. You must not communicate with other candidates when in the testing room. No food or beverages are allowed. You must not bring any paper or pencils (other than the ones provided to you) into the testing room. You will be directed to write your password (from your NTS) on the scratch paper so that it can be accounted for, i.e., you will be required to exchange the original supply for a new supply should you request it, and you must turn it in after the exam. See the Candidate Bulletin for a long list of prohibited items and other restrictions. Don't assume they will be what you may expect. For example, you are not allowed to have a watch; jewelry—pendant necklace or large earrings; an eyeglass case; or a container of any kind including a plastic bag. The Candidate Bulletin states that jackets and sweaters are also prohibited; however, if you require a separate sweater or a jacket due to room temperature, it must be worn at all times.

After checking in, you will be escorted to your workstation where you must remain seated during the exam except when given permission to leave the testing room for an authorized break. After you log in, proceed to the introductory screens without delay. THERE IS A TIME LIMIT ON THE INITIAL SCREENS AND, IF THAT TIME LIMIT IS EXCEEDED, YOUR TEST SESSION WILL AUTOMATICLLY TERMINATE. One of these screens presents the *Policy Statement and Agreement Regarding Exam Confidentiality and the Taking of Breaks*. (A copy of this statement is included in the Candidate Bulletin.) If you do not accept it you will not be allowed to take the exam and your fees will be forfeited. (See the "Breaks" and "The Nondisclosed Exam" topics within this Appendix.)

Breaks

Breaks are only allowed between testlets. A testlet (see next topic) is a segment of the exam. After each testlet, a candidate has the option to take a break, but **the exam's clock will keep running** so you should use any break time sparingly and judiciously. Breaks over 10 minutes may be reported to your board of accountancy. If you choose to take a break, the test center staff will confirm that you have completed a testlet and you will be asked to provide a fingerprint prior to leaving and again on your return. When you return to your computer you will be required to enter your exam password in order to continue the exam. If you leave the testing room at any other time, you will not be allowed to return and the incident will be reported to your board of accountancy. The break policy is part of the statement you must accept on your computer screen in order to begin the exam. (A copy of it is included in the Candidate Bulletin.)

EXAM FORMAT

Testlets

Multiple-choice questions and simulations are grouped into testlets. Typically a testlet has either 24 (only REG) or 30 multiple-choice questions or a single simulation. The FAR, AUD and REG exam sections have three multiple-choice question and two simulation testlets delivered in that order; BEC is comprised of three multiple-choice question testlets only. Candidates **cannot** pick the order in which they answer testlets, but *within* a testlet, questions (multiple-choice or simulation) can be answered in any order. Once you indicate you have completed a testlet, you **cannot** return to it.

While the exam sections cover materials from the AICPA's content specification outlines (CSOs), the questions in each testlet are delivered randomly, i.e., they are not in the some order as the CSOs. (The AUD CSO is included in the fifth section of this appendix.)

Adaptive Testing Model for FAR, AUD & REG Multiple-Choice Questions

After a candidate finishes a multiple-choice question testlet in the FAR, AUD, and REG exam sections, the software selects the next testlet based on the candidate's performance on the previous testlet. (The first testlet is always at the "moderately difficult" level.) If a candidate does well on a testlet, the next testlet will be a little more difficult. Otherwise, the next testlet will be at the same level of difficulty as the previous testlet. The intent is that analysis of adaptive testing statistics will eventually allow the examiners to reduce the number of questions, resulting in more time for testing skills. The BEC multiple-choice question testlets are not delivered in this manner; all of the BEC multiple-choice questions are at the "moderately difficult" level.

Multiple-Choice Questions

There are 3 multiple-choice question testlets in each of the four exam sections. Each testlet in an exam section will contain the same number of questions. REG multiple-choice testlets typically have 24 questions each; FAR, AUD and BEC testlets typically have 30 questions per testlet. In FAR, AUD, and REG the multiple-choice testlets account for 70% of the score. (BEC consists of these 3 multiple-choice question testlets only; the other exam sections also have 2 simulation testlets.) The tutorial on the AICPA's exam Web site at www.cpa-exam.org demonstrates how to select an answer, move to another question, etc. The sample tests (also on their Web site) allow you to practice answering a few questions using the exam software.

Simulations—FAR, AUD, & REG Only

A simulation is a condensed case study consisting of a variety of tasks, including searching databases, completing written communication exercises, and working with spreadsheets and forms. There are 2 simulation testlets (1 simulation makes up a testlet) on the FAR, AUD, and REG exam sections. BEC does not have simulations. Each simulation is designed to take between 30 and 50 minutes to complete. All simulations have a written communication exercise. Simulations account for 30% of the score—10% for the written communication exercise portion and 20% for the objective portions. The tutorial and sample tests on the AICPA's exam Web site (www.cpa-exam.org) afford candidates the opportunity to gain exposure to the exam software and the format of the simulations—there is 1 sample simulation included for each exam section.

Simulation Appearance Simulations appear as a collection of tabbed pages. Each tab requiring a candidate response will be designated by a pencil icon that changes appearance when any potion of the response is entered on that tab. The altered icon does **not** indicate a *completed* response.

Scenario Elements A simulation generally will have one or two scenarios providing the basis for the answers to all of the questions in that simulation.

Objective Response Elements Simulations may require candidates to select answers from drop-down lists or to enter numbers into worksheets or tax forms (for REG). Candidates don't need to know how to create a spreadsheet from scratch; however, they do need to know how to categorize, determine value, and add to a previously constructed worksheet.

Written Communication Elements These exercises typically require candidates to complete tasks such as writing a letter or memo. Only responses that address the topic will be graded. Responses that are off topic or offer clearly illegal advice will not receive any credit. Scores are based on three criteria: (1) organization (structure; ordering and linking of ideas); (2) development (presentation of supporting evidence); and (3) expression (use of standard business English). Additional information is included in the *Writing Skills* section of this text.

Word Processor Tool The word processor tool included has limited features which include "Undo," "Redo," "Cut," "Copy," and "Paste." It also has a spell-checker which you should use because spelling is part of the scoring criteria. Also the electronic scoring software may not recognize a key concept than includes a typo.

Spreadsheet Tool The exam has a blank spreadsheet tool for candidates to use as "electronic scratch paper." If you calculate an amount using the spreadsheet tool, you must transfer the result to the appropriate answer location to obtain credit.

Research Elements A research exercise requires a search of an electronic database of authoritative literature to identify the reference (for example, the section and paragraph number of the codification of a professional standard) for the guidance requested. No written analysis of the guidance is required; candidates merely provide the most appropriate reference as their response.

Finding the answer (reference) involves one of two possible approaches. A candidate can use the database's search engine and select the relevant guidance from the "hits" generated by that search. Alternatively, candidates may use the authoritative literature's table of contents; clicking on folders to expand the table of contents and "drilling down" to the appropriate section of the relevant guidance. Either approach ends with scrolling through (reading) a document to locate the specific guidance requested so that its reference number can be selected as the response. Taking the sample simulation test on the AICPA's exam Web site (www.cpa-exam.org) will allow you see firsthand how to navigate within the database and select an answer.

Candidates who have an NTS may get a **free** six-month subscription to the databases used in the FAR and AUD exam sections by subscribing at the AICPA's exam Web site (www.cpa-exam.org). The AICPA cautions candidates that the interface used by this package is **not** exactly the same as the one used in the exam. Only their sample tests reflect the actual exam's functionality and interfaces.

THE NONDISCLOSED EXAM

Exam Disclosure

The Uniform CPA Examination is nondisclosed. This means that candidates are not allowed to receive a copy of their exam questions after the test. Also, candidates are required to accept the terms of the exam which include a promise not to reveal questions or answers. Only the AICPA has access to the test questions and answers. (In the past, the AICPA has released a small number of questions with unofficial answers from each nondisclosed exam; it makes no guarantees that it will continue this practice.) Bisk Education's editors update the diagnostic, study, and practice questions, based upon content changes, items from previously disclosed tests, and the teaching expertise of our editors. Due to the nondisclosure requirements, Bisk Education's editors are no longer able to address questions about specific exam questions, although we continue to supply help with similar study problems and questions in our texts.

The AICPA no longer discloses the exam in order to increase consistency, facilitate computer administration of the test, and improve exam quality by pretesting questions. Because the exam is no longer completely changed every year, statistical equating methods are more relevant, and the usefulness of specific questions as indicators of candidates' knowledge can be tested.

Nonscored Pretest Questions

Each testlet (multiple-choice and simulation) may include pretest questions. Pretest questions in simulations may include written communication questions. Pretest questions are not included in a candidate's final score; they are presented only so the Board of Examiners may evaluate them for effectiveness and possible ambiguity. You will **not** know which questions will not be scored.

Postexam Diagnostics

The AICPA Board of Examiners' Advisory Grading Service provides boards of accountancy with individual diagnostic reports for candidates that fail an exam section. The accountancy boards may mail the diagnostic reports to candidates along with their scores. Candidates should contact the board in their jurisdiction to find out its policy on this issue.

Candidate Requests for Question Review

Candidates who believe they have identified a problem with an exam question should contact the AICPA Examinations Team in writing by fax or letter. See the Candidate Bulletin for the fax number or mailing address and the AICPA's specific instructions. Your fax or letter must be received within four days of taking the exam to ensure a timely review. The ACIPA asks that you include your exam section identification number and that you do not include the exact wording or attempt to outline the question or simulation—simply provide enough information for the examiners to identify the question, such as "question number 12 in the first testlet" or the tab name for a simulation question. They request that you include the nature of your concern, your rationale, and, if possible, references to support your position. According to the Candidate Bulletin, the AICPA is unable to respond directly to candidates, but reviews every fax or letter received by the deadline.

TEN ATTRIBUTES OF EXAM SUCCESS

1.	**Positive Mental Attitude**	6.	**Exam Strategies**
2.	**Development of a Plan**	7.	**Exam Grading**
3.	**Adherence to the Plan**	8.	**Solutions Approach™**
4.	**Time Management**	9.	**Focus on Ultimate Objective—Passing!**
5.	**Knowledge**	10.	**Exam Confidence**

We believe that successful candidates possess these ten characteristics that contribute to their ability to pass the exam. Because of their importance, we will consider each attribute individually.

1. Positive Mental Attitude

Preparation for the exam is a long, intense process. A positive mental attitude, above all else, can be the difference between passing and failing.

2. Development of a Plan

The significant commitment involved in preparing for the exam requires a plan. We have prepared a study plan in the *Getting Started* section of this text. Take time to read this plan. Amend it to your situation. Whether you use our study plan or create your own, the importance of this attribute can't be overlooked.

3. Adherence to the Plan

You cannot expect to accomplish a successful and comprehensive review without adherence to your study plan.

4. Time Management

We all lead busy lives and the ability to budget study time is a key to success. We have outlined steps to budgeting time in the personalized training plan found in the *Getting Started* section.

5. Knowledge

There is a distinct difference between understanding the material and knowing the material. A superficial understanding of accounting, auditing, and the business environment is not enough. You must know the material likely to be tested on the exam. Your Bisk Education text is designed to help you acquire the necessary knowledge.

6. Exam Strategies

You should be familiar with the format of the exam and know exactly what you will do when you enter the testing room. In Section Two, we discuss the steps you should take in preparation for the exam.

7. Exam Grading

An understanding of the exam written communication grading procedure will help you to maximize points on the exam. Remember that your objective is to score 75 points on each exam section. In Section Three, we explain AICPA grading procedures and show you how to tailor your answer to the grading guide and thus earn more points on the exam.

8. Solutions Approach™

The Solutions Approach™ is an efficient, systematic method of organizing and solving questions found on the exam. This approach will permit you to organize your thinking and your written answers in a logical manner that will maximize your exam score. Many candidates have never developed an effective problem-solving methodology. Our Solutions Approach™ teaches you to derive solutions independently and will help you avoid drawing "blanks" on the exam; with it, you always know where to begin.

9. Focus on the Ultimate Objective—Passing!

Your primary goal in preparing for the exam is to attain a score of 75 or better on all sections and, thus, pass the exam. Your review should be focused on this goal. Other objectives, such as learning new material or reviewing old material, are important only insofar as they assist you in passing the exam.

10. Exam Confidence

Exam confidence is actually a function of the other nine attributes. If you have acquired a good working knowledge of the material, an understanding of the grading system, a tactic for answering simulations, and a plan for taking the exam; you can go into the testing room confident that you are in control.

SECTION TWO: EXAM STRATEGIES

The exam is more than a test of your knowledge and technical competence. It is also a test of your ability to function under psychological pressure. You could easily be thrown off balance by an unexpected turn of events during the exam. Your objective is to avoid surprises and eliminate hassles and distractions that might shake your confidence. You want to be in complete control so that you can concentrate on the exam material, rather than the exam situation. By taking charge of the exam, you will be able to handle pressure in a constructive manner. The keys to control are adequate preparation and an effective exam strategy.

OVERALL PREPARATION

Advance preparation will arm you with the confidence you need to overcome the psychological pressure of the exam. As you complete your comprehensive review, you will cover most of the material that will be tested on the exam; it is unlikely that any multiple-choice question or simulation will deal with a topic you have not studied. But if an unfamiliar topic is tested, you will not be dismayed because you have learned to use the Solutions Approach™ to derive the best possible answer from the knowledge you possess. Similarly, you will not feel pressured to write "perfect" written communication responses, because you understand the grading process. You recognize that there is a limit to the points you can earn for each answer, no matter how much you write.

The components of your advance preparation program have previously been discussed in this appendix. Briefly summarizing, they include the following.

1.   Comprehensive review materials such as your Bisk Education CPA Review program.

2.   A method for prereview and ongoing self-evaluation of your level of proficiency.

3.   A study plan that enables you to review each subject area methodically and thoroughly.

4.   A Solutions Approach™ for each type of exam question.

5.   An understanding of the grading process and grader orientation skills.

EXAM STRATEGIES

The second key to controlling the exam is to develop effective strategies for the days you take the exam. Your objective is to avoid surprises and frustrations so that you can focus your full concentration on the questions and your answers.

You should be familiar with the format of the exam and know exactly what you will do when you enter the testing room. Remember to read all instructions carefully, whether general or specific to a particular question. Disregarding the instructions may mean loss of points.

On the following pages, we discuss the steps you should take on exam day. Planning in advance how you will spend your exam time will save you time and help you to avoid confusion.

EXAM TIME BUDGETING

All exam sections will have 3 multiple-choice testlets and (except for BEC) 2 simulation testlets. BEC is comprised of 3 multiple-choice testlets only. You must complete each testlet in the order it is presented. The multiple-choice testlets are always presented first. Each simulation is expected to take between 30 and 50 minutes, depending on the exam section—generally, FAR and AUD simulations are designed to take longer to complete than REG's. Budget your time for the FAR, AUD and REG exam sections by deducting the time needed to complete the two simulations from the total time allowed and then dividing the remainder between the 3 multiple-choice testlets. For example, on the 4½-hour AUD exam, you should set a goal to begin the first simulation testlet when there is at least 1½ hours of time remaining. This will allow you a little less than 1 hour for each of the multiple-choice testlets if you take a short break. If you can complete the multiple-choice testlets in a little less time you will have more time to organize your thoughts while working on the simulations.

You must plan how you will use your exam time and adhere faithfully to your schedule. If you budget your time carefully, you should be able to answer all parts of all testlets. Assuming you will use the Solutions Approach™, your time budgets may be similar to these. If you benefit by taking more breaks than are included in this schedule, your budget may differ from this scenario. Be sure to adjust your time budget to accommodate your individual needs and strengths.

	Minutes			
	FAR	AUD	REG	BEC
Answer multiple-choice question testlet	51	58	34	50
Answer multiple-choice question testlet	51	58	33	50
Answer multiple-choice question testlet	51	58	33	50
Break	7	6	0	0
Answer simulation testlet	40	45	40	n/a
Answer simulation testlet	40	45	40	n/a
	240	270	180	150

Your objective in time budgeting is to avoid running out of time to answer a question. Work quickly but efficiently; i.e., use the Solutions Approach™. Remember that when you are answering a written communication question, a partial answer is better than no answer at all.

ORDER OF ANSWERING QUESTIONS

The objective portions of each exam section comprise the majority of the point value of the FAR, AUD, and REG exam sections and 100% of BEC's.

By solving the objective portion of the simulations first, not only do you gain confidence, but you will find that they often involve the same topic or one related to the one covered in the written communication portion.

A very effective and efficient manner of answering the objective questions (in the simulations as well as the multiple-choice testlets) is to make two passes through the questions. Remember, *within* a testlet you can answer the questions in any order. On the first pass, you should answer those questions that you find the easiest. If you come across a question that you find difficult to solve, note it on your scratch paper during a simulation or click on the "Mark for review" button during a multiple-choice testlet and proceed to the next one. This will allow you to avoid wasting precious time and will enable your mind to clear and start fresh on your second pass. You should come up with an answer on the second pass, even if you have to guess. You are not penalized for wrong answers. Once you leave a testlet, you may not return to it. Before leaving a testlet, make sure you have answered all of the questions. Be careful not to overlook any items; use particular care in simulations.

Written communication responses should be worked only through the key word outlines on the first pass. Then take a fresh look at the question and return to write your written communication response.

PAGE NUMBERING

Identify and label your scratch paper pages to avoid confusing yourself during the exam.

PSYCHOLOGY OF EXAM SUCCESS

As stated previously, the exam is in itself a physical and mental strain. You can minimize this strain by avoiding all unnecessary distractions and inconveniences during your exam week. For example, consider the following.

- **Review the AICPA's free tutorial and sample tests** at www.cpa-exam.org at least a month before taking the exam and then again a week before your exam. Because the testing software is subject to change, revisit the site to be sure that you are familiar with it if you took an exam in a previous window. The site also has the most current edition of *The Uniform CPA Examination Candidate Bulletin: Information for Applicants,* a publication with useful information for candidates. This is **not** available at the test center.

- **Carefully register for the exam.** You must bring two forms of identification and your NTS to the test center on the day of your exam. The name you use to make the appointment must **exactly match** your name on your 2 IDs and your NTS.

- **Make any reservations for lodging well in advance.** If you are traveling, it's best to reserve a room for the preceding night so that you can check in, get a good night's sleep, and locate the exam site well before the exam.

- **Stick to your normal eating, sleeping, and exercise habits.** Eat lightly before the exam. Watch your caffeine and alcohol intake. If you are accustomed to regular exercise, continue a regular routine leading up to your exam day.

- **Locate the testing center** before the exam and familiarize yourself with the surroundings and alternate routes.

- **Arrive early for the exam.** Allow plenty of time for unexpected delays. Nothing is more demoralizing than getting caught in a traffic jam ten minutes before your exam is scheduled to begin. Your appointment time is the time that the actual exam process is scheduled to start, not the start of the test center check-in procedures which include identification verification, digital photography, storage locker assignment, etc. The examiners ask that you arrive at least 30 minutes before your scheduled appointment.

- **Avoid possible distractions,** such as friends and conversation, immediately before the exam.

- In general, you should not attempt serious study on the nights before exam sessions. It's better to relax. If you feel you must study, spend half an hour or so going over the chapter outlines in the text. Some candidates develop a single page of notes for each chapter throughout their review process to review for a few minutes during the evening before the exam. This single page may include only those things that are particularly troublesome for that candidate,

Avoid self-evaluation of your exam performance until after you receive your official score. Self-evaluation without an official score is unreliable. Not all of the examiners' questions are the same point value. Further, some of the questions are not scored and candidates have no way to identify these. Instead of speculating, focus on preparing for your next exam section.

AICPA GENERAL RULES GOVERNING EXAMS

1. Only the exam password on your NTS will be used on your exam for the purpose of identification. If a question calls for an answer involving a signature, do not use your own name or initials.

2. Use the exact same name as on your NTS when scheduling your appointment. Two pieces of identification are required; one must have a photo. The name on your 2 IDs must match your name on your NTS **exactly.**

3. Seating during the exam is assigned by Prometric.

4. Any reference during the exam to books or other matters or the exchange of information with other persons shall be considered misconduct sufficient to bar you from further participation in the exam.

5. The only aids most candidates are permitted to have in the testing room are supplied by the proctors. Wallets, briefcases, files, books, phones, watches, and other material brought to the exam site by candidates must be placed in a designated area before the start of the exam. Candidates are loaned a key to a small storage locker. The test center is not responsible for lost items.

6. Do not leave your workstation during a testlet. Breaks are allowed only between testlets.

7. Smoking is allowed only in designated areas away from the general exam area.

8. No telephone calls are permitted during the exam session.

9. Answers must be completed in the total time allotted for each exam section. The fixed time for each session must be observed by all candidates. The testing software will end the test at the end of the specified time.

EXAM WEEK CHECKLIST

What to <u>pack</u> for exam week:

1. NTS and 2 forms of acceptable matching identification; see the Candidate Bulletin

2. If traveling, your hotel confirmation and an alarm clock (Don't rely on a hotel wake-up call.)

3. Cash and/or a major credit card

4. An inexpensive watch to facilitate your timely arrival at the exam site (Watches are **not** allowed in the testing room—the computer screen displays the time remaining to complete the exam.)

5. Comfortable clothing that can be loosened to suit varying temperatures (What is worn into the testing room must be worn throughout the testing period; however, once at the testing center, you can remove a sweater or coat **before** entering the testing room.)

6. Appropriate review materials and tools for final reviews during the last days before the exam

7. Healthy snack foods (Food is not allowed in testing room.)

Evenings before exam sections:

1. Read through your Bisk Education chapter outlines for the next day's section(s).

2. Eat lightly and monitor your intake of alcohol and caffeine. Get a good night's rest.

3. Do not try to cram. A brief review of your notes will help to focus your attention on important points and remind you that you are well prepared, but too much cramming can undermine your self-confidence. If you have reviewed conscientiously, you are already well prepared for the exam.

The morning of each exam section:

1. Eat a satisfying meal before your exam. It will be several hours before your next meal. Eat enough to ward off hunger, but not so much that you feel uncomfortable.

2. Dress appropriately. Wear layers you can loosen to suit varying temperatures in the room. If you require a separate sweater or a jacket due to room temperature, it must be worn at all times.

3. Arrive at the exam center at least 30 minutes early.

What to bring to the exam:

1. Appropriate identification (two forms, one with a picture) and NTS. Your name on the identification must match your name on your NTS **exactly.** Use the exact same name when scheduling your appointment.

2. An inexpensive watch (to be left outside of the testing room) to ensure that you arrive 30 minutes early. The computer screen displays the time remaining to complete the exam.

3. Take only those articles that you need to get to and from the exam site. Avoid taking any articles that are not allowed in the testing room, especially valuable ones. There are small storage lockers outside of the testing room to hold purses, etc. The test center is not responsible for lost items. Watches, phones, pencils, purses, tissues, candy, and gum are not allowed in the testing room. Even medication is not allowed except by previous arrangement.

During the exam:

1. Always read all instructions and follow the directions of the exam administrator. Remember that an error in following directions could invalidate your entire exam.

2. Immediately report any computer problems to the test center staff.

3. Budget your time. Always keep track of the time and avoid getting too involved with one question.

4. **Satisfy the grader.** Remember that the grader cannot read your mind. You must explain every point in written communications. Focus on key words and concepts. Tell the grader what you know, don't worry about any points you don't know.

5. Answer every question, even if you must guess.

6. Use **all** the allotted time. If you finish a testlet early, go back and reconsider the more difficult questions.

7. Remember that you can only leave your workstation between testlets.

8. Take enough time to organize written answers. Well-organized answers will impress the grader.

9. Remember that you are well prepared for the exam, and that you can expect to pass. A confident attitude will help you overcome exam anxiety.

SECTION THREE: EXAM GRADING

The exam is prepared and graded by the AICPA Examinations Division. Candidates register for the exam through various boards of accountancy. It is administered by a commercial testing center, Prometric.

An understanding of the grading procedure will help you maximize grading points on the exam. Remember that your objective is to pass the exam. You cannot afford to spend time on activities that will not affect your score, or to ignore opportunities to increase your points. The following material abstracted from the AICPA's *The Uniform CPA Examination Candidate Bulletin: Information for Applicants* booklet summarizes the important substantive aspects of the Uniform CPA Examination itself and the AICPA grading procedures.

OBJECTIVE QUESTIONS

Objective questions consist of multiple-choice questions and objective answer format questions in simulations. It is important to understand that **you are not penalized for incorrect responses to objective questions—** your total objective question score is determined solely by the number of correct answers. Thus, **you should answer every question.** If you do not know the answer, make an intelligent guess.

The point to remember is to avoid getting "bogged down" on one answer. Move along and answer all the questions. This helps you avoid leaving questions unanswered or panic answering questions due to poor budgeting of test time.

WRITTEN COMMUNICATION EXERCISES

Every simulation includes a written communication exercise. Candidates must read a situation description and then compose an appropriate document. The instructions will state what form the document should take (such as a memo or letter) and its focus. The candidate's response should provide the correct information in writing that is clear, complete, and professional.

Written communication responses are graded for writing skills, but the content must answer the question. Only those answers that are generally responsive to the topic will be graded. If the response is off-topic, or offers advice that is clearly illegal, no credit will be given for the response. Scores will be based on three general writing criteria: organization, development, and expression.

Organization: the document's structure, ordering of ideas, and linking of one idea to another:

- Overview/thesis statement
- Unified paragraphs (topic and supporting sentences)
- Transitions and connectives

Development: the document's supporting evidence/information to clarify thoughts:

- Details
- Definitions
- Examples
- Rephrasing

Expression: the document's use of conventional standards of business English:

- Grammar
- Punctuation
- Word usage
- Capitalization
- Spelling

Scoring is fully automated for all exam components except the written communication portion of simulations. A combination of human graders and electronic scoring is used to score written communication responses. All scoring routines—whether automated or not—are verified at various stages of the scoring process.

RESEARCH QUESTIONS

In their current form, research questions are objective questions. The only response required is the selection of a paragraph reference from the professional literature obtained by a search of a database. The candidate doesn't provide any commentary or analysis of the guidance. The search can be made either by using the table of contents feature or the search engine. Most candidates will find the table of contents easier to use than the search engine, once they become familiar with the auditing literature database. (Candidates who have a NTS may get a complimentary six-month online subscription to this database by subscribing at the AICPA's exam Web site, www.cpa-exam.org). However, if you prefer using a search engine, make sure you practice using the exam's "Advanced Search" feature by taking the sample test on the AICPA's exam Web site. Click on "Help" within the research portion of the sample simulation (or take the site's tutorial) for more information about the search engine's advanced features. And regardless of which search method you prefer, keep in mind that the AICPA cautions candidates that the interface used by their complimentary subscription package is **not** exactly the same as the one used in the exam. Only their sample tests reflect the actual exam's functionality and interfaces.

GRADING IMPLICATIONS

To summarize this review of the AICPA's grading procedure, we can offer the following conclusions that will help you to satisfy the grader and maximize your score:

1. Attempt an answer on every question.

2. Respond directly to the requirements of the questions.

3. Use of a well-chosen example is an easy way of expressing an understanding of the subject or supporting a conclusion.

4. Use schedules and formats favored by the AICPA examiners.

5. Answer all requirements.

6. Develop a Solutions Approach™ to each question type.

7. Written communication exercises: Label your solutions parallel to the requirements. Offer reasons for your conclusions. Separate grading concepts into individual sentences or paragraphs. Use of a well-chosen example is an easy way of expressing an understanding of the subject or supporting a conclusion. Do **not** present your answer in outline format.

8. Allocate your exam time based on AICPA point value, if provided.

SECTION FOUR: THE SOLUTIONS APPROACH™

The Bisk Education Solutions Approach™ is an efficient, systematic method of organizing and solving questions found on the exam. Remember that all the knowledge in the world is worthless unless you can convey it to the grader. Conversely, a little knowledge can go a long way if you use a proper approach. Our Solutions Approach™ and grader orientation skills, when properly developed, can be worth at least 10 to 15 points for most candidates. These 10 to 15 points can often make the difference between passing and failing.

We will suggest a number of steps for deriving a solution that will help maximize your grade on the exam. Although you should remember the important steps in our suggested approach, don't hesitate to adapt these steps to your own taste and requirements. When you work the questions at the conclusion of each chapter, make sure you use your variation of the Solutions Approach™. However, DO NOT CONSULT THE ANSWER UNTIL YOU FINISH THE QUESTION. The worst thing you can do is look at a question and, before answering it, turn to the answer without working the problem. This will build false confidence and provide no skills in developing a Solutions Approach™. Therefore, in order to derive the maximum number of points from a written communication solution, you should first apply the Solutions Approach™ to reading and answering the question, and secondly, write an answer using the same organization and format illustrated by the sample AICPA unofficial answer included in this section.

SOLUTIONS APPROACH™ FOR WRITTEN COMMUNICATION EXERCISES

Our six steps are as follows:

1. Scan the text of the question for an overview of the subject area and content of the question.
2. Study the question requirements slowly and thoroughly. Note portions of the requirements on your scratch paper as needed.
3. Visualize the unofficial answer format based on the requirements of the question.
4. Carefully study the text of the question. Note important data on your scratch paper.
5. Outline the solution in key words and phrases. Be sure to respond to the requirements, telling the grader only what is relevant. You must explain the reasons for your conclusions.
6. Write the solution in the proper format based upon your key word outline. Write concisely in complete sentences. Do not forget to proofread and edit your solution.

Written Communication Exercise Example

To illustrate the Solutions Approach™ for written communication questions, we consider a question from a past exam.

Sample Question

Cook, CPA, has been engaged to audit the financial statements of General Department Stores, Inc., a continuing audit client, which is a chain of medium-sized retail stores. General's fiscal year will end on June 30, Year 1, and General's management has asked Cook to issue the auditor's report by August 1, Year 1. Cook will not have sufficient time to perform all of the necessary fieldwork in July Year 1, but will have time to perform most of the fieldwork as of an interim date, April 30, Year 1.

For the accounts to be tested at the interim date, Cook will also perform substantive tests covering the transactions of the final two months of the year. This will be necessary to extend Cook's conclusions to the balance sheet date.

Required:

a. Describe the factors Cook should consider before applying principal substantive tests to General's balance sheet accounts at April 30, Year 1.

b. For accounts tested at April 30, Year 1, describe how Cook should design the substantive tests covering the balances as of June 30, Year 1, and the transactions of the final two months of the year.

Applying the Solutions Approach™

Let's look at the steps you go through to arrive at your solution:

In **Step 1,** you scan the question. Do not read it thoroughly; simply get an overview of the subject area and content of the question. You notice the question deals with substantive testing.

In **Step 2,** you study the question requirements thoroughly. Part a asks about factors important to the reliance of substantive testing of the balance sheet accounts, while part b refers to the period between the date of testing and year-end. Note key phrases and words on your scratch paper.

In **Step 3,** you visualize the format of your solution. The solution will be in paragraph form. Part a will discuss the factors considered in the decision to rely on substantive testing. Part b will discuss the design of substantive tests to be used and the risks inherent to this area.

In **Step 4,** you carefully study the text of the question, given the requirements you want to satisfy, i.e., read the question carefully. You should note important information on your scratch paper.

In **Step 5,** you outline your answer in keyword form. In your exam preparation, as you work AUD written communication questions, notice that sometimes you are not asked to make a decision or reach a conclusion, but rather you are asked to identify and discuss all important factors in the situation.

Outline Answer

a. Assess difficulty in controlling incremental audit risk
   Consider:
      Reliability of accounting records
      Management integrity
      Business environment
      Predictability of year-end balances
      Internal control for cutoffs
      Availability of information for final two months
      Cost of substantive tests necessary to provide level of assurance
         Control risk assessed at < maximum: not required to extend audit conclusions to final two months
         If control risk = maximum—during final two months—will effectiveness be impaired?

b. Design of tests
      Level of assurance meets audit objectives
      Comparison of year-end information to comparable interim to identify and investigate unusual amounts
      Other analytical procedures to extend conclusions based on interim date to balance sheet date

In **Step 6,** you write your solution. These are the instructions that the AICPA includes as part of the "Communication" tab in the AUD sample test available on its exam Web site (www.cpa-exam.org): "REMINDER: Your response will be graded for both technical content and writing skills. Technical content will be evaluated for information that is helpful to the intended reader and clearly relevant to the issue. Writing skills will be evaluated for development, organization, and the appropriate expression of ideas in professional correspondence. Use a standard business memo or letter format with a clear beginning, middle, and end. Do not convey information in the form of a table, bullet point list, or other abbreviated presentation."

Use a format similar to the unofficial answer. Notice how clear and concise the AICPA unofficial answers are. There is no doubt as to their decision or the reasoning supporting the decision. Notice also how they answer each requirement separately and in the same order as in the question. Be sure to proofread and edit your response.

Sample Unofficial Answer

a. Before applying principal substantive tests to balance sheet accounts at April 30, Year 1, the interim date, the auditor should assess the difficulty in controlling incremental audit risk. The auditor should consider whether the reliability of the accounting records and management's integrity has been good in the auditor's experience. The auditor should also consider whether (1) rapidly changing business conditions or circumstances may predispose General's management to misstate the financial statements in the remaining period; (2) the year-end balances of accounts selected for interim testing will be predictable; (3) General's procedures for analyzing and adjusting its interim balances and for reestablishing proper accounting cutoffs will be appropriate; (4) General's accounting system will provide sufficient information about year-end balances and transactions in the final two months of the year to permit investigation of unusual transactions, significant fluctuations, and changes in balance compositions that may occur between the interim and balance sheet dates; and (5) the cost of the substantive tests necessary to cover the final two months of the year and provide the appropriate audit assurance at year-end is substantial.

Assessing control risk at below the maximum would not be required to extend the audit conclusions from the interim date to the year-end; however, if the auditor assesses control risk at the maximum during the final two months, the auditor should consider whether the effectiveness of the substantive tests to cover that period will be impaired.

b. The auditor should design the substantive tests so that the assurance from those tests and the tests to be applied as of the interim date, and any assurance provided from the assessed level of control risk, achieve the audit objectives at year-end. Such tests should include the comparison of year-end information with comparable interim information to identify and investigate unusual amounts. Other analytical procedures and/or substantive tests should be performed to extend the auditor's conclusions relative to the assertions tested at the interim date to the balance sheet date.

SOLUTIONS APPROACH™ FOR OBJECTIVE QUESTIONS

The Solutions Approach™ is also adaptable to objective questions. We recommend the following framework:

1. Your objective portion will be determined by the number of correct answers with no penalty for incorrect answers.

2. Read the question carefully, noting exactly what the question is asking. Negative requirements are easily missed. Note key words and when the requirement is an exception (e.g., "except for...," or "which of the following does **not**..."). Perform any intermediate calculations necessary for the determination of the correct answer.

3. Anticipate the answer by covering the possible answers and seeing if you know the correct answer.

4. Read the answers given.

5. Select the best alternative. Very often, one or two possible answers will be clearly incorrect. Of the other alternatives, be sure to select the alternative that best answers the question asked.

6. After completing all of the individual questions in a testlet, go back and double-check that you have answered each question.

7. Answer the questions in order. This is a proven, systematic approach to objective test taking. You generally will be limited to an average of 2 to 2½ minutes per multiple-choice question. Under no circumstances should you allow yourself to fall behind schedule. If a question is difficult or long, be sure you remain cognizant of the time you are using. If after a minute or so you feel that it is too costly to continue on with a particular question, select the answer you tentatively feel is the best;

mark it for review; and go on to the next question. Return to these questions at a later time and attempt to finally answer them when you have time for more consideration. If you cannot find a better answer when you return to the question, use your preliminary answer because your first impressions are often correct. However, as you read other question(s), if something about these subsequent questions or answers jogs your memory, return to the previous tentatively answered question(s) and make a note of the idea for later consideration (time permitting).

A simulation typically has a group of objective questions, generally based on one hypothetical situation. A simulation is a particularly challenging format for many candidates. In this case, you should consider skimming all the related questions (but not the answer possibilities) before you begin answering, since an overall view of the problem will guide you in the work you do.

Note also that many incorrect answer choices are based on the erroneous application of one or more items in the text of the question. Thus, it is extremely important to anticipate the answer before you read the alternatives. Otherwise, you may be easily persuaded by an answer choice that is formulated through the incorrect use of the given data.

Let's consider a multiple-choice question adapted from a past exam.

Sample Objective Question

Which of the following is an element of a CPA firm's quality control system that should be considered in establishing its quality control policies and procedures?
a.   Complying with laws and regulations
b.   Using statistical sampling techniques
c.   Relevant ethical requirements
d.   Considering audit risk and materiality   (5/94, Aud., #15, amended, 4680)

Applying the Solutions Approach™

Let's look at the steps you should go through to arrive at your objective question solution.

In **Step 1,** you must carefully read the directions that precede your particular objective exam portion.

In **Step 2,** you must read the question and its requirements carefully. Look out for questions that require you to provide those options **not** applicable, **not** true, etc...

In **Step 3,** you must anticipate the correct answer after reading the question but before reading the possible answers.

In **Step 4,** you must read the answer carefully and select the alternative that best answers the question asked. Ideally, the best alternative will immediately present itself because it roughly or exactly corresponds with the answer you anticipated before looking at the other possible choices.

In **Step 5,** you select the best alternative. If there are two close possibilities, make sure you select the best one in light of the facts and requirements of the question.

In **Step 6 and 7,** you must make sure you have selected an answer to all questions before you leave a testlet, with due regard to time constraints.

Unofficial Answer

Solution: The answer is (c). "Relevant ethical requirements" is one of the elements that should be addressed by a firm's system of quality control. Answer (a) is not an *element* of a system of quality control. Answers (b) and (d) would be associated with auditing requirements and procedures.

BENEFITS OF THE SOLUTIONS APPROACH™

The Solutions Approach™ may seem cumbersome the first time you attempt it; candidates frequently have a tendency to write as they think. Such a haphazard approach often results in a disorganized answer. The Solutions Approach™ will help you write a solution that parallels the question requirements. It will also help you recall information under the pressure of the exam. The technique assists you in directing your thoughts toward the information required for the answer. Without a Solutions Approach™, you are apt to become distracted or confused by details that are irrelevant to the answer. Finally, the Solutions Approach™ is a faster way to answer exam questions. You will not waste time on false starts or rewrites. The approach may seem time-consuming at first, but as you become comfortable using it, you will see that it actually saves time and results in a better answer.

We urge you to give the Solutions Approach™ a good try by using it throughout your review. As you practice, you may adapt or modify it to your own preferences and requirements. The important thing is to develop a system so that you do not approach exam questions with a storehouse of knowledge that you cannot express under exam conditions.

———————

SECTION FIVE: CONTENT SPECIFICATION OUTLINE

The AICPA Board of Examiners has developed a content specification outline of each section of the exam to be tested. These outlines list the areas, groups, and topics to be tested, and indicate the approximate percentage of the total test score devoted to each area. The content of the exam is based primarily on results of national studies of public accounting practice and the evaluation of CPA practitioners and educators.

AUDITING & ATTESTATION

I. **Plan the Engagement, Evaluate the Prospective Client and Engagement, Decide Whether to Accept or Continue the Client and the Engagement, and Enter Into an Agreement With the Client (22%-28%)**

A. Determine Nature and Scope of Engagement

   1. Auditing Standards Generally Accepted in the United States of America (GAAS)
   2. Standards for Accounting and Review Services
   3. Standards for Attestation Engagements
   4. Compliance Auditing Applicable to Governmental Entities and Other Recipients of Governmental Financial Assistance
   5. Other Assurance Services
   6. Appropriateness of Engagement to Meet Client's Needs

B. Assess Engagement Risk and the CPA Firm's Ability to Perform the Engagement

   1. Engagement Responsibilities
   2. Staffing and Supervision Requirements
   3. Quality Control Considerations
   4. Management Integrity
   5. Researching Information Sources for Planning and Performing the Engagement

C. Communicate With the Predecessor Accountant or Auditor
D. Decide Whether to Accept or Continue the Client and Engagement
E. Enter Into an Agreement With the Client About the Terms of the Engagement
F. Obtain an Understanding of the Client's Operations, Business, and Industry
G. Perform Analytical Procedures
H. Consider Preliminary Engagement Materiality

I. Assess Inherent Risk and Risk of Misstatements from Errors, Fraud, and Illegal Acts by Clients
J. Consider Other Planning Matters

   1. Using the Work of Other Independent Auditors
   2. Using the Work of a Specialist
   3. Internal Audit Function
   4. Related Parties and Related Party Transactions
   5. Electronic Evidence
   6. Risks of Auditing Around the Computer

K. Identify Financial Statement Assertions and Formulate Audit Objectives

   1. Significant Financial Statement Balances, Classes of Transactions, and Disclosures
   2. Accounting Estimates

L. Determine and Prepare the Work Program Defining the Nature, Timing, and Extent of the Procedures to be Applied

II. **Consider Internal Control in Both Manual and Computerized Environments (12%-18%)**

A. Obtain an Understanding of Business Processes and Information Flows
B. Identify Controls That Might Be Effective in Preventing or Detecting Misstatements
C. Document an Understanding of Internal Control
D. Consider Limitations of Internal Control
E. Consider the Effects of Service Organizations on Internal Control
F. Perform Tests of Control
G. Assess Control Risk

III. **Obtain and Document Information to Form a Basis for Conclusions (32%-38%)**

A.   Perform Planned Procedures

1.   Applications of Audit Sampling
2.   Analytical Procedures
3.   Confirmation of Balances and/or Transactions With Third Parties
4.   Physical Examination of Inventories and Other Assets
5.   Other Tests of Details
6.   Computer-Assisted Audit Techniques, Including Data Interrogation, Extraction and Analysis
7.   Substantive Tests Before the Balance Sheet Date
8.   Tests of Unusual Year-End Transactions

B.   Evaluate Contingencies
C.   Obtain and Evaluate Lawyers' Letters
D.   Review Subsequent Events
E.   Obtain Representations From Management
F.   Identify Reportable Conditions and Other Control Deficiencies
G.   Identify Matters for Communication With Audit Committees
H.   Perform Procedures for Accounting and Review Services Engagements
I.   Perform Procedures for Attestation Engagements

IV. **Review the Engagement to Provide Reasonable Assurance That Objectives are Achieved and Evaluate Information Obtained to Reach and to Document Engagement Conclusions (8%-12%)**

A.   Perform Analytical Procedures
B.   Evaluate the Sufficiency and Competence of Audit Evidence and Document Engagement Conclusions
C.   Evaluate Whether Financial Statements Are Free of Material Misstatements
D.   Consider Whether Substantial Doubt About an Entity's Ability to Continue as a Going Concern Exists

E.   Consider Other Information in Documents Containing Audited Financial Statements
F.   Review the Work Performed to Provide Reasonable Assurance That Objectives Are Achieved

V. **Prepare Communications to Satisfy Engagement Objectives (12%-18%)**

A.   Reports

1.   Reports on Audited Financial Statements
2.   Reports on Reviewed and Compiled Financial Statements
3.   Reports Required by Government Auditing Standards
4.   Reports on Compliance With Laws and Regulations
5.   Reports on Internal Control
6.   Reports on Prospective Financial Information
7.   Reports on Agreed-Upon Procedures
8.   Reports on the Processing of Transactions by Service Organizations
9.   Reports on Supplementary Financial Information
10.   Special Reports
11.   Reports on Other Assurance Services
12.   Reissuance of Reports

B.   Other Required Communications

1.   Errors and Fraud
2.   Illegal Acts
3.   Communication With Audit Committees
4.   Other Reporting Considerations Covered by Statements on Auditing Standards and Statements on Standards for Attestation Engagements

C.   Other Matters

1.   Subsequent Discovery of Facts Existing at the Date of the Auditor's Report
2.   Consideration After the Report Date of Omitted Procedures

SECTION SIX:
AUTHORITATIVE PRONOUNCEMENTS CROSS-REFERENCE
Auditing & Attestation

Section No.	Bisk CPA Review Auditing & Attestation Chapter Number(s)	AU Section Title / Statements on Auditing Standard Nos.
AU 110	21	*Responsibilities and Functions of the Independent Auditor* SAS 1, 78, 82
AU 120	21	*Defining Professional Requirements in Statements on Auditing Standards* SAS 102
AU 150	21	*Generally Accepted Auditing Standards* SAS 95, 98, 102, 105, 113
AU 161	21	*The Relationship of Generally Accepted Auditing Standards to Quality Control Standards* SAS 25, 98
AU 201	21	*Nature of the General Standards* SAS 1
AU 210	21	*Training and Proficiency of the Independent Auditor* SAS 1, 5
AU 220	21	*Independence* SAS 1
AU 230	21	*Due Professional Care in the Performance of Work* SAS 1, 41, 82, 99, 104
AU 311	22	*Planning and Supervision* SAS 108, 114
AU 312	22	*Audit Risk and Materiality in Conducting an Audit* SAS 107
AU 314	22, 23	*Understanding the Entity and Its Environment and Assessing the Risks of Material Misstatement* SAS 109
AU 315	21	*Communications Between Predecessor and Successor Auditors* SAS 84, 93
AU 316	22	*Consideration of Fraud in a Financial Statement Audit* SAS 99, 113
AU 317	22	*Illegal Acts by Clients* SAS 54

Section No.	Bisk CPA Review Auditing & Attestation Chapter Number(s)	AU Section Title / Statements on Auditing Standard Nos. (contd.)
AU 318	22, 23, 25	*Performing Audit Procedures in Response to Assessed Risks and Evaluating the Audit Evidence Obtained* SAS 110
AU 322	25	*The Auditor's Consideration of the Internal Audit Function in an Audit of Financial Statements* SAS 65
AU 324	30	*Service Organizations* SAS 70, 78, 88, 98
AU 325	23	*Communicating Internal Control Related Matters Identified in an Audit* SAS 115
AU 326	24	*Audit Evidence* SAS 106
AU 328	25	*Auditing Fair Value Measurements and Disclosures* SAS 101, 113
AU 329	24	*Analytical Procedures* SAS 56, 96
AU 330	25	*The Confirmation Process* SAS 67
AU 331	25	*Inventories* SAS 1, 43, 67
AU 332	25	*Auditing Derivative Instruments, Hedging Activities, and Investments in Securities* SAS 92
AU 333	24, 28	*Management Representations* SAS 85, 89, 99, 113
AU 334	24	*Related Parties* SAS 45
AU 336	24	*Using the Work of a Specialist* SAS 73
AU 337	24	*Inquiry of a Client's Lawyer Concerning Litigation, Claims, and Assessments* SAS 12
AU 339	24	*Audit Documentation* SAS 103
AU 341	28	*The Auditor's Consideration of an Entity's Ability to Continue as a Going Concern* SAS 59, 64, 77, 96, 113, 114

Section No.	Bisk CPA Review Auditing & Attestation Chapter Number(s)	AU Section Title / Statements on Auditing Standard Nos. (contd.)
AU 342	22, 25	*Auditing Accounting Estimates* SAS 57, 113
AU 350	26	*Audit Sampling* SAS 39, 43, 45, 111
AU 380	22	*The Auditor's Communication With Those Charged With Governance* SAS 114
AU 390	28	*Consideration of Omitted Procedures After the Report Date* SAS 46
AU 410	28	*Adherence to Generally Accepted Accounting Principles* SAS 1, 62
AU 411	28	*The Meaning of Present Fairly in Conformity With Generally Accepted Accounting Principles* SAS 69, 91, 93
AU 420	28	*Consistency of Application of Generally Accepted Accounting Principles* SAS 1, 43, 88
AU 431	28	*Adequacy of Disclosure in Financial Statements* SAS 32
AU 504	28	*Association With Financial Statements* SAS 26, 35, 72
AU 508	28	*Reports on Audited Financial Statements* SAS 58, 64, 79, 85, 93, 98
AU 530	28	*Dating of the Independent Auditor's Report* SAS 1, 29, 98, 103
AU 532	30	*Restricting the Use of an Auditor's Report* SAS 87
AU 534	30	*Reporting on Financial Statements Prepared for Use in Other Countries* SAS 51
AU 543	28	*Part of Audit Performed by Other Independent Auditors* SAS 1, 64
AU 544	28	*Lack of Conformity With Generally Accepted Accounting Principles* SAS 1, 2, 62, 77
AU 550	28	*Other Information in Documents Containing Audited Financial Statements* SAS 8, 98

Section No.	Bisk CPA Review Auditing & Attestation Chapter Number(s)	AU Section Title / Statements on Auditing Standard Nos. (contd.)
AU 551	30	*Reporting on Information Accompanying the Basic Financial Statements in Auditor-Submitted Documents* SAS 29, 52, 98
AU 552	30	*Reporting on Condensed Financial Statements and Selected Financial Data* SAS 42, 71
AU 558	28	*Required Supplementary Information* SAS 52, 98
AU 560	28	*Subsequent Events* SAS 1, 12, 98, 113
AU 561	28	*Subsequent Discovery of Facts Existing at the Date of the Auditor's Report* SAS 1, 98
AU 623	30	*Special Reports* SAS 62, 77
AU 625	30	*Reports on the Application of Accounting Principles* SAS Nos. 50, 97
AU 634	30	*Letters for Underwriters and Certain Other Requesting Parties* SAS 72, 76, 86
AU 711	30	*Filings Under Federal Securities Statutes* SAS 37

Section No.	Bisk CPA Review Auditing & Attestation Chapter Number(s)	AR Section Title / Statements on Standards for Accounting and Review Services Nos.
AU 722	30	*Interim Financial Information* SAS 100, 116
AU 801	29	*Compliance Auditing Considerations in Audits of Governmental Entities and Recipients of Governmental Financial Assistance* SAS 74, 75
AU 901	25	*Public Warehouses—Controls and Auditing Procedures for Goods Held* SAS 1, 43

Section No.	Bisk CPA Review Auditing & Attestation Chapter Number(s)	AR Section Title / Statements on Standards for Accounting and Review Services Nos.
AR 20	31	*Defining Professional Requirements in Statements on Standards for Accounting and Review Services* SSARS 16
AR 50	31	*Standards for Accounting and Review Services* SSARS 11
AR 100	31	*Compilation and Review of Financial Statements* SARS 1, 2, 3, 5, 7, 8, 9, 10, 12, 15, 17, 18
AR 110	31	*Compilation of Specified Elements, Accounts, or Items of a Financial Statement* SSARS 13, 17
AR 120	31	*Compilation of Pro Forma Financial Information* SSARS 14, 17

Section No.	Bisk CPA Review Auditing & Attestation Chapter Number(s)	AR Section Title / Statements on Standards for Accounting and Review Services Nos. (contd.)
AR 200	31	*Reporting on Comparative Financial Statements* SSARS 2, 3, 4, 5, 7, 11, 12 , 15, 17
AR 300	31	*Compilation Reports on Financial Statements Included in Certain Prescribed Forms* SSARS 3, 5, 7, 15, 17
AR 400	31	*Communications Between Predecessor and Successor Accountants* SSARS 4, 7, 9, 15, 17
AR 600	31	*Reporting on Personal Financial Statements Included in Written Personal Financial Plans* SSARS 6

Section No.	Bisk CPA Review Auditing & Attestation Chapter Number(s)	AT Section Title / Statements on Standards for Attestation Engagements
AT 20	31	*Defining Professional Requirements in Statements on Standards for Attestation Engagements* SSAE 13
AT 50	31	*SSAE Hierarchy* SSAE 14
AT 101	31	*Attest Engagements* SSAE 10, 11, 12, 14

Section No.	Bisk CPA Review Auditing & Attestation Chapter Number(s)	AT Section Title / Statements on Standards for Attestation Engagements
AT 201	31	*Agreed-Upon Procedures Engagements* SSAE 10, 11
AT 301	31	*Financial Forecasts and Projections* SSAE 10,11
AT 401	31	*Reporting on Pro Forma Financial Information* SSAE 10
AT 501	31	*An Examination of an Entity's Internal Control Over Financial Reporting That Is Integrated With an Audit of Its Financial Statements* SSAE No. 15
AT 601	31	*Compliance Attestation* SSAE No. 10
AT 701	31	*Management's Discussion and Analysis* SSAE No. 10
Section No.	Bisk CPA Review Auditing & Attestation Chapter Number(s)	QC Section Title / Statements on Quality Control Standards
QC 10	21	*A Firm's System of Quality Control* SQCS 7

Reference	Bisk CPA Review Auditing & Attestation Chapter Number(s)	Other Standards
GAGAS	29	*Government Auditing Standards ("Yellow Book")*
PCAOB AS 1	29	*References in Auditors' Reports to the Standards of the Public Company Accounting Oversight Board*
PCAOB AS 3	29	*Audit Documentation*
PCAOB AS 4	29	*Reporting on Whether a Previously Reported Material Weakness Continues to Exist*
PCAOB AS 5	29	*An Audit of Internal Control Over Financial Reporting That Is Integrated with An Audit of Financial Statements*
PCAOB AS 6	29	*Evaluating Consistency of Financial Statements*
PCAOB AS 7	29	*Engagement Quality Review*

Registration Process

To sit for the exam, candidates must apply to the appropriate board of accountancy or its exam administrator. (Some boards contract with an exam administrator to handle candidate applications.) Once a board or its exam administrator determines that a candidate is eligible to sit for the exam, they inform the National Association of State Boards of Accountancy (NASBA) and NASBA adds the candidate to its database. With a national database, NASBA is able to ensure that no candidate can sit for the same exam section more than once during a single exam window. NASBA then sends Prometric a notice to schedule (NTS). (The exam is given at test centers operated by Prometric.) When you receive your NTS (from whom you receive your NTS varies by jurisdiction), you can make your appointment to sit for the exam with Prometric.

Candidates may select any available date during the open window. If taking the exam on a particular day is important to you, it is advisable to schedule it at least 45 days in advance. **No appointment can be made fewer than 5 days (10 days, if you have been approved for special testing accommodations) in advance of a desired test date**. Your NTS will have an expiration date which is set by your board. After the expiration date, you must reapply and pay the fees again.

If any medical conditions exist or other special testing accommodations are needed, candidates must supply their information to their board or its exam administrator during the application process in order to obtain their approval so the information can be included on their NTS. Ordinarily, candidates may not bring anything into the exam room—including prescription medications.

See the ***Uniform CPA Examination Candidate Bulletin: Information for Applicants*** for more information. To download a copy, visit the AICPA's exam Web site (www.cpa-exam.org) or NASBA's (www.nasba.org).

APPENDIX C
WRITING SKILLS

CONTENTS

INTRODUCTION

Before skipping this appendix, review at least the following writing samples and the "Writing an Answer to an Exam Question" starting on page C-5. Be sure to take the Diagnostic Quiz on C-8.

An assessment of written communication skills is incorporated into simulations. The written communication elements require candidates to write memoranda, letters to clients, or other communications an entry-level CPA would write on the job. Simulations with written communication elements currently are presented in the Financial Accounting & Reporting, Auditing & Attestation, and Regulation exam sections, but not the Business Environment & Concepts (BEC) exam section. The examiners have yet to announce an implementation date for the current plan to have communication elements in the BEC exam section only.

For this element, candidates read a description of a situation and then write an appropriate document relating to it. The instructions will state in what form the document should be presented and its focus. The candidate's response should provide the correct information in writing that is clear, complete, and professional. Only those writing samples that are in your own words and responsive to the topic will be graded. Credit will not be given for a response that is off-topic or offers advice that clearly is incorrect.

Constructed responses will be scored holistically. Scores will be based on three general writing criteria: organization, development, and expression.

1. **Organization:** The document's structure, ordering of ideas, and linking of one idea to another:

> Overview/thesis statement
> Unified paragraphs (topic and supporting sentences)
> Transitions and connectives

2. **Development:** The document's supporting evidence/information to clarify thoughts:

> Details
> Definitions
> Examples
> Rephrasing

3. **Expression:** The document's use of conventional standards of business English:

> Grammar (sentence construction, subject/verb agreement, pronouns, modifiers)
> Punctuation (final, comma)
> Word usage (incorrect, imprecise language)
> Capitalization
> Spelling

WRITING SKILLS SAMPLES

The following questions taken from past exams are answered in various ways to illustrate good, fair, and poor writing skills.

Essex Company has a compensation plan for future vacations for its employees. What conditions must be met for Essex to accrue compensation for future vacations?   FAR Problem—From Chapter 7—Liabilities

Good: Essex must accrue compensation for future vacations if all of the following criteria are met. Essex's obligation relating to employees' rights to receive compensation for future vacations is attributable to employees' services already rendered. The obligation relates to rights that vest or accumulate. Payment of the vacation benefits is probable. The amount can be reasonably estimated.

Explanation: This essay is coherent, concise, and well organized. The first sentence uses the wording of the question to introduce the elements of the answer. Each point is then made clearly and concisely. There are no unnecessary words or elements. The language and vocabulary are appropriate, and there are no mistakes in grammar or spelling.

Fair: In order for Essex to accrue compensation for future vacations, they must attribute their obligation to employees services already rendered, recognize that the obligation relates to vested and accumulated rights, and that payment is probable and the amount can be reasonably estimated.

Explanation: This passage is also coherent and concise; however, it lacks the clarity and detail of the previous answer. The language is appropriate, but the grammatical construction is somewhat weak.

Poor: It is based on accrual. The employees must have vested or accumulated rights. They must be able to estimate amounts of compensation and their payment. Vested rights means that the employer must pay the employees even if he is fired or quits.

Explanation: This answer is so poorly worded and disorganized as to be virtually incoherent. There are also some grammar mistakes. The final sentence is additional information but not necessary to answer the question.

PARAGRAPHS

The kind of writing you do for the CPA exam is called **expository writing** (writing in which something is explained in straightforward terms). Expository writing uses the basic techniques we will be discussing here. Other kinds of writing (i.e., narration, description, argument, and persuasion) will sometimes require different techniques.

Consider a paragraph as a division that consists of one or more sentences, deals with one point, and begins on a new, indented line. Paragraphs provide a way to write about a subject one point or one thought at a time.

Usually, a paragraph begins with a **topic sentence.** The topic sentence communicates the main idea of the paragraph, and the remainder of the paragraph explains or illuminates that central idea. The paragraph sometimes finishes with a restatement of the topic sentence. This strategy is easily read by the exam graders.

Often the topic sentence of the first paragraph is the central idea of the entire composition. Each succeeding paragraph then breaks down this idea into subtopics with each of the new topic sentences being the central thought of that subtopic.

Let's take a look at a simple paragraph to see how it's put together.

> The deductibility of home mortgage interest has been under recent review by Congress as a way to raise revenue. There have been two major reasons for this scrutiny. First, now that consumer interest is nondeductible and investment interest is limited to net investment income, taxpayers have been motivated to rearrange their finances to maximize their tax deductions. Second, most voters do not own

homes costing more than $500,000 and, therefore, putting a cap on mortgage loans does not affect the mass of voters. Given the pressure to raise revenue, two major changes have occurred in this area.

The first sentence of the example is the **topic sentence.** The second sentence introduces the supporting examples which appear in the next two sentences beginning with *first* and *second.* The final sentence of the paragraph acts as a preview to the contents of the next paragraph.

Now, let's examine the makeup of a single paragraph answer to a written communication question from a previous CPA Exam.

Question: Dunhill fraudulently obtained a negotiable promissory note from Beeler by misrepresentation of a material fact. Dunhill subsequently negotiated the note to Gordon, a holder in due course. Pine, a business associate of Dunhill, was aware of the fraud perpetrated by Dunhill. Pine purchased the note for value from Gordon. Upon presentment, Beeler has defaulted on the note.

Required: Answer the following, setting forth reasons for any conclusions stated.

1. What are the rights of Pine against Beeler?
2. What are the rights of Pine against Dunhill?

Examples of possible answers:

1. The rights of Pine against Beeler arise from Pine's having acquired the note from Gordon, who was a holder in due course. Pine himself is not a holder in due course because he had knowledge of a defense against the note. The rule wherein a transferee, not a holder in due course, acquires the rights of one by taking from a holder in due course is known as the "shelter rule." Through these rights, Pine is entitled to recover the proceeds of the note from Beeler. The defense of fraud in the inducement is a personal defense and not valid against a holder in due course.

The first sentence of the paragraph is the topic sentence in which the basic answer to the question is given. The third and fourth sentence explains the rule governing Pine's rights. (The *shelter rule* would be considered a *key phrase* in this answer.) The final sentence of the paragraph is not really necessary to answer the question but was added as an explanation of what some might mistakenly believe to be the key to the answer.

2. As one with the rights of a holder in due course, Pine is entitled to proceed against any person whose signature appears on the note, provided he gives notice of dishonor. When Dunhill negotiated the note to Gordon, Dunhill's signature on the note made him secondarily liable. As a result, if Pine brings suit against Dunhill, Pine will prevail because of Dunhill's secondary liability.

The first sentence of this paragraph restates the fact that Pine has the rights of a holder in due course and what these rights mean. The second sentence explains what happened when Dunhill negotiated the note, and the third sentence states the probable outcome of these results.

Note that in both answers 1. and 2., the sentences hang together in a logical fashion and lead the reader easily from one thought to the next. This is called coherence, a primary factor in considerations of conciseness and clarity.

Transitions

To demonstrate how to use **transitions** in a paragraph to carry the reader easily from one thought or example to another, let's consider a slightly longer and more detailed paragraph. The transitions are indicated in italics.

A concerted effort to reduce book income in response to AMT could have a significant impact on corporations. *For example,* the auditor-client relationship may change. *Currently,* it isn't unusual for corporate management to argue for higher rather than lower book earnings, *while* the auditor would argue for conservative reported numbers. Such a corporate reporting posture may change as a consequence of the BURP adjustment. *Furthermore,* stock market analysts often rely on a price/earnings ratio. Lower earnings for essentially the same level of activity may have a significant effect on security prices.

The first sentence of the paragraph is the topic sentence. The next sentence, beginning with the transition *for example,* introduces the example with a broad statement. The following sentence, beginning with *currently,* gives a specific example to support the basic premise. The sentence beginning *furthermore* leads us into a final example. Without these transitions, the paragraph would be choppy and lack coherence.

What follows is a list of some transitions divided by usage. We suggest you commit some of these to memory so that you will never be at a loss as to how to tie your ideas together.

Transitional Words & Phrases

One idea plus one idea:

again	equally important	in addition	likewise	similarly
also	finally	in the same fashion	moreover	third
and	first	in the same respect	next	thirdly
and then	further	last	second	too
besides	furthermore	lastly	secondly	

To show time or place:

after a time	at that time	immediately	presently	thereafter
after a while	at the same time	in due time	second	thereupon
afterwards	before	in the meantime	shortly	to the left
as long as	earlier	lately	since	until
as soon as	eventually	later	soon	when
at last	finally	meanwhile	temporarily	while
at length	first	next	then	
	further	of late		

To contrast or qualify:

after all	at the same time	however	nevertheless	on the other hand
although true	but	in any case	nonetheless	otherwise
and yet	despite this fact	in contrast	notwithstanding	still
anyway	for all that	in spite of	on the contrary	yet

To introduce an illustration

for example	in particular	incidentally	specifically	to illustrate
for instance	in other words	indeed	that is	
in fact	in summary	namely	thus	

To indicate concession

after all	I admit
although this may be	naturally
at the same time	of course
even though	

To indicate comparison:

in a likewise manner
likewise
similarly

WRITING AN ANSWER TO AN EXAM QUESTION

Now that we have examined the makeup of an answer to an exam question, let's take another question from a past CPA Exam and see how to go about writing a clear, comprehensive answer, step by step, sentence by sentence. A question similar to the one that follows would very likely be one the examiners would choose to grade writing skills.

Question:

Bar Manufacturing and Cole Enterprises were arch rivals in the high technology industry, and both were feverishly working on a new product that would give the first to develop it a significant competitive advantage. Bar engaged Abel Consultants on April 1, for one year, commencing immediately, at $7,500 a month to aid the company in the development of the new product. The contract was oral and was consummated by a handshake. Cole approached Abel and offered them a $10,000 bonus for signing, $10,000 a month for nine months, and a $40,000 bonus if Cole was the first to successfully market the new product. In this connection, Cole stated that the oral contract Abel made with Bar was unenforceable and that Abel could walk away from it without liability. In addition, Cole made certain misrepresentations regarding the dollar amount of its commitment to the project, the state of its development, and the expertise of its research staff. Abel accepted the offer.

Four months later, Bar successfully introduced the new product. Cole immediately dismissed Abel and has paid nothing beyond the first four $10,000 payments plus the initial bonus. Three lawsuits ensued: Bar sued Cole, Bar sued Abel, and Abel sued Cole.

Required: Answer the following, setting forth reasons for any conclusions stated.

Discuss the various theories on which each of the three lawsuits is based, the defenses that will be asserted, the measure of possible recovery, and the probable outcome of the litigation.

Composing an Answer:

<u>Analyze</u> requirements.

<u>Plan</u> on one paragraph for each lawsuit. Each paragraph will contain four elements: theory, defenses, recovery, and outcome.

Paragraph one:

Step 1: Begin with the first lawsuit mentioned, Bar vs. Cole. Write a topic sentence that will sum up the theory of the suit.

    Topic sentence: Bar's lawsuit against Cole will be based upon the intentional tort of wrongful interference with a contractual relationship.

Step 2: Back up this statement with law and facts from the question scenario.

    The primary requirement for this cause of action is a valid contractual relationship with which the defendant knowingly interferes. This requirement is met in the case of Cole.

Step 3: State defenses.

    The contract is not required to be in writing since it is for exactly one year from the time of its making. It is, therefore, valid even though oral.

Step 4: Introduce subject of recovery (damages).

    Cole's knowledge of the contract is obvious.

Step 5: Explain possible problems to recovery.

The principal problem, however, is damages. Since Bar was the first to market the product successfully, it would seem that damages are not present. It is possible there were actual damages incurred by Bar (for example, it hired another consulting firm at an increased price).

Step 6: Discuss possible outcome.

It also might be possible that some courts would permit the recovery of punitive damages since this is an intentional tort.

Paragraph one completed:

Bar's lawsuit against Cole will be based upon the intentional tort of wrongful interference with a contractual relationship. The primary requirement for this cause of action is a valid contractual relationship with which the defendant knowingly interferes. The requirement is met in the case of Cole. The contract is not required to be in writing since it is for exactly one year from the time of its making. It is, therefore, valid even though oral. Cole's knowledge of the contract is obvious. The principal problem, however, is damages. Since Bar was the first to market the product successfully, it would seem that damages are not present. It is possible there were actual damages incurred by Bar (for example, it hired another consulting firm at an increased price). It also might be possible that some courts would permit the recovery of punitive damages since this is an intentional tort.

Paragraph two:

Step 1: Discuss second lawsuit mentioned, Bar vs. Abel. Write a topic sentence that will sum up the theory of the suit.

Topic sentence: Bar's cause of action against Abel would be for breach of contract.

Step 2: State defenses. [Same as for first paragraph; this could be left out.]

The contract is not required to be in writing since it is for exactly one year from the time of its making. It is, therefore, valid even though oral.

Step 3: Introduce subject of recovery (damages).

Once again, [*indicating similarity and tying second paragraph to first*] damages would seem to be a serious problem.

Step 4: Explain possible problems to recovery.

Furthermore, punitive damages rarely would be available in a contract action. Finally, Bar cannot recover the same damages twice.

Step 5: Discuss possible outcome.

Hence, if it proceeds against Cole and recovers damages caused by Abel's breach of contract, it will not be able to recover a second time.

Paragraph two completed:

Bar's cause of action against Abel would be for breach of contract. [The contract is not required to be in writing since it is for exactly one year from the time of its making. It is, therefore, valid even though oral.] Once again, damages would seem to be a serious problem. Furthermore, punitive damages rarely would be available in a contract action. Finally, Bar cannot recover the same damages twice. Hence, if it proceeds against Cole and recovers damages caused by Abel's breach of contract, it will not be able to recover a second time.

Paragraph three:

Step 1: Discuss third lawsuit mentioned, Abel vs. Cole. Write a topic sentence that will sum up the theory of the suit.

Topic sentence: Abel's lawsuit against Cole will be based upon fraud and breach of contract.

Step 2: State defenses.

There were fraudulent statements made by Cole with the requisite intent and that were possibly to Abel's detriment. The breach of contract by Cole is obvious.

Step 3: Back up these statements with law and facts from the question scenario.

However, the contract that Cole induced Abel to enter into and which it subsequently breached was an illegal contract, that is, one calling for the commission of a tort.

Step 4: Explain possible problems to recovery and possible outcome.

Therefore, both parties are likely to be treated as wrongdoers, and Abel will be denied recovery.

Paragraph three completed:

Abel's lawsuit against Cole will be based upon fraud and breach of contract. There were fraudulent statements made by Cole with the requisite intent and that were possibly to Abel's detriment. The breach of contract by Cole is obvious. However, the contract that Cole induced Abel to enter into and which it subsequently breached was an illegal contract, that is, one calling for the commission of a tort. Therefore, both parties are likely to be treated as wrongdoers, and Abel will be denied recovery.

Paragraph Editing:

After you have written your response, review your work to check for the six characteristics that the AICPA will be looking for; coherent organization, conciseness, clarity, use of standard English, responsiveness to the requirements of the question, and appropriateness to the reader.

DIAGNOSTIC QUIZ

The following quiz is designed to test your knowledge of standard English. The correct answers follow the quiz, along with references to the sections that cover that particular area. By identifying the sections that are troublesome for you, you will be able to assess your weaknesses and concentrate on reviewing these areas. If you simply made a lucky guess, you'd better do a review anyway.

Circle the correct choice in the brackets for items 1 through 17.

1. The company can assert any defenses against third party beneficiaries that [they have/it has] against the promisee.

2. Among those securities [which/that] are exempt from registration under the 1933 Act [are/is] a class of stock given in exchange for another class by the issuer to its existing stockholders without the [issuer's/issuer] paying a commission.

3. This type of promise will not bind the promisor [as/because/since] there is no mutuality of obligation.

4. Under the cost method, treasury stock is presented on the balance sheet as an unallocated reduction of total [stockholders'/stockholders/stockholder's] equity.

5. Jones wished that he [was/were] not bound by the offer he made Smith, while Smith celebrated [his/him] having accepted the offer.

6. [Non-cash/Noncash] investing and financing transactions are not reported in the statement of cash flows because the statement reports only the [affects/effects] of operating, investing, and financing activities that directly [affect/effect] cash flows.

7. Since [its/it's] impossible to predict the future and because prospective financial statements can be [effected/affected] by numerous factors, the accountant must use [judgment/judgement] to estimate when and how conditions are [likely/liable] to change.

8. A common format of bank reconciliation statements [is/are] to reconcile both book and bank balances to a common amount known as the "true balance."

9. Corporations, clubs, churches, and other entities may be beneficiaries so long as they are sufficiently identifiable to permit a determination of [who/whom] is empowered to enforce the terms of the trust.

10. None of the beneficiaries [was/were] specifically referred to in the will.

11. Either Dr. Kline or Dr. Monroe [have/has] been elected to the board of directors.

12. The letter should be signed by Bill and [me/myself].

13. Any trust [which/that] is created for an illegal purpose is invalid.

14. When the nature of relevant information is such that it cannot appear in the accounts, this [principal/principle] dictates that such relevant information be included in the accompanying notes to the financial statements. Financial reporting is the [principal/principle] means of communicating financial information to those outside an entity.

15. The inheritance was divided [between/among] several beneficiaries.

16. Termination of an offer ends the offeree's power to [accept/except] it.

17. The consideration given by the participating creditors is [their/there] mutual promises to [accept/except] less than the full amount of [their/there] claims. Because [their/there] must be such mutual promises [between/among] all the participating creditors, a composition or extension agreement requires the participation of at least two or more creditors.

Follow instructions for items 18 through 20.

18. The duties assigned to the interns were to accompany the seniors on field work assignments and the organization and filing of the work papers.

   Fix this sentence so that it will read more smoothly. _____

   _____

   _____

19. Circle the correct spelling of the following pairs of words.

   liaison laison   privilege priviledge   paralleled paraleled

   achieve acheive   occasion occassion   accommodate accomodate

20. Each set of brackets in the following example represents a possible location for punctuation. If you believe a location needs no punctuation, leave it blank; if you think a location needs punctuation, enter a comma, a colon, or a semicolon.

   If the promises supply the consideration [ ] there must be a mutuality of obligation [ ] in other words [ ] both parties must be bound.

ANSWERS TO DIAGNOSTIC QUIZ

Each answer includes a reference to the section that covers what you need to review.

1.	it has	Pronouns—Antecedents, p. C-27.
2.	that; is; issuer's	Subordinating Conjunctions, p. C-30; Verbs—Agreement, p. C-23; Nouns—Gerunds, p. C-26.
3.	because	Subordinating Conjunctions, p. C-30.
4.	stockholders'	Possessive Nouns, p. C-25.
5.	were; his	Verbs, Mood, p. C-22; Nouns—Gerunds, p. C-26.
6.	Noncash; effects; affect	Hyphen, p. C-20; Syntax: Troublesome Words, p. C-13.
7.	it's; affected; judgment, likely	Syntax: Troublesome Words, p. C-13; Spelling: Troublesome Words, p. C-22; Diction: List of Words, p. C-11.
8.	is	Verbs—Agreement, p. C-23.
9.	who	Pronouns, Who/Whom, p. C-26.
10.	were	Verbs—Agreement with Each/None, p. C-24.
11.	has	Verbs—Agreement, p. C-23.
12.	me	Pronouns, that follow prepositions, p. C-27.
13.	that	Subordinating Conjunctions, p. C-30.
14.	principle; principal	Syntax: Troublesome Words, p. C-12.
15.	among	Diction: List of Words, p. C-10.
16.	accept	Syntax: Troublesome Words, C-12

17. their; accept; their; there; among;   Syntax: Troublesome Words, p. C-12; Diction: List of Words, p. C-10.

18. Two possible answers: Parallelism: p. C-15.

The duties assigned to the interns were *accompanying* the seniors on field work assignments and *organizing* and filing the work papers.
or
The duties assigned to the interns were to accompany the seniors on field work assignments and *to organize* and *file* the work papers.

19. In every case, the **first choice** is the correct spelling.
Refer to Spelling: Troublesome Words, p. C-21.

20. If the promises supply the consideration [,] there must be a mutuality of obligation [;] in other words [,] both parties must be bound.   Refer to Punctuation, p. C-16.

Scoring

Count one point for each item (some numbers contain more than one item) and one point for question number 18 if your sentence came close to the parallelism demonstrated by the answer choices. There are a total of 40 points.

If you scored 37-40, you did very well. A brief review of the items you missed should be sufficient to make you feel fairly confident about your grammar skills.

If you scored 33-36, you did fairly well—better than average—but you should do a thorough review of the items you missed.

If you scored 29-32, your score was average. Since "average" will probably not make it on the CPA exam, you might want to consider a thorough grammar review, in addition to the items you missed.

If you scored below average (28 or less), you **definitely** should make grammar review a high priority when budgeting your exam study time. You should consider using resources beyond those provided here.

SENTENCE STRUCTURE

A sentence is a statement or question, consisting of a subject and a predicate. A subject, at a minimum is a noun, usually accompanied by one or more modifiers (for example, "The Trial Balance"). A predicate consists, at a minimum, of a verb. Cultivate the habit of a quick verification for a subject, predicate, capitalized first word, and ending punctuation in each sentence of an essay. A study of sentence structure is essentially a study of grammar but also moves just beyond grammar to diction, syntax, and parallelism. As we discuss how sentences are structured, there will naturally be some overlapping with grammar.

DICTION

Diction is appropriate word choice. There is no substitute for a diversified vocabulary. If you have a diversified vocabulary or "a way with words," you are already a step ahead. A good general vocabulary, as well as a good accounting vocabulary, is a prerequisite of the CPA exam. Develop your vocabulary as you review for the Exam.

An important aspect of choosing the right words is knowing the audience for whom you are choosing those "perfect words." A perfect word for accountants is not necessarily the perfect word for mechanics or lawyers or English professors. If a CPA exam question asks you to write a specific document for a reader other than another accountant or CPA, you need to be very specific but less technical than you would be otherwise.

Accounting, auditing, and related areas have a certain diction and syntax peculiar unto themselves. Promulgations, for instance, are written very carefully so as to avoid possible misinterpretations or misunderstandings. Of course, you are not expected to write like this—for the CPA exam or in other situations. Find the best word possible to explain clearly and concisely what it is you are trying to say. Often the "right word" is simply just not the "wrong word," so be certain you know the exact meaning of a word before you use it. As an accountant writing for accountants, what is most important is knowing the technical terms and the "key words" and placing them in your sentences properly and effectively. Defining or explaining key words demonstrates to graders that you understand the words you are using and not merely parroting the jargon.

The following is a list of words that frequently either are mistaken for one another or incorrectly assumed to be more or less synonymous.

Among—preposition, refers to more than two
Between—preposition, refers to two; is used for three or more if the items are considered severally and individually

If only part of the seller's capacity to perform is affected, the seller must allocate deliveries *among* the customers, and he or she must give each one reasonable notice of the quota available to him or her.
Between merchants, the additional terms become part of the contract unless one of the following applies. (This sentence is correct whether there are two merchants or many merchants.)

Amount—noun, an aggregate; total number or quantity
Number—noun, a sum of units; a countable number
Quantity—noun, an indefinite amount or number

The checks must be charged to the account in the order of lowest *amount* to highest *amount* to minimize the *number* of dishonored checks.
The contract is not enforceable under this paragraph beyond the *quantity* of goods shown in such writing.

Allude—verb, to state indirectly
Refer—verb, to state clearly and directly

She *alluded* to the fact that the company's management was unscrupulous.
She *referred* to his poor management in her report.

Bimonthly—adjective or adverb; every two months
Semimonthly—adjective or adverb; twice a month

Our company has *bimonthly* meetings.
We get paid *semimonthly*.

Continual—adjective, that which is repeatedly renewed after each interruption or intermission
Continuous—adjective, that which is uninterrupted in time, space, or sequence

The *continuous* ramblings of the managing partner caused the other partners to *continually* check the time.

Cost—noun, the amount paid for an item
Price—noun, the amount set for an item
Value—noun, the relative worth, utility, or importance of an item
Worth—noun, value of an item measured by its qualities or by the esteem in which it is held

The *cost* of that stock is too much.
The *price* of that stock is $100 a share.
I place no *value* on that stock.
That stock's *worth* is overestimated.

Decide—verb, to arrive at a solution
Conclude—verb, to reach a final determination; to exercise judgment

> Barbara *decided* to listen to what the accountant was saying; she then *concluded* that what he was saying was true.

Fewer—adjective, not as many; consisting or amounting to a smaller number (used of numbers; comparative of few)
Less—adjective, lower rank, degree, or importance; a more limited amount (used of quantity—for the most part)

> My clients require *fewer* consultations than yours do.
> My clients are *less* demanding than yours are.

Good—adjective, of a favorable character or tendency; noun, something that is good
Well—adverb, good or proper manner; satisfactorily with respect to conduct or action; adjective, being in satisfactory condition or circumstances

> It was *good* [adjective] of you to help me study for the CPA exam.
> The decision was for the *good* [noun] of the firm.
> He performed that task *well* [adverb].
> His work was *well* [adjective] respected by the other accountants.

Imply—verb, to suggest
Infer—verb, to assume; deduce

> Her report seems to *imply* that my work was not up to par.
> From reading her report, the manager *inferred* that my work was not up to par.

Oral—adjective, by the mouth, spoken; not written
Verbal—adjective, relating to or consisting of words
Vocal—adjective, uttered by the voice, spoken; persistence and volume of speech

> Hawkins, Inc. made an *oral* agreement to the contract.
> One partner gave his *verbal* consent while the other partner was very *vocal* with his objections.

State—verb, to set forth in detail; completely
Assert—verb, to claim positively, sometimes aggressively or controversially
Affirm—verb, to validate, confirm, state positively

> The attorney *stated* the facts of the case.
> The plaintiff asserted that his rights had been violated.
> The judge *affirmed* the jury's decision.

SYNTAX

Syntax is the order of words in a sentence. Errors in syntax occur in a number of ways; the number one way is through hasty composition. The only way to catch errors in word order is to read each of your sentences carefully to make sure that the words you meant to write or type are the words that actually appear on the page and that those words are in the best possible order. The following list should help you avoid errors in both diction and syntax and gives examples where necessary.

Troublesome Words

Accept—verb, to receive or to agree to willingly
Except—verb, to take out or leave out from a number or a whole; conjunction, on any other condition but that condition

> *Except* for the items we have mentioned, we will *accept* the conditions of the contract.

Advice—noun, information or recommendation
Advise—verb, to recommend, give advice

> The *accountant advised* us to take his *advice*.

Affect—verb, to influence or change (**Note:** affect is occasionally used as a noun in technical writing only.)
Effect—noun, result or cause; verb, to cause

> The effect [noun] of Ward, Inc.'s decision to cease operations affected many people.
> He quickly *effected* [verb] policy changes for office procedures.

All Ready—adjectival phrase, completely prepared
Already—adverb, before now; previously

> Although the tax return was *all ready* to be filed, the deadline had *already* passed.

All Right; Alright—adjective or adverb, beyond doubt; very well; satisfactory; agreeable, pleasing. (Although many grammarians insist that **alright** is not a proper form, it is widely accepted.)

Appraise—verb, set a value on
Apprise—verb, inform

> Dane Corp. *apprised* him of the equipment's age, so that he could *appraise* it more accurately.

Assure—verb, to give confidence to positively
Ensure—verb, to make sure, certain, or safe
Insure—verb, to obtain or provide insurance on or for; to make certain by taking necessary measures and precautions

> The accountant assured his client that he would file his return in a timely manner.
> He added the figures more than once to *ensure* their accuracy.
> She was advised to *insure* her diamond property.

Decedent—noun, a deceased person
Descendant—noun, proceeding from an ancestor or source

> The decedent left her vast fortune to her *descendants*.

Eminent—adjective, to stand out; important
Imminent—adjective, impending

> Although he was an *eminent* businessman, foreclosure on his house was *imminent.*

Its—possessive
It's—contraction, **it is**

> The company held *its* board of directors meeting on Saturday. *It's* the second meeting this month.

Lay—verb, to place or set
Lie—verb, to recline

> > He *lies* down to rest.
> > He *lays* down the book.

Percent—used with numbers only
Percentage—used with words or phrases

> > Each employee received 2 *percent* of the profits.
> > They all agreed this was a small *percentage.*

Precedence—noun, the fact of preceding in time, priority of importance
Precedent—noun, established authority; adjective, prior in time, order, or significance

> The board of directors meeting took *precedence* over his going away.
> The president set a *precedent* when making that decision.

Principal—noun, a capital sum placed at interest; a leading figure; the corpus of an estate; adjective, first, most important
Principle—noun, a basic truth or rule

> Paying interest on the loan's *principal* [noun] was explained to the company's *principals* [noun].
> The principal [adjective] part of…
> She refused to compromise her *principles.*

Than—conjunction, function word to indicate difference in kind, manner, or identity; preposition, in comparison with (indicates comparison)
Then—adverb, at that time; soon after that (indicates time)

> BFE Corp. has more shareholders *than* Hills Corp.
> First, we must write the report, and *then* we will meet with the clients.

Their—adjective, of or relating to them or themselves
There—adverb, in or at that place

> *There* were fifty shareholders at the meeting to cast *their* votes.

Modifier Placement

Pay close attention to where modifiers are placed, especially adverbs such as **only** and **even.** In speech, inflection aids meaning but, in writing, placing modifiers improperly can be confusing and often changes the meaning. The modifier should usually be placed before the word(s) it modifies.

> She *almost* finished the whole report.
> She finished *almost* the whole report.
>
> *Only* she finished the report.
> She *only* finished the report.
> She finished *only* the report.

Phrases also must be placed properly, usually, but not always, following the word or phrase they modify. Often, **reading the sentence aloud** will help you decide where the modifier belongs.

> Fleming introduced a client to John with a counter-offer. (*With a counter-offer* modifies *client,* not *John,* and should be placed after *client.)*
> The accountant recommended a bankruptcy petition to the client under Chapter 7. (*Under Chapter 7* modifies *bankruptcy petition,* not *the client,* and should be placed after *bankruptcy petition.)*

Split Infinitives

Infinitives are the root verb form (e.g., to be, to consider, to walk). Generally speaking, infinitives should not be split except when to do so makes the meaning clearer.

> Awkward: Management's responsibility is to clearly represent its financial position.
> Better: Management's responsibility is to represent its financial position clearly.
>
> Exception: Management's responsibility in the future is to better represent its financial position.

Sentence Fragments

To avoid sentence fragments, read over your work carefully. Each sentence needs at least (1) a subject and (2) a predicate.

> Unlike the case of a forged endorsement, a drawee bank charged with the recognition of its drawer-customer's signature. (The verb *is*, before the word *charged,* has been left out.)

PARALLELISM

Parallelism refers to a similarity in structure and meaning of all parts of a sentence or a paragraph. In parallelism, parts of a sentence (or a paragraph) that are parallel in meaning are also parallel in structure. Sentences that violate rules of parallelism will be difficult to read and may obscure meaning. The following are some examples of different **violations** of parallelism.

(1)   A security interest can be effected through a financing statement or the creditor's taking possession of it. (The two prepositional phrases separated by **or** should be parallel.)

Corrected: A security interest can be effected through a financing statement or through possession by the creditor.

(2)   The independent auditor should consider whether the scope is appropriate, adequate audit programs and working papers, appropriate conclusions, and reports prepared are consistent with results of the work performed. (The clause beginning with **whether** (which acts as the direct object of the verb **should consider**) is faulty. The items mentioned must be similarly constructed to each other.)

Corrected: The independent auditor should consider whether the scope is appropriate, audit programs and working papers are adequate, conclusions are appropriate, and reports prepared are consistent with results of the work performed.

(3)   The CPA was responsible for performing the inquiry and analytical procedures and that the review report was completed in a timely manner. (The prepositional phrase beginning with **for** is faulty.)

Corrected: The CPA was responsible for performing the inquiry and analytical procedures and ensuring that the review report was completed in a timely manner.

(4)   Procedures that should be applied in examining the stock accounts are as follows:

(1)   Review the corporate charter…
(2)   Obtain or preparing an analysis of…
(3)   Determination of authorization for… (All items in a list must be in parallel structure.)

Corrected:

1.   Review the corporate charter…
2.   Obtain or prepare an analysis of…
3.   Determine the authorization for…

There are many other types of faulty constructions that can creep into sentences—too many to detail here. Furthermore, if any of the above is not clear, syntax may be a problem for you and you might want to consider a more thorough review of this subject.

NUMBERS

1.   The basic rule for writing numbers is to write out the numbers ten and under and use numerals for all the others. More formal writing may dictate writing out all round numbers and numbers under 101. Let style, context of the sentence and of the work, and common sense be your guide.

The partnership was formed 18 years ago.
Jim Bryant joined the firm four years ago.
Baker purchased 200 shares of stock.

2.   When there are two numbers next to each other, alternate the styles.

three 4-year certificates of deposit   5 two-party instruments

3.   Never begin a sentence with numerals, such as:

1989 was the last year that Zinc Co. filed a tax return.

This example can be corrected as follows:

Nineteen hundred and eighty-nine was the last year that Zinc Co. filed a tax return. (For use only in very formal writing)
or
Zinc Co. has not filed a tax return since 1989.

CAPITALIZATION

This section mentions only areas that seem to cause particular difficulties.

1.   The first word **after a colon** is capped only when it is the beginning of a complete sentence.

We discussed several possibilities at the meeting: Among them were liquidation, reorganization, and rehabilitation.
We discussed several possibilities at the meeting: liquidation, reorganization, and rehabilitation.

2.   The capitalization of titles and headings is especially tricky. In general, the first word and all other important words, no matter what length they are, should be capped. Beyond this general rule, there are several variations relating to the capitalization of pronouns. The important thing here is to pick a style and use it consistently within a single document, article, etc.

For example, the following pair of headings would both be acceptable depending on the style and consistency of style:

Issues for Property other than Cash   **or**   Issues For Property Other Than Cash

PUNCTUATION

PERIOD

Probably the two most common errors involving periods occur when incorporating quotation marks and/or parentheses with periods.

1.   When a period is used with closing quotation marks, the period is always placed **inside,** regardless of whether the entire sentence is a quote or only the end of the sentence.

2.   When a period is used with parentheses, the period goes **inside** the closing parenthesis if the entire sentence is enclosed in parentheses. When only the last word or words is enclosed in parentheses, the period goes **outside** the closing parenthesis.

(See Chapter 34, Contracts.)
The answer to that question is in the section on contracts (Chapter 34).

EXCLAMATION POINT

An exclamation point is used for emphasis and when issuing a command. In many cases, this is determined by the author when he or she wants to convey urgency, irony, or stronger emotion than ordinarily would be inferred.

COLON

A colon is used to introduce something in the sentence—a list of related words, phrases, or items directly related to the first part of the sentence; a quotation; a **direct** question; or an example of what was stated in the first part of the sentence. The colon takes the place of **that is** or **such as** and should never be used **with** such phrases.

> The accountant discussed two possibilities with the clients: first, a joint voluntary bankruptcy petition under Chapter 7, and second,…

> The following will be discussed: life insurance proceeds; inheritance; and property.

> My CPA accounting review book states the following: "All leases that do not meet any of the four criteria for capital leases are operating leases."

Colons are used in formal correspondence after the salutation.

> Dear Mr. Bennett:
> To Whom it May Concern:

Note: When **that is** or **such as** is followed by a numeric list, it may be followed by a colon.

> When writing a sentence, if you're not sure whether or not a colon is appropriate, it probably isn't. When in doubt, change the sentence so that you're sure it doesn't need a colon.

SEMICOLON

A semicolon is used in a number of ways:

1. Use a **semicolon in place of a conjunction** when there are two or more closely related thoughts and each is expressed in a coordinate clause (a clause that could stand as a complete sentence).

    > A marketable title is one that is free from plausible or reasonable objections; it need not be perfect.

2. Use a **semicolon** as in the above example **with a conjunction** when the sentence is very long and complex. This promotes **clarity** by making the sentence easier to read.

    > Should the lease be prematurely terminated, the deposit may be retained only to cover the landlord's actual expenses or damages; *and* any excess must be returned to the tenant.

    > An assignment establishes privity of estate between the lessor and assignee; *[and]* therefore, the assignee becomes personally liable for the rent.

3. When there are commas in a series of items, use a **semicolon** to separate the main items.

    > Addison, Inc. has distribution centers in Camden, Maine; Portsmouth, New Hampshire; and Rock Island, Rhode Island.

COMMA

Informal English allows much freedom in the placement or the omission of commas, and the overall trend is away from commas. However, standard, formal English provides rules for its usage. Accounting "language" can be so complex that using commas and using them correctly and appropriately is a necessity to avoid obscurity and promote clarity. Accordingly, we encourage you to learn the basics about comma placement.

What follows is not a complete set of rules for commas but should be everything you need to know about commas to make your sentences clear and concise. Because the primary purpose of the comma is to clarify meaning, it is the opinion of the editors that in the case of a complex subject such as accounting, it is better to overpunctuate than to underpunctuate. If you are concerned about overpunctuation, try to reduce an unwieldy sentence to two or more sentences.

1. Use a comma to **separate a compound sentence** (one with two or more independent coordinate clauses joined by a conjunction).

    Gil Corp. has current assets of $90,000, but the corporation has current liabilities of $180,000. Jim borrowed $60,000, and he used the proceeds to purchase outstanding common shares of stock.

    Note: In these examples, a comma would **not** be necessary if the **and** or the **but** were not followed by a noun or pronoun (the subject of the second clause). In other words, if by removing the conjunction, the sentence could be separated into two complete sentences, it needs a comma.

2. Use a comma after an introductory word or phrase.

    During 1992, Rand Co. purchased $960,000 of inventory.
    On April 1, 1993, Wall's inventory had a fair value of $150,000.

    Note: Writers often choose to omit this comma when the introductory phrase is very short. Again, we recommend using the comma. It will never be incorrect in this position.

3. Use a comma after an introductory adverbial clause.

    Although insurance contracts are not required by the Statute of Frauds to be in writing, most states have enacted statutes that now require such.

4. Use commas to separate items, phrases, or clauses in a series.

    To be negotiable, an instrument must be in writing, signed by the maker or drawer, contain an unconditional promise or order to pay a sum certain in money on demand or at a specific time, and be payable to order or to bearer.

    Note: Modern practice often omits the last comma in the series (in the above example, the one before **and**). Again, for the sake of clarity, we recommend using this comma.

5. In most cases, use a comma or commas to separate **a series of adjectives.**

    Silt Co. kept their inventory in an old, decrepit, brick building.
    He purchased several outstanding shares of common stock. (*No* commas are needed.)

    When in doubt as to whether or not to use a comma after a particular adjective, try inserting the word **and** between the adjectives. If it makes sense, use a comma. (In the second example, above, **several and outstanding,** or **outstanding and several** don't make sense.)
    ---

6. Use a comma or commas to set off any **word or words, phrase, or clause that interrupts the sentence** but does not change its essential meaning.

    SLD Industries, as drawer of the instrument, is only secondarily liable.

7. Use commas to set off **geographical names** and **dates.**

    Feeney Co. moved its headquarters to Miami, Florida, on August 16, 1992.

QUOTATION MARKS

Quotation marks are used with **direct quotations; direct discourse and direct questions;** and **definitions or explanations of words.** Other uses of quotation marks are used rarely in the accounting profession and, therefore, are not discussed in this review.

HYPHEN

1. Use a hyphen to separate words into syllables. It is best to check a dictionary, because some words do not split where you might imagine.

2. Modern practice does not normally hyphenate prefixes and their root words, even when both the prefix and the root word begin with vowels. A common exception is when the root word begins with a capital letter or a date or number.

prenuptial	nonexempt	semiannual
pre-1987	nonnegotiable	non-American

3. Although modern practice is moving away from using hyphens for **compound adjectives** (a noun and an adjective in combination to make a single adjective), clarity dictates that hyphens still be used in many cases.

long-term investments	two-party instrument
a noninterest-bearing note	short-term capital losses

4. Use a hyphen **only** when the compound adjective or compound adjective-adverb **precedes the noun.**

    The well-known company is going bankrupt.
    The company is well known for its quality products.

Note: There are certain word combinations that are always hyphenated, always one word, or always two words. Use the dictionary.

5. **Suspended hyphens** are used to avoid repetition in compound adjectives. For example, instead of having to write **himself or herself,** especially when these forms are being used repeatedly as they often must be in our newly nongender-biased world, use **him- or herself.**

10-, 15-, and 18-year depreciation	first-, second-, and third-class

SPELLING

Just as many of us believe that arithmetic can be done always by our calculators, we also believe that spelling will be done by our word processors and, therefore, we needn't worry too much about it. There is no doubt that these devices are tremendous boons. However, sometimes a spell-checker cannot tell the difference between words that you have misspelled which are nonetheless real words, such as **there** and **their.** (See the list in this section of words often confused.)

Let's hit some highlights here of troublesome spellings with some brief tips that should help you become a better speller.

1. **IE** or **EI**? If you are still confused by words containing the **ie** or **ei** combinations, you'd better relearn those old rhymes we ridiculed in grade school.

    "**i** before **e** except after **c.**" (This works only for words where the ie-ei combination sounds like **ee.**)

ach**ie**ve	bel**ie**ve	ch**ie**f
ceiling	rece**i**ve	rece**i**pt

Of course there are always **exceptions** such as:

| either | neither | seize | financier |

When **ie** or **ei** have a different sound than **ee**, the above rule does not apply. For example:

| friend | sieve | efficient |
| foreign | sovereign | surfeit |

2.   **Doubling final consonants.** When an ending (**suffix**) beginning with a vowel is added to a root word that ends in a single consonant, that final consonant is **usually doubled**.

| lag—lagging | bid—bidding | top—topped |

The exceptions generally fall under three rules.

First, double only after a short vowel and **not** after a double vowel.

| big—bigger | tug—tugging | get—getting |
| need—needing | keep—keeping | pool—pooled |

Second, a **long** vowel (one that "says its own name"), which is almost always followed by a silent **e** that must be dropped to add the suffix, is **not** doubled.

| hope—hoping | tape—taped | rule—ruled |

Note: Sometimes, as in the first two examples above, doubling the consonants would create entirely new words.

Third, with root words of two or more syllables ending in a single consonant, double the consonant **only** when the last syllable is the **stressed syllable.**

Double:	be**gin**—beginning, beginner	pre**fer**—preferred, preferring
	re**gret**—**regretted**, regrettable	ad**mit**—admitted, admittance
Don't	pro**hib**it—prohibited, prohibitive	**ben**efit—benefited, benefiting
Double:	de**vel**op—developing	**pref**erence—preferable

3.   **Drop** the silent **e** before adding a suffix **beginning with a vowel.**

| store—storing | take—taking | value—valuing |

Keep the **e** before adding a suffix **beginning with a consonant,** such as:

| move—movement | achieve—achievement |

Again, there are **exceptions**.

| **e:** | mile—mileage | dye—dyeing |

| **No e:** | argue—argument | due—duly | true—truly |

4.   Change **y** to **ie** before adding **s** when it is the single final vowel.

| country—countries | study—studies | quantity—quantities |

Change **y** to **i** before adding other endings **except s.**

| busy—business | dry—drier | copy—copier |

Exceptions: Keep **y** for the following:

copying	studying	trying

Y is also usually preserved when it follows another vowel.

delays	joys	played

Exceptions:

day—daily	lay—laid	pay—paid	say—said

5. **Forming Plurals.** The formation of some plurals does not follow the general rule of adding **s** or **es** to the singular. What follows are some of the more troublesome forms.

   Some singular nouns that end in **o** form their plurals by adding **s**; some by adding **es**.

ratio**s**	zero**s**	hero**es**	potato**es**

   Many nouns taken directly from **foreign languages** retain their original plural. Below are a few of the more common ones.

alumnus—alumni	basis—bases	crisis—crises
criterion—criteria	datum—data	matrix—matrices

   Other nouns taken directly from foreign languages have **two acceptable plural forms:** the foreign language plural and the anglicized plural. Here are some of the more common:

medium—media, mediums	appendix—appendices, appendixes
formula—formulae, formulas	memorandum—memoranda, memorandums

   Finally, in this foreign language category are some commonly used Latin nouns that form their plurals by adding **es**.

census—censuses	consensus—consensuses
hiatus—hiatuses	prospectus—prospectuses

Troublesome Words: Spelling

Spelling errors occur for different reasons; probably the most common reason is confusion with the spelling of similar words. The following is a list of commonly misspelled words. You will find those you may have misspelled in taking the Diagnostic Quiz, and you may recognize others you have problems with. Memorize them. (Note: some of these words may have acceptable alternative spellings; however, the spellings listed below are the preferred form.)

accommodate	bankruptcy	irrelevant	paralleled	skillful
achieve	deferred	judgment	privilege	supersede
acknowledgment	existence	liaison	receivable	surety
balance	fulfill	occasion	resistance	trial

GRAMMAR

This section on grammar is intended to be a brief overview only. Consequently, the authors have chosen to focus on items that seem to cause the most problems. If you did not do well on the Diagnostic Quiz, you would be well advised to go over all the material in this section and consider a more thorough grammar study than provided here.

VERBS

The verb is the driving force of the sentence: it is the word or words to which all other parts of the sentence relate. When trying to analyze a sentence to identify its grammatical parts or its meaning, or when attempting to amend a sentence, you should always identify the verb or verbs first. A verb expresses action or being.

Action: The accountant *visits* his clients regularly.
Being: Kyle *is* an accountant.

Voice

1. The **active voice** indicates that the subject of the sentence (the person or thing) does something. The **passive voice** indicates that the subject is acted upon.

    Active: *The accountant worked* on the client's financial statements.
    Passive: The client's financial statements *were worked on by the accountant.*

2. The most important thing to understand about voice is that it should be consistent; that is, you should avoid shifts from one voice to another, especially within the same sentence as below.

    Taylor Corporation *hired* an independent computer programmer to develop a simplified payroll application for its new computer, and an on-line, data-based microcomputer system *was developed.*

    Use the active voice for the entire sentence:

    Taylor Corporation *hired* an independent computer programmer to develop a simplified payroll application for its new computer, and he *developed* an on-line, data-based microcomputer system.

Mood

1. Common errors in syntax are made when **more than one mood** is used in a single sentence. The first example that follows begins with the **imperative** and shifts to the **indicative.** The second example corrects the sentence by using the imperative in both clauses, and the third example corrects the sentence by using the indicative in both clauses. The fourth example avoids the problem by forming two sentences.

    Pick up (imperative) that work program for me at the printer, and then we will go (indicative) to the client.
    Pick up that work program for me at the printer, and then go to the client with me.
    After you pick up that work program for me at the printer, we will go to the client.
    Pick up that work program for me at the printer. Then we will go to the client.

2. There are three moods: the indicative, the imperative, and the subjunctive. We do not examine the subjunctive. Most sentences are **indicative:**

    The percentage of completion method is justified. Declarative indicative.
    Is the percentage of completion method justified? Interrogative indicative.

3. Sentences that give a command are called **imperative** sentences:

    Pick up your books!
    Be sure to use the correct method of accounting for income taxes.

Tense

1.   Tense is all about *time.* If the proper sequence of tenses is not used, confusion can arise as to what happened when. Consider:

> *Not getting* the raise he was expecting, John was unhappy about the additional work load. [???]
> *Having not gotten* the raise he was expecting, John was unhappy about the additional work load. [Much clearer]

2.   The **present tense** is used to express action or a state of being that is taking place in the present. The present tense is also used to express an action or a state of being that is habitual and when a definite time in the future is stated.

> Dan *is taking* his CPA exam.
> Robin *goes* to the printer once a week.
> The new computer *arrives* on Monday.

3.   The **present perfect tense** is used to indicate action that began in the past and has continued to the present.

> From the time of its founder, the CPA firm *has celebrated* April 16 with a fabulous dinner party.

4.   The **future tense** is used to indicate action that takes place in the indefinite future.

> A plan of reorganization *will determine* the amount and the manner in which the creditors *will be paid*, in what form the business *will continue,* and any other necessary details.

5.   The **future perfect tense** is used to indicate action that has not taken place yet but will take place before a specific future time.

> Before Susan arrives at the client's office, the client *will have prepared* the documents she needs.

6.   The **past tense** is used to indicate an action that took place in the past. The **past tense** is also used to indicate a condition or state occurring at a specific time in the past.

> The predecessor auditor *resigned* last week.
> The company *contacted* its auditor the first of every new year.

7.   The **past perfect tense** is used to indicate an action that is completed before another action that also took place in the past.

> The work load *had been* so heavy that she was required to work overtime. (Not *was*)

Agreement

1.   The first element of agreement to examine is **verb** and **subject.** These two components must agree **in number.** Number is just one of several things to consider when examining the agreement of the components of a sentence.

2.   The subject of the sentence is the noun or pronoun (person, place, or thing) doing the action stated by the verb (in the case of the active voice) or being acted upon by the verb (in the case of the passive voice). Although the subject normally precedes the verb, this is not always the case. Thus, you must be able to identify sentence elements no matter where they happen to fall. This is not a difficult matter, at least most of the time. Consider:

(1)   Lewis, Bradford, Johnson & Co. [is or are] the client with the best pay record.

(2)   For me, one of the most difficult questions on the exam [was or were] concerned with correcting weaknesses in internal controls.

In both examples, the first choice, the singular verb form, is correct. In sentence (1), Lewis, Bradford, Johnson & Co. is considered singular in number because we are talking about the company, not Lewis, Bradford, and Johnson per se. In sentence (2), the verb is also singular because **one** is the subject of the sentence, not **questions. Questions** is the object of the preposition **of.** If this seems confusing, rearrange the sentence so that the prepositional phrase appears first, and the agreement of subject and verb will be clearer. Thus:

Of the most difficult questions, one *was concerned* with correcting weaknesses in internal controls.

We will address special problems associated with prepositional phrases in other sections.

3.   Beware of the word **number.** When it is preceded by the word **the,** it is always singular, and when it is preceded by the word **a,** it is always plural.

The number of listings generated by the new EDP system *was* astounding.
A number of listings *were generated* by the new EDP system.

4.   A **compound subject,** even when made up of nouns singular in number, always takes a plural verb.

The balance sheet, the independent auditor's report, and the quarterly report *are lying* on the desk. (Not *is lying)*

5.   Continuing now with **compound subjects,** let's address the problem of when there are two or more subjects—one (or more) singular and one (or more) plural. When the sentence contains subjects connected by **or** or **nor,** or **not only…but also,** the verb should agree with the subject nearer to the verb.

Either the auditors or the partner *is going* to the client.
Not only the partner but also the auditors *are going* to the client.

In the case of the first example above, which sounds awkward, simply switch the order of the subjects **(the partner; the auditors)** and use the verb **are going** to make it read better.

6.   When one subject is **positive** and one is **negative,** the verb always agrees with the positive.

The partner, and not the auditors, *is going* to the client.
Not the partner but the auditors frequently *go* to the client.

7.   You should use singular verbs with the following: each, every, everyone, everybody, anyone, anybody, either, neither, someone, somebody, no one, nobody, and one.

Anybody who wants to go *is* welcome.
Neither the accountant nor the bookkeeper ever *arrives* on time.
One never *knows* what to expect.

Watch out for the words **each** and **none.** They can trip up even careful writers.

8.   Improper placement of **each** in the sentence will confuse the verb agreement.

The balance sheet, the income statement, and the statement of cash flows each [has/have] several errors.

In this example, we know that the verb must be **has** (to agree with **each**), but then again, maybe it should be **have** to agree with the subjects. The problem is that we have a sentence with a compound subject that must take a plural verb, but here it is connected with a singular pronoun (each). This is a very common error. This particular example may be fixed in one of two ways. First, if the word **each** is not really necessary in the sentence, simply drop it. Second, simply place the word **each** in a better position in the sentence. In the example below, placing the word **each** at the end of the sentence properly connects it to **errors;** also it no longer confuses verb agreement.

The balance sheet, the income statement, and the statement of cash flows *have* several errors *each*.

9. The word **none** has special problems all its own. Not too many years ago, it was the accepted rule that every time **none** was the subject of the sentence, it should take a **singular verb.** Most modern grammarians now agree that the plural may be used when followed by a prepositional phrase with a plural object (noun) or with an object whose meaning in the sentence is plural.

    None of the statements *were* correct.

    When **none** stands alone, some purists believe it should take the singular and others believe that the plural is the proper form when the meaning conveys plurality. Consequently, in the following example, either the singular or plural is generally acceptable.

    All the financial statements had been compiled, but none *was* **or** *were* correct.

When in doubt, use **not one** in place of **none** (with a singular verb, of course).

NOUNS

Nouns are people, places, and things and can occur anywhere in the sentence. Make sure that, when necessary, the nouns are the same in number.

Do the exercises at the end of each chapter by answering the *questions* true or false. (Not singular *question*)
At the end of the engagement, everyone must turn in their *time sheets*. (Not singular *time sheet*)

Possessive Nouns

1. The basic rule for making a **singular noun** possessive is to add an **apostrophe and an s.** If a singular noun ends in s, **add apostrophe and an s.** To make a **plural noun** possessive, add an **apostrophe alone** when the plural ends in **s** or an **apostrophe and an s** when the plural does not end in an **s.**

    | Singular: | client*'s* | system*'s* | beneficiary*'s* | *Chris'* |
    | Plural: | clients*'* | systems*'* | beneficiaries*'* | |

2. A common area of difficulty has to do with **ownership,** that is, when two or more individuals or groups are mentioned as owning something. If the ownership is **not common** to all, apostrophes appear after each individual or group. If the ownership **is common** to all, only the last individual or group in the series takes an apostrophe.

    Not common to all: The accountant's and the attorney's offices…
    Common to all: Robert, his brother, and their sons' company…

Most of the confusion associated with possessives seems to be with the plural possessive. Remember to make the noun **plural** first and **possessive** second.

---

3. Modern usage tends to make possessive forms into adjectives where appropriate. Thus:

    Company's (possessive) management becomes *company* (adjective) management.
    A *two weeks'* (possessive) vacation becomes a *two weeks* or *two-week* (both adjectives) vacation.

In most instances, either the possessive form or the adjectival form is acceptable. Go with the form that seems most appropriate for that particular sentence.

Gerunds

1.   A gerund is a verb changed to a noun by adding **ing.** A noun preceding a gerund must be possessive so that it may be construed as **modifying the noun.**

> *Caroline's telecommuting* was approved by the partner.

In this example, the subject of the sentence is **telecommuting,** not Caroline or Caroline's. Since we know that nouns cannot modify nouns, Caroline must become **Caroline's** to create a possessive form that can modify the noun **telecommuting.**

2.   The same holds true for **gerunds** used as **objects of prepositions:**

> The partner objected to *Caroline's telecommuting.*

In this example, **telecommuting** is the object of the preposition **to.** Caroline's is an appositive (or possessive) form modifying **telecommuting.**

PRONOUNS

Like Latin where most words have "cases" according to their function in the sentence, English **pronouns** also have cases. Sometimes you may be aware that you are using a case when determining the proper form of the pronoun and sometimes you may not.

> *He* met *his* partner at *their* office.

1.   Let's begin by tackling everybody's favorite: **who** and **whom.** We're going to take some time reviewing this one since it seems to be a major area of confusion. There is little or no confusion when **who** is clearly the **subject** of the sentence:

> *Who* is going with us?

And little or no confusion when **whom** is clearly (1) the **object** of the sentence or (2) the **object** of the preposition.

> (1)   Jenny audited *whom*? *Whom* did Jenny audit?

> (2)   Jenny is working for *whom*? For *whom* is Jenny working?

If you are having difficulty with **questions,** try changing them into declarative sentences (statements) and substituting another pronoun. Thus: Jenny audits **them** (objective), obviously not **they** (subjective), or Jenny is working for **her,** obviously not **she.**

---

2.   **Who** or **whoever** is the subjective case, and **whom** or **whomever** is the objective case. Common errors occur frequently in two instances: (1) when **who or whoever** is interrupted by a parenthetical phrase and (2) when an entire clause is the subject of a preposition.

> (1)   *Whoever* she decides is working with her should meet her at six o'clock.

In this example, **she decides** is a parenthetical phrase (one that could be left out of the sentence and the sentence would still be a complete thought). When you disregard **she decides,** you can see that **whoever** is the subject of the sentence, not **she.** The error occurs when **she** is believed to be the subject and **whomever,** the object of **decides.**

> (2)   Jenny will work with *whoever* shows up first.

This example represents what seems the most problematic of all the areas relating to who or whom. We have been taught to use the objective case after the preposition (in this case **with**). So why isn't **whomever** the correct form in this example? The answer is that it would be the correct form if the sentence ended with the word **whomever.** (**Whomever** would be the object of the preposition **with.**) In this case, it is not the last word but, rather, it is the **subject** of the clause **whoever shows up first.**

> Again, make the substitution of another pronoun as a test of whether to use the subjective or objective case.

Let's look at a few more examples. See if you are better able to recognize the correct form.

(1)   I'm sure I will be comfortable with [*whoever/whomever*] the manager decides to assign.

(2)   To [*who/whom*] should she speak regarding that matter?

(3)   He always chooses [*whoever/whomever*] in his opinion is the best auditor.

(4)   She usually enjoys working with [*whoever/whomever*] the partner assigns.

(5)   [*Who/Whom*] should I ask to accompany me?

Let's see how well you did.

(1)   **Whomever** is correct. The whole clause after the preposition **with** is the object of the preposition, and **whomever** is the object of the verb **to assign.** Turn the clause around and substitute another pronoun. Thus, **the manager decides to assign** *him.*

(2)   **Whom** is correct. **Whom** is the object of the preposition **to.** Make the question into a declarative sentence and substitute another pronoun. Thus, **She should speak to** *him* **regarding that matter.**

(3)   **Whoever** is correct. The entire clause **whoever is the best auditor** is the object of the main verb **chooses. Whoever** is the subject of that clause. **In his opinion** is a parenthetical phrase and doesn't affect the rest of the sentence.

(4)   **Whomever** is correct. The entire clause **whomever the partner assigns** is the object of the preposition **with,** and **whomever** is the object of the verb **assigns.** Again, turn the clause around and substitute another pronoun. Thus, **the partner assigns** *him.*

(5)   **Whom** is correct. **Whom** is the object of the main verb **ask.** Turn the question into a regular declarative sentence and substitute another pronoun. Thus, **I should ask** *her* **to accompany me.**

3.   Pronouns that follow prepositions are always in the **objective case,** except when serving as the subject of a clause, as discussed above. The most popular misuse occurs when using a pronoun after the preposition **between.** (**I, he, she, they,** are never used after **between,** no matter where the prepositional phrase falls in the sentence.)

> Between you and me, I don't believe our client will be able to continue as a going concern.
> That matter is strictly between her and them.

Antecedents

1.   An antecedent is the word or words for which a pronoun stands. Any time a pronoun is used, its antecedent must be clear and agree with the word or words for which it stands.

> *The accountant* placed *his* work in the file.

In this example, **his** is the pronoun with **the accountant** as its antecedent. **His** agrees with **the accountant** in person and number. **His** is used so as not to repeat **the accountant.**

2.   Confusion most often occurs when using indefinite pronouns such as **it, that, this,** and **which.**

> The company for *which* he works always mails *its* paychecks on Friday.

In this example, the pronouns **which** and **its** both clearly refer to **the company.** Consider the next example. Since it is not clear what the antecedent for **it** is, we can't tell for sure whether the company or the paycheck is small.

> The company always mails my paycheck on Friday and *it* is a small one.

3. So far in our discussion of antecedents, we have talked about agreement in person. We have not addressed agreement in **number.** The following examples demonstrate pronouns that **do not agree** in number with their antecedents.

> The company issued quarterly financial reports to *their* shareholders. (*Its* is the correct antecedent to agree in number with *company*.)

> Each of the methods is introduced on a separate page, so that the student is made aware of *their* importance. (*Its* is the correct antecedent to agree in number with *each*.) **Note: Importance** refers to **each,** the subject of the sentence, not to **methods,** which is the object of the preposition **of.**

4. When a pronoun refers to singular antecedents that are connected by **or** or **nor**, the pronoun should be **singular.**

> Joe or Buddy has misplaced *his* workpapers.

> Neither Joe nor Buddy has misplaced *his* workpapers.

5. When a pronoun refers to a singular and a plural antecedent connected by **or** or **nor**, the pronoun should be **plural.**

> Neither Joe nor his associates can locate *their* workpapers.

6. Pronouns must also agree with their antecedents in **gender.** Because English language has no way of expressing gender-neutral in pronoun agreement, it has been the custom to use **his** as a convenience when referring to both sexes. To avoid this "gender bias" in writing, there is a growing use of a more cumbersome construction in order to be more politically correct.

> **Old:** When a new partner's identifiable asset contribution is less than the ownership interest *he* is to receive, the excess capital allowed *him* is considered as goodwill attributable to *him.*

> **New:** When a new partner's identifiable asset contribution is less than the ownership interest *he or she* is to receive, the excess capital allowed *the new partner* is considered as goodwill attributable to *him or her.*

You will note in the above example that **he or she (he/she)** and **him or her (him/her)** have been used only once each and the antecedent **new partner** has been repeated once.

The idea is to not overload a single sentence with too many repetitions of each construction. When it seems that **he/she** constructions are overwhelming the sentence, repeat the noun antecedent where possible, even if it sounds a bit labored.

---

7. **Reflexive pronouns** are pronouns that are used for **emphasizing their antecedents** and should **not be used as substitutes** for regular pronouns. The reflexive pronouns are **myself, yourself, himself, herself, itself, ourselves, yourselves, and themselves.**

> The financing is being handled by the principals *themselves.* (Demonstrates emphasis)
> The partner *himself* will take care of that matter. (Demonstrates emphasis)
> My associate and *I* accept the engagement. (Not my associate and *myself*...)
> I am fine; how about *you*? (Not how about *yourself*?)

ADJECTIVES & ADVERBS

1. Most of us understand that adjectives and adverbs are **modifiers,** but many of us can't tell them apart. In fact, there are many words that can be used as either depending on their use. Consequently, differentiating adjectives from adverbs is really not very important as long as you know how to use them. Understanding, however, that **adjectives modify nouns or pronouns,** and **adverbs modify verbs** and adjectives will help you choose the correct form.

    > Falcone Co. purchased *two* computers from Wizard Corp., a very *small* manufacturer. (*two* is an adjective describing the noun *computers, very* is an adverb modifying the adjective *small,* and *small* is an adjective describing the noun *manufacturer.*)

    > Acme advised Mason that it would deliver the appliances on July 2 as *originally* agreed. (*originally* is an adverb describing the verb *agreed.*)

2. In writing for the CPA exam, avoid colloquial uses of the adjectives **real** and **sure.** In the following examples, adverbs are called for.

    > I am *very* (not *real*) sorry that you didn't pass the exam.
    > He will *surely* (not *sure*) be glad if he passes the exam.

3. **Comparisons** using adjectives frequently present problems. Remember that when comparing two things, the **comparative** (often **er**) form is used, and when comparing more than two, the **superlative** (often **est**) form is used.

    > This report is *larger* than the other one.
    > This report is the *largest* of them all.
    > This report is *more* detailed than the others.
    > This report is the *most* detailed of them all.

4. **Articles** are adjectives. **An** precedes most vowels, but when the vowel begins with a **consonant sound,** we should use **a.**

    > *a* usual adjustment…
    > *a* one in a million deal…

    Similarly, when **a** or **an** precedes abbreviations or initials, it is the next **sound** that we should consider, not the next letter. In other words, if the next sound is a vowel sound, **an** should be used. Usually, your reader will be reading the abbreviations or initials and not the whole term, title, etc.

    > *An S.A.* will be used to head up the field work on this engagement.
    > *An F.O.B.* contract is a *contract* indicating that the seller will bear that degree of risk and expense that is appropriate to the F.O.B. terms.

CONJUNCTIONS

There are three types of conjunctions: coordinating, subordinating, and correlative.

Coordinating Conjunctions

Coordinating conjunctions are conjunctions that connect equal elements in a sentence. These conjunctions include **and, but, for, yet, so, or,** and **nor.** Examples of common problems involving coordinating conjunctions:

1. Leaving out the **and,** leading to difficulties with comprehension and clarity.

    > The accountant studied some of management's representations, marked what she wanted to discuss in the meeting. (The word *and* should be in the place of the comma.)

Mike's summer job entails opening the mail, stamps it with a dater, routing it to the proper person. (Should be: ...opening the mail from other offices, *stamping* it with a dater, *and* routing it to the proper person. **This example also demonstrates a lack of parallelism,** which is addressed in an earlier section.)

2. Omission of **and** is correct when the sentence is a compound sentence (meaning that it contains two independent clauses), in which case a semicolon takes the place of **and.** When the semicolon is used, the ideas of each independent clause should be closely related.

    The security is genuine; it has not been materially altered.

3. Although the rules for **or** and **nor** have become less strict over time, you should understand proper usage for the sake of comprehension and clarity. Most of us are familiar with **either**...**or** and **neither**...**nor**:

    Either the creditor must take possession *or* the debtor must sign a security agreement that describes the collateral.

The company would neither accept delivery of the water coolers, nor pay for them, because Peterson did not have the authority to enter into the contract.

Subordinating Conjunctions

Subordinating conjunctions are conjunctions that introduce subordinate elements of the sentence. The most common and the ones we want to concentrate on here are **as, since, because, that, which, when, where,** and **while.**

1. **As; Since; Because**

    Because is the only word of the three that **always** indicates cause. **Since** usually indicates **time** and, when introducing adverbial clauses, may mean either **when** or **because.** **As** should be avoided altogether in these constructions and used only for comparisons. We strongly recommend using the exact word to avoid any confusion, especially when clarity is essential.

    Attachment of the security interest did not occur because Pix failed to file a financing statement. (Specifically indicates *cause.*)
    Green has not paid any creditor since January 1, 1992. (Specifically indicates *time.*)

    The following example is a typical misuse of the conjunction **as** and demonstrates why **as** should not be used as a substitute for **because:**

    As the partners are contributing more capital to the company, the stock prices are going up.

    The meaning of this sentence is ambiguous. Are the stock prices going up **while** the partners are contributing capital or are the stock prices going up **because** the partners are contributing more capital?

2. **That; Which**

    Many people complain about not understanding when to use **that** and when to use **which** more than just about anything else. The rule to follow requires that you know the difference between a restrictive and a nonrestrictive clause. A **restrictive clause** is one that must remain in the sentence for the sentence to make sense. A **nonrestrictive** clause is one that may be removed from a sentence and the sentence will still make sense.

    That is used with restrictive clauses; *which* is used with nonrestrictive clauses.

    (1) An accountant who breaches his or her contract with a client may be subject to liability for damages and losses *which* the client suffers as a direct result of the breach.

(2)   As a result, the accountant is responsible for errors resulting from changes *that* occurred between the time he or she prepared the statement and its effective date.

(3)   A reply *that* purports to accept an offer but which adds material qualifications or conditions is not an acceptance; rather, it is a rejection and a counter-offer.

In example (1) above, the clause beginning with **which** is nonrestrictive (sentence would make sense without it). In examples (2) and (3), the clauses that follow **that** are restrictive (necessary for the meaning of the sentence).

> If you can put commas around the clause in question, it is usually nonrestrictive and thus takes **which**. Occasionally, there will be a fine line between what one might consider restrictive or nonrestrictive. In these cases, make your choice based on which sounds better and, if there is another **which** or **that** nearby, let that help your decision. (Unless truly necessary, avoid two or three uses of **which** or two or three uses of **that** in the same sentence.)

3.   **When; Where**

The most common incorrect usage associated with these words occurs when they are used to define something.

(1)   Exoneration is *where* the surety takes action against the debtor, which seeks to force the debtor to pay his or her debts.

(2)   A fiduciary relationship is where the agent acts for the benefit of the principal.

(3)   Joint liability is *when* all partners in a partnership are jointly liable for any contract actions against the partnership.

The above three examples are **faulty constructions.** The verb **to be** (**is,** in this case) must be followed by a predicate adjective (an adjective modifying the subject) or a predicate nominative (a noun meaning the same as the subject), **not** an adverbial phrase or clause. These sentences should be rewritten as follows:

(1)   Exoneration is *an action* by the surety against the debtor, which seeks to force the debtor to pay his or her debts.

(2)   A fiduciary relationship is *the association* of the agent and the principal whereby the agent acts for the benefit of the principal.

(3)   Joint liability is *the liability* of all partners in a partnership for any contract actions against the partnership.

4.   **While**

Formerly, **while** was acceptable only to denote time. Modern practice accepts **while** and **although** as nearly synonymous. In example (1), either while or although is acceptable. In example (2), **while** is **not** a proper substitution for **although.**

(1)   *While/Although* Acme contends that its agreement with Mason was not binding, it is willing to deliver the goods to Mason.

(2)   Under a sale or return contract, the sale is considered as completed *although* it is voidable at the buyer's election.

Correlative Conjunction

The third type of conjunction is the **correlative conjunction.** We have briefly mentioned and presented examples of **either...or** and **neither...nor** earlier in connection with nouns, verbs, and agreement. Now we want to discuss these correlatives in connection with **parallelism.**

1.   **Not only** should be followed by **but (also).**

In determining whether a mere invitation or an offer exists, the courts generally will look *not only* to the specific language *but also* to the surrounding circumstances, the custom within the industry, and the prior practice between the parties.

2.   Watch out for **placement of correlatives.** Faulty placement leads to faulty construction and obstructs clarity.

The lawyer *either* is asked to furnish specific information *or* comment as to where the lawyer's views differ from those of management.

Below is the same sentence in much clearer form. Note that the phrases introduced by *either* and *or* are now in parallel construction: *either to furnish...or to comment.*

The lawyer is asked *either* to furnish specific information *or to* comment as to where the lawyer's views differ from those of management.

_____

APPENDIX D
FINANCIAL RATIOS

Analytical procedures consist of evaluations of financial information made by a study of plausible relationships among both financial and nonfinancial data. Plausible relationships among data may reasonably be expected to exist and continue in the absence of changes in conditions. Several common financial ratios are shown here for your reference.

When computing a ratio, consider the following factors:

1.   Net or gross amounts (e.g., receivables)

2.   Average for the period or year-end (e.g., receivables, inventories, common shares outstanding)

3.   Adjustments to income (e.g., interest, income taxes, preferred dividends)

Although not a ratio, *working capital* is a measure of the short-term solvency of an entity. It is equal to current assets less current liabilities.

1. Current Ratio
$$\frac{\text{Current Assets}}{\text{Current Liabilities}}$$

2. Acid Test or Quick Ratio
$$\frac{\text{Cash + Marketable Securities + Net Receivables}}{\text{Current Liabilities}}$$

3. Defensive Interval Ratio
$$\frac{\text{Cash + Marketable Securities + Net Receivables}}{\text{Average Daily Cash Expenditures}}$$

4. Debt to Equity
$$\frac{\text{Total Liabilities}}{\text{Owners' Equity}}$$

5. Times Interest Earned
$$\frac{\text{Income Before Income Taxes and Interest Charges}}{\text{Interest Charges}}$$

6. Times Preferred Dividends Earned
$$\frac{\text{Net Income}}{\text{Annual Preferred Dividend Requirement}}$$

7. Accounts Receivable Turnover
$$\frac{\text{Net Credit Sales}}{\text{Average Net Receivables}}$$

8. Number of Days' Sales in Average Receivables
$$\frac{360}{\text{Receivables Turnover}}$$

9. Inventory Turnover
$$\frac{\text{Cost of Goods Sold}}{\text{Average Inventory}}$$

10. Return on Total Assets
$$\frac{\text{Net Income + Interest Expense (Net of Tax)}}{\text{Average Total Assets}}$$

11. Number of Days' Supply in Average Inventory

$$\frac{360}{\text{Inventory Turnover}}$$

- The number of days' supply in average (ending) inventory can also be computed in the following manner:

$$\frac{\text{Average (Ending) Inventory}}{\text{Average Daily Cost of Goods Sold}}$$

- Average daily cost of goods sold is determined by dividing cost of goods sold by the number of business days in the year (e.g., 365, 360, 300, or 250).

12. Length of Operating Cycle

$$\textit{Number of days' sales in average receivables} + \textit{Number of days' supply in average inventory}$$

13. Book Value Per Common Share

$$\frac{\text{Common Stockholders' Equity}}{\text{Number of Common Shares Outstanding}}$$

- To determine common stockholders' equity, preferred stock is subtracted from total stockholders' equity at the greater of its liquidation, par or stated value. Cumulative preferred stock dividends in arrears are also similarly subtracted. Treasury stock affects the denominator as the number of common shares outstanding is reduced.

14. Book Value Per Preferred Share

$$\frac{\text{Preferred Stockholders' Equity}}{\text{Number of Preferred Shares Outstanding}}$$

- Preferred stockholders' equity is comprised of (a) preferred stock at the greater of its liquidation, par or stated value and (b) cumulative preferred stock dividends in arrears.

15. Return on Common Stockholders' Equity

$$\frac{\text{Net Income} - \text{Preferred Dividends}}{\text{Average Common Stockholders' Equity}}$$

16. Return on Stockholders' Equity

$$\frac{\text{Net Income}}{\text{Average Stockholders' Equity}}$$

17. Earnings Per Share

$$\frac{\text{Net Income} - \text{Preferred Dividends}}{\text{Average Number of Common Shares Outstanding}}$$

18. Price-Earnings Ratio

$$\frac{\text{Market Price Per Common Share}}{\text{Earnings Per Common Share}}$$

19. Dividend Payout Ratio

$$\frac{\text{Cash Dividend Per Common Share}}{\text{Earnings Per Common Share}}$$

20. Yield on Common Stock

$$\frac{\text{Dividend Per Common Share}}{\text{Market Price Per Common Share}}$$

APPENDIX E
RECENTLY RELEASED AICPA QUESTIONS

2008 RELEASED AICPA QUESTIONS AND ANSWERS

In September 2008, the AICPA released fifty multiple-choice questions and one simulation relating to the AUD section of the CPA Examination. These questions and their unofficial answers are reproduced here, along with the exclusive Bisk Education explanations. The multiple-choice questions in Problems 1 and 2 were labeled *moderate* and *hard*, respectively, by the AICPA examiners. Problem 3 is the one simulation that was disclosed.

2009 RELEASED AICPA QUESTIONS AND ANSWERS

In April 2009, the AICPA released fifty multiple-choice questions and one simulation relating to the AUD section of the CPA Examination. These questions and their unofficial answers are reproduced here, along with the exclusive Bisk Education explanations. The multiple-choice questions in Problems 4 and 5 were labeled *moderate* and *hard*, respectively, by the AICPA examiners. Problem 6 is the one simulation that was disclosed.

Editor note: The AICPA did not state if these questions ever appeared on any exam; whether they were assigned points or were merely being pretested and earned no points if they did appear on an exam; or if they were now obsolete for some reason. These questions are intended only as a study aid and should not be used to predict the content of future exams. It is the AICPA's policy that released questions will not appear on future exams. These questions have been reproduced as received from the AICPA examiners. If candidates encounter what they believe are errors or ambiguities in questions during their actual exams, they should bring them to the attention of the examiners in accordance with the procedures outlined on the AICPA's Uniform CPA Examination Web site (www.cpa-exam.org).

Problem 1 MULTIPLE-CHOICE QUESTIONS (2008 Moderate)

1. On March 1, Green, CPA, expressed an unqualified opinion on the financial statements of Ajax Co. On July 1, Green's internal inspection program discovered that engagement personnel failed to observe Ajax's physical inventory. Green believes that this omission impairs Green's ability to support the unqualified opinion. If Ajax's creditors are currently relying on Green's opinion, Green should first
a. Request Ajax's management to communicate to its creditors that Green's opinion should **not** be relied on.
b. Reissue Green's auditor's report with an explanatory paragraph describing the departure from GAAS.
c. Undertake to apply the alternative procedures that would provide a satisfactory basis for Green's opinion.
d. Advise Ajax's board of directors to disclose this development in its next interim report.
(R/08, AUD, 0600A, #1, 8607)

2. Which of the following procedures would best detect a liability omission by management?
a. Inquiry of senior support staff and recently departed employees
b. Review and check mathematical accuracy of financial statements
c. Review articles of incorporation and corporate bylaws
d. Review purchase contracts and other legal documents (R/08, AUD, C00046A, #2, 8608)

3. Evidence concerning the proper segregation of duties for receiving and depositing cash receipts ordinarily is obtained by
a. Completing an internal control questionnaire that describes the control activities
b. Observing the employees who are performing the control activities
c. Performing substantive tests to verify the details of the bank balance
d. Preparing a flowchart of the duties performed and the entity's available personnel
(R/08, AUD, 1249A, #3, 8609)

4. Which of the following documents are examples of audit evidence generated by the client?
a. Customer purchase orders and bank statements
b. Shipping documents and receiving reports
c. Vendor invoices and packing slips
d. Bills of lading and accounts receivable confirmations (R/08, AUD, A0548A, #4, 8610)

5. Which of the following procedures is ordinarily performed by an accountant during an engagement to compile the financial statements of a nonissuer?
a. Make inquiries of the employees and senior management regarding transactions with related parties.
b. Determine whether there is substantial doubt about the entity's ability to continue as a going concern.
c. Scan the entity's records for the period just after the balance sheet date to identify subsequent events requiring disclosure.
d. Consider whether the financial statements are free from obvious material mistakes in the application of accounting principles.
(R/08, AUD, 1362A, #5, 8611)

6. Which of the following best represents a key control for ensuring sales are properly authorized when accessing control risks for sales?
a. The separation of duties between the billing department and the cash receipts approval department
b. The use of an approved price list to determine unit selling price
c. Copies of approved sales orders sent to the shipping, billing, and accounting departments
d. Sales orders are sent to the credit department for approval (R/08, AUD, C00044A, #6, 8612)

7. When providing limited assurance that the financial statements of a nonissuer require no material modifications to be in accordance with GAAP, the accountant should
a. Assess the risk of material misstatement in the financial statements due to fraud.
b. Perform tests of controls to evaluate the effectiveness of the controls.
c. Understand the accounting principles of the industry in which the entity operates.
d. Communicate with the audit committee regarding material weaknesses in internal control.
(R/08, AUD, 1713A, #7, 8613)

8. In assessing the competence of internal auditors, an independent CPA most likely would obtain information about the
a. Influence of management on the scope of the internal auditors' duties
b. Policies limiting internal auditors from communicating with the audit committee
c. Quality of the internal auditors' working paper documentation
d. Entity's ability to continue as a going concern for a reasonable period of time
(R/08, AUD, 1443A, #8, 8614)

9. Which of the following procedures would an auditor most likely perform to assist in the evaluation of loss contingencies?
a. Checking arithmetic accuracy of the accounting records
b. Performing appropriate analytical procedures
c. Obtaining a letter of audit inquiry from the client's lawyer
d. Reading the financial statements, including footnotes (R/08, AUD, A0917A, #9, 8615)

10. A client maintains a large data center where access is limited to authorized employees. How may an auditor best determine the effectiveness of this control activity?
a. Inspect the policy manual establishing this control activity.
b. Ask the chief technology officer about known problems.
c. Observe whether the data center is monitored.
d. Obtain a list of current data center employees. (R/08, AUD, 0259A, #10, 8616)

11. Detection risk differs from both control risk and inherent risk in that detection risk
a. Exists independently of the financial statement audit
b. Can be changed at the auditor's discretion
c. Arises from risk factors relating to fraud
d. Should be assessed in nonquantitative terms (R/08, AUD, 1721A, #11, 8617)

12. To provide assurance that each voucher is submitted and paid only once, an auditor most likely would examine a sample of paid vouchers and determine whether each voucher is
a. Stamped *paid* by the check signer
b. Returned to the vouchers payable department
c. Supported by a vendor's invoice and purchase order
d. Prenumbered and accounted for (R/08, AUD, 1137A, #12, 8618)

13. In an engagement to review the financial statements of a nonissuer, the accountant most likely would perform which of the following procedures?
a. Physical inspection of inventory
b. Vouching of inventory purchase transactions
c. Analysis of inventory turnover
d. Evaluation of internal control over inventory (R/08, AUD, A0526A, #13, 8619)

14. An auditor requests a client to send letters of audit inquiry to attorneys who have been consulted concerning litigation, claims, and assessments. The primary reason for this request is to obtain
a. The attorneys' assurance that litigation, claims, and assessments that are probable of assertion are properly accounted for
b. Corroboration of the information furnished by management concerning litigation, claims, and assessments
c. A description of litigation, claims, and assessments that have a reasonable possibility of unfavorable outcomes
d. The opinion of an expert whether any loss contingencies are possible, probable, or remote (R/08, AUD, 0394A, #14, 8620)

15. Which of the following is an inherent limitation of internal controls?
a. Judgmental sampling
b. Collusion
c. Segregation of duties
d. Employee peer review (R/08, AUD, A1224A, #15, 8621)

16. If the objective of an auditor's test of details is to detect a possible understatement of sales, the auditor most likely would trace transactions from the
a. Sales invoices to the shipping documents
b. Cash receipts journal to the sales journal
c. Shipping documents to the sales invoices
d. Sales journal to the cash receipts journal (R/08, AUD, 0546A, #16, 8622)

17. An auditor believes that there is substantial doubt about an entity's ability to continue as a going concern for a reasonable period of time. In evaluating the entity's plans for dealing with the adverse effects of future conditions and events, the auditor most likely would consider, as a mitigating factor, the entity's plans to
a. Extend the due dates of existing loans.
b. Operate at increased levels of production.
c. Accelerate expenditures for research and development projects.
d. Issue stock options to key executives. (R/08, AUD, 0263A, #17, 8623)

18. Which of the following statements is correct regarding a compilation report on financial statements issued in accordance with *Statements on Standards for Accounting and Review Services* (SSARS)?
a. The report should **not** be issued if the accountant is **not** independent from the entity.
b. The report should include a statement indicating that the information is the representation of the accountant.
c. The report should include a description of other procedures performed during the compilation.
d. The date on the report should be the date of completion of the compilation.
(R/08, AUD, A1409A, #18, 8624)

19. The phrase *generally accepted accounting principles* is an accounting term that
a. Includes broad guidelines of general application but **not** detailed practices and procedures
b. Encompasses the conventions, rules, and procedures necessary to define accepted accounting practice at a particular time
c. Provides a measure of conventions, rules, and procedures governed by the AICPA
d. Is included in the audit report to indicate that the audit has been conducted in accordance with generally accepted auditing standards (GAAS)
(R/08, AUD, C00108A, #19, 8625)

20. Which of the following circumstances would permit an independent auditor to accept an engagement after the close of the fiscal year?
a. Issuance of a disclaimer of opinion as a result of inability to conduct certain tests required by generally accepted auditing standards due to the timing of acceptance of the engagement
b. Assessment of control risk below the maximum level
c. Receipt of an assertion from the preceding auditor that the entity will be able to continue as a going concern
d. Remedy of limitations resulting from accepting the engagement after the close of the end of the year, such as those relating to the existence of physical inventory
(R/08, AUD, A0325A, #20, 8626)

21. When issuing letters for underwriters, commonly referred to as comfort letters, an accountant may provide negative assurance concerning
a. The absence of any significant deficiencies in internal control
b. The conformity of the entity's unaudited condensed interim financial information with generally accepted accounting principles (GAAP)
c. The results of procedures performed in compiling the entity's financial forecast
d. The compliance of the entity's registration statement with the requirements of the Securities Act of 1933 (R/08, AUD, 0456A, #21, 8627)

22. An accountant is required to comply with the provisions of the *Statements on Standards for Accounting and Review Services* when performing which of the following tasks?
a. Preparing monthly journal entries
b. Providing the client with software to generate financial statements
c. Generating financial statements of a nonissuer
d. Providing a blank financial statement format or template (R/08, AUD, A0156A, #22, 8628)

23. Which of the following statements would be appropriate in an accountant's report on compiled financial statements of a nonissuer prepared in accordance with *Statements on Standards for Accounting and Review Services* (SSARS)?
a. We are not aware of any material modifications that should be made to the accompanying financial statements.
b. A compilation is substantially less in scope than an audit in accordance with generally accepted auditing standards (GAAS).
c. A compilation is limited to presenting in the form of financial statements information that is a representation of management.
d. A compilation is performed to obtain reasonable assurance about whether the financial statements are free from material misstatement.
(R/08, AUD, A0681A, #23, 8629)

24. Quality control policies and procedures that are established to decide whether to accept a new client should provide the CPA firm with reasonable assurance that

a. The CPA firm's duty to the public concerning the acceptance of new clients is satisfied.
b. The likelihood of associating with clients whose management lacks integrity is minimized.
c. Client-prepared schedules that are necessary for the engagement are completed on a timely basis.
d. Sufficient corroborating evidence to support the financial statement assertions is available.

(R/08, AUD, 1705A, #24, 8630)

25. For the fiscal year ending December 31, previous year and the current year, Justin Co. has net sales of $1,000,000 and $2,000,000; average gross receivables of $100,000 and $300,000; and allowance for uncollectible accounts receivable of $30,000 and $50,000, respectively. If the accounts receivable turnover and the ratio of allowance for uncollectible accounts receivable to gross accounts receivable are calculated, which of the following best represents the conclusions to be drawn?

a. Accounts receivable turnovers are 10.0 and 6.6 and the ratios of uncollectible accounts receivable to gross accounts receivable are 0.30 and 0.16, respectively. Examine allowance for possible overstatement of the allowance.
b. Accounts receivable turnovers are 10.0 and 6.6 and the ratios of uncollectible accounts receivable to gross accounts receivable are 0.30 and 0.16, respectively. Examine allowance for possible understatement of the allowance.
c. Accounts receivable turnovers are 14.3 and 8.0 and the ratios of uncollectible accounts receivable to gross accounts receivable is 0.42 and 0.20, respectively. Examine allowance for possible overstatement of the allowance.
d. Accounts receivable turnovers are 14.3 and 8.0 and the ratios of uncollectible accounts receivable to gross accounts receivable are 0.42 and 0.20, respectively. Examine allowance for possible understatement of the allowance.

(R/08, AUD, C00096A, #25, 8631)

Problem 2 MULTIPLE-CHOICE QUESTIONS (2008 Hard)

26. Which of the following would be a consideration in planning an auditor's sample for a test of controls?

a. Preliminary judgments about materiality levels
b. The auditor's allowable risk of assessing control risk too high
c. The level of detection risk for the account
d. The auditor's allowable risk of assessing control risk too low

(R/08, AUD, C04951A, #26, amended, 8632)

27. An auditor is auditing a mutual fund company that uses a transfer agent to handle accounting for shareholders. Which of the following actions by the auditor would be most efficient for obtaining information about the transfer agent's internal controls?

a. Review reports on internal control placed in operation and its operating effectiveness produced by the agent's own auditor.
b. Review prior year workpapers to determine whether the number of transactions processed by the agent has materially increased.
c. Perform an audit on the internal control function of the agent.
d. Perform tests of controls on a sample of the audited firm's transactions through the agent.

(R/08, AUD, A1071A, #27, 8633)

28. Which of the following statements is true regarding analytical procedures in a review engagement?
a. Analytical procedures are **not** required to be used as a substantive test.
b. Analytical procedures do **not** involve comparisons of recorded amounts to expected amounts.
c. Analytical procedures are required to be used in the final review stage.
d. Analytical procedures involve the use of both financial and nonfinancial data.
(R/08, AUD, C00095A, #28, 8634)

29. In reviewing the financial statements of a nonissuer, an accountant is required to modify the standard review report for which of the following matters?

	Inability to assess the risk of material misstatement due to fraud	Discovery of significant deficiencies in the design of the entity's internal control
a.	Yes	Yes
b.	Yes	No
c.	No	Yes
d.	No	No

(R/08, AUD, 1276A, #29, 8635)

30. An auditor is determining if internal control relative to the revenue cycle of a wholesaling entity is operating effectively in minimizing the failure to prepare sales invoices. The auditor most likely would select a sample of transactions from the population represented by the
a. Cash receipts file
b. Shipping document file
c. Customer order file
d. Sales invoice file
(R/08, AUD, 1447A, #30, 8636)

31. A CPA concludes that the unaudited financial statements on which the CPA is disclaiming an opinion are **not** in conformity with generally accepted accounting principles (GAAP) because management has failed to capitalize leases. The CPA suggests appropriate revisions to the financial statements, but management refuses to accept the CPA's suggestions. Under these circumstances, the CPA ordinarily would
a. Express limited assurance that **no** other material modifications should be made to the financial statements.
b. Restrict the distribution of the CPA's report to management and the entity's board of directors.
c. Issue a qualified opinion or adverse opinion depending on the materiality of the departure from GAAP.
d. Describe the nature of the departure from GAAP in the CPA's report and state the effects on the financial statements, if practicable.
(R/08, AUD, 1883A, #31, 8637)

32. Which of the following procedures would an auditor most likely perform prior to the balance sheet date?
a. Review subsequent events
b. Perform search for unrecorded liabilities
c. Send inquiry letter to client's legal counsel
d. Review detail and test significant travel and entertainment expenses
(R/08, AUD, C04989A, #32, 8638)

33. An audit client failed to maintain copies of its procedures manuals and organizational flowcharts. What should the auditor do in an audit of financial statements?
a. Issue a qualified opinion on the basis of a scope limitation.
b. Document the auditor's understanding of internal controls.
c. Assess control risk at the maximum level.
d. Restrict the auditor's responsibility to assess the effectiveness of controls in the audit engagement letter. (R/08, AUD, A2097A, #33, 8639)

34. Which of the following factors most likely would assist an independent auditor in assessing the objectivity of the internal auditor?
a. The organizational status of the director of internal audit
b. The professional certifications of the internal audit staff
c. The consistency of the internal audit reports with the results of work performed
d. The appropriateness of internal audit conclusions in the circumstances
(R/08, AUD, A0584A, #34, 8640)

35. Auditors try to identify predictable relationships when applying analytical procedures. Relationships involving transactions from which of the following accounts most likely would yield the highest level of evidence?
a. Interest expense
b. Allowance for doubtful accounts
c. Accounts receivable
d. Accounts payable
(R/08, AUD, 2048A, #35, 8641)

36. An accountant is required to comply with the provisions of *Statements on Standards for Accounting and Review Services* when

I. Reproducing client-prepared financial statements, without modification, as an accommodation to a client
II. Preparing standard monthly journal entries for depreciation and expiration of prepaid expenses

a. I only
b. II only
c. Both I and II
d. Neither I nor II (R/08, AUD, 0040A, #36, 8642)

37. Which of the following procedures would an auditor most likely perform regarding litigation?
a. Confirm directly with the clerk of the court that the client's litigation is properly disclosed.
b. Discuss with management its policies and procedures for identifying and evaluating litigation.
c. Inspect the legal documents in the client's lawyer's possession regarding pending litigation.
d. Confirm the details of pending litigation with the client's adversaries' legal representatives.
(R/08, AUD, 2169A, #37, 8643)

38. Before reissuing a compilation report on the financial statements of a nonissuer for the prior year, the predecessor accountant is required to
a. Obtain an updated management representation letter from the entity's management.
b. Compare the prior year's financial statements with those of the current year.
c. Review the successor accountant's working papers for matters affecting the prior year.
d. Make inquiries of the entity's lawyers concerning continuing litigation.
(R/08, AUD, 0697A, #38, 8644)

39. Which of the following procedures would an accountant most likely perform during an engagement to review the financial statements of a nonissuer?
a. Review the predecessor accountant's working papers.
b. Inquire of management about related party transactions.
c. Corroborate litigation information with the entity's attorney.
d. Communicate internal control deficiencies to senior management.
(R/08, AUD, 0487A, #39, 8645)

40. Which of the following situations represents a risk factor that relates to misstatements arising from misappropriation of assets?
a. A high turnover of senior management
b. A lack of independent checks
c. A strained relationship between management and the predecessor auditor
d. An inability to generate cash flow from operations (R/08, AUD, A0254A, #40, 8646)

41. Which of the following actions should an accountant take when engaged to compile a company's financial statements in accordance with *Statements on Standards for Accounting and Review Services* (SSARS)?
a. Perform analytical procedures.
b. Express negative assurance on the financial statements.
c. Make management inquiries and examine internal controls.
d. Perform the engagement even though independence is compromised.
(R/08, AUD, A1127A, #41, 8647)

42. Which of the following procedures would a CPA most likely perform when reviewing the financial statements of a nonissuer?
a. Verify that the accounting estimates that could be material to the financial statements have been developed.
b. Obtain an understanding of the entity's internal control components.
c. Assess the entity's ability to continue as a going concern for a reasonable period of time.
d. Make inquiries about actions taken at the board of directors meetings.

(R/08, AUD, 1865A, #42, 8648)

43. In evaluating the reasonableness of an entity's accounting estimates, an auditor most likely concentrates on key factors and assumptions that are
a. Stable and **not** sensitive to variation
b. Objective and **not** susceptible to bias
c. Deviations from historical patterns
d. Similar to industry guidelines

(R/08, AUD, 1438A, #43, 8649)

44. A client decides **not** to make an auditor's proposed adjustments that collectively are **not** material and wants the auditor to issue the report based on the unadjusted numbers. Which of the following statements is correct regarding the financial statement presentation?
a. The financial statements are free from material misstatement, and **no** disclosure is required in the notes to the financial statements.
b. The financial statements do **not** conform with generally accepted accounting principles (GAAP).
c. The financial statements contain unadjusted misstatements that should result in a qualified opinion.
d. The financial statements are free from material misstatement, but disclosure of the proposed adjustments is required in the notes to the financial statements.

(R/08, AUD, A1383A, #44, 8650)

45. A client is a defendant in a patent infringement lawsuit against a major competitor. Which of the following items would **least** likely be included in the attorney's response to the auditor's letter of inquiry?
a. A description of potential litigation in other matters or related to an unfavorable verdict in the patent infringement lawsuit
b. A discussion of case progress and the strategy currently in place by client management to resolve the lawsuit
c. An evaluation of the probability of loss and a statement of the amount or range of loss if an unfavorable outcome is reasonably possible
d. An evaluation of the ability of the client to continue as a going concern if the verdict is unfavorable and maximum damages are awarded

(R/08, AUD, A1562A, #45, 8651)

46. In using the work of a specialist, an auditor may refer to the specialist in the auditor's report if, as a result of the specialist's findings, the auditor
a. Desires to disclose the specialist's findings, which imply that a more thorough audit was performed
b. Makes suggestions to management that are likely to improve the entity's internal control
c. Corroborates another specialist's findings that were consistent with management's assertions
d. Adds an explanatory paragraph to the auditor's report to emphasize an unusually important subsequent event

(R/08, AUD, 1736A, #46, 8652)

47. When an accountant is **not** independent with respect to an entity, which of the following types of compilation reports may be issued?
a. The standard compilation report may be issued, regardless of independence.
b. A compilation report with negative assurance may be issued.
c. A compilation report with special wording that notes the accountant's lack of independence may be issued.
d. A compilation report may be issued if the engagement is upgraded to a review.

(R/08, AUD, A0494A, #47, 8653)

48. Which of the following items would most likely require an adjustment to the financial statements for the year ended December 31, year 1?
a. Uninsured loss of inventories purchased in year 1 as a result of a flood in year 2
b. Settlement of litigation in year 2 over an event that occurred in year 2
c. Loss on an uncollectible trade receivable recorded in year 1 from a customer that declared bankruptcy in year 2
d. Proceeds from a capital stock issuance in year 2 which was being approved by the board of directors in year 1

(R/08, AUD, A2346A, #48, 8654)

49. Which of the following is an element of a CPA firm's quality control policies and procedures applicable to the firm's accounting and auditing practice?
a. Information processing
b. Engagement performance
c. Technology selection
d. Professional skepticism

(R/08, AUD, 1513A, #49, 8655)

50. Which of the following procedures would an auditor most likely perform in obtaining evidence about subsequent events?
a. Examine changes in the quoted market prices of investments purchased since the year-end.
b. Compare the latest available interim financial information with the financial statements being reported upon.
c. Apply analytical procedures to the details of the balance sheet accounts that were tested at interim dates.
d. Inquire about payroll checks that were recorded before the year-end but cashed after the year-end.

(R/08, AUD, 0395A, #50, 8656)

Problem 3 SIMULATION (2008)

Based on the company and its environment, including its internal control, the auditors assessed the risk of material misstatements to the financial statements, whether due to error or fraud, and designed the nature, timing, and extent of further audit procedures to be performed.

As a result of conducting the above risk assessment procedures, the audit program for year 2 includes the following changes from the audit program for year 1. The company has a calendar year-end and operates only on weekdays.

In conducting the audit procedures for the search for unrecorded liabilities, the materiality/scope for this area was assessed by the auditors at $6,000. Adjustments are only recorded for items equal to, or exceeding materiality. The last day of fieldwork is estimated to be February 1, year 3.

For the items reflected in the following check register, which are **not** recorded in the accounts payable subsidiary ledger at December 31, year 2, determine if each potential liability is recorded in the proper accounting period and also determine the amount that should be journalized, if any. If no action is required, you must enter $0.

For each of the check numbers in the table below, double click on each of the associated shaded cells and select from the lists provided if any action or adjustment is required, as well as, the dollar value of the required adjustment. Each selection may be used once, more than once, or not at all.

Check Register				
Vendor	**Check #**	**Check Date**	**Amount**	**Nature of Expense**
Water World Distributors, Inc.	1333	1/6/year 3	$ 3,500	Water coolers in office and warehouse delivered 12/31/year 2
Daniel Breen, Esquire	1334	1/6/year 3	$ 6,000	Corporate legal services for December, year 2
Telephone Services, Inc.	1335	1/8/year 3	$ 6,500	December, year 2 telephone and computer services
Payroll processing— Paychecks	1336	1/10/year 3	$25,500	Biweekly payroll (12/25/year 2 -1/7/year 3)
Pitt Ohio Trucking Company	1337	1/10/year 3	$45,601	Trucking services 12/4/year 2 - 1/3/year 3, deliveries made evenly throughout the period
Petty cash	1338	1/17/year 3	$ 2,002	Replenish petty cash box
Smith's Forklift Repairs	1339	1/22/year 3	$11,000	Received new forklift on 12/29/year 2, ordered on 12/18/year 2
Glenn's Glass Distribution Center	1340	1/23/year 3	$12,230	Specialty goods ordered 12/20/year 2, delivered 12/31/year 2
Payroll processing— Paychecks	1341	1/24/year 3	$25,500	Biweekly payroll (1/8/year 3 -1/15/year 3)
Daniel Breen, Esquire	1342	2/6/year 3	$ 6,800	Corporate legal services for January, year 3

Check #	Adjustment needed?	Amount
1333		
1334		
1335		
1336		
1337		
1338		
1339		
1340		
1341		
1342		

Selection List for Adjustment Needed

No action required
Adjustment

Selection List for Amount

$0	$7,650
$2,002	$9,900
$2,970	$11,000
$3,500	$12,230
$4,413	$12,750
$6,000	$25,500
$6,500	$41,188
$6,800	$45,601

| Unrecorded Liabilities | Substantive Tests | Audit Adjustments | Communication |

The auditor determines that each of the following objectives will be part of the company's audit. For each objective, double click on the shaded area and select **two** different substantive tests that provide the best support for the audit objective. A substantive test may be used once, more than once, or not at all.

Audit Objective	Substantive Tests
1. Receivables at the end of year 2 are properly cut off with respect to sales made in year 2.	
2. The aggregate of net receivables in the balance sheet is fairly stated at estimated net realizable value.	
3. Depreciation expense is fairly stated.	
4. Fixed assets included in the balance sheet exist.	

Selection List

A. Request positive confirmation directly from the customer of its balance owed to the company.	I. From the fixed assets subledger, trace a selection of fully depreciated assets from the ledger to the manufacturing floor and check the associated identification number.
B. Test that the income statement agrees to the change of assets minus liabilities and owner's equity.	J. Recalculate the year's depreciation expense.
C. Test the aging in the accounts receivable trial balance.	K. Review the process of assigning expected useful life to machinery with the controller and ask if any assumptions have changed.
D. Trace shipping documents to the related sales invoices and orders, and to entries in the sales journal and accounts receivable subsidiary ledger.	L. Foot the fixed asset subledger.
E. Analyze the historical relationship of bad debt write-offs in comparison with sales and accounts receivable.	M. Vouch additions to the property, plant and equipment subsidiary ledger.
F. Foot the accounts receivable trial balance.	N. Make a physical inspection of major property, plant and equipment acquisitions
G. Foot and cross-foot the sales journal.	O. Foot and cross-foot the purchases journal
H. Identify the last number used in year 2 and the first number used in year 3 for prenumbered shipping documents and prenumbered sales invoices. Trace the respective numbers to postings in the sales journal and accounts receivable subsidiary ledger.	P. Investigate and review cash receipts related to retirements and sales of property, plant and equipment during the year.

Unrecorded Liabilities	Substantive Tests	Audit Adjustments	Communication

The year under audit is year 2.

During the course of the year 2 audit of the company, the auditor discovered the following situations that may or may not require an adjusting journal entry. Each audit finding is independent of any of the other findings. Double click on a shaded space and select the account or accounts that would comprise the adjusting journal entry, if required, to correct the audit finding. Accounts may be used once, more than once, or not at all.

Audit Finding	Adjusting Journal Entry	
	Dr.	**Cr.**
1. The bank's confirmation reply regarding the company's line of credit indicated that the December, year 2, interest was unpaid at year-end. Accruals for monthly interest expense have been made for 11 months in year 2 by the company.		
2. Employee overtime pay for hours worked before year-end, but paid in the following year, were **not** recorded in year 2.		
3. In the last week of year 2, the company recorded revenue for services rendered to some clients in year 3.		
4. During year 2, a former client sued the company for inappropriate work. Legal counsel has advised that it is *reasonably possible* that the company will be assessed damages. An amount can be estimated.		
5. At the end of year 2, a major customer filed for bankruptcy.		

Selection List for Audit Findings

Cash	Allowance for Doubtful Accounts
Accounts Receivable	Operating Expenses
Other Current Assets	Interest Expense
Property and Equipment	Other Income
Accounts Payable	Accumulated Depreciation
Accrued Liabilities	
Common Stock	Disclosure but **no** entry required
Revenues	**No** entry or disclosure required

Your CPA firm has been auditing the financial statements of XYZ Company for several years. Your assistants have approached you and asked if they can omit the confirmation of XYZ's accounts receivable. In a memorandum to your audit team, describe the circumstances under which the confirmation of accounts receivable may be omitted.

Type your communication in the response area below the horizontal line using the word processor provided.

REMINDER: Your response will be graded for both technical content and writing skills. Technical content will be evaluated for information that is helpful to the intended reader and clearly relevant to the issue. Writing skills will be evaluated for development, organization, and the appropriate expression of ideas in professional correspondence. Use a standard business memo or letter format with a clear beginning, middle, and end. Do **not** convey information in the form of a table, bullet point list, or other abbreviated presentation.

During the year-end audit of Client Mfg., the lead auditor in charge of the audit asks you to provide guidance for discovering material transactions with related parties. What are examples of procedures to recognize material transactions with related parties?

Reminder: On the actual exam, you will use an electronic database of authoritative literature to find and select the reference (appropriate section and paragraph of the relevant guidance). Please see the AICPA's tutorial and sample test on their exam Web site (www.cpa-exam.org).

Paragraph reference answer: _____   (R/08, AUD, 8657)

Solution 1 MULTIPLE-CHOICE ANSWERS (2008 Moderate)

1. (c) If the auditor concludes that the omission of a procedure considered necessary at the time of the audit impairs the auditor's present ability to support the previously expressed opinion and there are persons currently relying (such as Ajax's creditors), or likely to rely, on the report, the auditor should promptly *apply* the omitted procedure or *alternative procedures that would provide a satisfactory basis for the opinion.* Only if the auditor discovers, after performing these procedures, that the audit report cannot be supported, would other actions such as the other answer alternatives come into play, depending on the circumstances. (Chapter 28-7-4; 8607; CBT Skill: analysis; CSO: 5.3.2)

2. (d) This is an instance of testing for completeness, i.e., that all transactions and events that should have been recorded have been recorded. The best test for this would be to trace (*review*) information contained in source documents (*purchase contracts and other legal documents*) to the financial statements. Inquiry is not as effective as this tracing procedure. Reviewing the financial statements for mathematical accuracy would not detect an unrecorded liability; this would only provide evidence about recorded liabilities. A company's articles of incorporation and corporate bylaws generally do not contain liability information and they would prove an even less likely source of evidence of recent omissions. (Chapter 25-3-6; 8608; CBT Skill: judgment; CSO: 3.1.5)

3. (b) The best way to obtain evidence about the proper segregation of duties is by *observing the employees who are performing the control activities.* Procedures to verify the details of the bank balance, if they included examining signatures on deposit slips, could indicate which employees prepared the deposits, but this would not provide conclusive evidence as to which employees actually collected (physically handled) the receipts. Flowcharts and internal control questionnaires speak more to the effectiveness of the design rather than the operation of this control, but even if they are based on inquiries about the operation of the control, they do not provide as high a degree of evidence as simply actually observing who does what. (Chapter 23-5-3; 8609; CBT Skill: analysis; CSO: 2.6.0)

4. (b) *Shipping documents* (records of goods shipped by the client) *and receiving reports* (records of goods received by the client) are generated by the client. Customer purchase orders and bank statements are generated externally by the client's customers and the client's financial institutions, respectively. Vendor invoices and packing slips (records of goods shipped to the client) are generated externally by the client's vendors. Bills of lading (records of receipt of goods by a shipper) are generated externally usually by common carriers used by the client. Accounts receivable confirmation *requests* are sent out by the auditor or the client; the confirmations are completed (generated) by the client's customers and returned directly to the auditor by the client's customers. (Chapter 23-5-2; 8610; CBT Skill: understanding; CSO: 3.1.5)

5. (d) When engaged to compile the financial statements of a nonissuer, an accountant should read the *financial statements* and consider whether they appear to be appropriate in form and *free from obvious material* errors. This would include mistakes in the compilation of the financial statements, including arithmetical or clerical mistakes; and *mistakes in the application of accounting principles,* including inadequate disclosure. A compilation does **not** contemplate performing inquiry, analytical procedures or other procedures performed in a review. Accordingly, it would not include performing procedures regarding related party transactions, going concern issues, or subsequent events. (A compilation does **not** provide a basis for expressing any level of assurance on the financial statements.) Note: Even though an accountant is not required to perform these procedures, if going concern or subsequent event issues come to the accountant's attention, the accountant should request that management consider the possible effects on the financial statements. The accountant should then evaluate management's response and consider its effect on the compilation report. (Chapter 31-1-2; 8611; CBT Skill: analysis; CSO: 3.8.0)

6. (d) *Sending sales orders to the credit department for approval* is a key control for ensuring that sales are properly authorized. Although the billing and cash receipts departments should be separate (to reduce the opportunity for any one person to both perpetrate and conceal fraud or errors in the normal course of their duties), their separation does not impact whether sales are properly authorized. Use of an approved price list is a control to ensure the accuracy of sales transactions rather than proper authorization. The receipt of *approved* sales orders by the shipping, billing, and accounting departments occurs after the fact. (Chapter 23-7-1; 8612; CBT Skill: judgment; CSO: 2.7.0)

7. (c) This question states the objective of a review engagement. For a review engagement, an accountant should *possess a level of knowledge of the accounting principles* and practices *of the industry*

in which the entity operates and an understanding of the entity's business that will provide through the performance of inquiry and analytical procedures, a reasonable basis for expressing limited assurance that there are no material modifications that should be made to the financial statements in order for them to be in conformity with GAAP or OCBOA. A review does **not** include assessing fraud risk or evaluating the effectiveness of controls—a review does not even contemplate obtaining an understanding of the entity's internal control. The accountant is not required to communicate the existence of material weaknesses in internal control to the entity's audit committee. (Chapter 31-1-3; 8613; CBT Skill: understanding; CSO: 1.6.0)

8. (c) The assessment of the competence of internal auditors by the auditor should include obtaining information about the *quality of working paper documentation,* reports, and recommendations. Information about the influence of management on the scope of the internal auditor's duties and the policies limiting their communication with the audit committee bear on the assessment of their objectivity rather than their competence. Information about the entity's ability to continue as a going concern would not reflect on the competence of the internal auditors. (Chapter 24-2-2; 8614; CBT Skill: understanding; CSO: 1.10.3)

9. (c) Loss contingencies include those arising from litigation, claims and assessments. A *letter of inquiry to the client's lawyer* is the auditor's primary means of corroboration of the information furnished by management about such matters. The financial statements (including footnotes), which may include accrual or disclosure of loss contingencies, are part of the information furnished by management. Performing appropriate analytical procedures and checking the arithmetic accuracy of the accounting records are not likely to provide information about the evaluation of loss contingencies. (Chapter 24-6-2; 8615; CBT Skill: judgment; CSO: 3.2.0)

10. (c) *Observation* of the application of the control, i.e., *whether the data center is monitored* to limit access, yields the most reliable audit evidence about the effectiveness of this control. The control may not be practiced as it is described in the policy manual. Inquiry of the chief technology officer does not provide as reliable evidence as the auditor's observation of the control's application. Obtaining a list of current data center employees by itself does not provide evidence of the effectiveness of the control's application. (Chapter 23-3-2; 8616; CBT Skill: analysis; CSO: 2.6.0)

11. (b) Detection risk differs from control risk and inherent risk in that it *can be changed at the auditor's discretion.* Detection risk, control risk, and inherent risk make up audit risk. *Detection risk* is the risk that the auditor will not detect a misstatement that exists in a relevant assertion. It is a function of an audit procedure's effectiveness and how the auditor applies the procedure. Accordingly, it can be changed at the auditor's discretion. *Control risk* is the risk that a misstatement that could occur in a relevant assertion will not be prevented or detected on a timely basis by the entity's internal control. *Inherent risk* is the susceptibility of a relevant assertion to a misstatement assuming that there are no related controls. Thus, inherent risk and control risk, rather than detection risk, are the entity's risks, i.e., they exist independently of the audit and cannot be changed at the auditor's discretion. Detection risk arises from the fact that the auditor does not examine 100 percent of an account balance or a class of transactions and other factors (which include the possibility that an auditor might select an inappropriate audit procedure, misapply an appropriate audit procedure, or misinterpret the audit result) rather than from fraud risk factors. All three risks can be assessed in quantitative terms, such as percentages, or nonquantitative terms, such as high, medium, or low risk. (Chapter 22-2-4; 8617; CBT Skill: understanding; CSO: 1.9.0)

12. (a) The voucher and all supporting documents should be canceled (*stamped paid*) *by the check signer* to avoid duplicate payments. The return of the voucher to the vouchers payable department provides no control to prevent it from being paid more than once. Confirmation that each voucher is supported by a vendor's invoice and purchase order provides evidence that the payment is based on a valid purchase, but would not stop a duplicate payment. Prenumbering and accounting for vouchers allows confirmation that all vouchers were recorded and should allow the discovery of a duplicate payment, but it would not prevent it. (Chapter 23-7-5; 8618; CBT Skill: judgment; CSO: 2.6.0)

13. (c) In a review, the accountant must apply analytical procedures, such as the *analysis of inventory turnover.* A review does **not** include tests of accounting records through inspection, observation, confirmation, or examination of source documents; or other procedures ordinarily performed in an audit. So the accountant would not perform a physical inspection of inventory or vouch inventory purchase transactions. Nor does a review include obtaining an understanding of the entity's internal control, so the accountant would not evaluate internal control over inventory. (Chapter 31-1-3; 8619; CBT Skill: analysis; CSO: 3.8.0)

14. (b) The primary reason for a letter of audit inquiry to the client's attorneys is to obtain *corroboration of the information furnished by management concerning litigation, claims, and assessments*. The attorney's legal expertise is sought by the auditor, not the assurance that matters are properly *accounted* for. The letter of inquiry should address two lists; one comprised of *pending* or threatened litigation, claims, and assessments; and the other, *unasserted claims and assessments* that would, if asserted, have a reasonable possibility of an unfavorable outcome. The pending matters list is not limited to those that management believes have a reasonable possibility of an unfavorable outcome. And although an attorney's response does include addressing the description of matters and the evaluation of their likely outcome, the *primary* reason for the auditor's request is to corroborate management's information. The attorney is asked to evaluate the likelihood of an unfavorable outcome, not give an opinion using the terms *possible*, *probable* or *remote*. (Chapter 24-6-2; 8620; CBT Skill: understanding; CSO: 3.3.0)

15. (b) *Collusion* is an inherent limitation of any system of internal control. An internal control system, no matter how well designed and operated, cannot give an entity absolute assurance that its objectives will be met because any system has inherent limitations. Other inherent limitations of internal control are faulty human judgment, human failures that lead to errors or mistakes, and inappropriate management override of controls. Judgmental sampling is part of the application of an auditing procedure; not an inherent limitation of internal control. Segregation of duties and employee peer reviews are examples of controls; not inherent limitations. (Chapter 23-2-1; 8621; CBT Skill: understanding; CSO: 2.4.0)

16. (c) To discover understated (unrecorded) sales, the auditor would most likely trace transactions from *shipping documents to sales invoices*. This would reveal orders that have been shipped, but not billed and is an example of testing for completeness. Vouching from sales invoices to shipping documents (the opposite direction) is a test to substantiate that sales are not overstated (verify their occurrence or existence). Comparing entries between the cash receipts journal and the sales journal would verify that the entries were posted correctly, but it would not locate an unrecorded sale. Note: The sales and cash receipts journals are often combined in one journal. (Chapter 25-3-2; 8622; CBT Skill: analysis; CSO: 3.1.5)

17. (a) The auditor would most likely consider, as a mitigating factor, the entity's plans to *extend the due dates of existing loans.* The extension would immediately allow the entity more time to raise cash and more flexibility in planning expenditures. The auditor would need to conclude that it would be granted by the lender and would provide enough of an increase in available funds to be effective. The auditor would be less likely to consider increased levels of production as a mitigating factor. This would definitely mean an increase of expenditures which might not result in increased profitability. Accelerating expenditures for R & D is even more risky especially when the auditor considers that the benefit would need to occur soon enough to meet the reasonable period criteria, i.e., not to exceed one year beyond the date of the financial statements being audited. Although issuing stock options to key executives is often used to attract talent and motivate management (aligning their interests with those of the shareholders), it is unlikely this would be considered a mitigating factor even though upon their granting the options involve no cash outlay and if exercised, generally produce tax savings. Most plans do not allow the employee to exercise the options for at least a year and then often only a portion of them. (Chapter 28-9-4; 8623; CBT Skill: judgment; CSO: 4.4.0)

18. (d) *The date on the report should be the date of completion of the compilation.* An accountant need **not** be independent with respect to an entity to issue a compilation report. In such a case, the accountant should specifically disclose the lack of independence in the last paragraph of the report; however, the reason for the lack of independence should **not** be included. One of the basic elements of a compilation report is a statement that a compilation is limited to presenting in the form of financial statements information that is the representation of *management* (owners); not the accountant. Any other procedures that the accountant might have performed before or during the compilation engagement should **not** be described in the report. (Chapter 31-1-2; 8624; CBT Skill: understanding; CSO: 5.1.2)

19. (b) The phrase *generally accepted accounting principles* is a technical accounting term that *encompasses the conventions, rules, and procedures necessary to define accepted accounting practice at a particular time.* It includes not only broad guidelines of general application, but also detailed practices and procedures. No single reference source, such as the AICPA, exists for all of GAAP. The first sentence of the scope paragraph of the standard report explicitly states that the audit was conducted in accordance with GAAS; the inclusion of a phrase about adherence to GAAP in the opinion paragraph of the report is not an indirect reference

to GAAS. (Chapter 28-1-1; 8625; CBT Skill: judgment; CSO: 1.1.1)

20. (d) *Remedy of limitations resulting from accepting the engagement after the close of the end of the year, such as those relating to the existence of physical inventory* would permit the auditor to accept such an engagement. Although early appointment is preferable, an auditor may accept an engagement near or after the close of the fiscal year. The taking of the inventory could be postponed or failing that, another could be taken for the auditor to observe. If the auditor believes that circumstances are such that acceptance after the close of the fiscal year would preclude an unqualified opinion, the auditor should discuss the possible necessity of a qualified or disclaimer of opinion with the client. This is an example of when candidates need to choose the best answer on the exam. It is much more likely that an auditor would accept an engagement after the close of the client's fiscal year if the determination was made that the resultant limitations could be remedied. The assessment of control risk below the maximum level cannot be determined prior to the acceptance of an engagement and is also not relevant to the issue of whether to accept the engagement after the close of the fiscal year. An auditor cannot rely on a predecessor auditor's assertion about a client's ability to continue as a going concern, setting aside the unlikelihood of receiving such a communication. Further, this is not relevant to the issue of whether to accept the engagement after the close of the fiscal year. (Chapter 22-1-1; 8626; CBT Skill: understanding; CSO: 1.4.0)

21. (b) An accountant may give negative assurance as to whether any material modifications should be made to an entity's *unaudited condensed interim financial information for it to be in conformity with GAAP* when the accountant has conducted a review of the interim financial information in accordance with SAS 100, *Interim Financial Information.* Accountants should **not** mention reports related to internal control in a comfort letter, thus negative assurance regarding the absence of any significant deficiencies in internal control should not be made. Accountants may **not** provide negative assurance on the results of procedures performed in compiling an entity's financial forecast. Accountants provide assistance regarding the financial information contained in a registration statement, not the compliance of the registration statement with the Securities Act of 1933. (Chapter 30-3-2; 8627; CBT Skill: understanding; CSO: 5.2.4)

22. (c) An accountant is required to comply with the provisions of the SSARS when *submitting unaudited financial statements of a nonissuer* to a client or third parties. *Submission of financial statements* is defined as presenting to a client or third parties financial statements that the accountant has prepared either manually or through the use of computer software. The other three answer alternatives do not meet this definition. (Chapter 31-1-1; 8628; CBT Skill: judgment; CSO: 1.1.2)

23. (c) One of the basic elements of a report on compiled financial statements is a statement that *a compilation is limited to presenting in the form of financial statements information that is the representation of management* (owners). A statement that the accountant is not aware of any material modifications that should be made to the financial statements in order for them to be in conformity with GAAP, other than those modifications, if any, indicated in the report (similar to answer *a*), is a basic element of a *review* report rather than a compilation report. A compilation does **not** provide a basis for expressing any level of assurance on the financial statements being compiled. A statement that a *review* is substantially less in scope than an audit, the objective of which is the expression of an opinion regarding the financial statements taken as a whole and, accordingly, no such opinion is expressed (similar to answer *b*), is also an element of a review rather than a compilation report. The basic element in a compilation report that addresses the scope of the engagement is a statement that the financial statements have not been audited or reviewed and, accordingly, the accountant does not express an opinion or any other form of assurance on them. Answer *d* is similar to the statement included in the scope paragraph of the standard *audit* report. Again, a compilation does **not** provide any level of assurance. (Chapter 31-1-2; 8629; CBT Skill: understanding; CSO: 5.1.2)

24. (b) One of the elements of a system of quality control is the *acceptance and continuance of client relationships and specific engagements.* Addressing this includes establishing policies and procedures designed to provide a firm with reasonable assurance that it will *accept or continue relationships with clients only when it has considered the integrity of the client*, including the identity and business reputation of the client's principal owners, key management, related parties, and those charged with its governance; and the risk associated with providing professional services in the particular circumstances. A firm's duty to the public may come into play within this element of quality control in the consideration of the withdrawal from an engagement under certain circumstances, but generally not in regard to the acceptance of a new client. However, the public interest is directly addressed in two other elements of a quality control system: *relevant ethical requirements* and *engagement performance.*

Whether the client will meet any agreed-upon obligations such as the timely completion of schedules would probably not yet be known when the acceptance of a new client is being considered and is unlikely to be a factor in any event. Nor is it a quality control issue. Prior to the acceptance of a new client, the auditor can only try to ascertain if there will be sufficient corroborating evidence. Although this would be a consideration in whether to accept a new client and it could be posed that having personnel capable of making this judgment is part of this element of quality control, it is not as important an issue as the integrity of the client. (Chapter 21-4-2; 8630; CBT Skill: understanding; CSO: 1.2.3)

25. (b) Accounts receivable turnovers are 10.0 and 6.6 and the ratios of uncollectible accounts receivable to gross accounts receivable are 0.30 and 0.16, respectively. The auditor should examine the allowance account for possible *understatement.* The calculations are as follows. Prior year accounts receivable turnover: net sales of $1,000,000 divided by average receivables of $100,000 = 10.0. Current year accounts receivable turnover: net sales of $2,000,000 divided by average receivables of $300,000 = *6.6. Prior year ratio of allowance for uncollectible accounts receivable to average accounts receivable: allowance for uncollectible accounts receivable of $30,000 divided by average receivables of $100,000 = 0.30. Current year ratio of allowance for uncollectible accounts receivable to average accounts receivable: allowance for uncollectible accounts receivable of $50,000 divided by average receivables of $300,000 = *0.16. Thus accounts receivable turnover decreased from 10.0 to 6.0 and the ratio of allowance for uncollectible accounts receivable to average accounts receivable also decreased; from 0.30 to 0.16. The lower the rate of accounts receivable turnover, the longer the accounts receivable are being held and thus the less likely they are to be collected. In this situation, one would expect the ratio of the allowance of uncollectible accounts receivable to average accounts receivable to increase. Because it decreased, the auditor should examine the allowance account for possible understatement. *Note: Rather than rounding, the examiners truncated these calculations. (Chapter 24-4-4; 8631; CBT Skill: analysis; CSO: 4.1.0)

Solution 2 MULTIPLE CHOICE ANSWERS (2008 Hard)

26. (d) When planning an audit sample for a test of controls, the auditor should consider *the auditor's allowable risk of assessing control risk too low*; not too high. The auditor should also consider the relationship of the sample to the objective of the test of controls; the maximum rate of deviations from prescribed controls that would support the planned assessed level of control risk; and characteristics of the population, i.e., the items comprising the account balance or class of transactions of interest. Preliminary judgments about materially levels and the level of detection risk are considerations for planning a sample for a substantive test of details. (Chapter 26-1-6; 8632; CBT Skill: judgment; CSO: 3.1.1)

27. (a) The most efficient method to obtain information about the transfer agent's internal control would be to *review reports on internal control placed in operation and its operating effectiveness produced by the agent's own auditor.* Answers c and d describe methods of obtaining information that are not as efficient as answer a. While a significant increase in the number of transactions processed may bear on the planning of the audit procedures, it doesn't reveal any information about internal controls. (Chapter 30-4-2; 8633; CBT Skill: judgment; CSO: 2.5.0)

28. (d) The analytical procedures the accountant may consider performing when conducting a review of financial statements include *comparing current financial information with relevant nonfinancial information.* In order to obtain a reasonable basis for the expression of limited assurance, the accountant must apply analytical procedures to the financial statements, as well as make inquiries and obtain representations from management. Analytical procedures include comparing recorded amounts, or ratios developed from recorded amounts, to expectations developed by the accountant. Although analytical procedures are required by GAAS to be included in the both the planning and the final review stage of an audit, this is not a requirement of a review. (Chapter 31-1-3; 8634; CBT Skill: analysis; CSO: 4.1.0)

29. (d) A review does **not** include assessing fraud risk nor does it contemplate obtaining an understanding of the entity's internal control, so the report would not speak to these matters. (Chapter 31-1-3; 8635; CBT Skill: understanding; CSO: 5.1.2)

30. (b) The auditor should make the selection from the *shipping document file.* Attempting to match shipping documents to invoices would reveal goods shipped that were not invoiced. The cash receipts file contains evidence of payments, so it would be

highly unlikely to discover payments received from customers who weren't billed. The customer order file would be a workable but inefficient choice by the auditor because normally goods are not invoiced until they are shipped, so it would involve checking shipping documents as well to confirm the sale. The sales invoice file would not be used because the auditor is looking for sales that were not invoiced. (Chapter 23-7-1; 8636; CBT Skill: analysis; CSO: 2.6.0)

31. (d) If the accountant concludes that the unaudited financial statements on which the accountant is disclaiming an opinion are **not** in conformity with GAAP, the accountant should suggest appropriate revision; failing that, the accountant should *describe the nature of the departure in the report and, if practicable, state the effects on the financial statements* or include the necessary information for adequate disclosure. When disclaiming an opinion, no assurance can be expressed. Restricting the distribution of the report is not an adequate remedy. The accountant cannot issue a qualified or adverse opinion on unaudited financial statements. (Chapter 28-8-5; 8637; CBT Skill: analysis; CSO: 5.1.1)

32. (d) The *review of travel and entertainment expenses* can be done *prior* to the balance sheet date; however, when substantive procedures are performed at an interim date, the auditor should perform further audit procedures to cover the remaining period that provide a reasonable basis for extending the audit conclusion from the interim date to the balance sheet date. Various phases of an audit are completed during the subsequent period that extends from after the balance sheet date to the date of the audit report. These include the other answer alternatives: review of subsequent events (self-explanatory), the search for unrecorded liabilities, and inquiry of the client's legal counsel. Certain procedures are applied to transactions occurring after the balance sheet date such as the examination of data to assure that proper cutoffs have been made and the examination of data that would provide information to aid the auditor in the evaluation of the assets and liabilities as of the balance sheet date. These procedures would include the search through these post balance sheet transactions for evidence of liabilities that existed at the balance sheet date, but were not recorded. The attorney's response should include coverage of as much of this subsequent period as possible, i.e., have an effective date (the latest date of the period covered by the response) as close to the date of the auditor's report as practicable. Note: As a practical matter, an auditor may choose to send an initial request to the attorney earlier in the audit, so that the completion of the audit is not delayed, with the understanding that

an update will be needed close to the report date. (Chapter 25-1-3; 8638; CBT Skill: analysis; CSO: 3.1.7)

33. (b) *The auditor should document key elements of her/his understanding of internal control* regardless of the client's records. The client's failure to do so does not constitute a scope limitation; necessitate that the auditor assess control risk at the maximum level; nor restrict the auditor's responsibility to assess the effectiveness of controls. (Chapter 23-2-5; 8639; CBT Skill: judgment; CSO: 2.3.0)

34. (a) When assessing the internal auditors' objectivity, the auditor should obtain information about such factors as *the organizational status of the director of the internal audit* function. The professional certifications of the internal audit staff is a factor to consider when assessing their competence; not their objectivity. Answer alternatives *c* and *d* are factors to consider when developing evaluation procedures for testing the effectiveness of internal auditors' work rather than their objectivity. (Chapter 24-2-2; 8640; CBT Skill: understanding; CSO: 1.10.3)

35. (a) Relationships involving income statement accounts, such as *interest expense,* tend to be more predictable than relationships involving only balance sheet accounts because income statement accounts represent transactions over a period of time, whereas balance sheet accounts represent amounts as of a point in time. (Chapter 24-4-4; 8641; CBT Skill: analysis; CSO: 3.1.2)

36. (d) *Neither I nor II.* An accountant is required to comply with the provisions of the SSARS when submitting unaudited financial statements of a nonissuer to a client or third parties. *Submission of financial statements* is defined as presenting to a client or third parties financial statements that the accountant has prepared either manually or through the use of computer software. Neither I nor II meets this definition. (Chapter 31-1-1; 8642; CBT Skill: understanding; CSO: 1.1.2)

37. (b) The auditor's procedures should include a *discussion with management about the policies and procedures adopted for identifying, evaluating,* and accounting *for litigation,* claims, and assessments. The events or conditions that should be considered in the financial accounting for and reporting of litigation, claims, and assessments are matters within the direct knowledge and, often, control of management of an entity. Accordingly, management is the primary source of information about such matters. It is the auditor's responsibility to conclude whether the client's litigation is properly disclosed. The auditor requests the client's attorney's opinion on this, not the clerk of the court. The clerk of the court would

not have the information needed. The auditor would examine documents in the client's possession; not the lawyer's possession. The auditor would not likely inspect documents in the client's lawyer's possession due to confidentiality considerations. If the attorney's response does not provide enough information, the auditor would arrange a conference with the attorney rather than request documentation. It would not be appropriate for the auditor to contact the client's adversaries' legal representatives. (Chapter 24-6-1; 8643; CBT Skill: analysis; CSO: 3.2.0)

38. (b) Before reissuing a compilation (or a review report) of a nonissuer on the financial statements of a prior period, the predecessor accountant should read the financial statements of the current period and the successor's report; *compare the prior period financial statements* with those previously issued and *with those of the current period;* and obtain a letter from the successor that indicates whether s/he is aware of any matter that might have a material effect on the financial statements, including disclosures, reported on by the predecessor. The other answer alternatives are not required. Note: The predecessor should **not** refer to the letter from the successor or the successor's report in the reissued report. (Chapter 31-2-4; 8644; CBT Skill: understanding; CSO: 5.1.2)

39. (b) A review does include making *inquiries of management which should include asking about related party transactions*. The successor accountant may wish to review the predecessor's working papers relating to matters of continuing accounting significance and those relating to contingencies. As this is not a requirement, as are inquiries of management, it is not as likely to be performed. In a review the accountant is ordinarily **not** required to corroborate management's responses with other evidence, so it is not likely that the accountant would contact the entity's attorney. A review does **not** contemplate obtaining an understanding of the entity's internal control, thus communication of internal control deficiencies to senior management would not be likely. (Chapter 31-1-3; 8645; CBT Skill: analysis; CSO: 3.8.0)

40. (b) *A lack of independent checks* or inadequate segregation of duties is one of the risk factors associated with misstatements arising from misappropriation of assets. The other answer alternatives are risk factors relating to misstatements arising from fraudulent financial reporting. (Chapter 22-4-2; 8646; CBT Skill: understanding; CSO: 1.9.0)

41. (d) *An accountant need **not** be independent* with respect to an entity to issue a compilation report. In such a case, the accountant should specifically disclose the lack of independence in the last paragraph of the report; however, the reason for the lack of independence should **not** be included. A compilation does **not** include performing analytical procedures. A compilation does **not** provide a basis for expressing any level of assurance on the financial statements being compiled. A compilation does **not** include making management inquiries nor does it contemplate gaining an understanding of an entity's internal control. (Chapter 31-1-2; 8647; CBT Skill: understanding; CSO: 1.1.2)

42. (d) When reviewing the financial statements of a nonissuer, an accountant should *make inquiries about actions taken at the board of directors meetings*. Making inquiries of management along with applying analytical procedures and obtaining representations from management are required in order to obtain a reasonable basis for the expression of limited assurance. A review does **not** include verification of accounting estimates or tests of accounting records and procedures ordinarily performed in an audit. A review does **not** contemplate obtaining an understanding of an entity's internal control. A review does **not** include the assessment of an entity's ability to continue as a going concern; however, during the performance of a review (or a compilation) it may come to the attention of the accountant that there may be such an uncertainty. If so, the accountant should request that management consider the possible effects on the financial statements, including related disclosures. (Chapter 31-1-3; 8648; CBT Skill: analysis; CSO: 3.8.0)

43. (c) In evaluating the reasonableness of an estimate, the auditor normally concentrates on key factors and assumptions that are *deviations from historical patterns;* sensitive to variations (not stable and insensitive to variations); subjective and susceptible to misstatement and bias (not the opposite); and, of course, significant to the accounting estimate. The auditor would expect the estimates to be consistent with industry guidelines, so estimates that did not conform would bear more scrutiny to obtain evidence that the variation was reasonable under the circumstances. (Chapter 25-3-10; 8649; CBT Skill: understanding; CSO: 1.11.2)

44. (a) In the situation described, *the financial statements are free from material misstatement, and **no** disclosure is required in the notes to the financial statements.* An unqualified opinion states that the financial statements present fairly, *in all material respects,* the financial position, results of operations, and cash flows of the entity in conformity with GAAP. (Chapter 28-2-1; 8650; CBT Skill: judgment; CSO: 4.3.0)

45. (d) *An auditor would not seek an evaluation of the client's ability to continue as a going concern from an attorney* regardless of the cause of the client's financial difficulties; that is the auditor's responsibility and does not involve legal expertise. Answer alternatives *a-c* would be likely to be covered in the client's attorney's response to a letter of audit inquiry. (Chapter 24-6-2; 8651; CBT Skill: understanding; CSO: 3.3.0)

46. (d) The auditor may, as a result of the report or findings of the specialist, decide to *add explanatory language to a standard report (for example, to emphasize an unusually important subsequent event)* or depart from an unqualified opinion. Reference to and identification of the specialist may be made in the auditor's report if the auditor believes such reference will facilitate an understanding of the reason for the explanatory paragraph or the departure from the unqualified opinion. *Otherwise*, the auditor should **not** refer to the work or findings of the specialist. Such a reference might be misunderstood to be a qualification of the auditor's opinion or a division of responsibility, neither of which is intended. Further, there may be an inference that the auditor making such reference performed a more thorough audit than an auditor not making such reference. (Chapter 24-5-5; 8652; CBT Skill: judgment; CSO: 1.10.2)

47. (c) When an accountant is **not** independent with respect to an entity, *a compilation report with special wording that notes the accountant's lack of independence may be issued.* The accountant should specifically disclose the lack of independence in the last paragraph of the report. However, the reason for the lack of independence should **not** be described. Regardless of the accountant's independence, a compilation does **not** provide a basis for expressing any level of assurance on the financial statements being compiled. There is no point in upgrading the engagement when the accountant lacks independence. Upgrading the engagement does **not** change the requirement for disclosure of the lack of independence in a compilation report. (An accountant is *precluded* from issuing a *review* report for an entity with respect to which the accountant is **not** independent.) (Chapter 31-1-2; 8653; CBT Skill: understanding; CSO: 5.1.2)

48. (c) *A loss on an uncollectible trade receivable recorded in year 1 from a customer that declared bankruptcy in year 2* would most likely require an adjustment to the financial statements. Auditors must consider two types of subsequent events. The first type requires adjustment of the financial statements because it provides evidence about conditions that existed at the balance sheet date. A loss on an uncollectible trade account receivable as a result of a customer's deteriorating financial condition leading to bankruptcy subsequent to the balance sheet date would be indicative of conditions existing at the balance sheet date. A bankruptcy after the balance sheet date is the classic example of an event that represents the culmination of conditions that existed over a relatively long period of time as opposed to a sudden event like a fire or flood that occurred after the balance sheet date. The second type of subsequent event provides evidence about conditions that did **not** exist at the balance sheet date and does **not** require adjustment of the financial statements, however due to their nature; some of them may require disclosure to keep the financial statements from being misleading. The other answer alternatives are examples of the second type of subsequent event and they are all also examples of events that would require disclosure. (Chapter 28-7-2; 8654; CBT Skill: analysis; CSO: 3.4.0)

49. (b) *Engagement performance* is one of the elements of a firm's system of quality control. The firm's quality control system should include policies and procedures addressing it and the other elements which are: leadership responsibilities for quality within the firm; relevant ethical requirements; acceptance and continuance of client relationships and specific engagements; human resources; and monitoring. Information processing, technology selection, and professional skepticism are not defined elements of a firm's quality control system. (Chapter 21-4-2; 8655; CBT Skill: understanding; CSO: 1.2.3)

50. (b) The auditor generally should *compare the latest available interim financial information with the financial statements being reported upon.* This is an example of a procedure to find events occurring in the period subsequent to the balance sheet date, but prior to the issuance of the audit report, which may require adjustment to or disclosure in the financial statements. Changes in the market prices of investments purchased and recorded after the year-end are not relevant because the investments are appropriately not a part of the current year's financial statements. The application of analytical procedures to the details of balance sheet accounts that were tested at interim dates is done so that evidence can be obtained for the extension of the conclusions made at the time of the interim tests to the period end—it is not part of the subsequent period testing. When payroll checks (appropriately recorded as expense in the current year) were cashed does not affect the financial statements. (Chapter 28-7-2; 8656; CBT Skill: analysis; CSO: 3.4.0)

Solution 3 SIMULATION ANSWER (2008)

Response #1: Unrecorded Liabilities

Check # 1333 $0

The amount of this check ($3,500) is lower than the $6,000 materiality level for adjustments set by the auditors for unrecorded liabilities; otherwise an adjustment would have been needed.

Check # 1334 $6,000

This represents an expense for year 2, paid in year 3, which is equal to the materiality level; an adjustment (accrual of expense) is needed.

Check # 1335 $6,500

This represents an expense for year 2, paid in year 3, which exceeds the materiality level; an adjustment (accrual of expense) is needed.

Check # 1336 $12,750

The portion of this check that represents the salary expense for the period December 25 through December 31, year 2 is an expense for year 2, paid in year 3. The only information the problem gives you is that it is a biweekly payroll. Halving the amount of the check ($25,500/2 = $12,750) is a reasonable assumption to arrive at the amount of the adjustment (accrual of expense) needed.

Check # 1337 $41,188

The portion of this check that represents the delivery expense for the period December 4 through December 31, year 2 is an expense for year 2, paid in year 3. The problem states that deliveries are made evenly throughout the period. The expense covers a period of 31 days (December 4, year 2 through January 3, year 3), 28 of which were part of year 2; thus the calculation for the amount of the adjustment (accrual of expense) needed would be (($45,601 / 31) × 28) = $41,188.

Check # 1338 $0

This amount of this check ($2,002) is lower than the $6,000 materiality level for adjustments set by the auditors for unrecorded liabilities; no adjustment is needed.

Check # 1339 $11,000

This represents an unrecorded liability for year 2 (when the forklift was ordered and received), which exceeds the materiality level; an adjustment

(recording of the asset and related payable) is needed.

Check # 1340 $12,230

This represents an unrecorded liability for year 2 (when the goods were ordered and received) which exceeds the materiality level; an adjustment (recording of the purchase and related payable) is needed.

Check # 1341 $0

No adjustment is needed; this represents year 3 salary expense, paid in year 3.

Check # 1342 $0

No adjustment is needed; this represents an expense for year 3, paid in year 3.

Response #2: Substantive Tests

1. D, H

    - Any shipping documents dated year 3 should not be invoiced (recorded as sales) in year 2; any shipping documents dated year 2 should be posted to the year 2 sales journal and accounts receivable subsidiary ledger.

    - Accounting for the prenumbered documents in each year's postings will determine if proper cutoff occurred.

2. C. E

    - If the aging of accounts receivable is not accurate, the allowance for uncollectible accounts receivable won't be either; thus the net realizable value of receivables will not be fairly stated.

    - Comparison and the resulting analysis of the current year's relationship to prior years is a test of the reasonableness of the current year's relationship.

3. J, K

    - The recalculation of depreciation expense will confirm its mathematical accuracy and that the expense is allocated to the correct year.

- This review will confirm that the methods and estimates are appropriate, reasonable, and consistently applied.

4. N. M

- Testing (vouching) for existence by physically inspecting the acquisitions which are included in the balance sheet will confirm that fixed assets are not overstated,

- This is another procedure to determine if the assets included in the balance sheet actually exist.

Response #3: Audit Adjustments

1. Dr. Interest Expense
      Cr. Accrued Liabilities
   To record interest expense for December

2. Dr. Operating Expenses
      Cr. Accrued Liabilities
   To record year 2 salary expense paid in year 3

3. Dr. Revenues
      Cr. Accounts Receivable
   To adjust revenue for year 3 sales recorded in year 2

4. Disclosure, but no entry required.

   When the loss is *reasonably possible*, rather than *probable*, accrual would be inappropriate, but disclosure of the nature of the contingency is required.

5. Dr. Operating Expenses
      Cr. Allowance for Doubtful Accounts
   To record the increase in bad debt expense

Response #4: Communication

To: Audit Team

From: Senior Auditor

Re: Conditions for the Allowable Omission of Accounts Receivable Confirmations

Confirmation of accounts receivable is a **generally accepted auditing procedure.** Generally, evidence obtained from **third parties** will provide us with **higher**-quality **audit evidence** than we would typically find available within our client's records. Thus, there is a **presumption** that we should confirm accounts receivable unless we find one of the following conditions to be the case.

If accounts receivable are **immaterial to the financial statements**, then it would be acceptable not to confirm them.

Or, if we knew that the use of confirmations would be **ineffective**, we could omit them. For example, if our prior years' working papers indicated that last year's **response rate** was unsatisfactory or we had reason to believe that the responses would probably be **unreliable**.

And finally, we could omit them if our combined assessed level of **inherent risk** and **control risk** was **low** enough that when combined with **other substantive tests of details** or **analytical procedures**, we concluded that **audit risk** would be reduced sufficiently for the applicable financial statement **assertions**. However, usually it takes both confirmations *and* other substantive procedures combined to reduce audit risk for these assertions to an acceptably low level.

Additionally, should we omit them; we would need to document how we overcame the presumption to perform them.

Response #5: Research

Paragraph Reference Answer: AU 334.08

"The following procedures are intended to provide guidance for identifying material transactions with parties known to be related and for identifying material transactions that may be indicative of the existence of previously undetermined relationships:

   a. Provide audit personnel performing segments of the audit or auditing and reporting separately on the accounts of related components of the reporting entity with the names of known related parties so that they may become aware of transactions with such parties during their audits.

   b. Review the minutes of meetings of the board of directors and executive or operating committees for information about material transactions authorized or discussed at their meetings.

   c. Review proxy and other material filed with the Securities and Exchange Commission and comparable data filed with other regulatory agencies for information about material transactions with related parties.

d. Review conflict-of-interests statements obtained by the company from its management.

e. Review the extent and nature of business transacted with major customers, suppliers, borrowers, and lenders for indications of previously undisclosed relationships.

f. Consider whether transactions are occurring, but are not being given accounting recognition, such as receiving or providing accounting, management or other services at no charge or a major stockholder absorbing corporate expenses.

g. Review accounting records for large, unusual, or nonrecurring transactions or balances, paying particular attention to transactions recognized at or near the end of the reporting period.

h. Review confirmations of compensating balance arrangements for indications that balances are or were maintained for or by related parties.

i. Review invoices from law firms that have performed regular or special services for the company for indications of the existence of related parties or related party transactions.

j. Review confirmations of loans receivable and payable for indications of guarantees. When guarantees are indicated, determine their nature and the relationships, if any, of the guarantors to the reporting entity."

2009 RELEASED AICPA QUESTIONS AND ANSWERS

Problem 4 MULTIPLE-CHOICE QUESTIONS (2009 Moderate)

1. Which of the following is an analytical procedure that an auditor most likely would perform during the final review stage of an audit?
a. Comparing each individual expense account balance with the relevant budgeted amounts and investigating any significant variations
b. Testing the effectiveness of internal control procedures that appear to be suitably designed to prevent or detect material misstatements
c. Reading the financial statements and considering whether there are any unusual or unexpected balances that were **not** previously identified
d. Calculating each individual expense account balance as a percentage of total entity expenses and comparing the results with industry averages
(R/09, AUD, 0258A, #1, 8801)

2. Accepting an engagement to compile an entity's financial projection most likely would be inappropriate if the projection is to be included in a(an)
a. Mortgage application for the purpose of expanding the entity's facilities
b. Offering statement of the entity's initial public offering of common stock
c. Comprehensive document to be used in negotiating a new labor contract
d. Report to the audit committee that is **not** sent to the stockholders
(R/09, AUD, 1105A, #2, 8802)

3. Which of the following procedures is an accountant required to perform when reviewing the financial statements of a nonpublic entity in accordance with Statements on Standards for Accounting and Review Services (SSARS)?
a. Assess control risk
b. Obtain a management representation letter
c. Confirm account balances
d. Perform a physical inventory observation
(R/09, AUD, A0416A, #3, 8803)

4. A CPA firm is completing the fieldwork for an audit of Swenson Co. for the current year ended December 31. The manager in charge of the audit is performing the final steps in the evidence accumulation phase of the audit and notes that there have been several changes in Swenson during the year under audit. Which of the following items would indicate there could be substantial doubt about Swenson's ability to continue as a going concern for a reasonable period of time?
a. Cash infusion by a venture capital firm
b. Recurring working capital shortages
c. A lack of significant contracts with new customers
d. Term debt refinanced with a new bank
(R/09, AUD, C00099A, #4, 8804)

5. The blank form of accounts receivable confirmations may be **less** efficient than the positive form because
a. Shipping documents need to be inspected.
b. Recipients may sign the forms without proper investigation.
c. More nonresponses to the requests are likely to occur.
d. Subsequent cash receipts need to be verified.
(R/09, AUD, 1554A, #5, 8805)

6. An accountant agrees to the client's request to change an engagement from a review to a compilation of financial statements. The compilation report should include
a. No reference to the original engagement
b. Reference to a departure from GAAS
c. Scope limitations that may have resulted in the change of engagement
d. Information about review procedures already performed
(R/09, AUD, A0298A, #6, 8806)

7. Which of the following describes a weakness in accounts payable procedures?
a. The accounts payable clerk files invoices and supporting documentation after payment.
b. The accounts payable clerk manually verifies arithmetic on the vendor invoice.
c. The accounts payable system compares the receiving report to the vendor invoice.
d. The accounts payable manager issues purchase orders.
(R/09, AUD, A2440A, #7, 8807)

8. A successor auditor's inquiries of the predecessor auditor should include questions regarding
a. The predecessor's evaluation of audit risk and judgment about materiality
b. Subsequent events that occurred since the predecessor's audit report was issued
c. The predecessor's understanding as to the reasons for the change in auditors
d. The predecessor's knowledge of accounting matters of continuing significance

(R/09, AUD, 1609A, #8, 8808)

9. Which of the following most likely would cause an auditor to consider whether a client's financial statements contain material misstatements?
a. Management did **not** disclose to the auditor that it consulted with other accountants about significant accounting matters.
b. The chief financial officer will **not** sign the management representation letter until the last day of the auditor's fieldwork.
c. Audit trails of computer-generated transactions exist only for a short time.
d. The results of an analytical procedure disclose unexpected differences.

(R/09, AUD, C05022A, #9, 8809)

10. Which of the following statements is correct regarding accounting estimates?
a. The auditor's objective is to evaluate whether accounting estimates are reasonable in the circumstances.
b. Accounting estimates should be used when data concerning past events can be accumulated in a timely, cost-effective manner.
c. An important accounting estimate is management's listing of accounts receivable greater than 90 days past due.
d. Accounting estimates should **not** be used when the outcome of future events related to the estimated item is unknown.

(R/09, AUD, A0670A, #10, 8810)

11. A practitioner has been engaged to apply agreed-upon procedures in accordance with Statements on Standards for Attestation Engagements (SSAE) to prospective financial statements. Which of the following conditions must be met for the practitioner to perform the engagement?
a. The prospective financial statement includes a summary of significant accounting policies.
b. The practitioner takes responsibility for the sufficiency of the agreed-upon procedures.
c. The practitioner and specified parties agree upon the procedures to be performed by the practitioner.
d. The practitioner reports on the criteria to be used in the determination of findings.

(R/09, AUD, A1603A, #11, 8811)

12. A test of a payroll system involved comparing an individual's number of overtime hours a week with an average of weekly overtime during a similar period in a prior year and evaluating the results. This is an example of what type of test?
a. Range test
b. Detail test
c. Category test
d. Reasonableness test

(R/09, AUD, C04942A, #12, 8812)

13. Which of the following is an analytical procedure that an auditor most likely would perform when planning an audit?
a. Confirming a sample of accounts payable
b. Scanning payroll files for terminated employees
c. Comparing current year balances to budgeted balances
d. Recalculating interest expense based on notes payable balances

(R/09, AUD, C04973A, #13, 8813)

14. Which of the following statements is correct concerning an auditor's use of the work of an actuary in assessing a client's pension obligations?
a. The auditor is required to understand the objectives and scope of the actuary's work.
b. The reasonableness of the actuary's assumptions is strictly the auditor's responsibility.
c. The client is required to consent to the auditor's use of the actuary's work.
d. If the actuary has a relationship with the client, the auditor may **not** use the actuary's work.

(R/09, AUD, 0925A, #14, 8814)

15. Which of the following titles would be considered suitable for financial statements that are prepared on a cash basis?
a. Income statement
b. Statement of operations
c. Statement of revenues collected and expenses paid
d. Statement of cash flows

(R/09, AUD, A0108A, #15, 8815)

16. Which of the following could be difficult to determine because electronic evidence may **not** be retrievable after a specific period?
a. The acceptance level of detection risk
b. The timing of control and substantive tests
c. Whether to adopt substantive or reliance test strategies
d. The assessed level of inherent risk

(R/09, AUD, A2086A, #16, 8816)

17. The purpose of establishing quality control policies and procedures for deciding whether to accept or continue a client relationship is to
a. Monitor the risk factors concerning misstatements arising from the misappropriation of assets
b. Provide reasonable assurance that personnel are adequately trained to fulfill their responsibilities
c. Minimize the likelihood of associating with clients whose management lacks integrity
d. Document objective criteria for the CPA firm's responses to peer review comments

(R/09, AUD, 0811A, #17, 8817)

18. Which of the following situations most likely could lead to an embezzlement scheme?
a. The accounts receivable bookkeeper receives a list of payments prepared by the cashier and personally makes entries in the customers' accounts receivable subsidiary ledger.
b. Each vendor invoice is matched with the related purchase order and receiving report by the vouchers payable bookkeeper who personally approves the voucher for payment.
c. Access to blank checks and signature plates is restricted to the cash disbursements bookkeeper who personally reconciles the monthly bank statement.
d. Vouchers and supporting documentation are examined and then canceled by the treasurer who personally mails the checks to vendors.

(R/09, AUD, 0197A, #18, 8818)

19. Independence is **not** required on which of the following types of engagements?
a. Audit
b. Review
c. Compilation
d. Agreed-upon procedures

(R/09, AUD, C01154A, #19, 8819)

20. An accountant's compilation report on a financial forecast should include a statement that
a. The hypothetical assumptions used in the forecast are reasonable in the circumstances.
b. The forecast should be read only in conjunction with the audited historical financial statements.
c. The accountant expresses only limited assurance on the forecasted statements and their assumptions.
d. There will usually be differences between the forecasted and actual results.

(R/09, AUD, 0382A, #20, 8820)

21. Which of the following actions should the auditor take in response to discovering a deviation from the prescribed control procedure?
a. Make inquiries to understand the potential consequence of the deviation
b. Assume that the deviation is an isolated occurrence without audit significance
c. Report the matter to the next higher level of authority within the entity
d. Increase sample size of tests of controls

(R/09, AUD, A3061A, #21, 8821)

22. Which of the following events **least** likely would indicate the existence of related party transactions?
a. Making a loan with **no** scheduled date for the funds to be repaid
b. Maintaining compensating balance arrangements for the benefit of principal stockholders
c. Borrowing funds at an interest rate significantly below prevailing market rates
d. Writing off obsolete inventory to net realizable value just before year-end

(R/09, AUD, 0354A, #22, 8822)

23. As part of the process of observing a client's physical inventories, an auditor should be alert to
a. The inclusion of any obsolete or damaged goods
b. Any change in the method of pricing from prior years
c. The existence of outstanding purchase commitments
d. The verification of inventory values assigned to goods in process

(R/09, AUD, 0234A, #23, 8823)

24. After issuing an auditor's report, an auditor has **no** obligation to make continuing inquiries concerning audited financial statements **unless**
a. Information about a material transaction that occurred just after the auditor's report was issued is deemed to be reliable.
b. A final resolution is made of a contingent liability that had been disclosed in the financial statements.
c. Information that existed at the report date and may affect the report comes to the auditor's attention.
d. An event occurs just after the auditor's report was issued that affects the entity's ability to continue as a going concern.
(R/09, AUD, 0299A, #24, 8824)

25. Which of the following statements is correct regarding a review of a nonpublic entity's financial statements in accordance with Statements on Standards for Accounting and Review Services (SSARS)?
a. The accountant is required to assess the risk of fraud.
b. It is **not** necessary for the accountant to obtain a management representation letter.
c. An opinion is expressed in the review report.
d. The accountant must be independent to issue the review report.
(R/09, AUD, A0465A, #25, 8825)

Problem 5 MULTIPLE-CHOICE QUESTIONS (2009 Hard)

26. In obtaining written representations from management, materiality limits ordinarily would apply to representations related to
a. Amounts concerning related party transactions
b. Irregularities involving members of management
c. The availability of financial records
d. The completeness of minutes of directors' meetings (R/09, AUD, 0251A, #26, 8826)

27. As a result of sampling procedures applied as tests of controls, an auditor incorrectly assesses control risk higher than appropriate. The most likely explanation for this situation is that
a. The deviation rate in the auditor's sample is **less** than the tolerable rate, but the deviation rate in the population exceeds the tolerable rate.
b. The deviation rate in the auditor's sample exceeds the tolerable rate, but the deviation rate in the population is **less** than the tolerable rate.
c. The deviation rates of both the auditor's sample and the population exceed the tolerable rate.
d. The deviation rates of both the auditor's sample and the population are **less** than the tolerable rate. (R/09, AUD, 0065A, #27, 8827)

28. An accountant has been engaged to compile the financial statements of a nonpublic entity. The financial statements contain many departures from GAAP because of inadequacies in the accounting records. The accountant believes that modification of the compilation report is not adequate to indicate the deficiencies. Under these circumstances, the accountant should
a. Inform management that the engagement can proceed only if distribution of the accountant's report is restricted to internal use
b. Withdraw from the engagement and provide **no** further service concerning these financial statements
c. Quantify the effects of the departures from GAAP and describe the departures from GAAP in a special report
d. Obtain written representations from management that the financial statements will **not** be used to obtain credit from financial institutions
(R/09, AUD, 1687A, #28, 8828)

29. Under which of the following circumstances would the expression of a disclaimer of opinion be inappropriate?
a. The auditor is unable to obtain the audited financial statements of a consolidated investee.
b. Management does **not** provide reasonable justification for a change in accounting principles.
c. The company failed to make a count of its physical inventory during the year and the auditor was unable to apply alternative procedures to verify inventory quantities.
d. Management refuses to allow the auditor to have access to the company's canceled checks and bank statements. (R/09, AUD, 0668A, #29, 8829)

30. According to the third standard of fieldwork, which of the following terms identifies a requirement for audit evidence?
a. Appropriate
b. Adequate
c. Reasonable
d. Disconfirming (R/09, AUD, A2527A, #30, 8830)

31. When performing analytical procedures in the planning stage, the auditor most likely would develop expectations by reviewing which of the following sources of information?
a. Unaudited information from internal quarterly reports
b. Various account assertions in the planning memorandum
c. Comments in the prior year's management letter
d. The control risk assessment relating to specific financial assertions
(R/09, AUD, A0387A, #31, 8831)

32. An auditor's decision whether to apply analytical procedures as substantive tests usually is determined by the
a. Availability of documentary evidence that should be verified
b. Extent of accounting estimates used in preparing the financial statements
c. Precision and reliability of the data used to develop expectations
d. Number of transactions recorded just before and just after the year-end
(R/09, AUD, 1846A, #32, 8832)

33. In a financial statement audit, inherent risk is evaluated to help an auditor assess which of the following?
a. The internal audit department's objectivity in reporting a material misstatement of a financial statement assertion it detects to the audit committee
b. The risk that the internal control system will **not** detect a material misstatement of a financial statement assertion
c. The risk that the audit procedures implemented will **not** detect a material misstatement of a financial statement assertion
d. The susceptibility of a financial statement assertion to a material misstatement assuming there are **no** related controls
(R/09, AUD, C04944A, #33, 8833)

34. Which of the following statements most likely would be included in an engagement letter from an auditor to a client?
a. The CPA firm will provide absolute assurance about whether the financial statements are free of material misstatement.
b. The CPA firm is responsible for ensuring that the client complies with applicable laws.
c. The CPA firm will involve information technology specialists in the performance of the audit.
d. The CPA firm will adjust the financial statements to correct misstatements before issuing a report.
(R/09, AUD, A2728A, #34, 8834)

35. A CPA is engaged to examine an entity's financial forecast. The CPA believes that several significant assumptions do not provide a reasonable basis for the forecast. Under these circumstances, the CPA should issue a(an)
a. Adverse opinion
b. Pro forma opinion
c. Qualified opinion
d. Unqualified opinion with an explanatory paragraph (R/09, AUD, 1592A, #35, 8835)

36. Which of the following represents an inherent limitation of internal controls?
a. Bank reconciliations are **not** performed on a timely basis.
b. The CEO can request a check with **no** purchase order.
c. Customer credit checks are **not** performed.
d. Shipping documents are **not** matched to sales invoices. (R/09, AUD, A2099A, #36, 8836)

37. An auditor's tests of controls for completeness for the revenue cycle usually include determining whether
a. Each receivable is collected subsequent to the year-end.
b. An invoice is prepared for each shipping document.
c. Each invoice is supported by a customer purchase order.
d. Each credit memo is properly approved.
(R/09, AUD, 1449A, #37, 8837)

38. Which of the following prospective financial statements is(are) appropriate for general use?

	Financial forecast	Financial projection
a.	Yes	Yes
b.	Yes	No
c.	No	Yes
d.	No	No

(R/09, AUD, 0045A, #38, 8838)

39. Which of the following procedures most likely would assist an auditor to identify litigation, claims, and assessments?
a. Inspect checks included with the client's cutoff bank statement
b. Obtain a letter of representations from the client's underwriter of securities
c. Apply ratio analysis on the current year's liability accounts
d. Read the file of correspondence from taxing authorities (R/09, AUD, 1869A, #39, 8839)

40. Which of the following is the primary objective of probability proportional to sample (PPS) size?
a. To identify overstatement errors
b. To increase the proportion of smaller-value items in the sample
c. To identify items where controls were **not** properly applied
d. To identify zero and negative balances
(R/09, AUD, A1442A, #40, 8840)

41. When assessing the competence of the internal auditors, an independent CPA should obtain information about the
a. Organizational level to which the internal auditors report
b. Quality of the internal auditors' working paper documentation
c. Policies prohibiting internal auditors from auditing sensitive matters
d. Internal auditors' preliminary assessed level of control risk (R/09, AUD, 1636A, #41, 8841)

42. An auditor is testing the reasonableness of dividend income from investments in publicly-held companies. The auditor most likely would compute the amount that should have been received and recorded by the client by
a. Reading the details of the board of directors' meetings
b. Confirming the details with the investee companies' registrars
c. Electronically accessing the details of dividend records on the Internet
d. Examining the details of the client's most recent cutoff bank statement
(R/09, AUD, 1462A, #42, 8842)

43. Analytical procedures used in the planning phase of an audit should focus on
a. Documenting the risk factors relating to the susceptibility of assets to misappropriation
b. Identifying the internal control activities that could reduce the assessed level of control risk
c. Discovering uncorrected misstatements that should be communicated to the audit committee
d. Enhancing the auditor's understanding of the transactions and events that have occurred since the last audit (R/09, AUD, 2212A, #43, 8843)

44. In auditing an entity's computerized payroll transactions, an auditor would be **least** likely to use test data to test controls concerning
a. Overpayment of employees for hours **not** worked
b. Control and distribution of unclaimed checks
c. Withholding of taxes and Social Security contributions
d. Missing employee identification numbers
(R/09, AUD, 0364A, #44, 8844)

45. Which of the following factors is most relevant when an auditor considers the client's organizational structure in the context of control risk?
a. Management's attitude toward information processing and accounting departments
b. The organization's recruiting and hiring practices
c. Physical proximity of the accounting function to upper management
d. The suitability of the client's lines of reporting
(R/09, AUD, A2774A, #45, 8845)

46. An auditor who uses the work of a specialist may refer to the specialist in the auditor's report if the
a. Auditor believes that the specialist's findings are reasonable in the circumstances.
b. Specialist's findings support the related assertions in the financial statements.
c. Auditor modifies the report because of the difference between the client's and the specialist's valuations of an asset.
d. Specialist's findings provide the auditor with greater assurance of reliability about management's representations.
(R/09, AUD, 0352A, #46, 8846)

47. Which of the following ratios would an engagement partner most likely consider in the overall review stage of an audit?
a. Total liabilities/net sales
b. Accounts receivable/inventory
c. Cost of goods sold/average inventory
d. Current assets/quick assets
(R/09, AUD, 1368A, #47, 8847)

48. In attribute sampling, a 25% change in which of the following factors will have the smallest effect on the size of the sample?
a. Tolerable rate of deviation
b. Number of items in the population
c. Degree of assurance desired
d. Planned assessed level of control risk
(R/09, AUD, 1748A, #48, 8848)

49. Which of the following is a conceptual similarity between generally accepted auditing standards and the attestation standards?
a. Both sets of standards require the CPA to report on the adequacy of disclosure in the financial statements.
b. All of the standards of fieldwork in generally accepted auditing standards are included in the attestation standards.
c. The requirement that the CPA be independent in mental attitude is included in both sets of standards.
d. Both sets of standards are applicable to engagements regarding financial forecasts and projections.
(R/09, AUD, 1401A, #49, 8849)

50. What is an auditor's responsibility for supplementary information, such as disclosure of pension information, which is outside the basic financial statements but required by the GASB?
a. The auditor should engage a specialist, such as an actuary, to verify that management's assertions are reasonable.
b. The auditor's only responsibility for supplementary information is to determine that such information has **not** been omitted.
c. The auditor should perform tests of transactions to the supplementary information to verify that it is reasonably comparable to the prior year's information.
d. The auditor should apply certain limited procedures to the supplementary information and report deficiencies in, or omissions of, such information.
(R/09, AUD, 1895A, #50, 8850)

Problem 6 SIMULATION (2009)

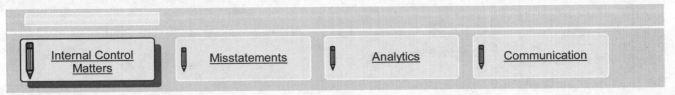

You have been asked by the audit partner to draft a letter to the client on internal control related matters. You were informed that the written communication regarding significant deficiencies and material weaknesses identified during an audit of financial statements should include certain statements.

For each of the significant deficiencies and material weaknesses reflected in the table below, select from the list provided the appropriate disposition of each statement in regard to the letter to the client on internal control related matters. Each selection may be used once, more than once, or not at all.

Internal Controls	Related Matters
1. State that the purpose of the audit was to express an opinion on the financial statements, and to express an opinion on the effectiveness of the entity's internal control over financial reporting.	
2. Identify, if applicable, items that are considered to be material weaknesses.	
3. State that the author is not expressing an opinion on the effectiveness of internal control.	
4. Include the definition of the term significant deficiency.	
5. Include the definition of the term material weakness, where relevant.	
6. State that the author is expressing an unqualified opinion on the effectiveness of internal control.	
7. State that the communication is intended solely for management and external parties.	
8. Identify the matters that are considered to be significant deficiencies.	

Selection List:

- Included
- Excluded
- Included, but only with client management's approval
- Communicated orally with no need to document the communication

The year under audit is year 2.

During the audit of accounts payable, you detected misstatements previously undetected by the client. All misstatements were related to year 2. For each of the liability misstatements shown below, select the most appropriate item from the list provided.

- In column B, indicate the audit procedure that was most likely used to detect the misstatement.
- In column C, select the internal control that most likely could prevent or detect this type of misstatement in the future.

Audit procedures and internal controls may be selected once, more than once, or not at all.

Misstatement	Column B Audit Procedure Used to Detect Misstatement	Column C Internal Control That Could Prevent or Detect Misstatement in the Future
1. An accounts payable clerk misplaces year-end invoices for raw materials that were received on December 21, year 2, and, therefore, liabilities were not recorded.		
2. The company tends to be careless in recording payables in the correct period.		
3. The company has the same person approving pay requests and cutting checks.		
4. The company's receiving department mis-places receiving reports for purchases of raw materials at year-end and, therefore, liabilities were not recorded.		

Column B Selection List

1. From the January, year 3, cash disbursements journal, select payments and match to corresponding invoices.
2. Review the cash disbursements journal for the month of December, year 2.
3. On a surprise basis, review the receiving department's filing system, and test check quantities entered on December, year 2, receiving reports to packing slips.
4. Identify open purchase orders and vendors' invoices at December 31, year 2, and investigate their disposition.
5. Request written confirmation from the accounts payable supervisor that all vendor invoices have been recorded in the accounts payable subsidiary ledger.

6.	Investigate unmatched receiving reports dated prior to January 1, year 3.
7.	Compare the balances for selected vendors at the end of year 2 and year 1.
8.	Determine that credit memos received 10 days after the balance sheet date have been recorded in the proper period.
9.	Select an unpaid invoice and ask to be walked through the invoice payment process.

Column C Selection List

1.	The purchasing department supervisor forwards a monthly listing of matched purchase orders and receiving reports to the accounts payable supervisor for comparison to a listing of vouched invoices.
2.	The accounts payable supervisor reviews a monthly listing of open purchase orders and vendors' invoices for follow-up with the receiving department.
3.	Copies of all vendor invoices received during the year are filed in an outside storage facility.
4.	All vendor invoices are reviewed for mathematical accuracy.
5.	On a daily basis, the receiving department independently counts all merchandise received.
6.	All vendor invoices with supporting documentation are canceled when paid.
7.	At the end of each month, the purchasing department confirms terms of delivery with selected vendors.
8.	Accounts payable personnel are assigned different responsibilities each quarter within the department.
9.	A clerk is responsible for matching purchase orders with receiving reports and making certain they are included in the proper month.

The table below presents ratios that the company uses to track its performance. During fieldwork, the auditors determined that the ratios were inaccurate due to significant errors, described below, made by the company in year 2. The company has agreed to make adjusting journal entries for year 2 to correct the errors.

After you have determined the appropriate adjusting journal entry (entries) to correct each error, select the impact, if any, that the adjusting journal entry (entries) would have on the erroneous ratio.

Ratio	Year 2 Erroneous Ratio	Ratio	Year 2 Erroneous Ratio
Inventory turnover	4.38	Return on equity	17.53%

Impact of Adjusting Journal Entries on the Inventory Turnover Ratio	Company Errors	Impact of Adjusting Journal Entries on the Return on Equity Ratio
	1. Inventory stored at a distribution center on December 31, year 2, was inadvertently omitted during the year 2 physical inventory count, to which the general ledger was adjusted.	
	2. During the physical inventory, the company included inventory that it was holding on consignment.	
	3. The company failed to record the materials in transit accrual for late supplier/vendor invoices.	
	4. The company declared and paid a cash dividend on December 30, year 2, but failed to record the transaction in year 2.	

Selection List:

- Increases
- Decreases
- No impact

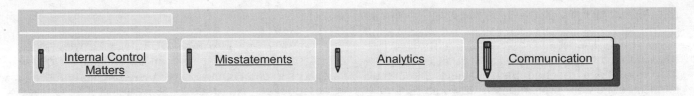

During your audit of Wagner Corp., you uncover paid invoices for material fixed assets. However, the purchase of the assets was charged to expenses. Prepare a memo to the engagement partner raising the possibility that this constitutes either a misstatement arising from fraudulent financial reporting or a misstatement arising from a misappropriation of assets. Recommend the next steps to be taken to determine which, if any, of these forms of fraud may have been committed.

REMINDER: On the actual exam your response will be graded for both technical content and writing skills. Technical content will be evaluated for information that is helpful to the intended reader and clearly relevant to the issue. Writing skills will be evaluated for development, organization, and the appropriate expression of ideas in professional correspondence. Use a standard business memo or letter format with a clear beginning, middle, and end. Do not convey information in the form of a table, bullet point list, or other abbreviated presentation.

You and your staff have completed an audit of a nonissuer for the calendar year ended December 31, year 2. The audit report date of the financial statement was March 11, year 3, and on March 26, year 3, the client issued the financial statements.

On April 15, year 3, as you are ascertaining that the workpapers and related audit programs are complete and properly signed off, you notice that the financial statements include a material misstatement subsequent to the issuance of an unqualified report. The misstatement was determined to be the inclusion of material nonexistent sales.

Your audit team issued the financial statements. Information regarding nonexistent sales was not known at the date of the audit report. The auditors find the subsequently discovered information is both reliable and existed at the date of the auditor's report. The team determines that the inclusion of the material nonexistent sales would have affected the audit report. The audit team believes there are persons currently relying on, or likely to rely on, the financial statements. Is the auditor's responsibility with respect to the nonexistent sales different if the auditor has resigned or been discharged prior to undertaking or completing the investigation than if he were the continuing auditor?

Reminder: On the actual exam, you will use an electronic database of authoritative literature to find and select the reference (appropriate section and paragraph of the relevant guidance). Please see the AICPA's tutorial and sample test on their exam Web site (www.cpa-exam.org).

Paragraph reference answer: _____   (R/09, AUD, 8942)

_____

Solution 4 MULTIPLE-CHOICE ANSWERS (2009 Moderate)

1. (c) The objective of analytical procedures used in the final review stage of the audit is to assess the conclusions reached and evaluate the overall financial statement presentation. It would generally include *reading the financial statements* and notes *and considering* the adequacy of the evidence gathered in response to unusual or unexpected balances identified and *any unusual or unexpected balances* or relationships *that were not previously identified*. Comparing each individual expense account balance with the relevant budgeted amounts and investigating any significant variations; and calculating each individual expense account balance as a percentage of total entity expenses and comparing the results with industry averages are analytical procedures that would be performed during the course of the audit (used as substantive procedures), not during the final review stage. Analytical procedures are not applicable to tests of controls. (Chapter 24-4-2; 8801; CBT Skill: analysis; CSO: 4.1.0)

2. (b) Inclusion of an entity's compiled financial *projection* in an *offering statement of the entity's initial public offering of common stock* would be *inappropriate* because this is an example of a general use distribution. A financial forecast is the only type of prospective financial statement appropriate for general use. The other three answer alternatives are examples of limited use distributions and could appropriately include either a financial projection or a financial forecast. A financial projection, unlike a financial forecast, is not confined to the presentation of (to the best of the responsible party's knowledge and belief) the expected results. Instead, a projection incorporates one or more hypothetical assumptions. A general use distribution will include parties who will not be able to directly ask the responsible parties questions about the presentation and were not involved in negotiating the terms of the engagement for its preparation. Deprived of this type of involvement, it is best that they receive prospective financial statements that contain only the expected results, i.e., a financial forecast. (Chapter 31-4-2; 8802; CBT Skill: understanding; CSO: 1.1.6)

3. (b) When reviewing the financial statements of a nonpublic entity in accordance with SSARS, the accountant is required to *obtain a management representation letter*. A review differs significantly from an audit of financial statements in which the auditor provides reasonable assurance that the financial statements, taken as a whole, are free of material misstatement. The objective of a review is to express limited assurance that there are no material modifications that should be made to the financial statements in order for them to be in conformity with GAAP or OCBOA. A review does not contemplate obtaining an understanding of the entity's internal control, thus assessing control risk is not required. Nor does it involve tests of accounting records by obtaining sufficient, appropriate audit evidence via inspection, observation, confirmation or examination of source documents or other procedures usually performed in an audit, so confirmation of account balances and observation of the physical inventory would also not be required. Chapter 31-1-3; 8803; CBT Skill: analysis; CSO: 3.8.0)

4. (b) Ordinarily, information that significantly contradicts the going concern assumption relates to the entity's inability to continue to meet its obligations (*recurring working capital shortages*) as they become due without substantial disposition of assets outside of the ordinary course of business, restructuring of debt, externally forced revisions of its operations, etc. As this definition indicates, some items (all of the other answer alternatives) are usually a concern only when considered in conjunction with other financial difficulties or negative trends and depending on the circumstances. *Recurring working capital shortages* is a stand-alone indication that there could be a going concern issue, thus it is the best answer. The cash infusion would be a concern if was needed to meet current obligations. Lack of new customers would be a concern if the company needed to maintain a certain rate of growth to meet its current obligations. Term debt refinanced with a new bank would be reviewed by an auditor for other reasons, but on the surface, is not an indicator of a going concern problem. It would be if the refinancing was done under less favorable terms due to working capital shortages. (Chapter 28-9-3; 8804; CBT Skill: judgment; CSO: 4.4.0)

5. (c) The blank form of accounts receivable confirmation does not include the amount or other information; the recipients are requested to provide it. This form may provide a greater degree of assurance about the information confirmed, however it may be less efficient than the other positive form because *more nonresponses to the requests are likely to occur* due to the extra effort required of the recipients. Neither inspection of shipping documents or verification of subsequent cash receipts are dictated by the use of the blank form; however, they may be part of the alternative procedures the auditor uses if the response rate to the confirmation process is too low. That recipients may sign the forms without proper investigation is an issue with the other type of positive confirmation that includes the amounts and/or other information. Editor note: The blank form is a type of positive confirmation. The question

indicates that it is not which may have been why the examiners released this question. They may not intend to use it again for this reason. (Chapter 25-3-2; 8805; CBT Skill: judgment; CSO: 3.1.3)

6. (a) The compilation report should *not include a reference to the original engagement*, any review procedures that may have been performed, or scope limitations that resulted in the changed engagement. A reference to a departure from GAAS is not related to the question because an accountant must perform a compilation or review of a nonpublic entity in accordance with SSARS, not GAAS. (Chapter 31-1-5; 8806; CBT Skill: analysis; CSO: 5.1.2)

7. (d) If *the accounts payable manager issues purchase orders*, incompatible functions of authorization and record keeping are combined creating a weakness in internal control. A person should not be in the position to both perpetrate and conceal errors or fraud in the normal course of their duties, thus the duties of authorization, record keeping, and custody of assets should be separated. The other answer alternatives describe appropriate internal controls. (Chapter 23-5-2; 8807; CBT Skill: analysis; CSO: 2.4.0)

8. (c) A successor auditor's inquiries of the predecessor auditor should include questions regarding *the predecessor's understanding as to the reasons for the change in auditors.* The purpose of the inquiries is to assist the successor auditor in determining whether to accept the engagement. (The other answer alternatives do not directly relate to that.) Other matters subject to inquiry for this purpose are information that might bear on the integrity of management; disagreements with management as to accounting principles, auditing procedures, or other similarly significant matters; communications to those charged with governance regarding fraud and illegal acts by clients; and communications to management and those charged with governance regarding significant deficiencies and material weaknesses in internal control An auditor should not accept an engagement until the appropriate communications with the predecessor auditor have been evaluated. The predecessor's evaluation of audit risk and judgment about materiality would have limited if any value for the current audit; additionally these are matters of judgment that are the sole responsibility of the successor auditor. After the date of the report, an auditor has no obligation to make any further or continuing inquiry or perform any other auditing procedures with respect to the audited financial statements covered by that report, unless new information which may affect the report comes to the auditor's attention. The question did not indicate that was the case, so subsequent events that occurred since the predecessor's audit report was issued would generally not be appropriate subject matter for successor inquiries. The predecessor's knowledge of accounting and auditing matters of continuing significance may be of interest to the successor auditor as revealed by the successor's auditor's review of the predecessor's workpapers for purposes of planning the engagement but not for determining to accept the engagement. (Chapter 21-5-2; 8808; CBT Skill: understanding; CSO: 1.3.0)

9. (d) An auditor would most likely consider the possibility that a client's financial statements contained material misstatements if *the results of an analytical procedure disclosed unexpected differences*. An auditor should evaluate significant unexpected differences. If an explanation for the difference cannot be obtained, the auditor should design further audit procedures to determine whether the difference is a likely misstatement. Whenever an auditor becomes aware that management has consulted with other accountants about significant accounting matters (whether or not this was disclosed to the auditor by management) the auditor should discuss with those charged with governance the auditor's views about those same matters. Whether this would cause the auditor to consider that the financial statements might be materially misstated would depend on the circumstances. The delivery of the management representation letter is an issue that should be explained to the client during the initial stage of the planning stage of the audit and documented in an engagement letter along with other understandings with the client. The representations should be dated as of the date of the auditor's report. (The reference to completion of fieldwork is based on superseded guidance.) At any rate the CFO is not refusing to sign and although such representations are part of the audit evidence, they complement, rather than serve as a substitute for, other audit procedures; thus any issue with them would be less of a concern regarding material misstatements than an unexpected difference disclosed by analytical procedures. Audit trails of computer-generated transactions existing for a short time are not an indication of a material misstatement. The auditor should be aware of the client's record retention policies and either arrange to test the transactions during their existence or develop alternative auditing procedures. (Chapter 24-4-3; 8809; CBT Skill: analysis; CSO: 4.3.0)

10. (a) The auditor's objective when evaluating accounting estimates is to determine if all accounting estimates that could be material to the financial statements have been developed; *are reasonable in the circumstances;* and are presented in conformity

with GAAP and are properly disclosed. The opposite is true of alternatives "b" and "d", i.e., accounting estimates should be used when data concerning past events can**not** be accumulated in a timely, cost-effective manner; and accounting estimates **should** be used when the measurement of some amounts or the valuation of some accounts is uncertain, pending the outcome of future events. Obviously, there is no need to use an estimate for accounts receivable greater than 90 days past due or any other account / amount that can be readily calculated using actual data (Chapter 25-3-10; 8810; CBT Skill: understanding; CSO: 1.11.2)

11. (c) One of the conditions that must be met by a practitioner who accepts an engagement to apply agreed-upon procedures in accordance with SSAE to prospective financial statements is that *the practitioner and specified parties agree upon the procedures to be performed by the practitioner.* The prospective financial statements must include a summary of significant assumptions, not account ting policies. The specified parties, not the practitioner, must take responsibility for the sufficiency of the agreed-upon procedures for their purpose. The practitioner does not report on the criteria to be used in the determination of findings, rather the criteria must be agreed upon between the practitioner and the specified parties. (Chapter 31-4-2; 8811; CBT Skill: understanding; CSO: 3.9.0)

12. (d) This question describes an analytical procedure known as a *reasonable test* which is a comparison of an estimated amount, calculated by the use of relevant financial and nonfinancial information, with a recorded amount. (Chapter 24-4-4 8812; CBT Skill: judgment; CSO: 2.7.0)

13. (c) The analytical procedure that an auditor most likely would perform when planning an audit is *comparing current year balances to budgeted balances.* Recalculating interest expense based on notes payable balances is an analytical procedure, but not one that would generally be performed during the planning phase. Analytical procedures used in planning the audit generally use data aggregated at a high level The other answer alternatives are examples of tests of details, not analytical procedures. (Chapter 24-4-1; 8813; CBT Skill: analysis; CSO: 1.7.0)

14. (a) The auditor should obtain an understanding of the nature of the work performed by a specialist, such as an actuary. This understanding should include the *objectives and scope of the* specialist's [*actuary's*] *work.* The appropriateness and reasonableness of methods and assumptions used and their application are the responsibility of the specialist, not the auditor. The client is not required to consent to the auditor's use of the actuary's work; the auditor decides if there are matters that require special skill or knowledge and thus require using the work of a specialist to obtain appropriate audit evidence. Naturally, the auditor enjoys greater assurance of reliability if a specialist does not have a relationship with the client, however if the auditor can attain satisfaction that the specialist's objectivity will not be impaired, such a specialist can be acceptable. (Chapter 24-5-3; 8814; CBT Skill: understanding; CSO: 1.10.2)

15. (c) Titles such as balance sheet, statement of financial position, statement of income (or income statement), statement of operations, and statement of cash flows are generally understood to be applicable only to financial statements that are presented in accordance with GAAP. Financial statements prepared in conformity with a comprehensive basis of accounting other than GAAP (OCBOA) should not use these "GAAP" titles. Examples of suitable titles for cash basis financial statements are statement of assets and liabilities arising from cash transactions, or *statement of revenues collected and expenses paid.* (Chapter 30-2-2; 8815; CBT Skill: understanding; CSO: 5.1.10)

16. (b) *The timing of control and substantive tests* could be difficult to determine because electronic evidence may not be retrievable after a specific period if files are changed and if backup files do not exist. The auditor must consider the entity's data retention policies when determining the timing of some procedures. The determination of the other answer alternatives is not made more difficult because electronic evidence may not be retrievable after a specific period. (Chapter 27-2-3; 8816; CBT Skill: judgment; CSO: 1.10.5)

17. (c) One of the purposes of establishing quality control policies and procedures for deciding whether to accept or continue a client relationship is to *minimize the likelihood of associating with clients whose management lacks integrity.* Monitoring the risk factors concerning misstatements arising from the misappropriation of assets is not an aspect of a CPA's firm quality control system. Providing reasonable assurance that personnel are adequately trained to fulfill their responsibilities is part of both the human resources element and the engagement performance element of a quality control system rather than the acceptance and continuance of client relationships and specific engagements element. Documenting objective criteria for the CPA firm's responses to peer review comments is part of the engagement performance element of a firm's quality

control system. (Chapter 21-4-2; 8817; CBT Skill: understanding; CSO: 1.2.3)

18. (c) *Access to blank checks and signature plates is restricted to the cash disbursements bookkeeper who personally reconciles the monthly bank statement* is the situation that most likely could lead to an embezzlement scheme. Bank reconciliations should not be prepared by persons who sign checks or keep the records for receipts or disbursements. This is an example of incompatible functions which place a person in the position to both perpetrate and conceal errors or fraud in the normal course of their duties. The duties of authorization, record keeping, and custody of assets should be separated. Additionally, bank reconciliations should not be done by persons with responsibility for handling cash receipts. The other answer alternatives are examples of appropriate duties / control practices. (Chapter 23-1-2; 8818; CBT Skill: understanding; CSO: 2.2.0)

19. (c) An accountant is not required to be independent to perform a *compilation* engagement. The lack of independence should be specifically disclosed (by adding a statement to the last paragraph of the report) without describing the reason for the lack of independence. Independence is required for the other answer alternatives. (Chapter 31-1-2; 8819; CBT Skill: understanding; CSO: 3.8.0)

20. (d) An accountant's compilation report on a financial forecast should include a caveat that the prospective results may not be achieved, such as *there will usually be differences between the forecasted and actual results* because events and circumstances frequently do not occur as expected, and those differences may be material. Answers "a" and "c" are not correct because the report should also include a statement that a compilation is limited in scope and does not enable the accountant to express an opinion or any other form of assurance on the prospective financial statements or the assumptions. There is no requirement that the forecast be read in conjunction with the audited historical financial statements. (Chapter 31-4-2; 8820; CBT Skill: understanding; CSO: 5.1.6)

21. (a) When deviations from prescribed controls are discovered the auditor should *make inquiries to understand the potential consequences of the deviation*. The auditor should never assume that a deviation is an isolated occurrence without audit significance. Answer alternatives "c" and "d" may or may not be determined to be appropriate actions after the auditor has gained an understanding of the potential consequences. (Chapter 23-4-3; 8821; CBT Skill: judgment; CSO: 2.6.0)

22. (d) The event that is the least likely indicator of the existence of related party transactions is the writing off obsolete inventory to net realizable value just before year-end. A company should have policies and procedures in place to do this and it would be considered by an auditor searching for related party transactions. The other three answer alternatives are indicators of the existence of related party transactions. (Chapter 24-8-1; 8822; CBT Skill: judgment; CSO: 1.10.4)

23. (a) As part of the process of observing a client's physical inventories, an auditor should be alert to *the inclusion of any obsolete or damaged goods.* The other answer alternatives are auditing considerations for inventories, but they do not directly relate to the observation of the client's physical count of inventory quantities. (Chapter 25-3-3; 8823; CBT Skill: understanding; CSO: 3.1.4)

24. (c) After the date of the report, the auditor has no obligation to make any further inquiry or perform any other auditing procedures concerning audited financial statements, unless new *information that existed at the report date and may affect the report comes to the auditor's attention.* (Chapter 28-7-3; 8824; CBT Skill: understanding; CSO: 5.3.1)

25. (d) *The accountant must be independent to issue the review report* because although the accountant is not expressing an opinion, limited assurance is being given. The other answer alternatives are not true. (Chapter 31-1-3; 8825; CBT Skill: understanding; CSO: 3.8.0)

Solution 5 MULTIPLE-CHOICE ANSWERS (2009 Hard)

26. (a) Materiality limits ordinarily would apply to management representations related to *amounts concerning related party transactions.* Materiality considerations would not apply to those representations that are not directly related to amounts included in the financial statements such as the availability of financial records or the completeness of minutes of directors' meetings. Other items of this nature are management's acknowledgement of its responsibility for the fair presentation of financial statements in conformity with GAAP and communications from regulatory agencies concerning noncompliance with or deficiencies in financial reporting practices. Nor would materiality apply to irregularities involving members of management because of the possible effects of fraud on other aspects of the audit. (Chapter 24-3-3; 8826; CBT Skill: judgment; CSO: 3.5.0)

27. (b) The tolerable rate is the maximum rate of deviation from the prescribed internal control policies and procedures that would support the auditor's assessed level of control risk. In this case, the auditor has assessed control risk too high. The risk of assessing control risk too high is the risk that the assessed level of control risk based on the sample is greater (*the deviation rate in the auditor's sample exceeds the tolerable rate,...*) than the true operating effectiveness of the control (*...but the deviation rate in the population is less than the tolerable rate*). The situation described in answer "a" would result in assessing control risk too low. Answers "c" and "d" would support the auditor's assessment of control risk. (Chapter 26-1-4; 8827; CBT Skill: analysis; CSO: 3.1.1)

28. (b) If the accountant believes that modification of the standard report is not adequate to indicate the deficiencies in the financial statements, taken as whole, the accountant should *withdraw from the* compilation (or review) *engagement and provide no further services concerning those financial statements*. It may also be advisable for the accountant to consult with an attorney. (Chapter 31-1-4 8828; CBT Skill: analysis; CSO: 5.1.2)

29. (b) If *management does not provide reasonable justification for a change in accounting principle*, the auditor should express a qualified opinion or, if the effect of the change is sufficiently material, the auditor should express an adverse opinion. A disclaimer of opinion should not be expressed because there are material departures from GAAP. All of the other answer alternatives are examples of scope limitations. Restrictions on the scope of an audit, whether imposed by the client or by circumstances, may require the auditor to qualify the opinion or to disclaim an opinion. (Chapter 28-4-3; 8829; CBT Skill: analysis; CSO: 5.1.1)

30. (a) The third standard of fieldwork states: "The auditor must obtain sufficient *appropriate* audit evidence by performing audit procedures to afford a reasonable basis for an opinion regarding the financial statements under audit." (Chapter 24-1-1; 8830; CBT Skill: understanding; CSO: 4.2.0)

31. (a) The purpose of analytics in the planning stage of the audit is to assist in planning the audit procedures that will be used to obtain audit evidence for specific account balances or classes of transactions. To accomplish this one of the things the auditor should focus on is the transactions and events that have occurred since the last audit date. The *unaudited information from internal quarterly reports* would be the best source of information for developing expectations. Expectations, in this context, are the auditor's predictions of recorded accounts or ratios. The effectiveness of analytical procedures depends on developing expectations that can reasonably be expected to identify unexpected relationships. Account assertions in the planning memorandum would not provide the needed data to develop such expectations. The auditor is interested in transactions and events that have occurred since the last audit date, so comments in the prior year's management letter would have limited usefulness and again would probably not include data needed to derive expectations. Control risk affects the reliability of data and thus the precision of the expectation, but it would not be considered a source for developing expectations. (Chapter 24-4-1; 8831; CBT Skill: understanding; CSO: 3.1.2)

32. (c) The decision about which procedure to use (analytics or tests of details, or a combination) is based on the auditor's judgment of their effectiveness and efficiency in identifying potential misstatements in the given situation. The effectiveness and efficiency of analytical procedures is based on the nature of the assertion; the plausibility and predictability of the relationship; the availability and *reliability of the data used to develop expectations*; and the *precision* of the expectation. The other answer alternatives are not relevant considerations. (Chapter 24-4-3; 8832; CBT Skill: understanding; CSO: 3.1.2)

33. (d) Inherent risk is *the susceptibility of a* relevant *financial statement assertion to a misstatement* that could be *material*, either individually, or when aggregated with other misstatements, *assuming that there are no related controls*. If the auditor

decides it would be efficient to consider how the internal auditors' work might affect the nature, timing and extent of audit procedures, the auditor should assess the competence and objectivity of the internal auditors. This evaluation affects detection risk, not inherent risk. The risk that the internal control system will not prevent or detect a material misstatement on a timely basis is control risk, not inherent risk. The effectiveness of an audit procedure or its application by the auditor is detection risk, not inherent risk. (Chapter 22-2-4 8833; CBT Skill: judgment; CSO: 1.9.0)

34. (c)   The statement most likely to be included in an engagement letter from an auditor to a client is that *the CPA firm will involve information technology specialists in the performance of the audit.* Involvement of specialists or internal auditors, if applicable, is something the auditor may choose to include in the letter. The engagement letter should include a statement that the auditor will obtain reasonable (not absolute) assurance about whether the financial statements are free of material misstatement, whether caused by error or fraud; accordingly a material misstatement may remain undetected. The letter should state that management (not the auditor) is responsible for identifying and ensuring that the entity complies with the laws and regulation applicable to its activities. The letter should also state that management (not the auditor) is responsible for adjusting the financial statement to correct material misstatements. (Chapter 22-1-2; 8834; CBT Skill: judgment; CSO: 1.5.0)

35. (a)   If the CPA believes the assumptions do not provide a reasonable basis for the forecast, the CPA should issue an *adverse opinion.* The opinion paragraph should include a statement to that effect. (Chapter 31-4-2; 8835; CBT Skill: understanding; CSO: 5.1.6)

36. (b)   One of the inherent limitations of internal control is inappropriate management override of internal control. An example of this would be if *the CEO can request a check with no purchase order.* The other answer alternatives describe weaknesses in internal control, but they are not *inherent* limitations. Inherent limitations are intrinsic—no matter how well designed and operated, internal control can only provide an entity with reasonable, not absolute, assurance. (Chapter 23-2-1; 8836; CBT Skill: judgment; CSO: 2.4.0)

37. (b)   When testing for completeness for the revenue cycle, the auditor is checking to see that all sales have been recorded. Tracing ("up the house") from a *shipping document* to an invoice tests that goods that were shipped were also invoiced. The

auditor would also need to confirm that the invoice was recorded. Testing receivables to see if they were collected subsequent to the year-end is done to determine if there was proper cutoff. Checking to see that each invoice is supported by a customer purchase order and that credit memos are properly authorized is testing for occurrence (validity). (Chapter 23-5-2; 8837; CBT Skill: analysis; CSO: 2.6.0)

38. (b)   A financial *forecast* is the only type of prospective financial statement appropriate for *general use. General use* refers to use of the statements by parties who are not negotiating directly with the responsible party. Because recipients of prospective financial statements distributed for general use are unable to ask the responsible party directly about the presentation, the presentation most useful to them is one that portrays, to the best of the responsible party's knowledge and belief, the expected results, i.e., a financial *forecast.* Any type of prospective financial statements that would be useful in the circumstances would normally be appropriate for limited use. Thus, a limited use distribution could include either a financial forecast or a projection. (Chapter 31-4-2; 8838; CBT Skill: understanding; CSO: 1.1.3)

39. (d)   Management is the primary source of information about litigation, claims and assessments, however most audits include other procedures (usually for other purposes) that may also assist the auditor in identifying such matters. These include reading minutes of meetings of stockholders, directors, and appropriate committees held during and subsequent to the period being audited; reading contracts, loan agreements, leases, and *correspondence from taxing* or other governmental *authorities*, and similar documents; obtaining information concerning guarantees from bank confirmation forms, and inspecting other documents for possible guarantees by the client. Answers "a" and "b" could possibly reveal evidence of litigation, claims, and assessments, but correspondence from taxing authorities is a more likely source. Applying ratio analysis on the current year's liability accounts is the least likely procedure of the alternatives to disclose such information. (Chapter 24-6-2; 8839; CBT Skill: analysis; CSO: 3.2.0)

40. (a)   In PPS sampling, because the sample is selected proportional to size, larger dollar amounts have a higher probability of being selected, thus *overstatements (errors)* are more likely to be selected than understatements. An auditor will normally use PPS sampling when testing for material overstatements. For the reason just stated, PPS sampling is unlikely to select smaller-value items and these amounts may be significantly understated in the

sample, not increased. PPS sampling is a form of variables sampling which is normally used in substantive testing where the auditor is usually interested in the selection of dollar amounts, not attributes as is usually the case in tests of controls. Additionally, samples taken to test the operating effectiveness of controls (to provide a basis for the auditor to conclude whether the controls are being properly applied) should be selected in a manner such that the sample is representative of the population, thus all items in the population should have an opportunity to be selected which is not the case with PPS sampling. Zero balances are not subject to PPS selection and negative balances would have to be segregated into a separate population for testing. (Chapter 26-5-1; 8840; CBT Skill: analysis; CSO: 3.1.1)

41. (b) When assessing the competence of internal auditors, one of the factors a CPA should consider is *the quality of the internal auditors' working paper documentation,* reports, and recommendations. The organizational level to which they report is an indicator of their objectivity, not their competence. Alternative "c" is a nonsense answer. Obviously, you would not want to bar internal auditors from auditing sensitive matters. However, a policy prohibiting them from auditing areas where **relatives** are employed in important or audit-sensitive positions is a measure of their objectivity, but again, not their competence. The evaluation of internal auditor's preliminary assessed level of control risk would be an indicator of their competence because monitoring the performance of an entity's controls is one of internal audit's major responsibilities. However, it is more likely that an independent CPA would obtain information about this matter to assess the relevance of internal audit activities. The "best", in this case, the most clear-cut answer, is "b". (Chapter 24-2-2; 8841; CBT Skill: understanding; CSO: 1.10.3)

42. (c) Published dividend records provide the strongest evidence supporting dividends earned on marketable equity securities. (Chapter 25-3-5; 8842; CBT Skill: analysis; CSO: 3.1.5)

43. (d) Analytical procedures used in the planning phase of an audit should focus on *enhancing* the auditor's understanding of the client's business and *the auditor's understanding of the transactions and events that have occurred since the last audit*, and identifying areas that may represent specific risks relevant to the audit. The other answer alternatives do not describe activities that would occur during the planning phase of an audit. (Chapter 24-4-1; 8843; CBT Skill: analysis; CSO: 1.7.0)

44. (b) In auditing an entity's computerized payroll transactions, an auditor would be least likely to use test data to test controls concerning control and distribution of unclaimed checks. The other answer alternatives are examples of data that can be accessed and tested via computer applications while controls over unclaimed checks are more likely to be manual. (Chapter 27-5-2 8844; CBT Skill: analysis; CSO: 3.1.6)

45. (d) Control risk is a function of the effectiveness of the design and operation of internal control in achieving a company's objectives relevant to the preparation of the financial statements. One of the five components of internal control is the control environment. One of the elements of the control environment is a company's organizational structure. As it provides the framework for accomplishing the company's objectives, a relevant organizational structure includes considering key areas of authority and responsibility and appropriate (*suitable*) *lines of reporting*. The key to selecting the best answer was to determine which was most related to a company's organizational structure. Management's attitude and recruiting and hiring practices are not directly related to organizational structure, as is the case with lines of reporting. The physical proximity of the accounting function to upper management could be completely unrelated to organizational structure. (Chapter 23-1-2; 8845; CBT Skill: analysis; CSO: 2.7.0)

46. (c) An auditor who uses the work of a specialist may refer to the specialist in the auditor's report if the *auditor modifies the report because of the difference between the client's and the specialist's valuations of an asset* **and the auditor believes such reference will facilitate the understanding of the reason for the modification**. The modification may take the form of either the addition of an explanatory paragraph to a standard report or the departure from an unqualified opinion. If the auditor believes that the specialist's findings are reasonable in the circumstances, ordinarily the auditor would use the findings, but this does not speak to whether a reference in the auditor's report is appropriate because there is no indication of whether the findings support the related assertions in the financial statements and thus do or do not require modification of the auditor's report. If the specialist's findings support the related assertions in the financial statements or provide the auditor with greater assurance of reliability about management's representations, it follows that the auditor will be able to conclude that sufficient appropriate audit evidence has been obtained. As no modification of the auditor's report is needed as a result of the specialist's findings, no reference should be made to the specialist because

it could be misinterpreted as either a qualification or a division of responsibility. (Editor note: This question is an example of when candidates must choose the best answer. The other answer alternatives are clearly wrong and answer "c" is at least partially correct.) (Chapter 24-5-5; 8846; CBT Skill: analysis; CSO: 1.10.2)

47. (c) An engagement partner would most likely consider *cost of goods sold/average inventory* in the overall review stage of an audit. Known as *inventory turnover,* it measures the number of times inventory is acquired and sold during a period and is thus used as an indicator of the efficiency of the operations of a company. The other answer alternatives are not meaningful financial statement analysis calculations. (Chapter 24-4-2; 8847; CBT Skill: analysis; CSO: 4.1.0)

48. (b) The *number of items in the population* has virtually no effect on the sample size unless the population is very small. (Chapter 26-3-3; 8848; CBT Skill: understanding; CSO: 3.1.1)

49. (c) *The requirement that the CPA be independent in mental attitude is included in both sets of standards.* Only GAAS require the CPA to report on the adequacy of disclosure in the financial statements. The attestation standards do not include a standard similar the GAAS second standard of fieldwork: "The auditor must obtain a sufficient understanding of the entity and its environment, including its internal control, to assess the risk of material misstatement of the financial statements whether due to error or fraud, and to design the nature, timing, and extent of further audit procedures." Only the attestation standards are applicable to engagements regarding financial forecasts and projections. (Chapter 31-3-3; 8849; CBT Skill: understanding; CSO: 1.1.3)

50. (d) The auditor has no responsibility to audit information outside the basic financial statements in accordance with GAAS. However, the auditor does have certain responsibilities with respect to it. The nature of this responsibility varies with the nature of the information and the document containing the financial statements. With respect to supplementary information required by the FASB, GASB or FASAB, *the auditor should apply certain limited procedures to it and report deficiencies in, or the omission of, such information.* Required supplementary information differs from other types of information outside the basic financial statements because the FASB, GASB, or FASAB considers the information an essential part of the financial reporting of certain entities and accordingly authoritative guidelines for the measurement and presentation of the information have been established. (Chapter 28-11-2; 8850; CBT Skill: understanding; CSO: 5.1.9)

Solution 6 SIMULATION ANSWER (2009)

Response #1: Internal Control Matters

1. Excluded

The written communication regarding significant deficiencies and material weaknesses identified during the audit of financial statements should include a statement that indicates the purpose of the auditor's consideration of internal control was to express an opinion on the financial statements, **but not** to express an opinion on the effectiveness of the entity's internal control.

2. Included

The complete statement is: Identify the matters that are considered to be significant deficiencies and those that are considered to be material weaknesses.

3. Included

Self-explanatory.

4. Included

The complete statement is: Include the definition of the term material weakness and, where relevant, the definition of the term significant deficiency.

5. Included

See the explanation for item 4.

6. Excluded

There should be a statement that the auditor is **not** expressing an opinion on the effectiveness of internal control.

7. Excluded

There should be a statement that the communication is intended solely for the information and use of management, those charged with governance, and others within the organization and is **not** intended to be and should **not** be used by anyone other than these specified parties.

8. Included

See the explanation for item 2.

1. Column B: 6

   A search for unrecorded liabilities would include the investigation of unmatched receiving reports.

   Column C: 1

   The process of comparing the receiving reports to the voucher packages would have revealed the missing invoices.

2. Column B: 1

   A review for proper cutoff of purchases is accomplished by comparing year 3 cash disbursement entries with the dates on the corresponding invoices to see if any invoices received in year 2 were recorded in year 3.

   Column C: 9

   This procedure would help to ensure that the liability was recorded in the month the goods were received.

3. Column B: 9

   A walk-through would allow the auditor to observe that incompatible functions were being performed by the same person.

   Column C: 8

   This procedure is the best choice from the available ones. A better control would simply be not to allow the same person to perform both functions.

4. Column B: 4

   A search for unrecorded liabilities would include the investigation of unmatched invoices.

   Column C: 2

   Following up on unmatched invoices with the receiving department should help to identify unreported received goods.

$$\text{Inventory turnover} = \frac{\text{Cost of Goods Sold}}{\text{Average Inventory}}$$

$$\text{Return on equity} = \frac{\text{Net Income}}{\text{Average Stockholders' Equity}}$$

1. Dr. Inventory
      Cr. Inventory Over and Short

   To reverse erroneous reduction of inventory; inventory at distribution center should not have been omitted in physical inventory count

   Impact on inventory turnover ratio: Decreases

   This journal entry caused cost of goods sold to decrease by a greater proportion than average inventory increased, so the ratio decreased.

   Impact on return on equity ratio: Increases

   This journal entry caused net income to increase by a greater proportion than average stockholder's equity, so the ratio increased.

2. Dr. Inventory Over and Short
      Cr. Inventory

   To reverse erroneous increase of inventory; consigned goods should not have been included in physical inventory count

   Impact on inventory turnover ratio: Increases

   This journal entry caused cost of goods sold to increase by a greater proportion than average inventory decreased, so the ratio increased.

   Impact on return on equity ratio: Decreases

   This journal entry caused net income to decrease by a greater proportion than average stockholder's equity, so the ratio decreased.

3. Dr. Inventory
      Cr. Accounts Payable

   To adjust for materials in transit not recorded

   Impact on inventory turnover ratio: Decreases

   This journal entry caused cost of goods sold to decrease by a greater proportion than average inventory increased, so the ratio decreased.

   Impact on return on equity ratio: Increases

   This journal entry caused net income to increase by a greater proportion than average stockholder's equity, so the ratio increased.

4. Dr. Retained Earnings
      Cr. Cash

   To record cash dividend paid

Impact on inventory turnover ratio: No impact

The payment of the dividend did not affect either component of the ratio.

Impact on return on equity ratio: Increases

This journal entry had no effect on net income while it decreased average stockholder's equity, so the ratio increased.

Response #4: Communication

To: Engagement Partner

From: Senior Auditor

Re: Audit of Wagner Corporation Financial Statements; Investigation of Material Misstatement Due to Failure to Capitalize Expenditures for Fixed Assets

Our audit has uncovered a material misstatement of the financial statements of Wagner Corporation due to their failure to capitalize expenditures for fixed assets. We discovered invoices documenting purchases of equipment that we have determined were expensed.

Our investigation of this matter is in the initial stages so we have not yet determined whether this misstatement was intentional and thus involves fraud or was unintentional, i.e., due to an error. We will expand our further audit procedures to make this determination and reevaluate our risk assessment.

We will be alert to both types of fraud: fraudulent financial reporting and the misappropriation of the equipment.

If the equipment can be located we will try to determine through interviews with the persons responsible for recording the purchases why the company's capitalization vs. expense policy was not followed. If our investigation identifies that this is the only issue, it is unlikely this is a case of fraudulent financial reporting because management is under pressure to increase profits. Expensing these items, of course, substantially lowered net income. Nor does the company's tax situation create undue pressure for lowering recorded income. However, we will review the entire process to see if inappropriate management override of reporting controls occurred that has the appearance of fraud. And unless we find that management override was the only factor, we will make suggestions as to how internal controls can be improved to prevent this from happening in the future.

If the equipment cannot be located we will determine if it was returned or destroyed. It may have also been disposed of for appropriate reasons, but in any case, there was a failure to properly record the event. We will investigate why controls failed in the same manner as described in the preceding paragraph. We may decide to examine the company records regarding claims filed with their insurance carrier to see if in conjunction with whatever our investigation reveals, irregularities exist there that support our concerns. This may or may not lead to the need to confirm issues directly with their insurance carrier.

If the absence of the equipment cannot be explained, we will try to determine if there was any collusion between the vendors' employees and Wagner employees in order to determine the nature of the theft. This may inform our investigation by revealing whether it was a "paper" theft involving only funds or if the equipment was actually stolen. We will seek to confirm that the invoices are valid by contacting the vendors. This will, of course, necessitate gaining beforehand as much assurance as possible under the circumstances that we are not communicating with a vendor employee who could have been involved in the possible fraudulent scheme. If we determine that any of the vendors are related parties we will scrutinize those transactions first. We will examine the canceled checks that were written for all the purchases of the expensed equipment and follow up on any irregularities or patterns we may discover. We will send copies of the cancelled checks to the vendors and ask them to verify that the bank stamps are appropriate and the endorsements are both appropriate and authentic.

We will attempt to walk-through the entire purchase process of the missing equipment. The identification and interviewing of these individuals may reveal a pattern that indicates there was collusion among Wagner employees.

We will seek to authenticate any other documents we are able to locate in the audit trail as well by examining signatures; reviewing the sequence of any date stamps; looking for alterations or missing information; matching with other documents we may have been able to authenticate, etc.

If we find evidence that the goods were received— are able to authenticate and match receiving reports to the invoices—we will interview the employees that signed the receiving reports. We will then try to find records that will allow us to trace the disposition of the equipment after it left the receiving department. If we find proof that procedures were followed and the equipment was placed in storage we will determine if there are records of who had access to the equipment. Additionally, we will examine the physical and procedural security for the stored equipment. This may indicate whether outsiders could have stolen the equipment or if it was more likely to have been an employee,

We will interview other members of management and other appropriate employees not involved in purchasing to determine if they suspect fraud. We will also discuss our concerns with their internal auditors for the same purpose.

I will keep you apprised of our progress and would like to meet with you as soon as possible concerning our formal communications with management and those charged with governance about this matter.

Response #5: Research

Paragraph Reference Answer: AU 9561.02

"Interpretation—No. Section 561, *Subsequent Discovery of Facts Existing at the Date of the Auditor's Report,* requires the auditor to undertake to determine whether the information is reliable and whether the facts existed at the date of his report. This undertaking must be performed even when the auditor has resigned or been discharged."

INDEX

A

S

W

Y

Bisk Education
CPA Review™

AMERICA'S BEST CPA REVIEW SINCE 1971

TURN DOWNTIME INTO
STUDY TIME
WITH AUDIO TUTORS

AUDIO TUTOR SERIES

Make every minute count! This popular lecture series, covering over 40 hours of vital exam information, puts a personal CPA review expert at your side while you drive... while you jog...whenever you can listen to a CD.

"Using your CPA Review Audio Tutor helped fill idle time that would have been unproductive – like driving to work and doing household chores. I needed a different study program to help me over the hump. Bisk CPA Review did it."

Craig Woods
NEW YORK

THE PERFECT COMPLEMENT FOR OFFLINE STUDYING CONVENIENCE
Bisk CPA Review Audio Tutor Series

Bisk Education
CPA REVIEW™

BISK CPA REVIEW VIDEOS

2

GREAT WAYS TO WATCH, LISTEN AND LEARN
TO PASS THE CPA EXAM

1 HOT•SPOT™ DVDs

Weak in a specific area? Master it with your choice of 35 topic-specific videos ... they're perfect for rounding out those rough spots before you sit for the exam!

These videos provide extensive coverage of the toughest, most challenging and most frequently tested topics within each of the four sections of the computer-based CPA exam – Financial Accounting & Reporting, Auditing & Attestation, Business Environment & Concepts, and Regulation.

Featuring America's best CPA review instructor – Bob Monette, JD, CPA, who uses humor to help you remember his problem-solving tips – each video is packed with valuable exam strategies and comes with a comprehensive viewer's guide for easy reference.

- Order just the titles you need (35 topic-specific videos available)

- Each video provides extensive coverage of a specific topic area

- Each video focuses on the toughest, most challenging and most frequently tested topics on the computer-based CPA exam

- Each video comes with a comprehensive viewer's guide

www.CPAexam.com/10

2 INTENSIVE DVDs

The Intensive Video Series is specifically designed to help you master all four sections of the exam during the weeks right before you sit.

This "Intensive" video review is packed with 24 hours of tips, tricks and techniques from America's best CPA review instructor, Bob Monette, JD, CPA, whose entertaining approach makes it easy to master his proven problem-solving techniques. This powerful video program will not only increase your retention of the most heavily tested exam topics (according to AICPA specifications), it will also teach you what to study and how to most effectively prepare for the computer-based CPA exam.

Leave nothing to chance ... find out what you absolutely need to know to pass with our clear, concise Intensive Video Series – if you can find 24 hours of study time between now and the exam, our instructors can help you pass!

- Cram for the exam with guidance from America's leading CPA review instructors
- Learn from lively experts who use humor to teach problem-solving
- Increase your retention of the most heavily tested exam topics with helpful memory aids
- Refresh your memory on subjects you covered in previous classes
- Clarify topics you didn't quite grasp the first time around
- Target the information you must know to pass the exam
- Find information fast with a comprehensive viewer's guide

POWERFUL LAST-MINUTE STUDY TOOL

AVAILABLE BY SECTION OR COMPLETE SET

Bisk Education
CPA REVIEW™

NO OTHER VIDEO SERIES IS THIS COMPREHENSIVE

AVAILABLE HOT • SPOT™ DVDs:

▶ ▶ **Financial Accounting & Reporting Section**
- Bonds & Other Liabilities
- Cash, Receivables & Marketable Securities
- Consolidations
- Statement of Cash Flows
- Accounting for Income Taxes
- Government & Nonprofit Accounting
- Inventory, Fixed Assets & Intangible Assets
- Leases & Pensions
- Owners' Equity & Miscellaneous Topics
- Revenue Recognition & Income Statements

▶ ▶ **Auditing & Attestation Section**
- Audit Evidence
- Audit Standards & Planning
- Statistical Sampling
- Internal Control
- Standard Audit Reports
- Other Reports, Reviews & Compilations

*Titles subject to change

▶ ▶ **Regulation Section**
- Bankruptcy & Suretyship
- Commercial Paper & Documents of Title
- Contracts
- Corporate Taxation
- Fiduciary Relationships
- Government Regulation of Business
- Gross Income, Tax Liabilities & Credits
- Individual Taxation
- Partnerships & Other Tax Topics
- Professional & Legal Responsibilities
- Property & Insurance
- Property Taxation
- Sales
- Secured Transactions

▶ ▶ **Business Environment & Concepts Section**
- Business Entities
- Cost & Managerial Accounting
- Economics
- Financial Management
- Information Technology

"I am thrilled to let you know that I passed all four parts of the exam on the first try. I wanted to tell your company, 'Thanks for the great Hot•Spot DVDs.' The instructors were extremely knowledgeable and I believe their exam tips were the difference in passing or failing for me. Without your videos, I would not have been a success."

Tracy Wang
LOUISIANA

TARGETED TRAINING THAT LETS YOU MASTER ANY EXAM TOPIC
Bisk CPA Review Videos